A WRITER'S COMPANION

. . . . .

A WRITER'S COMPANION

EDITED BY
LOUIS D. RUBIN, JR.
· · · · ·
IN ASSOCIATION WITH
JERRY LEATH MILLS
· · · · ·

You could look it up
—CHARLES DILLON STENGEL

HarperPerennial
A Division of HarperCollinsPublishers

First HarperPerennial edition published 1997.

Library of Congress Cataloging-in-Publication Data

A writer's companion / edited by Louis D. Rubin, Jr.,
in association with Jerry Leath Mills.
p.   cm.
Includes bibliographical references (p.   ).
ISBN 0-06-273472-5
1. Handbooks, vade-mecums, etc.   2. Literary curiosa—
Handbooks, manuals, etc.
I. Rubin, Louis Decimus. 1923–   .   II. Mills, Jerry Leath.
AG105.W97   1997
031.02—dc21   96-45543

97 98 99 00 ❖/RRD 10 9 8 7 6 5 4 3 2

CONTENTS

. . . . .

PREFACE AND APOLOGIA: WHY THIS PARTICULAR REFERENCE BOOK?

. . . . .

REFERENCE BOOKS GET COMPILED BECAUSE SOMEBODY THINKS THEY WILL BE useful. Upon the occasion of publishing yet another such, it seems proper to say why it was prepared and what purposes it is designed to serve.

To do that, a modicum of background is in order. As the late Casey Stengel remarked, "You could look it up"—and throughout most of my life I have been doing just that. I have been a writer for sixty years, and an editor for almost that long. For forty-two years I was also a teacher. Doing those things required the constant checking of facts. No matter how well one might know a particular subject, there is always something to be verified; and inevitably I often had only a general acquaintance with much of the subject matter of the material that came across my desk.

There were certain reference works I came to depend upon. Yet although I regularly consult dictionaries, encyclopedias, and any number of other reference books, they were never sufficient—and of course never could be. So I frequently had to go looking in all kinds of books and places to find out what I needed to know.

I found myself wishing that I might compile a reference book of my own and for myself, one which would bring together within the covers of a single volume a great deal of the particular kind of information that I was apt to need and want—a kind of personal writer's and editor's companion.

It would not be a "how-to" book, with names and addresses of publishing houses and magazines, advice on preparing manuscripts, suggested stylistic guidelines, and the like. What I had in mind was a book with substantive material in it—events, dates, places, opinions, glossaries, checklists, information of various kinds.

I wanted to design a book that would be of particular use to writers and editors. It seemed to me that, from having been for so long in the writing and editing trade myself, I might be in a position to know at least some of the things that it would be handy to have included in a desk-sized reference work. To compile and edit such a book might be an appropriate way to wrap up my own editing career.

It would be fun to prepare, too. I had been involved in compiling and editing a few reference books in the past, and although I certainly wouldn't want to make compiling, rather than writing, my principal retirement activity, there is an undoubted fascination in searching out and bringing useful information together. To quote Robert Frost in a different context, "The fact is the sweetest dream that labor knows."

My own set of interests and reference needs would not be everybody's; far from it. Naturally I would seek the help of other writers and editors in deciding what should go in the book. Even then, no single volume, however inclusive, could possibly accommodate the reference needs of all or even of most writers and editors. Still, I thought it would be possible to provide information on a number of topics that others would appreciate having available.

So, early in 1991, after I had retired from my teaching position at the University of North Carolina at Chapel Hill and as I got ready to retire from Algonquin Books of Chapel Hill, I began making plans for the book. I drew up a list of possible subjects for inclusion, and I sent it to more than a hundred active American and British writers, many though by no means all of them acquaintances of mine. They included novelists, poets, journalists, scholars, and writers about art, music, literature, sports, science, history, philosophy, archaeology, the classics, folklore, politics and government, theology, psychoanalysis, the outdoors.

I asked them to suggest topics not on my list that would be useful to them if compiled for reference, and to cite the particular reference books they most often used. I explained that the kind of book I had in mind obviously could not accommodate the detailed requirements of their specialized professional needs, but that I wanted to know what each would find useful for quick reference purposes.

Fifty-five authors responded, many at considerable length. When I added the topics they proposed to those I had thought of, I found that I had several hundred suggested subjects for inclusion.

In making the final choices for my book, I proceeded with certain assumptions in mind. As noted, it would be a general work, and it would not be designed to replace specialized reference sources. I would seek to gather material, and in sufficient detail, on a variety of topics—topics about which, from my own experience and that of others, it seemed to me that writers and editors would find it useful to have information available within the covers of a single volume.

Another assumption was that although it was to be a single-volume work, it would be preferable to have the individual categories presented in reasonably detailed form, even if doing so would necessarily restrict the number and range of topics included. Presentations that were too greatly abridged and truncated would be of little use to anyone. (As for what "reasonably detailed" would constitute, I should have to decide that myself.)

My original idea had been for a book that could more or less stand by itself, without reference to what could be found in any other books. The object, after all, was to draw together, within a single volume, information much of which was presented elsewhere but only within a number of separate books. But when I examined the lists of reference works that the fifty-five authors who responded cited as being in steady use by them, I quickly reached several conclusions.

There were two kinds of books that almost everybody used. One was an almanac, usually the *World Almanac and Book of Facts*. There was no point in duplicating what was available in that highly useful and easily accessible work, unless I could add significantly to what it provided.

The other kind of books, naturally enough, were word books—dictionaries, a *Roget* or other books of synonyms and antonyms. Most of those replying reported making regular use of unabridged dictionaries. So no etymologies and word lists should be included. However, specialized glossaries would be useful because of their compactness, and a modest compilation of slang and informal expressions, as suggested by several writers, would be appropriate.

I also decided that, given the current rage for detailed statistical information on almost every variety of athletic competition, and the abundant reference compilations now readily available on newsstands as well as bookstores, I would omit almost all material about sports from my book. I made only two exceptions. One was a compilation that, astoundingly, no one seems ever to have bothered to make for major league baseball. The other was a listing, in handy, quick-reference form, of something that is so often the subject of debate in professional football.

That, in any event, is how this book came to be.

I have called it a "writer's companion," or an "editor's vade mecum," and a "browsing reader's treasure chest"—the last because I'm sure there are numerous readers like myself who sometimes enjoy looking at compilations without any particular object in mind. Some of the material in it, such as the compilations showing the rise and fall of the downtown hotel in

America, the shrinkage of the daily newspaper over the years, the decades when numerous consumer products came into general use, the years when major league teams were and were not pennant contenders, the homes of the famous, and so on, is not to my knowledge elsewhere available in handy format.

Still, I believe that above all this book will be of use to writers—very much including fiction writers, whose needs, for purposes of verisimilitude, tend to be especially eclectic. Without the appropriate factual reference, the authentic example, the specific proper noun, what literary critics call the "suspension of disbelief" can be imperiled.

Novelists know this, as do other writers. So do editors, including copy editors. So do book reviewers. It is, in any event, the principal justification I can offer for having prepared *A Writer's Companion*, and I believe it is sufficient.

To help in compiling and presenting so extensive and disparate an assortment of material, I secured the collaboration of a longtime colleague and friend, Jerry Leath Mills, professor of English at the University of North Carolina at Chapel Hill, a Renaissance scholar, editor of *Studies in Philology*, and a man of far-ranging interests and avocations. As associate editor he assumed responsibility for preparing approximately one-fourth of the topics to be covered.

Another colleague, Connie Eble, whose specialty is the American language, agreed to prepare a glossary of some commonly used colloquial expressions, a task that was beyond my capabilities. One of the writers whose suggestions I sought for topics to be included in the book, George A. Kennedy, is not only a distinguished classical-languages scholar but a railroad buff of the first magnitude, and he not only proposed inclusion of a roster of famous American and European trains and their routes, but volunteered to compile it himself.

To the writers who responded so generously to my request for suggestions for possible inclusions and information on reference books frequently consulted, I am greatly indebted. Many of their suggestions are reflected in the subjects chosen for presentation. Their willingness to help has made this venture into truly a *writers'* companion. The pages which follow are enormously richer in scope and variety for their participation.

They are Jeffry J. Andresen, Noel Annan, Russell Baker, John Barth, Joseph Blotner, Walter Dean Burnham, Jackson Cope, Robert W. Creamer, Guy Davenport, Carlo D'Este, Ellen Douglas, Leon Edel, Clyde Edgerton, John S. D. Eisenhower, John R. Elting, Wallace Fowlie, Frank Freidel, Henry Louis Gates, Jr., Herbert Gold, Robert B. Heilman, Steven Hess, Christopher

Hill, Fred C. Hobson, Josephine Humphreys, Blyden Jackson, Alfred Kazin, George A. Kennedy, James LeaSor, Walton Litz, Katie Letcher Lyle, Nick Lyons, Maynard Mack, Jay Martin, Jill McCorkle, Helen Hill Miller, J. Hillis Miller, Paul C. Nagel, Edwin Newman, Jaroslav Pelikan, J. Roland Pennock, Nelson W. Polsby, Julia Randall, A. L. Rowse, Karl Shapiro, Joseph C. Sloane, David G. Smith, Lee Smith, Elizabeth Spencer, Anthony Storr, John Updike, Richard Wilbur, Joel Williamson, Jules Witcover, and the late Howard Nemerov and John Hersey.

For the shortcomings of compilation, judgment, and presentation, and for the absence of material that someone else might think should have been included but wasn't, the responsibility throughout is my own.

In preparing a substantial number of the sections I was fortunate to be able to draw upon the research and editorial talents of Dr. Ian Crump, scholarly son of a scholarly father, and of Jesma Reynolds, an experienced researcher. Others who helped to prepare, either in part or *in toto*, sections of this book, or to check them for accuracy, include David Sisk, Claire Sanders, Martha Fawbush, Benita Muth, Margaret Campbell, Andrew John Kirkendall, Mark Litle, Timothy J. Henderson, Gus Fraser, John Sepich, and Al Benthall. At the end of each piece those responsible for primary preparation of the data are identified. The introductory paragraphs are largely my own.

For aid in much of the research of the material contained in this book I am indebted to the staffs of the Walter Royall Davis and Louis Round Wilson Libraries of the University of North Carolina at Chapel Hill, and in particular Dr. James F. Govan, now the retired university librarian. Not only did we have at our disposal the several million volumes of a major research library and depository, but I was provided with an office throughout the most active period of the book's preparation.

I was in no way hesitant, either, to call upon the assistance of friends more knowledgeable than I in various of the topics covered. In particular Edward L. Beach and John Rousmaniere saved me from grievous error in the presentation of types of ships and boats. Others include Carolyn Wallace, John S. D. Eisenhower, Donald Kennedy, Maynard Pearlstine, P. Geoffrey Feiss, Maurice M. Bursey, and John A. Redfield. I am grateful, too, to Jeffry A. Andresen for his good offices in helping to arrange for the preparation of the glossary of psychoanalytical terms.

My friend Edmund Fuller, literary critic and longtime book reviewer for the *Wall Street Journal,* prepared a lengthy critique of this manuscript that was of invaluable use. As a self-confessed generalist, he responded to the various sections in precisely the spirit with which they were compiled, coming up again and again with extremely useful suggestions, notations, and comments drawn from his wide range of interests.

There are numerous others who have helped. One in particular merits prominent acknowledgment. Robert Alden Rubin, senior editor of Algonquin Books of Chapel Hill, has on numerous occasions cheerfully rescued his aging, Underwood No. 5-reared father from the otherwise fatal results of appalling ineptitude in the use of a Macintosh word-processor.

LOUIS D. RUBIN, JR.

Chapel Hill, North Carolina
September 1, 1994

I

TRAVEL AND

TRANSPORTATION

I

BOATS, SHIPS, AND OTHER WATERCRAFT

. . . . .

Anyone who has ever done much writing about watercraft knows that those who read it tend to be extremely persnickety about nomenclature. Write "bark" when you mean "barkentine," or "battleship" when you mean "battle cruiser," and you are asking for all kinds of trouble. Yet there is by no means general agreement among the experts about such matters; quite the contrary.

What is the difference between a "boat" and a "ship"? Good question; authorities disagree. A rule-of-thumb distinction has to do with size; that is, you can put a boat on a ship, but you can't put a ship on a boat. Think of it this way. A "ship's boat" is a small craft kept aboard and lowered for use in harbor; a "boat's ship" is the larger vessel that the boat belongs to and can be hoisted onto. Yet that doesn't make a sailboat that keeps a dinghy on the cabin roof into a ship. And in the United States Navy, submarines, which certainly function independently both atop and underneath the surface of the ocean, are traditionally referred to as boats, not ships.

In short, there is no such thing as unanimous agreement on terminology. In particular, aficionados of sailing vessels can and frequently do dispute at length over exactly what was a brig, a brigantine, a bark, a barkentine, and so on. One man's prau is another man's proa, and so on. Moreover, boats and ships have evolved over the centuries, and their conformations have changed.

There have been thousands of different kinds of watercraft, ranging from rafts and simple log canoes to full-rigged sailing vessels and giant ocean liners and warships. The compilation that follows describes only a few of the most commonly known types, including modern craft and some older craft frequently encountered in books. We have relied in particular on two excellent compilations, Graham Blackburn's *Illustrated Encyclopedia of Ships, Boats, Vessels, and Other Water-Borne Craft* and

Björn Landström's *Sailing Ships* (see Sources, below).

For their generous help in making this descriptive compilation as accurate as possible, we are indebted to Capt. Edward L. Beach, USN ret., and John Rousmaniere.

Aircraft carrier. Flat-decked Navy ship designed to transport, launch, and land airplanes. Known in U.S. Navy as *attack carrier*. The earliest carriers date from World War I, and were converted naval or cargo vessels which carried seaplanes aboard and lowered them into the water with cranes. The Royal Navy might well have ambushed and trapped the German High Seas Fleet at Jutland in 1916 if Admiral Jellicoe hadn't declined to make use of a seaplane carrier. The "flat-top" with a deck for launching and landing airplanes came soon afterward. The *Langley* was the first U.S. aircraft carrier. World War II battle fleets in the Pacific developed into fast carrier fleets, with battleships in effect relegated to functioning as antiaircraft protection for carriers and bombarding shore installations. See also **Escort carrier**.

Ark. (1) Large vessel of refuge, without means of propulsion, modeled on the biblical ark of Noah; (2) early flat-bottomed vessel on U.S. inland waters for transporting produce.

Armed merchant cruiser. Large merchant vessel, usually fast, taken over by navy during wartime, armed, and used primarily for convoying and blockading. The *Jervis Bay* of World War II was an armed merchant cruiser. Also known as *auxiliary cruiser*; see below.

Attack transport. Fast Navy ship designed to carry and put ashore troops and equipment, including landing craft.

Auxiliary cruiser. Armed passenger or cargo vessel converted to naval duty for convoying and patrolling during wartime; see **Armed merchant cruiser**.

Banker. Large cod-fishing vessel of the offshore North Atlantic banks. Present-day bankers are motorized; earlier they were schooner rigged. Commonly they carried dories, from which crewmen fished with long lines. Kipling's *Captains Courageous* is set aboard a banker.

Barca-longa. Large lugsail-rigged Spanish fishing boat carrying two or three sails.

Barco de mer. See **Fishing boat**.

Barge. (1) Roomy flat-bottomed boat used for transporting goods or passengers in harbors, canals, or waterways, offshore, etc., usually towed but sometimes self-propelled; also known as *lighter*; (2) older term for any small sailing vessel; also *bark*; (3) admiral's barge, large Navy boat, earlier rowed but now powered, for harbor transport of flag officers; (4) highly ornamented ceremonial craft; "The barge she sat in, like a burnished throne"—Shakespeare; (5) coastal trading vessel; the *Thames barge* was flat bottomed, with leeboards, ketch or yawl rigged;

(6) formerly a double-decked towed vessel for pleasure parties. "Don't barge in on me"—Anon.

Bark. Three-masted sailing vessel, with foremast and mainmast square rigged, mizzenmast fore and aft rigged; also *barque*. Earlier the term was used for any small sailing craft. The *jackass-bark* has square top- and topgallant sails on the mainmast but the lower main is fore and aft rigged. The *four-masted bark* carries square-rigged fore-, main-, and mizzenmasts, and fore-and-aft sails on the aftermast. "Yond tall anchoring bark/Diminish'd to her cock, her cock a buoy/Almost too small for sight"—Shakespeare, *King Lear.*

Barkentine. Three-masted sailing vessel similar to a bark but with only the foremast square rigged. Also *barquentine*.

Bassboat. Fast motor craft for inland pleasure fishing developed in 1960s, cathedral hulled with very low freeboard, decked-over blunt bow, very stable, with high pedestal seats at bow and stern, powered by outboard engine.

Bathysphere. Diving sphere for deep-sea observation and study.

Batteau. (1) Light flat-bottomed skiff, rowed or poled, tapering to blunt ends; (2) double-ended flat-bottomed rowing craft, sharp raked, used on lakes and rivers of northern North America. Also *bateau*.

Battle-cruiser. Large warship built by British and Germans for First World War, similar to battleship and with long-range guns, but faster and with lighter protective armor. The lack of protection proved disastrous; wrongly used as part of the battleline, three were sunk in a couple of hours at Jutland in 1916. The HMS *Hood,* sunk by a single salvo fired by the *Bismarck* in 1942, was Great Britain's most famous battle-cruiser.

Battleship. Largest, most heavily armed and armored of a navy's warships. Early battleships, which were direct descendants of the sailing *ships-of-the-line* or *line-of-battle-ships,* were known as *ironclads*. The British HMS *Dreadnought,* launched in 1906 at the instigation of Admiral Sir John Fisher, displaced 17,900 tons, and its big guns were all of the same caliber. Its advent rendered all earlier battleships obsolete, and its name became generic for the largest battleships; but by World War I, the heyday of the battleship, it too was outdated by larger and more formidable craft. The last major surface engagement of battleship fleets was Jutland, in 1916, in which the British Grand Fleet, although suffering greater damage, drove the German High Seas Fleet back to cover. In World War II, battleship fleets fought no major surface engagements. The German *Bismarck,* after sinking the British battle-cruiser *Hood* in the North Atlantic, was ultimately disabled and slowed by aerial attack and sunk by torpedoes, bombing, and shelling. In 1942 the USS *Washington* disabled the Japanese battleship *Kirishima* to the point where she was scuttled by her own forces. The largest battleships ever built were Japan's 72,000-ton *Yamato* and *Musashi;* both were sunk by aerial attack. During the Korean, Vietnam, and Desert

Storm conflicts, American battleships of World War II vintage such as the *Missouri, Iowa,* and *Wisconsin* were restored to service, modernized, and stripped of all but big guns and antiaircraft batteries, and used to shell shore installations. "Sailors, who pitch this portent at the sea/Where dreadnoughts shall confess/Its hell-bent deity"—Robert Lowell.

Bergantina. Small Mediterranean rowing or sailing vessel often carried dismantled aboard larger sailing ships in the fifteenth and sixteenth centuries.

Billy-boat. Merchant ship of the seventeenth and eighteenth centuries, with square-rigged foremast and cut-off lateen mainsail. Also *bilander.*

Bireme. Galley with oars on two banks or in groups of two, usually with outriggers, used in the Mediterranean from the seventh century B.C.E. onward.

Block Island boat. Cat-rigged yawl or ketch, with masts of equal height, with short keel.

Bomb-ketch. Sturdily constructed sailing vessel with main- and mizzenmasts, and with foremast removed to accommodate heavy mortars.

Brig. Two-masted square-rigged naval vessel; originally, *brig* was short for *brigantine,* but it evolved into a separate type of ship. A *collier brig* was an English coaling vessel with a very large headsail and spanker and large topsails. A *hermaphrodite brig* carried a square-rigged foremast and topsails and a fore-and-aft gaff-rigged mainsail. A *brig-sloop* was a small English naval vessel ranking just below a *frigate.* ". . . the mate of the *Nancy* brig"—W. S. Gilbert.

Brigantine. Two-masted vessel with square-rigged foremast, and a mainmast usually of two parts, carrying square topsails and a fore-and-aft spanker mainsail. (When the main topsail was fore and aft, this craft was also sometimes called a *hermaphrodite brig.)*

Bug-eye. Ketch-rigged Chesapeake Bay sailing vessel of shoal draft, often double ended, with raked masts. See also **Skipjack.**

Bulk carrier. Merchant vessel, often equipped with heavy overhead lifts, designed to carry dry bulk cargo such as grain, ore, and minerals. See also **Great Lakes bulk carrier.**

Bum boat. Small harbor craft used for peddling and ferrying ships' crews. Little Buttercup, in Gilbert and Sullivan's *HMS Pinafore,* was proprietor of a bum boat.

Buss. Beamy square-rigged North Sea fishing boat.

Buy-boat. Stern-cabined Chesapeake Bay workboat, low-hulled, 50–75 foot, with ample open space forward, for buying and transporting crab catches.

Cabin cruiser. Pleasure craft, gasoline or diesel powered, with live-aboard accommodations; also *power cruiser.* See also **Yacht.**

Cable-ship. Large ship specially fitted out for laying and repairing electric cable underwater. The *Great Eastern,* built as a passenger liner, turned out to be an excellent cable-ship.

Caique. (1) Light Turkish rowboat; (2) working sailboat of the eastern Mediterranean, short masted with extended gaff-rig loose-footed mainsail.

Canal boat. Long, low-roofed craft used on inland canals. The canal boat could be rowed or poled, carry sail, or be pulled by teams of horses or mules operating alongside on the canal bank. Motorized canal boats are used to carry cargo or passengers in Europe and the British Isles today. Canal boats are often narrow beamed for negotiating locks, and low cabined to fit under bridges. "I've got a mule, her name is Sal,/Fifteen miles on the Erie Canal"—folk song.

Canoe. Narrow, light open boat. The Indian canoe after which most small American pleasure canoes are modeled was of skins or birchbark, and was paddled. Indians also fashioned canoes of logs, with burnt-out interiors. Canoes in the South Pacific and Indian Oceans used outriggers, frequently with sails. The Chesapeake Bay *log canoe,* also known as a *cunner,* was a sailing craft with its hull formed of hewn sections of logs fitted together lengthwise. The *Accra canoe* is a West African fishing craft. "Every man paddle his own canoe"—Captain Marryat.

Captain's gig. Small ship's boat for the use of its captain, similar to an *admiral's barge.* See **Tender**.

Caravel. Sailing vessel, also *carvel,* used in the Mediterranean and later by the Spanish and Portuguese on voyages of discovery in the fifteenth, sixteenth, and seventeenth centuries. Early caravels were two masted; later they were of three and four masts, the fore- and mainmasts with square sails and the aftermasts lateen rigged. Caravels were usually square sterned, and smaller and of shallower draft than carracks and galleons. Columbus' *Nina* was a lateen-rigged *caravela latina.*

Cargo liner. Large freight-carrying ship, sometimes with accommodations for passengers (because of maritime regulations usually twelve or fewer), following a regularly scheduled route. See **Freighter**.

Carrack. Large European merchant vessel, fourteenth to seventeenth century, with high fore- and aftcastles, two and later three, sometimes four masted. Foremast and main were typically square sailed; aftmasts generally carried lateen or spritsail rigs. Carracks were often heavily armed, and evolved into the galleons and other warships of the sixteenth and seventeenth centuries.

Catamaran. Twin-hulled vessel. Small, fast-sailing catamarans which can be launched from beaches are very popular today.

Cat-boat. Beamy centerboard sailboat, with large mainsail and no jib. "Cat-rigged" on any craft means without a jib.

Chebacco boat. Eighteenth-century New England two-masted sailing vessel, cat-rigged, with overhanging stern and without bowsprit or headsails.

Clipper ship. Clippers varied in shape and rig, but the fully developed American clipper of the mid-nineteenth century was long, fast, deep hulled, and full-rigged, with tall raked masts heavily sparred, an overhanging bow, concave waterlines, and a large sail area; "the noblest of all sailing vessels, and the most beautiful creation of man in America"—Samuel Eliot Morison. The English *tea-clipper*, used in the China trade and typified by the *Cutty Sark*, was a response to the American clippers. The iron- and steel-hulled *wool-clippers*, the last full-rigged sailing ships, were basically bark rigged. The German *Preussen*, the only five-masted full-rigger, built in 1902, carried 47 sails including both upper and lower topgallants. The *Baltimore clipper* was not a full-rigged ship but a small, fast schooner, with gaff-rigged fore-and-aft mainsails, a sharp bow, and a deep aft-hull. "You're off from some clipper that flies the Black Ball"—folk song, "Blow the Man Down." See also **Pole-and-line craft**.

Coaster. Earlier, any sailing craft engaged primarily in coastal trade. Later a small freighter, often with cabin and propulsion machinery aft, used in North European coastwise traffic. "Dirty British coaster with a salt-caked smokestack"—John Masefield.

Coble. Flat-bottomed English fishing boat, with single lugsail, shaped with deep forefoot for bow-first launching from shore or beach. The coble was fitted for three sets of oars.

Cockboat. Dinghy or rowboat carried aboard a ship. See **Tender**.

Cog. Northern European merchant ship, thirteenth to fifteenth centuries, clinker-built, straight ended, single masted and with loose-footed square sail, forecastle and large aftercastle for defense, and with tall, narrow stern rudder.

Collier. Ship, originally sail, later power, used to carry coal. See also **Brig**.

Container ship. Large ship, now the predominant cargo vessel on the oceans, designed expressly to carry freight preloaded in standard-sized containers, usually truck trailers, which are stacked in holds and on deck. Many container ships carry no cargo-handling equipment, and are off- and on-loaded by overhead wharfside cranes at specially equipped container ports. Smaller container-type craft, with sterns that can be lowered to serve as ramps, are now extensively used in coastal and island freight traffic; the trailers are driven aboard and ashore by tractor-trucks.

Coracle. Very small, light, one-man fishing boat, usually oval shaped or rounded, made of skin stretched over wicker frames, used in British Isles from ancient Celts onward. In Stevenson's *Treasure Island*, Ben Gunn builds a coracle.

Corbita. Large round-bottomed merchant ship of ancient Rome, with square-sail-rigged mainmast and steering-sail set on yardarm beneath angled spar at bow.

Corvette. (1) Flush-decked, ship-rigged naval vessel, with single tier of guns, ranking just below a frigate; also *sloop-of-war*; (2) in World War II an anti-submarine convoy escort vessel.

Crab boat. Also *crab skiff*. See **Fishing boat**.

Cruise liner. Large passenger ship especially designed for cruising; also *cruise ship*. By comparison with the transatlantic liners of earlier years, ships specifically designed to be cruise liners have less enclosed deck space, much more open space, passenger cabins designed for single or double rather than multiple occupancy, and in most instances one-class accommodations. (The British *Queen Elizabeth II* is almost the only exception.) Most cruise liners built since the 1960s have eliminated the traditional large dummy funnels of the modern ocean liner in order to gain open deck space atop.

Cruiser. (1) Fast, powerful naval ship, larger than a destroyer but smaller than a battleship. Modern cruisers are essentially the same as destroyers (*e.g.*, the Aegis-class cruiser is built on the same hull and power-plant as the Spruance-class destroyer). *Light cruisers* are generally less heavily armored than *heavy* or *armored cruisers*. In the U.S. Navy of World War II, "light" cruisers carried 6-inch guns, whereas "heavy" cruisers carried 8-inch guns. The *missile cruisers* of the present-day Navy are its major surface warships, armed with guided missile launchers and extensive antiaircraft weaponry. See also **Battle-cruiser**; Armed merchant cruiser. (2) Small pleasure craft with overnight accommodations are also known as *cabin* or *power cruisers*. (3) A cruising boat is a sailboat used wholly or mainly for cruising, not racing.

Currach. Irish craft, skins (now canvas) over wicker framing, similar to a coracle but more pointed and often larger, with multiple eight oars and a square-sail. Also *curragh*. See also **Irish wicker vessel**.

Cutter. (1) Small-sized oceangoing ship, fast and rugged, used by the Coast Guard for patrol or rescue duty; (2) fast sailing craft with gaff mainsail, square topsail, and two jibs, used to collect government revenues from merchant ships or as naval auxiliaries; (3) ship's large square-sterned rowboat, for multiple banked oars, with lugsail-rigged mast that can be unstepped and stored aboard (if motor powered, it is usually called a launch). "He jumped into the wave,/As o'er the cutter's edge he tried to cross"—Byron; (4) pleasure boat with mainsail and both jib and forestaysail, and with single mast stepped one-third to one-half of the way back.

Daysailer. Small sailing sloop, up to 30 feet in length, either open hulled or with a small cuddy-cabin.

Destroyer. Originally a torpedo-boat destroyer designed to guard battle fleets against attacks by small, fast powerboats armed with torpedoes. But destroyers soon took over the torpedo functions and came also to be used for antisubmarine duty and protecting convoys and battle fleets. The destroyer, called a "tin can" in the Navy, was a very fast unarmored ship armed with guns, torpedo tubes, and depth charges. Today's destroyers are often as large as World War II cruisers, and the cruiser designation is fading out. Some destroyer-type ships, armed with missiles, are also called guided missile frigates. *Radar picket destroyers* carry heavy electronic gear. The *destroyer escort* was a smaller World War II vessel turned out in large numbers for patrol and escort duty.

Dhow. Arab boat of the Indian Ocean, usually with overhanging bow, high square poop, and from one to three masts. Though there are numerous variants in hull configuration, the dhow is characterized by its large-sailed lateen rig.

Dinghy. Small boat towed behind or hoisted upon a larger vessel. Dinghys can be rowed, sailed, or powered with outboard motors. The *Bahama dinghy* is a workboat, usually cat rigged. See **Tender**.

Dogger. Two-masted ketch-rigged Dutch fishing vessel working the Dogger Bank of the North Sea.

Dory. Traditional dory was a flat-bottomed, hard-chine, sharp-bowed rowboat, sometimes also a sailboat, with V-shaped transom, which was stacked aboard bankers and other craft and used to fish the Grand Banks. Today the term is given to small hard-chine, sharp-bow craft, particularly if double ended, whether rowed, sailed, or outboard powered.

Double canoe. South Pacific sailing craft of the past made by joining together two canoes.

Down Easter. Any large sailing ship built on Maine coast in mid-nineteenth to early twentieth century.

Dragger. Fishing boat used to drag nets along harbor and ocean floors.

Drakar. Danish Viking fighting-ship, oared and with loose-footed square sail, and with carved dragon head on stemhead.

Dreadnought. See **Battleship**.

Dredge. (1) Shallow-draft craft equipped with powerful suction pumps or bucket chains, used to remove silt and deepen channels and harbors; (2) fishing vessel, sail or engine powered, used to dredge oysters, clams, scallops, etc., from bay or harbor bottom. See **Dragger; Skipjack**.

Drifter. Seagoing fishing boat which sets out lengthy buoyed fish nets to take herring and other shoaling fish.

Dromon. Byzantine craft of Middle Ages, with tiers of 100 to 200 or more oars, outriggers, and lateen-rigged sails. War dromons were equipped with rams. Also *dromond*.

Dugout canoe. Primitive paddled vessel made from burnt-out or hollowed-out logs.

DUKW. Amphibious truck used in World War II.

East Indiaman. Large Dutch and English merchant craft, heavily armed. Earlier ships were galleons, with two-masted square-sail rigging; eighteenth-century Indiamen were full-rigged three-masters with fore-and-aft mainsail on mizzenmast, and rectangular bowsprit sail. "An India ship of fame was she,/Spices and shawls and fans she bore"—Herman Melville.

E-boat. Very fast torpedo boat developed by Germany in World War II, used extensively in English Channel operations. See **Torpedo boat**.

Escort carrier. Medium-length ship, originally converted from merchant use, with flight deck for launching airplanes, designed for convoy use in World War II. Escort carriers played a key role in the Battle of Leyte Gulf in 1944. Carriers of this size now carry helicopters. See **Aircraft carrier**.

Factory ship. Sizable offshore and oceangoing commercial motor vessel used to render and process whales and fish taken by smaller craft.

Fast combat support ship. Fast Navy ship developed to carry ammunition, fuel oil, aviation fuel, missiles, and general provisions in support of combat operations.

Fast patrol boat. Very fast U.S. motor gunboat, larger than the PT boat of World War II, aluminum hulled, powered by combined diesel and gas turbine engine, and variously armed with torpedoes and guided missiles.

Felucca. Narrow, fast-sailing vessel, lateen rigged, usually with three masts, primarily Mediterranean.

Ferry. Boat designed to carry people, vehicles, goods, etc., across rivers, bays, or other relatively narrow bodies of water. Depending on traffic volume and water conditions, ferries can range from very small flat-decked open craft, powered by sail or cable or even rowed, to large seagoing vessels with overnight accommodations, as in the English Channel ferries. *Car ferries* are usually double ended. Some large ferries can carry two hundred cars and several thousand passengers at a time. "On the ferry-boats the hundreds and hundreds that cross"—Walt Whitman.

Fireship. Vessel, usually old, loaded with combustibles or explosives, designed to drift down upon wooden sailing ships and set them afire. The English used fireships to good effect against the Spanish Armada at Calais.

Fishing boat. Any boat designed for fishing. Myriads of distinctive types have evolved in various locales over the years. In the United States, the East Coast *lobster boat* and *crab boat* both have shelter cabins far forward and a low, decked-over stern for handling "pots" (wooden-stripped, now wire traps), but the lobster boat is round bottomed while the crab boat, which works the Chesapeake Bay and Southeast coast, is either flat or broadly V bottomed with deadrise. The *Puget Sound crabber* is larger with sleeping quarters and a live well. The British and Scottish lobster boat is extremely high bowed, with cabin aft and a short steadying sail at the stern. The Portuguese *barco de mer*, double ended with its tall stem and stern posts, is flat bottomed. The *Accra canoe* of West Africa is a long dugout canoe with a single square lugsail and sprit. Mediterranean fishing boats are wide beamed and double ended, low sided with whaleboat lines. Various other kinds of fishing craft are noted throughout this list.

Floating drydock. Drydock with tanks that can be flooded, thus lowering the drydock area to receive a ship, then be pumped out to allow the external portion of the ship's hull to be scraped, painted, or repaired. It can be towed to where it is needed. Floating drydocks are often built in sections which can be joined together.

Fluyt. Round-sterned, flat-bottomed, relatively narrow Northern European merchant sailing vessel of seventeenth and eighteenth centuries, sometimes armed, characteristically with sides sloping inward. Also *flute*.

Freighter. Coastal or oceangoing vessel used to carry cargo, formerly steam powered, now steam-turbine, oil, or diesel powered. By "freighter" is usually meant a general-purpose merchant vessel, carrying cargo in holds with hatch-covers. Although there were many varieties of freighters, typically the ocean-going freighter of World War II vintage or earlier was three islanded, with raised forecastle, bridge and central cabin, and poop, with masts and cargo booms for the fore and aft holds. Nowadays the old general-purpose freighter of Joseph Conrad's and William McFee's day has been largely superceded by more specialized merchant craft. See **Bulk carrier**; **Cargo liner**; **Coaster**; **Container ship**; **Liberty ship**; **Tramp steamer**; **Victory ship**, etc.

Friendship sloop. Originally a single-masted, fore-and-aft-rigged fishing vessel built in Friendship, Maine, now a popular wooden, gaff-rigged pleasure craft. The working Friendship sloop was hard bilged and thus weak in the garboards, with a radically swooped sheer to get the crew closer to the water. Many a good man has come to grief trying to restore an old Friendship sloop.

Frigate. (1) Fast, mid-sized warship with two gundecks, three masted and ship rigged. A U.S. frigate such as the *Constitution* was larger and heavier than frigates in the British Navy, and was rated at 44 guns, although she usually carried 10 or 12 more. Frigates were used for patrol, blockade, and commerce raiding. The mid-nineteenth-century *steam frigate* carried both sails and steam propulsion, and was the standard warship of most navies. "There is no frigate like a book . . . "—Emily Dickinson. (2) In today's navy a large destroyer-type warship, often nuclear powered, armed with guided missiles and 5-inch guns.

Galleas. Combination rowing vessel/sailing warship of the Renaissance period, common in the Mediterranean. A large galleas such as those which fought at Lepanto in 1571 had several banks of oars and three lateen-rigged masts, and was armed with a ram and twenty or more guns.

Galleon. Large sixteenth- and seventeenth-century sailing warship and merchant ship, round hulled and of deep draft, earlier with high forecastle extended over prow, three and four decked, and lofty aftcastle. Both the Spanish ships of the Armada and their English opponents were galleons, although the term itself was used only in Spain and Portugal. The *ship-of-the-line* of eighteenth-century navies evolved directly from the galleon. "O minstrel galleons of Carib fire"—Hart Crane.

Galley. Vessel propelled by banks of oars, often in tiers, and sometimes with auxiliary sail. See also **Barge; Bireme; Trireme; Quadrireme, quinquireme; Shell**. Mediterranean war vessels from ancient times through the sixteenth century were oared galleys. "Over the sea our galleys went"—Robert Browning. (A ship's kitchen, where meals are prepared, is also called a galley.)

Gig. Rowing craft assigned to the commanding officer of a naval ship.

Gloucester fishing schooner. Two-masted sailing vessel of several types, characteristically with pronounced rise from stern to bow. See **Schooner**.

Gondola. (1) High-prowed, long, narrow, flat-bottomed boat used in the canals of Venice, propelled by a standing oarsman; (2) coastal Italian passenger vessel, oar powered; also *gundalow*. "Our gondola, that four swift oarsmen ply"— John Addington Symonds; (3) heavy, flat-bottomed river and lake boat, oar and sail propelled, in northern United States, with cannon mounted, used during Revolutionary War.

Great Lakes bulk carrier. Long cargo vessel without loading and discharging gear, with bridge at bow and engine room at stern, developed for carrying ore and grain under the peculiar weather and visibility difficulties of the Great Lakes. For years these boats were usually exactly 600 feet long, and built with vertical bow, without flare, and with anchors recessed in pockets in order to negotiate locks. Because the ship was steered almost from the point of the bow, a long spar led out from the prow to aid in holding a course. See also **Whaleback**.

Great Lakes schooner. Two- and three-masted cargo-carrying sailing vessel, sharp ended with long bowsprit. "Come all you bold sailors that follow the Lakes/On an iron ore vessel your living to make"—folk song.

Gunboat. Small, heavily armed naval vessel of light draft, for use in rivers and coastal waters. "Where the Lincoln gunboats lay"—H. C. Work. The use of warships to intimidate unruly native populations gave rise to the term *gunboat diplomacy*.

Hermaphrodite brig. See **Brig**.

Hog Island ship. Cargo vessel, built in the United States in large numbers during World War I to a standard design originated at Hog Island Shipyard near Philadelphia, to replace ships lost to German submarines. The Hog Islander was an ugly vessel which after the war was used in merchant service.

Houseboat. Floating house for living aboard. Although in the United States many houseboats are powered by engines and designed to serve essentially

as roomy cabin cruisers, especially on inland waters, the houseboat is characteristically a dwelling built on a barge, without means of self-propulsion.
Also called *shanty boat*.

Hovercraft. Vessel powered by large air screws, which moves atop the water on
a cushion of air. Large hovercraft are used as ferries across the English
Channel.

Hydrofoil. Power vessel which, once it reaches a certain speed, lifts up from the
surface of the water and rides on foils or skids, thereby attaining very high
speeds. In rough waters and at low speeds the hydrofoil operates as a normal
power boat. There are also a few sailing hydrofoils.

Icebreaker. Navy or Coast Guard motor vessel with strong, reinforced armored
bow and powerful engines, designed to break a channel through ice for
other vessels. Some icebreakers also mount propellers forward for pushing
floes and have a rounded forefoot to allow the vessel to be driven upon the
ice and crush it by its weight.

Irish wicker vessel. Ancient Irish craft, resembling a *currach*, made of wicker
thatch, to be rowed and sailed. Saint Brendan is said to have sailed a currach
to Greenland.

Ironclad. Although any modern vessel of iron or steel is technically an ironclad,
basically the term is used to denote mid-nineteenth-century wooden-
hulled steam frigates and other craft whose sides and superstructure were
reinforced by iron plate, and later any warship constructed of iron instead of
wood. The *Merrimac* and *Monitor* of the American Civil War were iron-
clads. "The rivets clinch the iron-clads,/Men learn a deadlier lore"—
Herman Melville.

Jacht. See **Yacht**.

Jackass-bark. See **Bark**.

Jollyboat. Small- to medium-sized boat carried by sailing ship, usually on stern
davits, for assorted jobs. See also **Dinghy**.

Jon boat. Small, light, rectangular-shaped craft of low freeboard, to be paddled,
rowed, or poled.

Junk. Far Eastern, especially Chinese, flat-bottomed vessel of various kinds,
with bluff lines, very high poop, overhanging stern, often with high squared
bow, and pole masts. The junk sail is lug rigged with a curved leech and
stiffened with battens running entirely across. Junks typically have little or
no keel. The *motor junk* is widely used today.

Kayak. Small Eskimo canoe, made of animal skins over wooden frames, and
covered atop except for a small opening in which the paddler fits; the skins
are then laced about him. Kayaks built of fiberglass are now widely used for
pleasure on swift-flowing inland streams.

Keelboat. Flat-bottomed covered freight craft, powered by poles or sweeps, formerly used on western U.S. rivers.

Ketch. (1) Fore-and-aft-rigged vessel, with mainmast and small aftmast stepped forward of rudder post and cockpit; see **Yawl**; (2) small seventeenth-century two-masted square-rigged coastal trading vessel. See also **Bomb-ketch**.

Landing craft. Vessel, extensively used in World War II for amphibious operations in the Pacific, the Mediterranean, Normandy, etc., equipped with a bow ramp which was lowered onto shores and beaches. There were and are a number of varieties of landing craft. The *LCI—Landing Craft, Infantry* was a small craft for setting infantry ashore from larger vessels. The *LCM—Landing Craft, Medium* was a larger vessel capable of discharging men, tanks, and vehicles. The *LCT—Landing Craft, Tank* carried tanks ashore. The *LSI—Landing Ship, Infantry* and *LSM—Landing Ship, Medium* were larger vessels which brought troops or vehicles ashore by bow ramps or via LCIs. The *LST—Landing Ship, Tank* was a large seagoing ship, originally converted from merchant use, capable of traversing hundreds of miles of ocean, and bearing troops and amphibious tanks and vehicles, as well as smaller landing craft. Today's U.S. Navy uses the *LSD—Landing Ship, Dock, LPD—Amphibious Transport Dock, LPH—Amphibious Assault Ship, LST—Landing Ship, Tank,* and smaller craft.

Launch. Small powerboat, technically a ship's boat, but more generally any small powered harbor craft.

Liberty ship. Cargo vessel of 7,000 to 10,000 tons, of which 2,770 were built in U.S. yards to a standardized design during World War II. They were widely used after the war as merchant ships. The Liberty ship was flush decked with a short, high superstructure and three masts. See also **Hog Island ship**; **Victory ship**.

Lifeboat. (1) Generic term for ship's boat carried on davits, for use in emergencies at sea; (2) strong, buoyant, oared open boat capable of being launched through surf, for rescuing persons aboard shipwrecked vessels; (3) modern engine-powered rescue craft. See also **Whaleboat**.

Liferaft. Buoyant platform raft for use in emergencies at sea, originally built of cork but now of inflatable rubber.

Lighter. Flat-bottomed boat or barge for conveying passengers and cargo between anchored ships and shore installations and for general harbor use. Although originally the term meant a towed vessel, it can also signify a powered craft. "The hay-boat, the belated lighter"—Walt Whitman.

Lightship. Vessel equipped with powerful light, stationed offshore to warn ships of dangerous shoals and obstructions. Most lightships have now been replaced by beacons and radio buoys. "Blast my eyes, but the light-ship is hid by the mist, lads"—Herman Melville.

Liner. Large seagoing passenger vessel; an *ocean liner*. The heyday of the *transatlantic liner* was the period from the late nineteenth century through the mid–1960s; among the largest and best known of these were the

Aquitania, Mauretania, Queen Mary, Queen Elizabeth, Normandie, Ile de France, United States, Leonardo da Vinci, and, earlier, the ill-fated *Titanic* and *Lusitania.* When jet aircraft service supplanted passenger ships on the North Atlantic, some transatlantic liners were adapted for cruising use. *Coastal liners* were smaller passenger vessels operating between coastal seaports. "The Liner she's a lady"—Rudyard Kipling. Also see **Cruise liner**.

Lobster boat. See **Fishing boat**.

Longboat. Largest boat carried by a merchant vessel. "Put him in the longboat 'til he's sober"—folk song, "What Shall We Do with the Drunken Sailor?"

Longliner. Fishing vessel, principally for tuna, which uses lines up to 50 miles in length with baited hooks strung with floats, released over the stern and then reeled in across a roller mounted on the stern.

Longship. Long Viking war galley, with places for up to 80 oarsmen and a loose-footed square sail. Norse longships raided along the coasts of Europe and the British Isles, into the Mediterranean, and perhaps as far as the North American continent. See also **Drakar; Viking ship**.

Lugger. Lugsail-rigged harbor and coastal merchant vessel, typically two masted.

Man-of-war. Any sizable fighting craft, but the term is generally used to designate a large, full-rigged warship, whether a frigate or a ship-of-the-line. The man-of-war evolved from the carrack and the galleon. "Yon black man-of-war hawk that wheels in the light/O'er the black ship's white sky-s'l"—Herman Melville.

Minelayer. Naval vessel especially equipped to plant mines. Destroyers, corvettes, patrol boats, submarines, converted merchant ships and trawlers have been used for mine laying, as have aircraft. The celebrated 230-mile-long North Sea mine barrage of 1918 was laid mainly by converted U.S. coastal vessels and obsolete warships. Today's navies include craft designed specifically for coastal mine laying.

Minesweeper. Naval vessel, with hull of wood, bronze, fiberglass, or other non-magnetic materials, designed to locate and to remove or detonate acoustic, contact, and magnetic mines. Minesweepers are classified into three types: ocean, coastal, and inshore. Also known as *mine-craft*.

Monitor. Shallow-draft, heavily-armored warship of very low freeboard, with turreted heavy guns, for coastal bombardment and defense. The original *Monitor*, from which this class of warship takes its name, was described as a "cheesebox on a raft" because of its low flat deck and single revolving gun turret, and was slow and unseaworthy. "The *Monitor* was ugly, but she served us right well"—Herman Melville.

Mosquito boat. See **Torpedo boat**. Also, small sail-powered fishing craft working out of ports for shrimping and other such activities were sometimes known as the "mosquito fleet."

Motor sailer. Pleasure craft designed for regular use under either sail or power, with a relatively large engine. The motor sailer is essentially a compromise, slower than the powered cabin cruiser and less efficient but roomier and faster under power than sailing craft equipped with auxiliary engines.

MTB—motor torpedo boat. Small, fast English craft armed with torpedo tubes. See **Torpedo boat**.

Multihull. See **Catamaran**; **Trimaran**.

Oiler. Naval tanker equipped with pumps for refueling ships at sea. See **Tanker**.

Ore carrier. See **Bulk carrier**; **Great Lakes bulk carrier**.

Outboard motorboat. Small craft, usually but not always open decked, powered by a removable motor on the transom or in a well.

Packet. Originally a swift government sailing vessel of medium size used to deliver dispatches and mail. The term came in the nineteenth century to mean any fast, smartly fitted-out passenger or cargo vessel adhering to a schedule. A *steam packet* was a fast, medium-sized passenger vessel following a regular run. The term persisted through the nineteenth and into the early twentieth centuries for scheduled inland and coastal passenger craft, high-sided and of wooden construction with overnight accommodations. "Beware these packet ships, I say—"—folk song, "Across the Western Ocean."

Paddlewheeler. Steam vessel propelled by paddlewheels located at the sides or on the stern. Seagoing and harbor paddlewheel vessels were almost always *sidewheelers*. *Sternwheelers* were used primarily on inland waters. Although the development of the screw propeller rendered paddlewheel propulsion obsolete, sidewheeler harbor tugs and excursion boats remained in service long after the paddle steamer had disappeared from the high seas.

Pilot boat. Fast, seaworthy boat, formerly sail, now power, to transport harbor and river pilots to and from ships.

Pink. Sailing craft with narrow, overhanging stern, common in the seventeenth and eighteenth centuries. Baltic and North Sea pinks were variously rigged; Mediterranean pinks were lateen rigged.

Pinky. Also *pinkie*; two-masted, fore-and-aft-rigged fishing boat, named after the pink. The *New England pinky* had a narrow, raised stern and sharply raked masts, and was schooner rigged. The *Yarmouth pinky* of the east coast of England had a less-pronounced lift to the narrow stern and flatter lines.

Pinnace. (1) Small, flat-sterned oceangoing sailing vessel, originally square and later schooner rigged, which could be rowed. "And a pinnace, like a flutter'd bird, came flying from far away"—Alfred Tennyson; (2) ship's boat, sometimes with double-banked oars, single sail.

Pirogue. (1) Originally a West Indian dugout canoe, later a hollowed-out log canoe used in Cajun areas of Louisiana; (2) large multipaddle canoe used for loading and unloading ships through surf in Senegal.

Pocket battleship. German naval warships, armed like battleships but theoretically limited to 10,000 tons by the Treaty of Versailles, which saw action in World War II as commerce raiders. The *Graf Spee,* scuttled off the River Plate in 1939 after a duel with three British cruisers, was a pocket battleship. See also **Battleship.**

Pole-and-line craft. Large fishing vessel which uses hooks and lines to catch tuna by chumming, with two or three poles and lines, manned by fishermen, to each unbaited hook; a *tuna clipper.*

Pontoon boat. Boat, usually small pleasure craft, with deck and superstructure mounted upon hollow cylinders or tanks. Outboard-powered pontoon boats with canopies have become very popular on inland lakes and reservoirs.

Power cruiser. See **Cabin cruiser.**

Pram. Small blunt-ended dinghy.

Prau. Malayan sailing craft of various kinds, which may be rowed or sailed. Also *prao, prahu.*

Pre-position ship. Large arklike but fast ship developed by the United States for swift delivery and unloading of a supply of tanks, vehicles, artillery, etc., to a trouble spot for use by troops.

Proa. Swift-sailing double-ended canoe of the Orient carrying lateen sail and with outrigger sailed to leeward.

PT boat—patrol torpedo boat. Small, fast U.S. Navy craft equipped with torpedo tubes. A PT boat evacuated General Douglas MacArthur from Bataan in 1942. PT–109 became famous as the craft aboard which President John F. Kennedy served during World War II. See **Torpedo boat.**

Puget Sound crab boat. See **Fishing boat.**

Pungy. Chesapeake Bay working schooner used for dredging oysters.

Punt. Small flat-bottomed, square-ended workboat which can be rowed or poled. "As the slow punt swings round"—Matthew Arnold.

Purse-seiner. Any workboat which draws purse seines—large cylindrical nets open at the front, which can be closed by pulling drawstrings. Purse-seiners are used in ocean fishing throughout the world for taking salmon, herring, pilchard, tuna, mackerel, and menhaden.

Pushboat. Tugboat which pushes rather than pulls barges, widely used on inland waterways, with square bow and two large knees which rest against stern of rearmost barge. Pushboats have very high wheel-houses in order to permit the helmsman to see ahead over the barges being pushed. Also *towboat.*

Q-ship. Antisubmarine craft of World War I, disguised as merchantman but with concealed guns, torpedoes, etc., designed to lure submarine to surface. A few were used in World War II but to little effect. Also *Q-boat.*

Quadrireme, quinquireme. Galleys of the Classical period. Björn Landström and Graham Blackburn both doubt that four- and five-banked vessels were used, and assume that the terms refer to the number of rowers. A quadrireme would have two banks of two-man oars, a quinquireme a top and bottom bank of two-man oars and a middle bank of one-man oars. "Quinquireme of Nineveh from distant Ophir"—John Masefield.

Raft. Water-borne platform, open or sheltered. "You feel mighty free and easy and comfortable on a raft"—Mark Twain.

Ram. Warship with sharply pointed beak projecting from bow. The Laird rams being built for the Confederacy in England during the American Civil War, but never delivered, were steam ironclad vessels designed to break the Union blockade of southern ports. "Under the waterline a *ram*'s blow is dealt"—Herman Melville.

Reefer. Refrigerated ship for carrying perishable goods such as tropical fruit.

Roman trader. Merchant vessel, with single loose-footed square sail, steering sail at prow, broad and round with high carved gooseneck stern post. See also **Corbita**.

Rowboat. Although there are dozens of different kinds of rowboats, when used today the term generally denotes a small flat-bottomed skiff with a single set of oars.

Sampan. Light boat of the Orient, sculled or sail powered.

Schooner. Originally a Dutch fishing vessel. All schooners have fore-and-aft rigging, to allow them to sail close to the wind. The characteristic schooner, whether for pleasure or for work, is double masted, the aftermast being taller than the foremast. Schooners have also carried square-rigged topsails. Late-nineteenth- and early-twentieth-century merchant schooners were often steel hulled, and carried four, five, or six masts. The *Thomas W. Lawson*, a 5,000-ton schooner built in 1902 and lost in 1907, was seven masted, with identical, easily exchanged sails on the five middle masts, and could be handled with a 16-man crew. As late as the 1930s, long after the steamship had taken over, multimasted schooners were still used along the North American coast for transporting lumber. There were numerous varieties of schooners, among the better-known American types being the *Gloucester fishing schooner*, the *Great Lakes schooner*, and the *pungy*. Although two-masted schooners are still used as pleasure craft, they have largely given way to the sloop, ketch, and cutter. "There's a schooner in the offing,/With her topsails shot with fire"—Richard Hovey.

Scow. (1) Square-ended, flat-bottomed working craft, used to load and unload cargo, to transport garbage offshore, etc.; (2) fast, blunt-ended, broad-beamed racing sloop with long overhangs.

Scull. Very light, narrow oared single- or two-person racing boat. See also **Shell**. There is a famous oil painting by Thomas Eakins, *Max Schmitt in a Single Scull*.

Shallop. (1) Small two-masted European vessel, fore and aft or lugsail rigged, of the seventeenth, eighteenth, and nineteenth centuries; (2) light open pleasure or fishing boat, also used sometimes as a tender on large sailing warships.

Sharpie. Shallow-draft, flat-bottomed centerboard craft, most often with two cat-rigged masts.

Shell. Oared racing boat, very light and fast, wide enough only for a single oarsman, with outriggers. Eight-oared shells, with a coxswain, are used in intercollegiate racing. "On Boston Basin, shells/Hit water by the Union Boat Club wharf"—Robert Lowell. See also **Scull**.

Ship-of-the-line. Full-rigged warship, of a size large enough to participate in the line of battle during a naval engagement between fleets. British usage of the eighteenth century and Napoleonic Wars rated warships by the number of guns, the first three categories being ships-of-the-line. At the time of the battle of Trafalgar, 1805, a first-rate ship such as Nelson's *Victory* carried 100 guns or more, a second rater from 84 to 100 guns, a third rater 70 to 90. Later these figures were increased. "The full-sailed fleets, the shrouded show/of Ships-of-the-Line"—Herman Melville.

Skiff. (1) Flat-bottomed rowboat; (2) earlier, any light sailing vessel.

Skipjack. Chesapeake Bay and Atlantic Coast sailing workboat, sharp chined with single raked mast and centerboard. Skipjacks are of shallow draft, with a wide V bottom.

Sloop. (1) Single-masted, fore-and-aft-rigged boat, Marconi (Bermudan)- or gaff-rigged main, usually with a single jib. The mast of a sloop is stepped farther forward than that of a cutter, but farther aft than a cat-boat's. ". . . The white sails of schooners and sloops"—Walt Whitman. See also **Friendship sloop**. (2) The *Sloop-of-war* was a sailing warship used for convoying, scouting, and privateering, with a single deck of guns, usually below a frigate in size, though some later sloops-of-war were as big as frigates and more powerful because they carried heavy guns. The *ship-sloop* was three masted, the *brig-sloop* two masted. The sloop-of-war could also be rowed. (3) In World War II, a small antisubmarine escort naval craft was called a sloop.

Smack. Small fore-and-aft-rigged fishing boat. "Not a skiff, nor a yawl, or a mackerel boat,/Nor a smack across Neptune's face"—Thomas Hood.

Snow. (pronounced to rhyme with *cow*). Sailing ship, similar to a brig with square-sail-rigged fore- and mainmasts, but somewhat larger and with a third mast stepped very close to the second or mainmast, carrying a spanker sail. See **Brig**.

Sportfisherman. Cabin cruiser, but with smaller cabin accommodations and a large open stern cockpit. Most sportfishermen have flying bridges and often tuna towers.

Steam schooner. Single- or double-ended wooden vessel used in the Pacific Northwest to carry lumber during the late nineteenth and early twentieth centuries.

Submarine. Diesel- or nuclear-powered craft designed for underwater service, armed with torpedoes and missiles. In the U.S. Navy a submarine is usually, and with some affection (and affectation), called a boat rather than a ship, despite greatly increased size. In World War II the submarine became the U.S. Navy's most successful weapon against the Japanese fleet and merchant marine. "We all live in a yellow submarine"—the Beatles.

Submarine rescue ship. Naval craft especially designed to rescue trapped submarines. Some later models are twin hulled, to facilitate launching a rescue submarine, the Deep Sea Rescue Vessel, or DSRV, between them.

Tanker. Vessel designed to transport bulk liquid, especially oil. *Coastal tankers* are smaller than oceangoing tankers, which include *supertankers* of up to 500,000 tons. There are also tanker *barges* for transporting bulk liquid on waterways and rivers. Older tankers have a bridge amidships and engines aft, but the latest designs have the bridge and living quarters for the crew concentrated right over the engines. Coastal tankers have always had the superstructure and engines located at the stern. Also see **Oiler**.

Tea clipper. Mid- to late-nineteenth-century sailing ship used to transport tea or other high-priority cargo from the Orient to England. See **Clipper ship**.

Tender. Vessel designed to service or to carry people and cargo to and from other vessels, lighthouses, buoys, etc. (1) A naval *destroyer tender* or *submarine tender*, a large seagoing ship, equipped with extensive repair facilities; (2) a *buoy tender* designed for maintaining harbor, seaway, and waterway buoys and markers; (3) a small craft, such as a dinghy, carried aboard a larger vessel. See **Cockboat**; **Cutter**; **Dinghy**; **Dory**; **Gig**; **Jollyboat**; **Launch**; **Longboat**; **Pinnace**; **Punt**; **Whaler**; **Yawl boat**, *etc.*

Torpedo boat. Small, very fast naval vessel equipped with torpedo tubes, originally designed to be used for coastal defense; sometimes referred to as a *mosquito boat*. The PT boat, the German E-boat, the British MTB—Motor torpedo boat, etc., are all developed from the torpedo-boat prototype.

Torpedo boat destroyer. See **Destroyer**.

Towboat. (1) Tugboat; (2) pushboat, with high knees at bow for pushing barges along rivers and waterways. See **Pushboat**; **Tugboat**.

Tramp steamer. Merchant ship without a regular route, picking up and delivering cargo from port to port as offered. "And I'd sell my tired soul for the bucking beam-sea roll/Of a black Bilbao tramp"—Rudyard Kipling. See **Freighter**.

Transport. A *troopship*. By a transport is sometimes meant a ship built or maintained by the U.S. Army or Navy for the specific purpose of transporting troops, as distinguished from a peacetime passenger vessel converted into temporary troopship service during hostilities. See **Attack transport**; **Troopship**.

Trawler. Fishing vessel rigged to drag trawl nets through water. Sailing trawlers were of various kinds. Trawlers today are motorized. *Stern trawlers,* such as shrimp trawlers, tend to be wide beamed and square sterned, with high bow, wheelhouse well forward, with masts, outriggers, and booms to handle nets. *Side trawlers,* which tend to be larger, oceangoing craft, have their wheelhouse and engines aft, with open deck amidships and with cranes for working nets over either side.

Trawler yacht. Wide-beamed pleasure craft with displacement rather than planing hull, powered, taking its hull configuration from the commercial fishing trawler. A trawler yacht trades speed through the water for comfort and roominess.

Trimaran. Vessel with three hulls. See also **Catamaran**.

Trireme. Galley with three banks of oars. See **Galley**; **Bireme**, etc.

Troller. Fishing craft, commercial or pleasure, which takes fish by trailing a lure or baited hook behind a slowly moving boat. See **Sportfisherman**.

Troopship. Passenger ship, often a *liner,* designed or converted to carry troops. During World War II the *Queen Mary* and *Queen Elizabeth* could carry all or most of an entire army division. The *Queen Elizabeth II* and the *Canberra* were temporarily converted to troopship service during the Falkland Islands fighting in 1982.

Tugboat. Craft designed to pull or push ships, barges, etc. Tugs have powerful engines, with high gear ratios for producing power rather than speed. *Harbor tugs* work inshore, docking and undocking ships, performing waterfront duties. *Oceangoing tugs* are larger craft designed to make extensive sea voyages towing barges and other craft. *Salvage tugs* are slow but rugged and especially seaworthy vessels which take disabled ships and other watercraft in tow, sometimes during storm conditions. "The big steam-tug closely flank'd on each side by the barges"—Walt Whitman. See also **Pushboat**; **Towboat**.

Tuna clipper. See **Pole-and-line craft**.

U-Boat. German submarine. See **Submarine**.

Victory ship. U.S. cargo ship of 7,500 tons or larger, built in large numbers during World War II. The Victory ship was three knots faster than the Liberty ship, with larger superstructure and a longer forecastle. Like the Liberty ship it saw widespread commercial use after 1945. See also **Freighter**; **Hog Island ship**; **Liberty ship**.

Viking ship. Long, usually open-hulled Scandinavian galley, for rowing and sailing, with high stem and stern posts. There were numerous types of such ships, for merchant and war use, dating from many centuries before the Christian Era through the early Middle Ages. They were masted, with a loose-footed square sail. The *longship* was the dreaded war galley. The *cog* of Northern Europe was the direct descendant of the Viking merchant ship. See **Cog**; **Drakar**; **Longship**.

Water scooter. Abominable and dangerous small jet-powered one-person pleasure craft designed to allow teenagers to crisscross bows and wakes of larger
craft.

Whaleback. Long bulk-carrying vessel designed for use on the Great Lakes, with
spoon bow and with decks and topsides rounded to permit self storing of
cargoes and to minimize cargoes shifting during storms. As with other
Great Lakes bulk carriers, the wheelhouse was located at the bow and the
engines at the stern. See **Great Lakes bulk carrier**.

Whaleboat. (1) Small open, double-ended rowing craft, carried aboard whaling
ships and lowered in pursuit of whales; (2) thereafter, any open, double-
ended oared boat used for coastal work. The lifeboat is built along whaleboat lines. "The hurt beast/Bobbing by Ahab's whaleboats in the East"—
Robert Lowell. Also see **Lifeboat**.

Whale-killer. Motor-powered vessel equipped with a harpoon gun.

Whaler. (1) Warship's boat; (2) whaling ship; (3) *trade name for small, open,
cathedral-hulled craft of fiberglass construction, outboard powered*.

Whaling ship. Also called *whaler*. The term refers to vessels of various kinds,
formerly of sail, now motorized, used to hunt whales. The American whaling ship, of which the *Pequod* in Melville's *Moby-Dick* was an example,
was square rigged, and two or three masted, and lowered whaleboats from
davits when whales were sighted. As described in *Moby-Dick*, the whaling
ship carried equipment for rendering the whale and storing sperm oil in barrels. "A whaleship was my Yale College and my Harvard"—Herman
Melville.

Wherry. (1) Small, open rowing craft of the British Isles; (2) British coastal cargo
sailing vessel.

Windjammer. Any square-rigged sailing ship.

Windsurfer. Surfboard with single lateen-rigged sail. Also called *sailboard*.

Xebec. Mediterranean sailing vessel, with overhanging bow and stern, typically
three masted with lateen-rigged sails but often with square sails on foremast. The xebec, heavily armed with cannon, saw extensive use as a corsair
ship by the Barbary pirates and others.

Yacht. (1) Originally *jacht*, a fast Dutch dispatch boat, single masted with fore-
and-aft mainsail, topsail, and several headsails—essentially a *cutter*—and
with leeboards rather than keels for use in shoal water and the Zuider Zee;
(2) from the mid-seventeenth century onward a pleasure boat, either a sailing vessel or, after the mid-nineteenth century, motor powered. As John
Rousmaniere writes in *The Golden Pastime*, leisure and love of luxury are
two of the prime components of classical yachting: "his ancestors and
friends, his reputation and works, his land and horses, his yacht and bank
account"—William James. Generally speaking, a yacht may be defined as
any pleasure vessel of 50 feet or longer. There were yachts, of course, long

before the term was invented; the barge on which Cleopatra entertained Mark Antony was by any plausible definition a yacht.

Yawl. (1) Cruising fore-and-aft-rigged sailboat, with mainmast and a small mizzen stepped abaft of the cockpit, rather than forward of it as with the ketch. "His nine-knot yawl/Was auctioned off to lobstermen"—Robert Lowell. (2) Any of several Northern European coastal sailing craft.

Yawl boat. Small round-bottomed, flat-stern craft carried on davits at the stern of a coastal sailing vessel. See **Tender**.

SOURCES

Baker, W. A., and Tre Tryckare. *The Engine Powered Vessel.* New York: Grosset and Dunlap, 1965.

Blackburn, Graham. *The Illustrated Encyclopedia of Ships, Boats, Vessels, and Other Water-Borne Craft.* Woodstock, N.Y.: Overlook Press, 1978.

Blair, Carvel Hall, and Willits Dyer Ansel. *A Guide to Fishing Boats and Their Gear.* Cambridge, Md.: Cornell Maritime Press, Inc., 1968.

Culver, Henry B. *The Book of Old Ships.* New York: Dover Publications, 1992.

Dodman, Frank E. *Observer's Book of Ships.* London: Frederick Warne & Co., editions for 1966 and 1990.

Knight, Austin M. *Modern Seamanship.* 14th ed. Revised by Captain John V. Noel, Jr., assisted by William J. Miller. Princeton, N.J.: D. Van Nostrand Co., 1966.

Landström, Björn. *Sailing Ships.* New York: Doubleday and Co., 1969.

Moloney, Elbert S. *Chapman's Piloting, Seamanship, and Small Boat Handling.* 58th ed. New York: Hearst Marine Books, 1987.

Noel, John V., Jr., and Edward L. Beach. *Naval Terms Dictionary.* 5th ed. Annapolis: U.S. Naval Institute Press, 1988.

Rogers, John G. *Origins of Sea Terms.* 2nd ed. Mystic, Conn.: Mystic Seaport Museum, 1985.

Rousmaniere, John. *The Golden Pastime: A New History of Yachting.* New York: W. W. Norton, 1986.

"Ship," "History of Shipping." *Encyclopaedia Britannica.* 14th ed. Chicago: Encyclopaedia Britannica Co., Inc., 1957.

Webster's New International Dictionary of the English Language. 2nd ed., unabridged. Vols. I–III. Springfield, Mass.: G. and C. Merriam Co., 1959.

—L.D.R.

2

GREYHOUNDS OF THE NORTH ATLANTIC: THE GREAT LINERS

· · · · ·

SINCLAIR LEWIS ARRIVES IN NEW YORK ABOARD THE AQUITANIA. TO THE waiting ship-news reporters he sounds off about the snobbery and clannishness of British writers, and the terrible poverty in the slums of English cities.

Ernest Hemingway comes home from his African safari aboard the *Ile de France*. He tells the ship-news reporters he is headed for Key West for a "season of intensive writing" in order to earn enough money to return to Africa.

Thomas Wolfe returns to New York aboard the *Bremen* on the Fourth of July, is met by Maxwell Perkins, tells the host of ship-news reporters his impressions of conditions in Nazi Germany.

There is nothing comparable nowadays to the glamor of the arrival of the great transatlantic ocean liners at the Hudson River piers, with the celebrities being interviewed, the flashguns popping, and the general bustle and excitement. Nor, for that matter, can one imagine so much attention being paid any more to mere literary figures and what they might have to say about anything.

The heyday of the transatlantic luxury liner began at the turn of the twentieth century, when ships became really large and fast. The two British lines, Cunard and White Star, competed with two German lines, Hamburg-America (HAPAG) and North German Lloyd, for the blue riband for swift crossing between Europe and America. The First World War removed German liners from the high seas, and the larger German ships were taken over by the victorious Allies and renamed.

Few large ships were built in the 1920s; the 1930s, however, despite the showdown caused by the Great Depression, saw the advent of larger and faster liners than ever before. After World War II, air travel began siphoning off passengers from the sea lanes. Not until the advent of jet service in the 1960s, however, reducing passage time from what had been at least five days to a matter of five or six hours, was the day of the transatlantic liner done. By the mid–1970s only the Cunard Line's *Queen Elizabeth II* was still making transatlantic runs, and then only a few times each summer.

Some of the liners were adaptable for tropical cruising, and remained in service after their transatlantic days ended. The onetime *France*, for example, is now the *Norway* and a regular caller at Caribbean ports. More typically, however, the decline of North Atlantic passenger service meant the boneyard for the onetime greyhounds of the sea.

The list that follows is a selection of some of the best-known, most memorable liners from the great days of passenger travel on the North Atlantic run. They have been chosen for various reasons—length of service, speed, popularity, fame, occasionally tragedy (*e.g.*, the *Titanic*, or the Anchor-Donaldson Line's *Athenia*, the first ship to be torpedoed in World War II). All ships chosen were of 10,000 gross registered tonnage or more. Most were in service between New York City and northern European ports.

When ships were renamed, the new names have been given, but have been cross-listed only when such names were used while the ship was in transatlantic service. The most complete and thoroughgoing guide to the transatlantic liners is Arnold Kludas' magnificent five-volume compilation, *Great Passenger Ships of the World*, translated by Charles Hodges, with illustrations to show all phases of each ship's history. See Sources, below.

Albert Ballin. 627 ft., 20,815 gross tons (GRT). Hamburg-America Line. Launched, 1922. Renamed *Hansa*, 1935. German training ship, 1940. Struck mine, sank, 1945. Raised, 1949. Renamed *Sovietski Sojus*, 1953.

America. 723 ft., 26,454 GRT. United States Lines. Launched, 1939. Renamed U.S. Navy transport *West Point*, 1942. Returned to United States Lines, renamed *America*, 1946. Sold, 1964, renamed *Australis*. Sold, 1978, renamed *Americabut*. Wrecked, 1994.

Amerika. 700 ft., 22,225 GRT. Hamburg-America Line. Launched, 1905, largest ship in world when built. Interned, Boston, 1914. Renamed U.S. Navy transport *America*, 1917. Sank, 1918. Raised, back in service, United States Lines, 1919. Laid up, 1931. Renamed U.S. Maritime Commission accommodation ship *Edmund B. Alexander*, 1941. Troop transport, 1941. Laid up, 1949. Broken up, 1958.

Andrea Doria. 700 ft., 29,083 GRT. "Italia" S.A.N. Launched, 1951. Rammed by *Stockholm* and sank, 1956.

Aquitania. 901 ft., 45,647 GRT. Cunard Line. Launched, 1913. Troop transport, 1915–18; 1939–45. Sold for breaking up, 1949.

Athenia. 538 ft., 13,465 GRT. Anchor-Donaldson Line. Launched, 1922. Torpedoed and sunk, September 3, 1939, first submarine victim of World War II.

Baltic. 726 ft., 23,884 GRT. White Star Line. Launched, 1903, largest ship in world when built. Laid up, 1932, sold for breaking up, 1933.

Batory. 526 ft., 14,287 GRT. Gdynia-America Line. Launched, 1935. British troop transport, 1939. Returned to Gdynia-America Line, 1946. Sold for hotel ship, 1969. Sold for breaking up, 1971.

Berengaria. See **Imperator**.

Bergensfjord. 578 ft., 18,739 GRT. Norwegian-American Line. Launched, 1955. Sold, 1971, renamed *DeGrasse*. Sold, 1973, renamed *Rasa Sayang*.

Berlin. (1) 572 ft., 15,286 GRT. North German Lloyd Line. Launched, 1925. Laid up, 1938. Hospital ship, 1939. Sank after hitting mine, 1945. Raised, renamed *Admiral Nachimow*, 1949. (2) See **Gripsholm**.

Bismarck. 956 ft., 56,551 GRT. Hamburg-America Line. Launched, 1914. Completed by British, 1922. Largest ship in world when built. Sold to White Star Line, 1921, renamed *Majestic*. Laid up, 1936. Renamed British training ship *Caledonia*, 1937. Burned out, sank, 1939. Sold for scrap, 1940.

Bremen. (1) 938 ft., 51,656 GRT. North German Lloyd Line. Launched, 1928. Blue riband, 1929, 1930. Naval accommodation ship, 1940. Burnt out, 1941, scrapped. (2) 697 ft., 29,253 GRT. Launched, 1938, as *Pasteur* for Cie Sudatlantique. British troopship, 1940. Sold, 1957. Renamed *Bremen*, 1959. Sold, 1971. Renamed *Regina Magna*, 1972. Laid up, 1974.

Britannic. 712 ft., 26,943 GRT. White Star Line. Launched, 1929. Troop transport, 1939. Returned to Cunard-White Star Line, 1947. Broken up, 1961.

Campania. 622 ft., 12,950 GRT. Cunard Line. Launched, 1892. Blue riband, 1893, 1894. Rebuilt as aircraft carrier HMS *Campania*, 1916. Sank after collision, 1918.

Carinthia. 608 ft., 21,947 GRT. Cunard Line. Launched, 1955. Sold, 1968, renamed *Fairland*. Renamed *Fairsea*, 1971. Renamed *Fair Princess*, 1984.

Carmania. (1) 675 ft., 19,524 GRT. Cunard Line. Launched, 1905. First turbine-driven Cunard liner. Broken up, 1932. (2) See **Saxonia**.

Caronia. (1) 678 ft., 19,594 GRT. Cunard Line. Launched, 1904. Broken up, 1933. (2) 715 ft., 34,183 GRT. Cunard-White Star Line. Launched, 1947. Sold, 1968, renamed *Columbia*, then *Caribia*. Laid up after explosion, 1969. Sold for breaking up, 1974.

Carpathia. 558 ft., 13,564 GRT. Cunard Line. Launched, 1902. Rescued 700 survivors of *Titanic*, 1912. Torpedoed, sank, 1914.

Celtic. 700 ft., 20,904 GRT. White Star Line. Launched, 1901. Largest ship in world when built. Stranded in storm, 1928, sold for breaking up.

Champlain. 641 ft., 28,124 GRT. Compagnie Générale Transatlantique. Launched, 1931. Struck mine, sank, scrapped, 1940.

City of New York. 560 ft., 10,499 GRT. Inman Line. Launched, 1888. First twin-screw express steamer. Blue riband, 1892. Sold, 1893, renamed *New York*. Renamed U.S. Navy auxiliary cruiser *Harvard*, 1898. Returned to American Line, 1901. Renamed U.S. Navy transport *Plattsburg*, 1917. Broken up, 1923.

City of Paris. 560 ft., 10,499 GRT. Inman Line. Launched, 1888. Blue riband, 1889, 1892. Sold, 1893, renamed *Paris*. Renamed U.S. Navy auxiliary cruiser *Yale*, 1898. Renamed *Philadelphia*, 1901. Renamed U.S. Navy transport *Harrisburg*, 1917. Broken up, 1923.

Columbus. See **Homeric**.

Constitution. 682 ft., 23,754 GRT. American Export Lines. Launched, 1950. Laid up, 1968. Sold, 1974, renamed *Oceanic Constitution*. Laid up, 1974. Later renamed *Constitution*.

Conte di Savoia. 815 ft., 48,502 GRT. "Italia" Flotta Riunite. Launched, 1931. Laid up, 1939. Bombed, sank, 1943. Raised, 1945, but not rebuilt; sold for scrap, 1950.

Cristoforo Colombo. 700 ft., 29,191 GRT. "Italia" S.A.N. Launched, 1953. Sold for hotel ship, 1977.

Deutschland. 684 ft., 16,502 GRT. Hamburg-America Line. Launched, 1900. Blue riband, 1900, 1901. Renamed *Victoria Luise*, 1917. Renamed *Hansa*, 1921. Broken up, 1925.

Duchess of Atholl. 601 ft., 20,119 GRT. Canadian Pacific Line. Launched, 1927. Troop transport, 1939. Torpedoed, sank, 1942.

Duchess of Bedford. 601 ft., 20,123 GRT. Canadian Pacific Line. Launched, 1929. Troop transport, 1939. Refitted, renamed *Empress of India*, then *Empress of France*, 1947. Broken up, 1960.

Duchess of Richmond. 600 ft., 20,022 GRT. Canadian Pacific Line. Launched, 1928. Troop transport, 1940. Renamed *Empress of Canada*, 1947. Burnt out, sank, 1953. Sold for breaking up, 1954.

Duchess of York. 601 ft., 20,021 GRT. Canadian Pacific Line. Launched, 1928. Troop transport, 1940. Bombed, set on fire, sank, 1943.

Empress of Britain. (1) 760 ft., 42,348 GRT. Canadian Pacific Line. Launched, 1930. Troop transport, 1939. Bombed, torpedoed, sank, 1940. (2) 640 ft., 25,516 GRT. Canadian Pacific Line. Launched, 1955. Sold, 1964, renamed *Queen Anna Maria*. Sold, 1975, renamed *Carnivale*.

Empress of Canada. (1) See Duchess of Richmond. (2) 650 ft., 27,284 GRT. Canadian Pacific Line. Launched, 1960. Sold, 1972, renamed *Mardi Gras*.

Empress of France. See Duchess of Bedford.

Empress of Scotland. See Kaiserin Auguste Victoria.

Europa. 941 ft., 49,746 GRT. North German Lloyd Line. Launched, 1928. Blue riband, 1930. Naval ship, 1939. U.S. Navy transport, 1945. Handed over to France, renamed *Liberté*, 1946. Sank, 1946. Refitted, 1950. Scrapped, 1962.

Flandre. 600 ft., 20,469 GRT. Compagnie Générale Transatlantique. Launched, 1951. Sold, 1968, renamed *Carla Costa*.

France. (1) 713 ft., 23,666 GRT. Compagnie Générale Transatlantique. Launched, 1910. Troopship, 1914, renamed *France IV*. Returned to Compagnie Générale Transatlantique, 1919, renamed *France*. Laid up, 1934. Sold for breaking up, 1934. (2) 1035 ft., 66,348 GRT. Compagnie Générale Transatlantique. Launched, 1960. Largest passenger ship in world since 1972. Sold, renamed *Norway*, 1979.

Franconia. See **Ivernia**.

Friedrich der Grosse. 546 ft., 10,531 GRT. North German Lloyd Line. Launched, 1896. Interned, New York, 1914, renamed U.S. Navy troop transport *Huron*, 1917. Renamed *City of Honolulu*, 1922. Caught fire, 1922, sank.

George Washington. 723 ft., 25,570 GRT. North German Lloyd Line. Launched, 1908. Interned, New York, 1914. U.S. troop transport, 1917. Sold, 1920. Sold to United States Lines, 1921. Laid up, 1932. U.S. troop transport, 1943. Laid up, 1947. Destroyed by fire, 1951.

Georgic. 711 ft., 27,759 GRT. White Star Line. Launched, 1931. Troop transport, 1940. Badly damaged, 1941. Returned to service, 1949. Sold for breaking up, 1955.

Great Eastern. 689 ft., 18,915 GRT. Eastern Steam Navigation Company. Launched as *Leviathan*, 1858. Sold, renamed *Great Eastern*, 1858. Largest ship in world when built; length not exceeded until 1899. Fitted for cable laying, 1864. Broken up, 1889–91.

Gripsholm. (1) 573 ft., 17,993 GRT. Swedish-American Line. Launched, 1924. Sold, 1954. Sold, renamed *Berlin*, 1955. Broken up, 1966. (2) 631 ft., 23,191 GRT. Swedish-American Line. Launched, 1956. Sold, 1974, renamed *Navarino*.

Homeric. 774 ft., 34,351 GRT. Built for North German Lloyd Line as *Columbus*, launched, 1913. Handed over to Great Britain, 1919, purchased by White Star Line. Completed, renamed *Homeric*, 1920. Laid up, 1935. Sold for breaking up, 1936.

Ile de France. 792 ft., 43,153 GRT. Compagnie Générale Transatlantique. Launched, 1926. Laid up, 1939. Troop transport, 1940. Returned to Compagnie Générale Transatlantique, 1946. Sold for breaking up, 1958.

Imperator. 909 ft., 52,117 GRT. Hamburg-America Line. Launched, 1912. Largest ship in world when built. Handed over to Great Britain, 1920, sold to Cunard Line, 1921, renamed *Berengaria*. Fire, 1938, sold for breaking up.

Independence. 682 ft., 23,719 GRT. American Export Lines. Launched, 1950. Laid up, 1969. Sold, 1974, renamed *Oceanic Independence*. Laid up, 1976. Renamed *Sea Luck I*, 1976; later renamed *Independence*.

Italia. See **Kungsholm**.

Ivernia. 608 ft., 21,717 GRT. Cunard Line. Launched, 1954. Renamed *Franconia*, 1963. Laid up, 1971. Sold, 1973, renamed *Fedor Shalyapin*.

Kaiser Wilhelm der Grosse. 655 ft., 14,349 GRT. North German Lloyd Line. Launched, 1897. Blue riband, 1897. Largest ship in world when built. Auxiliary cruiser, German navy, 1914. Scuttled off Spanish West Africa, 1914.

Kaiser Wilhelm II. 707 ft., 19,361 GRT. North German Lloyd Line. Launched, 1902. Blue riband, 1906. Interned, New York, 1914, renamed U.S. Navy transport *Agamemnon*, 1917. Laid up, 1919. Renamed *Monticello*, 1929; broken up, 1940.

Kaiserin Auguste Victoria. 705 ft., 24,581 GRT. Hamburg-America Line. Launched, 1905. Largest ship in world when built. Handed over to Great Britain, 1919. Sold, renamed *Empress of Scotland*, 1921. Burnt out, sank, 1930, scrapped, 1931.

Kronzprinzessin Cecilie. 707 ft., 19,360 GRT. North German Lloyd Line. Launched, 1906. Had largest steam-reciprocating machinery ever built into a ship. Interned, Boston, 1914. Renamed U.S. Navy transport *Mount Vernon*, 1917. Torpedoed, 1918. Laid up, 1919. Broken up, 1940.

Kungsholm. (1) 609 ft., 20,223 GRT. Swedish-American Line. Launched, 1928. Sold to U.S. War Shipping Administration, renamed *John Ericsson*, 1942. Bought back by Swedish-American Line, sold, 1947. Renamed *Italia*, 1948. Sold for floating hotel, renamed *Imperial Bahama*, 1964. Broken up, 1965. (2) 600 ft., 21,141 GRT. Swedish-American Line. Launched, 1952. Sold, 1964. Renamed *Europa*, 1965.

Laconia. 623 ft., 19,680 GRT. Cunard Line. Launched, 1921. Troop transport, 1940. Torpedoed, sank, 1942.

Lafayette. 613 ft., 25,178 GRT. Compagnie Générale Transatlantique. Launched, 1929. Caught fire, destroyed, 1938.

Laurentic. 600 ft., 18,724 GRT. White Star Line. Launched, 1927. Armed cruiser, 1939. Torpedoed, sank, 1940.

Leonardo da Vinci. 767 ft., 33,340 GRT. "Italia" S.A.N., Genoa. Launched, 1958. Sold, 1976.

Leviathan. See **Vaterland**.

Liberté. See **Europa**.

Lucania. 622 ft., 12,952 GRT. Cunard Line. Launched, 1893. Blue riband, 1893, 1894. Largest ship in world when built. Burnt out, 1909, sold for scrap.

Lusitania. 787 ft., 31,550 GRT. Cunard Line. Launched, 1906. Blue riband, 1907, 1908. Torpedoed, sank, 1915.

Maasdam. 502 ft., 15,024 GRT. Holland-America Line. Launched, 1952. Badly damaged, 1963. Sold, renamed *Stefan Batory*, 1968.

Majestic. (1) 582 ft., 10,147 GRT. White Star Line. Launched, 1889. Blue riband, 1891. Broken up, 1914. (2) See **Bismarck**.

Manhattan. 705 ft., 24,289 GRT. United States Lines. Launched, 1931. Renamed U.S. Navy transport *Wakefield,* 1941. Reserve ship, 1946. Sold for breaking up, 1964.

Mauretania. (1) 790 ft., 31,938 GRT. Cunard Line. Launched, 1906. The "Greyhound of the Atlantic." Blue riband, 1907, 1908, 1909. Held blue riband until 1929. Broken up, 1935. (2) 772 ft., 35,738 GRT. Cunard-White Star Line. Launched, 1938. Laid up, 1939. Troop transport, 1940. Returned to Cunard-White Star, 1946. Sold for breaking up, 1965.

Media. 531 ft., 13,345 GRT. Cunard-White Star Line. Launched, 1946. Sold, renamed *Flavia,* 1961. Sold, 1969.

Megantic. 565 ft., 14,878 GRT. White Star Line. Launched, 1908. Troop transport, 1914. Returned to White Star Line, 1919. Laid up, 1931. Sold for breaking up, 1933.

Michelangelo. 906 ft., 45,911 GRT. "Italia" S.A.N. Launched, 1962. Laid up, 1975. Sold, 1976.

New York. See **City of New York**.

Nieuw Amsterdam. (1) 615 ft., 16,967 GRT. Holland-America Line. Launched, 1905. Broken up, 1932. (2) 759 ft., 36,287 GRT. Holland-America Line. Launched, 1937. Laid up, 1939. British troop transport, 1940. Returned to Holland-America Line, 1946. Sold for breaking up, 1974.

Normandie. 1,030 ft., 79,280 GRT. Compagnie Générale Transatlantique. Launched, 1932. Largest ship in world when built. Blue riband, 1935, 1937. Laid up, 1939. Renamed U.S. transport *Lafayette* 1941. Caught fire, heeled over on side, 1942. Sold for scrapping, 1946.

Oceanic. 704 ft., 17,272 GRT. White Star Line. Launched, 1899. Largest ship in world when built. Grounded, 1914, broken up.

Olympia. 612 ft., 22,979 GRT. Greek Line. Launched, 1955. Laid up, 1974.

Olympic. 882 ft., 45,324 GRT. White Star Line. Launched, 1910, largest ship in world when built. Laid up, 1935. Scrapped, 1937.

Oslofjord. 577 ft., 16,844 GRT. Norwegian-American Line. Launched, 1949. Chartered, renamed *Fulvia,* 1969. Caught fire, sank, 1970.

Paris. (1) See City of Paris. (2) 764 ft., 34,569 GRT. Compagnie Générale Transatlantique. Launched, 1916. Maiden voyage, 1921. Caught fire, heeled over at berth, 1939. Scrapped, 1947.

Parthia. 532 ft., 13,362 GRT. Cunard-White Star Line. Launched, 1947. Sold, 1961, renamed *Remuera,* 1962. Sold, renamed *Aramac,* 1964. Sold for breaking up, 1969.

Pasteur. See **Bremen**.

Philadelphia. See **City of Paris**.

Pilsudski. 526 ft., 14,294 GRT. Gdynia-America Line. Launched, 1934. British troop transport, 1939. Struck mine, sank, 1939.

Queen Elizabeth. 1,029 ft., 83,673 GRT. Cunard-White Star Line. Launched,

1938. Troop transport, 1940. Returned to Cunard-White Star, 1946. Sold for convention center, 1969. Sold for floating university, 1970. Caught fire, sank, 1972.

Queen Elizabeth II. 963 ft., 65,863 GRT. Cunard Line. Launched, 1968.

Queen Mary. 1,019 ft., 80,774 GRT. Cunard-White Star Line. Launched, 1934. Maiden voyage, 1936. Blue riband, 1936, 1938. Laid up, 1939. Troop transport, 1940. Return to passenger service, 1947. Sold for museum and convention center, 1967.

Raffaello. 904 ft., 45,933 GRT. "Italia" S.A.N. Launched, 1963. Laid up, 1975. Sold, 1976.

Rex. 880 ft., 51,062 GRT. "Italia" Flotta Riunite. Launched, 1931. Blue riband, 1933. Laid up, 1940. Bombed, sank, 1944.

Roma. 709 ft., 32,583 GRT. Navigazione Generale Italiana. Launched, 1926. Laid up, 1939. Taken over by Italian navy for conversion to aircraft carrier, 1940. Bombed, 1944, sunk, 1945, to prevent German use for blocking harbor of Genoa. Scrapped, 1951.

Rotterdam (1) 667 ft., 24,149 GRT. Holland-America Line. Launched, 1908. Broken up, 1940. (2) 748 ft., 38,645 GRT. Holland-America Line. Launched, 1958.

Ryndam. 502 ft., 15,015 GRT. Holland-America Line. Launched, 1950. Transferred, renamed *Waterman*, 1968. Returned to Holland-America, renamed *Ryndam*, 1968. Laid up, 1971. Sold, 1972, rebuilt, renamed *Atlas*.

Saturnia. 632 ft., 23,940 GRT. Cosulich Soc Triestina di Nav. Launched, 1925. Troop transport, 1935–36. Laid up, 1940. Transport, U.S. Navy, 1943. Renamed hospital ship *Frances Y. Slanger*, 1945. Returned to Italy, renamed *Saturnia*, 1946. Laid up, 1965. Broken up, 1966.

Saxonia. 497 ft., 21,637 GRT. Cunard Line. Launched, 1954. Renamed *Carmania*, 1962. Laid up, 1971. Sold, 1973, renamed *Leonid Sobinov*.

Statendam. 697 ft., 29,511 GRT. Holland-America Line. Launched, 1924. Maiden voyage, 1929. Laid up, 1939. Bombed, caught fire, scrapped, 1940.

Stavangerfjord. 553 ft., 12,977 GRT. Norwegian-American Line. Launched, 1917. Laid up, 1939. German accommodation ship, 1940. Returned to Norwegian-American Line, 1945. Sold for breaking up, 1963.

Sylvania. 608 ft., 21,989 GRT. Cunard Line. Launched, 1956. Sold, 1968, renamed *Fairwind*.

Titanic. 883 ft., 46,329 GRT. White Star Line. Launched, 1911. Largest ship in world when built, and supposedly "unsinkable." On maiden voyage struck iceberg, 11:40 P.M., April 14, 1912; sank 2:10 A.M., April 15.

United States. 990 ft., 53,329 GRT. United States Lines. Launched, 1951. Blue riband, 1952. Fastest commercial ship ever built. Laid up, 1969. Sold and towed to Turkey, 1993.

Vaterland. 948 ft., 54,282 GRT. Hamburg-America Line. Launched, 1913. Interned, New York, 1914. Renamed U.S. Navy transport *Leviathan*, 1917. Rebuilt for United States Lines, 1923. Laid up, 1934. Sold for breaking up, 1937.

Veendam. 579 ft., 15,450 GRT. Holland-America Line. Launched, 1922. Seized by Germany, 1940. Resumed Holland-America transatlantic service, 1947. Broken up, 1953.

Virginian. 538 ft., 10,754 GRT. Allan Line. Launched, 1904. Troop transport, 1914. Sold, 1920, renamed *Drottningholm*. Red Cross service, 1940. Sold, 1945. Renamed *Brasil*, 1948. Renamed *Homeland*, 1951. Broken up, 1955.

Volendam. 472 ft., 15,434 GRT. Holland-America Line. Launched, 1922. Taken over as transport by British, 1940. Torpedoed, 1940. Repaired, 1941. Resumed Holland-America transatlantic service, 1947. Sold for breaking up, 1952.

Vulcania. 632 ft., 23,970 GRT. Cosulich Soc Triestina di Nav. Launched, 1926. Troop transport, 1935. Troop transport, 1941. Laid up, Trieste, 1942. U.S. Army transport, 1943. Returned to "Italia" S.A.N., 1946. Sold, renamed *Caribia*, 1965. Laid up, 1972. Sold, 1974.

Washington. 705 ft., 24,289 GRT. United States Lines. Launched, 1932. Renamed U.S. Navy transport *Mount Vernon*, 1941. Renamed *Washington*, 1945. Chartered by United States Lines, 1948. Laid up, 1951. Sold for breaking up, 1964.

SOURCES

Bowen, Frank C. *A Century of Atlantic Travel, 1830–1930.* Boston: Little, Brown and Co., 1930.

Braynard, Frank O., and William H. Miller. *Fifty Famous Liners.* New York: W. W. Norton, 1982.

Cairis, Nicholas T. *Passenger Liners of the World Since 1893.* Rev. ed. New York: Bonanza Books, 1979.

Kludas, Arnold. *Great Passenger Ships of the World.* Translated by Charles Hodges. 5 vols. Wellingborough, Eng.: Patrick Stephens, 1975–77.

Maxtone-Grahame, John. *The Only Way to Cross.* New York: Macmillan, 1972.

Various issues of *Steamboat Bill*, published by American Steamship Historical Society.

—L.D.R.

3

SOME FAMOUS TRAINS

I am riding on a limited express,
one of the crack trains of the nation.
—CARL SANDBURG, "Limited"

·　·　·　·　·

IT WOULD BE DIFFICULT FOR ANYONE WHO IS LESS THAN, SAY, FIFTY YEARS OLD to understand the imaginative importance that the railroad exercised on the minds of writers. But one need only consult many of the important American novels written between Nathaniel Hawthorne's *The House of Seven Gables* (1851) and Eudora Welty's *The Optimist's Daughter* (1972) to find vivid portraits of trains in action and passengers riding aboard them whenever travel is appropriate to the story.

To cite only a few examples among many, consider the train leaving Chicago for the West and the holidays in Fitzgerald's *The Great Gatsby*, the numerous train trips in Thomas Wolfe's fiction, Carrie Meeber's trip to Chicago and Hurstwood's and Carrie's escape to Canada in Dreiser's *Sister Carrie*, the railroad machinations in Samuel L. Clemens' and Charles Dudley Warner's *The Gilded Age*, the Marches' trip to New York in Howell's *A Hazard of New Fortunes*, Quentin Compson's return home to Mississippi from Harvard for the holidays in Faulkner's *The Sound and the Fury*, the departure of Jack Burden's mother for the West at the close of Warren's *All the King's Men*, Hazel Motes's journey to Atlanta in Flannery O'Connor's *Wise Blood*, among others. All those authors were provincials; it was the train that would transport them to the metropolis, where literary careers, fame, and fortune supposedly awaited them.

The present-day Amtrak system can give little idea of the prevalence, and importance, of trains. The major railroads all had crack passenger trains of their own, bearing names, and there was competition among them. The traveler between New York City and Chicago could choose from among the Pennsylvania Railroad's Broadway Limited and Pennsylvania Limited, the New York Central's Commodore Vanderbilt and Twentieth Century Limited, and a half dozen lesser trains on those and the Erie system. The traveler between Chicago and Los Angeles debated the merits of the Santa Fe's Super Chief and the Union Pacific's City of Los Angeles.

One could journey to Florida from the Northeast via either the Atlantic Coast Line's Champions and Florida and Havana Specials, or the Seaboard Air Line's Silver Meteor or Orange Blossom Special. Between Chicago and Minneapolis the choice was between the Rockets of the Rock Island, the 400 of the Milwaukee Road, and the Burlington Zephyr. And so on.

In the British Isles and Europe there were crack trains too, and although rail service there has also experienced competition from automobiles and air travel, because of the short distances involved between major cities, intercity passenger travel has survived better there than in the United States. The same is true in Japan.

The oldest named train in the world is probably the Irish Mail, dating from 1842. In the United States, the Fall River Boat Train (1847–1937) may have been the first to acquire a name. The oldest American train names still in use by Amtrak are "Sunset Limited," with an ancestry reaching back to 1884, and "Empire State Express," dating from 1891. Many names originated informally with employees or the public, then were officially taken up by a railroad in its advertising.

Until the middle of the nineteenth century most passenger trains made all stops; "express" trains then began to appear. "Limited" indicated a limited number of stops, though the number of passengers carried was also limited. "Special" emphasized special services, such as parlor cars, diners, sleepers, or an observation car. In the twentieth century the majority of these in the United States, and some in Britain, were owned and operated by the Pullman Company. On the European continent most famous trains were owned and operated over the international network of railways by La Compagnie Internationale des Wagons-Lits, founded in 1872 by Georges Nagelmachers in Belgium.

The compilation that follows was prepared by George Kennedy of the University of North Carolina at Chapel Hill. It lists some of the best-known name trains and, if ascertainable, when they first went into service, together with the cities along their routes. Except as noted, most trains here listed operated in the period from 1920 or 1930 to 1960, and some still continue in service.

Railroads over which the trains operated are abbreviated as follows:

ACL: Atlantic Coast Line
B & O: Baltimore & Ohio
C & NW: Chicago and North Western
CB & Q: Chicago, Burlington, & Quincy
CIWL: La Compagnie Internationale des Wagons-Lits
D & RGW: Denver & Rio Grande Western
FEC: Florida East Coast
LMS: London, Midland, & Scottish
LNER: London & North Eastern
MIL: Chicago, Milwaukee, St. Paul, and Pacific
MP: Missouri Pacific
NH: New York, New Haven, & Hartford
NYC: New York Central
PRR: Pennsylvania
RF & P: Richmond, Fredericksburg, and Potomac
SAL: Seaboard Air Line
SF: Atcheson, Topeka, & Santa Fe
SP: Southern Pacific
SR: Southern Ry (U.K.) and Southern Ry (U.S.)
TEE: Trans-Europe Express
UP: Union Pacific

AUSTRALIA

Indian Pacific. (1970): Australian National Rys. Four days a week, Sydney–Kalgoolie–Perth in 65 hours.

BRITISH ISLES

Boat Train. Any of several scheduled trains between London and Channel ports with connections for the Continent; also special trains operated in connection with transatlantic steamships. SR: London (Waterloo) to Southampton or Plymouth; LMS: London (Euston) to Liverpool.

Brighton Belle. London, Brighton, & South Coast, later SR, British Rail: London (Victoria)-Brighton, as many as four round trips a day. Originally (1882) called Pullman Limited Express; name Brighton Belle officially given in 1934.

Cornish Riviera Express (1902). Great Western Ry, later SR, British Rail: London (Paddington)–Bristol–Plymouth–Cornwall.

Flying Scotsman (began 1862, named 1923). LNER, later British Rail: London (Kings Cross)–York–Newcastle–Edinburgh.

Golden Arrow/Flèche d'Or. CIWL: London (Victoria)-Dover, with Channel steamer and connecting train to Paris (Nord).

Irish Mail (1842). London & North Western Ry, later LMS, later British Rail: London (Euston)–Chester–Holyhead, then by steamer to Dublin. Until Irish independence carried nightly a watch set to Greenwich Mean Time in London as standard time for Dublin.

Night Ferry. CIWL: London (Victoria)–Paris (Nord) or Brussels. (Sleeping cars carried on Channel steamer.)

Queen of Scots. LNER, later British Rail: London (King's Cross)–Leeds–Edinburgh–Glasgow.

Royal Scot. LMS, later British Rail: day train, London (Euston)–Carlisle–Glasgow.

EUROPE

Arlberg Express. CIWL: night train, Paris–Zurich–Innsbruck–Vienna.

Aurora. Russian Natl. Rys: Leningrad–Moscow, summer only.

Blauer Enzian. TEE: Hamburg–Hannover–Munich (in summer to Salzburg and Klagenfurt).

Catalan. TEE: Geneva–Grenoble–Avignon–Narbonne–Barcelona.

Cisalpin. TEE: day train, Paris–Dijon–Lausanne–Milan (in summer to Venice).

Edelweiss. CIWL/TEE: day train, Amsterdam–Antwerp–Brussels–Luxembourg–Metz–Strasbourg–Mulhouse, later to Basel and Zurich.

Gottardo. TEE: Basel–Zurich–Lugano–Como–Milan.

Mistral. TEE: Paris–Dijon–Lyon–Avignon–Marseille–Cannes–Nice.

Orient Express (1883). CIWL: Calais–Paris–Munich–Vienna; extended (1888) to Budapest, Bucharest, Sofia, and Istanbul. Reduced to one car, Paris–Bucharest, 1962. See also **Simplon Orient Express**.

Palatino. Italian State Rys: (Naples)–Rome–Pisa–Genoa–Turin–(Paris).

Parsifal. TEE: day train, Paris–Cologne–Hamburg.

Puerta del Sol. TEE: night train, Paris–Madrid.

Reingold. CIWL/TEE: London (Liverpool Sta.)–Harwich-steamer to Hook of Holland–Rotterdam–Cologne–Bonn–Basel.

Rome Express (1883). CIWL: Calais–Paris–Turin–Bologna–Florence–Rome.

Simplon Orient Express (1919). CIWL: Calais–Paris–Lausanne–Simplon Tunnel–Milan–Venice–Trieste–Belgrade–Bucharest–Sofia–Istanbul. Also cars Paris–Belgrade–Thessalonica–Athens. Reduced to one car, Paris–Istanbul, 1962; revived under private management, 1982.

Sud Express (1890). CIWL: Paris–Bordeaux–Biarritz–Hendaye, with connections for Madrid, Lisbon, and North Africa.

Talgo. Spanish National Rys: Madrid–Port Bou, where gauge is changed for operation in France to Grenoble and Geneva and to Bordeaux and Paris. Also Barcelona–Paris cars.

TEE (Trans-Europe Expresses). Network of first-class trains in Western Europe. Many altered to ordinary trains, 1978.

Train Bleu. CIWL/TEE: Paris (Gare de Lyon)–Lyon–Marseille–Nice–Ventimiglia.

Trains à Grande Vitesse (TGV) (1981). Paris (Gare de Lyon)–Lyon and Paris–Geneva several times a day. Fastest trains in the world, regularly operating at 160 mph; February 26, 1981, special train attained 235.6 mph.

Trans-Siberian Express (1900). CIWL until World War I: Paris–Berlin–Warsaw–Moscow–Lake Baikal–Manchuria (connections to Peking and Shanghai)–Vladivostok (with steamer to Japan) in about two weeks' time. Continues in operation Moscow–Pacific.

INDIA (INDIAN STATE RYS)

Decan Queen. Day train, Bombay–Poona.

Frontier Mail. Bombay–Amritsar; before 1947 continued to Peshawar in Pakistan.

Rajdhanis. Air-conditioned expresses, Bombay–Delhi and Bombay–Calcutta.

Taj Express. New Delhi–Agra.

JAPAN

Shinkansen or Bullet (1964). Japanese National Rys: Tokyo–Osaka, also to Hakata and elsewhere. Numerous trains; cruising speed about 130 mph.

SOUTH AFRICA

Bloutrein (Blue Train). South African State Rys: Capetown–Johannesburg twice a week in 25 hours. (One of the most luxurious trains in the world.)

UNITED STATES AND CANADA

Unless otherwise indicated, most trains were discontinued in the 1960s. Amtrak continued some names after taking over intercity passenger trains in 1971. Via Rail took over operation of Canadian trains in 1978. Timetables can be found in the Official Guide of the Railways, published monthly by the National Railway Publishing Company, New York, since 1868.

Abraham Lincoln. Alton (later Gulf, Mobile, & Ohio): Chicago (Union Sta.)–Springfield, Ill.–Alton–St. Louis.

Airway Limited (1928–30). Coordinated through service overnight PRR: New York (Penn Sta.)–Newark–North Philadelphia–Pittsburgh–Port Columbus, Ohio; then all day by Transcontinental Air Transport plane: Port Columbus–Wynona, Okla.–Clovis, N.M.; then second night SF: Clovis–Los Angeles.

Ann Rutledge. Same route as Abraham Lincoln.

Aristocrat. CB & Q: Chicago (Union Sta.)–Omaha–Lincoln–Denver.

Atlantic Limited. Canadian Pacific: Montreal (Mt. Royal)–Sherbrooke–Brownsville, Maine–St. John, N.B.–Halifax. Continued by Via Rail.

Bar Harbor Express. Summer train, originally daily, later only weekends. PRR: Washington–New York (Penn Sta.)*; NH: New York–New Haven–New London–Worcester; Boston & Maine: Worcester–Portland; Maine Central: Portland–Bangor–Ellsworth, Maine.

Birmingham Special. PRR: New York–Washington; SR: Washington–Lynchburg; Norfolk & Western: Lynchburg–Roanoke–Bristol; SR: Bristol–Knoxville–Chattanooga–Birmingham.

Black Diamond (1896). Day train, Lehigh Valley: New York (Penn Sta.)–Bethlehem–Allentown–Wilkes-Barre–Ithaca–Buffalo; also Philadelphia–Buffalo cars to and from Reading Co. at Bethlehem.

Bluebird. Wabash: Chicago (Dearborn Sta.–Decatur–St. Louis.

Blue Bird and **Red Bird.** Chicago Great Western: Minneapolis–St. Paul–Rochester, Minn. (Mayo Clinic).

Bluebonnet. Frisco: St. Louis–Springfield, Mo.–Dallas; Missouri–Kansas–Texas: Dallas–Austin–San Antonio.

Blue Comet (1929–41). Central RR of NJ: New York (Jersey City)–Atlantic City.

Boat Train. See **Fall River Boat Train**.

Boll Weevil. Unofficial name in the 1930s and 1940s of SAL gas-electric train: Hamlet, N.C.–Charleston, S.C.–Savannah, Ga.

Broadway Limited. (Inaugurated November 24, 1912; all sleeping cars until taken over by Amtrak.) Successor to the Pennsylvania Special. PRR: New York (Penn Sta.)–Newark–North Philadelphia–Pittsburgh–Fort Wayne–Chicago (Union Sta.).

Burlington Zephyr. See **Zephyr Streamlined Trains**.

California Limited. SF: Chicago (Dearborn Sta.)–Kansas City–Albuquerque–Flagstaff–Los Angeles.

Canadian/Canadienne. Canadian Pacific: Montreal (Mt. Royal) and Toronto–Winnipeg–Calgary–Banff–Vancouver. Continued by Via Rail until 1989.

Cannonball or **Cannon Ball.** Popular term used by several RRs including Long Island (New York–Montauk) and Norfolk & Western (Richmond–Norfolk). See also **Wabash Cannonball**.

Capitol Limited. B & O: New York (Jersey City)*–Philadelphia–Baltimore–Washington–Pittsburgh–Youngstown–Akron–Chicago (Grand Central). Continued by Amtrak: Washington–Pittsburgh–Chicago (Union Sta.).

Carolina Special. SR: Charleston–Columbia–Spartanburg–Asheville–Knoxville–Lexington–Cincinnati, with sleeper to and from Chicago (Central Sta.) on

---

*Most New York–Washington trains on PRR stopped at Newark, Trenton, North Philadelphia, Philadelphia (30th St.), Wilmington, and Baltimore. Before the opening of Penn Station (1910), PRR trains left from Jersey City, with ferry connections to Manhattan. The Hell Gate Bridge connection between Penn Station and New England opened in 1917. From 1919 to 1926, B&O trains to New York used Penn Station; before and after that time, they used the Jersey City terminal of Central RR of New Jersey.

NYC; also Goldboro, N.C.–Raleigh–Durham–Greensboro–Winston-Salem–Asheville–Cincinnai section.

Cascade. SP: (San Francisco ferry)–Oakland–Klamath Falls–Eugene–Portland–Tacoma–Seattle.

Champion streamlined trains of the Atlantic Coast Line. East Coast Champion, PRR: New York–Washington*; RF & P: Washington–Richmond; ACL: Richmond–Rocky Mount–Florence–Charleston–Savannah–Jacksonville; FEC: Jacksonville–West Palm Beach–Miami. West Coast Champion, same route New York–Jacksonville, ACL: Jacksonville–Orlando–Tampa and St. Petersburg.

Chief and Super Chief. SF: Chicago (Dearborn Sta.)–Kansas City–Albuquerque–Flagstaff–Barstow–Los Angeles. Continued by Amtrak as Southwest Chief. San Francisco Chief: same route to Barstow, then Bakersfield–Fresno–Oakland (San Francisco ferry). Texas Chief: Chicago–Kansas City–Oklahoma City–Fort Worth–Houston.

City of Miami. Ill. Central: Chicago (Central Sta.)–Birmingham; Central of Ga.: Birmingham–Albany; ACL: Albany–Jacksonville; FEC: Jacksonville–Miami.

City of New Orleans. Ill. Central: Chicago (Central Sta.)–Memphis–Jackson–New Orleans.

City of trains of the Union Pacific. UP trains to and from Chicago (C & NW; in 1960s MIL: Chicago–Council Bluffs) or St. Louis (Wabash: St. Louis–Kansas City). City of Denver: Chicago–Omaha–Julesburg–Denver; City of Los Angeles: Chicago–Omaha–Cheyenne–Ogden–Salt Lake City–Las Vegas–Los Angeles; City of San Francisco: Omaha–Cheyenne–Ogden; SP: Ogden–Reno–Sacramento–Oakland (San Francisco ferry); City of St. Louis: St. Louis–Kansas City–Denver–Cheyenne–Green River, Wyo.; there cars to or from (1) Pocatello–Boise–Portland; (2) Ogden–Reno–Oakland–(San Francisco ferry); (3) Ogden–Salt Lake City–Las Vegas–Los Angeles. City of Portland: See **Streamline(r)**.

Columbine. C & NW: Chicago–Council Bluffs; UP: Council Bluffs–Omaha–Topeka–Denver.

Commodore Vanderbilt. NYC: New York (Grand Central)–Albany–Buffalo–Cleveland–Toledo–South Bend–Chicago (LaSalle Sta.).

Congressional Limited (December 7, 1885). All-parlor-car train, PRR: New York–Washington.*

Continental and Super Continental. Canadian National: Montreal (Central Sta.) and Toronto–Winnipeg–Edmonton–Vancouver. Continued by Via Rail.

Crescent. PRR: New York–Washington*; SR: Washington–Charlotte–Spartanburg–Atlanta; Atlanta & West Point: Atlanta–West Point, Ga.; Western Ry of Alabama: West Point–Montgomery; Louisville & Nashville: Montgomery–Mobile–New Orleans. Continued by Amtrak.

Crusader. Reading Co.: Philadelphia–Jenkintown–New York (Jersey City).

Daylight. SP: Los Angeles–Santa Barbara–San Jose–San Francisco.

Dixie Flagler and other "Dixie"-named trains of the Chicago & Eastern Illinois.
Chicago (Dearborn Sta.)–Evanston; Louisville & Nashville: Evanston–
Nashville–Chattanooga–Atlanta; ACL: Atlanta–Jacksonville–Orlando–
Tampa–St. Petersburg; FEC: Jacksonville–Miami.

Dominion. Canadian Pacific: Montreal (Mt. Royal) and Toronto–Winnipeg-
Calgary–Banff–Vancouver. Replaced by Canadian (1949). Soo Dominion:
C & NW: Chicago–Milwaukee–St. Paul; Soo Line: St. Paul–Minneapolis–
Winnipeg, with through cars for Vancouver.

Eagle streamlined trains of the Missouri Pacific. MP to and from St. Louis:
Missouri River Eagle for Kansas City; Texas Eagle for Little Rock–Dallas–
Fort Worth–Houston (continued by Amtrak); Aztec Eagle for San Antonio–
Laredo–Mexico City (National of Mexico); Colorado Eagle for Kansas City–
Topeka–Pueblo–Colorado Springs–Denver.

El Capitan. All-coach train of SF: Chicago (Dearborn Sta.)–Kansas City–
Albuquerque–Flagstaff–Bakersfield–Stockton–Oakland (San Francisco ferry).

Empire Builder. Great Northern: Seattle/Portland–Spokane–Glacier Park–Fargo–
Minneapolis; CB & Q to and from Chicago (Union Sta.). Continued by
Amtrak.

Empire State Express (October 26, 1891). Day train, NYC: New York (Grand
Central)–Albany–Utica–Syracuse–Rochester–Buffalo. In later years sections continued Buffalo–Cleveland and Buffalo–Detroit. May 10, 1893,
attained 112 mph. with locomotive No. 999 west of Rochester, first time
man had attained over 100 mph. Continued by Amtrak: New York-Buffalo.

Erie Limited. Erie RR: New York (Jersey City)-Binghamton–Elmira–Akron–
Huntington, Ind.–Chicago (Dearborn Sta.).

Fall River Boat Train (1847–1937). New York–Fall River, Mass. (at some periods,
Newport, R.I.) by overnight steamer; Old Colony (later NH): Fall River (or
Newport)–Boston.

Fast Mail. Term often used by railroads in nineteenth and early twentieth centuries for fast overnight train, sometimes with sleeping cars. Amtrak uses
the name for one of its Washington–New York–Boston trains. The SR train
in the "Wreck of the Old 97" was a Fast Mail.

Federal Express. First through train from Boston to Washington, operated
1890–93 via Springfield, Mass., Poughkeepsie, N.Y., Bethlehem, Pa., and
Philadelphia. It was then replaced by the Federal Express via Providence,
New Haven, and New York, utilizing a car ferry from the Bronx to Jersey
City and PRR: Jersey City–Washington. From 1917 via Hell Gate Bridge and
Penn Sta., New York.*

Florida Special (1888). First luxury train between the Northeast and Florida, win-
ter season only; continued operation until the 1960s. PRR: New York–
Washington*; RF & P: Washington–Richmond; ACL: Richmond–Rocky
Mount–Florence–Charleston–Savannah–Jacksonville; FEC: Jacksonville–

West Palm Beach–Miami; also section to Orlando–Tampa and St. Petersburg via ACL.

Floridian. Ill. Central: Chicago (Central Sta.)–Jackson, Miss.–Birmingham; Central of Ga.: Birmingham–Albany, Ga.; ACL: Albany–Jacksonville; FEC: Jacksonville–West Palm Beach–Miami.

Flying Crow. Kansas City Southern: Kansas City–Shreveport–Port Arthur, Tex.

Flying Yankee (1883–99, revived 1926; as lightweight streamlined train, 1935). Boston & Maine: Boston (North Sta.)–Portland; Maine Central: Portland–Bangor.

400 Trains of the Chicago and North Western. Twin Cities 400: Chicago–Milwaukee–Eau Claire–St. Paul–Minneapolis (400 miles in 400 minutes). Other 400 trains included Kate Shelley 400: Chicago–Clinton, Ia.; Peninsula 400: Chicago–Milwaukee–Fond du Lac–Green Bay–Escanaba, Mich.–Ishpeming.

Georgian. Louisville & Nashville: Atlanta–Chattanooga–Nashville–Evansville, Ind.–St. Louis; Chicago & Eastern Illinois: Evansville–Chicago (Dearborn Sta.).

George Washington. Chesapeake & Ohio: Washington–Charlottesville–Charleston, W.V.–Ashland, Ky.–Lexington–Louisville; also Ashland–Cincinnati; through cars New York (PRR)* to Cincinnati, Chicago, and St. Louis (NYC); also Norfolk (ferry to Phoebus)–Newport News–Richmond section, connecting at Charlottesville.

Golden State Limited. Rock Island: Chicago (LaSalle Sta.)–Kansas City–Tucumcari, N.M.; SP: Tucumcari–El Paso–Tucson–Phoenix–Los Angeles.

Green Diamond (1936). Early streamlined diesel train of the Ill. Central: Chicago (Central Sta.)–Springfield–St. Louis.

Havana Special. PRR: New York–Washington*; RF & P: Washington–Richmond; ACL: Richmond–Rocky Mount–Florence–Charleston–Savannah–Jacksonville; FEC: Jacksonville–West Palm Beach–Miami; continued to Key West (1920–35) until causeway destroyed by hurricane.

Hiawatha (1935). Streamlined trains of the MIL: Chicago (Union Sta.)–Milwaukee–La Crosse–St. Paul–Minneapolis. Other later Hiawatha trains included North Woods Hiawatha to Wausau and Minocqua, Wis.; Oympian Hiawatha: See **Olympian**.

International Limited (1900). Grand Trunk Western: Montreal (Central Sta.)–Toronto–Pontiac–Battle Creek–Chicago (Dearborn Sta.).

James Whitcomb Riley. NYC: Cincinnati–Indianapolis–Chicago (Central Sta.).

Laker. Soo Line: Chicago (Grand Central)–Oshkosh–Duluth.

Lark. SP day train: Los Angeles–Santa Barbara–San Jose–San Francisco.

Laurentian. Delaware & Hudson: Montreal (Mt. Royal)–Saratoga–Troy; NYC: Troy–Harmon–New York (Grand Central).

Lone Star Limited. Cotton Belt: Memphis–Shreveport–Dallas–Fort Worth.

Merchants Limited (1903). All-parlor-car day train until taken over by Amtrak as a Washington–Boston train. NH: New York (Grand Central)–New Haven–New London–Providence–Boston (South Station).

Mercury. NYC (Mich. Cent.): Chicago (Central Sta.)–Battle Creek–Jackson–Ann Arbor–Detroit.

Montrealer. Overnight train, PRR: Washington-New York*; NH: New York–Springfield, Mass.; Boston & Maine: Springfield–White River Jct.; Central Vermont: White River Jct.–Montreal (Central Sta.). Southbound train originally called Washingtonian; under Amtrak both called Montrealer and now operated via New London, Conn., and Amherst, Mass., instead of Springfield.

Mountaineer. Summer season only, New York, Ontario, & Western: New York (Weehawken)–Middletown, N.Y.–Catskill Mountain points.

Nancy Hanks (1893 only); **Nancy Hanks II** (1948–71). Central of Ga.: Atlanta–Macon–Savannah. Named for a race horse.

National Limited. B & O: New York (Jersey City)*–Philadelphia–Baltimore–Washington–Parkersburg, W.Va.–Cincinnati–Vincennes, Ind.–St. Louis. First all air-conditioned train, 1932.

Nellie Bly. PRR: New York–Newark–Trenton–Atlantic City.

New England Limited (1885). NH: New York–New Haven–Middleton–Willimantic, Conn.; New York and New England: Willimantic–Boston. Known as the White Train or Ghost Train, 1891–95, when its cars were painted white and gold.

New England States. Boston & Albany: Boston–Albany; NYC: Albany–Toledo–South Bend–Chicago.

Nickel Plate Limited. Nickel Plate Road: Chicago (La Salle Sta.)–Fort Wayne–Cleveland–Buffalo, with through cars via Delaware, Lackawanna & Western to and from New York (Hoboken).

North Coast Limited (1900). Northern Pacific: Seattle/Tacoma–Spokane–Butte–Missoula–Bismarck–Minneapolis–St. Paul; CB & Q: St. Paul–Chicago (Union Sta.).

North Shore Limited. NYC: New York (Grand Central)–Albany–Buffalo–Detroit–Jackson–Chicago (Central Sta.).

Ocean Limited. Canadian National: Montreal (Central Sta.)–Leavis–Edmundston–St. John or Moncton-Halifax.

Ohio State Limited. NYC: New York (Grand Central)–Harmon–Albany–Syracuse–Buffalo–Cleveland–Columbus–Cincinnati.

Olympian. MIL: Chicago (Union Sta.)–Milwaukee–St. Paul–Minneapolis–Aberdeen, S.D.–Butte–Spokane–Seattle/Tacoma.

Orange Blossom Special (1925). Winter-season sleeping-car train, PRR: New York–Washington*: RF & P: Washington–Richmond; SAL: Richmond–Raleigh–Columbia–Savannah–Jacksonville–Palm Beach–Miami; also section to Tampa and St. Petersburg.

Oriental Limited. Great Northern: Seattle/Portland–Spokane–Glacier Park–Fargo–Minneapolis–St. Paul; CB & Q : St. Paul–Chicago (Union Sta.).

Overland Limited (1899). C & NW: Chicago–Council Bluffs; UP: Omaha–Cheyenne–Ogden; SP: Reno–Sacramento–Oakland (ferry to San Francisco).

Owl. Name for midnight train on several roads, including (1898) SP: Los Angeles–Santa Barbara–San Jose–San Francisco. Also NH: New York (Grand Central)–Boston, continued as Night Owl by Amtrak: Boston–Providence–New York–Philadelphia–Baltimore–Washington.

Panama Limited. Ill. Central: Chicago (Central Sta.)–Memphis–Jackson–New Orleans.

Pan-American. Louisville & Nashville: Cincinnati–Louisville–Nashville–Birmingham–Mobile–New Orleans.

Pennsylvania Limited (1891–1971). PRR: New York (Penn Sta.)*–Newark–Philadelphia–Pittsburgh–Fort Wayne–Chicago (Union Sta.).

Pennsylvania Special (1902–12). Predecessor of the Broadway Limited. PRR: New York*–Newark–Philadelphia–Pittsburgh–Fort Wayne–Chicago. The unofficial world's record for speed by a steam-powered train was set by the Special in June 1905, between Ada and Crestline, Ohio, 127 mph.

Penn Texas. PRR: New York–Newark–North Philadelphia–Harrisburg–Pittsburgh–Columbus–Indianapolis–Terre Haute–St. Louis, with through sleeping cars via Frisco and Missouri–Kansas–Texas Rwy: New York–St. Louis–Dallas–San Antonio or Missouri Pacific and Texas & Pacific: New York–St. Louis–Little Rock–Dallas–Fort Worth–El Paso or Dallas–Houston.

Pere Marquette. Pere Marquette RR, later Chesapeake & Ohio: Chicago (Grand Central)–Grand Rapids–Detroit.

Phoebe Snow. Delaware, Lackawanna, & Western: day train, New York (Hoboken)–Scranton–Binghamton–Elmira–Buffalo. Successor to the Lackawanna Ltd.

Piedmont Limited. SR: day train, Washington–Charlottesville–Lynchburg–Greensboro–Charlotte–Spartanburg–Atlanta.

Pocahontas. Norfolk & Western: night train, Norfolk–Petersburg–Lynchburg–Roanoke–Bluefield–Portsmouth–Cincinnati and Portsmouth–Columbus.

Powhattan Arrow. Norfolk & Western: day train, Norfolk–Petersburg–Lynchburg–Bluefield–Portsmouth–Cincinnati.

Queen & Crescent. SR: Cincinnati–Chattanooga–Birmingham–New Orleans.

Rebel (1935). First lightweight, streamlined train in the South. Gulf, Mobile, and Northern: New Orleans–Jackson, Miss., later extended to St. Louis. Gulf Coast Rebel (1940). Gulf, Mobile, and Ohio: Mobile–Jackson, Miss.–St. Louis.

Red Bird. See **Blue Bird and Red Bird**.

Red Wing. Boston & Maine: Boston (North Sta.)–Welles River; Canadian Pacific: Welles River–Newport–Sherbrooke–Montreal (Mt. Royal).

Rocket streamlined trains of the Chicago, Rock Island, and Pacific. Rock Island, to and from Chicago (LaSalle Sta.): Rocky Mountain Rocket for Des Moines–Omaha–Topeka and Denver or Colorado Springs; Peoria Rocket for Peoria. Twin Star Rocket: Minneapolis–Kansas City–Fort Worth–Dallas–Houston; Zephyr Rocket: Minneapolis–Burlington, Ia.–St. Louis, in conjunction with CB & Q.

Royal Blue. In 1890 the Baltimore & Ohio opened the "Royal Blue Route": New York (Jersey City)*–Philadelphia–Wilmington–Baltimore (Mt. Royal and Camden Sta.)–Washington. The premier day train was originally called the Royal Limited, but in 1935 became the Royal Blue. Discontinued in 1958.

Royal Gorge. D & RGW: Denver–Colorado Springs–Pueblo–Leadville–Grand Junction–Salt Lake City. Carried through sleepers from Chicago (CB & Q at Denver) and St. Louis (MP at Pueblo) to Oakland (San Francisco ferry). Successor to the Scenic Limited.

Royal Palm. NYC: Chicago (Central Sta.)–Indianapolis–Cincinnati and Detroit–Toledo–Cincinnati and Cleveland–Columbus–Dayton–Cincinnati; SR: Cincinnati–Chattanooga–Atlanta–Macon–Jacksonville; FEC: Jacksonville–West Palm Beach–Miami.

San Juan (1934–51). D & RGW narrow-gauge deluxe train: Alamosa–Durango, Colo.; standard-gauge connections at Alamosa to and from Denver on Colorado and New Mexico Express.

Senator. Day train, PRR Washington–New York* (Penn Sta.); NH: New York–Stamford–Bridgeport–New Haven–New London–Providence–Boston (South Sta.). Continued by Amtrak.

Silver streamlined trains of the Seaboard Air Line. Silver Comet, PRR: New York–Washington*; RF & P: Washington–Richmond; SAL: Richmond–Raleigh–Hamlet–Greenwood, S.C.–Athens, Ga.–Atlanta–Birmingham. Silver Meteor, PRR: New York–Washington*; RF & P: Washington–Richmond; SAL: Richmond–Raleigh–Hamlet, N.C.–Columbia–Savannah–Jacksonville–Ocala–West Palm Beach–Miami. Name used by Amtrak for train to both coasts of Florida via ACL route through Charleston. Silver Star, same route New York–Ocala; SAL: Ocala–Tampa–St. Petersburg. Continued by Amtrak to both coasts of Florida.

Silverton. D & RGW narrow-gauge line, opened 1882: Durango–Silverton, Colo. Operation as a tourist train began in 1953.

Southern Belle. Kansas City Southern: Kansas City–Shreveport–New Orleans.

Southwestern Limited. NYC: New York (Grand Central)–Albany–Buffalo–Cleveland–Indianapolis–St. Louis.

South Wind. PRR: Chicago (Union Sta.)–Louisville; Louisville & Nashville:

Louisville–Nashville–Chattanooga–Atlanta; ACL: Atlanta–Waycross–Jacksonville; FEC: Jacksonville–West Palm Beach–Miami.

Sportsman. Chesapeake & Ohio: Norfolk (ferry to Phoebus)–Newport News–Richmond–Charlottesville or Washington–Charlottesville–Charleston, W.Va.–Ashland, Ky.–Cincinnati; through sleeper: Washington–Indianapolis–Chicago (Central Sta.) via NYC to and from Cincinnati.

Streamline(r) (1934). UP: Lightweight, three-car experimental train, exhibited nationally and put into service Kansas City–Topeka–Salina, Kans., as the City of Salina. A six-car Streamliner (1934) became the City of Portland on the Chicago & North Western: Chicago–Council Bluffs; UP: Omaha–Cheyenne–Pocatello–Boise–Portland.

Sunset Limited (1884). SP: New Orleans-Houston–San Antonio–El Paso–Phoenix–Los Angeles.

Sunshine Special. MP: St. Louis–Little Rock–Texarkana; Texas & Pacific: Texarkana–Dallas–Fort Worth–El Paso; also through sleepers (MP) St. Louis–San Antonio–Laredo (connections for Mexico City), St. Louis–Houston, and St. Louis or Memphis–El Paso–Los Angeles (SP).

Tennessean. PRR: New York–Washington*; SRR: Washington–Lynchburg; Norfolk & Western: Lynchburg–Bristol, Tenn.; SRR: Bristol–Knoxville–Chattanooga–Memphis.

Texas Special. Frisco: St. Louis–Springfield, Mo.–Dallas; Missouri–Kansas–Texas Line: Dallas–Austin–San Antonio.

Thoroughbred. Monon: Chicago (Dearborn Sta.)–Lafayette, Ind.–Bloomington–French Lick–Louisville.

Tippecanoe. Monon: Chicago (Dearborn Sta.)–Indianapolis.

Twentieth Century Limited (1902–70). NYC: New York (Grand Central)–Harmon–Albany–Syracuse–Buffalo–Cleveland–South Bend–Chicago (LaSalle Sta.). At some periods non-stop Harmon–Chicago. All Pullman until 1962.

Wabash Cannonball. Detroit–Fort Wayne–St. Louis day train of the Wabash, apparently named in the 1950s and 1960s from the song of this name which, however, envisions operation "to the wide Pacific shore."

White Train. See **New England Limited**.

Yankee Clipper. Day train, NH: Boston (South Sta.) Providence–New London–Bridgeport–Stamford–New York (Grand Central). Until after World War II, all parlor cars, named for clipper ships. Continued by Amtrak.

Zephyr streamlined trains of the Chicago, Burlington, and Quincy. Pioneer (or Burlington) Zephyr (1934), first lightweight, streamlined train, exhibited nationally; in service (1936) as Denver Zephyr: Chicago (Union Sta.)–Omaha–Denver (and later Colorado Springs); Twin Zephyr: Chicago (Union Sta.)–La Crosse–St. Paul–Minneapolis; California Zephyr, CB & Q: Chicago (Union Sta.)–Omaha–Denver; Denver & Rio Grande Western: Denver–Grand Junction–Salt Lake City; Western Pacific: Salt Lake City–

Sacramento–Stockton–Oakland (San Francisco), continued by Amtrak (1971) as San Francisco Zephyr; Rocky Mountain Zephyr (on subsidiaries Colorado & Southern and Forth Worth and Denver City): Denver–Colorado Springs–Pueblo–Amarillo–Fort Worth–Houston.

—George Kennedy

4

SOME NOTABLE AIRCRAFT

· · · · ·

WHAT SEEMS AMAZING ABOUT THE DEVELOPMENT OF AVIATION IS HOW rapidly it has all taken place. Consider that Orville Wright, for example, who with his brother Wilbur built the first workable heavier-than-air craft, was still in his seventies when he died, yet he had seen jet aircraft in action. In less than a century we have moved from cloth-and-stick kitelike crates with crude gasoline engines attached to manned flights in space. The casual traveler thinks nothing of boarding a Boeing 747 in the evening and alighting in Paris six hours later.

Lena Grove, in William Faulkner's *Light in August*, had a somewhat different concept of time and distance. "My, my," she declares. "A body does get around. Here we aint been coming from Alabama but two months, And now it's already Tennessee." And Flannery O'Connor has her character Tarwater tell his uncle in *The Violent Bear It Away* that "I wouldn't give you nothing for no airplane. A buzzard can fly." (Flannery O'Connor herself always flew when she traveled; she didn't care for trains, she said, because they rattled her bones. As for Faulkner, he piloted an airplane of his own for a while.)

In the late 1930s Lefty Gomez of the Yankees held up the World Series game he was pitching to watch an airplane as it passed over the ball park. Nowadays, across the East River, on certain days when the flight pattern from LaGuardia Field is right, all conversation halts in Shea Stadium and at Forest Hills every couple of minutes while another jet aircraft blasts past overhead. So you win a few, and you lose a few, but almost no scheduled flights get rained out any more—visibility means nothing, for it's all done with instruments. (Snow and ice are another matter.)

Whatever one thinks of them in terms of the noise they make, airplanes are part of our experience, and for not a few of us who grew up and have lived out our lives while the history of aviation has been taking place, the very model numbers and names have a resonance to them, much as an inhabitant of Camelot must have felt when King Arthur and his Round Table knights came clanking by on horseback.

The compilation that follows is of a few—a very few—of the better-known aircraft from Kill Devil Hills onward. Emphasis has been placed on American aircraft. Rockets and spacecraft are not included.

A-29. See **Lockheed A-29 Hudson**.

Aeronca. Various models; U.S. single-engine high-wing light plane (1930).

Aerospatiale Ecureuil (Twinstar) 350. Large French helicopter (1967); earlier known as "Astar" in the United States.

Aichi D3A1. "Val"; Japanese carrier-based dive bomber of World War II (1941).

Airbus A300. European multicountry twin-engine jet passenger aircraft (1974); other models thereafter.

Airspeed Oxford. British two-engine low-wing Royal Air Force advanced trainer (1927).

Air Tractor. Various models; U.S. single-wing plane designed for crop dusting (1972).

Akron. U.S. Navy dirigible (1931); crashed April 4, 1933, killing 73 persons.

Albatros. Various models; German fighters of World War I; the DII and DIII (1917–18) saw heavy duty.

Alpha Jet. See **Dassault-Breguet/Dornier Alpha Jet**.

Antonov AN-24V. Soviet Russian twin-engine turbojet passenger aircraft (1960).

AT-6. See **North American AT-6**.

AT-17. See **Cessna UC-78 Bobcat**.

Autogiro. See **Cierva C-30 Autogyro**.

Avro Lancaster. Four-engine British bomber (1942) used extensively in bombing of Germany in World War II.

B-1. See **North American Rockwell B-1B**.

B-17. See **Boeing B-17 Flying Fortress**.

B-24. See **Consolidated B-24 Liberator**.

B-25. See **North American B-25 Mitchell**.

B-26. See **Martin B-26G Marauder**.

B-29. See **Boeing B-29 Superfortress**.

B-36. See **Convair B-36D**.

BAC Canberra B. 1 Mk. 8. British twin-engine jet light bomber (1954).

Beechcraft Airliner. Various models; U.S. twin-engine passenger aircraft (1968).

Beechcraft B90 King Air. U.S. twin-engine turboprop passenger aircraft (1966).

Beechcraft Bonanza. Various models; U.S. light aircraft (1947).

Beechcraft C-45. U.S. twin-engine, twin-tail transport of World War II (1937); civilian model called Beechcraft 18.

Bell Model 47. U.S. helicopter (1945); military version called AH–1 Sioux.

Bell 206 Ranger. U.S. helicopter (1968), widely used for ambulance, police, traffic reporting; military version is OH-58 Kiowa.

Bell P-39 Airacobra. U.S. fighter of World War II (1939), cannon armed.

Bellanca Cruisemaster. Popular U.S. light aircraft (1946).

Betty. See **Mitsubishi G4MI.**

Blériot VI. Louis Blériot's tractor-propeller airplane of 1907.

Blériot XI. Louis Blériot's plane which crossed English Channel in 1909.

Bloch 174. Two-engine French bomber-reconnaissance plane (1939).

Boeing 314 Clipper. U.S. flying boat (1938) used on Atlantic passenger service; flew throughout World War II.

Boeing 377 Stratocruiser. U.S. four-engine passenger aircraft (1948); military version known as C-97.

Boeing 707-320C. U.S. four-engine jet passenger aircraft (1958); first U.S.-built jetliner.

Boeing 727-200. U.S. three-engine jet passenger aircraft (1967).

Boeing 737-200. U.S. twin-engine jet passenger aircraft (1967).

Boeing 747. Various models; U.S. four-engine passenger jumbo jet (1970).

Boeing 757. U.S. twin-engine jet passenger aircraft (1982).

Boeing B-17 Flying Fortress. U.S. Army Air Force four-engine heavy bomber of World War II (1938); the B-17 bore the brunt of the daylight bombing of Germany beginning in 1942.

Boeing B-29 Superfortress. U.S. Army Air Force long-range heavy bomber of World War II (1943), used against Japan; the B-29 *Enola Gay* dropped the atom bomb on Hiroshima August 6, 1945.

Boeing B-47 Stratojet. U.S. six-engine long-range jet bomber (1951).

Boeing B-52H. U.S. eight-engine long-range bomber (1956).

Boeing P-12. U.S. fighter biplane (1930) with fuselage of bolted light alloy.

Boeing P-26A. First U.S. monoplane fighter (1933); known as "Peashooter."

Boeing-Vertol CH-47C Chinook. U.S. military cargo transport helicopter (1964).

Breguet III. Early (1912) French biplane used by French and British air forces before World War I.

Brewster F2A-3 Buffalo. U.S. Navy's first single-wing carrier fighter (1938).

Bristol Beaufighter Mk. X. British twin-engine night fighter of World War II (1940), much used during Battle of Britain.

Bristol Blenheim Mk. 1. British patrol bomber (1937).

Bristol Scout C and D. British escort fighter of early years of World War II.

British Aerospace 125. British twin-engine jet business aircraft (1962); numerous models.

Britten-Norman BN2-A Islander. British light twin-engine business plane (1967).

C-45. See **Beechcraft C-45.**

C-46. See **Curtiss C-46 Commando.**

C-47. See **Douglas DC-3.**

C-53. See **Douglas DC-3**.

C-54. See **Douglas DC-4**.

C-124. See **Douglas C-124 Globemaster**.

Campini N-1. World's first jet aircraft (1940); made 311-mile flight between Milan and Rome.

Canadair CL-215. Canadian two-engine amphibian (1969); much used to fight forest fires.

Canberra. See **BAC Canberra B. 1 Mk. 8**.

Caproni CA-3. Italian bombing plane of World War I.

Caravelle. See **Sud-Aviation SE-210 Caravelle**.

Catalina. See **Consolidated PBY Catalina**.

Caudron G-IV. Two-engine French bomber and reconnaissance plane of early World War I years.

Cessna C-34 Airmaster. U.S. single-engine high-wing light plane; various models followed; three-wheeled single-engine high-wing light plane (1956) has been widely used.

Cessna Citation. Various models; U.S. twin-engine jet business aircraft (1969).

Cessna Skymaster 337. U.S. twin-inline-engine, twin-boom high-wing business aircraft (1961); military version called O-2.

Cessna UC-78 Bobcat. U.S. twin-engine business aircraft (1941); used by U.S. Army as trainer, AT-17.

Chance-Vought F4U-1 Corsair. Heavily used U.S. Navy carrier-based fighter of World War II; also used in Korea. See **Vought 02U Corsair**.

Cherokee. See **Piper Cherokee**.

Cierva C-30 Autogyro. Predecessor to helicopter (1930); used unpowered rotors and conventional propeller propulsion.

Comet. See **DeHavilland DH 106 Comet**.

Concorde SST. British-French four-engine supersonic passenger aircraft (1969).

Consolidated B-24 Liberator. U.S. Army Air Force four-engine bomber (1941); also used for transport and reconnaissance; the most heavily produced U.S. plane of World War II.

Consolidated Commodore. U.S. flying boat (1929) used by predecessor of Pan American Airways between United States and South America.

Consolidated PBY Catalina. U.S. Navy flying boat (1936), widely used in World War II for patroling and bombing; also used by Royal Air Force.

Constellation. See **Lockheed L-749 Constellation**.

Convair. Various models; U.S. twin-engine passenger aircraft (1948).

Convair B-36D. U.S. six-engine long-range bomber (1946).

Corsair. See **Chance-Vought F4U-1 Corsair**.

Curtiss C-46 Commando. U.S. Army Air Force twin-engine transport (1940) widely used in World War II; paratroops customarily were transported in the C-46.

Curtiss Condor. U.S. twin-engine biplane passenger airliner (1930); several models.

Curtiss H-4, H-12. Two-engine U.S. Navy flying boat (1915 etc.) also used by British navy in World War I.

Curtiss JN-3 Jenny. American trainer (1915), widely used by barnstormers in 1920s.

Curtiss NC. U.S. Navy flying boat (1919); the NC-4 flew from Newfoundland to England via the Azores and Portugal.

Curtiss P-40 Warhawk. Earlier models called Tomahawk; U.S. fighter of World War II (1939); widely used, especially in Pacific.

Curtiss R-1. U.S. Navy plane piloted by Bert Acosta which won the 1921 Pulitzer Trophy.

Curtiss Robin. American single-engine high-wing light plane (1927).

Curtiss SB2C4 Helldiver. Superior U.S. Navy carrier-based dive bomber of World War II (1943).

Dash 7. See **DeHavilland DHC7 Dash 7**.

Dassault-Breguet/Dornier Alpha Jet. French-German military trainer and close support/reconnaissance twin-engine jet (1973).

Dassault Falcon. French twin- and tri-engine jet business aircraft (1965); known as "Mystère" in France; various models.

Dassault Mirage. Various models; French twin-engine jet fighter (1964).

DC. See **Douglas and McDonnell-Douglas models**.

DeHavilland B-IV Mosquito. Fast British light bomber and night fighter (1941) of World War II; built almost entirely of wood.

DeHavilland DH 88 Comet. Twin-engine British plane (1934) which won England–Melbourne race in 1934.

DeHavilland DH 106 Comet. English four-engine passenger jet aircraft (1952); first passenger jet.

DeHavilland DHC3 Otter. Canadian single-engine passenger aircraft (1952); frequently used as floatplane.

DeHavilland DHC7 Dash 7. Canadian four-engine passenger aircraft (1973).

DeHavilland Gypsy Moth. British single-engine biplane (1928).

DeHavilland Vampire FB 5. British three-engine jet fighter (1949).

Dornier DO X. German six-motored flying boat (1929).

Douglas. See also **McDonnell-Douglas**.

Douglas C-124 Globemaster. U.S. four-engine military transport (1950).

Douglas DC-3. Twin-engine U.S. passenger craft of 1935 used throughout world for next three decades and more; the U.S. Army version was designated the C-47 and C-53; most popular commercial plane ever built.

Douglas DC-4. U.S. four-engine passenger aircraft (1938); military transport version was the C-54 Skymaster.

Douglas DC-6B. U.S. four-engine passenger aircraft (1946).

Douglas SBD-5 Dauntless. U.S. Navy carrier-based bomber (1941) used throughout World War II.

Duperdussin Racer. 1912 French monoplane which broke the speed record in 1913.

Empire Boat. See **Short S23-C Empire Boat.**

F-4E Phantom. See **McDonnell-Douglas F-4E Phantom.**

F-14B. See **Grumman F-14B.**

F-15. See **McDonnell-Douglas F-15.**

F-16. See **General Dynamics F-16 Fighting Falcon.**

F-86. See **North American F-86 Sabre.**

F-104G. See **Lockheed F-104G Starfighter.**

F.E.2b. British two-seater fighter of World War I (1915).

Fairchild C-119 Flying Boxcar. U.S. twin-engine military transport (1949).

Fairchild FH227. U.S. two-engine turboprop passenger aircraft (1966); built to design licensed by Fokker (Netherlands).

Fairchild PT. Various models; U.S. military basic training aircraft (1940).

Fairchild Republic A-10 Thunderbolt. "Warthog"; U.S. Air Force twin-engine jet close-support aircraft (1972).

Fairey Swordfish. British torpedo bomber single-engine biplane (1934); helped sink battleship *Bismarck* in 1942.

Farman F-60 Goliath. French twin-engine passenger aircraft (1919). See also **Henri Farman HF 20, HF 40; Maurice Farman MF-11.**

Flyer I. Wright brothers' first heavier-than-air plane, which achieved flight on December 17, 1903, at Kill Devil Hills, N.C.; it was followed by a series of other models.

Flying Boxcar. See **Fairchild C-119 Flying Boxcar.**

Flying Fortress. See **Boeing B-17 Flying Fortress.**

Focke-Wulf FW 200A Condor. Four-engine German airliner (1937); much used as transport in World War II.

Focke-Wulf FW-190. German fighter plane of World War II (1940), extremely effective; also used as bomber.

Fokker D-VII. Germany's best World War I fighter (1918).

Fokker Dr-1 Triplane. German fighter (1917); Richthofen was flying one when he was shot down.

Fokker E-111. German fighter (1915) widely used on Western Front; first plane to have machine guns synchronized with propeller.

Fokker F-27 Friendship. Netherlands' two-engine turboprop passenger aircraft (1957).

Fokker F-VIIb-3m. Three-motored passenger plane (1927) used throughout Europe in 1930s; various models.

Ford Trimotor. "Tin Goose"; passenger plane built by Henry Ford in 1929; popular in North and South America; some were still flying decades later.

Gee-Bee Model SZ Super Sportster. American racing plane of early 1930s, noted for killing pilots.

General Dynamics F-16 Fighting Falcon. U.S. jet fighter-bomber-interceptor (1975).

Globemaster. See **Douglas C-124 Globemaster**.

Gloster Gladiator. British military biplane fighter (1937).

Gloster Meteor. First British jet fighter (1944), used against V-1 bombs in last stages of World War II.

Golden Flyer. Glenn Curtiss' plane which won the Gordon Bennett Cup and Prix de la Vitesse in 1909. In 1910 it took off from the deck of a ship at Hampton Roads, Va.

Gotha. Various models; German bombing plane of World War I; the G-IV and G-V bombed London in 1917–18.

Graf Zeppelin. German dirigible (1929) which made historic round-the-world flight.

Grumman E2 Hawkeye. U.S. Navy twin-engine carrier-based early-warning aircraft (1961); has large radar pancake atop.

Grumman F-14B. U.S. Navy carrier-based jet fighter (1972).

Grumman F4F-4 Wildcat. U.S. Navy carrier-based fighter (1940) of World War II.

Grumman F6F-3 Hellcat. Highly successful U.S. Navy carrier-based fighter of World War II (1942); also used by British.

Grumman F9F Panther. U.S. Navy carrier-based jet fighter (1949).

Grumman G-21 Goose. U.S. two-engine amphibious aircraft (1937).

Grumman Gulfstream. U.S. twin-engine jet business aircraft (1967); various models.

Grumman TBF-1 Avenger. Widely used U.S. Navy carrier-based torpedo bomber of World War II (1942).

Gypsy Moth. See **DeHavilland Gypsy Moth**.

Halberstadt CL-11. German escort fighter and strafer of World War I (1917).

Halifax. See **Handley-Page Halifax Mk. III**.

Handley-Page. Several models; British bombers of World War I; the V-1500 was the first four-motored British aircraft.

Handley-Page Halifax Mk. III. Four-engined British bomber (1940) used throughout World War II.

Harrier. See **Hawker Siddeley Harrier Mk. 1**.

Hawker Hurricane Mk. I-IV. British fighter plane of World War II (1937) which bested German bombers during Battle of Britain.

Hawker Siddeley Harrier Mk. 1. British twin-engine vertical-takeoff fighter (1969); U.S. Marine version manufactured with McDonnell-Douglas.

Hawker Typhoon Mk. 1B. "Tiffy"; widely used British World War II ground-attack fighter (1941).

Heinkel He-111. Various models; German medium bomber of World War II (1936); used mainly as night and torpedo bomber.

Hellcat. See **Grumman F6F-3 Hellcat**.

Henri Farman HF 20, HF 40. World War I French observation planes.

Hindenburg LZ-129. German dirigible (1936) which offered scheduled passenger service across Atlantic; it caught fire May 6, 1937, while landing at Lakehurst, N.J., killing 35 people.

Hughes (McDonnell-Douglas) 500. Various models; U.S. helicopter (1965); military version is OH-6A.

Hughes Hercules. Enormous eight-engine wooden seaplane, known as the "Spruce Goose," developed by Howard Hughes in early 1940s, designed to carry 700 passengers. It flew only once, in 1947, for one mile.

Hurricane. See **Hawker Hurricane Mk. I-IV**.

Hydravion. French floatplane (1907); first successful floatplane.

Ilyushin I1-2 Shturmovik. Soviet Russian ground-attack and antitank aircraft of World War II (1941).

Ilyushin I1-4. Twin-engine medium bomber of Soviet Russia during World War II (1940).

Ilyushin I1-62 Classic. Soviet Russian four-engine jet passenger aircraft (1967).

Ilyushin I1-76M Candid. Soviet Russian four-engine jet military transport (1971).

Jenny. See **Curtiss JN3 Jenny**.

Junkers Ju-52. German trimotor passenger aircraft (1936), adapted for use as heavy bomber and paratrooper transport in World War II.

Junkers Ju-87 Stuka. German single-engine dive bomber (1938), highly effective in Battle of France in 1940; used throughout World War II.

Junkers Ju-88. German two-engine medium bomber (1936) used in various roles in World War II.

Kawasaki Ki-45 KA1c. Twin-engine Japanese night fighter and ground-attack aircraft of World War II (1942).

Kiowa. See **Bell 206 Ranger**.

Laird Super-Solution. Winner of 1921 Bendix Trophy with Jimmy Doolittle as pilot.

Lancaster. See **Avro Lancaster**.

Learjet. Various models; U.S. two-engine jet business aircraft (1963).

Liberator. See **Consolidated B-24 Liberator**.

Lockheed 10A Electra. All-metal twin-motor American passenger airplane (1935); several models.

Lockheed A-29 Hudson. U.S. Navy two-engine light bomber of World War II (1939), also used extensively by British Coastal Command.

Lockheed C-5A Galaxy. U.S. four-engine military transport jet (1971); largest North American aircraft.

Lockheed C-130 Hercules. U.S. four-engine turboprop military transport (1954); civilian version L-100-20 (1968).

Lockheed F-104G Starfighter. U.S. twin-engined jet fighter (1960).

Lockheed F-117A Stealth Fighter. U.S. twin-engine long-range jet bomber, not fighter (1981).

Lockheed L-749 Constellation. U.S. four-engine passenger aircraft (1943); military transport version known as C-69.

Lockheed L-1011 Tristar. U.S. three-engine jet passenger aircraft (1970).

Lockheed L-1049E Super Constellation. Widely used U.S. four-engine passenger aircraft (1951).

Lockheed Lodestar. U.S. twin-engine airliner (1940); for military use became the PV-1 Ventura, widely used in World War II.

Lockheed Orion. U.S. single-engine passenger plane (1932).

Lockheed P-38 Lightning. Fork-tailed twin-engine U.S. fighter of World War II (1940); very fast.

Lockheed P-80 Shooting Star. U.S. twin-engine jet fighter (1945); first American jet.

Lockheed SR-71A. U.S. two-engine high-altitude reconnaissance aircraft (1966).

Lockheed U-2. U.S. high-altitude jet reconnaissance aircraft (1956).

Lockheed Vega Model 1. U.S. passenger aircraft (1928); Wiley Post and Harold Gatty flew one around the world in 1931, Post in the *Winnie Mae* did it solo in 1933, and Amelia Earhart flew solo from Newfoundland to London in 1932 in a Vega.

Los Angeles. U.S. dirigible built in Germany (1924).

Luscombe. Various models; U.S. single-engine high-wing light plane (1937).

Macchi-Gastoldi MC-72. Italian seaplane which broke speed record for seaplanes at 441 mph in 1934 Schneider Cup race.

Marauder. See **Martin B-26G Marauder**.

Martin 130 China Clipper. U.S. four-engine flying boat (1934) used between Orient and California by Pan American Airlines.

Martin B-10. U.S. two-engine bomber (1933); the all-metal single-wing Martin Bomber of the Army Air Corps in the 1930s.

Martin B-26G Marauder. U.S. Army Air Force twin-engine medium bomber of World War II (1942).

Martin MB-1. U.S. twin-engine biplane bomber (1918); first U.S. bomber.

Maurice Farman MF-11. French reconnaissance plane used by Allies in early years of World War I.

McDonnell-Douglas 500. See **Hughes (McDonnell-Douglas) 500**.

McDonnell-Douglas DC-8. U.S. four-engine jet passenger aircraft (1958).

McDonnell-Douglas DC-9. U.S. twin-engine jet passenger aircraft (1965); longer version known as Super 80 built in 1979.

McDonnell-Douglas DC 10. U.S. three-engine jet passenger aircraft (1971).

McDonnell-Douglas F-4E Phantom. U.S. twin-engine jet fighter (1967).

McDonnell-Douglas F-15. U.S. jet fighter (1973).

Messerschmitt Bf-109. Various models; German fighter (1938) used in Spanish Civil War and throughout World War II.

Messerschmitt Bf-110C. German long-range fighter of World War II (1939).

Messerschmitt Me-16b Komet. German rocket-propelled fighter of World War II (1944).

Messerschmitt Me-262A Sturmvogel. German jet fighter and bomber of World War II (1944); first jet warplane.

MiG. See **Mikoyan-Gurevich (MiG).**

Mikoyan-Gurevich (MiG). Various models; Russian fighter plane of World War II (1940) and thereafter, including MiG-15, jet fighter used in Korea, the MiG-21PF (1960), and the MiG-31 Foxhound (1975).

Miles M14A Magister. British single-engine low-wing Royal Air Force trainer (1937).

Mirage. See **Dassault Mirage**.

Mitchell. See **North American B-25 Mitchell**.

Mitsubishi A6M3. "Zero"; widely deployed Japanese navy and army fighter plane of World War II (1939).

Mitsubishi G4MI. Japanese medium bomber of World War II (1941), known as "Betty" to Americans.

Mitsubishi Ki-46-II. "Dinah"; long-range Japanese reconnaissance plane of World War II (1941).

Monocoupe 90. U.S. single-engine high-wing light plane (1930).

Montgolfière. Hot-air balloon of Montgolfière brothers that carried two men aloft, November 21, 1793.

Mosquito. See **DeHavilland B-IV Mosquito**.

Mustang. See **North American P-51 Mustang**.

Nakajima B5N2. Japanese carrier-based torpedo bomber of World War II (1937).

Nieuport. Various models; French fighter plane, used by Billy Bishop, Albert Ball, Charles Nungesser, and other aces.

Norge (Dirigible No. 1). Dirigible designed by Umberto Nobile, which Roald Amundsen and Lincoln Ellsworth flew over the North Pole May 12, 1926.

North American AT-6. Advanced U.S. trainer of World War II (1938).

North American B-25 Mitchell. U.S. Army Air Force twin-engine light bomber of World War II (1941); led by Jimmy Doolittle, B-25s from carrier *Hornet* bombed Tokyo, April 18, 1942.

North American F-86 Sabre. U.S. jet fighter (1949).

North American P-51 Mustang. U.S. fighter plane (1941) used extensively by British and U.S. Army Air Force; one of most successful planes of World War II.

North American Rockwell B-1B. U.S. long-range four-engine jet aircraft (1976).

Northrop P-61 Black Widow. U.S. twin-engine night fighter of World War II (1942).

Otter. See **DeHavilland DHC3 Otter**.

P-38. See **Lockheed P-38 Lightning**.

P-39. See **Bell P-39 Airacobra**.

P-40. See **Curtiss P-40 Warhawk**.

P-47. See **Republic P-47 Thunderbolt**.

P-51. See **North American P-51 Mustang**.

Panavia Tornado IDS. Italian-British-German multirole twin-engine jet combat aircraft (1975).

PBY. See **Consolidated PBY Catalina**.

Peashooter. See **Boeing P-26A**.

Phantom. See **McDonnell-Douglas F-4E Phantom**.

Piper Cherokee. Various models; U.S. light aircraft (1961).

Piper Cub. U.S. high-wing light plane, used as trainer by Civilian Pilot Training Program and by U.S. Army for artillery spotting; originally known as "Taylor Cub" (1931).

Piper L-4 Grasshopper. U.S. Army artillery observer and liaison plane of World War II (1941).

Pitcairn PA-5 Super Mailwing. U.S. single-engine biplane (1927).

R-34. British dirigible which crossed Atlantic Ocean in 1919.

R.E. 8. British reconnaissance plane, sometimes used as bomber, 1916 and after.

Republic P-47 Thunderbolt. U.S. fighter plane (1941) used extensively for escort duty on bombing raids over Germany, 1944–45.

Ryan NYP. U.S. single-engine high wing (1927); Lindbergh's *Spirit of St. Louis* which he flew solo from New York to Paris May 20–21, 1927.

Ryan ST. Various models; U.S. single wing (1933); the Ryan PT (1939) was widely used as trainer during World War II.

S.E.5a. Very successful British World War I fighter used in 1917–18.

Santos-Dumont No. 6. Lighter-than-air craft which flew seven miles in France (1901).

Savoia-Marchetti S-55. Italian flying boat (1925); Italo Balbo led 24 S-55s on a cruise of 12,430 miles around the North Atlantic in 1933.

Savoia-Marchetti SM-7911 Sparviero. Italian light twin-engine bomber (1936) of Spanish Civil War and World War II.

Shenandoah. U.S. Navy dirigible (1923); crashed in storm September 3, 1925.

Short S23-C Empire Boat. English four-engine flying boat (1936) much used on overseas flights to Africa and Australia.

Short Sunderland Mk. V. Heavily-armed four-engine British flying boat (1938) developed from Short S-2b-C and widely used during World War II.

Sikorsky CH-54 Skycrane. U.S. large helicopter designed for lifting large objects (1964); S-64 is military version.

Sikorsky S-42. U.S. flying boat (1934) used in Caribbean and Great Lakes passenger service.

Sikorsky S-61. U.S. military transport and rescue helicopter (1961); known as "Jolly Green Giant"; civilian version is the HH-3E.

Sikorsky S-70 Blackhawk. U.S. Army and Navy combat helicopter (1974); Army version is UH60; Navy version is CH-60 Seahawk.

Sopwith F-l Camel. British World War I fighter, widely used after 1917.

Sopwith Pup. British World War I fighter (1916).

Sopwith Triplane. World War I British fighter of 1917.

Spad. Various models; leading French and Allied fighter of World War I, flown by Georges Guynemer, René Fonck, Eddie Rickenbacker, etc.

Spirit of St. Louis. Ryan NYP monoplane which Charles A. Lindbergh flew alone nonstop from New York to Paris, May 20–21, 1927.

Spitfire. See **Supermarine Spitfire**.

Spruce Goose. See **Hughes Hercules**.

SST. See **Concorde SST**.

Starfighter. See **Lockheed F-104G Starfighter**.

Stearman PT-13. U.S. single-engine biplane (1935); Army Air Force trainer; more produced than any other biplane in history.

Stinson Reliant. U.S. single-engine high-wing business plane (1935); Army trainer model of World War II called AT-19.

Stinson Trimotor SM-6000. Popular U.S. airliner (1931).

Stratocruiser. See **Boeing 377 Stratocruiser**.

Stuka. See **Junkers Ju-87 Stuka**.

Sud-Aviation SE-210 Caravelle. French twin-engine passenger jet aircraft (1959).

Sunderland. See **Short Sunderland Mk. V**.

Super Constellation. See **Lockheed L-1049E Super Constellation**.

Supermarine S-5, S-6, S-6B. British seaplanes, winners of Schneider Cup (1927–31); forerunners of Spitfire fighter.

Supermarine Spitfire. Foremost British fighter plane of World War II (1938), which played leading role in stopping the Luftwaffe in 1940; produced throughout war.

Swordfish. See **Fairey Swordfish**.

Taube. Etrich A-11 German plane (1910) used during World War I as trainer.

Taylorcraft Model B. U.S. high-wing light plane (1938); widely used as primary trainer.

Taylor Cub. U.S. high-wing light plane (1931); see also **Taylorcraft Model B and Piper Cub**; various models.

Tin Goose. See **Ford Trimotor**.

Tornado. See **Panavia Tornado IDS**.

Travel Air 2000. U.S. single-engine three-seat biplane (1925); followed by Model 4000 in 1926; both widely used.

Travel Air "R" Mystery Ship. U.S. single-engine monoplane (1929); winner of 1929 U.S. National Air Races.

Tupolev Tu-22 Blinder. Soviet Russian twin-engine medium bomber (1960).

Tupolev Tu-114 Rossiya. Soviet Russian four-engine passenger aircraft (1957).

U-2. See **Lockheed U-2**.

Vickers-Vimy IV. First plane to fly Atlantic nonstop, 1919; piloted by Capt. John Alcock and Lt. A. W. Brown.

Vickers Viscount. British four-engine turbo-prop passenger aircraft (1953).

Vickers Wellington III. British medium bomber (1938) used throughout World War II.

Voisin 5. French bomber with pusher-propeller of early World War I.

Vought 02U Corsair. U.S. Navy reconnaissance plane (1926).

Vultee BT-13A Valiant. Standard U.S. trainer of World War II (1940).

Waco F. Various models, beginning with Waco 9 (1925); U.S. single-engine biplane of 1930s and thereafter.

Wellington. See **Vickers Wellington III**.

Wildcat. See **Grumman F4F-4 Wildcat**.

Yakovlev Yak. Various models; Soviet Russian fighter of World War II (1940); over 30,000 were produced; also used in Korean War.

Yankee Clipper. See **Boeing 314 Clipper**.

Zeppelin I. Count von Zeppelin's 426-foot dirigible of 1900.

Zero. See **Mitsubishi A6M3**.

SOURCES

Angelucci, Enzo. *Airplanes: From the Dawn of Flight to the Present Day*. New York: McGraw-Hill, 1973.

———. *World Encyclopedia of Civil Aircraft, from Leonardo da Vinci to the Present*. New York: Crown Publishers, 1982.

Avery, Derek, ed. *Modern Civil Aircraft*. Stamford, Conn.: Longmeadow Press, 1988.

Daniels, Jeff, ed. *Modern Combat Aircraft*. Stamford, Conn.: Longmeadow Press, 1988.

The International Encyclopedia of Aviation. New York: Crown Publishers, 1977.

Jane's All the World's Aircraft, 1993–1994. Surrey, Eng.: Jane's Information Group, 1993.

Jane's Encyclopedia of Aviation. 5 vols. Danbury, Conn.: Grolier Educational Corp., 1980.

Montgomery, M. R., and Gerald Foster. *A Field Guide to Airplanes of North America*. 4th ed. Boston: Houghton Mifflin Co., 1992.

Riley, Gordon. *Vintage Aircraft of the World*. Shepperton, Surrey, Eng.: Ian Allen Ltd., 1983.

—L.D.R.

5

FAMOUS AUTOMOBILES

. . . . .

FROM JAY GATSBY'S RESPLENDENT VEHICLE WITH ITS GREEN LEATHER SEATS and handsome boxes in F. Scott Fitzgerald's *The Great Gatsby* to the dilapidated old Essex that the state trooper shoves over the side of the road in Flannery O'Connor's *Wise Blood,* varieties of automobiles have figured prominently and often importantly in modern letters. To quote Ms. O'Connor again, via Mr. Shiflet in "The Life You Save May Be Your Own," "The body, lady, is like a house; it don't go anywhere; but the spirit, lady, is like a automobile: Always on the move, always . . . "

In the early decades of this century, the variety of automobile makes on sale in the United States was sizable indeed. By the 1920s the range had narrowed some; the Depression years cut it down even further; and by the 1960s there were really only five or six different American manufacturers. For a time after World War II the English made a run for it on the American market, but except for sportscars the quality was poor, and once the Germans and then the Japanese cars arrived in force, the Hillman Minxes, Morris Minors, and Ford Anglias disappeared.

During all these decades—the 1940s, 1950s, 1960s—the American Big Three manufacturers enjoyed tidy profits and little competition. "See the U.S.A./In your Chevrolet/America is the Greatest Land of All" sang Dinah Shore on radio and TV commercials, the assumption being that the one was roughly identical with the other. Or as "Engine Charlie" Wilson, ex–GM head and at the time President Eisenhower's secretary of defense, put it, "What's good for General Motors is good for the nation."

Then came the Japanese. It was in the 1970s that Japan-made cars began not only crowding out the other imports (except for the Volvo and selected sport and luxury German cars) but cutting seriously into the sales of American cars. This is no place to rehearse the combined stupidity and complacent arrogance that put General Motors, Ford, and Chrysler, with the help of the United Auto Workers, on the ropes. Suffice it to say that only within the past several years have American models begun appearing that didn't have what *Consumer Reports* listed as "worse than average" frequency of repair records. It remains to be seen whether the lesson has been properly learned; there is still no small amount of rhetoric to the effect that it is an act of patriotism to drive a car that needs repairs more often.

What follows is a list of some of the more notable automobiles of our century, domestic and foreign. The inclusive dates for various models are not usually given, because many models have changed so radically under the same name that dates beyond the date of introduction have little meaning. A Ford Thunderbird, for example, meant something far more special and classy when first introduced in 1955 than it does today. On the other hand (and atypically so far as most cars go), the Volkswagen "Beetle," the "people's car" that the Führer promised would be available for all good Germans to drive in peace once *Lebensraum* was attained and the *Untermenschen* eradicated, remained almost the same reliable little "Bug" from 1938 until its discontinuance forty years later. Indeed, there is even talk now of bringing it back onto the market.

Information is given in the following format: Name of car (country of manufacture)—date of first production. No. of cylinders, horsepower when known [some companies, *e.g.*, Rolls-Royce after 1925, do not specify power]. Brief description with any distinctive details. Name and location of manufacturer.

Abbreviations used are: cyl = cylinders; hp = horsepower; mph = miles per hour; wlb = wheelbase; CC = Chrysler Corporation (Detroit); FMC = Ford Motor Company (Detroit); GMC = General Motors Corporation (Detroit). "Seater" (as in "4-seater") refers to the number of people a car will seat, not to the number of separate seats.

Alco touring car (U.S.)—1912. 6 cyl, 60 hp. Large touring car on 134-inch wlb. American Locomotive Company, Providence, R.I.

Alfa 12 (Italy)—1911. 4 cyl, 12 hp. Produced in limousine (4-seater) and sportscar versions. Anonima Lombarda Fabbrica Automobili, Milan.

Alfa Romeo RL Sport (Italy)—1922. 6 cyl, 84 hp. Produced in touring and racing versions, the latter capable of 90+ mph. SA Alfa Romeo, Milan.

Argyll 12 (G.B.)—1910. 4 cyl, 12 hp. Open touring car. Argyll Motor Ltd., Strathclyde, Scotland.

Auburn 120 Speedster (U.S.)—1929. 8 cyl. Supercharged high-speed 2-seater sportscar with rakish lines and chrome headers; each car supplied with certification that it had been tested at 100+ mph. Central Mfg. Co., Connersville, Ind.

Austin 7 (G.B.)—1923. 4 cyl, 105 hp. Known as "the Baby Austin"; short-wlb (75 inches) convertible 4-seater. Austin Motor Co. Ltd., Birmingham, Eng.

Bentley Le Mans (G.B.)—1931. 8 cyl, 200 hp. Racing car capable of 115 mph, winner of several prestigious European races in the early 1930s; large for a racing model, boxy with very long louvered hood; 4-seater in road model. Bentley Motors Ltd., Derby, Eng. (subsidiary of Rolls-Royce).

Bentley Silent Sports Car (G.B.)—1933. 6 cyl, 25 hp. Capable of 90 mph; offered in 2-seater and sedan models on 126-inch wlb. Bentley Motors Ltd., Derby, Eng. (subsidiary of Rolls-Royce).

BMW 328 (Germany)—1937. 6 cyl, 80 hp. Convertible 2-seater utility runabout, racy and streamlined. Bayerische Motorwerke AC, Munich.

BMW 520 (Germany)—1972. 6 cyl. Among the most popular of the numerous BMW models available in the United States since the late 1960s. Bayerische Motoren Werke AG., Munich.

BMW Dixi (Germany)—1928. 4 cyl, 15 hp. Sporty 2-seater, later made in a limousine version. Dixi-Werke (absorbed by BMW in 1928), Eisenbach.

Bugatti 35B (France)—1930. 8 cyl. Elegant racing convertible 2-seater famed for steering and handling qualities. E. Bugatti, Molsheim.

Buick 24/30 (U.S.)—1911. Open 5-seater. Buick Motor Co., Flint, Mich.

Buick Century (U.S.)—1936. 8 cyl, 116 and 120 hp options. Available in a variety of body styles; named after a famous long-distance railroad train in order to stress its virtues as a heavy cruising car. GMC.

Buick Riviera (U.S.)—1964. V-8 cyl, 325 hp. Available in various body styles. GMC.

Buick Roadmaster Series 80 (U.S.)—1936. 8 cyl, 37.8 hp. Coupe and sedan body styles available on 131-inch wlb. [The distinctive 4-hole simulated ventilation ports for the Roadmaster were introduced, along with the 3-hole ports for the Special and Super models, in the 1949 models.] GMC.

Cadillac 314 (U.S.)—1927. V-8 cyl, 80 hp. Convertible 4–5-seater touring car of luxury class. Cadillac Motor Co., Detroit.

Cadillac Coupe de Ville (U.S.)—1949. V-8, 160 hp. The industry's first "pillarless" hardtop coupe, *i.e.*, without a center post or door frame between the front and rear side windows; a distinctive feature was the "tailfin" rear fender introduced that year. Production of models designated "Coupe de Ville" continued for 44 years, until the spring of 1993. GMC.

Cadillac Eldorado (U.S.)—1953. V-8 cyl, 325 and 345 hp options. Large luxury car once described by its own makers as the most ostentatious vehicle they had ever produced; carried the famous tailfin rear fenders to new extremes; eventually made in hardtop coupe, Brougham hardtop sedan, and convertible coupe body styles. GMC.

Camaro. See **Chevrolet Z-28 Camaro**.

Chevrolet Bel Air (U.S.)—1953. V-8 cyl, 180 hp. One of the more successful "facelift" cars offering major appearance changes in 1953; available in convertible, hardtop coupe, sedan, and station-wagon body styles. GMC.

Chevrolet Capitol (U.S.)—1927. 4 cyl, 26 hp. 2-door 4-seater. GMC.

Chevrolet Corvette (U.S.)—1955. First in 6 cyl, then V-8 cyl, 283 hp. Made in convertible and split-window coupe models; a fast, powerful car restyled in major ways in 1984. GMC.

Chevrolet Impala (U.S.)—1958. 6 cyl, 145 hp and V-8 cyl, 185 hp options. Originally available only as sport coupe or convertible, later expanding to include other body styles. GMC.

Chevrolet Z–28 Camaro (U.S.)—1967. 6 and 8 cyl options, 140 and 155 hp. Sports and racing-style "muscle car"; GMC's answer to the Ford Mustang; 2-door hardtop with sliding top in later models. GMC.

Chrysler Imperial (U.S.)—1928. 6 cyl, 92 hp. Large car available in several body styles, designed to compete with Cadillac and Lincoln in the American big-car market. CC.

Chrysler New Yorker (U.S.)—1939. 8 cyl, 130 hp. Available in 2-passenger coupe, 5-passenger club coupe, sedan, and special-order Victoria Coupe, all on 125-inch wlb. CC.

Chrysler Royal Six Town & Country Wagon (U.S.)—1941. 6 cyl, 108, 112, and 115 hp options. Chrysler's first station wagon, a 9-passenger wood-paneled vehicle also available in a less popular 6-passenger model. CC.

Citroen B2 (France)—1921. 4 cyl, 20 hp. Closed 4-seater with 3 doors and oval rear-side windows. SA Andre Citroen, Paris.

Columbia (U.S.)—1904. 4 cyl, 24 hp. Touring car with open-sided front seats and enclosed rear compartment. Electric Vehicle Co., Hartford, Conn.

Cord 810 (U.S.)—1935. V-8 cyl, 125 hp. A sleek front-wheel-drive auto with distinctive wraparound grille bars encompassing the fore-end from front door to front door (the so-called coffin-nose effect) and tilting headlights; in 1937 the 812, a supercharged version, was added to the line. Auburn Automobile Co., Auburn, Ind.

Cord L-29 (U.S.)—1932. 8 cyl, 125 hp. Closed 2-seater coupe with sophisticated instrument panel, front-wheel drive, and ground clearance some 10 inches lower than usual for the time; popular among gangsters of the 1930s. Auburn Automobile Co., Auburn, Ind.

Coupe de Ville. See **Cadillac Coupe de Ville.**

De Dion-Bouton Voiturette (France)—1903. 1 cyl, 8 hp. Open 2-seater. De Dion-Bouton, Paris.

De Soto Custom Sedan (U.S.)—1946. 6 cyl, 109 hp. Large, comfortable 4-door sedan very similar in lines and mechanical details to other Chrysler cars of that era; also available as a convertible coupe. CC.

De Soto Sportsman (U.S.)—1958. V-8 cyl, 280 and 315 hp options. Backswept, "spaceship" lines with the exaggerated tailfins of the period; a long (126-inch wlb), rakish hardtop coupe. CC.

Duesenberg Model J (U.S.)—1929. 8 cyl, 265 hp. Large 4-door closed sedan with engine built by Lycoming (Duesenberg made bodies only); among the most coveted and expensive cars of the 1930s; nicknamed "the Cooper" because movie star Gary Cooper owned one; furnished with an elaborate and advanced-design instrument panel; capable of *ca.* 120 mph. Duesenberg Motor Co., Indianapolis, Ind.

Duesenberg Model SJ (U.S.)—1935. 8 cyl, 325 hp. Supercharged engine by Lycoming; billed as the fastest road car in America. Duesenberg Motor Co., Indianapolis, Ind.

Edsel (U.S.)—1958. V-8 cyl, 303 hp. Offered in several body styles on 118-inch wlb to rival Pontiac, Buick, and Dodge, but notoriously unsalable and in production for only two years; today, a collector's item in any model. FMC.

Eldorado. See **Cadillac Eldorado**.

Fiat 501 (Italy)—1923. 4 cyl. Convertible 4-seater capable of *ca.* 45 mph; over 70,000 made through 1926. Fiat SA, Turin.

Fiat Zero (Italy)—1912. 4 cyl, 15 hp. Large touring car. Fiat SA, Turin.

Ford Crown Victoria (U.S.)—1955. 6 cyl, 162 hp and V-8 cyl, 182 hp options. Sporty 2-door hardtop with chromed steel bar wrapped across the roof and along the sides of the rear deck. FMC.

Ford Custom (U.S.)—1949. 6 cyl, 95 hp and V-8 cyl, 100 hp options. Introduced the postwar Ford squared-off shape, a radical departure from the appearance of earlier models; available in a variety of body styles on 114-inch wlb. FMC.

Ford Model A (U.S.)—1927. 4 cyl, 40 hp. An extremely durable car produced in several body styles (coupe, sedan, convertible touring car) for five years; many still in regular use as late as the 1950s. FMC.

Ford Model K (U.S.)—1906. 6 cyl, 40 hp. High-powered open touring car on 114-inch wlb. FMC.

Ford Model T (U.S.)—1908. 4 cyl, 20 hp. Famous all-steel "Tin Lizzie" first produced by manual construction and later by assembly line; over 15 million produced in touring town car, runabout, and coupe styles up to discontinuance in 1927. FMC.

Ford Mustang (U.S.)—1965. 6 cyl and V-8 cyl options. Small, sporty 4-seater on 108-inch wlb with convertible and hardtop versions; many later changes, especially in 1969 and 1970, in engine and body specifications. FMC.

Ford Roadster (U.S.)—1932. 4 cyl, 50 hp. Convertible roadster in 2-seater and 4-seater models, the former with rumble seat; a few made as Model 18 with the then-new V-8 engine. FMC.

Ford Thunderbird (U.S.)—1955. V-8 cyl, 202 hp. Originally a 2-seater sportscar on 114-inch wlb available in convertible and hardtop styles; later enlarged and modified in many ways over its long, successful career. FMC.

Ford V-8. See **V-8 Ford**.

Franklin (U.S.)—1927. 12 cyl. Fast (*ca.* 95 mph) 2-seater coupe with closed passenger compartment. Franklin Automobile Co., Syracuse, N.Y.

Frazer (U.S.)—1947. 6 cyl, 100 hp. Available only in 4-door sedan; introduced with its almost identical though slightly less expensive companion car, the Kaiser; both with rounded boxy shape predictive of much postwar automotive styling. Kaiser-Frazer Corp., Willow Run, Mich.

Henry J (U.S.)—1950. 4 cyl, 68 hp and 6 cyl, 80 hp options. Small economy car capable of a 30 miles-per-gallon gasoline consumption rate; 2-door model only. Kaiser-Frazer Corp., Willow Run, Mich.

Hispano-Suiza Alfonso (Spain)—1912. 4 cyl, 65 hp. Sports/racing car. Hispano-Suiza SA, Barcelona.

Honda Civic (Japan)—1962. 4 cyl, 61 hp. Available in a variety of models and styles in succeeding years. Honda Motor Co. Ltd., Tokyo.

Horch 951 A (Germany)—1938. 8 cyl, 120 hp. Heavy luxury car chiefly in 4-door sedan models. Horch Werke AG, Zwicken.

Hudson Commodore (U.S.)—1948. 6 cyl, 121 hp and 8 cyl options. Large (121-inch wlb) sedan in 2- and 4-door styles with floorboards suspended between sides of the frame and lowered in order to lower the center of gravity; "step down into a Hudson" was the company's advertising slogan. Hudson Motor Co., Detroit, Mich.

Hudson Hornet (U.S.)—1951. 6 cyl, 145 hp. Available as sedan, club coupe, hardtop, and convertible; body styles similar to the basic 1948 plans but with improved engine. Hudson Motor Co., Detroit, Mich.

Itala 35/45 (Italy)—1907. 4 cyl, 45 hp. Open touring car; winner of the Peking-to-Paris race in 1907 (see **Spyker**). Itala Fabbrica Automobili SA, Turin.

Jaguar XK-120 (G.B.)—1950. 6 cyl, 190 hp. Long (104-inch wlb), sleek convertible 2-seater, also in hardtop model; the car that established the Jaguar's immense appeal in the United States, although earlier models had been available since the 1930s; most distinctive features were the very long hood and assertive front fenders. Jaguar Car Co. of British Motor Corp., London, Eng.

Jeep (U.S.)—1941. Light 4-wheel-drive General Purpose (GP) vehicle, enormously popular, designed by Karl K. Pabst for U.S. Army and built by Willys-Overland and Ford; during World War II some 650,000 were manufactured and used throughout the world. Jeeps are still made for civilian use. Named for a remarkable little animal in O. C. Segar's comic strip, "Popeye," which possessed the ability to disappear into the fourth dimension. See also **Willys Jeep Station Wagon**.

Kaiser. See **Frazer**.

Lancia Lambda 214 (Italy)—1923. 4 cyl, 49 hp. Large closed 4-door sedan *ca.* 16 feet in overall length. Fabbrica Automobili Lancia, Turin.

Land Rover (G.B.)—1948. 4 cyl., 60 hp; 4-wheel drive. Very popular all-terrain vehicle by Rover; various models thereafter.

La Salle V-8 (U.S.)—1927. V-8 cyl, 86 hp. Smaller and in some ways more advanced version of the Cadillac; available in coupe, convertible coupe, roadster, phaeton, and sedan, all on 125-inch wlb. GMC.

Lincoln Continental (U.S.)—1940. V-12 cyl, 120 hp. Luxury sedan and cabriolet models; inaugurated the distinctive Lincoln feature of the "continental" spare tire ring case outside the trunk. FMC.

Lincoln Zephyr (U.S.)—1936. V-12 cyl, 110 hp. Large (122-inch wlb) fastback sedan in 2- and 4-door models with streamlined appearance and headlights integral with front fenders; produced for five years. FMC.

Locomobile Type D (U.S.)—1904. 4 cyl, 16 hp. Luxury open touring car, 4-seater on 84-inch wlb. Locomobile Co., Chicopee, Mass.

Mercedes 630 (Germany)—1926. 6 cyl, 100 hp. Very large convertible 7-passenger touring car, supercharged, with 138-inch wlb. Daimler-Benz AG, Stuttgart-Unterturkheim.

Mercedes-Benz 500K (Germany)—1935. 8 cyl, 160 hp. Offered in roadster, sports coupe, cabriolet, convertible tourer, and limousine versions, all luxury cars; fewer than 400 built in this model designation. Daimler-Benz AG, Stuttgart-Unterturkheim.

Mercedes-Benz SS (Germany)—1929. 6 cyl, 170 hp. Racing car adapted for passenger use as a stylish convertible 2-seater with long louvered hood and side-mounted spare tire. Daimler-Benz, Stuttgart-Unterturkheim.

Mercedes Simplex (Germany)—1902. 4 cyl, 22 hp. Open touring car adapted for racing; set a new speed record of 69 mph in 1902. Daimler Motoren AG, Cannstatt.

Mercer Raceabout Type 35 (U.S.)—1911. 4 cyl. Open 2-seater racer with wooden spoke wheels and "Monocle" windshield similar to that of the Stutz Bearcat; factory guaranteed to cover a mile in 51 seconds. Roebling and Kuser, Mercer County, N.J.

Mercury (U.S.)—1939. V-8 cyl, 95 hp. Designed as a midrange car between Ford and Lincoln; built on 116-inch wlb; major changes made in 1949, 1952, 1967, and later. FMC.

Mercury Monterey (U.S.)—1957. V-8 cyl, 255 hp. Introduced in several body styles with the 2-door sedan at the bottom of its medium-price range. FMC.

MG Midget J2 (G.B.)—1932. 4 cyl, 60 hp. Convertible 2-seater sportscar with cutaway doors and fold-down windshield; made with numerous changes over the years to date. MG Car Co. Ltd., Abington, Eng.

Minerva Torpedo (Belgium)—1927. Large convertible luxury-class touring car, 4-seater. Minerva Motors, Antwerp.

Morris Oxford (G.B.)—1912. 4 cyl. Light 2-seater known for reliability and economy of operation. Morris Motor Co., Oxford, Eng.

Mustang. See **Ford Mustang**.

Nash Ambassador (U.S.)—1934. 8 cyl, 125 hp. Large car (124 and 132 wlb models) in several body styles. Nash Motors Co., Kenosha, Wis.

Nash Rambler (U.S.)—1950. 6 cyl, 82 hp. Small car available in convertible (later, hardtop) and station-wagon versions on 100-inch wlb; a big seller for several years. Nash Motors Co., Kenosha, Wis.

Nissan Stanza (Japan)—1977. 4 cyl, 88 hp. One of numerous Nissan (formerly Datsun) models, available in several body styles. Nissan Motor Co. Ltd., Tokyo.

Oldsmobile 98 (U.S.)—1949. V-8 cyl, 135 hp. The "rocket-engine" Olds available in several body styles, celebrated for advanced engine design. GMC.

Oldsmobile Curved Dash (U.S.)—1902. 1 cyl, 4.5 hp. Inexpensive 2-seater on a short (66-inch) wlb. Olds Motor Co., Lansing, Mich.

Packard Model L (U.S.)—1904. 4 cyl, 20 hp. Open 4-seater in roadster and sedan models, both without doors. Packard Motor Car Co., Detroit.

Packard Twelve (U.S.)—1933. V-12 cyl. Convertible 4-seater touring car capable of 100 mph. Packard Motor Car Co., Detroit.

Packard Twin Six (U.S.)—1915. V-12 cyl. Luxury car in convertible coupe and sedan models. Packard Motor Car Co., Detroit.

Peerless Model F Green Dragon (U.S.)—1903. 4 cyl, 60 hp. Racing car made famous by driver Barney Oldfield, who set several records with it in 1903–04. Peerless Motor Car Co., Cleveland.

Peugeot Bebe (France)—1913. 4 cyl. Convertible 2-seater, popular despite steering problems. SA des Automobiles Peugeot, Sochaux.

Pierce-Arrow (U.S.)—1919. 6 cyl, 75 hp. Luxury convertible 4-seater; headlights sunk into front fenders produced a streamlined effect unusual at the time. Pierce-Arrow Motor Co., Buffalo, N.Y.

Pierce-Arrow 41 (U.S.)—1931. 8 cyl, 132 hp. Closed 4-door sedan of luxury class; built after the company had become a subsidiary of Studebaker. Pierce-Arrow Motor Co., Buffalo, N.Y.

Pierce-Arrow Silver Arrow (U.S.)—1933. 12 cyl, 175 hp. 4-door sedan built for 1933 Chicago World Exhibition; offered at the then-astronomical price of $10,000. Pierce-Arrow Motor Co., Buffalo, N.Y.

Plymouth Belvidere (U.S.)—1951. 6 cyl, 97 hp. Hardtop coupe version of the top-line Cranbrook; two-tone color schemes in which the trunk was the color of the roof; offered in several body styles in succeeding years. CC.

Plymouth Sport Fury (U.S.)—1959. V-8 cyl, 230 hp. Available in sports coupe and convertible models; large, lowslung cars with "windswept" lines and exaggerated tailfins. CC.

Pontiac Bonneville (U.S.)—1957. V-8 cyl, 300 hp. Fuel-injected, fast road model available originally in convertible only, though a hardtop version was added in 1958. GMC.

Pontiac Catalina Vista (U.S.)—1959. V-8 cyl, 330 and 345 hp options. Large (122-inch wlb) 4-door hardtop with wraparound rear window and V-formation tailfins. GMC.

Pontiac GTO (U.S.)—1964. V-8 cyl, 333 and 360 options. Successful example of "muscle car" type, with large, powerful engine in midsize body; distinguished for speed on road and track; made in convertible and hardtop models with various style changes over the years. GMC.

Pontiac Star Chief (U.S.)—1954. 8 cyl, 122 hp. Top-of-the-line Pontiac for that and succeeding years; 124-inch wlb. GMC.

Porter Model 45 (U.S.)—1920. 4 cyl, 120 hp. Large (132-inch wlb) automobile in 7-passenger convertible touring car and five other body styles; most expensive of American cars in 1920, starting at $9,200. American & British Mfg. Co., Bridgeport, Conn.

Renault AX (France)—1909. 2 cyl, 14 hp. Originally a 2-seater but modified to produce a popular Paris taxi version with enclosed passenger compartment to separate riders from driver. Société Renault Freres, Billancourt.

Reo Royale (U.S.)—1932. 8 cyl, 125 hp. Large auto available in closed sedan and touring-car models with high-quality coachwork. Reo Motor Co., Lansing, Mich.

Rolls-Royce Phantom I (G.B.)—1925. 6 cyl, 75 hp. Open 4-seater; an American version with left-hand steering was built at Springfield, Mass. Rolls-Royce Ltd., London and Crewe, Eng.

Rolls-Royce Silver Ghost (G.B.)—1907. 6 cyl, 50 hp. Open touring car with silver-colored body and mahogany dashboard; over 6,000 built in the period 1907–25. Rolls-Royce Ltd., London and Crewe, Eng., and Rolls-Royce of America, Springfield, Mass.

Rolls-Royce Silver Wraith (G.B.)—1947. 6 cyl. Manufactured for eleven years and considered by many the finest Rolls-Royce ever built; available in a variety of body styles with interiors by various coachmakers on 127-inch wlb. Rolls-Royce Ltd., London and Crewe, Eng.

Royal Tourist 4-440 (U.S.)—1906. 4 cyl, 75 hp. Large touring car on 114-inch wlb. Royal Motor Car Co., Cleveland.

Russo-Balt K (Russia)—1913. 4 cyl, 24 hp. Convertible 2-seater. Russko-Baltskij vagonnyj, Riga.

Spyker (Holland)—1906. 4 cyl, 15 hp. Convertible 4-seater touring car; participated in a 61-day race/rally in 1907 from Peking to Paris. Jacob and Henrik Spijker, Trompenburg.

SS Jaguar 100 (G.B.)—1937. 6 cyl, 102 hp. 2-seater sports and racing convertible. SS Cars Ltd., Coventry, Eng.

Studebaker (U.S.)—1940. 6 cyl. Economical auto with 110-inch wlb and advanced designs, especially in the 1949 adaptations, which spawned many jokes about not being able to tell which way it was going because the hood and rear deck looked so much alike. Studebaker Corp., South Bend, Ind.

Stutz Bearcat (U.S.)—1912. 4 cyl, 60 hp. 2-seater racer with single monocle-shaped windshield on driver's side only and large barrel-shaped rear-mounted fuel tank. Ideal Motor Car Co., Indianapolis, Ind.

Tatra 11 (Czechoslovakia)—1923. 2 cyl, 12 hp. 2- and 4-seater closed-cab models, the former also in a racing version that won first prize in the 1924 Stuttgart Solitude race. Tatra Works Shareholding Co., Koprivnice, Czechoslovakia.

Thomas Flyer (U.S.)—1907. 6 cyl, 72 hp. Open 4-seater; winner of the New York-to-Paris race across three continents (via Siberia) in 168 days in 1908. E. R. Thomas Motor Co., Buffalo, N.Y.

Thunderbird. See **Ford Thunderbird**.

Toyota Corolla 1100 (Japan)—1966. 4 cyl, 75 hp. One of numerous Toyota models available in several body styles. Toyota Motor Corp. Ltd., Toyota City.

V–8 Ford (U.S.)—1932 and thereafter. Generic term for the many models of Ford cars using the highly successful V–8 engine; chiefly applied to roadsters and sporty models over the years. FMC.

Vauxhall (G.B.)—1905. 3 cyl, 9 hp. Inexpensive open 2-seater; first Vauxhall auto to use a steering wheel instead of a tiller. Vauxhall Motors Ltd., Bedfordshire, Eng.

Vauxhall Prince Henry (G.B.)—1914. 4 cyl, 75 hp. Named after the Prince Henry races in Germany; open 4-seater. Vauxhall Motors Ltd., Bedfordshire, Eng.

Volkswagen (Germany)—1938. 4 cyl, 24 hp. The classic "Beetle" or "Bug"; 2-door 5-seater with air-cooled rear-mounted engine; over 19 million produced before discontinuance in 1978. Volkswagenwerk GmbH, Wolfsburg.

Volkswagen Corrado SLC (Germany)—1993. V-6 cyl, 178 hp. High-performance sports coupe with top speed of *ca.* 140 mph. Volkswagenwerk GmbH, Wolfsburg.

Volvo OV (Sweden)—1927. 4 cyl, 28 hp. Convertible 4-seater (some closed models later made under the designation PV). AB Volvo Car Division, Goteborg.

Willys Jeep Station Wagon (U.S.)—1948. 4 cyl, 63 hp and 6 cyl, 70 hp options. Boxy, imitation wood-paneled wagons with overdrive standard on most models. Willys-Overland Co., Toledo, Ohio.

SOURCES

Bennett, Martin. *Rolls-Royce: The History of the Car.* 2nd ed. Sparkford, Eng.: Oxford Illustrated Press, 1983.

Dammann, George H. *Seventy Years of Chrysler.* Rev. ed. Sarasota, Fla.: Crestline Publishing Co., 1974.

Dunham, Terry B., and Lawrence R. Gustin. *The Buick: A Complete History.* Princeton, N.J.: Princeton Publishing Co., 1980.

Hendry, Maurice D. *Cadillac, Standard of the World: The Complete History.* 3rd ed. Princeton, N.J.: Princeton Publishing Co., 1979.

Hirsch, Jay. *Great American Dream Machines: Classic Cars of the 50s and 60s.* New York: Macmillan, 1985.

Norbye, Jan P. *The 100 Greatest American Cars*. Blue Ridge Summit, Pa.: Tab Books, Inc., 1981.

Norbye, Jan P., and Jim Dunne. *Pontiac: The Postwar Years*. Osceola, Wis.: Motorbooks International, 1979.

Porazik, Juraj. *Motor Cars, 1770–1940*. Leicester, Eng.: Galley Press, 1981.

Stein, Ralph. *The Great Cars*. New York: Grosset and Dunlap, 1967.

—J.L.M.

6

THE DOWNTOWN HOTEL
IN AMERICA

. . . . .

TO A CHILD GROWING UP IN A SMALL CITY A HALF CENTURY AND MORE AGO, far from any place remotely resembling a metropolis, hotels and railroad trains were among the more glamorous of human institutions. They represented the great world beyond the town boundaries, the means of escape from the mundane, the ordinary. I doubt whether anyone reared in places such as New York City, Chicago, Boston, San Francisco, and Philadelphia can imagine how such matters were once viewed by those of us who grew to maturity in the provinces. What one yearned to do was to go aboard the train, travel to the big city, and check into a downtown hotel.

Of railroads, more elsewhere in this volume. For now, let us consider the hotel. There were hotels in one's own town, of course. These too had their lure. One walked by the entrance, observed the resplendently uniformed porter standing outside, stared through the ornate portals into the dark recesses within, caught a glimpse perhaps of potted palms, overstuffed sofas, brass-ornamented elevator doors. A taxicab pulled up in front, the porter hurried to open the rear door, a traveler from afar stepped out onto the sidewalk, the porter received the luggage, traveler and porter disappeared inside the hotel—fortunate visitor, to be staying in so glamorous a place.

Motels? They were unheard of; there were only certain low-class, even disreputable affairs called tourist cabins at the edges of the city or beyond the limits. The hotels that mattered were downtown. That was where the action was. That was where any traveler of any importance wanted to be.

The American hotel developed with the American railway system. Hotels were located where the stores, offices, and public buildings were located, and convenient to railway stations. The golden age of the urban hotel was the late nineteenth and early twentieth centuries. The downtown hotel as we know it in the United States was a development of the decades immediately preceding the Civil War, and its hegemony lasted until after World War II, when expanding automobile and air traffic, the decline of rail transportation, and the development of surburban motor courts and motels brought an end to the primacy of the center-city in all but the largest metropolitan centers.

The first luxury hotel in the United States was the Tremont in Boston (1829). It was swiftly followed by others. Thereafter the social history of American cities can be traced and defined in important ways by the development of hotels, their flourishing, their obsolescence, their decline, and their replacement by newer hotels.

Then after World War II everything changed. Today only in the very largest American cities, where it still remains more practical to get around by public conveyance than private automobile, does the downtown hotel ordinarily thrive in anything resembling its onetime splendor.

The essence of a hotel's attraction was its ability to offer travelers the latest in comfort and convenience. As successive developments were made in the facilities and conveniences of the burgeoning nineteenth and early twentieth centuries, hotels were pressed to keep pace. Each new amenity— running water, gas and then electric lighting, private bathrooms, elevators, steam heat, fireproof buildings, telephone service, air conditioning, radios, more recently television—could mean expensive remodeling and replacement, or else swift decline in patronage. Without costly improvements, the first-class hotel of one generation became the second-line hotel of the next, and the flophouse of the generation following that. Thus a hotel's rise and fall could be a brief business indeed.

Until after the First World War relatively few hotels were chain operated. In the 1920s and 1930s, the Sheraton, Hilton, Menger, and other chains began building hotels in various cities. Only after World War II did chain ownership become the norm.

The compilation that follows is an effort to trace the rise and fall of the American downtown hotel as an institution. (Hotels located in resort areas and designed primarily for more lengthy stays are another matter entirely, and are not included.) It begins with the pre-Civil War period, and ends with the period immediately preceding World War II. After that, the automobiles, interstate highways, and airlines took over, and except in the largest cities little or no meaningful continuity with the once-regnant downtown hotel listings could thereafter be recorded.

To facilitate comparison, hotels are grouped in four different periods, each in a different style of typography:

(1) IN CAPITAL LETTERS, PRE-CIVIL WAR.

(2) In Roman type, the early 1880s, following the massive post–1865

railroad expansion across the length of the continent.

(3) In underlined type, in or about 1910, before the beginning of extensive intercity automobile travel.

(4) *In italic type, immediately before World War II, in 1940–41, when railroad passenger service was still the dominant mode of intercity transport, and downtown was still the place for the traveler to stay.*

Various guidebooks and other works have been drawn on, some of which were more selective than others. In smaller cities, especially in pre–Civil War days, the number of available hotels with decent facilities was limited, as the numerous accounts of European travelers to the then-young United States of America testify. *Appleton's Hand-Book* for 1860, the earliest city-by-city directory used in this compilation, frequently left the hotel listings blank for numerous cities, as if to advise the traveler that all bets were off, and local advice had better be sought.

In each chronological listing, the names of hotels continuing to operate as reasonably good hotels from one historical era into the next precede those of the newer hotels; otherwise the order of appearance is alphabetical. Obviously what constituted a "first-class" hotel varied from community to community and from era to era. No attempt has been made to rate hotels in order of quality or popularity.

Albany, N.Y.

(1) Congress Hall; Crosby's; Delavan House; Stanwix Hall. (2) Delavan House; Stanwix Hall; Kenmore. (3) Stanwix Hall; New Kenmore; Ten Eyck; Hampton; Globe. (4) *New Kenmore; Ten Eyck; Hampton; DeWitt Clinton; Farnham's; Wellington.*

Albuquerque, N.M.

(3) Alvarado. (4) *Alvarado; El Fidal; Franciscan.*

Atlanta, Ga.

(1) Trout House. (2) Kimball House; Markham; National. (3) Kimball House; Aragon; Ballard; Majestic; Piedmont. (4) *Piedmont; Atlanta-Biltmore; Ansley; Clermont; Cox-Carlton; Georgian Terrace; Henry Grady; Robert Fulton; Winecoff.*

Austin, Tex.

(2) Avenue; Raymond House; Stringer's. (3) Avenue; Driskill; Hancock. (4) *Driskill; Stephen F. Austin.*

Baltimore, Md.

(1) BARNUM'S CITY; EUTAW HOUSE; FOUNTAIN; GILMOR HOUSE; MALTBY HOUSE; NATIONAL. (2) Barnum's; Eutaw House; Maltby; Carrollton House; Howard; Mt. Vernon. (3) Eutaw House; Howard; Belvedere; Caswell; Keenan; Rennert; St. James; Sherwood; Stafford. (4) *New Howard; Belvedere; Stafford; Emerson; Lord Baltimore; Mt. Royal; Southern.*

Bangor, Maine

(1) BANGOR HOUSE. (2) Bangor House; Franklin House; Penobscot Exchange. (3) Bangor House; Penobscot Exchange; Windsor. (4) *Bangor House; Penobscot Exchange.*

Baton Rouge, La.

(2) Harney's. (3) Mayer. (4) *Heidelberg; King.*

Birmingham, Ala.

(2) Florence; Relay House. (3) Florence; Hillman; Metropolitan; New Morris. (4) *Bankhead; Claridge; Empire; Molton; Redmond; Thomas Jefferson; Tutwiler.*

Boise, Idaho

(2) Overland. (3) Idanha; Oxford. (4) *Boise; Owyhee.*

Boston, Mass.

(1) Adams; American House; Boylston; Coolidge; Parker House; Reverse House; Shawmut House; Tremont; United States. (2) Adams House; American House; Boylston; Parker House; Revere; Tremont; United States; Belmont; Brunswick; Clarendon; Commonwealth; Crawford House; Creighton House; Evans House; Metropolitan; National; New England; Quincy House; Young's. (3) American House; Parker House; Revere House; United States; Brunswick; Commonwealth; Crawford House; Quincy House; Young's; Bellevue; Brewster; Clare's; Copley Square; Essex; Franklin Square House; Langham; Lenox; Maverick; Somerset; Thorndike; Touraine; Vendome; Victoria. (4) *Parker House; Bellevue; Copley Plaza; Somerset; Vendome; Bradford; Kenmore; Lincolnshire; Manger; Myles Standish; Puritan; Ritz Carlton; Sheraton; Statler; Tournine; Westminster.*

Bridgeport, Conn.

(1) STANLEY HOUSE. (2) Atlantic; Elm House; Sterling. (3) Atlantic House; Windsor. (4) *Arcade; Barnum.*

Brooklyn, N.Y.

(1) GLOBE; MANSION HOUSE; PIERREPONT HOUSE; (2) Mansion House; Pierrepont House. (3) Mansion House; Pierrepont; Brevoort; Clarendon; Margaret; St. George. (4) *Pierrepont; Margaret; St. George; Bossert; Half Moon; Towers.*

Buffalo, N.Y.

(1) AMERICAN. (2) Bonney's; Continental; Mansion House; Pierce's; Tifft House. (3) <u>Mansion House; Broezel House; Genesee; Iroquois; Lafayette; Lenox; Niagara; Stafford; Statler; Touraine.</u> (4) *Lenox; Statler; Touraine; Buffalo; Fairfax; Fillmore; Ford; Lafayette; Park Lane; Stuyvesant; Tudor Arms; Westbrook.*

Burlington, Iowa

(1) BASSETT HOUSE. (2) Bassett House; Duncan; Gorham; Grand Central. (3) <u>Delano; Union.</u> (4) *Burlington.*

Cedar Rapids, Iowa

(2) Grand; Northwestern; Pullman; Southern. (3) <u>Grand; Delavan.</u> (4) *Allison; Commonwealth; Magnus; Montrose; Roosevelt.*

Charleston, S.C.

(1) CALDER HOUSE; CHARLESTON; MILLS; PAVILION; PLANTER. (2) Charleston; Mills; Pavilion; Waverly House. (3) <u>Charleston; St. John's (Mills); Argyle.</u> (4) *Charleston; St. John's; Francis Marion; Fort Sumter.*

Charleston, W.Va.

(1) HALE HOUSE; ST. JAMES. (2) Hale House; Ruffner. (3) <u>Ruffner.</u> (4) *Daniel Boone.*

Charlotte, N.C.

(1) CAROLINA INN; CENTRAL. (2) Central; Belmont; Mansion House. (3) <u>Selwyn; Buford.</u> (4) *Selwyn; Charlotte; Mecklenburg.*

Chattanooga, Tenn.

(2) Chattanooga; Crutchfield; Read House; Stanton House. (3) <u>Read House; Patten; Southern; Williams.</u> (4) *Read House; Patten.*

Cheyenne, Wyo.

(2) Inter-Ocean; M. P. Railroad. (3) <u>Inter-Ocean; Normandie.</u> (4) *Frontier; Plains.*

Chicago, Ill.

(1) American Temperance Union; Briggs House; Lake House; Mansion; Metropolitan; Richmond House; Sherman House; Tremont House; Western. (2) Briggs House; Metropolitan; Sherman House; Tremont House; Atlantic; Brevoort; Brunswick; Burdick House; Burke's; Commercial; Grand Pacific; Kuhn's; Massasoit House; Palmer House; Southern. (3) <u>Briggs House; Sherman; Brevoort; Grand Pacific; Palmer House; Auditorium; Bismarck; Chicago Beach;</u>

Congress Apartments; Del Prado; Galt House; Grace; Great Northern; Hyde Park; Kaiserhof; Kenwood; LaSalle; Lexington; Majestic; McCoy's; Metropole; Morrison; Ontario; Saratoga; South Side; Stratford; Victoria; Wellington; Windemere; Windsor-Clifton. (4) *Atlantic; Palmer House; Sherman; Auditorium; Bismarck; Chicago Beach; Congress; Del Prado; LaSalle; Morrison; Windemere; Allerton; Ambassador; Ambassador West; Baker; Belmont; Blackstone; Central Plaza; Crillon; Drake; Eastgate; Edgewater Beach; Fairfax; Guyon; Harrison; Hayes; Knickerbocker; Maryland; New Lawrence; Pearson; St. Clair; Seneca; Sheridan Beach; Shoreland; Sovereign; Stevens; Walker.*

Cincinnati, Ohio

(1) BURNET HOUSE; HENRIE HOUSE; PEARL STREET HOUSE; SPENCER HOUSE; WALNUT STREET HOUSE. (2) Burnet House; Walnut Street House; Crawford House; Denison; Emery; Galt; Gibson House; Grand; Keppler's; Merchant's; Palace; St. James; St. Nicholas. (3) Burnet House; Gibson House; Grand; St. Nicholas; Alms; Havlin; Honing; Lackman; Martin's; Munro; Sinton; Stag. (4) *Gibson; Alms; Sinton; Fountain Square; Kemper Lane; Metropole; Netherland Plaza.*

Cleveland, Ohio

(1) ANGIER HOUSE; WEDDELL HOUSE. (2) Weddell House; American House; Forest City House; Hollenden; Kennard House; Stillman. (3) Forest City; Hollenden; Baldwin; Colonial; Euclid; Gillsy. (4) *Hollenden; Lake Shore; Allerton; Auditorium; Belmont; Bolton Square; Carter; Cleveland; Olmstead; Park Lane Villa; Sovereign; Statler; Wade Park Manor; Westlake.*

Columbia, S.C.

(1) CONGAREE. (2) Columbia House; Grand Central; Wheeler House. (3) Columbia; Wright's; Colonial; Jerome. (4) *Columbia; Jefferson; Wade Hampton.*

Columbus, Ga.

(2) Central; Planters; Rankin House. (3) Rankin House; Racine; Springer. (4) *Ralston; Waverly.*

Columbus, Ohio

(1) NEIL HOUSE. (2) Neil House; American House; Park; St. Charles; United States. (3) Neil House; Park; Crittenden; Grand Southern; Hartman. (4) *Neil House; Crittenden; Deshler Wallick; Fort Hayes; Seneca; Virginia.*

Concord, N.H.

(1) EAGLE HOUSE. (2) Eagle; Phoenix. (3) Eagle; Phoenix. (4) *Eagle; Phoenix.*

Dallas, Tex.

(2) Grand Windsor; Lamar; St. George's. (3) Imperial; Lakeside; Oriental; Southland. (4) *Southland; Adolphus; Ambassador; Baker; Cliff Towers; Ervington; Jefferson; Melrose; Sanger; Stoneleigh Court.*

Davenport, Iowa

(1) Le Claire House. (2) Ackley House; Burtis House; Kimball House; Newcomb; St. James. (3) Kimball House; St. James. (4) *Blackhawk.*

Denver, Colo.

(1) Broadwell House; Denver House. (2) Alvord; American; Charpiot's; Grand Central; Inter-Ocean; St. James; Wentworth; Windsor. (3) St. James; Windsor; Adams; Albany; Brown Palace; Metropole; New Markham; Oxford; Shirley. (4) *Albany; Brown Palace; Oxford; Shirley; Colburn; Cory; Cosmopolitan; Lancaster; Olin; Park Lane; Savoy.*

Des Moines, Iowa

(2) Aborn House; Capitol; Kirkwood. (3) Kirkwood; Savery; Victoria. (4) *Brown; Commodore; Fort Des Moines.*

Detroit, Mich.

(1) American; Biddle House; Michigan Exchange; Woodworth's. (2) Biddle House; Michigan Exchange; Brunswick; Cass; Griffin; Griswold; Russell House; Stanwix. (3) Brunswick; Griswold; Cadillac; Claire; Metropolis; Normandie; Oriental; Pontchartrain; Tuller; Washington Inn; Wayne. (4) *Book-Cadillac; Barlum; Briggs; Detroit-Leland; Detroiter; Fort Shelby; Fort Wayne; Lee Plaza; Roosevelt; Statler; Strathmore; Webster Hall; Whittier; Wolverine.*

Dubuque, Iowa

(1) Julien House; Washington. (2) Julien House; European; Tremont. (3) Julien House; Merchants. (4) *Julien Dubuque; Canfield.*

Duluth, Minn.

(2) Clark House. (3) Lenox; McKay; St. Louis; Spalding. (4) *Spalding; Duluth; Holland.*

El Paso, Tex.

(2) Angelus; Sheldon. (3) Sheldon; Orndorff; Pierson; St. Regis. (4) *Cortez; Hilton; Paso del Norte.*

Fort Wayne, Ind.

(1) Washington Hall. (2) Aveline House; Mayer. (3) Wayne. (4) *Indiana; Keenan.*

Fort Worth, Tex.

(2) El Paso; Grand Central; Mansion; Metropolitan; Planters. (3) <u>Metropolitan;</u> <u>Delaware; Worth.</u> (4) *Worth; Blackstone; Texas.*

Galveston, Tex.

(1) ISLAND CITY HOUSE. (2) Island City; Girardin; Tremont House. (3) <u>Tremont;</u> <u>Palmetto; Royal; Seaside; Washington.</u> (4) *Buccaneer; Coronado Court; Galvez;* *Jean Lafitte.*

Greensboro, N.C.

(1) BLAND'S; SOUTHERN. (2) McAdoo House; Piedmont. (3) <u>Benbow; Guilford.</u> (4) *King Cotton; O. Henry; Sedgefield Inn.*

Hannibal, Mo.

(1) PLANTER'S HOUSE. (2) Planter's House; Ketterings; Park. (3) <u>Mark Twain;</u> <u>Union Depot.</u> (4) *Mark Twain.*

Harrisburg, Pa.

(1) COVERLEY'S. (2) Bolton's; Jones; Kirkwood House; Lochiel House; United States. (3) <u>Lochiel House; Commonwealth.</u> (4) *Penn-Harris.*

Hartford, Conn.

(1) UNITED STATES. (2) United States; Allyn House; American; Brower House; City; Park Central; Trumbull. (3) <u>Allyn House; Garde; Hartford; Heublein; New</u> <u>Dom.</u> (4) *Garde; Heublein; Bond.*

Helena, Mont.

(3) <u>Helena; Grandon.</u> (4) *Placer.*

Houston, Tex.

(1) FANNIN HOUSE. (2) Fannin; State Capitol; Tremont House. (3) <u>Tremont;</u> <u>Brazos; Bristol; Rice.</u> (4) *Rice; Bon Milam; Lamar; Sam Houston; Texas State;* *Warwick; William Penn.*

Indianapolis, Ind.

(1) AMERICAN; BATES HOUSE. (2) Bates House; Grand; Occidental; Remy House; Sherman House. (3) <u>Grand; Claypool; Denison; English; Spencer.</u> (4) *Claypool;* *Antlers; Lincoln; Mariott; Pennsylvania; Severin; Sheffield Inn; Warren;* *Washington.*

Jackson, Miss.

(2) Bowman House; Edwards House. (3) <u>Edwards House.</u> (4) *Edwards;* *Heidelberg; R. E. Lee; Walthall.*

Jacksonville, Fla.

(1) Judson House. (2) Carlton; Everett; Metropolitan; Moncrieff House; Nicholls House; St. James; St. John's; Tremont; Windsor. (3) <u>Windsor; Aragon; Duval; Grand View; Roseland.</u> (4) *Windsor; George Washington; Mayflower; Roosevelt; Seminole.*

Kansas City, Mo.

(1) Western. (2) Blossom; Centropolis; Coates House; Lindell; Metropolitan; Pacific House; St. James; Union Depot. (3) <u>Coates; Baltimore; Kupper; Densmore; Midland; Savoy; Victoria.</u> (4) *Aladdin; Ambassador; Bellerive; Commonwealth; Continental; LaSalle; Muehlebach; Netherlands; Park Lane; Pickwick; Ponce de Leon; President; State.*

Knoxville, Tenn.

(2) Atkin; Lamar House. (3) <u>Colonial; Cumberland; Imperial; Stratford.</u> (4) *Andrew Johnson; Farragut.*

Lancaster, Pa.

(1) North American. (2) City; Michael's Grape; Stevens House. (3) <u>Stevens House; Wheatland.</u> (4) *Stevens House; Brunswick.*

Laramie, Wyo.

(2) Laramie House. (3) <u>Johnson; Kuster; Pacific.</u> (4) *Connor.*

Lexington, Ky.

(1) Phoenix House. (2) Phoenix House; Ashland House. (3) <u>Phoenix; Leland.</u> (4) *Phoenix; Lafayette.*

Lincoln, Nebr.

(2) Arlington; Commercial; Grand Central; Windsor. (3) <u>Windsor; Capitol; Lincoln; Lindell.</u> (4) *Capitol; Lincoln; Cornhusker.*

Little Rock, Ark.

(1) Anthony House. (2) Anthony House; Capitol; Deming; Grand Central; Robinson House. (3) <u>Capitol; Gleason; Marion.</u> (4) *Marion; Albert Pike; McGehee.*

Los Angeles, Calif.

(2) Pico House; St. Charles. (3) <u>Alexandria; Alvarado; Angelus; Fremont; Hayward; Hershey Arms; Hollenbeck; Lankershim; Leighton; Melrose; Nadeau; Pepper; Rosslyn; Van Nuys; Westminster.</u> (4) *Lankershim; Ambassador; Beverly*

Hills; Beverly-Wilshire; Biltmore; Clark; Garden of Allah; Gaylord; Hollywood; Hollywood-Plaza; Knickerbocker; Mayfair; New Rosslyn; Park-Wilshire; Roosevelt; Savoy; Town House.

Louisville, Ky.

(1) GALT HOUSE; LOUISVILLE. (2) Galt House; Louisville; Alexander's; Central; Commercial House; Fifth Avenue; National; United States; Willard. (3) <u>Galt House; Louisville; Fifth Avenue; Willard's; Seelbach's.</u> (4) *Seelbach; Brown; Henry Clay; Henry Watterson; Kentucky; Tyler.*

Macon, Ga.

(1) LANIER HOUSE. (2) Lanier House; Brown's; National. (3) <u>New Lanier House; Brown.</u> (4) *Lanier House; Dempsey.*

Madison, Wis.

(1) CAPITOL HOUSE. (2) Capitol House; Park; Ton-ya-wa-tha. (3) <u>Capitol; Park; Avenue; Sherlock.</u> (4) *Capitol; Park; Belmont; Loraine.*

Memphis, Tenn.

(1) GAYOSO. (2) Gayoso; Clarendon; Commercial; Gaston; Peabody; Worsham. (3) <u>Gayoso; Clarendon; Gaston; Peabody.</u> (4) *Gayoso; Peabody; Claridge; William Len.*

Miami, Fla.

(3) <u>Gralyn House; Halcyon Hall; Iroquois; Royal Palm; San Carlos.</u> (4) *Alcazar; Columbus; El Comodoro; Everglades; McCallister; Miami Colonial.*

Milwaukee, Wis.

(1) NEWHALL HOUSE. (2) Newhall House; Grand Central; Kirby House; Metropolitan; Plankinton; Republican; St. Charles. (3) <u>Kirby; Plankinton House; Republican House; St. Charles; Aberdeen; Blatz; Pfister; Schlitz.</u> (4) *Plankinton House; Pfister; Ambassador; Astor; Knickerbocker; Schroeder.*

Minneapolis, Minn.

(2) Bellevue; Clark; First National; Merchants; Nicollet House; Pauley House; St. James; West. (3) <u>Nicollet House; West; Brunswick; Holmes; Hyser; Majestic; Plaza; Vendome.</u> (4) *Nicollet; Andrews; Buckingham; Curtis; Dyckman; Francis Drake; Leamington; Radisson.*

Mobile, Ala.

(1) BATTLE HOUSE. (2) Battle House; Laclede; St. James. (3) <u>Battle House; Bienville; Cawthon; Southern.</u> (4) *Battle House; Cawthon; Admiral Semmes.*

Montgomery, Ala.

(1) EXCHANGE. (2) Exchange; Central. (3) <u>Exchange; Glenmore; Mabson; Windsor.</u>
(4) *Jefferson Davis; Whitley.*

Nashville, Tenn.

(1) NASHVILLE. (2) Gilchrist; Maxwell House; Nicholson; Stacey House; St. Cloud; Scott's. (3) <u>Maxwell House; Duncan; Hermitage; Tulane; Utopia.</u> (4) *Hermitage; Andrew Jackson; James Robertson; Noel; Sam Davis.*

Newark, N.J.

(1) CITY; EAGLE. (2) Continental; Newark; Park. (3) <u>Continental.</u> (4) *Douglas; Riviera; Robert Treat; St. Francis.*

New Haven, Conn.

(1) TONTINE. (2) Tontine; Elliot; New Haven House; Tremont. (3) <u>Tontine; New Haven House; Davenport; Garde.</u> (4) *Bishop; Taft.*

New Orleans, La.

(1) CRESCENT CITY; EXCHANGE; ST. CHARLES; ST. LOUIS; VERANDAH. (2) St. Charles; St. Louis; Cassidy; City; Denechaud; Royal; St. James; Windsor. (3) <u>St. Charles; New Denechaud; Cosmopolitan; Fabachers; Grunewald; Monteleone.</u> (4) *St. Charles; Monteleone; DeSoto; Jung; New Bienville; New Orleans; Roosevelt.*

New York, N.Y.

(1) American; Astor House; Brevoort; Carlton House; Clarendon; Clinton; Exchange; Fifth Avenue; Holt's; Howard; Irving House; Lovejoy's; Metropolitan; New York; Prescott House; St. Nicholas; Tammany; Taylor's International. (2) Astor House; Brevoort House; Clarendon; Fifth Avenue; Metropolitan; New York; St. Nicholas; Brunswick; Buckingham; Everett House; Gilsey; Gramercy Park House; Grand; Grand Central; Grand Union; Hoffman House; Murray Hill; Park Avenue; Rossmore; St. Cloud; Sturtevant; Union Square; Westminster; Windsor. (3) <u>*Downtown (from Battery to Canal St.):* Astor House; Cosmopolitan; Smith and McNells. *Between Canal St. and 14th St.:* Lafayette-Brevoort House; Albert; Broadway Central; St. Denis. *From 14th St. to 26th St.:* Hoffman House; Albemarle; Chelsea; Margaret Louisa Home; New Amsterdam; Westminster. *Above Madison Square:* Astor; Clarendon; Gramercy Park; Grand Union; Murray Hill; Park Avenue; Albany; Algonquin; Belleclaire; Belmont; Breslin; Bristol; Buckingham; Cadillac; Cumberland; Earlington; Empire; Endicott; Flanders; Gerard; Gilsey House; Gotham; Grenoble; Herald Square; Holland House; Imperial; King Edward; Knickerbocker; Latham; Majestic; Manhattan; Marie Antoinette; Marseille; Martha Washington House;</u>

Martinique; Navarre; Netherland; New Florence; New Grand; New Plaza; New Weston; Normandie; Pierrepont; Prince George; Roland; St. Andrew; St. Regis; San Remo; Savoy; Seville; Sherman Square; Victoria; Waldorf-Astoria; Webster; Winthrop; Woodward. (4) *Uptown: Savoy Plaza; Barbizon; Barbizon Plaza; Carlyle; Empire; Essex House; Hampshire House; Park Central; Pierre; Plaza; Ritz Tower; St. Moritz South. Central: Astor; Algonquin; Ambassador; Gotham; Gramercy Park; Prince George; St. Regis; Waldorf-Astoria; Winthrop; Barclay; Beekman Tower; Berkshire; Biltmore; Claridge; Commodore; Edison; Fifth Avenue; Lexington; Lincoln; Madison; McAlpin; New Yorker; Park Lane; Pennsylvania; Piccadilly; Ritz-Carlton; Roosevelt; Taft; Times Square; Vanderbilt; Warwick; Weylin; Winslow.*

Norfolk, Va.

(1) NATIONAL. (2) National; Atlantic; Purcell House. (3) Atlantic; Fairfax; Gladstone; Monticello. (4) *Atlantic; Fairfax; Monticello; Southland.*

Ogden, Utah

(2) Beardsley House; Ogden House; Utah. (3) Broom House; Depot House; Reed House. (4) *Ben Lomond.*

Oklahoma City, Okla.

(4) *Oklahoma Biltmore; Skirvin.*

Omaha, Nebr.

(1) DOUGLAS HOUSE; HERNDON HOUSE. (2) Grand Central; Metropolitan; Whithnell House. (3) Drexel; Henshaw; Loyal; Merchant's; Millard; Murray; Paxton House; Rome. (4) *Paxton; Blackstone; Fontenelle; Logan.*

Pensacola, Fla.

(2) Bedell House; City; European; St. Mary's Hall; Winter House. (3) Continental; Escambia; Merchants'. (4) *San Carlos.*

Philadelphia, Pa.

(1) American House; Continental; Francis's Union; Girard; Indian Queen; La Pierre; Marshall House; Washington House. (2) Continental; Girard House; La Pierre; Aldine; Bellevue; Bingham; Colonnade; Guy's; Lafayette; St. Cloud; West End. (3) Continental; Aldine; Bellevue-Stratford; Bingham; Colonnade; Dooner's; Green's; Hanover; Lorraine; Majestic; Normandie; Rittenhouse; St. James; Stenton; Vendig; Walton; Windsor. (4) *Bellevue-Stratford; Adelphia; Barclay; Benjamin Franklin; Chateau Crillon; Drake; Mayfair House; Philadelphia; Ritz-Carlton; Walnut Park Plaza; Warwick; Wellington.*

Phoenix, Ariz.

(3) <u>Adams House; Commercial; Ford.</u> (4) *Adams; Arizona Biltmore; Camelback Inn; Jokake Inn; San Carlos.*

Pittsburgh, Pa.

(1) MONONGAHELA HOUSE. (2) Monongahela House; Anderson; Bayer; Central; Robinson; St. Charles; Seventh Avenue. (3) <u>Monongahela; Anderson; St. Charles; Seventh Avenue; Colonial; Duquesne; Fort Pitt; Griswold; Henry; Lincoln; Lorraine; Newell's; Schenley.</u> (4) *Schenley; Pittsburgher; Roosevelt; Webster Hall; William Penn.*

Portland, Maine

(1) AMERICAN; ELMS. (2) City; Falmouth House; Preble; St. Julian; United States. (3) <u>Falmouth House; Preble House; Columbia; Congress Square; Jefferson; Lafayette; West End.</u> (4) *Lafayette; Eastland and Congress Square.*

Portland, Oreg.

(2) Clarendon; Esmond; Holton House; Merchants; St. Charles. (3) <u>Eaton; Grand Central; Imperial; Lenox; Perkins.</u> (4) *Benson; Congress; Heathman; Multnomah; Portland.*

Providence, R.I.

(1) ALDRICH; CITY; MANSION HOUSE. (2) Aldrich; City; Central; Dorrance; Narragansett; Perrine; Providence. (3) <u>Dorrance; Narragansett; Crown; Newman.</u> (4) *Narragansett; Providence-Biltmore.*

Raleigh, N.C.

(1) WASHINGTON; YARBOROUGH HOUSE. (2) Yarborough House; National. (3) <u>Yarborough House; Park.</u> (4) *Carolina; Sir Walter.*

Reno, Nev.

(2) Depot. (3) <u>Golden Eagle; Riverside.</u> (4) *Golden Eagle; Riverside; El Cortez.*

Richmond, Va.

(1) BALLARD HOUSE; EXCHANGE; SPOTSWOOD. (2) Exchange and Ballard; American; Ford's; St. Charles. (3) <u>Ford's; Jefferson; Lexington; Murphy's; Park; Richmond.</u> (4) *Jefferson; Murphy's; Richmond; John Marshall; William Byrd.*

Roanoke, Va.

(3) <u>Ponce de Leon; Roanoke; Stratford.</u> (4) *Roanoke; Patrick Henry.*

Rochester, N.Y.

(1) EAGLE; CONGRESS. (2) Congress Hall; Brackett House; Clinton House; National; New Osburn House; Powers; Reed's; Whitcomb House; Windsor. (3) Osburn House; Powers; Whitcomb; Rochester; Seneca. (4) *Powers; Rochester; Sagamore.*

Sacramento, Calif.

(1) JONES'; ORLEANS. (2) Orleans; Capitol House; Golden Eagle; Grand; Langhorn. (3) Capitol; Golden Eagle; Sacramento. (4) *Sacramento; Californian; Senator.*

St. Joseph, Mo.

(1) PATEE HOUSE. (2) Bacon House; Commercial; Pacific House; Saunders House; Union Depot. (3) Metropole; St. Charles. (4) *Robidoux.*

St. Louis, Mo.

(1) CITY; MISSOURI; MONROE; NATIONAL; PLANTERS; UNITED STATES; VIRGINIA. (2) Planters; Barnum's; Broadway; Everett House; Grand Central; Laclede; Lindell; Olive Street; St. James; St. Nicholas; Southern. (3) Planters; Grand Central; Laclede; New St. James; Southern; Beers; Benton; Berlin; Garni; Grand Avenue; Hamilton; Jefferson; Marquette; Maryland; Merchants; Muckingham; Rosier; Stratford; Terminal; Usona; Washington; West End. (4) *Jefferson; Chase; Claridge; Congress; Coronado; Forest Park; Mayfair; Lennox; Park Plaza; Statler.*

St. Paul, Minn.

(1) BARLOW HOUSE; FULLER HOUSE; RICE; WINDSOR HOUSE. (2) Windsor; Clarendon Exchange; Grand Central; Merchants'; Metropolitan; Ryan; St. James; Sherman House. (3) Merchants'; Ryan; Aberdeen; Angus; Euclid; Frederick; Magee's Bachelors. (4) *Commodore; Lowry; St. Paul.*

Salt Lake City, Utah

(2) Cliff House; Continental; Townsend. (3) Cullen; Grand Pacific; Kenyon; Knutsford; New Wilson. (4) *Newhouse; Temple Square; Utah.*

San Antonio, Tex.

(1) MENGER. (2) Menger; Central; Hord House; Maverick; Plaza; St. Leonard. (3) Menger; New Maverick; Bexar; Hot Sulphur; Mahncke; St. James; Southern. (4) *Menger; Aurora; Blue Bonnet; Gunter; Plaza; St. Anthony.*

San Diego, Calif.

(2) Horton House. (3) Brewster; Helix; Robinson; U.S. Grant. (4) *U.S. Grant; El Cortez; Park Manor; Pickwick; San Diego.*

San Francisco, Calif.

(1) American Exchange; Cosmopolitan; Graham House; International House; Irving House; Occidental; Oriental; Parker House; Rasette House; Union; Ward House. (2) American Exchange; International; Occidental; Baldwin House; Brooklyn; Grand; Lick House; Palace; Russ House. (3) <u>Palace; Audubon; Fairmont; Grand Central; Imperial; Jefferson; Majestic; Savoy; St. Francis; St. James.</u> (4) *Palace; Fairmont; St. Francis; Canterbury; Chancellor; Clift; Drake-Wiltshire; Empire; Mark Hopkins; Pickwick; Sir Francis Drake; Whitcomb.*

Santa Fe, N.M.

(1) SANTA FE. (2) Palace. (3) <u>Palace; Clare.</u> (4) *La Fonda.*

Savannah, Ga.

(1) City; Pulaski House; Screven House. (2) Pulaski House; Screven House; Marshall House. (3) <u>Pulaski; Screven; DeSoto; Martinique.</u> (4) *DeSoto; Savannah-Oglethorpe.*

Scranton, Pa.

(1) Forest House; Wyoming. (2) Forest House; Wyoming House; Commercial; Lackawanna Valley; Parker House. (3) <u>Coyne; Jermyn; Terrace.</u> (4) *Casey.*

Seattle, Wash.

(1) FELKER HOUSE. (2) Occidental. (3) <u>Butler; Lincoln; New Washington; Rainier-Grand; Savoy.</u> (4) *New Washington; Benjamin Franklin; Claremont; Edmond Meany; Mayflower; Olympic; Roosevelt; Wilsonian.*

Spokane, Wash.

(2) California. (3) <u>Halliday; Spokane; Victoria.</u> (4) *Davenport.*

Springfield, Ill.

(1) AMERICAN. (2) Leland House; Palace; Revere; St. Nicholas. (3) <u>Leland House; St. Nicholas; Ridpath.</u> (4) *Leland; St. Nicholas; Abraham Lincoln.*

Springfield, Mass.

(1) COOLEY'S; MASSASOIT HOUSE. (2) Cooley; Massasoit House; Hayne's; Warwick. (3) <u>Cooley's; Massasoit House; Haynes; Worthy.</u> (4) *Bridgeway; Highland.*

Stockton, Calif.

(2) Commercial; Grand; Mansion; Yosemite House. (3) <u>Yosemite; Imperial.</u> (4) *Clark; Stockton.*

Syracuse, N.Y.

(1) GLOBE; ONONDAGA; SYRACUSE. (2) Globe; Burns; Congress Hall; Europe House; Vanderbilt House. (3) <u>Jefferson; St. Cloud; Warner; Yates.</u> (4) *Onandaga; Syracuse.*

Tacoma, Wash.

(2) Tacoma. (3) <u>Tacoma; Bonneville; Donnelly.</u> (4) *Walker; Winthrop.*

Tallahassee, Fla.

(2) City; Leon. (3) <u>Leon; St. James.</u> (4) *Cherokee; Floridan.*

Tampa, Fla.

(2) Orange Grove; Tampa. (3) <u>Tampa Bay; Almeria; City; DeSoto; Palmetto.</u> (4) *Floridan; Hillsboro; Tampa Terrace; Thomas Jefferson.*

Terre Haute, Ind.

(1) TERRE HAUTE HOUSE. (2) Terre Haute House; National; Ohmer's Depot. (3) <u>Terre Haute House; Filbeck.</u> (4) *Terre Haute House; Deming.*

Toledo, Ohio

(1) AMERICAN; OLIVER. (2) Oliver House; Boody House; Burnet; Jefferson; Madison. (3) <u>Boody House; Jefferson; Madison; St. Charles; Secor; Wayne.</u> (4) *New Secor; Belvedere; Commodore Perry; Fort Meigs; Hillcrest.*

Topeka, Kans.

(1) GARVEY'S. (2) Copeland; Fifth Avenue; Gordon House; Taft House; Windsor. (3) <u>Throop; National.</u> (4) *Jayhawk.*

Trenton, N.J.

(1) FRENCH ARMS; MANSION HOUSE; TRUE AMERICAN INN; UNITED STATES. (2) American House; United States; Joy's; National; Trenton. (3) <u>Trenton; Windsor.</u> (4) *Hildebrecht; Stacy-Trent.*

Troy, N.Y.

(1) MANSION HOUSE; NORTHERN; TEMPERANCE HOUSE; TROY; ST. CHARLES; UNION HALL; WASHINGTON. (2) Mansion House; Troy House; American House; Revere House. (3) <u>Mansion House; Troy; Fifth Avenue; Rensselaer; Windsor.</u> (4) *Troy; Hendrick; Hudson.*

Tucson, Ariz.

(1) PHILLIPS HOUSE. (2) Cosmopolitan; Hodges; Orndorff; San Xavier. (3) <u>Heidel; San Augustin; Santa Rita; Windsor.</u> (4) *Santa Rita; Pioneer.*

Tulsa, Okla.

(3) <u>New State, Robinson, Tulsa House.</u> (4) *Adams, Alvin, Bliss, Mayo.*

Utica, N.Y.

(1) Bagg's. (2) Bagg's; American; Butterfield House; Central. (3) <u>Bagg's;</u> <u>Butterfield; Yates.</u> (4) *Martin; Utica.*

Washington, D.C.

(1) Brown's; Ebbitt House; National; Willard's. (2) Ebbitt House; National; Willard's; Arlington; Arno; Congressional; Continental; Globe; Imperial; Metropolitan; Riggs House; St. James; St. Marc; Washington; Wormley's. (3) <u>Ebbitt House; National; New Willard; Arlington; Metropolitan; Riggs House; St.</u> <u>James; Bancroft; Cairo; Cochran; Dewey; Dolly Madison House; Driscoll; Fetra's</u> <u>Temperance; Grafton; Hamilton; Normandie; Raleigh; Regent; Richmond;</u> <u>Shoreham.</u> (4) *Willard; Washington; Raleigh; Shoreham; Ambassador; Annapolis; Carlton; Dodge; DuPont Circle; Fairfax; Francis Scott Key; Hamilton; Hay-Adams; Lafayette; Lee House; Mayflower; New Amsterdam; Roger Smith; Roosevelt; Wardman Park.*

Wheeling, W.Va.

(2) Grant House; McLure House; St. James; Stanton House. (3) <u>McLure; Windsor.</u> (4) *McLure; Windsor.*

Wichita, Kans.

(2) Occidental. (3) <u>Carey.</u> (4) *Allis; Broadview; Lassen.*

Wilmington, Del.

(1) Washington House. (2) Clayton House; Dickinson; Felton; Grand Union. (3) <u>Clayton House; Wilmington.</u> (4) *Du Pont.*

Winston-Salem, N.C.

(1) Salem Tavern. (2) Salem Tavern. (3) <u>Zinzendorf.</u> (4) *Robert E. Lee.*

Worcester, Mass.

(1) Lincoln House. (2) Lincoln House; Bay State House; Waldo House. (3) <u>Lincoln; Bay State; New Park; Standish; Warren.</u> (4) *Bancroft.*

SOURCES

Appleton's Handbook to the United States and Canada. New York: D. Appleton and Co., 1879.

Baedeker, Karl. *The United States: Handbook for Travellers.* New York: Charles Scribner's Sons, 1909.

Englishman's Illustrated Guide Book to the United States and Canada. 2nd ed. London: Longman, 1875.

Hall, Edward H., ed. *Appletons' Hand-Book of American Travel.* New York: D. Appleton and Co., 1869.

Hillyard, M. B. *The New South.* Baltimore: Manufacturers' Record Co., 1887.

Lathrop, Elise. *Early American Inns and Taverns.* New York: Robert M. McBride and Co., 1926.

Ludy, Robert B. *Historic Hotels of the World.* Philadelphia: David McKay Co., 1927.

Richards, T. Addison, ed. *Appleton's Companion Hand-Book of Travel.* New York: D. Appleton and Co., 1860.

Travel America Guide. New York: Ahrens Publishing Co., 1940.

Where to Eat, Sleep and Play in the U.S.A. Bronxville, N.Y.: Traveler's Windfall Association, 1941.

Williamson, Jefferson. *The American Hotel: An Anecdotal History.* New York: Alfred A. Knopf, 1930.

—**L.D.R.**

HOMES OF THE FAMOUS
IN THE BRITISH ISLES
AND THE UNITED STATES

· · · · ·

ACCORDING TO THE LATE EDGAR A. GUEST, IT TOOK A HEAP O' LIVIN' IN A house to make it home, but a good question is, At what point does a home become a House? What makes a residence, whether urban or rural, eligible to be known to others by a name rather than merely by its street or R.F.D. address? Apparently there is nothing logical about the process; it seems to involve the way in which the owner thinks of himself or herself. It is a kind of harking back, as it were, to seventeenth- and eighteenth-century England. Members of the rising middle class became wealthy through trade or manufactures or politics, were ennobled, and purchased rural seats to confirm their elevated status.

Expanse of acreage and wealth usually have something to do with it, but not always. Andrew Carnegie called his estate near Pittsburgh, Braemur Cottage, which was a kind of reverse snobbery; as well, he called the Carnegie Steel Company the Village Smithy. The nineteenth-century South Carolina poet Paul Hamilton Hayne, the family wealth almost all having been lost in the Civil War, moved into a tiny dwelling near Augusta, Georgia, which he called by the imposing name of Copse Hill. Hayne's motive was probably not status but picturesqueness, just as Joel Chandler Harris, with an eye toward the Roman poet, called his place in the Atlanta suburbs Snapbean Farm.

Samuel L. Clemens built an imposing, elaborately ornate house in Hartford, Connecticut; it is said to resemble a Mississippi River steamboat. Yet, although located in a subdivision called Nook Farm, it has been known since then simply as the Mark Twain House. On the other hand, he did give a name to his later house in Redding, Connecticut; it was called after one of his fictional characters, Captain Stormfield.

In William Styron's novel *Set This House on Fire* a sign is painted on a wall along the winding road to Sambucco: BEHOLD ABOVE YOU THE PALACIAL VILLA OF EMILIO NARDUCCI OF WEST ENGLEWOOD, N.J., U.S.A. (The original was and perhaps still is visible en route to Ravello from Amalfi, on the Tyrrhenian coast of Italy.) The motives that set it there are scarcely very different from those that prompted John Churchill, Duke of Marlborough, and his wife Sarah to give the name of Blenheim to the huge new palace awarded to them by Queen Anne, in honor of the famous victory over the French in 1704.

A certain amount of etiquette seems to be involved in bestowing names upon dwelling places. For example, it is all right to give a summer place, whether at the shore or in the mountains, a name, even though it already has a perfectly good street or road address; but to call one's year-round city residence by a name would be considered pretentious, unless it is located well out in the suburbs. (Yet some have done so, and gotten away with it.)

If Abraham Lincoln had survived his second term and gone back to Springfield, Illinois, to live, would he have given his house there a name? One doubts it, even though Mrs. Lincoln would probably have liked the idea. When Harry Truman returned to Independence, Missouri, he didn't give his house a name, not even Dewey Dell. If Jimmy Carter's peanut farm in Georgia has a name, I haven't heard of it; perhaps Hostage House would do. But Mount Vernon, Monticello, Sagamore Hill, Hyde Park, the LBJ Ranch—these are all right, because somehow they seem to fit the personalities involved. And there is certainly no law against someone buying or even renting a modest split-level in Lower Suburbia and entitling it The Pits, or Brazenface Manor, Disorderly House, or Deere Abbey, or Bach Haus, or, if an owner of dogs, Tickbourne House—whatever looks good on letterhead.

Below are some famous persons and the names of their residences.

Acheson, Dean. Harewood, Sandy Spring, Md.
Adams, Henry. Pitch Pine Hill, Beverly, Mass.
Adams, John and Abigail. Peacefield, Quincy, Mass.
Albert, Prince. Osborne House, East Cowes, Eng.
Astor, John Jacob. Astor Villa, Hoboken, N.J.
Astor, Lady Nancy. Cliveden, Buckinghamshire, Eng.
Barnum, P. T. Court Marina, Bridgeport, Conn.
Beckford, William. Fonthill Abbey, near Fonthill Bishop, Eng.
Beecher, Henry Ward. Boscobel, Peekskill, N.Y.
Biddle, Nicholas. Andalusia, near Philadelphia, Pa.
Booth, Edwin. Boothden, Middletown, R.I.

Brontë, Anne, Charlotte, and Emily. Haworth Parsonage, Haworth, Eng.

Brown, Margaret ("Molly"). Mon Etui, Newport, R.I.

Bryant, William Cullen. Cedarmere, Roslyn, N.Y.

Buck, Pearl. Green Hills Farm, Dublin, Pa.; Mountain Haunt, Winhall, Vt.

Bulwer-Lytton, Sir Edward. Knebworth, near Stevenage, Eng.

Burke, Edmund. The Gregories, Beaconsfield, Eng.

Byrd, Adm. Richard E. Wickyup, East Sullivan, Maine.

Byrd, William, II. Westover, Charles City County, Va.

Cabell, James Branch. Dumbarton Grange, near Richmond, Va.

Cable, George W. Tarryawhile, Northampton, Mass.

Calhoun, John C. Fort Hill, near Clemson, S.C.

Campbell-Bannerman, Sir Henry. Belmont Castle, Meigle, Scotland.

Carnegie, Andrew. Braemar Cottage, Cresson, Pa.; Skibo Castle, Dornoch Firth, Scotland; Shadowbrook, Lenox, Mass.

Carroll, Charles. Carrollton, near Frederick, Md.

Cavendish, Sir William. Chatsworth House, near Bakewell, Eng.

Cecil, Robert, Earl of Salisbury. Hatfield House, Hatfield, Eng.

Cecil, William, Lord Burghley. Burghley House, near Stamford, Eng.

Churchill, John, Duke of Marlborough. Blenheim Palace, Woodstock, Eng.; Marlborough House, London, Eng.

Churchill, Sir Winston. Chartwell, Westerham, Eng.

Clay, Henry. Ashland, Lexington, Ky.

Clemens, Samuel L. Stormfield, Redding, Conn.; Wave Hill House, New York City, N.Y.

Cleveland, Grover. Gray Gables, Bourne, Mass.

Coke, Thomas. Holkham Hall, Wells, Eng.

Coolidge, Calvin. The Beeches, Northampton, Mass.

Cooper, James Fenimore. Otsego Hall, Cooperstown, N.Y.; Angevine Farm, Scarsdale, N.Y.

Copley, John Singleton. Mount Pleasant, Boston, Mass.

Cornell, Katherine. Chip Chop, Vineyard Haven, Mass.; Peter Rock, Palisades, N.Y.

Cowper, William. Orchard Side, Olney, Eng.

Darwin, Charles. Down House, Downe, Eng.

Davis, Jefferson. Beauvoir, Biloxi, Miss.; Rosemont, Woodville, Miss.

DeMille, Cecil B. Paradise, near Cottonwood Glen, Calif.

Dewey, Thomas E. Dapplemere, Pawling, N.Y.

Diana, Princess of Wales. Althorp, near Northampton, Eng.

Dickens, Charles. Gadshill, near Rochester, Eng.

Disraeli, Benjamin. Hughenden Manor, near High Wycomb, Eng.

Douglas, Stephen. Oakenwald, Chicago, Ill.

Douglas, William O. Prairie House, Goose Prairie, Wash.

Douglass, Frederick. Cedar Hill, Washington, D.C.
Doyle, Sir Arthur Conan. Windlesham Manor, Crowborough, Eng.
Dreiser, Theodore. Iroki, Mount Kisco, N.Y.
Eddy, Mary Baker. Pleasant View, Concord, N.H.
Edison, Thomas A. Glenmont, West Orange, N.J.
Eliot, George, and George Henry Lewes. The Heights, Wormley, Eng.
Fairbanks, Douglas, and Mary Pickford. Pickfair, Beverly Hills, Calif.
Fairfax, Baron Thomas. Appleton House, Nunappleton, Yorkshire, Eng.
Faulkner, William. Rowan Oak, Oxford, Miss.
Ferber, Edna. Treasure Hill, Easton, Conn.
Fitzgerald, F. Scott. La Paix, Towson, Md.
Ford, Henry. Fair Lane, Dearborn, Mich.
Friddell, Guy R. The Gin House, Norfolk, Va.
Frost, Robert. Pencil Pines, South Miami, Fla.
Garfield, James A. Lawnfield, Mentor, Ohio.
Gore-Booth, Constance. Lissadell, near Drumcliff, Ireland.
Gregory, Lady Augusta. Coole Park, near Gort, Ireland.
Hammerstein, Oscar. Highland Farm, Doylestown, Pa.
Hardy, Thomas. Max Gate, Dorchester, Eng.
Harris, Joel Chandler. Snapbean Farm, near Atlanta, Ga.
Harrison, Benjamin. Point Farm, North Bend, Ohio.
Hayes, Rutherford B. Spiegel Grove, Fremont, Ohio.
Hearst, William Randolph. La Cuesta Encantada, San Simeon, Calif.
Hogg, James. Eldinhope, near Selkirk, Scotland.
Holmes, Oliver Wendell. Canoe Meadows, Pittsfield, Mass.
Holmes, Oliver Wendell, Jr. Beverly Farms, Beverly, Mass.
Hughes, Ted. Lumb Bank House, Hebden Bridge, South Pennines, Eng.
Humphrey, Hubert. Triple H Ranch, Waverly, Minn.
Irving, Washington. Sunnyside, Tarrytown, N.Y.
Jackson, Andrew. Hermitage, Nashville, Tenn.
James, Henry. Lamb House, Rye, Eng.
Jeffers, Robinson. Tor House, Carmel, Calif.
Jefferson, Thomas. Monticello, near Charlottesville, Va.
Johnson, Lyndon B. LBJ Ranch, near Burnet, Tex.
Kaufman, George S. Barley Sheaf Farm, Holicong, Pa.
Kipling, Rudyard. Batemans Burwash, Eng.; Naulakha, Brattleboro, Vt.
Lardner, Ring. The Mange, Kings Point, N.Y.; Still Pond, East Hampton, N.Y.
Lauderdale, the Duke and Duchess of. Ham House, near Richmond, Eng.
Laurel, Stan. Fort Laurel, Canoga Park, Calif.
Lawrence, T. E. Clouds Hill, Bovington Camp, near Moreton, Eng.
Lee, Robert E. Arlington, Arlington, Va.
London, Jack. Wolf House, Glen Ellen, Calif.

McClellan, Gen. George B. Maywood, West Orange, N.J.

McCormick, Cyrus. Clayton Lodge, Richfield Springs, N.Y.

Madison, James. Montpelier, near Orange, Va.

Marquand, John P. Nervana, Hobe Sound, Fla.

Marshall, Gen. George C. Dodona Manor, Leesburg, Va.

Marshall, John. Oak Hill, Delaplane, Va.

Mason, George. Gunston Hall, Fairfax County, Va.

Monroe, James. Ash Lawn, near Charlottesville, Va.

Morrell, Ottoline. Garsington Manor, near Oxford, Eng.

Morris, Robert. Lemon Hill, Philadelphia, Pa.

Murrow, Edward R. Glen Arden, Pawling, N.Y.

Nast, Thomas. Harlem Lane, New York, N.Y.; Villa Fontana, Morristown, N.J.

Nation, Carry A. Hatchet Hall, Eureka Springs, Ark.

Newton, Sir Isaac. Woolsthorpe Manor, near Grantham, Eng.

Nightingale, Florence. Embley House, near Wellow, Eng.

Nimitz, Adm. Chester. Longview, Berkeley, Calif.

Noyes, John Humphrey. Mansion House, Kenwood, N.Y.

O'Hara, John. Linebrook, Princeton, N.J.

Olmsted, Frederick Law. Tosomock Farm, Staten Island, N.Y.

O'Neill, Eugene. Brook Farm, Ridgefield, Conn.; Casa Genotta, Sea Island, Ga.; Peaked Hill Bar, Provincetown, Mass.; Tao House, Danville, Calif.

Page, John. Rosewell, Gloucester County, Va.

Parker, Dorothy. Fox Hollow Farm, near Tinicum, Pa.

Parr, Katherine. Sudeley Castle, Winchcombe, Eng.

Parrish, Maxfield. The Oaks, Plainsfield, N.H.

Peary, Adm. Robert. Sawungun, Eagle Island, Maine.

Peirce, Charles S. Arisbe, near Milford, Pa.

Perelman, S. J. Rising Gorge, near Erwinna, Pa.

Pope, Alexander. Crossdeep, Twickenham, London, Eng.

Potter, Beatrix. Hill Top, near Sawrey, Eng.

Presley, Elvis. Graceland, Memphis, Tenn.

Pulitzer, Joseph. Chatwold, Bar Harbor, Maine.

Randolph, John. Roanoke, near Charlotte Court House, Va.

Rayburn, Sam. Home Place, Bonham, Tex.

Ringling, John. Ca'd'zan, Sarasota, Fla.

Rockefeller, John D. The Casements, Ormond Beach, Fla; Forest Hill and Homestead, East Cleveland, Ohio; Kykuit, North Tarrytown, N.Y.

Rockefeller, Nelson. The Eyrie, Seal Harbor, Maine.

Roosevelt, Franklin Delano and Eleanor. The Big House, Hyde Park, N.Y.; Val-Kill, Hyde Park, N.Y.

Roosevelt, Theodore. Sagamore Hill, Oyster Bay, N.Y.

Rothschild, Baron Ferdinand de. Waddesdon Manor, near Aylesbury, Eng.

Runyon, Damon. Las Melaleuccas, Miami, Fla.

Ruskin, John. Brantwood, Coniston, Eng.

Ruth, George Herman ("Babe"). Home Plate, Sudbury, Mass.

Sackville-West, Vita, and Harold Nicolson. Sissinghurst Castle, near Cranbrook, Eng.

Sandburg, Carl. Chikaming Goat Farm, Harbert, Mich.; Connemara Farm, near Flat Rock, N.C.

Sanger, Margaret. Willowlake, Fishkill, N.Y.

Scott, Sir Walter. Abbotsford, near Melrose, Scotland.

Shakespeare, William. New Place, Stratford-upon-Avon, Eng.

Shaw, George Bernard. Shaw's Corner, Ayot St. Lawrence, Eng.; Charleston Farm, Firle, Eng.; Torca Cottage, Dalkey, Ireland.

Sidney, Sir Philip. Penshurst, Kent, Eng.

Simms, William Gilmore. Woodlands, near Barnwell, S.C.

Sterne, Laurence. Shandy Hall, Coxwold, Eng.

Stuyvesant, Peter. White Hall, New Amsterdam, N.Y.

Sullivan, Ed. Kettletown Farm, Southbury, Conn.

Tate, Allen. Benfolly, near Clarksville, Tenn.

Tennyson, Alfred Lord. Aldworth, Haslemere, Eng.

Terry, Ellen. Smallhythe Place, near Tenterden, Eng.

Toscanini, Arturo. Villa Pauline, Bronx, N.Y.

Tyler, John. Sherwood Forest, Charles City County, Va.

Valentino, Rudolph. Falcon Lair, Bel Air, Calif.

Victoria, Queen. Balmoral Castle, near Crathie, Scotland.

Walpole, Horace. Strawberry Hill, Twickenham, Eng.

Walpole, Sir Robert. Houghton Hall, Houghton, Eng.

Washington, George. Mt. Vernon, Mt. Vernon, Va.

Waugh, Evelyn. Piers Court, Stinchcombe, Eng.

Webster, Daniel. Green Harbor, Marshfield, Mass.

Weill, Kurt, and Lotte Lenya. Brook House, New York City, N.Y.

Wellington, Duke of. Apsley House, London, Eng.; Stratford Saye House, near Basingstoke, Eng.

Westinghouse, George. Erskine Park, Lenox, Mass.; Solitude, Pittsburgh, Pa.

White, Stanford. Box Hill, St. James, N.Y.

Wolfe, James. Quebec House, Westerham, Eng.

Woolf, Virginia and Leonard. Monks House, Rodmell, Eng.

Wordsworth, William. Dove Cottage, Grasmere, Eng.

Wright, Orville. Hawthorne Hill, Dayton, Ohio.

Yeats, William Butler. Thoor Ballylee, near Gort, Ireland.

Ziegfeld, Florenz. Burkeley Crest, Hastings-on-Hudson, N.Y.

SOURCES

American Automobile Association Tourbooks. Heathrow, Fla.: American Automobile Association, 1991.

Bence-Jones, Mark. *Great English Homes: Ancestral Homes of England and Wales and the People Who Lived in Them.* New York: British Heritage Press, 1984.

Burton, Neil. *The Historic Houses Handbook.* New York: Facts on File, 1982.

Drabble, Margaret. *A Writer's Britain: Landscape in Literature.* New York: Alfred A. Knopf, 1979.

Eagle, Dorothy, and Hilary Carnell, eds. *The Oxford Literary Guide to the British Isles.* Oxford: Clarendon Press, 1977.

Eastman, John. *Who Lived Where: A Biographical Guide to Homes and Museums.* New York: Facts on File, 1983.

———. *Who Lived Where in Europe: A Biographical Guide to Homes and Museums.* New York: Facts on File, 1985.

Fedden, Robin, and Rosemary Joekes, eds. *National Trust Guide to England, Wales and Northern Ireland.* Rev ed. New York: W. W. Norton, 1977.

Hilowitz, Beverley, and Susan Eikov Green, eds. *Historic Houses of America: Open to the Public.* Rev. ed. New York: Simon and Schuster, 1980.

Jacobs, Michael, and Paul Stirton. *The Knopf Traveler's Guides to Art: Britain and Ireland.* New York: Alfred A. Knopf, 1984.

Lees-Milne, James, *et. al. Writers at Home: National Trust Studies.* New York: Facts on File, 1985.

Mobil Travel Guides to the United States for 1989. 7 vols. New York: Prentice-Hall, 1989.

—Ian Crump; L.D.R.

8

SOME FAMOUS MONUMENTS
OF THE WORLD

· · · · ·

THE POET SHELLEY, WHO WAS NO WORSHIPER OF REPUTATIONS, EXPRESSED HIS opinion of the efficacy of monuments to the great and famous in his poem "Ozymandias." In a desert lie the broken ruins of a statue, on the pedestal of which are the words, "My name is Ozymandias, King of Kings, Look on my Works, ye Mighty, and despair!" Now only the "lone and level sands stretch far away." (In point of fact the statue was that of Ramses II.) The most famous monument of antiquity, the bronze Colossus of Rhodes, apparently a hundred feet high, hasn't even fared as well as that; it has disappeared entirely, without even a memorial poem.

Heroic statuary, tablets, memorial columns, parks and shrines, and the like have intrigued writers. Ralph Waldo Emerson wrote one of his better poems to mark the setting of a stone commemorating the battle of Concord. Henry Timrod wrote his best poem about a monument to the Confederate dead that hadn't been erected yet but should have been (it has since). Allen Tate's best poem is about the monuments and gravestones in a Confederate cemetery. Robert Lowell's "To the Union Dead" commemorates, wryly, statuary in Boston. It is generally agreed, however, that words tend to outlast statuary, and this belief is particularly strong among those who deal professionally in language rather than statues; thus Shakespeare's "Not marble, nor the gilded monuments/Of princes, shall outlive this powerful rime . . . "

James Joyce built a chapter of *Ulysses* around a pillar in Dublin honoring Admiral Horatio Nelson's victory at Trafalgar; it cannot be seen anymore, however, for the Irish, no admirers of Britain, blew it up a few years ago. Ralph Ellison's *Invisible Man* has a memorable depiction of a statue to The Founder (Booker T. Washington) of a school for African Americans in the South (Tuskegee Institute); he is shown lifting the veil of ignorance from the face of his recently emancipated people, but Ellison's narrator wonders whether he isn't fastening it in place more securely.

Perhaps the most unusual monument in the United States is to be found in the town of Enterprise, in southeastern Alabama. It is a large replica of a boll weevil. The townsfolk erected it to express their appreciation of the bug which devastated the cotton crops in the early twentieth century; in so doing, it supposedly forced farmers to diversify, which turned out to be a good thing.

Here are the locations of a few of the better-known monuments of the world.

AFRICA

El Alamein, Egypt. Site of the Second World War battle and the Allied War Cemetery.

Fez, Morocco. Zaouia de Moulay Idriss, with the tomb of Moulay Idriss II, who established the capital of Morocco here in 808.

Meknes, Morocco. Tomb of Moulay Ismail.

Pretoria. Voortrekker Monument, honoring the 12,000 Boers who engaged in the Great Trek inland (1835–43) to escape British control in the Cape Colony; equestrian statue of Andries Pretorius, honoring one of the leaders of the Great Trek; statue of Marthinus Pretorius, honoring the founder of the city.

Rabat, Morocco. Mausoleum of Muhammad V, who brought about his country's independence from France and Spain.

ASIA

Agra, India. Taj Mahal, built by the Moghul emperor Shah Jehan in 1631–48 as a mausoleum for himself and his wife.

Ankara, Turkey. Tomb of Ataturk, commemorating the founder of the modern Turkish state.

Baghdad, Iraq. Victory Arch, erected in 1989 to commemorate Iraq's victory in the war with Iran.

Beijing, China. Monument to the People's Heroes and the Memorial Hall of Chairman Mao, in Tiananmen Square; 13 magnificent tombs from the Ming Dynasty are located in a valley outside the city.

Bethlehem. Rachel's Tomb, Judaism's third holiest site.

Bodrum (formerly Halicarnassus), Turkey. Tomb of King Mausolus of Caria, who gave his name to the word *mausoleum*; it was one of the seven wonders of the ancient world.

Bombay. Gateway of India, erected in 1911 to honor the landing of King George V and Queen Mary.

Bursa, Turkey. Yesil Turbe, or Green Tomb, the mausoleum of Mehmet I (Äelebi), who reigned from 1413 to 1421.

Hiroshima, Japan. Hiroshima Peace Memorial Park, containing the Atomic Bomb Memorial Dome (the ruins of the only building to withstand the atomic bomb explosion of August 6, 1945) and cenotaph inscribed with the names of those who died in the explosion.

Jerusalem. Golgotha (Calvary), in the Church of the Holy Sepulchre, believed to be the site of Jesus Christ's crucifixion; Garden Tomb, alternative site for the crucifixion; Holocaust Memorial to those who died in Hitler's "Final Solution," located on Mt. Zion.

Kanchanaburi, Thailand. Cemetery for Allied soldiers who died during the building of the infamous Bridge over the River Kwai.

Nablus, Israeli-occupied West Bank. Joseph's Tomb.

AUSTRALIA

Brisbane. Queenslands National War Memorial, honoring the state's war dead, in Anzac Square.

Canberra. Australian War Memorial, honoring dead from all wars since 1900, dedicated in 1941; Anzac Parade, completed in 1965 for the fiftieth anniversary of Gallipoli, leading from War Memorial to Lake Burley Griffin; carillon bell tower, given by the British government to mark the city's fiftieth jubilee in 1963.

Kalgoorlie, Western Australia. Lifesize statue of Paddy Hannan, commemorating discoverer of the Kalgoorlie Gold Fields.

Melbourne. Shrine of Remembrance, honoring dead of First World War, dedicated in 1934.

BRITISH ISLES

Dublin, Ireland. Children of Lir, statue honoring Irish patriots, erected in 1971 in National Garden of Remembrance; statue of Death of Cuchulainn, erected in 1929 in General Post Office to honor Easter 1916 Rebellion; Wellington Testimonial, 60-meter obelisk in Phoenix Park, highest such monument in Europe.

Edinburgh, Scotland. "Edinburgh's Disgrace," unfinished monument honoring Scottish dead from the Napoleonic Wars.

London, England. Statue of Achilles erected in Hyde Park to honor Duke of Wellington; Albert Memorial, erected in 1863 to honor Queen Victoria's consort; statue of Queen Boadicea erected on Victoria Embankment; replica of *Burghers of Calais,* by Rodin, set in Victoria Tower Gardens in 1915; the Cenotaph, war memorial designed by Edwin Lutyens, unveiled in 1920; equestrian statue of Charles I, erected in 1633 in what is now Trafalgar Square; statue of Sir William Churchill, Parliament Square; Eros, erected in

Piccadilly Circus in 1893 as a monument to Earl of Shaftesbury; Marble Arch, built by John Nash and moved to present site in Hyde Park (near site of Tyburn Tree) in 1852; monument, Doric column designed by Christopher Wren and Robert Hooke, commemorating 1666 Great Fire of London; statue of Rima, by Jacob Epstein, located in Hyde Park, honoring W. H. Hudson; Shakespeare Monument, Leicester Square; Temple Bar Memorial, marking boundary between cities of London and Westminster; Trafalgar Square, public square containing Nelson's Pillar, honoring Admiral Horatio Nelson's naval victory in 1805; Queen Victoria Monument, designed by Thomas Brock, erected on Mall in 1911; the Wellington Arch, erected in Hyde Park in 1825; Wellington Memorial, equestrian statue of the Duke of Wellington, near Wellington Arch in Hyde Park; in Westminster Abbey, numerous tombs of royalty and historic personages, monument to notable authors in Poets' Corner; Duke of York Column, in Waterloo Place, honoring Frederick, second son of George II.

Runnymede, England. Memorial commemorating signing of Magna Carta; memorial to John F. Kennedy, unveiled in 1965.

Stirling, Scotland. William Wallace Monument, 220-foot column commemorating Scottish patriot.

Stratford-upon-Avon, England. Shakespeare's Tomb, in Holy Trinity Church.

EUROPE

Auschwitz Concentration Camp. Site in southern Poland preserved as monument to the Holocaust.

Barcelona, Spain. Columbus Monument.

Berlin, Germany. Brandenburg Gate, monumental arch erected in 1791 marking former entrance to German capital; Soviet War Memorial, massive promenade built with marble from Nazi chancellory.

Birkenau Concentration Camp. Site in southern Poland preserved as monument to the Holocaust.

Brussels, Belgium. Mannekin-Pis statue, "oldest citizen" of Belgian capital, executed by Jerome Duquesnoy in 1619; nearby, on site of Battle of Waterloo (fought June 18, 1815), the Belgian Monument, Brunswick Monument, French Memorial, Gordon Memorial, Hanoverian Memorial, Lion Mound, Prussian Memorial, and General Schwerin Monument.

Bucharest, Romania. Triumphal Arch, honoring Romania's dead in First World War.

Budapest, Hungary. Statue of Joseph Bem, site of beginning of 1956 Hungarian uprising; Millennial Monument, commemorating thousandth anniversary of Magyar conquest of Hungary.

Caen, France. Beaches of June 6, 1944, Normandy invasion, "Utah" and "Omaha" for Americans, "Gold," "Juno," and "Sword" for British and Canadians; U.S. military cemetery at Omaha Beach, containing allegorical bronze figure by Donald de Luc; British cemetery at Sword Beach.

Calais, France. Rodin's statue of Burghers of Calais, installed in the city in 1895.

Copenhagen, Denmark. Little Mermaid statue in Copenhagen harbor, honoring Hans Christian Andersen.

Dijon, France. Tomb of Philip the Bold, erected between 1385 and 1410, and Tomb of John the Fearless and Margaret of Bavaria, erected between 1443 and 1470, in Palace of Dukes of Burgundy.

Florence, Italy. Several civic statues, in the Piazza della Signoria, including Cellini's *Perseus*, Giambologna's *Rape of the Sabines*, and copies of Michelangelo's *David* and Donatello's *Marzocco*; Medici Chapels, part of San Lorenzo Church, including unfinished tombs designed and sculpted by Michelangelo.

Gdansk, Poland. Three crosses of Solidarity Monument, commemorating violently suppressed 1970 shipworkers' strike.

Guernica, Spain. Tree of Guernica, former meeting place for local lords, symbol of liberty.

Helsinki, Finland. Jean Sibelius Monument, honoring Finnish composer.

Kiev, Ukraine. Nearby 15-meter memorial statue erected in 1976 to honor victims of Nazi concentration camp at Babi Yar.

Madrid, Spain. Alcalá Arch, honoring entrance of Charles III into city; Valle de los Cáidos, near Madrid, honoring dead in Spanish civil war; Francisco Franco's tomb.

Moscow, Russia. Lenin's Tomb, massive mausoleum in Red Square, containing body of founder of Soviet state; Tomb of the Unknown Soldier, honoring dead in Second World War.

Nuremberg, Germany. Nuremberg Rally Grounds, built for 1935 Nazi Party Congress.

Padua, Italy. Equestrian statue of Gattemelata, in Piazza del Santo, cast by Donatello in 1450.

Paris, France. Arc de Triomphe, designed by Jean Chalgrin, erected in 1836 in what is now Place Charles de Gaulle (also known as l'Etoile), and including Tomb of the Unknown Soldier; the Column of July in Place de la Bastille, on site of the notorious prison; Eiffel Tower, 984-foot tower of iron framework erected for International Exposition of 1889; Napoleon's Tomb, erected in 1861 in the Hôtel des Invalides; the Luxor Obelisk, presented by viceroy of Egypt to Charles X in 1829, in Place de la Concorde; Rodin's statue of Balzac, installed in 1939; Panthéon, containing tombs of Voltaire, Rousseau, and Zola; Monument to Marshal Ney, cast by François Rude in 1853; Tomb of Henri II, by Francesco Primaticcio and Germain Pilon, in Abbey Church of St.-Denis.

Prague, Czech Republic. Jan Hus statue, erected in 1915.

Rome, Italy. Augustus' Altar of Peace, monumental altar, erected by Senate in 9 b.c.e. to honor peace Augustus brought to Roman Empire; Caius Cestus' pyramid, tomb dating to 12 B.C.E.; Constantine's Arch, built in 315 C.E. after Constantine defeated his rival Maxentius at the Milvian bridge; equestrian statue of Marcus Aurelius, Capitol Square; Septimus Severus' Arch, dating to 203 C.E., commemorating victories over Parthians; Titus' Arch, raised in 81 C.E., commemorating capture of Jerusalem; Trajan's Column, erected in Rome in 113 C.E., commemorating Trajan's victories over the Dacians; Victor Emmanuel II Monument, dedicated in 1911, honoring the king who unified Italy.

Rotterdam, Netherlands. "Destroyed City" Monument, commemorating destruction of city by German bombers in Second World War.

St. Petersburg, Russia. Equestrian statue of Peter the Great, erected in 1782 in what is now Decembrists' Square.

St.-Remy-de-Provence, France. Roman mausoleum and triumphal arch.

Sofia, Bulgaria. Monument to Liberators, commemorating Russian aid in liberating Bulgaria from Turkish rule, including equestrian statue of Czar Alexander II; Tomb of Unknown Soldier, erected in 1981.

Tirgu Jiu, Romania. Three Brancusi monuments to First World War dead: *Kissing Gate, Table of Silence,* and *Endless Column.*

Venice, Italy. Equestrian statue of Colleoni, in Campo SS. Giovanni e Paolo cast by Andrea del Verrocchio from 1481 to 1488.

Vienna, Austria. Pestsäule, or Plague Column, commemorating citizens who died from bubonic plague in 1690s; Tomb of Countess Maria Christina, in Church of Augustinians, designed by Antonio Canova in 1798.

Warsaw, Poland. Monument to the Heroes of the Warsaw Ghetto, commemorating Jewish revolt against Nazis in 1944; Monument to Heroes of Warsaw, erected in 1964 to commemorate citizens killed between 1939 and 1945; Tomb of the Unknown Soldier; statue of Sigismund II Vasa, erected in 1644, honoring king who made city capital of Poland; Mermaid Monument, symbol of city, on banks of Vistula River.

LATIN AMERICA

Caracas, Venezuela. Panteón Nacional, with tomb of Simon Bolivar.

Mexico City, Mexico. Monumento de la Revolución, begun by Porfirio Diaz as a new legislative building; only dome was completed when 1910 revolution halted construction; afterward converted to present monument, containing remains of Francisco Madero and Venustiano Carranza.

Rio de Janeiro, Brazil. Statue of Christ the Redeemer, Corcovado Mountain, erected in 1931.

UNITED STATES

Alamogordo, N.M. Nearby cairn marks "Trinity Site," first atomic explosion, July 16, 1945.

Andersonville, Ga. Andersonville National Historic Site, Confederate prison and cemetery for Union dead.

Appomattox, Va. Appomattox Court House National Historic Park, where Confederate general Robert E. Lee surrendered to Gen. Ulysses S. Grant, April 9, 1865.

Astoria, Oreg. Astoria Column, honoring first settlement in the state.

Atlanta, Ga. Equestrian statues of Confederate president Jefferson Davis, Generals Thomas "Stonewall" Jackson and Robert E. Lee carved on side of Stone Mountain.

Baltimore, Md. Fort McHenry National Monument and Historic Shrine, in Baltimore harbor, honoring defense which inspired "The Star-Spangled Banner"; first major George Washington statue, Mt. Vernon Place.

Blaine, Wash. International Peace Arch, erected at Canadian border in 1921.

Boston, Mass. Boston Massacre Monument, commemorating shooting of unarmed colonists by British soldiers in 1770; Bunker Hill Monument, commemorating Revolutionary War battle of June 17, 1775; Benjamin Franklin statue by Richard Greenough, 1856; USS *Constitution,* "Old Ironsides," at Charlestown Navy Yard; bronze relief by Augustus St. Gaudens, commemorating Union army dead at Massachusetts State House.

Bradenton, Fla. De Soto National Memorial, marking site where Hernando de Soto and 600 conquistadors are believed to have landed on May 30, 1539.

Bridgeport, Conn. Lifesize statue of Tom Thumb on grave in Mountain Grove Cemetery.

Brigham City, Utah. Golden Spike National Monument, marking junction point of Union Pacific and Central Pacific railroads.

Charleston, S.C. Fort Sumter National Monument, commemorating bombardment of April 12–13, 1861; statues of William Pitt the Elder, John C. Calhoun, and William Gilmore Simms.

Charlotte, N.C. Captain James Jack Monument, honoring officer who carried Mecklenberg Declaration to Continental Congress.

Chattanooga, Tenn. Chickamauga and Chattanooga National Military Park at sites of Civil War battles of September–November, 1863.

Chinook, Mont. Chief Joseph Battleground State Monument.

Columbus, Ohio. Statue of Cornelia, the mother of the Gracchi, displaying her Ohio jewels: U. S. Grant, Philip Sheridan, James A. Garfield, W. T. Sherman, Edwin M. Stanton, Salmon P. Chase, and Rutherford B. Hayes.

Concord, Mass. Minute Man National Battlefield Park with reconstructed "rude bridge that arched the flood" (Emerson) and Minute Man Statue, executed by Daniel Chester French; cairn marking site of Henry David Thoreau's cabin on Walden Pond.

Council Bluffs, Iowa. Monument marking city's role as eastern terminus of transcontinental railroad; Lewis and Clark Monument; Mormon Trail Memorial, marking site where Mormons left Iowa.

Custer, N.D. Unfinished Crazy Horse Memorial, an equestrian statue.

Dallas, Tex. John F. Kennedy Memorial, designed by Philip Johnson to honor assassinated president.

Edison, N.J. Edison Memorial Tower, marking site where first incandescent electric bulb was made.

Fredericksburg and Spotsylvania National Military Park, Va. Sites of Civil War battles of Fredericksburg, Chancellorsville, the Wilderness, and Spotsylvania Court House.

Fulton, Mo. Churchill Memorial, marking site where Winston Churchill delivered his Iron Curtain speech on March 5, 1946.

Gettysburg, Pa. Gettysburg National Military Park, at site of Civil War battle fought July 1–3, 1863, and Lincoln's Gettysburg Address, November 19, 1863.

Gnadenhutten, Ohio. Monument marking site where soldiers massacred 90 Christian Indians in 1782.

Hardin, Mont. Custer Battlefield National Monument at site of Battle of Little Big Horn, June 25, 1876.

Harlingen, Texas. Iwo Jima War Memorial model for Marine Corps War Memorial in Arlington National Cemetery.

Hodgenville, Ky. Log cabin at Lincoln's Birthplace National Historic Site, commemorating president's birth on February 12, 1809.

Hopkinsville, Ky. Obelisk marking birthplace of Confederate president Jefferson Davis.

Hyannis, Mass. John F. Kennedy Memorial, consisting of a 4-meter-high circular fieldstone wall with the presidential seal, a fountain, and a small pool.

Kealakekua, Hawaii. Monument to James Cook, honoring the English explorer who died here in 1779.

Kent, Ohio. May 4th Site and Memorial, honoring the four students killed by Ohio National Guardsmen during a Vietnam War protest at Kent State University on May 4, 1970.

Kill Devil Hills, N.C. Wright Brothers National Memorial, honoring Orville and Wilbur Wright, who conducted, on the Outer Banks, the first powered flight on December 17, 1903.

Lafayette, Ind. Tippecanoe Battlefield, marking the site of the 1811 Indian battle.

Laramie, Wyo. Site of the Lincoln Head, the world's largest bronze head (3.8 meters high, 3 metric tons).

Lexington, Mass. Old Monument and Boulder on Battle Green, marking the site of the Minutemen's stand against the British in the Revolutionary War battle fought on April 19, 1775.

Manassas National Battlefield Park. Site in northern Virginia of Civil War battles fought on July 21, 1861, and August 29–30, 1862.

Marquette, Mich. Site of the statue of Father Marquette honoring the French missionary and explorer.

Mobridge, S.D. Sitting Bull Monument, executed by Korczak Ziolkowski.

Montgomery, Ala. Civil Rights Memorial, dedicated on November 5, 1989.

Mount Rushmore National Memorial. Located near Rapid City, S.D., this memorial, sculpted on a mountain, honors Presidents Washington, Jefferson, Lincoln, and Theodore Roosevelt; conceived and begun by Gutzon Borglum, it was finished by his son Lincoln in October, 1941.

New Orleans, La. Equestrian statue of Andrew Jackson, standing in Jackson Square.

New York, N.Y. 46-meter-high Statue of Liberty, given by the French nation to the United States and located on Liberty Island in New York Harbor; Grant's Tomb, containing the remains of the Civil War general and eighteenth president; the Washington Arch, designed by Stanford White and completed in 1895; statues throughout downtown Manhattan, including that of Gen. William Tecumseh Sherman and his horse, fabled in song.

Pearl Harbor, Honolulu, Hawaii. USS *Arizona* National Memorial Shrine, moored over the sunken battleship, honoring the dead from the Japanese attack on December 7, 1941.

Philadelphia, Pa. Liberty Bell, the bell of Independence Hall, rung on July 8, 1776, to announce U.S. independence (it did not crack until 1835); the William Penn Memorial Landing Stone, in nearby Chester, marking where Penn set foot in North America on October 28, 1682; the National Memorial Arch, erected in 1917 at nearby Valley Forge to commemorate the encampment by Continental troops from December 19, 1777, to June 19, 1778.

Plymouth, Mass. Plymouth Rock, marking traditional site of the Pilgrims' landing on December 21, 1620.

Princeton, N.J. Princeton Battle Monument, a 15-meter block, commemorating the Revolutionary War victory in 1777.

Put-in-Bay, Lake Erie, Ohio. 352-foot Memorial to Oliver Hazard Perry's Victory and International Peace on South Bass Island, commemorating 1813 U.S. naval victory.

Richmond, Va. Statue of George Washington, executed by Jean-Antoine Houdon in 1792, standing in the rotunda of the Virginia State Capitol; nearby, in Capitol Square, the Washington Monument, an equestrian statue of the first American president, surrounded by statues of Jefferson, Patrick Henry,

John Marshall, Andrew Lewis, and other famous Virginians; along Monument Avenue, statues of Robert E. Lee, J. E. B. Stuart, Jefferson Davis, Stonewall Jackson, and Matthew Fontaine Maury.

Ripon, Wis. Little White School House, marking the site where the Republican Party was born on March 20, 1854.

Roanoke Island, N.C. Fort Raleigh National Historic Site, marking first English settlement in New World.

Rome, N.Y. Tomb of the Unknown Soldier of the Revolution, designed by Lorimar Rich.

St. Louis, Mo. Gateway Arch, a 630-foot stainless-steel arch commemorating the gateway for western expansion, designed by Eero Saarinen and built between 1962 and 1965.

Salt Lake City, Utah. Brigham Young Monument, honoring the Mormon leader, unveiled in 1897; the Seagull Monument, commemorating the gulls that saved crops from crickets in 1848.

San Antonio, Tex. Alamo mission used as fort in Texan war of independence against Mexico; it fell to Santa Anna's troops on March 6, 1836.

San Francisco, Calif. Coit Memorial Tower, on Telegraph Hill, honoring the city's volunteer firefighters.

Saratoga National Historic Park. Site in northern New York State of Revolutionary War battles fought on September 19 and October 7, 1777.

Sharpsburg, Md. Antietam National Battlefield site, bloodiest one-day battle fought on U.S. soil, September 17, 1862.

Shiloh National Military Park. Site in Tennessee of Civil War battle fought on April 6–7, 1862.

Sioux City, Iowa. Sergeant Floyd Tomb, the first national historic landmark in the United States.

Springfield, Ill. Abraham Lincoln's Tomb.

Stones River National Battlefield, Murfreesboro, Tenn. Site in central Tennessee of Civil War battle fought from December 31, 1862, to January 2, 1863.

Vicksburg, Miss. Vicksburg National Military Park and Cemetery, honoring the dead from the Civil War battle and siege ending July 4, 1863.

Washington, D.C. Grant Memorial, one of the largest equestrian statues in the world; Thomas Jefferson Memorial, a circular domed and columned edifice that shelters the bronze statue of Jefferson by Rudolph Evans; Lincoln Memorial, a colonnaded structure that contains Daniel Chester French's statue of Lincoln; the Memorial to the Signers of the Declaration of Independence, in Constitution Gardens, consisting of large granite blocks carved with 56 signatures of the signers; the Vietnam Veterans Memorial, dedicated in 1982, consisting of V-shaped walls of black marble inscribed with names of dead from Vietnam conflict; the 555-foot Washington

Monument, built between 1848 and 1884 (the six monuments mentioned above are located on the Mall); the Emancipation Statue, erected in 1876; Arlington National Cemetery, in northern Virginia, containing the Tomb of the Unknown Soldier, the Tomb of the Unknown Soldier of the Civil War, John F. Kennedy's grave, the Tomb of Pierre L'Enfant, the Marine Corps War Memorial, the Confederate Memorial, and the mast of the battleship *Maine.*

West Point, N.Y. Battle Monument, honoring the dead from both sides of the Civil War.

Wounded Knee Battlefield. Site near Pine Ridge, S.D., of Indian mass grave and monument.

Yorktown, Va. Yorktown Battlefield, at which Lord Cornwallis surrendered his British troops to George Washington on October 19, 1781, thus effectively ending the Revolutionary War.

SOURCES

American Automobile Association Tourbooks. Heathrow, Fla.: American Automobile Association, 1991.

Bisignani, J. D. *Japan Handbook.* Victoria, Australia: Bookwise, 1983.

China Travel and Tourism Press, ed. *Official Guidebook of China.* New York: Lee Publishers, 1982.

Fodor's 91: Eastern Europe. New York: Fodor's Travel Publications, 1991.

Fodor's 91: Europe. New York: Fodor's Travel Publications, 1991.

Great Britain and Ireland: A Phaidon Cultural Guide. Englewood Cliffs, N.J.: Prentice-Hall, 1985.

Hale, Sheila. *The American Express Pocket Guide to Florence and Tuscany.* New York: Prentice-Hall, 1983.

Harvard Student Agencies, Inc. 1986 *Let's Go: The Budget Guide to Britain and Ireland.* New York: St. Martin's Press, 1986.

———. 1986 *Let's Go: The Budget Guide to Europe.* New York: St. Martin's Press, 1986.

Hurley, Frank. *Australia: A Camera Study.* Sydney: Angus and Robertson, 1955.

Jacobs, Michael, and Paul Stirton. *The Knopf Traveler's Guides to Art: Britain and Ireland.* New York: Alfred A. Knopf, 1984.

———. *The Knopf Traveler's Guides to Art: France.* New York: Alfred A. Knopf, 1984.

Janson, H. W. *History of Art: A Survey of the Major Visual Arts from the Dawn of History to the Present Day.* 2nd ed. Englewood Cliffs, N.J.: Prentice-Hall, 1977.

Jones, P. H. M., ed. *Golden Guide to South and East Asia.* Hong Kong: Far East Economic Review, 1969.

Kutcher, Arthur. *Looking at London: Illustrated Walks Through a Changing City.* London: Thames and Hudson, 1978.

Michelin Green Guide: Burgundy. London: Michelin Tyre Public Limited Co., 1988.

Michelin Green Guide: Netherlands. London: Michelin Tyre Public Limited Co., 1990.

Michelin Green Guide: Rome. London: Michelin Tyre Public Limited Co., 1985.

Michelin Green Guide: Spain. London: Michelin Tyre Public Limited Co., 1987.

Mobil Travel Guides to the United States for 1989. 7 vols. New York: Prentice-Hall, 1989.

Peterson, Vicki. *Australia*. London: Cassell, 1980.

Robertson, Ian. *The Blue Guide to France*. New York: W. W. Norton, 1988.

———. *The Blue Guide to Ireland*. New York: W. W. Norton, 1987.

Weinreb, Ben, and Christopher Hibbert, eds. *The London Encyclopedia*. Bethesda, Md.: Adler and Adler, 1986.

Wheeler, Tony. *South-East Asia on a Shoestring*. Berkeley, Calif.: Lonely Planet, 1989.

Wiencek, Henry. *The Smithsonian Guide to Historic America: Virginia and the Capital Region*. New York: Stewart, Tabori and Chang, 1989.

—Ian Crump; L.D.R.

9

A GUIDE TO THE RUINS

$\cdot\ \ \cdot\ \ \cdot\ \ \cdot\ \ \cdot$

RUINS ARE NOT WHAT THEY USED TO BE. THE HEYDAY FOR CONTEMPLATING them was the eighteenth century, when writers and savants were taking prodigious delight in the broken-down remains of the past—so much so that persons of wealth such as Horace Walpole sometimes had imitation Gothic ruins constructed on their estates.

The sense of the past that could come to Western man from observing the broken columns, walls, and foundations of an earlier epoch intrigued the ancient world, in particular the Greeks. But as a way of thinking it began to take hold with the waning of the medieval view of man as existing not in time but in eternity. Hitherto, what humans did and thought had been conceived not in terms of past and future so much as in relationship to heaven or hell. But with the Renaissance, human life began to be seen historically, as occupying a specific place in time between past and future. The present was now viewed as having been caused by the past, and affecting the future. (However, the centrality of all the above to the way that people think and have thought can be exaggerated. It was, after all, King Nabonidus of Babylon, 555–39 B.C.E., who was known as "the archaeologist on the throne.")

This sense of being inheritors of past ages came along with another important development: the perception of the boundaries of society as existing beyond Europe, in new continents and very different conditions. No longer was history confined to classical Greece and Rome and Christian Europe. People were eager to read accounts of distant places and to learn more about the past, and writers proceeded to supply them.

It was in the eighteenth century that travel books achieved wide popularity and the science of archaeology began developing. One thinks of Samuel Johnson and James Boswell contemplating the ruins of the cathedral and monastery on the remote Hebrides island of Iona, from which Scotland had been Christianized in the sixth century and where the graves of the Scottish kings lay, and of Johnson's response: "That man is little to be envied whose patriotism would not gain fervor upon the plains of Marathon or whose piety would not grow warmer among the ruins of Iona."

Perhaps the most celebrated account of an enthrallment with ancient ruins is Edward Gibbon's famous account of visiting the ruins of the Roman forum and being inspired to write *The Decline and Fall of the Roman Empire:* "It was at Rome, on the 15th of October, 1764, as I set musing amidst the ruins of the Capitol, while the bare-footed friars were singing vespers in the Temple of Jupiter, that the idea of writing the decline and fall of the city first started in my mind." Gibbon had the wrong ruins—the friars were installed in the temple of Juno, not Jupiter—but the moment is unforgettable: the fallen grandeur of Imperial Rome, the sense of historical change, the eighteenth-century Englishman overwhelmed by the ruin of the great work of time.

The decades that followed have vastly expanded our knowledge of the past, and archaeologists have discovered and learned how to excavate and use the sites and artifacts of earlier civilizations to understand and interpret the events of history in ways that would have astounded Johnson, Gibbon, and their contemporaries. If the shock and excitement of the initial confrontation with the sense of the historical past have receded somewhat, not so our interest in history or our penchant for reading and writing about journeys to the sites of long-ago—and not-so-long-ago—events. The steamship and the jet airplane have provided us with easy access to the scenes of ancient civilizations, so that arduous journeys such as Johnson and Boswell were forced to make in order to view the antiquities of Scotland two centuries ago can be negotiated in comfort and ease. Tourism, once the privilege of the few, is now a massive and thriving industry.

The compilation that follows is of some of the more notable sites of ruins available to travelers today. Some places, needless to say, are rather more accessible than others—the area between the Tigris and Euphrates rivers, for example, is not exactly wide open to tourism just now. All dates given are for the Common Era unless otherwise specified.

AFRICA

Abu Simbel. Egyptian temple site in Nubia dating from *ca.* 1250 B.C.E.; structures moved in 1960s because of flooding from Aswan Dam.

Abydos. City in Upper Egypt (fl. 3200–1085 B.C.E.); includes great temple of Seti I (*ca.* 1300 B.C.E.).

Alexandria. Egyptian city founded by Alexander the Great in 332 B.C.E.; contained library since destroyed; remains include Pompey's Pillar and Roman amphitheater.

Axum. City in northern Ethiopia and center of Axum Kingdom (500 B.C.E.–first millennium C.E); contains tall, thin funerary steles.

Beni Hassan. Site, in Middle Egypt, of a rock-cut temple (*ca.* 1500 B.C.E.) and several tombs (*ca.* 1900 B.C.E.).

Carthage. Phoenician city founded in eighth century B.C.E., near modern Tunis; destroyed by Rome.

Dendera. City in Upper Egypt notable for the Temple to Hathor (the goddess of women) and Sixth Dynasty tombs.

Elephantine. Rock island in Nile with fortified harbor from the Twelfth Dynasty and the Temple to Hekayeb.

Gedi. Site on Indian Ocean in modern Kenya (*ca.* thirteenth–fifteenth centuries).

Giza. Egyptian burial site across the Nile from Cairo; includes the Great Sphinx, and pyramids of Cheops, Chephron, and Mykerinus.

Heliopolis. Second-millennium B.C.E. Egyptian city 5 miles northeast of Cairo.

Karnak. Site in Upper Egypt that includes the Temple of Amon and an enormous entry gate.

Le Kef. Site of ancient fortified town in northern Tunisia.

Lepcis Magna. Roman colony on the Lybian coast.

Luxor. Temple site in Upper Egypt, near ancient Thebes and Karnak; includes Temple to Amon built during reign of Amenhotep III.

Meidum. Old Kingdom site in Egypt; notable for the Tomb of Atet (*ca.* 2600 B.C.E.).

Memphis. Major city of ancient Egypt; little remains.

Meroe. Capital of Kush kingdom in Nubia; the ruins include temples, palaces, and baths.

Nagada. Large predynastic cemetery in Upper Egypt (used between *ca.* 3800 and 3200 B.C.E.).

Oxyrhynchus. Roman colony located 120 miles south of Cairo.

Saqqarah. Egyptian necropolis near Memphis; includes many mastaba tombs and the Step Pyramid of Zoser (*ca.* 2800 B.C.E.).

Sethi Tomb. Tomb of Seti I in the Valley of the Kings, Egypt.

Tanis. Egyptian city at mouth of eastern branch of Nile; ruins include temple to Ramses II and tombs from Twenty-First and Twenty-Second Dynasties.

Timgad. Roman colony in modern Algeria; ruins include monumental gates, colonnaded roadways, temples, and baths.

Tutankhamon's Tomb. Located in the Valley of the Kings, the only nearly intact Egyptian tomb.

Yeha. Northeast Ethiopian site with several massive limestone structures of unknown origin (*ca.* fifth century B.C.E.?).

Zimbabwe. Ruins of an ancient African culture in country of same name; extensive ruins include massive stone enclosure known as the Temple.

THE AMERICAS

Anse au Meadow. Site of Viking settlement in northwest Newfoundland.

Aztec Ruins National Monument. Site in northwest New Mexico, of pueblo structures.

Bandelier National Monument. Site of pueblo ruins in northern New Mexico.

Big Horn Medicine Wheel. Rock circle and possible astronomical device in Wyoming.

Bonampak. Mayan ceremonial site with several ruined temples; located in Mexico near the Guatemalan border.

Cahokia. Site, near East St. Louis, Ill., of several earthen pyramids, including the largest in the U.S.A., the Monk's Mound.

Chaco Culture National Historic Park. Site in western New Mexico; ruins include prehistoric traces thought to be roads.

Chanchan. Capital of Chimu Empire and largest city of ancient Peru; located near modern Trujillo.

Chelly, Canyon de. Pueblo site in east Arizona; ruins include Antelope House, Mummy Cave, and White House.

Chichen Itza. Mayan and Toltec ceremonial center near modern Merida, Mexico; includes the so-called Nunnery complex, the Iglesia, the Caracol, the Courtyard of a Thousand Columns, the Ball Court, and the Temple of the Warriors.

Cholula. Religious center in pre-Hispanic Mexico; located near present Puebla.

Copan. Site, in modern Honduras, of large Mayan city; includes Hieroglyphic Stairway.

Cuzco. Capital of Incan Empire; located in south-central Peru.

Emerald Mound. Third largest temple mound in the United States; located in Mississippi.

Etowah Mounds Archaeological Area. Temple mounds in Georgia dating from *ca.* 1000.

Gila Cliff Dwellings National Monument. Site, in southwest New Mexico, of pueblo structures.

Machu Picchu. Incan city northwest of Cuzco; situated at 9,000-ft. elevation.

Mesa Verde. Region in southwest Colorado famous for numerous pueblo villages built into overhanging cliffs (fl. eleventh–thirteenth centuries); ruins include Cliff Palace and Square Tower ruin.

Mitla. Sacred burial places for Zapotecs and Mixtecs; located 20 miles from Oaxaca, Mexico.

Monte Alban. Major Zapotec ceremonial center near Mitla, in Mexico; ruins include the Great Plaza and tombs.

Montezuma Castle National Monument. Pueblo ruin in central Arizona.

Navajo National Monument. Ruins of pueblo villages in northern Arizona.

Palenque. Mayan site in state of Chiapas, Mexico; includes palace complex with a 3-story tower and five temple pyramids.

Piedras Negras. Mayan site in Guatemala near the Mexican border; includes only known Mayan sweat baths.

Remojadas. Olmec site in Mexican state of Veracruz.

Salinas National Monument. Pueblo site in central New Mexico; ruins include Gran Quivira, Quarai, and Abo.

Salmon Ruins. Pueblo ruins in northwest New Mexico.

Serpent Mound. Burial mound located south of Hillsboro, Ohio.

Tajin, El. Totonac ceremonial center near Veracruz, Mexico; includes Pyramid of the Niches.

Tenochtitlán. Capital of the Aztec Empire; modern Mexico City founded on its ruins.

Teochuatihuacan. Site, 25 miles north of Mexico City, of Pyramids of the Moon and of the Sun (*ca.* second century).

Tikal. Mayan city in Guatemala; ruins include pyramid temples.

Tlatilco. Grave site (*ca.* 1000 B.C.E.) near Mexico City.

Tula. Site near Mexico City of Toltec capital; ruins include colonnades and Atlantean columns, often of warriors.

Wupatki National Monument. Pueblo ruins in northeast Arizona; ruins include Tall House, amphitheater, ball court, and citadel.

Xochicalco. Fortified hilltop site (fl. seventh–eleventh centuries) in Mexican state of Morelos.

ASIA

Aihole. Site, in central India, of more than 70 Hindu temples dating from *ca.* fifth–seventh centuries.

Ajanta. Site, near Aurangabad, India, of 29 rock-carved caves, mostly Buddhist (*ca.* second–sixth centuries).

Amaravati. Site near Nagpur, India, of capital of Satavahana Empire from first century B.C.E. to third century C.E.; includes the Great Stupa.

Angkor. Site, in Cambodia, of several Khmer capitals between ninth and sixteenth centuries; includes Angkor Wat and Angkor Thom.

Arikamedu. Iron Age settlement site in south India.

Ayuthia. Center of early Thai Kingdom (fl. thirteenth–sixteenth centuries); located 50 miles north of Bangkok.

Begram. Kushan capital (fl. second century B.C.E.–241); located in modern Afghanistan.

Caves of the Thousand Buddhas. Site of vast number of wall paintings from before the seventh century; located at Kizil, Turkestan.

Changsha. Capital of Chu Kingdom in China; site of several tombs.

Cheng Chou. Early capital of Chinese Shang culture.

Chiahsiang Hsien. Site of Han Dynasty tombs; located in Shantung province, China.

Elephanta. Island site, in Bombay Harbor, of cave temples (eighth–ninth centuries).

Ellora. Site, near Aurangabad, India, of 34 cave temples carved from rock between fifth and ninth centuries; the temples are Hindu, Buddhist, and Jainist.

Great Wall of China. 1,400-mile-long fortification built in north China from southwest Kansu to southern Manchuria.

Harappa. Site, in modern Pakistan, of Indus Valley civilization which ended in 1500 B.C.E.

Hoabinh. Prehistoric settlement 50 miles west of Hanoi, Vietnam.

Hsiangtanshan. Buddhist shrine from the Han Dynasty; located in Shantung province, China.

Kanchi. Coastal city in south India; site of several temples (*ca.* sixth–eighth centuries) of Dravidian origin.

Khajuraho. Site, in north Madhya Pradesh, India, of 28 Hindu and Jain temples built between 950 and 1050.

Konarak. Site, in the Indian state of Orissa, of a Hindu temple dedicated to Surya.

Loyang. North China city on the Yellow River; ruins include earthen walls and tombs.

Lungmen. Site, in China, of decorated Buddhist cave shrines.

Mohenjo-Daro. Site, in modern Pakistan (400 miles southwest of Harappa), of Indus Valley civilization which ended in 1500 B.C.E.

Nara. Ancient cultural and religious center in Japan, site of Todai-ji and Horyu-ji temples.

Nikko Temple. Shinto memorial shrine and mausoleum located in Nikko, Japan.

Oceo. Site of Funan royal port in Mekong Delta, Vietnam; ruins include Indian-style temples.

Pagan. Capital of Burma founded in 849; includes numerous Buddhist shrines and temples.

Pazyryk. Multitomb site in the Altai Mountains in western Siberia (*ca.* fifth–third centuries B.C.E.).

Polonnaruwa. Capital of Ceylon from 781 to 1290; ruins include numerous temples and monastery buildings.

Sanchi. Ancient religious center near modern Bhilsa in central India; ruins include the hemispherical Great Stupa.

Sigiriya. Site, on Lion Mt. in central Ceylon, of ruined palace and fortress dating from early sixth century.

Taj Mahal. Islamic mausoleum in Agra, India; built by Moghul emperor Shah Jehan in 1630–48.

Tanjore. Site, in southeast India, of capital of Chola Dynasty (900–1150); includes huge Rajajesvara temple dedicated to Shiva.

Tooth, Temple of the. Repository, in Kandy, Ceylon, of a tooth of the Buddha.

Trakieu. Site in central Vietnam of Cham capital.

Tunhuang. Site, in north-central China, of Buddhist temple caves with wall paintings.

Vat Phra Keo. Royal temple (*ca.* eighteenth century) in the eastern portion of Thai Royal Palace area in Bangkok.

Yunkang. Buddhist cave temple site (460–93) in Shansi province, China.

ASIA MINOR

Alaca Huyuk. Site, in north-central Turkey, of thirteen so-called royal tombs (*ca.* 2500 B.C.E.).

Aleppo. City in northwest Syria settled *ca.* 2000 B.C.E.; also known as Khalap or Haleb.

Amman. Capital of Jordan and site of Roman theater, Nymphaeum, Jebel Quala'a, fortifications, and temple to Heracles.

Atchana. Settlement in southeast Turkey (fl. mid-third millennium to 1200 B.C.E.); also known as Alalakh.

Avdat. Nabatean city in modern Israel.

Baalbek. Roman city in Lebanon; includes Temple of Jupiter, Temple of Bacchus, and circular Temple of Venus.

Behistun. Site in Iran of cliff bas relief of Darius' victories; carved in 516 B.C.E.

Brak. Site in east Syria (fl. prehistoric times to mid-second millennium B.C.E.).

Carchemish. Hittite city-state located on west bank of Euphrates at the Turkish-Syrian border.

Catal Huyuk. Site in central Turkey; inhabited from *ca.* 6700 to 5650 B.C.E.

Crac des Chevaliers. Crusader castle in Syria.

Ctesiphon. City and summer residence of the Parthian kings on the east bank of the Tigris in modern Iraq; includes the Arch of Ctesiphon.

Dorak. Site in northwest Turkey of two royal tombs from *ca.* 2480 B.C.E.

Ecbatana. Persian city and capital of Medes in western Iran; captured by both Cyrus the Great and Alexander the Great.

Enkomi. Bronze Age site on the east coast of Cyprus.

Ephesus. Greek port city in western Asia Minor; the extensive ruins include the Temple of Artemis (one of the seven wonders of the ancient world), the theater, and the library.

Eridu. Oldest city of Sumer; located 12 miles south of Ur in Iraq.

Gezer. Canaanite city south of Lydda, Israel.

Ghassul. Site northeast of the Dead Sea in Palestine; inhabited *ca.* 3800–3350 B.C.E.

Gordion. Capital of Phrygians; located in central Turkey.

Göreme. Site of frescoed Byzantine churches in central Turkey.

Hacilar. Site in southwest Turkey (fl. from seventh millennium B.C.E.).

Hattusas. Site, in central Turkey, of Hittite capital (fl. 3000–1230 B.C.E.).

Hazor. Canaanite site in northern Israel.

Ishtar Gate. One of the few monumental remains of Babylon; located 50 miles south of Baghdad.

Jerash. Roman city in modern Jordan.

Jericho. One of the oldest continuously occupied sites in the world (8000–1300 B.C.E.); located at the north end of the Dead Sea.

Jerusalem. City in Israel, holy to Jews, Moslems, and Christians; ruins include Wailing Wall and the Burnt House.

Karak. Site in east Jordan of Crusader castle.

Karatepe. Fortress-settlement in south Turkey dating from *ca.* eighth century B.C.E.

Khorsabad. Site near Mosul, Iraq, of Dur Sharrukin (Sargon's fort).

Kish. Sumerian city-state (fl. 3200–2600 B.C.E.) 50 miles south of Baghdad.

Mari. City in Syria near the Iraqi border (fl. *ca.* 1760 B.C.E.).

Masada. Natural rock fortress in Israel; site of Zealots' last stand against Romans and subsequent mass suicide.

Megiddo. Site of fortifications (*ca.* 3500 B.C.E.) in north Palestine.

Miletus. Greek town in western Asia Minor; founded *ca.* 1500 B.C.E. and sacked in fifth century B.C.E.

Mt. Carmel. Ridge in Israel and site of Wadi el Mugharah (Valley of Caves), which has been inhabited from prehistoric times.

Nimrud. One of three great capitals of the Assyrian Empire; located 20 miles south of Mosul, Iraq.

Nineveh. Site near Mosul, Iraq; ruins include the palaces of Sennacherib, Ashurbanipal, and Ashurnasirpal II and the temples of Ishtar and Nabu.

Nippur. Chief religious center of the Sumer; located near Baghdad.

Qalat al Rabadh. Islamic castle near Ajlun, Jordan.

Palmyra. Site northeast of Damascus formerly known as Tadmor; includes a temple to Baal.

Pasargadae. Early dynastic capital of the Achaemenids; located 60 miles southeast of Shiraz, Iran; ruins include Cyrus' residence and tomb, the audience hall, and the gate.

Pergamon. Greek city in west Asia Minor (fl. third–second centuries B.C.E.).

Persepolis. Capital of Achaemenid Dynasty; founded by Darius I *ca.* 520 B.C.E. and looted by Alexander the Great in 330 B.C.E.

Petra. Site, in southern Jordan, of Nabataean capital; ruins include the so-called Treasure House, the amphitheater, and palace.

Sardis. Chief city of Lydia in west Asia Minor; site of King Croesus' mint.

Susa. Site, in southwest Iran, of capital of Elam; ruins include palace of Darius I.

Troy. Site, near modern Hissarlik, Turkey, of nine successive cities; Homeric Troy is identified as Troy VII.

Ur. Center, in southern Iraq, of Sumerian civilization and of a so-called royal cemetery.

Uruk. Site, in southern Iraq, of ancient Sumerian city-state; ruins include city walls and the White Temple.

BRITISH ISLES

Antonine Wall. Northernmost Roman frontier wall in Scotland; built in 142.

Avebury. Site of Megalithic stone circles in Wiltshire, England.

Brugh na Boinne. Bronze Age cemetery in eastern Ireland.

Cadbury. Neolithic hill fort in Somerset, England; traditionally identified as Camelot.

Caernarvon Castle. Castle in north Wales dating to 1283.

Carrowkeel. Passage grave cemetery in Ireland (*ca.* 2500–2000 B.C.E.).

Cashel. Site in southern Ireland of founding of Catholic church in Ireland.

Dover Castle. Important castle in southeast England.

Dowris. Bronze Age site near Athlone, Ireland.

Dowth. Passage grave in Ireland dating from third millennium B.C.E.

Dunn Aengus. Cliffside fortress on Inishmore Island, Ireland.

Glastonbury. Site in western England of ruined abbey popularly believed to contain tombs of King Arthur and Queen Guinevere.

Grianan of Aileach. Circular stone fort (*ca.* 1700 B.C.E.) in Co. Donegal, Ireland.

Gur, Lough. Iron Age site of a menhir circle in Co. Limerick, Ireland.

Hadrian's Wall. 74-mile Roman frontier wall in England; built in 122–26.

Harlech Castle. Ruined castle in north Wales.

Iona. Island in Hebrides, site of seventh-century monastery, ruins of thirteenth-century monastery and cathedral, graves of many ancient Scottish kings.

Maes Howe. Orkney Island site of Megalithic tomb.

Maiden Castle. Large hill fort in Dorset, England.

New Grange. Site of Megalithic passage grave near Dublin, Ireland.

Ossian's Grave. Megalithic tomb in Northern Ireland.

Silbury Hill. Site of unknown purpose in Wiltshire, England; dates from after 2000 B.C.E.

Skara Brae. Well-preserved Neolithic village on main Orkney island.

Stanwick. Site, near Richmond, of largest Celtic fortifications in England; stronghold of rebel Brigantes.

Stonehenge. Bronze Age stone circle and possible observatory in Wiltshire, England; built *ca.* 2000–1400 B.C.E.

Tara. Site, near Dublin, of Bronze Age fort and royal residence; coronation site for Irish High Kings until sixth century.

Tintagel. Castle on Cornish coast of England; supposed birthplace of King Arthur.

Tintern Abbey. Ruins, in England, of twelfth-century Cistercian abbey; inspiration for Wordsworth's poem.

Trim Castle. Largest Anglo-Norman castle in Ireland.

White Horse of Uffington. Colossal chalk engraving in Berkshire, England; cut between third and first centuries B.C.E.

Windmill Hill. Site of Neolithic causeway or causewayed corral in Wiltshire, England.

EUROPE

Agrigento. Greek site, in southern Sicily, of Temple of Concordia.

Aigle Castle. Late Gothic castle in Switzerland.

Aigues-Mortes. Medieval fortified town in southern France.

Alise-la-Reine. Possible site in eastern France of Caesar's siege of Vercingetorix and Gauls at Alesia.

Almería Castle. Moorish-Christian castle in Spain.

Altamira Cave. Site, near Santander, Spain, of Cro-Magnon cave paintings.

Anghelu Ruju. Copper Age cemetery of rock-cut tombs in Sardinia.

Anlo. Neolithic settlement site on Drentho Heath in Holland.

Aosta. Roman town, 50 miles north of Turin, with preserved fortifications.

Arles. City in southeast France; ruins include Roman theater, amphitheater, Bath of Constantine and Cryptoporticus.

Athens. Greek city-state; site includes the Parthenon, the Erechtheum, the Athena Nike, the Propylaea, the Chalkotheke, the theater of Dionysus, the Theseum in the Agora, and the Kermeikos Cemetery.

Autun. City in eastern France; ruins include Roman theater, two city gates, and the temple of Janus.

Avignon. City in southern France; site of Papal Palace (built 1335–45).

Avila. Medieval fortified city in central Spain.

Baux, Les. Ruined medieval walled town in southern France.

Beauvais. City in northern France; site of tallest Gothic cathedral; roof collapsed in 1284.

Bernardini Tomb. Etruscan burial vault at Palestrina, Italy.

Bernous Cave. Located near Bourdeilles, France; contains cave art from Aurignacian Period.

Birka. Island site in Malar Lake, Sweden, of 1,200 Viking graves.

Biskupin. Iron Age village near Poznan, Poland.

Bodrogkeresztur. Prehistoric cemetery site in eastern Hungary.

Byzantium. City in modern Turkey (later known as Constantinople; now known as Istanbul); founded seventh century B.C.E.; contains Aya Sophia, city walls. Memet's Fort is nearby.

Caere. Etruscan city 30 miles north of Rome (fl. seventh–fifth centuries B.C.E.).

Calatrava Castle. Fortification in central Spain, finished 1217.

Carcassone. Medieval walled city (since restored) in southwest France.

Carnac. Site in southwest Brittany, France, of long avenues of standing stones (*ca.* 4000–3000 B.C.E.).

Castillo Cave. Site near Santander, Spain, of prehistoric cave art.

Cayla de Mailhac. Hilltop site in southwest France; inhabited from *ca.* 700 to 100 B.C.E.

Chertomlyk Burial. Scythian burial mound in Ukraine.

Chillon Castle. Ninth–thirteenth-century Swiss castle on Lake Geneva; made famous by Lord Byron's poem.

Chinon. Town in northwest France surmounted by three ruined castles.

Chiusi. One of twelve Etruscan cities in central Italy.

Ciempozuelos. Beaker culture settlement near Madrid, Spain.

Cluny. Site in eastern France of abbey destroyed in French Revolution.

Coca Castle. Fifteenth-century Spanish castle.

Cordoba. City in southern Spain and site of Moorish mosque.

Corinth. City located on the isthmus between mainland Greece and the Peloponnesus.

Crotona. Greek colony founded in eighth century B.C.E. on the "toe" of Italy.

Cuba, La. Norman castle in Sicily.

Cumae. Earliest Greek colony in Italy, near Naples (founded 750 B.C.E.).

Danilo. Neolithic village on Dalmatian coast.

Delphi. Site in Greece of Apollo's oracle and the omphalos (the navel stone of the world); remains include the temple of Apollo.

Diocletian's Palace. Retreat built in 300 near Split, Croatia.

Dolni Vestonice. Ice Age grave site in Moravia.

Domme. Fine example, in southwest France, of the bastide towns built during the Hundred Years' War.

Dubrovnik. Fortified coastal city in Croatia.

Elateia. Earliest known Neolithic site in central Greece.

Entremont. Celtic settlement near modern Aix-en-Provence, France.

Epidauros. Site in eastern Peloponnesus of Asklepieion and the Great Theater.

Esquiline. One of the seven hills of Rome; used as a cemetery.

Evora. Town in southern Portugal with Roman temple.

Fatyanovo Cemetery. Burial ground (*ca.* 1800 B.C.E.) near modern Yaroslavl, Russia.

Filitosa. Prehistoric fortress in Corsica.

Font-de-Gaume Cave. Site with Magdalenian painting in the Perigord region of France.

Fontenay. Site in eastern France of abbey destroyed in French Revolution.

François Tomb. Multichambered Etruscan tomb at Vulci, Italy.

Gaillard, Chateau. Medieval castle in northern France.

Gigantija. Site on island of Gozo near Malta with double temple dating from *ca.* 3000 B.C.E.

Glasinac. Cemetery site near Sarajevo.

Gonnesa. Site of Bronze Age village in Sardinia.

Gournia. Minoan town on the Gulf of Merabello, Crete.

Granada. City in southern Spain and site of fourteenth-century Moorish fort, the Alhambra.

Gravensteen Castle. Castle of the Counts in Ghent, Belgium.

Hadrian's Villa. Roman country villa built at Tibur (Tivoli) between 125 and 138.

Hagia Triada. Site, in southern Crete, of luxurious Minoan palace.

Herculaneum. Roman town buried during the eruption of Mount Vesuvius in 79.

Heuneburg. Celtic hilltop fort near Sigmaringen, Germany.

House of Tiles. At Lerna on the Gulf of Argos in the Peloponnesus; dates from late third millennium B.C.E.

Hunebed Road. Road between Emmen and Nordlaren, Holland, lined with hunebeds (prehistoric funerary monuments).

Jordanova. Neolithic settlement in Polish Silesia.

Kaiser-Wilhelm-Gedächniskirke. Church ruin in Berlin, bombed in World War II.

Karanovo. Neolithic site in eastern Bulgaria.

Kivik. Site of decorated Bronze Age funerary slab in southern Sweden.

Klein-Aspergle. Site of Celtic grave mound near Ludwigsburg, Baden-Württemberg, Germany.

Knossos. Major Minoan center near modern Herakleion, Crete.

Koln-Lindenthal. Neolithic village near Cologne, Germany.

Kos. Greek island in western Aegean; site of Hippocrates' Asklepion.

Kuban Royal Tombs. Scythian grave site in the Caucasus Mountains.

Kul Oba. Scythian burial site in the Crimea.

Lascaux Cave. Cave near Montignac, France, with paintings dating from *ca.* 15,000 B.C.E.

Lepenski Vir. Mesolithic village located on Danube near Belgrade.

Leubingen. Bronze Age site in Saxony, Germany.

Lindos. City on Rhodes with a Greek acropolis and a Hospitaler's Castle.

Maikop. South Russian site of Kuban tomb dating to *ca.* 2300 B.C.E.

Mallia. Minoan port on northeast coast of Crete.

Malta Temples. Series of great stone temples (*ca.* 3000 B.C.E.).

Marvao. Medieval castle in eastern Portugal.

Merida. Town in western Spain; site of Roman theater and amphitheater.

Metapontum. Greek seaport in southern Italy; founded *ca.* 680 B.C.E.

Methoni. Site of Venetian fortress in the southern Peloponnesus.

Millares, Los. Fortified Copper Age site near southeast Spanish coast.

Mnajdra. Site of temple on the southern coast of Malta.

Monemvassia. Medieval fortified Greek town in southern Peloponnesus.

Moussa. Broch or citadel in the Shetland Islands; occupied 300 B.C.E. to 400.

Munsingen. Large Helvetii cemetery site in Switzerland.

Mycenae. Chief city of Mycenean civilization; located in northeast Peloponnesus; ruins include the Lion Gate, the citadel, and the royal tombs.

Mystra. Three-tiered Byzantine city in the central Peloponnesus.

Neapolis. Latin name for Greek port on site of modern Naples; traces of city walls, temples, and a theater remain.

Niaux Cave. Site in Ariège Department, France, with cave paintings dating from 12,000 B.C.E.

Nimes. City in southern France; ruins include the so-called Maison Carée and the amphitheater.

Noin Ula. Site of Hun burial ground (*ca.* first century) near Lake Baikal, Russia.

Nora. Phoenician city in Sardinia; site includes temple to Tamit.

Obidos. Medieval walled town in central Portugal.

Olympia. Major Greek religious site in the northwest Peloponnesus; ruins include Sanctuary of Zeus and site of Olympic Games.

Orange. City in southern France; ruins include Roman triumphal arch and best-preserved theater in Europe.

Orchomenos. Ancient Boeotian town on Greek mainland; includes acropolis.

Ostia. Ancient port of Rome: ruins include fort, baths, forum, and oldest Jewish synagogue in Europe.

Paestum. Roman name for Poseidonia, a Greek city in southwest Italy; extensive ruins include three impressive Doric temples.

Panagurishte. Bulgarian site of Thracian burial mounds (*ca.* fourth–third centuries B.C.E.).

Peche Merle Cave. Site in southwest France with prehistoric paintings.

Pella. Site, in Macedonia, of Philip's and Alexander's capital; ruins include town walls and floor mosaics.

Penafiel Castle. Fifteenth-century Spanish castle.

Phaestos. Minoan palace in southern Crete.

Pompeii. Roman town in southern Italy near Naples buried in the eruption of Mt. Vesuvius (79); extensive and well-preserved ruins include forum, temples, two theaters, and amphitheater.

Pont du Gard. Roman aqueduct near Nimes, in southern France.

Predmost. Prehistoric grave site near Prerov, Moravia.

Pylos. Mycenean palace on west coast of the Peloponnesus.

Raknehaugen. Site of Norse burial mound in Romerike, Norway.

Rhodes. Greek port city on island of same name; ruins include temples to Zeus, Apollo, and Dionysus and a Crusader Castle of the Knights of St. John.

Rome. Capital of the Roman Empire; ruins include Appian Way (312), Ara Pacis Augustae (9 B.C.E.), the Capitol, Caracalla's Baths (third century), Catacombs, Circus Maximus (ca. sixth century B.C.E.), the Colosseum, Constantine's Arch (312–15), Diocletian's Bath (ca. 302), the Forum, Golden House (64), the Pantheon (ca. 126), Titus' Arch (81), Trajan's Column; Capitoline, smallest of the seven Roman hills, with sites of temples to Jupiter, Juno, and Minerva; Palatine, one of seven hills, traditionally associated with Romulus and Remus; Quirinal, northernmost of seven Roman hills.

St.-Remy-de-Provence. Village in southern France and site of Roman mausoleum and triumphal arch and Celtic city of Glanum.

San Gimignano. Medieval walled town in Tuscany with 13 of 70 palace towers remaining.

Santa Lucia. Large cemetery (ca. ninth–second centuries B.C.E.) near Ljubljana, Slovenia.

Segovia. City in central Spain and site of Roman aqueduct.

Somme-Bionne. Important Celtic burial ground in northern France; includes 5 royal graves and 80 graves of tribesmen.

Sparta. City in southern Peloponnesus; the few remains include the temple to Artemis.

Stabiae. Roman spa buried in eruption of Mt. Vesuvius (79).

Syracuse. Greek city on southeast coast of Sicily; remains include temples to Apollo and Athena and the theater.

Taormina. Greek city in northeast Sicily with theater.

Tarentum. Spartan colony on southern coast of Sicily.

Tarquinia. Chief of twelve Etruscan cities and site of necropolis with frescoed tombs, Italy.

Tarragona. City in eastern Spain; ruins include Roman arena, city walls, Ferreres Aqueduct, Centcelles Mausoleum, Berà Triumphal Arch, Scipios Tower, and a paleo-Christian necropolis.

Tarxien. Site in eastern Malta of four stone temples (ca. 3000–1500 B.C.E.).

Thebes. City in central Greece; ruins include the royal palace, the Elektra Gate, and the Temple of Apollo.

Thera. Volcanic island in the Aegean Sea now known as Santorini; site of ruins speculatively identified as Atlantis.

Tiryns. Mycenean fortress-town located on Gulf of Argos.

Tornus. Site in eastern France of ruined abbey.

Trelleborg. Site in western Zealand, Denmark, of Viking fortification.

Trialeti. Site, in the Republic of Georgia, of Bronze Age kurgans, or barrow graves.

Trier. Site in eastern Germany of Porta Nigra (Roman gate dating to 115).

Trois Freres Cave. Complex with prehistoric engravings in the Ariege Department, France.

Vaison-la-Romaine. Town in southern France with ruins of Roman settlement.

Veii. Etruscan rival of Rome and site of several tombs.

Vinca. Neolithic settlement near Belgrade, Serbia.

Waldalgesheim. Celtic princely tomb on the Rhine in Germany.

Zakros. Minoan palace site in eastern Crete.

INDONESIA AND PACIFIC ISLANDS

Borobudur. Buddhist temple in central Java (*ca.* eighth century).

Easter Island. Pacific island site of gigantic stone statues of human heads.

SOURCES

Anderson, William. *The Castles of Europe from Charlemagne to the Renaissance.* London: Elek Books, 1970.

Birnbaum, Stephen, ed. *Birnbaum's Italy: 1987.* Boston: Houghton Mifflin Co., 1987.

Folsom, Franklin. *America's Ancient Treasures: A Guide to Archaeological Sites and Museums in the United States and Canada.* Albuquerque: University of New Mexico Press, 1983.

Geldard, Richard G. *The Traveler's Key to Ancient Greece: A Guide to the Sacred Places of Ancient Greece.* New York: Alfred A. Knopf, 1989.

Hale, Sheila. *The American Express Pocket Guide to Florence and Tuscany.* New York: Prentice-Hall, 1983.

Harvard Student Agencies, Inc. *1986 Let's Go: The Budget Guide to Europe.* New York: St. Martin's Press, 1986.

Hawkes, Jacquetta, ed. *Atlas of Ancient Archaeology.* New York: McGraw-Hill, 1974.

Jacobs, Michael, and Paul Stirton. *The Knopf Traveler's Guides to Art: France.* New York: Alfred A. Knopf, 1984.

Kurtz, Seymour. *The World Guide to Antiquities.* New York: Crown Publishers, 1975.

Michelin Green Guides to various places. London: Michelin Tyre Public Limited Co., various dates.

Robertson, Ian. *The Blue Guide to France.* New York: W. W. Norton, 1988.

—Ian Crump; L.D.R.

II

HISTORY AND

POLITICS

IO

HISTORIC BATTLES
AND CAMPAIGNS

· · · · ·

WHEN THE POET SIEGFRIED SASSOON, AN OFFICER IN THE BRITISH EXPEDI-
tionary Force, met Winston Churchill in France late in the First World War,
he expressed shock at Churchill's remark that war was the natural state of
humankind. Yet anyone who consults a book such as Ernest and Trevor
Dupuy's *Encyclopedia of Military History* might be able to see Churchill's
point. For the double-columned pages of the Dupuys's massive chronology
of warfare from earliest times onward record tens of thousands of battles,
sieges, and campaigns fought, won, or lost from the dawn of recorded history to the present.

We are assured that the pen is mightier than the sword; unfortunately,
this works out only over the very long haul. All things considered, the
ancient Hebrews were mightier writers than the Assyrians, and it is true
that very few Assyrians have been seen around in recent centuries.
However, it is doubtful that this was of any particular comfort to the citizens of Israel and Judea during the ninth and eighth centuries B.C.E.

The relationship of writing to warfare, and of writers to warriors, has
always been highly complex. When Stephen Dedalus, who has gotten himself very drunk and then been knocked out by a British soldier, is painfully
sobering up at the Cabmen's Shelter in James Joyce's *Ulysses*, he stares at a
table knife and asks Leopold Bloom to take it away. It reminds him, he says,
of Roman history. Joyce was a peaceable man, and did not think very highly
of warriors, whether Roman, British, or whatever.

Ernest Hemingway, by contrast, was of a different school of thought—
or maybe emotion is a better word for it. He was a writer, but he very much
feared that being a writer meant being a sissy, and so he went out of his way
to write and to behave toughly. About bullfighting he wrote that "killing
cleanly and in a way which gives you aesthetic pleasure and pride has
always been one of the greatest enjoyments of a part of the human race.

Because the other part, which does not enjoy killing, has always been the more articulate and has furnished most of the good writers, we have had very few statements of the true enjoyment of killing." What one has to ask is, Who is trying to convince whom of what?

In any event, one outcome of the psychological hang-up embodied in that remark is some of the finest prose ever written about war, hunting, and fishing. Another outcome, alas, is that the author of it took his own life when in his early sixties. There have been no small number of authors, however, who finessed nicely what was for Hemingway psychologically an either/or affair—Stendhal, for example, or Tolstoy.

General James Wolfe is famed for two things: for defeating the French under Montcalm at Quebec, and for having declared after reading Gray's "Elegy" that he would rather have written it than take Quebec. Would Hemingway have rather cleared out the St. Mihiel Salient than written *The Sun Also Rises*? In both instances, I doubt it.

William Faulkner, whose "The Bear" is arguably the greatest hunting story ever written, when young also felt himself deficient in masculinity for not having been a war hero in 1917–18. Unlike Hemingway, he came to realize the absurdity of the comparison. He knew exactly how to get Hemingway's goat, however; in the 1950s he gave an interview in which he declared that Hemingway had "no courage" because he had never used words that readers needed to look up in a dictionary. Hemingway, who had started the sniping earlier, was so upset that he asked the U.S. general with whose outfit he had served as a war correspondent in 1944 to write Faulkner and tell him how brave he was.

Whatever the difficulties of equating the vocations of penmanship and swordsmanship, it cannot be gainsaid that there are very few writers who do not, at some point or the other, have to concern themselves with warfare. The list that follows is a selection of certain significant military and naval engagements, beginning with the battle of Megiddo in present-day Palestine in the fifteenth century B.C.E. and concluding with the Russian suppression of the Chechnan revolt. In preparing it we have relied upon the Dupuys' exhaustive work, David Eggenberger's *Dictionary of Battles*, Michael Sanderson's *Sea Battles: A Reference Guide*, and William E. Langer's *Encyclopedia of World History*, as well as more specialized studies and compilations. See Sources, below.

Megiddo, 1469 B.C.E. Egyptian army under Thutmosis defeats Palestinian chieftains led by King of Qadesh at Megiddo, north of present-day Jerusalem.

Qadesh, 1294. Ramses of Egypt fights Hittites at Qadesh on Orontes River in present-day Syria.

Nile Delta, 1190. Ramses III defeats invading eastern Mediterranean sea peoples.

Troy, ca. 1180. Greek and Asiatic forces besiege and conquer Mycenean city of Troy; Homer's *Iliad* is based on this campaign.

Mt. Gilboa, 1012. Israelites under Saul fight Philistines at Mt. Gilboa; Saul is killed.

Qardar, 854. Shalmaneser III of Assyria defeats "Damascus coalition" of twelve kings on Orontes River near present-day Lebanon.

Samaria, 722. Assyrians under Sargon II besiege and conquer Samaria, exiling King Hoshea and people of Israel to Media.

Raphia, 716. Sargon II defeats Egyptian pharoah Osorkon at Raphia (Raffa) in Sinai on coast of Palestine.

Elteqeh, 701. Sennacherib of Assyria defeats Egyptians under Shabaka at Elteqeh in present-day Palestine.

Babylon, 689. Babylon is taken and the city sacked by Assyrians under Sennacherib.

Nineveh, 612. Assyrian capital of Nineveh, on Tigris River near present-day Mosul, Iraq, is captured by Nabopolassar of Chaldea and Cyaxares of Medea.

Carchemish, 605. Egyptians under Necho II defeated by Nebuchadrezzar of Babylon, near Mediterranean coast of present-day Syria.

Jerusalem, July 586. Babylonians under Nebuchadrezzar II capture Jerusalem and carry people into exile, ending kingdom of Judah.

Thyreatis, 560. After battle in which each side is represented by three hundred champions ends with both sides claiming victory, Sparta defeats Argus and takes plain of Thyreatis on Peloponnesus.

Sepeia, 494. Cleomenes I of Sparta defeats Argives, establishing dominion over Peloponnesus.

Marathon, 490. Athenians and Plataeans under Callimachus defeat Persian army and check King Darius' invasion of Greece.

Thermopylae, 480. Spartan force under Leonidas is defeated by invading Persians after spirited stand.

Salamis, September 480. Persian flotilla of Xerxes is routed by Athenian fleet under Themistocles at island of Salamis.

Cumae, 474. Syracusan fleet under Hiero stops Etruscan expansion into southern Italy near present-day Naples.

Plataea, 479. Led by Pausanias and the Spartans, Greek army decisively defeats Xerxes and Persians on slope of Mt. Cithaeron in Boeotia, ending threat of Persian invasion.

Mantinea, 418. Spartans under Agis defeat coalition army of Athenians, Mantineans, and Argives in Peloponnesian War.

Syracuse, 413. After failing to take Syracuse, Athenian expedition in Sicily led by Nicias and Demosthenes is defeated by Syracusans and Spartans in land and sea battle.

Cynossema, autumn 411. Peloponnesian fleet under Mindarus encounters and is routed by Athenian fleet of Thrasylus and Thrasybulus off Cynossema Point on Asia Minor coast.

Aegospotami, 405. In decisive battle of Peloponnesian War, fought along shoreline of Hellespont, Spartan galleys under Lysander destroy Athenian fleet under Conon.

Cunaxa, 401. Artaxerxes II of Persia defeats rebel army of his brother Cyrus, including Greek mercenaries, at Cunaxa near Babylon. As chronicled in Xenophon's *Anabasis,* Greeks then fight their way across mountains of Armenia to Black Sea.

Cnidus, 394. Persian galleys under Pharnabazus and Athenians under Conon demolish Spartan fleet under Pisander off southwest Asia Minor coast near Rhodes, destroying Sparta's sea power.

Naxos, 376. Spartan fleet of Pollio blockading approaches to Saronic Gulf is defeated by Athenian galleys under Chabrias off island of Naxos in Cyclades Islands.

Leuctra, July 371. Thebans under Epaminondas outflank and defeat Spartan phalanxes of Cleombrotus at Leuctra in Thebes.

Mantinea, 362. Thebans smash coalition of Spartans, Athenians, and Mantineans at Mantinea in Peloponnesus, but Epaminondas is mortally wounded.

Chaeronea, 338. Philip of Macedon crushes Athenian-Boeotian-Theban army, with his son Alexander leading decisive cavalry charge.

Issus, October 333. Alexander the Great's Macedonian army routs Persian army of Darius III on coastal plain north of Pinarus River in Asia Minor.

Caudine Forks, 321. Roman army under Veturius and Postumus is routed near Caudium in Apennines east of present-day Naples by Samnite army led by Pontius.

Gaugamela (Arbela), October 1, 331. Alexander destroys army of Persians, Bactrians, Parthians, and others under Darius III on plain east of Arbela, near present-day Erbil, Iraq.

Ausculum, 279. Pyrrhus of Epirus defeats Roman army under Sulpicius Saverrio near present-day Ascoli in Italy, but suffers heavy losses. The term *Pyrrhic victory* is derived from this and previous battle at Heraclea.

Mylae, 260. In naval battle off northeast coast of Sicily near present-day Milazzo, Roman galleys under Gaius Dullius overpower Carthaginian fleet.

Trasimeno, April 217. Carthaginian army under Hannibal ambushes and routs Roman army under Gaius Flaminius at Lake Trasimeno in central Italy near present-day Perugia.

Cannae, August 2, 216. Roman army under Varro attacks Hannibal's waiting Carthaginian army on Adriatic coast in southeastern Italy and suffers crushing defeat, losing some 60,000 men.

Metaurus, 207. After crossing Alps to reinforce his brother Hannibal, Hasdrubal's Carthaginian force is annihilated by Roman army under Claudius Nero and Marcus Livius Salinator at Metaurus River near Sena in east-central Italy.

Zama, 202. Carrying war into Africa, Romans under Scipio defeat Hannibal's Carthaginian army inland from present-day Tunisian coast, ending Second Punic War.

Cynoscephalae, 197. Roman army under Flamininus defeats Macedonian army of Philip V in hills of southeast Thessaly, Greece.

Magnesia, December 190. Roman army under Lucius Cornelius Scipio and Scipio Africanus defeats Syrian army of Antiochus III near present-day Smyrna, gaining control of Asia Minor.

Arausio, 105. Cimbri and Teutones migrate into southern Gaul and destroy large Roman army under Caepio and Mallius Maximus at present-day Orange in Rhone Valley, France.

Aix-en-Provence, 102. Romans under Gaius Marius slaughter Teutones and Ambrones at Aquae Sextiae on Rhone River in present-day Provence. The year following, Marius joins Quintus Lutatius Catulus and annihilates Cimbri at Vercellae south of Milan in Po Valley, Italy, ending threat to Rome.

Chaeronea, 86. Sulla's Roman legions defeat forces of Mithridates of Pontus and Greek allies, led by Archeleus, in Boeotia, Greece.

Lemnos, 73. Roman galleys under L. Licinius Lucullus attack fleet of Mithridates of Pontus in Hellespont, pursue it to island of Lemnos in Aegean Sea, then win sea and land battle.

Bibracte, 58. Helvetii invading Gaul are defeated by Julius Caesar at hilltop town of Bibracte, capital of the Aedui, near present-day Autun, France.

Alesia, 52. Caesar attacks and besieges Gallic army under Vercingetorix at mountain fortress at present-day Alise-Ste.-Reine, in east-central France, and forces capitulation.

Pharsala, 48. In decisive battle of Roman civil war, Caesar's army defeats Pompey's forces at Enipeus River in present-day Thessaly.

Phillippi, 42. Following assassination of Caesar in Rome, Mark Antony's and Octavian's forces pursue Brutus and Cassius to Epirus, in present-day eastern Greece, and after indecisive battle on October 26 and Cassius' suicide, Brutus and Republican army are defeated.

Actium, 31. Octavian's war galleys, under direction of Agrippa, attack fleet of Mark Antony and Cleopatra on coast of Epirus; Cleopatra flees with 60 ships, Antony follows her, and remaining ships capitulate after seven days.

Teutoburg Forest, 9 C.E. German tribes under Arminius massacre three Roman legions under Publius Quintillius Varus in present-day Ems Valley, Germany.

Caer Caradoc, 50. Caractacus, British tribal chieftain and son of Cymbeline, is defeated by Romans under Ostorius Scapula on hill in Shropshire near Welsh border.

Towcester, 61. Revolt against Romans in Britain led by Queen Boadicea, whose forces sack Colchester, London, and Verulamium, is crushed by Suetonius Paulinus at site believed to be on Watling Street Highway near modern-day Tolchester.

Lugdunum, 197. Roman emperor Septimus Severius defeats British and Gallic legions of rival Clodius Septimius Albinius in battle near present-day Lyon, France.

Edessa, 260. Persian king Shapur I defeats Roman army of Emperor Valerian, taking him prisoner, near site of modern Urfa, Turkey.

Saxa Rubra (Mulvian Bridge), 312. In battle between armies of two of several rival claimants to Roman throne, Constantine defeats Maxentius north of Rome along Flaminian Way near bridge across Tiber River, with Maxentius drowning when pontoon bridge collapses.

Adrianople, July 3, 323. Constantine, "Augustus of the West," defeats Licinius, "Augustus of the East," and besieges Byzantium. In September he crushes Licinius at present-day Scutari, Turkey, and becomes sole emperor, establishing Christianity as official religion of empire.

Tanais River, ca. 372. Huns defeat Alani, Sarmatian tribe, in region of present-day Don River and begin westward push, with Ostrogoths and Visigoths retreating into north-central Europe.

Adrianople, August 9, 378. After Goths move into Thrace, Valens attempts to check them and is defeated by Gothic cavalry under Fritigern, and his Roman army is destroyed near present-day Edirne in European Turkey.

Fei River, 383. Chinese defeat invasion of Eastern Ch'in Empire territory by Ch'iang tribe of Tibet under emperor Fu Chien on Fei River in present-day central China.

Pollentia, April 6, 402. Roman army under Stilicho attacks Alaric's Visigoth army at present-day Pollenza, Italy, and drives it northward into Tuscany.

Rome, 410. After leaving vicinity of Rome in 409, Alaric and Visigoths return to storm Salarian Gate and to capture and sack city.

Hippo, 431. Vandals under Gaiseric twice defeat army under Roman-barbarian general Bonifacius, then besiege and take port city of Hippo, present-day Bône, Algeria.

Chalons, June 451. Hun ruler Attila (Atla), with Ostrogoth allies, is defeated by Visigoth-Frankish-Roman army under Aetius and Theodoric on Mauriac Plain east of Seine River near present-day Troyes, France.

Tolbiacum, 496. Merovingian king Clovis defeats Alemanni at present-day Zülpichon plain of Rhine River near Cologne, Germany.

Campus Vogladensis, 507. Clovis defeats Visigoths under Alaric II at present-day Vouillé, northwest of Poitiers, France, killing Alaric and forcing Visigoth retreat across Pyrenees into Spain.

Dara, 528. Byzantine general Belisarius, with Hun allies, defeats Persian-Arab army at new fort in northern Mesopotamia.

Tricameron, December 533. Belisarius defeats army of Gelimer at Tricameron, south of modern-day Tunis, bringing an end to Vandal kingdom in Africa.

Casilinum, 554. Byzantine army under Narses annihilates Frankish army under Buccelin near-present day Capua, north of Naples, Italy.

Catraeth, ca. 600. Invading Celtic army of King Mynyddog is defeated by English near present-day Catterick.

Nineveh, December 12, 627. Byzantine army under Heraclius defeats Persian army under Khosrau II on Tigris River near ruins of ancient Nineveh near Mosul in present-day Iraq.

Mecca, 630. Moslems under Mohammed march from Medina and storm Mecca on Red Sea in present-day Saudi Arabia.

Yarmuk, August 636. Muslim army under Khālid ibn al-Walid conquers Syria and Palestine by defeating Byzantine army under Theodorus Trithurius in Yarmuk River valley west of present-day Sea of Galilee.

Winn-waed, 655. Penda, king of Anglo-Saxon Mercia, is defeated by Oswy of Northumbria in present-day central England.

Wadi Bekka, 711. Moorish conquest of Spain is furthered by defeat of Visigoth king Roderick by Muslim army of Tarik ibn Ziyad near Medina Sidonia in Cadiz.

Hellespont, September 717. Armada under Suleiman, en route through Hellespont to join in Moslem siege of Constantinople, is attacked and routed at Sea of Marmora by Byzantine fleet under the Isaurian Leo III.

Tours, October 732. Charles Martel, "Hammer of the Franks," defeats invading Arab forces of Abd-ar-Rahmān at Tours, holy city of Gaul, in present-day east-central France.

Roncesvalles, August 15, 778. Baggage train and rear guard of Charlemagne's Frankish army, under Roland, are annihilated by Christian Basques of Pampeluna at pass through Pyrenees.

Edington, May 878. Alfred the Great, king of Wessex, defeats Danes under Guthrum in crucial battle near present-day Trowbridge in southern England.

Lechfeld, August 10, 955. German king Otto decisively defeats Magyar horse archers at Lech River near Augsburg, ending destructive raids into Germany.

Candia, March 961. Byzantine fleet under Gen. Nicephorus Phocas storms Saracen stronghold at Candia (Heraklion) and regains Crete.

Maldon, August 10–11, 991. Danish invaders under Olaf Tryggvason defeat Anglo-Saxons under Ealdorman Brithnoth of Essex near Maldon, East Anglia.

Swold, 1000. Olaf I of Norway is defeated and killed in naval battle with Olaf Skutkonung of Sweden and Sweyn I of Denmark off Swold Island in Baltic Sea.

Peshawar, 1001. Moslem army of Sultan Mahmud of Ghazni defeats Punjabis under Rajah Jaipal of Lahore on border of Kashmir in present-day Pakistan.

Clontarf, April 23, 1014. Irish under Brian Boru of Munster drive Danish invaders under Sweyn I back to ships near Dublin; Brian and son are killed.

Assandun, October 18, 1016. Danes under King Canute defeat Saxons under Edmund Ironside of Wessex at present-day Ashington, Essex.

Dunsinane, 1054. Malcolm III defeats Macbeth near present-day Perth, Scotland.

Stamford Bridge, September 25, 1066. Saxon king Harold II defeats Norse army under Harold Hardrada and Tostig on Derwent River near York.

Hastings, October 14, 1066. Norman army under Duke William defeats Saxon king Harold II's defending army on Senlac Hill north of Hastings, opening England to Norman conquest.

Manzikert, 1071. Seljuk Turks under Alp Arslan rout Byzantine army of Emperor Romanus IV in present-day eastern Turkey, opening Asia Minor to invasion.

Dyrrachium, October 18, 1081. Normans under Robert Guiscard besieging Dyrrachium (Durrës, or Durazzo) in Epirus, present-day Albania, defeat Byzantine relieving force sent from Constantinople, storm and sack city.

Dorylaeum, 1091. Ambushed by Seljuks under Kiliji Arslan at crossroads of Dorylaeum in Anatolia, Crusaders under Bohemund and Bishop of le Puy rally to defeat Turks.

Orontes, 1098. Crusaders under Bohemund cross Orontes River in northern Syria and defeat Turks under Emir Kerboga.

Ascalon, 1099. Crusaders under Godfrey de Bouillon defeat Egyptian army of al-Afdal Shahinshah on coast of Palestine.

Hundsfeld, 1109. Polish army of Boleslav III defeats army of Henry V of Germany near Breslau in Silesia.

Ourique, 1139. Alfonso I of Portugal defeats Moors. (Actual battle was fought at undetermined location in southeast Portugal.)

Ts'ai-shih, 1161. Sung General Yu Yun-wen defeats Ch'in emperor Liang's invasion at Yangtze River near Nanking.

Legnano, May 29, 1176. Hohenstaufen king Frederick Barbarossa defeated by army of Lombard League cities in northwest Italy northwest of Milan after infantry pikemen stand up to heavy cavalry charges.

Ishibashi, August 23, 1180. Minamoto clan army under Yorimoto is defeated by Taira in Sagami Province, Japan.

Danoura, 1184. War junks of Minamoto clan under Yoshitsune defeat Taira convoy in strait of Shimonoseki at western exit of Inland Sea of Japan.

Hattin, July 4, 1187. Moslem army under Saladin, Ayyubite sultan of Egypt, destroys Crusaders under Guy of Lusignan near Tiberias, close to Sea of Galilee.

Arsouf, September 7, 1191. Crusader army of Richard I, the Lion-Hearted, of England and Philip II of France defeats Saladin's Turkish army at Arsouf near coast of Palestine.

Navas de Tolosa, 1212. Alphonso VIII of Castile leads coalition army against Almohades at Navas de Tolosa in Andalusia and drives Moors from Castile and Andalusia.

Bouvines, July 27, 1214. Philip II Augustus of France defeats German-Flemish-English army led by Emperor Otto IV at plateau between Lille and Tournai in northern France.

Peking, 1214. Mongols under Genghis Khan capture Peking in China.

Bamian, 1221. Mongols under Genghis Khan defeat Turkish army under Jalal-ad-Din at pass between Kush and Koh-i-Baba in Afghanistan, razing city and massacring inhabitants, and ravage northern India.

Kalka, 1223. Russian army under Mitislav Udaloj of Halicz and Mitislav Romanovich, prince of Kiev, is routed by Mongols under Prince Subedai on Kalka River north of Gulf of Taganrog in southern Russia.

Pien Ching, 1233. Mongols under Prince Subedai besiege and take present-day Kaifeng and control northern China.

Neva River, 1240. Alexander Nevsky, Russian prince of Novgorod, defeats Swedes under Birgir Jarl on banks of Neva River near present-day St. Petersburg.

Liegnitz and Sajo River, April 9–11, 1241. In battles on April 9 and 11, Mongol army under Kaidu routs Silesian and Polish army under Henry II of Silesia near Breslau on Oder River, and another Mongol army under Batu and Prince Subedai defeats Hungarians under King Bela at Sajo River.

Lake Peipus, 1242. Alexander Nevsky, Russian prince of Novgorod, defeats Livonian order of Teutonic Knights on frozen surface of Lake Peipus in Estonia.

Fariskur, 1250. Moslems under Fakr-ed-din annihilate Crusader army of Louis IX of France at Fariskur (El Mansura) near Nile delta.

Baghdad, February 15, 1258. Mongols under Hulagu Khan defeat Arab defenders and sack Baghdad, ending rule of Abbassid caliphate.

Ayn Jalut, September 3, 1260. Mongol general Kitbugha's army advancing through Syria toward Egypt is defeated by Mamelukes under Sultan Qutuz.

Kenilworth and Evesham, August 2–4, 1265. Edward I of England crushes army of younger Simon de Montfort near Severn River August 2, then two days later routs elder Simon's army at bend of Avon River.

Kyushu, 1281. Kublai Khan's invasion of Japan is thwarted when Mongol invasion fleet is destroyed by severe storm (*kamikazi*—"divine wind") off north Kyushu.

Acre, May 15, 1291. Mamelukes under Khalil capture Acre on Palestine coast from Knights of St. John.

Curzola, September 7, 1298. Genoese fleet under Lamba Doria defeats Venetians under Andrea Dandolo at island of Curzola off Dalmatian coast in Adriatic Sea.

Falkirk, July 22, 1298. English army under Edward I defeats Scottish army under Sir William Wallace at Callender Wood, near head of Firth of Forth.

Courtrai, July 1, 1302. French cavalry under Comte d'Artois is routed by Flemish infantry under Guy de Dampierre at Day of the Spurs in Flanders; 4,000 gilt spurs are collected by victors.

Bannockburn, June 23–24, 1314. Scottish army under Robert Bruce routs Edward II's English army south of Stirling in central Scotland, lifting siege of Stirling Castle.

Morgarten, November 15, 1315. Swiss force defeats invading Austrian army under Archduke Leopold I in narrow mountain pass at Lake Aegeri on border of Schwyz and Zug cantons.

Sluys, June 24, 1340. English fleet of Edward III destroys fleet of French, Genoese, and Spanish ships under Hugh Quieret and Nicholas Bétuchet at mouth of Zwyn River while guarding Bruges in present-day Belgium.

Rio Salado, October 30, 1340. King Alfonso XI of Castile and Leon, in alliance with Alfonso IV of Portugal, decisively defeats Moslem army near Tarifa, on Rio Salado in Andalusia, Spain.

Crécy, August 26, 1346. English army of Edward III is caught by French of Philip VI while retreating through Flanders; in ensuing battle English longbowman infantry destroys vaunted French cavalry.

Poitiers, September 19, 1356. Edward III's English-Gascon army, led by the Black Prince, overcomes French army of John II at Poitiers on Clain River in west-central France, capturing French king and Philip the Bold of Burgundy, the Dauphin.

Helsingborg, 1362. Waldemar IV of Denmark defeats Hanseatic League fleets in Oresund Strait between Sweden and Zeeland, the Netherlands.

La Rochelle, June 22–23, 1372. English fleet of armed merchantmen under Earl of Pembroke is intercepted by Castilian galleys commanded by Ambrosio Bocanegra off La Rochelle in Bay of Biscay and is captured or destroyed.

Pola, May 7, 1379. Genoese galleys under Luciano Doria rout Venetian fleet under Vettore Pisani at Pola in Adriatic Sea.

Chioggia, December 23, 1379. Venetian fleet under Vettore Pisani blockades Genoan fleet of Pietro Doria at Chioggia, south of Venice, forcing surrender on June 24, 1380.

Kulikovo, September 8, 1380. Grand Duke Dmitri Donskoi of Vladimir and Moscow defeats Mongolian Tartars near source of Don River.

Navarette, April 3, 1367. Edward III of England, crossing Pyrenees, defeats French and Castilian army of Henry of Trastamara and Bertrand du Guesclin south of Ebro River in Spain.

Aljubarrota, August 14, 1385. Portuguese under Regent John, with help of English archers, defeat army of John of Castile 50 miles north of Lisbon.

Sempach, July 9, 1386. Leopold III's invading Swabian-Austrian army is defeated by Swiss in north-central Switzerland on Lake of Sempach.

Kossovo Polje, 1389. Murad I of Turkey defeats coalition of Serbs, Bulgarians, Albanians, Montenegrins, Wallachians, and Bosnians under Prince Lazar of Serbia at Kossovo Polje (Blackbird Field) in southwest Serbia, beginning more than 500 years of Turkish suzerainty in Balkans.

Nicopolis, September 25, 1396. Ottoman Turks under Sultan Bayazzid decisively defeat Crusader army under King Sigismund of Hungary south of Kicopolis at Danube River in present-day Romania.

Panipat, December 17, 1398. Tamerlane's Tartar army routs and massacres Indian army of Mahmud Tughluk at Panipat, then devastates northern India.

Ankara, July 20, 1402. Tamerlane's Tartars defeat Sultan Bayazzid and Ottoman Turks near Ankara in Anatolia, Asia Minor.

Shrewsbury, July 21, 1403. Henry IV's army, under future Henry V, defeats Henry Percy of Northumberland, "Harry Hotspur," in Shropshire, killing him and preventing union with Owen Glendower of Wales.

Tannenburg, 1410. Polish and Lithuanian forces under Jagiello defeat Teutonic Knights in battle between Tannenburg and Grünwald in northern Poland.

Agincourt, October 24, 1415. Brought to bay at Agincourt on Pas-de-Calais near Arras, Henry V of England defeats French army under Marshal Jean Boucicault, then massacres prisoners.

Harlech, 1409. Harlech Castle in Wales is recaptured by Prince Henry; Owen Glendower's revolt ends as Glendower flees into mountains.

Kutna Hora, December 19, 1421. Hussites under John Ziska, trapped outside Kutna Hora (Königratz) in Bohemia, smash through lines of Catholics under Emperor Sigismund.

Orléans, May 7, 1429. Joan of Arc leads forces of Dauphin Charles, captures key fortification of Tourelles, and lifts English siege of Orléans.

Kossovo Polje, October 17, 1448. Turkish sultan Murat II defeats Hungarian army under John Hunyadi in southern Serbia.

Constantinople, May 29, 1453. After 50-day siege, Turks under Mohammed II breach walls of Constantinople and Byzantine empire falls, with last emperor, Constantine Paleologus XI, killed during attack.

St. Albans, May 22, 1455. Duke of York and Earl of Warwick defeat Duke of Somerset in opening battle of War of the Roses at St. Albans in southeast England.

Northampton, July 18, 1460. Warwick defeats army of Henry VI and takes Lancastrian king prisoner at Northampton, 70 miles northeast of London.

Towton, March 29, 1461. Edward of York, having proclaimed himself Edward IV, defeats Lancastrian army at Towton, near York in northeast England; Henry VI flees to Scotland.

Barnet, April 14, 1471. Edward IV, after fleeing to Flanders, returns to defeat Warwick, now allied with Lancastrians, at Barnet, near London, with Warwick cut down and killed.

Morat, June 22, 1476. Besieged by Charles, Duke of Burgundy, at Morat, on lake in Fribourg canton, Swiss army attacks and routs Burgundians.

Bosworth, August 22, 1485. In climactic battle of War of the Roses at Bosworth Field in central England, Richard III, after usurping throne following Edward IV's death, is defeated by Henry Tudor, earl of Richmond; Richard is killed and Tudor becomes Henry VII.

Granada, January 2, 1492. After desperate sorties, Moslem forces under Boabdil surrender Granada to Christian army of Ferdinand of Aragon, ending Moorish sway on Iberian peninsula.

Cerignola, April 26, 1503. Spanish army under Gonzalo Fernàndez de Córdoba, the "Great Captain," defeats French under Louis XII in Apulia in southern Italy, opening Naples to recapture.

Garigliano, December 29, 1503. Spanish under Córdoba again defeat French of Louis XII at Rapido River below Cassino in south-central Italy.

Diu, February 3, 1509. Portuguese fleet under Francisco de Alameida destroys Gujarat-Egyptian fleet at Diu on northwest coast of India.

Merv, 1510. Shiite Moslem shah Ismail of Persia defeats Sunni Moslem army of Usbek Turks at Merv, present-day Bhayram-Ali, on Murghab River in Turkoman.

Flodden Field, September 9, 1513. Scotch under James IV cross Tweed River, attack English army under Thomas Howard, earl of Surrey, in northeast England, and are crushed.

Marignano, September 13–14, 1515. Francis I of France defeats Swiss south of Milan at present-day Melignano after timely arrival of Venetian cavalry, forcing evacuation of Duchy of Milan by Swiss.

Merj-Dabik, August 24, 1516. Turkish sultan Selim I defeats Mamelukes under Sultan Kansu al-Gauri north of Aleppo, Syria.

Otumba, July 7, 1520. Retreating Spanish under Hernando Cortés defeat Aztec army at Otumba east of present-day Mexico City.

Tenochtitlan, August 13, 1521. Spanish and Tlaxcala allies under Cortés capture Mexico City from Aztec defenders.

Rhodes, January 1, 1523. After six months of siege by Turks under Sultan Suleiman I, Knights Hospitalizers agree to evacuate Rhodes in Dodecanese Islands, off coast of Turkey.

Pavia, February 24, 1525. Army of Emperor Charles V of Austria and Spain under Charles de Lannoy and Marquis of Pescara defeats French of King Francis I at Pavia in Lombard, capturing Francis and establishing Habsburg rule in northern Italy.

Panipat, April 19, 1526. King Babar of Kabul, Kahir-el-din Mohammed, defeats army of Ibrahim, sultan of Delhi, at Panipat on Jumna River in Punjab.

Mohacs, August 29–30, 1526. Turkish army under Suleiman I destroys army under Louis II of Hungary and Bohemia at Mohacs on Duna River, killing Louis and securing Ottoman control of Hungary.

Vienna, October 15, 1529. Turkish army of Suleiman I retreats from Vienna after siege fails.

Kappel, October 11, 1531. Protestant army is defeated by army of Catholic cantons near Zurich in northern Switzerland, and Huldreich Zwingli is killed.

Ceresole, April 14, 1544. French army of Francis I, under Duc d'Enghien, with Swiss and Italians, defeats Spanish and Austrian army under Marqués del Vasto south of Turin.

Pinkie, September 10, 1547. English under Earl of Hertford defeat Scotch under Earl James Hamilton at Firth of Forth and devastate Edinburgh region.

Kazan, 1552. Tsar Ivan IV, "the Terrible," seizes Kazan from Tartars, opening Volga region to Russian control.

Astrakhan, 1554–1556. Tartar stronghold at head of Volga River delta on Caspian Sea in Russia falls to Ivan the Terrible.

Malta, September, 1565. Moslem siege of Knights of St. John under Jean de la Vallette at Malta by Turks under Mustapha Pasha and Admiral Piali is lifted when Christian relief fleet and army under Garcia of Toledo arrives at Mediterranean island fortress.

Lepanto, October 7, 1571. Italo-Spanish fleet under Don John of Austria checks Moslem sea power in Mediterranean with victory over Turks under Ochiali Pasha at Lepanto in Gulf of Patra off Greece.

Romerswael, January 29, 1574. Dutch "sea beggars" fleet under Adm. Louis Boisot defeats Spanish fleet off Romerswael in Schedlt River seeking to relieve siege of Middelburg by Zeelanders.

Antwerp, October 3, 1576. Mutinous Spanish troops capture and sack Antwerp.

Alcántara, August 25, 1580. Spanish under Duke of Alba defeat Portuguese under Don Antonio de Crato of Beja at Alcántara in Estramadura, near Lisbon, and Philip II becomes king of Portugal.

Cadiz, April 19, 1587. Forestalling Spanish naval preparations for attack on England, Francis Drake raids Cadiz and destroys numerous vessels of fleet being prepared by Philip II.

Spanish Armada, July–August 1588. Powerful armada under Medinia Sidonia moves upon England, is met off Devon coast by English under Lord Howard of Effingham, Drake, Sir John Hawkins, and Sir Martin Frobisher. English attack and harass Spanish, who fail to link up with Duke of Parma off Calais; driven northward, Spanish sail entirely around British Isles, lose more than sixty ships to storm, and shipwreck before returning to Spain.

Ivry, March 14, 1590. Henry of Navarre's Protestant-Bourbon army defeats Army of the Catholic League under Duc de Mayenne at Ivry-la-Bataille in northern France near Evreux.

Yellow Sea, July 9, 1592. Korean fleet under Yi Sung-sin destroys Japanese warships and transports off southwest coast of Korea.

Chinhae Bay, November 1598. Japanese fleet withdrawing invasion forces is attacked by Korean fleet under Yi Sung-sin; both sides lose heavily; Yi Sung-sin is killed.

Nieuport, July 2, 1600. Netherlands army under Maurice of Nassau defeats Spanish under Albert of Austria at Nieuport on Yser River in northeast Belgium.

Sekugahara, October 21, 1600. General Ieyasu, regent of Japan, defeats forces of three other regents and gains control of throne.

Weisser Berg, November 8, 1620. In first major battle of Thirty Years' War, Army of the Catholic League under Count Tilly, with Spanish under Marquis di Spinola, defeats Bohemians under Prince Christian of Anhalt-Bernberg near Prague.

Stadtlohn, August 5, 1623. Count Tilly's Catholic army defeats Christian of Brunswick's Protestant mercenaries near Dutch-German frontier.

Dessau, April 25, 1626. Protestant army under Ernst von Mansfeld is thoroughly defeated by Catholic League army under Wallenstein, duke of Friedland, at Dessau Bridge at Elbe River in central Germany.

Breitenfeld, September 17, 1631. Gustavus Adolphus of Sweden's Protestant army routs Count Tilly's Catholic League forces at Breitenfeld, north of Leipzig in Saxony.

Lützen, November 16, 1632. Adolphus' Protestant army attacks Wallenstein's Catholic mercenaries at Lützen, near Leipzig in Saxony; Gustavus is killed, but Wallenstein's army is driven from field.

Nördlingen, September 6, 1634. Swedish-German army under Gustavus Horn and Count Bernhard of Saxe-Weimar attacks Catholic army under Habsburg prince Ferdinand of Hungary and Spanish cardinal Infante Ferdinand in western Bavaria and is decisively beaten.

Stonington, July 28, 1637. Pequot Indians are defeated by Massachusetts and Connecticut colonists near Stonington.

The Downs, October 21, 1639. Dutch under Maarten Tromp defeat warships and transports of Spanish under Antonio de Oquendo at roadstead in English coastal waters off Kent.

Edgehill, October 23, 1642. English civil war begins with battle near Stratford-on-Avon, northeast of Banbury, between Royalist forces of Charles I and Parliamentary army under Earl of Essex; cavalry charge by Prince Rupert forces Essex to withdraw.

Rocroi, May 19, 1643. Spanish-Habsburg army under Don Francisco de Mello invades France and is trounced by French under Louis de Bourbon, duc d'Enghien, near Belgian border.

Marston Moor, July 2, 1644. "New Model" Parliamentary army under Oliver Cromwell and Lord Fairfax defeats Royalists under Prince Rupert and Duke of Newcastle near York; northern England lost to Charles I.

Freiburg, August 3, 1644. French under Duc d'Enghien and Vicomte de Turenne defeat Bavarians under Baron Franz von Mercy at Freiburg im Bresgau on Rhine River in Baden.

Naseby, June 14, 1645. Oliver Cromwell's New Model army crushes Royalists of Charles I near Northampton in central England.

Lens, August 10, 1648. In last major battle of Thirty Years' War, Duc d'Enghien, now Prince de Condé, repels Spanish army under Archduke Leopold William at Lens, in Pas-de-Calais.

Preston, August 17–19, 1648. Invading Scotch and Royalist allies under James, Duke of Hamilton, are decisively beaten by Oliver Cromwell in Lancashire, northern England.

Drogheda, September 12, 1649. English under Cromwell storm besieged Irish rebels at Drogheda in County Louth and massacre garrison.

Worcester, September 3, 1651. Army of Scotch and Royalists under Charles Stewart is defeated by Cromwell at Worcester, on Welsh border in central England.

Warsaw, July 18–20, 1656. Swedes of Charles X, with Brandenburg allies, defeat Poles under John Casimir and Stefan Czarniecki and occupy Polish capital.

Santa Cruz, April 20, 1657. English fleet under Adm. Robert Blake penetrates harbor of Santa Cruz de Tenerife in Canary Islands and destroys Spanish treasure galleons.

The Dunes, June 4, 1658. French and English army under Marshal Henri Turenne defeats Spanish under Don John of Austria and Prince of Condé near Dunkirk in Pas-de-Calais.

Oresund, October 29, 1658. Swedish fleet under Charles X besieging Copenhagen is defeated by Dutch fleet under Adm. Obham van Wassanaer.

Lowestoft, June 3, 1665. Dutch fleet under Wassanaer is defeated and routed by English fleet under James, duke of York, off coast of Suffolk in English Channel.

Orfordness, July 25–26, 1666. English fleet under Prince Rupert and Duke of Albemarle defeats Dutch under Adm. Micheil De Ruyter and Adm. Cornelis Tromp near mouth of Thames River estuary.

Solebay, May 28, 1672. Dutch fleet under De Ruyter catches and severely damages English fleet under Duke of York at Southwold Bay on Suffolk coast, thwarting Anglo-French invasion of Holland.

Texel, August 11, 1673. Anglo-French flotilla with troops for invasion of Holland, under command of Prince Rupert, is turned back by Dutch under De Ruyter off the Texel, in West Frisian Islands.

Hotin, November 11, 1673. Polish army under John Sobieski defeats Turks at Hotin, on Dniester River in Bessarabia, Ukraine.

Bloody Brook, September 18, 1675. Wampanoak and Nipmunk Indians under King Philip defeat New England colonists near Hadley, Mass.

Palermo, June 12, 1676. French fleet under Comte de Vivonne catches and destroys Dutch-Spanish squadron in harbor of Palermo, Sicily.

Hadley, June 12, 1676. Colonial force under Major Talcot defeats King Philip's Indians at Hadley, Mass.

Jamestown, September 18, 1676. Virginia colonists under Nathaniel Bacon attack and capture Jamestown from Gov. William Berkeley's forces.

Hjöge Bight, July 1, 1677. Danish fleet under Neils Juel routs Swedish fleet under Evert Horn at bay on coast of Sjaelland near Copenhagen.

Vienna, September 12, 1683. John Sobieski, now John II of Poland, arrives with Polish troops to join Austrian and German forces at besieged Vienna and defeat Turks under Kara Mustafa.

Boyne, July 11, 1690. William III of England defeats James II's Jacobite army of French and Irish Catholics at Boyne River near Drogheda in eastern Ireland.

Beachy Head, July 10, 1690. French fleet under Comte de Tourville defeats Anglo-Dutch fleet under Earl of Torrington in English Channel off East Sussex.

Barfleur, May 29–June 3, 1692. In naval battle at Cap Barfleur off Cotentin peninsula in Normandy, English and Dutch fleet under Adm. Edward Russell forces French fleet under Comte de Tourville to flee.

La Hogue, May 22–24, 1692. Anglo-Dutch fleet under Russell destroys French under de Tourville at bays of Cherbourg and La Hogue at tip of Cotentin peninsula.

Azov, July 28, 1696. Russian army of Peter the Great captures fortress commanding Sea of Azov and entrance to Black Sea from Turkish defenders.

Chiari, September 1, 1701. In opening campaign of War of Spanish Succession, Austrian army under Prince Eugene of Savoy defeats attacking French army under Marshal François de Villeroy at Chiari, west of Brescia in northern Italy.

Friedlinden, October 14, 1702. French army under Duc de Villars defeats Austrian army under Marquis Louis of Baden near Rhine River in Baden-Württemberg, Germany.

Hochstett, September 20, 1703. French under Villars and Bavarians under Elector defeat Austrians under Count Hermann Styrum on Danube near Dillingen in Bavaria.

Blenheim, August 13, 1704. Marching east to Danube with British and German forces, John Churchill, duke of Marlborough, unites with Eugene's Austrians to defeat French and Bavarians under Marshal Camille de Tallard at Blenheim, north of Danube in western Bavaria.

Ramillies, May 23, 1706. Allies under Marlborough defeat French under Villeroy northeast of Namur in Brabant, Belgium, opening up Brabant and Flanders.

Turin, September 7, 1706. Princes Eugene and Victor Amadeus of Savoy rout French under Philip of Orléans besieging Turin in Italian piedmont.

Alamansa, April 25, 1707. French and Spanish under Duke of Berwick defeat English and Portuguese under Lord Henry Galway at Almansa, southwest of Valencia in eastern Spain.

Oudenarde, July 11, 1708. Allies under Marlborough defeat French under Duc de Vendôme at Gavre, below Oudenarde on Scheldt River in Flanders.

Malplaquet, September 11, 1709. In battle northwest of Mauberge close to French-Belgian border, Marlborough and Eugene defeat French under Villars, who is wounded and replaced by Duc de Boufflers, with Allied losses considerably larger than those of French.

Poltava, July 8, 1709. Russians under Peter defeat army of Charles XII of Sweden and Mazeppa of Ukraine on Vorskla River in east-central Ukraine.

Peterwardein, August 5, 1716. Austrians under Eugene defeat large Turkish army on Danube River in Hungary.

Nam Tsho, 1717. Manchu army is trapped and annihilated by Dzungars near Nam Tsho in Tibet.

Belgrade, August 16, 1717. Austrian army under Eugene routs Turkish army under Khalil Pasha seeking to break siege of Belgrade; two days later Turks under Mustapha Pasha in Belgrade surrender.

Karnal, March 1739. Shah Nadir of Persia defeats Mogul army under Mohammed Shah north of Delhi in northwest India, occupying Delhi and seizing massive wealth including Koh-i-noor diamond and Peacock Throne.

Khotin, August 17, 1739. Russian army under Count Burkhard Christof Münnich defeats Turks at Stavutshina, near Khotin, in Moldavia, in eastern Romania.

Cartagena, March 4–May 6, 1741. British under Adm. Edward Vernon attack Spanish fortress of San Felipe at Cartagena in present-day Colombia and are repulsed with heavy losses.

Dettingen, June 27, 1743. English, Austrian, and Hanoverian troops under King George II defeat French under Marshal Jules de Noailles at Dettingen, on Main River in Bavaria.

Fontenoy, May 10, 1745. French under Louis XV and Marshal Maurice de Saxe defeat Anglo-Hanoverian army under Duke of Cumberland in western Belgium southeast of Tournai.

Hohenfriedberg, June 4, 1745. Frederick the Great of Prussia defeats Austrians and Saxons under Prince Charles in Silesia.

Louisburg, June 1745. Fort Louisburg, on Cape Breton Island near entrance to Gulf of St. Lawrence, is captured from French by New England expedition under William Pepperell supported by fleet under Sir Peter Warren.

Prestonpans, September 20, 1745. Scotch Highlanders under Charles Edward Stuart—"Bonnie Prince Charlie"—and Lord George Murray defeat British force under Gen. Sir John Cope in North Berwick, Scotland.

Kesselsdorf, December 14, 1745. Saxons and Austrians under Marshal Friedrich August Rutowsky are defeated by Prussians under Leopold of Anhalt-Dessau on Elbe River in Saxony, resulting in Peace of Dresden December 25.

Culloden, April 16, 1746. British army under Cumberland destroys Highlanders at Culloden, east of Inverness near Moray Firth, ending Bonnie Prince Charlie's foray; many prisoners are massacred.

Madras, September 21, 1746. French under Marquis Joseph François Dupleix repel attack on Madras in southeast India by Nawab Anwar-ud-Din.

Finisterre, October 14, 1747. French fleet under Adm. Desherbiers de l'Étanduère escorting convoy off Cape Finisterre at northeast tip of Spain engages more powerful British fleet under Adm. Edward Hawke, permitting convoy to escape safely.

Monongahela, July 9, 1755. British and American army under Maj. Gen. Edward Braddock is ambushed and routed by French and Indians east of Fort Duquesne in western Pennsylvania.

Minorca, May 20, 1756. British fleet under Adm. John Byng fails to drive French fleet from island of Minorca in Mediterranean Sea and land troops for invasion. Byng is later court-martialed and executed.

Prague, May 6, 1757. Prussians under Frederick defeat Austrians under Count Maximilian von Browne at Prague on Moldau River in Bohemia in early battle of Seven Years' War.

Kolin, June 18, 1757. Prussians under Frederick attack Austrians under Field Marshal Leopold von Daun at Kolin on Elbe River east of Prague and are defeated with heavy losses.

Plassey, June 23, 1757. English and Indian troops under Robert Clive defeat Indo-French army of Diraj-ud-Daula, nawab of Bengal, 80 miles north of Calcutta in west Bengal, opening way for British conquest of northeast India.

Rossbach, November 5, 1757. Prussians under Frederick catch French under Prince Charles, duke of Soubise, and Austrians under Prince of Saxe-Hulburghausen at Rossbach in Saxony and drive them from field with heavy losses.

Leuthen, December 6, 1757. Frederick strikes flank of Austrian army under Charles west of Breslau in Silesia and inflicts heavy casualties.

Louisburg, July 27, 1758. British and Americans under Gen. Jeffrey Amherst and Gen. James Wolfe capture fortress of Louisburg on Cape Breton Island from French.

Zorndorf, August 25, 1758. Russians under Count Wilhelm Fermor advancing upon Berlin are hit and driven off by Prussians under Frederick near Warthe River in Brandenburg.

Minden, August 1, 1759. Prussians under Prince Ferdinand of Brunswick, reinforced by British brigade under Lord George Sackville, defeat French under Marquis Louis de Contades near junction of Ems and Weser rivers in Westphalia, despite Sackville's refusal to make key cavalry charge.

Quebec, September 13, 1759. British under Wolfe, with help of naval squadron under Adm. Charles Saunders, scale cliffs north of Quebec and defeat French under Marquis Louis Joseph de Montcalm, securing control of Canada for English. Wolfe and Montcalm are both killed.

Quiberon Bay, November 20, 1759. British naval squadron under Adm. Edward Hawke follows French force under Adm. Hubert de Conflans into Quiberon Bay on Brittany coast of France and destroys it.

Torgau, November 3, 1760. Prussians under Frederick outlast Austrians under Daun in confused battle at Torgau on Elbe River in Saxony.

Panipat, January 7, 1761. Afghans under Ahmad Shāh Durāni defeat Mahratha Hindu army at Panipat in Karnal district of Punjab, north of Delhi.

Alamance, May 16, 1771. Gov. William Tryon defeats colonial force of Regulators at Alamance Creek near Hillsborough, N.C.

Lexington and Concord, April 19, 1775. Colonial militia attack British troops sent to seize arms at Lexington and Concord, Mass., driving them back to Boston.

Bunker Hill, June 17, 1775. British troops under Sir William Howe suffer considerable losses before ousting American force under Col. William Prescott from redoubt on Charlestown peninsula overlooking Boston.

Great Bridge, December 11, 1775. Loyalists under Earl of Dunmore, royal governor of Virginia, are attacked and defeated by patriot force at Great Bridge south of Norfolk.

Quebec, December 31, 1775. British and Canadian force under Sir Guy Carleton repels American attack under Gen. Benedict Arnold and Gen. Richard Montgomery.

Charleston, June 28, 1776. British assault on Charleston, S.C., is repelled when land attack on Sullivan's Island fails and naval squadron under Sir Peter Parker is driven off by batteries under Gen. William Moultrie.

Long Island, August 27, 1776. British and Hessian army under Howe outflanks and routs Americans under George Washington at Long Island.

White Plains, October 28, 1776. Howe defeats Washington's army at White Plains, N.J.

Trenton, December 26, 1776. American army under Washington crosses Delaware River and defeats and captures Hessian force under Col. Johann Rall at Trenton, N.J.

Princeton, January 3, 1777. Washington's army converges on British general Charles Cornwallis' advance force at Princeton, N.J., and drives it back on New Brunswick with heavy losses.

Oriskany, August 6, 1777. Patriot militiamen under Gen. Nicholas Herkimer marching to relieve siege of Fort Stanwix on Mohawk River in New York State are ambushed by Loyalists and Indians at Oriskany, but rally and drive off attackers.

Bennington, August 1, 1777. Americans under Gen. John Stark attack and destroy British-Hessian-Indian force under Col. Friedrich Baum at Bennington, Vt.

Brandywine, September 11, 1777. British and Hessians under Howe drive Americans under Washington from positions on Brandywine Creek southwest of Philadelphia.

Freeman's Farm (Saratoga), September 19, 1777. Americans under Gen. Horatio Gates and Col. Daniel Morgan stop British-Hessian-Loyalist army under Gen. John Burgoyne near Saratoga, N.Y., at Freeman's Farm.

Germantown, October 4, 1777. Americans under Washington attack British at Germantown, west of Philadelphia, Pa., but take severe casualties and are driven off.

Bemis Heights (Saratoga), October 7, 1777. Burgoyne advances and is decisively defeated by Americans under Gates, Arnold, and Morgan, and driven back upon Saratoga, N.Y.; Burgoyne surrenders October 17.

Monmouth, June 28, 1778. After Sir Henry Clinton abandons Philadelphia to move across New Jersey to New York City, Washington's army attacks at Monmouth and despite initial blundering by Gen. Charles Lee repels Clinton's counterattacks, with heavy losses to British.

Savannah, December 29, 1778. British forces under Lt. Col. Archibald Campbell land near Savannah, Ga., rout American militia under Gen. Robert Howe, and occupy Savannah.

Stony Point, July 15, 1778. Americans under Gen. Anthony Wayne attack and retake Stony Point on Hudson River in New York, capturing most of British garrison.

Newtown, August 29, 1779. Americans under Gen. John Sullivan and Gen. James Clinton defeat Loyalist-Iroquois force under Sir John Johnson and Joseph Brant at present-day Elmira, N.Y., ending Indian threat to Pennsylvania-New York frontier.

Savannah, October 9, 1779. Americans under Gen. Benjamin Lincoln and French under Comte d'Estaing attack British at Savannah, Ga., and are repulsed with heavy casualties.

Charleston, April–May, 1780. British under Gen. Henry Clinton besiege Charleston, S.C., capture Fort Moultrie on May 6; Lincoln surrenders on May 12.

Camden, August 16, 1780. British and Loyalists under Earl Charles Cornwallis defeat Americans under Gates at Camden, S.C.

King's Mountain, October 7, 1780. American militia under Col. Isaac Shelby and Col. William Campbell defeat and capture Loyalist force under Maj. Patrick Ferguson at King's Mountain near South Carolina-North Carolina border, ending British hopes of subduing Carolina backcountry and forcing Cornwallis to withdraw back into South Carolina.

Cowpens, January 17, 1781. American regulars and militia under Daniel Morgan destroy British force under Col. Banastré Tarleton at Cowpens in South Carolina.

Guilford Court House, March 15, 1781. After retreating across North Carolina, Americans under Gen. Nathanael Greene meet British at Guilford Court House, near Greensboro; British hold field but take severe casualties and Cornwallis is forced to retreat toward coast.

Chesapeake Capes, September 5, 1781. After British under Cornwallis move north into Virginia, Washington withdraws army from New York, joins French army and fleet at head of Chesapeake Bay, then moves to invest Cornwallis at Yorktown. French fleet under Comte de Grasse stands off British fleet under Adm. Thomas Graves in engagement off Virginia capes, causing Graves to withdraw toward New York.

Yorktown, October 19, 1781. Attempts to break out of encirclement by Washington's Americans and French under Vicomte de Rochambeau fail, and Cornwallis surrenders British army at Yorktown, ending British hopes of subduing Americans.

Les Saintes, April 12, 1782. British fleet under Adm. George Rodney defeats French under de Grasse off Les Saintes, islands between Guadeloupe and Dominica.

Trincomalee, September 3, 1782. After French under Adm. Pierre André de Suffren capture British base at Trincomalee in Ceylon, they are attacked by British under Adm. Sir Edward Hughes; British are forced to break off action, and Hughes withdraws to Madras.

Rimnik, September 22, 1789. Austro-Russian army under Count Aleksandr Suvórov and Francis, prince of Saxe-Coburg, defeats Turkish army in Moldavia, north of Danube in eastern Romania.

Svenskund, July 9–10, 1790. Swedish fleet under Duke of Sudermania repels attack by Russian fleet under Prince Nassau-Siegen at Svenskund Fjord on Baltic, then drives off Russians.

Petersham, February 4, 1787. Insurgents under Daniel Shays attack Massachusetts militia under Gen. William Shepherd guarding Federal arsenal at Petersham near Springfield, and are quickly routed.

Wabash, November 4, 1791. Indians attack and defeat American militia force under Gen. Arthur St. Clair on Wabash River in Ohio.

Valmy, September 20, 1792. French Revolutionary army under Gen. François de Kellermann uses artillery barrage to defeat invading coalition army of Germans, Austrians, and French *emigrés* under Duke of Brunswick at Valmy in northeastern France.

Toulon, December 19, 1792. English-Spanish-Neapolitan fleet under Adm. Samuel Hood is forced to withdraw from harbor of Toulon on Mediterranean coast after French under Gen. Jacques Dugonmier capture fortifications dominating harbor.

Neerwinden, March 18, 1793. Allied army under Prince of Saxe-Coburg repulses attack by French under Gen. Charles Dumouriez with heavy losses southeast of Louvain in Belgium.

Hondschoote, September 8, 1793. British-Hanoverian army under Duke of York is driven back by French army under Gen. Jean-Nicolas Houchard east of Dunkirk on French coast.

Menin, September 13, 1793. French under Houchard defeat Dutch under Prince of Orange at Menin on Franco-Belgian border in Flanders, but halt without attacking Austrians; Houchard is subsequently guillotined.

Wattignies, October 15–16, 1793. Austrians under Saxe-Coburg besieging Maubeuge south of Sambre River are attacked by French under Gen. Jean-Baptiste Jourdan and retreat toward Liège.

Tourcoing, May 18, 1794. Allied army under Saxe-Coburg is defeated by French under Gen. Joseph Souham at Tourcoing, north of Lille in Flanders.

Fleurus, June 26, 1794. Allies under Saxe-Coburg attack French under Jourdan and Gen. Jean Kléber at Fleurus, north of Charleroi in Belgium, are repulsed, and retreat.

Fallen Timbers, August 20, 1794. Indian and Canadian militia attack on American force under Gen. Anthony Wayne at Fallen Timbers in northwest Ohio is repulsed with heavy losses.

Lodi, May 10, 1796. French under Gen. Napoleon Bonaparte defeat Austrian and Piedmont army under Gen. Jean-Pierre Beaulieu at Adda River at Lodi.

Würzburg, September 3, 1796. Austrians under Archduke Charles defeat French under Jourdan at Würzburg on Main River in Unterfranken, Germany, forcing French to withdraw beyond Rhine.

Rivoli, January 14, 1797. Timely arrival of Marshal André Masséna's force at Rivoli on Adige River east of Lake Garda enables French under Bonaparte to drive Austrians under Alvintzy northward into Tyrol.

Cape St. Vincent, February 14, 1797. Spanish fleet under Adm. José de Cordova is defeated by British under Adm. Sir John Jervis off Cape St. Vincent at southwestern tip of Portugal.

Pyramids, July 21, 1798. French army under Bonaparte, crossing Mediterranean, defeats Mamelukes on Nile River between Embabeh and Giza, Egypt.

The Nile, August 1, 1798. British squadron under Adm. Horatio Nelson catches and devastates French fleet under Adm. François Brueys in Aboukir Bay at Rosetta mouth of Nile River in Egypt; Brueys is killed and Bonaparte's army is blocked from return to France.

Aboukir, July 25, 1799. Turkish army landed on Egyptian coast by British is defeated by Bonaparte at Rosetta mouth of Nile.

Seringapatam, May 4, 1799. English-Indian army under Sir George Harris storms Seringapatam, on island in Cauvery River in Mysore, southeast India, with defending Moslem ruler, Tippoo Sahib, killed during assault.

Trebbia, June 17–19, 1799. Russians and Austrians under Marshal Aleksandr Suvórov defeat French under Gen. Jacques Macdonald on Trebbia River south of Piacenza in northern Italy.

Novi, August 15, 1799. Allies under Suvórov defeat French under Gen. Barthéleme Joubert at Novi, in Italian piedmont; Joubert is killed.

Zurich, September 25, 1799. French army under Masséna defeats Allies under Gen. Aleksandr Korsakov at Zurich in north-central Switzerland.

Marengo, June 14, 1800. French under Bonaparte counterattack and rout Austrians under Baron Michael Melas at Marengo near Alessandria in Italian piedmont.

Hohenlinden, December 3, 1800. French under Gen. Jean-Victor Moreau defeat Austrians under Archduke John at Hohenlinden in southern Bavaria; Austrians sign armistice December 25.

Aboukir, March 20, 1801. British-Turkish army under Sir Ralph Abercromby defeats French under Gen. Jacques de Menou at Nile River delta; Abercromby is killed.

Copenhagen, April 2, 1801. British fleet under Sir Hyde Parker defeats Danes at Copenhagen after Adm. Horatio Nelson ignores order to disengage and moves in to destroy moored Danish fleet.

Assaye, September 23, 1803. British under Sir Arthur Wellesley defeat Mahratta army under Doulut Rau Sindhia and Rajah of Berar at Assaye 260 miles northwest of Hyderabad, southern India.

Ulm, October 14, 1805. French under Bonaparte, now Emperor Napoleon I, encircle and defeat Austrians under Baron Karl Mack at Elchingen; Mack surrenders at Ulm in Baden-Württemberg, southern Germany.

Trafalgar, October 21, 1805. British fleet under Nelson defeats French and Spanish under Adm. Pierre Villeneuve off Cape Trafalgar near entrance to

Mediterranean; Nelson is fatally wounded; victory assures British control of seas and permanently ends invasion threat.

Austerlitz, December 2, 1805. Napoleon strikes center of Austro-Russian army under Gen. Mikhail Kutuzov east of Brunn in Moravia, cutting it in two.

Jena and Auerstädt, October 14, 1806. French under Napoleon overwhelm Prussians under Prince Friedrich Ludwig Hohenlohe at Jena east of Weimar on Saale River, while fifteen miles to north, at Auerstädt, Marshal Louis-Nicolas Davout fights off Prussians under Duke of Brunswick, who is killed.

Eylau, February 8, 1807. Napoleon attacks Russians under Count Levin Bennigsen at Eylau in East Prussia on Polish border, and after sanguinary battle Bennigsen withdraws to east.

Friedland, June 14, 1807. After holding action, French under Napoleon smash Russians under Bennigsen at Friedland near foot of Sudetes Mountains in Bohemia, driving them across Alle River with heavy casualties; Napoleon, Tsar Alexander, and Prussian emperor sign peace treaty shortly thereafter.

Corunna, January 16, 1809. British army under Sir John Moore repulses attack by French under Marshal Nicolas-Jean Soult at Corunna in northwest Spain; Moore is mortally wounded, and British are evacuated by sea.

Regensburg (Ratisbon), April 23, 1809. Napoleon strikes Austrians under Archduke Charles at Eckmülf, just below Regensburg in east Bavaria, driving them across Danube and opening way to Vienna.

Talavera, July 28, 1809. British under Wellesley withstand two attacks by French under Gen. Claude Victor at Talavera on Tagus River in Toledo, central Spain, then upon arrival of French army under Soult retreat into Portugal.

Wagram, July 5–6, 1809. French under Napoleon defeat Austrians under Archduke Charles at Wagram in northeast Austria, on the Marshfeld, through massed artillery fire by 100 guns, forcing Austrians to make armistice.

Bussaco, September 27, 1810. British-Portuguese army under Wellesley, now Viscount Wellington, decisively checks French under Masséna at Bussaco on Mondego River in Portugal, gaining time to withdraw into fortified lines at Torres Vedras north of Lisbon.

Caldéron Bridge, January 17, 1811. Spanish under Gen. Felix Calleja del Rey defeat Mexican insurgents under Miguel Hidalgo y Costilla at Caldéron Bridge near Guadalajara.

Tippecanoe, November 7, 1811. American force under Gen. William Henry Harrison defeats Indians under Prophet at confluence of Tippecanoe and Wabash rivers in Indiana.

Salamanca, July 22, 1812. Wellington hits isolated left wing of French under Gen. Auguste Marmont at Salamanca on Tormes River in Leon in western Spain, inflicting heavy casualties.

Detroit, August 16, 1812. American general William Hull surrenders Detroit to British general Isaac Brock in opening engagement of War of 1812.

Borodino, September 7, 1812. Napoleon's Grand Army, now deep into Russia, attacks Russians under Kutuzov at Borodino, on Kalatscha River fifty miles from Moscow, driving Russians from field but suffering heavy casualties; week later French enter Moscow.

Berezina, November 26–29, 1812. Napoleon's army retreating from Moscow holds off Russian attacks and crosses Berezina River in Byelorussia, en route to Vilna; thereafter retreat becomes rout, Napoleon leaves for Paris, and tiny remnant of Grand Army straggles back to France.

Lützen, May 2, 1813. Attacked by Russians and Prussians under Gen. Ludwig Wittgenstein at Lützen, near Leipzig in Saxony, Napoleon counterattacks and drives off Allies.

Bautzen, May 20–21, 1813. Napoleon attacks Allies under Wittgenstein across Elbe River at Bautzen northeast of Dresden and drives them eastward, but fails to pursue.

Vittoria, June 21, 1813. British-Spanish-Portuguese army under Wellington defeats French under Joseph Bonaparte and Marshal Jean-Baptiste Jourdan at Vittoria, north of Ebro River in Alava, northern Spain, sending French retreating across Pyrenees into France.

Lake Erie, September 10, 1813. American fleet under Comdr. Oliver Hazard Perry defeats British squadron under Comdr. Robert H. Barclay at Put-In Bay on Lake Erie near present-day Sandusky, Ohio.

The Thames, October 5, 1813. Americans under Harrison defeat British and Indians under Col. Henry Proctor and Tecumseh on Thames River west of present-day London, Ontario.

Leipzig, October 16–19, 1813. Allied armies under Gebhard von Blücher, Jean-Baptiste Bernadotte, and Karl Philipp von Schwarzenberg defeat French under Napoleon east of Leipzig in Saxony, in "Battle of the Nations," forcing French westward toward Rhine.

Horseshoe Bend, March 27, 1814. Americans under Gen. Andrew Jackson and Gen. John Coffee defeat Creeks and Cherokees at Horseshoe Bend on Tallapoosa River in Alabama.

La Puerta, June 15, 1814. Insurrectionary army led by Simon Bolivar is defeated by loyalist army under Gen. José Tomás Boves southeast of Lake Maracaibo in Venezuela.

Chippewa, July 5, 1814. Americans under Gen. Winfield Scott defeat British and Indians under Gen. Phineas Riall on Chippewa River in Ontario across Niagara River from present-day Buffalo.

Lundy's Lane, July 25, 1814. Americans under Gen. Jacob Brown and British under Gen. Riall and Gen. Gordon Drummond fight desperate drawn battle at Lundy's Lane near Niagara Falls across river from present-day Buffalo; afterward Americans abandon field.

Bladensburg, August 24, 1814. British under Gen. Robert Ross defeat Americans under Gen. William H. Winder at Bladensburg, Md., northeast of Washington; thereafter British enter and burn Washington.

Lake Champlain, September 11, 1814. American fleet under Comdr. Thomas MacDonough defeats British fleet under Cap. George Downie in Plattsburg Bay on Lake Champlain in New York State.

Fort McHenry, September 12–14, 1814. Americans under Gen. John Stricker stop British advance east of Baltimore at Bread-and-Butter Creek, then bombardment of Fort McHenry by British fleet under Adm. Alexander Cochrane fails.

New Orleans, January 8, 1815. Two weeks after treaty ending War of 1812 is signed in Ghent, Belgium, Americans under Jackson repel British attack under Gen. Edward Pakenham below New Orleans on Mississippi River; Pakenham is killed.

Ligny and Quatre-Bras, June 16, 1815. Napoleon, returning to France from Elba after abdication in 1814, defeats Prussians under Blücher at Ligny northeast of Charleroi in Namur, while Marshal Michel Ney holds off British under Wellington at Quatre-Bras.

Waterloo, June 18, 1815. Napoleon attacks Wellington's army at Waterloo, in Brabant near Brussels, Belgium, but fails to crack British defenses before Prussians under Blücher arrive; Allies then rout French. On June 21 Napoleon surrenders to British.

Chacabuco, February 12–13, 1817. Argentinian and Chilean army under Gen. José de San Martin and Gen. Bernardo O'Higgins, after crossing Andes, defeats Spanish under Col. Maroto at Chacabuco, north of Santiago, Chile.

La Puerta, March 15, 1818. Bolivar's insurrectionary army is defeated by Spanish under Gen. Pablo Morillo in Venezuela southeast of Lake Maracaibo.

Maipú, April 5, 1818. Argentine-Chilean army under San Martin defeats Spanish under Gen. Mariano Osorio south of Santiago, Chile.

Boyaca, August 7, 1819. Bolivar defeats Spanish in decisive battle at Boyaca, near Tunja in central New Grenada, assuring independence of present-day Colombia.

Carabobo, June 24, 1821. Bolivar defeats Spanish under Manuel de Latorre at valley of Carabobo, north of Valencia in Venezuela, assuring independence of Venezuela.

Pichincha, May 24, 1822. Bolivar defeats Spanish at Pichincha, near Quito, Ecuador.

Junin, August 6, 1824. Bolivar's army of Colombians and Peruvians defeats Spanish under Gen. José Canterac at Junin, near Lake Junin, Peru, in Andes Mountains.

Ayacucho, December 9, 1824. Peruvian-Colombian army under Gen. Antonio José de Sucre defeats Spanish under Viceroy José de la Serna on plain of

Ayacucho near Huamanga (now Ayacucho), southeast of Lima, breaking back of Spanish dominion in South America.

Prome, November 30–December 2, 1825. British under Gen. Sir Archibald Campbell defeat Burmese on Irrawaddy River, south-central Burma.

Navarino, October 20, 1827. British, French, and Russian fleet under Adm. Sir Henry Codrington enters Navarino Bay on Peloponnesian coast and devastates Turkish fleet under Tahir Pasha.

Ostroleka, May 26, 1831. Poles under Gen. Jan Sigmunt Skrzneki are defeated by Russians under Count Dibich-Zabalanski at Ostroleka on Narew River in northeast Poland.

Alamo, March 6, 1836. Mexicans under Gen. Antonio Lopéz de Santa Anna storm Alamo mission in San Antonio, massacre Texas revolutionaries under Col. William Travis.

Goliad, March 20, 1836. Texans under Col. J. W. Fannin are captured and massacred by Mexicans under Santa Anna at Goliad, southeast of San Antonio.

San Jacinto, April 21, 1836. Texans under Sam Houston defeat Mexicans under Santa Anna on San Jacinto River near Galveston Bay; Santa Anna is captured.

Kissimmee, December 25, 1837. American force under Col. Zachary Taylor defeats Seminole Indians at Kissimmee on Lake Okeechobee in Florida.

Blood River, December 16, 1838. Boers under Andries Pretorius defeat Zulus under Chief Dingaan in Natal, South Africa.

Canton, May 24, 1841. After China attempts to interfere with British trading post and stop importation of opium from India, British expedition under Sir Hugh Gough captures Canton.

Isly, August 14, 1844. Algerians under Abd el Kader are defeated by French under Marshal Thomas R. Bugeaud at Isly near Moroccan-Algerian frontier.

Sobraon, February 10, 1846. British-Indian army under Gough attacks and defeats Sikhs at bend of Sutlej River in Punjab.

Palo Alto, May 8, 1846. American army under Gen. Zachary Taylor defeats Mexicans under Gen. Mariano Arista on road to Matamoros at waterhole of Palo Alto, near present-day Brownsville.

Resaca de la Palma, May 9, 1846. Taylor defeats and drives Mexicans under Arista across Rio Grande River at Resaca de la Palma above Fort Texas near Brownsville.

Monterey, September 21–24, 1846. Taylor attacks Mexicans under Gen. Pedro de Ampudia and captures Monterey on Santa Catarina River in northeast Mexico.

Buena Vista, February 22–23, 1847. Mexican army under Santa Anna attacks and is defeated by American army under Taylor north of Buena Vista, south of Saltillo.

Cerro Gordo, April 18, 1847. American army under Gen. Winfield Scott defeats Santa Anna at Cerro Gordo northeast of Vera Cruz on road to Mexico City.

Molino del Rey, September 8, 1847. American force under Gen. William J. Worth defeats Santa Anna three miles southeast of Mexico City.

Chapultepec, September 13, 1847. Scott defeats Santa Anna at outskirts of Mexico City.

Gujrat, February 21, 1849. British-Indian army under Sir Hugh Gough defeats Sikhs and Afghans north of Lahore in Punjab, ending second Sikh war.

Novara, March 23, 1849. Austrians under Marshal Josef Radetsky defeat Piedmontese under King Charles Albert of Sardinia at Novara.

Temesovar, August 9, 1849. Hungarians under Gen. Arthur von Görgei are defeated by Russians and Austrians under Gen. Julius von Haynau at Temesovar in southeastern Hungary.

Sinope, November 30, 1853. Rifled guns of Russian naval squadron under Adm. Paul S. Nahkimov destroy wooden-hulled Turkish squadron under Osman Pasha in harbor of Sinope in northern Turkey on Black Sea.

Balaklava, October 25, 1854. Russians under Prince Alexander Sergeievich Menshikov attack but fail to dislodge British, French, and Turks under overall command of Lord Raglan at Balaklava, below Sevastopol on Crimean peninsula.

Inkerman, November 5, 1854. Russians under Menshikov attack British and French under Lord Raglan at Inkerman, below Sevastopol, losing heavily.

Malakoff, September 8, 1855. French under Gen. Pierre F. J. Bosquet successfully storm Russian defenders under Prince Michael Gorchakov at Malakoff fortifications on Crimean peninsula; British assault on Redan fortifications fails, but gunfire from Malakoff drives out defenders, and Sevastopol is captured on September 9.

Fatshan Creek, June 1, 1857. British flotilla under Rear Adm. Sir Michael Seymour destroys fleet of Chinese armed war junks in Fatshan Creek south of Canton.

Delhi, September 14–20, 1857. English and Indian reinforcements under Gen. John Nicholson recapture Delhi on Jumma River in central India after Bengal army mutinies; Nicholson is mortally wounded.

Lucknow, November 16, 1857. British under Sir Colin Campbell storm Lucknow in Uttar Pradesh in northern India, relieving garrison besieged by Bengalis after mutiny.

Gwalior, June 19, 1858. British under Gen. Sir Hugh Rose defeat Bengalis under Tantia Topi and Rani of Jhansi at Gwalior in Madhya Pradesh, ending Great Mutiny.

Magenta, June 4, 1859. French and Sardinians under Emperor Napoleon III defeat Austrians under Count Franz Gyulai at Magenta, west of Milan in Lombardy, northern Italy.

Solferino, June 24, 1859. French and Sardinians under Napoleon III defeat Austrians under Emperor Franz Josef five miles south of Mincio River below Lake Garda in Lombardy, north Italy.

Calpulalpam, December 22, 1860. Mexican Liberal army under Jésus Gonzáles Ortega defeats Conservative army under Miguel Miramón at Calpulalpam, 40 miles northeast of Mexico City.

Chi-Hoa, February 25, 1861. Siege of French-Spanish garrison in Saigon is lifted when French force under Gen. Leonard Charner defeats Vietnamese.

Fort Sumter, April 12–14, 1861. Confederates under Gen. P. G. T. Beauregard bombard Fort Sumter in harbor of Charleston, S.C.; Union defenders under Maj. Robert Anderson surrender.

Bull Run (First Manassas), July 21, 1861. Confederate army under Gen. Beauregard and Gen. Joseph E. Johnston defeats Union army under Gen. Irvin McDowell on Bull Run at Manassas Junction in northern Virginia.

Wilson's Creek, August 10, 1861. Confederate force under Gen. Ben McCullough is attacked by Union force under Gen. Nathaniel Lyon and Gen. Franz Sigel at Wilson's Creek, southwest of Springfield, Mo.; in fierce fighting Lyon is killed and Maj. Samuel Sturgis orders withdrawal of Lyon's force.

Forts Henry and Donelson, February 6–16, 1862. Union army under Gen. Ulysses S. Grant and navy under Comdr. Andrew H. Foote take Forts Henry (February 6) and Donelson (February 16) from Confederates under overall command of Gen. Albert Sidney Johnston between Cumberland and Tennessee rivers in north-central Tennessee.

Pea Ridge (Elkhorn Tavern), March 7–8, 1862. Union army under Gen. Samuel Curtis defeats Confederate army under Gen. Earl Van Dorn at Elkhorn Tavern on Pea Ridge, north of Fayetteville in northwest Arkansas.

Hampton Roads, March 8–9, 1862. Confederate ironclad *Virginia*, formerly *Merrimack*, under Capt. Franklin Buchanan attacks Union flotilla in Hampton Roads, off Hampton, Va., on March 8, sinking one warship and grounding another; on March 9 *Virginia* and Union ironclad *Monitor* under Lt. John Worden fight inconclusive battle off Hampton, first engagement between ironclads in naval history.

Island No. 10, April 4–8, 1862. Union fleet under Andrew H. Foote runs Confederate batteries at Island No. 10 on Mississippi River south of New Madrid, Ky., at Kentucky–Tennessee border, permitting army under Gen. John Pope to seize island.

Shiloh, April 6–7, 1862. After Confederate attack under A. S. Johnston has seemingly driven Union army into Tennessee River at Shiloh in southwest Tennessee, Union army under Grant rallies and defeats Confederates under Beauregard, who takes command after Johnston is mortally wounded.

New Orleans, April 24–25, 1862. Union fleet under David Glasgow Farragut runs fortifications at Fort Jackson and captures New Orleans on Mississippi River.

Corinth, May 3–4, 1862. Confederates under Gen. Earl Van Dorn attack Union force under Gen. William S. Rosecrans at Corinth, Miss., near Tennessee border; after heavy fighting Confederates withdraw westward.

Cross Keys and Port Republic, June 8–9, 1862. Climaxing month-long campaign in Shenandoah Valley, Confederates under Gen. Thomas J. "Stonewall" Jackson defeat Union forces of Gen. John Charles Frémont at Cross Keys and James Shields at Port Republic southeast of Harrisonburg, Va.

Seven Days, June 25–July 1, 1862. In series of attacks from Oak Grove and Mechanicsville to Malvern Hill, Confederate army under Gen. Robert E. Lee stops advance of Union army under Gen. George B. McClellan on Richmond from east, ending in Union army's reembarkation on troopships at James River.

Cedar Mountain, August 9, 1862. Confederates under Jackson defeat vanguard of Union army under Gen. John Pope at Cedar Mountain southwest of Manassas Junction.

Bull Run (Second Manassas), August 29–30, 1862. Confederate army under Lee defeats Union army under Pope on Bull Run at Manassas Junction.

Antietam (Sharpsburg), September 17, 1862. Union army under McClellan attacks Confederate army under Lee at Sharpsburg on Antietam Creek north of Potomac River in Maryland; next day Confederates withdraw into Virginia.

Perryville, October 8, 1862. Confederate army under Gen. Braxton Bragg attacked by Union army under Gen. Don Carlos Buell at Perryville, Ky.; Confederates withdraw into Tennessee.

Fredericksburg, December 13, 1862. Union army under Gen. Ambrose Burnside attacks Confederate army under Lee at Fredericksburg on Rappahannock River in northern Virginia and after taking heavy casualties withdraws northward.

Stones River (Murfreesboro), December 31, 1862–January 3, 1863. Confederate army under Bragg attacks Union army under Rosecrans along Stones River at Murfreesboro, Tennessee; Confederates fail to drive enemy northward, and Bragg withdraws southward.

Port Hudson, March 14–July 9, 1863. Union fleet under Farragut runs past Confederate batteries at Port Hudson, La., 25 miles north of Baton Rouge; Port Hudson is attacked and besieged by Union army under Gen. Nathaniel Banks, and falls July 9.

Charleston, April 7, 1863. Union flotilla under Adm. Samuel F. du Pont attacks Confederate harbor fortifications at Charleston, S.C., but is driven off.

Chancellorsville, May 1–4, 1863. Union army under Gen. Joseph Hooker crosses Rappahannock River and is defeated by Confederate army under Lee at Chancellorsville west of Fredericksburg; Stonewall Jackson is wounded and dies eight days later.

Gettysburg, July 1–3, 1863. Confederate army under Lee attacks and is defeated by Union army under Gen. George G. Meade south of Gettysburg, in south-central Pennsylvania.

Vicksburg, May 19–July 4, 1863. After failing to take Confederate positions May 19 and 22, Union army under Grant besieges Vicksburg, on Mississippi River 30 miles east of Jackson, and Confederate army under Gen. John C. Pemberton surrenders on Fourth of July, opening entire length of river to Union navy and splitting Confederacy in two.

Chickamauga, September 19–20, 1863. Despite heavy losses, Confederate army under Bragg drives Union army under Rosecrans from field at Chickamauga Creek, south of Chattanooga in southeastern Tennessee.

Lookout Mountain (Chattanooga), November 24, 1863. Union army under Grant storms Lookout Mountain south of Chattanooga, driving Confederates under Bragg southward.

Missionary Ridge (Chattanooga), November 25, 1863. Union army under Grant ousts Confederates under Bragg from Missionary Ridge east of Chattanooga.

Wilderness, May 5–6, 1864. Union army under Grant attacks Confederate army under Lee in woods fifteen miles west of Fredericksburg in northern Virginia, but fails to dislodge Confederates.

Spotsylvania, May 8–12, 1864. After moving around Confederate right, Union army under Grant battles Confederate army under Lee for five days in area of Spotsylvania Court House southeast of Fredericksburg, with heavy casualties on both sides.

New Market, May 15, 1864. Confederates under Gen. John C. Breckenridge, including cadet corps of Virginia Military Institute, drive back Union army under Gen. Franz Sigel north of Harrisonburg, Va.

Cold Harbor, June 1–3, 1864. Union army under Grant assaults Lee's army northeast of Richmond, Va., absorbing heavy losses, but fails to dislodge entrenched Confederates.

Brice's Cross Roads, June 10, 1864. Confederates under Gen. Nathan Bedford Forrest rout Union force under Gen. Samuel D. Sturgis north of Tupelo in northeast Mississippi.

Petersburg, June 15–18, 1864. Confederates under Beauregard hold off Union army under Gen. Benjamin F. Butler at Petersburg, 25 miles south of Richmond, while Grant's army crosses James River and moves on Petersburg; when Grant attacks on June 18 he is met and stopped by Lee's army.

Kenesaw Mountain, June 27, 1864. Union army under Gen. William Tecumseh Sherman attacks Confederate army under Gen. Joseph E. Johnston at

Kenesaw Mountain northwest of Atlanta, Ga., and is repulsed with heavy losses.

Monocacy, July 9, 1864. Confederates under Gen. Jubal A. Early defeat Union force under Gen. Lew Wallace on Monocacy River southeast of Frederick, Md.; Union resistance, however, enables reinforcements to arrive in time to defend Washington.

Peachtree Creek, July 20, 1864. Confederate army under Gen. John Bell Hood attacks Sherman advancing on Atlanta at Peachtree Creek north of city, and is repulsed with sizable losses.

Atlanta, July 22, 1864. Union army under Sherman is attacked by Confederates under Hood outside Atlanta, with Confederates taking heavy casualties; on September 1 Hood evacuates Atlanta.

Crater, July 30, 1864. Federal engineers blow up mine beneath Confederate lines east of Petersburg, but Burnside fails to exploit opportunity and Confederates under Gen. William Mahone trap Union troops in crater and inflict heavy losses.

Mobile Bay, August 5, 1864. Union fleet under Farragut runs past Confederate defenses into Mobile Bay on Gulf Coast and forces surrender of Confederate ironclad *Tennessee* under Buchanan.

Shimonosekei, September 5–8, 1864. British, Dutch, and French warships bombard Shimonosekei on straits at southwestern tip of Honshu, Japan.

Opequon Creek (Winchester), September 19, 1864. Union army under Sheridan rallies to defeat Confederate army under Early west of Opequon Creek near Winchester, Va.

Fishers Hill, September 22, 1864. Union army under Sheridan crushes Confederate army under Early at Fishers Hill west of Strasburg, Va.

Cedar Creek, October 19, 1864. Confederate army under Early delivers surprise attack on Sheridan's Union army at Cedar Creek; Sheridan rallies his retreating forces and deals devastating blow to Early's army, opening up Shenandoah Valley to Union conquest.

Franklin, November 30, 1864. Confederate army under Hood attacks Union army under Gen. John M. Schofield at Franklin, in central Tennessee, and is thrown back with heavy losses.

Nashville, December 15–16, 1864. Union army under Gen. George H. Thomas routs Confederate army under Hood at Nashville, Tenn.

Savannah, December 13–21, 1864. Having marched from Atlanta southward for 300 miles, laying waste a 50-mile path through Georgia, Union army under Sherman reaches sea coast and storms Fort McCallister south of Savannah; Confederates evacuate city, which falls on December 21.

Fort Fisher, January 13–15, 1865. Union fleet under Adm. David Dixon Porter and army under Gen. Alfred H. Terry capture Fort Fisher at mouth of Cape Fear River in North Carolina, closing Confederacy's last important sea link.

Fort Stedman, March 25, 1865. Besieged in Petersburg by Union army under Grant, Confederate force under Gen. John B. Gordon takes Fort Stedman east of city, but Union counterattack regains fort with heavy Confederate losses.

Five Forks, April 1, 1865. Union army under Sheridan turns flank of Confederate lines at Petersburg, exposing Lee's army; on April 2 Grant orders general attack, and on April 3 Lee's army evacuates defenses, surrendering to Grant six days later at Appomattox Court House.

Custozza, June 24, 1866. Austrians under Archduke Albert defeat Italians under King Victor Emmanuel of Sardinia near Verona in Venezia, northern Italy.

Königgrätz (Sadowa), July 3, 1866. After invading Holstein, Prussian army under Gen. Helmuth von Moltke defeats Austrian army under Gen. Ludwig von Benedek at Sadowa, near Königgrätz, in eastern Bohemia.

Mentana, November 3, 1867. Italian insurgents under Giuseppe Garibaldi are defeated by papal troops and French at Mentana, ten miles northeast of Rome.

Wörth, August 6, 1870. Germans under Crown Prince Frederick Charles defeat French under Marshal Marie de MacMahon at Wörth, northeast of Strasbourg on Saar River in Alsace.

Spicheren, August 6, 1870. Germans under Gen. Karl von Steinmetz defeat French under Gen. Charles Auguste Frossard southeast of Saarbrücken on Saar River in Lorraine.

Gravelotte-St. Privat, August 18, 1870. French under Marshal Achille Bazaine are defeated by Germans under Frederick Charles east of Moselle River near Metz.

Sedan, September 1, 1870. Converging German armies under Moltke corner and defeat French under Gen. Auguste Ducrot at Sedan near Belgian border; Emperor Napoleon III surrenders.

Little Big Horn, June 25, 1876. Sioux Indians under Chiefs Sitting Bull and Crazy Horse wipe out U.S. cavalry force under Gen. George Armstrong Custer at Little Big Horn in south-central Montana.

Plevna, July 19–December 10, 1878. Russians under King Carol I of Rumania and Gen. Frants Todleben capture Plevna in north-central Bulgaria from Turks under Marshal Osman Nuri Pasha.

Isandhlwana, January 22, 1879. Zulus under King Cetywayo destroy British force under Viscount Chelmsford in Natal (Zululand).

Rorke's Drift, January 23, 1879. British force withstands repeated Zulu attacks at base camp on Buffalo River in Natal.

Ulundi, July 4, 1879. British army under Gen. Sir Garnet Wolseley defeats Zulus under King Cetywayo at Ulundi in Natal.

Sherpur, December 23, 1879. British-Indian army under Sir Frederick Roberts repels attack by Afghan tribesmen at Sherpur, north of Kabul.

Tacna, May 26, 1880. Chilean army under Gen. Manuel Baquedano defeats Bolivian-Peruvian army under Bolivian president Narciso Campero at Tacna on Bolivian litoral.

Kandahar, September 1, 1880. After 22-day march, British-Indian army under Roberts defeats Afghan tribesmen and relieves siege at Kandahar, near Arghandab River.

Majuba, February 27, 1881. Boers under Gen. Petrus Joubert wipe out British force under Gen. Sir George Colley at Majuba in Transvaal.

Tel-el-Kebir, September 13, 1882. British under Wolseley defeat Egyptians under Ahmet Arabi at Tel-el-Kebir in northeast Egypt.

Khartoum, January 26, 1885. Moslem dervish army under Mahdi Mohammed Ahmet takes Khartoum, at confluence of Blue and White Nile rivers in Sudan, massacring British garrison including Gen. Charles "Chinese" Gordon.

Batoche, May 12, 1885. Canadian insurgents under Louis Riel are defeated by government army under Gen. Frederick Middleton at Batoche in south-central Saskatchewan.

Slivnitsa, November 17, 1885. Bulgarians under Prince Alexander defeat Serbian army under King Milam at Slivnitsa near Iskür River north of Sofia in Bulgaria.

Wounded Knee, December 29, 1890. In last major Indian campaign, Sioux under Chief Big Foot are massacred by U.S. 7th Cavalry in southwestern South Dakota.

Pyongyang, September 15, 1894. Japanese expedition defeats Chinese at Pyongyang, Korea.

Yalu River (Haiyang), September 17, 1894. Japanese fleet under Adm. Yuko Ito defeats Chinese under Adm. Ting Ju-chang in Gulf of Korea off Yalu estuary.

Weiheiweh, February 2–12, 1895. After stubborn fight, Chinese fleet under Ting Ju-chang, in harbor of naval base at Weiheiweh near tip of Shantung peninsula, is defeated by Japanese fleet under Ito and artillery from captured fortifications ashore.

Adowa, March 1, 1896. Ethiopian army under King Menelik II thwarts Italian conquest by defeating army under Gen. Oreste Baratiera in mountains south of Asmara in northern Ethiopia.

Manila Bay, May 1, 1898. American naval squadron under Comdr. George Dewey destroys Spanish squadron under Adm. Patricio Montojo in Manila Bay, Philippine Islands.

San Juan Hill, July 1, 1898. After taking village of El Caney on June 31, U.S. army under Gen. William Shafter defeats Spanish army under Gen. Arsenio Linares at San Juan Hill near coast of southeastern Cuba.

Santiago Bay, July 3, 1898. U.S. fleet under Adm. William T. Sampson blockading Santiago harbor destroys Spanish fleet under Adm. Pascal Cervera off southeastern coast of Cuba.

Omdurman, September 2, 1898. British and Egyptian force under Gen. Herbert Horatio Kitchener decisively defeats Moslem dervish army under Khalifa Abdullah at Omdurman, opposite Khartoum on White Nile River in Sudan.

Magersfontein, December 10–11, 1899. Boers under Gen. Piet A. Cronje defeat British under Gen. Lord Paul Methuen between upper Modder River and Kimberly in Natal, South Africa.

Colenso, December 15, 1899. Boers under Gen. Louis Botha defeat British under Gen. Sir Redvers Buller at Colenso, on Tugela River south of Ladysmith in Natal.

Spion Kop, January 23, 1900. British under Buller are defeated by Boers at Spion Kop on North Tugela River west of Ladysmith.

Paardeberg, February 27, 1900. British under Roberts besiege and capture Boer force under Cronje at Paardeberg, on Modder River west of Bloemfontein in Orange Free State.

Port Arthur, February 8, 1904. Japanese fleet under Adm. Heihachiro Togo stages surprise attack on Russian base at Port Arthur (Lu-Shun) on Kwangtung peninsula, Manchuria, on Yellow Sea.

Yalu, April 30–May 1, 1904. Japanese under Gen. Tamesada Kuroki defeat Russians under Gen. Zasulich at Wiju on Yalu River near Bay of Korea.

Yellow Sea, August 10, 1904. Russian fleet under Adm. Vilgelm Vitgeft attempts to break out of blockade at Port Arthur (Lu-Shun) and is defeated by Japanese fleet under Togo.

Sha-ho, October 5–17, 1904. After severe fighting, Japanese under Marshal Iwao Oyama fail to drive Russians under Gen. Alexsei Kuropatkin from positions south of Mukden.

Port Arthur, August 7, 1904–January 2, 1905. Attacks by Japanese under Gen. Maresuke Nogi force Russians under Gen. Anatoli Stësel southward down Wotang peninsula, finally capturing Port Arthur on January 2, 1905.

Mukden, March 6–8, 1905. Japanese under Oyama drive back right flank of Russians under Kuropatkin, forcing evacuation of Mukden two days later.

Tsushima, May 27–28, 1905. After 17,000-mile voyage from Baltic Sea, Russian fleet under Adm. Zinovy Rozhdestvenski arrives at Tsushima Strait between Korea and Japan and is devastated by Japanese fleet under Togo.

Monastir, November 5, 1912. Serbs under Crown Prince Alexander defeat Turks at Monastir (Bitola) in southwestern Macedonia.

Liège, August 4–15, 1914. As First World War begins, Germans under Gen. Karl von Bülow attack across frontier and hit Belgians under Gen. Gérard Mathieu Leman; Liège falls after ten days.

Jadar, August 16–24, 1914. Invading Austrians under Gen. Oskar Potiorek are attacked and defeated by Serbians under Marshal Radomir Putnik west of Belgrade and driven back into Austro-Hungary.

Sambre River, August 22–23, 1914. French and Belgian army under Gen. Charles Lanrezac is driven eastward from Namur by German armies under Gen. Max von Hausen.

Mons, August 23, 1914. British under Gen. Sir John French stop advancing Germans under Gen. Alexander von Kluck at Mons in southeast Belgium, then fall back after French retreat from Sambre River.

Lemburg (Lvov), August 23–September 10, 1914. In series of engagements in Galicia, Austrians under Marshal Franz Conrad von Hötzendorf attack advancing Russians under Gen. Nikolai Ivanov; after heavy losses on both sides Austrians withdraw to Carpathian Mountains.

Le Cateau, August 25–27, 1914. British army under Sir John French fights off attack by Germans under Kluck on Western Front at Le Cateau, southwest of Maubeuge in northeast France.

Tannenberg, August 26–31, 1914. Russian army under Gen. Aleksandr Samsonov advancing into East Prussia is encircled and routed by German army under Gen. Paul von Hindenburg and Gen. Erich Ludendorff at Tannenberg, southwest of Allenstein.

Marne, September 5–10, 1914. When German army under Kluck turns southeastward north of Paris, French under Gen. Joseph S. Gallieni attack its right flank; Kluck wheels westward to drive French off, and British under Sir John French and French under Gen. Franchet d'Esperay strike at gap between Kluck's and Bülow's armies northeast of Paris, sending Germans into full retreat to Aisne River.

Masurian Lakes, September 9–14, 1914. German army under Hindenburg and Ludendorff strikes Russian army under Gen. Pavel Rennenkampf near Mazurian Lakes in present-day northeast Poland, driving it across Niemen River with heavy losses.

Yser, October 18–31, 1914. Allied and German armies on Western Front in northern France begin "race to the sea." Belgian army under King Albert is forced westward along Channel coast, while British under Sir John French are withdrawn from east of Paris and sent northwest into Flanders to defend Channel ports. Meanwhile French army under Marshal Joseph-Jacques Joffre moves into positions northwest of Paris, while Germans under Gen. Erich von Falkenhayn establish front from Yser River on Channel coast to Oise River north of Paris.

Ypres, October 20–November 22, 1914. British army under Sir John French, reinforced by French under Gen. Ferdinand Foch, contains drive by Germans centered on Ypres in Pas-de-Calais. Western Front is stabilized, with trenches running from Channel to Alps.

Coronel, November 1, 1914. German naval squadron under Adm. Graf von Spee destroys British squadron under Adm. Sir Christopher Cradock off Chilean coast at Coronel in Pacific Ocean.

Lödz, November 3–December 6, 1914. Germans under Gen. August von Mackensen attack advancing Russians under Grand Duke Nicholas in western Poland, then after heavy Russian losses are counterattacked and forced back.

Drina River-Kolubara, November 6–December 15, 1914. Austrians under Gen. Oskar Potiorek cross Drina River and hit Serbians under Marshal Radomir Putnik, driving Serbs across Kolubara River and forcing evacuation of Belgrade; Serbs then regroup, drive Austrians across Sava River and out of Serbia.

Falkland Islands, December 8, 1914. British battle cruiser force under Adm. Sir Doveton Sturdee intercepts German squadron under Spee at Falkland Islands in southern Atlantic Ocean, sinking all but one German ship.

U-Boat Campaign, 1914–18. German submarines in Atlantic Ocean and Mediterranean Sea begin unrestricted attacks on all shipping in waters around Great Britain February 18, 1915, take heavy toll; sinking of liner *Lusitania* off Irish coast with heavy loss of life May 7 brings strong American protest, and after sinking of *Arabic* August 19 Germans announce large passenger ships will be spared; loss of merchant ships in 1916–17 creates food crisis in England; Germans resume unrestricted sinkings February 1, 1917, bringing United States into war; convoy system greatly reduces sinkings; new ship building in 1918 exceeds rate of losses.

Dogger Bank, January 24, 1915. British battle-cruiser squadron under Adm. David Beatty attacks German squadron under Adm. Franz von Hipper near Dogger bank in North Sea; British sink one battle cruiser but fail to destroy Hipper's force.

Masurian Lakes, February 7–21, 1915. German offensive under Hindenburg inflicts heavy casualties on Russians under appalling conditions in "Winter Battle" in eastern Poland, but Russian counterattack under Gen. Wensel von Plehve halts advance.

Dardanelles, February 19–March 18, 1915. British-French fleet under Adm. Sackville Carden bombards Turkish fortifications in Dardanelles straits and silences outer batteries; on March 18, under Adm. John de Robeck, attack is called off when one Allied ship is sunk by gunfire and two hit mines and sink.

Gallipoli, April 25, 1915. British and Australian-New Zealand force under Gen. Sir Ian Hamilton lands at Cape Helles at southeastern tip of Gallipoli Peninsula on European side of Dardanelles but is kept from advancing by savage Turkish resistance.

Neuve-Chapelle, March 10–13, 1915. British under Sir John French dislodge Germans east of Lille, but fail to exploit breakthrough and Germans quickly reestablish line.

Woevre, April 6–15, 1915. Attack by French army under Gen. Auguste Dubail along north face of St. Mihiel Salient east of Verdun fails to dislodge Germans.

Ypres, April 22–May 25, 1915. As Allied armies prepare to launch offensive on Western Front in Flanders, Germans under Falkenhayn unleash surprise attack after chlorine gas bombardment near Ypres, Belgium, routing French; Allied counterattacks stabilize line.

Gorlice-Tarnow, May 2–June 27, 1915. Germans and Austrians under Mackensen break through Russian positions in Galicia, southern Poland; subsequent offensive captures Warsaw and drives 300 miles eastward into Russia by late September.

Artois, May 9–June 30, 1915. British and French attack Germans in Artois in northeastern France; British under Gen. Sir Douglas Haig are stopped at Festubert; French corps under Gen. Philippe Pétain penetrates two miles at Souchez, then is halted; losses are heavy.

Isonzo, June–December, 1915. Italian armies under Gen. Luigi Cadorno stage series of attacks—June 23–July 7, July 18–August 3, October 18–November 4, November 10–December 2—against Austrians under Gen. Svetosan Borojevic von Bojna along Isonzo River north of Trieste, suffering heavy casualties and failing to dislodge Austrians.

Gallipoli, August 6, 1915–January 9, 1916. British and Anzac forces under Hamilton land at Sulva Bay on Gallipoli Peninsula while forces ashore at Cape Helles also attack; Allies fail to dislodge Turks, and after heavy losses are evacuated in early January.

Western Front, September 25–November 8, 1915. Allies under Joffre and Sir John French make series of attacks on Germans under Falkenhayn in Artois and Champagne on Western Front in effort to reduce Noyon salient; British hit Germans at Loos, September 25–October 14; French attack at Vimy Ridge, September 25–October 30, and at Champagne, September 25–November 8; minor gains are made, with heavy losses.

Verdun, February 21–December 18, 1916. Germans under Falkenhayn undertake massive offensive against French under Pétain centered on Verdun, on Marne River in Lorraine, northeastern France, 150 miles east of Paris on Western Front; French lose 460,000 men and Germans 278,000, but no breakthrough is achieved.

Lake Narotch, March 18–26, 1916. Russians under Gen. Alexei Kuropatkin attack Germans under Hindenburg at Lake Narotch east of Vilna in Lithuania, suffering heavy casualties and failing to dislodge Germans.

Trentino, May 15–June 17, 1916. Austrian offensive under Archduke Eugen in Trentino northeast of Brescia breaks lines of Italians under Cadorna, then is counterattacked and contained.

Brusilov Offensive, June 4–September 20, 1916. Russians under Gen. Alexei Brusilov attack and rout Austrians under Archduke Joseph along 300-mile front in eastern Poland and Galicia; German reinforcements stabilize front near Carpathian Mountains; casualties are massive.

Jutland, May 31–June 1, 1916. British Grand Fleet under Adm. Sir John Jellicoe and Adm. David Beatty fight series of actions with German High Seas Fleet under Adm. Reinhard Scheer and Adm. Franz von Hipper in North Sea off Jutland; British losses are greater, but German fleet flees to its base at Wilhelmshaven, leaving British in control of sea.

Somme, June 24–November 25, 1916. British under Haig, aided by French under Foch, fail to achieve breakthrough against Germans under Falkenhayn on Western Front along Somme River in Picardy; British suffer 453,000, French 194,000 casualties; German losses are estimated at 650,000.

Isonzo, August 6–November 14, 1916. Italians under Cadorno attack Austrians under Count Franz Conrad in series of offensives—August 16–17, September 14–26, October 10–12, November 1–14—along Isonzo River north of Trieste in northeast Italy, advancing lines but with heavy casualties on both sides.

Arges River, December 1–4, 1916. German army under Falkenhayn and Bulgarian army under Mackensen join to defeat Romanian army under Gen. Alexandru Averescu along Arges River west of Bucharest.

Kut-el-Amara and Baghdad, December 13, 1916–March 11, 1917. British army under Gen. Sir Frederick S. Maude attacks Turks at Kut-el-Amara on Tigris River southeast of Baghdad in Mesopotamia; Turks are ousted on February 16, retreating to Baghdad; British attack on March 7 and enter Baghdad March 11.

Gaza-Beersheba-Jerusalem, March 26–December 9, 1917. After crossing Sinai Peninsula from Egypt, British-Australian army fights series of battles against Turks along coast of Palestine; Turks under Gen. Kress von Kressenstein twice repel attacks on Gaza by Gen. Sir Archibald Murray; Gen. Sir Edmund Allenby, replacing Murray, defeats Turks at Beersheba and captures Jerusalem on December 9.

Arras, April 9–15, 1917. British and Canadians under Haig attack Germans under Falkenhausen on Western Front east of Arras in Artois, northeastern France, but fail to exploit breakthrough.

Aisne, April 16–20, 1917. French under Gen. Robert Nivelle attack Germans under Hindenburg and Ludendorff on Western Front along Aisne River northeast of Soissons in northern France; despite heavy losses, attack fails to break through and is followed by mutinies in French army.

Isonzo, May 12–September 15, 1917. Italians under Cadorna attack Austrians along Isonzo River north of Trieste in northeast Italy; first attack, May 12-June 8, fails, with heavy casualties, but second attack, August 18-September 15, brings important gains.

Ypres (Passchendaele), July 31–November 6, 1917. British and Canadians under Gen. Sir Hubert Gough and Gen. Sir Herbert Plumer attack Germans under Gen. Sixt von Arnim on Western Front east of Ypres, Belgium, in Flanders; Passchendaele Ridge is captured by Canadians, but casualties on both sides are massive.

Riga, September 1–21, 1917. Germans under Gen. Oscar von Hutier attack Russians across Dvina River below Gulf of Riga in Latvia; Russian army dissolves, Germans take Riga and threaten Petrograd, provisional Russian government of Alexander Kerensky flees Petrograd for Moscow.

Caporetto (Isonzo), October 24–November 12, 1917. German-Austrian army under Gen. Otto von Below breaks through Italian army under Cadorna, forcing general retreat from Isonzo River north of Trieste in northeastern Italy across Tagliamento River to line of Piave River north of Venice.

Cambrai, November 20–December 3, 1917. British under Gen. Julian Byng, using massed tanks, attack Germans under Gen. Georg von der Marwitz on Western Front west of Cambrai on Scheldt River; German line is restored by counterattack November 30.

German Western Front Offensive, March 21–July 18, 1918. (1) **Somme, March 21–April 5.** German armies under Generals Below, Marwitz, and Hutier break through British positions on Western Front along Somme River in Picardy and drive 40 miles southeastward; French fail to counterattack; on March 27, at urging of Haig, Ferdinand Foch is made Allied commander-in-chief. (2) **Lys, April 9–30.** Germans under Arnim and Gen. Frederick von Quast strike British under Gen. Plumer and Gen. Sir Henry S. Horne south of Ypres, in Pas-de-Calais, driving ten miles toward railway junction at Hazebrouck. (3) **Aisne (Chemin des Dames), May 27–June 2.** Germans under Gen. Bruno von Mudra and Gen. Max von Boehn attack French and British under Gen. Denis Duchêne across Aisne River, driving 23 miles to Marne River; U.S. units help force Germans back across Marne. (4) **Belleau Wood, June 4–17.** U.S. Marine and Army force under Gen. Omar Bundy attacks Germans at Belleau Wood on Marne River. (5) **Noyon-Montdidier, June 9–13.** Germans under Boehn and Hutier attack French under Pétain below Noyon on Ouse River in Picardy, northern France, and after some gains are halted and driven back by French and American counterattack. (6) **Champagne-Marne, July 15–18.** German armies under Gen. Boehm, Gen. Mudra, and Gen. Karl von Einem attack French and Americans under Gen. Henri Gouraud and Gen. Henri Mathias Berthelot east and west of Reims, but are stopped at Marne River.

Piave, June 15–July 6, 1918. Italians under Gen. Armando Diaz turn back attack by Austrians under Conrad and Gen. Borojevic von Bojna along Piave River north of Venice.

Allied Western Front Counteroffensive, July 18–September 6, 1918. (1) **Aisne-Marne, July 18–August 5.** Four French armies, including nine American divisions, hit Germans under Ludendorff, eliminating Marne salient. (2) **Amiens, August 8–12.** British, Canadians, and Anzacs under Gen. Henry Rawlinson and French under Gen. Eugène Debeney and Gen. Georges Humbert hit Germans at Amiens salient between Somme and Ouse rivers in Picardy, driving them ten miles; Ludendorff calls August 8 "black day of the German army." (3) **Lys and Amiens, August 18–September 4.** British and French armies attack Germans from Flanders to Aisne, with Canadians and Anzacs breaking through across Somme River, forcing German retreat to Hindenburg Line. (4) **St. Mihiel, September 12–16.** Americans and French under Gen. John J. Pershing hit Germans evacuating St. Mihiel Salient south of Verdun in Champagne, clearing out salient; Americans immediately begin transfer to Argonne Forest area.

Megiddo, September 19–21, 1918. British-Indian-Arab army under Gen. Sir Edmund Allenby defeats Turkish army under Gen. Liman von Sanders at Megiddo, north of Jerusalem in Palestine; on October 1 Allies capture Damascus in Syria.

Allied Western Front Final Offensive, September 26–November 11, 1918. (1) **Meuse-Argonne, September 26–October 3.** In opening Allied offensive planned by Foch, Americans under Pershing and French under Gouraud attack Germans under Crown Prince Wilhelm III and Gen. Max von Gallwitz along Meuse River/Argonne Forest in Champagne and Lorraine. (2) **Hindenburg Line, September 27–October 17.** British-French armies under Haig and British-Belgian army under King Albert attack Germans under Boehm and Crown Prince Rupprecht of Bavaria in northeastern France and Belgium, driving through Hindenburg Line toward Le Cateau in Flanders. (3) **Meuse-Argonne, October 4–31.** Americans under Pershing, after heavy losses, drive through Argonne Forest while French under Gouraud attack to Aisne River in northern France against Germans under Gallwitz and Crown. (4) **Sambre and Scheldt, October 17–November 11.** British under Rawlinson and Byng break through German lines on Seele River and advance to Sambre and Scheldt rivers in northern France, while Belgians under Albert move eastward through Flanders; German army begins to crumble. (5) **Meuse River Valley, November 1–11.** American armies under Pershing and French army under Gen. Gouraud smash through Germans in Meuse Valley and move upon Sedan; Germans sue for armistice on November 5; on November 10 Kaiser Wilhelm II abdicates; armistice is signed on November 11.

Vittoria Veneto, October 24–November 4, 1918. Italians under Diaz attack across Piave River in northern Italy; on November 4 Austrians sue for armistice.

Warsaw, August 16–25, 1920. Poles under Marshal Joséf Pilsudski attack Russians under Marshal Mikhail Tukhachevski south of Warsaw in Poland, stopping Communist advance and driving Red Army eastward with heavy casualties.

Novorossiisk, March 28, 1920. White Russian army under Gen. Anton Denikin disintegrates after Red Army under Tukhachevski captures Novorossiisk on Black Sea.

Hunan, July 9, 1926–March 12, 1927. Chinese Nationalists under Gen. Chiang Kai-chek begin offensive against warlords in Hunan; Shanghai captured March 22, 1927.

China, September 18, 1931–May 31, 1933. Japanese attack Mukden, Manchuria, after manufactured "incident," expand hold on Manchuria. Japanese attack lays waste large area of Shanghai January 28-March 4, 1932.

Long March, October, 1934–November, 1935. Following defeat by Nationalists under Chiang at Kuangchang April 4–28, 1934, Chinese Communist army under Mao Tse-tung breaks out of Kiangsi-Fukien base area, marches and fights way 6,000 miles to Shensi province in northwest China.

P'inghsinkuan, September 25, 1937. Chinese Communist army under Gen. Nieh Jung-chen defeats Japanese army under Gen. Seishiro Itagaki in Wutai Mountains, northern Shensi, China.

Addis Ababa, May 5, 1936. Italian army under Marshal Pietro Badoglio captures Ethiopian capital of Addis Ababa in northeast Africa.

Guadalajara, March 11–20, 1937. Italian forces supporting Spanish Nationalists under Francisco Franco penetrate Spanish Loyalist lines at Brihuega, near Guadalajara, on Henares River in central Spain, then are routed by Russian dive bomber attack.

Nanking, December 13, 1937. Japanese capture Nanking from Chinese Nationalists, then ravage and loot city.

Teruel, December 5, 1937–February 20, 1938. Spanish Loyalist forces recapture Teruel, on Guadalaviar river in east-central Spain, then are driven out by Nationalist counterattack.

Ebro River, July 24–November 18, 1938. Spanish Loyalists under Gen. Juan Modisto cross Ebro River in Catalonia, southern Spain, and attack Nationalists under Franco; assault is repelled August 1; Nationalists counterattack October 1, clear right bank of Ebro November 8.

Barcelona, January 26, 1939. Spanish Nationalists under Franco capture Loyalist capital of Barcelona, in Catalonia, northeast Spain.

Khalka River, August 20, 1939. Russian army under Gen. Georgi Zhukov defeats Japanese army near Khalka River on Manchurian–Outer Mongolian border.

Poland, September 1–October 5, 1939. World War II begins as Adolf Hitler's German armies under Gen. Walther von Brauchitsch cross border and attack Poles under Marshal Edward Smigly-Ritz; on September 17 Soviet troops enter Poland from east; Warsaw surrenders to Germans September 27.

Finland, November 30, 1939–January 6, 1940. Soviet Russian armies invade Finland at points along border; Finns under Marshal Karl von Mannerheim repel attacks with heavy Soviet losses; Red Army spearheads are destroyed at Tolvajärvi December 11–13 and Suomussalmi January 8.

Plate River, December 13, 1939. British squadron under Comdr. Henry Harwood intercepts German pocket-battleship *Graf Spee* off mouth of Plate River near coast of Argentina; *Graf Spee* is driven into harbor of Montevideo, Uruguay, and on December 17 is scuttled outside port.

Battle of Atlantic, 1939–1942. Sinking of British liner *Athenia* September 3, 1939, opens six-year battle by British and United States against German U-boats under Adm. Erich Raeder and later Adm. Karl Doenitz; despite convoy system and development of radar British take heavy losses in 1940 and 1941 as Germans develop "wolfpack" tactics and mount bombing attacks from French and Norwegian coasts.

Finland, February 1–March 12, 1940. Reorganized Russian armies under Gen. Semyon Timoshenko launch massive all-out attack on Finns, ultimately breaking through Mannerheim Line on February 13; Finns surrender March 12.

Norway, April 9–June 9, 1940. German armies under Gen. Nikolaus von Falkenhorst invade Norway and Denmark; British and French land troops north of Trondheim and at Narvik April 14–19; on June 8 British aircraft carrier *Glorious* and two destroyers are sunk by German battle-cruisers *Scharnhorst* and *Gneisenau*; by June 9 all Allied forces are evacuated, and Norwegian resistance ceases.

Blitzkrieg, May 10–June 22, 1940. German armies under Gen. Gerd von Rundstedt and Gen. Fedor von Bock invade Low Countries and France; armored spearheads and air power of Blitzkrieg split Allied armies; Dutch surrender May 15, Belgians May 28; French general Maurice Gamelin is replaced by Gen. Maxime Weygand; French retreat, Germans reach Channel coast May 31, dividing Allies; British under Gen. Lord John Gort withdraw to Dunkirk, and together with some French forces are evacuated May 26-June 3; on June 14 Paris falls; on June 16 Marshal Philippe Pétain replaces Paul Reynaud as premier; on June 22 France capitulates.

Oran and Alexandria, July 3–7, 1940. Three French battleships under Adm. Maurice Gensoul are sunk by British fleet under Adm. Sir James F. Somerville in harbor of Oran, Algeria, July 3–4, after refusing to join British or be interned or scuttled; on July 7 French squadron at Alexandria, Egypt, under Adm. René Emile Godfroy agrees to be demobilized.

Battle of Britain, July 10–October 30, 1940. With France and Low Countries out of the war, Germans, in preparation for cross-Channel invasion, launch aerial assault on England; despite constant day and night Blitz attacks, Luftwaffe fails to wrest control of skies from Royal Air Force; nightly bombings continue, but on October 27–29 intelligence intercepts indicate invasion plans canceled.

Greece, October 28–December 28, 1940. Italians under Gen. Sebastiano Visconti-Prasca invade Greece from Albania, and are halted by Greeks under Gen. Alexander Papagos; Greek counteroffensive begins November 14 and by late December Italians, now under Gen. Ubaldo Soddu, have been thoroughly repulsed.

Taranto, November 11, 1940. British fleet under Adm. Sir Andrew Cunningham launches air attack from carrier *Illustrious* on naval base at Taranto, in southern Italy on Ionian Sea, sinking three Italian battleships.

British Desert Offensive, December 9, 1940–February 5, 1941. British desert army under Gen. Richard N. O'Connor December 9–10 strikes Italian army under Gen. Rudolfo Graziani at Sidi Barrani; Italians retreat westward; British capture Bardia on coast of Libya from Italians under Gen. Annibale Bergonzoli January 3–5; British capture Tobruk from Italians under Gen. Petassi Mannella January 22; remaining Italian force under Bergonzoli surrenders at Beda Fromm February 5.

El Agheila, March 24, 1941. German Afrika Korps and Italians under Gen. Erwin Rommel recapture El Agheila on coast of Lybia from British under Gen. Sir Philip Neame.

Matapan, March 28, 1941. British Mediterranean fleet under Cunningham catches Italian fleet under Adm. Angelo Iachino near Cape Matapan off southern Greece, sinking three cruisers and two destroyers.

Yugoslavia, April 6–17, 1941. German army under Marshal Wilhelm List invades Yugoslavia; Yugoslavians surrender April 17.

Greece, April 6–29, 1941. After British force under Gen. Sir Henry Maitland Wilson arrives in Greece March 7–27, German army under List invades Greece, drives through Greeks under Gen. Alexander Papagos to reach coast; last British troops leave April 29.

Crete, May 20–31, 1941. German airborne army under Gen. Kurt Student attacks Crete, and despite heavy losses forces withdrawal of British under New Zealand major general Bernard Freyberg; 15,000 troops are evacuated by British fleet under Cunningham by May 31, with four cruisers and six destroyers sunk, and capital ships severely damaged.

Tobruk, April 10–December 10, 1941. German Afrika Korps and Italians under Rommel besiege British in Tobruk; British counteroffensive June 15–17 fails; Gen. Sir Claude Auchinleck replaces Gen. Sir Archibald Wavell as British commander in Middle East and attacks south of Tobruk November

18–23; Rommel's counterattack is checked November 27; Tobruk garrison breaks out, and Rommel withdraws to El Agheila.

Bismarck, May 18–28, 1941. German battleship *Bismarck* leaves Bergens-fjord May 21, sinks battle-cruiser *Hood* and damages battleship *Prince of Wales* in Denmark Strait May 24. *Bismarck* is attacked by British aircraft 700 miles east of Brest May 27, and after being disabled by *Rodney* and *King George V* is torpedoed and sunk.

"Barbarossa" (Invasion of Russia), June 1941. On June 22 Adolf Hitler invades Soviet Russia in Operation Barbarossa, with German spearheads aimed at Leningrad, Smolensk, and Kiev; Finns under Marshal Karl von Mannerheim join attack on Karelian isthmus; Russians retreat on all fronts. Minsk and Smolensk fall in mid-July, Kiev on September 19. Leningrad is isolated September 15, Soviet forces in Crimea on September 20. On October 6 Germans reach Sea of Azov. Yalta in Crimea falls on November 9. Rostov, on Don River, falls on November 21. On December 2 Germans are within 20 miles of Moscow. In November Russians begin heavy counterattacks; subzero temperatures aid in stopping German advances. Major Soviet offensive begins on Moscow front December 6. By year's end Germans, although still attacking in Crimea, are being driven back in Ukraine and north and south of Moscow.

Pearl Harbor, December 7, 1941. Japanese fleet under Adm. Chuichi Nagumo launches carrier attack on Pearl Harbor, Hawaii; eight U.S. battleships are sunk, capsized, or seriously damaged.

Clark Field, December 8, 1941. Eight hours after attack on Pearl Harbor, Japanese planes hit Clark Field, near Manila, find U.S. planes lined up in rows on ground, and destroy major portion of American air forces in Philippines.

Philippines, December 10, 1941–May 6, 1942. Japanese forces under Gen. Masaharu Homma invade Philippines, landing on Luzon December 10–22, Mindanao December 20–31; Manila is declared open city December 27; American and Filipino troops under Gen. Douglas MacArthur withdraw to Bataan peninsula; on orders from Washington MacArthur leaves Philippines, arriving in Australia March 17. Japanese break through Bataan lines April 3, Gen. Edward P. King surrenders April 9. Japanese land on Corregidor May 5–6, and Gen. Jonathan Wainwright surrenders fortress May 6.

Hong Kong, December 8–25, 1941. Japanese invade Kowloon December 8, land on island of Hong Kong December 18; British under Gen. C. M. Maltby surrender December 25.

Malaysia, December 8, 1941–February 15, 1942. Japanese under Gen. Tomoyuki Yamashita land on Malay peninsula at Kota Bharu and at Singora and Patani in Thailand; British and Australians withdraw into Singapore January 31; Japanese land on Singapore February 8; British general A. E. Percival surrenders February 15.

***Prince of Wales* and *Repulse*, December 10, 1941.** British battleship *Prince of Wales* and cruiser *Repulse*, under Adm. Sir Tom Phillips, are bombed and sunk by Japanese in South China Sea off coast of Malaysia.

Submarines Against Japan, 1941–45. When war comes, U.S. submarines are handicapped by torpedoes with defective firing and depth-control mechanisms, not corrected until mid- and late 1943; in 1942, 182 Japanese ships totaling 725,000 tons are sunk; in mid-1943 rate of sinkings quickens; by end of 1944 half of Japanese merchant fleet and two-thirds of tanker fleet have been sunk; at war's end U.S. submariners, constituting no more than 2 percent of Navy personnel, have accounted for 1,300 ships including battleships and 8 aircraft carriers, or 55 percent of enemy's losses at sea, at cost of 22 percent of U.S. submarine personnel engaged.

Battle of Atlantic, 1942–45. Entry of United States into war finds American navy totally unprepared to defend Atlantic coastal shipping; heavy losses taken in winter and spring of 1942; in May activity shifts to Caribbean; in 1942 Allied convoys to Russia on Murmansk run in North Atlantic experience heavy losses; mid-Atlantic sinkings reach peak in winter of 1942–43, then U.S. and British air and escort ship protection takes heavy U-boat toll and action shifts to Bay of Biscay; by end of 1943 Germans are experiencing severe U-boat losses despite development of schnorkel, permitting long submerged operation, and U-boat menace is severely reduced; in all, 23,351 Allied ships are sunk by Germans, 17,000 of them in 1940–42, at cost of 782 U-boats.

Russian Front, January 18–May 12, 1942. Russian winter counteroffensive against Germans gains ground; Donets River crossed south of Kharkov January 24; Marshal Semyon Timoshenko's armies threaten Dnepopetrovsk in Ukraine; new push in Crimea begins March 1; mud and exhaustion slow advances.

East Indies, January 11–March 9, 1942. Japanese under Yamashita and Adm. Koremochi Takahashi land in Borneo and Celebes, move through Moluccas, Timor, and Strait of Macassar to Java and Sumatra; on March 9 Dutch surrender to Japanese in Java.

Rommel's Desert Offensive, January 21–February 7, 1942. New offensive by German Afrika Korps and Italians under Rommel against British Eighth Army under Auchinleck ousts British from El Agheila, and on January 29 Rommel retakes Benghazi, on coast of Cyrenaica, North Africa.

Burma, January 12–February 23, 1942. Japanese under Gen. Shojiro Iida invade Burma from Thailand, drive British under Gen. Thomas Hutton out of Moulmein January 31 and across Sittang River February 23.

Java Sea, February 27, 1942. Allied naval force under Dutch admiral Karel Doorman is defeated by Japanese fleet under Adm. Takeo Takagi in Java Sea on February 27.

Burma, March 21–May 15, 1942. Japanese under Iida begin new offensive against British under Gen. Sir William Slim and Chinese under U.S. general Joseph Stilwell; Mandalay falls May 1; Chinese forces disintegrate; British retreat into India.

Tokyo, April 18, 1942. U.S. B-25s under Col. James Doolittle, launched from carrier *Hornet* 650 miles east of Japan, bomb Tokyo.

Coral Sea, May 7–8, 1942. U.S. fleet under Adm. Frank Jack Fletcher and Japanese fleet under Takagi fight first all-carrier naval battle near Louisiade Archipelago in Coral Sea southeast of New Guinea; American ship losses are greater, but Japanese cancel assault on Port Moresby.

Crimea, May 8–July 2, 1942. German offensive under Gen. Erich von Manstein captures Kerch in southern Crimea May 15.

Bir Hacheim, May 26–June 13, 1942. Offensive by German Afrika Korps and Italians under Rommel against British Eighth Army and Free French under Gen. Neil M. Ritchie cracks Allied position at Bir Hacheim, inland from Gazala in Cyrenaica, forcing Eighth Army retreat toward Egyptian border.

Midway, June 3–6, 1942. U.S. aircraft carrier force under Adm. Raymond A. Spruance turns back attack on Midway Island by Japanese fleet under Nagumo, sinking four Japanese carriers and establishing U.S. naval control of Pacific Ocean.

Tobruk-Mersa Matruh, June 20–30, 1942. German Afrika Korps and Italians under Rommel attack British at Tobruk on coast of Cyrenaica; Tobruk falls June 21; British under Auchinleck fight delaying action at Mersa Matruh, then retreat inside Egyptian border.

Russian Front, July–September 1942. Massive German summer offensive drives deeply into south-central Russia; Sevastopol in Crimea falls July 2, Rostov July 28; Don River is crossed August 20, and Stalingrad besieged July 22; Stalingrad is entered September 13.

Port Moresby, July 21–September 13, 1942. Japanese under Gen. Tomitoro Horii cross Owen Stanley Mountains in Papua to within 30 miles of Port Moresby, then are stopped by Australian and American force under Australian general Edmond F. Herring.

Guadalcanal, August 7, 1942–February 7, 1943. U.S. Marines under Gen. Alexander A. Vandegrift invade Japanese-occupied Solomon Islands east of New Guinea, capture Henderson Field on Guadalcanal; Japanese fleet under Adm. Gunichi Mikawa sinks four American and Australian cruisers off Savo Island August 9; in subsequent six-month battle U.S. Marine and Army forces repel counterattacks, then clear Japanese from Guadalcanal; series of naval battles ends with U.S. fleet under Adm. Thomas C. Kinkaid defeating Japanese under Adm. Nobutake Kondo November 14–15.

Alam Halfa, August 31–September 7, 1942. British Eighth Army under Gen. Sir Bernard Montgomery repels attack by Rommel's German Afrika Corps and Italians at Alam Halfa near El Alamein on Egyptian eastern coast.

El Alamein, October 23–November 6, 1942. Eighth Army attacks Rommel's army between El Alamein and Qattara Depression; on November 5 Rommel orders Afrika Korps retreat.

North Africa, November 8–28, 1942. Americans and British under Gen. Dwight D. Eisenhower land in Morocco and Algeria in Operation Torch; Vichy French resist until French admiral Jean Darlan orders ceasefire; Allies advance eastward; German reinforcements from Italy pour into Tunisia; British Eighth Army under Montgomery begins advance westward from El Alamein as Afrika Korps retreats.

Stalingrad and Russian Front, November 19, 1942–March 1943. Russian counteroffensive under Gen. Georgi Zhukov begins on Stalingrad front; Stalingrad is encircled November 23; relieving attack by Germans under Manstein December 12 is halted December 23; Manstein is in full retreat by December 27; Soviet offensive in Caucasus proceeds steadily; siege of Leningrad in north is partially broken January 11; Germans within Stalingrad are split into two pockets January 25; southern pocket under Gen. Friedrich Paulus surrenders January 31; last Germans surrender February 2. Russian offensive continues.

Buna and Gona, November 20, 1942–January 22, 1943. After driving Japanese back across Owen Stanley Mountains, Americans and Australians under U.S. general Robert L. Eichelberger take Buna and Gona on coast of Papua in bitter jungle fighting.

Kasserine Pass, February 14–22, 1943. German Afrika Korps under Rommel hits Americans under Gen. Lloyd R. Fredendall at Kasserine Pass in western Tunisia; after rapid penetration advance is halted; Rommel withdraws February 22.

Kharkov, February 18–March 20, 1943. Counterattack by Germans under Manstein retakes Kharkov March 14.

Bismarck Sea, March 2–4, 1943. U.S. and Australian bombers under Gen. George C. Kenney attack Japanese convoy in Bismarck Sea north of Papua, sinking seven transports and four destroyers.

Tunisia, March 19–May 13, 1943. Americans under Gen. George S. Patton take El Guettar March 19; British under Montgomery attack Germans and Italians under Gen. Jürgen von Arnim at Mareth Line near Gulf of Gabès March 20, break through March 28; Germans retreat 200 miles, form new defensive line; Americans, British, and French under direction of Gen. Sir Harold Alexander open offensive May 3; Bizerte and Tunis fall May 7; von Arnim surrenders May 13.

Attu, May 11–29, 1943. American army amphibious force under Adm. Francis W. Rockwell lands on Attu in Aleutian Islands to oust Japanese placed there and on Kiska in 1942; island is cleared May 29. Attack on Kiska August 15 finds Japanese gone.

Sicily, July 9–August 17, 1943. Americans under Patton and British under Montgomery invade Sicily, defended by Germans and Italians under Gen. Alfred Guzzoni; after stubborn German resistance, Allies take Messina and Germans withdraw to mainland.

South Pacific, July 1–December 31, 1943. U.S. and Anzac Army and Air Force units under MacArthur, Navy and Marine units under Adm. William F. Halsey begin drive to roll back Japanese conquests of 1941–42 in southwest Pacific. Rendova Island is captured June 30, Munda on New Georgia August 7, Lae in eastern New Guinea September 12 and Salamaua September 16, Finschhafen October 2; Bougainville is invaded November 1. On December 30 U.S. Marines under Gen. William H. Rupertus capture Japanese air field at Cape Gloucester in New Britain.

Russian Front, July 5–November 26, 1943. German summer offensive launched July 5 makes little headway; Russians open massive offensive August 12. Kharkov is retaken August 23, Smolensk September 25; Dneiper River is reached by October, Kiev recaptured November 6. German army cut off in Crimea, pushed back to Pripet Marshes in Ukraine.

Salerno, September 9–18, 1943. After British Eighth Army under Montgomery lands in Calabria at tip of Italian peninsula and Italians sign armistice with Allies September 3, U.S. Fifth Army under Gen. Mark Clark invades mainland below Salerno, 30 miles south of Naples; Germans under Marshal Albert Kesselring counterattack, but Allies, reinforced by airborne units and heavy naval gunfire, secure beachhead; Eighth Army arrives from south September 16, and Germans withdraw.

Volturno and Trigno rivers, October 12–November 15, 1943. After capturing Naples on October 1, Allies under Gen. Sir Harold Alexander advance up Italian peninsula against stiff German opposition; U.S. Fifth Army under Clark crosses Volturno River October 12–14, while British Eighth Army under Montgomery crosses Trigno River October 27-November 1; by November 15 Allied advance has halted to regroup.

Tarawa and Makin, November 20–24, 1943. U.S. Marine and Army units under overall command of Spruance attack Tarawa and Makin in Gilbert Islands; Makin falls to army unit November 23; Marines take Tarawa November 24 after fanatical Japanese resistance.

Gustaf ("Winter") Line, November 20–December 31, 1943. Germans under Kesselring have established defensive line south of Rome from Garigliano and Rapido rivers to Adriatic coast along Sangro River; by November 30 British Eighth Army under Montgomery has crossed Sangro, but U.S. Fifth Army under Clark is held up at Rapido, where Germans occupy strong positions at Monte Cassino; at year's end Fifth Army has been stopped five miles southeast of Rapido, and Eighth Army under Gen. Sir Oliver Leese north of Ortona.

Russian Front, December 24, 1943–April 15, 1944. Russians attack Germans in Ukraine, cross Polish frontier January 4, attack on Leningrad front January 15–19; two German corps in Ukraine encircled February 3; portion of German army escapes from Korsun pocket February 17; German rail communications to Crimea severed March 6; Russian drive into Romania reaches Carpathian Mountains April 1; in Crimea Russians recapture Sevastopol May 9.

Marshall Islands, January 30–February 23, 1944. U.S. Seventh Fleet under Spruance lands marine and army units on Kwajalein, Roi, and Namur in Marshall Islands in south-central Pacific; Japanese resist fiercely, but islands are secured by February 7; Americans land on Eniwetok February 17, Engebi February 18, Parry February 22; resistance ends February 23.

Los Negros, February 29–March 30, 1944. U.S. Army forces under MacArthur land on Los Negros in Admiralty Islands north of New Guinea; by March 30 Japanese have been cleared from Admiralties and air bases set up.

New Guinea, April 22–August 5, 1944. Americans under Eichelberger, supported by carrier aircraft under Adm. Marc Mitscher, land in northeast New Guinea at Hollandia and Aitape; Aitape is taken April 24; Americans take island of Biak May 27-June 29 after strenuous fighting; Japanese under Gen. Hotaze Adachi push through jungle from Wewak, attack Americans under Gen. Charles P. Hall at Aitape beginning July 10; Americans counterattack, Japanese flee into jungle after heavy losses.

East China, May–November, 1944. Japanese under Gen. Yasuji Okamura attack Chinese in drives from Hankow and Canton, capturing Hengyang August 9 and eliminating seven U.S. air fields.

Anzio and Rapido, January 5–March 3, 1944. In effort by Allies to outflank Germans under Kesselring, British and Americans under Gen. John P. Lucas land at Anzio, below Rome 60 miles north of Gustaf Line on western coast of Italy; German counterattack pins Allies to beachhead; Allies hold on against repeated assaults. U.S. Fifth Army under Clark, including New Zealand Corps under Freyberg, fails to oust Germans under Gen. Heinrich von Vietinghoff from positions across Rapido River at Monte Cassino.

Rome, May 11–June 4, 1944. Allies under Alexander crack Gustav Line; Kesselring orders general German retreat May 17; British Eighth and U.S. Fifth armies fight way northward; Allied breakout from Anzio links up with advance May 25; instead of attacking eastward to cut off Germans, Fifth Army under Clark drives for Rome; Rome falls June 4, as Germans retire toward new defensive line along Arno River.

Normandy, June 6–August 30, 1944. Anglo-American invasion army under Eisenhower goes ashore on Normandy coast of France June 6, in Operation

Overlord; German defense is under Rommel; after initial advances British under Montgomery are held up before Caen, while Americans under Gen. Omar Bradley experience tough going in drive across Cotentin peninsula. On July 25 Americans break through west of St. Lô; German counterattack at Avranches under Gen. Günther von Kluge August 6–10 is halted; British and Canadians drive northeastward, Americans southward then eastward; Germans lose 500,000 men, flee across Seine River; Paris is liberated August 25.

Italy, June–September 1944. Germans under Kesselring retreat to positions along Gothic Line in north-central Italy; ten American and French divisions leave for Operation Anvil-Dragoon in southern France; Allies under Alexander capture Florence August 13, Pisa September 2, Rimini September 21.

Saipan, June 15–July 9, 1944. After heavy naval and air bombardment, Marines under Gen. Holland Smith go ashore at Saipan in Mariana Islands, east-central Pacific, June 15; U.S. Army units under Gen. Ralph Smith land June 18; Japanese under Nagumo and Gen. Yoshitsugo Saito resist desperately; organized resistance ends July 9.

Philippine Sea, June 18–20, 1944. Japanese fleet under Adm. Jisaburo Ozawa sorties from Philippines to attack U.S. fleet under Spruance protecting Saipan landings; on June 19–20 Japanese lose heavily in air battles, and three Japanese carriers are sunk; Ozawa withdraws June 20.

Russian Front, June 23–December 15, 1944. Russians under overall direction of Zkuhov attack Germans north of Pripet Marshes in White Russia; Minsk falls July 3, Vilna July 13, Kaunas, Lithuania, August 1; to north, Mannerheim Line is broken and Viipuri, Finland, is captured July 20; Russian offensives capture Riga, Latvia, October 15; Lublin, Poland, July 24; Constanta on Black Sea August 29; Bucharest September 1; Sofia, Bulgaria, falls September 16; Belgrade captured by Russians and Yugoslav partisans October 20; Budapest is attacked December 27.

Guam and Tinian, July 21–August 10, 1944. U.S. amphibious forces under Adm. Richmond Kelly Turner land on Guam July 21 and Tinian July 24 in Marianas, east-central Pacific; Tinian is cleared August 1; organized resistance on Guam ends August 10.

Warsaw, August 1–September 30, 1944. Polish uprising in Warsaw under Gen. Tadeusz Bor-Komoroski is savagely suppressed by German SS; Russians east of city do not renew attack, do not aid British-U.S. efforts to drop supplies to Poles.

Southern France, August 15–September 15, 1944. Americans and French under Gen. Alexander M. Patch land on French Mediterranean coast between Hyères and Cannes in Operation Anvil-Dragoon; French under Gen. de Lattre de Tassigny take Toulon and Marseilles, Americans under Gen.

Lucius Truscott, Jr., drive northward up Rhone Valley; by September 15 Americans and French have advanced into Vosges Mountains.

Northern France and Low Countries, September 1–December 15, 1944. British under Montgomery advance into Belgium, but attempt to clear Scheldt River estuary is held up by Germans; Americans, short of gasoline after rapid advance, move eastward toward German border; airborne assault under Montgomery northward into Netherlands September 17–26 fails to outflank Germans; Scheldt is opened to transport in late November. Americans open offensive against German Westwall and Roer River; Aachen is captured October 21; after heavy fighting Roer is reached December 3; Metz is captured December 13; French capture Strasbourg November 23, but fail to oust Germans from Colmar Pocket.

Leyte, October 20–December 25, 1944. U.S. Army forces under MacArthur go ashore on Leyte, Philippine Islands; Japanese under Gen. Sosaku Suzuki land reinforcements from Luzon; kamikaze aircraft attacks damage U.S. naval forces; after extended campaign, organized Japanese resistance ends by December 31.

Formosa, October 11–14, 1944. U.S. Third Fleet under Halsey attacks targets on Formosa; Japanese lose much of remaining naval air strength.

Leyte Gulf, October 23–26, 1944. In greatest naval battle of all time, Japanese fleet under Ozawa launches three-pronged attack on U.S. Third Fleet under Halsey protecting landings on Leyte; despite luring U.S. fast carrier fleet northward and achieving surprise at San Bernadino Straits, Japanese lose four battleships, three carriers, ten cruisers, and other ships, and fleet ceases to exist as effective unit.

Ardennes, December 16, 1944–January 25, 1945. On Hitler's orders, Germans launch counteroffensive through Ardennes in Belgium and Luxembourg; drive aimed at Meuse River creates 50-mile-deep bulge, but Americans hold firm along northern and southern shoulders, begin counterattacking; forward progress of German drive is halted December 24; Germans fail to dislodge Americans at Bastogne, December 19–January 5; Germans begin withdrawal January 8; Allied line is restored January 25. Offensive has delayed drive on Germany but costs Germans 250,000 men, 600 tanks and assault guns, 1,600 airplanes.

Alsace–Lorraine, January 1–February 9, 1945. Germans under Gen. Johannes von Blaskowitz launch Operation Nordwind against U.S. Sixth Army group under Gen. Jacob Devers in Alsace and Lorraine; drive is stopped by January 11; French and Americans attack Colmar Pocket January 20, advance to Rhine.

North Burma and China, January 1–May 2, 1945. Two Chinese armies converge on Japanese near Mongyu; Burma Road is reopened January 27; British and Indians under Gen. Sir William Slim cross Irrawaddy River February 12–14;

Japanese under Gen. Hoyotaro Kimura counterattack March 5; Indians take Mandalay March 20; British occupy Rangoon May 2.

Philippines, January 9–August 15, 1945. U.S. Army under MacArthur goes ashore at Lingayen Gulf, Luzon, January 6, moves against Japanese under Yamashita; U.S. forces land on Bataan January 29, south of Manila Bay January 31; attack Manila February 8; Corregidor falls February 26; resistance in Manila ends March 3; Japanese forces on Luzon hold out in mountains until end of war.

Russian Front, January 12–May 7, 1945. Russians under Marshals Zhukov, Ivan Konev, and Konstantin Rokossovski open final offensive; Warsaw is captured January 17; Baltic Sea is reached January 26, cutting off German forces in East Prussia; Budapest surrenders February 13; Poznan falls February 23; Germans counterattack in Hungary March 6; Russians capture Gdynia March 28; Vienna captured April 13, Stettin April 26.

Rhineland, February 9–March 10, 1945. British and Americans under Montgomery and Americans under Bradley clear out German resistance west of Rhine River.

Dresden, February 13–14, 1945. American and British bombers stage massive raids on Dresden, Germany; fire storms kill at least 70,000 people.

Iwo Jima, February 19–March 26, 1945. U.S. Marines under Gen. Harry Schmidt go ashore at Iwo Jima in Bonins, east-central Pacific Ocean; Japanese under Gen. Tadamichi Kuribayashi resist fiercely; organized resistance ends March 16; several hundred remaining defenders die in suicide charge March 26.

Japan, February–August 1945. U.S. bomber offensive against Japan from Saipan and bases goes into high gear; low-level raids March 9–10 destroy large area of Tokyo; fighter planes based on Iwo Jima after April 7 permit daylight raiding; industrial areas leveled.

Central China, March–May 1945. Japanese open offensive, capture U.S. air field at Laohokow; Chinese counterattack checks drive April 10.

Rhineland and Ruhr, March 7–April 18, 1945. Troops of U.S. First Army under Gen. Courtney Hodges capture bridge across Rhine River at Remagen; U.S. Third Army under Patton drives southward from Moselle River into Saar Basin, collapsing Siegfried Line defenses, crosses Rhine March 22; British and U.S. armies under Montgomery cross Rhine near Wesel March 23; U.S. Seventh Army under Patch and French under de Tassigny cross March 26; U.S. armies encircle Germans in Ruhr, drive toward Mulde and Elbe River.

Okinawa, April 1–June 30, 1945. U.S. Army and Marines under Gen. Simon Buckner land on Okinawa, in Ryukyu Islands south of Japan; Japanese under Gen. Mitsuru Ushijima put up suicidal resistance; kamikaze attacks do severe damage to U.S., British naval forces; U.S. carrier planes sink battleship *Yamato*; organized resistance ends June 22; mopping-up operations completed June 30.

Northern Italy, April 9–May 2, 1945. British Eighth Army under Gen. Richard McCreery (April 9) and U.S. Fifth Army under Truscott (April 14) attack Germans under Vietinghoff across Po River in northern Italy; German resistance collapses April 20; German representatives sign surrender terms April 29, which are accepted by Vietinghoff May 1.

Berlin, April 16–May 3, 1945. Russian attack on Berlin opens April 16; city is encircled April 25; Hitler commits suicide April 30; Berlin is captured May 2–3.

Germany, April 18–May 7, 1945. German resistance in west begins collapsing; British and Canadians under Montgomery drive across northern Germany to Baltic Sea; Americans under Bradley sweep across central and southern Germany and into Austria and Czechoslovakia; French under de Tassigny drive to Lake Constance on Swiss border; on April 25 U.S. and advancing Russian patrols meet at Torgau on Elbe Rive; Bremen falls to British April 26, Hamburg May 3; Germans surrender to Eisenhower May 7; Zhukov and British air marshal Sir Arthur Tedder ratify surrender May 8; war in Europe ends at midnight May 8.

Japan, July–August 1945. U.S. submarines destroy remainder of Japanese merchant marine and fleet; fast carrier fleet planes wipe out most of remaining Japanese air force; land forces under MacArthur and naval forces under Adm. Chester Nimitz prepare for massive invasion.

Hiroshima and Nagasaki, August 6–9, 1945. U.S. B-29s from Saipan drop atomic bombs on Hiroshima August 6, Nagasaki August 9; on August 10 Japan surrenders, and war in Pacific officially ends with surrender September 2.

Manchuria, August 9–15, 1945. Russians under Marshal Alexander M. Valisevsky attack Japanese under Gen. Otozo Yamada in Manchuria.

China, November 15–30, 1945. Chinese Nationalists attack Chinese Communists north of Tienstin, drive across Great Wall into Manchuria; Communist offensive begins November 30.

China, March 10, 1946–December 7, 1949. Civil war between Chinese Nationalists under Chiang Kai-chek and Communists under Mao Tse-tung resumes; Nationalists defeat Communists at Szeping April 16-May 20; in May, 1947, Communists begin offensive across Sungari River; Mukden falls November 1, 1948; Communists defeat Nationalists at Hwai Hai November, 1948-January, 1949; capture Peking January 22, Nanking April 22, Shanghai May 27, Canton October 15, Chungking November 30; in December, 1949, Nationalists withdraw across Strait of Formosa to Taiwan.

Israel, May 14, 1948–February 24, 1949. Britain mandate over Palestine ends; Jordan, Egypt, Syria, Iraq, Lebanon attack Israel; after initial Arab successes Israelis repel attacks; Egypt attacks July 8 after temporary truce; Israel captures Sinai; United Nations calls for ceasefire December 29; armistice accepted February 24, 1949.

Korea, June 25–September 15, 1950. Communist North Korea invades South Korea across 38th Parallel June 25; Seoul captured June 28, Inchon July 3; U.S. ground forces committed June 30; U.S. and U.N. forces under Gen. Douglas MacArthur are pushed into perimeter at Pusan July 30–September 1; renewed North Korean offensive against Pusan begins September 1.

Inchon, September 15–26, 1950. U.N. forces under MacArthur, predominantly American and Korean, land at Inchon on Yellow Sea, outflanking North Koreans; offensive breaks out Pusan encirclement; North Koreans flee north; Seoul recaptured September 26.

North Korea, October 7–December 15, 1950. U.N. forces under MacArthur enter North Korea, capture Pyongyang October 20; Chinese Communist forces begin entering North Korea from Yalu October 16; Chinese and North Koreans attack U.N. forces October 26–November 2; Chinese attack of November 26–27 in west sends U.N. Eighth Army into full retreat; U.S. Marines at Chosin Reservoir in east break out of trap, withdraw to Hungnam on east coast, where 10th Corps is evacuated by sea; new U.N. line is established at 38th Parallel.

38th Parallel, January 1–March 31, 1951. Chinese and North Koreans attack across 38th Parallel line; U.N. forces under Gen. Matthew Ridgway withdraw to prepared positions; Chinese and North Koreans recapture Seoul January 4; Chinese offensive is halted January 15; U.N. counteroffensive retakes Seoul March 14, drives Chinese north of 38th Parallel March 31.

38th Parallel, April 23–June 15, 1951. Chinese launch new offensive against U.N. forces under Gen. James Van Fleet April 23, are halted May 3; U.N. launches counteroffensive May 21, drives Chinese north of 38th Parallel; thereafter line from Kaesong and Panmunjon on 38th Parallel to eastern seacoast of Korean peninsula 50 miles north of Parallel is maintained until armistice is signed July 27, 1953.

Dienbienphu, March 14–May 7, 1954. Following several years of fighting, Viethminh begin siege of French fortress of Dienbienphu near Laos border in northern Vietnam; fortress falls May 7.

Israel, October 29, 1956–March 4, 1957. After Egypt nationalizes Suez Canal, Arab raids on Israel increase; in agreement with Great Britain and France, Israelis attack and take Mitla in Sinai October 29, 40 miles from canal; French and British jets bomb air fields near Suez October 31; Israelis occupy Rafa November 1, seize much Russian military equipment, capture Sharm-el-Sheikh November 4; French and British capture Port Said November 5–6; United States demands ceasefire November 6; British and French withdraw November 22; Israelis leave Sharm-el-Sheikh March 4, 1957.

Vietnam, 1961–1973. Communists in North Vietnam under Ho Chi Minh in Hanoi begin infiltration of South Vietnam after 1954 Geneva agreement;

first U.S. advisers arrive to assist Vietnam government in Saigon December 31, 1961; U.S. airplanes bomb North Vietnam after PT boats attack destroyer in Gulf of Tonkin August 2, 1964; Communists attack Bien Hoa air base November 1, 1964; U.S. compound in Pleiku is attacked February 7, 1965; U.S. bomber offensive Rolling Thunder begins February 13, 1965; U.S. land forces arrive in Vietnam March 8, 1965, by end of year are at 190,000; B-52s bomb North Vietnam April 12, 1966; U.S.-Vietnam offensive under Gen. William C. Westmoreland begins February 23, 1967; Communist Tet offensive begins January 1968, Saigon, Hué, numerous towns attacked; 543,400 U.S. troops are in Vietnam by January 31, 1969; U.S. withdraws 115,000 troops during 1969; Vietnam army attacks in Cambodia March 27, 1970, U.S. troops join in attack April 30; Vietnamese attack Ho Chi Minh Trail in Laos February 8, 1971; U.S. troops in Vietnam are down to 140,000 by end of 1971; Communist offensive begins March 30, 1972; U.S. resumes bombing of north April 15; last U.S. combat troops depart August 11, 1972; last U.S. troops leave March 29, 1973.

China–India Border, October 20–November 21, 1962. Chinese armies attack India at points along 1,000-mile front, gain disputed territories.

Kashmir, September 1–23, 1965. Pakistan bombers hit Indian forces in Kashmir September 1; Indian army unleashes three-pronged offensive, drives to within four miles of Lahore; U.N. ceasefire accepted September 23; Indians withdraw February 25, 1966.

Six-Day War, June 5–10, 1967. As Arabs prepare to attack, Israelis stage pre-emptive strike June 5; 320 Egyptian, 416 Syrian, Jordanian, and Iraqi planes are destroyed June 5–6; Gaza, Sinai, Jerusalem, and West Bank of Jordan River captured June 5–9; Golan Heights captured June 9–10.

Yom Kippur War, October 6–November 16, 1973. Arabs attack Israel October 6; Syrians penetrate Golan Heights October 6; Egyptians attack across Suez Canal October 6–7; Israeli counterattack stops Syrians October 9; Israel attacks toward Damascus October 11; new Egyptian offensive October 14 fails; Egyptian Third Army trapped south of Little Bitter Lake in Sinai; Israelis take Suez and Abadiye October 23; Russians threaten intervention, but after confrontation with United States agree to U.N. peacekeeping force without major power participation October 25.

Vietnam, December 13, 1974–April 30, 1975. Communists begin offensive December 13, 1974; Hué falls March 25, 1975; Saigon is surrounded April 21; South Vietnam government surrenders April 30.

Afghanistan, December 21, 1979–February 15, 1989. Soviet Russia invades Afghanistan December 21; Soviet-Afghan Communist army launches offensive against guerrillas in Panjsher Valley in early September, 1980; heavy fighting in western Afghanistan, June, 1981; Soviets launch assault in Farah Province, September 5, 1981; Soviets attack in Panjsher Valley northeast of Kabul May 10 and August 25, 1982; Soviets drive back guerrillas besieging Ali Khel August, 1984; guerrillas attack Kabul airport February 22, 1985, stage rocket attack on Kabul April 12; Soviet-Afghans attack near Pakistan border August 20; guerrilla stronghold at Zhawar near Pakistan border captured April 23, 1986; guerrillas take Nahrin in Baghlan November 14, 1986; Kabul is under rocket attack throughout much of 1988; Soviet troops begin withdrawing May 15, 1988; withdrawal completed February 15, 1989.

Iran-Iraq, September 22, 1980–August 20, 1988. Iraqis under Saddam Hussein invade Iran at eight points September 22, 1980; major Iranian offensive opens April 29, 1982, Iraqis driven back across border May 24; Iranian offensive to capture Basra July 13–28 fails; Iranian offensive captures Majnoon Island February 22-March 16, 1984; U.N. experts say Iraqis are using chemical weapons; Iraq intensifies attacks on oil tankers in Persian Gulf April 18, 1984; Iranians advance in Fao peninsula and Kurdistan February 9–25, 1986; Iranian offensive fails to capture Basra December 23–25; Iraqi missiles hit Teheran February 27, 1988; Iraqis drop chemical bombs on Halabja, killing 4,000 people, March 16; Iraqis recapture Fao peninsula, April 16–18, and Mehran, June 19–22; U.N. ceasefire takes effect August 20, 1988.

Falkland Islands, April 2–June 14, 1982. Argentine force invades Falkland Islands in south Atlantic Ocean; Argentine cruiser *Belgrano* is torpedoed May 2, British cruiser *Sheffield* sunk by Exocet missile May 4; British force lands at San Carlos Bay May 26, three British ships sunk; Port Stanley recaptured June 14 and islands cleared.

Grenada, October 25–27, 1983. U.S. and Caribbean-nations force lands in Grenada October 25, clears island of Cuban "construction workers" October 27.

Libya, April 15, 1986. U.S. bombers attack Libya from England and aircraft carriers in Mediterranean Sea.

Panama, December 20, 1989–January 3, 1990. U.S. troops land in Panama Canal Zone, attack Panama Defense Force of Gen. Manuel Noriega December 20, 1989; Noriega surrenders January 3, 1990.

Persian Gulf, August 1, 1990–February 28, 1991. Iraqis invade Kuwait August 1; United States sends forces to Saudi Arabia August 7; in Operation Desert Storm, U.S.-led forces under Gen. Norman Schwarzkopf begin air attack January 17, 1991; ground forces attack Iraqis February 14; Kuwait is cleared February 28.

Yugoslavia, January 1991. Following Bosnia-Herzegovina's declaration of independence from Yugoslavia, Serbian forces launch savage attacks, besiege Sarajevo; widespread atrocities reported against Muslim population; U.N. peacekeeping force deployed in Croatia in April, 1992; U.N. sanctions approved May 30; fighting escalates and United Nations authorizes multinational military force August 12 to convoy humanitarian aid to Bosnia-Herzegovina; Croatian forces attack Serbs January 22, 1993; Serbs counterattack January 23; shelling of Muslim and Croat enclaves by Serbians continues throughout 1993 and into 1994; Serbian president breaks with Bosnian Serbs after they reject terms for proposed Bosnian federation, August 5, 1994; in October Bosnian forces attack Bosnian Serbs, who counterattack and crush Bosnians at Bihac, mid-November; Bosnian forces launch offensive against Bosnian Serbs, March 20, 1995; Croatian troops push into Croatian Serbian enclave in central Croatia, May 1, 1995; Bosnian Serbs release last of 370 members of UN peacekeeping force being held hostage, June 18; Bosnian and Croatian forces drive Bosnian Serbs from Bihac, August 8; NATO planes begin air strikes on Bosnian Serb military targets, August 30; Bosnian Serbs begin withdrawing heavy weapons from Sarajevo area. September 16; presidents of Bosnia, Serbia, and Croatia initial UN-sponsored peace agreement, November 22; NATO takes control of peacekeeping force of 60,000 troops in Bosnia. December 21.

Yemen, May 7—July 7, 1994. Civil war breaks out in Yemen between northern and southern factions; southern faction declares independence, May 7; northern forces capture Aden, July 7.

Chechnya, December 1, 1994–. Russian troops invade breakaway republic of Chechnya, December 1, 1994; Russian troops push into Grozny, capital of Chechen region, December 30; Chechen defenders push back Russian forces, January 2, 1995; presidential palace in Grozny falls to Russian army, January 19; Russian forces launch offensive east of Grozny March 21, capture Gudermes March 30, Shali March 31; Chechen forces attack Russian town of Budyonnovsk, June 14; truce signed, July 30; week of fighting at Gudermes leaves more than a hundred civilians dead, December 23.

SOURCES

Boardman, John, *et al.*, eds. *The Cambridge Ancient History*. 2nd ed. Vol. III, Pt. I. Cambridge, Eng.: Cambridge University Press, 1982.

Boatner, Mark M., III. *The Civil War Dictionary*. New York: David McKay Co., 1959.

Bury, J. D. *A History of Greece*. New York: Modern Library, n.d.

Chandler, David. *Dictionary of Battles*. New York: Henry Holt and Co., 1987.

Dupuy, R. Ernest, and Trevor Dupuy. *An Encyclopedia of Military History*. New York: Harper and Row, 1970.

Eggenberger, David. *A Dictionary of Battles*. New York: T. Y. Crowell, 1967.

Eisenhower, John S. D. *Allies: Pearl Harbor to D-Day*. Garden City, N.Y.: Doubleday and Co., 1982.

———. *So Far from God: The U.S. War with Mexico, 1846–1848*. New York: Doubleday and Co., 1989.

Encyclopaedia Britannica. 14th ed. Chicago: Encyclopaedia Britannica Co., Inc., 1957.

Falls, Cyril. *The Great War*. New York: G. P. Putnam's Sons, 1959.

Hall, Walter Phelps, and Robert Greenhalgh Albion, with Jennie Barnes Pope. *A History of England and the British Empire.* Boston: Ginn and Co., 1937.

Harris, William H., and Judith S. Levey, eds. *The New Columbia Encyclopedia.* 4th ed. New York: Columbia University Press, 1975.

Hiro, Dilap. *The Longest War: The Iran-Iraq Military Conflict.* London: Grafton Books, 1989.

Hough, Richard. *The Great War at Sea, 1914–1918.* Oxford: Oxford University Press, 1986.

Kinder, Hermann, and Werner Hilgemann. *Anchor Atlas of World History.* Translated by Ernest A. Menze. 2 vols. New York: Anchor Books, 1978.

Langer, William L., comp. and ed. *An Encyclopedia of World History.* 5th ed. Boston: Houghton Mifflin Co., 1972.

Leckie, Robert. *Conflict: The History of the Korean War, 1950–1953.* New York: G. P. Putnam's Sons, 1962.

McEntee, Girard Lindsley. *Military History of the World War.* New York: Charles Scribner's Sons, 1937.

Markov, Walter, and Heinz Helmert. *Battles of World History.* Leipzig, Germany: Edition Leipsig, 1978.

Marshall, S. L. A. *World War I.* New York: American Heritage Press, 1985.

Morgan, Kenneth O. *The People's Peace: British History, 1945–1989.* Oxford: Oxford University Press, 1990.

Morris, Richard B., ed. *Encyclopedia of American History.* 6th ed. New York: Harper and Row, 1982.

Paschall, Rod. *The Defeat of Imperial Germany, 1917–1918.* Chapel Hill: Algonquin Books of Chapel Hill, 1989.

Robinson, Cyril E. *Apollo History of Rome.* New York: T. Y. Crowell, 1965.

Rostovtzeff. M. *A History of the Ancient World: Vol. I, The Orient and Greece.* Translated by J. D. Duff. Westport, Conn.: Greenwood Press, 1971.

Sachar, Howard M. *A History of Israel, from the Rise of Zionism to Our Own Time.* New York: Alfred A. Knopf, 1976.

Sanderson, Michael. *Sea Battles: A Reference Guide.* London: David & Charles, 1975.

Spector, Ronald H. *Eagle Against the Sun: The American War with Japan.* New York: Vintage Books, 1885.

Starr, Chester G. *A History of the Ancient World.* New York: Oxford University Press, 1965.

Tindall, George Brown. *America: A Narrative History.* New York: W. W. Norton, 1984.

Trager, James, ed. *The People's Chronology: A Year-by-Year Record of Human Events from Prehistory to the Present.* New York: Holt, Rinehart and Winston, 1979.

Trotter, William R. *A Frozen Hell: The Russo-Finnish War of 1939–1940.* Chapel Hill: Algonquin Books of Chapel Hill, 1991.

Urban, Mark. *War in Afghanistan.* 2nd ed. New York: St. Martin's Press, 1990.

Weinberg, Gerhard L. *A World at Arms: A Global History of World War II.* Cambridge, Eng.: Cambridge University Press, 1994.

Wood, W. J. *Battles of the Revolutionary War, 1775–1781.* Chapel Hill: Algonquin Books of Chapel Hill, 1990.

Young, Brigadier Peter, ed. *The Almanac of World War II.* London: Bison Books, 1981.

—L.D.R.

FIREARMS OF HISTORY: A GLOSSARY OF TERMS AND MODELS

· · · · ·

IT WILL BE REMEMBERED THAT WHEN JAMES THURBER'S WALTER MITTY, waiting in the car for his wife to be finished at the hairdresser's, imagines himself preparing to take a bomber alone over the enemy lines during World War I, one of the things that he has himself do is to strap on "his huge Webley-Vickers automatic." That there was in actuality no such weapon of precisely that name (see **Webley revolver**, below) is part of the joke; it sounds so impressive.

Since guns and pistols, however, of necessity figure prominently in much writing, for purposes of technical authenticity it is usually advisable to get them right. What would we have thought of Ernest Hemingway if he had gotten Francis Macomber's 6.5 Mannlicher and .30-06 Springfield and the hunter Wilson's big .505 confused in "The Short Happy Life of Francis Macomber"?

The earliest reference to gunfire in English literature occurs in Geoffrey Chaucer's poem "The House of Fame" (*ca.* 1369) as a term of comparison for a rumor that spreads "As swifte as pellet out of gunne/When fire is in the powdre runne." Since then, firearms have figured in literature at least as prominently as in life, developing a vast and often arcane terminology.

The following glossary deals with many of those terms and also records a number of the more representative of the vast array of guns that have affected human society—for good and ill alike—over the years.

Action. Mechanism by which a gun is loaded, fired, and unloaded.
AK-47. Most widely dispersed of the assault rifles commonly in military use, and until 1994 increasingly available to civilians in the United States. Others include the AKM, AK-74, and RPK-74. The AK-47 comes with a 30-

round "banana" clip. The RPK-74 can be equipped with a 75-round drum magazine, and theoretically can be fired either automatically (at up to 600 rounds per minute, though more than 80 rounds per minute causes the gun barrel to overheat) or semiautomatically. Its 7.62 mm bullet is effective at ranges up to 300 yards. It is or has been manufactured in the former Soviet Union, China, Bulgaria, former East Germany, Hungary, North Korea, Poland, Romania, and former Yugoslavia.

AR-15. See **Assault rifle**.

Arisaka. Bolt-action rifle of the Japanese army from 1906 to 1945. The 6.5 mm ammo was increased to 7.7 in a 1939 version. Many entered civilian life as trophies when servicemen returned from World War II, and some are still in use as hunting and target arms.

Arquebus or harquebus. Early military arm, usually of matchlock or wheel-lock design, common in France, Germany, and Austria in the sixteenth and early seventeenth centuries. Most were muskets, but a few were produced with rifled barrels. Heavy of barrel, they were usually equipped with folding bipod rests.

Assault rifle. Light, rapid-fire, small-caliber military rifle such as the AK-47, AR-15, or M-16, used currently in most modern armies. Assault rifles typically possess capability for both automatic and semiautomatic fire, although laws require a blocking of the automatic function for civilian possession. See **AK-47**.

Autoloader. See **Semiautomatic**.

Automatic. (1) Firearm such as the "tommy gun" or unaltered AK-47 that continues to fire, eject, and load successive cartridges as long as the trigger is depressed. The term is often (perhaps usually) employed erroneously for semiautomatic weapons. Theoretically the average hand-held automatic can fire 600–700 rounds per minute with a single pull of the trigger, though at more than 100 rounds a minute the barrel would overheat; (2) popularly, a semiautomatic pistol with the magazine clip within the handle, as distinguished from a revolver with cylindrical magazine.

Ball. (1) Round lead projectile, forerunner of the bullet, used in muzzle-loading firearms; (2) jacketed military ammunition.

Ballard. Breech-loading American rifle developed and produced by C. H. Ballard for some thirty years after 1861.

Bar pistol. Handgun designed, for maximum concealability, as a flat rectangular metal bar containing two chambers and barrel channels, briefly popular in the first decade of the twentieth century.

Belly gun. Slang term for a firearm concealable in belt or waistband.

Beretta automatic pistol. Semiautomatic pistol available in a variety of calibers, including .22, .25, .32, and 9 mm from the 1920s to date. The 9 mm model was the official Italian military sidearm from 1934 to 1955.

Big bore. In the United States, a term for cartridges of .30 or larger; in Great Britain, for .450 or larger.

Birdshot. Small shotgun pellets (sizes 9 through 2 are the most common) for small game, as opposed to the larger pellets of buckshot.

Black powder. High-residue, relatively slow-burning gunpowder used in muzzle-loaders and other guns up to the end of the nineteenth century and still employed by hobbyists and antique-weapons enthusiasts for sporting purposes. For most uses, black powder has been replaced by smokeless powder since about 1884, although the U.S. Army was still using it during the Spanish-American War.

Blunderbuss. Smoothbore muzzle-loader with a bell- or trumpet-shaped muzzle, in use from the early seventeenth to the early nineteenth centuries and designed to fire a scattering of variously sized and composed missiles at close range.

Bolt action. Firearm action, commonly of rifles but also of a few shotgun models, operated by lifting, pulling back, and pushing forward the handle of a bolt that ejects a spent shell and loads a new one into the breech. The first successful bolt action was designed in Germany in 1837.

Boot pistol. Small handgun, usually of Deringer type, concealable in a boot, usually by means of a clip holster.

Bore. Interior of a gun barrel.

Bottleneck cartridge. Cartridge whose case tapers to a smaller diameter at the neck where the bullet is fitted, as with the .30-06 and most other modern high-powered rifle cartridges, so that a larger amount of powder may be loaded without increasing the size of the bullet.

"Boy Scout Rifle." Remington .22 caliber single-shot military model rifle made from 1913 to *ca.* 1923 and designated the official rifle of the Boy Scouts of America.

Breech. End of the barrel which receives the cartridge.

Breech-loader. Firearm with any one of the many actions in which the cartridge is loaded directly into the breech. *Cf.* **Muzzle-loader.**

Brown Bess. Flintlock muzzle-loading musket used by the British military from 1690 through the period of the American Revolution, so called because of the brown hue of its iron barrel.

Browning Automatic-5. Five-shot recoil-operated semiautomatic shotgun available in a wide range of models and in 12, 16, and 20 gauges from the 1900s to date. The Browning Automatic is a somewhat refined version of the Remington Model 11 (1905–49); both weapons are on a model designed by John Browning.

Browning Automatic .22. Semiautomatic rifle with 11-shot capacity made in Belgium and introduced to the United States in 1956; currently in production.

Browning automatic pistol. Semiautomatic pistol in .25, .380, and 9 mm models made from 1954 to date.

Browning Superposed. Over/under shotgun in a variety of models, formerly produced for Browning in Belgium and currently produced in Japan; available in 12, 20, 28, and .410 gauge and in several grades of ornate engraving.

Buckshot. Pellets, larger than birdshot, loaded in shotgun shells for larger game such as deer, boar, and black bear. Common sizes are designated, from largest to smallest, oo, o, 1, 2, 3, and 4.

Buffalo gun. Common term for the Sharps and Spencer rifles, used extensively after 1848 for buffalo hunting in the American West. The Sharps came in .45 and .52 caliber, the larger popularly known as the "Big Fifty." Both calibers were highly accurate at the long ranges that such hunting required. The early Sharps models employed paper cartridges, the later, metal. The Spencer was a .52 caliber repeater in carbine length, lighter and thus more punishing in its recoil. Prolonged shooting destroyed the hearing of most of the commercial buffalo hunters, who came to regard deafness as an occupational inevitability.

Bulldog revolver. Term applied to a variety of snub-nosed, large-caliber (usually .44) revolvers, most of them having rounded handle grips and 2- or 3-inch barrels to facilitate pocket concealment.

Bullet. Ballistic projectile of elongated shape, as opposed to a ball.

Buntline Special. Extremely long-barreled (*ca.* 18–19 inches) revolver, usually a version of the .45 Colt Single Action, manufactured in the late nineteenth century after a design by Ned Buntline (pseudonym of Edward Z. C. Judson), a writer of Western adventure novels.

Burp gun. World War II slang term for submachine gun.

Butt. Bottom end of stock of revolver; rear end of rifle stock.

Caliber. Diameter of a ballistic projectile, and also the designation of the weapon sized to accommodate it. Because caliber terms have developed historically and internationally, they exhibit a sometimes puzzling inconsistency, several systems being in use simultaneously. British and American designations usually specify decimal fractions of an inch: thus .30 caliber in American usage denotes a bullet diameter of .3000 (in British writing, given as .300). Continental designations are usually in millimeters: 7 mm, 9 mm, etc. So the same bullet may be 7.62 mm in one system and .308 caliber in another. But equivalences are not always absolute; .38 caliber, for example, is actually .357, while the term .22 *caliber* encompasses variations from .214 to .223. Cartridge designations derive from so many systems that some can be explicated only in terms of individual examples. The 7 x 57 Mauser, for instance, reflects the logical German system of describing both bullet diameter and cartridge length: it is a 7 mm bullet in a case 57 mm long. But the American

.30-06 applies to the bullet-cartridge combination developed for the .30 caliber bullet in [19]06, while .30-30 tells us that we have a .30 caliber bullet with the equivalent in smokeless powder of 30 grains of the older black powder propellant for which the combination was first devised.

Cane gun. Walking stick that conceals a barrel from which a bullet can be fired, usually by pressing a trigger on the handle; formerly made in England, France, and Belgium and in use around the turn of this century.

Carbine. Shortened and lighter version of a rifle, usually with a barrel length of less than 22 inches, intended for easy portability in battle or on horseback.

Cartridge. Complete unit of a round of ammunition, consisting of bullet, powder, case, and primer.

Center-fire. Cartridge such as most modern rifle and handgun ammunition employs, in which the primer is housed in the center of the cartridge base and struck by a firing pin for ignition of the powder within. See, by contrast, Rimfire.

Charles Daly shotguns. Line of side-by-side and over/under double-barreled shotguns made in Germany and Belgium and imported by Charles Daly, Inc., from the early 1930s to date.

Choke. Degree of constriction at the muzzle of a shotgun barrel, designed to compress the load of shot as it exits in order to produce a desirable pattern at the target. American choke designations are: cylinder bore (no constriction); improved cylinder (constriction of $^{19}/_{1000}$ inch); modified ($^{20}/_{1000}$ inch); improved modified ($^{30}/_{1000}$ inch); full choke ($^{40}/_{1000}$ inch). British terms for the same are, respectively, cylinder; quarter choke; half choke; three-quarter choke; full choke.

Clip. Mechanical device, usually a spring-loaded elongated metal box, that holds a number of cartridges and feeds them into the magazine as the firearm is operated.

Coffee-mill carbine. Sharps carbine with a small coffee grinder built into its butt stock, issued in small numbers to Union troops during the Civil War.

Colt automatic .45. Common, though inaccurate, term for the 1911 model Colt Military or Government .45 caliber semiautomatic pistol, the standard sidearm of the U.S. military from 1911 forward; perhaps the most famous and easily recognized modern handgun. It is sometimes designated the .45 ACP (for "automatic Colt pistol").

Colt Detective Special. Pocket double-action .38 Special revolver with 2-inch barrel, made from 1926 to date.

Colt double-action army revolver. Handgun made from 1877 to 1905 in a variety of calibers including .38-40, .44-40, and .45.

Colt Lightning rifle. Bolt-action repeating arm with a 26-inch barrel, made 1885–1900 in calibers .32-20, .38-40, and .44-40.

Colt navy revolver. Large, heavy revolver of .36 caliber, first manufactured in the 1850s and used extensively in the Civil War by ground as well as naval forces.

Colt Official Police. Double-action revolver made from 1928 to date in several calibers but most commonly occurring in .38 Special.

Colt Python. Double-action revolver of .357 magnum caliber, a favorite of sheriff's departments and highway patrol forces, available in 4- or 6-inch barrel lengths from 1954 to date.

Colt .45 single-action army revolver. See **Peacemaker**.

Colt Woodsman. Ten-shot, .22 caliber semiautomatic pistol with 6 ½-inch barrel, first produced as a target pistol in 1915 and sold as the "Woodsman" after 1927. [This was Ernest Hemingway's favorite knockabout or plinking pistol.]

Creedmore match rifle. Highly accurate version of the Sharps single-shot buffalo rifle used in international shooting competition in the late nineteenth century.

Culverin. Hand-cannon of the fifteenth century that required two men to fire a ball of *ca.* .80 caliber.

Cylinder. Rotating component of a revolver that holds the cartridges and presents them in succession for chambering as it rotates.

Deringer or derringer. Type of small, concealable pistol designed by Henry Deringer of Philadephia in 1825 and produced by numerous makers, including, in recent times, Colt, Remington, and Marlin. Various calibers have been employed by Deringers, including .22 and .30, but the most common is .41 Rimfire. Barrel length is usually *ca.* 3 inches in single- or double-barrel (over/under) versions. The Deringer was the typical self-protection weapon of travelers, gamblers, businessmen, and other citizens in the late nineteenth century; because of its small size and very short range it was seldom the choice of those engaged in aggressive criminality, although two U.S. presidents, Lincoln and McKinley, were assassinated with Deringer-type pistols.

Double action. Revolver action in which a single pull of the trigger rotates the cylinder and cocks and fires the weapon. The hammer does not have to be pulled back manually in a separate operation, as it does with a single-action handgun.

Double-barreled rifle. Large-caliber rifle with side-by-side barrels used chiefly by the British for dangerous African and Indian game such as lion, tiger, and buffalo, preferred for such duty because of its reliability and the speed with which two shots can be fired as compared to any of the single-barrel breechloaders.

Double-barreled shotgun. Shotgun having two parallel barrels, mounted either side by side or superposed ("over/under"). The double-barrel antedates all the repeating single-barrels and accounts for almost all examples before *ca.*

1895, including both muzzle- and breech-loading guns. In the first half of the twentieth century the most popular side-by-side doubles were made by Greener, Fox, Parker, L. C. Smith, Ithaca, and Winchester. Today the custom-made Winchester 21 is the only side-by-side double manufactured in the United States, though there are several European producers, especially in Spain, Italy, and England. The superposed or over/under remains very popular, especially for skeet and trap shooting, and is produced by Browning, Winchester, Ithaca, and Remington as well as by a number of foreign firms.

Drilling. Three-barrel arm consisting of side-by-side shotgun barrels, usually 16 gauge, with a single rifle barrel below. Most examples are of German, Belgian, and French pre-World War II manufacture. Many were brought into the United States by servicemen returning from the Second World War.

Dueling pistols. Matched pairs of single-shot flintlock or percussion pistols, introduced for gentlemanly dueling in late-eighteenth-century Europe and America.

Dum-dum. Soft-nosed bullet designed to expand or break up after entering its target, so called because of the British-operated arsenal at Dum Dum, India, where it was first introduced in the .303 Enfield cartridge around 1895.

Elephant gun. Any large-caliber rifle capable of stopping an elephant or rhinocerous, typically employing such heavy ammunition as the .458 Winchester Magnum, the .460 Weatherby Magnum, and the .600 Nitro Express. Only double-barreled and bolt-action rifles are sturdy enough to accommodate such loads. Winchester makes an "African" version of the bolt-action Model 70 chambered for the .458.

Elgin cutlass pistol. Combination breech-loading single-shot pistol and heavy knife (the blade mounted below and parallel to the barrel) made for several years after 1837.

Enfield revolver. Six-shot .38 caliber revolver carried as the official British army sidearm from 1932 to 1957.

Enfield rifle. Any of a number of military rifles produced by the Royal Enfield firm of England from 1853 forward, including the .303 bolt-action Lee-Enfield standard in the two world wars. During World War I, because of the shortage of Springfield rifles, Enfield rifles were manufactured in the United States for use by the U.S. Army.

Flintlock. Firearms ignition system, invented *ca.* 1615, that involves firing the gunpowder with sparks from a flint struck by a falling hammer at the breech. The flintlock mechanism was the system of widest use from its inception to *ca.* 1815 and powered such venerable weapons as the British Brown Bess musket and the Kentucky or Pennsylvania rifles of the American Revolution.

Fowling piece. Old term for a shotgun, considered primarily as a weapon for bird hunting.

Fox Sterlingworth. Double-barreled side-by-side shotgun popular in the 1920s, 1930s, and early 1940s in 12-, 16-, and 20-gauge models. Plain and deluxe models were offered up to the line's discontinuance in 1942. Many are still in use, especially among nostalgic southern quail hunters.

Garand. U.S. military semiautomatic .30 caliber M-1 rifle, designed by John Garand and adopted as the official U.S. Army rifle in 1936. World War II and the Korean conflict were fought with this arm and its diminutive, the .30 caliber carbine.

Gas-operated actions. Actions of some semiautomatic firearms, such as the M–1 Garand rifle and the Remington 1100 shotgun, which harness escaping gas from the fired cartridge to power the autoloading and cocking mechanism for the next shot.

Gauge. Diameter of a shotgun bore, after an archaic system of measurement denoting the number of lead balls of its diameter required to weigh one pound. Thus, a 12-gauge shotgun is one that has a bore the diameter of that of a lead ball weighing ¹⁄₁₂ pound, and so on through 16, 20, and 28 gauges (the modern survivors of what was once a large number of sizes) to the .410, an exception because it is a caliber instead of a gauge. Gauges larger than 10 are outlawed for hunting in the United States today (see **Punt gun**), though the huge 4, 6, and 8 gauges were once used for commercial shooting of waterfowl.

Grease gun. Nickname for the stubby U.S. submachine guns M3 and M3A1 of World War II and the Korean conflict.

Hall rifle. Flintlock (later percussion) rifle of .54 caliber developed in 1811 by John H. Hall and used to some extent against the Seminole Indians in Florida and in the Mexican War of 1846–48.

Handgun. Pistol or revolver capable of being carried and operated with one hand.

Harpers Ferry flint pistol. Flintlock handgun with 10 ½-inch barrel made at the Harpers Ferry Arsenal for several years after 1806, with design improvements in 1807 and 1808.

Harpers Ferry rifle. Model 1803 U.S. Flintlock Rifle produced at the Harpers Ferry Arsenal 1804–1807 and later, in a percussion version, 1846–*ca*. 1855.

Harquebus. See **Arquebus**.

Harrington & Richardson Topper. Inexpensive single-barrel shotgun, modified in 1948 from patterns going back to 1908; perennially popular with young hunters and as an all-purpose farm gun; made, to date, in 12, 16, 20, and .410 gauges.

Henry rifle. Lever-action .44 caliber rifle used in limited quantities in the Civil War and adapted by Winchester as the basis for models 1866 and 1873. The Henry held 16 cartridges in a tubular magazine.

Hog-leg. Slang term for any large, long-barreled revolver such as the Colt navy revolver or the Buntline Special.

Holland & Holland double rifle. Heavy-caliber double-barreled rifle for use in Africa and India, manufactured by the London firm since colonial days in several magnum calibers including .300, .375, and .465.

Horse pistol. Large heavy handgun of any make, such as those carried by cavalry troops at various times; capable of being used as a club at close quarters.

Ithaca Model 37 Featherlight. Lightweight pump-action shotgun made since 1937 in 12-, 16-, and 20-gauge models with a variety of barrel-length options.

Iver Johnson Champion. One of numerous brands of inexpensive single-shot shotguns (see **Harrington & Richardson Topper**); made since 1909 in 12, 16, 20, and .410 gauge.

Kentucky rifle. Long-barreled, muzzle-loading flintlock rifle made in several calibers (especially .32, .36, and .50), usually with octagonal iron barrel and short, sharply angled buttstock. This accurate rifle was developed in the late eighteenth century from German models and was the main American rifle of the early frontier and of the American Revolution. Also known as the Pennsylvania rifle and the long rifle, it was made by numerous talented gunsmiths, such as A. Gumpf, T. Grubb, N. Boyer, C. Birll, and Henry Deringer. Some remained in use up to and during the Civil War.

Krag-Jorgensen. 8 mm bolt-action military rifle, standard arm of the Danish army from 1889 to 1945. In its American adaptation of 1892 it was produced in .30 caliber and used in the Spanish-American War.

Lahti. 8-shot semiautomatic pistol of the Finnish and Danish armies after 1935.

Large bore. See **Big bore**.

L. C. Smith shotguns. Series of side-by-side double-barreled shotguns made in 12, 16, 20, and .410 gauges and a variety of grades from the 1920s to 1951.

Lebel rifle. 8 mm rifle used by French army from 1886 through World War II.

Lever action. Action used in several rifles and a few shotguns, in which a lever beneath the grip opens the breech, extracts a spent shell, and chambers a new cartridge, usually from a tubular magazine under the barrel. This is the "cavalry rifle" of the American West, still popular today as the Winchester 94 (.30-30 and .32) and the Marlin 336 (.30-30, .35, and .44 Magnum).

Llama automatic pistol. Semiautomatic handgun in .380 and 9 mm, manufactured in Spain.

Lock. Firing mechanism of a muzzle-loading firearm, whose essential components are memorialized in the phrase "lock, stock, and barrel." In a breech-loading arm the lock is usually integral with the sealing assembly. See **Flintlock; Matchlock; Wheel-lock**.

Luger. German 9 mm semiautomatic pistol utilizing the toggle lock system invented by the American Hugo Borchardt, produced for many years after 1900 and carried as the official German sidearm in World War I and early World War II before being supplanted by the Walther P-38.

M-1. See **Garand**.

M-1 carbine. Light, .30 caliber semiautomatic American carbine used in World War II and the Korean conflict.

M-16. Military rifle of U.S. forces in Vietnam and thereafter, a .223 caliber (5.56 mm) gas-operated repeater capable of either fully automatic or semiautomatic operation with a 20- or 30-round ammunition clip in standard issue.

Magnum. Cartridge of power and velocity greater than usual for its caliber; also, a firearm made to shoot magnum ammunition. There are magnum versions of several calibers, including .22, .38 (.357), 7 mm, .300, .41, and .44, achieved by increasing the size and powder capacity of the cases, and also magnum versions of shotgun loads in 10, 12, and 20 gauge.

Mannlicher-Carcano. Six-shot 6.5 mm bolt-action rifle used by the Italian armed forces from 1891 to 1945. This was the weapon used by Lee Harvey Oswald to kill President John F. Kennedy.

Marlin Model 336. Lever-action carbine made in .30-30, .35, and .44 magnum chamberings from 1950 to date. Earlier versions of the Marlin carbine date from 1891; the 39A is the oldest shoulder gun still being manufactured.

Martini-Henry. .45 rifle of the British army from 1871 to 1891, later adapted to .303 for use by the Home Guard in World War II.

Matchlock. Ancient (*ca.* 1411) firearms ignition system in which a slow-burning match or fuse was used to fire priming powder at the breech.

Mauser rifle. Term applied generically to a variety of bolt-action rifles modeled on the German military arm.

Minie ball. Cone-shaped bullet with a hollowed-out base that expanded upon firing and increased the bullet's ability to take on spin from the rifling in the barrel; used by both sides in the Civil War.

Mule-eared gun. Slang expression for a firearm with exposed side hammers.

Musket. Any of the smoothbore muzzle-loading firearms in use from early times to the late nineteenth century, designed to shoot a single lead ball. Lacking the grooved bore of a rifle, it was much less accurate; but its advantage for military purposes was that, not having the resistance such grooves presented to each new ball as it was loaded from the muzzle, it could be reloaded more quickly than a rifle under battle conditions, in which the rifle's advantage in accuracy was often negated anyway by necessary haste. There were also rifled muskets.

Muzzle-loader. Any firearm loaded by tamping the powder, projectile, and retaining patches down the barrel with a ramrod, as opposed to the various actions that load directly into the breech.

Nambu. 8 mm semiautomatic pistol, used by the Japanese military from 1914 to 1945.

Needlegun. Bolt-action, breech-loading rifle using paper cartridges invented by J. N. von Dreyse in 1829; the rifle designed by A. A. Chassepot and adopted as the official French army rifle in 1866 was based on it but used metallic cartridges.

Peacemaker. Colt .45 single-action army revolver, first produced in 1872; the classic sidearm of the American West.

Pennsylvania rifle. See **Kentucky rifle.**

Pepperbox revolver. Small percussion-cap handgun in .31 caliber consisting of from three to six fused-together rotating barrels fired by a bar hammer, manufactured by the firms of Darling and Robbins & Lawrence in the 1840s, as well as by others.

Percussion primer or cap. Small metal cap containing a priming mixture which, when struck by a hammer, ignites the main charge and fires the weapon. Firearms with this ignition mechanism were in wide use for several decades after 1816.

Pistol. Handgun of fixed or semiautomatic action, as opposed to a revolver.

Pistols and revolvers before 1900. See **Bar pistol; Buntline Special; Colt navy revolver; Colt .45 single-action army revolver; Deringer; Dueling pistols; Elgin cutlass pistol; Harpers Ferry flint pistol; Pepperbox revolver; Remington Double Deringer Model 95; Remington revolvers; Springfield pistol 1818; Starr revolver; Webley revolver.**

Pistols and revolvers since 1900. See **Beretta automatic pistol; Browning automatic pistol; Colt automatic .45; Colt Detective Special; Colt double-action army revolver; Colt Official Police; Colt Python; Colt Woodsman; Enfield revolver; Lahti; Llama automatic pistol; Luger; Nambu; Ruger Blackhawk; Ruger Single Six; Smith & Wesson Chief's Special; Smith & Wesson Combat Magnum; Smith & Wesson Regulation Police; Walther automatic pistol; Walther Pocket Automatic Model 8.**

Plains rifle. Heavier, large-caliber development of the Kentucky or Pennsylvania rifle, adapted for the larger game and greater distances of the West and shortened in overall length for horseback transportation.

Primer. Detonating mechanism that ignites the propelling powder in a firearm. In older actions the primer is a mixture added to the breech; in self-contained cartridges it is incorporated into the base of the shell. See **Center-fire; Rimfire.**

Pump action. Shotgun action also used in some rifles, in which the weapon is operated by a sliding forearm that opens and closes the breech, ejecting the spent shell and chambering a new one; also known as slide action and trombone action. Popular twentieth-century pump-action shotguns are the Winchester Model 12 (since 1912), Ithaca Model 37 (since 1937), and Remington 870 (since 1950). Rifles with pump actions are usually .22 or .30–30 caliber, but the Remington "Gamemaster" is made in several more powerful calibers.

Pump gun. Pump-action shotgun or rifle.

Punt gun. Very large shotgun of 4 to 8 gauge, usually mounted on the bow of a small boat, or punt, for waterfowling in the days of market shooting; illegal since the Migratory Bird Treaty of 1918.

Recoil operation. Process by which some semiautomatic weapons such as the Browning Automatic-5 and Remington Models 11 and 11-48 shotguns are operated, using the energy of the recoil to activate ejection, cocking, and chambering of the next round.

Remington Double Deringer Model 95. Single-action, .41 Rimfire deringer with superposed 3-inch double barrels, made from 1866 to 1935.

Remington "Gamemaster" Model 760A. Pump-action rifle in .257 Roberts, .270 Winchester, .30-06, .300 Savage, and .35 Remington calibers, made from 1952 to date.

Remington Model 11. 5-shot semiautomatic shotgun designed by John Browning and very similar to the modern Browning Automatic–5; made by Remington from 1911 to 1949.

Remington Model 11-48. Recoil-operated semiautomatic shotgun, made in 5-shot and 3-shot versions between 1948 and 1958.

Remington Model 1100. Gas-operated semiautomatic shotgun made in all gauges from 1963 to date; successor to the recoil-operated Models 11 and 11-48.

Remington revolvers. Small revolvers first made by Remington in 1856 and popular for several decades in .31, .36, and .44 calibers.

Remington "Wingmaster" Model 870. Pump-action shotgun made in all gauges from 1950 to date.

Remington "Woodsmaster" Model 740A. Gas-operated semiautomatic rifle in .270, .30–06, and .308, made from 1955 to date.

Revolver. Repeating handgun, patented by Samuel Colt in 1835, that uses a rotating cylinder with a series of firing chambers (usually six; thus "six-shooter"). In a single-action revolver, cocking by pulling back the hammer for each shot rotates the cylinder and aligns the chambers successively with the barrel for firing. In a double-action revolver, the cocking and rotation are both accomplished simply by pulling the trigger. *Cf.* **Pistol**.

Rifle. Long-barreled shoulder arm whose bore contains a series of spiraling grooves designed to impart a stabilizing spin on the bullet or ball to improve accuracy and increase range. All modern rifles and pistols have such "rifled" barrels. See, for contrast, **Musket**.

Rifles, muskets, and shotguns before 1900. See **Arquebus; Ballard; Blunderbuss; Brown Bess; Buffalo gun; Colt Lightning rifle; Coffee-mill carbine; Creedmore match rifle; Culverin; Enfield rifle; Fowling piece; Hall rifle; Harpers Ferry rifle; Henry rifle; Kentucky rifle; Krag-Jorgensen; Lebel rifle; Martini-Henry; Musket; Needlegun; Pennsylvania rifle; Plains rifle; Ross rifle; Spencer rifle; Springfield musket 1795; Stagecoach gun; Trapdoor Springfield; Winchester Model 73; Winchester Model 94 lever-action rifle.**

Rifles since 1900. See AK-47; AR-15; Arisaka; Assault rifle; "Boy Scout Rifle"; Browning Automatic .22; Burp gun; Elephant gun; Garand; Grease gun; Holland & Holland double rifle; M-1 carbine; M–16; Mannlicher-Carcano; Marlin Model 336; Mauser rifle; Remington "Gamemaster" Model 760A; Remington "Woodsmaster" Model 740A; Savage utility gun; Springfield rifle 1903; Tommy gun; Weatherby Magnum rifles; Winchester Model 70.

Rimfire. Cartridge fired by the firing pin striking the rim of the case, inside which the priming mixture is housed, as opposed to a center-fire cartridge with the primer centered in the base. The most common rimfire cartridge today is the .22, though others exist from older periods, such as the .41 Rimfire used in many deringers in the nineteenth century.

Riot gun. Short-barreled shotgun, usually of pump-action design, used for guard duty and riot control. Most current makers of pump-action shotguns produce a riot gun model.

Rolling block action. Very strong single-shot action found in some pistols and rifles of the late nineteenth century, in which the breech block moves backward to expose the chamber when the firearm is cocked, allowing for manual insertion of a cartridge, which is thereafter locked in place. The Remington rolling block rifle of 1865 was highly successful as a military and target arm.

Ross rifle. 5-shot, straight-pull bolt-action .303 rifle produced in Canada from *ca.* 1890 to 1917.

Round. Single cartridge or shot shell; used in plural.

Ruger Blackhawk. Heavy-frame, single-action frontier-style revolver available in .357 and .44 magnum calibers from 1955 to date.

Ruger Single Six. Single-action .22 revolver with barrel of 4 ⅝ to 9 ½ inches, made from 1951 to date.

Saturday Night Special. Slang term for any cheap, concealable pistol or revolver, usually of the smaller calibers such as .22, .25, or .32.

Savage utility gun. Single-shot .30-30 rifle with interchangeable 12-gauge shotgun barrel, made from 1938 to 1949.

Scope. Shortened term for a telescopic sight on a rifle or, occasionally, pistol.

Semiautomatic. Firearm that is self-loading, *i.e.*, chambers a new round automatically after each shot, but requires a separate trigger pull for each shot fired, as opposed to a fully automatic weapon (illegal for civilian possession) which continues to fire as long as the trigger is held back. Pistols, shotguns, and rifles are all made in semiautomatic versions.

Service pistol. See **Colt automatic .45.**

Sharps rifle. See **Buffalo gun.**

Shell. Commonly, a shotgun cartridge, but sometimes used loosely for pistol and rifle ammunition as well.

Shotgun. Smoothbore firearm designed to fire a charge of multiple pellets as opposed to the single projectile of a rifle; also known as scattergun. The pellets range in size from the smallest birdshot to the largest buckshot. Shotguns come in a variety of styles and actions: single-shot, double-barreled (side-by-side or over/under), pump action, bolt action, and semiautomatic.

Shotguns before 1900. See **Rifles, muskets,** and **shotguns before 1900.**

Shotguns since 1900. See **Browning Automatic-5; Browning Superposed; Charles Daly shotguns; Fox Sterlingworth; Harrington & Richardson Topper; Ithaca Model 37 Featherlight; Iver Johnson Champion; L. C. Smith shotguns; Punt gun; Remington Model 11; Remington Model 11-48; Remington "Wingmaster" Model 870; Winchester Model 12; Winchester Model 21.**

Single-action. See **Revolver.**

Six-gun or six-shooter. Term for a revolver, especially the Colt .45, popular in the American West.

Skeet gun. Shotgun designed for the sport of skeet shooting, *i.e.*, shooting at clay targets thrown by hand or springloaded device. Most skeet guns are pump-action, semiautomatic, or over/under double-barreled shotguns in 12, 20, 28, or .410 gauge, with open chokes intended to throw wide patterns of shot at the swiftly moving targets ("clay pigeons").

Smith & Wesson Chief's Special. Light (especially in the "airweight" model), snub-nosed double-action revolver with 2- and 3-inch barrel options, made from 1952 to date.

Smith & Wesson Combat Magnum. Large-frame double-action revolver in magnum calibers of .357, .41, and .45, manufactured from 1956 to date with available barrel lengths of 4 ½ and 6 inches.

Smith & Wesson Regulation Police. Double-action revolver made in .32 and .38 calibers from 1917 to date; widely used by police and constabulary officers.

Smokeless powder. Modern, fast-burning gunpowder introduced in 1884 to replace black powder as a firearms propellant. Smokeless powder is cleaner and faster burning, and more powerful in less volume than its predecessor.

Smokepole. Slang usage for shotgun or rifle.

Smoothbore. Firearm such as a shotgun or musket whose bore does not contain rifling grooves.

Spencer rifle. Repeating .52 caliber carbine used by the U.S. cavalry 1862–73 and later by buffalo hunters in the West. See **Buffalo gun.**

Springfield musket 1795. .69 caliber musket produced at the Springfield Armory in Massachusetts and adopted as the first standard U.S. military weapon, made by several contractors up to 1830, among them Eli Whitney, who developed the principle of the assembly line in order to produce them in volume.

Springfield pistol 1818. Large flintlock military pistol whose size and bludgeoning capability made it popular as a cavalry arm and naval boarding weapon.

Springfield rifle 1903. Bolt-action .30 caliber rifle produced for the U.S. armed services in 1903, employing a cartridge that evolved into the .30–06 three years later.

Stagecoach gun. Sawed-off 12-gauge shotgun used by stagecoach guards in nineteenth-century Europe and America. "Riding shotgun" referred to sitting next to the driver with such a weapon to thwart robbery.

Starr revolver. Handgun produced by E. T. Starr and sold for many years after 1856.

Stock. Part of gun that holds the barreled action and allows shooter to hold and aim the gun; wooden, plastic, metal.

Tommy gun. Common name for the .45 caliber Thompson submachine gun designed for military use in 1921 but quickly finding its way into the civilian criminal subculture, where it became the weapon of choice in the prohibition-days gang wars. Its distinctive visual feature, familiar to everyone from gangster movies, is its round box or drum magazine from which bullets feed into the chamber to fire up to 700 rounds per minute.

Trade guns. Flintlock muskets and rifles made cheaply for trade with Native Americans and Africans by European traders in the seventeenth and eighteenth centuries.

Trapdoor Springfield. .45 caliber rifle, also made in carbine length, used by Union troops in the Civil War. It was first chambered for paper cartridges and later adapted for the metal-cased .45-70 round.

Trap gun. Shotgun designed for the sport of trap shooting, *i.e.*, shooting at clay targets at longer ranges than those in the sport of skeet shooting. The typical trap gun has a long barrel and tight choke.

Varmint rifle. Highly accurate type of rifle designed for shooting light, high-velocity bullets at small targets such as prairie dogs, groundhogs, and foxes. Almost always in bolt action and employing telescopic sights, the varmint rifle appears mainly in calibers such as .220, .222, .223, .22-250, .243, 6 mm, .264, and light-bullet versions of the .270 and .30-06.

Ventilated rib. Narrow, flat sighting rib atop a shotgun barrel, slotted where it joins the barrel to allow air to circulate under it and avoid distorting heat waves when the barrel is hot from shooting.

Walther automatic pistol. 9 mm, 8-shot semiautomatic pistol that replaced the Luger as German army sidearm in 1938. Its production was discontinued in 1945 but resumed in 1953 and continues to date. Also known as the *P-38*.

Walther Pocket Automatic Model 8. Small-caliber (.25) semiautomatic pistol available in the United States since 1920.

Weatherby Magnum rifles. Line of currently manufactured high-quality bolt-action rifles in magnum calibers such as the .200 Rocket, .257 Weatherby Magnum, .300 Winchester Magnum, and .460 Weatherby Magnum, as well as standard calibers .270 and .30-06.

Webley revolver. British .455 double-action revolver made by the firm of Webley and Scott, used in British military and detective work from 1887 to post-

World War II. After World War I the Mark IV of .38 caliber was substituted for the .455 by the British army.

Wheel-lock. Firearms ignition system that involved a wheel striking flint to produce the spark that fired the gun. Developed about 1515, it was common in sixteenth-century warfare.

Winchester Model 12. Extremely popular 6-shot pump-action shotgun made in all gauges and several grades from 1912 to 1964, and currently in limited production (12 gauge only).

Winchester Model 21. Side-by-side double-barreled shotgun of very high quality, made in several grades in 12, 16, and 20 gauge from 1930 forward; currently produced only by custom order.

Winchester Model 70. World's most popular bolt-action high-powered rifle, made from 1936 to date in calibers from .22 Hornet to .458 Winchester Magnum.

Winchester Model 73. "Rifle that won the West," memorialized as such in, among other places, a famous movie with James Stewart in the leading role (*Winchester 73*, 1950). The 73 was a lever-action rifle with 24-inch octagonal barrel with a tubular magazine that held up to 15 cartridges, depending on caliber. It was made from 1873 to 1924 in various calibers, including .32–20, .38-40, and .44-40. This was the first rifle to use smokeless powder after its introduction in 1884.

Winchester Model 94 lever-action rifle. World's most popular lever action since 1894, once available in several calibers but currently produced only in .30-30 and .32. Also made in a carbine version.

Zip gun. Term for a crudely fashioned homemade pistol encountered in youth-gang and prison cultures, often fired by a nail driven by heavy rubber bands.

SOURCES

Abels, Robert. *Early American Firearms.* Cleveland: World Publishing Co., 1950.

Camp, Raymond R., *et al.*, eds. *The New Hunter's Encyclopedia.* 3rd. ed. New York: Galahad Books, 1972.

Mueller, Charles, and John Olson, eds. *Shooter's Bible Small Arms Lexicon and Concise Encyclopedia.* South Hackensack, N.J.: Shooter's Bible, Inc., 1968.

Pollard, Hugh B. C. *Pollard's History of Firearms.* Edited by Claude Blair. Feltham, Eng.: Country Life Books, 1983.

Sell, DeWitt E. *Collector's Guide to American Cartridge Handguns.* Harrisburg, Pa: The Stackpole Co., 1963.

Steindler, R. A. *The Firearms Dictionary.* Harrisburg, Pa.: The Stackpole Co., 1970.

Tarassuk, Leonid, and Claude Blair. *The Complete Encyclopedia of Arms and Weapons.* New York: Simon and Schuster, 1982.

Wahl, Paul. *Gun Trader's Guide.* 2nd rev. ed. Philadelphia: Chilton Co., 1957.

—J.L.M.

12

TREATIES, AGREEMENTS, AND CONCORDATS

· · · · ·

WILL ROGERS USED TO SAY THE UNITED STATES OF AMERICA HAD NEVER LOST a war and never won a peace conference. Neither contention is true anymore; we lost our war in Vietnam, while we seem to have done very well with the NATO agreement, which was not a peace treaty, to be sure, but certainly appears to have been of considerable use in helping to bring about the end of the Cold War.

Some treaties turn out to be to the advantage of the supposed disadvantaged party. For example, the Treaty of Paris between Great Britain and France in 1783 was made with the French seemingly in a strong position vis-à-vis the English, who had lost the American colonies and faced widespread war weariness at home. Yet the economic provisions resulted in a decided boost for the British, and the damage suffered by French business interests helped bring on the Revolution of 1789.

The extent to which treaties are supposed to mean very much varies. Napoleon, Hitler, and Josef Stalin, among others, were adept at negotiating treaties that they never really intended to keep. The United States negotiated agreements with Native American tribes, then went right on occupying more western land because the federal government could not control its citizens along the frontier.

What it is important to keep in mind about treaties is not so much what their provisions for the future are as that they serve to recognize and codify a then-current situation. They constitute a way for nations to agree on how things now stand; what happens to their provisions in the future will depend upon future developments. A "good" treaty is one that successfully recognizes the realities of an international situation. The Treaty of Versailles that ended World War I failed because it did not recognize the underlying realities of Germany's potential strength, despite military defeat, and sought to convert a momentary Allied ascendancy into a permanent advantage unwarranted by the actual situation. In so doing the Allies played into the hands of German militarism. By contrast, the treaties that concluded World War II, for all their inadequacies, appear to have lasted for almost a half century.

Perhaps the best-known peace treaty in literature is that of Utrecht (1713), which by ending the War of the Spanish Succession left Tristram Shandy's Uncle Toby without vocation. He could never hear the name mentioned, Laurence Sterne tells us, without heaving a sigh.

Here are some of the more important treaties, agreements, and concordats since the Middle Ages. They are listed chronologically rather than by name, because most people don't recall the name so much as the war or historical occasion that brought it about.

843 C.E. Treaty of Verdun. Carolingian empire is divided up between Lothair (Italy, northern France, and Low Countries), Louis the German (Teutonic regions from Rhineland to eastern frontier), and Charles the Bald (southern and western France).

1258. Treaty of Corbeil. Louis IX of France renounces claims to Barcelona, Urgel, Cerdagne, Roussillon, other cities; James I of Aragon cedes to France Carcassonne, Nimes, Toulouse, Foix, Bézier, Narbonne, other cities. Margaret, wife of Louis IX, inherits all rights in Provence.

1360. Treaty of Brétigny-Calais. Edward III of England is recognized as sole ruler of Calais and Aquitaine, but relinquishes all claim to the throne of France.

1420. Treaty of Troyes. In an agreement between England, Burgundy, and France, the dauphin, later Charles VII, is disinherited. Henry V of England is designated regent of France and successor to mad King Charles VI of France, given control of northern France, and weds Catherine, daughter of Charles VI.

1435. Treaty of Arras. Philip the Good's dukedom of Burgundy is recognized by Charles VII of France; Philip receives extensive territories and agrees to join Charles, thereby enabling remodeled French army to recapture Paris in 1436 and oust England from Normandy and Aquitaine.

1479. Treaty of Constantinople. Venetian Republic gives up Scutari, Negroponte, Lemnos, and other coastal stations, agrees to pay annual tribute to Turks for right to trade in Black Sea.

1494. Treaty of Tordesillas, June 7. Spain and Portugal, the dominant European colonial nations, agree to revise an earlier decree secured from Pope Alexander VI, and to divide the new realms along a line 370 leagues west of the Azores and Cape Verde Islands, with Portugal holding rights to the east and Spain to the west.

1559. Peace of Cateau-Cambresis, April 3. End of the series of wars between the two leading European Catholic monarchies, the Habsburgs and the Valois kings of France.

1560. Treaty of Edinburgh, July 6. After English forces aided the lowland Scot rebellion against French-Catholic regent Francis II, whose wife, Mary Stuart, had been declared "Queen of England and Scotland," a treaty between England, France, and Scotland virtually eliminates French influence in Scotland.

1648. Treaties of Westphalia, October 24. Concluded at Münster, between the Holy Roman Empire and France, and at Osnabrück between the Holy Roman Empire and Sweden and Protestant states of the empire, these treaties bring an end to the Thirty Years' War. Sweden obtains control of the Baltic Sea regions and a footing on the North Sea. France's control over Alsace and other Rhineland areas formerly claimed by the Habsburgs is recognized. Dutch independence from Habsburg control is acknowledged. Although none of the war-ravaged German states gain importantly, Brandenburg wins control of East Pomerania on the Baltic, and Bavaria receives the Upper Palatinate but is obliged to yield the Rhenish Palatinate. The settlement in effect eliminates the sovereignty of the Habsburgs and the Holy Roman Empire over the German principalities, and facilitates the subsequent growth of Bavaria and Brandenburg (Prussia) and the development of Austria as a nation-state. Habsburg Spain loses most of the Low Countries and almost all its remaining wealth and power.

1659. Treaty of the Pyrenees, November 7. War between France and Spain ends. Spain cedes frontier fortresses in Flanders and Artois and other territories, and Louis XIV weds Maria Teresa, oldest daughter of King Philip IV of Spain, thus setting up France's claim to the Spanish succession.

1667. Treaty of Breda, July 21. Agreement between England, Holland, France, and Denmark. England gets Antigua, Montserrat, and St. Kitts in West Indies; France gets Acadia in Canada. England retains New York, and the Dutch keep Surinam. Dutch ships may transport goods brought down the Rhine River to England.

1670. Treaty of Dover, May. Secret agreement between Charles II of England and Louis XIV of France whereby, in return for a cash subsidy, England would help France attack Holland. If provided with additional cash and, if necessary, troops, Charles will be willing to turn Catholic and convert England into a Catholic nation.

1678–79. Treaties of Nimwegen. France receives the Franche-Comté from Spain, but Holland wins the right to garrison a series of fortifications in the Spanish Netherlands for protection against France. France also receives Habsburg territories elsewhere, and is left in a commanding position in western Europe.

1697. Treaty of Ryswick, September 30. An agreement marking a temporary halt in the wars of Louis XIV against Austria, Spain, England, and

Holland. France keeps Strasbourg but surrenders Freiburg, Breisach, and Phillipsburg. France regains Pondicherry in India and Nova Scotia in America. Spain regains Catalonia. France abandons its claim to Cologne and some areas in Rhineland. Holland's right to garrison Namur, Ypres, and other fortresses is confirmed. William III is acknowledged as the rightful king of England, and France will no longer give aid to the deposed James II.

1713. Peace of Utrecht, April 11–July 13. Ending the war of the Spanish Succession, the treaties signed at Utrecht effectively mark the termination of Louis XIV's efforts to dominate western Europe. France cedes Newfoundland, Nova Scotia, St. Kitts, and Hudson Bay area to England, retains Quebec, and agrees to demolish the fortifications of Dunkirk on the English Channel. The Duke of Savoy regains Savoy and Nice, and acquires Sicily. France receives the principality of Orange, gives up other areas to Prussia. Philip V is recognized as king of Spain, thus formally separating the crowns of France and Spain. England receives Gibraltar and Minorca from Spain. From Utrecht dates the maritime and commercial ascendancy of England.

1748. Peace of Aix-la-Chapelle, October. The War of the Austrian Succession ends. Maria Teresa's right to the Habsburg throne is confirmed; the fortress of Louisburg on Cape Breton is returned to France; Madras in India is returned to England; Frederick the Great of Prussia retains Silesia; Parma, Piacenza, and Guastalla are ceded to the Spanish infant, Don Philip; and the House of Hanover, now established on the English throne, is to retain its German lands.

1763. Treaty of Paris, February 10. Concluding the Seven Years' War, this treaty between England, France, and Spain, together with that at Hubertusburg between Austria and Prussia (February 15), brings to an end some twenty-five years of warfare among the major European powers. France is divested of her empire in mainland North America; England receives Canada, Cape Breton Island, the remainder of Nova Scotia, and the region between the Alleghenies and the Mississippi River. France also cedes Grenada, St. Vincent, Dominica, and Tobago in the West Indies to England, but retains Gaudeloupe, Martinique, and Haiti. Spain cedes Florida to England, and receives Cuba back from England, which had captured Havana, and New Orleans and the trans-Mississippi from France. The slaving post at Senegal in Africa goes to England, with France retaining Gorée. France also retains Pondicherry and other trading posts in India. At Hubertusburg, Frederick the Great's title to Silesia is confirmed, and Prussia emerges as a major power alongside Austria.

1782–83. Treaty of Paris. In a preliminary treaty with the United States, November 30, 1782, Britain recognizes American independence, with boundaries along the St. Croix River, St. Lawrence watershed, and the 45th

Parallel, down the Mississippi River south to the 31st Parallel, and along the Apalachicola and St. Mary's rivers. The United States has the right to fish off Newfoundland and Nova Scotia. All depts due creditors of England or the United States by citizens of the other are validated. The U.S. Congress will "earnestly recommend" the full restoration of the rights and property of Loyalists by each state. British land and sea forces will evacuate American territory "with all convenient speed." The general treaty, September 3, 1783, provides for Britain to surrender Senegal and Tobago to France, and for Spain to retain Florida and Minorca.

1794. Jay's Treaty, November 19. Britain agrees to withdraw from its Northwest military posts, and to admit American ships to British East India ports on a nondiscriminatory basis. The West Indian trade is opened to U.S. ships of up to 70 tons, on condition that the United States renounce its carrying trade in cotton, molasses, and sugar. The disputed pre-Revolutionary War debt, northeastern boundary question, and compensation for illegal maritime searches are referred to joint commissions. British trade with the United States is placed on a most-favored-nation basis. After considerable resistance, the treaty, minus its West Indies trade provisions, is ratified by the U.S. Senate.

1795. Pinckney's Treaty, October 27. Confronting the imminence of war with England, Spain seeks to placate the United States by signing a treaty guaranteeing free navigation of the Mississippi River and the right to deposit goods at New Orleans for transshipment, setting the boundary of Florida at the 31st Parallel, and promising to restrain the Indians on the frontier.

1797. Peace of Campo-Formio, October 17. Austria cedes its possessions in the Lowlands to France, receives Venice, Istria, Dalmatia, and Venetian territory as far as the Adige. Bergamo and Brescia are assigned to the newly formed Cisalpine Republic. France receives the Ionian Islands. In secret provisions of the treaty, Austria agrees to the cession to France of the left bank of the Rhine from Basel to Andernach, and France will help Austria to secure Salzburg and part of Bavaria. Both sides agree that Prussia is not to be given any territory in return for cession of the Rhine territory to France.

1801. French Concordat with Papacy. Roman Catholicism is recognized as the church of the "majority of Frenchmen." New bishops and archbishops are to be installed, nominated by the government and consecrated by the pope. Bishops are to appoint parish priests, subject to government approval. Confiscated church property will not be restored, but the government is to support the clergy. Pope Pius VII is awarded possession of the Papal States, but without Ferrara, Bologna, and the Romagna.

1802. Treaty of Amiens, March 27. This treaty, constituting only a brief interlude during the continuing warfare between Great Britain and France, provides for England to give up most of its naval conquests, including the Dutch East Indies, the Cape of Good Hope, Minorca, Guadeloupe, and Martinique, retaining only Trinidad and Ceylon. Malta is to be restored to the Order of the Knights of Malta. France will evacuate Portugal, Naples, Egypt, and the Papal States. The Ionian Islands become an independent republic. The treaty does nothing to open European markets to British goods. Within two years, using the British failure to give up Malta as an excuse, hostilities are renewed by Napoleon.

1803. Louisiana Purchase, May 2. Having caused Spain to cede the Louisiana territory to France, Napoleon, realizing that its possession by France would draw the United States and Great Britain together, sells it to the United States for 60 million francs (approximately $15,000,000).

1805. Treaty of Pressburg, December 26. After Russia and Prussia withdraw from the coalition against Napoleon, Austria is forced to make peace with France. France receives Piedmont, Parma, and Piacenza; the Venetian territories are transferred to the Italian kingdom; Bavaria gains the Tyrol and other areas; and Württenberg and Baden receive what is left of Austria's western lands.

1807. Treaties of Tilsit, July 7–9. Following Napoleon's victory at Friedland, Russia and Prussia sign treaties with Napoleon. Russia recognizes the Grand Duchy of Warsaw; Danzig becomes a free city; and Russia accepts Napoleon's brothers as kings of Naples, Holland, and Westphalia. Napoleon will mediate the war between Russia and Turkey, while Tsar Alexander will seek to arrange peace between France and England—and, if England refuses, will ally Russia with France. Prussia cedes all lands between the Rhine and Elbe rivers, which become part of a new kingdom of Westphalia. Polish lands held by Prussia will become part of the new Grand Duchy of Warsaw under the king of Saxony. Prussia recognizes Napoleon's brothers as sovereigns. All Prussian ports are closed to trade with England. Prussia will maintain a standing army of no more than 42,000, and join France and Russia against England.

1809. Treaty of Schönbrunn, October 14. Napoleon, having defeated Austria at Wagram, signs a treaty with Austria in which Austria's Illyrian provinces are transferred to France, western Galicia becomes part of the Grand Duchy of Warsaw, Russia receives parts of eastern Galicia, and Salzburg and the northern Tyrol become part of Bavaria. Austria, its army limited to 150,000, will break off all ties with Great Britain.

1814. Treaty of Paris, May 30. After Napoleon has abdicated as emperor of France and been given the island of Elba as a sovereign principality, Louis XVI is restored to the French throne. To strengthen the Bourbon monarchy, the Allies at the first Peace of Paris do not exact monetary indemnities from France, and set French boundaries at those of 1792. Malta becomes British;

Mauritius, Tobago, and Santa Lucia are ceded to England; San Domingo is restored to Spain; Belgium becomes part of Holland; the German states form a federation; Prussia recovers Neuchâtel; and Switzerland remains an independent state.

1814. Peace of Ghent, December 24. After protracted negotiations, a treaty is signed beteeen Great Britain and the United States in which none of the issues over which the Americans had gone to war in 1812 are addressed. All prisoners are to be released, all conquered territory is to be restored, a commission will arbitrate the northeastern boundary between the United States and Canada, and the question of the Great Lakes and Newfoundland fisheries is left open for future negotiation.

1815. Treaty of Vienna, June 9. Austria receives Galicia, Thorn, and the surrounding region. The remainder of the Grand Duchy of Warsaw is incorporated as a kingdom under the tsar's sovereignty. Prussia receives two-thirds of Saxony and territory in Westphalia and the Rhineland. Austria gets Lombardy, Venice, and most of the Tyrol. Hanover is enlarged. A loose confederation is drawn up for Germany. Denmark loses Norway to Sweden but receives Lauenberg. Prussia gets Swedish Pomerania. Piedmont absorbs Genoa. Tuscany and Modena go to an Austrian archduke. Parma is given to Marie Louise of Austria, Napoleon's ex-empress. Papal territories are restored to the Pope. Naples receives the Sicilian Bourbons. Rights to free navigation of international rivers and conditions of diplomatic precedence are set. All the Allies except Spain sign the agreement.

1815. Treaty with Algiers, June 30. An American squadron under Stephen Decatur sails into the harbor of Algiers and exacts a treaty whereby the Dey renounces further molestation of American commerce and demands for payment of tribute, agrees to release all U.S. prisoners without ransom, and pays an indemnity for previous seizures. Similar guarantees are secured from Tunis (July 26) and Tripoli (August 5).

1815. Peace of Paris, November 20. Following Napoleon's escape from Elba and his defeat at Waterloo, a second Peace of Paris sets new terms. Prussia acquires the Rhineland, including the fortresses at Saarbrücken and Saarlouis. The Netherlands get the fortresses at Philippeville and Marienburg; Landau becomes a fortress of the German confederation and Bavaria acquires the surrounding region; part of Savoy is ceded to Sardinia; France must pay an indemnity of 700 million francs as well as the cost of an army of occupation along its frontiers, and her boundaries are now essentially those of 1790.

1817. Rush-Bagot Treaty, April 28–29. The United States and Great Britain agree to limit naval vessels on inland waters to one apiece on Lakes Champlain and Ontario and two apiece on the Upper Lakes. No warship will be of more than one hundred tons or mount more than one 18-pound gun.

1819. Adams-Onís Treaty, February 22. The United States receives the Floridas from Spain. The boundaries of the Louisiana Purchase are set along a line beginning at the mouth of the Sabine River and zigzaging northward to the 42nd Parallel, then westward to the Pacific. Spain thus cedes its claims to the Oregon country and America relinquishes its shadowy claims to Texas. The United States also agrees to assume the claims of American citizens against Spain, amounting to $5,000,000.

1829. Treaty of Adrianople, September 14. This treaty, ending the Russo-Turkish War, gives Russia the mouth of the Danube River and additional territory on the Black Sea. The Dardanelles are opened to all commercial traffic. Serbia receives autonomy from Turkey. Russia will occupy Moldavia and Walachia until Turkey pays a large indemnity. Turkey agrees to accept the London Protocol of March 29, whereby Greece will be an autonomous, tributary state under a prince. In 1832 a Bavarian prince, Otto, is chosen for the Greek throne.

1839. Treaty of London, April 19. Belgium's independence is accepted by Holland. The Schelde estuary is opened to ships of both countries, and the national debt is divided. Eastern Luxembourg becomes a grand duchy. England, France, Austria, Russia, and Prussia sign an agreement guaranteeing Belgian neutrality.

1842. Webster-Ashburton Treaty, August 9. American and Canadian boundaries are settled. The line between Maine and New Brunswick is fixed along its present-day border. The New York and Vermont border is set a half mile north of the 45th Parallel. The United States receives navigation rights along the St. John River. England agrees to a line between Lake Superior and the Lake of the Woods. Britain and the United States will maintain naval squadrons along the African coast to suppress the slave traffic.

1842. Treaty of Nanking, August 29. Following a dispute over British use of the port of Canton for its opium trade, British forces seize Chinese coastal forts and dictate a treaty whereby Hong Kong is ceded to England; Shanghai, Canton, and other ports are opened to British and American trade; and foreign nationals are to be under the jurisdiction of their own laws and courts. A uniform import tariff is set, and China is to pay Britain an indemnity of £21,000,000 for confiscated opium.

1844. Treaty of Wanghia, July 3. China grants most-favored-nation trading status to the United States, and extraterritorial legal jurisdiction for American citizens is secured.

1846. Oregon settlement, June 15. Great Britain and the United States agree that the U.S.–Canadian border line will be extended along the 49th Parallel to the middle of the channel between Vancouver Island and the mainland, then southward through the Strait of Juan de Fuca. The channel and the strait will be open to free navigation, and the British will have the right to use the mouth of the Columbia River below the 49th Parallel.

1846. Treaty of New Granada, December 12. New Granada (Colombia) and the United States sign a commercial treaty granting the right of transit across the Isthmus of Panama, and committing the United States to the "perfect neutrality" of the route.

1848. Treaty of Guadalupe-Hidalgo, February 2. New Mexico and California are ceded outright to the United States, and the American title to Texas is confirmed as far as the Rio Grande. Mexico will be paid $15,000,000, and $3,250,000 in claims by American citizens against Mexico will be assumed by the United States.

1850. Clayton-Bulwer Treaty, April 19. England and the United States agree to cooperate in making possible a canal across the Isthmus of Panama, and bind themselves never to fortify or exercise exclusive control over such a waterway.

1853. Gadsden Purchase, December 30. To facilitate the building of a railroad across the Southwest to California, the United States pays $10,000,000 to Mexico for territory south of the Gila River now comprising the southern portions of New Mexico and Arizona.

1854. Treaty of Kanagawa, March 31. Commodore Matthew C. Perry's expedition results in a treaty of friendship and commerce between the United States and Japan. The ports of Shimodo and Hakodate are to be open to U.S. trade, and shipwrecked American sailors, hitherto treated as felons, are to be protected.

1854. British-American Reciprocity Treaty, June 5. Negotiated following considerable dispute, this treaty provides for American fishing rights along the shores of Canada, Newfoundland, Nova Scotia, Prince Edward Islands, and elsewhere, and similar British rights along the Atlantic coast as far south as the 36th Parallel. A lengthy list of agricultural and other commodities can be shipped across the U.S.–Canadian border duty-free.

1856. Treaty of Paris, March 30. Meeting to conclude the Crimean War, representatives of England, France, Turkey, Russia, Austria, and Sardinia admit Turkey into the "public law and concert of Europe," and pledge to refrain from interfering in Turkey's internal affairs. The sultan of Turkey promises not to discriminate against Christians. The Black Sea will be neutral and open to trade, and its coasts will not be fortified. Kars will be returned to Turkey, and the Crimea to Russia. The Danube will be open to the ships of all nations, under the control of an international tribunal. Russia will cede southern Bessarabia to Moldavia, and renounce its protectorate over Moldavia and Wallachia, which will remain under Turkish supervision. The liberties of Serbia are to be guaranteed. A declaration is also signed, setting forth four rules of international law: (1) Privateering is outlawed. (2)

Except for contraband, an enemy's goods cannot be seized when under a neutral flag. (3) Neutral goods not under contraband cannot be captured when under an enemy's flag. (4) To be binding, a blockade must be effective.

1858. Treaties of Tientsin, June 18. The Western nations—England, France, Russia, and the United States—continue to force trading concessions from China. Eleven more ports are opened. Legations are permitted at Peking, and Christian missions in the interior. A maritime customs service with a foreign inspector-general and staff is established. The importation of opium is legalized.

1858. Townsend Harris Treaty, July 29. A commercial treaty between Japan and the United States opens five more ports to American trade, grants greater trade and residential rights, provides for reciprocal diplomatic representation, prohibits the importation of opium, and sets up a kind of extraterritorial legal status for Americans. A Japanese mission is to be taken for a visit to the United States aboard an American man-of-war.

1860. Treaty of Turin, March 24. After plebiscites in Parma, Modena, Romagna, and Tuscany produce a vote to oust the Austrian rulers and be annexed to Piedmont, Napoleon III of France and Camillo Cavour, premier of Piedmont, negotiate a treaty whereby, following a plebiscite, Nice and Savoy are ceded to France.

1864. Geneva Convention on the Red Cross, August 22. Sixteen nations meet in Geneva to draw up a Convention for the Amelioration of the Condition of the Wounded and Sick of Armies in the Field. Twelve nations sign. The provisions call for neutrality for the persons of the medical services of the armed forces, humane treatment of wounded, neutrality of citizens who voluntarily assist them, and an international emblem to mark personnel and supplies. A red cross on a white field is selected for the emblem.

1867. North German Confederation, July 1. Twenty-two North German states accept a treaty proposed by Prussia. The King of Prussia is hereditary president, assisted by a federal chancellor. Participating with Prussia are Saxony, Mecklenburg-Schwerin, Strelitz, Oldenburg, Saxe-Weimar, Brunswick, Anhalt, Saxe-Coburg-Gotha, Hamburg, Bremen, Lubeck, and smaller duchies and principalities. The princes retain certain sovereign rights, but foreign affairs, the raising and control of the army, and the decision of peace and war rest with the president. The legislature will consist of a federal council, or Bundesrat, appointed by the confederate states, and an elected Reichstag. Otto von Bismarck as chancellor is the president's first appointment.

1867. Alaskan Purchase, April 9. Russia sells the entire territory of Alaska to the United States for $7,200,000.

1871. Treaty of Washington, May 8. England and the United States agree to arbitration by an international tribunal of claims against British violations of neutrality during the American Civil War. American fisheries rights are expanded. The dispute over ownership of the San Juan Islands will be adjudicated by the emperor of Germany.

1871. Treaty of Frankfurt, May 10. The Germans, victors in the Franco-Prussian War, acquire all of Alsace except Belfort, as well as eastern Lorraine with the fortresses of Metz and Strasbourg. France must pay an indemnity of 5 million francs, with an army of occupation to remain in place until it is paid.

1872. Geneva Tribunal, September 14. Swiss, Brazilian, and Italian arbitrators award the United States $15,500,000 damages from England for the *Alabama* claims. On October 21, the German emperor upholds United States ownership of the San Juan Islands. In 1877 a commission will rule that Great Britain is entitled to $5,500,000 compensation for extension of fishing rights off the northeast Atlantic coast. These settlements resolve all the outstanding differences between Great Britain and the United States.

1878. Treaty of San Stefano, March 23. With Russian forces entrenched outside Constantinople, a Russo-Turkish treaty is signed that virtually eliminates the Ottoman Empire in Europe. Montenegro is to be enlarged and given the port of Andivari. Montenegro and Serbia are to receive territory and be independent of Turkey. Bosnia and Herzegovina will be granted reforms. Romanian independence of Turkey is acknowledged. Turkish fortresses on the Danube River are to be razed. Bulgaria will be an autonomous province, occupied by Russian troops for two years, and to extend from the Danube to the Aegean Sea. Russia will receive Ardahan, Kars, Batum, and Bayazid, and Turkey will pay Russia a large indemnity.

1878. Treaty of Berlin, July 13. With Count Otto von Bismarck acting as an "honest broker," agreement is reached by Great Britain, Austria-Hungary, Russia, Turkey, France, and Italy, sharply modifying the Treaty of San Stefano. Montenegro, Serbia, and Romania will be independent. Russia acquires Bessarabia from Romania, and retains Batoum, Ardahan, and Kars. Austria will control Bosnia and Herzegovina. England will occupy and administer Cyprus, with Turkey receiving its surplus revenues. Turkey will carry out reforms in its Asiatic territories. Bulgaria is divided into a northern province under nominal Turkish suzerainty; eastern Rumelia, with autonomous rights and a Christian governor; and Macedonia, under Turkish rule. Crete is to receive constitutional government, the Greco-Turkish border is to be rectified, the lower Danube River is to be demilitarized, and Armenians and other religious minorities controlled by Turkey are to be protected.

1883. Treaty of Ancón, October 20. With Chile victorious in the War of the Pacific, Peru cedes Tarapacá, and Chile will keep possession of Tacna and Arica for ten years.

1888. Treaty of Constantinople, October 29. An international convention, signed by Great Britain, France, Germany, Italy, Austria, Spain, the Netherlands, Russia, and Turkey, specifies that the Suez Canal is to be open to all nations in peace and in war.

1890. Anglo-German Colonial Agreement, July 1. Great Britain transfers the island of Heligoland to Germany and recognizes German claims to territories north of Lake Nyassa. Germany acknowledges England's claim to the northern areas of Lake Victoria Nyanza, the upper Nile Valley, and the Indian Ocean coast of Africa from Visu to Kismayu. Germany also recognizes the British protectorate over the islands held by the sultan of Zanzibar.

1893. Bering Sea arbitration, August 15. An international tribunal to mediate a dispute between Great Britain and the United States over sealing rights in the Bering Sea rejects U.S. claims to exclusive rights, assesses damages against the United States for seizing Canadian sealing ships, and prohibits pelagic sealing off the Pribilof Islands during a specified period each year.

1895. Treaty of Shimonosekei, April 17. Japan, having destroyed the Chinese military forces, compels China to accept a treaty recognizing the independence of Korea, ceding Formosa, the Pescadores, and the Liaotung peninsula to Japan, opening four more ports to foreign commerce, and calling for an indemnity to Japan of 200,000,000 taels. For a further indemnity, Japan, at the insistence of Russia, Germany, and France, returns Port Arthur and the Liaotung peninsula to China.

1897. British-Venezuelan Treaty, February 2. After a dispute over the boundary between Venezuela and British Guiana, Great Britain and Venezuela, through the mediation of the United States, sign an agreement to have the claims arbitrated. On October 3, 1899, the verdict generally supports the English contentions, but secures territory and control of the mouth of the Orinoco River for Venezuela.

1898. Treaty of Paris, December 10. Following the American victory in the Spanish-American War, Spain agrees to relinquish sovereignty over Cuba and cede the Philippines, Guam, and Puerto Rico to the United States, which will pay Spain $20,000,000 for the Philippines.

1899. Hague Convention, July 29. Twenty-six nations extend the provisions of the Geneva Convention to prohibit the use of poison gas and expanding bullets in war, ban the use of aerial explosives, safeguard neutral shipping rights, and provide for better treatment of prisoners of war. Establishment of a permanent court of international arbitration is authorized.

1899. Samoan Treaties. By an agreement signed on November 14, Great Britain relinquishes to Germany its claims to Samoan territory, receiving in turn rights in West Africa and islands in the Solomons group. Another treaty signed by Germany, Great Britain, and the United States, on December 2, abolishes the earlier protectorate and gives Germany the two largest islands in the group. The United States gains the rest of the islands, including the harbor of Pago Pago.

1901. Peace of Peking, September 7. Twelve nations sign the protocol ending the Boxer Rebellion, with China paying indemnities of $333,000,000, razing forts, and accepting foreign garrisons along a strategic railway. The United States subsequently reduces its share and later remits the unpaid balance.

1901. Hay-Pauncefote Treaty, November 18. Great Britain agrees to renounce joint rights to an Isthmian canal, which the United States will construct and operate. The neutrality of the canal will be maintained, and it will not be fortified.

1903. Hay-Bunau-Varilla Treaty, November 18. Following Panama's revolt from Colombia several weeks earlier, the United States and Panama agree to American control in perpetuity of a ten-mile strip across the Isthmus, construction of a canal, and full U.S. sovereignty including the right to fortify and defend the canal. The United States guarantees Panamanian independence, and will pay Panama $10,000,000 and an annual fee of $250,000 after nine years.

1904. Anglo-French Accord, April 8. France recognizes British occupation of Egypt, receives debt guarantees; Britain will recognize the Suez Canal convention; Britain surrenders its claim to Madagascar; Britain recognizes French interests in Morocco; France gives up Newfoundland shore claims but retains the right to fish; France receives territory east of the Niger and near French Gambia; spheres of interest on Siamese frontier are set.

1904. Treaty between Chile and Bolivia, October 20. Bolivia and Chile formally end the War of the Pacific. Chile's possession of the Pacific shore is recognized, and a railway linking Arica and La Paz will be constructed by Chile, which will relinquish the Bolivian portion after fifteen years.

1905. Treaty of Portsmouth, September 5. Through mediation by the United States, Japan and Russia end their war. Russia cedes the northern part of Sakhalin with Port Arthur, recognizes Japan's predominance in Korea, cedes railway lines in southern Manchuria, and turns over its lease on the Liaotung peninsula to Japan.

1906. Algeciras Convention, April 7. At a multipower conference called to defuse the menacing situation on the Moroccan coast, the independence of Morocco is reaffirmed. France will police the Morocco-Algerian border. Elsewhere the police are to be under French and Spanish control. German economic interests will be respected.

1909–12. Anglo-American Fisheries. The United States and Great Britain agree on January 27, 1909, to submit the longstanding fisheries dispute to the Hague Court, which on September 7, 1910, issues a decision sustaining Newfoundland's claim of local jurisdiction but providing safeguards for

New England fishermen. The Anglo-American Convention of July 20, 1912, sets up a permanent commission to adjust all future disputes.

1911. Franco-German Convention, November 4. After a confrontation between Germany, England, and France, Germany acknowledges a French protectorate over Morocco in exchange for being ceded half of the French Congo.

1913. Treaty of London, May 30. The first Balkan War ends with Turkey abandoning all claim to Crete and ceding other territory to Greece.

1913. Treaty of Bucharest, August 10. Ending the second Balkan War, Bulgaria loses Monastir, Ochridia, and Kossovo to Serbia, and Salonika, Epirus, and Kavala to Greece. The Serbs and Greeks retain portions of Macedonia held by them, and Romania receives the Dobrudja area along the Danube River.

1914. Bryan-Chamorro Treaty, August 5, not ratified by U.S. Senate until February 18, 1916. Nicaragua grants the United States exclusive rights to a canal route and naval base, in exchange for $3,000,000.

1916. Virgin Islands Treaty, August 4. Denmark sells the Virgin Islands to the United States for $25,000,000.

1918. Treaty of Brest-Litovsk, March 3. Following the Bolskevik Revolution, Russia signs a peace treaty with Germany, Austria-Hungary, Bulgaria, and Turkey, removing itself from the war, relinquishing all rights in Poland, Finland, and Lithuania, agreeing to evacuate Estonia, Livonia, the Ukraine, and occupied Turkish territories, and to demobilize its army.

1918. Austria-Hungary Armistice, November 3. Austria-Hungary will demobilize armies, withdraw troops fighting with Germans, surrender half its military equipment, evacuate all occupied and disputed territories, surrender its fleet, and allow Allies to occupy strategic points.

1918. German Armistice, November 11. Germany will evacuate occupied French and Belgian territory, the left bank of the Rhine and bridgeheads at Cologne, Mainz, and Coblenz; surrender its submarines and allow its fleet to be interned; destroy its aircraft, tanks, and heavy artillery; return prisoners of war and deported civilians; and turn over railroad rolling stock and trucks. Allies reserve the right to make claims for damages.

1919. League of Nations Covenant, April 28. The league will consist of the states ratifying the Treaty of Versailles, and others admitted by a two-thirds vote. Member nations will afford each other mutual protection against aggression, submit disputes to arbitration, and abstain from war for three months after an award. A permanent headquarters will be located at Geneva, Switzerland. There will be a general assembly, with each nation holding one vote, and a council made up of the five great powers and four others chosen periodically by the assembly.

1919. Treaty of Versailles, June 28. The League of Nations is established. Alsace-Lorraine is restored to France. Allies will occupy left bank of Rhine for fifteen (reduced to ten) years. Right bank of Rhine will be demilitarized zone. Saar Basin is internationalized for fifteen years, with coal mines under French control, then to decide its status by plebiscite. Belgian frontier is augmented. Luxembourg's independence will be affirmed by Germany. Central and northern Schleswig will decide by plebiscite whether to join Denmark or Germany. Poland will be an independent nation. Danzig will be a free city, with Poland given a corridor to Baltic Sea. German rivers will be internationalized, and Kiel Canal opened to ships of all nations. Germany will hand over all large and many smaller merchant ships to Allies, and build 200,000 tons of shipping annually for five years for Allies. Germany will deliver large quantities of coal to France, Belgium, and Italy for ten years, bear costs of occupying armies, and pay for all civilian damage during the war. German colonies will become Allied mandates under the League of Nations. Germany's army will be limited to 100,000 men, without large guns, and its navy to six warships. It will have no submarines or military aircraft. Heligoland fortifications will be dismantled.

1919. Treaty of Saint-Germain, September 10. The Austro-Hungarian monarchy is dissolved. Austria recognizes the independence of Czechoslovakia, Yugoslavia, Poland, and Hungary. The Trentino, the South Tyrol, Trieste, Istria, Friuli, and islands are ceded to Italy. Austria's army will be limited to 30,000, and Austria will pay reparations for thirty years. Union with Germany is forbidden without consent of the Council of the League of Nations.

1920. Treaty of Trianon, June 4. Hungary gives up Slovakia to Czechoslovakia, western Hungary to Austria, Croatia-Slavonia and part of the Banat to Yugoslavia, and the remainder of the Banat, Transylvania, and part of the Hungarian plain to Romania. Hungary will assume its share of the Austro-Hungarian debt, pay reparations, and restrict its army to 35,000 men.

1920. Statute of the Permanent Court for International Justice, June 25; ratified by League of Nations, December 13. Ultimately some fifty-nine nations adhere to the World Court, empowered to render judgment in international disputes submitted to it and give advisory opinions in any matter referred to it by the League of Nations.

1921. Treaty of Riga, March 18. Russia and Poland reach agreement on frontier boundaries, with Poland receiving portions of Byelorussia and Ukraine.

1921. U.S. Congress resolution, July 2. Following rejection of the Treaty of Versailles and membership in the League of Nations, the U.S. Congress declares by joint resolution that the war with Germany and Austro-Hungary is over. Separate treaties with Germany, Austria, and Hungary are ratified on October 18.

1921. Colombian Conciliation, April 20. United States emends and ratifies the Thomson-Urrutia Treaty of 1914, paying $25,000,000 to Colombia for forcing Panamian independence in order to build the Panama Canal.

1921. British-Irish Treaty, December 6. Ireland receives dominion status and becomes the Irish Free State, with entire control of finances, laws, and police. It assumes a proportion of the United Kingdom's debt, and the exclusion of Ulster is recognized.

1922. Five-Power Naval Agreement, February 6. United States, Great Britain, Japan, France, and Italy agree to a ten-year moratorium on building new warships, and maintenance of a capital ships ratio of 5 each for the United States and Great Britain, 3 for Japan, and 1.67 each for France and Italy. The same nations also sign a treaty subjecting the use of submarines in war to the accepted rules of naval warfare.

1923. Central American Conference, February 7. The United States and all Central American republics draw up a treaty of neutrality, providing for a Central American court of justice and limitation of armaments.

1925. Locarno Treaties, December 1. The Franco-German and Belgo-German frontiers are mutually guaranteed by France, Germany, Belgium, the Netherlands, Great Britain, and Italy. Germany signs arbitration treaties with Poland, Czechoslovakia, Belgium, and France. Franco-Polish and Franco-Czechoslovakian treaties in case of attack by Germany are signed.

1928. (Kellogg-Briand) Pact of Paris, August 27. Representatives of the United States, France, and thirteen other powers sign an agreement renouncing war as an instrument of national policy. Ultimately sixty-five nations, including the Soviet Union, ratify the pact.

1929. Lateran Treaties, February 11. Ending a half century's dispute over the temporal status of the Vatican, Italy and the Roman Catholic church conclude treaty arrangements whereby the pope will reign independently over Vatican City, retain Church property throughout Italy, and possess uncontrolled spiritual authority. The Italian government will pay an indemnity of 750,000,000 lire in cash and 1 billion lire in government bonds.

1929. Washington Treaty for Inter-American Arbitration, January 5. The Pan-American nations pledge themselves to seek arbitration and conciliation of disputes, and appoint commissions to deal with future problems as they arise.

1930. London Naval Disarmament Treaty, April 22. The United States, Great Britain, and Japan adopt an agreement on cruiser limitation, with Japan restricted to a 10–6 ratio. An upper limit of 52,700 submarine tons is accepted. No new capital ships are to be built before 1936.

1936. Egyptian-British Treaty, August 27. British forces will be withdrawn from Egypt except for 10,000 troops in the Suez Canal area. A British naval base will be maintained at Alexandria for not more than eight years. Unrestricted Egyptian immigration into the Sudan will be permitted, and Egyptian troops will be stationed there. Egypt will join the League of Nations, and sign a twenty-year alliance with Great Britain.

1939. Russo-German Agreement, September 29. Following Nazi Germany's invasion of Poland on September 1, the Soviet Unions move in from the east. The two dictatorships agree to divide Poland. Germany annexes Danzig and either annexes or takes control of 72,866 square miles of Polish territory. Russia occupies 77,620 square miles of eastern Poland.

1940. Russo-Finnish Treaty, March 12. After the Red Army breaches the Finnish defenses, the Soviet Union and Finland sign a treaty ceding the Karelian isthmus, the shores of Lake Ladoga, the city of Viipuri, and a naval base at Hangoe to Russia.

1940. German-French Armistice, June 22. With the French army defeated and the British Expeditionary Force evacuated from the Continent via Dunkirk, France signs an armistice agreement with Nazi Germany at Compiegne in which the nation is divided into a northern zone under German occupation and including the city of Paris, and a smaller southern zone with its capital at Vichy, functioning as a German satellite state.

1940. Act of Havana, July 30. The twenty-one nations of the Pan-American Union declare that the American republics, collectively or individually, may take over and administer any European possession in the New World endangered by aggression.

1940. U.S.-British Defense Agreement, September 3. Fifty over-age American destroyers are transferred to Britain, and in exchange the United States receives 99-year leases on naval bases in Newfoundland, Bermuda, the Bahamas, Jamaica, Antigua, St. Lucia, Trinidad, and British Guiana.

1941. Atlantic Charter, August 14. Meeting aboard warships at Argentia Bay, the heads of the governments of Great Britain and the United States issue a joint declaration of peace aims, which will later become the basis for the charter of the United Nations.

1945. Act of Chapultepec, March 3. Delegates of nineteen American republics sign a pact pledging joint action to guarantee all American states against aggression.

1945. Allied Control Committee, June 5. Germany is divided into four zones of occupation, under American, British, Russian, and French administration, and an Allied Control Commission assumes overall control.

1945. United Nations Charter, June 26. Delegates of fifty nations approve the charter for the United Nations. Provisions include the General Assembly, with each nation having one vote; the eleven-member Security Council, made up of the United States, Great Britain, the Soviet Union, France, and China, with six other members elected by the General Assembly for two-year terms; the Economic and Social Council of eighteen members to deal with human welfare and fundamental rights and freedoms; the International Court of Justice, located at The Hague; the Trusteeship Council; and the Secretariat, headed by a secretary-general.

1945. Potsdam Conference, August 2. Heads of U.S., British, and Russian governments plan a German peace settlement. Germany will be disarmed and demilitarized, war criminals will be tried, democratic ideals encouraged, local self-government and democratic political parties restored, and freedom of speech, press, and religion permitted subject to security needs. Economic restrictions will involve decentralization of cartels, syndicates, and trusts, prohibition on manufacture of war materials, and control of exports, imports, and scientific research. Germany will be compelled to compensate the nations it victimized.

1945. Japanese surrender, September 2. Japanese home islands will be under U.S. military occupation, the emperor will remain the head of state, the Japanese military structure will be dismantled, Korea will be under American and Soviet occupation, the Kurile Islands and southern part of Sakhalin ceded to Russia, Outer Mongolia placed under Russian control, and Russia and China will share facilities of Port Arthur and Manchurian railroads.

1947. European Peace Treaties, February 10. Italy loses four border regions to France, Adriatic Islands and Venezia Guilia to Yugoslavia, and Dodecanese Islands to Greece. Trieste will be a free territory, and Italian colonies in Libya and Somaliland will be given up. Italy will pay $360,000,000 reparations, and its armed forces will be limited to 300,000. Hungary will pay $300,000,000 in reparations to Soviet Union, Czechoslovakia, and Yugoslavia. Romania loses Bessarabia and northern Bukovina to Soviet Union, receives Transylvania back, and will pay $300,000,000 reparations to Soviet Union. Bulgaria retains southern Dobrudja, and will pay $70,000,000 reparations to Greece and Yugoslavia. Finland cedes Petsamo, part of the Rybachi peninsula, and the Karelian isthmus to Russia.

1947. Indian Independence Act, July 18. By act of the British Parliament, India and Pakistan become independent dominions within the British Commonwealth. Pakistan will consist of two widely separated areas. India will have access to Kashmir.

1948. Organization for European Economic Cooperation, April 16. In response to American formulation of the Marshall Plan for economic aid, sixteen European nations establish a committee for joint economic action, which becomes the Organization for European Economic Cooperation (OEEC), and will serve as the principal instrument in western Europe's transition from war to peace, reviving European production and trade.

1949. North Atlantic Treaty Organization, April 4. Great Britain, France, Belgium, the Netherlands, Canada, Luxembourg, Italy, Norway, Iceland, Portugal, and the United States sign a pact setting up a joint military and naval organization for mutual cooperation against aggression (NATO). Greece, Turkey, and West Germany will later join. On December 19, 1950, headquarters for North Atlantic Treaty forces are established, with Gen. Dwight D. Eisenhower, commander-in-chief.

1949. Council of Europe, May 5. A statute creating the Council of Europe, with a committee of ministers and a consultative assembly, is signed by Great Britain, France, Belgium, Netherlands, Italy, Denmark, Sweden, Norway, Luxembourg, and Ireland. Greece, Iceland, and Turkey subsequently join.

1951. Japan Peace Treaty and Japan-U.S. Security Treaty, September 8. Japan and forty-eight nations sign a peace treaty. Japan renounces Korea, Taiwan, and the Pescadores, cedes the northern Kuriles and southern Sakhalin to Russia, gives up the mandated islands, accepts temporary American occupation of the Ryukyus, including Okinawa and the Bonins. Japan and the United States sign a security treaty in which U.S. troops will be stationed in Japan.

1951. European Coal and Steel Agreement, April 18. France, West Germany, Italy, Belgium, the Netherlands, and Luxembourg sign a treaty in Rome setting up a single coal and steel authority for western Europe, to be directed by a High Authority consisting of nine individuals.

1953. Korean Armistice, July 26. U.N. and Communist delegates agree to an armistice providing for a demilitarized zone along the North and South Korean boundary, a joint military armistice commission, and a supervisory commission staffed by neutral nations.

1954. Southeast Asia Treaty, September 8. A defense treaty is signed establishing the Southeast Asia Treaty Organization (SEATO), with the United States, Great Britain, France, Australia, the Philippines, New Zealand, Thailand, and Pakistan taking part. The member nations will take joint action against aggression within a designated area of the Southwest Pacific to 20° 30' north.

1954. Trieste Agreement, October 5. Impasse over status of Trieste is settled by partition, Italy receiving one zone which includes the city of Trieste, and Yugoslavia the other.

1954. Geneva Conference, July 20. France, China, and the Viet Minh agree on an armistice dividing Vietnam at the 17th Parallel, with the Communists controlling the northern section.

1954. Indo-China Agreements, December 29. France grants independence to South Vietnam, Laos, and Cambodia.

1955. Warsaw Pact, May 14. Eight Communist nations sign a twenty-year mutual defense treaty.

1955. Treaty of Vienna, May 15. The United States, Russia, Britain, and France sign a treaty for Austrian independence.

1956. Japan-Soviet Treaty, October 19. The Soviet Union and Japan sign a peace declaration, omitting mention of the Kuriles, recognizing Japanese sovereignty over the Habomai and Shikotan Islands, calling for repatriation of Japanese prisoners, relinquishing of reparations by Soviet Union, and establishment of diplomatic relations.

1957. Rome Treaty, March 25. France, West Germany, Italy, Belgium, the Netherlands, and Luxembourg establish a common market designed to eliminate intramember tariffs, establish a uniform external tariff, eliminate quotas, ban cartels, and ensure mobility of labor and capital.

1959. Cyprus Agreement, February 19. British, Turkish, Greek, Greek Cypriot, and Turkish Cypriot leaders sign an agreement making Cyprus an independent state. Britain will retain two military enclaves, the president of the new republic will be a Greek Cypriote and vice-president a Turkish Cypriote, and legislature will be 70 percent Greek Cypriote and 30 percent Turkish Cypriote.

1959. Antarctica Treaty, December 1. The United States, the Soviet Union, and ten other nations sign a treaty reserving Antarctica for scientific and other peaceful purposes.

1960. European Free Trade Association, May 3. Great Britain, Norway, Denmark, Sweden, Switzerland, Austria, and Portugal form a marketing group.

1962. Cuban Missile Agreement, October 28. After the United States imposes an air and naval quarantine on shipments to Cuba, the Soviet Union agrees to halt construction of missile bases and to remove weapons under U.N. supervision, and the United States agrees to end the quarantine and give assurances that Cuba will not be invaded.

1963. Nuclear Test Ban Treaty, August 5. The United States, Great Britain, and the Soviet Union agree to prohibit nuclear testing in space, in the atmosphere, and under water. Underground testing will continue.

1967. Outer Space Treaty, January 27. Sixty-three nations, including the United States and the Soviet Union, sign a treaty prohibiting the orbiting of weapons in space and disallowing territorial claims on celestial bodies.

1968. Nuclear Non-Proliferation Treaty, July 1. The United States, Britain, the Soviet Union, and fifty-nine other nations sign a nuclear nonproliferation treaty.

1971. Seabed Treaty, February 11. The United States, the Soviet Union, and eighty-five other states agree to bar deployment of nuclear weapons from the floors of the world's oceans beyond the twelve-mile territorial limits.

1971. Okinawa Treaty, June 17. The United States and Japan sign an agreement for return of Okinawa to Japan. The U.S.-Japan Security Agreement will be extended to include Okinawa, American forces can still use bases on the island, and Japan will pay $320,000,000 for U. S. assets.

1972. Strategic Arms Limitations Treaties, May 26. The United States and the Soviet Union sign a treaty providing a five-year limitation on atomic missiles. No more than two hundred antiballistic missiles may be deployed by either country, and no more than one hundred around each national capital. The Soviet Union will have 1,618 intercontinental ballistic missiles, and 950 submarine-launched ballistic missiles aboard 62 nuclear-powered submarines. The United States will have 1,054 ICBMs, and 710 SLBMs aboard 44 submarines. The arrangement will give the United States 5,700 warheads to the Soviet Union's 2,500, and 500 long-range bombers to the Soviet Union's 140.

1973. Vietnam Ceasefire, January 27. Marking an end to American involvement in the Vietnam War, the United States, South and North Vietnam, and the Vietcong agree to a ceasefire to be monitored by an international control commission made up of representatives of Canada, Indonesia, Poland, and Hungary, with supervisory military commissions in the field. U.S. forces will be withdrawn, U.S. prisoners of war will be released, and the United States will remove mines from North Vietnam harbors. On March 2, at an international conference in Paris, the parties involved in the fighting, together with representatives of the control commission, Great Britain, France, China, and the Soviet Union, sign an agreement reaffirming the January 27 arrangements and declaring respect for the sovereignty and territorial integrity of Vietnam and the right to self-determination of its people.

1975. Helsinki Declaration, August 1. A thirty-five-nation summit Conference on Security and Cooperation in Europe draws up a declaration of intent, in which the signers commit themselves to accept the territorial status quo in Europe, to respect the sovereignty and sanctity of borders, and to ease the flow of people, ideas, publications, and commerce across national frontiers and the Iron Curtain.

1977. Panama Canal Treaty, September 7. The United States and Panama agree upon a new treaty, calling for gradual assumption of canal operation and defense by Panamanians before the year 2000. The Canal Zone will be permanently neutral, with the United States possessing the right to defend its neutrality. U.S. naval forces will have permanent and unconditional access to the canal. Panama will be paid an annuity of up to $10,000,000, and receive up to $10,000,000 from tolls.

1979. Egypt-Israel Peace Treaty, March 26. Following the Camp David initiative of 1978, Israel and Egypt sign a peace treaty calling for exchange of ambassadors, opening of the Suez Canal to Israeli ships, and return of the Sinai Peninsula to Egypt.

1987. U.S.-Russian Missile Agreement, December 8. U.S. president Ronald Reagan and Soviet leader Mikhail Gorbachev sign agreement calling for dismantling of 1,752 U.S. and 859 Russian missiles with a 300–3,400-mile range.

1991. First Strategic Arms Reduction Treaty, July 31. Soviet Union leader

Mikhail Gorbachev and U. S. President George Bush sign START 1—First Strategic Arms Reduction Treaty—restricting numbers of nuclear weapons delivery systems, effecting a 33 percent overall reduction in strategic nuclear forces and providing for monitoring of Inter-Continental Ballistic Missile assembly facilities.

1991. Commonwealth of Independent States, December 8. President Boris Yeltsin of Russia and leaders of the Ukraine and Byelorussia sign an agreement establishing a Commonwealth of Independent States to replace the Union of Soviet Socialist Republics.

1992. Open Skies Treaty, March 25. Twenty-five nations, including former members of the U.S.S.R., sign an Open Skies Treaty in Helsinki, Finland, providing for mutual airborne inspections to monitor arms control agreements.

1993. Second Strategic Arms Reduction Treaty, January 3. Russian President Boris Yeltsin and U.S. President George Bush sign START 2—Second Strategic Arms Reduction Treaty—to reduce number of long-range missiles over ten-year period and eliminate land-based missiles.

1993. International Space Station Agreement, September 5. U.S. and Russia sign agreement to design and build an international space station.

1993. Israel-PLO Agreement, September 13. Israel and the Palestine Liberation Organization sign an agreement for Palestinian self-government, to begin in Gaza Strip and Jericho.

1993. North American Free Trade Agreement, September 14. U.S. President Bill Clinton signs supplements to NAFTA—the North American Free Trade Agreement—linking U.S., Canada, Mexico.

1994. Israel-Jordan Treaty, October 26. Israel and Jordan sign a treaty formally ending state of war.

SOURCES

Bailey, Thomas A. *A Diplomatic History of the American People.* 3rd ed. New York: F. S. Crofts, 1946.

Calvocoressi, Peter. *World Politics Since 1945.* 4th ed. London: Longman, 1982.

Chernow, Barbara A., and George Valasi, eds. *The Columbia Encyclopedia.* 5th ed. New York: Columbia University Press, 1993.

Encyclopedia Americana. Yearbooks for the years 1972 through 1991.

Encyclopedia of American Facts and Dates. 8th ed. New York: Harper and Row, 1987.

Hall, Walter Phelps, and Robert Greenhalgh Albion, with Jennie Barnes Pope. *A History of England and the British Empire.* Boston: Ginn and Co., 1937.

Hexter, J. H., and Richard Pipes, with Anthony Molho. *Europe Since 1500.* New York: Harper-American Heritage, 1971.

Langer, William L., comp. and ed. *An Encyclopedia of World History.* 5th ed. Boston: Houghton Mifflin Co., 1972.

McKinney, Loren Carey. *The Medieval World.* New York: Farrar and Rinehart, 1938.

Marriott, Sir J. A. R. *The History of Europe from 1815 to 1939*. 5th edition. London: Methuen and Co., 1948.

Morris, Richard B., ed. *Encyclopedia of American History*. 6th ed. New York: Harper and Row, 1982.

Reddaway, W. F. *A History of Europe from 1715 to 1814*. 3rd ed. London: Methuen and Co., 1948.

Tindall, George Brown. *America: A Narrative History*. New York: W. W. Norton, 1984.

Williams, Neville. *A Chronology of the Modern World, 1763 to the Present Time*. New York: David McKay Co., 1967.

—L.D.R.

13

PRESIDENTIAL CANDIDATES
AND WOULD-BE CANDIDATES

. . . . .

WINNING THE NOMINATION OF A MAJOR POLITICAL PARTY TO RUN FOR PRESI-
dent is usually no easy business. Many are called, but few are chosen. And
once the choice is made, those losing out often recede from public view very
rapidly indeed. Who now remembers the names of those who contested so
heatedly with Herbert Hoover and Al Smith for the Republican and
Democratic party nominations in 1928?

Surprisingly enough, some of the information offered in this section on
U.S. presidential elections, which one would think would be frequently in
demand, is fairly hard to come by. It is no trick at all to find out the winning
and losing candidates for president and vice-president of the United States
over the years; most general reference works list that. What is less easy is
learning who contested with them for the party nominations. General reference works don't give that information.

Until 1831, there were no national political conventions. Party candidates were usually chosen through caucuses of senators and representatives. The convention method came into full use for the 1832 elections, and
thereafter candidates for president have normally been selected by the delegates to party political conventions. Not always, however—as the candidacy of Ross Perot showed in 1992.

American presidents are chosen by electoral rather than direct popular
vote. Each state is allocated one elector for each senator and for each representative in Congress. If no presidential candidate receives a majority of
electoral votes, the House of Representatives selects the president from
among the candidates with the three highest numbers of electoral votes.
Since the 1800 election this has happened only once, in the election of 1824.

The Constitution does not prescribe a method for selection of presidential electors by the states, and it was not until the election of 1824
that a total of popular votes cast for candidates became meaningful. Nor

does the Constitution provide for proportional selection of presidential electors within the states; in most states the candidate gaining a majority of votes receives all the electoral votes. A president may be elected even though gaining fewer popular votes than his principal opponent—*e.g.,* Rutherford B. Hayes and Benjamin Harrison. There is also no constitutional requirement that presidental electors cast their votes for the candidates for whom they were elected to vote, although most states have such laws.

The tabulation that follows lists the leading contenders for the nominations, the places and dates of party caucuses and conventions, the presidential and vice-presidential candidates selected, and the outcome of each national election. Names of particular interest are in boldface type.

1789

George Washington of Virginia was the unanimous choice for president under the new Constitution; there were no opposing candidates. Sixty-nine electoral votes were cast for Washington, and 34 for **John Adams** of Massachusetts, who became vice-president.

1792

George Washington was reelected unanimously, receiving 132 votes, with 3 abstentions. **John Adams** was reelected vice-president with 77 votes; 50 electoral votes were cast for George Clinton of New York by Anti-Federalist electors.

1796

John Adams of Massachusetts, the Federalist candidate, was elected president with 71 electoral votes; **Thomas Jefferson** of Virginia, the Democratic-Republican candidate, received 68 electoral votes, and was elected vice-president. Thomas Pinckney of South Carolina, Federalist, received 59 electoral votes; Aaron Burr of New York, 30; and 48 electoral votes were divided among others.

1800

A Democratic-Republican congressional caucus in Philadelphia nominated **Thomas Jefferson** of Virginia for president. There was a tie vote between **Aaron Burr** of New York and **Pierce Butler** of South Carolina for vice-president; Butler's supporters walked out of the caucus and no formal Democratic-Republican nomination for vice-president was made. A Federalist congressional caucus reluctantly renominated **John Adams** of Massachusetts for president, and **Charles Cotesworth Pinckney** of South Carolina for vice-president.

On the assumption that Adams and Pinckney would receive the same number of electoral votes and that the Federalists would outpoll the

Jeffersonian Democratic-Republican candidates, it was the intention of Alexander Hamilton's faction to persuade one presidential elector not to vote for Adams, so that Pinckney would then succeed to the presidency. When the electoral college ballot count was tabulated early in 1801, however, Jefferson and Burr each received 73 votes, Adams 65 votes, and Pinckney 64. Federalists in the House of Representatives saw an opportunity to thwart their enemies by supporting Burr, even though the intention of the Democratic-Republicans that Jefferson should be president was clear. Thirty-five ballots were held, with each state voting as a unit, without breaking the deadlock. It appears that finally Alexander Hamilton, believing Burr to be a more dangerous man than Jefferson, arranged for three Federalists to cast blank ballots, making possible **Jefferson**'s election by a majority of two states. **Burr** became vice-president. To forestall another such eventuality, the Twelfth Amendment to the Constitution was enacted.

1804

The Democratic-Republican congressional caucus unanimously renominated **Thomas Jefferson** for president. **George Clinton** of New York was nominated for vice-president over John Breckenridge of Kentucky. An informal caucus of Federalists nominated Charles Cotesworth Pinckney of South Carolina for president, Rufus King of New York for vice-president. In the election **Jefferson** and **Clinton** won with 162 electoral votes to Pinckney's and King's 14.

1808

The Democratic-Republican congressional caucus in January of 1808 nominated **James Madison** of Virginia for president over George Clinton of New York and James Monroe of Virginia. **Clinton** was nominated for vice-president over John Langdon of New Hampshire. The Federalists held a secret meeting in New York City in August, nominating **Charles Cotesworth Pinckney** of South Carolina for president, after considering supporting George Clinton. **Rufus King** was the Federalist choice for vice-president. **Madison** was elected president with 122 electoral votes to Pinckney's 47 and 6 for George Clinton. **Clinton** was chosen vice-president.

1812

James Madison of Virginia was renominated for president at the Democratic-Republican congressional caucus in May; John Langdon of New Hampshire was nominated for vice-president over Elbridge Gerry of Massachusetts. When Langdon declined the nomination, a second caucus held in June chose **Elbridge Gerry**. In New York State an anti-Madison group nominated **DeWitt Clinton** of New York for president, and at a secret meeting in New York City the Federalists endorsed Clinton's candidacy, with **Charles Jared Ingersoll** of

Pennsylvania as vice-president. **Madison** was elected president, with 128 votes to DeWitt Clinton's 89, and **Gerry** was elected vice-president.

1816

The Democratic-Republican congressional caucus in March nominated **James Monroe** of Virginia for president over William Harris Crawford of Georgia. **Daniel D. Tompkins** of New York received the vice-presidential nomination over Simon Snyder of Pennsylvania. The moribund Federalist party made no nominations. **Monroe** and **Tompkins** were elected, Madison receiving 183 electoral votes to 34 for Rufus King of New York.

1820

The Democratic-Republican congressional caucus selected **James Monroe** of Virginia and **Daniel D. Tompkins** of New York for reelection, although no formal nominations were made. The Federalists were no longer functioning as a political party. **Monroe** and **Tompkins** received 231 electoral votes. One electoral vote was cast for **John Quincy Adams** of Massachusetts.

1824

Only 66 of 261 Democratic-Republican congressmen took part in the party caucus in February; **William H. Crawford** of Georgia received 64 votes. Four other candidates sought the presidency. **John Quincy Adams** of Massachusetts was nominated at a meeting in Boston. **Andrew Jackson** of Tennessee was nominated by that state's legislature and at a meeting in Harrisburg, Pennsylvania. **Henry Clay** of Kentucky was nominated by the Kentucky legislature. **John C. Calhoun** of South Carolina announced his candidacy. Calhoun withdrew from the race to run for vice-president on both the Jackson and Adams tickets, and Crawford was eliminated from the campaign when he suffered a paralytic stroke. Richard Rush of Pennsylvania was named for vice-president as Adams's running mate on some state ballots.

In the presidential election, Jackson received 99 electoral votes and 151,271 popular votes, which were tabulated for the first time. Adams received 84 electoral and 113,122 popular votes. Clay won 37 electoral and 47,531 popular votes, and Crawford 41 electoral and 40,856 popular votes. Because no candidate had a majority of electoral votes, the election therefore went to the House of Representatives, which voted by states. **Adams** was chosen president by the votes of 13 states, with 7 for Jackson and 4 for Crawford, and **Calhoun** was named vice-president. After Adams selected Clay for secretary of state, a "corrupt bargain" charge was made by Jackson's adherents. The election of 1824 virtually eliminated the congressional caucus as a means of selecting nominees, and saw the end of one-party politics. Thereafter there were two increasingly distinct party organizations, the National Republicans, who became the Whigs, and the Democrats.

1828

Andrew Jackson of Tennessee, nominated by the legislature of that state, was the presidential candidate of the Jacksonian Democrats, and **John C. Calhoun** of South Carolina the vice-presidential candidate. Several state conventions nominated **John Quincy Adams** of Massachusetts for president and **Richard Rush** of Pennsylvania for vice-president. **Jackson** was elected president and **Calhoun** vice-president, with 178 electoral votes and 642,553 popular votes, over Adams' and Rush's 83 electoral and 500,897 popular votes.

Beginning with the presidential election of 1832, the political convention became the established mode for party nominations. The listings that follow give the contenders for the nomination for each party polling 2 percent or more of the popular vote in the subsequent election. The place and date for each party convention are listed.

Results of the presidential election are given in electoral votes, popular votes, and percentage of total popular votes.

1832

"National Republicans" (Whigs)—Baltimore, Md., December 12–14, 1831
>President—**Henry Clay**, Kentucky
>Vice-President—**John Sergeant**, Pennsylvania

"Anti-Masons"—Baltimore, Md., September 26–28, 1831
>President—**William Wirt**, Maryland
>Vice-President—**Amos Ellmaker**, Pennsylvania

Democrats—Baltimore, Md., May 21–23
>President—**Andrew Jackson**, Tennessee (not formally nominated; convention concurred in state nominations)
>Vice-President—**Martin Van Buren**, New York

ELECTION

Andrew Jackson, 219 electoral votes; 701,780 popular (54.2%)
Henry Clay, 49; 484,205 (37.4%)
William Wirt, 7; 100,715 (7.8%)
John Floyd (Virginia), 11 electoral votes

1836

Democrats—Baltimore, Md., May 20–23, 1835
>President—**Martin Van Buren**, New York
>Vice-President—**Richard Mentor Johnson**, Kentucky

Whigs—No convention. Regional candidates.
>President—**Daniel Webster**, New Hampshire, in Massachusetts; **Hugh L. White**, Tennessee, in South; **William Henry Harrison**, Ohio, elsewhere.

Vice-President—**Francis Granger**, New York, as Harrison's and Webster's running mate; **John Tyler**, Virginia, as White's.

ELECTION
Martin Van Buren, 170 electoral votes; 764,176 popular (50.8%)
William Henry Harrison, 73; 550,866 (36.7%)
Hugh L. White, 26; 146,107 (9.7%)
Daniel Webster, 14; 41,207 (2.7%)

1840

Whigs—Harrisburg, Pa., December 4–7, 1839
  President—**William Henry Harrison**, Ohio; Winfield Scott, New Jersey; Henry Clay, Kentucky
  Vice-President—**John Tyler**, Virginia (succeeded to presidency when Harrison died in office)
Democrats—Baltimore, Md., May 5–6
  President—**Martin Van Buren**, New York
  Vice-President—No party nominee chosen

ELECTION
William Henry Harrison, 234 electoral votes; 1,275,390 popular (52.9%)
Martin Van Buren, 60; 1,128,854 (46.8%)

1844

Liberty Party—Buffalo, N.Y., August 30–31, 1843
  President—**James G. Birney**, Michigan
  Vice-President—**Thomas Morris**, Ohio
Whigs—Baltimore, Md., May 1
  President—**Henry Clay**, Kentucky; John Tyler, Virginia (President Tyler's supporters held a separate convention to renominate him, on May 27, 1844, in Baltimore, but Tyler withdrew in favor of the Democratic candidate.)
  Vice-President—**Theodore Frelinghuysen**, New Jersey
Democrats—Baltimore, Md., May 27–29
  President—Martin Van Buren, New York; Lewis Cass, Michigan; **James K. Polk**, Tennessee
  Vice-President—Silas Wright, New York (declined); **George M. Dallas**, Pennsylvania

ELECTION
James K. Polk, 170 electoral votes; 1,339,494 popular (49.5%)
Henry Clay, 105; 1,300,004 (48.1%)
James G. Birney, 0; 62,103 (2.3%)

1848

Democrats—Baltimore, Md., May 22–25
    President—**Lewis Cass**, Michigan; James Buchanan, Pennsylvania; Levi Woodbury, New Hampshire
    Vice-President—**William O. Butler**, Kentucky; John A. Quitman, Mississippi
Whigs—Philadelphia, Pa., June 7–9
    President—Henry Clay, Kentucky; **Zachary Taylor**, Virginia; Winfield Scott, New Jersey
    Vice-President—**Millard Fillmore**, New York (succeeded to presidency when Taylor died in office); Abbott Lawrence, Massachusetts
Free-Soilers—Buffalo, N.Y., August 9
    President—**Martin Van Buren**, New York; John P. Hale, New Hampshire
    Vice-President—**Charles Francis Adams**, Massachusetts

ELECTION
Zachary Taylor, 163 electoral votes; 1,361,393 popular (47.3%)
Lewis Cass, 127; 1,223,460 (42.5%)
Martin Van Buren, 0; 291,501 (10.1%)

1852

Democrats—Baltimore, Md., June 1–5
    President—Lewis Cass, Michigan; James Buchanan, Pennsylvania; William L. Marcy, New York; Stephen A. Douglas, Illinois; **Franklin Pierce**, New Hampshire
    Vice-President—**William R. King**, Alabama
Whigs—Baltimore, Md., June 16–21
    President—Millard Fillmore, New York; **Winfield Scott**, New Jersey; Daniel Webster, Massachusetts
    Vice-President—**William A. Graham**, North Carolina
Free Democrats—Pittsburgh, Pa., August 11
    President—**John P. Hale**, New Hampshire
    Vice-President—**George W. Julian**, Indiana

ELECTION
Franklin Pierce, 254 electoral votes; 1,607,510 popular (50.8%)
Winfield Scott, 42; 1,386,942 (44%)
John P. Hale, 0; 155,210 (4.9%)

1856

Republicans—Pittsburgh, Pa., June 17–19
    President—Salmon P. Chase, Ohio; William H. Seward, New York; John McLean, Ohio; **John C. Fremont**, California

Vice-President—**William L. Dayton**, New Jersey; Abraham Lincoln, Illinois

American (Know-Nothings)—Philadelphia, Pa., February 22
President—**Millard Fillmore**, New York
Vice-President—**Andrew Jackson Donelson**, Tennessee

Anti-Slavery Know-Nothings—New York, N.Y., June 12–19
President—**Nathaniel P. Banks**, Massachusetts (dropped out of race after nomination of Fremont by Republicans)
Vice-President—**William F. Johnston**, Pennsylvania (dropped out of race in favor of William L. Dayton)

Democrats—Cincinnati, Ohio, June 2–6
President—Franklin Pierce, New Hampshire; **James Buchanan**, Pennsylvania; Stephen A. Douglas, Illinois
Vice-President—John A. Quitman, Mississippi; **John C. Breckenridge**, Kentucky

ELECTION
James Buchanan, 174 electoral votes; 1,838,072 popular (45.3%)
John C. Fremont, 114; 1,342,345 (33.1%)
Millard Fillmore, 8; 873,053 (21.5%)

1860
Democrats—Charleston, S.C., April 23-May 3; reconvened Baltimore, Md., June 18–23
President—**Stephen A. Douglas**, Illinois; Robert M. T. Hunter, Virginia; James Guthrie, Kentucky
Vice-President—**Herschel Johnson**, Georgia

Southern Democrats—Baltimore, Md., June 28
President—**John C. Breckenridge**, Kentucky
Vice-President—**Joseph Lane**, Oregon

Republicans—Chicago, Ill., May 16–18
President—William H. Seward, New York; **Abraham Lincoln**, Illinois; Simon Cameron, Pennsylvania; Salmon P. Chase, Ohio; Edward Bates, Missouri
Vice-President—**Hannibal Hamlin**, Maine; Cassius M. Clay, Kentucky

Constitutional Union—Baltimore, Md., May 9
President—**John Bell**, Tennessee; Sam Houston, Texas
Vice-President—**Edward Everett**, Massachusetts

ELECTION
Abraham Lincoln, 180 electoral votes; 1,865,908 popular (39.8%)
Stephen A. Douglas, 12; 1,380,202 (29.5%)

John C. Breckenridge, 72; 848,019 (18.1%)
John Bell, 39; 590,901 (12.6%)

1864

Republicans (Union)—Baltimore, Md., June 7–8
President—**Abraham Lincoln**, Illinois; Salmon P. Chase, Ohio; U. S. Grant, Illinois
Vice-President—Hannibal Hamlin, Maine; **Andrew Johnson**, Tennessee (succeeded to presidency after Lincoln was assassinated); Samuel S. Dickinson, New York
Democrats—Chicago, Ill., August 29–31
President—**George B. McClellan**, New Jersey; Thomas H. Seymour, Connecticut
Vice-President—James Guthrie, Kentucky; **George H. Pendleton**, Ohio

ELECTION
Abraham Lincoln, 212 electoral votes; 2,218,388 popular (55%)
George B. McClellan, 21; 1,812,807 (45%)

1868

Republicans—Chicago, Ill., May 20–21
President—**Ulysses S. Grant**, Illinois
Vice-President—Benjamin F. Wade, Ohio; Reuben E. Fenton, New York; Henry Wilson, Massachusetts; **Schuyler Colfax**, Indiana
Democrats—New York, N.Y., July 4–9
President—George H. Pendleton, Ohio; Andrew Johnson, Tennessee; Winfield Scott Hancock, Pennsylvania; Thomas A. Hendricks, Indiana; **Horatio Seymour**, New York
Vice-President—**Francis P. Blair, Jr.**, Missouri

ELECTION
Ulysses S. Grant, 214 electoral votes; 3,013,650 popular (52.7%)
Horatio Seymour, 80; 2,708,744 (47.3%)

1872

Liberal Republicans—Cincinnati, Ohio, May 1–3
President—Charles Francis Adams, Massachusetts; Lyman Trumbull, Illinois; David Davis, Illinois; **Horace Greeley**, New York; B. Gratz Brown, Missouri
Vice-President—**B. Gratz Brown**, Missouri

Democrats—Baltimore, Md., July 9–10
  President—**Horace Greeley**, New York
  Vice-President—**B. Gratz Brown**, Missouri
Republicans—Philadelphia, Pa., June 5–6
  President—**U. S. Grant**, Illinois
  Vice-President—Schuyler Colfax, Indiana; **Henry Wilson**, Massachusetts

ELECTION

Ulysses S. Grant, 286 electoral votes; 3,598,235 popular (55.6%)
Horace Greeley, (63—Greeley died before the Electoral College was convened, and
his electoral votes were cast for Thomas A. Hendricks, 42; B. Gratz Brown, 18;
Charles J. Jenkins, 2, and David Davis, 1); popular vote 2,834,761 (43.8%)

1876

Republicans—Cincinnati, Ohio, June 14–16
  President—James G. Blaine, Maine; Roscoe Conkling, New York; Oliver P.
    Morton, Indiana; Benjamin H. Bristow, Kentucky; **Rutherford B. Hayes**,
    Ohio
  Vice-President—**William A. Wheeler**, New York
Democrats—St. Louis, Mo., June 27–29
  President—**Samuel J. Tilden**, New York; Thomas J. Hendricks, Indiana
  Vice-President—**Thomas J. Hendricks**, Indiana

ELECTION

Rutherford B. Hayes, 185 electoral votes; 4,034,311 popular (48%)
Samuel J. Tilden, 184; 4,288,546 (51%)

1880

Republicans—Chicago, Ill., June 2–8
  President—U. S. Grant, Illinois; **James A. Garfield**, Ohio; James G. Blaine,
    Maine; John Sherman, Ohio
  Vice-President—**Chester A. Arthur**, New York (succeeded to presi-
    dency after Garfield was assassinated); Elihu B. Washburn, Illinois
Greenback-Labor—Chicago, Ill., June 9–11
  President—**James B. Weaver**, Ohio
  Vice-President—**B. J. Chambers**, Texas
Democrats—Cincinnati, Ohio, June 22–24
  President—**Winfield Scott Hancock**, Pennsylvania; Thomas F. Bayard,
    Delaware; Henry G. Payne, Ohio; Samuel J. Randall, Pennsylvania
  Vice-President—**William H. English**, Indiana

ELECTION

James A. Garfield, 214 electoral votes; 4,446,158 popular (48.2%)
Winfield S. Hancock, 155; 4,444,260 (48.2%)
James B. Weaver, 0; 305,987 (3.4%)

1884

Republicans—Chicago, Ill., June 3–6
    President—**James G. Blaine**, Maine; Chester A. Arthur, New York; George
        F. Edmunds, Vermont
    Vice-President—**John A. Logan**, Illinois
Democrats—Chicago, Ill., July 8–11
    President—Thomas A. Hendricks, Indiana; **Grover Cleveland**, New York;
        Thomas F. Bayard, Delaware; Allen G. Thurman, Ohio
    Vice-President—**Thomas A. Hendricks**, Indiana

ELECTION

Grover Cleveland, 219 electoral votes; 4,874,621 popular (48.5%)
James G. Blaine, 182; 4,848,936 (48.2%)

1888

Prohibition—Indianapolis, Ind., May 31-June 2
    President—**Clinton B. Fisk**, New Jersey
    Vice-President—**John A. Brooks**, Missouri
Democrats—St. Louis, Mo., June 5–7
    President—**Grover Cleveland**, New York
    Vice-President—**Allen G. Thurman**, Ohio; Isaac P. Gray, Indiana; John C.
        Black, Illinois
Republicans—Chicago, Ill., June 19–25
    President—John Sherman, Ohio; Walter Q. Gresham, Indiana; Russell A.
        Alger, Michigan; Chauncey Depew, New York; **Benjamin Harrison**,
        Indiana
    Vice-President—**Levi P. Morton**, New York; William Walter Phelps, New
        Jersey; William O. Bradley, Kentucky

ELECTION

Benjamin Harrison, 233 electoral votes; 5,443,892 popular (47.8%)
Grover Cleveland, 168; 5,534,488 (48.6%)
Clinton B. Fisk, 0; 249,813 (2.2%)

1892

Republicans—Minneapolis, Minn., June 7–10
  President—**Benjamin Harrison**, Indiana; James G. Blaine, Maine; William McKinley, Ohio
  Vice-President—Levi P. Morton, New York; **Whitelaw Reid**, New York
Democrats—Chicago, Ill., June 21–23
  President—**Grover Cleveland**, New York; David B. Hill, New York; Horace Boies, Iowa
  Vice-President—**Adlai E. Stevenson**, Illinois; Isaac P. Gray, Indiana
Prohibition—Cincinnati, Ohio, June 29–July 1
  President—**John Bidwell**, California
  Vice-President—**James B. Cranfill**, Texas
People's Party (Populists)—Omaha, Neb., July 2–4
  President—**James B. Weaver**, Iowa; James H. Kyle, South Dakota
  Vice-President—**James G. Field**, Virginia; Ben Terrell, Texas

ELECTION

Grover Cleveland, 277 electoral votes; 5,551,883 popular (46%)
Benjamin Harrison, 145; 5,179,244 (43%)
James B. Weaver, 22; 1,024,280 (8.5%)
John Bidwell, 0; 270,770 (2.2%)

1896

Republicans—St. Louis, Mo., June 16–18
  President—**William McKinley**, Ohio; Thomas B. Reed, Maine
  Vice-President—**Garret A. Hobart**, New Jersey; Henry Clay Evans, Tennessee
Democrats—Chicago, Ill., July 7–11
  President—Richard P. Bland, Missouri; **William Jennings Bryan**, Nebraska; Robert E. Pattison, Pennsylvania
  Vice-President—John C. Sibley, Pennsylvania; John B. McLean, Ohio; **Arthur Sewall**, Maine; Richard P. Bland, Missouri

ELECTION

William McKinley, 271 electoral votes; 7,108,480 popular (51%)
William Jennings Bryan, 176; 6,511,495 (46.7%)

1900

Republicans—Philadelphia, Pa., June 19–21
  President—**William McKinley**, Ohio
  Vice-President—**Theodore Roosevelt**, New York (succeeded to presidency after McKinley was assassinated)

Democrats—Kansas City, Mo., July 4–6
   President—**William Jennings Bryan**, Nebraska
   Vice-President—**Adlai Stevenson**, Illinois; David B. Hill, New York

ELECTION

William McKinley, 292 electoral votes; 7,218,039 popular (51.7%)
William Jennings Bryan, 155; 6,358,345 (45.5%)

1904

Socialists—Chicago, Ill., May 5
   President—**Eugene V. Debs**, Indiana
   Vice-President—**Benjamin Hanford**, New York
Republicans—Chicago, Ill., June 21–23
   President—**Theodore Roosevelt**, New York
   Vice-President—**Charles W. Fairbanks**, Indiana
Democrats—St. Louis, Mo., July 6–9
   President—Francis M. Cockrell, Missouri; **Alton B. Parker**, New York;
      William Randolph Hearst, New York
   Vice-President—**Henry G. Davis**, West Virginia

ELECTION

Theodore Roosevelt, 336 electoral votes; 7,626,593 popular (56.4%)
Alton B. Parker, 140; 5,082,898 (37.6%)
Eugene V. Debs, 0; 402,489 (3.0%)

1908

Socialists—Chicago, Ill., May 10–17
   President—**Eugene V. Debs**, Indiana
   Vice-President—**Benjamin Hanford**, New York
Republicans—Chicago, Ill., June 16–19
   President—**William Howard Taft**, Ohio; Philander C. Knox, Pennsylvania
   Vice-President—**James S. Sherman**, New York; Franklin Murphy, New
      Jersey
Democrats—Denver, Colo., July 7–10
   President—**William Jennings Bryan**, Nebraska; George Gray, Delaware;
      John A. Johnson, Minnesota
   Vice-President—**John W. Kern**, Indiana

ELECTION

William Howard Taft, 321 electoral votes; 7,676,258 popular (51.6%)
William Jennings Bryan, 162; 6,406,801 (43.1%)
Eugene V. Debs, 0; 420,380 (2.8%)

1912

Socialists—Indianapolis, Ind., May 12

President—**Eugene V. Debs**, Indiana

Vice-President—**Emil Seidel**, Wisconsin

Republicans—Chicago, Ill., June 18–22

President—Theodore Roosevelt, New York; **William Howard Taft**, Ohio; Robert M. La Follette, Wisconsin

Vice-President—**James S. Sherman**, New York; William E. Borah, Idaho

Democrats—Baltimore, Md., June 25-July 2

President—John Beauchamp "Champ" Clark, Missouri; **Woodrow Wilson**, New Jersey; Judson Harmon, Ohio; Oscar W. Underwood, Alabama

Vice-President—**Thomas R. Marshall**, Indiana; John Burke, North Dakota

Progressives—Chicago, Ill., August 5–7

President—**Theodore Roosevelt**, New York

Vice-President—**Hiram W. Johnson**, California

ELECTION

Woodrow Wilson, 435 electoral votes; 6,293,152 popular (41.8%)

Theodore Roosevelt, 88; 4,119,207 (27.4%)

William Howard Taft, 8; 3,486,333 (23.2%)

Eugene V. Debs, 0; 900,369 (6%)

1916

Republican—Chicago, Ill., June 7–10

President—**Charles Evans Hughes**, New York; John W. Weeks, Massachusetts; Elihu Root, New York; Theodore Roosevelt, New York (nominated at Progressive convention held simultaneously in Chicago, but declined in favor of Hughes)

Vice-President—**Charles W. Fairbanks**, Indiana; Elmer J. Burkett, Nebraska.

Democrats—St. Louis, Mo., June 14–16

President—**Woodrow Wilson**, New Jersey

Vice-President—**Thomas R. Marshall**, Indiana

Socialists—No convention

President—**Allan L. Benson**, New York

Vice-President—**George R. Kirkpatrick**, New Jersey

ELECTION

Woodrow Wilson, 277 electoral votes; 9,126,300 popular (49.2%)

Charles Evans Hughes, 254; 8,546,789 (46.1%)

Allan L. Benson, 0; 589,924 (3.2%)

1920

Socialists—New York, N.Y., May 8–15

    President—**Eugene V. Debs**, Indiana

    Vice-President—**Seymour Stedman**, Ohio

Republicans—Chicago, Ill., June 8–12

    President—Leonard Wood, New Hampshire; Hiram Johnson, California; Frank Lowden, Illinois; Herbert C. Hoover, California; **Warren G. Harding**, Ohio

    Vice-President—Irvine L. Lenroot, Wisconsin; **Calvin Coolidge**, Massachusetts (succeeded to presidency when Harding died in office)

Democrats—San Francisco, Calif., June 28-July 6

    President—William G. McAdoo, California; Edward I. Edwards, New Jersey; A. Mitchell Palmer, Pennsylvania; **James M. Cox**, Ohio; Alfred E. Smith, New York

    Vice-President—**Franklin D. Roosevelt**, New York

ELECTION

Warren G. Harding, 404 electoral votes; 16,133,314 popular (60.3%)

James M. Cox, 127; 9,140,884 (34.2%)

Eugene V. Debs, 0; 913,664 (3.4%)

1924

Republicans—Cleveland, Ohio, June 10–12

    President—**Calvin Coolidge**, Massachusetts; Robert M. La Follette, Wisconsin; Hiram W. Johnson, California

    Vice-President—Frank O. Lowden, Illinois; **Charles G. Dawes**, Nebraska; Herbert C. Hoover, California

Democrats—New York, N.Y., June 24-July 9

    President—Alfred E. Smith, New York; William G. McAdoo, California; **John W. Davis**, West Virginia; Samuel M. Ralston, Indiana; Oscar W. Underwood, Alabama

    Vice-President—**Charles W. Bryan**, Nebraska; George L. Berry, Tennessee

Progressives—Cleveland, Ohio, July 4–7

    President—**Robert M. La Follette**, Wisconsin

    Vice-President—**Burton K. Wheeler**, Montana

ELECTION

Calvin Coolidge, 382 electoral votes; 15,717,553 popular (54%)

John W. Davis, 136; 8,386,169 (28.8%)

Robert M. La Follette, 13; 4,814,050 (16.5%)

1928

Republicans—Kansas City, Mo., June 12–15
> President—**Herbert C. Hoover**, California; Frank O. Lowden, Illinois; George W. Norris, Nebraska
> Vice-President—**Charles Curtis**, Kansas

Democrats—Houston, Tex., June 26–29
> President—**Alfred E. Smith**, New York; Thomas Walsh, Montana; James A. Reed, Missouri
> Vice-President—**Joseph T. Robinson**, Arkansas; Alben W. Barkley, Kentucky

ELECTION

Herbert C. Hoover, 444 electoral votes; 21,411,991 popular (58.2%)

Alfred E. Smith, 87; 15,000,185 (40.8%)

1932

Socialists—Milwaukee, Wis., May 22–24
> President—**Norman Thomas**, New York
> Vice-President—**James H. Maurer**, Pennsylvania

Republicans—Chicago, Ill., June 14–16
> President—**Herbert Hoover**, California
> Vice-President—**Charles Curtis**, Kansas; James G. Harbord, New York; Hanford MacNider, Iowa

Democrats—Chicago, Ill., June 27-July 2
> President—**Franklin D. Roosevelt**, New York; Alfred E. Smith, New York; Albert C. Ritchie, Maryland; John N. Garner, Texas
> Vice-President—**John N. Garner**, Texas

ELECTION

Franklin D. Roosevelt, 472 electoral votes; 22,825,016 popular (57.4%)

Herbert Hoover, 59; 15,758,397 (39.6)

Norman Thomas, 0; 883,990 (2.2%)

1936

Republicans—Cleveland, Ohio, June 9–12
> President—**Alfred M. Landon**, Kansas; William E. Borah, Idaho; Frank Knox, Illinois
> Vice-President—**Frank Knox**, Illinois

Democrats—Philadelphia, Pa., June 23–27
> President—**Franklin D. Roosevelt**, New York
> Vice-President—**John N. Garner**, Texas

Union Party—No party convention
> President—**William Lemke**, North Dakota
> Vice-President—**Thomas O'Brien**, Massachusetts

ELECTION

Franklin D. Roosevelt, 523 electoral votes; 27,747,636 popular (60.8%)
Alfred M. Landon, 8; 16,679,543 (36.5%)
William Lemke, 0; 892,492 (2%)

1940

Republicans—Philadelphia, Pa., June 24–28
> President—**Wendell Willkie**, Indiana; Thomas E. Dewey, New York; Robert
> A. Taft, Ohio
> Vice-President—**Charles McNary**, Oregon; Dewey Short, Missouri

Democrats–Chicago, Ill., July 15–18
> President—**Franklin D. Roosevelt**, New York; John N. Garner, Texas; James
> A. Farley, New York
> Vice-President—**Henry A. Wallace**, Iowa; William B. Bankhead, Alabama

ELECTION

Franklin D. Roosevelt, 449 electoral votes; 27,263,448 popular (54.7%)
Wendell Willkie, 82; 22,336,260 (44.8%)

1944

Republicans—Chicago, Ill., June 26–28
> President—**Thomas E. Dewey**, New York; John W. Bricker, Ohio; Harold
> Stassen, Minnesota; Douglas MacArthur, Wisconsin
> Vice-President—**John W. Bricker**, Ohio

Democrats—Chicago, Ill., July 19–21
> President—**Franklin D. Roosevelt**, New York; Harry F. Byrd, Virginia
> Vice-President—Henry A. Wallace, Iowa; **Harry S Truman**, Missouri (suc-
> ceeded to presidency when Roosevelt died in office); William O.
> Douglas, Washington; James F. Byrnes, South Carolina

ELECTION

Franklin D. Roosevelt, 432 electoral votes; 25,611,936 popular (53.4%)
Thomas E. Dewey, 99; 22,013,372 (46%)

1948

Republicans—Philadelphia, Pa., June 21–25
> President—**Thomas E. Dewey**, New York; Robert A. Taft, Ohio; Harold E.
> Stassen, Minnesota; Earl Warren, California; Arthur Vandenburg,
> Michigan; Douglas MacArthur, Wisconsin
> Vice-President—**Earl Warren**, California

Democrats—Philadelphia, Pa., July 12–14
> President—**Harry S Truman**, Missouri; Richard B. Russell, Georgia
> Vice-President—**Alben W. Barkley**, Kentucky

States Rights (Dixiecrats)—Birmingham, Ala., July 17
    President—**J. Strom Thurmond**, South Carolina
    Vice-President—**Fielding L. Wright**, Mississippi
Progressives—Philadelphia, Pa., July 23-25
    President—**Henry A. Wallace**, Iowa
    Vice-President—**Glen Taylor**, Idaho

ELECTION

Harry S Truman, 303 electoral votes; 24,105,587 popular (49.5%)
Thomas E. Dewey, 189; 21,970,017 (45.1%)
J. Strom Thurmond, 39; 1,169,134 (2.4%)
Henry A. Wallace, 0; 1,157,057 (2.4%)

1952

Republicans-Chicago, Ill., July 7–11
    President—Robert A. Taft, Ohio; **Dwight D. Eisenhower**, Texas; Douglas
        MacArthur, New York; Harold E. Stassen, Minnesota; Earl Warren,
        California
    Vice-President—**Richard M. Nixon**, California
Democrats—Chicago, Ill., July 21–26
    President—Estes Kefauver, Tennessee; **Adlai E. Stevenson**, Illinois; Richard
        B. Russell, Georgia; W. Averill Harriman, New York; Alvin W. Barkley,
        Kentucky
    Vice-President—**John J. Sparkman**, Alabama

ELECTION

Dwight D. Eisenhower, 442 electoral votes; 33,936,137 popular (55.1%)
Adlai E. Stevenson, 89; 27,314,649 (44.4%)

1956

Democrats—Chicago, Ill., August 13–17
    President—**Adlai E. Stevenson**, Illinois; W. Averell Harriman, New York;
        Estes Kefauver, Tennessee; Lyndon B. Johnson, Texas
    Vice-President—**Estes Kefauver**, Tennessee; John F. Kennedy, Massachusetts;
        Albert A. Gore, Tennessee; Robert F. Wagner, New York; Hubert H.
        Humphrey, Minnesota; Lyndon B. Johnson, Texas
Republicans—San Francisco, Calif., August 20–23
    President—**Dwight D. Eisenhower**, Texas
    Vice-President—**Richard M. Nixon**, California; Christian A. Herter,
        Massachusetts

ELECTION
Dwight D. Eisenhower, 457 electoral votes; 35,585,245 popular (57.4%)
Adlai E. Stevenson, 73; 26,030,172 (42%)

1960

Democrats—Los Angeles, Calif., July 11–15
> President—**John F. Kennedy**, Massachusetts; Lyndon B. Johnson, Texas;
> Adlai E. Stevenson, Illinois; Stuart Symington, Missouri; Wayne
> Morse, Oregon
> Vice-President—**Lyndon B. Johnson**, Texas (succeeded to presidency after
> assassination of Kennedy)

Republicans—Chicago, Ill., July 25–28
> President—**Richard M. Nixon**, California; Barry Goldwater, Arizona;
> Nelson Rockefeller, New York
> Vice-President—**Henry Cabot Lodge**, Massachusetts

ELECTION
John F. Kennedy, 303 electoral votes; 34,221,344 popular (49.7%)
Richard M. Nixon, 219 electoral votes; 34,106,671 (49.5%)

1964

Republicans—San Francisco, Calif., July 13–16
> President—**Barry Goldwater**, Arizona; Nelson Rockefeller, New York;
> William W. Scranton, Pennsylvania; George Romney, Michigan; Henry
> Cabot Lodge, Massachusetts
> Vice-President—**William E. Miller**, New York

Democrats—Atlantic City, N.J., August 24–27
> President—**Lyndon B. Johnson**, Texas
> Vice-President—**Hubert H. Humphrey**, Minnesota; Thomas J. Dodd,
> Connecticut; Eugene McCarthy, Minnesota

ELECTION
Lyndon B. Johnson, 486 electoral votes; 43,126,584 popular (61%)
Barry Goldwater, 52; 27,177,838 (38.5%)

1968

Republicans—Miami Beach, Fla., August 5–8
> President—**Richard M. Nixon**, California; Nelson Rockefeller, New York;
> Ronald Reagan, California
> Vice-President—**Spiro T. Agnew**, Maryland; George Romney, Michigan

Democrats-Chicago, Ill., August 26–29
> President—**Hubert H. Humphrey**, Minnesota; Eugene McCarthy,

Minnesota; Robert Kennedy, Massachusetts (assassinated during nomination campaign, June 5); George S. McGovern, South Dakota

Vice-President—**Edmund S. Muskie**, Maine; Julian Bond, Georgia

American Independent—No convention

President—**George C. Wallace**, Alabama

Vice-President—Marvin Griffin, Georgia ("interim" candidate); **Curtis E. LeMay**, Ohio

ELECTION

Richard M. Nixon, 301 electoral votes; 31,785,148 popular (43.4%)

Hubert H. Humphrey, 191; 31,274,503 (42.7%)

George C. Wallace 46; 9,901,151 (13.5%)

1972

Democrats–Miami Beach, Fla., July 10–13

President—**George S. McGovern**, South Dakota; Hubert H. Humphrey, Minnesota; George C. Wallace, Alabama; Edmund S. Muskie, Maine; Henry M. Jackson, Washington; Eugene McCarthy, Minnesota

Vice-President—**Thomas F. Eagleton**, Missouri; Frances T. Farenthold, Texas; Mike Gravel, Alaska (Eagleton withdrew from ticket July 31, and **R. Sargent Shriver**, Maryland, was named by Democratic National Committee meeting, Washington, D.C., August 8.)

Republicans—Miami Beach, Fla., August 21–23

President—**Richard M. Nixon**, California; Paul N. McCloskey, California; John M. Ashbrook, Ohio

Vice-President—**Spiro T. Agnew**, Maryland (After Agnew resigned from office in 1973, Gerald R. Ford, Michigan, was appointed vice-president; Ford became president upon resignation of Nixon in 1974, and Nelson Rockefeller, New York, was appointed vice-president.)

ELECTION

Richard M. Nixon, 520 electoral votes; 47,170,179 popular (60.7%)

George S. McGovern, 17; 29,171,791 votes (37.5%)

1976

Democrats—New York, N.Y., July 12–15

President—**Jimmy Carter**, Georgia; Edmund Muskie, Maine; Henry M. Jackson, Washington; Morris K. Udall, Arizona; George C. Wallace, Alabama; Lloyd C. Bentsen, Texas; Edmund (Jerry) Brown, California; Frank Church, Utah; George McGovern, South Dakota.

Vice-President—**Walter Mondale**, Minnesota

Republicans—Kansas City, Mo., August 16–19
   President—**Gerald R. Ford**, Michigan; Ronald Reagan, California
   Vice-President—**Robert Dole**, Iowa

ELECTION
Jimmy Carter, 297 electoral votes; 40,830,763 popular (50.1%)
Gerald R. Ford, 240; 39, 147,793 (48%)

1980
Republicans-Detroit, Mich., July 14–17
   President—**Ronald Reagan**, California; Howard H. Baker, Jr., Tennessee;
      George Bush, Texas; John Connolly, Texas; Robert Dole, Kansas; Philip
      M. Crane, Illinois; Gerald R. Ford, Michigan; John B. Anderson, Illinois
      (Anderson subsequently ran for president as an independent candidate.)
   Vice-President—**George Bush**, Texas
Democrats–New York, N.Y., August 11–14
   President—**Jimmy Carter**, Georgia; Edmund (Jerry) Brown, California;
      Edward M. (Teddy) Kennedy, Massachusetts
   Vice President—**Walter Mondale**, Minnesota
National Unity Party—No convention
   President—**John B. Anderson**, Illinois
   Vice-President—**Patrick J. Lucey**, Wisconsin

ELECTION
Ronald Reagan, 489 electoral votes; 43,904,153 popular (50.7%)
Jimmy Carter, 49; 35,483,883 (41%)
John B. Anderson, 0; 5,720,060 (6.7%)

1984
Democrats—San Francisco, Calif., July 16–19
   President—**Walter Mondale**, Minnesota; Gary Hart, Colorado; John Glenn,
      Ohio; Lloyd Bentsen, Texas; George McGovern, South Dakota; Rev.
      Jesse Jackson, Illinois; Reuben Askew, Florida; Alan Cranston,
      California; Ernest Hollings, South Carolina
   Vice-President—**Geraldine Ferraro**, New York; Thomas Bradley, California
Republicans-Dallas, Tex., August 20–23
   President—**Ronald Reagan**, California
   Vice-President—**George Bush**, Texas

ELECTION
Ronald Reagan, 525 electoral votes; 54,455,074 popular (59%)
Walter Mondale, 13; 37,557,137 (41%)

1988

Democrats—Atlanta, Ga., July 18–21

President—**Michael Dukakis**, Massachusetts; Richard Gephardt, Indiana; Paul Simon, Illinois; Bruce Babbitt, Arizona; Jesse Jackson, Illinois; Gary Hart, Colorado

Vice-President—**Lloyd Bentsen**, Texas

Republicans—New Orleans, La., August 15–18

President—**George Bush**, Texas; Robert Dole, Iowa; Jack Kemp, New York; Alexander Haig, Pennsylvania; Pat Robertson, Virginia

Vice-President—**Dan Quayle**, Indiana

ELECTION

George Bush, 426 electoral votes; 48,881,221 popular (53.4%)

Michael Dukakis, 111; 41,805,422 (45.6%)

1992

Democrats—New York City, N.Y., July 13–16

President—**Bill Clinton**, Arkansas; Edmund (Jerry) Brown, California; Tom Harkin, Iowa; Paul Tsongas, Massachusetts; Bob Kerrey, Nebraska; Douglas Wilder, Virginia

Vice-President—**Albert Gore**, Tennessee

Republicans—Houston, Tex., August 17–21

President—**George Bush**, Texas; Pat Buchanan, District of Columbia; David Duke, Louisiana

Vice-President—**Dan Quayle**, Indiana

Independent—No convention

President—**H. Ross Perot**, Texas

Vice President—**Vice Adm. James Stockdale**, Illinois

ELECTION

Bill Clinton, 370 electoral votes; 44,908,254 popular votes (42.9%)

George Bush, 168; 39,102,343 (37.4%)

Ross Perot, 0; 19,217,213 (19%)

SOURCES

Figures for the popular vote totals in presidential elections differ from tabulation to tabulation. Those cited above have been taken from Robert A. Diamond, ed., *Congressional Quarterly's Guide to U.S. Elections* (Washington, D.C.: Congressional Quarterly, Inc., 1985), for the period 1832–1984; and from *The World Almanac and Book of Facts, 1993* (New York: Pharos Books, 1994), for the elections from 1976 through 1992.

Other books from which information has been drawn include the following:

Morris, Richard B., ed. *Encyclopedia of American History*. 6th ed. New York: Harper and Row, 1982.

National Party Conventions, 1831–1980. Washington, D.C.: Congressional Quarterly, Inc., 1983.

Prewitt, Kenneth, Sidney Verba, and Robert H. Salisbury. *An Introduction to American Government*. 5th ed. New York: Harper and Row, 1987.

Stoddard, Henry Luther. *Presidential Sweepstakes*. New York: G. P. Putnam's Sons, 1948.

Tindall, George Brown. *America: A Narrative History*. New York: W. W. Norton, 1984.

Wayne, Stephen J. *The Road to the White House*. New York: St. Martin's Press, 1980.

—L.D.R.

14

PROMINENT MEMBERS OF
THE U.S. CONGRESS

Congress is in session, and no man is safe.
—ANON.

· · · · ·

WRITERS OF HUMOR HAVE LONG TENDED TO DRAW UPON THE CONGRESS OF the United States for Grade-A Choice subject matter. Mark Twain declared that it could probably be shown that America has no distinctive criminal class except Congress. H. L. Mencken offered this hypothesis: "Suppose two-thirds of the members of the national House of Representatives were dumped into the Washington garbage incinerator tomorrow, what would we lose to offset our gain of their salaries and the salaries of their parasites?" And so on.

What makes a congressman effective doesn't necessarily make him or her popular, as witness the fact that the last genuinely important congressman to be elected president other than via the incumbent's being assassinated, dying in office, or getting kicked out was James A. Garfield in 1880. Nobody ever accused either Warren G. Harding or John F. Kennedy of being a central figure in congressional decision making. Clearly, if one is going to run for president it is far better to do so as a governor than as a senator or a representative.

Once a congressman retires, his or her contemporary renown swiftly ebbs. Who remembers, immediately and without coaching, Howard W. Smith, Pat Harrison, Claude Kitchin, Carl Vinson, even Carl Albert? Yet in their day, which was not so very long ago, they were men of much legislative power; presidents courted them. Ask the average reasonably well read citizen to give the names of a half dozen leading members of Congress during the Civil War years. The list offered will probably begin and end with

Thaddeus Stevens, and then only because he sought to oust Andrew Johnson from the White House.

It is time that something be done about this. So herewith follows a compilation of the names of no fewer than 250 United States senators and representatives who in their time were influential and prominent members of our national legislative branch. They have been selected in terms of their contemporary importance *as* congressmen, rather than for renown earned in other branches of government or in private life. Admittedly the choice of which congressmen to include is to a degree arbitrary. No persons still serving in Congress are listed. Congressmen are identified by important legislation, programs, or groups with which they were associated, and their particular interests as legislators.

The following abbreviations are used: D—Democrat; R—Republican; [Dem-] Repub.—Thomas Jefferson Democratic Republicans; Fed—Federalist; H—House of Representatives; S—Senate; Maj L—Majority party leader; Min L—Minority party leader.

Aiken, George David (1892–1984). R Vt. S 1941–75. *Agriculture and forestry.*

Albert, Carl Bert (1908–   ). D Okla. H 1947–77 (speaker 1971–77). *Maj L 1962–71.*

Aldrich, Nelson Wilmarth (1841–1915). R 1879–81, S 1881–1911. *Ranking Republican in House; "Old Guard" conservative; Aldrich-Vreeland Act; Payne-Aldrich Tariff Act; Gold Standard Act.*

Allison, William Boyd (1829–1908). R Iowa. H 1863–71, S 1873–1908. *Conservative; Bland-Allison Silver Act.*

Ames, Oakes (1804–73). R Mass. H 1863–73. *Credit Mobilier scandal; censured by House.*

Aspin, Les (1938–95). D. Wis. H. 1970–93. *Armed Services.*

Atchison, David Rice (1807–86). Whig Mo. S 1843–55. *Kansas-Nebraska Act.*

Bailey, Joseph Weldon (1862–1929). D Miss. H 1891–1901, S 1901–13. *Free Silver.*

Baker, Howard Henry, Jr. (1925–   ). R Tenn. S 1967–85. *Foreign relations; environment and public works; Watergate investigation; Min L 1977–81; Maj L 1981–85.*

Baldwin, Abraham (1754–1807). [Dem-] Repub. Ga. H 1789–99, S 1799–1807. *Jeffersonian.*

Bankhead, John Hollis II (1872–1946). D Ala. S 1931–46. *New Deal; Bankhead-Jones Farm Tenancy Act; rules.*

Bankhead, William Brockman (1874–1940). D Ala. H 1917–40 (speaker 1936–40). *New Deal; Bankhead Cotton Control Act; agriculture; Maj L 1935–36.*

Barkley, Alben William (1877–1956). D Ky. H 1913–27, S 1927–49. *New Deal; Democratic party policy; Maj L 1937–47; Min L 1947–49.*

Bayard, James Asheton, Jr. (1799–1880). D Del. S 1851–64, 1867–69. *Conservative; finances.*

Bayard, Thomas Francis (1828–98). D Del. S 1869–85. *Civil service; opposed railroads; opposed protective tariff.*

Benton, Thomas Hart, "Old Bullion" (1782–1858). D Mo. S 1821–51, H 1853–55. *Jacksonian; Specie Circular; "hard money."*

Beveridge, Albert Jeremiah (1862–1927). R Ind. S 1889–1911. *Progressive; reform.*

Bilbo, Theodore Gilmore, "The Man" (1877–1947). D Miss. S 1935–47. *New Deal; anti-civil rights; barred by Senate 1947 from taking oath of office.*

Black, Hugo Lafayette (1886–1971). D Ala. S 1927–37. *New Deal.*

Blaine, James Gillespie (1830–93). R Me. H 1863–76 (speaker 1869–75), S 1876–81. *U. S. Grant Stalwart; spoilsman.*

Bland, Richard Parks, "Silver Dick" (1835–99). D Mo. H 1873–95, 1897–99. *Free Silver.*

Bloom, Sol (1870–1949). D N.Y. H 1923–49. *Foreign affairs.*

Bolling, Richard Walker (1916–91) D Mo. H 1949–83. *Rules.*

Borah, William Edgar (1865–1940). R Idaho. S 1907–40. *Opposed League of Nations; Isolationist.*

Boutwell, George Sewall (1818–1905). R Mass. H 1863–69, S 1873–77. *Pre-Civil War Democrat; U. S. Grant Stalwart; active in Andrew Johnson impeachment.*

Bradley, Bill (1943–). D. N.J. S 1978–1997. *Energy; finance.*

Brewster, [Ralph] Owen (1888–1961). R Me. H 1935–41, S 1941–52. *Conservative.*

Bricker, John William (1893–1986). R Ohio. S 1946–59. *Conservative; atomic energy.*

Bridges, [Henry] Styles (1898–1961). R N.H. S 1937–61. *Appropriations; Min L 1952–53.*

Brooks, Jack Bacon (1922–). D. Tex. H 1967–1994. *Judiciary.*

Buchanan, James (1791–1868). D Pa. H 1821–31, S 1834–45. *Jacksonian.*

Butler, Benjamin Franklin (1818–93). R Mass. H 1867–75, 1877–79. *Pre-Civil War Democrat; Greenback party.*

Byrd, Harry Flood (1887–1966). D Va. S 1933–65. *Anti-New Deal; finance; anti-civil rights.*

Byrnes, James Francis (1879–1972). D S.C. H 1911–25, S 1931–41. *New Deal.*

Calhoun, John Caldwell (1782–1850). D S.C. H 1811–17, S 1832–43, 1845–50. *1812 War Hawk; proslavery leader.*

Cameron, Simon (1799–1889). R Pa. S 1845–49, 1857–61, 1867–77. *Pre-Civil War Democrat; opposed civil service reform.*

Cannon, Howard Walter (1912–). D Nev. S 1959–83. *Rules.*

Cannon, Joseph Gurney, "Uncle Joe" (1836–1926). R Ill. H 1873–91, 1893–1913, 1915–23 (speaker 1903–11). *"Old Guard" conservative; stripped of much of his power as Speaker in 1910.*

Capehart, Homer Earl (1897–1979). R Ind. S 1945–63. *Banking and currency.*

Capper, Arthur (1865–1951). R Kans. S 1919–49. *Agriculture and forests; banking and currency.*

Cass, Lewis (1782–1866). D Mich. S 1845–48, 1849–57. *Jacksonian; popular sovereignty.*

Celler, Emanuel (1888–1981). D N.Y. H 1923–73. *Judiciary.*

Chandler, Zachariah (1813–79). R Mich. S 1857–75. *Radical Republican leader; U. S. Grant Stalwart.*

Church, Frank Forrester (1924–84). D Idaho. S 1957–81. *Foreign relations.*

Clark, James Beauchamp "Champ" (1850–1921). D Mo. H 1893–95, 1897–1921 (speaker 1911–19). *Free Silver; Min L 1907–11, 1919–21.*

Clay, Henry (1777–1852). Whig Ky. S 1806–1807, 1810–11, 1831–42, 1849–52, H 1811–14, 1815–21, 1823–25 (speaker during House tenures). *1812 War Hawk; internal improvements; Missouri Compromise; Compromise of 1850.*

Clayton, Henry De Lamar (1857–1929). D Ala. H 1897–1914. *Clayton Anti-Trust Act.*

Clayton, John Middleton (1796–1856). Whig Del. S 1829–36, 1845–49, 1853–56. *Protectionist.*

Cobb, Howell (1815–68). D Ga. H 1843–51, 1855–57 (speaker 1849–51). *Compromise of 1850.*

Cockran, [William] Bourke (1854–1923). D N.Y. H 1887–89, 1891–95, 1904–1909, 1921–23. *Labor reform.*

Colfax, Schuyler (1823–85). R Ind. H 1855–69 (speaker 1863–69). *U. S. Grant Stalwart; Credit Mobilier scandal.*

Conkling, Roscoe (1829–88). R N.Y. H 1859–63, 1865–67, S 1867–81. *Radical Republican; U. S. Grant Stalwart; Credit Mobilier scandal.*

Connally, Thomas Terry (1877–1963). D Tex. H 1917–29, S 1929–53. *New Deal; Truman Doctrine; foreign affairs; United Nations.*

Cooper, John Sherman (1901–91). R Ky. S 1946–49, 1952–55, 1956–73. *Liberal; foreign affairs.*

Copeland, Royal Samuel (1868–1938). D N.Y. S 1923–38. *Pure food and drug laws.*

Corwin, Thomas (1794–1865). Whig, R Ohio. H 1831–40, 1859–61; S 1845–50. *Opposed Mexican War.*

Cox, Samuel Sullivan, "Sunset" (1824–89). D Ohio. N.Y. H 1857–65, 1869–73, 1873–85, 1886–89. *Tariff, civil service reform.*

Cranston, Alan (1914–). D Calif. S 1969–93. *Liberal; veterans' affairs; housing and urban affairs; censured for savings and loans scandal.*

Cummins, Albert Baird (1850–1926). R Iowa. S 1908–26. *Esch-Cummins Transportation Act; agriculture.*

Curtis, Charles (1860–1936). R Kans. H 1893–1907, S 1907–13, 1915–29. *Conservative; Maj L 1925–29.*

Davis, Henry Winter (1817–65). R Md. H 1855–61, 1863–65. *Radical Republican.*

Dawes, Henry Laurens (1816–1903). R Mass. H 1857–75, S 1875–93. *Protectionist; Dawes Act giving citizenship rights to Indians.*

Depew, Chauncey Mitchell (1834–1928). R N.Y. S 1889–1911. *"Old Guard" conservative; supported railroad interests.*

Dies, Martin, Jr. (1900–72). D Tex. H 1931–45, 1953–59. *Anti-subversive investigations.*

Dingley, Nelson (1832–99). R Maine. H 1881–99. *Protective tariff; Dingley Act.*

Dirksen, Everett McKinley (1896–1969). R Ill. H 1933–49, S 1951–69. *Conservative; appropriations; Min L 1959-69.*

Dole, Robert (1923–). R. Kan. H 1961–69; S 1969–1996. *Agriculture. Min L 1986–95; Maj L 1995–96.*

Douglas, Paul Howard (1892–1976). D Ill. S 1949–67. *Liberal; economy; labor.*

Douglas, Stephen Arnold, "Little Giant" (1813–61). D Ill. H 1843–47, S 1847–61. *Compromise of 1850; Kansas-Nebraska Act; popular sovereignty.*

Eastland, James Oliver (1904–86). D Miss. S 1941, 1943–78. *Judiciary; anti-civil rights.*

Edmunds, George Franklin (1828–1919). R Vt. S 1866–1901. *Civil rights; Sherman Anti-Trust Act.*

Elkins, Stephen Benton (1841–1911). R W.Va. S 1895–1911. *Elkins Act; Mann-Elkins Act extending powers of Interstate Commerce Commission.*

Ellender, Alan Joseph (1890–1972). D La. S 1937–72. *Conservative; anti-civil rights; agriculture and forestry; appropriations.*

Ervin, Samuel James, Jr. (1896–1985). D N.C. H 1946–47, S 1954–74. *Conservative; government operations; Watergate investigation.*

Fessenden, William Pitt (1806–69). Whig, R Maine. H 1841–43, S 1854–64, 1865–69. *Opposed Radical Republicans.*

Fish, Hamilton (1888–1991). R N.Y. H 1920–45. *Isolationist.*

Flanders, Ralph Edward [Unknown font 2: Book Antiqua](1880[End Font: Book Antiqua]–1970). R Vt. S 1946–59. *United Nations.*

Foley, Thomas Stephen (1929–). D. Wash. H 1969–1995 (speaker 1989–95). *Agriculture. Maj L 1987–89.*

Foot, Solomon (1802–66). Whig, R Vt. H 1843–47, S 1851–66. *Antislavery.*

Foraker, Joseph Benson (1846–1917). R Ohio. S 1897–1909. *"Old Guard" conservative.*

Ford, Gerald Rudolph, Jr. (1913–). R Mich. H 1949–73. *Conservative; appropriations; Min L 1965–73.*

Forsyth, John (1780–1841). D Ga. H 1813–18, 1823–27; S 1818–19, 1829–34. *Jacksonian.*

Frye, William Pierce (1830–1911). R Maine. H 1871–81, S 1881–1911. *Expansionist.*

Fulbright, [James] William (1905–1995). D Ark. H 1943–45, S 1945–74. *Foreign affairs; Fulbright Act for international scholar exchange; banking and currency; opposed Vietnam War.*

Garner, John Nance (1868–1967). D Tex. H 1903–33 (speaker 1931–33). *Ways and means; agriculture; anti-Ku Klux Klan; Min L 1930–31.*

George, Walter Franklin (1878–1957). D Ga. S 1922–57. *Conservative.*

Giddings, Joshua Reed (1795–1864). Whig, R Ohio. H 1838–42, 1842–59. *Abolitionist.*

Giles, William Branch (1762–1830). [Dem-] Repub. Va. H 1790–98, 1801–1803, S 1804–15. *Opposed Madison administration in War of 1812.*

Gillette, Guy Mark (1879–1973). D Iowa. H 1933–36, S 1936–45, 1949–55. *New Deal; agriculture; small business.*

Glass, Carter (1858–1946). D Va. H 1902–18, S 1920–46. *Federal Reserve Act; opposed New Deal.*

Goldwater, Barry Morris (1909–). R Ariz. S 1953–65, 1967–87. *Conservative; intelligence; armed services.*

Gore, Thomas Pryor (1870–1949). D Okla. S 1907–21, 1931–37. *Supported Woodrow Wilson.*

Gorman, Arthur Pue (1839–1906). D Md. S 1881–99, 1903–1906. *Wilson-Gorman Tariff Act.*

Green, Theodore Francis (1867–1966). D R.I. S 1937–61. *Liberal; rules; foreign relations.*

Grundy, Felix (1777–1840). D Tenn. H 1811–14, S 1829–38, 1839–40. *Jacksonian.*

Hale, Eugene (1836–1918). R Maine. H 1869–79, S 1881–1911. *Protectionist.*

Hale, John Parker (1806–73). D N.H. H 1843–45, S 1847–53, 1855–65. *Antislavery.*

Halleck, Charles Abraham (1900–86). R Ind. H 1935–69. *Conservative; rules; commerce; Maj L 1947–49, 1953–55; Min L 1959–65.*

Hanna, Marcus Alonzo, "Mark" (1837–1904). R Ohio. S 1897–1904. *Conservative.*

Harlan, James (1820–99). R Iowa. S 1855–57, 1857–65, 1867–73. *Free-Soiler; opposed Andrew Johnson; U. S. Grant Stalwart.*

Harrison, Byron Patton, "Pat" (1881–1941). D Miss. H 1911–19, S 1919–41. *New Deal.*

Hartley, Fred Allan, Jr. (1902–69). R N.J. H 1929–49. *Conservative; education and labor; Taft-Hartley Act.*

Hatch, Carl Atwood (1889–1963). D N. M. S 1933–49. *Hatch Act forbidding pressuring federal employees for campaign contributions.*

Hawley, Joseph Roswell (1826–1905). R Conn. H 1872–75, 1879–81, S 1881–1905. *Protectionist; civil service reform.*

Hawley, Willis Chatman (1864–1941). R Oreg. H 1897–1933. *Protectionist; Smoot-Hawley Tariff Act.*

Hayden, Carl Trumbull (1877–1972). D Ariz. H 1912–27, S 1927–69. *Rules; appropriations.*

Hayne, Robert Young (1791–1839). D S.C. S 1823–32. *Antitariff; Webster-Hayne debates.*

Hays, Wayne Levere (1911–89). D Ohio. H 1949–76. *Administration.*

Hendricks, Thomas Andrews (1819–85). D Ind. H 1851–55, S 1863–69. *Agriculture; Greenbacker.*

Hepburn, William Peters (1833–1916). R Ohio. H 1881–87, 1893–1909. *Hepburn Act regulating railroads; Pure Food and Drug Act.*

Hewitt, Abram Stevens (1822–1903). D N.Y. H 1875–79, 1881–86. *Reform.*

Hickenlooper, Bourke Blakemore (1896–1971). R Iowa. S 1945–69. *Atomic energy; foreign relations; banking and currency.*

Hill, [Joseph] Lister (1894–1984). D Ala. H 1923–38, S 1938–69. *New Deal; civil rights moderate; labor and public welfare.*

Hoar, George Frisbie (1826–1904). R Mass. H 1869–77, S 1877–1904. *Protectionist; civil service reform.*

Hull, Cordell (1871–1955). D Tenn. H 1907–21, 1923–31, S 1931–33. *Federal income tax law.*

Humphrey, Hubert Horatio, Jr. (1911–78). D Minn. S 1949–64, 1971–78. *Liberal; civil rights; health and education; agriculture and forestry.*

Ingalls, John James (1833–1900). R Kans. S 1873–91. *"Old Guard" conservative; opposed civil service, antitrust laws.*

Jackson, Henry Martin, "Scoop" (1912–83). D Wash. H 1941–53, S 1953–83. *International affairs; energy and natural resources.*

Javits, Jacob Koppel (1904–86). R N.Y. H 1947–54, S 1957–1981. *Foreign affairs; government operations.*

Jenner, William Ezra (1908–85). R Ind. S 1944–45, 1947–59. *Anti-Communist investigator; rules.*

Johnson, Andrew (1807–75). D Tenn. H 1843–53, S 1857–62, 1875. *Antisecession.*

Johnson, Hiram Warren (1866–1945). R Calif. S 1917–45. *Progressive 1912; opposed Woodrow Wilson; isolationist.*

Johnson, Lyndon Baines (1908–73). D Tex. H 1937–49, S 1949–61. *New Deal; aeronautical and space; Min L 1953–55; Maj L 1955–61.*

Johnson, Richard Mentor (1780–1850). D Ky. H 1807–19, 1829–37, S 1819–29. *Jacksonian.*

Jones, James Kimbrough (1839–1908). D Ark. H 1881–85, S 1885–1903. *Tariff reform.*

Jones, Wesley Livsey (1863–1932). R Wash. H 1899–1909, S 1909–32. *Prohibitionist; Jones Act.*

Julian, George Washington (1817–99). Whig, R Ind. H 1849–51, 1861–71. *Public lands.*

Kefauver, [Carey] Estes (1903–63). D Tenn. H 1939–49, S 1949–63. *Tennessee Valley Authority; Kefauver-Harris Drug Safety Act; crime investigations.*

Kelley, William Darrah, "Pig Iron" (1814–90). R Pa. H 1861–90. *Protectionist.*

Kerr, Robert Samuel (1896–1963). D Okla. S 1949–63. *Liberal; aeronautical and space.*

King, Rufus (1755–1827). Fed N.Y. S 1789–96, 1813–25. *Opposed Jefferson.*

King, William Rufus De Vane (1786–1853). D N.C., Ala. H (N.C.) 1811–16, S (Ala.) 1819–44, 1848–52. *Jacksonian.*

Kitchin, Claude (1869–1923). D N.C. H 1901–23. *Supported corporate profits tax; opposed U.S. entry into World War I; Maj L 1915–19; Min L 1921–23.*

Knowland, William Fife (1908–74). R Calif. S 1945–59. *Conservative; Maj L 1953–55, Min L 1955–59.*

Knutson, Harold (1880–1953). R Minn. H 1917–49. *Ways and Means.*

La Follette, Robert Marion (1855–1925). R Wis. H 1885–91, S 1906–25. *Progressive 1912, 1924; investigated Teapot Dome scandal; labor; agriculture.*

La Follette, Robert Marion, Jr. (1895–1953). R Wis. S 1925–47. *Labor; agriculture.*

LaGuardia, Fiorello Henry (1882–1947). R N.Y. H 1917–19, 1923–33. *Norris-LaGuardia Act forbidding injunctions against strikes.*

Lamar, Lucius Quintus Cincinnatus (1825–93). D Miss. H 1857–60, 1873–77, S 1877–85. *Sectional conciliator.*

Langer, William (1886–1959). R N.D. S 1941–59. *Isolationist; post office and civil service; judiciary.*

Lodge, Henry Cabot (1850–1924). R Mass. H 1887–93, S 1893–1924. *Conservative; opposed League of Nations membership; Min L 1918–19; Maj L 1919–24.*

Lodge, Henry Cabot, Jr. (1902–86). R Mass. S 1937–44, 1947–53. *Foreign affairs.*

Logan, John Alexander, "Black Jack" (1826–86). D Ill. H 1859–62, 1867–71, S 1871–77, 1879–86. *Became Republican; U. S. Grant Stalwart; "Bloody Shirt"; opposed civil service reform.*

Long, Russell Billiu (1918–). D La. S 1948–87. *Finance.*

Longworth, Nicholas (1869–1931). R Ohio. H 1903–13, 1915–31 (speaker 1925–31). *Conservative; Maj L 1923–25.*

Lovejoy, Owen (1811–64). R Ill. H 1857–64. *Abolitionist.*

Lowndes, William Jones (1782–1822). [Dem-] Repub. S.C. H 1811–22. *1812 War Hawk; Missouri Compromise.*

Lucas, Scott Wike (1892–1968). D Ill. H 1935–39, S 1939–51. *Agriculture; small business; Maj L 1949–51.*

McCarran, Patrick Anthony, "Pat" (1876–1954). D Nev. S 1933–54. *McCarran Act restricting immigration; judiciary.*

McCarthy, Joseph Raymond (1908–57). R Wis. S 1947–57. *Anti-Communist investigator; censured by Senate for contempt.*

McClellan, John Little (1896–1977). D Ark. H 1935–39, S 1943–77. *Conservative; executive branch expenditures; government operations; appropriations.*

McCormack, John William (1891–1980). D Mass. H 1928–71 (speaker 1962–71). *Liberal; ways and means; Maj L 1939–47, 1949–53, 1955–62.*

McDuffie, George (1790–1851). D S.C. H 1821–34, S 1842–46. *Nullification.*

McGovern, George Stanley (1922–). D S.D. H 1957–61, S 1963–81. *Opposed Vietnam involvement.*

McKellar, Kenneth Douglas (1869–1957). D Tenn. H 1911–17, S 1917–53. *New Deal; Tennessee Valley Authority; appropriations.*

McKinley, William, Jr. (1843–1901). R Ohio. H 1877–83, 1885–91. *McKinley Tariff Act.*

McNary, Charles Linza (1874–1944). R Ore. S 1917–18, 1918–44. *McNary-Haugen Farm Relief Bill; Min L 1933–44.*

Macon, Nathaniel (1757–1837). [Dem-] Repub. N.C. H 1791–1815 (speaker 1801–1807), S 1815–28. *Jeffersonian.*

Magnuson, Warren Grant (1905–89). D Wash. H 1937–44, S 1944–81. *Commerce.*

Mann, James Robert (1856–1922). R Ill. H 1897–1922. *Mann-Elkins Act for railroad regulation; Mann Act outlawing prostitution across state lines; Min L 1911–19.*

Mansfield, Michael Joseph, "Mike" (1903–). D Mont. H 1943–53, S 1953–77. *Rules; Maj L 1961–77.*

Martin, Joseph William, Jr. (1884–1968). R Mass. H 1925–67 (speaker 1947–49, 1953–55). *Conservative; protectionist; Min L 1939–47, 1949–53, 1955–59.*

Martin, Thomas Staples (1847–1919). D Va. S 1893–1919. *Conservative; Federal Reserve Act; Min L 1911–13, 1919; Maj L 1917–19.*

Mason, James Murray (1798–1871). D Va. H 1837–39, S 1847–61. *Jacksonian; Fugitive Slave Law.*

Metzenbaum, Howard (1917–). D. Ohio. S 1976–1995. *Labor.*

Mills, Wilbur Daigh (1904–1992). D Ark. H 1939–77. *Ways and means.*

Mondale, Walter Frederick, "Fritz" (1928–). D Minn. S 1964–76. *Liberal; budget.*

Monroney, Almer Stillwell, "Mike" (1902–80). D Okla. H 1939–51, S 1951–69. *Post office and civil service.*

Morgan, John Tyler (1824–1907). D Ala. S 1877–1907. *Expansionist; Isthmian canal.*

Morrill, Justin Smith (1810–98). R Vt. H 1855–67, S 1867–98. *Protectionist; Morrill Tariff Bill; Morrill Land Grant Act.*

Morse, Wayne Lyman (1900–74). R Ore. S 1945–69. *Became Democrat; small business; labor.*

Mundt, Karl Earl (1900–74). R S.D. H 1939–48, S 1948–73. *Conservative; "China Lobby."*

Muskie, Edmund Sixtus (1914–1996). D Maine. S 1959–80. *Budget.*

Nelson, Knute (1843–1923). R Minn. H 1883–89, S 1895–1923. *Supported establishment of Departments of Commerce, Labor.*

Norris, George William (1861–1944). R. Nebr. H 1903–13, S 1913–43. *Progressive 1912; Norris-LaGuardia Act forbidding injunctions against strikes; Tennessee Valley Authority; became Independent.*

Nunn, Sam (1938–). D. Ga. S 1972–1997. *Armed services.*

Nye, Gerald Prentice (1892–1971). R N.Dak. S 1925–45. *Isolationist; investigated World War I munitions sales.*

O'Mahoney, Joseph Christopher (1884–1962). D Wyo. S 1934–53, 1954–61. *Liberal; internal and insular affairs.*

O'Neill, Thomas Philip, Jr., "Tip" (1912–94). D Mass. H 1953–87 (speaker 1977–87). *Budget; Maj L 1973–77.*

Otis, Harrison Gray (1765–1848). Fed Mass. H 1797–1801, S 1817–22. *Opposed War of 1812.*

Owen, Robert Latham (1856–1947). D Okla. S 1907–25. *Federal Reserve Act; Farm Loan Act.*

Patman, [john William] Wright (1893–1976). D Tex. H 1929–76. *Small business; banking and currency.*

Payne, Sereno Elisha (1843–1914). R Ill. H 1883–87, 1889–14. *"Old Guard" conservative; Payne-Aldrich Tariff Act; Maj L 1901–11.*

Pendleton, George Hunt (1825–89). D Ohio. H 1857–65, S 1879–85. *Civil Service Act.*

Pepper, Claude Denson (1900–89). D Fla. S 1936–51, H 1963–89. *Liberal; rules.*

Percy, Charles Harting (1919–). R Ill. S 1967–85. *Foreign relations.*

Pickering, Timothy (1745–1829). Fed Mass. S 1803–11, H 1813–17. *Opposed War of 1812.*

Pittman, Key (1872–1940). D Nev. S 1913–40. *Silver, mining.*

Platt, Orville Hitchcock (1827–1905). R Conn. S 1879–1905. *Protectionist.*

Platt, Thomas Collier (1833–1910). R N.Y. H 1873–77, S 1881, 1897–1909. *"Old Guard" conservative; expansionist.*

Pomeroy, Samuel Clarke (1816–91). R Kans. S 1861–73. *Supported Salmon P. Chase for president against Lincoln in 1864; prohibitionist.*

Powell, Adam Clayton, Jr. (1908–72). D N.Y. H 1945–67, 1969–71. *Education and labor.*

Proctor, Redfield (1831–1908). R Vt. S 1891–1908. *"Old Guard" conservative.*

Proxmire, William (1915–). D Wis. S 1957–89. *Banking, housing, and urban affairs.*

Quay, Matthew Stanley (1833–1904). R Pa. S 1887–99, 1901–1904. *"Old Guard" conservative.*

Rainey, Henry Thomas (1869–1934). D Ill. H 1903–21, 1923–34 (speaker 1933–34). *Maj L 1931–33.*

Randall, Samuel Jackson (1828–1890). D Pa. H 1863–90 (speaker 1876–81.) *Protectionist.*

Randolph, Jennings (1902–). D W.Va. H 1933–47, S 1958–85. *Environment and public works.*

Randolph, John (1773–1833). [Dem-] Repub. Va. H 1799–1813, 1815–17, 1819–25, 1827–29, S 1825–27, 1833. *Opposed War of 1812; strict construc-tionist.*

Rankin, John Elliott (1882–1960). D Miss. H 1921–53. *Conservative; veterans affairs; anti-civil rights.*

Rayburn, Samuel Taliaferro (1882–1961). D Tex. H 1913–61 (speaker 1940–47, 1949–53, 1955–61). *Wheeler-Rayburn Act regulating holding company control of public utilities; Maj L 1937–40; Min L 1947–49, 1953–55.*

Reagan, John Henninger (1818–1905). D Tex. H 1857–61, 1875–87, S 1887–91. *Interstate Commerce Act.*

Reece, [Brazilla] Carroll (1889–1961). R Tenn. H 1921–31, 1933–47, 1951–61. *Conservative; commerce; rules.*

Reed, Thomas Brackett, "Czar" (1839–1902). R Maine. H 1877–99 (speaker 1889–91, 1891–95). *Protectionist; opposed Spanish-American War, imperi-alism.*

Rhett, Robert Barnwell (name originally Smith) (1800–76). D S.C. H 1837–49, S 1850–52. *Proslavery, secessionist.*

Ribicoff, Abraham Alexander (1910–). D Conn. H 1949–53, S 1963–81. *Government operations.*

Rivers, Lucius Mendel (1905–70). D S.C. H 1941–70. *Armed services.*

Rives, William Cabell (1793–1868). D, Va. H 1823–29, S 1832–34, 1836–39, 1841–45. *Jacksonian.*

Robinson, Joseph Taylor (1872–1937). D Ark. H 1903–13, S 1913–37. *New Deal; Min L 1923–33; Maj L 1933–37.*

Rogers, Edith Nourse (1881–1960). R Mass. H 1925–60. *Veterans' affairs.*

Rostenkowski, Dan (1928–). D. Ill. H 1958–1995. *Ways and Means. Health Reform. Indicted for Fraud, 1995.*

Russell, Richard Brevard, Jr. (1897–1971). D Ga. S 1933–37. *New Deal; anti-civil rights; armed services; appropriations.*

Sabath, Adolph Joachim (1866–1952). D Ill. H 1907–52. *Rules.*

Saltonstall, Leverett (1892–1979). R Mass. S 1945–67. *Armed services.*

Scott, Hugh Doggett, Jr. (1900–1994). R Pa. H 1941–45, 1947–59, S 1959–77. *Foreign affairs; judiciary; Min L 1969–77.*

Seward, William Henry (1801–72). Whig R N.Y. S 1849–61. *Antislavery.*

Sherman, John (1823–1900). R Ohio. H 1855–61, S 1861–77, 1881–97. *Sherman Anti-Trust Act; Sherman Silver Purchase Act.*

Simmons, Furnifold McLendell (1854–1940). D N. C. H 1887–89, S 1901–31. *Agriculture; Underwood-Simmons Tariff Act.*

Smith, Ellison DuRant, "Cotton Ed" (1864–1944). D S.C. S 1909–44. *Conservative.*

Smith, Howard Alexander (1880–1966). R N.J. S 1944–59. *Labor and public welfare.*

Smith, Howard Worth (1883–1976). D Va. H 1931–67. *Conservative; anti-civil rights; rules.*

Smith, Margaret Chase (1897–1995). R Maine. H 1940–49, S 1949–73. *Appropriations; armed services.*

Smith, Samuel (1752–1839). [Dem-] Repub. Md. H 1793–1803, 1816–22, S 1803–15, 1822–33. *Jacksonian.*

Smoot, Reed (1862–1941). R Utah. S 1903–33. *Conservative; protectionist; Smoot-Hawley Tariff Act.*

Sparkman, John Jackson (1899–1985). D Ala. H 1937–46, S 1946–79. *New Deal; small business; banking and currency; foreign relations.*

Spooner, John Coit (1843–1919). R Wis. S 1885–91, 1897–1907. *Supported railroads.*

Stennis, John Cornelius (1901–95). D Miss. S 1947–89. *Armed services; appropriations; anti-civil rights.*

Stephens, Alexander Hamilton (1812–83). Whig Ga. H 1843–59, 1873–82. *Antisecession; became Democrat.*

Stevens, Thaddeus (1792–1868). Whig, R Pa. H 1849–53, 1859–68. *Antislavery; led Andrew Johnson impeachment.*

Stewart, William Morris (1827–1909). R Nev. S 1864–75, 1887–1905. *Silver.*

Sumner, Charles (1811–74). Whig, R Mass. S 1851–74. *Abolitionist.*

Swanson, Claude Augustus (1862–1939). D Va. H 1893–1906, S 1910–33. *Supported Woodrow Wilson.*

Symington, Stuart (1901–88). D Mo. S 1953–76. *Armed services; foreign affairs.*

Taft, Robert Alphonso (1889–1953). R Ohio. S 1939–53. *Conservative; Taft-Hartley Act outlawing closed-shop labor union contracts; labor and public welfare; Maj L 1953.*

Talmadge, Herman Eugene (1913–). D Ga. S 1957–81. *Agriculture; finance; anti-civil rights.*

Thurman, Allen Granberry (1813–95). D Ohio. H 1845–47, S 1869–81. *Opposed railroad interests; Thurman Act.*

Tillman, Benjamin Ryan, "Pitchfork Ben" (1847–1918). D S.C. S 1895–1918. *Opposed Gold Democrats; white supremacy.*

Tobey, Charles William (1880–1953). R N.H. H 1933–39, S 1939–53. *Banking and currency; commerce.*

Toombs, Robert Augustus (1810–85). Whig, D Ga. H 1845–53, S 1853–61. *Unionist.*

Tower, John Goodwin (1925–91). R Tex. S 1961–85. *Conservative; armed services.*

Trumbull, Lyman (1813–96). R Ill. S 1855–73. *Antislavery; civil service reform; opposed impeachment of Andrew Johnson.*

Tydings, Millard Evelyn (1890–1961). D Md. H 1923–27, S 1927–51. *Anti-New Deal; armed services; opposed Joseph McCarthy witch hunting.*

Underwood, Oscar Wilder (1862–1929). D Ala. H 1895–96, 1897–1915, S 1915–27. *Agriculture; Underwood-Simmons Tariff Act; supported Woodrow Wilson; Maj L 1911–15; Min L 1920–23.*

Vandenburg, Arthur Hendrick (1884–1951). R Mich. S 1928–51. *Foreign relations; pre-1941 isolationist; later supported United Nations, Marshall Plan.*

Vinson, Carl (1883–1981). D Ga. H 1914–65. *Armed services.*

Voorhees, Daniel Wolsey (1827–97). D Ind. H 1861–66, 1869–73, S 1877–97. *Greenbacker.*

Wade, Benjamin Franklin (1800–78). Whig, R Ohio. S 1851–69. *Abolitionist; opposed Andrew Johnson; protectionist.*

Wadsworth, James Wolcott, Jr. (1877–1953). R N.Y. S 1915–27, H 1933–51. *Armed services.*

Wagner, Robert Ferdinand (1877–1953). D N.Y. S 1927–49. *New Deal; National Industrial Recovery Act; Social Security Act; Wagner Labor Relations Act; U.S. Housing Act.*

Walsh, David Ignatius (1872–1947). D Mass. S 1919–25, 1926–47. *Walsh-Healey Wage and Hour Act.*

Walsh, Thomas James (1859–1933). D Mont. S 1913–33. *Supported Woodrow Wilson; Teapot Dome investigation.*

Washburne, Elihu Benjamin (1816–87). R Ill. H 1853–69. *Supported Andrew Johnson impeachment.*

Webster, Daniel (1782–1852). Whig N.H., Mass. H (N.H.) 1813–17, (Mass.) 1823–27, S 1827–41, 1845–50. *Supported tariff, manufactures; Webster-Hayne debates; favored Compromise of 1850.*

Weicker, Lowell Palmer (1931–). R Conn. H 1969–71, S 1971–89. *Small business; Watergate investigation.*

Wheeler, Burton Kendall (1882–1975). D Mont. S 1923–47. *Progressive; isolationist; Wheeler-Rayburn Act regulating holding company control of public utilities.*

Williams, Harrison Arlington, Jr. (1919–). D N.J. H 1953–57, S 1959–82. *Labor, public works, and human resources; resigned to avoid censure for bribery.*

Wilmot, David (1814–68). Whig, R Pa. H 1845–51, S 1861–63. *Antislavery; Wilmot Proviso.*

Wilson, Henry (1812–75). R Mass. S 1855–73. *Abolitionist; opposed Andrew Johnson.*

Winthrop, Robert Charles (1809–94). Whig Mass. H 1840–50 (speaker 1848–49), S 1850–51. *Moderate during slavery controversy.*

Wright, James Claude, Jr. (1922–). D Tex. H 1955–89 (speaker 1987–89). *Commerce; Maj L 1977–87.*

SOURCES

Bailey, Stephen K., and Howard D. Samuel. *Congress at Work*. New York: Henry Holt and Co., 1952.

Baldwin, Leland D. *The Stream of American History*. New York: American Book Co., 1952.

Biographical Dictionary of the American Congress, 1774–1989. Washington, D.C.: U.S. Government Printing Office, 1989.

Congressional Quarterly's Guide to Congress. 4th ed. Washington, D.C.: Congressional Quarterly, Inc., 1991.

Josephson, Matthew. *The Politicos*. New York: Harcourt, Brace and Co., 1938.

Key, V. O. *Politics, Parties and Pressure Groups*. 4th ed. New York: T. Y. Crowell, 1958.

Martin, Michael, and Leonard Gelber. *The New Dictionary of American History*. New York: Philosophical Library, 1952.

Morison, Samuel Eliot. *The Oxford History of the American People*. New York: Oxford University Press, 1969.

Morris, Richard B., ed. *Encyclopedia of American History*. 6th ed. New York: Harper and Row, 1982.

Peterson, Merrill D. *The Great Triumvirate: Webster, Clay and Calhoun*. New York: Oxford University Press, 1987.

Roller, David C., and Robert W. Twyman, eds. *The Encyclopedia of Southern History*. Baton Rouge: Louisiana State University Press, 1979.

Webster's Biographical Dictionary. 1st ed. Springfield, Mass.: G. and C. Merriam Co., 1948.

Williams, T. Harry, Richard N. Current, and Frank Friedel. *A History of the United States*. New York: Alfred A. Knopf, 1959.

—L.D.R.

15

THE DAILY NEWSPAPER
IN THE UNITED STATES
IN THE TWENTIETH CENTURY

. . . . .

HERMAN MELVILLE'S ISHMAEL, IN *MOBY-DICK*, INFORMS READERS THAT A whaling ship "was my Yale College and my Harvard." For no small number of American authors, however, the newsroom performed that function. Among those who began their writing careers as journalists (earlier on, as compositors) were William Cullen Bryant, John Greenleaf Whittier, Walt Whitman, Henry Timrod, Mark Twain, William Dean Howells, Joel Chandler Harris, George W. Cable, Stephen Crane, Frank Norris, Theodore Dreiser, H. L. Mencken, Willa Cather, Eugene O'Neill, Maxwell Anderson, Ernest Hemingway, Carl Sandburg, Ring Lardner, John Dos Passos, Robert Sherwood, Katherine Anne Porter, Sinclair Lewis, James Thurber, John Steinbeck, James T. Farrell, J. P. Marquand, Kenneth Rexroth, James Agee, John Hersey, Elizabeth Spencer, Donald Barthelme, Thomas Pynchon, John Ashbery, and William Kennedy. Journalism represented, for numerous young men and women, the way that one could begin earning a living with words.

In the early nineteenth century strong opinions about politics, a sufficient flair in the use of the English language to assert it, and enough money to buy some type and a hand press were all that were necessary to start a newspaper. By the later decades of the century, however, daily newspapers were becoming expensive business ventures even in the smaller cities. Mechanical typesetting, high-speed rotary presses, photoengraving, stereotyping, dry mats and electrotyping, telegraph news, and larger news- and feature-writing staffs made the competition for circulation, advertising, and thus survival extremely costly, and the old-time editor-owner began giving way to the businessman-publisher.

The first half of the twentieth century saw the daily newspaper in the United States flourish, grow in the size and scope of its format and activities, consolidate with rival newspapers for greater strength and profitability, and attain its apogee of circulation and influence. There was much talk of the "one-party press," for in city after city competition was eliminated, and morning and afternoon newspapers were controlled by a single management, which more than often was politically conservative in editorial outlook.

Then, following the end of World War II, came the advent of television and the exodus to the suburbs and consequent decline of the center city. The downtown department store advertising on which newspapers depended for the bulk of their revenues underwent a relative decline. Instead of reading the newspaper after dinner, people took in the news on TV and then watched programs. Circulation, particularly for afternoon newspapers, dropped. The 1960s saw numerous once-profitable afternoon newspapers begin disappearing from the scene. By the 1990s such onetime giants of the industry as the Philadelphia *Bulletin*, Washington *Star*, St. Louis *Globe-Democrat*, New York *Herald-Tribune* and Dallas *Times-Herald* ceased publication. Meanwhile certain national newspapers such as the *Wall Street Journal* and *USA Today* expanded in circulation.

The compilation that follows charts the course of daily newspaper publishing in one hundred American cities during the twentieth century. Only English-language newspapers of general circulation, published for a local or regional rather than a national audience, are included.

Birmingham, Ala. 1900, *Age-Herald, Ledger, News;* 1925, *Age-Herald, News, Post;* 1950, *Age-Herald, News, Post;* 1975, *News, Post-Herald;* 1993, *News, Post-Herald.*

Mobile, Ala. 1900, *Herald, Item, News, Register;* 1925, *News-Item, Register;* 1950, *Press, Register;* 1975, *Press, Register;* 1993, *Press, Register.*

Montgomery, Ala. 1900, *Advertiser, Journal;* 1925, *Advertiser, Journal, Times;* 1950, *Advertiser, Journal;* 1975, *Advertiser, Journal;* 1993, *Advertiser, Journal.*

Phoenix, Ariz. 1900, *Gazette, Republican, Enterprise;* 1925, *Gazette, Republican;* 1950, *Gazette, Republic;* 1975, *Gazette, Republic;* 1993, *Gazette, Republic.*

Little Rock, Ark. 1900, *Democrat, Gazette, Tribune;* 1925, *Democrat, Gazette, News;* 1950, *Democrat, Gazette;* 1975, *Democrat-Gazette;* 1993, *Democrat-Gazette.*

Los Angeles, Calif. 1900, *Evening Express, Herald, Journal, Record, Times;* 1925, *Examiner, Express, Herald, Illustrated Daily News, Record, Times;* 1950, *Examiner, Herald and Express, Mirror, News, Times;* 1975, *Herald-Examiner, Times;* 1993, *News, Times.*

Oakland, Calif. 1900, *Enquirer, Times, Tribune;* 1925, *Post-Enquirer, Tribune;* 1950, *Post-Enquirer, Tribune;* 1975, *Tribune;* 1993, *Tribune.*

Sacramento, Calif. 1900, *Evening Bee, Record-Union;* 1925, *Bee, Star, Union;* 1950, *Bee, Union;* 1975, *Bee, Union;* 1993, *Bee, Union.*

San Diego, Calif. 1900, *Evening Tribune, San Diegan-Sun, Union, Vidette;* 1925, *Sun, Tribune, Union;* 1950, *Journal, Union, Tribune-Sun;* 1975, *Union, Tribune;* 1993, *Daily Transcript, Union-Tribune.*

San Francisco, Calif. 1900, *Call, Chronicle, Evening Post, Examiner, Report;* 1925, *Bulletin, Call and Post, Chronicle, Examiner, Illustrated Daily Herald, News;* 1950, *Call-Bulletin, Chronicle, Examiner, News;* 1975, Chronicle, Examiner;* 1993, *Chronicle, Examiner.*

Denver, Colo. 1900, *Evening Post, Republican, Rocky Mountain News, Times;* 1925, *Colorado Herald, Express, Post, Rocky Mountain News, Times;* 1950, *Post, Rocky Mountain News;* 1975, *Post, Rocky Mountain News;* 1993, *Post, Rocky Mountain News.*

Hartford, Conn. 1900, *Courant, Post, Telegram, Times;* 1925, *Courant, Times;* 1950, *Courant, Times;* 1975, *Courant, Times;* 1993, *Courant.*

New Haven, Conn. 1900, *Evening Leader, Morning Journal and Courier, Palladium, Union;* 1925, *Journal-Courier; Register, Times-Leader, Union;* 1950, *Journal-Courier, Register;* 1975, *Journal-Courier, Register;* 1993, *Register.*

Wilmington, Del. 1900, *Evening Journal, Every Evening, Morning News, Republican;* 1925, *Every Evening, Journal, News;* 1950, *Journal-Every Evening, News;* 1975, *Journal, News;* 1993, *News-Journal.*

Washington, D.C. 1900, *Evening Star, Post, Times;* 1925, *Herald, News, Post, Star, Times;* 1950, *News, Post, Star, Times-Herald;* 1975, *Post, Star-News;* 1993, *Post, Times.*

Jacksonville, Fla. 1900, *Evening Call, Florida Times-Union and Citizen, Metropolis;* 1925, *Florida Times-Union, Journal;* 1950, *Florida Times-Union, Journal;* 1975, *Florida Times-Union, Journal;* 1993, *Florida Times-Union.*

Miami, Fla. 1900, none; 1925, *Herald, News, Tribune;* 1950, *Herald, News;* 1975, *Herald, News;* 1993, *Herald.*

Tampa, Fla. 1900, *Herald, Morning Tribune, Times;* 1925, *Times, Tribune;* 1950, *Times, Tribune;* 1975, *Times, Tribune;* 1993, *Tribune.*

Atlanta, Ga. 1900, *Constitution, Journal;* 1925, *Constitution, Georgian, Journal;* 1950, *Constitution, Journal;* 1975, *Constitution, Journal;* 1993, *Constitution, Journal.*

Macon, Ga. 1900, *News, Telegraph;* 1925, *News, Telegraph;* 1950, *News, Telegraph;* 1975, *News, Telegraph;* 1993, *Telegraph.*

Savannah, Ga. 1900, *Morning News, Press;* 1925, *News, Press;* 1950, *News, Press;* 1975, *News, Press;* 1993, *News, Press.*

Honolulu, Hawaii. 1900, *Evening Bulletin, Hawaiian Star, Independent, Pacific Commercial Advertiser;* 1925, *Advertiser, Star-Bulletin;* 1950, *Advertiser, Hawaii Times, Star-Bulletin;* 1975, *Advertiser, Star-Bulletin;* 1993, *Advertiser, Star-Bulletin.*

Boise, Idaho. 1900, *Idaho Statesman;* 1925, *Capital News, Idaho Statesman;* 1950, *Idaho Statesman, Evening Statesman;* 1975, *Idaho Statesman;* 1993, *Idaho Statesman.*

Chicago, Ill. 1900, *Chronicle, Democrat, Evening Post, Inter-Ocean, Journal, News, Record, Republican, Tribune;* 1925, *American, Herald and Examiner, Journal, News, Post, Tribune;* 1950, *Herald-American, News, Sun-Times, Tribune;* 1975, *News, Sun-Times, Tribune;* 1993, *Herald, Sun-Times, Tribune.*

Peoria, Ill. 1900, *Evening Star, Herald-Transcript, Journal;* 1925, *Journal, Star, Transcript;* 1950, *Journal, Star;* 1975, *Journal-Star;* 1993, *Journal Star.*

Springfield, Ill. 1900, *Illinois State Journal, Illinois State Register, News;* 1925, *Illinois State Journal, Illinois State Register;* 1950, *Illinois State Journal, Illinois State Register;* 1975, *State Journal-Register;* 1993, *State Journal-Register.*

Evansville, Ind. 1900, *Courier, Evening News, Press;* 1925, *Courier, Journal, Press;* 1950, *Courier, Press;* 1975, *Courier, Press;* 1993, *Courier, Press.*

Fort Wayne, Ind. 1900, *Journal-Gazette, News, Sentinel;* 1925, *Journal-Gazette, News-Sentinel;* 1950, *Journal-Gazette, News-Sentinel;* 1975, *Journal-Gazette, News-Sentinel;* 1993, *Journal-Gazette, News-Sentinel.*

Indianapolis, Ind. 1900, *Indiana Tribune, Journal, News, Press, Sentinel, Sun;* 1925, *News, Star, Times;* 1950, *News, Star, Times;* 1975, *News, Star;* 1993, *News, Star.*

Des Moines, Iowa. 1900, *Iowa Capital, Iowa State Register, Leader, News;* 1925, *Capital, Register, Tribune;* 1950, *Register, Tribune;* 1975, *Register, Tribune;* 1993, *Register.*

Topeka, Kans. 1900, *Capital, Democrat, State Journal;* 1925, *Capital, State Journal;* 1950, *Capital, State Journal;* 1975, *Capital, State Journal;* 1993, *Capital-Journal.*

Wichita, Kans. 1900, *Beacon, Eagle, Star;* 1925, *Beacon, Eagle;* 1950, *Beacon, Eagle;* 1975, *Beacon, Eagle;* 1993, *Eagle.*

Louisville, Ky. 1900, *Commercial, Courier-Journal, Dispatch, Evening Post, News, Times;* 1925, *Courier-Journal, Herald, Post, Times;* 1950, *Courier-Journal, Times;* 1975, *Courier-Journal, Times;* 1993, *Courier-Journal.*

New Orleans, La. 1900, *Item, Picayune, States, Telegram, Times-Democrat;* 1925, *Item, States, Times-Picayune;* 1950, *Item, States, Times-Picayune;* 1975, *States-Item, Times-Picayune;* 1993, *Times-Picayune.*

Shreveport, La. 1900, *Caucasian, Evening Journal, Morning Progress, Times;* 1925, *Journal, Times;* 1950, *Journal, Times;* 1975, *Journal, Times;* 1993, *Times.*

Portland, Maine. 1900, *Advertiser, Eastern Argus, Evening Express, Press;* 1925,

Express and Advertiser, Press Herald; 1950, *Express, Press Herald;* 1975, *Express, Press Herald;* 1993, *Press Herald.*

Baltimore, Md. 1900, *American, Morning Herald, News, Sun, World;* 1925, *News, Sun, Evening Sun;* 1950, *News-Post, Sun, Evening Sun;* 1975, *News-American, Sun, Evening Sun;* 1993, *Sun, Evening Sun.*

Boston, Mass. 1900, *Advertiser, Evening Record, Evening Transcript, Globe, Herald, Journal, Post, Traveler;* 1925, *Advertiser, American, Globe, Herald, Post, Telegram, Transcript, Traveler;* 1950, *Ameri-can, Globe, Herald, Post, Traveler;* 1975, *Globe, Herald American;* 1993, *Globe, Herald.*

New Bedford, Mass. 1900, *Evening Standard, Morning Mercury;* 1925, *Mercury, Standard, Times;* 1950, *Standard-Times;* 1975, *Standard-Times;* 1993, *Standard-Times.*

Springfield, Mass. 1900, *News, Republican, Union;* 1925, *News, Republican, Union;* 1950, *News, Republican, Union;* 1975, *News, Union;* 1993, *Union-News.*

Worcester, Mass. 1900, *Evening Gazette, Evening Post, Spy, Telegram;* 1925, *Gazette, Post, Telegram;* 1950, *Gazette, Telegram;* 1975, *Gazette, Telegram;* 1993, *Telegram and Gazette.*

Detroit, Mich. 1900, *Evening News, Free Press, Journal, Tribune;* 1925, *Free Press, News, Times;* 1950, *Free Press, News, Times;* 1975, *Free Press, News;* 1993, *Free Press, News.*

Grand Rapids, Mich. 1900, *Democrat, Evening Press, Herald;* 1925, *Herald, Press;* 1950, *Herald, Press;* 1975, *Press;* 1993, *Press.*

Lansing, Mich. 1900, *Journal, State Republican;* 1925, *Capital News, State Journal;* 1950, *State-Journal;* 1975, *State Journal;* 1993, *State Journal.*

Duluth, Minn. 1900, *Evening Herald, News-Tribune;* 1925, *Herald, News-Tribune;* 1950, *Herald, News-Tribune;* 1975, *Herald, News-Tribune;* 1993, *News-Tribune.*

Minneapolis, Minn. 1900, *Journal, Times, Tribune;* 1925, *Journal, Star, Tribune;* 1950, *Star, Tribune;* 1975, *Star, Tribune;* 1993, *Star-Tribune.*

St. Paul, Minn. 1900, *Dispatch, Globe, Pioneer Press;* 1925, *Dispatch, News, Pioneer Press;* 1950, *Dispatch, Pioneer Press;* 1975, *Dispatch, Pioneer Press;* 1993, *Pioneer Press.*

Jackson, Miss. 1900, *Clarion-Ledger, Evening News;* 1925, *Clarion-Ledger, News;* 1950, *Clarion-Ledger, News;* 1975, *Clarion-Ledger, News;* 1993, *Clarion-Ledger.*

Kansas City, Mo. 1900, *Journal, Mail, Star, Times, World;* 1925, *Journal, Post, Star, Times;* 1950, *Star, Times;* 1975, *Star, Times;* 1993, *Star.*

St. Louis, Mo. 1900, *Chronicle, Evening Journal, Globe-Democrat, Post-Dispatch, Star;* 1925, *Globe-Democrat, Post-Dispatch, Star, Times;* 1950, *Globe-Democrat, Post-Dispatch, Star-Times;* 1975, *Globe-Democrat, Post-Dispatch;* 1993, *Post-Dispatch.*

Omaha, Nebr. 1900, *Bee, News, World-Herald;* 1925, *Bee, News, World-Herald;* 1950, *World-Herald;* 1975, *World-Herald;* 1993, *World-Herald.*

Manchester, N.H. 1900, *Mirror and American, Union;* 1925, *Leader, Mirror, Union;* 1950, *Leader, Union;* 1975, *Union Leader;* 1993, *Union Leader.*

Camden, N.J. 1900, *Courier, Post-Telegram, Review;* 1925, *Courier, Post-Telegram;* 1950, *Courier-Post;* 1975, *Courier-Post;* 1993, *Courier-Post.*

Jersey City, N.J. 1900, *Evening Journal, News;* 1925, *Jersey Journal;* 1950, *Jersey Journal;* 1975, *Jersey Journal;* 1993, *Jersey Journal.*

Newark, N.J. 1900, *Advertiser, Evening News;* 1925, *Ledger, News, Star-Eagle;* 1950, *News, Star-Ledger;* 1975, *Star-Ledger;* 1993, *Star-Ledger.*

Trenton, N.J. 1900, *State Gazette, Times, True American;* 1925, *State Gazette, Times;* 1950, *Times, Trentonian;* 1975, *Times, Trentonian;* 1993, *Times, Trentonian.*

Albuquerque, N.M. 1900, *Citizen, Journal-Democrat;* 1925, *Herald, Journal, Tribune;* 1950, *Journal, Tribune;* 1975, *Journal, Tribune;* 1993, *Journal, Tribune.*

Albany, N.Y. 1900, *Argus, Evening Journal, Press-Knickerbocker-Express, Times-Union;* 1925, *Journal, Knickerbocker Press, News, Times-Union;* 1950, *Knickerbocker News, Times-Union;* 1975, *Knickerbocker News-Union-Star, Times-Union;* 1993, *Times-Union.*

Buffalo, N.Y. 1900, *Commercial, Courier, Enquirer, Evening News, Evening Times, Review;* 1925, *Commercial, Courier, Enquirer, Express, News, Times;* 1950, *Courier-Express, News;* 1975, *Courier-Express, News;* 1993, *News.*

New York, N.Y. 1900, *Commercial Advertiser, Evening Post, Evening Telegram, Herald, Journal, Mail and Express, News, Press, Sun, Evening Sun, Times, Tribune, Evening Tribune, World;* 1925, *American, Graphic, Herald-Tribune, Journal, Mirror, Daily News, Post, Sun, Telegram and Mail, Times, World;* 1950, *Herald Tribune, Journal-American, Mirror, News, Post, Times, World Telegram & Sun;* 1975, *News, Post, Times;* 1993, *News, New York Newsday, Post, Times.*

Rochester, N.Y. 1900, *Democrat and Chronicle, Evening Times, Herald, Post-Express, Union and Advertiser;* 1925, *Democrat and Chronicle, Herald, Journal and Post-Express, Times-Union;* 1950, *Democrat and Chronicle, Times-Union;* 1975, *Democrat and Chronicle, Times-Union;* 1993, *Democrat and Chronicle, Times-Union.*

Syracuse, N.Y. 1900, *Evening Herald, Evening Telegram, Journal, Post-Standard;* 1925, *Herald, Journal, Post-Standard, Telegram;* 1950, *Herald-Journal, Post-Standard;* 1975, *Herald-Journal, Post-Standard;* 1993, *Herald-Journal, Post-Standard.*

Charlotte, N.C. 1900, *News, Observer;* 1925, *News, Observer;* 1950, *News, Observer;* 1975, *News, Observer;* 1993, *Observer.*

Greensboro, N.C. 1900, *Evening Telegram, Record;* 1925, *News, Record;* 1950, *News, Record;* 1975, *News, Record;* 1993, *News and Record.*

Raleigh, N.C. 1900, *Morning Post, News and Observer, Times-Visitor;* 1925, *News and Observer, Times;* 1950, *News and Observer, Times;* 1975, *News and Observer, Times;* 1993, *News and Observer.*

Winston-Salem, N.C. 1900, *Journal, Twin-City Daily Sentinel;* 1925, *Journal, Twin City Sentinel;* 1950, *Journal, Twin City Sentinel;* 1975, *Journal, Twin City Sentinel;* 1993, *Journal.*

Akron, Ohio. 1900, *Beacon Journal, Democrat;* 1925, *Beacon Journal, Press, Times;* 1950, *Beacon Journal;* 1975, *Beacon Journal;* 1993, *Beacon Journal.*

Cincinnati, Ohio. 1900, *Commercial Tribune, Enquirer, Post, Times-Star;* 1925, *Commercial Tribune, Enquirer, Post, Times-Star;* 1950, *Enquirer, Post, Times-Star;* 1975, *Enquirer, Post.*

Cleveland, Ohio. 1900, *News and Herald, Plain Dealer, Press, Recorder, World;* 1925, *News, Plain Dealer, Press, Times and Commercial;* 1950, *News, Plain Dealer, Press;* 1975, *Plain Dealer, Press;* 1993, *Plain Dealer.*

Columbus, Ohio. 1900, *Citizen, Evening Dispatch, Ohio State Journal, Press-Post;* 1925, *Citizen, Dispatch, Ohio State Journal;* 1950, *Citizen, Dispatch, Star;* 1975, *Citizen-Journal, Dispatch;* 1993, *Dispatch.*

Dayton, Ohio. 1900, *Evening Herald, Evening Press, Journal, News;* 1925, *Herald, Journal, News;* 1950, *Journal Herald, News;* 1975, *Journal Herald, News;* 1993, *News.*

Toledo, Ohio. 1900, *Bee, Blade, Commercial, News;* 1925, *Blade, News-Bee, Times;* 1950, *Blade, Times;* 1975, *Blade, Times;* 1993, *Blade.*

Oklahoma City, Okla. 1900, *Oklahoman, Times-Journal;* 1925, *Oklahoman, Oklahoma News, Times;* 1950, *Oklahoman, Times;* 1975, *Oklahoma Journal, Oklahoman, Times;* 1993, *Oklahoman.*

Tulsa, Okla. 1900, *Evening Democrat;* 1925, *Tribune, World;* 1950, *Tribune, World;* 1975, *Tribune, World;* 1993, *World.*

Portland, Oreg. 1900, *Evening Telegram, Morning Oregonian* 1925, *News, Oregonian, Oregon Journal, Telegram;* 1950, *Oregonian, Oregon Journal;* 1975, *Oregonian, Oregon Journal;* 1993, *Oregonian.*

Harrisburg, Pa. 1900, *Patriot, Star-Independent, Telegraph;* 1925, *News, Patriot, Telegraph;* 1950, *News, Patriot;* 1975, *News, Patriot;* 1993, *News, Patriot.*

Philadelphia, Pa. 1900, *Call, Evening Bulletin, Evening Herald, Evening Item, Evening Telegraph, Inquirer, News, North American, Press, Public Ledger, Record, Times;* 1925, *Bulletin, Inquirer, North American, Public Ledger, Record;* 1950, *Bulletin, Inquirer, News;* 1975, *Bulletin, Inquirer, News;* 1993, *Inquirer, Daily News.*

Pittsburgh, Pa. 1900, *Chronicle Telegraph, Commercial Gazette, Dispatch, Leader, News, Post, Press, Times;* 1925, *Chronicle Telegraph, Gazette-*

Times, Post, Press, Sun; 1950, *Post-Gazette, Press, Sun- Telegraph;* 1975, *Post-Gazette, Press;* 1993, *Post-Gazette.*

Providence, R.I. 1900, *Evening Bulletin, Evening Telegram, Journal, News;* 1925, *Bulletin, Journal, News, Tribune;* 1950, *Bulletin, Journal;* 1975, *Bulletin, Journal;* 1993, *Journal.*

Charleston, S.C. 1900, *Evening Post, News and Courier;* 1925, *Evening Post, News and Courier;* 1950, *Evening Post, News and Courier;* 1975, *Evening Post, News and Courier;* 1993, *Post and Courier.*

Columbia, S.C. 1900, *Record, State;* 1925, *Record, State;* 1950, *Record, State;* 1975, *Record, State;* 1993, *State.*

Chattanooga, Tenn. 1900, *News, Times;* 1925, *News, Times;* 1950, *News-Free Press, Times;* 1975, *News-Free Press, Times;* 1993, *News-Free Press, Times.*

Knoxville, Tenn. 1900, *Journal and Tribune, Sentinel;* 1925, *Journal and Tribune; News, Sentinel;* 1950, *Journal, News-Sentinel;* 1975, *Journal, News-Sentinel;* 1993, *News-Sentinel.*

Memphis, Tenn. 1900, *Commercial Appeal, Evening Scimitar;* 1925, *Commercial Appeal, News Scimitar, Press;* 1950, *Commercial Appeal, Press-Scimitar;* 1975, *Commercial Appeal, Press-Scimitar;* 1993, *Commercial Appeal.*

Nashville, Tenn. 1900, *American, Banner;* 1925, *Banner, Tennessean;* 1950, *Banner, Tennessean;* 1975, *Banner, Tennessean;* 1993, *Banner, Tennessean.*

Dallas, Tex. 1900, *Morning News, Times Herald* 1925, *Dispatch, Journal, News, Times Herald;* 1950, *News, Times-Herald;* 1975, *News, Times-Herald;* 1993, *News.*

El Paso, Tex. 1900, *Graphic, Herald, Times;* 1925, *Herald, Post, Times;* 1950, *Herald-Post, Times;* 1975, *Herald-Post, Times;* 1993, *Herald-Post, Times.*

Fort Worth, Tex. 1900, *Gazette, Mail-Telegram, Morning Register;* 1925, *Press, Record, Star-Telegram;* 1950, *Press, Star-Telegram;* 1975, *Press, Star-Telegram;* 1993, *Star-Telegram.*

Houston, Tex. 1900, *Evening Record, Herald, Post, Press;* 1925, *Chronicle, Post-Dispatch, Press;* 1950, *Chronicle, Post, Press;* 1975, *Chronicle, Post;* 1993, *Chronicle, Post.*

San Antonio, Tex. 1900, *Express, Light;* 1925, *Express, Light, News;* 1950, *Express, Light, News;* 1975, *Express, Light, News;* 1993, *Express-News.*

Salt Lake City, Utah. 1900, *Deseret Evening News, Reporter, Herald, Tribune;* 1925, *Deseret News, Telegram, Tribune;* 1950, *Deseret News, Telegram, Tribune;* 1975, *Deseret News, Tribune;* 1993, *Deseret News, Tribune.*

Norfolk, Va. 1900, *Dispatch, Landmark, Public Ledger, Virginian-Pilot;* 1925, *Ledger-Dispatch, Virginian-Pilot;* 1950, *Virginian-Pilot, Ledger-Dispatch;* 1975, *Ledger-Star, Virginian-Pilot;* 1993, *Ledger-Star, Virginian-Pilot.*

Richmond, Va. 1900, *Dispatch, Evening Leader, News, Times;* 1925, *News Leader, Times-Dispatch;* 1950, *News Leader, Times-Dispatch;* 1975, *News Leader, Times-Dispatch;* 1993, *Times-Dispatch.*

Roanoke, Va. 1900, *Evening World, Times;* 1925, *Times, World-News;* 1950, *Times, World-News;* 1975, *Times, World-News;* 1993, *Times and World-News.*

Seattle, Wash. 1900, *Post-Intelligencer, Star-Times;* 1925, *Post-Intelligencer, Star, Times;* 1950, *Post-Intelligencer, Times;* 1975, *Post-Intelligencer, Times;* 1993, *Post-Intelligencer, Times.*

Spokane, Wash. 1900, *Chronicle, Spokesman-Review;* 1925, *Chronicle, Press, Spokesman-Review;* 1950, *Chronicle, Spokesman-Review;* 1975, *Chronicle, Spokesman-Review;* 1993, *Spokesman-Review.*

Tacoma, Wash. 1900, *Evening News, Ledger;* 1925, *Ledger, News-Tribune, Times;* 1950, *News-Tribune;* 1975, *News-Tribune;* 1993, *News-Tribune.*

Charleston, W.Va. 1900, *Courier, Gazette, Mail-Tribune;* 1925, *Gazette, Mail;* 1950, *Gazette, Mail;* 1975, *Gazette, Mail;* 1993, *Gazette, Mail.*

Madison, Wis. 1900, *Democrat, Wisconsin State Journal;* 1925, *Capital Times, Wisconsin State Journal;* 1950, *Capital Times, Wisconsin State Journal;* 1975, *Capital Times, Wisconsin State Journal;* 1993, *Capital Times, Wisconsin State Journal.*

Milwaukee, Wis. 1900, *Evening Wisconsin, Journal, News, Sentinel;* 1925, *Journal, Leader, Sentinel, Wisconsin News and Evening Sentinel;* 1950, *Journal, Sentinel;* 1975, *Journal, Sentinel;* 1993, *Journal, Sentinel.*

SOURCES

Editor and Publisher: International Year Book Number for 1950, 1975, 1993.
Ayer's & Son's Newspaper Annual and Directory. Philadelphia: N. W. Ayer & Son, 1900, 1925.

—**L.D.R.**

III

ARCHITECTURE

16

GREAT
ARCHITECTURAL WORKS

. . . . .

No one has ever written better about architecture—not its technical aspects but its emotional content—than Marcel Proust. Very early in *Swann's Way*, the first volume of *Remembrance of Things Past*, he describes at considerable length the fictional church of Saint-Hilaire in Combray, modeled upon the actual church of Saint-Jacques at Illiers. At one point the narrator's grandmother, who prizes the steeple's "natural air and an air of distinction," remarks to the family: "My dears, laugh at me if you like; it is not conventionally beautiful, but there is something in its quaint old face which pleases me. If it could play the piano, I am sure it would really *play*."

Before and after that, Proust is much more specific in his description of the church, though always in terms of the way the narrator *feels* about what he is seeing. But the grandmother's remark, while thoroughly impressionistic and subjective, nevertheless does, when read within the context, convey something of the emotional impact of an edifice of wood, stone, glass, and metal upon one's sensibilities.

"Unlike the other arts," declares the *Encyclopedia Britannica* (1957), "architecture rose from a primary requirement of human life—the need for shelter." From the earliest tent made of animal hides to the Crystal Palace and the World Trade Center constitutes quite a leap, and the history of civilization can in effect be traced in the structures built for keeping out of the wind and rain, warding off the midday sun, crossing bodies of water, repelling foes, worshiping, administering government, conducting business, and watching football games.

"Form ever follows function," wrote the architect Louis Sullivan. So it does, or in any event ought to, but it had better not follow it too literally. Which is worse, building a post office to look like a church, or building it to look like a cracker box? The one proposes false and irrelevant emotions, the other no emotion at all: sterility. It's somewhere in between that successful architects must operate, and the great architectural works are those that, whether through conscious design or innate taste, not only perform a function but make an aesthetic statement.

A goodly selection of the world's great buildings and bridges appears below, with their locations, dates of construction, and architects or engineers (when known). When the name of the architectural work is also the location, it is not repeated; thus Ely Cathedral is in Ely, England. Names are given in terms of their more usual reference in English.

Abbaye St. Etienne. Caen, France, 1068–1115.

Abu Simbel, Temple of. Aswan, Egypt, *ca.* 1250 B.C.E.

Acropolis. Athens, begun *ca.* 700 B.C.E.

Aix-la-Chapelle (Aachen), Cathedral of. Aachen, Germany, 792–805.

Al Ahzar Mosque. Cairo, *ca.* 970.

Albert Memorial. Kensington Gardens, London, by Sir George Gilbert Scott, J. H. Foley, and others, 1863–72.

Alcazar. Toledo, by Covarrubias, 1537–53.

Alexandria, lighthouse at. *ca.* 300 B.C.E.

Al-Hakim Mosque. Cairo, 1013.

Alhambra Palace. Granada, Spain, 1228–1354.

Altes Museum. Berlin, by Friedrich Schinkel, 1823–47.

Amiens, Cathedral of. France, 1220–88.

Ammon, Temple of. Karnak, Egypt, *ca.* 1530–1323 B.C.E.

Ammon-Re, Temple of. Luxor, Egypt, *ca.* 1408–1300 B.C.E.

Amsterdam, Royal Palace at. Netherlands, 1648–65.

Angkor Wat, temple at. Cambodia, *ca.* 1150.

Angoulême, Cathedral of. France, *ca.* 1105–28.

Antwerp Cathedral. Belgium, 1352–1411.

Arc de Triomphe. Paris, by Jean-François-Thérèse Chalgrin and Jean-Armand Reymond, 1808–35.

Ashmolean Museum and Taylor Institution. Oxford, Eng., by Charles Robert Cockerell, 1841–45.

Attalos, Stoa of. Athens, reconstructed second century B.C.E.

Augustus' Altar of Peace. Rome, *ca.* 9 B.C.E.

Bacchus, Temple of. Baalbek, Lebanon, 160.

Bacon's Castle. Surry County, Va., *ca.* 1655.

Balleroy, Château de. France, by François Mansart, 1626–36.

Baltimore, Old Catholic Cathedral at. Maryland, by Benjamin Latrobe, 1806–18.

Bamberg Castle. Germany, *ca.* 547.

Banqueting House. Whitehall, London, by Inigo Jones, 1619–22.

Bath Abbey. England, by R. and W. Vertue, 1501–39.

Bauhaus. Dessau, Germany, by Walter Gropius, 1925–26.

Beauvais Cathedral. France, 1225–1568.

Belvedere of Prince Eugene. Vienna, by Johann Lucas von Hildebrandt, 1721–25.

Biltmore Estate. Asheville, N.C., by Richard Morrow Hunt, 1892–96.

Blenheim Palace. Oxfordshire, Eng., by Sir John Vanbrugh, 1705–24.

Blois, Château of. France, 1493–1524.

Bodleian Library. Oxford, Eng., by Thomas Holt, 1613–36.

Borobudur, Temple of. Java, *ca.* 800.

Bourges Cathedral. France, 1192–1275.

Brandenberg Gate. Berlin, by Carl Gotthard Langhans, 1788–91.

Brazil Parliament Buildings. Brasilia, by Lucio Costa and Oscar Niemeyer, 1960.

Brighton Pavilion. England, by John Nash, 1815–21.

Brihadisva Rasvamin Temple. India, *ca.* 1018.

Brooklyn Bridge. New York City, by J. A. and W. A. Roebling, 1869–83.

Burgos, Cathedral of. Spain, 1221–1457.

Ca' d'Oro. Venice, by Giovanni and Bartolomeo Bon, *ca.* 1421.

Caecilia Metalla, Tomb of. Rome, *ca.* 20 B.C.E.

Caernarvon, Castle of. Wales, 1298–1301.

Campanile. Pisa, 1063–1278.

Campidoglio. Rome, 1546.

Canadian Parliament. Ottawa, by Thomas Fuller and F. W. Stent, 1861–67; destroyed by fire, 1916, rebuilt by Jean O. Marchand and John A. Pearson, 1916–23.

Canterbury Cathedral. England, by William of Sens, 1071–1185.

Capitol. Washington, D.C., by William Thornton, Benjamin Latrobe, and others, 1793–1867.

Caracalla, Baths of. Rome, 211–17.

Carcassonne, walled city of. France, *ca.* 1285.

Casa Mila. Barcelona, by Antonio Gaudí, 1905–10.

Castel' S. Angelo (Hadrian's Tomb). Rome, *ca.* 135.

Castor and Pollux, Temple of. Rome, 484 B.C.E.

Centennial Hall. Breslau, Germany, by Max Berg, 1912–13.

Central Library. University City, Mexico, by Juan O'Gorman, 1951–53.

Cêntre Nationale d'Art. Paris, by Piano and Rogers, 1977.

Chambord, Château de. France, 1525–44.

Ch'ang-an Pagoda. China, 625–705.

Chartres Cathedral. France, 1194–1260.

Château Gaillard. Les Andelys, France, 1196–98.

Chenonceaux, bridge-castle of. France, by Philibert de l'Orme and Jean Bullant, 1515–76.

Cheops' Pyramid. Giza, Egypt, *ca.* 2700 B.C.E.

Chrysler Building. New York, by William Van Alen, 1930.

Clifton Suspension Bridge. England, by Marc Isambard Brunel, 1830.

Cloth Hall. Ypres, Belgium, 1202–1304.

Cluny, monastery church at. France, *ca.* 980.

Colleoni Chapel. Bergamo, Italy, by Giovanni Antonio Amadeo, 1470.

Cologne, Cathedral of. Germany, 1248–1322.

Colosseum. Rome, 70–82.

Constantine, Arch of. Rome, 315.

Coonley House. Riverside, Ill., by Frank Lloyd Wright, 1908–12.

Cordoba, mosque at. Spain, 785–987.

Cornaro Chapel. Santa Maria della Vittoria, Rome, by Bernini, *ca.* 1650.

Coventry Cathedral. England, reconstructed 1951–62.

Craigie-Longfellow House. Cambridge, Mass., 1759.

Crystal Palace. London, by Sir Joseph Paxton, 1850–51.

Ctesiphon, palace at. Iraq, *ca.* 400–300 B.C.E.

Damascus, Great Mosque at. Syria, 706–15.

Dilwarra Temple. Mount Abu, India, 1032.

Diocletian, Baths of. Rome, *ca.* 302.

Diocletian, Palace of. Split, Croatia, *ca.* 300.

Doges' Palace. Venice, by G. and B. Buon, 1309–84.

Dominican Monastery of La Tourette. Eveux, Lyons, France, by Edouard Le Corbusier, 1960.

Dublin Custom House. Ireland, by James Gandon, 1781–91.

Durham Cathedral. England, *ca.* 1100.

Dymaxion House. Wichita, Kans., by Buckminster Fuller, 1946.

Eads Bridge. St. Louis, Mo., by James Buchanan Eads, 1867–74.

Edinburgh, fort at. Scotland, 617.

Eiffel Tower. Paris, by Alexandre Gustave Eiffel, 1887–89.

El Djem Amphitheater. Carthage, Tunisia, *ca.* 200.

Ellora, Kaisala temple at. India, 780.

El Pilar Cathedral. Saragossa, Spain, 1677–1766.

Ely, Cathedral of. England, 1198–1215.

Empire State Building. New York City, N.Y., by Shreve, Lamb, and Harmon, 1930–31.

Epidauros, theater at. Greece, *ca.* 330 B.C.E.

Erechtheum. Athens, by Mnesicles, 420–393 B.C.E.

Escorial. Near Madrid, by Juan Bautista de Toledo and Juan de Herrera, 1563–89.

Exchange. Copenhagen, 1619–30.

Exeter Cathedral. England, *ca.* 1300.

Fagus Factory. Alfeld-an-der-Leine, Germany, by Walter Gropius and Adolf Meyer, 1911–14.

Familia Sagrada, La, Church of. Barcelona, by Antonio Gaudi i Cornet, 1882–1930.

Farnese Palace. Rome, by Antonio da Sangallo and Michelangelo, *ca.* 1515–34.

Federal Reserve Bank. Minneapolis, Minn., by Gunnar Birkerts, 1970–72.

Firth of Forth Railway Bridge. Scotland, by Sir John Fowler and Sir Benjamin Baker, 1883–90.

Flatiron Building. New York City, N.Y., by Daniel H. Burnham, 1902–1903.

Ford House. Lincoln, Mass., by Walter Gropius and Marcel Breuer, 1939.

Fortuna Virilis, Temple of. Rome, *ca.* 40 B.C.E.

Foundling Hospital. Florence, by Filippo Brunelleschi, 1421–45.

Four Heavenly Kings, Temple of. Osaka, Japan, 593.

Fragrant Hill Hotel. Beijing, by I. M. Pei, 1983.

Galla Placidia, Tomb of. Ravenna, Italy, 446.

Gare du Nord. Paris, by Jacques-Ignace Hittorff, 1858–66.

Gateway Arch. St. Louis, Mo., by Eero Saarinen, 1959–65.

Geller House. Lawrence, Long Island, N.Y., by Marcel Breuer, 1946.

General Motors Technical Institute. Warren, Mich., by Eliel and Eero Saarinen, 1946–55.

George Washington Bridge. Between Manhattan and New Jersey, by Cass Gilbert and Othmar Herman Ammann, 1927–31.

Glass House. New Canaan, Conn., by Philip Johnson, 1949.

Goetheanum I. Dornach, Switzerland, by Rudolph Steiner, 1913–20.

Golden Gate Bridge. San Francisco, Calif., by J. B. Strauss, 1933–37.

Grand Central Station. New York City, by Charles A. Reed and Allen H. Stem; Whitney Warren and Charles D. Wetmore, 1903–13.

Great Altar of Heaven. Beijing, *ca.* 1420.

Guaranty (now Prudential) Building. Buffalo, N.Y., by Louis Sullivan and Dankmar Adler, 1894–95.

Guild Houses, Grand' Palace. Brussels, 1690–1752.

Guir-i-Mir. Samarkand, Uzbek, 1404.

Hadrian's Wall. From Wallsend-on-Tyne to Bowness-on-Solway, Eng., 122–26.

Hagia Sophia. Istanbul, 532–37.

Hampton Court Palace. England, *ca.* 1520.

Hatshepsut, Temple of. Der el-Bahari, Egypt, *ca.* 1520 B.C.E.

Heinrichshof. Vienna, by Theophilus von Hansen, 1861–63.

Heraion. Olympia, Greece, *ca.* 590 B.C.E.

High Museum. Atlanta, Ga., by Richard Meier, 1984.

Himeji Castle. Japan, 1346–1610.

Holy Sepulchre, Church of the. Jerusalem, *ca.* 325.

Horiuji, Temple of. Nara, Japan, *ca.* 600.

Horus, Temple of. Edfu, Egypt, *ca.* 237–57 B.C.E.

Hôtel des Invalides Church. Paris, by Jules Hardouin-Mansart, 1680–91.

Hôtel de Soubise. Paris, by Pierre-Alexis Delamair, 1706.

Houses of Parliament. London, by Sir Charles Barry and Augustus Pugin, 1835–68.

Houses of Parliament. Melbourne, Australia, 1856–68.

Humayun, Tomb of. Delhi, 1565–66.

Imperial Hotel. Tokyo, by Frank Lloyd Wright, 1915–22.

Imperial Palace. Beijing, *ca.* 1100.

Imperial Villa. Katsura, Japan, by Prince Toshihito and Prince Toshitada, 1620–58.

Independence Hall. Philadelphia, Pa., 1731; demolished, 1781; rebuilt by William Strickland, 1832.

Isis, Temple of. Philae, Egypt, *ca.* 283–47 B.C.E.

Jami Masjid. Ahmahabad, India, 1411–24.

Jefferson Memorial. Washington, D.C., by John Russell Pope, 1943.

Jerusalem, temple at. Jerusalem, *ca.* 950 B.C.E.

Johnson Wax Co. Building. Racine, Wis., by Frank Lloyd Wright, 1936–39.

Julius III, Villa of. Rome, by Giacomo Barozzi da Vignola, 1550–55.

Jupiter, Temple of. Baalbek, Lebanon, *ca.* 10–249.

Jupiter, Temple of. Rome, *ca.* 509 B.C.E.

Katholikon. Mount Athos, Greece, *ca.* 1000–1200.

Kennedy Center. Washington, D.C., by Edward Durell Stone, 1971–73.

Kesava Temple. Somnathpur, India, *ca.* 1275.

Khons, Temple of. Karnak, Egypt, *ca.* 1198 B.C.E.

King's Chapel. Boston, Mass. by Peter Harrison, 1749–54.

King's College Chapel. Cambridge, Eng., 1446–1515.

King's Cross Station. London, by Lewis Cubitt, 1850–52.

Knossos, Palace of King Minos at. Crete, *ca.* 2000–1600 B.C.E.

Krak of the Knights. Syria, *ca.* 1110–1200.

Kubbet es-Sakhra. Jerusalem, 688–92.

Les Terraces. Near Paris, by Le Corbusier and Pierre Jeanneret, 1926–27.

Leuven (Louvain) Town Hall. Belgium, 1447–63.

Lever House. New York City, N.Y., by Gordon Bunshaft, 1953.

Liberia Vecchia. Venice, by Jacopo Sansovino, 1553.

Lincoln Memorial. Washington, D.C., by Henry Bacon, 1911–22.

Louvre. Paris, various sections by Philibert Delorme, Louis Le Vau, Claude Perrault, and others, 1546–1878.

M.I.T. Auditorium. Cambridge, Mass., by Eero Saarinen, 1952–55.

Machu Picchu. Peru, *ca.* 1500.

Magnus Martyr, Church of. London, by Christopher Wren, 1671–1705.

Mainz, Cathedral of. Germany, *ca.* 1009.

Maison Carré. Nimes, France, *ca.* 15 B.C.E.

Maisons-Jaoul. Paris, by Le Corbusier, 1954–56.

Mamellapuram Temple. India, 625–74.

Marcellus, Theater of. Rome, 23–13 B.C.E.

Marshall Field Warehouse. Chicago, Ill., by Henry H. Richardson, 1885–87.

Massachusetts, State House. Boston, Mass., by Charles Bullfinch, 1795–98.

Mausoleum. Halicarnassus, Turkey, 355–50 B.C.E.

Maxentius, Basilica of. (Basilica of Constantine). Rome, 310.

Medici Chapel of San Lorenzo. Florence, by Michelangelo, 1520–34.

Melrose Abbey. Scotland, 1450–1505.

Mexico City Cathedral. Mexico, 1563–1667.

Milan Cathedral. Italy, 1385–1485.

Monticello. Charlottesville, Va., by Thomas Jefferson, 1770–1808.

Mont St. Michel, abbey church and monastery at. France, 708; 1203–28; sixteenth century.

Montserrat. Near Barcelona, *ca.* eighth century.

Mormon Temple. Washington, D.C., by Fred L. Markham and others, 1970–74.

Mount Vernon. Fairfax County, Va., 1757–87.

Municipal Building. Portland, Oreg., by Michael Graves, 1983.

National Gallery. Edinburgh, by William Henry Playfair, 1850–54.

National Gallery of Art. Washington, D.C., by John Russell Pope, 1939–41.

New Scotland Yard. Victoria Embankment, London, by Richard Norman Shaw, 1887–88.

New York City, City Hall. By Joseph F. Mangin, 1803–1804.

North Carolina State Fair Pavilion. Raleigh, N.C., Matthew Nowicki and others, 1953–54.

Nôtre Dame, Cathedral of. Paris, *ca.* 1163–1260.

Nôtre Dame du Pont. Clermont-Ferrand, France, *ca.* 1100.

Opêra. Paris, by Jean-Louis-Charles Garnier, 1861–74.

Orange, theater at. France, *ca.* late first century B.C.E.

Our Lady of Guadalupe Church. Mexico City, by Pedro de Arrieta, 1695–1709.

Overseas-Chinese Banking Corp. Singapore, by B. E. P. Akitek and others, 1980.

Paestum, temples at. Italy, *ca.* 550–450 B.C.E.

Palace of Governors. Uxmal, Mexico, *ca.* 900.

Palais de Justice. Rouen, France, 1493–1508.

Palazetto della Sport. Rome, by P. L. Nervi, 1956–57.

Palazzo Barberini. Rome, by Carlo Maderna, 1628–38.

Palazzo Carignano. Turin, by Guarino Guarini, 1679.

Palazzo Chiericati. Vicenza, Italy, by Andrea Palladio, 1550-*ca.* 1580.

Palazzo della Ragione ("Il Salone"). Padua, 1218 to fifteenth century.

Palazzo Medici-Riccardi. Florence, by Michelozzo di Bartolomeo Michelozzi, 1444–60.

Palazzo Vecchio. Florence, 1298–1301.

Panthéon. Paris, by Jacques-Germain Soufflot, 1755–92.

Pantheon. Rome, *ca.* 125.

Papal Palace. Avignon, France, 1316–84.

Parthenon. Athens, by Ictinus and Callicrates, *ca.* 437–32 B.C.E.

Pearl Mosque. Agra, India, seventeenth century.

People's Bank. Bridgeport, Conn., by Richard Meier, 1989.

Persian Gate Palace. Persepolis, Iran, *ca.* 518–465 B.C.E.

Peterborough Cathedral. England, 1117–93.

Petit Palais. Paris, by Charles Girault, 1897–1900.

Philharmonie. Berlin, by Hans Scharoun, 1960–63.

Piacenza, Cathedral of. Italy, *ca.* 1050–1128.

Pitti Palace. Florence, by Filippo Brunelleschi (probably) and Bartolommeo Ammannati, 1458–1570.

Pokrov Cathedral. Moscow, by Postnik and Barma, 1555–60.

Pons Aemilius. Rome, 179 B.C.E.; arched superstructure, 142 B.C.E.

Pons Mulvius. Rome, 109 B.C.E.

Pont du Gard. Nimes, France, *ca.* 14.

Ponte di Rialto. Venice, by Antonio da Ponte, 1580–92.

Ponte Vecchio. Florence, by Taddeo Gaddi, 1345.

Portunus, Temple of. Rome, 35–39 B.C.E.

Potala. Tibet; massive palace of the Dalai Lama overlooking Lhasa; seventh to seventeenth century.

Prague Cathedral. Czech Republic, by d'Arras and Parler, 1344–96.

Pyramid of the Sun. Teotihuacan, Mexico, *ca.* 250.

Rathaus Portico. Cologne, Germany, by Wernickel, 1569–71.

Regensburg Cathedral. Germany, 1275–1564.

Reims, Cathedral of. France 1211–90.

Reliance Building. Chicago, Ill., by D. H. Burnham and J. W. Root, 1890–94.

Rhodes, Colossus of. Greece, *ca.* 275 B.C.E.

Rijksmuseum. Amsterdam, by P. J. H. Cuijpers, 1877–85.

Rio de Janeiro, Ministry of Education and Health. Brazil, by Edouard Le Corbusier, Lucio Costa, Oscar Niemeyer, and others, 1937–42.

Rockefeller Center. New York City, N.Y., by Max Abramovitz and Wallace K. Harrison, Harvey W. Corbett, Jacques A. Fouilhoux, Raymond M. Hood, William H. MacMurray, L. A. Reinhart, and Henry Hofmeister, 1929–33, 1941–74.

Rotonda (Villa Capri). Vicenza, Italy, by Andrea Palladio, begun 1550.

Royal Horticultural Hall. London, by Easton and Robertson, 1923–26.

S. Agnese Fuori le Mura. Rome, 625–38.

S. Theodore, church of. Athens, *ca.* 1060–1070.

Sacsahuaman Fortress. Peru, *ca.* 1475.

Saint-Denis, Ambulatory of. Near Paris, by Abbot Suger, 1140–44.

Saint Mark's, Cathedral of. Venice, 1063–1073; belfry by Bartolomeo Bon, 1510–14.

Saint Martin-in-the-Fields, Church of. London, by James Gibbs, 1722–26.

Saint Maurice, Church of. Angers, France, *ca.* 1020–1032.

Saint Michael's Church. Charleston, S.C., 1752–61.

Saint Patrick's Cathedral. New York City, N.Y., by James Renwick, 1858–79.

Saint Paul's Cathedral. London, by Christopher Wren, 1675–1710.

Saint Peter's, Cathedral of. Rome, 326.

Saint Peter's Basilica. Vatican City, Rome, by Bramante, Raphael, Michelangelo, Giacomo della Porta, Maderna, Giovanni Lorenzo Bernini, and others, *ca.* 1500–1750.

Saint Sabina, Church of. Rome, 422–32.

Saint Sernin Cathedral. Toulouse, France, 1077–1119.

Saint Sophia Cathedral. Novgorod, Russia, 1050.

Saint Trophîme. Arles, France, *ca.* 1100.

Salisbury Cathedral. England, 1220–58.

San Angelo Bridge. Vatican City, Rome, 136.

San Carlo alle Quattro Fontane. Rome, by Borromini, 1635–67.

San Lorenzo. Florence, by Filippo Brunelleschi, 1421–55.

San Lorenzo, New Sacristy. Florence, by Michelangelo Buonarroti, 1521–34.

San Stefano, Rotondo, Basilica of. Rome, 468–83.

San Vitale. Ravenna, Italy, 526–47.

Sant' Ambrogio, Cathedral of. Milan, 1080–1118.

Sant' Andrea. Mantua, Italy, by Alberti, 1470.

Sant' Apollinaire in Classe. Ravenna, Italy, by Anthemius of Tralles and Isidorus of Miletus, 534–39.

Santa Maria della Fiore Cathedral. Florence, by Arnolfo di Cambio, dome by Filippo Brunelleschi, 1296–1434.

Santa Maria Maggiore, Basilica of. Rome, 432.

Sargon II, Palace of. Khorsabad, Iraq, *ca.* 733 B.C.E.

Sas Bahu Temple. Gwalior, India, 1093.

Seagram Building. New York City, N.Y., by Ludwig Mies van der Rohe and Philip Johnson, 1956–58.

Second Bank of the United States. Philadelphia, Pa., by William Strickland, 1817–24.

Septimus Severus, Arch of. Rome, 203.

Seville Cathedral. Spain, 1402–1520.

Shah-i-Zinda Necropolis. Samarkand, Uzbek, 1300–1500.

Sher Shah, Tomb of. Sahsaran, India, 1542–45.

Shiwa or Siva Temple. Java, *ca.* 1000–1200.

Shogun Palaces. Japan, 1603–1868.

Shore Temple. Mamallapuram, India, 750.

Siena, Cathedral of. Italy, 1226–1380.

Solomon R. Guggenheim Museum. New York City, N.Y., by Frank Lloyd Wright, 1956.

Sorbonne Church. Paris, by Jacques Lemercier, 1635–38.

Speyer, Cathedral of. Germany, 1030–1061.

Sphinx. Giza, Egypt, *ca.* 1800 B.C.E.

Stazione Termini. Rome, by Angiolo Mazzoni, 1938; E. Montuori and others, 1947–51.

Stock Exchange. Amsterdam, by Hendrik Berlage, 1898–1903.

Stockholm, Royal Palace at. Sweden, by Nicodemus Tessin, 1690–1753.

Stockholm City Library. Sweden, by E. G. Asplund, 1924–27.

Stonehenge. Wiltshire, Eng., *ca.* 2000–1400 B.C.E.

Strawberry Hill. Twickenham, Eng., 1747.

Strozzi Palace. Florence, by Benedetto da Majano and Simone del Pollaiuolo 1489–1507.

Suleimaniye Mosque. Istanbul, 1551–58.

Sultan Ahmed I, Mosque of (the Blue Mosque). Istanbul, by Mehmet Aga, 1609–16.

Sung Yüeh Ssii Temple, pagoda. China, *ca.* 522.

Sun Temples. Orissa and Khajuraho, India, *ca.* 1000–1200.

Tagus Bridge. Alcántara, Spain, 106.

Taj Mahal. Agra, India, 1630–48.

Taliesin West. Phoenix, Ariz., by Frank Lloyd Wright, 1938.

Tavera Hospital. Toledo, by De Bustamente, 1542–79.

Temple of Warriors. Chichen Itza, Mexico, *ca.* 1000–1200.

Teotihuacan, citadel at. Mexico, *ca.* 600.

Thorncrown Chapel. Eureka Springs, Ark., by E. Fay Jones, 1990.

Titus, Arch of. Rome, 81.

Trajan's Column. Rome, completed by Apollodorus of Damascus, 114.

Transportation Building. Chicago, Ill., by Louis Sullivan, 1893.

Tribune Tower. Chicago, Ill., by J. M. Howells and Raymond Hood, 1923–25.

Trinity Church. Boston, Mass., by Henry H. Richardson, 1872–77.

Tugenhat House. Brnó, Czech Republic, by Ludwig Mies van der Rohe, 1930.

TWA Building. New York, by Eero Saarinen, 1956–62.

Unité d'Habitation. Marseilles, by Le Corbusier, 1946–52.

United States Pavilion (Geodesic Dome). Montreal, by Buckminster Fuller, 1967.

Uspenski Cathedral. Kremlin, Moscow, *ca.* 1326; rebuilt by Fioraventi, 1475–79.

Vaux-le-Vicomte, Château. Near Paris, by Louis Le Vau, 1656–61.

Vendramini Palace. Venice, by Pietro Lombardo (?), 1481–89.

Versailles, Palais de. France, by Salomon de Brosse, Louis Le Vau, André Lenôtre, Jules Hardouin-Mansart, Jacques-Ange Gabriel, and others, 1661–1756.

Vierzehnheiligen, Church of. near Bamberg, Germany, by Balthasar Neumann, 1743–72.

Villa Medici. Rome, 1574–80.

Villa Savoye. Poissy, France, by Le Corbusier, 1929–32.

Virginia State Capitol. Richmond, Va., by Thomas Jefferson, 1789–98.

Vishnu, Temple of. Deogarh, India, fifth century.

Vishnu, Temple of. Pranbanam, India, *ca.* 1000–1200.

Votivkirche. Vienna, by Heinrich von Ferstel, 1856–79.

Wainwright Building. St. Louis, Mo., by Dankmar Adler and Louis Sullivan, 1890–91.

Warwick Castle. England, 914–1087.

Washington Monument. Washington, D.C., by Robert Mills, 1848–84.

Westminster Abbey. London, 1245–69.

Whitehall Cenotaph. London, by Sir Edwin Landseer Lutyens, 1920.

White House. Washington, D.C., by James Hoban, 1792–1829.

White Tower of the Tower of London. By Gundulf, 1078–1087.

Williamsburg Capitol. Virginia, 1701–1705.

Wilton House. England; south façade by Inigo Jones, 1649–53.

Windsor Castle. England, *ca.* 1075–1125.

Winter Palace. St. Petersburg, Russia, by Bartolomeo Francesco Rastrelli, 1754–62.

Wollaton Hall. Nottinghamshire, Eng., 1580–88.

Woolworth Building. New York City, N.Y., by Cass Gilbert, 1911–13.

World Trade Center. New York City, N.Y., by Minoru Yamasaki and Emery Roth, 1961–73.

Worms, Cathedral of. Germany, *ca.* 1000–1200.

Yakushi Pagoda. Japan, *ca.* 680.

Zeus, Temple of. Olympia, Greece, by Libon of Elis, *ca.* 460 B.C.E.

Ziggurat. Ur, *ca.* 2125 B.C.E.

Zoser's Pyramid. Saqqura, Egypt, by Imhotep, *ca.* 2750 B.C.E.

SOURCES

"Architecture." *Encyclopaedia Britannica.* 14th ed. Chicago: Encyclopaedia Britannica Co., Inc., 1957.

"Architecture." *World Book Encyclopedia.* Chicago: World Book, 1984.

Baumgart, Fritz. *A History of Architectural Styles.* New York: Praeger, 1969.

Briggs, Martin S. *Everyman's Concise Encyclopedia of Architecture.* London: J. M. Dent, 1959.

Crouch, Dora P. *History of Architecture: Stonehenge to Skyscrapers.* New York: McGraw-Hill, 1985.

Esher, Lionel G. B. Brett, Fourth Viscount. *The World of Architecture.* London: Thomas Nelson, 1963.

Fletcher, Sir Banister. *A History of Architecture.* 18th ed. New York: Charles Scribner's
      Sons, 1975.
Gane, John F., ed. *American Architects Directory.* 3rd ed. New York: R. R. Bowker, 1970.
Gloag, John. *Architecture.* London: Cassell, 1963.
Hunt, William Dudley, Jr. *Encyclopedia of American Architecture.* New York: McGraw-
      Hill, 1980.
Mitchell, George. *Architecture of the Islamic World.* London: Thames and Hudson, 1978.
Placzek, Adolf K., *et al.,* eds. *Macmillan Encyclopedia of Architects.* 4 vols. New York:
      Free Press, 1982.
Randall, Alec. *Rediscovering Rome.* London: Heinemann, 1960.
Richards, J. M. *An Introduction to Modern Architecture.* New York: Penguin Books, 1947.

—J.L.M.

17

ARCHITECTURAL TERMS:
A GLOSSARY

· · · · ·

"I CALL ARCHITECTURE FROZEN MUSIC," WROTE GOETHE, WHO WAS POET, scientist, novelist, dramatist, and musician. But music, except perhaps for military marches, is of little practical use other than through association, whereas architecture has a utilitarian as well as an artistic function—and woe to the architect who emphasizes one to the exclusion of the other. The architect must be an engineer, thoroughly versed in the elements of structural design and the properties of materials used in construction, and at the same time what is created must be pleasing to the eye in an abstract, non-representational mode.

Architects commissioned to design buildings today, whether public, governmental, industrial, commercial, or residential, confront a problem that was largely unknown before the nineteenth century. For no longer is there a dominant period style, a more or less uniform set of expectations within which the architect can work, with its own rules and assumptions. When Sir Christopher Wren designed his magnificent churches and public buildings in London, he did not have to ask himself whether to build in Romanesque, or Gothic, or colonial, or Elizabethan, or Queen Anne, or baroque, or Georgian, or Mission, or Palladian, or Greek Revival, or neo-classical, or "natural," or "severely functional," or bauhaus, or Corbusian, or whatever.

Today's architect, by contrast, can draw on no such common set of expectations. Moreover, the variety of building materials, each with its own structural and technological properties, far exceeds what was available to earlier architects. Reinforced concrete, iron, steel, aluminum, glass, plastics, laminated wood, present choices that were previously unknown to builders. In earlier ages, too, whatever went into a building was produced on the site; today much of what the architect must work with is prefabricated.

If, however, the range of choices and decisions that confront the architect is far greater nowadays, so too are the opportunities, and the great creative architects and architectural firms of the twentieth century—Le Corbusier, Wright, Maillart, van der Rohe, Gropius, Breuer, the Saarinens, Fuller, Pei, Skidmore Owings & Merrill, Hardy Holzman & Pfeiffer, Portman, others—have designed and built buildings that combine "frozen music" with functional utility in ways that would have astounded and enthralled their predecessors.

The following is a glossary of some terms commonly used in architecture and architectural history. For help in compiling it we are grateful to Mr. Maynard Pearlstine, A.I.A., of Kiawah Island, South Carolina, who has designed a few good buildings himself in his time. For historical periods and schools the reader should consult the glossary on art schools, movements, styles, and periods.

Abacus. Uppermost member of a column capital.

Abbey. Church connected to a monastery.

Abutment. Part of a support that receives the lateral thrust of an arch or vault.

Acanthus. Ornamentation on Corinthian and composite column capitals, based on leaves of the Mediterranean plant of this name.

Acropolis. Elevated stronghold of an ancient Greek city.

Acrosolium. Canopied for a tomb, as in a catacomb.

Adobe. Sun-baked clay brick.

Aedicule. Sculpture niche or window framed by columns.

Agora. Greek central square or marketplace; the equivalent of a Roman forum.

Aisle. Longitudinal passage between rows of seats; space between columns of the nave and side walls of a church.

Alcove. Recessed space in a room; unlike a niche, this space extends to the floor.

Almshouse. Charity house constructed to shelter the indigent.

Ambulatory. Passageway in a church behind the high altar and behind the apse.

Amphitheater. Circular or oval structure with central arena surrounded by rising tiers of seats or benches; an outdoor theater.

Annulet. Small flat fillet encircling a column.

Anta. Pilaster with a base and capital at the end of a wall.

Anthemion. Honeysuckle or palmette ornament on columns and elsewhere in Greek and Roman buildings.

Apotropaion. Decorative image, usually ugly, placed on a building to protect it and its inhabitants against evil.

Apse. In churches, the semicircular or polygonal vaulted space intended to house an altar.

Aqueduct. Channel constructed, often with elevated portions, to convey water.

Arcade. Arched covered walk with shops along the sides.

Arch. Usually curved structure, composed of wedge-shaped solids, employed to span an opening; some of the more common types are the semicircular, the Gothic, the ogee, the stilted, the depressed, the horseshoe, the basket, and the Tudor.

Architectonic. Having or expressing the spatial qualities related to architectural design.

Architrave. In classical architecture, the main beam that spans from column to column and forms the lowest part of the entablature; more commonly, the ornamental molding around a doorway or opening.

Arris. Edge formed by junction of two surfaces.

Ashlar. Masonry or rectangular stones in regular ranges on the face of a building.

Atlantes. Muscular figures, modeled after Atlas, that serve as pillars.

Atrium. Open patio around which a house is built, or a multistoried court in a building, usually built with a skylight.

Axis. Imaginary straight line which passes through a building so that its two sides appear in symmetry.

Azulejos. Painted and glazed earthenware tiles popular in Spain, Portugal, and Latin America.

Balcony. Platform that projects from a building and is enclosed by a railing or a parapet.

Baldachin. Ornamental canopy over an altar.

Balloon frame. Construction of studs and plates held together by nails, superceding the ancient and expensive method of mortise and tenon joints; first used in Chicago in 1833.

Baluster. Short post or pillar to support a stair railing.

Balustrade. Railing supported by balusters.

Baptistry. Small building or part of a church where baptismal rites are performed.

Barbican. Small fortified outwork or a tower at a gate or a bridge.

Bar joists. Light steel members consisting of zigzag-shaped steel rods joining top and bottom members.

Bartizan. Small projecting turret with lookout holes on a parapet.

Base. Lowest visible part of a wall or bottom support of a pillar.

Basilica. Hall or church, usually oblong, with apse.

Bastion. Originally, projection from fortress wall that permitted greater firing range; now, any strongly fortified position.

Batten. Strip of material used to cover or attach a joint.

Bay. Vertical division of a structure.

Beam. Any horizontal member that supports weight in a roof, floor, or ceiling; also called *girder*.

Bearing wall. Wall capable of bearing the weight of the structure, as opposed to wall that supports no weight; also *load-bearing wall*.

Belfry. Tower in which bells are located.

Belvedere. Any building, such as a cupola or summerhouse, designed specifically to take advantage of its view.

Bema. Raised transverse space reserved for clergy in early Christian churches.

Béton brut. Concrete as it appears after the framework or shuttering has been removed.

Bevel. Rounding or smoothing of an acute angle.

Boss. Any projecting ornament; usually carved.

Boulevard. Walkway.

Brace. Structural material used diagonally to stiffen or support a portion of a building.

Breastsummer or bressummer. Horizontal beam spanning a wide opening in an external wall.

Breastwork. Any defensive wall that is thrown up quickly.

Brick bonds. Methods for laying of walls; they include the common, garden wall, English, stack, and Flemish bonds.

Brise-soleil. Louvered sunscreen incorporated into façade of a building to shade the window openings from the sun.

Broken pediment. Pediment split apart at the center and filled with an urn or other ornament.

Bulwark. Any fortified rampart, often made of earth.

Bungalow. One-level frame house with porch; houses in this style were originally built in Bengal.

Buttress. Internal or external wall support, frequently used to compensate for the lateral thrust of an arch or a vault.

Cabanas. Small porches, dressing rooms, and showers normally found at seaside areas.

Caisson. Sunken panel in a vaulted ceiling; also a watertight chamber.

Campanile. Free-standing belltower.

Canopy. Rooflike structure extending out from a wall.

Cantilever. Projecting, unsupported member that is counterbalanced by the weight of the anchoring structure.

Capital. Topmost member of a column, pier, pilaster, or pillar.

Caracol or caracole. Spiral staircase.

Caryatid. Supporting column in the form of a female figure.

Casement. (1) Vaulted chamber built within a fortress wall; (2) window opening on hinges.

Castle. Fortified residence of a prince or nobleman.

Castrum. Roman military camp built on a rectangular plan.

Catacombs. Underground cemeteries used by the early Christians; these consisted of tunnels with niches for tombs.

Cathedral. Church that is the official seat of a diocesan bishop.

Cavity wall. Masonry wall construction consisting of outer and inner wythes of brick separated by a cavity of several inches and joined by metal ties.

Cella. See **Naos**.

Cenotaph. Memorial raised to commemorate persons who are buried elsewhere.

Chalet. Originally, timbered house in the Alps; now, any house built in the Swiss style.

Chamfer. Diagonal bevel formed by two surfaces meeting at an angle; a hollow chamfer is concave, a sunk chamfer slightly sunk but flat.

Chancel. Part of a church containing seats for clergy and choir.

Chancery. Building or suite of rooms for legal or diplomatic use.

Chapel. Smaller structure, often attached to a church or cathedral, used for private worship.

Chapter house. Large room or house attached to a monastery or cathedral and used for meetings or "chapters" of the governing body.

Château. French country estate.

Chevet. Eastern end of a church that includes the apse, ambulatory, and radiating chapels.

Choir. Part of church reserved, during services, for the singers and the clergy.

Choir screen. Screen, often ornamented, separating choir and clergy from the congregation.

Cinquefoil. Ornamental foliation with five lobes divided by cusps.

Circus. Originally, a roofless Roman arena; in eighteenth- and nineteenth-century Britain, houses arranged in a circle or near circle.

Citadel. Fortified enclosure; usually located near a city.

Clapboard construction. Construction technique in which horizontal boards are overlapped to cover a wood frame.

Clapper bridge. Type of bridge constructed with stone slabs.

Clearstorey or clerestory. Wall with high row of windows.

Cloister. Covered arcade surrounding a cortile or quadrangle.

Cob. Building material made of unburnt clay, straw, and gravel.

Coffering. System of deep recesses in a ceiling, often ornamental.

Collar beam. Horizontal beam tying together and stiffening the two sides of a timber-framed roof near the ridge.

Colonnade. Columns arranged in order, supporting an entablature or a series of arches.

Column. Free-stranding pillar, usually cylindrical, supporting a load.

Composite order. One of the five Roman orders of architecture; a modification of the Corinthian order.

Console. Any decorative bracket.

Coping. Capping or covering to a wall or walkway.

Corbel. Projection from wall to support overhanging member.

Corian. Solid surfacing, manufactured by DuPont, for countertops and walls.

Corinthian order. One of the three Greek and five Roman orders of architecture; it can be identified by the acanthus leaves on the column capital.

Cornice. Highest part of the entablature; molded projection along the top of a building.

Corps de logis. Central part of a building that has smaller, attached structures.

Cortile. Open courtyard enclosed by walls in an Italian-style house.

Cottage. Small house in rural setting, traditionally for a retainer or farmer; now a small vacation house.

Crenellation. Notched parapet.

Crescent. Group of buildings with unified façades arranged in an arc.

Cresset. Metal bracket intended to hold a torch.

Cresting. Horizontal ornamentation along roof on top of wall.

Cromlech. Prehistoric circle of large upright stones or dolmens.

Crossing. Intersection in a church where the nave and the chancel cross the transepts; it is often surmounted with a dome or a spire.

Crown. Top of an arch.

Crucks. Curved timbers used in pairs to support ridge beams of Early English houses.

Crypt. Story under main floor of a church.

Cupola. Small dome, often on ridge of roof.

Curtain wall. Exterior wall with no structural function.

Dado. Part of a plinth or pedestal between the base and the cap or cornice; more commonly, the lower part of an exterior wall; also, groove cut into a piece of wood to receive another piece.

Dais. Raised platform, designed to give prominence to users.

Dentils. Toothlike cube ornamentation in classical cornices.

Dipteral. Temple with double range of columns on each side.

Dolmen. Prehistoric structure composed of two or more large stone slabs crowned with another, horizontal stone; commonly a tomb.

Dome. Curved vault, ceiling, or roof.

Domus. Roman house built for one family.

Doric order. One of the three Greek and five Roman orders of architecture, with tapered shafts and no bases for columns.

Dormer. Window in a sloping roof.

Drawbridge. Bridge, originally at the entrance of a castle or fortified town, that can be raised or lowered over a moat or body of water.

Eaves. Portion of roof projecting beyond the walls of a building.

Ell. Expansion to a building built at right angles to it.

Embrasure. Aperture with sides flared outward from the inner side of the wall in which it is constructed.

Enceinte. Encircling fortification of castle or town.

Enfilade. Series of doors aligned axially to create a view.

Entablature. Horizontal beam, composed of cornice, frieze, and architrave, and supported by pillars.

Entasis. Outward bulge in shaft of a column.

Extrados. Outside curve of an arch or a vault.

Façade. Main exterior face or front of a building.

Fanlight. Semicircular window above a door.

Fan vault. Vaulting in which all ribs have the same curve and resemble the framework of a fan, as in the Perpendicular period of late English Gothic architecture.

Fenestration. Arrangement and design of windows on a façade.

Ferroconcrete. Concrete construction reinforced with steel rods.

Fillet. Flat band separating moldings and ornaments from each other; also, uppermost member of a cornice concave junction where surfaces meet.

Flamboyant. Tracery in which bars of stonework are arranged in long flamelike columns.

Flèche. Slender wooden spire.

Fluting. Long, parallel grooves with rounded ends, used especially as ornamentation on columns.

Flying buttress. External, arched wall support, used especially in Gothic cathedrals.

Folly. Functionally useless, purely ornamental building, often constructed in parks or gardens; often a fake ruin.

Footing. Portion of foundation transmitting loads to ground.

Forum. Central public meeting-space in Roman cities and towns.

Fosse. Defense moat or ditch.

Foyer. Entry hall; lobby.

Frame construction. Method of construction that uses a wooden frame to support the building.

French window. Window that extends to the floor and has two panels that swing open.

Frieze. Originally, middle horizontal member of classical entablature, between the cornice and the architrave, often ornamented with reliefs; now, any horizontal member joining top of siding to understructure of a cornice.

Fronton. Any pediment crowning a door or window; commonly, a jai alai arena.

Functionalism. Theory that the form of a building should follow and express its function and material.

Fusuma. Wood or paper sliding door in a Japanese house.

Gable. Upper part of a wall enclosed by a double-sloping roof.

Gallery. Corridor or covered walk open on one or both sides.

Gargoyle. Rainspout carved in the shape of a grotesque, and usually mythical, beast.

Garret. Room just under the roof.

Gazebo. Small open turret or summerhouse from which one can enjoy the view.

Gibbs surround. Exterior door frame of alternating large and small stones, named after James Gibbs (1682–1754).

Gisant. Recumbent figure on a tomb.

Glacis. Raised slope in front of a fortification on which attackers are directly in the defenders' line of fire.

Gopura or gopuram. Monumental gateway to a Hindu temple.

Groin. Angle formed by two intersecting vaults.

Grotto. Manmade cave, usually including fountains.

Ha-ha. Wall constructed in a ditch so as not to block a view.

Half-timbered. Construction style, popular in northern Europe during the Renaissance, combining strong timber supports with wattle-and-daub, brick, or stone.

Harmonic proportions. System of balanced proportions, based upon the seemingly divine structures of music, developed by Renaissance architects.

Haunch. Portion of an arch between the crown and the springing line.

Herm. Rectangular post crowned with a bust or head, usually of Hermes; it was often used as a milestone by the Greeks and Romans.

Hip roof. Roof with four sides that slope upward.

Hollow metal. Framing for windows and doors consisting of light-gauge metal sections.

Hood molding. Projecting molding above a window or doorway; also known as dripstone.

Hotel. French term for any important townhouse; now a commercial establishment offering lodging.

Hypostyle. Pillared hall with flat roof resting on columns, as in Egyptian buildings.

Iconostasis. In a Greek Orthodox church, the screen separating the chancel from the congregation, and bearing icons.

Inglenook. Nook or recessed seat by a fireplace.

Intrados. Concave inner curve of an arch or a vault.

Ionic order. One of the three Greek and five Roman orders of architecture; it can be identified by the scrolls on its column capitals.

Jalousie. Door or window shade made from adjustable horizontal slats.

Jamb. Side post of a door frame.

Keep. Strongest tower in a castle; also called a donjon.

Keystone. Wedge-shaped stone at the top of an arch.

Kiblah wall. Wall of a mosque oriented toward Mecca.

Kiosk. Small open structure, often used for selling merchandise.

Kremlin. Citadel of a Russian city.

Lady chapel. Chapel dedicated to the Virgin Mary, on axis of church at the east end; also *axial chapel*.

Lancet. Sharply pointed arch.

Lantern. Windowed superstructure crowning the top of a dome.

Lattice. System of crossed metal or wood bars forming a screen.

Leader. Vertical downspout; also, hot air outlet duct.

Lift-slab. Construction method of casting reinforced concrete floor and roof slabs on top of each other at ground level and lifting to final position by hydraulic jack.

Lintel. Horizontal cross member placed above an opening to bear the weight of the structure above.

Log cabin. Small habitation built of rough-hewn logs; a familiar structure on the American frontier in the late eighteenth and nineteenth centuries.

Loge. Booth, stall, especially theater box.

Loggia. Columned gallery or arcade attached to larger building; characteristic of theaters.

Louvers. Moveable horizontal slats in a window to keep out rain and glare.

Lucarne. Small dormer window.

Lunette. Semicircular area enframed by an arch or vault.

Lych-gate. Roofed gate at entrance to a churchyard.

Machicolation. In a medieval fortification, a projecting parapet with floor openings through which boiling oil or rocks could be dropped upon attackers.

Madrasah. Mosque and theological school arranged around a courtyard.

Mansard roof. Roof with double slope on two or four sides.

Mantelpiece. Frame for a fireplace.

Martello tower. Squat, round coastal defense tower, named for Cape Mortella, Corsica; see opening chapter of James Joyce's *Ulysses*.

Mastaba. Rectangular Egyptian tomb resembling a small pyramid with a sheared top.

Mausoleum. Stately or magnificent commemorative tomb.

Megalith. Huge stone slab used to make cromlechs or dolmens; also *menhir*.

Member. Any component part of a building, structural or decorative.

Merlon. Part of a crenellation or battlement that projects upward.

Mews. Royal Stables in London; now, any English stables in an urban setting.

Mezzanine. Low-ceilinged floor between two main floors.

Mihrab. Niche in a mosque designating the kiblah wall.

Minaret. Tall, slender, balconied tower from which Moslems are called to prayer by the muezzin.

Minster. Church attached to a monastery.

Misericord. Room or separate building in a monastery, in which monastic's discipline could be eased; also, supportive ledge under hinged church seat.

Miter. Diagonal unit formed by meeting of moldings at right angles.

Moat. Protective trench, often filled with water, encircling a castle or fortified town.

Molding. Any ornamental strip or frame.

Mortice. Cavity in a material into which the tenon or tongue of another material is fitted to join them together.

Mosque. Moslem place of worship.

Motte-and-bailey. Wooden fortified tower built on a mound and encircled by an open space, surrounded by ditch and stakes; post-Roman and Norman.

Movable form. Framework for pouring concrete that can be reused.

Mullion. Vertical bar that divides windows or doors.

Mushroom column. Reinforced concrete column flared at the top.

Naos. Sanctuary in a classical temple or a Byzantine church; also known as a cella.

Narthex. Porch or large room leading into early nave of church.

Nave. Central aisle that forms main part of a church.

Newel. Central shaft of a spiral staircase; also, post into which the handrail of a staircase is framed.

Niche. Any wall recess, especially one used to hold a statue.

Obelisk. Tall, thin, four-sided stone pillar that ends in a pyramid.

Ogee. Molding or arch made up of convex and concave curves.

Oratory. Small chapel, located in a larger structure, used for private prayer.

Orders of architecture. System devised by Vitruvius in first century B.C.E. for classifying the three types of Greek architecture, Corinthian, Doric, and Ionic; the five Roman orders of architecture include those and the Tuscan and composite.

Oriel. Window corbeled out from face of a wall by means of projecting stones.

Orientation. Placement of a building in relation to rising sun; also, general location in terms of terrain, weather, etc.

Oubliette. Secret dungeon, with top opening through which prisoners were dropped.

Pagoda. Buddhist temple shaped as a tower, common in India and China; there is a famous pagoda in Kew Gardens, London.

Palace. Large, stately house, especially residence of nobility or a high ecclesiastic.

Palazzo. Italian term for a palace or an important building.

Pantheon. Temple dedicated to all the gods of a religion.

Parapet. Castle wall, often crenellated and placed on a rampart, that protects defenders from enemy fire; also, any wall projection entirely above the roof.

Parquet. Inlaid floor of geometrically arranged wood tiles.

Parterre. Decoratively patterned flower garden.

Patio. Open courtyard, adjoining or enclosed by walls.

Pavilion. Large open tent; also, partly open structure for entertaining.

Pedestal. Base of a classical column, or of a statue, vase, or the like.

Pediment. Gable decoration, usually triangular but sometimes curved, above a portico, window, or door.

Penthouse. Apartment that is constructed on the roof of a building.

Peripteral. Term describing a building which is surrounded by a single row of columns.

Peristyle. Colonnade surrounding a building or open space.

Perron. Outdoor stairway to a building entrance.

Pew. In a church, a bench reserved for the congregation.

Piazza. In Italy, an open public space enclosed by buildings; also, a porch or veranda.

Pickling. Finish on wood stripped of its coat of paint but with gesso coat remaining in the grain.

Pier. Column that supports weight.

Pilaster. Pier or column partially projecting from a wall.

Pile. Concrete, steel, or wood column driven into ground to support building.

Pillar. Evenly shaped, free-standing upright.

Pinnacle. Ornamental body or shaft at the top of a spire.

Pitch. Angle at which a roof slopes away from the horizontal.

Plan. Two-dimensional graphic representation showing the layout of a building as seen from above.

Platform framing. Evolution of the balloon frame, with vertical studs supporting each floor as the building rises.

Plinth. Projecting rectangular base of a column, pier, or vertical trim.

Podium. Low wall or supporting base for a building, a row of columns, or a terrace; also, an elevated platform.

Portal. Large or monumental entryway.

Porch. Covered approach or gallery attached to a building.

Portcullis. Heavy iron grate lowered in the gateway to a castle or a fortified town to bar entrance.

Portico. Roofed porch supported by columns and attached to a larger building.

Postern. Private entrance to a castle or monastery.

Presbytery. Sanctuary of a church reserved for use only by clergy.

Pronaos. In a classical temple, the inner portico in front of a naos; it is enclosed by side walls but has only columns in front.

Prostyle. Portico with columns in front of a building.

Pulpit. Elevated platform in which the preacher stands when officiating.

Purlin. Horizontal timber laid across principal rafters in a roof.

Pylon. Tall tower; also, gateway to Egyptian temple.

Pyramid. Structure with a square base and four sloping, triangular sides that meet at a peak.

Quadrangle. Space enclosed on four sides by buildings or a colonnade.

Quatrefoil. Panel divided by cusps into four leaf-shaped openings.

Quoins. Stone or brick designed to reinforce an external corner of a building.

Rabbet or rebate. Groove into which a tongue or a flange fits.

Radiating chapel. Chapel projecting radially from the curve of the ambulatory in a Romanesque or Gothic church.

Rafter. Inclined structural support for the covering of a roof.

Rampart. Earthen or masonry wall, topped with a parapet, that surrounds a castle or fortified town or place.

Ravelin. Small, V-shaped fortification that is detached from, and defends, the main fort; also known as a half moon.

Redoubt. Small fortification detached from the main fort.

Refectory. Dining hall of a monastery or college.

Reredos. Screen behind the altar in a church.

Respond. Corbel or pilaster attached to a wall to support end of an arch.

Retable. Decorative shelf behind an altar.

Rib. Long curved supporting member in an arch or vaulted roof.

Ridge or ridgepole. Beam that runs the length of a roof's apex.

Rise. Height of an arch from the springing line to the bottom or crown of the keystone; also, height between stairway steps.

Rood screen. In a church, the screen below the rood, or cross, dividing the chancel from the nave.

Rose window. Large, circular window with tracery; frequently used in medieval architecture.

Rotunda. Round building; also, circular hall inside a building.

Rusticated column. Column whose shaft contains deliberately rough-cut blocks.

Sacristy. Room attached to a church for storage of sacred objects, vestments, etc., and where participants in services are robed; also *vestry*.

Sally-port. Postern used by the defenders as a secret gate from which to sally out to fight the attackers.

Salon. Large, elegantly furnished drawing room.

Sanctuary. Part of a church or temple that contains the main altar and constitutes the sacred shrine.

Sarcophagus. Elaborately decorated coffin.

Sash. Window frame in which glass panes are fixed.

Scagliola. Imitation marble made of powdered gypsum, sand, loose stones, and an adhesive.

Scarp. Inner slope of a defensive ditch or moat.

Scriptorium. Room in a monastery for the copying of manuscripts.

Shaft. Portion of a column between the base and the capital; also, vertical space in a structure, such as an elevator shaft.

Shingle. Slab of wood, masonry, or metal used in roofing or as siding.

Shoji. Japanese sliding door made of rice paper on a wood frame.

Sill. Horizontal member forming the lowest part of a window or door frame.

Skeletal construction. Multistory buildings whose loads are supported by steel framework.

Skylight. Window placed in a roof to increase the amount of light in the room below.

Skyscraper. Very tall, multistoried building constructed on steel framework.

Soffit. Exposed underside of any overhead component of a building.

Solar. Upper living room or apartment in a castle or medieval house; also, derived from the sun, as in solar heat.

Sopraporta. Pediment placed over a door.

Spandrel. Triangular-shaped area between the upper curving portions of adjacent arches; also between the exterior of an arch and the rectangular frame enclosing the arch; paneled wall between the sill of a window and the head of a window below.

Spire. Tall, pointed roof placed on top of a tower; a steeple.

Springer. Wedge-shaped bottom stone of an arch.

Springing line. Imaginary line drawn from the undersides of the springers, from which the arch rises.

Squinch. Interior corner arch support.

Staffage. Small figures decorating an architectural drawing.

Stanchion. Upright beam used as a support.

Stele. Standing stone that is decoratively carved or bears an inscription, used as memorial or marker.

Stepped pyramid. Pyramid with its four sloping sides cut with steps.

Stereobate. Building's foundation or base.

Stile. (1) Upright member of a door or window frame; (2) set of steps used to cross over a fence.

Stilts. Pillars or posts that raise a building off the ground.

Stoa. In Greek architecture, a long covered arcade.

Stoop. Small porch or raised platform at the door of a house.

Story or storey. Space between floor levels in a building; a floor.

String course. Horizontal molding or projecting range along the face of a building.

Strut. Structural base or support, as in trusses.

Stucco. Quick-setting malleable material, usually cement, sand, and lime, used for finishing external walls; fine interior plasterwork.

Synagogue. Jewish religious structure for communal worship.

Tabernacle. House of worship; a temple.

Tebam. In a synagogue, the dais for the reader.

Tectonic. Of or pertaining to building or construction.

Temenos. Sacred structure surrounding a temple.

Tenon. Projecting tongue of material that fits into hole or mortice in another material to join the two materials.

Terrace. Open embankment or raised area connected to a building.

Terracotta. Unglazed hard clay baked or burnt in molds.

Terrazzo. Floor and wall material of marble chips and cement.

Thatch. Roofing material made from dried rushes or straw.

Thermae. Greek or Roman public baths.

Tholos. In classical architecture, a round building, often domed.

Thrust. Push or force exerted by the elements of a structure.

Tie beam. Beam used to connect the bottom ends of the rafters.

Tierceron. Secondary, intersecting rib in Gothic vaulting.

Tokonoma. In Japanese architecture, raised alcove for art works.

Torana. In Indian Buddhist architecture, a decorated gateway.

Trabeated. Constructed with beams or lintels.

Tracery. Decorative stonework used in windows or on walls.

Transept. Portion of a building crossing the main axis at a right angle.

Transom. Horizontal crosspiece that separates a door from a window over it.

Trefoils. Three-leaved tracery.

Triclinium. Ancient Roman dining room with couches on three sides of a low table.

Triforium. Small arcaded gallery located above the arches of a church.

Triglyphs. Blocks with vertical channels in the frieze of Doric entablature.

Triumphal arch. Commemorative arched gateway.

Trumeau. Pillar supporting the lintel of a monumental doorway.

Truss. Structural frame, usually triangular, supporting bridges, roofs, etc.

Turret. Small covered tower surmounting a larger tower or a corner in the castle walls.

Tuscan order. One of the five Roman orders of architecture; it can be identified by its plain columns.

Tympanum. Triangular space enclosed by the entablature and sloping cornices of the pediment.

Vault. Any arched roof; some common types of vaulting are barrel, groin, ribbed groin, domical, tunnel, fan, and oven.

Veranda or verandah. Covered porch or balcony attached to the outside of a building.

Vernacular architecture. Architecture, usually anonymous, that uses local materials and is based on local needs and conditions.

Vestibule. Anteroom serving as an entryway.

Vestry. See **Sacristy**.

Viaduct. Series of arches supporting a road, railroad tracks, water lines, etc.

Villa. Originally, a country house, especially Roman; now, any large suburban house.

Voussoir. Wedge-shaped stone used to build arches.

Wainscot. Wood paneling applied to the walls of rooms, usually the lower portion.

Wall plate. Horizontal beam that supports roof beams.

Ward. Central, open space in a castle, also called a bailey; also, a division, floor, or roof for a particular group, such as a hospital or prison ward.

Wattle-and-daub. Primitive technique of weaving sticks together and then plastering them with mud to make a wall.

Wing. Extension or annex of a building; offstage space adjoining the acting area of a theater.

Ziggurat. Terraced pyramid used as a temple by the ancient Assyrians and Babylonians.

SOURCES

Cowan, Henry J. *Dictionary of Architectural Science.* New York: John Wiley and Sons, 1973.

Elspass, Margy Lee. *The North Light Dictionary of Art Terms.* Fairfield, Conn.: North Light, 1984.

Fleming, John, Hugh Honour, and Nikolaus Pevsner. *Penguin Dictionary of Architecture.* 4th ed. Harmondsworth, Eng.: Penguin Books, 1991.

Fletcher, Sir Banister. *A History of Architecture.* 18th ed. New York: Charles Scribner's Sons, 1975.

Giedion, S. *Space, Time and Architecture.* Cambridge, Mass.: Harvard University Press, 1980.

Harris, Cyril M. *Dictionary of Architecture and Construction.* 2nd ed. New York: McGraw Hill, 1975.

Janson, H. W. *History of Art: A Survey of the Major Visual Arts from the Dawn of History to the Present Day.* 2nd ed. Englewood Cliffs, N.J.: Prentice-Hall, 1977.

Lucie-Smith, Edward. *The Thames and Hudson Dictionary of Art Terms.* London: Thames and Hudson, 1984.

Michelin Green Guide: Burgundy. London: Michelin Tyre Public Limited Co., 1988.

The Random House Dictionary of the English Language. New York: Random House, 1967.

Webster's New World Dictionary of the American Language. 2nd ed. New York: World Publishing Co., 1970.

—**Ian Crump; L.D.R.**

IV

PAINTING AND

SCULPTURE

18

GREAT ARTISTS

· · · · ·

"The supreme question about a work of art," James Joyce has A. E. (George Russell) declare in *Ulysses*, "is out of how deep a life does it spring." Others would reply that the artist's life as such has nothing to do with the question; it is rather a matter of how well the life is created, or recreated, in the medium being used, whether painting, literature, music, or whatever. What is undeniable is that when we speak of a painting as being a Rembrandt or a van Gogh, we have in mind not only the particular painting, but a particular set of artistic qualities that add up to a way of looking at the world, and that are uniquely present in that artist's canvases.

Fashions and tastes in painting change; the avant-garde of one generation is the next generation's academy. But time has a way of sorting out the merely novel (or the merely traditional) from the genuinely imaginative vision, and over the long run (and however imperfectly) the work of the great artists comes to be identified and recognized.

The following is a list of a hundred famous painters, together with representative works by each and where they may be seen. The roster of those selected comes up into contemporary times, and it may well be that a revised list, compiled at some future date, might omit some names and add others. Needless to say, dates of composition are usually only approximate.

Angelico, Fra (born Guido di Pietro; 1400–55). Florentine Renaissance painter; his works include *The Coronation of the Virgin* (1430–40, Louvre, Paris); *The Annunciation* (1436, Museo del Diocesano del Gesú, Cortona); a series of fifty frescoes in the Monastery of San Marco (1438–45, San Marco Museum, Florence); and the fresco series *The Lives of Saints Stephen and Laurence* (1447–50, Vatican).

Bellini, Giovanni (*ca.* 1430 or 1440–1516). Venetian painter who, with his father and older brother, transformed Venice into an important Renaissance art center; his works include *The Agony in the Garden* (1460, National

Gallery, London); *The Doge Loredano* (1503, National Gallery, London); *Madonna with the Doge Agostino Barbarigo* (1488, Sta. Maria degli Angeli, Murano, Italy); the San Zaccaria Altarpiece (1505, San Zaccaria, Venice); *Madonna of the Meadow* (1510, National Gallery, London); and *Woman with a Mirror* (1515, Kunsthistorisches Museum, Vienna).

Bosch, Hieronymus (*ca.* 1450–1516). Flemish painter whose real name was Jerome van Aken but who signed his works "Jheronimus Bosch" after his birthplace, 's Hertogenbosch; he is famous for his fantastic, almost surreal, works, such as *The Seven Deadly Sins* (*ca.* 1480, Prado, Madrid); *The Temptation of St. Anthony* (between 1485 and 1505, Museo Nacional de Arte Antiga, Lisbon); *The Haywain* (between 1485 and 1505, Prado); and *The Garden of Earthly Delights* (between 1485 and 1505, Prado).

Botticelli, Sandro (1445–1510). Florentine Renaissance painter whose real name was Alessandro di Mariano Filipepi, but his nickname, which means "little barrel," became the family name; his most famous works are *Primavera* (*ca.* 1478, Uffizi, Florence); *The Birth of Venus* (early 1480s, Uffizi); *Mars and Venus* (early 1480s, National Gallery, London); *Pietà* (early 1490s, Alte Pinakothek, Munich); and *Mystic Nativity* (1500, National Gallery, London).

Braque, Georges (1882–1963). French painter who, together with Picasso, developed cubism; his cubist works include *Houses at l'Estaque* (1908, Marguerite and Hermann Rupf Foundation, Bern); *Le Château de La Roche-Guyon* (1909, Collection of Rolf de Maré, Stockholm); and *The Portuguese* (1911, Kunstmuseum, Basel). After the First World War, his works became more figurative, such as the Canéphorae series (1923–26); *Woman with a Mandolin* (1937, Museum of Modern Art, New York); *Painter and Model* (1939, Collection of Walter P. Chrysler, Jr., New York); the Studio series (1949–56); *The Shower* (1952, Phillips Collection, Washington, D.C.); and the Bird series (1955–63).

Breughel or Brueghel, Pieter, called the Elder (*ca.* 1525–69). Flemish painter whose works include *Children's Games* (1560, Kunsthistorisches Museum, Vienna); *The Fall of Icarus* (1562–69, Musées Royaux des Beaux-Arts, Brussels); *Tower of Babel* (1563, Kunsthistorisches Museum); *Return of the Hunters* (1565, Kunsthistorisches Museum); *Wedding Banquet* (1566, Kunsthistorisches Museum); *Peasant Dance* (1566, Kunsthistorisches Museum); and *The Blind Leading the Blind* (1568, Museo di Capodimonte, Naples).

Campin, Robert (*ca.* 1378–1444). Flemish painter who is also known as the Master of Flémalle or the Master of the Mérode Altarpiece; he rejected the International Gothic style and is responsible for developing, with van Eyck, the more naturalistic Netherlandish style. His works include the Mérode Altarpiece (1420 or 1430, Cloisters, New York); *Virgin and Child before a*

Firescreen (1420 or 1430, National Gallery, London); *Madonna* (1420 or 1430, Hermitage, St. Petersburg); *Portrait of a Man* (1420 or 1430, National Gallery, London); and *Portrait of a Woman* (1420 or 1430, National Gallery, London).

Caravaggio (1573–1610). Italian painter whose real name was Michelangelo Merisi or Amerighi, but who took the name of his birthplace; he is renowned for his use of light and shadow and his realism, as in *Young Bacchus* (ca. 1595, Uffizi, Florence); *Supper at Emmaus* (1598–1600, National Gallery, London); *The Crucifixion of St. Peter* (1600–1601, S. Maria del Popolo, Rome); *The Conversion of St. Paul* (1600–1601, S. Maria del Popolo); *The Deposition of Christ* (1604, S. Maria in Vallicella, Rome); and *The Beheading of St. John the Baptist* (1608, Valetta Cathedral, Malta).

Cassatt, Mary or Marie (1845–1926). American impressionist painter who lived in Paris; her works include *The Cup of Tea* (1879, Metropolitan Museum, New York); *La Loge* (1882, National Gallery, Washington, D.C.); *Lady at the Tea Table* (1885, Metropolitan Museum); and *Young Women Picking Fruit* (1891, Carnegie Institute, Pittsburgh, Pa.).

Cézanne, Paul (1839–1906). French painter whose important innovations prepared the ground for fauvism and cubism; his works include *Self-Portrait* (1879, Tate Gallery, London); several versions of *The Card Players* (1890–92, Louvre, Paris; Barnes Foundation, Philadelphia, Pa., Courtauld Institute, London); *Mont Sainte-Victoire Seen from Bibemus Quarry* (1898–1900, Baltimore Museum of Art); and *Grandes Baigneuses* (1898–1905, Philadelphia Museum of Art).

Chagall, Marc (1887–1985). Russian painter who spent most of his career in Paris; he is known for his lyrical, dreamy paintings of Russian Jewish folk motifs, such as *I and the Village* (1911, Museum of Modern Art, New York); *Self-Portrait with Seven Fingers* (1911, Stedelijk Museum, Amsterdam); *Purim* (1917, Collection of Louis E. Stern, New York); *Portrait of Bella in Green* (1934–35, Stedelijk Museum); and *Around Her* (1937–44, Musée National d'Art Moderne, Paris).

Chardin, Jean-Baptiste-Siméon (1699–1779). French painter who made his reputation with still lifes, such as *Rayfish* (1728, Louvre, Paris), but who is remembered more for his realistic portrayals of bourgeois life, such as *Lady Sealing a Letter* (1733, Staatliche Museen, Berlin); *Washerwoman* (ca. 1733, Nationalmuseum, Stockholm); *House of Cards* (1734–35, Louvre); and *Back from Market* (1739, Staatliche Museen).

Cimabue (ca. 1240–1302). Florentine painter whose real name was Cenni di Pepi; he was the first painter to begin to move away from the rigid Byzantine style to the relatively more naturalistic Gothic style; his surviving works include the *Maestà* (ca. 1285, Uffizi, Florence); and the St. John mosaic (1301, Pisa Cathedral).

Constable, John (1776–1837). British landscape painter whose concern for light and his brush technique influenced nineteenth-century French landscape painters, including the impressionists; some of his works are *Malvern Hill, Warwickshire* (1808, National Gallery, London); *View of Dedham (Stour Valley and Dedham Village)* (1815, Museum of Fine Arts, Boston, Mass.); *Hay Wain* (1821, National Gallery, London); *Hampstead Heath* (1821, City Art Gallery, Manchester); *Hadleigh Castle* (1829, Tate Gallery, London); and *Stoke-by-Nayland* (1836, Art Institute of Chicago).

Corot, Jean-Baptiste-Camille (1796–1875). French landscape painter and member of the Barbizon school; his works include *Papigno* (1826, Collection of Dr. Fritz Nathan, Zurich); *Cathedral at Chartes* (1830, Louvre, Paris); *View of the Forest at Fontainbleau* (1831, National Gallery, Washington, D.C.); *Church of Marissel* (1867, Louvre); and *Cathedral of Sens* (1874, Louvre).

Courbet, Gustave (1819–77). French realist painter known for such works as *Burial at Ornans* (1850, Louvre, Paris); *The Bathers* (1853, Musée Fabre, Montpellier); *The Winnowers* (1854, Musée des Beaux-Arts, Nantes); *Artist's Studio (*1854–55, Musée d'Orsay, Paris); and *Demoiselles des Bords de las Seine* (1856, Musée de Petit Palais, Paris).

Cranach, Lucas, called the Elder (1472–1553). German Renaissance painter; his works include *Crucifixion* (1503, Kunsthistorisches Museum, Vienna); *Rest on the Flight into Egypt* (1504, Staatliche Museen, Berlin); *Judith* (1526, Staatsgalerie, Stuttgart); *The Duke of Saxony and The Duchess of Saxony* (1514, Gemäldegalerie, Dresden); *The Judgment of Paris* (1529, Metropolitan Museum, New York); and *Venus and Amor* (1531, Musées Royaux des Beaux-Arts, Brussels).

Dali, Salvador (1904–89). Spanish surrealist painter whose works include *The Accommodation of Desire* (1929, Julien Levy Gallery, Bridgewater, Conn.); *Apparition of Face and Fruit Dish* (1931, Wadsworth Atheneum, Hartford, Conn.); *Persistence of Memory* (1931, Museum of Modern Art, New York); *Mae West* (1936, Art Institute of Chicago); and *The Crucifixion of St. John on the Cross* (1951, Glasgow Art Gallery).

David, Jacques-Louis (1748–1825). French neoclassical painter who is best known for his historical paintings, such as *The Oath of the Horatii* (1784, Louvre, Paris); *The Death of Socrates* (1787, Metropolitan Museum, New York); *Brutus and His Dead Sons* (1789, Louvre); *The Death of Marat* (1793, Musées Royaux des Beaux-Arts, Brussels); *The Intervention of the Sabine Women* (1799, Louvre); and *The Coronation of Napoleon* (1805–1807, Louvre).

Degas, Edgar (1834–1917). French painter often associated with the impressionists; his works include *Portrait of the Bellelli Family* (1860–62, Musée d'Orsay, Paris); *Dancing Class* (1872, Musée de l'Impressionisme, Paris); *The Glass of Absinthe* (1876, Musée d'Orsay); *At the Seaside* (1877,

National Gallery, London); *Women Seated at a Café Terrace* (1877, Musée d'Orsay); *Edmond Duranty* (1879, Glasgow Art Gallery); *The Tub* (1886, Musée d'Orsay); *The Bath* (1890, Art Institute of Chicago); and *After the Bath* (1898, Musée d'Orsay).

de Kooning, Willem (1904–). Dutch-born American abstract expressionist painter whose works include *Queen of Hearts* (1943–46, Hirshhorn Collection, New York); *Woman I* (1950–52, Museum of Modern Art, New York); *Woman IV* (1952–53, Nelson Gallery—Atkins Museum, Kansas City, Mo.); *Merritt Parkway* (1959, Sidney Janis Gallery, New York); and *The Door to the River* (1960, Whitney Museum, New York).

Delacroix, Eugène (1798–1863). French romantic painter; his works include *Massacre at Chios* (1824, Louvre, Paris); *The Death of Sardanapalus* (1827, Louvre); *The Combat of the Giaour and the Pasha* (1827, Art Institute of Chicago); *Liberty Leading the People* (1830, Louvre); *Women of Algiers* (1834, Louvre); *Moroccan Kaid* (1837, Musée des Beaux-Arts, Nantes); *The Battle of Taillebourg* (1837, Louvre); *Jewish Wedding in Morocco* (1839, Louvre); *The Taking of Constantinople by the Crusaders* (1840, Louvre); and *Mulet-Abd-Ar-Rahman, the Sultan of Morocco, Surrounded by His Guards and Principal Officers* (1845, Musée des Augustins, Toulouse).

Duccio di Buoninsegna (ca. 1255-ca. 1318). Italian painter, the greatest of the Siennese school, although the only surviving examples of his art are *The Rucella Madonna* (ca. 1285, Uffizi, Florence) and *The Maestà* (1308–11, Museo dell' Opera del Duomo, Siena).

Duchamp, Marcel (1887–1968). French dadaist artist and one of the most influential artists of the twentieth century; his most famous—or infamous—works are *Nude Descending a Staircase #2* (1912, Philadelphia Museum of Art); *Bride Stripped Bare by Her Bachelors, Even, or The Large Glass* (1915–23, Philadelphia Museum of Art); *L.H.O.O.Q. (Mona Lisa)* (1919, Mary Sisler Collection, New York); and *Etant Donnés* (1946, assembled 1969, Philadelphia Museum of Art).

Dürer, Albrecht (1471–1528). German Renaissance painter and engraver; his paintings include *Self-Portrait as a Boy* (1484, Albertina, Vienna); *Self-Portrait* (1498, Prado, Madrid); *Young Man Wearing a Cap* (1500, Alte Pinakothek, Munich); *Self-Portrait (as Christ)* (1500 or 1504–1505, Alte Pinakothek); *The Adoration of the Magi* (1504, Uffizi, Florence); *Adam and Eve* (1507, Prado); and *The Adoration of the Trinity* (1511, Kunsthistorisches Museum, Vienna). His most famous engravings are *Knight, Death, and the Devil* (1513); *St. Jerome in His Study* (1514); and *Melancholia* (1514).

Eakins, Thomas (1844–1916). American realist painter who is best known for *Max Schmitt in a Single Scull* (1871, Metropolitan Museum of Art, New York); *Gross Clinic* (1875, Jefferson Medical College, Philadelphia, Pa.); and his portraits, such as that of Mrs. Edith Mahon (1904, Smith College Museum of Art, Northampton, Mass.).

Eyck, Jan van (d. 1441). Netherlandish painter and one of the greatest artists of the northern Renaissance; his works include *The Adoration of the Lamb*, commonly known as *The Ghent Altarpiece* (finished 1432; Ghent Cathedral); *The Man in a Red Turban*, which is possibly a self-portrait (1433, National Gallery, London); *The Ince Hall Madonna* (1433, National Gallery of Victoria, Melbourne); *The Arnolfini Wedding Portrait* (1434, National Gallery, London); *The Madonna of Chancellor Rolin* (ca. 1435, Louvre, Paris); and *The Madonna with Canon van der Paele* (1436, Groeningemuseum, Bruges).

Fragonard, Jean-Honoré (1732–1806). French rococo painter whose works include *Coresus Sacrificing Himself to Save Callirhoe* (1765, Louvre, Paris); *Sleeping Bacchante* (1765–72, Louvre); *The Swing* (1766, Wallace Collection, London); the four-painting series entitled *The Progress of Love: Pursuit, Meeting, Love Letters, Lover Crowned* (1771–72, Frick Collection, New York); *Women Bathing* (1775, Louvre); *Fête at St-Cloud* (1775, Banque de France, Paris); and *Boy as Pierrot* (1789–91, Wallace Collection).

Gainsborough, Thomas (1727–88). English landscape and portrait painter who is best known for such works as *Mr. and Mrs. Robert Andrews* (1748, National Gallery, London); *Charterhouse* (1748, Foundling Hospital Offices, London); *Blue Boy* (1770, Huntington Art Gallery, San Marino); *Harvest Wagon* (1771, Barber Institute of Fine Arts, Birmingham); *Mrs. Siddons* (1785, National Gallery, London); and *Country Boy with Dog and Pitcher* (1785, Sir Alfred Beit Collection, Russborough).

Gauguin, Paul (1848–1903). French postimpressionist painter who is best known for his Tahitian paintings, such as *Two Women on the Beach* (1891, Musée d'Orsay, Paris); *Vahine no te Tiare, or Woman with a Gardenia* (1891, Ny Carlsberg Glyptotek, Copenhagen); *Reverie, or Woman in a Red Dress* (1891, Nelson Gallery—Atkins Museum, Kansas City, Mo.); *Nafea Faa Ipoipo, or When Are You Getting Married?* (1892, Kunstmuseum, Basel); *Nevermore* (1897, Courtauld Institute, London); *Where Do We Come From? What Are We? Where Are We Going?* (1897, Museum of Fine Arts, Boston); *Riders on the Beach* (1902, Folkwang Museum, Essen, Germany).

Géricault, Théodore (1791–1824). French romantic painter; his works include *Light Cavalry Officer Charging* (1812, Louvre, Paris); *Race of the Riderless Horses* (1817, Louvre); *Raft of the Medusa* (1818–19, Louvre); *Derby at Epsom* (1821, Louvre); and *A Kleptomaniac* (1822–23, Musée des Beaux-Arts, Ghent).

Giorgione (born Giorgio Barbarelli or Giorgio del Castelfranco; 1476 or 1478–1510). Venetian Renaissance painter whose few authenticated works cannot be precisely dated; these include *Laura* (Kunsthistorisches Museum, Vienna); *The Tempest* (Accademia, Venice); *Three Philosophers* (Kunsthistorisches Museum); *Sleeping Venus* (Gemäldegalerie, Dresden); *Christ Carrying the* Cross (S. Rocco, Venice); *The Castelfranco Madonna* (Castelfranco Cathedral); *Concert Champêtre* (Louvre, Paris); *The Adoration of the Shepherds* (National Gallery, Washington, D.C.); and *Portrait of a Man* (Staatliche Museen, Berlin).

Giotto di Bondone (1266, 1267, 1276, or 1277–1337). Florentine painter who is generally held to be the founder of modern Western painting; he is best known for his frescoes *The Lives of Saints Anne and Joachim*; *The Life of the Virgin*; *The Annunciation*; *The Passion*; and *The Last Judgment* (1305–1306, Arena Chapel, Padua).

Goes, Hugo van der (ca. 1440–82). Netherlandish painter; because he did not sign his paintings, only the Portinari Altarpiece (1475–76, Uffizi, Florence) can be definitely ascribed to him; other works attributed to him include the Monforte Altarpiece (Staatliche Museen, Berlin); *The Fall of Adam and Eve* (Kunsthistorisches Museum, Vienna); *The Lamentation* (Kunsthistorisches Museum); and *The Death of the Virgin* (Groeningemuseum, Bruges).

Goya, Francisco de (1746–1828). Spanish painter and engraver; his paintings include *The Family of Charles IV* (1799, Prado, Madrid); *The Clothed Maja* and *The Naked Maja* (ca. 1804, Prado); *The Second of May, 1808*, and *The Third of May, 1808* (1814, Prado); and *Saturn Devouring his Children* (ca.1818, Prado); his two most famous series of engravings are *Los Caprichos* (1793–99) and *Los Desastres de la Guerra* (1810–14).

Greco, El (1541–1614). Cretan-born Spanish painter, sculptor, and architect whose real name was Domenikos Theotocopoulos; his works include *The Assumption of the Virgin* (1577, Art Institute of Chicago); *El Espolio* (1577–79, Toledo Cathedral); *Burial of Count Orgaz* (1586–88, S. Tomé, Toledo); *Laocöon* (1610, National Gallery, Washington, D.C.); *View of Toledo* (1608, Metropolitan Museum, New York); and *The Adoration of the Shepherds* (1612–14, Prado, Madrid).

Gris, Juan (born José Victoriano González; 1887–1927). Spanish painter who, influenced by Picasso, developed synthetic cubism in works such as *Lampe a pétrole* (1912, Kröller-Müller Museum, Arnhem); *Breakfast* (1914, Museum of Modern Art, New York); *Violin* (1916, Kunstmuseum, Basel); *Sunblind* (1924, Tate Gallery, London); and *Violin and Fruit Dish* (1924, Tate Gallery).

Grünewald, Matthias (1470 or 1480–1528). German painter whose real name was Mathis Gothart Neithardt (the change of name was made in a seventeenth-century biography and was discovered only recently); his masterpiece is the Isenheim Altarpiece (1512–15, Musée d'Unterlinden, Colmar, France).

Hals, Frans (1581 or 1585–1666). Dutch painter known for his portraits and portrait groups, such as *The Banquet of the Officers of the St. George Militia Company* (1616, Frans Hals Museum, Haarlem); *Laughing Cavalier* (1624, Wallace Collection, London); *Malle Babbe* (1630–33, Staatliche Museen, Berlin); *Lucas de Clerq* (1635, Rijksmuseum, Amsterdam); *Feytje van Steenkiste* (1635, Rijksmuseum); *The Regents of the St. Elizabeth Hospital* (1641, Frans Hals Museum); *The Regents of the Old Men's Alms House* and *The Regentesses of the Old Men's Alms House* (1664, Frans Hals Museum).

Hiroshige, Ando (1797–1858). Japanese painter and printmaker who was one of the last and greatest masters in the ukiyo-e style; his works include *Fifty-Three Stages of the Tokaido* (1833–34); *Views of Kyoto* (1834); and *One Hundred Views of Edo* (1856–58).

Hockney, David (1937–). British painter who has been associated with pop art; his works include *Flight into Italy—Swiss Landscape* (1962, Dufferin and Ava Collection, London); *Peter Getting Out of Nick's Pool* (1966, Walker Art Gallery, Liverpool); *Bigger Splash* (1967, Tate Gallery, London); *Christopher Isherwood and Don Bachardy* (1968, Private Collection); and *Mr. and Mrs. Clark Percy* (1970–71, Tate Gallery).

Hogarth, William (1697–1764). English painter and engraver who is best known for his series *The Rake's Progress* (ca. 1735, Sir John Soane's Museum, London) and *Marriage à la Mode* (ca. 1743, National Gallery, London).

Hokusai, Katsushika (1760–1849). Japanese painter whose works include *Amusements of the Eastern Capital* (1799); *Thirty-Six Views of Mount Fujiyama*, which includes the famous *Breaking Wave Off Kanagawa* (1825–31); *Views of Famous Bridges* (1827–30); and *Waterfalls of the Provinces* (ca. 1829).

Homer, Winslow (1836–1910). American realist painter known particularly for his seascapes, such as *Inside the Bar, Tynemouth* (1883, Metropolitan Museum, New York); *Eight Bells* (1886, Addison Art Gallery of American Art, Phillips Academy, Andover, Mass.); *Coast in Winter* (1892, Worcester Art Museum); *Nor'easter* (1895, Metropolitan Museum); *Rum Cay* (1898–99, Worcester Art Museum); and *Gulf Stream* (1899, Metropolitan Museum).

Hopper, Edward (1882–1967). American realist painter; his works include *Early Sunday Morning* (1930, Whitney Museum, New York); *Room in Brooklyn* (1932, Museum of Fine Arts, Boston); *Nighthawks* (1942, Art Institute of Chicago); *Approaching a City* (1946, Phillips Gallery, Washington, D.C.); and *Second-Story Sunlight* (1960, Whitney Museum).

Ingres, Jean-Auguste-Dominique (1780–1867). French painter whose works include *Mlle. Rivière* (1805, Louvre, Paris); *Napoleon as Emperor* (1806, Musée de l'Armée, Les Invalides, Paris); *Valpinçon Bather* (1808, Louvre); *La Grande Odalisque* (1814, Louvre); *Portrait of M. Bertin* (1832, Louvre);

Odalisque with a Slave (1839, Fogg Art Museum, Cambridge, Mass.); and *Turkish Bath* (1863, Louvre).

Johns, Jasper (1930–). American painter associated with pop art and minimalism; his works include *Target with Four Faces* (1955, Museum of Modern Art, New York); *Gray Alphabets* (1956, Ben Heller Collection, New York); *Three Flags* (1958, Mr. and Mrs. Barton Tremaine Collection, Madison, Conn.); and *False Start* (1959, Mr. and Mrs. Robert C. Scull Collection, New York).

Kahlo, Frida (1910–54). Mexican surrealist painter who is best known for her self-portraits, such as *Frida and Diego Rivera* (1931, Museum of Modern Art, San Francisco); *The Two Fridas* (1939, Museo de Arte Moderno, Mexico City); *Self-Portrait with Diego in My Mind* (1943, Private Collection); and *Self-Portrait with Loose Hair* (1947, Private Collection).

Kandinsky, Wassily (1866–1944). Russian-born expressionist painter who lived first in Germany, where he was a member of the Blaue Reiter group, and then in France; his works include *Blue Mountain No. 84* (1908, Guggenheim Museum, New York); *Black Lines* (1913, Thannhauser Gallery, Munich); *Fugue* (1914, Guggenheim Museum); *Shrill-Peaceful Rose Color* (1924, Wallraf-Richartz Museum, Cologne); *Et Encore* (1940, Museum of Fine Arts, Bern); and *Freshness* (1941, Galerie Maeght, Paris).

Kirchner, Ernst Ludwig (1880–1938). German expressionist painter and one of the founders of the Brücke group in Dresden; his works include *Self-Portrait with a Model* (1907, Kunsthalle, Hamburg); *Nude with a Hat* (1911, Wallraf-Richartz Museum, Cologne); *Five Women in the Street* (1913, Wallraf-Richartz Museum); *Street, Berlin* (1913, Museum of Modern Art, New York); *Self-Portrait as a Soldier* (ca. 1915, Allen Memorial Art Museum, Oberlin, Ohio); *Young Girl on a Blue Sofa* (1917–18), Minneapolis Institute of the Arts); *Moonlit Winter Night* (1918, Detroit Institute of Art); and *Amselfuh* (1923, Kunstmuseum, Basel).

Klee, Paul (1879–1940). Swiss-born German painter and member of the Blaue Reiter group whose works include *Motif of Hammamet* (1914, Doetsch-Benziger Collection, Basel); *Vocal Fabric of the Singer Rosa Silber* (1922, Museum of Modern Art, New York); *Twittering Machine* (1922, Museum of Modern Art); *Dance of the Red Skirts* (1924, Private Collection, Bern); *Family Outing* (1930, Paul-Klee-Stiftung, Basel); *In Suspense* (1930, Paul-Klee-Stiftung); *To Parnassus* (1932, Museum of Fine Arts, Bern); and *Flowering Harbor* (1938, Kunstmuseum, Basel).

Klimt, Gustav (1862–1918). Austrian Secession painter whose works include *Judith with the Head of Holofernes* (1901, Österreichische Galerie, Vienna); *Frau Fritsa Riedler* (1906, Österreichische Galerie); *Frau Adele Bloch-Bauer* (1907, Österreichische Galerie); and *The Kiss* (1908, Musée des Beaux-Arts, Strasbourg).

La Tour, Georges de (1593–1652). French painter known for his use of light and shadows in paintings such as *Magdalen at the Mirror* (*ca.* 1628, Private Collection, Paris); *The Penitent Magdalen* (*ca.* 1635–40, Louvre, Paris); *Jesus and St. Joseph in the Workshop* (*ca.* 1645, Louvre); and *The Denial of St. Peter* (1650, Musée des Beaux-Arts, Nantes).

Le Nain, Antoine (d. 1648), **Louis** (d. 1648), and **Mathieu** (1607–77). Three French brothers whose paintings cannot be distinguished from one another because all three signed themselves with only their last name; their works include *Cart, or Return from the Harvest* (1641, Louvre, Paris); *Family Reunion* (1642, Louvre); *Guard* (1643, Private Collection, Paris); *Peasants at Supper* (*ca.* 1645–48, Louvre); and *Portraits of an Interior* (1647, Louvre).

Leonardo da Vinci (1452–1519). Florentine painter and draughtsman who was one of the notable figures of the High Renaissance and one of the greatest artists of all time; his works include *Annunciation* (1475, Uffizi, Florence); *The Adoration of the Magi* (1481, Uffizi); *Lady with an Ermine* (1483–84, Krartoryski Gallery, Cracow); *The Last Supper* (1495–97, Sta. Maria delle Grazie, Milan); *The Mona Lisa* (1503–1507, Louvre, Paris); *The Virgin and Child with St. Anne* (1503–1507, Louvre [the cartoon is in the National Gallery, London]); and two versions of *The Virgin of the Rocks* (1506, National Gallery, London; 1508, Louvre).

Limbourg or Limburg, Herman, Jean or Jahnequin, and Paul or Pol (d. 1416). Three Flemish brothers who are famous for illustrating two manuscripts, "Les Belles Heures" (*ca.* 1403–23, Cloisters, New York); and "Les Tres Riches Heures du Duc de Berry" (*ca.* 1415–16, Musée Condé, Chantilly, France).

Malevich, Kasimir (1878–1935). Russian painter and the founder of the suprematist movement; his works include *Chiropodist in the Bathroom* (1908–1909, Stedelijk Museum, Amsterdam); *Woman with Buckets* (1910–11, Stedelijk Museum); *Peasants in Church* (1910–11, Stedelijk Museum); *Taking in the Harvest* (1911, Stedelijk Museum); *The Knife Grinder* (1912, Yale University Art Gallery, New Haven, Conn.); *Black Square* (1915, Russian Museum, St. Petersburg); *Suprematist Composition* (1917, Tate Gallery, London); and *Suprematist Composition: White on White* (1917–18, Museum of Modern Art, New York).

Manet, Edouard (1832–83). French painter who was associated with the impressionists and is generally considered to be the originator of modern, post-mimetic art; his works include *Le Déjeuner sur l'Herbe* (1863, Musée d'Orsay, Paris); *Olympia* (1863, Musée d'Orsay); *The Fifer* (1866, Musée de l'Impressionisme, Paris); *Emile Zola* (1868, Musée d'Orsay); and *The Bar at the Folies-Bergères* (1881, Courtauld Institute, London).

Mantegna, Andrea (*ca.* 1430–1506). Italian painter who is known for his use of extreme foreshortening and other illusionist techniques; his works include the *Camera degli Sposi* fresco cycle (1474, Palazzo Ducale, Mantua); a series of paintings entitled *Triumph of Caesar* (1486–94, Royal Collection, Hampton Court Palace, London); *Parnassus* (1497, Louvre, Paris); and *The Triumph of Virtue* (ca. 1500, Louvre).

Masaccio (1401–28). Name given to the Florentine Renaissance painter Tommaso di Ser Giovanni di Mone; his influential works include *The Virgin with St. Anne* (1422, Uffizi, Florence); the Brancacci Chapel fresco cycle (ca.1425–28, Sta. Maria del Carmine, Florence); *Madonna Enthroned* (1426, National Gallery, London); and *The Holy Trinity with the Virgin and St. John* (ca. 1428, Sta. Maria Novella, Florence).

Matisse, Henri (1869–1954). French painter who participated in the fauvist movement and was one of the most important artists of the twentieth century; his works include *The Open Window* (1905, Whitney Museum, New York); *Portrait with a Green Stripe* (1905, Royal Museum of Fine Arts, Copenhagen); *Joie de Vivre* (1905–1906, Barnes Foundation, Merion, Pa.); *La Desserte Rouge* (1908, Hermitage, St. Petersburg); *The Dance* (1910, Hermitage); *The Moroccans* (1916, Museum of Modern Art, New York); *Bathers by a River* (1916–17, Art Institute of Chicago); *La Danse* (1933, Barnes Foundation); the Chapelle du Rosaire (1949–51, Vence, France); and *Memory of Oceanie* (1953, Museum of Modern Art).

Memlinc or Memling, Hans (ca. 1430 or 1440–94). German-born Netherlandish painter whose works include *Virgin and Child with Donors, or The Donne of Kidwelly Triptych* (1468, National Gallery, London); *Martin van Nieuwenhove Diptych* (1487, Memlinc Museum, Bruges); and *St. Ursula Shrine* (1489, Memlinc Museum).

Michelangelo Buonarroti (1475–1564). Italian sculptor, poet, and painter; he was one of the foremost figures of the High Renaissance and one of the greatest artists of all time; his paintings include *The Doni Tondo* (ca. 1503, Uffizi, Florence); the Old Testament fresco cycle in the Sistine Chapel (1508–12, Vatican); and *The Last Judgment* (1536–41, Sistine Chapel, Vatican).

Modigliani, Amedeo (1884–1920). Italian painter who worked in Paris; he is best known for his elongated figures as in *Oscar Miestchaninoff* (1916, Private Collection, Bern); *Jeanne Hébuterne* (1919, Guggenheim Museum, New York); *Reclining Nude* (1919, Museum of Modern Art, New York); and *Self-Portrait* (1919, Museu d'Arts Contemporanea, Sao Paolo).

Mondrian, Piet (1872–1944). Dutch abstract painter and one of the founders of the De Stijl group; his works include *Red Tree* (1908, Gemeentemuseum, The Hague); *Composition in Line and Color* (1913, Kröller-Müller Museum, Arnhem); *Composition in Yellow and Blue* (1929, Boymans—van Beuningen Museum, Rotterdam); *Fox-Trot A* (Yale University Art Gallery, New Haven, Conn.); and *Broadway Boogie-Woogie* (1942–43, Museum of Modern Art, New York).

Monet, Claude Oscar (1840–1926). French painter, one of the most important of the impressionists; his works include *Women in the Garden* (1867, Musée d'Orsay, Paris); *The River* (1868, Art Institute of Chicago); *Impression: Sunrise* (1872, Musée Marmottan, Paris); *Gare St-Lazare* (1877, Musée d'Orsay); *Cliffs at Etretat* (1883, Musée d'Orsay); *Spring* (1886, Fitzwilliam Museum, Cambridge, Mass.); *Rouen Cathedral: Full Sunlight* (1894, Musée d'Orsay); *Water Lilies, Giverny* (1907, Jocelyn Walker Collection, London); and *Water Lilies* (1920–25, Museum of Modern Art, New York).

Munch, Edvard (1863–1944). Norwegian painter who was associated with the symbolists and was a precursor to the expressionists; his works include *Self-Portrait* (1881, Munch Museum, Oslo); *The Scream* (1893, National Gallery, Oslo); *Puberty* (1895, National Gallery, Oslo); and *In Hell* (1895, Munch Museum).

Nolde, Emil (1867–1956). Name assumed by the German expressionist painter Emil Hansen in 1904; his works include *The Last Supper* (1909, Stiftung Seebüll Ada und Emil Nolde, Neukirchen, Germany); *Dance Round the Golden Calf* (1910, Staatsgemäldesammlungen, Munich); and *Masks and Dahlias* (1919, Stiftung Seebüll Ada und Emil Nolde).

O'Keeffe, Georgia (1887–1986). American precisionist-influenced painter who is best known for her desert and flower paintings, such as *Black Iris* (1926, Metropolitan Museum, New York); *Ranchos Church Front* (1929, Jack Lawrence Collection, New York); *Near Abiquiu, New Mexico* (1930, Metropolitan Museum); *Summer Days* (1936, Mrs. Robert R. Young Collection, Newport, R.I.); and *Pelvis Series, Red with Yellow* (1945, Mrs. A. B. Windfohr Collection, Fort Worth, Tex.).

Picasso, Pablo (1881–1973). Spanish sculptor, ceramist, graphic artist, and painter; with Georges Braque, he developed cubism between 1907 and 1914; he was perhaps the best-known artist of the twentieth century; his numerous works include *La Vie* (1903, Cleveland Museum of Art); *The Frugal Repast* (1904, Bibliothèque Nationale, Paris); *Family of Saltimbanques* (1905, National Gallery, Washington, D.C.); *Les Demoiselles d'Avignon* (1907, Museum of Modern Art, New York); *Majolie* (1911, Museum of Modern Art); *Three Musicians* (1921, Museum of Modern Art); *Mother and Child* (1921, Art Institute of Chicago); *Three Dancers* (1925, Tate Gallery, London); and *Guernica* (1937, Reina Sofia Museum, Madrid).

Piero della Francesca (1410 or 1420–92). Italian painter who is now considered one of the greatest artists of the Quattrocento; his works include *The Flagellation* (1445 or 1456–57, Galleria Nazionale, Urbino); *The Dream of Constantine* (1452–59, S. Francesco, Arezzo); the series of frescoes *The Legend of the True Cross* (1452–65, S. Francesco, Arezzo); *Battista Sforza and Federigo da Montefeltro* (1465, Uffizi, Florence); and *Madonna and Child with Frederico da Montefeltro* (1475, Brera, Milan).

Pissarro, Camille (1830–1903). French impressionist painter whose works include *Jallais Hill: Pontoise* (1867, Metropolitan Museum, New York); *Lower Norwood: Snow Scene* (1870, Tate Gallery, London); *Red Roofs* (1877, Musée d'Orsay, Paris); *Orchard with Flowering Fruit Trees, Springtime, Pontoise* (1877, Louvre, Paris); *The Café au Lait* (1881, Art Institute of Chicago); and *Boulevard des Italiens, Morning, Sunlight* (1897, National Gallery, Washington, D.C.).

Pollock, Jackson (1912–56). American abstract expressionist painter famous for his "poured" paintings, such as *She-Wolf* (1943, Museum of Modern Art, New York); *Eyes in the Heat* (1946, Peggy Guggenheim Museum, Venice); *Full Fathom Five* (1947, Museum of Modern Art); *One (#31, 1950)* (1950, Museum of Modern Art); *Convergence* (1952, Albright-Knox Art Gallery, Buffalo); and *Blue Poles* (1953, National Museum, Canberra).

Poussin, Nicolas (1593 or 1594–1665). French neoclassical painter whose works include *Poet's Inspiration* (ca. 1628, Louvre, Paris); *Bacchanalian Revel* (ca. 1635, National Gallery, London); *The Rape of the Sabine Women* (ca. 1635, Louvre); *The Holy Family on the Steps* (1648, National Gallery, Washington, D.C.); *Landscape with the Funeral of Phocion* (1648, Oakley Park, Shropshire); and *The Four Seasons* (1660–64, Louvre).

Raphael (1483–1520). Name given to the Italian painter Raffaello Sanzio, who was one of the most important artists of the High Renaissance; his works include *The Marriage of the Virgin* (1504, Brera, Milan); *The School of Athens* (1510–11, Stanza della Segnatura, Vatican); *Galatea* (1511–12, Villa Farnesina, Rome); *The Sistine Madonna* (1513–14, Gemäldegalerie, Dresden); and *Baldassare Castiglione* (ca. 1516, Louvre, Paris).

Rauschenberg, Robert (1925–). American painter whose works include *Bed* (1955, Mr. and Mrs. Leo Castelli Collection, New York); *Monogram* (1959, Moderna Museet, Stockholm); and *Retroactive* (1964, Wadsworth Atheneum, Hartford, Conn.).

Rembrandt, Harmensz van Rijn (1606–69). Dutch painter who is considered one of the world's greatest artists; his works include *Balaam's Ass* (1626, Musée Cognacq-Jay, Paris); *The Anatomy Lesson of Dr. Tulp* (1632, Mauritshuis, The Hague); *Self-Portrait with Saskia* (ca. 1635, Gemäldegalerie, Dresden); *The Blinding of Samson* (1636, Städelsches Kunstinstitut, Frankfurt); *The Corporalship of Captain Banning Cocq's Civil Guards*, which is better known as *The Night Watch* (1642, Rijksmuseum, Amsterdam); *The Holy Family* (1645, Hermitage, St. Petersburg); *Bathsheba* (1654, Louvre, Paris); *The Syndics of the Drapers Guild* (1662, Rijksmuseum); and *The Jewish Bride* (1664, Rijksmuseum).

Renoir, Pierre-Auguste (1841–1919). French impressionist painter whose works include *La Grenouillère* (1869, Nationalmuseum, Stockholm); *La Loge* (1874, Courtauld Institute, London); *The Swing* (1876, Musée de l'Impressionisme, Paris); *La Moulin de la Galette* (1876, Louvre, Paris); *Mme. Charpentier and Her Daughters* (1878, Metropolitan Museum, New York); *The Umbrellas* (ca. 1881–84, National Gallery, London); *The Bathers* (ca. 1884–87, Philadelphia Museum of Art); *Mother and Child* (1914, Tate Gallery, London); and *Seated Bather* (1914, Art Institute of Chicago).

Rivera, Diego (1886–1957). Mexican painter who is known for his murals, such as *Creation* (1922, Escuela Nacional Preparatoria, Mexico City); *Fecund Earth* (1923–26, Agricultural School, Chapingo, Mexico); *Detroit Industry* (1932, Detroit Institute of Art); and *History Mexico* (1929–51, National Palace, Mexico City).

Rothko, Mark (1903–70). Russian-born American painter who was an important member of the New York school and one of the creators of color field painting; his works include *Baptismal Scene* (1945, Whitney Museum, New York); *Prehistoric Memories* (1946, Betty Parsons Gallery, New York); *Number 24* (1949, Hirshhorn Museum, Washington, D.C.); *Red, White, and Brown* (1957, Kunstmuseum, Basel); *Sassrom* (1958, Cardazzo Collection, Venice); and *Number 2* (1962, Mrs. Albert D. Lasker Collection, New York).

Rouault, Georges (1871–1958). French expressionist painter; his works include *The Mirror* (1906, Music National d'Art Moderne, Paris); *Little Olympia* (1906, Statens Museum for Kunst, Copenhagen); *Three Judges* (1913, Museum of Modern Art, New York); *Christ Mocked* (ca. 1932, Museum of Modern Art); *Old King* (1936, Carnegie Institute, Pittsburgh, Pa.); and *Head of a Clown* (1948, Museum of Fine Arts, Boston, Mass.).

Rousseau, Henri-Julien (1884–1910). French naïve painter known as "Le Douanier"; his works include *The Present and the Past* (1889, Barnes Foundation, Philadelphia, Pa.); *Child on the Rocks* (1895, National Gallery, London); *Sleeping Gypsy* (1897, Museum of Modern Art, New York); *Hungry Lion* (1905, Private Collection, Switzerland); *The Snake Charmer* (1907, Musée d'Orsay, Paris); and *The Dream* (1910, Museum of Modern Art).

Rubens, Peter Paul (1577–1640). Dutch baroque painter whose works include *Marchesa Brigida Spinola-Doria* (1606, National Gallery, Washington, D.C.); *Self-Portrait with His Wife* (1609, Alte Pinakothek, Munich); *The Raising of the Cross* (1610–11, Antwerp Cathedral); *The Descent from the Cross* (1611–14, Antwerp Cathedral); *The Rape of the Daughters of Leucippus* (ca. 1618, Alte Pinakothek); *The Garden of Love* (1630–34, Prado, Madrid); and *Hélène Fourment with Two of her Children* (ca. 1637, Louvre, Paris).

Schiele, Egon (1890–1918). Austrian Expressionist painter whose works include *Seated Male Nude* (1910, Dr. R. Leopold Collection, Vienna); *The Artist's*

Mother Sleeping (1911, Albertina, Vienna); *The Embrace* (1917, Österreichische Galerie, Vienna); and *Paris von Gütershol* (1918, Minneapolis Institute of the Arts).

Seurat, Georges (1859–91). French Neoimpressionist painter who is famous for his use of pointillist technique in such works as *A Bathing Scene at Asnières* (1883–84, National Gallery, London); *La Grande Jatte* (1884–86, Art Institute of Chicago); *The Parade* (1887–88, Metropolitan Museum, New York); *The Uproar* (1889–90, Kröller-Müller Museum, Arnhem); and *The Circus* (1891, Musée d'Orsay, Paris).

Stella, Frank (1936–). American abstract painter; his works include *Jill* (1963, Albright-Knox Art Gallery, Buffalo, N.Y.); *Empress of India* (1965, Irving Blum Collection, Los Angeles, Calif.); *Black Adder* (1965, Leo Castelli Gallery, New York); *Moultonboro III* (1966, Leo Castelli Gallery); *Sabra II* (1967, Leo Castelli Gallery); and *Guadaloupe Island* (1979, Tate Gallery, London).

Tiepolo, Giambattista (1696–1770). Venetian painter who is considered by many to be the greatest artist of the eighteenth century; his works include the *Antony and Cleopatra* fresco cycle (1745–50, Palazzo Labia, Venice); the *Kaisersaal* frescoes (1751–53, Würzburg, Germany); *The Apotheosis of the Pisani Family* (1761–62, Villa Pisani, Strà, Italy); *The Apotheosis of Spain* (1762–64, Royal Palace, Madrid); *The Apotheosis of Aeneas* (1764–66, Royal Palace, Madrid); *The Apotheosis of the Spanish Monarchy* (1764–66, Royal Palace, Madrid); and *The Immaculate Conception* (1767–69, Prado, Madrid).

Tintoretto, Jacopo (1518–94). Nickname of the Venetian painter Jacopo Robusti, derived from his father's working as a dyer (tintore); his works include *The Miracle of St. Mark Rescuing a Slave* (1548, Accademia, Venice); *The Finding of the Body of St. Mark* (1562, Brera, Milan); *Christ Before Pilate* (1566–67, Scuola di San Rocco, Venice); *Bacchus and Ariadne* (1578, Doges Palace, Venice); and *The Last Supper* (1592–94, S. Giorgio Maggiore, Venice).

Titian (ca. 1487–1576). Name given to the Venetian painter Tiziano Vecellio; his works include *The Assumption of the Virgin* (1516–18, Sta. Maria Gloriosa dei Frari, Venice); *Bacchanal* (ca. 1518, Prado, Madrid); *Bacchus and Ariadne* (1522–23, National Gallery, London); *Venus of Urbino* (1538, Uffizi, Florence); *Pope Paul III and His Grandsons* (1545–46, Museo di Capodimonte, Naples); *Charles V at Mühlberg* (1548, Prado); *The Rape of Europa* (1562, Isabella Stuart Gardiner Museum, Boston); and *Pietà* (1576, Accademia, Venice).

Toulouse-Lautrec, Henri-Marie-Raymond de (1864–1901). French postimpressionist painter; his works include *Au Cirque Fernando* (1888, Art Institute of Chicago); *In the Parlor at the Rue des Moulins* (1894, Musée Toulouse-

Lautrec, Albi, France); and *English Girl at "Le Star," Le Havre* (1899, Musée Toulouse-Lautrec); but he is probably best known for his posters and lithographs of Aristide Bruant, "La Goulie," Jane Avril, May Belfort, Loïe Fuller, and Yvette Guilbert.

Turner, Joseph Mallord William (1775–1851). English painter who is most famous for his seascapes, such as *Shipwreck* (1805, Tate Gallery, London); *The Wreck of a Transport Ship* (1810, Calouste-Gulbenkian Museum, Lisbon); *Bay of Baiae, with Apollo and the Sibyl* (1823, Tate Gallery); *Sunrise, with a Boat Between Headlands* (1835–45, Tate Gallery); *The Fighting Téméraire* (1839, National Gallery, London); *Rockets and Blue Lights* (1840, Sterling and Francine Clark Art Institute, Williamstown, Mass.); and *Sun of Venice Going into the Sea* (1843, Tate Gallery).

Utrillo, Maurice (1883–1955). French painter of cityscapes, such as *La Place du Tertre* (ca. 1910, Tate Gallery, London); *Rue des Poisonniers* (1930, Private Collection); and *Sacré-Coeur de Montmartre* (1937, Indianapolis Museum of Art).

van Gogh, Vincent (1853–90). Dutch postimpressionist painter whose works include *The Potato Eaters* (1885, van Gogh Museum, Amsterdam); *Café at Evening* (1888, Kröller-Müller Museum, Arnhem); *Postman Roulin* (1888, Museum of Fine Arts, Boston, Mass.); *Self-Portrait with a Severed Ear* (1889, Courtauld Institute, London); *Starry Night* (1889, Museum of Modern Art, New York); *Madame Ginoux or L'Arlésienne* (1890, Metropolitan Museum, New York); and *Cornfield with Crows* (1890, van Gogh Museum).

Velazquez or Velàsquez, Diego Rodriguez de Silva y (1599–1660). Spanish painter whose works include *The Immaculate Conception* (1618, National Gallery, London); *An Old Woman Cooking Eggs* (1618, National Gallery of Scotland, Edinburgh); *Luis de Góngora* (1622, Museum of Fine Arts, Boston, Mass.); *The Surrender of Breda* (1634–35, Prado, Madrid); *Pope Innocent X* (1650, Palazzo Doria, Rome); and *The Maids of Honor,* better known as *Las Meninas* (1656, Prado).

Vermeer, Jan (1632–75). Dutch painter whose works include *The Procuress* (1656, Gemäldegalerie, Dresden); *A Street in Delft* (1660, Rijksmuseum, Amsterdam); *A View of Delft* (1660s, Mauritshuis, The Hague); *A Woman in Blue Reading a Letter* (1664, Rijksmuseum); *A Woman Weighing Pearls* (ca. 1665, National Gallery, Washington, D.C.); and *The Letter* (1666, Rijksmuseum).

Veronese, Paolo (born Paolo Caliari; 1528–88). Italian painter whose works include *The Marriage at Cana* (1562–62, Louvre, Paris); *The Finding of Moses* (1570, Prado, Madrid); *The Feast at the House of Levi,* originally titled *The Last Supper* (1573, Accademia, Venice); *The Martyrdom of St. Giustina* (1575, S. Giustina, Padua); and *Annunciation* (1581, Accademia).

Watteau, Jean-Antoine (1684–1721). French rococo painter whose works include *Le Bal Champètre* (1714–15, Dulwich College Picture Gallery, London); *L'Amour Désarmé* (1714–16, Musée Condé, Chantilly, France); *Embarkation for Cythera* (1717, Louvre, Paris); *Mezzetin* (1718, Metropolitan Museum, New York); *Gilles* (ca. 1719, Louvre); *Italian Comedians* (1720, National Gallery, Washington, D.C.); and *Enseigne de Gesaint* (1721, Staatliche Museen, Berlin).

Weyden, Rogier van der (1399 or 1400–64). Netherlandish painter whose works include *Standing Madonna* (ca. 1430–32, Kunsthistorisches Museum, Vienna); *Annunciation* (1430 or 1440, Louvre, Paris); *Deposition* (ca. 1435, Prado, Madrid); *Crucifixion Triptych* (ca. 1441–42, Kunsthistorisches Museum); and *The Last Judgment* (ca. 1450, Hôtel Dieu, Beaune, France).

Whistler, James Abbot McNeill (1834–1903). American painter who worked in England; his works include *White Girl* (1862, National Gallery, Washington, D.C.); *The Artist in His Studio* (1864, Art Institute of Chicago); *Symphony in White, No. 3* (1867, Barber Institute of Fine Arts, Birmingham); *Chelsea: Nocturne in Blue and Green* (ca. 1870, Tate Gallery, London); *Arrangement in Gray and Black, No. 1: The Artist's Mother* (1872, Louvre, Paris); and *Peacock Room, Harmony in Blue and Gold* (1876, Freer Gallery, Washington, D.C.).

Zurbaràn, Francisco (1598–1664). Spanish painter whose works include *The Crucifixion* (1627, Art Institute of Chicago); *The Apostle Peter Appearing to S. Pedro Nolasco* (1628, Prado, Madrid); *St. Serapion* (1628, Wadsworth Atheneum, Hartford, Conn.); *The Triumph of Thomas Aquinas* (1631, Provincial Museum of Fine Arts, Seville); and *Hercules Seared by the Poisoned Robe* (1634, Prado).

SOURCES

Chilvers, Ian, and Harold Osborne. *The Oxford Dictionary of Art*. New York: Oxford University Press, 1988.

Jacobs, Michael, and Paul Stirton. *The Knopf Traveler's Guides to Art: Britain and Ireland*. New York: Alfred A. Knopf, 1984.

———. *The Knopf Traveler's Guides to Art: France*. New York: Alfred A. Knopf, 1984.

Janson, H. W. *History of Art: A Survey of the Major Visual Arts from the Dawn of History to the Present Day*. 2nd ed. Englewood Cliffs, N.J.: Prentice-Hall, 1977.

Myers, Bernard S., ed. *McGraw-Hill Dictionary of Art*. 5 vols. New York: McGraw-Hill, 1969.

Osborne, Harold, ed. *The Oxford Companion to Art*. Oxford, Eng.: Clarendon Press, 1970.

The Phaidon Dictionary of Twentieth-Century Art. Oxford, Eng.: Phaidon, 1973.

Piper, David. *The Illustrated Dictionary of Art and Artists*. New York: Random House, 1984.

—Ian Crump; L.D.R.

19

NOTABLE SCULPTORS

. . . . .

The young would-be writer Stephen Dedalus, in James Joyce's *A Portrait of the Artist as a Young Man*, is much concerned with artistic theory. At one point he proposes this hypothetical question: "If a man hacking in fury at a block of wood make there an image of a cow, is that image a work of art? If not, why not?" To which his then-friend Lynch replies, "That's a lovely one. That has the true scholastic stink."

Stephen's concern is for what it is that makes something "artistic"—with how, and in what way, beauty becomes involved with its perception. He could not, for his purposes, have chosen a more appropriate example than sculpture, because it is arguably the oldest of the fine arts, quite possibly antedating language itself, and one common to every race and civilization. In its origins sculpture was inextricably mixed with its usefulness; the prehistoric human who used a stone adze to fashion a replica of an animal sought to summon that animal, yet at the same time doubtless took pride in the object's proportions. Much the same is true today of the wood carver who fashions a decoy; it is meant to coax ducks to within shooting distance, yet its decorative qualities are highly valued.

Sculpture has enjoyed close relationships with both architecture and painting. For the ancient Greeks, sculpture in stone was the preeminent form of all the arts. Today sculptors use numerous materials and forms—not merely stone but metal, papier maché, terra-cotta, wood, junk, whatever. What sculpture lacks in subtlety it gains in immediacy; even in non-representational forms it retains its primitive three-dimensional strength.

The following is a listing of a few of the more important sculptors, ancient and modern, with representative works and their location. (The sculptors of many of the pieces of antiquity are of course not known; a few are listed below under unknown Egyptian and classical sculptors.)

Arp, Hans or **Jean** (1887–1966). Franco-Swiss painter and poet as well as sculptor; he was a prominent dadaist and later was affiliated with the surrealists; he turned to sculpture in the 1930s and produced works such as *Torso* (1931, Müller-Widmann Collection, Basel); *Shell and Head* (1933, Peggy Guggenheim Museum, Venice); *Hybrid Fruit Called Pagoda* (1934, Tate Gallery, London); *Human Concretion* (1935, Museum of Modern Art, New York); *Giant Pip* (1937, Musée National d'Art Moderne, Paris); and *Siren* (1942, Sidney Janis Gallery, New York).

Bernini, Gianlorenzo (1598–1680). Italian architect and painter as well as sculptor; he is known as one of the primary exponents of the baroque; his most important works include *Apollo and Daphne* (1622–25, Borghese Gallery, Rome); *Pope Urban VIII* (1640–42, Spoleto Cathedral); *The Ecstasy of St. Teresa* (1645–52, Sta. Maria della Vittoria, Rome); *Francesco I d'Este, Duke of Modena* (1650–51, Estense Gallery, Modena); and *Blessed Lodovica Albertoni* (1671–74, S. Francesco a Ripa, Rome).

Bologna, Giovanni, or **Giambologna** (born Jean Boulogne; 1529–1608). Italian sculptor born in Flanders; he was the most important mannerist sculptor and is known for his twisting figures; his works include *The Fountain of Neptune* (1563–66, Bologna), which earned him his reputation; *The Medici Mercury* (1580, Bargello, Florence); *The Rape of the Sabines* (1579–83, Loggia dei Lanzi); and *Hercules and the Centaur* (1594–1600, Loggia dei Lanzi).

Borglum, (John) Gutzon (1867–1941). American sculptor famous for such sculpture as *The Mares of Diomedes* (1904, Metropolitan Museum, New York), *Abraham Lincoln* (1901, Capitol, Washington, D.C.), and his mountainside bas-reliefs of American presidents at Mount Rushmore, South Dakota (begun 1927, finished by his son Lincoln Borglum in 1941), and Confederate generals at Stone Mountain, Georgia (begun 1916, never completed).

Brancusi, Constantin (1876–1957). Romanian-born sculptor who lived in Paris; he is known for the austere simplicity of his work, including *The Kiss* (1908, Museum of Modern Art, Philadelphia, Pa.); *Torso of a Young Man* (1922, Museum of Modern Art, Philadelphia, Pa.); several variations on *Bird in Space* (1925–40); *Endless Column* (1937, Tirgu Jiu, Romania); and *The Cock* (1941, Musée National d'Art Moderne, Paris).

Calder, Alexander (1898–1976). American sculptor who invented the mobile; his works include *Lobster Trap and Fish Tail* (1939, Museum of Modern Art, New York); *Spider* (1939, Museum of Modern Art, New York); *Mobile* (1950, Guggenheim Museum, New York); *Semaphore* (1959, Galerie Maeght, Paris); *Les Renforts* (1963, Foundation Maeght, St.-Paul, France); and *Red, Black, and Blue* (1967, Dallas Airport).

Canova, Antonio (1757–1822). Italian neoclassical sculptor; his most famous pieces are *Theseus and the Minotaur* (1781–83, Victoria and Albert

Museum, London); the Tomb of Countess Maria Christiana (1798–1805, Church of the Augustinians, Vienna); and *Pauline Bonaparte as Venus* (1800, Borghese Gallery, Rome).

Cellini, Benvenuto (1500–71). Italian goldsmith, sculptor, and biographer; his works include the Saltcellar of François I (1543, Kunsthistorisches Museum, Vienna); *The Nymph of Fontainebleu* (1545, Louvre, Paris); and *Perseus with the Head of Medusa* (1545–54, Loggia dei Lanzi, Florence).

Cornell, Joseph (1903–73). American sculptor who constructed assemblages inside framing boxes, including *Untitled (Habitat with Owl)* (1946, Collection of Arno Schefler, New York); *Untitled (Hotel de l'Etoile)* (1951–52, ACA Gallery, New York); *Untitled (Medici Princess)* (1953–54, Gatodo Gallery, Tokyo); *Untitled (Window Façade)* (1953, Collection of Michael M. Rea, Washington, D.C.); and *Observatory American Gothic* (1954, Collection of Mr. and Mrs. E. A. Bergman, Chicago).

Degas, Edgar (1834–1917). French painter and sculptor; although Degas is better known as a painter associated with the impressionist movement, Renoir considered him a greater sculptor than Rodin; his most famous piece, which exists in many versions, is *The Fourteen-Year-Old Dancer.*

Donatello (born Donato di Niccolo di Betto Bardi; 1386–1466). Italian sculptor who rejected the International Gothic style and was one of the foremost proponents of the Renaissance; his most important works are *St. Mark* (1411–13, Or San Michele, Florence); *St. George and the Dragon* (1415–17, Bargello, Florence); *David* (1433–43, Bargello); *Gattamelata* (1447–53, Piazza del Santo, Padua); and *St. Mary Magdalene* (1456, Baptistry, Florence).

Epstein, Sir Jacob (1880–1959). New York-born sculptor, studied under Rodin, worked largely in England. Among his important works are *Day* and *Night* (1929, Passenger Transport Building, London); *Christ Showing the Stigmata* (1919, Cheny-Garrand Collection, Wheathamstead, Eng.); *Madonna and Child* (1942, Cavendish Square, London); *The Oscar Wilde Memorial* (1909, Père-Lachaise Cemetery, Paris); *Joseph Conrad* (1924, National Portrait Gallery, London); and *Rima* (1925, Hyde Park, London).

French, Daniel Chester (1850–1931). Massachusetts-born American sculptor whose work in the beaux-arts style moved toward the grandly heroic. His best-known sculpture is the statue of Abraham Lincoln in the Lincoln Memorial in Washington, D.C. (1922). Other notable works are *The Minute Man* (1874, Concord, Mass.) and *The Angel of Death and the Sculptor* (1892, Forest Hills Cemetery, Roxbury, Mass.).

Ghiberti, Lorenzo (1378–1455). Italian goldsmith and sculptor; in 1403 he won the commission to cast a second set of doors, based on the New Testament, for the Baptistry in Florence (Andrea Pisano cast the first set in 1336); a year after he completed this set in 1424, he was commissioned to cast a third set based on the Old Testament; this set, which he finished in 1456, Michelangelo praised as worthy of being the Gates of Paradise.

Giacometti, Alberto (1901–66). Swiss painter and sculptor who is known for his attenuated figures; his works include *Palace at 4 A.M.* (1932–33, Museum of Modern Art, New York); *Man Pointing* (1947, Tate Gallery, London); *The Nose* (1947, Hirshhorn Museum, Washington, D.C.); *The Glade: Composition with Nine Figures* (1950, Collection of Mr. and Mrs. David A. Wingate, New York); *Large Head of Diego* (1954, Robert B. Mayer Family Collection, Chicago, Ill.); *Bust of Diego* (1957, Hirshhorn Museum); and *Walking Man I* (1960, Albright-Knox Art Gallery, Buffalo, N.Y.).

Gislebertus (fl. 1130s). French Romanesque sculptor who executed the tympanum of the Cathedral of St. Lazarus in Autun, France; he was one of the first sculptors to sign his work.

Houdon, Jean-Antoine (1741–1828). French sculptor of neoclassical portraits; his works include *Empress Catherine II of Russia* (1773, Hermitage, St. Petersburg); *Sophie Arnould as Iphigenia* (1775, Louvre, Paris); *Jean-Jacques Rousseau* (1778, Louvre); *Voltaire* (1781, Fabre Museum, Montpellier, France); *Comtesse de Sabran* (1785, Thuringen Museum, Eisenach, Germany); *George Washington* (1788–92, State Capitol, Richmond, Va.); and *Mirabeau* (1791, Louvre).

Maillol, Aristide (1861–1944). French sculptor who concentrated on the female nude; his works include *Seated Woman (Méditerranée)* (1901, Collection Oskar Reinhert, Winterthur, Switzerland); *Night* (1902–1909, Dina Vierny Collection, Paris); *Chained Action* (1905, Musée National d'Art Moderne, Paris); and *The Mountain* (1937, Musée National d'Art Moderne).

Michelangelo Buonarroti (1475–1564). Italian painter and poet as well as perhaps the greatest of sculptors; his works include *Bacchus* (1496–97, Bargello, Florence); *Pietà* (1498–99, Vatican); *David* (1501–1504, Accademia, Florence); *The Dying Slave* (1513–16, Louvre, Paris); *The Rebellious Slave* (1513–16, Louvre); *Moses* (1515, S. Pietro in Vincoli, Rome); and *Pietà Rondanini* (1555–64, Castello Sforesco, Milan).

Moore, Henry (1898–1986). English abstract sculptor whose works include the series *Reclining Figure* (1929, Leeds City Art Museum; 1957–58, UNESCO Building, Paris; 1963–65, Lincoln Center, New York); *Two Forms* (1936; Collection of Mrs. H. Gates Lloyd, Haverford, Pa.); *Recumbent Figure* (1938, Tate Gallery, London); *Family Group* (1945–49, Museum of Modern Art, New York); and *King and Queen* (1952–53, Tate Gallery).

Nevelson, Louise (1900–88). American painter and sculptor; her sculptures include *Wedding Feast at Dawn* (1959, Museum of Modern Art, New York); *An American Tribute to the British People* (1960–64, Tate Gallery, London); *Sky Gate—New York* (1978, World Trade Center, New York); and *Mrs. N's Palace* (1964–77, Pace Gallery, New York).

Oldenburg, Claes (1929–). Swedish-born American sculptor who has often been associated with the pop art movement because of his monumental works celebrating everyday objects, such as *Dual Hamburger* (1962, Museum of Modern Art, New York); *Bedroom Ensemble* (1963, Sidney Janis Gallery, New York); two *Giant Light Switches* (1964, Sidney Janis Gallery, and Collection of Leon Krausher, New York); *Soft Toilet* (1966, Collection of Mr. and Mrs. Victor Ganz, New York); and *Lipsticks in Piccadilly Circus* (1966, Tate Gallery, London).

Phidias (d. ca. 432 B.C.E.). Greek sculptor who supervised the construction of the Parthenon in Athens; he carved the chryselephantine statues of Athena for the Parthenon and of Zeus for the temple dedicated to him in Olympia (parts of both are known through copies).

Pisano, Andrea (ca. 1290–1348). Italian goldsmith and sculptor who worked in the International Gothic style; he cast the first set of doors for the Baptistry in Florence (1330–36). See **Ghiberti, Lorenzo**.

Pisano, Nicola (d. 1284?) and **Giovanni** (d. after 1314). Two Italian sculptors, father and son (no relation to Andrea Pisano), who revived sculpture as a distinct art form; they produced the neoclassical pulpits in the Baptistry in Pisa (1259) and in the Siena Cathedral (1265–68). Giovanni carved the Madonna and Child for the Arena Chapel in Padua (1305).

Praxiteles (fl. mid-fourth century B.C.E.). Greek sculptor; two of his sculptures are known through Roman copies: *Hermes and the Infant Diana* (Olympia Museum, Greece) and *Aphrodite of Cnidus* (Vatican).

Robbia, Luca della (1399–1482). Italian sculptor and ceramicist who invented glazed terra-cotta; he is noted for his *Cantoria, or Singing Gallery* (1431–38, Cathedral Museum, Florence) and his numerous terra-cotta tondos and reliefs, such as *Madonna and Angels* (1460, Bargello, Florence).

Rodin, Auguste (1840–1917). French romantic sculptor who made his reputation with *The Age of Bronze* (1878, Louvre, Paris); in 1880, he was commissioned to cast *The Gates of Hell* for the Musée des Art Décoratif and, although he never completed this project, it included many of his greatest works, such as *The Thinker* (1880), *The Kiss* (1886), and *Prodigal Son* (1889); he also cast *The Burghers of Calais* (1884–86) and modeled Balzac (1939), which was cast by public subscription after his death. (Casts of most of his works are in the Rodin Museum in Paris.)

Rude, François (1784–1855). French sculptor of the romantic school; his works include *The Departure of the Volunteers in 1792*, better known as *The Marseillaise* (1833–36, Arc de Triomphe, Paris); *The Awakening of Napoleon to Immortality* (1847, Fixin, France); *Joan of Arc* (1852, Louvre, Paris) and *Monument to Marshal Ney* (1853, Paris).

Saint-Gaudens, Augustus (1848–1907). Irish-born American sculptor, important for his underlying realistic technique in public statuary. His best-known works are the memorial to Clover Adams (1891, Rock Creek Cemetery, Washington, D.C.), *David Glasgow Farragut* (1881, Madison Square Park, New York City), *Robert Gould Shaw Memorial* (1896, Boston Common), *Abraham Lincoln* (1887, Lincoln Park, Chicago, Ill.); and the equestrian statue of William Tecumseh Sherman (1903, Central Park, New York City).

Segal, George (1924–). American sculptor who is known for his unpainted plaster figures or groups, including *Gas Station* (1963, National Gallery of Canada, Ottawa); *Cinema* (1963, Albright-Knox Art Gallery, Buffalo, N.Y.); *Restaurant Window* (1967, Wallraf-Richartz Museum, Cologne); *The Execution* (1967, Vancouver Art Gallery); *Hot Dog Stand* (1978, San Francisco Museum of Modern Art); *In Memory of May 4, 1970, Kent State: Abraham and Isaac* (1978, John B. Putnam, Jr., Memorial Collection, Princeton, N.J.); *Gay Liberation* (1980, Sidney Janis Gallery, New York); and *The Holocaust* (1982, Sidney Janis Gallery).

Sluter, Claus (d. 1405 or 1406). Flemish sculptor who was active in Dijon; he was the most important figure in the transition, in northern European sculpture, from the International Gothic to a Renaissance style; his works include *The Tomb of Philip the Bold* (1385–1410, Musée des Beaux-Arts, Dijon) and *The Well of Moses* (1395–1403, Chartreuse de Champmol, Dijon).

Smithson, Robert (1938–73). American conceptual and environmental sculptor; his work includes *Map of Glass (Atlantis)* (1969, Loveladies Island, New Jersey); *Asphalt Rundown* (1969, Rome); *Partially Buried Woodshed* (1970, Kent, Ohio); *Spiral Jetty* (1970, Great Salt Lake, Utah) and *Broken Circle* (1971, Emmen, Holland).

Unknown Egyptian and classical sculptors (all dates are B.C.E. unless otherwise indicated). *Menkaura and His Queen* (ca. 2600, Museum of Fine Arts, Boston, Mass.); *Sphinx of Amenemhet III* (ca. 1800, Cairo Museum), bust of Nofretete (ca. 1375, Egyptian Museum, Berlin); *Snake Goddess* (ca. 1500, Museum of Fine Arts, Boston, Mass.), *Dying Warrior of Aegina* (ca. 550, Glyptotek, Munich), *Winged Victory of Samothrace* (ca. 300, Louvre, Paris), *Aphrodite of Melos—Venus de Milo* (ca. 300–250, Louvre); *Dying Gaul* (ca. 240, Capitoline Museum, Rome); *Laocoön and His Sons* (ca. 50, Vatican); *Julius Caesar* (ca. 20 B.C.E.–50 A.D., Imperial Museum, Berlin); *Augustus in Prima Porta* (ca. 15, Vatican).

Verrocchio, Andrea del (1435–88). Italian goldsmith and sculptor; his sculptures include *Christ and St. Thomas* (1467–83, Or San Michele, Florence); *The Beheading of John the Baptist* (1477–80, Cathedral Museum, Florence); *David* (1475, Bargello, Florence); and *Colleoni* (1481–88, Campo dei SS. Giovanni e Paolo, Venice).

SOURCES

Arnason, H. H. *The Sculptures of Houdon.* London: Phaidon, 1975.

Chilvers, Ian, and Harold Osborne. *The Oxford Dictionary of Art.* New York: Oxford University Press, 1988.

Fletcher, Valerie J. *Alberto Giacometti, 1901–1966.* Washington, D.C.: Smithsonian Institution Press, 1988.

Giedion-Welcker, Carla. *Jean Arp.* New York: Harry N. Abrams, 1957.

Hobbs, Robert, *et al. Robert Smithson: Sculpture.* Ithaca, N.Y.: Cornell University Press, 1981.

Jacobs, Michael, and Paul Stirton. *The Knopf Traveler's Guides to Art: Britain and Ireland.* New York: Alfred A. Knopf, 1984.

———. *The Knopf Traveler's Guides to Art: France.* New York: Alfred A. Knopf, 1984.

Janson, H. W. *History of Art: A Survey of the Major Visual Arts from the Dawn of History to the Present Day.* 2nd ed. Englewood Cliffs, N.J.: Prentice-Hall, 1977.

Maillard, Robert, ed. *A Dictionary of Modern Sculpture.* London: Methuen, 1960.

Michelin Green Guide: Burgundy. London: Michelin Tyre Public Limited Co., 1988.

Nevelson, Louise. *Louise Nevelson: Atmospheres and Environments.* New York: Clarkson N. Potter, 1980.

The Phaidon Encyclopedia of Art and Artists. Oxford, Eng.: Phaidon, 1978.

Sweeney, James Johnson, and Daniel Lelong. *Calder: The Artist, the Work.* London: Lund Humpheries, 1971.

Tuchman, Phyllis. *George Segal.* New York: Abbeville Press, 1983.

—Ian Crump; L.D.R.

20

THE ART MUSEUMS
OF THE WORLD

· · · · ·

ELSEWHERE IN THIS VOLUME IT HAS BEEN NOTED THAT WRITERS OFTEN choose to write about painters. The analogy of writing with painting goes back at least as far as the Roman poet Horace's dictum *ut pictura poesis*—as in painting, so in poetry. There are legitimate theoretical objections to this, but certainly writers of prose and poetry alike have frequented museums and studied works of art in an effort to achieve some of its color and clarity. Perhaps the most famous statement of the affinity comes in the French novelist Marcel Proust's depiction, in *Remembrance of Things Past*, of the death of the novelist Bergotte (modeled in part on Anatole France), who despite his illness goes to a museum in order to see Vermeer's *View of Delft*. Staring at an area of wall depicted in the painting, he thinks, "That is how I ought to have written. . . . My last books are too dry. I ought to have gone over them with several coats of paint, made my language exquisite in itself, like this little patch of yellow wall." At that moment he is assailed by a stroke, and falls to the floor.

Most visits to art museums end less drastically. There are now excellent museums in most American cities, and traveling exhibitions from major repositories supplement local collections to make works by leading artists of the past and present available to large audiences. Therefore no longer must one travel to the great museums of the world to see examples of the art form that, as Proust wrote about another of his characters, an artist, offers "a sort of metamorphosis of the things represented in it, analogous to what in poetry we call metaphor . . . [so that], if God the Father had created things by naming them, it was by taking away their names or giving them other names that Elstir created them anew."

Below are the locations of a few of the more important art museums of the world, with some of their principal collections.

ASIA AND ASIA MINOR

Baroda, India. Museum and Picture Gallery, one of India's most significant, shows works by Romney, Reynolds, and Lely, Indian miniatures, and folk art.

Bombay, India. Prince of Wales Museum includes the Tata Collection of rare paintings of the Moghul school.

Cairo, Egypt. Coptic Museum displays Coptic religious art; Museum of Islamic Art houses one of the world's finest collections of Islamic art.

Haifa, Israel. Museum of Japanese Art has a fine collection.

Jerusalem, Israel. Billy Rose Sculpture Garden contains works by Moore, Picasso, and others; art-museum wing of the Israel Museum houses collections of ancient, modern, and Jewish ritual art; synagogue in the Hadassah Medical Center has twelve stained-glass windows by Chagall.

Kobe, Japan. Kobe Municipal Museum of Namban Art displays early Western-influenced Japanese painting.

Kurashiki, Japan. Ohara Museum of Art collection includes works by El Greco, Cézanne, van Gogh, and Renoir.

Kyoto, Japan. Kyoto National Museum collection includes Buddhist art and painting from the Kyoto school; National Museum of Modern Art focuses on contemporary art from Japan and the rest of the world.

Nagoya, Japan. Tokugawa Art Museum collection includes the picture scrolls from *The Tale of Genji.*

Nara, Japan. Shosoin, in the 1,200-year-old Imperial Treasure House, displays art from the Nara period and Asian porcelains.

Osaka, Japan. Osaka Municipal Museum of Art shows ancient and modern art.

Tel Aviv, Israel. Tel Aviv Museum displays Israeli and world art.

Tokyo, Japan. Bridgestone Museum of Art has strong collections of French impressionists and contemporary Western art; Kamakura Museum focuses on art from the twelfth through the sixteenth centuries; National Museum, founded in 1871, shows art from Japan, China, and India; National Museum of Modern Art displays Japanese art produced since 1907; National Museum of Western Art contains European and American painting; Nezu Institute of Fine Arts shows ancient Japanese art; Tokyo Metropolitan Art Museum displays contemporary Japanese art; Yamatane Museum of Art contains modern Japanese art from the Meiji and Showa periods.

AUSTRALIA

Melbourne. National Gallery of Victoria displays European, Asian, and Australian art, including works by Rubens, Goya, Tiepolo, Rembrandt, Cézanne, Picasso, Noland, French, Drysdale, and Roberts.

Sydney. Art Gallery of New South Wales focuses on nineteenth-century British, contemporary, and Australian art.

EUROPE

Agen, France. Museé des Beaux-Arts includes work by Goya and Corot.

Aix-en-Provence, France. Musée Granet displays works by Rembrandt and Ingres.

Albi, France. Musée Toulouse-Lautrec is devoted to the artist's work.

Amsterdam, Netherlands. Municipal Museum shows art from 1850 to the present, including works by Cézanne, Monet, Picasso, Léger, Malevitch, Chagall, Mondrian, and Van Doesburg; Rijksmuseum, founded by Louis Bonaparte, has an important fifteenth- to seventeenth-century Dutch collection, including Hals, Rembrandt, and Vermeer; Vincent van Gogh Museum offers extensive collection of the artist's works.

Antwerp, Belgium. Mayer van den Bergh Museum contains work of Breughel; Middelheim estate has an extensive sculpture garden; Royal Museum of Fine Arts has one of the world's best Flemish art collections; the Rubens Huis displays the artist's work.

Arnhem, Netherlands. Kröller-Müller National Museum contains works by Picasso, Mondrian, Marini, Braque, and Léger and a large van Gogh collection.

Athens, Greece. Benaki Museum houses Anthony B. Benaki's collection of Asian, Greek, and European art and two early works by El Greco; Byzantine Museum displays icons, frescoes, and mosaics.

Barcelona, Spain. Federico-Marés Museum displays sculpture from the tenth to the nineteenth centuries, including de la Cuada; Joan Miró Foundation presents many of the artist's works; Museum of Catalan Art includes works by Juan of Tarragona, Borrossà, Tintoretto, El Greco, Zurbarán, and Ribera.

Basel, Switzerland. Kunstmuseum has the world's largest collection of cubist art.

Bayeux, France. Musée de la Tapisserie de la Reine Mathilde houses the famous Bayeux Tapestry.

Bayonne, France. Musée Léon Bonnat exhibits several impressive oil sketches by Rubens and work by Vouet, Goya, and Ingres.

Beaune, France. Hôtel Dieu exhibits work by van der Weyden.

Berlin, Germany. Brücke Museum features works by artists of this expressionist school; Gemäldegalerie in the Dalhem Museum has collections of Flemish, Dutch, Italian, and German art; National Gallery shows expressionist and contemporary works.

Bern, Switzerland. Kunstmuseum has the world's largest collection of Klee's work.

Besançon, France. Museum of Fine Arts displays works by Bellini, Bronzino, Cranach, and Courbet.

Birmingham, England. Birmingham Museum and Art Gallery exhibits Christus, Dolci, Guercino, Caravaggio, Canaletto, Ramsay, and Degas.

Bonn, Germany. Städisches Kunstmuseum has one of the world's largest collections of expressionist and contemporary German art.

Bruges, Belgium. Groeningemuseum concentrates on Flemish art; Hôpital St.-Jean houses the Memlinc Museum.

Brussels, Belgium. Musée d'Art Ancien displays the works of early Flemish masters, including Breughel; Musée d'Art Moderne focuses on nineteenth- and twentieth-century Belgian art; Musées Royaux des Beaux-Arts include work by David.

Budapest, Hungary. Museum of Fine Arts has strong collections of Spanish, Italian, and Flemish art.

Cambridge, England. Fitzwilliam Museum exhibits Titian, Veronese, Ricci, Renoir, Cézanne, and Matisse.

Cardiff, Wales. National Museum of Wales has an important collection of nineteenth-century French and modern art.

Castres, France. Musée Goya is devoted to the artist's works.

Chantilly, France. Musée Condé houses work by the Limbourg brothers.

Colmar, France. Musée d'Unterlinden displays Schongauer and Grünewald altarpieces.

Cologne, Germany. Museum Ludwig displays art from the fourteenth through the nineteenth centuries; Wallraf-Richartz Museum contains works by expressionists, Russian constructionists, and pop artists.

Copenhagen, Denmark. Royal Museum of Fine Arts features collections of Danish and world art.

Dijon, France. Musée des Beaux-Arts displays work by Broederlam and Rodin.

Dresden, Germany. Gemäldegalerie der Alte Meister, in the Zwinger Palace, has one of the oldest and best collections in Europe, including Raphael; Gemäldegalerie der Neue Meister displays art from the nineteenth and twentieth centuries, including works by Gauguin and Monet.

Dublin, Ireland. Hugh Lane Municipal Gallery of Modern Art shares its collection of nineteenth-century French painting with the National Gallery in London; National Gallery of Ireland displays collections of Italian, Flemish, English, and Irish art as well as Russian and Greek icons.

Edinburgh, Scotland. National Gallery of Scotland contains works by Massys, van der Goes, Raphael, Rembrandt, Titian, Rubens, El Greco, Velazquez, Poussin, Constable, Turner, Monet, Pissarro, Renoir, Ramsay, Wilkie, Scott, Pettie, and Guthrie.

Eindhoven, Netherlands. Van Abbe Museum shows contemporary art, including works by Picasso, Braque, Chagall, Léger, Mondrian, Kokoschka, Kandinsky, Mirò, Bacon, and Stella.

El Escorial, Spain. New Museums, in the El Escorial Monastery and Palace commissioned by Philip II in 1563, contain work by van der Weyden, Titian, El

Greco, Gerard David, Bosch, Ribera, Velazquez, Tintoretto, Veronese, Bassano, and Reni.

Enschede, Netherlands. Twenthe Museum includes work by Breughel and Monet.

Florence, Italy. Baptistry displays Ghiberti's Gates of Paradise; Bargello Palace houses Renaissance sculpture by Donatello, Verrocchio, Michelangelo, Cellini, and Della Robbia; Monastary of San Marco contains more than forty frescoes by Fra Angelico; Brancacci Chapel contains frescoes by Masaccio; Galleria dell' Accademia contains work by Michelangelo as well as Renaissance painting; the Galleria degli Uffizi, which was designed by Vasari as an office building in 1560, turned into a private art gallery in 1581, and bequeathed to the citizens in 1757, has an extensive collection of Renaissance art, including Cimabue, Duccio's altarpiece, Giotto's altarpiece, Martini, Botticelli, Fabriano, van der Goes' altarpiece, Veneziano, da Vinci, Titian, Bronzino, Parmegianino, and Raphael; Medici Chapels were designed by Michelangelo and contain his sculptures; Palatine Gallery in the Pitti Palace exhibits works by Raphael, Rubens, Murillo, del Sarto, Lippi, Titian, Veronese, and Tintoretto.

Ghent, Belgium. Museum voor Schone Kunsten features Flemish and Belgian art; Sint-Baafskathedraal (Ghent Cathedral) displays van Eyck altarpiece.

Glasgow, Scotland. Burrell Collection at Glasgow Art Gallery displays Memlinc, Bellini, Rembrandt, Manet, Cézanne, and Degas.

Grenoble, France. Musée de Peinture et de la Sculpture exhibits Beert, Veronese, Rubens, Domenichino, Zurbarán, and Matisse.

Haarlem, Netherlands. Frans Hals Museum, installed in the former almshouse for old men, features eight of the artist's paintings.

The Hague, Netherlands. Mauritshuis, located in a seventeenth-century palace, has an important collection of Flemish and Dutch art that includes Metsys, van der Weyden, Memlinc, Vermeer, Rubens, and Rembrandt.

Innsbruck, Austria. Tiroler Landesmuseum Ferdinandeum features collections of Gothic art, stained glass, impressionism, and modern realism.

Istanbul, Turkey. Hagia Sophia, built by Emperor Justinian, contains Byzantine mosaics; Kariye Museum, in the Chora Church, preserves extensive late Byzantine mosaics.

Krakow, Poland. National Museum has an extensive collection of European art from the Renaissance to the eighteenth century, including work by da Vinci and Rembrandt.

Le Havre, France. Museum of Fine Arts includes among its collection works by Bronzino and Monet.

Lille, France. Lille Museum of Fine Arts contains work by Donatello, Bouts, Goya, and Sonia Delaunay.

Lisbon, Portugal. Calouste-Gulbenkian Museum includes its collections of fifteenth- to eighteenth-century European and medieval religious art and work by Bouts, Rubens, Corot, and Manet.

Liverpool, England. Walker Art Gallery exhibits Martini, Mostaert, van Cleve, Rembrandt, Elsheimer, Wilson, Wright, Millais, Hockney, and Albert Moore.

Locarno, Switzerland. Museo d'Arte Moderna has a large collection of dadaist art.

London, England. Courtauld Institute Galleries include among their collections of Renaissance, impressionist, and postimpressionist art Campin, Breughel, Monaco, Manet, Degas, Renoir, van Gogh, and Cézanne; Dulwich Picture Gallery concentrates on seventeenth-century Dutch and French art; gallery at Hampton Court Palace displays Italian art from the sixteenth to the eighteenth centuries; Kenwood House shows works by Hals, Vermeer, Rembrandt, Romney, and Gainsborough; National Gallery includes the Wilton Diptych, Masaccio, van Eyck, da Vinci, Raphael, Titian, Gainsborough, van Gogh, Picasso, and Matisse; National Portrait Gallery contains portraits of famous English men and women; Sir John Soane's Museum contains works by Hogarth; Tate Gallery exhibits British and modern art, including works by Hogarth, Blake, Constable, Turner, Seurat, van Gogh, Cézanne, and Picasso; Victoria and Albert Museum holds Hilliard, Raphael, and Constable; Wallace Collection exhibits French rococo and English painting.

Lucerne, Switzerland. Am Rhyn Haus contains a collection of Picassos.

Lugano, Switzerland. Thyssen-Bornemisza Gallery, one of Europe's finest private collections, contains works by Duccio, Raphael, Titian, Rembrandt, Rubens, and Velazquez.

Lyon, France. Museum of Fine Arts displays an extensive collection of French and European art, including works by Massys, Tintoretto, Zurbarán, Rembrandt, Poussin, and Claude.

Madrid, Spain. Reina Sofia Museum houses work by Picasso; Prado has important Flemish, Spanish, and Italian art collections, including Bosch, van der Weyden, Breughel, Raphael, Rubens, El Greco, Velazquez, Goya, Dürer, Cranach, Botticelli, del Sarto, Mantega, Zurburán, Rubens, and Van Dyck.

Mainz, Germany. St. Stephen's Church has stained-glass windows by Chagall.

Manchester, England. City Art Gallery shows works by Guardi, Reni, Claude, Boucher, Fragonard, Gainsborough, Reynolds, Hunt, Millais, and Brown.

Milan, Italy. Art gallery in the Brera Palace displays Italian painting; Poldi-Pezzoli Museum displays Italian art from the Renaissance to the seventeenth century and Asian porcelains; Santa Maria delle Grazie contains da Vinci's *Last Supper*; art gallery in the Castello Sforesco includes work by Michelangelo.

Moscow, Russia. Tretyakov Art Gallery houses Russian and Soviet art, including Rublev.

Munich, Germany. Alte Pinakothek features Italian and northern European art, including Dürer; Haus der Kunst and Staatsgalerie Moderner Kunst display modern and contemporary art; Lenbachhaus has an extensive collection of works by Kandinsky and artists of the Blaue Reiter school; Neue Pinakothek exhibits nineteenth-century German art.

Nantes, France. Musée des Beaux-Arts includes among its collection works by de La Tour, Courbet, Maroni, and Ingres.

Naples, Italy. Museo di Capodimonte features European art from the fourteenth to the sixteenth centuries.

Nuremberg, Germany. Germanisches Nationalmuseum displays medieval art and wood sculpture.

Orléans, France. Museum of Fine Arts exhibits Velazquez, Le Nain, and Gauguin.

Oslo, Norway. Munch Museum is devoted to the artist's work; National Gallery contains works of nineteenth-century Norwegian and European art; two Vigeland museums are devoted to the works of Gustav and Emanuel Vigeland.

Oxford, England. Ashmolean Museum, opened in 1683 and the first public museum in England, contains the Alfred Jewel, Uccello, Cosimo, Giorgione, Michelangelo, Bronzino, Millais, and Toulouse-Lautrec.

Padua, Italy. Arena Chapel contains an important fresco cycle by Giotto.

Paris, France. Musée Marmottan is devoted almost entirely to Monet's works; Musée Auguste Rodin, in the Hôtel Biron, where the sculptor had lived, is devoted to his work and art collection; Musée National d'Art Moderne, housed in the Centre National d'Art et de Culture Georges Pompidou, features in its collection of modern art Picasso, Matisse, Rousseau, De Chirico, and Pollock; Musée National du Louvre includes the Winged Victory of Samothrace, the Avignon Pietà, Clouet, Cimabue, Martini, Ghirlandaio, da Vinci, Michelangelo, Raphael, Rembrandt, de La Tour, Poussin, Watteau, Chardin, David, Ingres, Géricault, Courbet, Manet, and Whistler; Musée de l'Impressionisme, installed in the former Gare d'Orsay, houses the world's most important collection of impressionist works, including Manet, Monet, Renoir, Cézanne, and van Gogh; Musée des Thermes et de l'Hôtel de Cluny contains the Unicorn Tapestries.

Prague, Czech Republic. National Gallery in Prague Castle displays works by Dürer, Breughel, and others.

Ravenna, Italy. Battistero Neoniano displays Byzantine mosaic of the baptism of Christ; Sant' Apollinare Nuovo houses mosaics of notable Christian martyrs and virgins; Church of San Vitale contains mosaics of Justinian and Theodora.

Rome, Italy. Barberini Palace displays works of Italian and northern Renaissance art; Borghese Gallery includes sculptures by Canova and

Bernini, and works by Raphael, Correggio, Caravaggio, and Titian; San Luigi dei Francesi displays three works by Caravaggio; San Pietro in Vincoli houses Michelangelo's *Moses*; Santa Maria della Vittoria contains work by Bernini; Vatican Art Museum has an extensive art and sculpture collection, but its most famous works are *Laocoön and His Sons*, the Belvedere Torso, the Apollo Belvedere, and works by Michelangelo and Raphael.

Rotterdam, Netherlands. Boymans-van Beuningen Museum has collections of Flemish, Dutch, and modern art, including Brueghel, Rembrandt, Corot, and Magritte.

Rouen, France. Museum of Fine Arts exhibits Gerard David, Velazquez, Caravaggio, de La Tour, Poussin, Fragonard, and Gericault.

St.-Paul, France. Foundation Maeght exhibits a collection of modern and contemporary art, including works by Braque, Bonnard, Calder, Chagall, Soulages, Tapies, Léger, Matisse, Zadkine, Richier, and Kandinsky.

St. Petersburg, Russia. Hermitage Museum, founded as a court gallery by Catherine the Great in 1764 and now located in the Winter Palace, has excellent collections of Spanish, Dutch, Central Asian, French impressionist, and twentieth-century art, including Cranach, Giorgione, Raphael, da Vinci, Velazquez, Rembrandt, Hals, Monet, Renoir, Picasso, and Matisse.

St.-Tropez, France. Musée de l'Annonciade contains work by Signac, Matisse, Bonnard, and Vuillard.

Siena, Italy. Museo dell' Opera del Duomo contains a Duccio altarpiece; Palazzo Pubblico displays art from the Siennese school, including Martini; Pinacoteca Nazionale features Siennese art from the twelfth to the seventeenth centuries.

Southampton, England. Southampton Art Gallery shows Jordaens, Böethus, Gérard, Gainsborough, Brzeska, and Spencer.

Stockholm, Sweden. Swedish Museum of Modern Art features modern and contemporary art, including Kienholz.

Toledo, Spain. Santa Cruz Museum and Santo Tomé Church contain works by El Greco.

Toulouse, France. Musée des Augustins, which occupies the fourteenth-century monastery of the Augustins, exhibits Notre Dame de Grasse and works by Tournier, Caravaggio, and Ingres.

Valencia, Spain. Fine Arts Museum displays works by Jacomart, Reixach, and the Osonases of the fifteenth-century Valencia school as well as art by Bosch, Velazquez, and Goya.

Vence, France. Matisse designed the Chapelle du Rosaire and decorated it with drawings and stained glass.

Venice, Italy. Galleria dell' Accademia displays Veronese, Titian, Tintoretto, and Giorgione; Peggy Guggenheim Museum houses outstanding collection of modern art.

Vienna, Austria. Academy of Fine Arts displays Bosch; Albertina has the world's finest collection of drawings; Österreichische Gallerie shows medieval

Austrian art; Kunsthistorisches Museum includes among its extensive collection works by Breughel, Mantegna, Parmigianino, Vermeer, Rembrandt, Dürer, Titian, Rubens, and Velazquez.

Villeneuve-lès-Avignon, France. Musée Municipal contains work by Quarton.

Viseu, Portugal. Grao Vasco Museum shows a collection of work from the important but little-known Viseu school, including Fernandes and Vaz.

Warsaw, Poland. National Museum displays collections of Coptic, medieval, and Polish art.

Zurich, Switzerland. Kunsthaus features expressionist, dadaist, and surrealist art collections.

LATIN AMERICA

Buenos Aires, Argentina. Museo Nacional de Bellas Artes displays nineteenth-century French and Argentine painting.

Caracas, Venezuela. Museo de Bellas Artes contains a painting by El Greco and works by Venezuelan artists.

Lima, Peru. Museo Nacional de Anthropologia y Arqueologica has an important collection of seventeenth- and eighteenth-century Cuzco art.

Mexico City, Mexico. Escuela Nacional Preparatoria contains murals by Rivera, Orozco, and Siqueiros; Museo de Arte Alvar y Carmen T. Carrillo Gil also focuses on the work of Rivera, Orozco, and Siqueiros; Museo Diego Rivera, also known as the Anahuacalli or "House of Mexico," was designed by Rivera and contains his painting and his pre-Columbian art collection; Museo Frida Kahlo displays her art and her pre-Columbian art collection in her home; Museo de Arte Moderno contains works by Magritte, Delvaux, Guerrero, Bissier, Nay, O'Gorman, Hideo, Rivera, Kahlo, Orozco, and others; Museo Nacional de Arte displays Mexican art from 1525 to the present; Museo de San Carlos contains, in its collection of European and Mexican art, Cranach, Fragonard, and Mostaert; Rufino Tamayo Museum is devoted to that artist's work and to his collection of pre-Columbian, Mexican, and other art; Secretaría de Educación has murals by Rivera.

Oaxaca, Mexico. Rufino Tamayo Museum of Pre-Hispanic Art contains the collection Tamayo amassed for over twenty years.

Puebla, Mexico. Bello Museum, or Museum of Art, houses a fine collection from the seventeeth through the nineteenth centuries.

Quito, Ecuador. Museo de San Francisco focuses on religious art.

UNITED STATES AND CANADA

Akron, Ohio. Akron Art Museum displays art from 1850 to the present, including works by Chase, Hassam, Warhol, Stella, Segal, and Pearlstein.

Ames, Iowa. Parkes Library, at Iowa State University, contains murals by Grant Wood.

Baltimore, Md. Baltimore Museum of Art features a collection of early Christian mosaics, the Cone Collection of French postimpressionists, and the Wertzberger Sculpture Garden of twentieth-century sculpture with an emphasis on the human body; Walters Art Gallery has a fine Renaissance collection.

Berkeley, Calif. University Art Museum features contemporary and Asian art.

Boston, Mass. Isabella Stuart Gardiner Museum shows works by Raphael, Fra Angelico, Martini, Dürer, Vermeer, Rembrandt, Titian, Botticelli, and Sargent; Museum of Fine Arts includes Duccio, van der Weyden, Turner, and van Gogh.

Buffalo, N.Y. Albright-Knox Art Gallery has an important collection of modern American and European art.

Cambridge, Mass. Arthur M. Sackler Museum concentrates on Asian and Islamic art; Fogg Art Museum displays Romanesque, French, and Italian art; Busch-Reisinger Museum displays German art.

Charleston, S.C. Charleston City Hall has an outstanding collection of eighteenth- and nineteenth-century American portraiture, including work by Sully, Morse, and Trumbull; Gibbes Art Gallery features American works.

Chattanooga, Tenn. Hunter Museum of Art includes works by such American artists as Cassatt, Sully, and Benton.

Chicago, Ill. Art Institute of Chicago has one of the world's finest nineteenth- and twentieth-century French collections, and shows works from the thirteenth century to the present, including El Greco, Bosch, Rembrandt, Constable, Monet, van Gogh, Seurat, Toulouse-Lautrec, and Picasso; Smart Museum of Art at the University of Chicago displays Chinese, ancient, modern, and contemporary art; Martin D'Arcy Gallery of Art shows medieval, Renaissance, and baroque art; Museum of Contemporary Art houses contemporary American art; Terra Museum of American Art contains work from 300 years of American art, including Andrew Wyeth and Homer.

Cincinnati, Ohio. Cincinnati Art Museum has collections of American, Asian, and European art, including works by Botticelli, Rubens, Monet, van Gogh, and Picasso; Taft Museum exhibits works by Rembrandt, Gainsborough, Corot, Turner, and Whistler.

Cleveland, Ohio. Cleveland Museum of Art collection extends from ancient Egyptian to modern art and includes works by El Greco, Goya, Turner, Monet, Renoir, van Gogh, Picasso, Pollock, and Segal.

Columbia, S.C. Columbia Museum of Art houses the Kress Collection of Medieval, Renaissance, and Baroque art and also has works by Dürer, Monet, Renoir, Chagall, Matisse, Johns, and Allston.

Columbus, Ohio. Columbus Museum of Art contains works from sixteenth- to twentieth-century Europe, America, and Asia.

Coral Gables, Fla. Lowe Art Museum, at the University of Miami, contains the Kress Collection of Renaissance and Baroque art, the Barton Collection of primitive art, and the Barker Memorial Collection of American art; Metropolitan Museum and Art Center features twentieth-century, Asian, and African art.

Dallas, Tex. Dallas Museum of Art has collections of pre-Columbian, early African, impressionist, and contemporary art.

Davenport, Iowa. Davenport Museum of Art features collections of Mexican-colonial, naïve Haitian, Asian, and nineteenth- and twentieth-century art.

Denver, Colo. Museum of Western Art displays works by Bierstadt, Moran, Farny, Russell, Remington, Blumenschein, and O'Keeffe.

Detroit, Mich. Detroit Institute of Art has collections of African, Indian, American, and European art, including van Eyck, Breughel, Whistler, van Gogh, and Rivera's murals of Detroit Industry.

Elkhart, Ind. Midwest Museum of American Art houses works by Rockwell, Moses, and Calder.

Eugene, Oreg. Museum of Art houses the Warner Collection of Asian art, regional and contemporary works, and a collection of African art, mostly from Ghana and Nigeria.

Farmington, Conn. Hill-Stead Museum displays works by Degas, Cassatt, Manet, Monet, and Whistler.

Fort Dodge, Iowa. Blanden Memorial Art Museum contains American, European, and Japanese painting and nineteenth- and twentieth- century graphic arts.

Fort Worth, Tex. Kimbell Art Museum features works by El Greco, Ribera, Canaletto, Tintoretto, Tiepolo, Rubens, Van Dyck, Cuyp, Goya, Monet, Murillo, and Cézanne; Modern Art Museum of Fort Worth contains works by Picasso, Pollock, Louis, Rothko, Stella, Still, and Warhol.

Fredericton, New Brunswick. Beaverbrook Art Gallery shows Canadian, eighteenth- to twentieth-century British, and European art, including Dali.

Grand Rapids, Mich. Grand Rapids Art Museum has collections of Renaissance, German expressionist, French, and American painting.

Hartford, Conn. Wadsworth Atheneum displays twentieth-century art, Renaissance, Dutch, and Victorian painting; Wadsworth, El Greco, and Bierstadt.

Houston, Tex. Menil Collection displays Byzantine, medieval, European, Oceanic, and African collections and houses the Mark Rothko Chapel with murals and sculpture by the artist; Museum of Fine Arts has, along with its European, American, African, and Asian collections, one of the world's largest collections of Remingtons.

Indianapolis, Ind. Eiteljorg Museum of American Indian and Western Art includes works by Remington, Russell, O'Keeffe, and original members of the Taos Society of Artists; Indianapolis Museum of Art houses one of the finest African art collections in the United States as well as collections of Asian, pre-Columbian, American, and European art.

Kansas City, Mo. Nelson Gallery-Atkins Museum has an outstanding Asian art collection as well as paintings by European and American masters.

La Jolla, Calif. San Diego Museum of Contemporary Art features American art from 1955 to the present.

Lawrence, Kans. Spencer Museum of Art, one of the finest university museums in the United States, features collections of Renaissance, baroque, nineteenth- and twentieth-century American, and Japanese art.

Lincoln, Nebr. Christlieb Collection of Western Art contains works by Remington and Russell; Sheldon Memorial Art Gallery and Sculpture Garden has a fine collection of twentieth-century art.

Los Angeles, Calif. Los Angeles County Museum of Art shows European, American, Native American, and Islamic art and houses the Suin'enkan artworks in the Japanese Pavilion; Museum of Contemporary Art focuses on art from the 1940s to the present.

Memphis, Tenn. Memphis Brooks Museum of Art has fine collections of European art from the thirteenth through the nineteenth centuries and twentieth-century American art.

Miami Beach, Fla. Bass Museum of Art displays art from the fourteenth to the eighteenth centuries.

Midland, Tex. Museum of the Southwest houses the Hogan Collection, works by founding members of the Taos Society of Artists.

Milwaukee, Wis. Charles Allis Art Museum features art from America, Asia, and Europe; Milwaukee Art Museum contains old masters, American, and contemporary art.

Minneapolis, Minn. Minneapolis Institute of the Arts contains collections of American, European, Asian, and Oceanic art; Walker Art Center exhibits twentieth-century art.

Montreal, Quebec. Musée d'Art Neo-Byzantin is devoted to Byzantine-influenced works by Rosette Mociornitza; Montreal Museum of Fine Arts features European and Canadian art.

Moorhead, Minn. Plains Art Museum features African, Native American, and contemporary art.

Muncie, Ind. Fine Arts Gallery has collections of Italian Renaissance, nineteenth-century American, and contemporary art.

New Haven, Conn. Yale Center for British Art displays art from the Elizabethan Age to the present; Yale University Art Gallery includes work by Homer.

New Orleans, La. New Orleans Museum of Art has collections of thirteenth- to eighteenth-century Italian and nineteenth-century French art, eighteenth-century miniatures, and African, Asian, and pre-Columbian art.

New York, N.Y. Asia Society Galleries were founded by John D. Rockefeller III to exhibit his Asian collection; Brooklyn Museum has collections of Egyptian, Oceanic, American, Latin American, and Asian art; Cloisters, a branch of the Metropolitan Museum, features medieval art and includes a Campin altarpiece; Frick Museum includes Duccio, van Eyck, Bellini, Vermeer, Rembrandt, Velazquez, Ingres, and Constable; Metropolitan Museum of Art contains works by Giotto, van Eyck, van der Weyden, Mantegna, Cranach, Breughel, El Greco, Rembrandt, Poussin, Degas, Bingham, Homer, and Seurat; Museum of Modern Art includes Matisse, Rousseau, Picasso, Chagall, Orozco, Pollock, and Beckmann; Solomon R. Guggenheim Museum displays modern and contemporary art, including Kandinski and Mondrian; Studio Museum has one of the world's finest collections of African-American, Caribbean, and African art; Whitney Museum of American Art includes Hopper, Gorky, Demuth, and Sloan.

Norfolk, Va. Chrysler Museum features painting, decorative arts, and glass, including the Chrysler Institute of Glass Collection.

Oberlin, Ohio. Allen Memorial Art Museum, at Oberlin College, has concentrations in Flemish, Dutch, late nineteenth- and twentieth-century European, Japanese, and contemporary art.

Ogdensburg, N.Y. Frederic Remington Art Museum contains one of the world's largest collections of the artist's work.

Omaha, Nebr. Joslyn Art Museum features European, American, Western, and Native American art.

Oneonta, N.Y. van Ess Gallery features Renaissance, baroque, and nineteenth- and twentieth-century art.

Ottawa, Ontario. National Gallery of Canada displays European, Canadian, Inuit, and contemporary art.

Palm Beach, Fla. Edna Hibel Museum of Art is devoted to the artist's work; Norton Gallery exhibits nineteenth- and twentieth-century French painting, modern and contemporary American art, and Chinese porcelain.

Pasadena, Calif. Norton Simon Museum includes works by Monet, Renoir, van Gogh, Degas, and Modigliani in its collection of art from the Renaissance to the twentieth century.

Philadelphia, Pa. Barnes Foundation houses the Barnes Collection, which has an important group of impressionist works; Pennsylvania Academy of Fine Arts displays 300 years of American art; Jefferson Medical College shows work by Eakins; Philadelphia Museum of Art shows American, Asian, and European art, including Duchamp, and contains reconstructions of a Japanese teahouse, a Chinese palace hall, and an Indian temple; Rodin Museum houses the largest collection of the sculptor's work outside Paris.

Pittsburgh, Pa. Carnegie Institute contains work by Rouault; Frick Art Museum features Italian Renaissance, Flemish, and eighteenth- century French art.

Portland, Oreg. Portland Art Museum contains collections of European, nineteenth- and twentieth-century American, Northwest Native American and pre-Columbian art.

Princeton, N.J. John B. Putnam, Jr., Memorial Collection, on the Princeton University campus, includes works by Picasso, Moore, Noguchi, Calder, Segal, and Lipchitz.

Providence, R.I. Museum of Art at the Rhode Island School of Design contains classical, Asian, European, modern, Latin American, and American art.

Raleigh, N.C. North Carolina Museum of Art contains works by Raphael, Botticelli, Rubens, Van Dyck, Monet, Andrew Wyeth, Benton, O'Keeffe, and Homer.

Richmond, Va. Virginia Museum of Fine Arts includes extensive holdings of paintings, sculpture, prints from major world cultures, Russian jewelry and Easter eggs by Fabergé, art deco, and art nouveau exhibits.

Rochester, N.Y. Memorial Art Gallery includes works by Monet, Cézanne, Matisse, Homer, and Cassatt.

Rockland, Maine. William A. Farnsworth Art Museum features nineteenth- and twentieth-century American art.

St. Petersburg, Fla. Museum of Fine Arts exhibits European, American, and Asian art; Salvador Dali Museum contains the world's largest collection of the artist's work.

San Antonio, Tex. San Antonio Museum of Art, in the old Lone Star Brewing Company building, features art of pre-Columbian and Latin America.

San Francisco, Calif. Ansel Adams Center is devoted to the photographer's work; Asian Art Museum features art from Japan, China, and elsewhere in Asia; California Palace of the Legion of Honor includes works by Rembrandt, Rubens, Goya, El Greco, Cézanne, Manet, Monet, Renoir, and Degas; DeYoung Memorial Museum concentrates on American art from the colonial period to the present; San Francisco Museum of Modern Art displays contemporary American art.

San Marino, Calif. Henry E. Huntington Art Gallery exhibits works by Lawrence, Reynolds, Romney, and Gainsborough among its outstanding collection of English portraiture.

Santa Barbara, Calif. Museum of Art contains collections of contemporary American and European art and photography.

Santa Fe, N.M. Museum of Fine Arts concentrates on Santa Fe and Taos artists.

Sarasota, Fla. Ringling Museum has a fine collection of baroque art.

Seattle, Wash. Charles and Emma Frye Art Museum displays late nineteenth- and twentieth-century European and American art.

Southampton, N.Y. Parrish Art Museum displays Renaissance and nineteenth- and twentieth-century American art.

Toledo, Ohio. Toledo Museum of Art features works by Rembrandt, Rubens, El Greco, and van Gogh.

Toronto, Ontario. Art Gallery of Ontario displays Canadian and fourteenth- to twentieth-century European art, including the Henry Moore Collection; George R. Gardiner Museum of Ceramic Art features pre-Columbian, fifteenth- and sixteenth-century Italian, and seventeenth-century English porcelains; McMichael Canadian Art Gallery shows works by the Group of Seven, Thompson, Carr, Milne, and Gagnon; Royal Ontario Museum has Asian and classical art collections.

Trinidad, Colo. A. R. Mitchell Memorial Museum of Western Art displays works by Mitchell, Dunn, von Schmidt, and others.

Tucson, Ariz. Museum of Art at the University of Arizona contains the Kress Collection of Renaissance art, the Pfeiffer Collection of twentieth-century painting, and the Gallagher Collection of modern art; Tucson Museum of Art displays pre-Columbian, Spanish-colonial, and Western art.

Victoria, British Columbia. Art Gallery of Greater Victoria contains a fine collection of Japanese as well as Canadian and European art.

Washington, D.C. Arthur M. Sackler Gallery of Smithsonian Institution has Chinese, ancient Near Eastern, and South Asian collections; Corcoran Gallery of Art has an extensive American art collection and the Clark Collection of European art; Dumbarton Oaks displays pre-Columbian, early Christian, and Byzantine art; Hirshhorn Museum and Sculpture Garden features modern American and European art, including works by Calder, De Kooning, Eakins, Jetlovà, Kiefer, Moore, Pollock, Puryear, Rodin, and Rothko; National Gallery of Art, chartered by Congress in 1937 at the urging of Andrew W. Mellon, has one of the world's finest collections of European and American art, including Giotto, van Eyck, Grünewald, Memlinc, Botticelli, van der Weyden, da Vinci, Rembrandt, Raphael, Vermeer, Hals, Giorgione, El Greco, Fragonard, Manet, Monet, Cassatt, Picasso, Bellows, and Pollock; National Museum of African Art at the Smithsonian focuses on sub-Saharan art, especially Royal Benin art; National Museum of Women in the Arts includes in its collection work by Fontana and Claudel; National Portrait Gallery includes the Hall of Presidents, Brady's Civil War photographs, and work by Degas; Phillips Collection includes Renoir, Cézanne, van Gogh, Matisse, Sloan, and Marin.

Williamsburg, Va. Abby Aldrich Rockefeller Folk Art Center has a fine collection of early American work; DeWitt Wallace Decorative Arts Center features decorative arts of the seventeenth, eighteenth, and early nineteenth centuries.

Williamstown, Mass. Sterling and Francine Clark Art Institute contains works by della Francesca, Dürer, Fragonard, Gainsborough, Corot, Stuart, Manet, Degas, Monet, Goya, Homer, Sargent, Renoir, and Picasso.

Wilmington, Del. Delaware Art Museum has a collection of English Pre-Raphaelite painting and American work by the Wyeths, Eakins, Hooper,

Homer, Pyle, and Sloan; Winterthur Museum displays a large collection of early American decorative art.

Winnipeg, Manitoba. Winnipeg Art Gallery houses the largest collection of Inuit art in North America.

Worcester, Mass. Worcester Art Museum includes in its diverse collections work by El Greco, Massys, Monet, and Homer.

SOURCES

American Automobile Association Tourbooks. Heathrow, Fla: American Automobile Association, 1991.

Bisignani, J. D. *Japan Handbook*. Victoria, Australia: Bookwise, 1983.

Box, Ben, ed. 1991 *South America Handbook*. New York: Prentice-Hall, 1990.

China Travel and Tourism Press, ed. *Official Guidebook of China*. New York: Lee Publishers, 1982.

Christensen, Erwin O. *A Guide to Art Museums in the United States*. New York: Dodd, Mead and Co., 1968.

Fodor's 91: Eastern Europe. New York: Fodor's Travel Publications, 1991.

Hale, Sheila. *The American Express Pocket Guide to Florence and Tuscany*. New York: Prentice-Hall, 1983.

Harvard Student Agencies, Inc. 1986 *Let's Go: The Budget Guide to Europe*. New York: St. Martin's Press, 1986.

———. 1981–82 *Let's Go: The Budget Guide to Greece, Israel, and Egypt*. New York: E. P. Dutton, 1981.

IDA—International Dictionary of Arts. 21st ed. 2 vols. Munich: K. G. Saur, 1993.

Jackson, Virginia, *et al.*, eds. *Art Museums of the World*. New York: Greenwood Press, 1987.

Jacobs, Michael, and Paul Stirton. *The Knopf Traveler's Guides to Art: Britain and Ireland*. New York: Alfred A. Knopf, 1984.

———. *The Knopf Traveler's Guides to Art: France*. New York: Alfred A. Knopf, 1984.

Janson, H. W. *History of Art: A Survey of the Major Visual Arts from the Dawn of History to the Present Day*. 2nd ed. Englewood Cliffs, N.J.: Prentice-Hall, 1977.

Jones, P. H. M., ed. *Golden Guide to South and East Asia*. Hong Kong: Far East Economic Review, 1969.

Kopper, Philip. *America's National Gallery of Art: A Gift to the Nation*. New York: Harry N. Abrams, 1991.

Michelin Green Guides to Netherlands, Portugal, Spain, and Rome. London: Michelin Tyre Public Limited Co., various dates.

Mobil Travel Guides to the United States, 1989. 7 vols. New York: Prentice-Hall, 1989.

Perkins, Dorothy. *Encyclopedia of Japan*. New York: Facts on File, 1991.

Peterson, Vicki. *Australia*. London: Cassell, 1980.

Richardson, John, and Eric Zafran, eds. *Master Paintings from the Hermitage and the State Russian Museum: Leningrad*. New York: M. Knoedler, 1975.

Wheeler, Tony. *South-East Asia on a Shoestring*. Berkeley, Calif.: Lonely Planet, 1989.

Wiencek, Henry. *The Smithsonian Guide to Historic America: Virginia and the Capital Region*. New York: Stewart, Tabori and Chang, 1989.

—Ian Crump; L.D.R.

21

ART SCHOOLS, MOVEMENTS,
STYLES, AND PERIODS:
A GLOSSARY

. . . . .

ONE MAN'S PIET, IT HAS BEEN SAID, IS ANOTHER MAN'S POUSSIN; AND BEYOND doubt the styles and modes of painting have undergone rapid and constant change during the past two centuries. There is a cartoon by James Thurber showing a bearded man standing on a chair and studying a painting on the wall of an art gallery, while nearby another man is explaining, "He knows all about art, but he doesn't know what he likes."

Moveover, art critics being the folk that they are, there has been no shortage of names and labels applied to such alterations and allegiances. Pity the poor art lover who can't distinguish between Régence and Regency; it would be like a poetry lover mistaking Pope for Poe.

The glossary that follows is an effort to identify what is customarily meant by some of the more commonly used terms applied to schools, movements, phases, vogues, styles, and periods over the long history of visual and tactile art.

Abstract expressionism. American style of the 1940s and 1950s fusing automatism and ideas of "shallow space" with a rebellion against traditional ideas of style and technique; its primary exponents were Jackson Pollock, Mark Rothko, and Arshile Gorky.

Abstract illusionism. Tendency in American abstract painting technique in which, by devices such as shading, forms and brushstrokes are made to seem separate from the picture plane, as if floating above it.

Abstract image painting. Version of abstract expressionism that achieves its effect through use of color and form, not brushwork or other markings.

Abstraction-Création. Name adopted by group of abstract artists of various styles who assembled in Paris in the 1930s under the leadership of Auguste Herbin and Georges Vantongerloo.

Abstraction lyrique. European equivalent of American abstract expressionism, of which Georges Mathieu has been the primary exponent; also known as *tachisme* or *art informel*.

Achaean. Art created by the Achaeans from 2000 to 1100 B.C.E. in what is now southern and eastern Greece.

Achaemenian. Art produced by the Achaemenians from 550 to 330 B.C.E. in Persia and Near East.

Ada school. Group of Carolingian ivory carvers and manuscript illuminators under patronage of Ada, purportedly Charlemagne's sister.

Aegean. Art produced by the Cycladic, Minoan, Mycenean, and other cultures situated near Aegean Sea from the later Stone Age through the Bronze Age to 1400 B.C.E.

Aeropittura. Late development of Italian futurism in which artists sought to represent the sensations caused by such modern machines as the airplane.

Aestheticism. Theory, first formulated by Immanuel Kant in the eighteenth century, holding that the philosophy of art is distinct from all other forms of philosophy, and that art must be judged through aesthetic criteria.

Aesthetic movement. British artistic movement of latter part of the nineteenth century; an outgrowth of the Pre-Raphaelite Brotherhood, it advocated the doctrine of art as decorative; its foremost practitioners were Albert Moore, James McNeill Whistler, and Edward Burne-Jones.

Affichisme. Term used by Raymond Hains and Jacques de la Villegle in the 1950s to describe collages made from pieces of ripped posters.

Allied Artists Association. Name adopted by group of British painters who exhibited together between 1908 and 1911.

Amarma art. Style identified with the reign of the Egyptian pharaoh Akhenaten; it is more naturalistic than art from earlier or later periods of ancient Egyptian culture.

American abstract artists. Group of artists who gathered in 1936 to promote abstract art in New York City; members included Josef Alberts, Balcomb Greene, and Willem de Kooning.

American scene painting. Style of American figurative painting, dating to the 1920s and 1930s, naturalistically portraying midwestern small-town life; its primary exponents were Grant Wood, Thomas Hart Benton, and Charles Burchfield.

Angevin Gothic. Style of Gothic architecture characterized by dropped arches; it is associated with the Plantagenet period in Aquitaine (1154–1453).

Animal style. Style of zoomorphic decoration distinctive to nomadic tribes of eastern Europe and central Asia.

Antipodeans. Association of Australian figurative artists, founded in 1959.

Antwerp mannerists. Group of painters active in Antwerp region at beginning of sixteenth century.

Archaic. Ancient Greek art produced between 650 and 480 B.C.E.; statues in this style are characterized by their set smiles.

Armory Show. Watershed exhibition of modern art held at 69th Regiment Armory in New York City in late winter of 1913; it introduced the American public to impressionism and postimpressionism.

Art autre, un. Term, coined by critic Michel Tapié, for "alienated," non-geometrical art created by such postwar artists as Wols, Jean Dubuffet, Georges Mathieu, and Jean Fautrier; it is synonymous with art informel and tachisme.

Art brut. Term coined by Jean Dubuffet to describe seemingly "raw" art produced by people outside the art world, such as children, prisoners, and mental patients.

Art deco. Geometrical and elegant style of decorative art that succeeded art nouveau and was popular in the 1920s and 1930s.

Arte povera. Term coined by critic Germano Celant in 1970 to describe artworks created from worthless materials.

Art nouveau. Sinuously asymmetrical and stylized form of decorative art prevalent in Europe at turn of the twentieth century.

Arts and crafts movement. British movement founded in 1888 emphasizing craftsmanship in industry; its most important adherents were John Ruskin, A. W. N. Pugin, and William Morris.

Ashcan school. Group of American artists who produced naturalistic urban paintings during the years before World War I; its primary members were Robert Henri, John Sloan, George Luks, and George Bellows.

Auricular. Intricate northern European decorative style that preceded baroque; also known as *lobate*.

Avignon school. School of painters active in the Avignon region from arrival of papal court in 1309 to about 1460.

Backsteingotik. Term for Gothic style of architecture executed in brick that culminated in north Germany in the fourteenth century.

Barbizon school. French landscape painters centered in town of Barbizon during the late 1840s, including Jean-Baptiste-Camille Corot, Théodore Rousseau, and Jean-François Millet.

Baroque. Predominant style of western European art from about 1550 to the mid-eighteenth century; this overtly emotional style, making much use of curves, is characterized by its revolt against the intellectuality of the mannerism that was allied with the late Renaissance.

Bauhaus. German architecture and design school founded by Walter Gropius in Weimar in 1919; it influenced, and was much influenced by, industrial technology.

Beaux-arts. Artistic and architectural style furthered by the French Academy in the nineteenth century.

Biedermeier. Central European decorative style, popular from 1815 to 1860, emphasizing middle-class attitudes.

Black-figured. Dominant style in Greek vase painting before the sixth century B.C.E., originating in Corinth.

Blaue Reiter, Der, or the Blue Rider. Group of expressionist artists centered in Munich in 1911; its foremost members were Wassily Kandinsky, Paul Klee, August Macke, and Franz Marc.

Blaue Vier, or Blue Four. Four artists—Paul Klee, Wassily Kandinsky, Lyonel Feininger, and Alexei von Jawlensky—who exhibited together in Germany, the United States, and Mexico between 1924 and 1934.

Bloomsbury group. Loose association of British writers, artists, and critics who met frequently during the 1920s and 1930s; painters in the group included Roger Fry, Vanessa Bell, and Duncan Grant.

Blue Rose group. Group of Russian artists, active at the turn of the century, who were influenced by the Fauvists and were concerned with primitivist style; its primary representatives were Mikhail Larionov and Natalia Goncharova.

Bohemian school. Name for group of artists active in Prague region from the mid-fourteenth century to the beginning of the fifteenth century.

Bolognese classicism. Classically influenced art emphasizing forms of nature and robust drawing, centered in Bologna in the early seventeenth century.

Brücke, Die, or the Bridge. Name adopted by group of expressionist artists who gathered in Dresden in 1905–1906; including Ernst Kirchner, Karl Schmidt-Rottluff, Erich Heckel, Max Pechstein, Fritz Bleyl, Emil Nolde, and Otto Mueller.

Brutalism. Allison Smithson's term for stark, functional architectural approach of Le Corbusier and British contemporaries.

Byzantine art. Stylized Christian art produced by artists living in eastern Roman Empire (330–1453), centered in Byzantium (now Constantinople).

Camden Town group. Group of London-based postimpressionist artists under leadership of W. R. Sickert whose work frequently featured realistic working-class scenes.

Canadian group. Group of painters who worked from 1933 to 1969 to foster Canadian art.

Canton school. Style of art produced for Europeans by Chinese artists in the late eighteenth and early nineteenth centuries.

Caravaggisti. Loosely affiliated followers of Caravaggio working in seventeenth-century Rome.

Carolingian Renaissance. Western European revival in arts and learning fostered by Charlemagne and his successors in the late eighth and ninth centuries.

Celtic art. Art of the Celtic peoples of western Europe between about 450 B.C.E and 700 C.E.; it is characterized by geometric and spiral designs and stylized animals.

Cercle et Carré. Group of French artists founded by Michel Seuphor and Joaquin Torres-Garcia in 1929; symbolic and religious concepts were joined with geometric abstraction.

Chicago school. Group of architects, among them Louis Sullivan, Daniel Burnham, and William Le Baron Jenney, in Chicago between the 1870s and 1920s, who influenced development of the skyscraper.

Chinoiserie. Eighteenth-century decorative style employing motifs drawn from Chinese art.

Chippendale. Ornamented British furniture with strong French influence; the name derives from the British furniture maker Thomas Chippendale.

Churrigueresque. Highly wrought baroque style popular in Spain and Latin America during the eighteenth century.

Classicism. Art of ancient Greece and Rome; more generally, art that is emotionally balanced, rational, and in opposition to romanticism. Renaissance classicism was a self-conscious effort to revive the art of antiquity. The French Academy of the seventeenth and eighteenth centuries strongly influenced classical ideals.

COBRA. Group of expressionist-influenced Scandinavian and Dutch painters who gathered in Paris in 1948. Its primary members were Asger Jorn, Karel Appel, Corneille, Pierre Alechinsky, and Constant.

Cologne school. German painters of various styles who worked in and around Cologne from the fourteenth to sixteenth centuries.

Conceptual art. Style, prevalent since the 1960s, in which the basic idea, or concept, of a work is privileged above its execution; among exponents of this style are Sol LeWitt, Bruce Nauman, and Joseph Kosuth.

Concrete. Style of modern art that repudiates figurative reference, representing abstract ideas in tangible, geometrical forms. The movement, though short-lived, influenced such artists as Wassily Kandinsky and Ben Nicholson.

Constructivism. Style of abstract art, prevalent in Russia in the late 1910s and early 1920s that favored art forms for industrialized society.

Consulat. Style of French art inspired by Napoleon's expedition to Egypt from 1798 to 1799.

Coptic. Classically influenced art produced by the Copts (Egyptian Christians) from the third to eighth centuries.

Corrente. Antifascist association of Italian artists existing briefly during 1938 and 1939.

Cubism. Abstract style of modern art, developed by Pablo Picasso and Georges Braque between 1907 and 1914, which rejected the notion that art should imitate reality, and depicted three-dimensional objects two-dimensionally; other cubists were Juan Gris, Fernand Léger, and Robert Delaunay.

Cycladic. Art produced in Cyclades islands of Aegean Sea between 2500 and 1400 B.C.E.; centers included Naxos and Delos.

Dada or dadaism. Antiart movement that began in Zurich during World War I and spread to Paris and the U.S.; its primary members were Tristan Tzara, Hans Arp, Hugo Ball, and Marcel Duchamp.

Danube school. Name for loose grouping of artists in Germanic states along the Danube River in the early sixteenth century who pioneered in depiction of landscape.

Decadent movement. European art movement of end of the nineteenth century which was related to art nouveau, but was prone to offend bourgeois taste and morality.

De Stijl. Group of Dutch abstract artists, including Piet Mondrian and Theo van Doesburg, who painted between 1912 and 1928.

Deutscher Werkbund, or **German Association of Craftsmen.** Group of manufacturers, architects, and businessmen who operated in Germany beginning in 1907 and influenced the bauhaus.

Directoire. Neoclassical decorative art style popular in France at end of the eighteenth century.

Donkey's Tail. Name for 1912 exhibition by a group of Russian artists who rejected Western influences and advocated traditional Russian forms; its chief members were Mikhail Larionov, Natalia Goncharova, and Kasimir Malevich.

Earth art. Large outdoor sculptures composed of such natural materials as stones, dirt, or snow; a well-known example is Robert Smithson's *Spiral Jetty* (1970).

Ecological art. Movement, prevalent since the 1960s, that seeks to make its viewers enter and participate in its three-dimensional artworks; also known as *environmental art.*

Eight, the. American artists exhibiting in 1908 in opposition to then-current academic standards; they were Maurice Prendergast, Ernest Lawson, Robert Henri, George Luks, William Glackens, John Sloan, Arthur Davies, and Everett Shinn.

Elementarism. Modified form of neoplasticism that eased the strict rigidity advocated by the De Stijl group.

Elizabethan art. Art produced in England during reign of Elizabeth I (1551–1603).

Empire. Neoclassical decorative style popular in France during reign of Napolean I.

Entartete Kunst. Nazi exhibition, held in Munich in 1937, of so-called decadent art.

Etruscan. Art produced by the Etrurians, in what is now Tuscany, between the seventh and third centuries B.C.E.

Euston Road school. London art school, formed in 1937, that rejected modernist theories and favored objective depiction; its foremost representatives were William Coldstream, Victor Pasmore, Claude Rogers, Lawrence Gowing, and Rodrigo Moynihan.

Expressionism. Twentieth-century style of art which held, in opposition to impressionism, that the artist expressed subjective reactions to reality; its primary exponents were Oskar Kokoschka, Georges Rouault, James Ensor, Marc Chagall, and Emil Nolde.

Faiyum. Naturalistic portraits painted on Roman mummies in Egyptian cemeteries.

Fantastic realism. Group of post–1945 Austrian artists who fused elements of meticulous realism and fairy-tale fantasy.

Fauves, les. Term applied to a group of early twentieth-century French artists who used vivid, nonrealistic colors; foremost in the group were Henri Matisse, André Derain, Albert Marquet, and Maurice de Vlaminck.

Federal. Neoclassical style popular in United States between 1789 and the Jacksonian era.

Federal Art Project (F.A.P.). New Deal program of the 1930s that employed artists to produce art for public buildings and places.

Fin de siècle. The various artistic movements, such as art nouveau, in vogue at the end of the nineteenth century.

Flamboyant style. Final elaborate development of French Gothic architecture, characterized by double curves in tracery.

Fluxus. Name assumed in 1962 by international association of avant-garde artists, including Joseph Beuys, who revived dadaism.

Fontainebleau school. International group of artists working under patronage of François I at Palace of Fontainebleau in the mid-sixteenth century.

Funk. Type of art, often self-consciously distasteful and/or pornographic, originating in California during the 1950s and 1960s; its foremost exponent is Edward Kienholz.

Futurism. Italian art movement, founded in 1909, glorifying modern technology; its primary exponents were F. T. Marinetti, Umberto Boccioni, Carlo Carrà, Luigi Russolo, and Giacomo Balla.

Geometric art. Geometrically ornamented preclassical Greek art, especially pottery, produced in ninth to eighth centuries B.C.E.

Georgian. English style of architecture, popular during reigns of George I to George IV (1714–1830), combining aspects of rococo and neoclassicism; much employed in the United States in the late 1700s.

Glasgow school. Two different Scottish art movements dating from the turn of twentieth century; the first, the "Glasgow Boys," which included William MacGregor, John Lavery, and David Cameron, advocated open-air painting;

the second, founded by the architect Charles Rennie Mackintosh, developed a Scottish art nouveau.

Gothic. Term for art, especially architecture, produced in Europe between Romanesque and Renaissance periods (1150s to fifteenth century); architecturally it was a monumental and elaborately yet often delicately ornamented style; in painting, it was an expressively naturalistic style that developed the use of the third dimension.

Gothic revival. Self-conscious revival of Gothic architecture occurring in Britain and the United States from the mid-eighteenth century onward; often used for churches and university buildings.

Grand Manner. History painting of elevated subjects and style promulgated by Sir Joshua Reynolds.

Greek Revival. Revival of classical Greek architecture flourishing in Britain and the United States from the 1760s to the 1840s.

Groupe de Recherche d'Art Visuel (GRAV). Scientifically oriented kinetic art movement originating in Paris in 1958; its primary exponents were François Morellet, Yvaral, Joël Stein, Julio Le Parc, and Francisco Sobrino.

Group of Seven. Group of expressionist-influenced Canadian landscape painters who exhibited together between 1920 and 1931. They included Franklin Carmichael, Lawren Harris, A. Y. Jackson, Frank Johnston, Arthur Lisner, J. E. H. Macdonald, and Frederick Varley.

Gutai group. Association of Japanese artists, founded by Jiro Yoshihura in 1954, who engaged in dadaesque happenings and produced abstract expressionist paintings.

Hague school. Dutch realists of the second half of the nineteenth century who focused on landscape and peasant subjects; they included Anton Mauve, Johannes Bosboom, the Maris brothers, and Joseph Israels.

Helladic. Art dating from Bronze Age in Greece (2900–1100 B.C.E.).

Hellenic. Art dating from Iron Age to end of classical period in Greece (1100–323 B.C.E.).

Hellenistic. Art created during the reigns of successors to Alexander the Great (323–100 B.C.E.).

High Renaissance. Pinnacle of Renaissance art (1495–1520), exemplified in work of Raphael, Leonardo da Vinci, and Michelangelo.

Hispano-Moresque. Islamic art and architecture of Spain, *ca.* 1100–1500 C.E.

Hudson River school. Group of American landscape painters who worked between 1820 and 1870; its most important representatives were Thomas Cole, Thomas Doughty, Asher B. Durard, and Frederick Church.

Iconoclast. Type of Byzantine art produced between 710 and 843, when the representation of images was forbidden.

Impressionism. Late nineteenth-century French art movement using a variety of radical brush techniques to represent the momentary impression of light and color; its foremost practitioners included Claude Monet, Auguste Renoir, Camille Pissarro, Edward Degas, Mary Cassatt, and Berthe Morisot.

Independent Group. Informal group of British pop artists who gathered at the Institute of Contemporary Arts in London beginning in 1952.

Individualists. Chinese artists who rejected the standards of the official schools in the seventeenth century.

International Gothic. Movement toward greater elegance and naturalism in late Gothic painting and sculpture; it is exemplified in the work of Pisanello, Gentile da Fabriano, Bernardo Martorell, André Beauneveu, the Limbourg brothers, and Giovanni de Paolo.

International style. Major trend of European avant-garde architecture of the 1920s and 1930s favoring space over mass.

Jack of Diamonds. Group of Russian avant-garde artists, founded in 1910, who preceded the Donkey's Tail and Russian futurist groups.

Jacobean. Mannerist-influenced architectural style popular in England during reign of James I (1603–25).

Japonisme. Term for Japanese impact on European art in the nineteenth century, particularly impressionism and postimpressionism.

Jazz modern. Cubist-influenced decorative style of the 1920s and 1930s.

Jugendstil. Art nouveau, German and Austrian style.

Junk art. Term for art that Robert Rauschenberg made from ordinary trash in the 1950s; related to arte povera.

Kalighat painting. Nineteenth- and early twentieth-century school of Indian watercolorists associated with the cult of the goddess Kali.

Kangra. Delicate, refined school of Indian painting under patronage of Rajah Sansar Chand (1775–1823).

Kano. Hereditary school of Japanese painters from the fourteenth to nineteenth centuries.

Kitchen sink school. Name for group of British social realist artists in the 1950s.

Korin school. Japanese art movement, active between the sixteenth and eighteenth centuries, named after Ogata Korin (1658–1716).

Little Masters. German printmakers who specialized in small-sized works during the sixteenth century.

Louis XIV. Lavish, formal decorative style, marked by splendor of effect, popular in France during reign of Louis XIV (1643–1715).

Louis XV. French decorative rococo style popular during reign of Louis XV (1715–74).

Louis XVI. Austere neoclassical style popular in France during reign of Louis XVI (1774–92).

Louis Philippe. Term for eclecticism of artistic styles—including empire, troubadour, and rococo—popular in France during early and mid-nineteenth century.

Luminism. John Baur's term describing work of mid-nineteenth century American landscape painters fascinated with effects of light.

Lyrical abstraction. Lush, colorful variety of late abstract expressionism; its primary exponents are Jack Tworkov and Paul Jenkins.

Macchiaioli. Group of nineteenth-century Florentine painters who emphasized painterly freshness through use of patches of color; its primary members were Giovanni Fattori and Telemaco Signorini.

Mannerism. Style of art that succeeded High Renaissance (1515–1610); it exhibited a preference for stylistic devices, distorted forms, and discordant colors.

Marine painting. Art portraying ships and the sea; developed first in low countries in the late 1500s.

Mestizo. Term used to describe Andean ornamentation that fused Christian and Native American motifs; also known as *provincial highlands style.*

Migration period art. Art produced by Germanic tribes who invaded the Roman Empire between 370 and 800 C.E.

Minimalist. Term for art, prevalent since the 1960s, that has reacted to abstract expressionism by disregarding all expressiveness or illusion.

Minoan. Art produced on Crete during Bronze Age (2500–1100 B.C.E.).

Mir Iskusstva. Title of periodical published in St. Petersburg by Serge Diaghilev from 1898 to 1905; its adherents blended symbolism and Russian tradition.

Modernism. The avant-garde movements of the twentieth century, viewed as a whole.

Mogul. Style of art produced in Moslem India from the sixteenth to nineteenth centuries.

Mosan school. Name for group of northern French and Flemish manuscript illuminators and metalworkers active from the eleventh to thirteenth centuries.

Mound Builder. Term for artifacts produced by flourishing Native American culture in Ohio and Mississippi river basins between the third and seventeenth centuries.

Mozarabic. Style of art produced in Spain by Christians living under Moorish rule.

Mudéjar. Style of Spanish art exhibiting Moorish influences, produced by Moors and Christians.

Mycenean. Style of art produced by mainland Greek culture flourishing in the second millenium B.C.E.

Nabis. Group of French postimpressionist artists of the 1890s; among them were Pierre Bonnard, Edouard Vuillard, Maurice Denis, Paul Sérusier, and Aristide Maillol.

Nanga. School of gentleman-scholar Japanese painters in the seventeenth and eighteenth centuries.

Naturalism. Late nineteenth-century style of art emphasizing representation of everyday life from a scientific perspective, especially its more sordid aspects.

Nazarenes. Group of German artists, formed in Vienna and moving to Rome in the early nineteenth century, influenced by High Renaissance.

Neo-Attic. Late Hellenistic style of ornamentation, imitating archaic and classical Greek motifs, that emphasizes composition.

Neoclassicism. Decorative and architectural style, popular in the late eighteenth century, that reacted against rococo by reviving ancient Greek and Roman styles.

Neodadaism. Term used to describe dada-influenced art produced by Robert Rauschenberg, Jasper Johns, and others in the 1950s.

Neoexpressionism. International art movement that revived German expressionism in the 1970s; its foremost practitioners were Georg Baselitz, Rainer Fetting, Anselm Kiefer, Julian Schnabel, and Sandro Chia.

Neoimpressionism. Scientifically grounded development of impressionism, reacting against formlessness and subjectivity; its primary exponents were Georges Seurat, Paul Signac, and Camille Pissarro.

Neoplasticism. Austere style of abstract art, advocated by the De Stijl group, that used only rectangles, primary colors, and right angles.

Neoromanticism. Style of art, originating in Paris in the 1920s, exhibiting theatrical, lyrical, and escapist tendencies.

Neue Sachlichkeit, or **New Objectivity.** German art in the 1920s that reacted against expressionism and focused on depicting the face of evil; its primary exponents were George Grosz and Otto Dix.

New brutalism. Radically functionalist style of architecture prevalent in the United Kingdom during the 1950s.

New realism. Movement of American artists who rejected abstract expressionism in 1950s and 1960s and created collages using images from consumer culture and found objects; it is related to the French nouveau réalisme.

New York school. Abstract expressionists working in New York City in the 1940s and 1950s; some later moved toward pop art.

Norman. Romanesque style prevalent in Normandy and then England after Norman conquest.

Norwich school. Group of English painters centered on John Crone (1768–1821) who exhibited East Anglian landscapes in the early years of the nineteenth century.

Nouveau réalisme, or **new realism.** Movement of French artists who, in the 1960s, rejected abstraction and made assemblages.

Novecento Italiano. Group of Italian figurative artists, politically oriented, many of whom became identified with fascism.

November Group. Association of Finnish expressionist painters, founded in 1917.

Novembergruppe, or **November Group.** Group of socialist-linked German artists, active between 1918 and 1929, who combined expressionism with dadaism.

Omega Workshops. Workshops organized by Roger Fry in England in 1913 to employ young painters in decorative arts.

Op art. Style of abstract art, popular in the 1960s, concerned with exploiting optical effects.

Orphism. Guillaume Apollinaire's term for a "pure" abstract art influenced by cubism; also known as *Orphic cubism.*

Ottonian. Style of art named for Ottonian German emperors (919–1024).

Painters Eleven. Group of Canadian nonobjective painters centered in Toronto from 1953 to 1960.

Palladianism. Neoclassical architectural style that followed the work of the late Renaissance Venetian architect Andrea Palladio (1508–1580).

Paris school. General term for fauvist, cubist, surrealist, and other avant-garde artists working in Paris during first part of the twentieth century.

Patroon painters. Group of six or so anonymous artists who worked for Dutch settlers or patroons in New Amsterdam (late New York) between 1715 and 1730.

Pattern painting. Figurative school of decorative painters in New York City in the 1870s.

Peintres de la réalité, or **painters of reality.** Term coined to describe group of seventeenth-century French painters, among them George de La Tour, the Le Nain brothers, and Sebastien Stoskopff, who drew their subject matter from the everyday world.

Performance art. Art form combining aspects of stage, music, and visual art to program special but controlled events.

Pergamene. Strongly realistic, virtuoso school of Hellenistic sculpture associated with the kingdom of Pergamum in Asia Minor during the third and second centuries B.C.E.

Perpendicular style. Fifteenth century English Gothic architecture, characterized by rectilinear lines and soaring transoms.

Picturesque, the. Eighteenth century term for arrangement of picture-like scenic elements such as gardens, paintings, and sculptures.

Pittura metafisica. Italian art movement (1917–21) that emphasized mystery and incongruity beneath surface reality; its primary exponents were Giorgio de Chirico and Carlo Carra.

Plateresque. Spanish early Renaissance architectural style of the sixteenth century, characterized by intricate, profuse ornamentation.

Pont-Aven group. Postimpressionist painters who worked in Pont-Aven, Brittany, during the 1880s and 1890s, influenced by Paul Gauguin's non-naturalistic use of colors; the group included Paul Sérusier and Jan Verkade.

Pop art. Art style of the 1950s and 1960s, borrowing familiar images from consumer culture; its primary exponents were Andy Warhol, Roy Lichtenstein, Jim Dine, and Claes Oldenburg.

Postimpressionism. Term used loosely for French painters after the 1880s, especially Paul Cézanne, Paul Gauguin, Vincent van Gogh, Georges Seurat, and Henri Toulouse-Lautrec, who reacted against impressionism.

Postmodernism. Style of architecture, prevalent since the 1970s, seeking to fuse modernism and classicism.

Post-painterly abstraction. Term used to describe works of those artists who rejected abstract expressionism but did not return to figural painting, such as Morris Louis, Ellsworth Kelly, Jules Olitski, Frank Stella, Al Held, and Kenneth Noland.

Poussinism. Doctrine, espoused by late-seventeenth-century followers of Nicolas Poussin, emphasizing draftsmanship over color.

Precisionist painters. Style of twentieth-century American painting featuring industrial and technological scenes with sharp, formal realism so that the works to seem quasi-cubist or abstract; the foremost practitioners were Charles Demuth, Georgia O'Keeffe, Preston Dickinson, and Charles Sheeler.

Pre-Columbian. Art of the Americas before arrival of the Europeans in 1492.

Pre-Raphaelite Brotherhood. Mid-nineteenth-century English artists who imitated the style of early Italian Renaissance painting; important members and followers included Holman Hunt, Dante Gabriel Rossetti, John Millais, William Morris, Edward Burne-Jones, and Ford Madox Brown.

Primitivism. Art that imitates primitive techniques of representation and ornamentation; naive art.

Proto-Renaissance. Term used for any of several short-lived classical revivals that occurred between the twelfth and fourteenth centuries.

Pueblo art. Art produced by Hopi and Zuni tribes from the seventh century to the present.

Purism. Avant-garde movement, offshoot of cubism, that advocated clarity and objectivity and criticized the tendency toward decorative effects. Its primary exponents were Amédée Ozenfant and Le Corbusier, who published a manifesto, *After Cubism* (1918), urging that art accept the milieu of the machine age.

Queen Anne. Architectural and decorative style, popular in England from 1702 to 1714, combining elements of baroque and classical grace.

Rayism. Futurist-influenced abstract movement, founded by Mikhail Larionov and Natalia Goncharova in Russia in 1912, emphasizing manipulation of supposedly invisible beams of color that objects emitted; also known as *rayonism.*

Realism. Style of nineteenth-century art that rebelled against romantic idealism and turned to scenes from the everyday world; its principal practitioner was Gustave Courbet.

Red-figured. Technique of Greek vase painting in the sixth century B.C.E. using the red color of the pot for figures.

Régence. Decorative style, popular in France during the Regency (1715–33), combining aspects of baroque and rococo.

Regency. Neoclassical style popular in England during the Regency of George IV (1811–20).

Regionalism. American art movement of the Depression era and the 1940s that turned away from most European styles in favor of representational subject matter, typically of the rural and small-town Midwest; its primary exponents were Thomas Hart Benton, Grant Wood, Andrew Wyeth, Edward Hopper, and John Curry; it is also known as American Gothic.

Renaissance. European art of the fourteenth to sixteenth centuries, marked by revival of classical designs and concern for humanistic values.

Rococo. Delicate and playful style of European art prevalent in the eighteenth century; it began in France as a reaction against baroque grandeur and was characterized by asymmetry and graceful lightness, in which somber and heavy colors and forms were replaced by light shades and undulating lines.

Romanesque. Style of architecture and art flourishing throughout Europe from the ninth to twelfth centuries; it is strongly stylized, and is characterized by its use of sturdy walls and pillars and its revival of vaulted ceilings and sculpture.

Romanticism. European and American art movement, prevalent from the 1780s to 1830s, that reacted against neoclassical formalism and championed the power of the individual imagination; in painting its primary exponents were J. M. W. Turner, Caspar Friedrich, Eugene Delacroix, and Théodore Géricault. Use of landscapes and religious themes flourished. In architecture it produced a self-conscious return to medieval forms, especially in church design.

Romanists. Northern European artists of the sixteenth century.

Rosicrucians. Loose association of European religious artists, using the cross and rose for symbols, who exhibited in Paris in the 1890s.

Rubénisme. Doctrine, espoused by Peter Paul Rubens' followers, emphasizing the primacy of color as against design.

St. Ives painters. British abstract expressionist painters working in Cornwall in the 1940s, centered on Barbara Hepworth and Ben Nicholson.

Salon, the. Annual official exhibition of the Académie Française held in the Louvre from 1667 to 1881; it became increasingly academic in selection.

Salon d'Automne. Annual exhibition in Paris that became notorious when Matisse, Derain, and Vlaminck were attacked as "wild beasts" or fauves.

Salon des Indépendants. Annual exhibition, held in Paris from 1884 until 1914, of Seurat and others who rejected the official salon.

Salon des Refusés. Paris exhibition that showed Edouard Manet, Paul Cézanne, Camille Pissarro, James McNeill Whistler, and others who had been rejected by the official salon. The huge crowds that attended came mainly to ridicule the work displayed, but ultimately the result was to undermine the Académie's dominance.

Schildersbent, or **Band of Painters.** Name for group of Dutch and Flemish painters working in Rome in the seventeenth century; founded in 1623, it was outlawed by the pope in 1720 after its members engaged in drunken brawls.

Section d'Or. Group of French cubists who first exhibited together—without Pablo Picasso and Georges Braque—from 1912 to 1914; they included Jean Metzinges, Fernand Leger, Roger de La Fresnaye, Francis Picabia, and Juan Gris.

Severe style. Style in Greek sculpture that succeeded the archaic (480–450 B.C.E.) and led into the classical.

Sezession, or **Secession.** Name adopted by German and Austrian artists in the 1890s who rejected current academic conventions and worked in the modern styles, staging their own exhibitions in Munich and Berlin.

Shaker furniture. Plain, yet elegant furniture produced by Christian sect known as "Shaking Quakers."

Shingle. Domestic American architectural style, popular in the 1870s and 1880s, that derived from Colonial and Queen Anne modes.

Situation group. British abstract artists who exhibited together in 1960 and 1961; paintings all measured thirty square feet or larger.

Socialist realism. Official art of Soviet Union; it glorified the Communist state and its aims.

Soft style *(weicher Stil).* Northern German style of painting and sculpture; it flourished in the early fifteenth century.

Sondergotik. Late German development of Gothic architecture characterized by soaring vaulting and elaborate stained glass and tracings.

Sublime. Term, popularized in the late eighteenth century, used to describe any immense or wild scene that inspired awe or terror.

Sumerian. Art produced by the earliest Mesopotamian civilizations of Ur and Sumer (about 3000–2300 B.C.E.).

Superrealism. American and British art movement of the 1970s that produced works of minute verisimilitude; also known as photorealism.

Suprematism. Russian nonobjective style of painting founded in 1913.

Surrealism. European art and literary movement, founded by André Breton in 1924, that represented images from the unconscious; its foremost practitioners were Max Ernst, Salvador Dali, Yves Tanguy, André Masson, René Magritte, and Jean Miro.

Symbolism. Late nineteenth-century European art movement, originating in Paris, whereby direct representation of reality was discarded in favor of subjective representations; its primary exponents were Odilon Redon, Gustave Moreau, Jan Toorop, Puvis de Chavannes, and Gustav Klimt.

Synchromism. American equivalent of Orphism; its primary exponents were Stanton Macdonald-Wright and Morgan Russell, who exhibited together in 1913 and 1914.

Synthetism. Term used to describe the work of Paul Gauguin, Émile Bernard, and others who advocated the simplification of forms into large-scale patterns and represented objects in large areas of unmodulated colors.

Ten, the. (1) Group of American impressionist painters who exhibited together from 1898 to 1918; (2) group of American expressionists who exhibited between 1935 and 1940.

Tosa. Influential and long-lived fifteenth-century school of Japanese court artists who painted in yamato-e style.

Transitional. English architectural style that fused elements of the Norman style with aspects of early English Gothic.

Transitional art. Any work created from European junk by twentieth-century African artists.

Transition style. Restrained version of rococo art, popular in the 1760s, preceding French neoclassicism.

Troubadour. French style of gothic revival architecture; also known as *cathedral style.*

Tudor. Style of art and architecture popular in England during the sixteenth century, bridging late Gothic and Renaissance.

Utrecht school. Group of seventeenth-century Dutch painters, including Dirck van Baburen, Hendrick Terbrugghem, Paulus Bor, Abraham Bloemaert, and Gerit van Honthorst, some of whom visited Rome. They were influenced by Caravaggio's art, but modified that painter's dark subject matter with lighter colors.

Vingt, les (Les XX), or **the Twenty.** Group of Belgian and French postimpressionist painters and sculptors exhibiting during the 1880s and 1890s.

Viseu school. Manueline painters, centered in Viseu, Portugal, active between 1505 and 1550; its primary exponents were Vasco Fernandes (also known as Grao Vasco) and Gaspar Vaz.

Visigothic. Style of art prevalent in Iberian peninsula during the fifth to eighth centuries; its practitioners fused Roman and Byzantine styles.

Vorticism. English avant-garde movement influenced by cubism and futurism; its primary exponents were Wyndham Lewis, Henri Gaudier-Brzeska, and Ezra Pound.

Wanderers, the. Group of reform-oriented Russian social realists who showed
their works in traveling exhibitions during the 1880s and 1890s; their paintings depicted the poor and oppressed.

Washington color painters. Name given to Kenneth Noland, Gene Davis, Morris
Louis, and other artists who exhibited together at Gallery of Modern Art in
Washington, D.C., in 1965.

Wiener Werkstätte, or **Viennese Workshops.** Group of Austrian artisans who
combined aspects of arts and crafts movement with elements from art nouveau and Jugendstil styles.

Zero Group. Group of German kinetic artists flourishing from 1957 to 1966,
including Otto Peine and Heinz Mack.

SOURCES

Chilvers, Ian, and Harold Osborne. *The Oxford Dictionary of Art.* New York: Oxford
University Press, 1988.

Elspass, Margy Lee. *The North Light Dictionary of Art Terms.* Fairfield, Conn.: North
Light, 1984.

Hill, Ann, ed. *A Visual Dictionary of Art.* Greenwich, Conn.: New York Graphic Society,
1974.

Lucie-Smith, Edward. *The Thames and Hudson Dictionary of Art Terms.* London:
Thames and Hudson, 1984.

Myers, Bernard S., ed. *McGraw-Hill Dictionary of Art.* New York: McGraw-Hill, 1969.

The Phaidon Encyclopedia of Art and Artists. Oxford, Eng.: Phaidon, 1978.

Piper, Sir David, ed. *The Random House Dictionary of Art and Artists.* New York:
Random House, 1988.

Praeger Encyclopedia of Art. New York: Praeger Publishers, 1971.

Webster's New World Dictionary of the American Language. 2nd ed. New York: World
Publishing Co., 1970.

—**Ian Crump; L.D.R.**

22

THE LANGUAGE OF PAINTING:
A GLOSSARY

. . . . .

HAS IT EVER BEEN NOTICED THAT WHEN NOVELISTS WISH TO CENTER WORKS OF fiction on characters with artistic sensibility, but don't want to write so-called autobiographical fiction, they are likely to make such characters painters or sculptors rather than writers?

The reason for choosing not to make them writers is obvious: it automatically puts the character in question at a further remove from the writer, so that the tendency to slip into letting the character's fictional experience become the writer's own direct biographical experience is lessened.

Why, however, a painter or sculptor rather than a composer of music? For every fictional musician such as Romain Rolland's Jean-Christophe, Eudora Welty's Miss Eckhart, and Thomas Mann's Adrian Leverkühn there must be a dozen literary painters and sculptors. Nathaniel Hawthorne's people in *The Marble Faun*, D. H. Lawrence's Paul Morel, Ernest Hemingway's Thomas Hudson, William Styron's Cass Kinsolving, Henry James's numerous artists, Joyce Cary's Gulley Jimson, Virginia Woolf's Lillie Briscoe, Anthony Powell's Bomby, John Galsworthy's Jolyon Forsyte—it seems that if a writer wants to deal with an artist at work, what painters or sculptors do can be made understandable in language without requiring as much technical expertise on the writer's part as might be needed for music and musicians.

It also may have something to do with abstraction. That is, most painters deal in visual images, and even those who don't seek to be representational must put visible forms and colors on a canvas. Musical sounds imitate abstract relationships and emotions, and so cannot be particularized in language. It would be easier, wouldn't it, to write a description of what Rembrandt might do while painting *The Night Watch* than of Beethoven's actions when composing the Grosse Fugue?

Looking at the matter the other way around, it has obviously been far more common, and more practical, for painters to illustrate literary works than for musicians to compose program music about them. Until fifty years ago or so, it was standard practice for popular novels to be illustrated. Composers, it is true, often create musical works on literary subjects— Strauss's *Don Quixote*, Berlioz' *Harold in Italy*, Mendelssohn's *Fingal's Cave*, and so on—but the literary subject is really little more than an occasion for a musical statement that might just as readily be entitled something else.

To write about painting and sculpture requires some knowledge of the vocabulary of visual art. The compilation that follows gives some of the more commonly used terms. In preparing it we have made particular use of Edward Lucie-Smith's excellent and succinct *Thames and Hudson Dictionary of Art Terms*. See Sources below.

Abbozzo. First outline, drawing, or underpainting on a canvas.

Absorbent ground. In painting, untreated ground that absorbs the liquid from the paint.

Abstract art. Art that discards depiction of real objects and uses formal patterns, lines, and colors to express aesthetic content.

Academic art. Art strongly shaped by the standards of an official academy; usually conservative.

Academy. Institution that originated in the Renaissance and supplanted the medieval guild system; it trained its pupils to become professional artists rather than artisans, providing a thorough knowledge of theory as well as technique. Though of lesser importance today, academies still flourish.

Accent. Small dab of color used to contrast with another color.

Accidental color. Optical illusion created after one stares at a brightly colored area and then transfers his gaze to a white or neutrally colored area where he briefly sees the complementary color of the one he had initially stared at.

Accidental points. In perspective, additional vanishing points not on the horizon line.

Achromatic. White, blacks, and grays.

Acrylic paint. Synthetic color, soluble in water, used as a quick-drying paint; favored by many over oils.

Action. Term used since the 1960s, a development of the "happening" but less theatrical in its implications; it describes any structured sequence or combination of movements or sounds, manipulation of materials; sometimes viewed as a form of abstract expressionism.

Adoration. Scene or representation depicting the adoration of the infant Jesus by the Magi.

Advancing color. Tendency of a strongly saturated warm color to advance toward the viewer; the opposite of a retreating color.

Aesthete. One who prizes his artistic sensibility above all else.

Aestheticism. Theory, formulated by Immanuel Kant in the eighteenth century and current in the art for art's sake movement, that the philosophy of art is distinct from other forms of philosophy and that art need not necessarily embody extrinsic values.

Aesthetics. The study of the beautiful in art.

Airbrushing. Method of painting that employs a mechanical paint sprayer to achieve a smooth, gradations of tones and colors.

Ajouré. Openwork technique, usually employed in metalwork, in which material is pierced or perforated in elaborate patterns.

Albumen print. Photographic print made on paper coated with egg white (albumen), salt, and silver nitrate; this process was used throughout the second half of the nineteenth century.

All-over painting. Abstract expressionist painting, applied uniformly without a central focus or dominant area of interest.

Altarpiece. Work of sacred art, such as a tryptich, placed above or near the altar in a church.

Anaglyph. Sculpture or decoration developed in relief, such as a cameo; in photography, a superimposed stereoscopic image.

Anamorphosis. In painting, an image that appears distorted or unrecognizable except when observed from an angle or in a curved mirror; popular during the eighteenth century.

Ancona. Early Italian altarpiece with several painted panels but no folded wings.

Animal interlace. Ornamentation consisting of interwoven representations of stylized animals.

Anti-art. Term, apparently coined by Marcel Duchamp, for work that, although seemingly artistic, contradicts the conventions and assumptions ordinarily associated with artistic creation.

Anti-cernes. White spaces between colors used by the fauves in place of black outlines.

Appliqué. Method of decoration in which pieces of a material are placed on, or "applied" to, another surface to form a design.

Aquarelle. Watercolor done without inks or body white.

Aquatint. Intaglio process of printmaking in which resin is fused into a metal plate and steeped in acid to produce tones that provide a granulated or ink wash effect.

Arabesque. Linear decoration that involves intricately interlaced floral or geometrical designs; used from classical times onward.

Architectonic. Having or expressing the structural unity inherent in architectural design.

Armature. Frame or skeleton on which a sculptor builds up material.

Arras. Term for tapestry that derives from Arras, the French city which was the most important medieval weaving center.

Arricciato or **arriccio.** Second layer of plaster upon a wall on which the design of a fresco is set out.

Assemblage. Technique that involves combining "found" materials into integrated creations.

Atectonic. In sculpture, refers to shapes that reach out into space.

Atelier. Artist's studio or printmaker's workshop.

Aubusson. Name for tapestry or carpet made by hand in the French city of Aubusson; also a particular rug weave.

Aureole. In painting, halo or soft light that encircles the head or body of a sacred person.

Autograph. Picture identifiable as the work of a particular artist.

Automatism. Technique of using a brush or pencil without conscious control in order to gain access to unconscious urges.

Avant-garde. Experimental and startlingly unconventional artistic innovation in designs, ideas, or techniques during a particular period; also, the practitioners of such.

Axis. Imaginary straight line through a composition, along which the main points are balanced.

Azulejos. Painted and glazed wall tiles popular in Spain, Portugal, and Latin America.

Background. Area appearing behind something being represented, especially in a landscape or seascape.

Back light. Lighting that comes from behind a figure or object.

Balance. Elements of a composition that appear in equilibrium through the spatial arrangement of forms and use of color.

Banding. In furniture making, decorative wood inlay of a different color than the wood of the rest of the piece.

Barbotine. Primitive method of ornamenting pottery with soft clay.

Batik. Indonesian technique of coating textiles with wax in order to preserve the original colors when dyed.

Batten. Strip of wood used to attach tiles or to support plastering.

Beauvais. Type of tapestry made in French city of that name.

Bentwood. In furniture making, plywood bent into curved forms while under steam heat.

Bezel. Setting for a stone in jewelry, usually a ring.

Binder. In painting, liquid added to paint to make it adhere to a surface, such as canvas.

Biomorphic. Abstract form using configurations found in nature rather than geometric patterns.

Bistre. Brown pigment, made from boiled beechwood soot, frequently used in wash drawings.

Biting in. In etching, corrosive effect of acid bath on unprotected parts of a metal plate.

Bitumen. Asphalt, tar, etc., producing pigment that darkens with age and develops craquelure; employed as an underpaint in the late eighteenth and early nineteenth centuries, it caused severe damage to paintings.

Bleeding. Process whereby paint or ink migrates into an adjoining area of canvas or through a layer of paint.

Block. Engraved piece used to stamp a raised image onto paper.

Bloom. Cloudy or blanched effect that develops on varnished surfaces from moisture.

Blot drawing. In watercolor painting, technique that allows the image to grow out of an accidental ink or watercolor splotch on the paper.

Blow-up. Photographic enlargement.

Boasted work. In sculpture, piece of stone brought roughly into the shape of the finished carving with a two-edged chisel.

Bocage. Porcelain flowers or leaves, as if in hedge form.

Bodegón. Spanish type of still-life painting that often contains human figures.

Body art. Action or happening in which the body of the artist is literally the medium of expression.

Bolus clay. Decomposed granite, grayish white, used in porcelain.

Bone china. Low-fired porcelain containing ash secured from calcined bones; originally made in England in the eighteenth century.

Boss. Raised ornament formed from a protuberance.

Bottega. Workshop of an Italian master artist of the Middle Ages and Renaissance.

Braquette. Framing in which a picture is held in four corner clips.

Brocade. Fabric with a raised interwoven pattern.

Brush. Wood rod fixed at the end with horsehair or other types of hair, for applying paint.

Brushwork. Marks left on a painted surface by the paintbrush; these are often regarded as a type of signature.

Buffet. Piece of shelved furniture designed to stand against a wall; now, a sideboard.

Burin. Awl-like engraving tool with a diamond point.

Burr. Ragged edge of furrow metal raised on an engraving plate by the burin, often retained to produce a blurred line.

Bust. Sculpted portrait of head and shoulders of the sitter.

Busy. Term used to describe areas of an artwork that appear confusing or overactive.

Byobu. Japanese movable screen.

Cabochon. Convex or dome-shaped gem.

Cabriole leg. Double-curved, highly ornamental furniture leg that ends in a scroll, foot, or claw.

Calligraphic painting. (1) Style of abstract art that emphasizes the scriptural quality of the brushstroke; (2) Chinese and Japanese ink paintings made with a writing brush and composed with the writing strokes.

Callot figures. Grotesque dwarf figures used as decoration on goldwork and porcelain, after French engraver Jacques Callot (1592–1635).

Calotype. Early type of negative-and-positive photographic process on silver oxide paper.

Camaïeu, en. Technique of monochromatic painting or decoration in several shades of the same color.

Cameo. Gemstone carved in relief.

Camera lucida. Optical contrivance much like a camera obscura, except that a prism is used to focus an object's reflected light on a piece of paper as an image that can be traced, enlarged, or reduced.

Camera obscura. Darkened box with small aperture that focuses an object's reflected light onto a piece of paper as an inverted image.

Camp. Term, borrowed from theatrical and homosexual usage, denoting a style of ironic kitsch.

Canon of proportion. In art, especially sculpture, the formula that sets forth a ratio for the ideal proportions of the human body.

Canopic vase. Vase with lid fashioned in the form of an animal or human head.

Capriccio. Extravagantly conceived composition portraying imaginary as well as real features.

Carcass. Frame or skeleton of veneered furniture.

Caricature. Portrait or cartoon in which the sitter's features are exaggerated for comic or ironic effect.

Carnations. Flesh colors in painting.

Carpet page. Entire page of abstract patterning in illuminated manuscripts.

Cartellino. Piece of paper displayed within a larger painting, on which an inscription or a signature appears.

Cartoon. Originally, full-scale preparatory design for tapestry or painting; now, any humorous drawing or drawings, usually with accompanying monologue, dialogue, or tag line.

Casein paint. Binder made of hydrochloric acid and skimmed milk.

Casting. Creation of an object, or cast, by pouring liquid metal or wax into a mold.

Catalogue raisonné. Annotated catalog of an artist's life work.

Cave art. Painting, drawings, or carvings made in caves or rock outcroppings by prehistoric peoples.

Cavo-rilievo. Technique of hollow relief whereby a design is cut into the plate.

Ceramics. Term embracing pottery and porcelain.

Chalk. Powdery limestone substance molded into sticks.

Charcoal. Black porous carbon used as a drawing stick; also, the drawing thereby produced.

Chasing. Technique of ornamenting metal with hammered indentations.

Checkered. Decorative pattern of alternating shapes of contrasting color.

Cherub. In painting, a winged child or infant.

Chevron. Decorative pattern of inverted Vs.

Chiaroscuro. In painting, rendering of form through balanced contrast between light and shade; used extensively by da Vinci.

Chisel. Sharp metal wedge used to sculpt.

Chroma. Hue and saturation, or degree of vividness of a color other than black, white, or gray.

Chromolithography. Colored lithograph achieved by using a separate stone or plate for each color; typically clumsy in result.

Chryselephantine. Adorned with gold and ivory.

Cire perdue. Method of casting metal in which a wax model is enclosed in a clay mold; the wax is then melted under heat and replaced with liquid metal.

Ciselure. Smoothing out the surface of a cast metal form.

Cleavage. Paint that flakes and separates from its ground.

Cliché-verre. Photographic print created by engraving an image on a coated glass plate that is then used as a negative.

Clobbering. Enamel overpainting on already ornamented porcelain.

Cloisonné. Technique of enamel decoration in which metal lines are used to separate colors that are filled in as paste and the work is fired.

Cloisonnism. Postimpressionist technique using darker shades to surround and highlight bright colors.

Clunch. Soft limestone used in interior carving.

Coil method. Forming a pottery vessel by building up coils.

Cold-working. Shaping metal with hammers without using heat.

Collage. Technique, invented by Pablo Picasso and Georges Braque, of gluing found objects, such as newspaper, to canvas or paper.

Collotype. Early photographic printing technique using gelatin plates.

Color-field painting. Technique of abstract art in which color field appears to stretch to infinity.

Color wheel. Circular diagram showing relationships of primary and secondary colors.

Combine painting. Technique, invented by Robert Rauschenberg, in which the artist combines painting with collage objects.

Commercial art. Art created primarily to help sell a product.

Community art. Collaborative art produced in the 1970s and 1980s by specific, often disadvantaged, communities in conjunction with visiting artists.

Complementary colors. Colors in extreme contrast to each other.

Composition. Organization of the elements within an artwork.

Computer art. Art, mainly graphics, produced with the use of a computer.

Conceptual art. Style, prevalent since the 1960s, in which the basic idea, or concept, of a work is more important than the final product.

Concrete art. Modern style that represents abstract ideas in tangible forms.

Connoisseurship. Bernard Berenson's term for the process of deducing art-historical information and evaluating art from within the artwork itself, without any supporting material.

Content. Subject matter or motif of an artwork.

Contour. In painting, outline that bounds a form.

Contrapposto. Technique of balancing opposing body parts asymmetrically around an axis in order to avoid an appearance of stiffness in the represented figure.

Conversation piece. Group portrait of figures, especially a family.

Cool or **cold colors.** Colors in which blue is dominant, suggesting coolness.

Copper engraving. Print made from an inscribed copper plate.

Copperplate. Rounded calligraphy like that engraved on copper.

Coulisses. Elements along the sides of a painting arranged to move the viewer's eye to the center.

Craquelure. Cracks in the surface of an old oil painting caused by embrittlement of the film of paint over the years.

Crayon. Drawing material in stick form; also, a crayon drawing.

Cross-hatching. Technique of using two or more sets of parallel lines, usually perpendicular to each other, to render shadows in drawings or engravings.

Cybernetic art. Works that react to external stimuli.

Daguerreotype. First practicable photographic process, invented in 1839; it made positives directly on sensitized silvered copper plates.

Damask. Rich fabric woven in large, raised patterns.

Dead color. Neutral color applied to canvas or panel before painting is begun.

Deckle edge. Type of paper with ragged, unfinished edge.

Décollage. Art created by the breaking down of materials.

Découpage. Decoration of a surface by cut-out patterns in a collage.

Delft. Type of Dutch earthenware decorated with cobalt blue patterns on white tin enamel.

Depth. Degree of recession of the perspective.

Design. Combination of features and details of an artwork.

Dhurry. Cotton carpet or rug woven as if it were a tapestry.

Diamond-point engraving. Technique for inscribing glass or porcelain with a diamond-tipped tool.

Die. Plate used to stamp a design; hollow mold.

Diptych. Hinged pair of painted panels.

Doodle. Drawing made with little conscious intent.

Draftmanship. Ability to draw well.

Dragging. Technique of drawing a paintbrush full of pigment lightly across a rough surface to create a broken effect.

Drawing. Any representation composed of lines.

Drip painting. Dripping paint onto canvas laid on a floor.

Dry plate process. Photographic process in which a gelatin emulsion is used on a glass plate.

Dry-point. In printing, technique in which a design is engraved directly onto a copper plate with a sharp tool, producing a burr.

Earth art. Works, produced in the 1960s, composed of natural materials such as stones, dirt, or snow.

Earth colors. Pigments such as brown or yellow found naturally in clay or soil.

Earthenware. Coarse clay articles fired at low heat and remaining porous unless glazed.

Easel. Free-standing structure designed to hold a canvas while it is being painted.

Ecce Homo. Representation of Christ as crowned with thorns; Latin of John 19.5.

Eggshell porcelain. Extremely thin, translucent porcelain.

Emblem. Image with an allegorical or symbolic meaning.

Embossing. Technique of creating raised figures or designs.

Embroidery. Method of decorating cloth by stitching.

Empaquetage. Technique of wrapping objects, including those of great size, such as buildings, as an art form.

Emulsion. Mixture of two liquids that do not normally combine.

Enamel. Colored material bonded to a metal surface through heating.

Engraving. Incising lines on a hard plate with a graver or burin to produce intaglio prints; also, the print made therefrom.

Environmental art. Three-dimensional artworks, produced since the 1950s, to be moved through by the viewer.

Épreuve d'artiste. First, unnumbered impression separate from the main edition of prints.

Escallop. Emblem in the form of a shell.

Escutcheon. Shield or background for display of a coat of arms.

Etching. Making a design on a plate with acid; also, any print made from such a plate.

Eye level. In perspective drawing, the horizontal line where two parallel lines meet at the vanishing point.

Faïence. Tin-glazed pottery or porcelain.

Fake. Work, usually a copy, intended to be passed off as the genuine work of a master.

Fayum. Naturalistic portrait paintings discovered on mummies in Roman cemeteries in Egypt.

Fetish. In African art, representation of a spiritually powerful being.

Fictile. Capable of being molded.

Fictive sculpture. In trompe-l'oeil painting, monochromatic figures made to look like sculptures.

Figurative art. Art that represents figures or objects that are visible in the real world.

Figure painting. Painting depicting the human figure.

Filigree. Delicate metal designs made by soldering.

Finish. Treatment of a painted, photographic, or ceramic surface.

Firing. Technique of baking or vitrifying ceramic, glass, or enamel objects in a kiln to harden them or to set their glaze.

Fixative. Liquid used to bind loose elements such as chalk or charcoal on pictures.

Focal point. In perspective drawing or painting, the point to which the eye is naturally drawn.

Foliation. Decorative carving modeled after leaves.

Folk art. Naïve or unsophisticated art produced by untutored artists.

Foreground. Area in a painting, especially a landscape or seascape, that appears closest to the viewer.

Foreshortening. Technique of representing an object at a sharply angled perspective in order to give the illusion of correct relative size.

Form. The product of a work's design and composition.

Formalism. Art and art criticism that privilege the study of form above that of content.

Found object. Object discovered by the artist in his environment and used with no or little alteration as part of an, or as an entire, artwork; also called an *objet trouvé.*

Foxing. Yellow and brown spots that appear on damp paper, caused by mold.

Fractur. Pennsylvania Dutch folk ornamentation developed from the use of German fraktur or Gothic lettering.

Fresco. Wall painting executed with earth pigments on freshly laid lime or plaster.

Frontispiece. Illustration placed before, and often facing, a book's title page.

Frottage. Technique of producing an impression of a relief by placing paper over it and rubbing with a pencil or a crayon.

Fugitive colors. Pigments that lose color rapidly when exposed to daylight.

Gelatin print. Photographic print made with gelatin-coated paper.

Genre painting. Painting conforming to preset standards of content or subject matter.

Gesso. White primer used as a base in painting.

Gestural painting theory. Abstract expressionist theory that an artist's characteristic marks on a canvas record the emotions felt while painting by the artist's entire personality.

Gisant. Recumbent effigy of the deceased upon a tomb.

Glair. Egg white used as glaze in egg tempera.

Glaze. Fired coating fused to a ceramic object to make it impervious to water as well as ornamenting it.

Glory. Light that emanates from a saint.

Gobelins. Tapestry produced at Gobelins factory in Paris.

Gold ground. Gold leaf used as background in medieval and early Renaissance paintings.

Gouache. Painting made with opaque watercolors.

Graphic art. Art that emphasizes lines or marks instead of color; it is usually executed on paper.

Gravure. General name for intaglio printing processes.

Grisaille. Monochromatic painting executed in shades of gray.

Grotesque. Fantastic style of decoration derived from Roman examples found in underground ruins, or "grotte."

Ground. Specially prepared, even-toned surface upon which an artist paints.

Guild. In the Middle Ages, a hierarchical union of men specializing in the same craft or trade.

Haboku. Free-style ink painting made in China between 960 and 1270 and in Japan until the fifteenth century.

Half-length. Painting that portrays the upper half of the human figure.

Happenings. Planned and/or improvisational theatrical art events; they have been performed since the 1960s.

Hard-edged painting. Abstract art with sharply defined forms and flat colors.

Harmonic proportions. System of balanced proportions, based on the seemingly divine structures of music, developed by Renaissance architects.

Heroic sculpture. Larger-than-life figural sculpture.

High art. Art exhibiting a consciously elevated, stylized, and classical manner.

Highlight. Brightest spot in a painting.

Historiated initials. Large, intricately adorned initial letters in medieval illuminated manuscripts.

History painting. Figural art depicting historic incidents in a grand style.

Hologram. Three-dimensional image recorded on a sensitized plate in the form of an interference pattern produced by splitting a laser beam.

Horizon line. In perspective drawing, line at which the sky and the earth or ocean meet; the vanishing point is located on this line.

Hue. Actual color, shade, or tint of an object.

Icon. Byzantine-style religious painting on a wooden panel in two dimensions or very low relief.

Iconography. Investigation of an artwork's content or subject matter rather than its style.

Iconology. Culturally and historically informed study of an artwork's subject matter.

Ignudo. Male nude, especially the nudes painted by Michelangelo on the Sistine Chapel ceiling.

Illuminations. Painted illustrations in handwritten medieval manuscript books, making use of gold highlighting.

Impasto. Thick application of paint to a surface.

Impression. Copy of a print or engraving.

Inlay. Technique by which small objects are fitted into a larger object to make a design.

Intaglio. Design cut below the surface of a material.

Intaglio printing. Technique of making a print by placing paper on an inked intaglio plate that has been wiped so that the ink remains only in the cut lines.

Interlace. Type of ornamentation using crisscrossed lines.

Intimisme. Term for postimpressionist portrayals of small domestic subjects.

Intonaco. Last layer of plaster on which a fresco is painted.

Italianate. Pertaining to or derived from Italian Renaissance art and architecture.

Japanned work. European imitations of Asian laquerwork.

Japonaiserie. Late nineteenth-century European imitations of Japanese art and craft works.

Junk art. Assemblages, made since the 1950s, composed of garbage.

Kakemono. Japanese painting or print on a vertical scroll.

Kara-e. Painting by a Japanese artist in the Chinese style.

Kilim. Rug with floral patterning, made by Middle Eastern nomads, with the same design on both sides.

Kinesthetic art. Art which elicits more than purely visual responses in the viewer.

Kinetic. Art that incorporates moving elements.

Kit-cat. Three-quarter-length portrait that depicts the head, shoulders, and one hand of its subject; the term derives from a series of portraits of the members of the Kit-Cat Club, named after Christopher (Kit) Cat who owned the pastry shop where the club met in early eighteenth-century London.

Kitsch. Mass-produced art, blatantly sentimental or pretentious, designed for popular appeal.

Kore. Greek sculpture of a clothed girl or young woman.

Kouros. Greek sculpture of a nude youth.

Kunstkammer. Collections of art and curiosities popular in German palaces during the sixteenth and seventeenth centuries.

Kunstwollen. The artist's intention.

Lacquer. Hard, waterproof varnish, first used in Asia.

Landscape shape. A canvas wider than it is high; also *landscape format.*

Lay figure. Hinged wooden mannequin used by artists to study human proportions.

Lettrism. Words or letters that are used solely for visual effect, without reference to their meaning.

Life drawing. Drawing of a live nude.

Line. Continuous mark made by a pencil, pen, brush, etc.

Line engraving. Engraving in which a design is inscribed on a metal plate with a burin.

Linocut. Popular variety of relief print made from a design carved in a linoleum block.

Lithograph. Print made by applying damp paper to a stone or metal plate that has been marked with a greasy ink.

Luminism. Presentation of light or atmospheric effects as a major aspect of a painting.

Macramé. Technique of knotting rope or cord to create a design.

Maculature. Weak, second print made before a plate is reinked.

Maesta. Representation of the Virgin and Child enthroned and surrounded by saints.

Mahlstick. Padded stick used by a painter to support a painter's brush-holding arm; also called an *artist's bridge.*

Majolica. Renaissance Italian earthenware, enameled, glazed, and brightly colored.

Makimono or **emaki-mono.** Japanese painting or print on a horizontal scroll.

Maquette. Small, preliminary model for the finished sculpture; also known as a *bozzetto.*

Marine painting. Genre of painting depicting the sea and shipping, popular in seventeenth-century Holland; J. M. W. Turner and Winslow Homer were later practitioners.

Marouflage. Technique of attaching a painted canvas to a wall with an adhesive.

Marquetry. Decorative insertion of inlays in wood veneer in furniture.

Masterpiece. Originally, an artwork presented by an apprentice to prove his qualifications to be a master in his guild; now, any artwork of great merit.

Mat or **mat board.** Heavy cardboard used for mounting artworks.

Matière. Material of an artwork, especially the paint.

Medium. Material with which an artist works to express his intent.

Metal cut. Print produced from a metal plate carved in relief.

Metal point. Technique of drawing with a pointed rod of a soft metal, such as lead or gold, on an abrasive surface.

Mezzotint. Engraving technique by which a plate of rough copper is scratched and smoothed to produce the effect of light and shade.

Miniature. Painting, often a portrait, of small scale.

Minimal art. Term for art, prevalent since the 1960s, that makes no attempt at expressiveness or illusion.

Mixed media. Art encompassing more than one medium.

Mobile. Standing or hanging sculpture displaying carefully balanced movable parts that can be set in motion by air currents; associated with Alexander Calder's work.

Model. Person posing for a painter or a sculptor.

Modeling. Technique of using malleable material to produce a three-dimensional form.

Modello. Small version of a larger commissioned work that an artist shows to a patron.

Moiré. Watered or wavy, often shimmering, design.

Molding. Ornamental plane or curved strip used for decorating.

Monochrome. In gradations of a single color.

Monotype. Technique of printing by which the paper is pressed on a painted plate.

Montage. Composite picture made by combining various pictures or attaching layers of two-dimensional materials to a surface.

Mordant. Adhesive used to attach gold leaf to panel or paper.

Moresque. Elaborate surface ornamentation that derives from Moorish art.

Mosaic. Artwork produced by setting small colored cubes of glass, marble, or stone in wet plaster or any adhesive base.

Motif. Recurrent design or theme in an artwork.

Multiples. Artworks specifically intended to be mass produced.

Mural. Painting executed directly on a wall or ceiling.

Namban. Japanese art that reveals European influences.

Narrative painting. Painting that recounts a story.

Nature-morte. French term for still life.

Negative. Transparent photographic plate or film on which light and shadow are reversed for making a positive print.

Niello. Technique of ornamenting gold with black inlay.

Nihon-ga. Painting in the Japanese style.

Nimbus. In Christian art, disk or halo placed behind a person's head to indicate holy status.

Nishiki-e. Lavish, multicolored Japanese print.

Nocturne. Musical term used by James Whistler to describe his night paintings.

Nude. In painting, an unclothed figure, often depicted erotically.

Obelisk. Tall, rectangular stone pillar that tapers to pyramid.

Objet d'art. Article, usually small and exquisitely made, of artistic nature.

Odalisque. Representation, usually erotic, of a female slave in a harem.

Oeuvre. Artist's entire body of work.

Oil paint. Paint composed of pigments originally ground in oil, especially linseed oil.

Old Master. A distinguished European painter who worked between 1500 and 1800.

Oleograph. Chromolithograph produced on canvas with oil-based inks meant to resemble an oil painting.

Openwork. Ornamentation pierced to display openings through its substance.

Optical mixtures technique. Technique, used by impressionists and neoimpressionists, of juxtaposing small touches of primary colors so that they appear to blend and to create secondary colors.

Orans or **orant.** Figure shown at prayer.

Orthogonals. In perspective, lines that would, in reality, be perpendicular to the picture plane but that seem to preserve length and distance.

Outline. The outer boundary of an object or a figure.

Painterly. Use of light and shade rather than physical outlines to represent form.

Palette. Flat tray on which an artist sets out and mixes colors.

Palette knife. Small, flat trowel blade used to mix paint on a palette and often to apply it to the canvas.

Palimpsest. Inscribed or painted surface through which an earlier inscription or painting may still be seen.

Panorama. Circular, life-sized painting that surrounds the viewer and creates the illusion of extended space and landscape.

Pantograph. Mechanical device for tracing enlarged or smaller copies of an original.

Papier collé. Collage composed wholly of pieces of paper.

Papier-mâché. Substance, composed of ground paper mixed with glue or paste, that can be molded while damp.

Parergon. In painting, detail that is secondary to the main idea.

Pastel. Picture made with crayon of dry pigment mixed with a heavy bonding material such as gum, typically pale and light in hue.

Pastiche. Work that is composed of borrowings from other works; also, an imitation, often satirical.

Pastoral. Representation of a rural landscape as Arcadia, in contrast to an urban present.

Patent furniture. Ingeniously mechanical furniture that has more than one purpose.

Patina. Pleasing surface discoloration due to age or use.

Pencil. Writing or drawing instrument of graphite encased in strips of wood.

Pentimento. Appearance through a painting of a previous design.

Performance art. Style, popular since the 1960s, that presents happenings as ephemeral theatrical events.

Perspective. Technique of representing three-dimensional space on a two-dimensional surface; one-point perspective has one vanishing point, while two-point perspective has two.

Petroglyph. Carving on a rock or a wall.

Photogram. Shadowlike photograph produced by placing objects on light-sensitive paper.

Photomontage. Montage created by using photographs.

Pictograph. Highly simplified drawing or diagram that symbolizes an action or a thing.

Picture space. Area seeming to extend behind the picture plane because of the use of perspective.

Pietà. Representation, in painting or sculpture, of the Virgin Mary mourning the dead Christ.

Pigment. Coloring agent in paint or dye.

Planography. Technique for printing from a plane surface.

Plaster of paris. Mixture of gypsum and water that hardens when it dries.

Plastic arts. Three-dimensional arts, such as sculpture and ceramics, characterized by modeling.

Plasticity. True or apparent capacity of an artistic form for being molded or shaped.

Plate. Marked surface used for printing or engraving.

Platinotype. Nineteenth-century, platinum-based photographic printing process.

Plein air. Pictures, usually landscapes, executed outdoors.

Pointillism. In painting, the consistent use of optical mixtures in small dots and points so that they blend together to form images.

Polyptych. Painting made on four or more attached panels.

Porcelain. Type of fine-grained, white, translucent ceramicware made of kaolin, feldspar, and quartz or flint and fired at high temperatures.

Portrait shape. Term for a canvas higher than it is wide; also *portrait format.*

Positive. Photographic print produced from a negative.

Pottery. All fired earthenwares except porcelain.

Pouncing. Process of copying a design by poking holes in the outlines and then pouring a fine powder through the holes to transfer the outlines to the surface below.

Predella. Painting placed below the main panel of an altarpiece.

Primary colors. Blue, yellow, and red; they are called primary because all other colors are derived from them.

Priming. Substance, usually paint or gesso, applied to a surface in order to seal or protect it prior to being painted.

Primitive. Artwork produced by a naive or unsophisticated artist.

Print. Inked image produced from a plate, stencil, woodblock, etc.

Profile. A figure's face seen from the side.

Profil perdu. Figure's face which is more than half turned away from the viewer.

Proof. Trial impression of an etching or an engraving made to see if any design changes need to be made on the plate.

Proportion. Ratio between respective elements in a building or an artwork.

Provenance. Record of all ownerships of an artwork.

Psychedelic art. Art mirroring or interpreting the mental states induced by hallucinogenic drugs.

Pugging. Ceramic kneading process to make wet clay more malleable and free from air bubbles.

Putto. In painting, any naked boy, such as a cupid or an angel.

Pyramidal composition. Composition in which the represented figures or objects fill the volume of an imaginary pyramid.

Quadratura. Mural, popular in the eighteenth century, that represents architectural subjects in trompe-l'oeil fashion.

R.A. Royal Academician, a member of the Royal Academy of Arts in the United Kingdom.

Ready-made. Term coined by Marcel Duchamp for everyday objects that have been placed in a context of separate existence and presented as artworks.

Rebus. Term for a word represented by an image or images.

Recession. Depth in space, or the appearance of it, in an artwork.

Red figure. Ancient Greek ornamentation in which the background is painted on and then fired so that it appears black while the unpainted design appears red.

Reflected color. Alteration of hue caused when one color is reflected on another.

Relief. Sculptural composition made so that most or all of its parts project out into space from a flat surface.

Relief process. Printing process in which an inked surface cut in relief rather than intaglio stands out, *i.e.*, letterpress.

Relining. In restoration, the process of mounting an old painting and its original canvas onto a new supporting canvas.

Replica. Work that precisely duplicates another artwork.

Repoussé. Metal relief hammered into shape from behind.

Repoussoir. Object or figure set in the foreground of a composition, and generally to the sides, in order to direct the viewer's eye into the center of the picture.

Reproduction. Copy of an artwork, generally made mechanically.

Resist. Wax or varnish used to protect areas receiving dyes, inks, acids, or pigments.

Retardant. Substance added to paint to slow its drying.

Reticulated. Having a netlike decoration.

Retreating color. Color, usually a cool color, appearing to recede from the picture plane.

Rhyton. Drinking vessel in the shape of an animal's head.

Rinceau. Ornamental scrolls of plant leaves and stems.

Ronde-bosse. Sculpture in the round instead of in relief.

Roughcast. Granular first coat applied to a wall to prepare it for frescoing.

Rupestrian painting. Cave painting on earthen or stone walls.

Sacra Conversazione. Representation of the Virgin and Child in which they are aware of, or conversing with, the encircling saints.

Sacra Famiglia. Representation of the Virgin and Child, often with Joseph in attendance.

Salon painting. Artwork in the style of the official salons; academic art.

Sand painting. Designs created by using different colors of sand, practiced by the Navajos and aborigines, among other groups.

Saturation. Color's degree of brilliance.

Scagliola. Imitation of ornamented marble made of finely ground gypsum, sand, loose stones, and glue.

Scale. Proportion of the elements of an artwork in relative to the original.

Schema. Generalized sketch of a composition.

School. Group of artists working under a single master's influence or sharing a common style and subject matter.

Scratchboard. Chalk-covered cardboard inked and scratched out to produce a design.

Scrimshaw. Whale-bone sculptures made by American sailors in the nineteenth century; any carving or ornamental engraving on ivory, whale-bone, shell, etc.

Sculpture. Shaped artwork executed in three dimensions.

Scumbling. Thin, uneven layer of paint applied over another color so that the underlayer shows through.

Secco. Painting on dried plaster; *cf.* fresco.

Secondary colors. Green, violet, and orange, derived from an equal blending of two of the primary colors.

Sepia. Brown pigment made from cuttlefish ink; also, a photograph in brown that resembles sepia.

Serial imagery. Image repeated several times in a work or group of works by the same artist.

Serigraphy. Silk-screen printmaking technique that uses stencils.

Sfregazzi. In oil painting, delicate glaze of shadows over flesh tones, applied by tapping with fingertips.

Sfumato. In painting or drawing, delicate fusion of tones from light to shadow.

Sgraffito. Decoration achieved by scratching through one layer of color to reveal another color below.

Shallow space. Undefined space in cubist and abstract expressionist paintings in which forms appear to float.

Shaped canvas. Nonrectangular picture.

Shop picture. Painting made in a master's workshop by a student or apprentice.

Siccative. Material added to oil paint to speed drying.

Signature. Artist's name or initials on an artwork.

Significant form. Clive Bell's term for the capacity of an art work to evoke an emotional response through its formal significance.

Silhouette. Profile made of black paper.

Silver point. Technique of drawing with a silver-pointed rod on specially prepared paper.

Simultaneism. Fusion into one creative act of the totality of the artist's attitudes and intentions; a principle of cubism.

Simultaneous representation. Depiction of an object or figure from more than one viewpoint in the same picture.

Singeries. Representations of clothed monkeys acting out human roles, popular during the rococo period.

Sinking in. Dull, lusterless areas of oil paintings that occur when pigments are partially absorbed by the ground.

Sinopia. Underdrawing for a fresco.

Size. Weak solution of glue used to make canvas less absorbent.

Sketch. Preliminary or practice drawing, lacking in details.

Slip. Clay solution used to coat and waterproof pottery.

Soak-stain. Process of painting on unsized canvas to produce stains or blots of color.

Social realism. Art that directly illustrates social, political, and economic issues.

Soft-ground etching. Etching made by drawing on paper placed on a plate specially treated with tallow.

Soft sculpture. Sculpture produced from soft materials whose weight causes them to assume certain shapes.

Solder. Compound used when heated to join metal surfaces.

Spolvero. Copy of a cartoon made by tracing rather than pricking outlines, *cf.* pouncing.

Sprezzatura. Seemingly casual, careless manner with which a sketch is executed.

Squaring for transfer. Use of a grid to make a larger copy of an image. The original is covered, and the contents of each grid are repeated onto a second surface, which has been marked with a larger-scale grid.

Stabile. Abstract sculpture without moving parts.

Stained glass. Colored window glass, often arranged in designs.

Steel engraving. Technique by which steel is deposited by electrolysis onto a copper plate used for engraving.

Stele. Standing slab, often used to mark a grave or a site.

Stenciling. Technique of transferring a design by applying paint through a perforated card or stencil.

Stereometric. Artworks that appear to be tridimensional; also *stereoscopic.*

Still life. Picture of inanimate objects.

Stippling. Technique of applying paint in small dots with brush, as in pointillism.

Stoneware. Dense, durable pottery made of clay and fusible stone fired at a high temperature.

Stop-out. In intaglio printing, the resist that prevents the plate from being bit or etched by the acid.

Street art. Term, current since the 1970s, for performance art put on in streets or other informal settings.

Stretcher. Wood frame onto which a canvas is stretched taut and affixed.

Striation. Surface of closely parallel striae or stripes.

Striking. Technique of hammering a heated metal between two intaglio dies.

Study. Detailed preliminary representation of a section of a composition, used to check against the final work.

Stump. Cigar-shaped roll of paper used to smudge chalk or charcoal lines; also, *stomp.*

Stylus. Pointed tool used to make small indentations.

Suiboku. Japanese free-style ink painting in black and white.

Suite. Collection of pictures with common theme.

Sumi-e. Japanese painting executed with black ink but that gives the impression of color through tonal gradations.

Sunday painter. Amateur artist.

Support. Canvas, wood panel, plaster, or other structure on which a painting is executed.

Suri-mono. Small Japanese wood-block print in the ukiyo-e style.

Systemic painting. Type of abstract painting exhibiting an organized system, such as repetition of a geometric motif.

Table. Picture painted on a panel in the Middle Ages.

Tachisme. Abstract painting in which paint is applied in stains, blots, or dribbles.

Tactile values. Bernard Berenson's term for the painter's effort to suggest tridimensional form.

Tanka. Tibetan religious painting executed on fabric.

Tantra. Art in the Buddhist and Hindu traditions concerned with representing visions of a cosmic sexuality.

Tapa. Fabric made by beating the bark of certain trees; also known as *bark cloth.*

Tapestry. Decorative embroidered fabric used as a wall hanging.

Tectonic. Of or pertaining to building or construction.

Tempera. Originally, egg emulsion used as a medium for pigments; now, any gouache or other opaque water-soluble emulsion.

Tempering. In painting, combining of pigments to lighten or alter the impact of a color.

Template. Pattern cut from metal, cardboard, or plastic.

Tenebrism. Art emphasizing the contrast of light and darkness.

Terra-cotta. Earthenware that has not been glazed.

Tertiary colors. Colors created by combining two or more secondary colors.

Tessera. Small chip or cube of marble or glass used in mosaics.

Texture. Tactile surface of an artwork.

Throwing. Technique of forming clay on a potter's wheel.

Tie-dye. Technique of dyeing designs in a fabric by knotting before immersing it in dye.

Tin glaze. Opaque white crystalline glaze containing tin, used to make Majolica, Faïence, and Delft.

Tinsel painting. Painting sprinkled with bits of glass or metal, or done on glass backed with tin foil so that it appears to sparkle.

Tint. Gradation of a color with reference to its mixture with white.

Tintype. Photograph on a small plate of enameled tin or iron.

Tonal values. Relative lightness or shade of the parts of a painting.

Tondo. Painting, fresco, or relief on a circular base.

Tone. Prevailing impact of color in a picture.

Toning. In oil painting, the technique of glazing the ground to produce a unified tone.

Tooling. Removing the roughness on a stone or a metal surface; decorating leather with heated tools.

Tooth. Tactile texture of canvas or other material that helps paint to cling to it.

Toreutic. Metal surface that has been worked in relief or intaglio.

Torso. Sculpted figure without head and limbs.

Townscape. Urban scene.

Trefoil. Decoration made to resemble a three-lobed leaf.

Tribhanga. Sanscrit term, "three bendings," for sinuous pose typical of Hindu sculptures.

Triptych. Altarpiece painted on three hinged panels.

Trois crayons. Drawings made with black, white, and red chalks.

Trompe-l'oeil. Painting designed to deceive the viewer into believing that he sees real objects or into real architectural space.

Trophy. Representation of a group of weapons or instruments.

Turning. Technique of shaping wood as it spins in a lathe.

Typology. Study of types and symbols, especially from the bible.

Ukiyo-e. Japanese style of art, popular in the seventeenth and eighteenth centuries, depicting scenes from everyday life.

Underglaze. Painted ornamentation applied to a ceramic object before application of a transparent glaze and fired with it.

Uniface. On one side only.

Values. In painting, the degrees of intensity of hues.

Vanishing point. In perspective, the point of infinite distance on the horizon at which parallel lines appear to converge.

Vanitas. Still life with skull or other symbols of human mortality.

Variant. Version of an artwork, often by the original artist, with slight differences.

Varnish. Protective solution painted or sprayed on paintings.

Veduta. Realistically delineated landscape view.

Vehicle. Medium in which pigments are suspended, which carries the color so that it can spread onto the canvas.

Verdure. Tapestry ornamented with foliage.

Verism. Theory that art should reproduce everyday reality, including its sordid elements.

Video art. Artwork that uses television or video technology.

Vignette. Design without a definite border.

Virtue. Collective term for objets d'art; *virtù*.

Vitreous. Glasslike.

Volume. Space articulated by painting or sculpture.

Warm or **hot colors.** Colors suggesting the kinesthetic sensations of warmth; reds and yellows.

Warp. In woven fabric, threads used as lengthwise-running framework.

Wash. Thin, transparent layer of color and water.

Watercolor. Water-soluble pigment mixed with a gum arabic binder and water; also, the work thereby produced.

Weepers. Sculptures of hooded mourners before a tomb.

Wet plate. Photographic process in which a silver nitrate-coated glass plate is exposed to light; it was superseded by the dry plate process.

Whiplash. Long, extremely sinuous S curve.

White line. Relief print made from an inked intaglio woodblock so that the image appears in white lines on a black ground.

Woodblock. Woodcut print made from assorted blocks of wood, each inked with different colors.

Woodcut. Technique by which a print is made from a design cut into wood along the grain.

Wood engraving. Technique by which a print is made from a design cut across the grain on end-grain blocks, so as to create greater subtlety than in a woodcut.

Woof. In woven fabric, the thinner threads that interlace the warp.

Yamato-e. Japanese style of linear narrative painting.

Zoomorphic ornament. Ornamentation using stylized representations of animals; characteristic of early Germanic art.

SOURCES

Elspass, Margy Lee. *The North Light Dictionary of Art Terms*. Fairfield, Conn.: North Light, 1984.

Jacobs, Michael, and Paul Stirton. *The Knopf Traveler's Guides to Art: Britain and Ireland*. New York: Alfred A. Knopf, 1984.

———. *The Knopf Traveler's Guides to Art: France*. New York: Alfred A. Knopf, 1984.

Janson, H. W. *History of Art: A Survey of the Major Visual Arts from the Dawn of History to the Present Day*. 2nd ed. Englewood Cliffs, N.J.: Prentice-Hall, 1977.

Lucie-Smith, Edward. *The Thames and Hudson Dictionary of Art Terms*. London: Thames and Hudson, 1984.

Mayer, Ralph. *A Dictionary of Art Terms and Techniques*. 2nd ed. revised by Steven Sheehan. HarperCollins, 1991.

Mills, John FitzMaurice. *Pergamon Dictionary of Art*. Oxford, Eng.: Pergamon, 1965.

Murray, Peter, and Linda Murray. *The Penguin Dictionary of Art and Artists*. 5th ed. Harmondsworth: Penguin, 1983.

Myers, Bernard S., ed. *McGraw-Hill Dictionary of Art*. New York: McGraw-Hill, 1969.

Quick, John. *Artists' and Illustrators' Encyclopedia*. 2nd ed. New York: McGraw-Hill, 1977.

Webster's New World Dictionary of the American Language. 2nd ed. New York: World Publishing, 1970.

Wolf, Martin L. *Dictionary of the Arts*. New York: Philosophical Library, 1951.

—Ian Crump; L.D.R.

V

MUSIC, CLASSICAL AND POPULAR

23

SOME NOTED COMPOSERS

. . . . .

THE POET STEPHEN SPENDER, IN AN ESSAY ENTITLED "THE MAKING OF A Poem," uses composers of music to make a point about writers and about creative method in general. There are, he notes, basically two kinds of composers; he calls them the Mozarts and the Beethovens. The Mozarts write music in prolific fashion, producing a symphony or a quartet within a day's time, turning out the music for an entire opera—overture, arias, ensembles, marches, dances, and all—in little more than a week. What they write emerges almost full-blown from their heads, and once set down requires little or no revision.

The Beethovens, by contrast, begin with a phrase, a motif. We can follow the process in Beethoven's notebooks. In its original form the phrase can be trite, banal. They proceed to work on it, often over a considerable extent of time, returning to it at intervals. They try it one way, then another, developing it, changing it. Eventually it may achieve a form very different from its original appearance in the notebooks.

The culminating motif from the fourth movement of the *Eroica* Symphony is an example. Beethoven used it first as one in a set of six German contradances. It appears, with greater elaboration, in his ballet music, *The Creatures of Prometheus*. He uses it again in the "Eroica Variations" for piano, in which he develops it in a number of different, often contrasting ways. Finally it receives its ultimate statement in the great conclusion to the Symphony No. 3 in E-flat Major.

It is unlikely that anyone, seeing or hearing the first sketch of the *Eroica* theme as it appears in the notebooks, would have been able to guess that it would ever attain the tremendous resolution that Beethoven gives it. Nor, encountering it in its final form, would one necessarily surmise the extended and painstakingly laborious process of composition that was involved in getting it there. It bears no marks of its evolutionary development.

It is also true that only a trained musicologist, upon listening to the *Eroica* finale and, say, that of Mozart's *Jupiter* Symphony, might be able to identify any connection between what he is hearing and the differences in the methods of composition. For, as Stephen Spender points out, whether in music, poetry, or any other kind of artistic composition, the ultimate merits of the final product bear no relationship to the creative process being used. Which is not to say, however, that as writers or musicians, we need not find it essential to labor hard and long at our craft. Beethoven, for one, found that it was.

The following is a listing of some distinguished composers of music, together with a smattering of representative works and dates of composition, when known.

Albeniz, Isaac (Manuel Francisco) (1868–1909). *Suite espagnole,* 1886; *Pepita Jiminez,* 1896; *Suite Iberia,* 1907.

Bach, C. P. E. (Carl Philipp Emanuel) (1714–88). *Magnificat,* 1749; *Amalian Sonatas,* 1761; *Short and Easy Keyboard Pieces,* 1768; *Die Israeliten in der Wuste,* 1769; *Morgengesang am Schopfungsfest,* 1783.

Bach, Johann Sebastian (1685–1750). *The Art of the Fugue,* 1748–50. Choral music and oratorios: "Jesu, Joy of Man's Desiring," from Cantata No. 147 (*Herz und Mund*), 1716; *The Passion According to St. John,* 1724; *The Passion According to St. Matthew,* 1727; *Christmas Oratorio,* 1734–35; *Easter Oratorio,* 1735; *Ascension Oratorio,* 1735; *Mass in B Minor,* written over two decades, 1724–49 (1749 premiere). Orchestral, chamber, and solo instrument music: Six Suites (Sonatas) for Violoncello, *ca.* 1720; Six *Brandenburg* Concertos, 1721; Concerto in D Minor for Two Violins and Orchestra, 1717–23. Piano music: Six French Suites for Piano, *ca.* 1722; Six English Suites for Piano, *ca.* 1725; *Goldberg Variations,* 1742; *Das Wohltemperierte Clavier,* (*The Well-Tempered Clavier*) Book I—1722, Book II—1744. Organ music: Passacaglia in C Minor, 1708–17; Toccata and Fugue in D Minor, 1708–17; Fantasia and Fugue in G Minor, 1708–17; Toccata in C Major, 1708–17.

Barber, Samuel (1910–81). *Dover Beach,* 1931; *School for Scandal,* 1933; String Quartet, 1936; *Knoxville: Summer of 1915,* 1947; *Vanessa,* 1958.

Bartok, Bela (1881–1945). String Quartet No. 1, 1908; *Bluebeard's Castle,* 1918; *Mikrokosmos,* 1926–39; Divertimento for Strings, 1939; Concerto for Orchestra, 1943.

Beethoven, Ludwig van (1770–1827). Orchestral music: Symphony No. 1 in C Major, 1800; Symphony No. 2 in D Major, 1802; Symphony No. 3 in E-flat Major (*Eroica*), 1804; Symphony No. 4 in B-flat Major, 1806; Symphony No. 5 in C Minor, 1805–1807; Symphony No. 6 in F Major (*Pastoral*), 1807–1808; Symphony No. 7 in A Major, 1812; Symphony No. 8 in F Major, 1812;

Symphony No. 9 in D Minor; 1817–23 (1824 premiere); Concerto for Violin and Orchestra, 1806; Piano Concerto No. 4 in G Major, 1806; Concerto No. 5 in E-flat Major (*Emperor*), 1809. Opera: *Fidelio*, February 20, 1805, Vienna. Piano: Sonata No. 7 in D Major, 1798; Sonata No. 8 in C Minor (*Pathetique*), 1797–98; Sonata No. 14 in C-sharp Minor (*Moonlight*), 1801; Sonata No. 21 in C Major (*Waldstein*), 1804; Sonata No. 23 in F Minor (*Appassionata*), 1804–1805; Sonata No. 29 in B-flat Major (*Hammerklavier*), 1818. Chamber music: Sonata in A Minor (*Kreutzer*), Op. 47, 1803; Quartet in B-flat Major, Op. 130, 1826; String Quartet in C-sharp Minor, Op. 131, 1825; String Quartet in A Minor, Op. 132, 1825; String Quartet in F Major, Op. 135, 1826. Choral music: *Missa Solemnis*, 1818–23 (1823 premiere).

Bellini, Vincenzo (1801–35). *La sonnambula* (*The Sleepwalker*), 1831; *Norma*, 1831; *I puritani di Scozia*, 1835.

Berlioz, Hector (1803–69). *Symphonie fantastique*, 1830; *Romeo and Juliet*, 1839; *La Damnation de Faust* (*The Damnation of Faust*), 1846; *Les Troyens*, 1863 (2nd part), 1890 (full premiere).

Bizet, Georges (1838–75). *Les Pêcheurs de perles* (*The Pearl Fishers*), 1863; *L'Arlésienne*, Suite No. 1, 1872; *Carmen*, 1875.

Bloch, Ernest (1880–1959). *Schelomo*, 1916; Piano Quintet No. 1, 1923; Concerto Grosso No. 1, 1925; *Avodath Hakodesh*, 1933.

Boccherini, Luigi (1743–1805). Quintet in F Major for Strings, 1772; Quintet in E Major for Strings, 1772; Six Quintets for Flute and Strings, 1773; Quintet in D for Guitar and Strings, 1799; Quintettino in C Major for Guitar and Strings.

Borodin, Alexander Porfiryevich (1863–87). Symphony No. 2 in B Minor, 1876; *On the Steppes of Central Asia*, 1880; "Polovtsian Dances," from *Prince Igor*, 1890.

Brahms, Johannes (1833–97). Orchestral music: *Variations on a Theme by Haydn*, 1873; Symphony No. 1 in C Minor, 1876; Symphony No. 2 in D Major, 1877; Symphony No. 3 in F Major, 1883; Symphony No. 4 in E Minor, 1885; Piano Concerto No. 1 in D Minor, 1858; *Academic Festival Overture*, 1880; Concerto in D Major for Violin and Orchestra, 1878; *Tragic* Overture in D Minor, 1880; Piano Concerto No. 2 in B-flat Major, 1881; Concerto in A Minor, Double Concerto, 1887. Choral music: *A German Requiem*, 1867 (partial), 1868 (full premiere). Chamber music: Piano Quintet in F Minor, Op. 34, 1862; Clarinet Quintet in B Minor, Op. 115, 1891. Piano music: *Variations and Fugue on a Theme by G. F. Handel* in B-flat Major, Op. 24, 1861; *Variations on a Theme by Paganini* in A Minor, Op. 35, 1863; Waltz No. 15 in A-flat Major, 1865. Vocal music: *Weigenlied* (*Lullaby*), 1868.

Britten, Benjamin (1913–76). *Peter Grimes*, 1945; *Young Person's Guide to the Orchestra*, 1946; *Gloriana*, 1953; *Death in Venice*, 1973; String Quartet No. 3, 1975.

Bruckner, Anton (1824–96). Symphony No. 4 in E-flat Major (*Romantic*), 1881; Symphony No. 7 in E Major, 1884.

Buxtehude, Diderik (1637–1707). Ciacona in C Minor, *ca.* 1680–90; Ciacona in E Minor, *ca.* 1680–90; Passacaglia in D Minor, *ca.* 1680–90.

Byrd, William (1543–1623). *Caniones Sacrae,* Book I, 1589; Book II, 1591; *Psalmes, Songs, and Sonnets,* 1611.

Chausson, Ernest (1855–99). Symphony in B-flat Major, 1890.

Cherubini, Luigi (1760–1842). *Médée,* 1797; *Les Deux Journées,* 1800; *Faniska,* 1806; Requiem in C Minor, 1816.

Chopin, Frédéric (1810–49). Twelve Grand Studies, Op. 10, 1829–32; Twelve Studies, Op. 25, 1832–36; Fantaisie No. 137 in F Minor, Op. 49, 1840–41; Polonaise No. 147 in A-flat Major, Op. 53, 1842; Barcarolle No. 158 in F-sharp Major, Op. 60, 1845–46.

Coleridge-Taylor, Samuel (1875–1912). *Te Deum,* 1890; *Hiawatha,* 1898–1900.

Copland, Aaron (1900–80). *El Salon Mexico,* 1936; *Billy the Kid,* 1940; *Rodeo,* 1942; *Appalachian Spring,* 1944; Piano Quartet, 1950.

Corelli, Arcangelo (1653–1713). *Christmas* Concerto in G Minor, Op. 6, No. 8, 1714.

Czerny, Carl (1791–1857). *Complete Theoretical and Practical Pianoforte School,* Op. 500, 1839.

Debussy, Claude (1862–1918). *Pelléas et Mélisande,* 1892–1902 (1902 premiere); *Nocturnes,* 1893–99; Quartet in G Minor, 1893; *L'Après-midi d'un faune (The Afternoon of a Faun),* 1894.

Donizetti, Gaetano (1797–1848). *Lucia di Lammermoor,* 1835; *La Fille du regiment (The Daughter of the Regiment),* 1840; *Don Pasquale,* 1843.

Dowland, John (1563–1626). *First Booke of Songes or Ayres of Foure Partes with Tableture for the Lute,* 1597.

Dukas, Paul (1865–1935). *L'Apprenti sorcier (The Sorcerer's Apprentice),* 1897; *La Peri,* 1912.

Dvorak, Antonin (1841–1904). Concerto in A Minor for Violin and Orchestra, Op. 53, 1880; *St. Ludmilla,* Op. 71, 1886; *Slavonic Dances,* series I, Op. 46, 1878; series II, Op. 72, 1886; Symphony No. 9 in E Minor (*From the New World*), Op. 95, 1893; Quartet in F Major (*American*), Op. 96, 1893; Quintet in E-flat Major, Op. 97, 1893; *Humoresque,* Op. 101, 1894; Concerto in B Minor for Cello and Orchestra, Op. 104, 1895.

Elgar, Sir Edward (1857–1934). Variations on an Original Theme (*Enigma*), 1899; *The Dream of Gerontius,* 1899; March No. 2 in A Minor (*Pomp and Circumstance*), 1902.

Falla, Manuel de (1876–1946). *El amor brujo,* 1915; *El sombrero de tres picos (The Three-Cornered Hat),* 1919.

Fauré, Gabriel (1845–1924). Sonata No. 1 in A Major for Violin and Piano, 1876; Quartet No. 2 in G Minor for Piano and Strings, 1886; "Clair de lune," 1887; *La Bonne Chanson,* 1892; *Pelléas et Mélisande* Suite, 1898.

Franck, César (1822–90). Sonata for Violin and Piano in A Major 1886; Prelude,

Aria, and Finale, 1886–87; Symphony in D Minor, 1888; Three Chorales, 1890.

Gershwin, George (1898–1937). "Rhapsody in Blue," 1924; Concerto in F for Piano and Orchestra, 1925; *An American in Paris*, 1928; *Porgy and Bess*, 1935.

Glinka, Mikhail Ivanovich (1804–57). *Ruslan and Ludmilla*, 1837–42.

Gluck, Christoph Willibald (1714–87). *Orfeo ed Euridice*, 1762; *Alceste*, 1776.

Gounod, Charles (1818–93). *Faust*, 1859; *Roméo et Juliette*, 1867.

Grieg, Edvard (1843–1907). Concerto in A Minor for Piano and Orchestra, 1869; *Peer Gynt* Suite, Nos. 1 and 2, 1874–76; *Holberg* Suite, 1884; Norwegian Dance No. 2, 1898.

Handel, George Frideric (1685–1759). Choral works and oratorios: *St. John's Passion*, 1704; *Chandos Anthems*, 1716–38; *Coronation Anthems* for George II, 1727; *A Collection of English Songs* (Minuet songs), 1731 and earlier; *Israel in Egypt*, 1738; *Messiah*, 1741; *Samele*, 1744; *Judas Maccabeus*, 1747. Orchestral music: *Water Music, ca.* 1717; Twelve Concerti grossi, Op. 6, 1739; *Music for the Royal Fireworks*, 1749. Operas: *Rinaldo*, 1711; *Ottone*, 1723; *Tamerlano*, 1724; *Rodelinda*, 1725; *Orlando*, 1733; *Alcina*, 1735. Mass: *Dettingen Te Deum*, 1743.

Haydn, Franz Joseph (1732–1809). Choral works and oratorios: *The Seven Words of Jesus on the Cross* or *The Passion*, 1785; *Mass in Time of War*, 1796; *The Creation*, 1796–98; *Lord Nelson Mass*, 1798; *The Seasons*, 1798–1801; *Ariana a Naxos*, 1792. Opera: *Orfeo ed Euridice*, 1791. Orchestral works: Symphony in F-sharp Minor, 1772; Symphony No. 88 in G Major, 1786–87; Symphony No. 94 in G Major (*The Surprise*), 1791; Symphony No. 95 in C Minor, 1791; Symphony No. 96 in D Major (*The Miracle*), 1791; Symphony No. 100 in G Major (*The Military*), 1794; Symphony No. 101 in D Major (*The Clock*), 1794; Symphony No. 103 in E-flat Major (*The Drum Roll*), 1795; Symphony No. 104 in D Major (*London*), 1795; Concerto in D Major for Cello and Orchestra, 1783; Concerto in D Major for Harpsichord and Orchestra, Op. 21, 1783. String quartets: *Sun Quartets*, Op. 20, 1772; *Russian Quartets*, Op. 33, 1781; Quartet in D Minor, Op. 76, No. 2 (*Quinten*), 1799; Quartet in D Major Op. 76, No. 5 (*Largo*), 1799; Quartet in C Major, Op. 76, No. 3 (*Emperor*), 1799.

Hindemith, Paul (1895–1963). *Das Marianleben*, 1923; *Mathis der Maler* (*Mathias the Painter*), 1935; *Symphonic Metamorphosis on Themes of Carl Maria von Weber*, 1943.

Holst, Gustav (1874–1934). *The Planets*, Op. 32, 1914–16 (1918 premiere); First Choral Symphony, 1923–24 (1925 premiere); *At the Boar's Head*, 1924 (1925 premiere); *Egdon Heath, Homage to Hardy*, Op. 47, 1927 (1928 premiere).

Indy, Vincent d' (1851–1931). *Symphony on a French Mountain Air*, 1887; *Istar Variations*, 1896 (1897 premiere).

Ives, Charles (1874–1954). *Harvest Home* Chorales, 1902; *Three Places in New England*, 1903–14; Sonata No. 2 for Piano (*Concord*), 1924.

Janacek, Leos (1854–1928). *Jeji Patorkyna*, 1894–1903 (1904 premiere); *The Diary of One Who Vanished*, 1916–19; String Quartet No. 1, 1923; *Sarka*, 1887 (1925 premiere); String Quartet No. 2, 1927–28.

Kodály, Zoltán (1882–1967). *Harry Janos* (1926), *Psalmus hungaricus* (1923), *Peacock Variations* (1939), *Dances of Galánta* (1933)

Lalo, Edouard (1823–92). *Symphonie espagnole*, for violin and orchestra, 1873; Overture to *Le Roi d'Ys*, 1875–88.

Leoncavallo, Ruggiero (1858–1919). *I Pagliacci* (*Clowns*), 1892; *Zaza*, 1900.

Liszt, Franz (1811–86). Orchestral music: *Hungarian Fantasy*, for piano and orchestra, 1822; *Les Preludes*, 1848–54 (1854 premiere); *Mazeppa*, 1851 (1854 premiere); Concerto No. 1 in E-flat Major for Piano and Orchestra, 1849–56 (1855 premiere); *Tasso, Lamento e Trionfo*, 1849–54 (1857 premiere); *Faust* Symphony, 1854–57 (1857 premiere); *Second Mephisto Waltz*, 1880–81 (1881 premiere). Piano works: *Third Mephisto Waltz*, 1883; *Hungarian Rhapsodies*, 1846–85. Transcriptions and arrangements: *Etudes d'exécution transcendante d'après Paganini*, 1838; Mendelssohn's "*Wedding March*," 1849–50; *Polonaise brilliant* (Weber), 1851.

Mahler, Gustav (1860–1911). Symphony No. 1 in D Major (*The Titan*), 1889; Symphony No. 2 in C Minor (*Resurrection*), 1895; Symphony No. 3 in D Minor, 1895; Symphony No. 4 in C-Sharp Minor (*The Giant*), 1900 (1902 premiere); Symphony No. 5 in C Minor, 1902; Symphony No. 6 in A Minor, 1904; Symphony No. 7 in D Major, 1905; Symphony No. 8 in E-flat Major, 1907 (1910 premiere); Symphony No. 9 in D Minor, 1909; Symphony No. 10 (unfinished), 1910; *Das Lied von der Erde*, song cycle, 1908.

Mascagni, Pietro (1863–1945). *Cavalleria Rusticana*, 1890.

Massenet, Jules (1845–1912). *Manon*, 1884; *Thaïs*, 1894; *Le Jongleur de Nôtre-Dame* (*The Juggler of Notre Dame*), 1902.

Mendelssohn, Felix (1809–47). Orchestral music: *A Midsummer Night's Dream* Suite, 1826–43 (overture premiere 1827; full premiere 1843); Symphony No. 4 in A Major (*Italian*), 1830–32 (1833 premiere); Symphony No. 5 in D Major (*Reformation*), 1830; Concerto No. 1 in G Minor for Piano and Orchestra, 1831; Symphony No. 3 in A Minor (*Scottish*), 1842; Concerto in E Minor for Violin and Orchestra, 1844; *Fingal's Cave* Overture, 1830 (revised 1832); *Ruy Blas* Overture, 1839. Choral music: *St. Paul*, 1836; *Elijah*, 1846. Piano music: *Songs without Words*, Book I, Op. 19, 1829; Book II, Op. 30, 1834; Book III, Op. 38, 1837; Book IV, Op. 53, 1841; Book V, Op. 62, 1842–44; Book VI, Op. 67, 1843–45; Book VII, Op. 85, 1834–45; Book VIII, Op. 102, 1842–45; *Rondo capriccioso*, 1824; *Variations sérieuses*, 1841. Chamber music: String Quintet No. 1 in A Major, Op. 18, 1826 (revised 1832); String Quartet Nos. 3–5 in E-flat Major, Op. 44, No. 3, 1838.

Menotti, Gian Carlo (1911–). *Amelia Goes to the Ball*, 1937; *The Medium*, 1946; *Amahl and the Night Visitors*, 1951; *The Saint of Bleecker Street*, 1954.

Meyerbeer, Giacomo (1791–1864). *L'Africana*, 1838–43 (1845 premiere).

Moniuszko, Stanislaw (1819–72). *Halka*, 1858; *Straszny dwór* (The haunted manor), 1865.

Monteverdi, Claudio (1567–1643). *Orfeo*, 1607; *Ariadne*, 1608; *Sanctissimi Virginis Missa senis vocibus ad Ecclesiarum choros ac Vesperaae pluribus decantandae cum nonnullis concentibus (*Vespers), 1610.

Morales, Cristóbal de (*ca.* 1500–53). *Lamentabatur Jacob*, 1543; *Ave Maris stella*, 1544.

Moussorgsky, Modeste (1839–81). *Boris Godunov*, 1st version 1868–69, 2nd version 1871–72; *St. John's Night on Bald Mountain*, 1867.

Mozart, Leopold (1719–87). *Toy* Symphony in C Major, 1788 (originally attributed to Haydn).

Mozart, Wolfgang Amadeus (1756–91). Operas: *Die Entfuhrung aus dem Serail* (*The Abduction from the Seraglio*), 1782; *Cosi Fan Tutte*, 1790; *Don Giovanni (Don Juan)*, 1791; *Die Zauberflöte (The Magic Flute)*, 1791; *Le Nozze di Figaro, (The Marriage of Figaro)* 1786. Piano works: Sonata in A Major, K. 396, 1782; Sonata in C Minor, K. 457, 1784; Sonata in F Major, K. 533 (unfinished), 1788; Sonata in D Major, K. 576, 1789. Strings: Quartet in C (*Dissonance*), 1785; Divertimento in E-flat, K. 80, 1788; Quintet in C Major, K. 515, 1787; Quintet in G Minor, K. 516, 1787; Quintet in D Major, K. 593, 1790. Orchestral works: Serenade in D (*Posthorn*), 1779; Serenades for Winds in B-flat, K. 361, 1781–84; Divertimento for Strings and Horns (*Ein muiskalischer Spass—A Musical Joke*), K. 522, 1787; Symphony No. 14 in A, 1771; Symphony No. 21 in A, 1772; Symphony No. 18 in F, 1772; Symphony No. 35 in D (*Haffner*), 1782; Symphony No. 38 in D Major (*Prague*), 1786; Symphony No. 40 in G Minor, 1788; Symphony No. 41 in C (*Jupiter*), 1788; *Eine kleine Nachtmusik*, K. 525, 1787. Vocal works: Mass in C Major (*Coronation*), K. 317, 1779; Concerto in A for Clarinet and Orchestra, 1791; Requiem in D Minor, K. 626 (unfinished), 1791.

Offenbach, Jacques (1819–80). *Orphée aux enfers (Orpheus in Hades)*, 1858; *La Vie parisienne (Paris Life)*, 1866; *Contes d'Hoffmann (Tales of Hoffman)*, unfinished, 1881.

Paganini, Niccolò (1782–1840). 24 *Capricci*, Op. 1, published 1820.

Palestrina, Giovanni Pierluigi da (1525–94). *Missa Papaef Marcelli, ca.* 1555–60, published 1567; *Te Deum Mass*, 1599.

Pergolesi, Giovanni Battista (1710–36). *L'Olimpiade*, 1735.

Piccinni, Niccolò (1728–1800). *L'Olimpiade*, 1st setting 1768, 2nd setting 1774; *Iphigenie en Tauride*, 1781.

Porpora, Nicola (Antonio) (1686–1766). Twelve Concertos for Violin, 1754.

Poulenc, Francis (1899–1963). *Les Biches*, 1924; *Concert champêtre*, 1928; *Aubade*, 1929; *Figure humaine*, 1943; *Les Mamelles de Tirésias*, 1947; *Stabat Mater*, 1950.

Prokofiev, Sergei (1891–1953). Symphony No. 1 in D (*Classical*), 1917; *The Love of Three Oranges*, 1921; *Lieutenant Kijé*, 1933; *Peter and the Wolf*, 1936; *Alexander Nevsky*, 1939; *Voina y Mir (War and Peace)*, October 16, 1944.

Puccini, Giacomo (1868–1924). *La Bohème*, 1893; *Tosca*, 1900; *La Fanciulla del West (The Girl of the Golden West)*, 1911; *Madame Butterfly*, 1904; *Manon Lescaut*, 1893; *La Rondine (The Sparrow)*, 1917; *Trittico*, 1918; *Turandot*, 1925.

Purcell, Henry (ca. 1659–95). *Dido and Aeneas*, 1689; *The Fairy Queen*, 1692; "Hail, Bright Cecilia," 1692; *Timon of Athens*, 1694; "Save Me, O God," ca. 1680–82; Sonata No. 9 in F Major (*Golden Sonata*), 1697; Toccata in A Major, undated.

Rachmaninoff, Sergei Vassilievich (1873–1943). Piano Concerto in F-sharp, 1891; Symphony No. 1 in D Minor, 1895; Piano Concerto No. 2 in C Minor, 1901; Prelude in C-sharp Minor, 1903; *Isle of the Dead*, 1909; *Rhapsody on a Theme by Paganini for Piano and Orchestra*, 1934.

Rameau, Jean-Philippe (1683–1764). *La Princesse de Navarre*, 1745.

Ravel (Joseph) Maurice (1875–1937). *L'Heure espanole*, 1907; *L'Enfant et les sortilèges*, 1920–25 (1925 premiere); *Boléro*, 1927; *Tzigane*, 1925–26; Concerto in G Major, 1931; *La Valse*, 1919–20.

Reger, Max (1873–1916). Fantasy and Fugue on Bach, Op. 46, 1900; Symphonic Prologue to a Tragedy in A Minor, Op. 108, 1908.

Respighi, Ottorino (1879–1936). *Fontani di Roma (Fountains of Rome)*, 1916; *Pina di Roma (Pines of Rome)*, 1924; *La Fiamma (The Flame)*, 1932–34.

Rimsky-Korsakov, Nikolay Andreyevich (1844–1908). *Snegurochka (The Snow Maiden)*, 1880–82; *Sheherazade*, 1888; *Mozart and Salieri*, 1897; *Le Coq d'Or (The Golden Cockerel)*, 1906–1907.

Rossini, Gioacchino Antonio (1792–1868). *Tancredi*, 1813; *Il Barbiere di Siviglie (The Barber of Seville)*, 1816; *Otello*, 1816; *Guillaume Tell*, 1829; *Stabat Mater*, 1841.

Saint-Saëns, Camille (1835–1921). *Messe solennelle*, Op. 4, 1856; Concerto No. 2 in G Minor, 1868; *Danse macabre*, 1874; Concerto No. 3 in B Minor for Violin, 1880; Symphony No. 3 in C Minor, 1886; *The Carnival of Animals*, 1886.

Satie, Erik (Alfred Leslie) (1866–1925). *Danses de travers*, 1897; *Sports et divertissements*, 1914; *Socrate*, 1918.

Scarlatti, (Pietro) Alessandro (Gaspare) (1660–1725). *Eraclea*, 1700; *Laodicea e Berenice*, 1701; *Mitridate Eupatore*, 1707; *La principessa fedele*, 1710; *Tigrane*, 1715; *Telemaco*, 1718.

Scarlatti, (Giuseppe) Domenico (1685–1757). *XLII Suites de pieces pour le clavicin*, 1730–37.

Schoenberg, Arnold (1874–1951). Five Orchestral Pieces, Op. 16, 1909; *Pelleas und Melisande*, Op. 5, 1902–1903; Violin Concerto, Op. 36, 1935–36; Trio, Op. 45, 1946; *Moses and Aaron*, first two acts 1932, resumed 1951 (1954 premiere).

Schubert, Franz (Peter) (1797–1828). Orchestral works: Symphony No. 4 in C Minor (*Tragic*), 1816; Symphony No. 9 in C major (*Great*), 1828 (1938 premier); Symphony No. 8 in B Minor (*Unfinished*), 1822 (1865 premiere); *Rosamunde*, incidental music, 1823. Chamber works: Quartet in A Minor, 1824; Quartet in D Minor (*Death and the Maiden*), 1824, (1826 premiere); Quartet in G Major, 1826 (1828 premiere); Quintet in C Major, 1828; Quintet in A Major (*Trout*), 1819; Trio in B-flat Major, 1827; Trio in E-flat Major, 1827. Piano works: *Wanderer* Fantasy in C, 1822; Sonata in C Minor, 1828; Sonata in A Major, 1819 or 1825; Sonata in B-flat Major, 1828. Vocal works: "Ganymed," 1817; *Schöne Mullerin*, 1823; "Hark, Hark, the Lark," 1826; *Die Winterreise*, 1827; *Schwanengesang*, 1828.

Schumann, Robert (Alexander) (1810–56). *Le Carnaval*, 1834–35; *Fantasiestucke*, 1837; *Scenes from Childhood*, 1838; *Album for the Young*, 1848; Concerto in A Minor for Piano and Orchestra, one movement 1841, finished 1845; Concerto in A Minor for Cello and Orchestra, 1853; Quintet in E-flat Major for Piano and Strings; *Manfred*, incidental music, 1848–49 (1852 premiere); Symphony No. 1 in B-flat Major (*Spring*), 1841; Symphony No. 3 in E-flat Major (*Rhenish*), 1850.

Scriabin, Alexander (1872–1915). *Prometheus: Poem of Fire*, Op. 60, 1909–10.

Shostakovich, Dmitri (1906–75). *Katerina Ismailove/Ledi Makbet Mtsenskago Uezda* (*Lady Macbeth of the Mtsensk District*), 1934; Symphony No. 5 in D Minor, 1937; Symphony No. 7 in C (*Leningrad*), 1941; Symphony No. 10 in E Minor, 1953.

Sibelius, Jean (1865–1957). Symphony No. 1 in E, 1891; *Kullervo* Symphony, 1892; *A Saga*, 1892, revised 1901; Romance in D-flat, No. 4, 1895; *Lemmenkäinen* Suite, 1895; *Finlandia*, 1899, revised 1900; *The Origin of Fire*, 1902; Symphony No. 3 in C, 1907; Symphony No. 4 in A, 1911.

Smetana, Friedrich (1824–84). *The Bartered Bride*, 1863–66; *The Moldau (Vltava)*, 1874–79; Quartet No. 1 in E Minor (*From My Life*), 1876.

Spohr, Louis (1784–1859). Nonet in F for Wind and Strings, 1813; *Die Letzten Dinge*, 1826; String Sextet in C, 1842.

Stanford, (Sir) Charles (Villiers) (1852–1924). *The Revenge Cantata*, Op. 24, 1886; Irish Symphony in F Minor, Op. 28, 1887; *Irish Rhapsodies*, 1905–11; *Stabat Mater*, Op. 96, 1907.

Strauss, Johann (1804–49). *Viktoria Walzer*, Op. 103, 1838; "Radetsky March," 1848.

Strauss, Johann, II (1825–99). "Blue Danube Waltz," Op. 315, 1867; "Tales from the Vienna Woods," 1868; *Kaiserwalzer,* Op. 436, 1888; *Die Fledermaus (The Bat),* April 5, 1874; *Zigeunerbaron (Gypsy Baron),* 1885.

Strauss, Richard (1864–1949). *Don Juan,* 1888; *Death and Transfiguration,* 1889; *Till Eulenspiegel's Merry Pranks,* 1895; *Thus Spake Zarathustra,* 1897; *Don Quixote,* 1897; *A Hero's Life,* 1898; "Allerseelen," Op. 10, No. 8, 1882–83; "Zueignung," Op. 10, No. 1, 1882–83; "Morgen," Op. 27, No. 4, 1893–94; "Wiegenlied," Op. 41, No. 1, 1899; "Traum durch die Dammerung," Op. 29, No.1, 1894–95; *Salome,* 1905; *Elektra,* 1909; *Der Rosenkavalier (The Knight of the Rose),* 1911; *Intermezzo,* 1924.

Stravinsky, Igor Fyodorovich (1882–1971). *Scherzo fantastique,* 1908; *Fireworks,* 1908; *The Firebird,* 1910; *Petrushka,* 1911; *The Rite of Spring,* 1913; *Le Rossignol (The Nightingale),* 1914; Symphonies of Wind Instruments, 1920; *Pulcinella,* 1920; *The Wedding,* 1923; *Oedipus Rex,* 1927; *Symphony of Psalms,* 1930; Symphony in Three Movements, 1945; *The Rake's Progress,* 1951.

Sullivan, Sir Arthur Seymour (1842–1900). *The Tempest,* incidental music, 1862; *Irish Symphony,* 1864; "Onward! Christian Soldiers," 1872; *Trial by Jury,* 1875; "The Lost Chord," 1877; *HMS Pinafore, or The Lass That Loved a Sailor,* 1878; *The Pirates of Penzance, or The Slave of Duty,* 1879; *Patience, or Bunthorne's Bride,* 1881; *Iolanthe, or The Peer and the Peri,* 1882; *The Mikado, or The Town of Titipu,* 1885; *The Golden Legend,* cantata, 1886; *The Yeomen of the Guard, or The Merryman and His Maid,* 1888; *The Gondoliers, or The King of Barataria,* 1889.

Tchaikovsky, Peter Ilyich (1840–93). *Romeo and Juliet,* 1870–80; Concerto No. 1 in B-flat Minor for Piano and Orchestra, 1875; *Swan Lake,* 1875–76; *Francesca de Rimini,* 1876; *March Slave,* 1876; Concerto in D Major for Violin and Orchestra, 1878; Symphony No. 4 in F Minor, 1878; *Eugen Onegin,* 1879; *1812 Overture,* 1880; *Capriccio Italien,* 1880; *Mazeppa,* 1882–83; *Manfred Symphony,* 1885; Symphony No. 5 in E Minor, 1888; *Sleeping Beauty,* 1888–89; *Nutcracker Suite,* 1891–92; Symphony No. 6 in B Minor (*Pathetique*), 1893.

Telemann, Georg Philipp (1681–1767). *Pimpinone,* 1725; *Music de table,* 1733.

Vaughan Williams, Ralph (1872–1958). *Salve Festa Dies (Hail Thee Festival Day),* ca. 1905; *Sine Nomine (For all the Saints),* ca. 1905; *Sea Symphony,* 1905–10; *Fantasia on a Theme by Thomas Tallis for Double-String Orchestra,* 1910; *Hugh the Drover,* 1911–14 (1924 premiere); *A London Symphony,* 1913; *Mass in G Minor,* ca. 1922; *Pastoral Symphony,* 1922; Symphony No. 4 in F Minor, 1935; Symphony No. 6 in E Minor, 1947; *The Pilgrim's Progress,* 1948–49.

Verdi, Giuseppe (Fortunino Francesco) (1813–1901). *Nabucco,* 1842; *Jerusalem,* 1843; *Macbeth,* 1847, revised French version 1865; *Rigoletto,* 1851; *La*

Traviata, 1853; *Il Trovatore,* 1853; *I vespri siciliani,* 1857, revised French version, titled *Simon Boccanegra,* 1881; *Don Carlos,* 1867; Italian version, *Don Carlo,* 1881; *Aida,* 1871; *Otello,* 1887; *Falstaff,* 1893; "Stabat Mater," 1896–97; "Te Deum," 1895–96.

Victoria, Tomas Luis de (ca. 1548–1611). Mass, *O quam gloriosum,* 1572; Mass, *Vide speciosam,* 1572.

Villa-Lobos, Heitor (1887–1959). *Bachiana Brasileira No. 2, 1930; Bachiana Brasileira No. 5, 1938–45;* Choros No. 10, 1925.

Vivaldi, Antonio (ca. 1675–1741). *L'estri armonico,* 12 concertos, Op. 3, 1712; VI Sonate, Op. 5, 1716.

Wagner, Richard (1813–83). *Seven Compositions from Goethe's "Faust,"* 1832; *A Faust Overture for Orchestra,* 1840; *Rienzi,* 1842; *Die Fliegende Holländer (The Flying Dutchman),* 1843; *Tannhauser und der Sangerkrieg auf Wartburg (Tannhauser and the Song Contest at the Wartburg),* 1845; *Lohengrin,* 1850; *Tristan und Isolde,* 1865; *Die Meistersinger von Nürnberg (The Mastersingers of Nuremberg),* 1868; *Das Rheingold,* 1869 (written 1853); *Die Walkure,* 1870 (written 1852); *Siegfried Idyl,* 1870; *Siegfried,* 1876 (written 1852); *Parsifal,* 1882.

Walton, William (1902–83). *Façade,* 1922; *Belshazzar's Feast,* 1931; *Henry V,* 1944; *Troilus and Cressida,* 1954; *Variation on a Theme by Hindemith,* 1963; *Capriccio Burlesco,* 1968.

Warlock, Peter (Philip Heseltine) (1894–1930). *Saudades,* 1916–17; *Capriol Suite,* 1926.

Weber, Carl Maria von (Friedrich Ernst) (1786–1826). *Invitation to the Dance,* 1819; *Concerto in F Minor,* Op. 79, 1821; *Konzertstück,* 1821; *Der Freischütz (The Freeshooter),* 1821; *Euryanthe,* 1823; *Oberon, or The Elf-King's Oath,* 1826.

Wolf, Hugo (1860–1903). *Italian* Serenade for String Orchestra, 1887; *Morike Lieder,* 1888; *Goethe Lieder,* 1888–89; *Spanisches Liederbuch,* 1889–90; *Italienisches Liederbuch,* 1896.

Zingarelli, Niccolo Antonio (1752–1837). *Giulietta e Romeo,* 1796; *Berenice,* 1811.

SOURCES

Randel, Don Michael, comp. *Harvard Concise Dictionary of Music.* Cambridge, Mass.: Belknap Press, 1978.
Sadie, Stanley, ed. *The New Grove Dictionary of Music and Musicians.* London: Macmillan, 1980.
———. *The Norton/Grove Concise Encyclopedia of Music.* New York: W. W. Norton, 1991.

—Margaret Campbell; Jesma Reynolds; L.D.R.

24

FAMOUS OPERAS

. . . . .

IT IS A MATTER OF OPINION WHETHER GRAND OPERA IS MORE EFFECTIVELY produced with or without elaborately realistic stage sets. It can be argued (echo-
ing Samuel Johnson on Shakespeare and the neoclassical unities) that anyone
who believes that he is seeing a chorus of Nordic river nymphs instead of a
group of singers on a stage can as readily imagine that the stage is the Rhine
River in the Teutowald instead of a theater in New York or London. On the
other hand, spectacle as such can surely offer a welcome dimension for opera,
and sets and costumes are an active ingredient in the show.

All art is "let's pretend," and involves certain agreed-upon fictions, or
conventions, between artist and audience. Opera, combining as it does
music, dramatic performance, spectacle, and storytelling, may be said to
lean more heavily upon such conventions than, say, prose fiction. Yet for all
its realistic texture the novel likewise depends on the willingness of the
reader to suspend certain assumptions about the nature of everyday reality;
how could we possibly know, for example, the details of what someone
other than ourselves is thinking and feeling? In a biography we wouldn't
accept any such thing.

As a musical genre, opera developed from madrigals, the commedia del
arte, and pastoral drama. It came into something of its own in the seventeenth century; Claudio Monteverdi's *La Favola d'Orfeo* (1607) has been
described as the first full-fledged opera; it is certainly the first about which
the details of performance are known. Italians were the prime practitioners;
there were two kinds of operas, the *opera seria* and the *opera buffa*. Forms
such as operettas and musical comedies might be said to have descended
from the latter. In the eighteenth century Handel wrote operas in the Italian
style for English audiences and Gluck for Austrian and German audiences,
and these are sometimes revived, but the standard operatic repertory today
usually begins with Mozart.

It was in the mid-nineteenth century that the movement toward
"music drama" got going. In Mozart and Rossini the arias, ensembles,

marches, serenades, etc., are separated from the recitatives. Later composers, foremost among them Wagner, didn't like this, and substituted leitmotifs and continuing melody throughout, seeking a more unified and totally shaped form. In the twentieth century there has been a tendency to combine the opera and cantata forms.

Film has revealed itself as being an ideal medium for opera, whether on small or large screen, and for most listener-viewers the addition of subtitles has enhanced the detailed dramatic meaning, so that the present day might well be considered a golden age for opera.

The following are the dates and places of first performance of some of the better-known operas, with composers and librettists. The first listing of the title is in accordance with the way that the opera is customarily referred to in the United States. Thus, *The Flying Dutchman* but *Der Freischütz.*

Abduction from the Seraglio, The (Die Entfuhrung aus dem Serail), by Wolfgang Amadeus Mozart. Libretto by Gottlieb Stephanie, based on Cristoph Friedrich Bretzner's Belmont und Constanze. Goethe was particularly taken by this opera, although Bretzner, the author of the story, protested its becoming an opera. It premiered in the Vienna Burgtheater, July 16, 1782.

Aida, by Giuseppe Verdi. Libretto by François-Auguste Mariette, Camille du Locle, and Antonio Chislanzoni. This was first produced on December 24, 1871, in Cairo. Although it is commonly believed that *Aida* was commissioned to celebrate the opening of the Suez Canal, it was actually commissioned by Egyptian viceroy Ishmail Pasha to celebrate the opening of the Khedive's new opera house. The two dates are almost identical. Its first production in Italy was at La Scala, Milan, February 7, 1872.

Alceste, by Christoph Willibald Gluck. Libretto by Raniero Calzabigi, based on Euripedes' *Alcestis.* The original version premiered in Vienna at the Burgtheater, December 26, 1767. This opera was then translated and adapted into French by F. L. G. Lebland du Roulletis. There were significant changes in the score in this version. It premiered at the Académie Royale de Musique in Paris, on April 23, 1776. It is this latter version that is popular.

Alcina, by George Frideric Handel. Libretto by Antonio Marchi, based on thirty stanzas from Ariosto's *Orlando Furioso.* Premiered at Covent Garden Theatre in London, April 16, 1735.

Amahl and the Night Visitors, by Gian Carlo Menotti. This was commissioned by NBC Television, and was broadcast on the network on December 24, 1951. This was the first opera designed for television. Its first stage performance was at Indiana University, at Bloomington, February 21, 1952.

Andrea Chenier, by Umberto Giordano. Libretto by L. Illica. Premiered at La Scala, Milan, March 28, 1896. The opera was a spectacular success when produced.

Antony and Cleopatra, by Samuel Barber. Text by Franco Zeffirelli, based on Shakespeare's play. Commissioned for the opening of the new opera house at Lincoln Center, the opera premiered at the Metropolitan Opera House, New York, on September 16, 1966.

Ariadne (Arianna), by Claudio Monteverdi. Libretto by Ottavio Rinuccini. This opera premiered at and was commissioned for the marriage celebration of Prince Francesco Gonzaga to Margareta di Savoia at the Teatro della Cotte in Mantua, May 28, 1608. All but "Lamento d'Arianna" and "Lasciatemi morir" has been lost, but these were imitated by Pietro Francesco Cavalli and Henry Purcell. The opera was immensely successful at its premiere and later when it was the inaugural opera at the Teatro di San Moise in 1639.

Ariadne auf Naxos, by Richard Strauss II. Words by Strauss's frequent collaborator, Hugo von Hofmannsthal. *Ariadne auf Naxos* was first produced at the Court Theater, Stuttgart, October 25, 1912. It was later revised and repremiered at Hofoper, in Vienna, October 4, 1916.

Barber of Seville, The (Il Barbiere di Siviglie), Gioacchino Antonio Rossini's most famous opera. The text is by Cesare Sterbini, adapted from Pierre-Augustin Caron de Beaumarchais' comedy of the same name. There was an earlier opera based on the same text by Giovanni Paisiello (libretto by Giuseppe Petrosellini, premiered 1782). Rossini's version premiered February 20, 1816, at the Teatro Argentina in Rome. Although it was booed and hissed at the opening by supporters of Paisiello's opera, public opinion quickly swung to acclaim. Paisiello's version was virtually forgotten.

Bartered Bride, The, by Friedrich Smetana. Libretto by Karel Sabina. This was first produced on May 30, 1866, at the Prague Provisional Theatre. Smetana continued to add scenes and arias until the September 25, 1870, production at the Provisional Theatre, which was the final version.

Beggar's Opera, The, words by John Gay, music by John Christopher Peupsch. This well-known opera was first performed in London at the Lincoln's Inn Fields, on January 29, 1728. Modern revivals began in London in 1878, and it was made into a movie (adapted by Sir Arthur Bliss) in 1953, with Lawrence Olivier as Macheath.

La Belle Hélène, by Jacques Offenbach. Libretto by Henri Meilhac and Ludovic Halevy. Premiered in Paris at the Théâtre des Variétés, December 17, 1864. The opera was a sensational success, and recent revivals have been almost as successful.

La Bohème, by Giacomo Puccini. Text by Giuseppe Giacosa and Luigi Illica, based on Henri Murger's *Scènes de la vie de Boheme*. This very popular opera premiered February 1, 1896, at the Teatro Reggio, Turin. The original reception was lukewarm, and the opera was not as successful as *Manon Lescaut* in its initial run. It is now acclaimed Puccini's masterwork.

Bohemian Girl, The, by Michael William Balfe. Text by Alfred Bunn. Premiered at Drury Lane Theatre in London, November 27, 1843. *The Bohemian Girl* ran for over one hundred nights and was highly successful in Europe and South America.

Boris Godunov, composed originally by Modeste Moussorgsky. Libretto by Moussorgsky based upon Aleksandr Sergeyevich Pushkin's and Nikolay Mikhaylovich Karamzin's *History of the Russian Empire*. This opera, in its original form, was first produced in its entirety on January 24, 1875, at the Maryinsky Theatre, St. Petersburg. The opera was first submitted to the literary committee of the Maryinsky Theatre and rejected; concert performances and single scenes led to its eventual staging. After Moussorgsky's death, the opera was extensively revised and abridged by Nikolay Andreyevich Rimsky-Korsakov. The latter version is the more commonly performed.

Breasts of Tiresias, The, (Les Mamelles de Tirésias), by Francis Poulenc. Text by Guillaume Apollinaire. This modern surrealist comic opera was first performed at the Opéra Comique, Paris, June 3, 1947. The humor is frequently described as "very French."

Carmen, by Georges Bizet. Libretto by Henri Meilhac and Lodvic Halevy, based on the novel by Prosper Mérimée. *Carmen* premiered at the Opéra Comique, Paris, March 3, 1875. Although it is one of the most popular operas in current repertoire, *Carmen* was originally a failure, criticized for obscenity, a lack of theatrical sense, and an absence of melody. In 1943 Oscar Hammerstein II adapted it to a musical set in the American South, and renamed it *Carmen Jones*. In 1954 it was made into a movie with an African-American cast led by Harry Belafonte, directed by Otto Preminger, with music dubbed.

Cavalleria Rusticana (Rustic Chivalry), by Pietro Mascagni. Libretto by Giovanni Targioni-Tozzetti and Guido Menasci. The libretto is based on a one-act drama by Giovanni Verga, who based his play on his own short story. The opera won first place in a contest organized by *Teatro Illustrato*, and was first produced at the Teatro Constanzi, Rome, on May 17, 1890. It was a rousing success, with curtain calls on the first night.

Cosi Fan Tutte (full title **Cosi Fan Tutte, ossia La Scuola Degli Amanti**, or **They All Do It, or The School for Lovers**), by Wolfgang Amadeus Mozart. Libretto by Lorenzo Da Ponte. This was first produced at the Burgtheater, Vienna, on January 26, 1790. Although popular at its premiere, the opera was not to the taste of the nineteenth century, and was repeatedly adapted. Not until the twentieth century was the original version restaged.

Cunning Little Vixen, The, by Leos Janacek. Libretto by Janacek from verses by Rudolf Tesnohlidek. Premiered at Brno, Czechoslovakia, November 6, 1904.

Damnation of Faust, The (La Damnation de Faust), by Hector Berlioz. Libretto by Berlioz and Almire Gandonniére, after Gerald de Nerval's French version of Goethe's play. Originally an orchestral piece, it was adapted for operatic performance by Raoul Gunsberg. It was first performed in concert in Paris at the Opéra Comique, Salle Favart, on December 6, 1846, and first staged February 18, 1893, in Monte Carlo.

Daughter of the Regiment, The (La Fille du Regiment), by Gaetano Donizetti. Libretto by Jean-François Bayard and Jules-Henry Vernoy de Saint-Georges. Premiered at the Opéra Comique, Paris, February 11, 1840. This is a very successful and popular opera, with over 600 performances by 1875, and is still frequently revived.

Death in Venice, by Benjamin Britten. Libretto by Britten's frequent collaborator, Myfanwy Piper, based on a 1913 short story by Thomas Mann. The opera premiered June 16, 1973, at the Maltings, Aldeburgh. This was Britten's last opera.

Les Dialogues des Carmélites (Dialogues of the Carmelites), by Francis Poulenc. Libretto by Emmet Lavery. This was based on a drama by Georges Bernanos, inspired by the novel *Die Letzte am Schafott*, by Gertrud von Le Fort, and a film script by the Reverend Father Raymond Bruckberger and Philippe Agostini. The novel was inspired by the execution of sixteen Carmelite nuns from Compiègne on July 17, 1794, in Paris. The opera was first performed at La Scala, Milan, on January 26, 1957.

Dido and Aeneas, by Henry Purcell. Text by Nahum Tate, adapted from a previous text, *Brutus of Alba*. The opera premiered at Hosia Priest's Boarding School for Girls, London, in October or December, 1689. Written to be performed by girls, there are few male roles. This is Purcell's only full-scale opera.

Don Carlos, by Giuseppe Verdi. Text by François-Joseph Mery and Camille Du Clocle, based on a tragedy by Friedrich Schiller. Premiered at the Opéra, Paris, on March 11, 1867. In 1893 Verdi completed a new version of the opera with a new libretto. He later revised it again, but the second version is the most successful.

Don Giovanni (Don Juan), by Wolfgang Amadeus Mozart. Text by Lorenzo Da Ponte. The original title of the opera was *Il Dissoluto Punito, ossia il don Giovanni*. First produced at Prague's Tyle Theatre on October 28, 1787. The opera was inspired by three other operas on this theme. This version was originally planned to be performed in honor of Joseph II's sister, but it was not ready in time.

Don Pasquale, by Gaetano Donizetti. Libretto by Giovanni Ruffini (signed Michele Accursi), adapted from a libretto by Angelo Anelli for *Ser*

Mercantonio, by Stefano Pavesi. First produced at the Théâtre Italien, Paris, January 3, 1843.

Don Quichotte (Don Quixote), by Jules Massenet. Text by Henri Cain, after Jacques Le Lorrain's play *Le Chevalier de la longue figure (The Knight of the Doleful Countenance),* itself modeled after Cervantes' novel. It opened at Monte Carlo's Théâtre du Casino, February 19, 1910.

Elektra, by Richard Strauss. Libretto by Hugo von Hofmannsthal, based on Sophocles' tragedy. Premiered at Königliches Opernhaus, Dresden, January 25, 1909. Although the opera adheres closely to the original story, after the premiere some claimed that the opera was immoral and perverse.

L'elisir d'amore (The Elixir of Love), by Gaetano Donizetti. Libretto by Felice Romani, based on the libretto *Le Philtre.* Premiered at Teatro della Cannobiana, Milan, May 12, 1832. Donizetti composed this in fourteen days, and it was an astounding success.

Eugen Onegin, by Peter Ilyich Tchaikovsky. Text by the composer and Constantine Shilovsky, based on the poem by Aleksandr Sergeyevich Pushkin. This was first produced in a student performance at the Moscow Conservatory in March, 1879. It was officially premiered in Moscow at the Bolshoi Theatre, on April 23, 1881. This is probably Tchaikovsky's most popular opera.

Fairy Queen, The, by Henry Purcell. Libretto by Elkanah Settle, based on Shakespeare's *A Midsummer Night's Dream.* It premiered in London at the Dorset Gardens Theatre in April, 1692. Although the opera was a great success at the time, only an incomplete score survives.

Falstaff, by Giuseppe Verdi. Libretto by Arrigo Boito, after Shakespeare's *Henry IV, Parts I and II,* and *The Merry Wives of Windsor.* Verdi's last opera, *Falstaff* premiered at La Scala, in Milan, February 9, 1893.

Faust, by Charles Gounod. Text by Jules Barbier and Michel Carré, adapted from Goethe's *Faust.* It was first produced at the Théâtre Lyrique in Paris, on March 19, 1859. Mildly successful at first, Gounod revised the opera in 1869, adding a ballet in the last act. This latter version is more popular today.

La Fiamma (The Flame), by Ottorino Respighi. The libretto is by Claudio Guastalla, based on the play *The Witch,* by Hans Wiers Jenssen. Premiered at the Rome Opera on January 23, 1934. The librettist originally intended to write an opera about the Empress Theodora, but settled for this, which was an immediate success.

Fidelio (Fidelio, oder Die Eheliche Liebe; Fidelio, or Conjugal Love), by Ludwig van Beethoven. Libretto by Josef Sonnleithner, drawn from Jean-Nicolas Bouilly's *Lenore, ou L'Amour conjugal;* reduced to two acts by Stefan von Breuning, adapted into final form by Georg Friedrich Treitschke. First performance, Theater an der Wien, Vienna, November 20, 1805. First performance of the final version at Karntnertor Theater, Vienna, 1814. This was

Beethoven's first, and only complete, opera. The original version was a failure, and Beethoven revised it twice before it was successful. It is this third version that is usually performed now.

Fiery Angel, The (Ognennyj Angel, or L'Ange de feu), score and text by Sergei Prokofiev. Libretto based on the novel by Valery Bryusov. This was first performed as an orchestral piece in Paris at the Théâtre des Champs-Elysées on November 25, 1954. It was first staged in Venice, at the Teatro La Fenice, September 14, 1955. The opera was written in 1925, but the score was lost, rediscovered in 1952, and revised.

Die Fledermaus (The Bat), by Johann Strauss II. Original book and lyrics by Henri Meilhac and Ludovic Hálevy, based on a German comedy by Roderich Benedix, adapted by Karl Haffner and Richard Genée. It was first staged in Vienna, at the Theater an der Wien, on April 5, 1874. Apparently due to the Vienna Stock Exchange problems of May 9, 1873, the opera closed after only sixteen performances, but later was a triumph.

Flying Dutchman, The (Der Fliegende Holländer), by Richard Wagner. Libretto by Wagner, based on Heinrich Heine's *Memoirs of Herr von Schnabelewopski*, and possibly inspired by a sea storm Wagner encountered in the summer of 1839 while traveling from Königsberg to London. First produced at Hofoper, Dresden, January 2, 1843.

Four Saints in Three Acts, by Virgil Thomson. Libretto by Gertrude Stein. First produced by Societies of Friends and Enemies of Modern Music, in Hartford, Connecticut, February 8, 1934.

Der Freischütz (The Freeshooter), by Carl Maria von Weber. Text by Friedrich Kind, based on Johann August Apel and Friedrich Laun's *Gespensterbuch*. First produced on June 18, 1821, at Schauspielhaus, Berlin. The opera was not very successful at its premiere, but when restaged in Vienna's Kartnertor Theater it was acclaimed.

La Gioconda (The Joyful Girl), by Amilcare Ponchielli. The libretto was taken from Victor Hugo's drama *Angelo, tyran de Padoue,* by Arrigo Bioto, under the anagrammatic pseudonym Tobia Gorrio. This was first produced at La Scala, Milan, on April 8, 1876, but Ponchielli continued to revise it, producing interim versions leading up to the final version, produced at La Scala, February 12, 1880. The opera is best known for its ballet, "The Dance of the Hours."

Girl of the Golden West, The (La Fanciulla del West), by Giacomo Puccini. Libretto by Carlo Zangarini and Guelfo Civinini, after the play of the same name by David Belasco. Premiered in New York City, at the Metropolitan Opera House on December 10, 1911. A popular success, with forty-six curtain calls on opening night.

Gloriana, by Benjamin Britten. Libretto by William Plomer, based on Lytton Strachey's *Elizabeth and Essex*. This opera, composed in honor of

Elizabeth II's coronation, premiered at Covent Garden, in London, on June 8, 1953.

Hansel and Gretel (Hansel ünd Gretel), by Engelbert Humperdinck. Text by Adelheid Wette, Humperdinck's sister. This, the best known of Humperdinck's operas, was first produced on December 23, 1893, at Hoftheater, Weimar, with Richard Strauss conducting.

Henri VIII, by Camille Saint-Saëns. Libretto by Leonce Detroyat and Armand Silvestre. The opera is a tale of the historical Henry, not Shakespeare's. First performed at the Opéra, Paris, March 5, 1883.

HMS Pinafore, or The Lass that Loved a Sailor, by Arthur Sullivan. Libretto by W. S. Gilbert. Premiered in London, at the Opéra Comique, May 25, 1878. Unsuccessful at first, Sullivan played selections from it at a promenade concert, and the songs and clever lyrics quickly caught the public's attention. This was Sullivan's first international success.

Les Huguenots, by Giacomo Meyerbeer. Libretto by Eugene Scribe, after Emile Deschamps. First produced at the Opéra, Paris, February 29, 1836. Wagner considered the fourth act one of the finest moments in opera.

Intermezzo, by Richard Strauss. The opera is based on a true episode in Strauss's life. Premiered at Dresden, at Staatsoper, November 4, 1924.

Iolanthe, or the Peer and the Peri, by Arthur Sullivan. Libretto by W. S. Gilbert. Simultaneous premieres in London, Savoy Theatre, and New York, Standard Theater, on November 25, 1882.

Iphigenia in Aulis (Iphigénie en Aulide), by Christoph Willibald Gluck. Gluck's opera, with libretto by du Roullet, follows Racine's play, which is based on Euripides' tragedy. First produced in Paris, April 19, 1774.

Jenufa (Her Stepdaughter), by Leos Janacek. Libretto by Janacek after the story by Gabriela Preiskova. First produced at Deutsches Nationaltheater, Brno, Czechoslovakia, January 21, 1904.

Le Jongleur de Nôtre Dame (The Juggler of Notre Dame), by Jules Massenet. *Libretto* by Maurice Lena. The libretto is based on the short story "Le Tombeor de Nostre Dame," by Gaston Paris. The story was later included in Anatole France's *Etui de Nacre.* The opera was first produced at Théâtre du Casino, Monte Carlo, on February 18, 1902.

Jumping Frog of Calaveras County, The, by Lukas Foss. Text by Jean Karsavina, based on Mark Twain's story of the same name. The opera premiered at Indiana University in Bloomington, May 18, 1950. This was Foss's first opera.

Katerina Ismailove/Lady MacBeth of the Mtsensk District (Ledi Makbet Mtsenskago Uezda), by Dmitri Shostakovich. The libretto is by Shostakovich and A. Preis, after a story by Nikolay Leskov. The opera, popular at first, was later criticized for being ideologically faulty. First produced at Leningrad's Maly Theatre, January 22, 1934.

Lakmé, by Leo Delibes. Libretto by Edmond Gondinet and Phillip Gille, based on the story by Pierre Loti, "Le Mariage de Loti." The opera was first produced at the Opéra Comique, Paris, on April 14, 1883.

Last Savage, The, (Le Dernier Sauvage), score and text by Gian Carlo Menotti. Although commissioned by the Paris Opéra, its theme was considered more suitable to the Opéra Comique, and it premiered there on October 21, 1962.

Lohengrin, score and text by Richard Wagner. The opera premiered at Weimar, Germany, on August 28, 1850. At the time Wagner was in political exile, and Franz Liszt directed the opera. Wagner did not hear *Lohengrin* performed until 1861, commenting at one point that he was the only German who had not done so.

Louise, by Gustave Charpentier. Text by Charpentier. Premiered in Paris at the Opéra Comique on February 2, 1900. The realistic setting and approach helped make *Louise* an enormous success, with almost a thousand performances during its first fifty years.

Love of Three Oranges, The (Lyubov k tryom Apelsinam), by Sergei Prokofiev. Libretto by Prokofiev based on a story by C. Gozzi. Produced in Chicago, Illinois, at the Chicago Opera, December 30, 1921.

Lucia di Lammermoor, by Gaetano Donizetti. Text by Salvatore Cammarano, based on Sir Walter Scott's *Bride of Lammermoor*. Very successful at its premiere and since, it is considered Donizetti's masterpiece. It was first performed at the Teatro San Carlo, Naples, on September 26, 1835.

MacBeth, by Ernest Bloch. Libretto by Edmond Fleg, modeled after Shakespeare. This is Bloch's only opera. First produced at the Opéra Comique, Paris, November 30, 1910.

Madame Butterfly (Madama Butterfly), by Giacomo Puccini. Libretto by Luigi Illican and Giuseppe Giacosa, based on David Belasco's play, from a story by John Luther Long. An earlier version, premiered at La Scala, was shouted down. The version now played opened at the Teatro Grande in Brescia, on March 28, 1904; it had been divided into three acts, and was a resounding success.

Magic Flute, The (Die Zauberflöte), by Wolfgang Amadeus Mozart. Libretto by Johann Emanuel Schikaneder. Mozart had become involved with a freemason group, and used their principles and rites to enhance what was originally a rather light fairy tale, "Lulu, oder die Zauberflöte," by August Jakob Lieveskind. First staged in the Theater auf der Wieden, Vienna, September 30, 1791.

Manon, by Jules Massenet. Libretto by Henri Meilhac and Philippe Gille, after the novel *Histoire du chevalier des Grieux et de Manon Lescaut*, by Abbé Antoine François Prevost. It was first produced at the Opéra Comique, Paris, January 19, 1884. The opera was not critically well received, and it was only after some years that it became popular.

Manon Lescaut, by Giacomo Puccini. Libretto by Ruggerio Leoncavallo, Marco Praga, Domenico Oliva, Giuseppe Giacosa, Luigi Illica, Giulio Ricordi, and others, although their names were not listed. Based on the novel by the Abbé Antoine François Prevost, *Histoire du chevalier des Grieux et de Manon Lescaut.* Unlike Massenet's version, Puccini's was wildly popular from the start. First performed at the Teatro Reggio, Turin, February 1, 1893.

Marriage of Figaro, The (Le Nozze di Figaro), by Wolfgang Amadeus Mozart. Libretto by Lorenzo Da Ponte, based on *La Folle Journée, ou Le Mariage de Figaro,* the second of a trilogy of Figaro comedies by Beaumarchais. Others in the trilogy are *The Barber of Seville* and *The Culpable Mother.* The opera was so popular that Joseph II was forced to issue a decree banning encores for ensemble passages. First produced at the Burgtheater, Vienna, with Mozart conducting, May 1, 1786.

Martha, oder Der Markt zu Richmond, by Friedrich Flotow. Text by F. W. Riese, based on an earlier ballet-pantomime by V. de Saint-Georges, Flotow, and others entitled *Lady Henriette, ou Le Servante de Greenwich.* Premiered at the Kartnertor Theater in Vienna November 25, 1847.

Masked Ball, The (Un Ballo in Maschera), by Giuseppe Verdi. Libretto by A. Somma, based on Eugene Scribe's *Gustave III, ou Le Bal masque.* Premiered at the Teatro Apollo in Rome, February 17, 1859. The story is based on an actual incident in which King Gustavus III of Sweden was shot in the back at a masked ball in Stockholm in 1792. To avoid political unrest Roman authorities insisted that the locale of Verdi's opera be changed from Sweden to colonial Boston.

Mathis der Maler (Mathias the Painter), by Paul Hindemith. The opera, very successful at its premiere, was eventually interpreted as a statement against national socialism. Premiered in Zurich at the Stadttheater, May 28, 1938.

Medea (Médée), by Luigi Cherubini. Libretto by François-Benoît Hoffman, based on Corneille's tragedy, inspired by Euripides and Seneca. First staged in Paris, at the Théâtre Feydeau, March 13, 1797, it was not particularly successful. In 1800 it opened in Berlin and was acclaimed by Beethoven, Weber, and later Wagner and Brahms.

Mefistofele, score and text by Arrigo Boito, based on Goethe's *Faust.* Premiered at La Scala, Milan, March 5, 1868. It was originally booed, but was revised and broken into two performances for a production at the Teatro Comunale in Bologna on October 4, 1875, and was successful.

Die Meistersinger von Nürnberg (The Mastersingers of Nuremberg), score and libretto by Richard Wagner. This is Wagner's only comedy. Premiered at Hoftheater, Munich, June 21, 1868.

Merry Wives of Windsor, The (Die Lustigen Weiber von Windsor), by Otto Nicolai. Libretto by S. H. Mosenthal, based on Shakespeare's play. It was produced at the Berlin Opera March 9, 1849.

Mignon, by Ambroise Thomas. Libretto by Michel Carré and Jules Barbier, based on Goethe's *Wilhelm Meister's Lehrjahre*. The first performance was at the Opéra Comique, Paris, November 17, 1866.

Mikado, The, or The Town of Titipu, by Arthur Sullivan. Libretto by W. S. Gilbert. Premiered at the Savoy Theatre, London, March 14, 1885. This is arguably Gilbert and Sullivan's most popular operetta.

Nabucco, by Giuseppe Verdi. Libretto by Temistocle Solera. Premiered at La Scala, Milan, March 9, 1842. Originally titled *Nabucodonosor*, this opera, Verdi's third, was his most successful thus far.

Norma, by Vincenzo Bellini. Text by Felice Romani, based on Alexandre Soumet's tragedy *Norma, ou L'Infanticide*. First performed December 26, 1831, at La Scala, Milan. Opening night was a dismal failure, but by the second performance the response became more positive.

Oberon, or The Elf-King's Oath, by Carl Maria von Weber. Text in English by James Robinson Planche, based on Sotheby's translation of Christoph Martin Wieland's poem "Oberon." First produced at Covent Garden, London, April 12, 1826. The overture is currently the most performed section. This was Weber's last opera.

Oedipus Rex, by Igor Stravinsky. Text, after Sophocles, by Jean Cocteau, translated into Latin by Jean Danielou. Premiered at the Théâtre Sarah Bernhardt, Paris, with Stravinsky conducting, May 30, 1927.

Orfeo, by Claudio Monteverdi. Libretto by Alessandro Striggio. *Orfeo* is sometimes called the first great opera. First produced at the Mantua Carnival, February 24, 1607.

Orestia, by Darius Milhaud, based on Paul Claudel's translation and arrangement of Aeschylus. This is a trilogy of operas: *Agamemnon* was composed in 1913, first performed in Paris, April 16, 1927. *Les Choëphores* was performed in concert in Brussels at the Théâtre de la Monnaie. It was first staged March 27, 1935. *Les Eumenides* was first performed in Antwerp, November 27, 1927. The first complete performance of the opera was in West Berlin, April 1963.

Orfeo ed Euridice, by Christoph Willibald Gluck. Text by Raniero di Calzabigi. First performed October 5, 1762, Vienna Burgtheater. The opera opened with the lead being sung by a castrato. In the early 1770s, Gluck rewrote the opera, adding some dances and making Orpheus a tenor. Modern productions usually give the role to a female contralto.

Otello, by Giuseppe Verdi. Libretto by Arrigo Boito, after Shakespeare. First produced February 5, 1887, at La Scala, Milan. This was Verdi's first opera since *Aida* in 1871.

I Pagliacci (Clowns), by Ruggiero Leoncavallo. First performed May 21, 1892, at the Teatro dal Verme, Milan. Leoncavallo based the story on an incident in Calabria, where his father was a judge.

Parsifal, by Richard Wagner. First produced at the Bayreuth Festspeilhaus, July 26, 1882. This was Wagner's last opera. Wagner did not want *Parsifal* to appear in opera houses. He wished it only to be performed at Beyreuth, but due to a copyright mistake it was produced at the Metropolitan Opera House in New York on December 24, 1903. Nevertheless, no European house would stage the opera until 1913, when the copyright expired.

Pearl Fishers, The (Les Pêcheurs de perles), by Georges Bizet. Libretto by Michel Carré and Eugene Cormon under the name Pierre Etienne Piestre. First produced September 29, 1863, at the Théâtre Lyrique, Paris. The opera was denounced early for being too derivative, but, with the backing of Berlioz, it soon won approval.

Pelleas and Melisande (Pelléas et Mélisande), by Claude Debussy. Text by Maurice Maeterlinck. First performed at the Opéra Comique, Paris, April 30, 1902. This is Debussy's only opera. Impressionistic in style, it was violently rejected at its opening. The support of a few critics and the backing of the theater kept the production open until the hostility ebbed.

Peter Grimes, by Benjamin Britten. Libretto by Montagu Slater, based on George Crabbe's poem "The Borough." It was immensely popular from the start, and helped reestablish a vogue for English opera. Premiered at Sadler's Wells Theatre in London, June 7, 1945.

Il Pirata (The Pirate), by Vincenzo Bellini. Libretto by Felice Romani, after Raimond's *Bertram, ou Le Pirate,* based on a play by Charles Robert Maturin. First produced in Milan, at La Scala, on October 27, 1827.

Pirates of Penzance, The, or The Slave of Duty, by Arthur Sullivan. Libretto by W. S. Gilbert. Premiered in Paignton, Devon, at the Bijou Theatre, December 30, 1879. This premiere was staged in order to secure the English copyright. The operetta had a full premiere the next night in New York at the 5th Avenue Theater.

Porgy and Bess, by George Gershwin. Story by DuBose Heyward, founded on the play of the same name and the novel *Porgy.* Libretto by Heyward, Dorothy Heyward, and Ira Gershwin. First performed in Boston, October 30, 1935. The New York production of the opera, shortly after the Boston premiere, was not very successful. When later revived, however, it broke Broadway records. It has been termed by some the first truly American opera, whatever that means.

Prince Igor, by Alexander Borodin. Libretto by Borodin after Vladimir Stasov. Left unfinished at his death, completed by Rimsky-Korsakov and Glazounov. First performed at St. Petersburg, November 4, 1890.

I Puritani di Scozia (The Puritans of Scotland), by Vincenzo Bellini. Libretto by Count Carlo Pepoli. Premiered in Paris, at the Théâtre Italien, January 25, 1835. Bellini's last opera is noted for the demands it places on singers.

Rake's Progress, The, by Igor Stravinsky. Libretto by Wystan Hugh Auden and Chester Kallman. Premiered in Venice, at the Teatro La Fenice, September 11, 1951.

Rape of Lucretia, The, by Benjamin Britten. Text by Ronald Duncan, after André Obey's *Le Viol de Lucrece* and passages from Livy, Shakespeare, Thomas Heywood, Nathaniel Lee, and F. Ponsard. First produced in Glyndebourne, on July 12, 1946. This opera was very successful, in part because of its reduced staging, thereby cutting production costs.

Rigoletto, by Giuseppe Verdi. Libretto by Francesco Maria Piave, based on Victor Hugo's play *Le Roi S'amuse.* Verdi had to rework the libretto in order to pass the censors. First produced in Venice, March 11, 1851, at the Teatro La Fenice.

Der Ring des Nibelungen, four-opera cycle by Richard Wagner. *Das Rheingold* was written in 1853, and premiered September 22, 1869, at the Munich Hoftheater. *Die Walküre* was written in 1852, and first produced June 25, 1870, at the Munich Hoftheater. *Siegfried* was written in 1848–51, and premiered August 16, 1876 at the Bayreuth Festspielhaus. *Die Götterdämmerung,* the last written of the cycle, was first produced at the Bayreuth Festspielhaus, August 17, 1876. Wagner began work on the full score in the proper order in 1853, and by 1857 was up to the second act of the final draft of *Siegfried.* At this point he set the work aside, returning to it in 1869. The entire *Ring* was completed in 1874. The first full performance of the cycle was at Bayreuth, August 13–17, 1876. This was the premiere performance of *Siegfried* and *Die Götterdämmerung.*

Robert, le Diable (Robert the Devil), by Giacomo Meyerbeer. Libretto by Eugene Scribe and Germain Delavigne. Produced in Paris at the Académie Royale de Musique on November 21, 1831. The lavish spectacle and cast have caused this opera, which was extremely successful, to be called the first grand opera.

Roberto Devereux, Conte di Essex, by Gaetano Donizetti. Libretto by Salvatore Cammarano, based on François Ancelot's *Elisabeth d'Angleterre.* First performed in Naples, at the Teatro San Carlo, October 29, 1837. This opera was enormously popular, enjoying regular performances until 1882.

Roméo et Juliette, by Charles Gounod. Libretto by Jules Barvier and Michel Carré, after Shakespeare's tragedy. Premiered at the Théâtre Lyrique, Paris, April 27, 1867.

La Rondine (The Sparrow), by Giacomo Puccini. Libretto by Giuseppe Adami. First produced March 27, 1917, at the Théâtre du Casino, Monte Carlo. This opera was very successful at first, but is seldom produced today.

Der Rosenkavalier (The Knight of the Rose), by Richard Strauss. Text by Hugo von Hofmannsthal. Premiered January 26, 1911, at the Königliches Opernhaus, Dresden.

Le Rossignol (The Nightingale), by Igor Stravinksy. Libretto by Stravinsky and Stephan Mitusov, drawn from a Hans Christian Andersen fairy tale. Premiered in Paris at the Opéra, May 26, 1914.

Ruddigore, or The Witch's Curse, by Arthur Sullivan. Libretto by William Gilbert. Premiered at the Savoy Theatre, London, January 22, 1887.

Rusalka, by Antonin Dvorak. Libretto by J. Krapil. First produced at the National Opera House, Prague, March 31, 1901.

Ruslan and Ludmilla, by Mikhail Ivanovich Glinka. Libretto by Glinka and Valeryan Shirkov, after Alexander Pushkin's poem of the same title. First produced at the St. Petersburg Imperial Theater, December 9, 1842.

Salome, by Richard Strauss. The libretto is based on the Oscar Wilde poem. Premiered at the Königliches Opernhaus, Dresden, December 9, 1905. The Dresden opening was arranged in reaction to fears that it would be censored in Vienna or Berlin.

Samson et Dalila, by Camille Saint-Saëns. Libretto by Ferdinand Lemaire, after the biblical story. First performed at the Hoftheater, Weimar, December 2, 1877, with Franz Liszt conducting.

Satyricon, by Bruno Maderna. Libretto from the prose work of the same name by Petronius Arbiter. First produced at the Nederlandse Operastichting, Amsterdam, March 16, 1973.

Sleeping Beauty (La Bella Addornmentata Nel Bosco), score by Ottorino Respighi. Libretto by Gian Bistolfi based on Charles Perrault's story. Premiered in Rome at the Teatro Odescalchi, April 13, 1922. The opera was composed between 1907 and 1909.

Snow Maiden, The (Snegurochka), written by Nikolay Andreyevich Rimsky-Korsakov, based on a comedy by Alexander N. Ostrovsky. Rimsky-Korsakov considered this his most successful opera. It opened in St. Petersburg at the Maryinsky Theatre, February 10, 1882.

La Sonnambula (The Sleepwalker), by Vincenzo Bellini. Libretto by Felice Romani. First performed at the Teatro Carcano, Milan, March 5, 1831. The opera was wildly successful at first, but has since fallen out of the standard operatic repertory.

Student Prince, The, by Sigmund Romberg. Libretto by Dorothy Donnelly. Premiered at the Jolson Theater, New York, December 2, 1924.

Tales of Hoffmann, (Contes d'Hoffmann), by Jacques Offenbach. Text by Jules Barbier and Michel Carré, based on stories by Ernst Theodor Amadeus Hoffman. First performed at the Opéra Comique, Paris, February 10, 1881. Offenbach died before finishing the orchestrations, which were completed by Ernest Guiraud.

Tannhauser (Tannhauser und der Sangerkrieg auf Wartburg, or Tannhauser and the Song Contest at the Wartburg), by Richard Wagner. When first produced at the Hofoper, Dresden, October 19, 1845, it was not a success, nor was it when premiered at Paris March 13, 1861, but thereafter it became perhaps the most popular of all Wagner's operas.

Thaïs, by Jules Massenet. The libretto, after Anatole France's novel, is by Louis Gallet. The opera premiered at the Opéra, Paris, March 16, 1894. Although not as warmly acclaimed critically as Massenet's *Manon,* when first presented it enjoyed considerable success.

Threepenny Opera, The (Die Dreigroschenoper), by Kurt Weill. Text by Bertolt Brecht. Adapted from John Gay's *The Beggar's Opera.* First performed at the Theatre am Schiffbauerdamm, Berlin, August 31, 1928. The orchestra's function in this work is closer to that of a jazz ensemble than a standard orchestra.

Tosca, by Giacomo Puccini. The text is after Victorien Sardou's drama, adapted by Luigi Illica and Giuseppe Giacosa. First performed at the Teatro Constanzi, Rome, January 14, 1900. Due to political and artistic factionalism, the premiere was not a critical success, but the audience adored it.

La Traviata, by Giuseppe Verdi. Text by Francesco Maria Piave, after the play *La Dame aux Camélias (Camille),* by Alexandre Dumas fils. First performed March 6, 1853, at the Teatro La Fenice, Venice. The opera was originally set in the nineteenth century, but Verdi moved the action to the seventeenth century the following year to please public taste.

Treemonisha, by Scott Joplin. Composed in 1908. First partial performance was at Morehouse College, Atlanta, Georgia, January, 1972. Although Joplin had the opera published in 1911, illness prevented his pursuing a production. The manuscript was rediscovered in 1970 by Vera Brodsky Lawrence.

Trial by Jury, by Arthur Sullivan. Libretto by W. S. Gilbert. Premiered at the Royalty Theatre, London, in 1875. This is Gilbert and Sullivan's second composition, and their first for D'Oyly Carte.

Tristan und Isolde, by Richard Wagner. First produced June 10, 1865, at the Hoftheater, Munich. This opera is frequently considered the greatest love drama of the genre.

Troilus and Cressida, by William Walton. Adapted from Geoffrey Chaucer's "Troylus and Cryseyde" by Christopher Hassall. Premiered at Covent Garden, London, December 3, 1954. Unlike Chaucer's Cressida, Walton's is faithful, even up to her suicide in the last scene.

Il Trovatore, by Giuseppe Verdi. Libretto by Salvatore Cammanaro, based on the drama Antonio García Gutiérrez' *El trovador.* First performed at the Teatro Apollo, Rome, January 19, 1853. The libretto was completed by Leone Emanuel Bardare after Cammarano's unexpected youthful death.

Les Troyens, by Hector Berlioz. The libretto, by Berlioz, is drawn from Virgil's *Aeneid.* Premiered at the Théâtre Lyrique, Paris, November 4, 1863 (second part only). First performance in its entirety at the Hoftheater in Karlsruhe over two nights, December 6 and 7, 1890.

Turandot, by Giacomo Puccini. Libretto by Renato Simoni and Giuseppe Adami, based on Carlo Gozzi's fairy tale. Premiered at La Scala, Milan, April 25, 1926. Puccini died before completing the opera. Although Franco Alfano, at Arturo Toscanini's suggestion, completed the third act from Puccini's notes, at the first performance at La Scala Toscanini came to the break between Puccini's and Alfano's work, laid down the baton, turned to the audience, and stated that the composer died at that point, and therefore the opera ended there.

Turn of the Screw, The, by Benjamin Britten. Libretto by Myfanwy Piper, based on Henry James's novel of the same name. First produced at the Teatro La Fenice, Venice, September 14, 1954. Unlike James's story, the central focus of the opera is on the children.

Undine, by Ernst Theodor Amadeus Hoffman. Libretto by Friedrich Heinrich Karl de la Motte-Fouque. First staged at the Schauspielhaus, Berlin, August 3, 1816. Quite successful at its premiere, the opera was presented regularly until the theater burned down. It was not revived successfully until 1922.

Vampire, The (Der Vampyr), by Heinrich Marschner. Libretto by Wilhelm August Wohlbruck. Premiered in Leipzig, March 29, 1828. This opera was a tremendous success at its premiere, and later in London. Richard Wagner liked the opera and eventually donated an aria for it. The vampire in question is J. W. Polidori's Ruthven, not Bram Stoker's Dracula.

La Wally, by Alfredo Catalani. Libretto by Luigi Illica, based on Wilhelmine von Hillern's novel *Die Geyer-Wally*. First produced at La Scala, Milan, January 20, 1892. Arturo Toscanini liked this opera so much that he named one of his daughters after it.

War and Peace (Voina y Mir), by Sergei Prokofiev. Libretto by Prokofiev and Mira Mendelson, based on Tolstoy's novel. The opera was first given in concert form at the Writers' Club in Moscow on October 16, 1944. The first performance, including only the first eight scenes, was given at Leningrad's Maly Theatre June 12, 1946.

William Tell (Guillaur ˮ Tell), by Gioacchino Rossini. Libretto by V. J. E. du Joy and H. L. F. Bis, based on Schiller's drama. Produced in Paris at the Opéra on August 3, 1829.

Zaza, by Ruggiero Leoncavallo. Text by Leoncavallo after a play by Charles Simon and Pierre Berton. Premiered at the Teatro Lirico, Milan, November 10, 1900. After *I Pagliacci*, *Zaza* is Leoncavallo's most popular opera. It is especially acclaimed in Italy.

SOURCES

Duckles, Vincent H., and Michael A. Keller. *Music Reference and Research Materials: An Annotated Bibliography.* 4th ed. New York: G. Schirmer, 1988.

Harewood, Earl of, ed. *The New Kobbé's Opera Book.* New York: G. P. Putnam's, 1976.

Mondadori, Arnoldo, ed. *The Simon and Schuster Book of the Opera.* New York: Simon and Schuster, 1977.

O'Connell, Charles, ed. *The Victor Book of the Opera: Stories of the Operas with Illustrations and Descriptions of Victor Opera Records.* Camden, N.J.: Victor Talking Machine, 1929.

Orrey, Leslie, ed. *The Encyclopedia of Opera.* New York: Charles Scribner's Sons, 1976.

Randel, Don Michael, comp. *Harvard Concise Dictionary of Music.* Cambridge, Mass.: Belknap Press, 1978.

Sadie, Stanley, ed. *The New Grove Dictionary of Music and Musicians.* London: Macmillan, 1980.

Slonimsky, Nicolas. *Lectionary of Music.* New York: Doubleday Anchor Books, 1990.

Thompson, Oscar, and Bruce Buhle, eds. *The International Cyclopedia of Music and Musicians.* 11th ed. New York: Dodd, Mead and Co. 1985.

Thorton, Weldon. *Allusions in Ulysses: An Annotated List.* Chapel Hill: University of North Carolina Press, 1968.

Warrack, John, and Ewan West, *The Oxford Dictionary of Opera,* New York: Oxford University Press, 1992.

Wier, Albert E., comp. and ed. *Macmillan Encyclopedia of Music and Musicians.* New York: Macmillan, 1938.

—Margaret Campbell; L.D.R.

25

SOME FAMOUS BALLETS

. . . . .

BALLET BEGAN WITH THE ROMANS, FLOURISHED WITH THE FRENCH, REACHED new heights with the Russians, and underwent much innovation with the Americans and the English. It involves elements of music, dance, drama, and spectacle. The music seems to be what makes it endure, but the dancing is what constitutes its greatest attraction for the audience. Listening to a ballet on the phonograph is something like reading a play.

The golden age of ballet is generally held to be the seventeenth century in France. Louis XIV sponsored it and enjoyed dancing in it; when the Sun King grew too fat to dance, ballet went into a decline at Versailles, but it retained its popularity in France and elsewhere. In the mid-nineteenth century St. Petersburg, in Russia, became a center for ballet, and beginning in 1909 a Russian company under Sergei Diaghilev and the dancer-choreographer Michel Fokine won acclaim for their art in Paris and elsewhere. In the early twentieth century the American danceuse Isadora Duncan introduced a new naturalness and grace to ballet, with traditional garb giving way to bare feet and flowing costume and movement.

The greatest musical composers have written some works expressly for ballet—Gluck, Mozart, Beethoven, Tchaikovsky, Richard Strauss, Rimsky-Korsakov, Stravinsky, Ravel, Prokofiev, Bartok, others—and their music, including even Johann Sebastian Bach's, has also been adapted for ballet by others. Numerous operas contain ballet sequences; French audiences in particular have insisted upon its inclusion. Wagner composed the Venusberg music for the Paris production of *Tannhauser*.

The compilation below lists some of the more popular ballets from the repertory, with composers, and the locations, dates, and casts of first performances.

Agon. Music by Igor Stravinsky. Choreographer ("Ch." hereafter): George Balanchine. New York, City Center, November 27, 1957. Principal dancers: Diana Adams, Melissa Hayden, Barbara Walczak, Barbara Milberg, Todd Bolender, Roy Tobias, Jonathan Watts, Arthur Mitchell.

Alexandre le grand. Music by Philippe Gaubert. Ch.: Serge Lifar. Paris, Opéra, June 21, 1937. Principal dancers: Serge Lifar, Yvette Chauviré, Suzanne Lorcia, Solange Schwarz.

Anna Karenina. Music by Rodion K. Scedrin. Chs.: Maya Plisetskaya, Natalia Ryzhenko, Vladimir Smirnov-Golovanov. Moscow, Bolshoi Theater, June 10, 1972. Principal dancer: Maya Plisetskaya.

Apollo in Musagète. Music by Igor Stravinsky. Ch.: George Balanchine. Washington, Library of Congress, April 27, 1928. Principal dancers: Adolph Bolm, Ruth Page, Elise Reiman, Berenice Holmes.

Appalachian Spring. Music by Aaron Copland. Ch.: Martha Graham. Washington, Library of Congress, October 30, 1944. Principal dancers: Martha Graham, Eric Hawkins, May O'Donnell, Merce Cunningham, Nina Fonaroff, Pearl Lang, Marjorie Mazia, Yuriko.

L'Après-midi d'un faune (The Afternoon of a Faun). Music by Claude Debussy. Ch.: Vaslav Nijinsky. Paris, Théâtre du Châtelet, May 29, 1912. Principal dancer: Vaslav Nijinsky.

Astarte. Music by Crome Syrcus. Ch.: Robert Joffrey. New York, City Center, September 20, 1967. Principal dancers: Trinette Singleton, Maximiliano Zomosa.

Autumn Leaves. Music by Frédéric Chopin. Ch.: Anna Pavlova. Río de Janeiro, 1918. Principal dancers: Anna Pavlova, Alexander Volinine, Hubert Stowitts.

La Bayadère. Music by Ludwig Minkus. Ch.: Marius Petipa. St. Petersburg, Maryinsky Theater, January 23, 1877. Principal dancers: Ekaterina Vazem, Pavel Gerdt, Lev Ivanov, Maria Gorshenkova, Maria M. Petipa.

Billy the Kid. Music by Aaron Copland. Ch.: Eugene Lohring. Chicago, Opera House, October 16, 1938. Principal dancers: Eugene Lohring, Marie-Jeanne, Lew Christensen, Todd Bolender.

La Boutique fantastique (The Fantastic Toyshop). Music by Gioacchino Rossini, arranged by Ottorino Respighi. Ch.: Léonide Massine. London, Alhambra Theatre, June 5, 1919. Principal dancers: Lydia Lopokova, Léonide Massine, Lydia Sokolova, Stanislas Idzikovsky, Leon Woizikovsky, Enrico Cecchetti.

Le Carnaval (Carnival). Music by Robert Schumann. Ch.: Michel Fokine. St. Petersburg, Pavlova Hall, March 5, 1910. Principal dancers: Leonid Leontiev, Tamara Karsavina, L. Schollar, B. Nijinski, V. Meyerhold, A. Bekefi, V. Kiselev.

Cinderella. Music by Varon Fittinghof-Schell. Chs.: Marius Petipa, Enrico Cecchetti, and Lev Ivanov. St. Petersburg, Maryinsky Theater, December 1,

1893. Principal dancers: Pierina Legnani, Pavel Gerdt, Enrico Cecchetti, Matilda Kschessinskaya II, M. Andersen.

Cinderella. Music by Sergei Prokofiev. Ch.: Frederick Ashton. Moscow, Bolshoi Theater, November 21, 1945. Principal dancer: Olga Lepeschinskaia.

Cléopâtre. Music by Anton Arensky. Ch.: Michel Fokine. Paris, Théâtre de Châtelet, June 2, 1909. Principal dancers: Ida Rubenstein, Anna Pavlova, Michel Fokine, Tamara Karsavina, Vaslav Nijinsky.

Concert, The, or The Perils of Everybody. Music by Frédéric Chopin. Ch.: Jerome Robbins. New York, City Center, March 6, 1956. Principal dancers: Tanaquil LeClercq, Todd Bolender, Yvonne Mounsey, Robert Barnett, Wilma Curley, John Mandia, Shaun O'Brien, Patricia Savoia, Richard Thomas.

Coppelia (The Girl with the Enamel Eyes). Music by Léo Delibes. Ch.: Arthur Saint-Léon. Paris, Opéra, May 25, 1870. Principal dancers: Giuseppina Bozzacchi, Eugénie Fiocre, François Dauty.

Le Coq d'Or (The Golden Cockerel). Music by Nikolai Rimsky-Korsakov. Ch.: Michel Fokine. Paris, Opéra, May 21, 1914. Principal dancers: Tamra Karsavina, Alexis Bulgakov, Enrico Cecchetti.

Le Corsaire. Music by Robert Bochsa. Chs.: Jules Perrot and others. London, King's Theatre, June 29, 1837. Principal dancers: François Decomb "Albert," Hermine Elssler, Pauline Duvernay.

Le Création du monde (The Creation of the World). Music by Darius Milhaud. Ch.: Jean Börlin. Paris, Théâtre des Champs-Elysées, October 25, 1923. Principal dancers: Jean Börlin, Evon Strandin.

Creatures of Prometheus, The. Music by Ludwig van Beethoven. Ch.: Salvatore Viganò. Vienna, Hoftheater, March 28, 1801. Principal dancers: Maria Casentini, Salvatore Viganò, Cesari, Ferdinando Gioja, Aichinger, Mlle. Brendi, Mlle. Cesari, Mlle. Renth.

Dances at a Gathering. Music by Frédéric Chopin. Ch.: Jerome Robbins. New York, New York State Theater, May 8, 1969. Principal dancers: Allegra Kent, Sara Leland, Kay Mazzo, Patricia McBride, Violette Verdy, Anthony Blum, John Clifford, Robert Maiorano, John Prinz, Edward Villella.

Daphnis and Chloë. Music by Maurice Ravel. Ch.: Michel Fokine. Paris, Théâtre du Châtelet, June 8, 1912. Principal dancers: Tamara Karsavina, Vaslav Nijinsky, A⁻⁻l Bolm.

Dark Elegies. Music by Gustav Mahler. Ch.: Antony Tudor. London, Duchess Theatre, February 19, 1937. Principal dancers: Dame Peggy van Praagh, Agnes de Mille, Maude Lloyd, Antony Tudor.

Deuce Coupe. Music by the Beach Boys. Ch.: Twyla Tharp. New York, City Ballet, March 1, 1973. Principal dancers: Erika Goodman, Twyla Tharp.

Don Juan. Music by Christoph Willibald Gluck. Ch.: Pietro Angiolini. Vienna, Burgtheater, October 17, 1761. Principal dancers: Gasparo Angiolini, Clerc, Pagani, Reggiano, Dupré, Turchi, Salvatore Viganò.

Don Quixote. Music by Ludwig Minkus. Ch.: Marius Petipa. Moscow, Bolshoi
Theater, December 14, 1869. Principal dancers: Anna Sobeshanskaja, Sergei
Sokolov, Wilhelm Vanner, Vasili Gellser.

The Dream. Music by Felix Mendelssohn, arranged by John Lanchbery. Ch.:
Frederick Ashton. London, Royal Opera House, April 2, 1964. Principal
dancers: Antoinette Sibley, Anthony Dowell, Keith Martin, Alexander
Grant.

La Esmeralda. Music by Cesar Pugni. Ch.: Jules Perrot. London, Her Majesty's
Theatre, March 9, 1844. Principal dancers: Carlotti Grisi, Jules Perrot,
Arthur Saint-Léon, Louis-François Gosselin, Antoine Coulon, Adelaide
Frassi, Mme. Copère.

Esplanade. Music by Johann Sebastian Bach. Ch.: Paul Taylor. Washington,
Lisner Auditorium, March 1, 1975. Principal dancers: Bettie de Jong,
Carolyn Adams, Eileen Croply, Nicholas Gunn, Monica Morris, Elie Chaib,
Lila York, Greg Reynolds, Ruth Andrien.

Eugen Onegin. Music by Peter Ilyich Tchaikovsky. Ch.: John Crenko. Stuttgart,
Germany, Württembergische Staatstheater, April 13, 1965. Principal
dancers: Marcia Haydée, Ray Barra, Egon Madsen, Ana Cardu.

Excelsior. Music by Romualdo Marenco. Ch.: Luigi Manzotti. Milan, La Scala,
January 11, 1881. Principal dancers: Bice Vergani, Carlo Montanara, Rosina
Viale, Carlo Coppi, Angelo Cuccoli.

Fancy Free. Music by Leonard Bernstein. Ch.: Jerome Robbins. New York,
Metropolitan Opera House, April 18, 1944. Principal dancers: John Kriza,
Harold Lang, Jerome Robbins, Muriel Bentley, Janet Reed, and Shirley
Eckl.

La Fille mal gardée (The Wayward Daughter). Music by Peter Ludwig Hertel.
Ch.: Jean Dauberval. Bordeaux, July 1, 1789. Revived in 1828 at the Paris
Opéra with music by Louis-Joseph-Ferdinand Hérold. Principal dancer:
unknown.

Filling Station, The. Music by Virgil Thompson. Ch.: Lew Christensen.
Hartford, Conn., Avery Memorial Theater, January 6, 1938. Principal
dancers: Lew Christensen, Marie-Jeanne, Eric Hawkins, Michael Kidd,
Todd Bolender, Eugene Lohring.

Firebird, The. Music by Igor Stravinsky. Ch.: Michel Fokine. Paris, Opéra, June
25, 1910. Principal dancers: Michel Fokine, Tamara Karsavina, Enrico
Cecchetti.

For the Sweet Memory of That Day, or The Triumphs of Petrarch. Music by
Luciano Berio. Ch.: Maurice Béjart. Florence, Boboli Gardens, July 7, 1974.
Principal dancers: Jorge Dann, Suzanne Farrell, Rita Poelvoorde.

Frankie and Johnny. Music by Jerome Moross. Chs.: Ruth Page and Bentley
Stone. Chicago, Great Northern Theater, June 19, 1938. Principal dancers:
Ruth Page, Bentley Stone, Ann Devine, Sean Marino.

La Giara (The Jar). Music by Alfredo Casella. Ch.: Jean Börlin. Paris, Théâtre des Champs-Elysées, November 19, 1924. Principal dancers: Axel Witzansky, Inger Friis, Eric Viber, Jean Börlin.

Giselle. Music by Adolphe Adam. Chs.: Jules Perrot and Jean Coralli. Paris, Académie Royale de Musique, June 28, 1841. Principal dancers: Carlotta Grisi, Lucien Petipa, Adèle Dumilâtre, M. Simon.

Glagolitic Mass. Music by Leos Janacek. Ch.: Jiri Kylián. Florence, Teatro della Pergola, June 5, 1979. Performed by the Netherlands Dance Theater. Principal dancers: Roslyn Anderson, Gerald Tibbs.

Green Table, The. Music by Frederic (Fritz) Cohen. Ch.: Kurt Jooss. Paris, Théâtre des Champs-Elysées, July 3, 1932. Principal dancer: Kurt Jooss.

Harbinger. Music by Sergei Prokofiev. Ch.: Eliot Field. New York, New York State Theater, May 11, 1967. Principal dancers: Christine Sarry, Edward Verso, Paula Tracy, Cynthia Gregory, Marcos Paredes, Eliot Feld.

Jardin aux lilas (The Lilac Garden). Music by Ernest Chausson. Ch.: Antony Tudor. London, Mercury Theatre, January 26, 1936. Principal dancers: Antony Tudor, Maude Lloyd, Hugh Laing, Peggy van Praagh.

Jeux (Games). Music by Claude Debussy. Ch.: Vaslav Nijinsky. Paris, Théâtre des Champs-Elysées, May 15, 1913. Principal dancers: Tamara Karsavina, Ludmilla Schollar, Vaslav Nijinsky.

Jewels. Music by Gabriel Fauré and others. Ch.: George Balanchine. New York, New York State Theater, April 13, 1967. Principal dancers: Violette Verdy, Conrad Ludlow, Mimi Paul, Francisco Moncion, Patricia McBride, Edward Villella, Patricia Neary, Suzanne Farrell, Jacques d'Amboise.

Magic Flute, The. Music by Riccardo Drigo. Ch.: Lev Ivanov. St. Petersburg, Little Theater of the Imperial Ballet School, March 10, 1893. Principal dancers: S. Belinskaya, Michel Fokine, S. Legat, C. Christerson.

Marguerite and Armand. Music by Franz Liszt, orchestrated by Humphrey Searle. Ch.: Frederick Ashton. London, Royal Opera House, March 12, 1963. Principal dancers: Rudolph Nureyev, Michael Somes, Leslie Edwards.

Miraculous Mandarin, The. Music by Béla Bartòk. Ch.: Todd Bolender. Milan, La Scala, October 12, 1942. Principal dancers: Aurel Milloss, Attilia Radice, Filippo Morucci, Guido Lauri, Giovanni Brinati, Teofilo Giglio, Adriano Vitale.

Le Molière Imaginaire (Moliere Imagined). Music by Nino Rota. Ch.: Maurice Béjart. Paris, Comédie Française, December 3, 1976. Principal dancers: Robert Hirsch, Bertrand Pie, Maurice Béjart, Jorge Donn, Rita Poelvoorde, Jan Nuyts, Catherine Verneuil.

Month in the Country, A. Music by Frédéric Chopin, arranged by John Lanchbery. Ch.: Frederick Ashton. London, Royal Opera House, February 12, 1976. Principal dancers: Lynn Seymour, Alexander Grant, Wayne Sleep,

Derek Rencher, Denise Nunn, Marguerite Porter, Anthony Conway, Anthony Dowell.

Moor's Pavane, The. Music by Henry Purcell, arranged by Simon Sadoff. Ch.: José Limón. New London, Conn., Connecticut College, August 17, 1949. Principal dancers: José Limón, Betty Jones, Lucas Hoving, Pauline Koner.

Mutations. Music by Karlheinz Stockhausen. Ch.: Glen Tetley. Scheveningen, Germany, Circus Theater, July 3, 1970. Principal dancers: Anja Licher, Gerard Lémaire.

Napoli (The Fisherman and His Bride). Music by Holger Simon Paulli, Edvard Helsted, Niels Wilhelm Gade, and Christian Lumbye. Ch.: Auguste Bournonville. Copenhagen, Theater Royal, March 29, 1842. Principal dancers: Caroline Fjeldsted, August Bournonville, Stromboe.

Les Noces (The Wedding). Music by Igor Stravinsky. Ch.: Bronislava Nijinska. Paris, Gaîté-Lyrique, June 14, 1923. Principal dancers: Felia Dubrovska, Leon Woizikovsky.

Nôtre Faust. Music by Johann Sebastian Bach, Ludwig Minkus, Harry Warren, and Argentinian tangos. Ch.: Maurice Béjart. Brussels, Théâtre de la Monnaie, December 12, 1975. Principal dancers: Maurice Béjart, Yann Le Gac, Jorge Donn, Bertrand Pié, Patrice Touron, Monet Robier, Shonach Mirk.

Nutcracker, The. Music by Peter Ilyich Tchaikovsky. Ch.: Lev Ivanov. St. Petersburg, Maryinsky Theater, December 5, 1892. Principal dancers: Antonietta Dell'Era, Pavel Gerdt, Olga Preobrajenska, Nicholas Legat.

Orpheus. Music by Igor Stravinsky. Ch.: George Balanchine. New York, City Center, April 28, 1948. Principal dancers: Nicholas Magallanes, Maria Tallchief, Francisco Moncion, Beatric Tompkins, Tanaquil LeClercq, Herbert Bliss.

Le Papillon (The Butterfly). Music by Jacques Offenbach. Ch.: Marie Taglioni. Paris, Opéra, November 26, 1860. Principal dancers: Emma Livry, Louise Marquet, Louis Mérante, Berthier.

Parade. Music by Erik Satie. Ch.: Léonide Massine. Paris, Théâtre du Châtelet, May 18, 1917. Principal dancers: Léonide Massine, Maria Chabelska, Lydia Lopokova, Nicholas Zvere, Leon Woizikowsky.

Pas de Quatre. Music by Cesare Pugni. Ch.: Jules Perrot. London, Her Majesty's Theatre, July 12, 1845. Principal dancers: Maria Taglioni, Fanny Cerrito, Lucile Grahn, Carlotta Grisi.

Les Patineurs (The Skaters). Music by Giacomo Meyerbeer, arranged by Constant Lambert. Ch.: Frederick Ashton. London, Sadler's Wells Theatre, February 16, 1937. Principal dancers: Harold Turner, Mary Honer, Elizabeth Miller, June Brae, Pamela May, Margot Fonteyn, Robert Helpmann.

La Péri. Music by Norbert Burgmüller. Ch.: Jean Coralli. Paris, Académie Royale de Musique, July 17, 1843. Principal dancers: Carlotta Grisi, Lucien Petipa, J. B. Barret, Jean Coralli, Delphine Marquet.

La Péri. Music by Paul Dukas. Ch.: Frederick Ashton. Paris, Théâtre du Châtelet, April 22, 1912. Principal dancers: Natlia Truhanova, W. Bekefi.

Petrouchka. Music by Igor Stravinsky. Ch.: Michel Fokine. Paris, Théâtre du Châtelet, June 13, 1911. Principal dancers: Vaslav Nijinsky, Tamara Karsavina, Alexander Orloff, Enrico Cecchetti.

Primitive Mysteries. Music by Louis Horst. Ch.: Martha Graham. New York, Craig Theater, February 2, 1931. Principal dancer: Martha Graham.

Prodigal Son, The. Music by Sergei Prokofiev. Ch.: George Balanchine. Paris, Théâtre Sarah Bernhardt, May 21, 1929. Principal dancers: Serge Lifar, Felia Dubrovska, Michael Federov, Leon Woizikovsky, Anton Dolin.

Prometheus. Music by Ludwig van Beethoven, Wolfgang Amadeus Mozart, Franz Joseph Haydn, Joseph Weigl, and Salvatore Viganó. Milan, La Scala, May 22, 1813. Principal dancers: Antonietta Pallerini, Gaetana Abrami, Luigi Costa, Giuseppe Villa, Giuseppe Paccini, Giovanni Bianchi, Francesca Venturi, Giuseppe Bertelli, M. Chouchous, Amalia Brugnoli.

Pulcinella (Punchinello). Music by Igor Stravinsky, after Giovanni Battista Pergolesi. Ch.: Léonide Massine. Paris, Opéra, May 15, 1920. Principal dancers: Léonide Massine, Tamara Karsavina, Lubov Tchernicheva, Vera Nemchinova, Sigmund Novak, Stanislas Idzikovsky, Nicholas Zverev, Enrico Cecchetti, Stanislas Kostetsky.

Raymonda. Music by Alexander Glazunov. Ch.: Marius Petipa. St. Petersburg, Maryinsky Theater, January 19, 1898. Principal dancers: Pierina Legnani, Sergei Legat, Nicholas Lega, Paul Gerdt.

Revelations. Music: Traditional African-American spirituals. Ch.: Alvin Ailey. New York, 92nd St. YM-YWHA, January 31, 1960. Principal dancers: Joan Derby, Minnie Marshall, Merle Derby, Dorene Richardson, Jay Fletcher, Nathaniel Horne, Carmen Howell.

Robert Schumann's "Davidsbündlertänze." Music by Robert Schumann. Ch.: George Balanchine. New York, New York State Theater, June 19, 1980. Principal dancers: Karin von Aroldingen, Suzanne Farrell, Kay Mazzo, Heather Watts, Adam Lüders, Jacques d'Amboise, Ib Andersen, Peter Martins.

Rodeo, or The Courting at Burnt Ranch. Music by Aaron Copland. Ch.: Agnes de Mille. New York, Metropolitan Opera House, October 16, 1942. Principal dancers: Agnes de Mille, Frederic Franklin, Casimir Kokitch, Milada Mladova.

Romeo and Juliet. Music by Constant Lambert. Monte Carlo, Opéra, May 4, 1926. Principal dancers: Tamara Karsavina, Serge Lifar, Tadeo Slavinsky, Lydia Sokolova, Leon Woizikovsky, Alexandra Danilova, Felia Dubrovska, Constantin Tcherkas.

Romeo and Juliet. Music by Sergei Prokofiev. Ch.: Leonid Levrosky. Leningrad, Kirov Theater, January 11, 1940. Principal dancers: Galina Ulanova, Konstantin Sergeyev, A. V. Lopukov, S. G. Karen.

Le Rossignol (The Nightingale). Music by Igor Stravinsky. Ch.: Léonide Massine. Paris, Opéra, February 2, 1920. Principal dancers: Tamara Karsavina, Stanislas Idzikovsky, Lydia Sokolova.

Le Sacre du printemps (The Rite of Spring). Music by Igor Stravinsky. Ch.: Vaslav Nijinsky. Paris, Théâtre des Champs-Elysées, May 29, 1913. Principal dancer: Maria Piltz.

Scheherazade. Music by Nikolai Rimsky-Korsakov. Ch.: Michel Fokine. Paris, Opéra, June 4, 1910. Principal dancers: Ida Rubinstein, Vaslav Nijinsky, Alexis Bulgakov, Basil Kissilev, Enrico Cecchetti.

Serenade. Music by Peter Ilyich Tchaikovsky. Ch.: George Balanchine. Hartford, Conn., Avery Memorial Theater, December 6, 1934 (first public performance). Principal dancers: Kathryn Mullowney, Heidi Vosseler, Charles Laskey.

Seventh Symphony, The. Music by Ludwig van Beethoven. Ch.: Léonide Massine. Monte Carlo, Opéra, May 5, 1938. Principal dancers: Frederick Franklin, Alicia Markova, Igor Youskevich, Nini Theilade, Natalia Krasovska.

Sleeping Beauty, The. Music by Peter Ilyich Tchaikovsky. Ch.: Marius Petipa. St. Petersburg, Maryinsky Theater, January 3, 1890. Principal dancers: Carlotte Brianza, Pavel Gerdt, Maria M. Petipa, Enrico Cecchetti, Varvara Nikitina, F. I. Kshesinsky, Giuseppina Cecchetti.

Spartacus. Music by Aram Khachaturian. Ch.: Yuri Grigorovich. Moscow, Bolshoi Theater, April 9, 1968. Principal dancers: Vladimir Vasiliev, Ekaterina Maximova, Maris Liepa, Nina Timofeyeva.

Le Spectre de la rose (The Spirit of the Rose). Music by Carl Maria von Weber. Ch.: Michel Fokine. Théâtre de Monte Carlo, April 19, 1911. Principal dancers: Tamara Karsavina, Vaslav Nijinsky.

Stars and Stripes. Music by John Philip Sousa. Ch.: George Balanchine. New York, City Center, Janury 17, 1958. Principal dancers: Allegra Kent, Diana Adams, Robert Barnett, Melissa Hayden, Jacques d'Amboise.

Summerspace. Music by Morton Feldman. Ch.: Merce Cunningham. New London, Conn., Connecticut College, August 17, 1958. Principal dancers: Merce Cunningham, Carolyn Brown, Viola Farber, Cynthia Stone, Marilyn Wood, Remy Charlip.

Swan Lake. Music by Peter Ilyich Tchaikovsky. Chs.: Lev Ivanov and Marius Petipa. St. Petersburg, Maryinsky Theater, January 15, 1895. Principal dancers: Pierina Legnani, Pavel Gerdt, Giuseppina Cecchetti, P. A. Bulgakov.

La Sylphide. Music by Jean Schneitzhoeffer. Ch.: Philippe Taglioni. Paris, Opéra, March 12, 1832. Principal dancers: Maria Taglioni, Joseph Mazilier, Lise Noblet, Mme. Elie, M. Elie.

Les Sylphides. Music by Frédéric Chopin. Ch.: Michel Fokine. Paris, Théâtre du

Châtelet, June 2, 1909. Principal dancers: Anna Pavlova, Vaslav Nijinsky, Tamara Karsavina, Alexandra Baldina.

Sylvia (Diana's Nymph). Music by Léo Delibes. Ch.: Louis Mérante. Paris, Opéra, June 14, 1876. Principal dancers: Rita Sangalli, Louis Mérante, Marco Magri, Marie Sanlaville, Louise Marquet.

Symphonic Variations. Music by César Franck. Ch.: Frederick Ashton. London, Royal Opera House, April 24, 1946. Principal dancers: Margot Fonteyn, Michael Somes, Pamela May, Brian Shaw, Moira Shearer, and Henry Danton.

Symphonie fantastique. Music by Hector Berlioz. Ch.: Léonide Massine. London, Covent Garden Opera House, July 24, 1936. Principal dancers: Tamara Toumanova, Léonide Massine, Nina Verchinina, George Sorich.

Taming of the Shrew, The. Music by Domenico Scarlatti, arranged by Kurt-Heinz Stolze. Ch.: John Cranko. Stuttgart, Germany, Württembergische Staatstheater, March 16, 1969. Principal dancers: Marcia Haydée, Richard Cragun, Susanne Hanke, Egon Madsen.

Tempest, The. Music by Arne Nordheim. Ch.: Glen Tetley. Schwetzingen Festival, Germany, Rokoko Theater, May 3, 1979. Principal dancers: Christopher Bruce, Gianfranco Paoluzi, Thomas Yang, Mark Wraith, Lucy Burge.

Theme and Variations. Music by Peter Ilyich Tchaikovsky. Ch.: George Balanchine. New York, City Center, November 26, 1947. Principal dancers: Alicia Alonso, Igor Youskevitch.

Three-Cornered Hat, The (El sombrero de tres picos). Music by Manuel de Falla. Ch.: Léonide Massine. London, Alhambra Theatre, July 22, 1919. Principal dancers: Léonide Massine, Tamara Karsavina, Leon Woizikovsky, Stanislas Idzikovsky.

Trinity. Music by Alan Raph and Lee Holdridge. Ch.: Gerald Arpino. New York, City Center, October 9, 1969. Principal dancers: Christian Holder, Donna Cowen, Starr Danias, Rebecca Wright, Dermot Burke, Gary Chryst, James Dunne.

Untitled. Music by Robert Dennis. Ch.: Pilobolus Dance Theater. New London, Conn., Connecticut College, August 2, 1975. Principal dancers: Alison Chase, Moses Pendleton, Robby Barnett, Jonathan Wolken, Martha Clarke, Michael Tracy.

Vienna Waltzes. Music by Johann Strauss, Jr., Franz Lehár, and Richard Strauss. Ch.: George Balanchine. New York, New York State Theater, June 23, 1977. Principal dancers: Karin von Aroldingen, Sean Lavery, Patricia McBride, Helgi Tomasson, Sara Leland, Bart Cook, Kay Mazzo, Peter Martina, Suzanne Farrell, Jorge Donn.

Voluntaries. Music by Francis Poulenc. Ch.: Glen Tetley. Stuttgart, Germany, Württembergische Staatstheater, December 22, 1973. Principal dancers: Marica Haydée, Richard Cragun, Birgit Keil, Reid Anderson, Jan Stripling.

SOURCES

Balanchine, George, and Francis Mason. *Balanchine's Complete Stories of the Great Ballets*. Rev. ed. Garden City, N.Y.: Doubleday and Co., 1977.

Clarke, Mary, and Clement Crisp. *The Ballet Goer's Guide*. New York: Alfred A. Knopf, 1981.

Clarke, Mary, and David Vaughan, eds. *The Encyclopedia of Dance and Ballet*. New York: G. P. Putnam's Sons, 1977.

Gruen, John. *The World's Great Ballets*. New York: Harry N. Abrams, 1981.

Mezzanotte, Riccardo, ed. *Phaidon Book of Ballet*. Oxford, Eng.: Phaidon, 1981.

Montadori, Arnoldo. *The Simon and Schuster Book of the Ballet*. New York: Simon and Schuster, 1980.

Robert, Grace. *The Borzoi Book of Ballets*. New York: Alfred A. Knopf, 1946.

Terry, Walter. *Ballet Guide*. New York: Dodd, Mead and Co., 1976.

Wilson, G. B. L. *A Dictionary of Ballet*. 3rd ed. New York: Theatre Arts Books, 1974.

—Jesma Reynolds; L.D.R.

26

THE INSTRUMENTS OF
THE SYMPHONY ORCHESTRA

· · · ·

ANYONE WHO HAS ATTENDED A CONCERT BY A SYMPHONY ORCHESTRA IN which a composition by Mozart or Beethoven was followed by a work composed by Wagner or Strauss has probably noticed that when time came for the latter work to be performed, a number of musicians not previously on stage now took their places in the orchestra.

What this indicates is the extent to which orchestras grew in size over the course of the nineteenth century. In the time of Mozart, Haydn, or early Beethoven, a standard orchestra might consist of some forty or so musicians. By the late nineteenth century an orchestra, by contrast, might include upwards of ninety to a hundred, a figure which is close to what holds true today. The earlier orchestra was conducted by one of the performing musicians, typically from a harpsichord or piano keyboard or as first violinist (konzertmeister); it is believed that the first conductor to stand before the orchestra and use a baton was Ludwig Spohr, in 1820.

The symphony orchestra as we know it evolved from small ensembles performing in churches or at courts in the sixteenth century; it took its present form in the eighteenth century, and over the years various instruments were added, some of them becoming standard components, others fading out after a time. Throughout most of the eighteenth century an orchestra contained harpsichords, furnishing the chorded harmonic continuo; as instrumental scoring became more detailed the harmonic function performed by the keyboard continuo became distributed among the various instruments. Full orchestral scoring, specifying which particular instruments were to play specific notes and passages, developed over the course of the eighteenth century.

The compilation that follows lists basic instruments of the evolving symphony orchestra.

Basset horn. Single-reed instrument, related to the clarinet, which dates from 1760. It was not always available to orchestras of the late eighteenth century, but Mozart occasionally scored for it. It is now occasionally used in modern orchestras.

Bassoon. Bass wind instrument developed in the seventeenth century from the curtal. It was very often used in the early baroque orchestra (seventeenth century) and remains a standard instrument in the modern orchestra. A contrabassoon, developed from an earlier version which appeared in 1739, is also sometimes added to a modern orchestra.

Celeste. Keyboard glockenspiel invented by Auguste Mustel in 1886. It first appeared in the orchestra for Tchaikovsky's *Nutcracker Suite* in 1892 and continues to be used occasionally in the twentieth century.

Cello. Bass member of the violin family, developed in the 1500s. It was part of Monteverdi's orchestra for *Orfeo* in 1607; and since the second half of the seventeenth century, the cello has been established as part of an orchestra's basic string group. See also **Double bass**.

Chalumeau. Simple, single-reed instrument, the direct ancestor of the orchestral clarinet, which appeared in the late seventeenth century. Even after the development of the clarinet, it continued to be used in opera orchestras, but it disappeared from the orchestra around 1770.

Cittern. Bass of the guitar family, with four pairs of double strings. Two archcitterns appeared in Monteverdi's *Orfeo* in 1607. Although citterns were still an alternative for providing a continuo in the first half of the eighteenth century, they were being increasingly replaced by keyboard instruments such as the harpsichord or the organ, until they disappeared from orchestras completely.

Clarinet. Single-reed instrument developed around 1700 from the chalumeau by J. C. Denner. It was added to the orchestra by C. W. Gluck but became indispensable to orchestras through Jean-Philippe Rameau in the mid-eighteenth century. Today the B-flat and the A clarinets are most commonly used in the orchestra. An E-flat clarinet may be used for special effects, as in Berlioz' *Symphonie fantastique.* An alto clarinet rarely appears in orchestral scores.

Clavichord. Keyboard instrument, with strings struck with small metal wedges, dating from medieval times. In the orchestra it was replaced during the late eighteenth century by the pianoforte, which offered considerably greater volume.

Cornet. Valved brass instrument, shaped like a trumpet but with a more conical bore, which is descended from the post horn, developed in France about 1830. Due to the slow acceptance of the valve trumpet by the French, the cornet was used in the nineteenth-century orchestra of Berlioz. An earlier instrument, the cornett, made of hard wood with fingerholes, dates from medieval times; it was used often through about 1650.

Cymbal. Brass percussion instrument, consisting of a pair of concave metal disks, introduced to the orchestra in the mid-eighteenth century owing to the interest in Turkish (Janissary) music. It is among the most important percussion instruments of the modern orchestra.

Double bass. Deepest member of the violin family, developed in the 1500s from the violone. The string bass violin appeared in Monteverdi's *Orfeo* in 1607, and has been a part of the orchestra's basic string group from the latter half of the seventeenth century onward.

Drum, bass. Adaption of the Turkish tabl turki, which appeared early in the sixteenth century. It was introduced to the orchestra in the mid-eighteenth century because of the interest in Turkish (Janissary) music and remains part of the percussion section of the modern orchestra, and an essential feature of military bands.

Drum, snare (side drum). Small, double-headed drum with snares which, except in the last movement of Handel's *Music for the Royal Fireworks*, did not enter the orchestra until the nineteenth century. It continues to be used in the modern orchestra.

Drum, tenor. Double-headed drum used primarily in military bands.

Electronic instruments. Instruments such as synthesizers, electric organs, electric guitars and zithers, theremins, vibraphones, ondes martenots, etc. They have been occasionally used in the twentieth-century orchestra, but are not considered basic instruments. In popular music they have become standard instruments.

English horn (Cor anglais). Woodwind instrument, the improved version of the older oboe da caccia, which appeared sporadically in orchestras between 1740 and 1780. It reentered the orchestra in the early nineteenth century.

Euphonium. Type of tuba with a large bugle and three to five valves, invented in 1843 by Sommer of Weimar. Although it is mainly important as a brass band instrument, it was occasionally used in the late nineteenth century and sometimes is used in modern orchestras.

Flute. Side-blown (transverse) flute, called a "German flute" in the seventeenth century, which was used by Jean-Baptiste Lully instead of recorders during his composing in France between 1660 and 1687. By the end of the seventeenth century, it was used in orchestras throughout western Europe. It is one of the modern orchestra's basic woodwinds. The fife, a small transverse flute which was a feature of military bands, has now been replaced by the piccolo.

French horn. Horn with a lengthened tube curled into a large, single coil. Introduced to the opera orchestra by Cavalli in a hunting scene in 1639, by 1691 it was differentiated from other horns by the name *French horn* and by the eighteenth century was commonly used in orchestras. Valves were added in the nineteenth century. The most usual current orchestral horns are double horns in F and B-flat.

Glockenspiel. Set of graded steel bars arranged in two rows and struck by very hard beaters. The early glockenspiel, with keyboard rather than beaters, was used in the eighteenth century but then dropped out of the standard ensemble. It returned to the orchestra in the late nineteenth century with beaters, and it continues to be used in the twentieth century.

Gong. Metal percussion instrument used for orchestral effects in the late nineteenth century, as in Tchaikovsky's *Pathetique* Symphony. It remains part of the twentieth-century percussion section.

Harmonium. Small reed organ patented in 1842 and first manufactured by A. F. Debain in Paris. It was used in light music arrangements and occasionally added to the orchestra until the first half of the twentieth century.

Harp. Stringed instrument, dating from ancient times; strings are plucked with the fingers. During the seventeenth century and the first half of the eighteenth century, harps were used in the orchestra for harmonic support. They entered the opera orchestra in the second half of the eighteenth century. During the nineteenth century, interest in harps as orchestral instruments was revived by composers such as Wagner and Tchaikovsky, and they continue to be used in the modern orchestra.

Harpsichord. Keyboard instrument which produces tones by plucking strings. It dates back to the fourteenth century, and was used in orchestras for harmonic continuo through most of the eighteenth century. As a solo instrument it gave way to the pianoforte, but it was revived in the early twentieth century.

Heckelphone. Form of the oboe, usually pitched at baritone range, invented in 1904. It was used in the orchestra for Richard Strauss's *Salome* in 1905, although it is not considered one of the standard instruments of current orchestras.

Horn. See **French horn**.

Kettledrum. See **Timpani**.

Lute. Stringed instrument generally used for basso continuo in baroque music. Three archlutes appeared in Monteverdi's *Orfeo* in 1607, and lutes were still being used occasionally in the 1700s. They were gradually dropped from the orchestra in the eighteenth century and replaced by keyboard instruments.

Oboe (hautboy). Wind instrument developed from the treble shawm in the seventeenth century, probably by the Hotteterre family. By the end of the century, oboes were found in orchestras throughout western Europe. The oboe remains one of the standard instruments of the modern orchestra.

Oboe da caccia. Early version of the cor anglais. It was used in Germany from around 1720 but was gradually eliminated from orchestras in the eighteenth century.

Oboe d'amore. One of several sizes of the oboe added to the orchestra in the early eighteenth century. Although its use declined in the same century, it was revived in the nineteenth century for performances of J. S. Bach's music and has been used by twentieth-century composers.

Ophicleide. Brass instrument of baritone range developed in nineteenth-century France from the key bugle as a replacement for the serpent. Introduced to the orchestra early in the same century, it appeared in Mendelssohn's overture to *A Midsummer Night's Dream* in 1826. Ophicleide solos were very popular in the mid-nineteenth century. The ophicleide was gradually made obsolete by the bass tuba.

Organ. Wind instrument controlled by a keyboard. The modern organ dates from medieval times. Two positive organs (fixed chamber organs) and a regal (small, portable reed organ) were used in Monteverdi's *Orfeo* in 1607. Organs continued to provide harmonic support throughout the seventeenth and early eighteenth centuries. Their use as an orchestral instrument declined after the mid-eighteenth century.

Percussion, occasional. Percussion instruments which, although not a normal part of a modern percussion section, have sometimes been added to the orchestra of the twentieth century for special effects. They include an anvil, can shaker, cog rattle, cowbell, cuckoo whistle, flexatone, gong, iron chains, maracas, multiple "whip," sandpaper blocks, shaker, sleighbells, Swannee whistle, switch, thundersheet, typewriter, xylophone, and wind machine.

Piano (pianoforte). Instrument whose strings are struck by hammers operated from a keyboard, which was developed during the early eighteenth century. Because it could be played both softly and loudly and possessed far greater range, it came to supersede the harpsichord and clavichord. The use of iron frames in the nineteenth century permitted greater tension, thicker strings, and a more ringing tone. Incorporated into the orchestra soon after its appearance, it continued to be used as harmonic continuo into the nineteenth century. The piano returned to the orchestra in the twentieth century as an obbligato instrument and continues to be used in modern orchestras.

Piccolo. Small flute with a range an octave above an ordinary flute. The piccolo is associated with the mid-eighteenth-century interest in Turkish (Janissary) music. During the late eighteenth century, it was added to opera orchestras in Germany. It continues to be used in the modern orchestra, and has generally replaced the fife in military bands.

Recorder. Wind instrument, blown through a whistle mouthpiece, which during the Renaissance underwent widespread development. The recorder was still in use in the orchestras of the mid-eighteenth century, but it was gradually being replaced by the transverse flute. It has been revived in the twentieth century as a solo and ensemble instrument.

Saxophone. Hybrid of the clarinet and oboe, played with a single reed but conical in bore, invented around 1840 by Adolphe Sax. The saxophone ranges in size from the sopranino and soprano to the baritone, bass, and contrabass. Its impact on the composers of the nineteenth century was widespread (for example, four saxophones appear in Strauss's *Sinfonia Domestica*, 1903), but although a staple in popular music it appears only selectively in the modern symphonic orchestra.

Serpent. Wind instrument with cupped mouthpiece, named for its long, sinuous tube shape, which is believed to have been invented about 1590 in France for use in church music. It was introduced to the orchestra by Mendelssohn in his oratorio "St. Paul" (1836). Like the ophicleide, it was gradually made obsolete by the bass tuba.

Tambourine. Shallow, one-headed drum with loose disks at the side. It was introduced to the orchestra in the late eighteenth century. The tambourine continues to be used in twentieth-century orchestras.

Tam-tam. Unpitched gong, of Malay origin, suspended in a frame and struck with a soft beater. It sometimes appears in the percussion sections of modern orchestras.

Theorbo. Large member of the lute family. It was used in orchestras, particularly as a continuo instrument, throughout the seventeenth and eighteenth centuries.

Timpani. Set of drums descended from the medieval naker, a small kettledrum of Arabic origin, introduced to the West in the fifteenth century. They can be tuned to precise pitch, and altered during performances. In the late seventeenth century, Jean-Baptiste Lully was one of the first to introduce them to the orchestra. Timpani continued to be used in the eighteenth century; and by the end of that century they were considered standard orchestral instruments, and they remain so in modern orchestras.

Triangle. Metal percussion instrument, in the form of a bent steel rod, named for its shape. It entered the orchestra in the late eighteenth century, and it remains an important modern orchestral instrument.

Trombone. Conical brass instrument similar to the trumpet, but with a telescopic slide for lengthening the tube, which first appeared in Europe in the 1400s. It was in wide use in the late 1600s, especially in sacred music and in bands, but it did not become a normal part of the symphonic orchestra until the nineteenth century. Thereafter it has been a standard brass orchestral instrument. The valve trombone was developed during the nineteenth century, but is little used today.

Trumpet. Lip-vibrated brass instrument, dating from ancient times. During the 1600s trumpets, although not a standard instrument, could be added to orchestras. Five trumpets without valves ("natural" trumpets) appeared in the orchestra of Monteverdi's *Orfeo*. New techniques, including extensions of length, bending, and mouthpieces, which allowed the instrument to diversify and to climb higher in its register, expanded its uses; by the end of the eighteenth century the trumpet was considered a normal orchestral instrument. During the early nineteenth century Stolzel and Bluhmel produced the first valved trumpet, which swiftly became standard; a B-flat valved trumpet is used in orchestras today. See also **Cornet**.

Tuba. Bass brass instrument developed in the 1820s and 1830s. During the nineteenth century it gradually superseded the ophicleide and the serpent as a bass instrument to become one of the orchestra's standard instruments. The three modern orchestral tubas are the E-flat bass, contrabass, and F bass tubas. John Philip Sousa extended the coil to fit around the body for use in marching bands, creating the sousaphone.

Tubular bells. Set of suspended metal tubes which are struck to produce sound. They were first brought into percussion sections during the late nineteenth century.

Viol. Bowed string instrument, usually held on the lap, which appeared in orchestras by the sixteenth century. By the mid-seventeenth century they had mostly disappeared from orchestras, replaced by the violin family, although in England they lasted late into the century. In chamber music the viol continued to be used into the mid-eighteenth century, and it has been revived in the twentieth.

Viola. Alto member of the violin family, structurally identical to the violin but slightly larger and tuned a fifth lower. It was in use by the later sixteenth century, and as the viola da brazzo became the middle instrument in the basic group of strings established in the second half of the seventeenth century.

Viola da gamba. Bass member of the viol family ("leg viol"). It appeared in orchestras of the seventeenth century but was gradually eliminated from the orchestra during the eighteenth century.

Viola d'amore. Tenor viol which appeared in baroque orchestras during the late seventeenth and early eighteenth centuries, and offered an especially soft, sweet sound. However, it gradually disappeared from the orchestra during the eighteenth century.

Violin. String instrument which emerged around 1550 from the medieval fiddle, the rebec, and the lira de braccio, and is the central instrument of the symphony orchestra and the chamber group, as well as for solo use. Since the eighteenth century the form and technique of the violin have become standardized, with only minor modifications.

Violoncello. See **Cello**.

Wagner tuba. Instrument related to the horn but with the conical bore increasing throughout its length and culminating in a bell rising obliquely from the body, devised by Richard Wagner for use in *The Ring*. It is sometimes added to the modern orchestra.

Xylophone. A percussion instrument which appeared in the early sixteenth century. The orchestral xylophone consists of two rows of wooden bars suspended over hollow tube resonators. It was added to the orchestra in the late nineteenth century in the scores of Tchaikovsky and Saint-Saëns.

SOURCES

Ammer, Christine. *The Harper Dictionary of Music.* 2nd ed. New York: Harper & Row, 1987.
Butler, Gregory G. "Instruments and Their Use: Early Times to the Rise of the Orchestra." In *The Orchestra: Origins and Transformations,* edited by Joan Peyser. New York: Charles Scribner's Sons, 1986.
Cummings, David, ed. *The New Everyman Dictionary of Music.* 6th ed. Originally comp. by Eric Bloom. London: Dent and Sons, Ltd., 1988.
Hadley, Benjamin, ed. *Britannica Book of Music.* Garden City, N.Y.: Doubleday and Co., 1980.
Randel, Don Michael, ed. *The New Harvard Dictionary of Music.* Cambridge, Mass.: Belknap Press, 1986.
Raynor, Henry. *The Orchestra.* New York: Charles Scribner's Sons, 1978.
Sadie, Stanley, ed. *The New Grove Dictionary of Musical Instruments.* London: Macmillan, 1984.
———. *The Norton/Grove Concise Encyclopedia of Music.* New York: W. W. Norton, 1991.
Sturrock, Susan, ed. *The Longman Handbook of Orchestral Instruments.* Burnt Mill, Eng.: Longman House, 1984.

—**Benita Muth; L.D.R.**

27

THE FORMS OF
CLASSICAL MUSIC

. . . . .

"Music," concludes Anthony Storr, "is an irreplaceable, unde-served, transcendental blessing." He is writing primarily of classical Western "art" music, and, as he points out, a chasm has developed between that and "popular" music. Persons with a strong interest in classical music can also enjoy much popular music, but it seldom works the other way around (this was, however, probably true in Handel's and Mozart's day as well).

Except for certain liturgical pieces, the body of classical music per-formed today is mostly a product of the last 350 years or so. More of it is available to more people nowadays than ever before in history, by virtue of recordings, FM radio, and (though not very often) television.

There are many, many hundreds of forms of classical music, ranging from simple songs to complex operatic, choral, and orchestral composi-tions. Obviously, just as the language of music is *sound*, and cannot be reproduced in language symbols, so any attempt to express the form and shape of musical compositions in words can only be partial and of a very general sort.

Moreover, the forms themselves have changed over the years; what the youthful Haydn called a symphony barely resembles a symphony by Shostakovich, and so on. As in all things, innovation can offend mightily; each generation tends to believe its own assumptions immutable. Carl Maria von Weber, upon hearing some of the later works of his contemporary Beethoven, pronounced him mad. What might Beethoven have thought of John Cage?

The compilation that follows offers brief descriptions of some of the more frequently encountered forms of classical music, principally those performed today, and insofar as possible without resort to technical musical terminology.

Air. Tune or song, vocal or instrumental.

Allemande. Baroque dance, originally in duple (two units to the measure) meter; *Allemande* means "German."

Ambrosian chant. Syllabic plainchant hymns of fourth century, identified with St. Ambrose, bishop of Milan.

Anglican chant. Harmonized singing of psalms and canticles, associated with the Church of England and later with New England churches.

Anthem. Hymned choral work performed in Protestant services in England.

Antiphon. Work sung by chorus prior to or following a psalm or canticle.

Arabesque. Melodic, rhythmic piece with elaborate ornamentation, popular during romantic period.

Aria. Solo for voice, part of an operatic or other extended work or sung independently.

Arrangement. Adaptation of a musical work for performance in a style or medium other than its original form; typically a version of an orchestral or operatic work adapted for piano.

Art song. Song written for artistic, as distinguished from folk or popular, performance.

Aubade. Composition of morning music, as contrasted with the evening music of the nocturne or serenade.

Bacchanale. Piece designed for sensuous singing and revelry; from Bacchus, the Greek god of wine.

Bagatelle. Short, light, rapidly paced piece, usually for piano.

Ballad. Song, simple and typically of folk origin, based on a simple verse.

Ballade. Originally a French song of three stanzas, based on a poem; later a musical narrative, with or without words.

Ballad opera. Stage dramatic presentation in which spoken dialogue is interwoven with music from folk songs, popular tunes, well-known melodies, etc., sung to lyrics written for the drama; popular in eighteenth-century England.

Ballet. Theatrical group dance, performed to music, without words; its great impetus came in France at the court of Louis XIV, and later in Vienna.

Barcarole. Boating song, with lilting rhythm, supposedly based on singing by Venetian gondoliers.

Battaglia. Orchestral piece, with drum rolls, trumpet flourishes, fanfares, imitations of gunfire, etc., describing a battle.

Bel canto. Elegant, ornamental form of singing, originating in Italy.

Berceuse. Lullaby imitating the rocking of a cradle.

Bergamasca. Italian dance, originally from Bergamo, typically in rapid tempo.

Bolero. Spanish dance, with castanets, in moderate tempo and triple time.

Byzantine chant. Unaccompanied liturgical music of Byzantine (Greek Orthodox) Church of Middle Ages, often nonscriptural but in the style of religious texts.

Caccia. Fourteenth-century Italian song and verses involving one voice "chasing" another.

Cancan. Rapid, "naughty" dance, developed on French vaudeville stage in mid-nineteenth century, in which the female performers hoisted their skirts above the knee as they stepped forward.

Canon. Composition in which a voice or melodic line is followed by one or more imitating voices or melodic lines.

Cantata. Work to be sung, with arias, duets, recitatives, choruses, and instrumental sections, for voices and orchestra or keyboard accompaniment, which flowered in the seventeenth and eighteenth centuries; shorter in length than the oratorio, the cantata can be religious or secular.

Canticle. Liturgical hymn of praise, other than a psalm, drawn from the Bible.

Canzone or canzona. Lyrical work, particularly of Italian origin, originally based on the stanzas of a poem, which later became instrumental rather than vocal, and evolved into the sonata.

Capriccio. Lively, whimsical, free-styled musical composition.

Carol. Song, in strophes, nowadays identified with Christmas.

Cassation. Eighteenth-century orchestral composition resembling a suite, serenade, or short symphony.

Catch. Composition for unaccompanied voices, originally three in number, with the lines overlapping; by careful syllabic coordination, unusual and sometimes risqué phrases can be made briefly audible.

Cavatina. Brief operatic or cantata solo piece.

Chaconne. See **Passacaglia**.

Chanson. French version of Renaissance canzone.

Chant. Liturgical plainsong.

Character piece. Romantic composition with a title, expressing a topic, usually written for piano.

Chorale. Congregational hymn first sung in Lutheran churches.

Commedia dell'arte. Renaissance Italian play, with stylized characters, which could involve music and dance.

Concerto. Composition for one or more solo instruments—piano, violin, cello, flute, oboe, clarinet, trumpet, etc.—and orchestra; a double concerto is for two solo instruments, and so on; the seventeenth- and earlier eighteenth-century concerto was in three movements; later four movements were included.

Concerto grosso. Composition in which a small group of solo instruments plays antiphonally (in alternating groups) with the full orchestra; popular during the early eighteenth century, it evolved into the symphony.

Contradance, or contredanse. Dance, usually lively, in which couples face each other and perform a variety of steps; the word itself is thought to have come from the English "country dance."

Cotillion. Eighteenth-century ballroom dance for couples, similar to the quadrille, in which one couple executes steps and the others duplicate them.

Cycle. Set of songs with common narrative structure or theme; see also **song cycle**.

Dance. Music to which rhythmic steps or body movements are performed.

Dirge. Song sung or played at funerals.

Divertimento. Composition, usually light and for keyboard instruments or an ensemble, with a number of units, including marches, minuets, dances, etc.

Doxology. Hymn of praise to God; the hymn beginning "Praise God from whom all blessings flow" is called "Old Hundred" or the "Doxology" in Protestant churches.

Duet. Composition for two performers, with or without accompaniment.

Ecossaise. English country dance, possibly of Scottish origin.

Elegy. Instrumental or vocal composition mourning a death.

Étude. Exercise or study designed to enhance technical ability through various kinds of techniques and devices.

Fandango. Spanish courtship dance, for guitar and castanets, ranging from moderately slow to fast tempo, in triple (three units to the measure) time.

Fanfare. Brief introductory ceremonial flourish for trumpets.

Fantasia. Instrumental piece in which conventional forms are set aside and the composer's fancy and inventiveness are emphasized.

Flamenco. Dance of southern Spain, characterized by use of semitones (half notes), and with guitar accompaniment.

Forlana. Italian dance in 6/4 or 6/8 meter.

Fugue. Polyphonic composition, developed from a given theme, which is stated first in one voice alone and then successively extended by imitative counterpoint in different octaves by all the other voices. Sections in which the thematic subject is stated at least once in all voices are called *expositions*; they alternate with *episodes*, in which the subject is not stated. The formal structure of the fugue involves exposition, development, and recapitulation.

Galliarde. Triple-meter court dance of sixteenth and seventeenth centuries.

Gavotte. Pastoral dance in 4/4 time, originally folk, later orchestral.

Gigue. Dance of baroque period in moderate to fast tempo, derived from the "jig" of Britain and Ireland.

Glee. Chordal unaccompanied song for three or more voices.

Gregorian chant. Roman Catholic liturgical chant of unharmonized plainsong, governed by speech rhythm, codified by or for Pope Gregory I, who established the Schola Cantorum in Rome in the sixth century.

Habanera. Dance and song in moderate 2/4 rhythm, named after the city of Havana, Cuba.

Hornpipe. Sailor's dance, usually solo with dancer's arms folded, in 3/2 or 4/4 time.

Humoresque. Brief, merry instrumental composition of nineteenth century.

Hymn. Song of religious praise or thanksgiving; early hymns were psalms or canticles.

Impromptu. Brief inventive piano piece.

Improvisation. Completely spontaneous music; in the eighteenth and nineteenth centuries it was common practice to give performers a theme for improvisation and elaboration.

Incidental music. Music composed to accompany the scenes of a dramatic performance; more often than not, it outlasted the dramatic performance.

Intermezzo. Originally a composition inserted between scenes and acts of an opera; later, an instrumental character piece.

Lament. Dirge.

Lied. (plur. *Lieder*). German art song, typically with simple development, and with the melody and accompaniment not linked musically to those of a larger composition.

Litany. Liturgical prayer, recited, with set responses from the congregation.

Madrigal. Originally, an Italian song for two or three voices, religious or secular; later, verse set to music, with four to six such settings; the madrigal is important in the evolution of opera.

Malagueña. Spanish dance in triple time.

March. Music for walking; the military march is designed to facilitate the quickstep of troops; it is also used in operas, symphonies, at funerals, etc., with appropriately varied rhythm.

Masque. Extended entertainment of sixteenth and seventeenth centuries, with poems, speeches, dances, and musical numbers.

Mass. Roman Catholic church service; the *missa solemnis*, the high mass, is sung with choral pieces and instrumental support; in the nineteenth century and thereafter masses were composed for other high ceremonial occasions and performed in concert halls. The major divisions of the mass are the Kyrie, Gloria, Credo, Sanctus, and Agnus Dei.

Mazurka. Polish folk dance, in triple time.

Minuet. Stately court dance, in 3/4 rhythm, of French origin; in the late seventeenth and eighteenth centuries minuets were inserted into orchestral suites and symphonies.

Morris dance. Traditional Renaissance English dance for masked men; its origins lie in Spanish dances pantomiming the battles between Christians and Moors.

Motet. Unaccompanied polyphonic (several simultaneous musical lines) choral composition, sung to a sacred text.

Musical comedy. Popular musical theater, derived from opera and featuring plot, dialogue, songs, and dances, with the mode and approach less formal and drawing more closely on the vernacular than operetta.

Nocturne. Composition of music for nighttime, as contrasted with day music, or aubade.

Octet. Composition for eight performers.

Opera. Musical play, with overture, arias, duets, ensembles, recitatives, marches and instrumental numbers, and sometimes ballets. Italian in origin and early development, it evolved from the madrigal and from pastoral dramatic works with musical settings; Monteverdi's *Orfeo* (1607) is often said to be the first full-fledged opera. The operatic form attained its mature form with the operas of Mozart. In the mid-nineteenth century the *music drama*, with leitmotifs and continuing melody throughout, replaced the earlier separation of arias and recitatives. *Opera seria* could be tragic or comic in nature; from *opera buffa* evolved light opera, operetta, musical comedy, etc.

Opera buffa. Italian comic opera, with recitatives and without dialogue.

Operetta. Originally a light opera; later a popular theater piece with music, dialogue, and dancing: *i.e.*, nineteenth and early twentieth-century style of musical comedy.

Oratorio. Extended narrative or dramatic composition, with arias, ensembles, recitatives, and instrumental compositions, performed in concert rather than staged; the subject matter is traditionally biblical.

Overture. Originally, the instrumental prelude to an opera, ballet, or play; the operatic overture often announced the melodies to be heard in the ensuing work; the concert overture, developed in the nineteenth century, is an expanded orchestral composition designed to be performed in its own right.

Parody. Earlier, replacement of the spoken text of a composition by another; later, the substitution of comic, usually vernacular text and situation for the original operatic libretto, for purposes of mockery.

Passacaglia. Baroque-period composition, a ritornello in which a theme is repeated with variations in harmonic progression; the historical distinction between passacaglia and chaconne is not clear, other than that the former was usually in a minor mode.

Passion music. Setting, for voice and instrumentation, of the text of the Passion.

Pasticcio. Work containing a variety of tunes of diverse origin, woven together loosely if at all.

Pastorale. Composition depicting or suggesting rural life.

Patter song. Rapid comic song with crowded verses.

Pavane or pavan. A court dance, stately and processional in form, in 4/4 or 4/2 rhythm.

Plainsong. Monophonic (single-voiced) chanted liturgical music, nonmetrical; also plainchant.

Polonaise. Polish dance, in moderate 3/4 time and with slow, stately movements.

Prelude. Originally a composition which introduced a larger work; in the nineteenth century it became an independent form.

Program music. Musical work, narrative or descriptive, intended to suggest a nonmusical idea.

Psalm. In music, a biblical poem which is sung, often with instrumental accompaniment.

Quadrille. Five-part French square dance in which two or four couples move about, usually in 6/8 or 2/4 time.

Quartet. Composition for four performers, vocal or instrumental; the string quartet, in four movements and usually with first and second violins, viola, and cello, received extensive development under Haydn, and through the example of that composer and Boccherini, Mozart, and Beethoven it became the most important instrumental chamber composition of the eighteenth and nineteenth centuries. Piano and guitar quartets substitute those instruments for a violin.

Quintet. Composition for five performers, vocal or instrumental; the instrumental quintet—string, piano, wind—follows the musical form of the quartet.

Quodlibet. Work with segments of well-known compositions combined in idiosyncratic fashion.

Recitative. Musical narrative which is spoken rather than sung, and is designed to move the action from one aria, ensemble, or other musical unit to the next.

Requiem mass. Mass for mourning, in which joyful sections of the mass are omitted; usually liturgical.

Revue. Theatrical presentation featuring a random variety of unconnected musical numbers, including vocal, instrumental, dance, and brief comic scenes.

Rhapsody. Nineteenth-century composition, instrumental or vocal, involving free fantasies, often illustrative of national music.

Ricercar, ricercare, or **ricercata.** Instrumental piece of sixteenth and seventeenth centuries, in imitative sequential style, resembling a fugue.

Ritornello. Section of a musical composition in which an earlier passage is repeated in a different rhythm; the ritornello form, important in the baroque concerto and concerto grosso, is based on recurring alternation between the solo or ensemble and the full orchestra.

Romance. The Spanish and French romance is a poem, in stanzas or strophes; the German is a lyrical instrumental composition.

Rondeau. Seventeenth-century French instrumental form with couplets and reiterated refrain.

Rondo. Instrumental form, whether independent or part of a larger work, in which the theme is repeated at least three times, with intervening episodes.

Round. Canon, usually in three following parts; the lines are sung sequentially.

Saraband. Slow, dignified dance of seventeenth and eighteenth centuries in 3/2 time.

Scherzo. Originally, light vocal composition; later, instrumental composition in rapid 3/4 meter, which largely replaced the minuet as the second movement of a symphony.

Septet. Instrumental composition for seven performers.

Serenade. Originally, evening song, sung by a lover to his beloved; later, multipart instrumental composition of a lighter nature.

Sextet. Vocal or instrumental work for six performers.

Siciliana. Song or instrumental work, of Italian origin, slow, in flowing 6/8 or 12/8 time.

Sinfonietta. Symphony on a reduced scale and scope.

Sonata. Composition, usually for one or two instruments, normally in three or four movements; the first movement is in sonata form, which is the basic structural development for much eighteenth- and nineteenth-century instrumental music of whatever kind, including the symphony; the first section, the exposition, opens with two contrasting themes in contrasting keys, and is followed by the second section, offering the development of each in various ways, then their recapitulation in the same key, and ending with a coda. As such, it provides the musical equivalent of "plot," the dramatic development of the composition constituting an exploration and a return home.

Sonatina. Short sonata.

Song. Short vocal composition.

Song cycle. See **Cycle.**

Suite. (1) Instrumental work consisting of a number of pieces in the same key; (2) work in which vocal and instrumental numbers from an opera or ballet are adapted for instrumental concert performance.

Symphonic poem. Nineteenth- and twentieth-century instrumental composition, usually in one movement, with a narrative or illustrative nonmusical subject; a form of program music; also called *tone poem.*

Symphonie concertante. Eighteenth-century orchestral composition in several movements, with one or more solo instruments; it is closer to the concerto grosso than the symphony.

Symphony. Composition, in movements, for full symphonic orchestra, based on the sonata form; as such it represents the culminating development of instrumental ensemble music; in Nicolas Slonimsky's words, the "supreme achievement of Western music." The symphony evolved out of the early eighteenth century concerto grosso; the three movements became four, and under Haydn and Mozart the form developed in depth and complexity. Beethoven's Symphony No. 3 in E-flat Major, the Eroica, opened the symphonic form to vastly greater range and intensity of expression, and, indeed, all subsequent symphonic music may be said to date from it.

Tarantella. Fast-moving Neapolitan dance in 6/8 meter.

Te Deum. Song of religious praise and rejoicing.

Toccata. Composition for keyboard instruments, in running idiomatic style.

Tombeau. Instrumental composition written in reverence for—"at the tomb of"—a dead person.

Trio. Composition for three vocal or instrumental performers; the instrumental trio customarily follows the sonata form. A string trio is written for violin, viola, and cello, or for two violins and cello; a piano trio is for violin, cello, and piano.

Trio sonata. Baroque composition for three or four instruments, written in three parts, with melody instruments and continuo.

Variations. Set of instrumental or chorale restatements, in which such devices as ornamentation, rephrasing, change of tempo, transposition (from one key to another), altered settings, and the like, are used in successive assertions of a given theme.

Voluntary. Composition in free, improvised style, for organ or other instruments, played during an Anglican church service.

Waltz. Ballroom dance in triple time.

Zarzuela. Spanish operatic form, interweaving spoken dialogue with music.

SOURCES

Randel, Don Michael, comp. *Harvard Concise Dictionary of Music.* Cambridge, Mass.: Belknap Press, 1978.

Sadie, Stanley, ed. *The New Grove Dictionary of Music and Musicians.* London: Macmillan, 1980.

———. *The Norton/Grove Concise Encyclopedia of Music.* New York: W. W. Norton, 1991.

Slonimsky, Nicolas. *Lectionary of Music.* New York: Doubleday Anchor Books, 1989.

Storr, Anthony. *Music and the Mind.* New York: Free Press, 1992.

—L.D.R.

28

MUSICAL TERMS: A GLOSSARY

. . . . .

THERE IS THAT DELICIOUS MOMENT IN JAMES JOYCE'S ULYSSES WHEN LEO-pold Bloom is en route with Stephen Dedalus to get some coffee, and he hears some men arguing in Italian. "A beautiful language," says Bloom. "I mean, for singing purposes. Why not write your poetry in that language? *Bella poetria!* it is so melodious and full. *Belladonna voglio.*" To which Stephen, who has shortly before been knocked out in a fight and is terribly hung over, replies, "To fill the ear of a sow elephant. They were haggling over money."

Italian may or may not be an especially musical language; a good argu-ment can be made that, with its prominently voiced consonants and indi-vidually sounded vowels, it is very much so. What is indisputable, however, is that it was the Italians who developed the major part of the terminology of music, so that to this day the expression marks that a composer writes upon his music to guide singers and instrumentalists in the proper approach to performance are written mostly in Italian.

Such language is not exactly measurable in its exactitude; to a consid-erable extent it depends upon a commonly shared sense of time and even emotional attitude—in which respect it can said to be artistic rather than scientific in its assumptions. What is the precise difference between *allegro non troppo,* which means "lively, but not too much so," and *allegretto,* or "rapidly, but gracefully"? There *is* a difference, but the ability to determine it comes from long hours of practice and experience, and there is always the danger that one person's *precisamente*—"precisely" (not a musical term)— may be another's *troppo,* "too much."

The glossary that follows is an effort to provide, for nonmusicians, an approximate explanation of some of the more often used musical terms relating to composition and performance.

A cappella. Vocal music without instrumental accompaniment.

Absolute pitch. See **Perfect pitch**.

Accelerando. Gradually accelerating tempo.

Accented note. Musical note receiving special stress or emphasis

Accidental. Mark, such as a flat or a sharp, placed before a note in a score to change its pitch.

Accompaniment. Subsidiary musical part designed to enhance a primary part; thus, piano accompaniment for a vocal solo.

Acoustics. Pertaining to the properties of sound; also, generally used to mean nonelectric: thus, an *acoustical recording* is one made before the introduction of electric recording methods.

Adagio. Slowly and gracefully.

Ad libitum. Freely; phrase indicating that the performer should feel free to introduce individual interpretation.

Alla breve. In duple measure (*i.e.*, two at a time); to be played twice as fast, usually two beats to the bar instead of four.

Alla turca. In Turkish style; in imitation of Turkish military music.

Allegretto. Rather rapidly, yet gracefully; tempo between adagio and allegro.

Allegro. Lively, quickly; music marked *allegro vivace* is to be played quite briskly.

Alternativo. One section within a composition alternated with another; much used in eighteenth-century dances.

Alto. (1) Vocally, the highest male voice or lowest female (contralto); (2) instrumentally, the high-middle range.

Andante. Moderately slow and even-paced (from the Italian for "plain"); the tempo of walking; it is by no means an exact term, and is typically modified, as in *andante moderato*, "somewhat faster"; *andante molto*, "quite slowly"; and so on.

Andantino. Typically for shorter compositions, signifying a bit quicker than straight andante; but it has also been used to mean a little slower than andante.

Antiphonal. Chanting or singing in alternation by chorus divided into two groups.

Appoggiatura. Embellishment to a tone in the form of a note preceding—in Italian, "leaning upon"—another and taking up part of its time; in the score it is written in smaller size.

Arpeggio. Spreading out the musical notes in a chord in sequential succession instead of sounding them all at once.

Atonal. Music lacking a tonal center or any relationship to a single key or scale, composed without reference to harmony or counterpoint.

Augmentation. Repetition of a note or theme with the time value increased, usually to twice the original length.

Bar. Vertical line marking the division between measures of music; also, the measure itself, made up of the notes between the vertical bars.

Baritone. Male voice in middle range, between tenor and bass.

Baroque. Characteristic music of period 1600–1750, originating earlier in Italy, and typified by ornamentation and extensive development of tonality and harmony, as in Bach and Handel; for system of musical notation, see **Thoroughbass**, below.

Bass. Lowest pitch of male voice; also, vocally and instrumentally, a deep sound.

Battaglia. Musical composition imitating the sounds of battle, with drumrolls, fanfares, imitations of musketry, bombardment, etc.; Beethoven's *Wellington's Victory* includes a battaglia.

Beat. Regularly repeated tempo of a musical composition; the conductor of an orchestra marks the beat with the rise and fall of baton or hand.

Bel canto. Italian for "beautiful song," a style of singing emphasizing a smooth, flowing melodic virtuosity.

Biedermeier. Used to signify derivative, unadventurous middle-class musical taste; in popular music, for example, Lawrence Welk might be said to have offered *biedermeier* for many years.

Bourdon. Monotonous, drawn-out, droning note, as in bagpipe music.

Bowing. Technique of applying a bow to strings, involving various kinds of strokes and pressures.

Broken chord. Splitting up of notes within a chord, as in arpeggio.

Cadence. Strain or sequence of chords concluding a musical composition or a passage within one.

Cadenza. Elaborate virtuoso passage for a vocal or instrument soloist near the close of a composition or a movement; designed to display technique, earlier cadenzas were improvised, but from Beethoven's time onward the composer customarily wrote them into the score.

Castrato. Male singer castrated before puberty to preserve his soprano voice; widely used in opera and Roman Catholic church music through eighteenth century and to a lesser extent later; castrati parts are now usually sung by countertenors.

Chamber music. Music for small instrumental groups, for performance in rooms rather than concert halls, customarily with a different part for each instrument, as for example string or piano trios, quartets, quintets, etc.

Choir. Group of church singers; can also be instrumental, as in a brass choir.

Chord. Combination of two or more—usually three—tones which blend harmoniously.

Chromatic. Use of all or most of the half tones—sharps and flats—within a given scale to produce richness and color.

Classical. Although classical music is commonly used to denote art music, historically it signifies the music of the late eighteenth and early nineteenth centuries, written between the baroque and the romantic periods, and characterized by clarity and simplicity, such as that of Haydn and Mozart.

Clef. Sign at the beginning of a musical composition designating the absolute pitch—*i.e.*, degree of vibration—of the notes; in piano music there are the G or treble clef and the F or bass clef; in instrumental or vocal music the C clef, based on middle C, can be soprano, alto, or tenor.

Coda. Concluding passage of a composition.

Col legno. "With wood"; the violinist is to tap the strings lightly with the wood of the bow.

Coloratura. Lyric. ation in general; a *col* lity.

Concert pitch. Pi l instruments perfor sposing while being p e piano key being str struck always produ nts are tuned in relat

Con grandezza. "With grandeur"; to be played in the grand style.

Continuo. See **thoroughbass**.

Counterpoint. "Note against note": music in which one musical line is juxtaposed with another for purposes of harmony, dissonance, and resolution, with the character of both lines being firmly retained; the great age of counterpoint was the first half of the eighteenth century.

Countertenor. Highest range of a full masculine voice; much used in medieval and early Renaissance music, scoring for the countertenor gave way to that for the castrato in the sixteenth through the eighteenth centuries, then was restored to some use in compositions.

Crescendo. Gradual increase in volume of tone.

Da capo. "From the beginning"; instruction to musician to return to the start of the part and repeat.

Development. Elaboration and exploration of a theme through melodic variations, greater complexity, etc.; in the sonata form the development follows the statement and moves toward the recapitulation.

Diapason. The full range of vocal tone; also, an organ stop.

Diatonic. Major and minor notes of a scale, without semitones.

Diminuendo. Gradually decreasing volume.

Diminution. Shortening and multiplying of a group of notes, in response to their previous assertion as long notes.

Dotted note. Dot placed next to a note: if under, to be slurred; if above, to be played staccato; if to the right, to be increased in length by one-half.

Due. (pronounced dou'-ai). To be played on two strings of the violin.

Encore. Short additional piece played in response to audience applause; a piece can also be repeated as an encore.

Episode. Digressive passage in a composition, to provide variety.

Exposition. Presentation of the themes of a composition.

Expression marks. Words or signs to indicate how music is to be performed, as in *allegro, andante,* dotted notes, etc.

Falsetto. Voice which is sung higher than its normal range.

Figural. Florid, decorative; music which is embellished; also used earlier to distinguish polyphonic music from plainsong.

Flat. Sign, ♭, indicating that a note is to be played a half tone lower.

Forte. To be played loudly, strongly rather than softly (*piano*); the pianoforte was so named because, unlike the harpsichord, it could be played either softly or loudly according to touch.

Glissando. Sliding effect produced by drawing a fingernail over groups of adjacent piano keys or harp strings.

Grace note. Musical note, not essential to melody or harmony, added for embellishment, without enlarging the tempo, as in appoggiatura.

Ground bass. Melody which is steadily repeated in the bass while the treble is constantly varied.

Harmony. Simultaneous sounding of tones to produce chords; *i.e.,* to function as one sound.

Homophonic music. Music in which all the parts move in the same rhythm, or in which the melodic lead is accompanied by chords.

Imitation. Repetition of a motif or portion of a theme through inversion, rhythmic change, different pitch or key, or other embellishments.

Improvisation. Extemporaneous, impromptu development of a tune; nowadays a feature of jazz music.

Interval. The distance between two notes—*i.e.,* between two frequencies of vibration, whether sounded simultaneously (harmonic) or successively (melodic).

Inversion. "Turning upside down": *harmonic inversion* involves placing the bass note on the top rather than the bottom of a chord; in *melodic inversion* the intervals between tones of a tune are made to ascend rather than descend, or vice versa.

Key. (1) In keyboard instruments a lever, and in reed or wind instruments a valve, activated by a finger to produce a particular sound; (2) the tonality of a scale, based on the main pitch, or tonal center; there are 24 keys, comprised of a major and a minor key for each pitch class.

Larghetto. Rather slowly.

Largo. Slowly, broadly; to be played in very stately fashion.

Legato. Without interruption; the notes to be played smoothly, as if bound together.

Leggero. Nimbly, in lively style.

Leitmotif. Particular phrase or passage, associated in Wagnerian opera with a character or idea and repeated upon each reappearance.

Major, minor. Two modes of tone, based on the intervals between notes (*i.e.*, units of vibration) in an octave, which are dominant in Western music; a *major scale*, or *key*, consists of tones and semitones in the ascending pattern T – T – S – T – T – T – S; the ascending *minor* pattern is T – S – T – T – S – T – T.

Measure. Music contained between two bar lines; *i.e.*, a bar.

Melody. Succession, or pattern, of single tones; a tune.

Meter. Rhythmic beat of music, as arranged in equal units.

Mezzo. Middle; moderate; thus the mezzo-soprano's range is midway between soprano and contralto.

Microtone. Interval between tones smaller than a semitone; although receiving some use in both very early and twentieth-century Western music, it has been characteristic of non-Western tonality.

Middle C. Key near the middle of the piano; notes above are in treble staff, below are in bass staff.

Moderato. At moderate speed; between andante (moderately slow) and allegro (brisk).

Modulation. Shift from one key into another during the performance of a composition.

Monophony. Single toned; a single line of melody, as in plainchant or unaccompanied solo.

Motif. Distinct phrase or passage which reappears within a composition.

Movement. Complete section of a composition.

Multimetric. Musical work written with differing meters.

Natural note. Note that is neither sharpened nor flatted.

Neoclassicism. Twentieth-century music written in high classical style; *i.e.*, imitative of the manner of composition prior to the romantic movement.

Neumes. System of written signs used in the Middle Ages to indicate relative pitch.

Non troppo. See **troppo.**

Notation. Act of writing down music on paper with signs that indicate the pitch and duration of tones; also, the system for doing so; the staff system now in use utilizes the vertical position of notes on horizontal lines to show relative pitch, and the shape and density of the notes to indicate duration.

Note. Written character which by placement and shape designates the relative pitch of musical sounds; see **Notation**, above.

Obbligato. Obligatory, required; the designated instrument must play these notes; paradoxically, the word has come to be used popularly to signify just the reverse, as in optional.

Octave. Interval between two notes that are seven diatonic scale degrees apart, thus eight notes in all; the pitch—*i.e.*, rate of sound vibration—of the higher note is exactly twice that of the lower.

Open notes. Instrumental notes not requiring manipulation; thus, the tone produced if a string is not depressed, a key or valve is not used, or holes are left uncovered.

Opus. Work; the opus number identifies the composer's works, usually by chronological sequence.

Orchestration. Instrumentation of a musical work, specifying which instruments are to play which notes.

Ostinato. Persistently—in Italian, "obstinately"—repeated fragment or passage.

Paraphrase. Freely adapted transcription of a composition.

Parlando. To be sung or played as if it were being declaimed.

Part. (1) Portion of a composition assigned to a particular instrument or voice; (2) one of the melodic lines in counterpoint.

Passage. Distinctive phrase or segment of a composition.

Perfect pitch. Ability to identify the pitch of a musical note by ear, without relationship to any other note; also known as *absolute pitch*.

Phrase. Brief division of a composition, typically four measures.

Pianissimo. Very softly.

Piano. Softly; also, the pianoforte.

Pitch. Sound of a note of music, as determined by the rate of vibration of the sound waves; the greater the number of vibrations, the higher the pitch.

Piu tosto. More quickly.

Polychoral. Multiple groups playing or singing within an ensemble.

Polyphony. Music with two or more distinctly shaped lines of melody, whether for harmony or contrast; counterpoint is a form of polyphony.

Prestissimo. With the utmost rapidity.

Presto. Quite rapidly; more so than allegro.

Quarter tone. One-fourth of a full tone; half of a semitone.

Range. Full register of a voice or instrument, from lowest to highest notes.

Recapitulation. In the sonata form, the restatement of the themes.

Recitativo. Recitatives; vocal passages which are delivered with the rhythm and intonation of speech and with harpsichord or, later, piano accompaniment, and which lack melody; used in opera through Rossini to develop the story between arias.

Register. The range of a voice or an instrument; also, a portion of that range, as in *upper register*, etc.

Repeat. Passage to be played a second time; indicated in the score by a series of two or four vertical dots.

Resonance. Resounding; transmission of sound vibration from one vibrating entity to another, as for example the strings of a piano, thus adding intensification and richness.

Rhythm. Regularly repeated beat pattern.

Ritardando. Retardation; in gradually slackening tempo.

Ritenuto. Retention, reduction; immediate slowdown of tempo.

Romantic. Musical era succeeding the classical, from last decade of eighteenth century to early twentieth; romantic music is expansive, more overtly emotional, less formally restrictive than baroque and classical; Beethoven's Symphony No. 3 in E-flat, the *Eroica,* has sometimes been called the first great romantic orchestral composition, although Beethoven's music has also been characterized as preromantic.

Scale. Succession of tones in fixed order of rising pitch; a scale is identified by the first note in the progression, and so is said to be in the key of C Major, E-flat, etc.

Scherzando. Playful, sporting.

Scordatura. Artificial tuning of a musical instrument to achieve a special audial effect.

Score. Musical notation for an entire composition, specifying which instruments are to play and which singers are to sing which notes.

Segue. To follow; the performing musician is to move straight into the next section of the composition without a separating break.

Semi. Half; a *semitone* lasts one-half as long as a full tone in tempo, a *quarter tone* one-half a *semitone.*

Sequence. Musical phrase repeated in a different pitch; in *melodic sequence* the repetition is in the melody line alone; in *harmonic sequence* in other parts as well.

Sforzando. Violently, compellingly; sudden, emphatic sounding of a note or chord.

Sharp. Sign, ♯, indicating that a given note is to be played a half note higher.

Sight reading. Performing a composition at first seeing.

Signature. Sign at beginning of a composition indicating key and tempo.

Soprano. Highest female voice range.

Sostenuto. Sustained, prolonged.

Staccato. Short, separate notes, clearly detached from each other.

Staff. Also called *stave;* a set of horizontal lines atop each other, upon and between which sequences of notes are placed to indicate their pitch and tempo; see **Notation**.

Stretto. Contracted; in close succession; increased tempo at the climax of a work.

Syncopation. Shifting the beat regularly in a measure to a position before or after where it would normally be sounded, to achieve a rhythmic effect of delaying and hurrying, as in dancing.

Tanto. Not too much; just enough.

Tardo. Slowly.

Tempo. Beat; rate of rhythmic speed at which a piece is to be performed.

Tenor. Highest normal range of a male voice.

Theme. Principal melodic subject of a composition.

Thoroughbass. In baroque music, the chordal accompaniment with only the bass notes given, and the intervals and chords indicated in figures; also known as *continuo* or *figured bass.*

Tonality. Basic principle of tonal organization in Western music, in which the affinity of groups of tones is organized by the tonic key note, or tonic key, as A Major, B-flat, etc.

Tone. Sound, or rate of vibration of the sound waves, of a note of music.

Transition. Movement from one musical key to another; also, the notes, or *bridge,* used to effect the move.

Transposing instruments. Instruments whose natural pitch differs from the musical notation indicating that pitch, so that to produce the desired sound through identical fingering or positioning on all instruments of the same family the notation must be changed. Thus, since the natural tone of the clarinet is B-flat, in order to get that tone played the composer writes the note for C Major. Today, however, most composers prefer to score the note they wish sounded, and leave the transposing to the performer.

Transposition. Changing a composition from one key into another; frequently done to accommodate singers with differing voice ranges.

Treble. Highest natural range of which a voice or instrument is capable, *i.e., soprano;* the *treble clef,* however, while the higher of the two piano clefs, is otherwise the second-highest instrument and vocal clef, the *soprano clef* being higher.

Tremolo. Trembling, tremulous; rapidly fluttered single note; also rapidly varying repetition in pitch.

Trill. Continuous alternation of two consecutive notes.

Troppo. "Too much"; *non troppo* is "not too much," or "not excessively so."

Tune. Melody; a pattern of tones.

Tutti. To be played by everyone in the ensemble.

Twelve-tone. System of composition, pioneered independently by Josef Matthias Hauer and Arnold Schoenberg, in which all twelve tones of the chromatic scale are used, without being grouped around a particular tone and those vibrating sympathetically with it, and so in no relationship to harmony.

Unison. Identical pitch; instruments and/or voices performing the same tone simultaneously.

Variations. Repetition of a theme with changes and embellishments of melody, harmony, tempo, etc.

Velato. Veiled; subdued.

Veloce. With velocity; rapid and dashing.

Vibrato. Vibrating; repeated slight alteration of pitch, but not to the degree of trembling; see **Tremolo.**

Voice. Sound uttered by human beings; in music the normal range of voices runs in descending order from *soprano* to *mezzo-soprano* to *alto* (or *contralto*) in female voices, and from *tenor* to *baritone* to *basso* in male voices; normally the male voice is an octave lower in pitch than the female; a male *counter-tenor* sings in approximately the same range as a female *alto*.

Volante. Flying along; rushing.

SOURCES

Randel, Don Michael, comp. *Harvard Concise Dictionary of Music.* Cambridge, Mass.: Belknap Press, 1978.

Sadie, Stanley, ed. *The New Grove Dictionary of Music and Musicians.* London: Macmillan, 1980.

———. *The Norton/Grove Concise Encyclopedia of Music.* New York: W. W. Norton, 1991.

Slonimsky, Nicolas. *Lectionary of Music.* New York: Doubleday Anchor Books, 1989.

Webster's New International Dictionary of the English Language. 2nd ed., unabridged. Vols. I-III. Springfield, Mass.: G. and C. Merriam Co., 1959.

—**L.D.R.**

29

FAMOUS MUSICALS
AND OPERETTAS

· · · · ·

WHAT IS THE DIFFERENCE BETWEEN A COMIC OPERA AND A LIGHT OPERA? OR between an operetta and a musical? Or between a musical comedy and a musical play? It is something like sex; we know what it is, but when it comes to defining it, there are marked differences of opinion.

One way of going about drawing the distinctions is through concrete examples. *The Marriage of Figaro* is a comic opera. *Der Fledermaus* is a light opera. *HMS Pinafore* is an operetta; so is *Desert Song*. *Annie, Get Your Gun* is a musical. *South Pacific* is a musical comedy. *West Side Story* is a musical play. So where are we now? Where do *Porgy and Bess* or *The Beggars' Opera* fit in?

The truth is that there are no hard-and-fast definitions. We could say that of the examples above, only *The Marriage of Figaro* is "serious" music—well, maybe *Porgy and Bess* too. Serious, though, to whom? To use "serious" like that is to make a value judgment; it implies that only Mozart's opera is important as a work of musical composition; the others are "popular" music. Still, value judgments can't be avoided, and as between Mozart and Richard Rodgers, I know where I stand. (But what about Rodgers vs. Puccini? Go it bear, go it dame!)

When Ezio Pinza's bass-baritone voice became too frail for continued performance as a member of the Metropolitan Opera Company, he turned to Rodgers and Hammerstein's *South Pacific*, and achieved far more widespread renown—and earned considerably more money—than he had ever known when singing Mozart roles. Still, that is hardly very helpful.

There is a legitimate, if less than entirely consistent, difference between grand opera and "popular" music. (But where do the Gilbert and Sullivan operettas belong? We decided they fitted into our Operas category more appropriately than into Musicals and Operettas.) One authority defines *operetta* as "a theatrical piece of light and sentimental character in simple and popular style, containing spoken dialogue, and dancing" (Don Michael Randel, *Harvard Concise Dictionary of Music*). An operetta is a more formal work than a musical in the way it is staged, in the nature of the spoken dialogue and the language convention, in the division between the music and the spoken words. The musical is more "realistic," less "artificial" in its presentation (yet how many people do you know who burst into extended song at important points in their lives?). And it is true that the songs from musicals can become popular hits without being adapted—*e.g.*, "Hello, Dolly," "Give My Regards to Broadway," "I Get a Kick Out of You."

So much for distinctions. Here are a few famous musicals and operettas and whatever, with the dates and places of first production, and best-known songs. (See also the essay on operas, in which you may find works that also might plausibly be listed here. To repeat, there are no hard-and-fast rules.)

Annie, by Charles Strouse. Lyrics by Martin Charnin. Premiered April 21, 1977, at Alvin Theatre in New York City. Songs include: "It's the Hard-Knock Life," "Tomorrow," "Easy Street."

Annie, Get Your Gun, by Irving Berlin. Lyrics by Dorothy and Herbert Field. Premiered May 16, 1946, at Imperial Theatre in New York City. Songs include: "I Got the Sun in the Morning," "Doin' What Comes Natur'lly," "You Can't Get a Man With a Gun," "There's No Business Like Show Business," "Anything You Can Do."

Anything Goes, by Cole Porter. Lyrics by Howard Lindsay, Russell Crouse, Guy Bolton, P. G. Wodehouse. Premiered November 21, 1934, at Alvin Theatre in New York City. Songs include: "You're the Top," "I Get a Kick Out of You," "Blow, Gabriel, Blow."

Babes in Toyland, by Victor Herbert. Libretto by Glen MacDonough. Premiered June 17, 1903, at the Opera House in Chicago. Songs include: "March of the Toys," "I Can't Do That Sum," "Toyland."

Brigadoon, by Frederick Loewe. Libretto by Alan Jay Lerner. Premiered March 13, 1947, at Ziegfeld Theatre in New York City. Songs include: "The Heather on the Hill," "Come to Me, Bend to Me," "Almost Like Being in Love," "Brigadoon."

Bye Bye Birdie, by Charles Strouse. Lyrics by Lee Adams. Premiered April 14, 1960, at Martin Beck Theatre in New York City. Songs include: "How Lovely to Be a Woman," "Put on a Happy Face," "Baby, Talk to Me," "Rosie."

Cabaret, by John Kander. Lyrics by Fred Ebb. Premiered November 20, 1966, at Broadhurst Theatre in New York City. Songs include: "Perfectly Marvelous," "Tom Belongs to Me," "The Money Song," "If I Could See Her," "Cabaret."

Camelot, by Frederick Loewe. Lyrics by Alan Jay Lerner. Based on T. H. White's *The Once and Future King.* Premiered December 3, 1960, at Majestic Theatre in New York City. Songs include: "I Wonder What the King Is Doing Tonight," "If Ever I Would Leave You," "Camelot."

Can-Can, by Cole Porter. Libretto by Abe Burrows. Premiered May 7, 1953, at Shubert Theatre in New York City. Songs include: "C'ést Magnifique," "I Love Paris," "It's All Right With Me."

Candide, by Leonard Bernstein. Lyrics by John Latouche, Richard Wilbur, Dorothy Parker, Lillian Hellman, Leonard Bernstein. Premiered December 1, 1956, at Martin Beck Theatre in New York City. Songs include: "Glitter and Be Gay."

Carousel, by Richard Rodgers. Lyrics by Oscar Hammerstein II. Adapted from Ferenc Molnar's *Liliom.* Premiered April 19, 1949, at Majestic Theatre in New York City. Songs include: "June Is Bustin' Out All Over," "You'll Never Walk Alone."

Cats, by Andrew Lloyd Webber. Based on T. S. Eliot's book of poetry. Premiered May 11, 1981, at New London Theatre in London. Songs include: "Jellicle Songs for Jellicle Cats," "The Rum Tum Tugger," "Old Deuteronomy," "Macavity," "Memory," "Mr. Mistoffelees."

Chorus Line, A, by Marvin Hamlisch. Lyrics by Edward Kleban. Premiered April 15, 1975, at Public Theatre in New York City. Songs include: "I Hope I Get It," "Nothing," "One," "What I Did for Love."

Connecticut Yankee, A, by Richard Rodgers. Lyrics by Lorenz Hart. Premiered November 3, 1927, at Vanderbilt Theatre in New York City. Songs include: "My Heart Stood Still," "Thou Swell," "I Feel at Home With You," "On a Desert Island with Thee."

Damn Yankees, by Richard Adler. Libretto by George Abbott and Douglass Wallop. Adapted from Douglass Wallop's book *The Year the Yankees Lost the Pennant.* Premiered May 5, 1955, at 46th Street Theatre in New York City. Songs include: "Shoeless Joe From Hannibal, Mo.," "Whatever Lola Wants," "Those Were the Good Old Days."

Desert Song, The, by Sigmund Romberg. Lyrics by Frank Mandel, Otto Harbach, Oscar Hammerstein II. Premiered November 30, 1926, at Casino Theatre in New York City. Songs include: "The Desert Song," "It."

Evita, by Andrew Lloyd Webber. Lyrics by Tim Rice. Premiered June 21, 1978, at Prince Edward Theatre in London. Songs include: "On This Night of a Thousand Stars," "Buenos Aires," "I'd Be Surprisingly Good for You," "Don't Cry for Me Argentina," "A New Argentina," "High Flying Adored," "And the Money Kept Rolling In."

Fanny, by Harold Rome. Lyrics by Harold Rome. Premiered November 4, 1954, at Majestic Theatre in New York City. Songs include: "Never Too Late for Love," "I Like You," "Love Is a Very Light Thing," "Fanny."

Fantasticks, The, by Harvey Schmidt. Lyrics by Tom Jones. Premiered May 3, 1960, at Sullivan Street Playhouse in New York City. Songs include: "Try to Remember."

Fiddler on the Roof, by Jerry Bock. Lyrics by Sheldon Harnick. Based on Sholom Aleichem's stories. Premiered September 22, 1964, at Imperial Theatre in New York City. Songs include: "Tradition," "Matchmaker, Matchmaker," "If I Were a Rich Man," "To Life," "Sunrise, Sunset."

Finian's Rainbow, by Burton Lane. Lyrics by E. Y. Harburg. Premiered January 10, 1947, at 46th Street Theatre in New York City. Songs include: "How Are Things in Glocca Morra?," "Something Sort of Grandish."

Firefly, The, by Rudolf Friml. Lyrics by Otto Harbach. Premiered December 2, 1912, at Lyric Theatre in New York City. Songs include: "Giannina Mia," "Sympathy," "Love Is like a Firefly."

42nd Street, by Harry Warren. Lyrics by Al Dubin. Premiered August 25, 1980, at Winter Garden Theatre in New York City. Songs include: "You're Getting to Be a Habit With Me," "We're in the Money," "Lullaby of Broadway," "Forty-second Street."

Funny Face, by George Gershwin. Lyrics by Ira Gershwin. Premiered November 22, 1927, at Alvin Theatre in New York City. Songs include: "'S Wonderful," "The Babbitt and the Bromide."

Gentlemen Prefer Blondes, by Jule Styne. Lyrics by Leo Robin. Based on the novel by Anita Loos. Premiered December 8, 1949, at Ziegfeld Theatre in New York City. Songs include: "Diamonds Are a Girl's Best Friend," "Bye, Bye, Baby."

Grease, by Jim Jacobs and Warren Casey. Lyrics by Jim Jacobs and Warren Casey. Premiered February 14, 1972, at Eden Theatre in New York City. Songs include: "Summer Nights," "Greased Lightnin'," "Beauty School Dropout," "There Are Worse Things I Could Do."

Gypsy, by Jule Styne. Lyrics by Stephen Sondheim. Premiered May 21, 1959, at Broadway Theatre in New York City. Songs include: "Let Me Entertain You," "Small World," "Everything's Coming Up Roses."

Hair, by Galt McDermot. Lyrics by Gerome Ragni and James Rado. Premiered (on Broadway) April 29, 1968, at Biltmore Theatre in New York City. Songs include: "Aquarius," "Hair," "LBJ," "Where Do I Go," "Good Morning Starshine."

Hello, Dolly!, by Jerry Herman. Lyrics by Jerry Herman. Premiered January 16, 1964, at St. James Theatre in New York City. Songs include: "It Takes a Woman," "It Only Takes a Moment," "Before the Parade Passes By," "Hello, Dolly!"

Jesus Christ Superstar, by Andrew Lloyd Webber. Lyrics by Tim Rice. Premiered October 12, 1971, at Mark Hellinger Theatre in New York City. Songs include: "Heaven on Their Minds," "I Don't Know How to Love Him," "King Herod's Song," "Superstar."

King and I, The, by Richard Rodgers. Lyrics by Oscar Hammerstein II. Based on Margaret Langdon's *Anna and the King of Siam*. Premiered March 29, 1951, at St. James Theatre in New York City. Songs include: "Getting to Know You," "Hello, Young Lovers," "Shall We Dance?"

Kismet, adapted from Alexander Borodin's *Prince Igor*. Lyrics by Robert Wright and George Forrest. Based on the play by Edward Knoblock. Premiered December 3, 1953, at Ziegfeld Theatre in New York City. Songs include: "Stranger in Paradise," "Baubles, Bangles, and Beads."

Kiss Me, Kate, by Cole Porter. Lyrics by Cole Porter. Premiered December 30, 1948, at New Century Theatre in New York City. Songs include: "Why Can't You Behave?," "Too Darn Hot."

La Cage aux Folles, by Jerry Herman. Lyrics by Jerry Herman. Based on film and play by Jean Poiret. Premiered August 21, 1983, at Palace Theatre in New York City. Songs include: "A Little More Mascara," "Song on the Sand," "La Cage aux Folles," "I Am What I Am," "Best of Times."

Les Misérables, by Claude-Michel Schönberg and Alain Boubil. Lyrics by Herbert Kretzmer. Premiered October 8, 1975, at Barbican Theatre in London. Songs include: "At the End of the Day," "I Dreamed a Dream," "Lovely Ladies," "Castle on a Cloud," "Do You Hear the People Sing," "A Little Fall of Rain," "In My Life."

Little Johnny Jones, by George M. Cohan. Lyrics by George M. Cohan. Premiered November 7, 1904, at Liberty Theatre in New York City. Songs include: "Yankee Doodle Dandy," "Give My Regards to Broadway."

Little Shop of Horrors, by Alan Mencken. Lyrics by Howard Ashman. Premiered May 20, 1982, at WPA Theatre in New York City. Songs include: "Little Shop of Horrors," "Grow for Me," "Somewhere That's Green."

Mame, by Jerry Herman. Lyrics by Jerry Herman. Premiered May 24, 1966, at Winter Garden Theatre in New York City. Songs include: "It's Today," "My Best Girl," "We Need a Little Christmas," "Bosom Buddies," "Mame."

Man of La Mancha, by Mitch Leigh. Lyrics by Joe Darion. Premiered November 22, 1965, at ANTA Washington Square Theatre in New York City. Songs include: "The Impossible Dream," "Knight of the Woeful Countenance," "Little Bird, Little Bird," "I Really Like Him."

Most Happy Fella, The, by Frank Loesser. Lyrics by Frank Loesser. Premiered May 3, 1956, at Imperial Theatre in New York City. Songs include: "The Most Happy Fella," "Standing on the Corner," "Rosabella," "Abbondanza," "Warm All Over."

Music Man, The, by Meredith Willson. Lyrics by Meredith Willson. Based on story by Meredith Willson and Franklin Lacey. Premiered December 19, 1957, at Majestic Theatre in New York City. Songs include: "Seventy-Six Trombones," "Marian, the Librarian," "Wells Fargo Wagon," "Trouble," "Lida Rose," "Gary, Indiana," "Goodnight, My Someone."

My Fair Lady, by Frederick Loewe. Lyrics by Alan Jay Lerner. Based on play *Pygmalion* by George Bernard Shaw. Premiered March 15, 1956, at Mark Hellinger Theatre in New York City. Songs include: "Wouldn't It Be Loverly," "I'm an Ordinary Man," "Just You Wait," "The Rain in Spain," "I Could Have Danced All Night," "Get Me to the Church on Time," "Hymn to Him," "Without You," "I've Grown Accustomed to Her Face."

No, No, Nanette, by Vincent Youmans. Lyrics by Irving Caesar and Otto Harbach. Premiered September 16, 1925, at Globe Theatre in New York City. Songs include: "Tea for Two," "I Want to Be Happy."

Of Thee I Sing, by George Gershwin. Lyrics by Ira Gershwin. Premiered December 26, 1931, at Music Box Theatre in New York City. First musical to win Pulitzer Prize. Songs include: "Of Thee I Sing," "Because, Because."

Oklahoma!, by Richard Rodgers. Lyrics by Oscar Hammerstein II. Premiered March 31, 1943, at St. James Theatre in New York City. Songs include: "Oh, What a Beautiful Morning," "The Surrey With the Fringe on Top," "Kansas City," "I Cain't Say No," "People Will Say We're in Love."

Pajama Game, The, by Richard Adler. Lyrics by Richard Adler. Based on Richard Bissell's book *7 ½ Cents*. Premiered March 13, 1954, at St. James Theatre in New York City. Songs include: "Steam Heat," "Hernando's Hideaway."

Peter Pan, by Mark Charlap and Jule Styne. Lyrics by Carolyn Leigh, Betty Comden, and Adolph Green. Based on play by James Barrie. Premiered October 20, 1954, at Winter Garden Theatre in New York City. Songs include: "I'm Flying," "I've Got to Grow," "Neverland."

Phantom of the Opera, The, by Andrew Lloyd Webber. Lyrics by Charles Hart. Premiered October 9, 1986, at Her Majesty's Theatre in London. Songs include: "The Phantom of the Opera," "The Music of the Night," "All I Ask of You," "Wishing You Were Somehow Here Again," "The Point of No Return."

Rose Marie, by Rudolf Friml and Herbert Stothart. Lyrics by Otto Harbach and Oscar Hammerstein II. Premiered September 2, 1924, at Imperial Theatre in New York City. Songs include: "Indian Love Call," "The Song of the Mounties."

Show Boat, by Jerome Kern. Lyrics by Oscar Hammerstein II. Adapted from Edna Ferber's novel. Premiered December 27, 1924, at Ziegfeld Theatre in New York City. Songs include: "Make Believe," "Ol' Man River," "Can't Help Lovin' Dat Man," "Bill."

Shuffle Along, by Eubie Blake. Lyrics by Noble Sissle. Premiered May 23, 1921, at 63rd Street Music Hall in New York City. Songs include: "I'm Just Wild About Harry," "Swanee Moon."

Sound of Music, The, by Richard Rodgers. Lyrics by Oscar Hammerstein II. Adapted from Maria Augusta Trapp's book *The Trapp Family Singers*.

Premiered November 16, 1959, at Lunt-Fontaine Theatre in New York City. Songs include: "My Favorite Things," "Do Re Mi," "Climb Every Mountain," "Edelweiss," "You Are Sixteen."

South Pacific, by Richard Rodgers. Lyrics by Oscar Hammerstein II. Adapted from James Michener's book *Tales of the South Pacific*. Premiered April 7, 1949, at Majestic Theatre in New York City. Songs include: "Some Enchanted Evening," "There Is Nothing like a Dame," "Bali Hai," "I'm Gonna Wash That Man Right Outa My Hair."

Sweet Charity, by Cy Coleman. Lyrics by Dorothy Fields. Premiered January 29, 1966, at Palace Theatre in New York City. Songs include: "Big Spenda," "If My Friends Could See Me Now," "Sweet Charity," "I'm a Brass Band."

This Is the Army, by Irving Berlin. Premiered July 4, 1942, at Broadway Theatre in New York City. Songs include: "Oh, How I Hate to Get Up in the Morning," "This Is the Army, Mr. Jones."

Threepenny Opera, The, by Kurt Weill. Lyrics by Marc Blitzstein. Premiered March 10, 1954, at Theatre de Lys in New York City. Songs include: "The Ballad of Mack the Knife," "Love Song," "Pirate Jenny," "Useless Song."

Vagabond King, The, by Rudolf Friml. Lyrics by Brian Hooker. Adapted from Justin Huntly McCarthy's *If I Were a King*. Premiered September 21, 1925, at Casino Theatre in New York City. Songs include: "Love for Sale," "Song of the Vagabonds," "Some Day."

West Side Story, by Leonard Bernstein. Lyrics by Stephen Sondheim. Premiered September 26, 1957, at Winter Garden Theatre in New York City. Songs include: "Something's Coming," "Maria," "Tonight," "America," "I Feel Pretty," "Somewhere."

Wiz, The, by Charles Smalls. Lyrics by Charles Smalls. Premiered January 5, 1979, at Majestic Theatre in New York City. Songs include: "Ease on Down the Road," "If You Believe," "He's the Wizard."

Zorba, by John Kander. Lyrics by Fred Ebb. Premiered November 17, 1968, at Imperial Theatre in New York City. Songs include: "Life Is," "The First Time," "Y'assou," "I Am Free," "Only Love."

SOURCES

Burton, Jack. *The Blue Book of Broadway Musicals*. New York: Century House, 1969.

Granze, Kurt. *The Broadway Musical Theatre*. Vol. II. New York: Oxford University Press, 1986.

Green, Stanley. *Broadway Musicals Show by Show*. Milwaukee: Hal Leonard Books, 1985.

Krasker, Tommy, and Robert Kimball. *Catalog of the American Musical*. New York: National Institute for Opera and Musical Theatre, 1988.

Lewine, Richard, and Alfred Simon. *Songs of the Theater*. New York: H. W. Wilson Co., 1984.

Randel, Don Michael, comp. *Harvard Concise Dictionary of Music.* Cambridge, Mass.: Belknap Press, 1978.

Walsh, Michael. *Andrew Lloyd Webber: His Life and Works.* New York: Harry N. Abrams, 1989.

—Jesma Reynolds; L.D.R.

30

POPULAR SONGS AND BALLADS

. . . . .

THERE IS A CERTAIN KIND OF NOVEL WHICH, SET IN THE RECENT PAST, GETS loaded up with song titles to provide period authenticity, in a highly self-conscious and artificial fashion. In such matters, chronological accuracy is important. Beyond doubt one doesn't need or want to have Christy Mathewson whistling "Take Me Out to the Ball Game" (1908) while on the way to pitch in the 1905 World Series, or Sigmund Freud humming "I Want a Girl Just like the Girl That Married Dear Old Dad" (1911) at the First International Psychoanalytic Conference in Salzburg in 1908.

The associations that one makes with all musical compositions are personal and subjective; doubtless there are retired morticians who become nostalgic when they hear the Chopin Funeral March. But popular music, whose audience is largest when in the late teens and the twenties, is especially liable to the workings of nostalgia, because the period when one listens to it with the greatest intensity is that in which one is first entering upon adult life and exploring its possibilities. In later years, hearing a song again brings back the emotions and attitudes associated with having encountered it when young.

The popular-music industry in America became commercialized in the decades before the Civil War. Minstrel shows and musical comedy developed. The sentimental ballad came into its own. The prospering middle class acquired pianos or organs, and the sale of sheet music flourished. Stephen Foster was its most successful practitioner, but he was victimized by musical publishers and unskilled at the accumulation and use of money, so that he was frequently in want. When the Civil War came along he tried repeatedly to produce a popular war song, but by then he had lost the knack.

Since then, popular music has undergone various stages, beginning with the sentimental ballad and the musical comedy tune, which developed into the songs of Tin Pan Alley. Jazz, beginning as the creation of African-American musicians and quickly commercialized, brought ragtime, classic

New Orleans two-beat, and swing. Folk music developed into the commercialized country-and-western of the Grand Old Opry. Rock and roll produced reggae and other varieties tied in with the drug culture. And so on, sometimes *ad nauseam*.

The listing that follows is of some of the more popular compositions from the year 1850 to the present. It should be pointed out that authorities disagree as to the dates and details of some of them; the recording and crediting of song titles has never been an exact science.

1850
"Camptown Races" (Stephen C. Foster)
"Cheer, Boys, Cheer" (Henry Russell and Charles Mackay)

1851
"Old Folks at Home" (Stephen C. Foster)

1852
"Massa's in de Cold Cold Ground" (Stephen C. Foster)

1853
"Goodnight, Ladies"
"Old Dog Tray" (Stephen C. Foster)
"Old Kentucky Home" (Stephen C. Foster)

1854
"Hard Times, Come Again No More" (Stephen C. Foster)
"Jeanie with the Light Brown Hair" (Stephen C. Foster)

1855
"Come Where My Love Lies Dreaming" (Stephen C. Foster)
"Listen to the Mockingbird" (Richard Milburn and Alice Hawthorne, pseud. of Septimus Winner)
"The Lone Fish (Meat) Ball" (Richard Storrs Willis; also attributed to George Martin Lane)

1856
"Darling Nelly Gray" (Benjamin Russell Hanby)

1857
"Jingle Bells" (James Pierpont)
"Lorena" (Joseph Philbrick Webster and H. D. L. Webster)

1858

"Get Out of the Wilderness" ("The Old Gray Mare," 1917) (J. Warner)

"Yellow Rose of Texas" ("J.K.")

1859

"Dixie" (Daniel Decatur Emmet)

"La Paloma" (Sebastian Yradier)

1860

"Far Above Cayuga's Waters"—"Annie Lisle" (H. S. Thompson; the familiar words of the Cornell University alma mater were written in 1872 by Archibald Weeks and Wilmot Smith)

"Old Black Joe" (Stephen C. Foster)

"The Glendy Burke" (Stephen C. Foster)

"When I Saw Sweet Nellie Home" ("Aunt Dinah's Quilting Party"; "I was seeing Nellie home") (Frances Kyle and L. J. Fletcher)

1861

"Aura Lee" (George R. Poulton and William Whiteman Fosdick)

"The Vacant Chair" (George Frederick Root and H. S. Washburn)

1862

"Taps" (Gen. Daniel Butterfield)

"The Bonnie Blue Flag" (lyrics by Harry B. McCarthy, to tune of "The Irish Jaunting Car")

"We Are Coming, Father Abraham" (Patrick Sarsfield Gilmore and James Sloan Gibbons)

1863

"Just Before the Battle, Mother" (G. F. Root)

"The Battle Cry of Freedom" (G. F. Root)

"The Rock Island Line"

"When Johnny Comes Marching Home" (P. S. Gilmore; adapted from "Johnny Fill Up the Bowl")

1864

"All Quiet Along the Potomac Tonight" (John Hill Hewitt; attributed to Lamar Fontaine)

"Beautiful Dreamer" (Stephen C. Foster)

"Come Home, Father" ("Father, dear father, come home from the bar") (H. C. Work)

"Der Deitcher's Dog" ("Where, O where has my little dog gone") (Septimus Winner, adapted via Beethoven's Symphony No. 6 from German folk song)

"Tenting on the Old Camp Ground" (Walter Kittredge)

"Tramp! Tramp! Tramp!" (G. F. Root)

1865

"Johnny Is My Darling"

"Marching Through Georgia" (H. C. Work)

1866

"Come Back to Erin" (Claribel, pseud. of Charlotte Allington Barnard)

"When You and I Were Young, Maggie" (J. A. Butterfield and George Washington Johnson)

1867

"Angel's Serenade" (Gaetano Braga and Harrison Millard)

"Champagne Charlie Was His Name" (Alfred Lee and H. J. Whymark)

1868

"The Daring Young Man (on the Flying Trapeze)" (Alfred Lee and George Leybourne)

"Sweet By and By" (Joseph Webster and S. Fillmore)

"Whispering Hope" (Alice Hawthorne, pseud. of Septimus Winner)

1869

"Little Brown Jug" (R. A. Eastburn, pseud. of Joseph Eastman Winner)

"Shoo Fly, Don't Bother Me" (Frank Campbell and Billy Reeves)

"Sweet Genevieve" (Henry Tucker and George Cooper)

ca. 1870

"Paddle Your Own Canoe" (H. Clifton and M. Hobson)

1871

"Goodbye, Liza Jane"

"Reuben and Rachel" ("Reuben, Reuben, I've been thinking") (William Gooch and W. Harry Birch)

1873

"The Mulligan Guard" (David Bragan and Edward Harrigan)

"Silver Threads Among the Gold" (Hart Pease Danks and Eben E. Rexford)

1876

"Grandfather's Clock" (H. C. Work)

"I'll Take You Home Again, Kathleen" (Thomas P. Westendorf)

"The Hat Me Father Wore" ([?] Ferguson and Daniel McCarthy)

1877

"Abdulla Bulbul Ameer" (Percy French)

"Chopsticks"—"The Celebrated Chop Waltz" (Arthur de Lulli, pseud. of Euphemia Allen)

"In the Gloaming" (Annie Fortesque Harrison and Meta Orred)

"The Lost Chord" (Arthur Sullivan and Adelaide Procter)

"Where Is My Wand'ring Boy Tonight" (Robert Lowry)

1878

"Baby Mine" (Archibald Johnston and Charles Mackay)

"Carry Me Back to Old Virginny" (James A. Bland)

"In the Evening by the Moonlight" (James A. Bland)

"Where Was Moses When the Lights Went Out" (Max Vernor)

1879

"Alouette"

"The Babies on the Block" (David Bragan and Edward Harrigan)

"Golden Slippers" ("Oh dem golden slippers") (Bland)

1880

"Cradle's Empty, Baby's Gone" (Harry Kennedy)

"Funiculi, Funicula" (Luigi Denza and G. Turco)

"Sailing" ("Sailing, sailing over the bounding Main") (Godfrey Marks, pseud. of James Frederick Swift)

1881

"My Bonnie Lies Over the Ocean"

"Peek-a-Boo" (William J. Scanlan)

"The Spanish Cavalier" (William D. Hendrickson)

1882

"Sweet Violets" (Joseph Emmet)

1883

"A Handful of Earth from (My Dear) Mother's Grave" (Joseph Murphy)

"My Nellie's Blue Eyes" (William J. Scanlan)

"There Is a Tavern in the Town" (published in 1883; much older)

1884

"A Boy's Best Friend Is His Mother" (Joseph P. Skelly)

"Always Take Mother's Advice" (Jennie Lindsay)

"Love's Old Sweet Song" ("Just a song at twilight") (James Lyman Molloy and G. Clifton Bingham)

"My Darling Clementine" (Percy Montross)

"Otchi Tchorniya"

"The Fountain in the Park" ("While strolling through the park one day") (Ed Haley and Robert A. Keiser)

1885

"Remember Boy, You're Irish" (William J. Scanlan)

"The Big Rock Candy Mountain"

1886

"The Letter That Never Came" (Paul Dresser, pseud. of Paul Dreiser)

1887

"Comrades" (Felix McGlennon)

"If You Love Me, Darling, Tell Me With Your Eyes" (Hubbard T. Smith and Samuel Minturn Peck)

1888

"Over the Waves" (Juventino Rosas)

"Where Did You Get That Hat?" (Joseph J. Sullivan)

"With All Her Faults I Love Her Still" (Monroe H. Rosenfeld)

1889

"Down Went McGinty" (Joseph Flynn)

"Playmates" (Harry Dacre)

"Slide Kelly Slide" (John W. Kelly)

1890

"Gambler's Blues" (see "St. James Infirmary," 1930)

"Little Annie Roonie" (Michael Nolan)

"O, Promise Me" (Reginald DeKoven and Clement Scott)

"Throw Him Down, McCloskey" (John W. Kelly)

1891

"Ta-ra-ra Boom-der-ré" (Henry J. Sayers)

"The Pardon Came Too Late" (Paul Dresser)

"The Picture That's Turned To(ward) the Wall" (Charles Graham)

"The Sweetest Story Ever Told" (R. M. Stults)

1892

"After the Ball" (Charles K. Harris)

"Daddy Wouldn't Buy Me a Bow-Wow" (Joseph Tabrar)

"Daisy Bell" ("A Bicycle Built for Two") (Harry Dacre)

"My Sweetheart's the Man in the Moon" (James Thornton)

"The Bowery" (Percy Gaunt and Charles H. Hoyt)

1893

"Do, Do, My Huckleberry Do" (John and Harry Dillon)

"Good Morning to All" ("Happy birthday to you") (Mildred Hill and Patty Smith Hill)

"See, Saw, Margery Daw" (Arthur West)

"Two Little Girls in Blue" (Charles Graham)

1894

"And Her Golden Hair Was Hanging Down Her Back" (Felix McGlennon and Monroe H. Rosenfeld)

"Forgotten" (Eugene Cowles and Flora Wulschner)

"Levee Song" ("I've been working on the railroad") (publ. in *Carmina Princetoniana*)

"She Is More to Be Pitied Than Censured" (William B. Gray)

"She May Have Seen Better Days" (James Thornton)

"The Sidewalks of New York" (Charles B. Lawlor and James W. Blake)

1895

"The Bully Song" (Charles E. Travathan, from popular tune)

"Down in Poverty Row" (Arthur Trevelyan and Gussie L. Davis)

"Just Tell Them That You Saw Me" (Paul Dresser)

"The Band Played On" (John E. Palmer and Charles B. Ward)

1896

"A Hot Time in the Old Town Tonight" (Theodore M. Metz and Joe Hayden)

"All Coons Look Alike to Me" (Ernest Hogan)

"Going for a Pardon" (James Thornton and Clara Havenschild)

"In the Baggage Coach Ahead" (Gussie L. Davis)

"My Gal's a High-Born Lady" (Barney Fagan)

"Sweet Rosie O'Grady" (Maude Nugent)

"You're Not the Only Pebble on the Beach" (Stanley Carter and Harry Braisted)

1897

"Asleep in the Deep" (Henry W. Petrie and Arthur J. Lamb)

"Beautiful Isle of Somewhere" (John S. Fearis and Jessie Brown Pounds)

"Break the News to Mother" (Charles K. Harris)

"Storyville Blues" (Tom Turpin)

1898

"Because" (Frederick V. Bowers and Charles Horwitz)

"Gypsy Love Song" (Victor Herbert and Harry B. Smith)

"She Was Bred in Old Kentucky" (Stanley Carter and Harry Braisted)

"The Rosary" (Ethelbert Nevin and Robert Cameron Rogers)

"When You Were Sweet Sixteen" (James Thornton)

1899

"Hello, Ma Baby" (Joseph E. Howard and Ida Emerson)

"Mandy Lee" (Thurland Chattaway)

"Maple Leaf Rag" (Scott Joplin)

"My Wild Irish Rose" (Chauncey Olcott)

"On the Banks of the Wabash Far Away" (Paul Dresser)

"She Was Happy Till She Met You" (Monroe H. Rosenfeld and Charles Graham)

1900

"A Bird in a Gilded Cage" (Harry von Tilzer and Arthur J. Lamb)

"Goodbye Dolly Gray" (Will D. Cobb and Paul Barnes)

"Just Because She Made Dem Goo-Goo Eyes" (John Queen and Hughie Cannon)

"Tell Me Pretty Maiden" (Leslie Stuart, pseud. of Thomas A. Barrett, and Owen
    Hall)

1901

"Boola Boola" (Anon.; based on a song by Bob Cole and Billy Johnson, "La Hoola
    Boola," 1897)

"Down Where the Cotton Blossoms Grow" (Harry von Tilzer and Andrew B.
    Sterling)

"Hello, Central, Give Me Heaven" (Charles K. Harris)

"I Love You Truly" (Carrie Jacobs-Bond)

"Just A-Wearyin' for You" (Carrie Jacobs-Bond and Frank L. Stanton)

"Mighty Lak a Rose" (Ethelbert Nevin and Frank L. Stanton)

"That's Where My Money Goes" (Walter Daniels and R. P. Lilly)

1902

"Bill Bailey, Won't You Please Come Home" (Hughie Cannon)

"In the Good Old Summertime" (George Evans and Ren Shields)

"Oh, Didn't He Ramble" (Bob Cole and J. Rosamond Johnson)
"Please Go 'Way and Let Me Sleep" (J. Tim Bryman)
"Under the Bamboo Tree" (Bob Cole and J. Rosamond Johnson)

1903

"Bedelia" (Jean Schwartz and William Jerome)
"Dear Old Girl" (Theodore F. Morse and Richard Henry Buck)
"Home on the Range" ("Arizona Annie") (tune revised by William Goodwin from
    melody by Daniel E. Kelly to lyrics published in 1873 by Bruce "Brewster"
    Higley entitled, "Oh, Give Me a Home Where the Buffalo Roam")
"Ida, Sweet as Apple Cider" (Eddie Leonard)
"Sweet Adeline" (Richard H. Gerard and Henry W. Armstrong)
"Toyland" (Victor Herbert and Glen MacDonough)
"Under the Anheuser Bush" (Harry von Tilzer and Andrew B. Sterling)
"Waltzing Matilda" (Marie Cowan, adapted from "Craigielea," by Robert
    Tsannahill, words by A. B. "Banjo" Patterson; has also been credited to
    "Thou Bonnie Wood of Craigie Lee," by James Barr and Andrew Barton
    Peterson, from Australian bush ballad)

1904

"Frankie and Johnny" (Hughie Cannon; based on folk song, "Frankie and Albert")
"Give My Regards to Broadway" (George M. Cohan)
"Goodbye, My Lady Love" (Joseph E. Howard)
"I Guess I'll Have to Telegraph My Baby" (George M. Cohan)
"Meet Me in St. Louis, Louis" (Kerry Mills and Andrew B. Sterling)
"Yankee Doodle Boy" (George M. Cohan)

1905

"Everybody Works But Father" (Jean Havez)
"I Want What I Want When I Want It" (Victor Herbert and Henry Blossom)
"In My Merry Oldsmobile" (Gus Edwards and Vincent Bryan)
"In the Shade of the Old Apple Tree" (Egbert van Alstyne and Harry Williams)
"Kiss Me Again" (Victor Herbert and Henry Blossom)
"My Gal Sal" (Paul Dresser)
"Rufus Rastus Johnson Brown" (Harry von Tilzer and Andrew B. Sterling)
"Wait 'Til the Sun Shines, Nellie" (Harry von Tilzer and Andrew B. Sterling)
"Will You Love Me in December As You Do in May" (Ernest R. Ball and James
    J. Walker)

1906

"Anchors Aweigh" (Charles A. Zimmerman, Alfred H. Miles, and R. Lovell)
"At Dawning" (Charles Wakefield Cadman and Nelle Richmond Eberhart)

"Because You're You" (Victor Herbert and Henry Blossom)
"Chinatown, My Chinatown" (Jean Schwartz and William Jerome)
"Every Day Is Ladies Day With Me" (Victor Herbert and Henry Blossom)
"Love Me and the World Is Mine" (Ernest R. Ball and Dave Reed, Jr.)
"Mary's a Grand Old Name" (George M. Cohan)
"School-Days" (Will D. Cobb and Gus Edwards)
"Sunbonnet Sue" (Gus Edwards and Will D. Cobb)
"Waltz Me Around Again, Willie" (Ren Shields and Will D. Cobb)
"You're a Grand Old Flag" (George M. Cohan)

1907
"Dark Eyes" ("Serenade Espagnole") (Neil Moret)
"Glow Worm" (Paul Lincke and Lilla Cayley Robinson)
"Harrigan" (George M. Cohan)
"On the Road to Mandalay" (Oley Speaks and Rudyard Kipling)

1908
"Cuddle Up a Little Closer" (Karl Hoschma and Otto Abels Harbach)
"Down in Jungle Town" (Theodore F. Morse and Edward Madden)
"Shine On, Harvest Moon" (Nora Bayes and Jack Norworth)
"Take Me Out to the Ball Game" (Harry von Tilzer and Jack Norworth)
"You Tell Me Your Dream" ("I had a dream, dear") (Charles N. Daniels, Jay
    Blackton, Albert H. Brown, and Seymoure Rice)

1909
"By the Light of the Silvery Moon" (Gus Edwards and Edward Madden)
"Casey Jones" (Eddie Newton and T. Lawrence Seibert)
"From the Land of the Sky Blue Water" (Charles Wakefield Cadman and Nelle
    Richmond Eberhart)
"Has Anybody Here Seen Kelly" (C. W. Murphy, Will Letters, John Charles
    Moore, and William C. McKenna)
"Heaven Will Protect the Working Girl" (A. Baldwin Sloane and Edgar
    Smith)
"I Wonder Who's Kissing Her Now" (Joseph E. Howard, Harold Orlob, William
    M. Hough, and Frank R. Adams)
"Meet Me Tonight in Dreamland" (Leo Friedman and Beth Slater Whitson)
"Mistress Mumbo Jumbo Jijjiboo J. O'Shea" ("I've got rings on my fingers, bells
    on my toes") (Maurice Scott, F. J. Barnes, and R. P. Weston)
"On, Wisconsin" (W. T. Purdy and Carl Beck)
"Put On Your Old Grey Bonnet" (Percy Wenrich and Stanley Murphy)
"That's a Plenty" (Bert A. Williams and Henry Creamer)

1910

"A Perfect Day" (Carrie Jacobs Bond)

"Ah, Sweet Mystery of Life" (Victor Herbert and Rida Johnson Young)

"Any Little Girl, That's a Nice Little Girl, Is the Right Little Girl for Me" (Fred Fisher and Thomas J. Gray)

"Come, Josephine, in My Flying Machine" (Fred Fisher and Alfred Bryan)

"Down by the Old Mill Stream" (Earl K. Smith and Tell Taylor)

"Let Me Call You Sweetheart" (Leo Friedman and Beth Slater Whitson)

"Mother Machree" (Chauncey Olcott, Ernest R. Ball, and Rida Johnson Young)

"Some of These Days" (Shelton Brooks)

"Stein Song"—" 'Opie': The University of Maine Stein Song" (E. A. Fenstad and Lincoln Colcord)

"Washington and Lee Swing" (Thornton W. Allen, M. W. Sheafe, and C. A. Robbins)

"What's the Matter With Father" (Egbert van Alstyne and Harry H. Williams)

1911

"Alexander's Ragtime Band" (Irving Berlin)

"Everybody's Doin' It" (Irving Berlin)

"Goodnight Ladies" (Egbert van Alstyne and Henry Williams)

"I Want a Girl Just Like the Girl That Married Dear Old Dad" (Harry von Tilzer and Will Dillon)

"Little Grey Home in the West" (Herman Löhr and Wilmot D. Eardley)

"Oh You Beautiful Doll" (Nathaniel Davis Ayer and Seymour Brown)

"Roamin' in the Gloamin" (Harry Lauder)

"Whiffenpoof Song" (Tod B. Galloway, Meade Minnigerode, and George S. Pomeroy)

1912

"Down South" (W. H. Myddleton; Sigmund Spaeth lyrics added in 1927)

"It's a Long Way to Tipperary" (Harry Williams and Jack Judge)

"Memphis Blues" (W. C. Handy and George A. Norton)

"Moonlight Bay" (Percy Wenrich and Edward Madden)

"My Melancholy Baby" (Ernie Burnett and George A. Norton)

"The Missouri Houn' Dawg Song" ("They gotta quit kickin' my dog around") (Cy Perkins and Webb M. Oungst)

"The Sweetheart of Sigma Chi" (F. Dudleigh Vernor and Bryan D. Stokes)

"Waiting for the Robert E. Lee" (Lewis F. Muir and L. Wolfe Gilbert)

"When Irish Eyes Are Smiling" (Ernest R. Ball, Chauncey Olcott, and George B. Grapf, Jr.)

"When It's Apple Blossom Time in Normandy" (Harry Gifford, Huntley Trevor, and Tom Mellor)

1913

"Ballin' the Jack" (Chris Smith and James Henry Burns)

"Brighten the Corner Where You Are" (Charles H. Gabriel and Ina Duley Ogdon)

"If I Had My Way" (James Kendis and Lou Klein)

"Now Is the Hour" ("Maori Farewell Song") (Maewa Kaihan, Clement Scott, and Dorothy Stewart)

"Panama" (Raymond Hubbell)

"Peg o' My Heart" (Fred Fisher and Alfred Bryan)

"The Trail of the Lonesome Pine" (Henry Carroll and Ballard MacDonald)

"You Made Me Love You" (James V. Monaco and Joe McCarthy)

1914

"Are You From Dixie ('Cause I'm from Dixie Too)" (Jack Yellen and George L. Cobb)

"By the Beautiful Sea" (Harry Carroll and Harold R. Atteridge)

"By the Waters of Minnetonka" (Thurlow Lieurance and J. M. Cavanass)

"Can't Yo' Heah Me Callin', Caroline" (William H. Gardner and Caro Roma)

"Play a Simple Melody" (Irving Berlin)

"St. Louis Blues" (W. C. Handy)

"The Aba Daba Honeymoon" (Arthur Fields and Walt Donovan)

"There's a Long Long Trail A-Winding" (Alonzo "Zo" Elliott and W. Stoddard King)

"They Didn't Believe Me" (Jerome Kern and Herbert Reynolds)

"Too-Ra-Loo-Ra-Loo-Ral, That's an Irish Lullaby" (James Royce Shannon)

"When You Wore a Tulip" (Percy Wenrich and Jack Mahoney)

"Yellow Dog Blues" (W. C. Handy; originally "Yellow Dog Rag")

1915

"Hesitating Blues" (W. C. Handy)

"I Didn't Raise My Boy to Be a Soldier" (Al Piantadosi and Alfred Bryan, taken from Harry Haas)

"In a Monastery Garden" (Albert William Ketèlbey)

"Keep the Home Fires Burning" (Ivor Novello and Lena Guilbert Ford)

"Missouri Waltz" (Frederick K. Logan and James R. Shannon, based on tune by John Valentine Eppel)

"M-O-T-H-E-R, a Word That Means the World to Me" (Theodore Morse, pseud. of Dorothy Terriss, and Howard Johnson)

"Neapolitan Love Song" (Victor Herbert and Henry Blossom)

"Pack Up Your Troubles in Your Old Kit Bag" (Felix Powell and George Asaf)

"Paper Doll" (Johnny Black)

1916

"Beale Street Blues" (W. C. Handy)

"Down in Honky Tonk Town" (Chris Smith and Charles McCarron)

"I Ain't Got Nobody" (Spencer Williams, Roger Graham, and Dave Peyton)

"If You Were the Only Girl in the World" (Nat D. Ayer and Clifford Grey)

"Ireland Must Be Heaven for My Mother Came From There" (Fred Fisher, Joe McCarthy, and Howard E. Johnson)

"La Cucaracha"

"La Cumparsita" (G. H. Matos Rodriguez; lyrics added in 1932 by W. Carol Raven)

"Li'l Liza Jane" (Countess Ada de Lachau)

"Nola" (Felix Arndt)

"Pretty Baby" (Tony Jackson, Egbert van Alstyne, and Gus Kahn)

"Roses of Picardy" (Haydn Wood and Fred E. Weatherly)

1917

"For Me and My Gal" ("The bells are ringing") (George W. Meyer, Edgar Leslie, and E. Ray Goetz)

"Hail, Hail, the Gang's All Here" (D. A. Esrom and Theodora Morse, adapted from Gilbert and Sullivan's *Pirates of Penzance*)

"Indiana" ("Back home again in Indiana") (James F. Hanley and Ballard MacDonald)

"MacNamara's Band" (Shamus O'Connor, John J. Stamford, and Harry DeCosta)

"Over There" (George M. Cohan)

"Smiles" (Lee G. Roberts and J. Will Callahan)

"The Bells of St. Mary's" (A. Emmett Adams and Douglas Furber)

"The Darktown Strutters Ball" (Shelton Brooks)

"The Johnson Rag" (Guy Hall and Henry Kleinauf)

"Tiger Rag" (Original Dixieland Band and Harry DeCosta)

"You're in the Army Now" (Isham Jones, Tell Taylor, and Ole Olsen)

1918

"After You've Gone" (Henry Creamer and Turner Layton)

"Good Morning, Mr. Zip-Zip-Zip" (Robert Lloyd)

"Hindustan" (Oliver G. Wallace and Harold Weeks)

"I'm Always Chasing Rainbows" (Harry Carroll and Joseph McCarthy, adapted from Chopin)

"Ja-Da" (Bob Carleton)

"Just a Baby's Prayer at Twilight" (M. K. Jerome, Sam M. Lewis, and Joe Young)

"K-K-K-Katy" (Geoffrey O'Hara)

"Mandy" (Irving Berlin)

"Marines' Hymn" ("From the halls of Montezuma") (from Jacques Offenbach's "Geneviève de Brabant," 1868)

"Oh, How I Hate to Get Up in the Morning" (Irving Berlin)

"Original Dixieland One-Step" (J. Russell Robinson, Joe Jordan, and James D. LaRocca)

"Somebody Stole My Gal" (Leo Wood)

"The Caissons Go Rolling Along" (Edmund L. Gruber)

"Till We Meet Again" (Richard A. Whiting and Raymond B. Egan)

1919

"A Pretty Girl Is Like a Melody" (Irving Berlin)

"Blues My Naughty Sweetie Gives to Me" (Charles McCarron, Carey Morgan, and Arthur Swanstrom)

"Cielito Lindo" (Quirino Mendoza y Cortez)

"Dardanella" (Felix Bernard, Johnny Black, and Fred Fisher)

"How Ya Gonna Keep 'Em Down on the Farm" (Walter Donaldson, Sam L. Lewis, and Joe Young)

"I'm Forever Blowing Bubbles" (John William Kellette, Jean Kenbrovin)

"Indian Summer" (Victor Herbert; lyrics by Al Dubin in 1940)

"In My Sweet Little Alice Blue Gown" (Harry Tierney and Joseph McCarthy)

"Missouri Waltz" (Frederick Knight Logan and J. R. Shannon, pseud. of James Royce)

"Royal Garden Blues" (Spencer and Clarence Williams)

"Sippin' Cider Through a Straw" (Carey Morgan and Lee David)

"Swanee" (George Gershwin and Irving Caesar)

"The World Is Waiting for the Sunrise" (Ernest Seitz and Eugene Lockhart)

1920

"Aunt Hagar's Blues" (W. C. Handy)

"Avalon" (Al Jolson, Vincent Rose, and B. G. DeSylva, taken from Puccini)

"Hold Me" (Art Hickman and Ben Black)

"I'll Be with You in Apple Blossom Time" (Harry von Tilzer and Neville Fleeson)

"Look for the Silver Lining" (Jerome Kern and B. G. DeSylva)

"Mah Lindy Lou" (Lily Strickland)

"My Mammy" (Walter Donaldson, Joe Young, and Sam M. Lewis)

"Margie" (Con Conrad, J. Russel Robinson, and Benny Davis)

"The Japanese Sandman" (Richard Whiting and Raymond Egan)

"When My Baby Smiles at Me" (Bill Munro, Harry von Tilzer, Andrew Sterling, and Ted Lewis, pseud. of Theodore Leopold Friedman)

1921

"Ain't We Got Fun" (Richard A. Whiting, Gus Kahn, and Raymond Egan)

"April Showers" (Louis Silvers and Jack Yellen)

"I'll See You in My Dreams" (Isham Jones and Gus Kahn)

"I'm Just Wild About Harry" (Eubie Blake and Noble Sissle)
"Kitten on the Keys" (Edward "Zez" Confrey)
"Peggy O'Neil" (Harry Pease, Edward G. Nelson, and Gilbert Dodge)
"Say It with Music" (Irving Berlin)
"The Sheik of Araby" (Ted Snyder, Harry B. Smith, and Francis Wheeler)
"There'll Be Some Changes Made" (Benton Overstreet and Billy Higgins)

1922
"A Kiss in the Dark" (Victor Herbert and B. G. DeSylva)
"Carolina in the Morning" (Walter Donaldson and Gus Kahn)
"China Boy" (Dick Winfree and Philip Boutelje)
"Georgia" (Walter Donaldson and Howard Johnson)
"Limehouse Blues" (Philip Braham and Douglas Furber)
"Runnin' Wild" (A. Harrington Gibbs, Joe Grey, and Leo Wood)
"Three O'Clock in the Morning" (Julian Robeldo and Theodora Morse, pseud. of
    Dorothy Terriss)
"Toot Toot Tootsie, Goodbye" (Ernie Erdman, Dan Russo, and Gus Kahn)
"Water Boy" (Avery Robinson and Howard Johnson)
" 'Way Down Yonder in New Orleans" (J. Turner Layton and Henry Creamer)

1923
"Barney Google" (Con Conrad and Billy Rose)
"I Cried for You" (Gus Arnheim, Abe Lyman, and Arthur Freed)
"I Love Life" (Mana Zucca and Irwin M. Cassel)
"It Ain't Gonna Rain No Mo" (Wendell Woods Hall, adapted from folk song)
"Mexicali Rose" (Jack B. Tenny and Helen Stone)
"Nobody Knows You When You're Down and Out" (Jimmy Cox)
"Sugar Blues" (Clarence Williams and Lucy Fletcher)
"That Old Gang of Mine" (Ray Henderson, Mort Dixon, and Billy Rose)
"Tin Roof Blues" (Roppolo, Mares, Brunies, Pollack, Stitzel, and Melrose)
"Weary Blues" (Artie Matthews, Mort Greene, and George Cates)
"Who's Sorry Now?" (Ted Snyder, Bert Kalmar, and Harry Ruby)
"Yes, We Have No Bananas" (Frank Silver and Irving Cohn)
"You've Gotta See Mamma Every Night or You Can't See Mamma at All" (Con
    Conrad and Billy Rose)

1924
"Amapola" (James M. LaCalle)
"California, Here I Come" (Joseph Meyer, Al Jolson, and B. G. DeSylva)
"Fascinating Rhythm" (George and Ira Gershwin)
"Hard-Hearted Hannah" (Milton Ager, Bob Bigelow, Charles Bates, and Jack
    Yellen)

"I Wonder What's Become of Sally" (Milton Ager and Jack Yellen)

"Indian Love Call" (Rudolf Friml, Otto Harbach, and Oscar Hammerstein II)

"It Had to Be You" (Isham Jones and Gus Kahn)

"King Porter Stomp" (Jelly Roll Morton, pseud. of Ferdinand LeMenthe)

"Nobody's Sweetheart Now" (Elmer Schoebel, Billy Meyers, Ernie Erdman, and Gus Kahn)

"Oh, Lady Be Good" (George and Ira Gershwin)

"Rose Marie" (Rudolf Friml, Otto Harbach, and Oscar Hammerstein II)

"Somebody Loves Me" (George Gershwin, B. G. DeSylva, and Ballard MacDonald)

"Tea for Two" (Vincent Youmans, Irving Caesar, and Clifford Grey)

"The Man I Love" (George and Ira Gershwin)

"When My Sugar Walks Down the Street" (Gene Austin, Jimmy McHugh, and Irving Mills)

1925

"Alabamy Bound" (Ray Henderson, B. G. DeSylva, and Bud Green)

"Always" (Irving Berlin)

"Dinah" (Harry Akst, Sam M. Lewis, and Joe Young)

"Don't Bring Lulu" (Ray Henderson, Billy Rose, and Lew Brown)

"Five Foot Two, Eyes of Blue" ("Has anybody seen my girl?") (Ray Henderson, Sam M. Lewis, and Joe Young)

"I Want to Be Happy" (Vincent Youmans, Irving Caesar, and Otto Harbach)

"I'm Sitting on Top of the World" (Ray Henderson, Sam M. Lewis, and Joe Young)

"If You Knew Susie Like I Know Susie" (Joseph Meyer and B. G. DeSylva)

"Jalousie" (Jacob Gade and Winifred May; English lyrics by Vera Bloom)

"Moonlight and Roses" (Ben Black and Neil Moret, adapted from Edward H. Lemare's "Andantino")

"Paddlin' Madelin' Home" (Harry Woods)

"Show Me the Way to Go Home" (Irving King, pseud. of Reg Connelly, and Jimmy Campbell)

"Sleepy Time Gal" (Ange Lorenzo, Richard A. Whiting, Joseph R. Alden, and Raymond Egan)

"Sweet Georgia Brown" (Kenneth Casey and Maceo Pinkard)

"Who Takes Care of the Caretaker's Daughter While the Caretaker's Busy Taking Care?" (Chick Endor)

"Why Do I Love You" (George and Ira Gershwin and B. G. DeSylva)

"Yes, Sir! That's My Baby" (Walter Donaldson and Gus Kahn)

1926

"Baby Face" (Harry Akst and Benny Davis)

"Big Butter and Egg Man" (Sidney Clare, Cliff Friend, and Joseph H. Santley)

"Black Bottom" (Ray Henderson, B. G. DeSylva, and Lew Brown)

"Bye Bye Blackbird" (Ray Henderson and Mort Dixon)

"If I Could Be with You One Hour Tonight" (Henry Creamer and Jimmy Johnson)

"Muskrat Ramble" (Kid Ory and Ray Gilbert)

"Rio Rita" (Harry Tierney and Joe McCarthy)

"Someone to Watch over Me" (George and Ira Gershwin)

"Tiptoe Through the Tulips" (Joe Burke and Al Dubin)

"What Can I Say, Dear (After I Say I'm Sorry)" (Walter Donaldson and Abe Lyman)

1927

"Ain't She Sweet" (Milton Ager and Jack Yellen)

"Blue Heaven" (George Whiting and Walter Donaldson)

"Blue Skies" (Irving Berlin)

"Can't Help Lovin' Dat Man" (Jerome Kern and Oscar Hammerstein II)

"Chloe" (Gus Kahn and Charles N. Daniels, pseud. of Neil Moret)

"Girl of My Dreams" (Sunny Clapp)

"I'm Looking Over a Four-Leaf Clover" (Harry Woods and Mort Dixon)

"Me and My Shadow" (Al Jolson, Dave Dreyer, and Billy Rose)

"Mississippi Mud" (Harry Barris)

"My Heart Stood Still" (Richard Rodgers and Lorenz Hart)

"Ol' Man River" (Jerome Kern and Oscar Hammerstein II)

"Struttin' With Some Barbecue" (Louis Armstrong and Lil Hardin)

"The Best Things in Life Are Free" (Ray Henderson, B. G. DeSylva, and Lew Brown)

"Why Do I Love You" (Jerome Kern and Oscar Hammerstein II)

1928

"Button Up Your Overcoat" (Ray Henderson, B. G. DeSylva, and Lew Brown)

"Constantinople" (Harry Carlton)

"Diga Diga Do" (Jimmy McHugh and Dorothy Fields)

"I'll Get By" (Fred E. Ahlert and Roy Turk)

"Lover Come Back to Me" (Sigmund Romberg and Oscar Hammerstein II)

"Shortnin' Bread" (Jacques Wolfe)

"There's a Rainbow Round my Shoulder" (Al Jolson, Dave Dreyer, and Billy Rose)

"When You're Smiling" (Mark Fisher, Joe Goodwin, and Larry Shay)

"I Can't Give You Anything but Love" (Jimmy McHugh and Dorothy Fields)

"Makin' Whoopee" (Walter Donaldson and Gus Kahn)

"Sweet Sue" (Victor Young and Will J. Harris)

"Sweet Lorraine" (Cliff Burwell and Mitchell Parish)

"Carolina Moon" (Joe Burke and Benny Davis)

1929

"Ain't Misbehavin' " (Fats Waller, Harry Brooks, and Andy Razaf)

"Am I Blue" (Harry Akst and Grant Clarke)

"Basin Street Blues" (Spencer Williams)

"Happy Days Are Here Again" (Jack Yellen and Milton Ager)

"Honeysuckle Rose" (Fats Waller and Andy Razaf)

"If I Had a Talking Picture of You" (Ray Henderson, B. G. DeSylva, and Lew Brown)

"Star Dust" (Hoagy Carmichael and Mitchell Parish)

"They Cut Down That Old Pine Tree" (William Raskin, Edward Eliscu, and George Brown)

"What Is this Thing Called Love" (Cole Porter)

1930

"Betty Co-ed" (J. Paul Fogarty and Rudy Vallee)

"Bidin' My Time" (George and Ira Gershwin)

"Body and Soul" (Johnny Green, Robert Sour, Edward Heyman, and Frank Eyton)

"Embraceable You" (George and Ira Gershwin)

"Georgia on My Mind" (Hoagy Carmichael and Stuart Gorrell)

"I Got Rhythm" (George and Ira Gershwin)

"I'm Confessing—That I Love You" (Doc Dougherty, Ellis Reynolds, and A. J. Neiburg)

"Little White Lies" (Walter Donaldson)

"On the Sunny Side of the Street" (Jimmy McHugh and Dorothy Fields)

"St. James Infirmary" (Joe Primrose; based on 1890 song, "Gambler's Blues")

"Three Little Words" (Bert Kalmar and Harry Ruby)

"Time on My Hands" (Vincent Youmans, Harold Adamson, and Mack Gordon)

"Walkin' My Baby Back Home" (Roy Turk, Fred E. Ahlert, and Harry Richman)

"When It's Sleepy Time Down South" (Leon and Otis Rene and Clarence Muse)

"Would You Like to Take a Walk" (Harry Warren, Billy Rose, and Mort Dixon)

1931

"All of Me" (Seymour Simons and Gerald Marks)

"Dancing in the Dark" (Arthur Schwartz and Howard Dietz)

"Good Night, Sweetheart" (Ray Noble, James Campbell, and Reginald Connelly)

"I Found a Million-Dollar Baby—in a Five-and-Ten-Cent Store" (Harry Warren, Billy Rose, and Mort Dixon)

"I Love a Parade" (Harold Arlen and Ted Koehler)

"I'll Be Glad When You're Dead (You Rascal You)" (Charles Davenport)

"Mood Indigo" (Duke Ellington, Albany Bigard, and Irving Mills)

"That Silver-Haired Daddy of Mine" (Gene Autry and Jimmy Long)

"That's My Desire" (Helmy Kresa and Carroll Loveday)

"When It's Sleepy Time Down South" (Leon and Otis Rene and Clarence Muse)

"Where the Blue of the Night Meets the Gold of the Day" (Fred E. Ahlert, Roy Turk, and Bing Crosby)

1932

"A Shanty in Old Shanty Town" (Little Jack Little, John Siras, and Joe Young)

"April in Paris" (Vernon Duke and E. Y. Harburg)

"How Deep Is the Ocean" (Irving Berlin)

"I'm Getting Sentimental over You" (George Bassman and Ned Washington)

"I've Got the World on a String" (Harold Arlen and Ted Koehler)

"Let's Have Another Cup of Coffee" (Irving Berlin)

"Let's Put Out the Lights and Go to Sleep" (Herman Hupfeld)

"Night and Day" (Cole Porter)

"Say It Isn't So" (Irving Berlin)

1933

"Annie Doesn't Live Here Any More" (Harold Spina, Joe Young, and Johnny Burke)

"Did You Ever See a Dream Walking" (Harry Revel and Mack Gordon)

"Easter Parade" (Irving Berlin)

"Everything I Have Is Yours" (Burton Lane and Harold Adamson)

"Have You Ever Been Lonely" (Bill Hill)

"I Like Mountain Music" (Frank Weldon and James Cavanaugh)

"It's a Sin to Tell a Lie" (Billy Mayhew)

"Shuffle Off to Buffalo" (Al Dubin and Harry Warren)

"Smoke Gets in Your Eyes" (Jerome Kern and Otto Harbach)

"Sophisticated Lady" (Duke Ellington, Irving Mills, and Mitchell Parish)

"Stormy Weather" (Harold Arlen and Ted Koehler)

"Temptation" (Nacio Herb Brown and Arthur Freed)

"The Last Roundup" (Bill Hill)

"The Old Spinning Wheel" (Bill Hill)

"Who's Afraid of the Big Bad Wolf" (Frank E. Churchill and Ann Rowell)

1934

"Alla en el Rancho Grande" (Sylvano R. Ramos and Bartley Costello)

"Blue Moon" (Richard Rodgers and Lorenz Hart)

"Carry Me Back to the Lone Prairie" (Carson Robison)

"Cocktails for Two" (Arthur Johnston and Sam Coslow)

"Deep Purple" (Peter DeRose and Mitchell Parish)

"I Get a Kick Out of You" (Cole Porter)

"Isle of Capri" (Will Grosz and Jimmy Kennedy)

"Mr. and Mrs. Is the Name" (Allie Wrubel and Mort Dixon)

"On the Good Ship Lollipop" (Richard A. Whiting and Sidney Clare)

"Santa Claus Is Coming to Town" (J. Frank Coots and Haven Gillespie)

"Stars Fell on Alabama" (Frank Perkins and Mitchell Parish)

"The Gypsy in Me" (Cole Porter)

"The Very Thought of You" (Ray Noble)

"What a Difference a Day Makes" ("Cuando vuelva a tu lada") (Maria Grever and Stanley Adams)

1935

"Begin the Beguine" (Cole Porter)

"Cheek to Cheek" (Irving Berlin)

"East of the Sun and West of the Moon" (Brooks Bowman)

"I Got Plenty o' Nuttin' " (George and Ira Gershwin and DuBose Heyward)

"I'm Gonna Sit Right Down and Write Myself a Letter" (Fred E. Ahlert and Joe Young)

"I'm in the Mood for Love" (Jimmy McHugh and Dorothy Fields)

"In a Sentimental Mood" (Duke Ellington, Irving Mills, and Manny Kurtz)

"Isn't This a Lovely Day" (Irving Berlin)

"It Ain't Necessarily So" (George and Ira Gershwin and DuBose Heyward)

"Just One of Those Things" (Cole Porter)

"Red Sails in the Sunset" (Hugh Williams, pseud. of Will Grosz, and Jimmy Kennedy)

"Summertime" (George and Ira Gershwin and DuBose Heyward)

"The Music Goes 'Round and 'Round" (Edward Farley, Michael Riley, and "Red" Hodgson)

"When I Grow Too Old to Dream" (Sigmund Romberg and Oscar Hammerstein II)

1936

"Empty Saddles" (Bill Hill)

"Good Night, Irene" (Huddie Ledbetter and John Lomax)

"I'm an Old Cowhand From the Rio Grande" (Johnny Mercer)

"I've Got a Feeling You're Fooling" (Arthur Freed and Nacio Herb Brown)

"I've Got You Under My Skin" (Cole Porter)

"Is It True What They Say About Dixie" (Sammy Lerner and Irving Caesar)

"Let Yourself Go" (Irving Berlin)

"Stompin' at the Savoy" (Benny Goodman, Edgar Sampson, Chick Webb, and Andy Razaf)

"The Glory of Love" ("That's the story of, that's the glory of love") (Bill Hill)

"The Night Is Young and You're So Beautiful" (Dana Suesse, Billy Rose, and Irving Kahal)

"The Way You Look Tonight" (Jerome Kern and Dorothy Fields)

1937

"Bei Mir Bist du Schön" (Sholom Secunda, Sammy Cahn, and Sol Chaplin)

"Blue Hawaii" (Ralph Rainger and Leo Robin)

"I've Got My Love to Keep Me Warm" (Irving Berlin)

"In the Still of the Night" (Cole Porter)

"Rosalie" (Cole Porter)

"The Dipsy Doodle" (Larry Clinton)

"The Nearness of You" (Hoagy Carmichael and Ned Washington)

"Vieni, Vieni" (Vincent Scotto and Rudy Vallee)

"Where or When" (Richard Rodgers and Lorenz Hart)

1938

"God Bless America" (Irving Berlin; written in 1917)

"Heigh-Ho" (Frank Churchill and Larry Morey)

"I Let a Song Go Out of My Heart" (Duke Ellington, Irving Mills, Henry Nemo, and John Redmond)

"Jeepers Creepers" (Harry Warren and Johnny Mercer)

"Love Walked In" (George and Ira Gershwin)

"My Heart Belongs to Daddy" (Cole Porter)

"One O'Clock Jump" (Count Basie and Harry James)

"Some Day My Prince Will Come" (Frank Churchill and Larry Morey)

"Thanks for the Memory" (Ralph Rainger and Leo Robin)

"The Flat-Foot Floogie" (Slim Gaillard, Sam Stewart, and Bud Green)

"Whistle While You Work" (Frank Churchill and Larry Morey)

"You Must Have Been a Beautiful Baby" (Harry Warren and Johnny Mercer)

1939

"All the Things You Are" (Jerome Kern and Oscar Hammerstein II)

"Ciribiribin" (A. Pestalozza, Rudolf Thaler, and Jack Lawrence, from folk tune, *ca.* 1898)

"Friendship" (Cole Porter)

"In the Mood" (Joe Garland and Andy Razaf)

"Moonlight Serenade" (Glenn Miller and Mitchell Parish)

"Over the Rainbow" (Harold Arlen and E. Y. Harburg)

"South of the Border" (Jimmy Kennedy and Michael Carr)

"Sunrise Serenade" (Frankie Carle and Jack Lawrence)

"The Beer Barrel Polka"—"Skoda Lasky" (Taromir Vejvoda, Wladimir A. Timm, and Vasek Zeman; 1939 English lyrics, Lew Brown)

"There'll Always Be an England" (Ross Parker and Hughie Charles)
"We're Off to See the Wizard" (Harold Arlen and E. Y. Harburg)

1940
"All or Nothing at All" (Arthur Altman and Jack Lawrence)
"All the Things You Are" (Jerome Kern and Oscar Hammerstein II)
"Back in the Saddle Again" (Ray Whiteley and Gene Autry)
"Between 18th and 19th on Chestnut Street" (Dick Rogers and Will Osborne)
"Bewitched, Bothered, and Bewildered" (Richard Rodgers and Lorenz Hart)
"Big Noise from Winnetka" (Bob Haggart, Ray Bauduc, Bob Crosby, and Gil
	Rodin)
"Blueberry Hill" (Al Lewis, Larry Stock, and Vincent Rose)
"How High the Moon" (Morgan Lewis and Nancy Hamilton)
"I'll Never Smile Again" (Ruth Lowe)
"South Rampart Street Parade" (Bob Haggart, Ray Bauduc, and Steve Allen)
"Taking a Chance on Love" (Vernon Duke, John LaTouche, and Fred Fetter)
"The Woodpecker's Song" (Eldo di Lazzaro and Harold Adamson)
"Tuxedo Junction" (Erskine Hawkins, William Johnson, Julian Dash, and Buddy
	Feyne)
"When You Wish Upon a Star" (Leigh Harline and Ned Washington)
"You Are My Sunshine" (Jimmie Davis and Charles Mitchell)

1941
"Anniversary Waltz" (Al Dubin and Dave Franklin)
"Blues in the Night" (Harold Arlen and Johnny Mercer)
"Buckle Down, Winsocki" (Hugh Martin and Ralph Blane)
"Chattanooga Choo-Choo" (Harry Warren and Mack Gordon)
"Deep in the Heart of Texas" (June Hershey and Don Swander)
"I Got It Bad and That Ain't Good" (Duke Ellington and Paul Francis Webster)
"Lili Marlene" (Norbert Schultze and Hans Leip)
"Take the A Train" (Billy Strayhorn)
"Why Don't You Do Right" (Joe McCoy)

1942
"Don't Get Around Much Anymore" (Duke Ellington and Bob Russell)
"Jingle Jangle Jingle" (Joseph J. Lilley and Frank Loesser)
"Moonlight Becomes You" (Jimmy Van Heusen and Johnny Burke)
"Moonlight Cocktail" (Kim Gannon and Luckeyth Roberts)
"Serenade in Blue" (Harry Warren and Mack Gordon)
"That Old Black Magic" (Harold Arlen and Johnny Mercer)
"Warsaw Concerto" (Richard Addinsell)
"White Christmas" (Irving Berlin)

1943

"(It Seems to Me) I've Heard That Song Before" (Jule Styne and Sammy Cahn)

"Besame Mucho" (Consuelo Velazquez, Eng. lyrics by Sunny Skylar)

"I Want to Be Happy" (Irving Caesar and Vincent Youmans; orig. 1924)

"I'm Thinking Tonight of My Blue Eyes" (Don Marcotte and A. P. Carter)

"Kansas City" ("Everything's up to date in Kansas City") (Richard Rodgers and Oscar Hammerstein II)

"Oh, What a Beautiful Morning" (Richard Rodgers and Oscar Hammerstein II)

"People Will Say We're in Love" (Richard Rodgers and Oscar Hammer- stein II)

"San Fernando Valley" (Gordon Jenkins)

"Taking a Chance on Love" (Vernon Duke, John LaTouche, and Ted Fetter)

"The Surrey with the Fringe on Top" (Richard Rodgers and Oscar Hammerstein II)

"You'd Be So Nice to Come Home to" (Cole Porter)

1944

"Ac-cen-tchu-ate the Positive" (Harold Arlen and Johnny Mercer)

"Don't Fence Me In" (Cole Porter)

"Evelina" (Harold Arlen and E. Y. Harburg)

"I'll Walk Alone" (Jule Styne and Sammy Cahn)

"Is You Is or Is You Ain't My Baby" (Louis Jordan and Billy Austin)

"Rum and Coca-Cola" (Jeri Sullavan, Paul Baron, and Morey Amsterdam, based on calypso song by Lionel Belasco published in 1906)

"Sentimental Journey" (Ben Homer, Bud Green, and Les Brown)

"You Always Hurt the One You Love" (Allan Roberts and Doris Fisher)

1945

"If I Loved You" (Richard Rodgers and Oscar Hammerstein II)

"It Might as Well Be Spring" (Richard Rodgers and Oscar Hammerstein II)

"It's Been a Long Long Time" (Jule Styne and Sammy Cahn)

"June Is Bustin' Out All Over" (Richard Rodgers and Oscar Hammerstein II)

"Let It Snow! Let It Snow! Let It Snow!" (Jule Styne and Sammy Cahn)

"The Atchison, Topeka, and the Santa Fe" (Harry Warren and Johnny Mercer)

1946

"Doin' What Comes Natur'lly" (Irving Berlin)

"The Girl That I Marry" (Irving Berlin)

"To Each His Own" (Jay Livingston and Ray Evans)

"You Call Everybody Darling" (Sam Martin, Ben Trace, and Clem Watts)

1947

"Civilization (Bongo, Bongo, Bongo)" (Bob Hilliard and Carl Sigman)

"Cool Water" (Bob Nolan)

"Feudin' and Fightin' " (Burton Lane and Al Dubin)
"I Love You (for Sentimental Reasons)" (William Best and Deke Watson)
"I'll Dance at Your Wedding" (Ben Oakland and Herb Magidson)
"Managua, Nicaragua" (Albert Gamse and Irving Fields)
"Open the Door, Richard" (Jack McVea, Dan Howell, Dusty Fletcher, and John
    Mason)
"Too Fat Polka" (Ross MacLean and Arthur Richardson)
"Woody Woodpecker" (George Tibbles and Ramey Idriss)

1948
"Always True to You in My Fashion" (Cole Porter)
"Baby, It's Cold Outside" (Frank Loesser)
"Buttons and Bows" (Jay Livingston and Raymond Evans)
"Mañana—Is Soon Enough for Me" (Peggy Lee and Dave Barbour)
"Nature Boy" (Eden Ahbez)
"On a Slow Boat to China" (Frank Loesser)
"Once in Love With Amy" (Frank Loesser)
"Red Roses for a Blue Lady" (Sid Tepper and Roy Brodsky)
"Tennessee Waltz" (Redd Stewart and Pee Wee King)

1949
"Bali Hai" (Richard Rodgers and Oscar Hammerstein II)
"Bonaparte's Retreat" (Pee Wee King, from folk tune)
"Cigareets, Whusky, and Wild Wild Women" (Tim Spencer)
"Diamonds Are a Girl's Best Friend" (Jule Styne and Leo Robin)
"Let's Take an Old-Fashioned Walk" (Irving Berlin)
"Mule Train" (John Lange, Hy Heath, and Fred Glickman)
"Rudolph the Red-Nosed Reindeer" (Johnny Marks)
"Some Enchanted Evening" (Richard Rodgers and Oscar Hammerstein II)
"That Lucky Old Sun" (Beasley Smith and Haven Gillespie)
"Wunderbar" (Cole Porter)

1950
"A Bushel and a Peck" (Frank Loesser)
"Music! Music! Music!" (Stephen Weiss and Bernie Baum)
"Ragg Mopp" (Johnny Lee Wills and Deacon Anderson)
"Silver Bells" (Jay Livingston and Ray Evans)
The Third Man Theme (Anton Karas)

1951
"Because of You" (Arthur Hammerstein and Dudley Wilkinson)
"Cold, Cold Heart" (Hank Williams)

"Come On-A My House" (Ross Bagdasarian and William Saroyan)
"How High the Moon" (Nancy Hamilton and Morgan Lewis)
"If" (Robert Hargreaves, Stanley J. Damerell, and Tolchard Evans)
"Mocking Bird Hill" (Vaughn Horton)
"My Heart Cries for You" (Percy Faith and Carl Sigman)
"It's No Sin" (Chester R. Shull and George Hoven)
"Tennessee Waltz" (Redd Stewart and Pee Wee King)
"Too Young" (Sylvia Dee and Sid Lippman)

1952
"Auf Wiederseh'n Sweetheart" (John Sexton, John Turner, and Eberhard Storch)
"Blue Tango" (Leroy Anderson)
"Cry" (Churchill Kohlman)
"Here in My Heart" (Pat Genaro, Lou Levinson, and Bill Borrelli)
"I Went to Your Wedding" (Jessie Mae Robinson)
"Kiss of Fire" (Lester Allen and Robert B. Hill)
"Slow Poke" (Pee Wee King, Redd Stewart, and Chilton Price)
"Wheel of Fortune" (Bennie Benjamin and George Weiss)
"Why Don't You Believe Me?" (Lew Douglas, King Laney, and Roy Rodde)
"You Belong to Me" (Pee Wee King, Redd Stewart, and Chilton Price)

1953
"Rags to Riches" (Richard Adler and Jerry Ross)
"Don't Let the Stars Get in Your Eyes" (Slim Willet)
"Eh, Cumpari" (Julius LaRosa and Archie Bleyer)
"How Much Is That Doggie in the Window" (Bob Merrill)
"I Believe" (Ervin Drake, Irvin Graham, Jimmy Shirl, and Al Stillman)
"I'm Walking Behind You" (Billy Reid)
"No Other Love" (Oscar Hammerstein II and Richard Rodgers)
"Song From 'Moulin Rouge' " (William Engvick and Georges Auric)
"Till I Waltz Again with You" (Sidney Prosen)
"Vaya Con Dios" (Larry Russell, Inez James, and Buddy Pepper)
"Why Don't You Believe Me?" (Lew Douglas, King Laney, and Roy Rodde)
"You, You, You" (Robert Mellin and Lotar Olias)

1954
"Hernando's Hideaway" (Richard Adler and Jerry Ross)
"I Need You Now" (Jimmie Crane and Al Jacobs)
"If I Give My Heart to You" (Jimmie Crane, Al Jacobs, and Jimmy Brewster)
"Little Things Mean a Lot" (Edith Lindeman and Carl Stutz)
"Oh, Mein Papa" (Paul Burkhard, John Turner, and Jeffrey Parsons)
"Secret Love" (Paul Francis Webster and Sammy Fain)

"Sh-Boom" (James Keyes, Claude Feaster, Carl Feaster, Floyd F. McRae, and
    James Edwards)
"Stranger in Paradise" (Robert Wright and George Forrest)
"Three Coins in the Fountain" (Sammy Kahn and Jule Styne)
"Wanted" (Jack Fulton and Lois Steele)

1955
"Sincerely" (Harvey Fuqua and Alan Freed)
"Autumn Leaves" (Joseph Kosma, Jacques Prevert, and Johnny Mercer)
"Cherry Pink and Apple Blossom White" ("Louiquy") (French lyrics, Jacques
    Larue; English lyrics, Mack David)
"Hearts of Stone" (Rudy Jackson and Edward Ray)
"Let Me Go, Lover" (Jenny Lou Carson and Al Hill)
"Love Is a Many-Splendored Thing" (Sammy Fain and Paul Francis Webster)
"Melody of Love" (Tom Glazer and H. Engelmann)
"Mr. Sandman" (Pat Ballard)
"Rock Around the Clock" (Max Freedman and Jimmy DeKnight)
"Sixteen Tons" (Merle Travis)
"The Ballad of Davy Crockett" (Tom Blackburn and George Burns)
"The Crazy Otto Rag" (Edward R. White and Mack Wolfson)
"Unchained Melody" (Hy Zaret and Alex North)
"Yellow Rose of Texas" (Don George)

1956
"Don't Be Cruel" (Otis Blackwell and Elvis Presley)
"Heartbreak Hotel" (Mae Boren Axton, Tommy Durden, and Elvis Presley)
"Hot Diggity" (Al Hoffman and Dick Manning)
"Hound Dog" (Jerry Leiber and Mike Stoller)
"Lisbon Antigua" (Raul Portela; Portuguese lyrics, José Galhardo and Amadeu
    do Vale; English lyrics, Harry Dupree)
"Love Me Tender" (Vera Matson and Elvis Presley)
"Memories Are Made of This" (Terry Gilkyson, Richard Dehr, and Frank
    Miller)
"Moonglow" and "Picnic" medley: "Moonglow" (Will Hudson and Eddie de
    Lange), "Picnic" (George W. Duning and Steve Allen)
"My Prayer" (Jimmy Kennedy and Georges Boulanger)
"Poor People of Paris" (from "La Goulant du pauvre Jean") (Marguerite Monnot
    and René Rouzaud; English lyrics, Jack Lawrence)
"Rock and Roll Waltz" (Dick Ware and Shorty Allen)
"Singing the Blues" (Melvin Endsley)
"The Great Pretender" (Buck Ram)
"The Wayward Wind" (Stan Lebowsky and Herb Newman)

1957

"All Shook Up" (Otis Blackwell and Elvis Presley)

"April Love" (Paul Francis Webster and Sammy Fain)

"Honeycomb" (Bob Merrill)

"Jailhouse Rock" (Jerry Leiber and Mike Stoller)

"Love Letters in the Sand" (Nick and Charles Kenny and J. Fred Coots)

"Round and Round" (Lou Stallman and Joe Shapiro)

"Tammy" (Jay Livingston and Ray Evans)

"Teddy Bear" (Kal Mann and Bernie Lowe)

"Too Much" (Lee Rosenberg and Bernard Weinman)

"Wake Up Little Susie" (Felice and Boudleaux Bryant)

"You Send Me" (L. C. Cooke)

"Young Love" (Carole Joyner and Ric Cartey)

1958

"All I Have to Do Is Dream" (Boudleaux Bryant)

"At the Hop" (Arthur Singer, John Medora, and David White)

"Chipmunk Song" (Ross Bagdasarian)

"Don't" (Jerry Leiber and Mike Stoller)

"Get a Job" (Earl T. Beal, Raymond W. Edwards, William F. Horton, and Richard
    A. Lewis)

"Hard-Headed Woman" (Claude De Metruis)

"He's Got the Whole World in His Hands" (based on black spiritual)

"It's All in the Game" (Gen. Charles Gates Dawes and Carl Sigman; based on
    instrumental by Dawes from 1912)

"It's Only Make-Believe" (Conway Twitty and Jack Nance)

"Nel Blu Dipinto di Blu" ("Volare") (Domenico Modugno; Italian lyrics,
    Modugno and Francesco Migliacci)

"Patricia" (Perez Prado)

"Poor Little Fool" (Shari Sheeley)

"Purple People Eater" (Sheb Wooley)

"Tequila" (Chuck Rio)

"The Stroll" (Nancy Lee and Clyde Otis)

"Tom Dooley" (Alan Lomax and Frank Warner; traditional folk song with adap-
    tations of words and music)

"Twilight Time" (Buck Ram, Al Nevins, Morton Nevins, and Artie Dunn)

1959

"A Big Hunk of Love" (Aaron Schroeder and Sid Wyche)

"Battle of New Orleans" (Jimmy Driftwood)

"Come Softly to Me" (Gary Troxel, Gretchen Christopher, and Barbara Ellis)

"Don't You Know" (Bobby Worth)

"Heartaches by the Number" (Harlan Howard)

"Kansas City" (Jerry Lieber and Mike Stoller)

"Mack the Knife," or Theme from *The Threepenny Opera*; also known as "Morit'at" (Kurt Weill, 1928; German lyrics, Berthold Brecht; English lyrics, Marc Blitzstein)

"Sleep Walk" (Don Wolfe, Johnny Santo, and Ann Farina)

"Stagger Lee" (Harold Logan and Lloyd Price)

"The Happy Organ" (Ken Wood, pseud. of Walter R. Moody, and David Clowney)

"Three Bells" ("While the angelus was ringing") ("Les Trois Cloches") (Bert Reisfeld; French lyrics, Jean Villard [Gilles]; English lyrics, Reisfeld); also known as "The Jimmy Brown Song," with different lyrics

"Venus" (Ed Marshall)

1960

"Are You Lonesome Tonight?" (Roy Turk and Lou Handman)

"Cathy's Clown" (Don and Phil Everly)

"El Paso" (Marty Robbins)

"Everybody's Somebody's Fool" (Jack Keller and Howard Greenfield)

"I'm Sorry" (Ronnie Self and Dub Albritton)

"It's Now or Never" (Aaron Schroeder and Wally Gold)

"My Heart Has a Mind of Its Own" (Howard Greenfield and Jack Keller)

"Running Bear" (J. P. Richardson)

"Save the Last Dance for Me" (Doc Pomus and Mort Shuman)

"Stuck on You" (Aaron Schroeder and J. Leslie McFarland)

"Teen Angel" (Jean and Red Surrey)

"The Twist" (Hank Ballard)

Theme from *A Summer Place* (Max Steiner)

"Why" (Bob Marcucci and Peter DeAngelis)

1961

"Big Bad John" (Jimmy Dean)

"Blue Moon" (Richard Rodgers and Lorenz Hart)

"Calcutta" (Heino Gaze, Paul Vance, and Lee Pockriss)

"Hit the Road, Jack" (Percy Mayfield)

"Michael" (Dave Fisher and Albert Gamsé; based on folk song)

"Pony Time" (Don Covey and John Berry)

"Quarter to Three Waltz" (Gene Barge, Frank Guida, Gary Anderson, and Joe Royster)

"Runaround Sue" (Dion DiMucci and Ernie Maresca)

"Runaway" (Charles Westover and Max Crook)

"Surrender" (Doc Pomus and Mort Shuman)

"Take Good Care of My Baby" (Gerry Goffin and Carole King)

"The Lion Sleeps Tonight"; originally entitled "Wimoweh" (Hugo Peretti, Luigi
     Creatore, George Weiss, and Albert Stanton)
"Tossin' and Turnin' " (Ritchie Adams and Malou Rene)
"Travelin' Man" (Jerry Fuller)
"Will You Love Me Tomorrow" (Gerry Goffin and Carole King)
"Wonderland by Night" (Lincoln Chase and Klauss-Günter Neuman)

1962
"Big Girls Don't Cry" (Bob Crewe and Bob Gaudio)
"Breaking Up Is Hard to Do" (Neil Sedaka and Howard Greenfield)
"Duke of Earl" (Bernie Williams, Eugene Dixon, and Earl Edwards)
"Good Luck Charm" (Aaron Schroeder and Wally Gold)
"He's a Rebel" (Gene Pitney)
"Hey! Baby" (Margaret Cobb and Bruce Channel)
"I Can't Stop Loving You" (Don Gibson)
"Johnny Angel" (Lee Pockriss and Lyn Duddy)
"Monster Mash" (Bobby Pickett and Leonard Capizzi)
"Peppermint Twist Part I" (Joey Dee and Henry Glover)
"Roses Are Red (My Love)" (Paul Evans and Al Byron)
"Sheila" (Tommy Roe)
"Sherry" (Bob Gaudio)
"Soldier Boy" (Luther Dixon and Florence Green)
"Telstar" (Joe Meek)

1963
"Blue Velvet" (Bernie Wayne and Lee Morris)
"Dominique" (Soeur Sourire; English lyrics by Noel Regney)
"Easier Said Than Done" (William Linton and Larry Huff)
"Fingertips, Part 2" (Henry Cosby and Clarence Paul)
"Go Away Little Girl" (Gerry Goffin and Carole King)
"He's So Fine" (Ronnie Mack)
"Hey Paula" (Ray Hildebrand)
"I Will Follow Him" (J. W. Stole, Del Roma, Arthur Altman, and Norman Gimbel)
"I'm Leaving It All Up to You" (Don Harris and Dewey Terry, Jr.)
"If You Wanna Be Happy" (Frank and Carmela Guida and Joseph Royster)
"It's My Party" (John Gluck, Jr., Wally Gold, and Herb Weiner)
"My Boyfriend's Back" (Robert Feldman, Gerald Goldstein, and Richard Gottehrer)
"Sugar Shack" (Keith McCormack and Faye Voss)
"Sukiyaki" (El Rohusuke Hachidai and Hochidai Nakamura)
"Surf City" (Jan Berry and Brian Wilson)
"Walk like a Man" (Bob Crewe and Bob Gaudio)
"Walk Right In" (Gus Cannon and Hosie Woods)

1964

"A Hard Day's Night" (John Lennon and Paul McCartney)

"Baby Love" (Brian and Eddie Holland and Lamont Dozier)

"Can't Buy Me Love" (John Lennon and Paul McCartney)

"Chapel of Love" (Jeff Barry, Ellie Greenwich, and Phil Spector)

"Come See About Me" (Brian and Eddie Holland and Lamont Dozier)

"Do Wah Diddy Diddy" (Jeff Barry and Ellie Greenwich)

"I Feel Fine" (John Lennon and Paul McCartney)

"I Get Around" (Brian Wilson)

"I Want to Hold Your Hand" (John Lennon and Paul McCartney)

"My Guy" (William "Smokey" Robinson)

"Oh, Pretty Woman" (Roy Orbison and Bill Dees)

"Rag Doll" (Bob Crewe and Bob Gaudio)

"She Loves You" (John Lennon and Paul McCartney)

"The House of the Rising Sun" (Alan Price)

"There! I've Said It Again" (Redd Evans and Dave Mann)

"Where Did Our Love Go" (Brian and Eddie Holland and Lamont Dozier)

1965

"(I Can't Get No) Satisfaction" (Mick Jagger and Keith Richard)

"Downtown" (Tony Hatch)

"Eight Days a Week" (John Lennon and Paul McCartney)

"Get Off My Cloud" (Mick Jagger and Keith Richard)

"Help Me Rhonda" (Brian Wilson)

"Help!" (John Lennon and Paul McCartney)

"I Can't Help Myself (Sugar Pie Honey Bunch)" (Brian and Eddie Holland and
    Lamont Dozier)

"I Hear a Symphony" (Brian and Eddie Holland and Lamont Dozier)

"I'm Telling You Now" (Freddie Garrity and Mitch Murray)

"I've Got You Babe" (Sonny Bono)

"Mrs. Brown You've Got a Lovely Daughter" (Trevor Peacock)

"Stop! In the Name of Love" (Brian and Eddie Holland and Lamont Dozier)

"This Diamond Ring" (Al Kooper, Bobby Brass, and Irwin Levine)

"Turn! Turn! Turn!" (Pete Seeger)

"Yesterday" (John Lennon and Paul McCartney)

"You've Lost That Lovin' Feeling" (Phil Spector, Barry Mann, and Cynthia
    Weil)

1966

"(You're My) Soul and Inspiration" (Barry Mann and Cynthia Weil)

"Cherish" (Terry Kirkman)

"Hanky Panky" (Jeff Barry and Ellie Greenwich)

"I'm a Believer" (Neil Diamond)

"Monday, Monday" (John Phillips)

"My Love" (Tony Hatch)

"Paint It Black" (Mick Jagger and Keith Richard)

"Paperback Writer" (John Lennon and Paul McCartney)

"Reach Out, I'll Be There" (Brian and Eddie Holland and Lamont Dozier)

"Summer in the City" (John Sebastian, Steve Boone, and Mark Sebastian)

"The Ballad of the Green Berets" (Barry Sadler and Robin Moore)

"The Sounds of Silence" (Paul Simon)

"We Can Work It Out" (John Lennon and Paul McCartney)

"When a Man Loves a Woman" (Calvin Lewis and Andrew Wright)

"Wild Thing" (Chip Taylor)

"Winchester Cathedral" (Geoff Stevens)

"You Can't Hurry Love" (Brian and Eddie Holland and Lamont Dozier)

"You Keep Me Hangin' On" (Brian and Eddie Holland and Lamont Dozier)

1967

"Daydream Believer" (John Stewart)

"Groovin' " (Felix Cavaliere and Eddie Brigati)

"Happy Together" (Garry Bonner and Alan Gordon)

"Hello Goodbye" (John Lennon and Paul McCartney)

"Judy in Disguise (with Glasses)" (John Fred and Andrew Bernard)

"Kind of a Drag" (Jim Holvay)

"Light My Fire" (Robbie Krieger, Ray Manzarek, John Densmore, and Jim Morrison)

"Ode to Billie Joe" (Bobbie Gentry)

"Respect" (Otis Redding)

"Somethin' Stupid" (C. Carson Parks)

"The Letter" (Wayne Carson Thompson)

"To Sir with Love" (Don Black and Mark London)

"Windy" (Ruthann Friedman)

1968

"(Sittin' on) the Dock of the Bay" (Otis Redding and Steve Cropper)

"Grazing in the Grass" (Philemon Hou and Harry Elston)

"Honey" (Bobby Russell)

"Love Is Blue" (Andre Popp, Pierre Cour, and Bryan Blackburn)

"Mrs. Robinson" (Paul Simon)

"People Got to Be Free" (Felix Cavaliere and Eddie Brigati)

"This Guy's in Love with You" (Burt Bacharach and Hal David)

"Tighten Up" (Archie Bell and Billy Buttier)

1969

"Aquarius" ("Let the Sunshine In") (James Rado, Gerome Ragni, and Galt McDermot)

"Crimson and Clover" (Tommy James and Peter Lucia)

"Dizzy" (Tommy Roe and Freddy Weller)

"Everyday People" (Sylvester Stewart)

"Get Back" (John Lennon and Paul McCartney)

"Hello, I Love You" (Jim Morrison, Ray Manzarek, Robbie Krieger, and John Densmore)

"Hey Jude" (John Lennon and Paul McCartney)

"Honky Tonk Women" (Mick Jagger and Keith Richard)

"I Can't Get Next to You" (Norman Whitfield and Barrett Strong)

"I Heard It Through the Grapevine" (Norman Whitfield and Barrett Strong)

"In the Year 2525" ("Exordium & Terminus") (Rick Evans)

"Love Child" (Pam Sawyer, R. Dean Taylor, Frank Wilson, and Deke Richards)

Love Theme from *Romeo and Juliet* (Nino Rota, Larry Kusik, and Eddie Snyder)

"Na Na Hey Hey Kiss Him Goodbye" (Gary De Carlo, Dale Frashver, and Paul Leka)

"Sugar, Sugar" (Jeff Barry and Andy Kim)

"Wedding Bell Blues" (Laura Nyro)

1970

"ABC" (Freddie Perren, Fonce Mizell, Deke Richards, and Berry Gordy, Jr.)

"Ain't No Mountain High Enough" (Nicholas Ashford and Valerie Simpson)

"American Woman (No Sugar Tonight)" (Randy Bachman, Burton Cummings, Garry Peterson, and Jim Kalel)

"Bridge Over Troubled Waters" (Paul Simon)

"Everything Is Beautiful" (Ray Stevens)

"I Think I Love You" (Tony Romeo)

"I'll Be There" (Berry Gordy, Jr., Hal Davis, Willie Hutch, and Bob West)

"Let It Be" (John Lennon and Paul McCartney)

"Mama Told Me (Not to Come)" (Randy Newman)

"My Sweet Lord (Isn't It a Pity)" (George Harrison)

"Raindrops Keep Fallin' on My Head" (Burt Bacharach and Hal David)

"Thank You (Falettin Me Be Mice Elf Again)" (Sylvester Stewart)

"The Long and Winding Road" (John Lennon and Paul McCartney)

"The Love You Save" (Freddie Perren, Fonce Mizell, Deke Richards, and Berry Gordy, Jr.)

"The Tears of a Clown" (Henry Cosby, William "Smokey" Robinson, and Stevie Wonder)

"(They Long to Be) Close to You" (Burt Bacharach and Hal David)

"War" (Norman Whitfield and Barrett Strong)

1971

"Brand New Key" (Melanie Safka)

"Brown Sugar" (Mick Jagger and Keith Richard)

"Family Affair" (Sylvester Stewart)

"Go Away Little Girl" (Gerry Goffin and Carole King)

"Gypsies, Tramps, and Thieves" (Bob Stone)

"How Can You Mend a Broken Heart" (Barry and Robin Gibb)

"It's Too Late" ("I Feel the Earth Move") (Toni Stern and Carole King)

"Joy to the World" (Hoyt Axton)

"Just My Imagination (Running Away with Me)" (Norman Whitfield and Barrett Strong)

"Knock Three Times" (L. Russel Brown and Irwin Levine)

"Maggie May" (Rod Stewart and Ron Quittenton)

"Me and Bobby McGee" (Kris Kristofferson)

"One Bad Apple" (George Jackson)

Theme from *Shaft* (Isaac Hayes)

1972

"A Horse with No Name" (Lee Bunnell)

"Alone Again (Naturally)" (Gilbert O'Sullivan)

"American Pie" (Don McLean)

"Baby Don't Get Hooked on Me" (Mac Davis)

"Candy Man" (Leslie Bricusse and Anthony Newley)

"I Can See Clearly Now" (Johnny Nash)

"Lean on Me" (Bill Withers)

"Me and Mrs. Jones" (Kenny Gamble, Leon Huff, and Cary Gilbert)

"My Ding-a-Ling" (Chuck Berry)

"The First Time Ever I Saw Your Face" (Ewan MacColl)

"Without You" (Pete Ham and Tom Evans)

1973

"Bad, Bad Leroy Brown" (Jim Croce)

"Brother Louie" (Errol Brown and Tony Wilson)

"Crocodile Rock" (Elton John and Bernie Taupin)

"Half-breed" (Mary Dean and Al Capps)

"Keep on Truckin' " (Anita Poree, Frank Wilson, and Leonard Caston)

"Killing Me Softly With His Song" (Norman Gimbel and Charles Fox)

"Let's Get It On" (Marvin Gaye and Ed Townsend)

"Midnight Train to Georgia" (Jim Weatherly)

"My Love" (Paul and Linda McCartney)

"The Morning After" (Al Kasha and Joel Hirshhorn)

"The Most Beautiful Girl" (Norro Wilson, Billy Sherrill, and Rory Bourke)

"The Night the Lights Went Out in Georgia" (Bobby Russell)

"Tie a Yellow Ribbon Round the Ole Oak Tree" (Irwin Levine and L. Russell Brown)

"Time in a Bottle" (Jim Croce)

"Top of the World" (Richard Carpenter and John Bettis)

"Will It Go Round in Circles" (Billy Preston and Bruce Fisher)

"You're So Vain" (Carly Simon)

1974

"(You're) Having My Baby" (Paul Anka)

"Annie's Song" (John Denver)

"Billy, Don't Be a Hero" (Mitch Murray and Pete Callander)

"I Can Help" (Billy Swan)

"I Honestly Love You" (Peter Allen and Jeff Barry)

"Kung Fu Fighting" (Carl Douglas)

"Rock Your Baby" (Harry Wayne Casey and Richard Finch)

"Seasons in the Sun" (Jacques Brel and Rod McKuen)

"The Loco-Motion" (Gerry Goffin and Carole King)

"The Streak" (Ray Stevens)

"The Way We Were" (Marvin Hamlisch and Alan and Marilyn Bergman)

"TSOP" (Kenny Gamble and Leon Huff)

1975

"Bad Blood" (Neil Sedaka and Phil Cody)

"Fame" (David Bowie, John Lennon, and Carlos Alomar)

"Fly, Robin, Fly" (Silvester Levay and Stephen Prager)

"He Don't Love You (like I Love You)" (Calvin Carter and Curtis May-field)

"Island Girl" (Elton John and Bernie Taupin)

"Jive Talkin' " (Barry, Robin, and Maurice Gibb)

"Love Will Keep Us Together" (Neil Sedaka and Howard Greenfield)

"Lucy in the Sky with Diamonds" (John Lennon and Paul McCartney)

"Philadelphia Freedom" (Elton John and Bernie Taupin)

"Rhinestone Cowboy" (Larry Weiss)

"That's the Way (I Like It)" (Harry Wayne Casey and Richard Finch)

1976

"Afternoon Delight" (Bill Danoff)

"December 1963 (Oh, What a Night)" (Bob Gaudio and Judy Parker)

"Disco Lady" (Harvey Scales, Albert Vance, and Don Davis)

"Don't Go Breaking My Heart" (Elton John and Bernie Taupin)

"Fifty Ways to Leave Your Lover" (Paul Simon)

"If You Leave Me Now" (Peter Cetera)

"Kiss and Say Goodbye" (Winfred "Blue" Lovett)

"Love Hangover" (Pam Sawyer and Marilyn McLeod)

"Play That Funky Music" (Robert Parissi)

"Silly Love Songs" (Paul and Linda McCartney)

"Tonight's the Night (Gonna Be Alright)" (Rod Stewart)

1977

"Best of My Love" (Maurice White and Al McKay)

"How Deep Is Your Love" (Barry, Robin, and Maurice Gibb)

"I Just Want to Be Your Everything" (Barry Gibb)

Love Theme from *A Star Is Born* ("Evergreen") (Barbra Streisand and Paul Williams)

"Rich Girl" (Daryl Hall)

"Sir Duke" (Stevie Wonder)

Star Wars Theme ("Cantina Band") (John Williams)

"Torn Between Two Lovers" (Phil Jarrell and Peter Yarrow)

"You Light Up My Life" (Joe Brooks)

1978

"(Love Is) Thicker Than Water" (Barry and Andy Gibb)

"Boogie Oogie Oogie" (Janice Marie Johnson and Perry Kibble)

"Grease" (Barry Gibb)

"If I Can't Have You" (Barry, Robin, and Maurice Gibb)

"Kiss You All Over" (Mike Chapman and Nicky Chinn)

"Le Freak" (Nile Rodgers and Bernard Edwards)

"MacArthur Park" (Jimmy Webb)

"Night Fever" (Barry, Robin, and Maurice Gibb)

"Shadow Dancing" (Barry, Robin, Maurice, and Andy Gibb)

"Three Times a Lady" (Lionel Richie)

"With a Little Luck" (Paul McCartney)

"You Don't Bring Me Flowers" (Neil Diamond and Alan and Marilyn Bergman)

1979

"Babe" (Dennis DeYoung)

"Bad Girls" (Donna Summer, Eddie Hokenson, Bruce Subano, and Joe "Bean" Esposito)

"Do Ya Think I'm Sexy?" (Rod Stewart and Carmine Appice)

"Escape (Pina Colada Song)" (Rupert Holmes)

"Hot Stuff" (Pete Bellotte, Harold Faltermeier, and Keith Forsey)

"I Will Survive" (Dino Fekaris and Freddie Perren)

"My Sharona" (Doug Fieger and Berton Averre)

"No More Tears (Enough Is Enough)" (Paul Jabara and Bruce Roberts)

"Reunited" (Dino Fekaris and Freddie Perren)
"Ring My Bell" (Frederick Knight)
"Rise" (Andy Armer and Randy Badazz)
"Too Much Heaven" (Barry, Robin, and Maurice Gibb)
"Tragedy" (Barry, Robin, and Maurice Gibb)

1980
"Another Brick in the Wall" (Roger Waters)
"Another One Bites the Dust" (John Deacon)
"Call Me" (Giorgio Moroder and Deborah Harry)
"Coming Up (Live at Glasgow)" (Paul McCartney)
"Crazy Little Thing Called Love" (Freddie Mercury)
"Funkytown" (Steven Greenberg)
"It's Still Rock and Roll to Me" (Billy Joel)
"(Just Like) Starting Over" (John Lennon)
"Lady" (Lionel Richie)
"Magic" (John Farrar)
"Rock with You" (Rodney Temperton)
"Upside Down" (Bernard Edwards and Nile Rodgers)
"Woman in Love" (Barry and Robin Gibb)

1981
"9 to 5" (Dolly Parton)
"Arthur's Theme" ("Best That You Can Do") (Burt Bacharach, Christopher
    Cross, and Peter Allen)
"Bette Davis Eyes" (Donna Weiss and Jackie DeShannon)
"Celebration" (Ronald Holt and Kool and the Gang)
"Endless Love" (Lionel Richie)
"I Love a Rainy Night" (Eddie Rabbitt, Even Stevens, and David Malloy)
"Jessie's Girl" (Rick Springfield)
"Kiss on My List" (Janna Allen and Daryl Hall)
"Morning Train (Nine to Five)" (Florrie Palmer)
"Physical" (Steve Kipner and Terry Shaddick)
"Private Eyes" (Daryl Hall, Warren Pash, and Sara and Joanna Allen)
"Rapture" (Chris Stein and Deborah Harry)

1982
"Abracadabra" (Steve Miller)
"Centerfold" (Seth Justman)
"Don't You Want Me" (Jo Callis, Phil Oakey, and Adrian Wright)
"Ebony and Ivory" (Paul McCartney)
"Eye of the Tiger" (Frankie Sullivan and Jim Peterik)

"Hard to Say I'm Sorry" (Peter Cetera and David Foster)

"I Love Rock and Roll" (Alan Merrill and Jerry Mamburg)

"Jack and Diane" (John Cougar Mellencamp)

"Maneater" (Daryl Hall, John Oates, and Sara Allen)

"Truly" (Lionel Richie)

"Up Where We Belong" (Jack Nitzsche, Will Jennings, and Buffy Sainte-Marie)

1983

"All Night Long (All Night)" (Lionel Richie)

"Baby, Come to Me" (Rod Temperton)

"Beat It" (Michael Jackson)

"Billie Jean" (Michael Jackson)

"Down Under" (Colin Hay and Ron Strykert)

"Every Breath You Take" (Sting)

"Flashdance (What a Feeling)" (Irene Cara, Giorgio Moroder, and Keith Forsey)

"Islands in the Stream" (Barry, Robin, and Maurice Gibb)

"Maniac" (Michael Sembello and Dennis Matkosky)

"Total Eclipse of the Heart" (Jim Steinman)

1984

"Caribbean Queen (No More Love on the Run)" (Keith Diamond, Billy Ocean, and Leslie Charles)

"Footloose" (Kenny Loggins and Dean Pitchford)

"Ghostbusters" (Ray Parker, Jr.)

"Hello" (Lionel Richie)

"I Just Called to Say I Love You" (Stevie Wonder)

"Jump" (Edward and Alex Van Halen, Michael Anthony, and David Lee Roth)

"Karma Chameleon" (George O'Dowd, Jon Moss, Roy Hay, Mikey Craig, and Phil Pickett)

"Let's Go Crazy" (Prince)

"Let's Hear It for the Boy" (Tom Snow and Dean Pitchford)

"Like a Virgin" (Billy Steinberg and Tom Kelly)

"Out of Touch" (Daryl Hall and John Oates)

"Owner of a Lonely Heart" (Trevor Rabin, Jon Anderson, Chris Squire, and Trevor Horn)

"Say, Say, Say" (Paul McCartney and Michael Jackson)

"The Reflex" (Duran Duran)

"Wake Me Up Before You Go-Go" (George Michael)

"What's Love Got to Do with It" (Terry Britten and Graham Lyle)

"When Doves Cry" (Prince)

1985

"A View to a Kill" (Simon LeBon, Nick Rhodes, Andy, John, and Roger Taylor, and John Barry)

"Against All Odds (Take a Look at Me Now)" (Phil Collins)

"Broken Wings" (Richard Page, Steven George, and John Lang)

"Can't Fight This Feeling" (Kevin Cronin)

"Careless Whisper" (George Michael and Andrew Ridgeley)

"Crazy for You" (John Bettis and Jon Lind)

"Everybody Wants to Rule the World" (Roland Orzabal and Ian Stanley)

"Everything She Wants" (George Michael)

"Heaven" (Bryan Adams and Jim Vallance)

"I Want to Know What Love Is" (Mick Jones)

"Money for Nothing" (Mark Knopfler and Sting)

"One More Night" (Phil Collins)

"Say You, Say Me" (Lionel Richie)

"Shout" (Roland Orzabal and Ian Stanley)

"St. Elmo's Fire (Man in Motion)" (David Foster and John Parr)

"The Power of Love" (Chris Hayes, Huey Lewis, and Johnny Colla)

"We Are the World" (Michael Jackson and Lionel Richie)

"We Built This City" (Bernie Taupin, Martin Page, Dennis Lambert, and Peter Wolf)

1986

"Amanda" (Tom Scholz)

"Glory of Love" (Theme from *The Karate Kid, Part II*) (Peter Cetera, David Foster, and Diane Nini)

"Greatest Love of All" (Michael Masser and Linda Creed)

"How Will I Know" (George Merrill, Shannon Rubicam, and Narada Michael Walden)

"Kiss" (Prince)

"Kyrie" (Richard Page, Steven George, and John Lang)

"On My Own" (Carole Bayer Sager)

"Papa Don't Preach" (Brian Elliott)

"Rock Me Amadeus" (Robert Bolland, Ferdinand Bolland, and Johnny Hoelfel)

"Stuck with You" (Christopher Hayes and Huey Lewis)

"That's What Friends Are For" (Burt Bacharach and Carole Bayer Sager)

"There'll Be Sad Songs (To Make You Cry)" (Wayne Brath Waite, Barry Eastmond, and Billy Ocean)

"True Colors" (Tom Kelly and Billy Steinberg)

"Walk like an Egyptian" (Liam Sternberg)

"When I Think of You" (James Harris III, Terry Lewis, and Janet Jackson)

1987

"Alone" (Billy Steinberg and Tom Kelly)
"At This Moment" (Billy Vera)
"Bad" (Michael Jackson)
"Didn't We Almost Have It All" (Michael Masser and Will Jennings)
"Faith" (George Michael)
"I Just Died in Your Arms" (Nick Van Eede)
"I Knew You Were Waiting for Me" (Simon Climie and Dennis Morgan)
"I Still Haven't Found What I'm Looking For" (U2)
"I Think We're Alone Now" (Ritchie Cordell)
"I Wanna Dance with Somebody" (George Merrill and Shannon Rubicam)
"La Bamba" (Ritchie Valens)
"Lean on Me" (Bill Withers)
"Livin' on a Prayer" (Jon Bon Jovi, Richie Sambora, and Desmond Child)
"Nothing's Gonna Stop Us Now" (Diane Warren and Albert Hammond)
"With or Without You" (U2)

1988

"Anything for You" (Gloria Estefan)
"Could've Been" (Lois Blaisch)
"Don't Worry, Be Happy" (Bobby McFerrin)
"Every Rose Has Its Thorn" (B. Dall, C. C. Deville, B. Michaels, and R. Rockett)
"Father Figure" (George Michael)
"Get Outa My Dreams, Get into My Car" (Robert John Lange and Billy Ocean)
"Groovy Kind of Love" (T. Wine and Carole Bayer Sager)
"Look Away" (Diane Warren)
"Man in the Mirror" (Siedah Garrett and Glen Ballard)
"Monkey" (George Michael)
"Never Gonna Give You Up" (Mike Stock, Matt Aitken, and Pete Waterman)
"One More Try" (George Michael)
"Roll With It" (Steve Winwood and Will Jennings)
"The Flame" (B. Mitchell and N. Graham)
"Where Do Broken Hearts Go" (Frank Wildhorn and Chuck Jackson)

1989

"Another Day in Paradise" (Phil Collins)
"Blame It on the Rain" (Diane Warren)
"Forever Your Girl" (O. Leiber)
"Girl I'm Gonna Miss You" (Farian, Kawohl, and Bischof-Fallenstein)
"Like a Prayer" (Madonna and Patrick Leonard)
"Lost in Your Eyes" (Debbie Gibson)
"Miss You Much" (James Harris III and Terry Lewis)

"Right Here Waiting" (Richard Marx)

"Straight Up" (E. Wolff)

"Toy Soldiers" (Martika and M. Jay)

"Two Hearts" (Phil Collins and Lamont Dozier)

"When I See You Smile" (Diane Warren)

1990

"Black Velvet" (C. Ward and D. Tyson)

"Escapade" (Janet Jackson, James Harris III, and Terry Lewis)

"How Am I Supposed to Live Without You" (Michael Bolton and D. James)

"It Must Have Been Love" (P. Gessle)

"Nothing Compares 2 U" (Prince)

"Opposites Attract" (O. Leiber)

"Release Me" (Wilson Phillips)

"She Ain't Worth It" (A. Armato, Ian Prince, and B. Brown)

"Vision of Love" (Mariah Carey and B. Margulies)

"Vogue" (Madonna and S. Pettibone)

1991

"(Everything I Do) I Do It for You" (from *Robin Hood*) (Bryan Adams, Robert John Lange, and Michael Kamen)

"All the Man That I Need" (Dean Pitchford and M. Gore)

"Baby Baby" (Amy Grant and Keith Thomas)

"Black or White" (Michael Jackson and B. Bottrell)

"Coming Out of the Dark" (Gloria Estefan, E. Estafan, Jr., and J. Secada)

"Emotions" (Mariah Carey, R. Clivillis, and D. Cole)

"Gonna Make You Sweat" (R. Clivillis and Frederick B. Williams)

"I've Been Thinking About You" (Londonbeat)

"Justify My Love" (Madonna, L. Kravitz, and Ingrid Chavez)

"Someday" (Mariah Carey and B. Margulies)

"The First Time" (B. Jackson and B. Simpson)

"You're in Love" (Wilson Phillips and Glen Ballard)

SOURCES

Agay, Denes, ed. *Best Loved Songs of the American People*. Garden City, N.Y.: Doubleday and Co., 1975.

ASCAP Biographical Dictionary. 4th ed. Prepared for the American Society of Composers, Authors, and Publishers by the Jacques Cattell Press. New York: R. R. Bowker, 1980.

Billboard Magazine. 1988–.

Bronson, Fred, comp. *The Billboard Book of Number One Hits*. New York: Billboard Publications, 1988.

Havlice, Patricia Pate. *Popular Song Index*. Metuchen, N.J.: Scarecrow Press, 1980.

Hoffman, Frank, comp. *The Cash Box Singles Charts, 1950–1981*. Metuchen, N.J.: Scarecrow Press, 1983.

Lax, Roger, and Frederick Smith, eds. *The Great Song Thesaurus*. 2nd ed. New York: Oxford University Press, 1989.

Shapiro, Nat, and Bruce Pollock, eds. *Popular Music, 1920–1979: A Revised Cumulation*. 3 vols. Detroit, Mich.: Gale Research Co., 1985.

Trager, James, ed. *The People's Chronology: A Year-by-Year Record of Human Events from Prehistory to the Present*. New York: Holt, Rinehart and Winston, 1979.

—Martha Forbush; L.D.R.

31

THE BIG BANDS

. . . ./.

JAZZ MUSIC BECAME POPULAR IN THE FIRST DECADE OF THE TWENTIETH CEN-tury; it became respectable in the 1920s. In the 1930s it developed into the form known as swing, and during the 1930s and 1940s it was enormously popular. By the late 1940s something known as bop or progressive jazz moved to the forefront, and jazz began to lose its popular audience. In the 1950s bop declined, and avant-garde jazz developed its own intense but special clientele. Popular music, meanwhile, split into rock and roll and folk blues. This is roughly where things stand today.

The big band era that people in their sixties and seventies remember with such fondness began in the early 1930s, and while it lasted the leading maestros and vocal and instrumental soloists were household names, particularly among the college-age set. Like all jazz its roots were African American, yet it was predominantly, though by no means exclusively, an affair of white musicians and white audiences. The nostalgia it evokes today is for the era of drugstore jukeboxes, the Lucky Strike Hit Parade, college proms, and Saturday night dancing at fashionable hotels and night-clubs.

Big band music was ballroom dance music. At the cutting edge were musicians such as Benny Goodman, Duke Ellington, Count Basie, Tommy Dorsey, Harry James, and Glenn Miller; at many a dance in many a city or town, or, during World War II, at the Officers' Club on many an Army base, Basie's "One O'Clock Jump" became the last number played, signifying that the party was over.

It was arranged music; the big bands did not often improvise, in the way that the jazz virtuosi of the 1920s and the post–World War II eras did. Many of the great jazz musicians, although some of them played in big bands and a few successfully fronted them, never fitted comfortably into it, and preferred instead to work in smaller combos. The greatest of them all, Louis Armstrong, appeared with big bands and had his own band at various times during the period, but his best music was played in smaller groups.

The vogue for the big bands faded after World War II, though many of the bands continued to play successfully during the 1950s and into the 1960s, and some few survived beyond that.

The listing that follows is of some of the major big bands, the decades when they were active, and representative tunes that are associated with them.

Ray Anthony. 1940s–70s; "The Man With the Horn."

Louis Armstrong. 1920s–60s; "When It's Sleepy Time Down South," "Strutting With Some Barbeque," "Old Rocking Chair's Got Me," "The Bucket's Got a Hole in It," "Blueberry Hill," "Mac the Knife," "Hello Dolly."

Charlie Barnet. 1930s–50s; "Cherokee," "Red Skin Rumba."

Blue Barron. 1930s–50s; "Sometimes I'm Happy."

Count Basie. 1930s–70s; "One O'Clock Jump."

Bunny Berigan. 1930s–40s; "I Can't Get Started."

Ben Bernie. 1920s–30s; "It's a Lonesome Old Town," "Au Revoir."

Les Brown. 1930s–80s; "Leap Frog," "Sentimental Journey," "I've Got My Love to Keep Me Warm."

Henry Busse. 1930s–50s; "Hot Lips," "When Day Is Done."

Cab Calloway. 1930s–60s; "Minnie the Moocher."

Frankie Carle. 1940s–70s; "Sunrise Serenade."

Casa Loma Orchestra. See **Glen Gray**.

Carman Cavallaro. 1930s–50s; "My Sentimental Heart."

Larry Clinton. 1930s–50s; "Deep Purple," "The Dipsy Doodle."

Bob Crosby. 1930s–70s; "South Rampart Street Parade," "Big Noise From Winnetka," "Summertime."

Xavier Cugat. 1940s–60s; "My Shawl."

Dorsey Brothers. 1930s; "Stop, Look and Listen."

Jimmy Dorsey. 1930s–50s; "I Get Along Without You Very Well," "Marie Elena," "Contrasts."

Tommy Dorsey. 1930s–50s; "Marie," "Song of India," "I'll Never Smile Again," "I'm Getting Sentimental Over You."

Eddy Duchin. 1930s–40s; "My Twilight Dream."

Billy Eckstine. 1940s; "Jelly, Jelly."

Duke Ellington. 1920s–70s; "Perdido," "Take the A Train," "Mood Indigo," "In a Sentimental Mood," "I Got It Bad and That Ain't Good."

Shep Fields. 1930s–70s; "Rippling Rhythm."

Ted Fio Rito. 1920s–40s; "Toot, Toot, Toot, Tootsie."

Jan Garber. 1920s–60s; "My Dear."

Dizzy Gillespie. 1940s–80s; "Woodyn You."

Benny Goodman. 1930s–60s; "King Porter Stomp," "After You're Gone," "Body and Soul," "Sing Sing Sing," "Heigh Ho, Nobody Home," "Let's Dance," "Stompin' at the Savoy."

Glen Gray (the Casa Loma Orchestra). 1920s–50s; "Casa Loma Stomp," "It's the Talk of the Town," "Smoke Rings."

Mal Hallett. 1920s–40s; "Boston Tea Party."

Lionel Hampton. 1940s–80s; "Flying Home."

Phil Harris. 1920s–30s; "That's What I Like About the South," "Rose Room."

Erskine Hawkins. 1930s–60s; "Tuxedo Junction."

Horace Heidt. 1930s–40s; "I'll Love You in My Dreams."

Fletcher Henderson. 1920s–40s; "Christopher Columbus."

Woody Herman. 1930s–80s; "Blue Prelude," "Blue Flame," "Woodchopper's Ball," "Blues in the Night," "Caldonia."

Earl (Fatha) Hines. 1930s–40s; "Rosetta," "Boogie-Woogie on St. Louis Blues," "Deep Forest."

Harry James. 1930s–70s; "Ciribiribin," "All or Nothing at All," "Flight of the Bumble Bee," "You Made Me Love You," "I'll Get By," "I Don't Want to Walk Without You," "I've Heard That Song Before."

Isham Jones. 1920s–40s; "I'll See You in My Dreams," "It Had to Be You," "You're Just a Dream Come True."

Spike Jones. 1940s–60s; "Temptation," "Der Fuehrer's Face," "You Always Hurt the One You Love."

Sammy Kaye. 1930s–60s; "Daddy," "Harbor Lights," "It Isn't Fair," "Kaye's Melody."

Hal Kemp. 1930s; "You're the Top," "It's Easy to Remember," "Got a Date With an Angel."

Stan Kenton. 1940s–70s; "Artistry in Rhythm," "Eager Beaver," "And Her Tears Flowed Like Wine."

Wayne King. 1920s–60s; "The Waltz You Saved for Me."

Gene Krupa. 1930s–60s; "Drum Boogie," "Let Me Off Uptown," "Stardust."

Kay Kyser. 1930s–50s; "Thinking of You," "Three Little Fishes," "Praise the Lord and Pass the Ammunition."

Enoch Light. 1930s–70s; "You're the Only Star."

Guy Lombardo. 1930s–70s; "Seems like Old Times," "September in the Rain," "Auld Lang Syne."

Johnny Long. 1930s–60s; "A Shanty in Old Shanty Town," "The White Star of Sigma Nu."

Jimmy Lunceford. 1920s–40s; "My Blue Heaven," "Organ Grinder's Swing," "Uptown Blues."

Clyde McCoy. 1930s–60s; "Sugar Blues."

Ray McKinley. 1940s–50s; "Hard-Hearted Hannah," "You've Come a Long Way From St. Louis," "Howdy, Friends."

McKinney's Cotton Pickers. 1920s–30s; "If I Could Be With You," "Baby, Won't You Please Come Home."

Freddy Martin. 1930s–70s; "The Hut-Sut Song," "Why Don't We Do This More Often," "Tonight We Love."

Frankie Masters. 1930s–50s; "Scatterbrain."

Glenn Miller. 1930s–40s; "Sunrise Serenade," "Moonlight Serenade," "Little Brown Jug," "In the Mood," "Chattanooga Choo Choo," "Serenade in Blue."

Vaughn Monroe. 1940s–50s; "Racing with the Moon."

Russ Morgan. 1930s–60s; "So Tired," "Somebody Else Is Taking My Place," "Does Your Heart Beat for Me."

Ozzie Nelson. 1930s–50s; "Loyal Sons of Rutgers."

Red Nichols. 1920s–40s; "Wail of the Winds."

Ray Noble. 1930s–40s; "The Very Thought of You," "The Touch of Your Lips," "Goodnight, Sweetheart."

Tony Pastor. 1930s–50s; "Let's Do It," "Blossoms," "I'm Confessin'."

Louis Prima. 1930s–50s; "Oh Ma-ma, The Butcher Boy for Me," "Way Down Yonder in New Orleans."

Alvino Rey. 1930s–50s; "Blue Rey," "Nighty Night."

Jan Savitt. 1930s–40s; "It's a Wonderful World," "Quaker City Jazz."

Artie Shaw. 1930s–50s; "Frenesi," "Indian Love Call," "Nightmare," "Rosalie," "Nightmare," "What Is This Thing Called Love."

Phil Spitalny. 1930s–40s; "My Isle of Golden Dreams."

Charlie Spivak. 1940s–50s; "Stardreams," "Dream."

Jack Teagarden. 1930s–40s; "The Sheik of Araby," "Basin Street Blues," "Red Wing," "I Gotta Right to Sing the Blues."

Claude Thornhill. 1940s–50s; "Where or When," "There's a Small Hotel," "Let's Call It a Day," "Snowfall."

Tommy Tucker. 1930s–50s; "I Don't Want to Set the World on Fire," "I Love You (Oh, How I Love You)."

Fats Waller. 1920s–30s; "Honeysuckle Rose," "Ain't Misbehavin'."

Fred Waring. 1920s–60s; "Sleep."

Chick Webb. 1930s–40s; "A Tisket, a Tasket," "Let's Get Together."

Ted Weems. 1930s–60s; "Nola," "Stardust," "Heartaches," "Out of the Night."

Lawrence Welk. 1920s–70s; "Bubbles in the Wine."

Paul Whiteman. 1910s–40s; "Rhapsody in Blue," "I've Found a New Baby."

SOURCES

Kinkle, Roger D., ed. *The Complete Encyclopedia of Popular Music and Jazz.* 4 vols. New Rochelle, N.Y.: Arlington House, 1974.

Simon, George T. *The Big Bands.* New York: Schirmer Books, 1981.

Simon, George T., and Friends. *The Best of the Music Makers.* Garden City, N.Y.: Doubleday and Co., 1979.

Shapiro, Nat, and Bruce Pollock, eds. *Popular Music, 1920–1979: A Revised Cumulation.* 3 vols. Detroit, Mich.: Gale Research Co., 1985.

—L.D.R.

32

ROCK MUSIC: THE MAJOR PERFORMERS

· · · · ·

THE WIDE RANGE OF MUSICAL STYLES GATHERED CURRENTLY UNDER THE heading of "rock" began to appear in something recognizably akin to modern forms in the early 1950s, with the emergence of a kind of music called rhythm and blues. At first exclusively African American (trade publications and record catalogs cited it as "race music"), rhythm and blues had evolved from many sources, including gospel and church music, country blues, jazz, and black pop.

Its early artists included individuals such as Johnny Ace, Big Joe Turner, Willie Mae ("Big Mama") Thornton, and Ruth Brown, as well as groups like the Dominoes, the Clovers, the Drifters, and the Five Royales. By the mid–1950s white musicians—chief among them Bill Haley, the Crew Cuts, and, especially, Elvis Presley—began a practice of copying and adapting themes and conventions of black music that not only broadened the audience base for rhythm and blues but also began forging that combination of black and white styles soon and permanently to be known as rock and roll.

After rhythm and blues begat rock and roll, the tribe increased exponentially, eventually dividing into overlapping subgenres with catchy labels such as doo-wop, rockabilly, soul, surfing music, psychedelic rock, and heavy metal. Along came Memphis, Manhattan, and Motown sounds, along with British beat, punk rock, art rock, jazz rock, new wave, reggae, southern rock, and swamp rock. And, as the slogan insists, the beat goes on.

The list that follows is of some of the major figures in rock history, the decades when they were most active (some performers, like Bo Diddley and Nappy Brown, are still touring after forty years), and representative tunes that are associated with them.

Johnny Ace. 1950s; "Pledging My Love," "My Song," "The Clock."

Faye Adams. 1950s; "Shake a Hand."

Allman Brothers Band. 1970s; "Ramblin' Man."

Paul Anka. 1950s; "Diana," Lonely Boy," "Put Your Head on My Shoulder."

Frankie Avalon. 1950s; "Venus," "Bobby Sox to Stockings," "Why."

LaVern Baker. 1950s; "Tweedle Dee," "Jim Dandy."

The Band. 1960s–80s; Albums: *Cahoots, The Last Waltz, Northern Lights, Southern Cross.*

The Beach Boys. 1960s–80s; "Surfin'," "I Get Around," "Help Me Rhonda," "Do You Wanna Dance?"

The Beatles. 1960s–70s; "I Want to Hold Your Hand," "Ticket to Ride," "Strawberry Fields Forever," "Sgt. Pepper's Lonely Hearts Club Band."

Chuck Berry. 1950s–70s; "Maybelline," "Brown-Eyed Handsome Man," "Roll Over Beethoven," "Johnny B. Goode."

Richard Berry. 1950s; "Louie, Louie" [possibly the most popular rock and roll song of all, it was subsequently recorded by, among others, the Kingsmen, Rockin' Robin Roberts, the Sonics, the Sandpipers, the Last, Black Flag, Wilbert Harrison, Les Danz and the Orchestra, the Impossibles, and the Rice University Marching Owl Band].

Blondie. 1970s; "The Tide Is High," "Rip Her to Shreds."

The Bobbettes. 1950s; "Mr. Lee."

Bo Diddley (E. McDaniels). 1950s–90s; "Bo Diddley," "Oh Yeah," "Who Do You Love?"

Booker T. and the MGs. 1960s; "Green Onions," "Time Is Tight."

Pat Boone. 1950s–60s; "I Almost Lost My Mind," "Friendly Persuasion," "Love Letters in the Sand."

Earl Bostic. 1950s; "Mambolina," "Flamingo."

David Bowie. 1970s–80s; "Changes," "Young Americans," "Golden Years."

James Brown. 1950s–80s; "Please, Please, Please," "Papa's Got a Brand New Bag," "It's Too Funky in Here."

Nappy Brown. 1950s–90s; "Don't Be Angry."

Ruth Brown. 1950s; "Mama, He Treats Your Daughter Mean," "So Long," "5–10–15 Hours."

Jackson Browne. 1970s–80s; "For Everyman," "The Pretender," "Running on Empty."

The Byrds. 1960s; "Mr. Tambourine Man," "You Ain't Going Nowhere."

The Cadets. 1950s; "Stranded in the Jungle."

Ray Charles. 1950s–80s; "I've Got a Woman," "What'd I Say?," "Don't Change on Me."

Chicago. 1970s–80s; "Does Anybody Really Know What Time It Is?"

The Chords. 1950s; "Sh-Boom" [the first rhythm and blues record ever to make the national pop-song chart of sales (1954); Carl Belz (see Sources) calls this "the first rock record"].

Eric Clapton. 1970s–90s; "I Shot the Sheriff," "Lay Down Sally."

The Clash. 1970s–80s; "White Riot," "Complete Control."

The Clovers. 1950s; "Good Lovin'," "One Mint Julep," "Your Cash Ain't Nothin' But Trash," "Love Potion Number 9."

The Coasters. 1950s; "Along Came Jones," "Poison Ivy," "Searching," "Yackety-Yack."

Sam Cooke. 1950s–60s; "You Send Me," "Chain Gang," "Bring It on Home to Me."

Country Joe and the Fish. 1960s; Albums: *Together, Here We Go Again.*

Cream. 1960s; Albums: *Fresh Cream, Wheels of Fire.*

Credence Clearwater Revival. 1960s–70s; "Proud Mary," "Green River," "Have You Ever Seen the Rain?"

The Crew Cuts. 1950s; "Sh-Boom," "Don't Be Angry," "Story Untold."

Crosby, Stills, and Nash. 1970s, 1990s; "Suite: Judy Blue Eyes."

Dell-Vikings. 1950s; "Come Go With Me," "Whispering Bells."

Dion and the Belmonts. 1950s–60s; "A Teenager in Love," "Runaround Sue."

Dire Straits. 1980s–90s; "Sultans of Swing," "Telegraph Road."

Fats Domino. 1950s–60s; "Blueberry Hill," "The Fat Man," "Goin' to the River," "Blue Monday," "Walkin' to New Orleans."

The Dominoes. 1950s; "Sixty-Minute Man," "Have Mercy Baby."

The Doors. 1960s–70s; "Light My Fire," "Riders on the Storm."

The Drifters. 1950s–60s; "Money Honey," "Such a Night," "Honey Love."

Bob Dylan. 1960s–90s; "Like a Rolling Stone," "Rainy Day Women," "Tangled Up in Blue."

The Eagles. 1970s, 1990s; "Desperado," "One of These Nights," "Hotel California."

Earth, Wind, and Fire. 1970s–80s; "Shining Star," "Got to Get You Into My Mind."

The Everly Brothers (Phil and Don). 1950s–60s; "Bye-Bye Love," "Cathy's Clown," "Bird Dog."

Fleetwood Mac. 1960s–90s; "Don't Stop," "Go Your Own Way," "Rhiannon."

The Fleetwoods. 1950s; "Mr. Blue," "Come Softly to Me."

Connie Francis. 1950s–60s; "Who's Sorry Now?," "Lipstick on Your Collar," "Everybody's Somebody's Fool."

Aretha Franklin. 1960s–80s; "Chain of Fools," "I Say a Little Prayer."

Lowell Fulson. 1950s; "Blue Shadows," "Three O'Clock Blues," "Took a Long Time."

Funkadelic. 1960s–80s; "I'll Bet You," "You and Your Folks, Me and My Folks."

The Grateful Dead. 1960s–90s; Albums: *Anthem of the Sun, Aoxomoxoa, American Beauty.*

Bill Haley and His Comets. 1950s; "Crazy Man Crazy," "Rock Around the Clock," "Dim, Dim the Lights."

Wilbert Harrison. 1950s–70s; "Don't Drop It," "Kansas City," "Let's Work Together."

Jimi Hendrix. 1960s; Albums: *Are You Experienced?, Rainbow Bridge.*

Herman's Hermits. 1960s; "Mrs. Brown, You've Got a Lovely Daughter," "I'm Henry the Eighth I Am."

John Hiatt. 1980s–90s; "Fallen Angel," "Memphis in the Meantime," "Thank You Girl."

Buddy Holly and the Crickets. 1950s; "That'll Be the Day," "Peggy Sue," "Maybe Baby."

Ivory Joe Hunter. 1950s; "I Almost Lost My Mind."

Michael Jackson. 1970s–90s; "Blame It on the Boogie," "Shake Your Body (Down to the Ground)," "Billie Jean," "Beat It."

Jefferson Airplane. 1960s–70s; Albums: *Bless Its Pointed Little Head, Early Flight.*

Billy Joel. 1970s–90s; "Piano Man," "Just the Way You Are," "New York State of Mind."

Elton John. 1970s–90s; "Honky Cat," "Daniel," "Bennie and the Jets."

Janis Joplin. 1960s; "Bobby McGee."

B. B. King. 1950s–70s; "You Know I Love You," "Rock Me Baby," "The Thrill Is Gone."

Kool and the Gang. 1970s–80s; "Funky Stuff," "Slick Superchick."

Cyndi Lauper. 1980s–90s; "Time After Time," "She Bop."

Led Zeppelin. 1970s–80s; "Stairway to Heaven," "Whole Lotta Love."

Brenda Lee. 1960s; "Break It to Me Gently," "Losing You."

Jerry Lee Lewis. 1950s–70s; "Whole Lot of Shakin' Goin On," "Great Balls of Fire," "What Made Milwaukee Famous Has Made a Fool Out of Me."

Little Richard. 1950s–70s; "Tutti-Frutti," "Long Tall Sally," "Slippin' and Slidin'," "Good Golly Miss Molly."

Little Walter. 1950s; "My Babe," "Juke."

Lovin' Spoonful. 1960s; "You Didn't Have to Be So Nice," "Summer in the City," "Nashville Cats."

Madonna. 1980s–90s; "Burning Up," "Like a Virgin," "Material Girl."

The Mamas and the Papas. 1960s; "California Dreamin'," "Monday, Monday," "Words of Love."

Bob Marley and the Wailers. 1970s; "Concrete Jungle," "Natty Dread."

Stick McGhee. 1950s; "Wine Spo-de-o-dee."

Marvin and Johnny. 1950s; "Cherry Pie," "Tic Toc."

Mickey and Sylvia. 1950s; "Love Is Strange."

The Midnighters. 1950s; "Work With Me Annie," "Annie Had a Baby," "Annie's Aunt Fannie," "Sexy Ways."

The Moody Blues. 1960s–90s; "Nights in White Satin."

Van Morrison. 1960s–80s; "Brown Eyed Girl," "Tupelo Honey," "It Fills You Up."

Randy Newman. 1960s–80s; "Short People," "Rednecks," "Political Science."

Roy Orbison. 1950s–70s; "Ooby Dooby," "Crying," "Oh, Pretty Woman."

The Orioles. 1950s; "Crying in the Chapel."

The Penguins. 1950s; "Earth Angel."

Wilson Pickett. 1960s; "Land of 1000 Dances," "Mustang Sally," "In the Midnight Hour."

Pink Floyd. 1960s–90s; Albums: *The Wall, Dark Side of the Moon.*

Elvis Presley. 1950s–70s; "Hound Dog," "Blue Suede Shoes," "Love Me Tender," "Return to Sender," "Let Me Be Your Teddy Bear."

Lloyd Price. 1950s; "Lawdy Miss Clawdy," "Stagger Lee," "Personality."

Prince. 1970s–90s; "Ronnie Talk to Russia," "Little Red Corvette," "Purple Rain."

Otis Redding. 1960s; "Try a Little Tenderness," "A Lover's Question," "(Sittin' on) The Dock of the Bay."

Smokey Robinson and the Miracles. 1960s; "More Love," "The Love I Saw in You Was Just a Mirage," "I Second That Emotion."

The Rolling Stones. 1960s–90s; "Heart of Stone," "(I Can't Get No) Satisfaction," "Let's Spend the Night Together," "Jumping Jack Flash," "Beast of Burden."

The Ronnettes. 1960s; "Be My Baby," "Baby I Love You," "Walkin' in the Rain."

Linda Ronstadt. 1970s–90s; "Long Long Time," "You're No Good."

Santana. 1970s; "Black Magic Woman."

Neil Sedaka. 1950s–60s; "Calendar Girl," "Breaking Up Is Hard to Do."

The Sex Pistols. 1970s–80s; "God Save the Queen," "Pretty Vacant."

The Shirelles. 1960s; "Dedicated to the One I Love," "Mama Said."

Shirley and Lee. 1950s–60s; "Let the Good Times Roll," "Feel So Good," "I'm Gone."

Simon and Garfunkel. 1960s–70s; "Parsley, Sage, Rosemary, and Thyme," "Bridge Over Troubled Water."

Lynyrd Skynyrd. 1970s; "Saturday Night Special," "Sweet Home Alabama," "Tuesday's Gone."

Percy Sledge. 1960s; "When a Man Loves a Woman," "Take Time to Know Her."

Sly and the Family Stone. 1960s–70s; "Dance to the Music," "Everyday People," "I Get High on You."

Patti Smith. 1970s–80s; "Piss Factory," "Radio Ethiopia (live)."

Sonny and Cher. 1960s; "I Got You, Babe," "Baby Don't Go," "Just You."

The Spaniels. 1950s; "Goodnight, Sweetheart, Goodnight."

Bruce Springsteen. 1970s–90s; "Born to Run," "Rosalita (Come Out Tonight)," "Born in the USA."

Steely Dan. 1970s; "Rikki Don't Lose That Number," "Black Friday," "Josie."

Rod Stewart. 1970s–90s; "Maggie May," "You Wear It Well," "Tonight's the Night."

The Supremes. 1960s; "Stop! In the Name of Love," "Forever Came Today," "Someday We'll Be Together."

James Taylor. 1970s–80s; "Handy Man," "Fire and Rain," "You've Got a Friend," "Rainy Day Man."

The Temptations. 1960s–70s; "The Way You Do the Things You Do," "Since I Lost My Baby," "Superstar."

Willie Mae ("Big Mama") Thornton. 1950s; "Hound Dog," "I Smell a Rat."

Joe Turner. 1950s; "Shake, Rattle, and Roll," "Money, Marbles, and Chalk."

Tina Turner. 1950s–90s; "It's Only Love," "What's Love Got to Do With It?"

Richie Valens. 1950s; "La Bamba," "Ooh My Head!," "Donna."

Bobby Vee. 1960s; "Devil or Angel," "Take Good Care of My Baby," "The Night Has a Thousand Eyes."

Velvet Underground. 1960s–70s; "European Son," "I Heard Her Call My Name."

The Village People. 1970s–80s; "Macho Man," "Y.M.C.A."

Gene Vincent. 1950s; "Be-Bop-A-Lula," "Dance to the Bop."

Tom Waits. 1970s–80s; "Sixteen Shells From a 30.06," "Big Black Maria," "Gun Street Girl."

The Who. 1960s–80s; "Happy Jack," "Pinball Wizard," "Summertime Blues," "Who Are You."

Maurice Williams and the Zodiacs. 1960s; "Stay."

Neil Young. 1970s–80s; "Only Love Can Break Your Heart," "Heart of Gold."

Frank Zappa. 1960s–80s; "Don't Eat the Yellow Snow," "Dancin' Fool," "Valley Girl."

ZZ Top. 1970s–80s; "Fandango."

SOURCES

Belz, Carl. *The Story of Rock.* 2nd ed. New York: Oxford University Press, 1972.

Chapple, Steve, and Reebee Garofalo. *Rock 'n' Roll Is Here to Pay.* Chicago: Nelson-Hall, 1977.

Curtis, Jim. *Rock Eras.* Bowling Green, Ohio: Bowling Green State University Popular Press, 1987.

Miller, Jim, ed. *The Rolling Stone Illustrated History of Rock and Roll.* New York: Random House, 1980.

Ward, Ed, Geoffrey Stokes, and Ken Turner. *Rock of Ages.* New York: Rolling Stone Press, 1986.

—J.L.M.

VI

LITERATURE AND LANGUAGE

33

SOME FAMOUS NOVELS

. . . . .

Nobody has ever succeeded in defining exactly what a novel is, but that it has become the preeminent and most popular of today's literary forms, there can be little argument. Although Thomas Jefferson urged young persons not to waste their time reading novels, he doubtless had in mind popular sentimental romances, not what Defoe, Sterne, Smollett, and Fielding had written. In any event, his advice was not commonly followed, either at the time or later. By the mid-nineteenth century the novel was reaching enormous audiences, and if there has been any falling off in popularity in recent years, as has been claimed, neither novelists nor readers nor publishers have noticed it.

The novel does have one omnipresent characteristic: It is always dying. The death of the novel has been regularly proclaimed by critics. If the principle of Gresham's Law—that bad money drives out good—were applied to the novel, it would indeed have expired some time back. But it doesn't seem to work that way; Maria Cummins didn't drive out Nathaniel Hawthorne, Henry James survived Gene Stratton Porter, and Eudora Welty can somehow coexist with Judith Krantz.

About thirty years ago the late Truman Capote, ever expert at self-promotion, announced that the "non-fiction novel," one of which he had supposedly just written, had replaced the (fictional) novel. Academics being ever on the lookout for new subject matter, doctoral dissertations were written and even published on the demise of the novel and the rise of the Capote-type model. Now as the turn of the century nears, the latter is, as a supposedly recognizable genre distinct from good narrative prose in general, as dead as the masque, the medieval morality play, and the rondel, *i.e.*, very dead indeed. The novel, by contrast, is as thriving a concern as ever.

It was also fashionable several decades ago to write off storytelling, in favor of the "anti-novel." Unfortunately for the practitioners of same, nobody much wanted to read anti-novels. Nowadays even the French have largely given them up.

The compilation that follows has been assembled on the assumption that the novel remains a valid literary entity. The author, date of publication, setting, and principal characters of a number of novels are given in that order.

Absalom, Absalom!, by William Faulkner (1936). Settings: nineteenth- and twentieth-century Yoknapatawpha (Lafayette) County, Miss., and Cambridge, Mass. Principal characters: Quentin Compson, Shreve McCannon, Rosa Coldfield, Thomas Sutpen, Henry Sutpen, Judith Sutpen, and Charles Bon.

Adventures of Augie March, The, by Saul Bellow (1953). Settings: Chicago, Canada, Mexico. Principal characters: Augie March, Simon March, Charlotte Magnus, Georgie March, William Einhorn, Mrs. Renling, Thea Fenchel, and Stella Chesney.

Age of Innocence, The, by Edith Wharton (1920). Settings: New York City, Newport, R.I., Washington, D.C., and Paris. Principal characters: Newland Archer, Ellen Olenska, May Welland, Aunt Medora.

Alexandria Quartet, The, by Lawrence Durrell (1957–60: *Justine* [1957]; *Balthazar* [1958]; *Mountolive* [1958]; and *Clea* [1961]). Setting: Alexandria, Egypt. Principal characters: L. G. Darley, Melissa, Mountolive, Pursewarden, Clea, Justine, and Nessim.

Alice's Adventures in Wonderland (first published as *Alice's Adventures Under Ground*), by Lewis Carroll (pseud. of Charles Lutwidge Dodgson) (1865). Setting: Alice's dreamworld. Principal characters: Alice, the White Rabbit, the Mad Hatter, the March Hare, the Duchess, the King and Queen of Hearts, the Mock Turtle, and the Cheshire Cat.

All Quiet on the Western Front (German title: *Im Westen nichts Neues*), by Erich Maria Remarque (1929). Settings: Germany and the Western Front in World War I. Principal characters: Paul Bäumer, Albert Kropp, Müller, Tjaden, Haie Westhus, and Stanislaus Katczinsky (Kat).

All the King's Men, by Robert Penn Warren (1946). Setting: identifiably the state of Louisiana. Principal characters: Jack Burden, Willie Stark, Tiny Duffy, Sadie Burke, Anne Stanton, Adam Stanton, and Judge Irwin.

Ambassadors, The, by Henry James (1903; first published serially in the *North American Review* [1903]). Settings: Paris, England, and Woollett, Mass. Principal characters: Lambert Strether, Chad Newsome, Maria Gostrey, Madame de Vionnet, Little Bilham, and Sarah and Jim Pocock.

American Tragedy, An, by Theodore Dreiser (1925). Settings: Kansas City, Chicago, New York City, and upstate New York. Principal characters: Clyde Griffiths, Samuel Griffiths, Sondra Finchley, and Roberta Alden.

Animal Farm, by George Orwell (pseud. of Eric Arthur Blair) (1945). Setting: Mr. Jones's farm in England. Principal characters: Napoleon, Snowball, Boxer, Squealer, and Mr. Jones.

Anna Karenina, by Lev Nikolayevich Tolstoy (1873–78). Settings: Moscow, St. Petersburg, and Levin's country estate. Principal characters: Prince Stephen Arkedyevich (Stiva) Oblonsky, Princess Darya Alexandrovna (Dolly) Oblonskaya, Anna Arkadyevna Karenina, Alexis Alexandrovich Karenin, Constantine Dmitrich (Kostya) Levin, Sergius Ivanich (Sergey) Koznyshev, Prince Alexander Shcherbatsky, Princess Shcherbatskaya, Prince Nicholas Shcherbatsky, Princess Nataly Alexandrovna Lvova, Prince (Arseny) Lvov, Nicholas Levin, Count Alex Kirilich Vronsky, Countess Nordston, Countess Vronskaya, Sergey Alexeyich (Serezha, Kutik) Karenin, Mary Nikolaevna (Masha), Countess Lydia Ivanovna, Princess Elizabeth Fedorovna Tverskaya (Betsy), Lieutenant Petrítsky, Baroness Shilton, Prince Tverskoy, Captain Prince Yashvin, Petrov, Anna Pavlovna Petrova, General Prince Serpuknovskoy, and Nicholas Ivanich Sviyazhsky.

As I Lay Dying, by William Faulkner (1930). Setting: Yoknapatawpha (Lafayette) County, Miss. Principal characters: Addie Bundren, Anse Bundren, Cash, Darl, Jewel, Dewey Dell, Vardaman, Reverend Whitfield, and Vernon and Cora Tull.

At Swim-Two-Birds, by Flann O'Brien (pseud. of Brian O'Nolan) (1939). Setting: Dublin. Principal characters: an unnamed male student, his uncle, Dermot Trellis, the Pooka Fergus MacPhellimey, the Good Fairy, John Furriskey, Finn MacCool, King Sweeny, and Orlick.

Awakening, The, by Kate Chopin (1899). Settings: New Orleans and Grand Isle, La. Principal characters: Edna Pontellier, Léonce Pontellier, Robert Lebrun, Alcée Arobin, and Adèle Ratignolle.

Barchester Towers, by Anthony Trollope (1857). Setting: the fictional city of Barchester, England. Principal characters: Dr. Proudie, Mrs. Proudie, Obadiah Slope, Mr. Quiverful, Archdeacon Grantly, Eleanor Bold, Mr. Harding, Dr. Vesey Stanhope, Signora Vesey-Neroni, and Francis Arabin.

Beloved, by Toni Morrison (1987). Settings: Cincinnati, Ohio, and Sweet Home Plantation, Ky. Principal characters: Sethe, Baby Suggs, Denver, Paul D, and Beloved.

Betrothed, The (Italian title: *I promessi sposi*), by Alessandro Manzoni (1825–27; rev., 1840–42). Setting: Milan. Principal characters: Lorenzo, Lucia, Don Rodrigo, the Un-Named, Don Abbondio, and Fra Christoforo.

Billy Budd, Foretopman (An Inside Narrative), by Herman Melville (1924; begun in 1886 and left unfinished). Setting: HMS *Bellipotent*. Principal characters: Billy Budd, Captain Vere, and John Claggart.

Bleak House, by Charles Dickens (1853; first published in monthly parts from March, 1852, to September, 1853). Setting: England, primarily London at the High Court of Chancery. Principal characters: Esther Summerson, Ada Clare, Richard Carstone, John Jarndyce, Sir Leicester Dedlock, Lady Dedlock, Tulkinghorn, Mademoiselle Hortense, Inspector Bucket, Allan Woodcourt, Krook, and Jo.

Blithedale Romance, The, by Nathaniel Hawthorne (1852). Settings: Blithedale Farm and Boston, Mass. Principal characters: Miles Coverdale, Hollingsworth, Zenobia Fauntleroy, Mr. Moodie, Priscilla Moodie, and Mr. Westervelt.

Brave New World, by Aldous Huxley (1932). Setting: England [?] in the year 632 After Ford (*i.e.,* after the twenty-sixth century). Principal characters: Bernard Marx, the Savage, Helmholtz Watson, and World Controller Mustapha Mond.

Bridge of San Luis Rey, The, by Thornton Wilder (1927). Setting: Peru, 1714. Principal characters: Brother Juniper, Marquesa de Montemayor, Pepita, Estaban, Uncle Pio, and Jaimé.

***Brothers Karamazov, The (Russian title:* Brat'ya Karamazovy),** by Fyodor Dostoyevsky (1879–80). Setting: Russia. Principal characters: Fyodor Pavlovich Karamazov, Dmitri Karamazov, Ivan Karamazov, Alyosha Karamazov, Smerdyakov, Grushenka, Katerina Ivanovna, Zosima, Rakitin, and Kolya Krassotkin.

Buddenbrooks, by Thomas Mann (1901). Setting: northern Germany. Principal characters: Johann Buddenbrook, Sr., Johann Buddenbrook, Jr., Toni, Christian, Thomas, and Hanno.

Burger's Daughter, by Nadine Gordimer (1979). Settings: South Africa, the Côte d'Azur, and London. Principal characters: Rosemarie (Rosa) Burger, Lionel Burger, Cathy Burger, Katya Bagnelli, Baasie, Conrad, and Bernard Chambalier.

***Caleb Williams, The Adventures of, or* Things As They Are,** by William Godwin (1794). Setting: England. Principal characters: Caleb Williams and Squire Falkland.

Call It Sleep, by Henry Roth (1934). Setting: Lower East Side (New York City). Principal characters: David Schearl, Albert Schearl, Genya Schearl, and Bertha.

Call of the Wild, The, by Jack London (1903). Settings: California and Alaska. Principal characters: Buck, a spitz (Buck's enemy), and John Thornton.

Cancer Ward, The (Russian title: *Rakovy korpus*), by Aleksandr Solzhenitsyn (1968). Setting: a hospital cancer ward in Soviet Asia. Principal characters: Oleg Filimonovich Kostoglotov, Pavel Nikolayevich Rusanov, Dr. Vera Kornilyevna Gangart, Dr. Lyudmila Afanasyevna Dontsova, Zoya, Dyomka, Sharaf Sibgatov, Alexey Fillipovich Shulubin, Vadim Zatsyrko, Yefrem Podduyev, Dr. Dormidont Tikhonovich Oreshchenkov, Avieta Pavlovna Rusanova, Lev Leonidovich, Asya, Prokofy Semyonovich, Elizaveta Anatolyevna, Rodichev, Kapitolina Matveyevna Rusanova, Yuri Rusanov, Maxim Petrovich Chaly, Nikolay Ivanovich Kadmin, Yelena Alexandrovna Kadmina, Auntie Styofa, Lavrenty Pavlovich Rusanov, and Maika Rusanova.

Candide, by Voltaire (pseud. of François-Marie Arouet) (1759). Settings: Westphalia, Lisbon, South America, France, Portsmouth, Venice, and Constantinople. Principal characters: Candide, Pangloss, and Cunégonde.

Castle, The (German title: *Das Schloss)*, by Franz Kafka (1926). Setting: village below the Castle of Count Westwest. Principal character: K.

Castle of Otranto, The: A Gothic Story, by Horace Walpole (1764). Setting: a castle in Italy. Principal characters: Manfred, Isabella, Theodore, and Matilda.

Castle Rackrent, by Maria Edgeworth (1801). Setting: an estate in Ireland. Principal characters: Thady Quirk, Sir Patrick Rackrent, Sir Murtagh Rackrent, Sir Kit Rackrent, his Jewish wife, Sir Condy Rackrent, Isabella Moneygawl, Judy Quirk, and Jason Quirk.

Catcher in the Rye, The, by J(erome) D(avid) Salinger (1951). Settings: prep school in Pa., and New York City. Principal characters: Holden Caulfield, Sally Hayes, Phoebe Caulfield, and Mr. Antolini.

Catch–22, by Joseph Heller (1961). Setting: U.S. Army Air Force base hospital on the fictional Italian island of Pianosa during World War II. Principal characters: Captain John Yossarian, Doc Daneeka, Milo Minderbinder, Major Major Major, Colonel Cathcart, Major de Coverly, Captain Black, Chief White Halfoat, Captain R. O. Shipman, Nurse Sue Ann Duckett, Havermeyer, Kid Sampson, McWatt, Aardvaark (Aarfy), Hungry Joe, Snowden, Clevinger, Orr, Dobbs, Nately, Nately's whore, General Dreedle, General Peckem, and Ex-P.F.C. Wintergreen.

Charterhouse of Parma, The (French title: *La Chartreuse de Parme)*, by Stendhal (pseud. of Henri Beyle) (1839). Settings: Battle of Waterloo, and Parma, Italy. Principal characters: Fabrizio del Dongo, Clelia Conti, Gina Pietranera, Count Mosca, Father Blanès, Ludovico, Marietta Valsera, Fausta, Count Conti, Rassi, and Giletti.

Clarissa, or, The History of a Young Lady, by Samuel Richardson (1747–48). Settings: Harlowe country home and London. Principal characters: Clarissa Harlowe, Robert Lovelace, John Belford, Miss Anna Howe, Mr. Solmes, and Mrs. Sinclair.

Clockwork Orange, A, by Anthony Burgess (pseud. of John Anthony Burgess Wilson) (1962). Setting: England. Principal characters: Alex, F. Alexander, the Prison Chaplain, Dr. Brodsky, Georgie, Pete, and Dim.

Cloister and the Hearth, The, by Charles Reade (1861). Settings: fifteenth-century Rome and Gouda, Holland. Principal characters: Gerard Eliason, Elias, Katherine, Margaret Van Eyck, Reicht Heynes, Peter Brandt, Margaret Brandt, Gerard (later Erasmus), Ghysbrecht Van Swieten, Giles, Kate, Denys, Martin, Hans Memling, Pietro, Fra Colonna, and Luke Peterson.

Color Purple, The, by Alice Walker (1982). Settings: Georgia and Africa. Principal characters: Celie, Shug, Albert, Nettie, Harpo, and Sophia.

Confessions of Nat Turner, The, by William Styron (1967). Setting: Southampton County, Va., in the 1820s and 1830s. Principal characters: Nat Turner, Hark, Thomas R. Gray, Margaret Whitehead, Benjamin Turner, Samuel Turner, Nelson, Will, Reverend Eppes.

Confessions of Zeno, The (Italian title: *La conscienza di Zeno*), by Italo Svevo (pseud. of Ettore Schmitz) (1923). Setting: Trieste. Principal characters: Zeno Cosini, Giovanni Malfenti, Ada Malfenti Speier, Augusta Malfenti Cosini, Alberta Malfenti, Anna Malfenti, Guido Speier, Olivia, and Carla.

Connecticut Yankee in King Arthur's Court, A, by Mark Twain (pseud. of Samuel L. Clemens) (1889). Settings: Hartford, Conn., and Arthurian England. Principal characters: the Connecticut Yankee (also called "the Boss"), Clarence, King Arthur, Sir Kay, Sir Sagramor, Merlin, Alisande (Sandy), and Hello-Central.

Counterfeiters, The (French title: *Les Faux-monnayeurs*), by André Gide (1926). Settings: Paris and Switzerland. Principal characters: Edouard, Olivier, Bernard, Georges, Laura, Passavant, and Boris.

Count of Monte Cristo, The (French title: *Le Comte de Monte Cristo*), by Alexandre Dumas père (1844–45). Settings: Château d'If prison, Monte Cristo island, and Paris. Principal characters: Edmond Dantès (with aliases Lord Wilmore and Abbé Busoni), Mercédès, Danglars, the Abbé Faria, Louis Dantès, Gaspard Caderousse, Fernand Mondego, Count de Morcerf, M. Morrel, Haydée, the Marquis de Saint-Méran, the Marchioness de Saint-Méran, Renée, M. Villefort, Emmanuel Herbaut, Julie Morrel, Maximilian Morrel, Viscount Albert de Morcerf, Baron Franz d'Epinay, Luigi Vampa, Peppino (Rocca Priori), Countess Guiccioli, Giovanni Bertuccio, Lucien Debray, Beauchamp, Count Château-Renaud, Eugénie Danglers, Assunta, Benedetto (Andrea Cavalcanti), Baptistin, Hermine Danglars, Héloise de Villefort, Edouard de Villefort, Valentine de Villefort, Nortier de Villefort, the Marquis Bartolomeo Cavalcanti, Barrois, Ali Tebelen, and Louise d'Armilly.

Cranford, by Elizabeth Gaskell (1851–53; first published serially in *Household Words*). Setting: Cranford (Knutsford), England. Principal characters: Miss Matilda Jenkyns, Peter Jenkyns, Mrs. Jamieson, Mulliner, Captain Brown, Miss Deborah Jenkyns, and Martha.

Crime and Punishment (Russian title: *Prestupleniye i nakazaniye*), by Fyodor Dostoyevsky (1866). Setting: St. Petersburg, Russia. Principal characters: Raskolnikov, Sonya Marmeladova, Porfiri Petrovich, Svidrigailov, and Marmeladov.

Daisy Miller, by Henry James (1878). Setting: Europe, chiefly Switzerland and Rome. Principal characters: Annie P. (Daisy) Miller, Frederick Winterbourne, Giovanelli, Mrs. Walker, Randolph Miller, Mrs. Costello, and Eugenio.

David Copperfield (full title: *The Personal History, Experience and Observations of David Copperfield the Younger, of Blunderstone Rookery [Which He Never Meant to Be Published on Any Account]*), by Charles Dickens (1849–50; first published serially between May, 1849, and November, 1850). Settings: London and Dover. Principal characters: David Copperfield, Mr. Murdstone, Betsy Trotwood, Dora Spenlow, James Steerforth, Emily Peggotty, Mr. Peggotty, Agnes Wickfield, Uriah Heep, Wilkins Micawber, Clara Peggotty, Miss Murdstone, Mr. Dick, and Rosa Dartle.

Dead Souls (Russian title: *Myortvye Dushi*), by Nikolai Gogol (1842). Setting: Russia. Principal characters: Pavel I. Chichikov, Manilov, Sobakevich, Korobochka, Plyushkin, and Nozdryov.

Death Comes for the Archbishop, by Willa Cather (1927). Setting: what is now New Mexico. Principal characters: Fr. Jean-Marie Latour, Fr. Joseph Vaillant.

Death in Venice (German title: *Der Tod in Venedig*), by Thomas Mann (1913). Setting: Venice. Principal characters: Gustav von Aschenbach and Tadzio.

Delta Wedding, by Eudora Welty (1946). Settings: Shellmound and Marmion plantations in the Mississippi Delta. Principal characters: Laura McRaven, Dabney Fairchild, Battle Fairchild, Ellen Fairchild, George Fairchild, Robbie Fairchild, Shelley Fairchild, and Troy Flavin.

Dr. Jekyll and Mr. Hyde, The Strange Case of, by Robert Louis Stevenson (1886). Setting: London. Principal characters: Dr. Henry Jekyll and Mr. Edward Hyde (the same person), Mr. Richard Enfield, Mr. Utterson, Dr. Hastie Lanyon, Sir Danvers Carew, and Poole.

Doctor Zhivago (Russian title: *Doktor Zhivago*), by Boris Pasternak (1957). Settings: Moscow, the Eastern Front in World War I, and Siberia. Principal characters: Dr. Yurii Andreievich Zhivago, Larisa Feodorovna Guishar (Lara), Nikolai Nikolaievich Vedeniapin (Uncle Kolya), Evgraf Andreievich Zhivago, Antonia Alexandrovna Gromeko (Tonia), Pavel Pavlovich Antipov (Pasha), Innokentii Dudorov (Nika), Misha Gordon, Victor Ippolitovich Komarovsky, Liberius Averkievich Mikulitsyn, and Tania.

Don Quixote de la Mancha (full Spanish title: *El Ingenioso Hidalgo don Quijote de la Mancha*), by Miguel de Cervantes Saavedra (pt. 1 [1605], pt. 2 [1615]). Setting: La Mancha, Spain. Principal characters: Don Quixote (Alonso Quijano), Sancho Panza, Rocinante (Don Quixote's horse), Dapple (Sancho's donkey), Dulcinea del Toboso, Ginés, Sansón Carrasco, and the barber.

Dracula, by Bram Stoker (1897). Settings: Transylvania, Whitby, and London. Principal characters: Count Dracula, Jonathan Harker, Mina Harker (née Murray), Lucy Westenra, Dr. John Seward, Van Helsing, Arthur Holmwood (later Lord Godalming), and Quincey P. Morris.

Egoist, The, by George Meredith (1879). Setting: fictional English hall. Principal characters: Sir Willoughby Patterne, Laetitia Dale, Constantia Durham, Clara Middleton, Vernon Whitford, Harry Oxford, and Crossjay.

Emma, by Jane Austen (1816). Setting: English country town. Principal characters: Emma Woodhouse, George Knightley, Harriet Smith, Mr. Elton, Frank Churchill, Jane Fairfax, and Mr. Woodhouse.

Erewhon, by Samuel Butler (1872). Setting: fictional country of Erewhon. Principal characters: Higgs, Yram, Mr. Nosnibor, and Arowhena.

Ethan Frome, by Edith Wharton (1911). Setting: rural New England. Principal characters: Ethan Frome, Zenobia Frome, and Mattie Silver.

Eugene Onegin: A Novel in Verse (Russian title: *Evgeni Onegin*), by Alexander Pushkin (1831). Settings: St. Petersburg and Onegin's country estate. Principal characters: Eugene Onegin, Tatyana, and Lenski.

Evelina, or A Young Lady's Entrance into the World, by Fanny Burney (1778). Settings: Berry Hill and London. Principal characters: Evelina, the Reverend Arthur Villars, Mrs. Mirvin, Lady Howard, Lord Orville, Sir John Belmont, Mme. Duval, and Sir Clement Willoughby.

Farewell to Arms, A, by Ernest Hemingway (1929). Settings: northern Italy (especially around Caporetto), Milan, and Lausanne during World War I. Principal characters: Frederic Henry and Catherine Barkley.

Fathers, The, by Allen Tate (1938). Settings: northern Virginia and Georgetown, Md., on eve of Civil War. Principal characters: Lacy Gore Buchan, Major Lewis Buchan, Semmes Buchan, Susan Buchan Posey, George Posey, Jane Posey, and Yellow Jim.

Fathers and Sons (Russian title: *Ottzy i deti*), by Ivan Turgenev (1862). Setting: Russia. Principal characters: Yevgeny Vassilyitch Bazarov, Arkady Kirsanov, Nikolai Petrovitch Kirsanov, Pavel Kirsanov, Katya Loktiv, Anna Odintsov, Vasily Bazarov, Arina Bazarov, and Fenitchka Savishna.

Finnegans Wake, by James Joyce (1939; sections were issued as *Work in Progress* between 1924 and 1932). Settings: a Chapelizod pub, Phoenix Park, and elsewhere in Ireland. Principal characters: HCE (or Humphrey Chimpden Earwicker), ALP (or Anna Livia Plurabelle), Shem, Shaun, and Issy (or Isabel).

Forsyte Saga, The, by John Galsworthy (1922; *The Man of Property* [1906]; *In Chancery* [1920]; *To Let* [1921]). Setting: London. Principal characters: Soames Forsyte, Old Jolyon Forsyte, Young Jolyon Forsyte, Philip Baines Bosinney, June Forsyte, Irene Forsyte, James Forsyte, Emily Forsyte, Montague Dartie, Winifred Forsyte Dartie, Val Dartie, Jolly and Holly Forsyte, Jon Forsyte, Annette Lamott Forsyte, Fleur Forsyte, and Michael Mont.

Fortunes of Richard Mahony, The, by Henry Handel Richardson (Ethel Richard Robertson) (1930; *Australia Felix* [1917], *The Way Home* [1925], and

Ultima Thule [1929]). Setting: Australia in nineteenth century. Principal characters: Richard Mahony, Mary Mahony, Purdy Smith, John Turnham, Henry Ocock.

For Whom the Bell Tolls, by Ernest Hemingway (1940). Setting: Spain during Civil War. Principal characters: Robert Jordan, Maria, Pilar, Pablo, Anselmo, El Sordo, and General Golz.

Frankenstein, or The Modern Prometheus, by Mary Shelley (1818). Settings: Geneva, the Alps, the University of Ingolstadt, Scotland, Ireland, Russia, and the Arctic. Principal characters: Victor Frankenstein, his Creature, Elizabeth Lavenza, Henry Clerval, and Robert Walton.

French Lieutenant's Woman, The, by John Fowles (1969). Settings: Lyme Regis, Exeter, and London in the nineteenth century. Principal characters: Charles Smithson, Sarah Woodruff, Ernestina Freeman, Mrs. Poulteney, Sam Farrow, Uncle Bob, and Dr. Grogan.

Gargantua (full French title: *La Vie très horrificque du grand Gargantua et Pantagruel*), by François Rabelais (under the pseud. Alcofribas Nasier) (*Gargantua* [1534], *Pantagruel* [1532 or 1533], *Le Tiers Livre* [1546], *Le Quart Livre* [1548 and 1552], and *Le Cinquième Livre* [1564]). Settings: France and Utopia. Principal characters: Gargantua, Pantagruel, Grandgousier, Gargamelle, Panurge, Picrochole, Frère Jean des Entommeures, Epistemon, Eusthenes, and Carpalim.

Gentlemen Prefer Blondes: The Illuminating Diary of a Professional Lady, by Anita Loos (1925). Settings: London and Paris. Principal characters: Lorelei Lee, Mr. Gus Eisman, Dorothy, Sir Francis Beekman ("Piggy"), Henry H. Spoffard, and H. Gilbertson Montrose.

Germinal, by Emile Zola (1885). Setting: mining region of northern France. Principal characters: Etienne Lantier, Souvarine, and Catherine.

Gil Blas de Santillane, by Alain-René Lesage (or Le Sage) (Vols. I and II [1715], Vol. III [1724], Vol. IV [1735]). Setting: Spain. Principal characters: Gil Blas, Dr. Sangrado, the Duke of Lerma, and Olivares.

Golden Bowl, The, by Henry James (1904). Setting: London. Principal characters: Adam Verver, Maggie Verver, Fanny Assingham, Amerigo, and Charlotte Stant.

Golden Notebook, The, by Doris Lessing (1962). Settings: London and southern Rhodesia. Principal characters: Anna Freeman Wulf, Molly Jacobs, Tommy Jacobs, Ella, and Saul Green.

Gone With the Wind, by Margaret Mitchell (1936). Settings: fictional Tara Plantation and Atlanta during and after the Civil War. Principal characters: Scarlett O'Hara, Rhett Butler, Ashley Wilkes, Charles Hamilton, Frank Kennedy, Melanie (Hamilton) Wilkes, Gerald O'Hara, Ellen O'Hara, Bonnie Blue Butler, Suellen O'Hara, Miss Pittypat, India Wilkes, and Mammy.

Grapes of Wrath, The, by John Steinbeck (1939). Settings: Oklahoma and California. Principal characters: Tom Joad, Jr., Tom Joad, Sr. ("Pa"), Ma Joad, Rose of Sharon Rivers (Rosasharn), Noah, Al, Ruthie, Winfield, Uncle John, Grampa Joad, Granma Joad, Jim Casey, Connie Rivers, Floyd Knowles, Muley Graves, Jim Rawley, Willy Feely, Ivy Wilson, Sairy Wilson, Timothy Wallace, and Aggie Wainwright.

Gravity's Rainbow, by Thomas Pynchon (1973). Settings: England and occupied Germany. Principal characters: Tyrone Slothrop, Captain Geoffrey (Pirate) Prentice, Ned Pointsman, Roger Mexico, Captain Weissman (Blicero), Enzian, Katje Borgesius, Jessica Swanlake, Seaman Bodine, Franz Pokler, Leni Pokler, Tchitcherine, and Major Duane Marvey.

Great Expectations, by Charles Dickens (1861; published serially in *All the Year Round* from December, 1860, to August, 1861). Settings: marsh country of Kent and London. Principal characters: Pip (Philip Pirrip), Joe Gargery, Mrs. Joe Gargery, Abel Magwitch, Miss Havisham, Estella, Jaggers, Herbert Pocket, Wopsle, Pumblechook, Wemmick, Biddy, and Orlick.

Great Gatsby, The, by F(rancis) Scott (Key) Fitzgerald (1925). Settings: East Egg and West Egg on Long Island and New York City. Principal characters: Nick Carraway, Jay Gatsby (formerly Jimmy Gatz), Tom Buchanan, Daisy Buchanan, Jordan Baker, and Myrtle Wilson.

Gulliver's Travels (full title: *Travels Into Several Remote Nations of the World, in Four Parts, by Lemuel Gulliver*), by Jonathan Swift (1726). Settings: Lilliput, Brobdingnag, Laputa, Lagado, Glubbdubrib, and the Land of the Houyhnhms and the Yahoos. Principal character: Lemuel Gulliver.

Heart Is a Lonely Hunter, The, by Carson McCullers (1940). Setting: city in Georgia. Principal characters: John Singer, Mick Kelly, Biff Brannon, Jake Blount, Dr. Benedict Mady Copeland, Portia, Willie, Spiros Antonapoulos, Charles Parker, and Alice Brannon.

Heart of Darkness, The, by Joseph Conrad (1902). Settings: a boat anchored in the Thames and an unnamed African river (the Congo). Principal characters: Marlow, Kurtz, and Kurtz's fiancée.

Henry Esmond, by William Makepeace Thackeray (1852). Setting: early eighteenth-century England. Principal characters: Henry Esmond, Third Viscount Castlewood, Lady Castlewood, Beatrix Castlewood, Lord Mohun, and Tom Tusher.

Hero of Our Time, A (Russian title: *Geroy nashego vremeni*), by Mikhail Lermontov (1840). Setting: Russia. Principal characters: the narrator, Grigori Aleksandrovich Pechorin, Maksim Maksimych, Bela, Azamat, Kazbich, Yanko, Princess Mary, Grushnitski, Vera, and Lieutenant Vulich.

High Wind in Jamaica, by Richard Hughes (1929). Settings: Jamaica, Caribbean Sea, and England. Principal characters: Mr. Bas-Thornton, Mrs. Bas-Thornton, John Bas-Thornton, Emily Bas-Thornton, Edward Bas-Thornton,

Rachel Bas-Thornton, Laura Bas-Thornton, Margaret Fernandez, Harry Fernandez, Captain Jonsen, and Captain Marple.

Hound of the Baskervilles, The, by Sir Arthur Conan Doyle (1902; published serially in *The Strand* between August, 1901, and April, 1902). Settings: fictional Baskerville Hall and Dartmoor, England. Principal characters: Sherlock Holmes, Dr. Watson, Sir Henry Baskerville, John Stapleton, and Dr. James Mortimer.

House Made of Dawn, by N(avarre) Scott Momaday (Tsoai-talee) (1968). Settings: Walatowa, N.M., and Los Angeles. Principal characters: Abel, Francisco, Fray Nicolás, Father Olguin, Angela St. John, Juan Reyes Fragua, John Big Bluff Tosamah, Milly, Ben Benally, and Martinez.

House of the Seven Gables, The, by Nathaniel Hawthorne (1851). Setting: Salem, Mass. Principal characters: Colonel Pyncheon, Matthew Maule, Thomas Maule, Judge Jaffrey Pyncheon, Clifford Pyncheon, Hepzibah Pyncheon, Phoebe Pyncheon, Mr. Holgrave, and Uncle Venner.

Huckleberry Finn, The Adventures of, by Mark Twain (pseud. of Samuel L. Clemens) (1884). Settings: pre-Civil War St. Petersburg (Hannibal), Mo., and various locales on the Mississippi River. Principal characters: Huckleberry (Huck) Finn, Jim, Tom Sawyer, the Widow Douglas, Miss Watson, Uncle Silas, Aunt Sally Phelps, the King, the Duke, Colonel Sherburn, Colonel Grangerford, and Buck Grangerford.

Humphrey Clinker, The Expedition of, by Tobias Smollett (1771). Settings: Bristol, Bath, Harrogate, York, Scarborough, and Durham. Principal characters: Humphrey Clinker, Matthew Bramble, Tabitha, Jerry, Lydia, Winifred Jenkins, and Lieutenant Obadiah Lismahago.

Idiot, The, by Fyodor Dostoyevsky (1868). Setting: St. Petersburg, Russia. Principal characters: Prince Myshkin, Rogozhin, Natasya Filipovna, and Aglaya Epanchin.

Invisible Man, by Ralph Ellison (1952). Settings: southern city, southern black college (Tuskegee Institute), and Harlem. Principal characters: the narrator, Dr. Bledsoe, Mr. Norton, Brother Jack, Rinehart, Ras the Destroyer, and Sibyl.

Ivanhoe, by Sir Walter Scott (1819). Setting: medieval England. Principal characters: Wilfred of Ivanhoe, Cedric, Rowena, Athelstane of Coningsburgh, King Richard Coeur de Lion, Sir Brian de Bois-Guilbert, Rebecca, Isaac, and Locksley (Robin Hood).

Jacques the Fatalist and His Master (French title: *Jacques le fataliste et son maître*), by Denis Diderot (1796). Setting: France. Principal characters: the narrator, Jacques, his Master, and the innkeeper's wife.

Jane Eyre, by Charlotte Brontë (under the pseud. Currer Bell) (1847). Settings: Gateshead, Lowood, Thornfield Hall, Marsh End or Moor House, and Ferndale (all fictional) in British Midlands. Principal characters: Jane Eyre,

Edward Rochester, Bertha Rochester, St. John Rivers, Mrs. Reed, John Reed, Helen Burns, Maria Temple, and Richard Mason.

Jean-Christophe, by Romain Rolland (1904–12, 10 vols.). Settings: Germany, Switzerland, and Paris. Principal characters: Jean-Christophe Krafft, Melchior Krafft, Louisa, Jean Michel, Ada, Lorchen, Colette Stevens, Grazia, Antoinette, Olivier, Jacqueline, and Anna.

Joseph Andrews, The History of the Adventures of, and of His Friend Mr. Abraham Adams, by Henry Fielding (1742). Settings: London, the road to Somersetshire, and Somersetshire. Principal characters: Joseph Andrews, Fanny Goodwill, Parson Abraham Adams, Lady Booby, Mrs. Slipslop, Pamela Booby, Squire Booby, Peter Pounce, Mr. Wilson, Mrs. Wilson, Mrs. Adams, Beau Didapper, Grammer Andrews, Gaffer Andrews, Parson Trulliber, Mr. Tow-Wouse, Mrs. Tow-Wouse, Betty, and Mr. Scout.

Journey to the End of Night (French title: *La Voyage au bout de la nuit*), by Louis-Ferdinand Céline (pseud. of Louis-Ferdinand Destouches) (1932). Setting: the Paris slums. Principal characters: Ferdinand Bardamu, Léon Robinson, Madelon, Lola, Musyne, Mme. Hérote, Dr. Bestombes, Roger Puta, Lieutenant Grappa, Molly, the Abbé Protisle, Tania, Dr. Baryton, Gustave Mandamour, Sophie, Bébert, Dr. Serge Parapine, and the Henrouilles.

Jude the Obscure, by Thomas Hardy (1895). Settings: Alfredston (Wantage) and Christminster (Oxford), England. Principal characters: Jude Fawley, Sue Bridehead, Arabella Donn, Phillotson, and "Father Time."

Julie, ou La Nouvelle Héloise, by Jean-Jacques Rousseau (1761). Setting: France. Principal characters: Julie d'Etanges, Saint-Preux, Lord Edward Bomston, Admiral Anson, Claire, Baron Wolmar, Baron d'Etange, and Mme. d'Etange.

Justine, or The Misfortunes of Virtue (French title: *Justine, ou Les Malheurs de la vertu*), by the Marquis de Sade (Comte Donatien-Alphonse-François de Sade) (1791; expanded 1797). Setting: France. Principal characters: Justine, Juliette, Saint-Florent, M. de Corville, M. de Gernande, M. du Harpin, La Dubois, Coeur-de-Fer, the Count de Bressac, his mother, his valet, Rodin, Rosalie, Clement, Omphale, Roland, Suzanne, Dubreuil, and Mme. Bertrand.

Kidnapped, by Robert Louis Stevenson (1886). Setting: mid-eighteenth-century Scotland. Principal characters: David Balfour, Ebenezer Balfour, Captain Hoseason, Alan Breck Stewart, Mr. Riach, Mr. Shuan, Mr. Rankeillor, Mr. Campbell, and Colin of Glenure (the "Red Fox").

Kim, by Rudyard Kipling (1901). Settings: Lahore, Umballa, Lucknow, Simla, the Grand Trunk Road, and the northern mountains of India. Principal characters: Kimball (Kim) O'Hara, Mahbub Ali, the Tibetan Lama, Colonel Creighton, and Lurgan.

Lady Chatterley's Lover, by D(avid) H(erbert) Lawrence (1928). Setting: estate in British Midlands. Principal characters: Constance (Connie) Chatterley, Sir

Clifford Chatterley, Oliver Mellors, Michaelis, Arnold Hammond, Tommy Dukes, Charles May, Hilda, Sir Malcolm Reid, Duncan Forbes, Wragby, and Tevershall.

Last Gentleman, The, by Walker Percy (1966). Settings: New York City, fictional southern cities, ranch and hospital in New Mexico. Principal characters: Will Barrett, Mr. and Mrs. Chandler Vaught, Jamie Vaught, Sutter Vaught, Kitty Vaught, Rita Vaught, Valentine Vaught, Fannin Barrett, D'Lo, Father Boomer.

Last of the Mohicans, The: A Tale of 1757, by James Fenimore Cooper (1826). Setting: Lake Champlain region of colonial New York State. Principal characters: Natty Bumppo (Hawkeye), Cora Munro, Alice Munro, Uncas, Chingachgook, Magua, Major Duncan, Heyward, and David Gamut.

Lazarillo de Tormes (full Spanish title: *La Vida de Lazarillo de Tormes y de sus Fortunas y Aduersidades*), anon. (1554). Setting: central Spain. Principal character: Lázaro.

Leopard, The (Italian title: *Il Gattapardo*), by Giuseppe Tomasi di Lampedusa (1956). Setting: medieval Sicily. Principal characters: Don Fabrizio Corbera, Tancredi Falconeri, Princess Maria Stella, Paolo, Francesco Paolo, Carolina, Concetta, Caterina, Don Calogero Sedàra, Angelica, Count Carlo Cavriaghi, and Father Pirrone.

Liaisons dangereuses, Les, by Pierre Choderlos de Laclos (1782). Setting: Paris. Principal characters: Vicomte de Valmont, the Marquise de Merteuil, the Comte de Gercourt, Cécile de Volanges, Chevalier Danceny, Mme. de Tourvel, Mme. de Volanges, Mme. de Rosemonde, and Sophie Carney.

Lie Down in Darkness, by William Styron (1951). Settings: Port Warwick (Newport News) and Charlottesville, Va., New York City. Principal characters: Peyton Loftis, Milton Loftis, Helen Loftis, Maudie Loftis, Harry Miller, Dolly Bonner, Ella Swan, and the Rev. Carey Carr.

Light in August, by William Faulkner (1932). Setting: Yoknapatawpha (Lafayette) County, Miss. Principal characters: Joe Christmas, Lena Grove, Byron Bunch, the Rev. Gail Hightower, Lucas Burch (alias Joe Brown), Joanna Burden, Percy Grimm, Mr. and Mrs. Simon McEachern, Eupheus (Doc) Hines, and Mrs. Hines.

Lolita, by Vladimir Nabokov (1955). Settings: New England and across the United States. Principal characters: Humbert Humbert, Lolita (Lo, Lola, Dolly, Dolores Haze), Charlotte Haze, Clare Quilty, Richard (Dick) F. Schiller, Gaston Godin, and John Ray, Jr., Ph.D.

Look Homeward, Angel: A Story of the Buried Life, by Thomas Wolfe (1929). Settings: Altamont (Asheville) and Pulpit Hill (Chapel Hill), N.C., and Norfolk and Langley Field, Va. Principal characters: Eugene Gant, W. O. Gant, Eliza Gant, Steve Gant, Ben Gant, Luke Gant, and Helen Gant.

Lord Jim, by Joseph Conrad (1900). Settings: Indian Ocean, Aden, and Patusan. Principal characters: Jim (Tuan or Lord Jim), Marlow, Doramin, Jewel, and Gentleman Brown.

Lord of the Flies, by William Golding (1954). Setting: uninhabited ocean island. Principal characters: Jack, Piggy, Simon, and Ralph.

Lord of the Rings, The, by J(ohn) R(onald) R(euel) Tolkien (1954–55; Vol. I: *The Fellowship of the Ring* [1954]; Vol. II: *The Two Towers* [1954]; Vol. III: *The Return of the King* [1955]). Settings: fictional landscapes. Principal characters: Frodo, Bilbo Baggins, Gandalf the Gray, Merry, Pippin, Aragorn, Sam, Sauron, and Gollum.

Losing Battles, by Eudora Welty (1970). Setting: Mississippi in the 1930s. Principal characters: Granny Vaughn, Jack Renfro, Beulah Renfro, Gloria Short Renfro, Miss Julia Percival Mortimer, Miss Lexie Renfro, Nathan Beecham, Curly Stovall, Curtis Beecham, Dolphus Beecham, Percy Beecham, Noah Webster Beecham, Judge Oscar Moody, Mrs. Maud Moody, Brother Bethune, and Willy Trimble.

Lucky Jim, by Kingsley Amis (1954). Setting: English provincial university. Principal characters: Jim Dixon, Prof. Welch, Margaret Peel, Mr. Catchpole, Bertrand Welch, Christine Callaghan, and Julius Gore-Urquhart.

Madame Bovary, by Gustave Flaubert (1857; originally published in *Le Revue de Paris* [1856]). Settings: fictional town of Yonville-l'Abbaye and Rouen. Principal characters: Emma Bovary (née Rouault), Charles Bovary, M. Homais, M. Léon, and Rodolphe Boulanger.

Magic Mountain, The (German title: *Der Zauberberg*), by Thomas Mann (1924). Setting: Haus Berghof sanatorium in the Swiss Alps before World War I. Principal characters: Hans Castorp, Joachim Ziemssen, Settembrini, Peeperkorn, Dr. Behrens, Clavdia Chauchat, Leo Naphta, and Dr. Krokowski.

Main Street, by Sinclair Lewis (1920). Setting: fictional town of Gopher Prairie, Minn. Principal characters: Carol Kennicott, Dr. Will Kennicott, Guy Pollock, Vida Sherwood, Raymond Wutherspoon, Erik Valborg, Bea Sorenson, Miles Bjornstam, Mrs. Bogart, Sam Clark, Percy Bresnahan, James Blauser, and Hugh Kennicott.

Manon Lescaut (full French title: *L'Histoire du chevalier des Grieux et de Manon Lescaut*), by Antoine-François, L'Abbé Prévost (1731). Settings: France and New Orleans. Principal characters: the Chevalier des Grieux, his father, Manon Lescaut, M. Lescaut, Tiberge, M. de B_____, M. de G_____ M_____, M. de G_____ M_____, Jr., M. de T_____, the Governor of New Orleans, and M. Synnelet.

Man's Fate (French title: *La Condition humaine*), by André Malraux (1933). Setting: Shanghai. Principal characters: Ch'en, Kyo, Gisors, May, Baron de Clappique, Katov, Hemmelrich, Ferral, König, Valerie, and Chiang Kai-shek.

Man Without Qualities, A (German title: *Der Mann ohne Eigenshaften*), by Robert Musil (1930–43). Setting: Vienna. Principal characters: Ulrich, Walter, Clarisse, Herr Dr. Paul Arnheim, Diotima, Bonadea, Agathe, General Stumm von Bordwehr, Moosbrugger, Count Leinsdorf, Rachel, and Soliman.

Marianne (full French title: *La Vie de Marianne*), by Pierre Carlet de Chamblain de Marivaux (1731–41, 11 parts). Setting: France. Principal characters: Marianne, M. de Climal, M. de Valville, Mme. de Valville, Mlle. Varthon, Mlle. de Tervire, and Mme. Dutour.

Master and Margarita, The (Russian title: *Master i Margarita*), by Mikhail Bulgakov (1966–67; unexpurgated ed., 1973). Settings: Palestine and Russia. Principal characters: the Master, Margarita, Woland (or Satan, Messire, the Devil), Ivan Nikolayevich Ponyrev (pen name "Homeless"), Yeshua Ha-Nozri, Matthu Levi, Pontius Pilate (or Hegemon), Yehudah of Kerioth, Koroviev (or Fagot), Azazello, Behemoth (or Tom), Hella, Mikhail Alexandrovich Berlioz, Styopa Likhodeyev, Professor Stravinsky, Grigory Danilovich Rimsky, Ivan Savelievich Varenukha, Arkady Apollonovich Sempleyarov, Nikanor Ivanovich Bosoy, Latunsky, and Aphranius.

Memoirs of a Woman of Pleasure (also called *Fanny Hill*), by John Cleland (1748–49). Setting: London. Principal characters: Fanny Hill, Charles, Mr. ———, Will, Mrs. Brown, and Mrs. Cole.

Metamorphosis, The (German title: *Die Verwandlung*), by Franz Kafka (1915). Setting: the Samsa apartment, Prague. Principal characters: Gregor Samsa, Mr. Samsa, Mrs. Anna Samsa, Grete Samsa, and the Chief Clerk.

Middlemarch: A Study of Provincial Life, by George Eliot (pseud. of Mary Anne or Marian Evans) (1871–72). Setting: fictional English community of Middlemarch. Principal characters: Dorothea Brooke, Dr. Edward Casaubon, Will Ladislaw, Dr. Tertius Lydgate, Rosamund Vincy, Fred Vincy, Mary Garth, Caleb Garth, Bulstrode, Mr. Brooke, Mrs. Cadwallader, Sir James Chettam, Celia Brooke, Mrs. Bulstrode, and Rev. Camden Farebrother.

Mill on the Floss, The, by George Eliot (pseud. of Mary Anne or Marian Evans) (1860). Setting: fictional English community of St. Ogg's. Principal characters: Maggie Tulliver, Tom Tulliver, Philip Wakem, Lucy, and Stephen Guest.

Misérables, Les, by Victor Hugo (1862). Setting: France. Principal characters: Jean Valjean (with aliases M. Madeleine and M. Fauchelevent), Javert, Monseigneur Myriel, Fantine, Cosette, Thénardier, Marius, and Gavroche.

Moby-Dick, or The Whale, by Herman Melville (1851). Settings: New Bedford and Nantucket, Mass., and aboard a whaling vessel. Principal characters: Ishmael, Captain Ahab, Queequeg, Moby-Dick (the white whale), Starbuck, Stubb, Flask, Tashtego, Daggoo, Fedallah, and Pip.

Moll Flanders: The Fortunes and Misfortunes of the Famous, by Daniel Defoe (1721). Settings: London, rural England, and colonial Virginia. Principal characters: Moll Flanders; her mother; Robin; Robin's older brother; Humphry; Jeremy E.; "Mother Midnight"; a gentleman of Bath; a linen draper; a clergyman in Newgate Prison; and a London bank clerk.

Monk, The, by M(atthew) G(regory) Lewis (1796). Setting: Spain. Principal characters: Ambrosio, his mother, Matilda, Antonia, Raymond, Agnes, and the Devil.

Moonstone, The, by Wilkie Collins (1868; published serially in *All the Year Round* between January and August, 1868). Setting: England. Principal characters: Rachel Verinder, Franklin Blake, Rosana Spearman, Godfrey Abelwhite, Colonel John Herncastle, Superintendent Seegrave, and Sergeant Cuff.

Moviegoer, The, by Walker Percy (1961). Setting: New Orleans and nearby. Principal characters: Binx Bolling, Kate Cutrer, Emily Cutrer, Jules Cutrer, Lonnie Smith, and Mercer.

Mrs. Dalloway, by Virginia Woolf (1925). Setting: London. Principal characters: Clarissa Dalloway, Richard Dalloway, M.P., Peter Walsh, Septimus Warren Smith, Sally Seton, Elizabeth, Miss Kilman, and Lady Bruton.

Murphy, by Samuel Beckett (1938). Settings: Dublin and London. Principal characters: Murphy, Celia, Neary, Miss Counihan, Cooper, and Wylie.

My Antonia, by Willa Cather (1918). Setting: Black Hawk, Nebr. Principal characters: James (Jim) Quayle Burden, Antonia Shimerda, Mr. Shimerda, Mrs. Shimerda, Ambroz (Ambrosch) Shimerda, Yulka Shimerda, Marek Shimerda, Mr. Burden, Mrs. Burden, Wycliffe (Wick) Cutter, Mrs. Cutter, Larry Donovan, Cuzak, Rudolph Cuzak, Anton Cuzak, Leo Cuzak, Jan Cuzak, Anna Cuzak, Yulka Cuzak, Nina Cuzak, Lucie Cuzak, Lena Lingard, Tiny Soderball, Mrs. Steavens, Otto Fuchs, Jake Marpole, Christian Harling, Peter, Pavel, Anton Jelinek, Martha, Gaston Cleric, and Genevieve Whitney Burden.

Naked and the Dead, The, by Norman Mailer (1948). Setting: the fictional Pacific island of Anopopei during World War II. Principal characters: General Cummings, Lieutenant Hearn, Sergeant Croft, Red Valsen, Gallagher, Julio Martinez, Joey Goldstein, and Wilson.

Naked Lunch, by William S(eward) Burroughs (Paris, 1959; New York, 1966). Settings: New York City and the fictional Freeland Republic, Mexico, and Interzon. Principal characters: William Lee, Doctor Benway, A. J., the Mugwumps, Ali Hassan, the Liquefactionists, the Senders, the Divisionists, and the Factualists.

Nana, by Emile Zola (1880). Setting: Paris. Principal characters: Nana, Gervaise, M. Fauchery, M. Steiner, Georges Hugon, Philippe Hugon, Mme. Hugon, Fontan, the Comte Muffatt de Beuville, Sabine de Beuville, the Marquis de

Chouard, the Comte Xavier de Vandeuvres, Hector de la Faloise, Mignon, Rose Mignon, Bordenave, Daguenet, Estelle, Satin, Prullière, Labordette, Lucy Stewart, Mme. Maloir, Zoé, Mme. Lerat, and Louis.

Native Son, by Richard Wright (1940). Setting: Chicago. Principal characters: Bigger Thomas, Mary Dalton, Jan Erlone, Boris A. Max, Bessie Mears, Mr. Dalton, Mrs. Dalton, Britten, and Buckley.

Nausea (French title: *La Nausée*), by Jean-Paul Sartre (1938). Settings: fictional French town of Bouville and Paris. Principal characters: Antoine Roquentin, Anny, Ogier P., and Françoise.

New Grub Street, by George Gissing (1891). Setting: London. Principal characters: Edwin Reardon, Jasper Milvain, Alfred Yule, Marian Yule, Amy Reardon (later Milvain), Harold Biffen, and Whelpdale.

Nightwood, by Djuna Barnes (1936). Settings: Berlin, Vienna, Paris, and New York City. Principal characters: Felix Volkbein, Robin Vote, Dr. Matthew O'Connor, Nora Flood, Jenny Petherbridge, Guido Volkbein, and Sylvia.

Nineteen Eighty-Four, by George Orwell (pseud. of Eric Arthur Blair) (1949). Setting: Airstrip One (England). Principal characters: Winston Smith, Julia, O'Brien, and "Big Brother."

Oblomov, by Ivan Goncharov (1859). Setting: St. Petersburg, Russia. Principal characters: Ilya Ilyich Oblomov, Zakhar, Andrey Stolz, Olga Ilyinsky, and Agat'ya Pshenitzyna.

Octopus, The, by Frank Norris (1901). Settings: ranches of the San Joaquin Valley and San Francisco. Principal characters: Governor Magnus Derrick, Annie Derrick, Lyman Derrick, Harran Derrick, Presley, Annixter, Hilma Tree, S. Behrman, Vanamee, Dyke, Hooven, and Osterman.

Of Human Bondage, by W(illiam) Somerset Maugham (1915). Settings: London, Germany, Paris, and an English country town. Principal characters: Philip Carey, William Carey, Louisa Carey, Miss Wilkinson, G. Etheridge Hayward, Mildred Rodgers, Fanny Price, Cronshaw, Norah Nesbit, Harry Griffiths, Thorpe Athelney, and Sally Athelney.

Of Time and the River: A Legend of Man's Hunger in His Youth, by Thomas Wolfe (1935). Settings: Altamont (Asheville), N.C., Cambridge, Mass., New York City, France. Principal characters: Eugene Gant, Eliza Gant, Helen Gant, Luke Gant, Bascom Pentland, Prof. Hatcher, Francis Starwick, Ann, Elinor, Robert Weaver, and the Countess.

Old Goriot (French title: *Le Père Goriot*), by Honoré de Balzac (1834). Setting: Paris. Principal characters: Eugène de Rastignac, Vautrin, M. Goriot, Anastasie de Restaud, Delphine de Nucingen, and Bianchon.

Old Wives' Tale, The, by Arnold Bennett (1908). Settings: fictional English town of Bursley and Paris. Principal characters: Sophia Baines, Constance Baines, John Baines, Mrs. Baines, Sam Povey, Charles Critchlow, Aunt Maria, Harriet Maddock, Gerald Scales, Maggie, Aline Chetwynd, Elizabeth

Chetwynd, Lily Holl, Dick Povey, Cyril Povey, Maria Insull, and Matthew Peel-Swynnerton.

Oliver Twist, by Charles Dickens (1837–38). Settings: English workhouse and London. Principal characters: Oliver Twist, Mr. Brownlow, Mrs. Maylie, Rose Maylie, Harry Maylie, Fagin, Bill Sikes, Nancy, Jack Dawkins (the Artful Dodger), Charles Bates, Monks (Edward Leeford), Mr. Bumble, Mrs. Corney, Mr. Grimwig, Mrs. Bedwin, Mr. Losberne, Mrs. Mann, Mr. Sowerberry, Mrs. Sowerberry, Noah Claypole, Charlotte, Mr. Fang, Toby Crackit, and Old Sally.

Once and Future King, The, by T(erence) H(ambury) White (1940; *The Sword in the Stone* [1939], *The Witch in the Wood* [1940], *Ill-Made Knight* [1941], *The Circle in the Wind* [1958.]) Setting: Arthurian England. Principal characters: "The Wart" (Arthur), Sir Ector, Sir Kay, Queen Morgause, Modred, Guenever, Lancelot, Elaine, Galahad, Sir Meliagrace, Agrivaine, and Merlyn.

One Day in the Life of Ivan Denisovich (Russian title: *Odin den Ivana Denisovicha*), by Aleksandr Solzhenitsyn (1962). Setting: Soviet labor camp. Principal characters: Ivan Denisovich (Shukov), Tyurin, Fetyukov, the Captain, Caesar Markovich, Alyosha the Baptist, Pavlo, and Der.

One Hundred Years of Solitude (Spanish title: *Cien Años de Soledad*), by Gabriel García Márquez (1967). Setting: the fictional village of Macondo. Principal characters: José Arcadio Buendía, Melquíades, Ursula Iguarán, José Arcadio, Rebeca, Colonel Aureliano Buendía, Amaranta, Pietro Crepsi, Pilar Ternera, Arcadio, Santa Sofia de la Piedad, Remedios the Beauty, José Arcadio Segundo, Aureliano Segundo, Fernanda del Carpio, Renata Remedios (Meme), José Arcadio, Amaranta Ursula, Gaston, and Aureliano.

On the Road, by Jack Kerouac (1957). Settings: United States and Mexico. Principal characters: Sal Paradise and Dean Moriarty.

Oroonoko, or The Royal Slave, by Aphra Behn (ca. 1688). Settings: Africa and Surinam. Principal characters: Oroonoko (Caesar), Imoinda, and Byam.

Our Mutual Friend, by Charles Dickens (1865; first published serially between May, 1864, and November, 1865). Setting: London. Principal characters: John Harmon (alias John Rokesmith), Bella Wilfer, Mr. Nicodemus Boffin, Mrs. Henrietta Boffin, Eugene Wrayburn, Lizzy Hexam, Bradley Headstone, and Jenny Wren.

Pamela, or Virtue Rewarded, by Samuel Richardson (1740–41). Setting: B_____ Hall, England. Principal characters: Pamela Andrews, Mr. B., Mrs. Jervis, Mr. Longman, Mrs. Jewkes, Mr. Williams, and Lady Davers.

Passage to India, A, by E(dward) M(organ) Forster (1924). Settings: Chandrapore, the Marabar Caves, and Mau, India. Principal characters: Dr. Aziz, Mrs. Moore, Adela Quested, Cyril Fielding, Professor Godbole, and Ronald Heaslop.

Petersburg, by Andrey Bely (pseud. of Boris Nikolayevich Bugaev) (1913–14, 1916, 1922). Setting: Petersburg, Russia. Principal characters: Nikolai Apollonovich Ableukhov, Apollon Ableukhov, Alexander Ivanovich, Lippanchenko, Pavel Yakovlevich, Sergy Likhutin, and Sophia Likhutin.

Picture of Dorian Gray, The, by Oscar Wilde (1891). Setting: England. Principal characters: Dorian Gray, Basil Hallward, and Lord Henry Wotton.

Pilgrimage, by Dorothy M. Richardson (1915–1938; Vol. I: *Pointed Roofs* [1915], *Backwater* [1916], and *Honeycomb* [1917]; Vol. II: *The Tunnel* [February, 1919] and *Interim* [December, 1919]; Vol. III: *Deadlock* [1921], *Revolving Lights* [1923], and *The Trap* [1925]; Vol. IV: *Oberland* [1927], *Dawn's Left Hand* [1931], *Clear Horizon* [1935], *Dimple Hill* [1938], and *March Moonlight* [1938]). Settings: England, Germany, and Switzerland. Principal characters: Miriam Henderson, her father, her mother, "Hypo" Wilson, Harriet Henderson, Sarah Henderson, Eve Henderson, Gerald, Pastor Lahmann, the Misses Perne, Grace Bloom, Florrie Bloom, Ted, Max, Dr. Orly, Sr., Dr. Orly, Jr., Dr. Hancock, Mrs. Bailey, Alma Eleanor Dear, Dr. Densley, Shatov, Selina Holland, Amabel, and the Rescorlas.

Pioneers, The, by James Fenimore Cooper (1823). Setting: Templeton, N.Y. Principal characters: Judge Marmaduke Temple, Elizabeth Temple, Natty Bumppo (Leatherstocking), Oliver Edwards (alias of Oliver Edward Effingham), Indian Joe (Chingachgook), Hiram Doolittle, Richard Jones, Major Edward Effingham, Mr. Grant, Louisa Grant, Benjamin Penguillan (Ben Pump), Elnathan Todd, Monsieur le Quoi, Major Hartmann, Jotham Riddel, Remarkable Pettibone, Squire Lippet, Mr. Van der School, and Agamemnon.

Plague, The (French title: *La Peste*), by Albert Camus (1947). Setting: Oran, French Algeria. Principal characters: Dr. Bernard Rieux, Mme. Rieux, Raymond Rambert, Father Paneloux, Jean Tarrou, Joseph Grand, M. Cottard, Dr. Richard, M. Othon, Jacques Othon, Mme. Rieux (Bernard Rieux's mother), Garcia, Raoul, Gonzales, Marcel, and Louis.

Portrait of a Lady, The, by Henry James (1881). Settings: England and Italy. Principal characters: Isabel Archer, Gilbert Osmond, Lord Warburton, Caspar Goodwood, Mrs. Touchett, Mme. Merle, Henrietta Stackpole, Pansy Osmond, Edward Rosier, Countess Gemini, and Ralph Touchett.

Portrait of the Artist as a Young Man, A, by James Joyce (1916; first published in *The Egoist* [1914–15]). Setting: Dublin. Principal characters: Stephen Dedalus, Simon Dedalus, Lynch, and Cranly.

Power and the Glory, The, by Graham Greene (1940). Setting: Mexico. Principal characters: a drunken priest (alias Montez), Father José, a mestizo, a police lieutenant, Marcia, Brigida, and Mr. Tench.

Pride and Prejudice, by Jane Austen (1813). Setting: English country town. Principal characters: Elizabeth Bennet, Fitzwilliam Darcy, Mr. Bennet, Mrs. Bennet, Jane Bennet, Charles Bingley, and Lady Catherine de Bourgh.

Princesse de Clèves, La, by the Comtesse de La Fayette (Marie Madeleine Pioche de la Vergne) (1678). Setting: France. Principal characters: the Princess de Clèves, the Prince de Clèves, the Duc de Nemours, the Queen Dauphine, the Vidame de Chartres, Mme. de Chartres, Henri II, and Diane de Poitiers.

Rainbow, The, by D(avid) H(erbert) Lawrence (1915). Setting: Derbyshire-Nottinghamshire border region. Principal characters: Tom Brangwen, Lydia Brangwen, Anna Brangwen, Will Brangwen, Ursula Brangwen, Gudrun Brangwen, and Anton Skrebensky.

Raj Quartet, The, by Paul Scott (1976; *The Jewel in the Crown* [1966], *The Day of the Scorpion* [1968], *The Towers of Silence* [1971], *A Division of the Spoils* [1975]). Setting: India. Principal characters: Ronald Merrick, Daphne Manners, Hari Kumar, Edwina Crane, Mabel Layton, Sara Layton, Susan Layton, Mildred Layton, Guy Perron, Barbie Batchelor, Mohammed Ali Kasim (known as MAK), Ahmed Kasim, and Count Bronowsky.

Rameau's Nephew (French title: *Le Neveu de Rameau*), by Denis Diderot (1805 in German; 1823 in French). Setting: Paris. Principal characters: Rameau and Denis Diderot.

Rasselas, by Samuel Johnson (1759.) Setting: Africa. Principal characters: Rasselas, Imlac, and Nekayah.

Red and the Black, The: A Chronicle of 1830 (French title: *Le Rouge et le noir: Chronicle de 1830*), by Stendhal (pseud. of Henri Beyle) (1830). Settings: Verrières (a town in the Franche-Comté), Paris, and Besançon. Principal characters: Julien Sorel (later M. de la Vernaye), Mme. de Rênal (Louise), Marquis de La Mole, Mathilde de La Mole, and M. de Rênal.

Red Badge of Courage, The: An Episode of the Civil War, by Stephen Crane (1895). Setting: a Civil War battle. Principal characters: Henry Fleming and Jim Conklin.

Remembrance of Things Past (French title: *À la recherche du temps perdu*), by Marcel Proust (1914–27; Vol. I: *Du Côté de chez Swann* [1913]; Vol. II: *À L'Hombre des jeunes filles en fleurs* [1919]; Vol. III: *Le Côté de Guermantes I* [1920]; Vol. IV: *Le Côté de Guermantes II, Sodome et Gomorrhe I* [1921]; Vol. V: *Sodome et Gomorrhe II* [1922]; Vol. VI: *La Prisonnière* [1923]; Vol. VII: *Albertine disparue* [1925]; Vol. VIII: *Le Temps retrouvé* [1927]). Settings: Paris, Combray (Illiers), Balbec (Cabourg), France, and Venice, Italy. Principal characters: Marcel, his father, his mother, his grandmother, Lèonie, Charles Swann, Odette de Crécy, de Forcheville, Gilberte Swann, Duke and Duchess of Guermantes; Albertine Simonet; Andreé; Jupien; Baron de Charlus, Prince and Princess of Guermantes, Robert de Saint-Loup, M. and Mme. Verdurin, Morel, Bergotte, Vinteuil, Elstir, Bloch, Mme. Villeparisis, M. de Norpois, Saniette, Rachel, M. LeGrandin, Françoise, and Dr. and Mrs. Cottard.

Return of the Native, The, by Thomas Hardy (1878). Setting: Egdon Heath, England. Principal characters: Damon Wildeve, Thomasin Yeobright, Eustacia Vye, Diggory Venn, and Clym Yeobright.

Rise of Silas Lapham, The, by William Dean Howells (1885). Setting: Boston. Principal characters: Silas Lapham, Persis Lapham, Penelope Lapham, and Tom Corey.

Robinson Crusoe, The Life and Strange Surprising Adventures of, by Daniel Defoe (1719). Setting: small, deserted island (Juan Fernandez). Principal characters: Robinson Crusoe and Friday.

Scarlet Letter, The, by Nathaniel Hawthorne (1850). Settings: Salem and Boston, Mass. Principal characters: Hester Prynne, Arthur Dimmesdale, Roger Chillingworth, and Pearl.

Siddhartha, by Hermann Hesse (1922). Setting: Indian subcontinent. Principal characters: Siddhartha, Govinda, Kamala, Vasudeva, and Gotama.

Sister Carrie, by Theodore Dreiser (1900). Settings: Chicago and New York City. Principal characters: Caroline Meeber, George Hurstwood, Charles Drouet, Bod Ames, Minnie Hanson, Sven Hanson, Mrs. Hurstwood, Mr. Vance, Mrs. Vance, Jessica Hurstwood, and George Hurstwood, Jr.

Slaughterhouse-Five, or The Children's Crusade, by Kurt Vonnegut, Jr. (1969). Settings: Ilium, N.Y., Dresden, Germany, and the planet of Tralfamadore. Principal characters: Billy Pilgrim, Kurt Vonnegut, Jr., Montana Wildhack, Valencia Merble Pilgrim, Howard W. Campbell, Jr., Edgar Derby, Roland Weary, Paul Lazzaro, and Kilgore Trout.

Sons and Lovers, by D(avid) H(erbert) Lawrence (1913). Setting: fictional Nottinghamshire coal-mining village of Bestwood. Principal characters: Paul Morel, Mrs. Gertrude Morel, Walter Morel, William Morel, Miriam Leivers, Clara Dawes, and Baxter Dawes.

Sorrows of Young Werther, The (German title: *Die Leiden des jungen Werthers*), by Johann Wolfgang von Goethe (1774; final version, 1787). Setting: Walheim, Germany. Principal characters: Werther, Charlotte (Lotte) S., and Albert.

Sot-Weed Factor, The, by John Barth (1960; rev., 1966). Settings: England and colonial Maryland, primarily on the Eastern Shore. Principal characters: Ebenezer Cook, Henry Burlingame III, Joan Toast, and Anna Cook.

Sound and the Fury, The, by William Faulkner (1929). Settings: Yoknapatawpha (Lafayette) County, Miss., and Cambridge, Mass. Principal characters: Jason Compson, Benjy Compson, Quentin Compson, Candace (Caddy) Compson, Quentin Compson (Caddy's daughter), Jason Compson, Herbert Head, Dalton Ames, Shrevelin McCannon, Gerald Bland, Dilsey, and Luster.

Story of an African Farm, The, by Olive Schreiner (first published under the pseud. Ralph Iron) (1883). Setting: farm on the Great Karoo in southern

Africa. Principal characters: Lyndall, Em, Waldo, Bonaparte Blenkins, Tant' Sannie, Uncle Otto, and Gregory Rose.

Stranger, The (French title: *L'Etranger*), by Albert Camus (1942). Setting: French Algeria. Principal characters: Meursault, his mother, and Marie.

Sun Also Rises, The, by Ernest Hemingway (1926). Settings: Paris, Spanish Pyrenees, and Pamplona. Principal characters: Jake Barnes, Lady Brett Ashley, Robert Cohn, Mike Campbell, Bill Gorton, and Pedro Romero.

Surfacing, by Margaret Atwood (1972). Setting: small lake near the Ontario-Quebec border. Principal characters: female narrator, Joe, Anna, and David.

Swiss Family Robinson, The (German title: *Der schweizerische Robinson*), by Johann Rudolf Wyss (1812–13). Setting: an island near New Guinea. Principal characters: Mr. Robinson, Mrs. Robinson, Fritz Robinson, Emily Montrose, Ernest Robinson, Jack Robinson, and Francis Robinson.

Tale of a Genji, The (Japanese title: *Genji monogatari*), by Lady Murasaki Shikibu (real name unknown) (*ca.* 1001–15). Setting: imperial Japanese court. Principal characters: Prince Genji, the Emperor of Japan, Lady Kokiden, Kiritsubo, Princess Aoi, Fujitsubo, Utsusemi, Ki no Kami, Yugao, and Lady Murasaki.

Tale of Two Cities, A, by Charles Dickens (1859). Settings: Paris and London. Principal characters: Charles Darnay, Lucie Manette, Sydney Carton, Dr. Manette, Mme. Defarge, M. Defarge, and Jerry Cruncher.

Temple of the Golden Pavilion, The (Japanese title: *Kinkakuji*), by Yukio Mishima (1956). Settings: Temple of the Golden Pavilion and Otani University. Principal characters: Mizoguchi, Kashiwagi, Tsurukawa, Father Tayama Dosen, Uiko, Mizoguchi's father and mother, Father Kuwai Zenkai, and Mariko.

Tess of the D'Urbervilles: A Pure Woman, by Thomas Hardy (1891). Settings: Blackmore Vale, Sandbourne (Bournemouth), and Stonehenge. Principal characters: Tess Durbeyfield, Alec D'Urberville, and Angel Clare.

Their Eyes Were Watching God, by Zora Neale Hurston (1937). Settings: Eatonville and Belle Glade, Fla. Principal characters: Janie Killicks, Starks Woods (née Crawford), Nanny Crawford, Logan Killicks, Joe Starks, Vergible (Tea Cake) Woods, and Phoeby Watson.

Things Fall Apart, by Chinua Achebe (1958). Setting: colonial Nigeria. Principal characters: Okonkwo, Nwoye (later Isaac), Ikemefuna, Unoka, Chielo, Ekwefi, Ezinma, Obierika, Mr. Brown, and the Rev. James Smith.

Three Musketeers, The (French title: *Les Trois Mousquetaires*), by Alexandre Dumas père (1844–45). Setting: Paris. Principal characters: D'Artagnan, Athos, Porthos, Aramis, Anne of Austria, the Duke of Buckingham, Milady, and Felton.

Through the Looking-Glass and What Alice Found There, by Lewis Carroll (pseud. of Charles Lutwidge Dodgson) (1871). Setting: Alice's dreamworld.

Principal characters: Alice, the Red Queen, the White Queen, Tweedledum and Tweedledee, the White Knight, the Walrus, the Carpenter, and Humpty Dumpty.

Tin Drum, The (German title: *Die Blechtrommel*), by Günter Grass (1959). Settings: Danzig and West Germany. Principal characters: Oskar Matzerath, Agnes Matzerath, Alfred Matzerath, Jan Bronski, Mr. Bebra, Roswitha Raguna, Herbert Truczinski, Maria Truczinski, Greff, Lina Greff, Sister Dorothea Köngetter, and Gottfried von Vittlar.

To Kill a Mockingbird, by Harper Lee (1960). Setting: town in Ala. Principal characters: Atticus Finch, Jean-Louise (Scout) Finch, Jeremy Atticus (Jem) Finch, Calpurnia, Charles Baker (Dill) Harris, Arthur (Boo) Radley, Tom Robinson, Robert (Bob) E. Lee Ewell, and Mayella Ewell.

Tom Jones, a Foundling, The History of, by Henry Fielding (1749). Settings: Somersetshire, road to London, and London. Principal characters: Tom Jones, Squire Allworthy, Bridget Allworthy, Squire Western, Sophia Western, Master Blifil, Lady Bellaston, Lord Fellamar, Jenny Jones (Mrs. Waters), Partridge, Thwackum, Square, Captain Blifil, Black George Seagrim, and Molly Seagrim.

Tom Sawyer, The Adventures of, by Mark Twain (pseud. of Samuel L. Clemens) (1876). Setting: St. Petersburg (Hannibal), Mo. Principal characters: Tom Sawyer, Sid Sawyer, Huck Finn, Aunt Polly, Becky Thatcher, Judge Thatcher, Muff Potter, Joe Harper, and Injun Joe.

To the Lighthouse, by Virginia Woolf (1927). Setting: old house in the Hebrides. Principal characters: Mrs. Ramsay, Mr. Ramsay, James Ramsay, Camilla (Cam) Ramsay, Lily Briscoe, Minta Doyle, Paul Rayley, Mr. Augustus Carmichael, and Charles Tansley.

Treasure Island, by Robert Louis Stevenson (1883; first published serially as "The Sea Cook or Treasure Island" in *Young Folks* between July, 1881, and June, 1882). Settings: Admiral Benbow Inn, England, the Hispaniola, and fictional island. Principal characters: Jim Hawkins, Long John Silver, Pew, Squire Trelawney, Dr. Livesey, and Ben Gunn.

Trial, The (German title: *Der Prozess*), by Franz Kafka (1925). Setting: central European city. Principal characters: Joseph K., Frau Grubach, Fräulein Bürstner, and Leni.

Tristram Shandy, The Life and Opinions of, by Laurence Sterne (1759–67). Setting: fictional Shandy Hall, England. Principal characters: Tristram Shandy, Walter Shandy, Mrs. Shandy, Uncle Toby, Corporal Trim, Yorick, the widow Wadman, Dr. Slop, and Obadiah.

Turn of the Screw, The, by Henry James (1898). Setting: Bly, an English country house. Principal characters: the Governess, Miles, Flora, Miss Jessel, and Peter Quint.

Ulysses, by James Joyce (1922). Setting: Dublin. Principal characters: Stephen Dedalus, Leopold (Poldy) Bloom, Molly Bloom, Hugh (Blazes) Boylan,

Haines, Malachi (Buck) Mulligan, the Citizen, Simon Dedalus, Martin Cunningham, Mr. Deasy, John Eglinton, Richard Best, AE, Myles Crawford, Lenahan, and Gertie McDowell.

Uncle Tom's Cabin, or Life Among the Lowly, by Harriet Beecher Stowe (1852; first published in *The National Era* between 1851 and 1852). Settings: plantations in Kentucky and Louisiana. Principal characters: "Uncle Tom" Shelby, Evangeline (Eva) St. Clare, Miss Ophelia St. Clare, Augustine St. Clair, Eliza Harris, George, Topsy, Marks, and Simon Legree.

Under the Volcano, by Malcolm Lowry (1947). Setting: Quauhnahuac (Cuernavaca), Mexico. Principal characters: Geoffrey Firmin, Yvonne Constable, Hugh Firmin, Jacques Laruelle, and Dr. Arturo Diaz Vigil.

U.S.A., by John Dos Passos (1938; *The Forty-Second Parallel* [1930], *1919* [1932], *The Big Money* [1936]). Settings: United States, Mexico, Paris, and Moscow. Principal characters: Fenian O'Hara McCreary (Fainy Mac), Maisie Spencer, Janey Williams, Joe Williams, Della Williams, J. Ward Morehouse, Annabelle Strang, Gertrude Staple, Eleanor Stoddard, Eveline Hutchins, Paul Johnson, Charley Anderson, Margo Dowling, Agnes Mandeville, Frank Mandeville, Tony de Carrida, Sam Margolies, Richard (Dick) Ellsworth Savage, Anna Elizabeth Trent ("Daughter"), Mary French, Don Stevens, Benny Compton, and Webb Cruthers.

Vanity Fair: A Novel Without a Hero, by William Makepeace Thackeray (1848; first published serially as "Pen and Pencil Sketches of English Society" between January, 1847, and July, 1848). Settings: England, Brussels, and Battle of Waterloo. Principal characters: Rebecca (Becky) Sharp, Amelia Sedley, Joseph (Jos) Sedley, Sir Pitt Crawley, Miss Crawley, Rawdon Crawley, George Osborne, William Dobbin, and Lord Steyne.

Vicar of Wakefield, The, by Oliver Goldsmith (1766). Setting: England. Principal characters: Dr. Charles Primrose, Deborah Primrose, George Primrose, Moses Primrose, Olivia Primrose, Sophia Primrose, Arabella Wilmot, Mr. Burchell (alias of Sir William Thornhill), and Squire Thornhill.

Villette, by Charlotte Brontë (1853). Setting: Villette (Brussels). Principal characters: Lucy Snowe, Madame Beck, John Bretton, Ginevra Fanshawe, Paulina Home, and M. Paul Emmanuel.

Virginian, The, by Owen Wister (1902). Setting: Wyoming. Principal characters: the Virginian, Molly Wood, Trampas, Steve, Judge Henry, and Shorty.

Virginians, The, by William Makepeace Thackeray (1857–59). Settings: colonial Virginia and England. Principal characters: George Esmond Warrington, Harry Esmond Warrington, Madame Rachel Esmond Warrington, the Baroness Beatrix Bernstein, Lady Maria Esmond, William Esmond, Fanny Esmond, Lord Castlewood, Mr. Sampson, Gumbo, Colonel Lambert, Mrs. Lambert, Hetty Lambert, Theo Lambert, Fanny Mountain, Mrs. Mountain, Sir Miles Warrington, Lady Warrington, Dora Warrington, Flora

Warrington, Tom Claypool, Mademoiselle Cattarina, George Washington, Mr. Dempster, Lord March, Lord Morris, the Countess of Yarmouth Walmoden, Mrs. Betty, Case, and Mr. Draper.

Voyage Out, The, by Virginia Woolf (1915). Setting: fictional South American resort of Santa Marina. Principal characters: Rachel Vinrace, Helen Ambrose, Terrence Hewet, and St. John Alaric Hirst.

Waiting for the Barbarians, by J(ohn) M(axwell) Coetzee (1980). Setting: colonial outpost on the frontier of a fictional empire. Principal characters: the Magistrate, Colonel Joll, the barbarian girl, and Warrant Officer Mandel.

War and Peace (Russian title: *Voina i mir*), by Lev Nikolayevich Tolstoy (1868–69). Setting: Napoleonic-era Russia. Principal characters: Count Pierre Bezukhov, Count Cyril Bezukhov, Princess Catiche (Catherine Semenovna), Count Ilya Rostov, Countess Nataly Rostova, Count Nicholas Rostov, Count Peter (Petya) Rostov, Countess Vera Rostova, Countess Nataly (Natasha) Rostova, Sonia, Lieutenant Alphonse Karlich Berg, Prince Andrew Bolkonski, Princess Mary Bolkonskaya, Princess Elizabeth (Lise) Bolkonskaya, Prince Nicholas (Koko) Andreevich Bolkonski, Prince Vasili Kuragin, Prince Hippolyte Kuragin, Prince Anatole Kuragin, Princess Helene Kuragina, Princess Anna Mikhaylovna Drubetskaya, Prince Boris (Bory) Drubetskoy, and Julie Karagina.

Warden, The, by Anthony Trollope (1855). Setting: fictional city of Barchester, England. Principal characters: Rev. Septimus Harding, Eleanor Harding, Reverend Theophilus Grantly, Susan Grantly, Bishop Grantly, John Bold, Mary Bold, John Bunce, Abel Handy, Tom Towers, Sir Abraham Haphazard, Mr. Finney, Doctor Pessimist Anticant, Mr. Popular Sentiment, Chadwick, Charles James Grantly, Henry Grantly, Samuel Grantly, Florinda Grantly, and Grizzel Grantly.

Waterfall, The, by Margaret Drabble (1969). Settings: London and Yorkshire. Principal characters: Jane Gray, James Otford, Malcolm Gray, Lucy Goldsmith Otford, Laurie Gray, and Bianca Gray.

Way of All Flesh, The, by Samuel Butler (1903). Setting: England. Principal characters: Ernest Pontifex, Edward Overton, John Pontifex, George Pontifex, Theobald Pontifex, Christina Pontifex, Towneley, Ellen, and Aunt Alethea.

Well of Loneliness, The, by Radclyffe Hall (1928). Settings: England and Paris. Principal characters: Stephen Gordon, Lady Anna Gordon, Sir Philip Gordon, Collins, Mlle. Duphot, Miss Puddleton, Jonathan Brockett, Angela Crossby, Ralph Crossby, Mary Llewellyn, Valerie Seymour, Dupont, Margaret Roland, Adolphe Blanc, Jamie, Wanda, and Barbara.

Wide Sargasso Sea, by Jean Rhys (pseud. of Ella Gwendolen Rees Williams) (1966). Settings: Dominica, Jamaica, and England. Principal characters: Antoinette (Bertha) Mason, Edward Rochester, Annette Cosway Mason, and Christophine.

Wilhelm Meister's Apprenticeship (German title: *Wilhelm Meisters Lehrjahre*), by Johann Wolfgang von Goethe (1795–96). Setting: Germany. Principal characters: Wilhelm Meister, Mariana, Philina, Aurelia, Natalia, and Mignon.

Wilhelm Meister's Travels, or The Renunciants (German title: *Wilhelm Meisters Wanderjahre oder Die Entsagenden*), by Johann Wolfgang von Goethe (1829). Setting: Germany. Principal characters: Wilhelm Meister, Felix, Lenardo, Hersilia, Flavio, Makaria, Joseph, Mary, Jarno, Fitz, Hilaria, and Julietta.

Wind in the Willows, The, by Kenneth Grahame (1908). Setting: animal land. Principal characters: Mole, Water Rat, Toad, Badger, Otter, and Sea-Farer.

Wings of the Dove, by Henry James (1902). Setting: London. Principal characters: Milly Theale, Susan Stringham, Kate Croy, and Merton Densher.

Women in Love, by D(avid) H(erbert) Lawrence (1920). Settings: Beldover, a British Midlands coal town, and the Swiss Alps. Principal characters: Ursula Brangwen, Gudrun Brangwen, Rupert Birkin, Gerald Crich, Loerke, and Hermione Roddice.

Wuthering Heights, by Emily Brontë (under the pseud. Ellis Bell) (1847). Settings: Wuthering Heights and Thrushcross Grange, two fictional halls on the Yorkshire moors. Principal characters: Heathcliff, Catherine, Edgar Linton, Hindley, Nelly Dean, Isabella, Hareton, Cathy, and Lockwood.

SOURCES

Adey, David, Ridley Beeton, Michael Chapman, and Ernest Pereira. *A Companion to South African English Literature.* Craighall, Eng.: A. D. Donker, 1986.

Barnhart, Clarence L., ed. *The New Century Handbook of English Literature.* New York: Appleton-Century-Crofts, 1956.

Benét, William Rose. *The Reader's Encyclopedia.* 2nd ed. New York: T. Y. Crowell, 1955.

Bleiler, Everett F. *The Guide to Supernatural Fiction.* Kent, Ohio: Kent State University Press, 1983.

Drabble, Margaret, ed. *The Oxford Companion to English Literature.* 5th ed. New York: Oxford University Press, 1985.

Herzberg, Max J., *et al.,* eds. *The Readers Encyclopedia of American Literature.* New York: T. Y. Crowell, 1962.

Magill, Frank, ed. *Cyclopedia of Literary Characters.* Vol. II of 4 vols. Englewood Cliffs, N.J.: Salem Press, 1990.

———. *Masterplots: Cyclopedia of Literary Characters.* 2 vols. Englewood Cliffs, N.J.: Salem Press, 1963.

———. *Masterplots II: American Fiction Series.* 4 vols. Englewood Cliffs, N.J.: Salem Press, 1986.

———. *Masterplots II: British Fiction Series.* 4 vols. Englewood Cliffs, N.J.: Salem Press, 1987.

———. *Survey of Contemporary Literature.* 7 vols. Englewood Cliffs, N.J.: Salem Press, 1971.

Ousby, Ian, ed. *The Cambridge Guide to Literature in English*. Cambridge, Eng.: Cambridge University Press, 1988.

Perkins, George, Barbara Perkins, and Phillip Leininger, eds. *Benét's Reader's Encyclopedia of American Literature*. New York: HarperCollins, 1991.

Reid, Joyce M. H., ed. *The Concise Oxford Dictionary of French Literature*. Oxford: Clarendon Press, 1976.

Tuck, Dorothy. *Crowell's Handbook of Faulkner*. New York: T. Y. Crowell, 1964.

Ward, A. C. *Longman Companion to Twentieth-Century Literature*. 2nd ed. London: Longman, 1975.

Ward, Philip. *The Oxford Companion to Spanish Literature*. Oxford: Clarendon Press, 1978.

Wilde, William H., Jay Hooten, and Barry Andrews. *The Oxford Companion to Australian Literature*. Melbourne: Oxford University Press, 1985.

Wynne-Davies, Marion, ed. *The Bloomsbury Guide to English Literature*. London: Bloomsbury Publishing, 1989.

—Ian Crump; L.D.R.

34

OCCUPATIONS OF FAMOUS
BRITISH, IRISH, AND
AMERICAN WRITERS

· · · · ·

TO WRITE WELL HAS NEVER BEEN A NOTABLY REMUNERATIVE ACTIVITY. IF IN Samuel Johnson's famous dictum, no one but a blockhead ever writes but for money—which repeatedly throughout his career he demonstrated wasn't so—then usually it hasn't been for very much money. The number of important writers who could earn a living entirely upon the proceeds of what they wrote has always been small, and is scarcely larger today than in the past. Indirect earnings are another matter.

Up until the eighteenth century, successful writers could generally depend upon the patronage of the aristocracy. In more recent times there have been governmental subsidies, political sinecures, and nowadays teaching appointments in universities. There is debate as to whether our literature is better off when our writers are teaching, or when they must write journalism, edit magazines, or work in hardware stores and banks for their daily bread and lodging. Generally those who don't teach believe that those who do shouldn't. The theory is that when employed in banks, newsrooms, or advertising agencies, as writers they would be less academic and in closer touch with everyday reality.

Nowadays many writers, particularly poets, do teach in creative writing programs. The late Flannery O'Connor reported that students sometimes complained to her that creative writing teachers at colleges and universities discouraged young writers; her own complaint was that they didn't discourage enough of them. Be that as it may, it is difficult to believe that, say, Edgar Allan Poe would have been a less effective writer had he taught at Columbia instead of writing hack journalism, or that William Golding's fiction would have been less in touch with the real world had he not taught at Bishop Wordsworth's School. It all depends on the particular writer.

What follows is a list of what an assortment of British and American authors have done at various times in their careers in order either to earn a living on a regular basis or else because they thought it needed doing.

A.E. (pseud. of George W. Russell). Agricultural editor.

Adams, Henry. Journalist, teacher.

Addison, Joseph. English government official, editor.

Agee, James. Journalist.

Alger, Horatio, Jr. Clergyman.

Ammons, A. R. Elementary school principal, biological glassware manufacturer, teacher.

Anderson, Maxwell. Teacher, newspaper reporter, magazine editor.

Anderson, Sherwood. Advertising writer, newspaper publisher.

Apple, Max. Teacher.

Arnold, Matthew. Inspector of schools, teacher.

Ashbery, John. Art journal critic, editor, teacher.

Auchincloss, Louis. Attorney.

Auden, W. H. Teacher.

Baldwin, James. Minister.

Barlow, Joel. Teacher, attorney, land agent, U.S. consul.

Barth, John. Teacher.

Beckett, Samuel. Teacher.

Beckford, William. Member of Parliament for Wells, Hindon.

Beddoes, Thomas Lovell. Physician.

Beerbohm, Max. Journalist.

Behn, Aphra. Spy.

Bellamy, Edward. Journalist.

Bellow, Saul. Teacher.

Benchley, Robert. Journalist, actor.

Bennett, Arnold. Solicitor's clerk, journalist.

Berry, Wendell. Farmer, teacher.

Berryman, John. Teacher.

Bierce, Ambrose. Night watchman, journalist.

Bishop, Elizabeth. Teacher.

Blake, William. Engraver and illustrator.

Bontemps, Arna. Librarian, teacher.

Boswell, James. Barrister.

Brontë, Anne. Governess.

Brontë, Charlotte. Governess, teacher.

Brooks, Gwendolyn. Publicist, teacher.

Brooks, Van Wyck. Journalist.

Brown, Charles Brockden. Editor.

Brown, Larry. Fireman.

Bryant, William Cullen. Lawyer, newspaper editor.

Buchan, John. Government official, governor-general of Canada.

Bunyan, John. Tinker, itinerant preacher.

Burke, Edmund. Government official, member of Parliament for Wendover, Bristol, Malton, Yorkshire.

Burns, Robert. Excise officer.

Burton, Robert. Rector.

Butler, Samuel. Sheep breeder.

Bynner, Witter. Journalist.

Cabell, James Branch. Genealogist, journalist.

Cable, George W. Journalist, clerk in cotton exchange.

Caldwell, Erskine. Journalist.

Callaghan, Morley. Attorney, journalist.

Carlyle, Thomas. Teacher.

Carroll, Lewis (pseud. of Charles Lutwidge Dodgson). Teacher.

Cary, Joyce. District officer in Nigerian civil service.

Cather, Willa. Journalist, teacher, magazine editor.

Chandler, Raymond. Oil company executive.

Chaucer, Geoffrey. Courtier, diplomat, knight of the shire (*i.e.*, M.P.) for Kent.

Chesnutt, Charles. Court stenographer, teacher, attorney.

Cibber, Colley. Actor.

Coleridge, Samuel Taylor. Journalist, editor.

Congreve, William. Government official.

Conrad, Joseph. Seaman.

Coward, Noel. Actor.

Crabbe, George. Surgeon, clergyman.

Crane, Stephen. Journalist.

Cullen, Countee. Editor, teacher.

Davie, Donald. Teacher.

Defoe, Daniel. Journalist and political writer, government agent.

De la Mare, Walter. Businessman.

De Quincey, Thomas. Journalist.

Dickens, Charles. Editor.

Dickey, James. Advertising writer, teacher.

Donne, John. Royal chaplain and dean of St. Paul's Cathedral, justice of the peace.

Dos Passos, John. Journalist.

Dove, Rita. Teacher.

Dowson, Ernest. Assistant manager of a dock.

Doyle, Arthur Conan. Physician.

Dreiser, Theodore. Journalist, magazine editor.

Durrell, Lawrence. Foreign service officer.

Eberhart, Richard. Teacher, vice-president of wax company.

Edgerton, Clyde. Teacher.

Eliot, T. S. Bank clerk, publisher.

Ellison, Ralph. Teacher.

Emerson, Ralph Waldo. Clergyman, optimist.

Empson, William. Teacher.

Etheridge, Sir George. Diplomat.

Farrell, James T. Assorted jobs.

Faulkner, William. Film scriptwriter.

Fielding, Henry. Magistrate.

Fitzgerald, F. Scott. Film scriptwriter.

Franklin, Benjamin. Printer, postmaster, diplomat.

Freneau, Philip. Journalist.

Frost, Robert. Farmer, teacher.

Garrett, George. Teacher.

Gass, William. Teacher.

Gay, John. Silk mercer.

Gibbon, Edward. Military officer, member of Parliament for Liskeard, Lymington, secretary to board of trade.

Gold, Herbert. Editor.

Golding, William. Teacher.

Goldsmith, Oliver. Physician, journalist.

Gordon, Caroline. Teacher.

Graves, Robert. Teacher.

Gray, Thomas. Don, Cambridge University.

Green, Henry. Managing director, business.

Greene, Graham. Journalist, magazine editor.

Haley, Alex. Coast Guardsman.

Hall, Donald. Teacher.

Halleck, Fitz-Greene. Banker.

Hammett, Dashiell. Detective.

Hardy, Thomas. Architect.

Harper, Michael. Teacher.

Harris, George Washington. Jeweler, railroad superintendent.

Harris, Joel Chandler. Journalist.

Harte, Bret. Miner, journalist, U.S. consul.

Hayden, Robert. Teacher.

Hazlitt, William. Journalist.

Hearn, Lafcadio. Journalist, teacher.

Hemingway, Ernest. Journalist.

Henry, O. (pseud. of William Sidney Porter) Bank teller, journalist.

Herbert, George. Member of Parliament for Montgomery; deacon, priest.

Herrick, Robert. Vicar.

Hersey, John. Journalist, teacher.

Hill, Geoffrey. Teacher.

Hilton, James. Journalist, teacher.

Hoffman, Daniel. Teacher.

Holmes, Oliver Wendell. Physician, professor of medicine.

Hopkins, Gerard Manley. Jesuit priest, teacher.

Housman, A. E. Teacher.

Howells, William Dean. Journalist, editor, U.S. consul.

Hughes, Langston. Seaman, dishwasher, busboy.

Hugo, Richard. Industrial writer, teacher.

Hurston, Zora Neale. Anthropologist, housekeeper.

Irving, Washington. Lawyer, diplomat.

James, Henry. Journalist.

Jarrell, Randall. Teacher.

Johnson, James Weldon. Attorney, teacher, U.S. consul, NAACP organizer.

Johnson, Samuel. Teacher, journalist, lexicographer.

Jones, David. Engraver, painter, illustrator.

Jonson, Ben. Actor.

Joyce, James. Language teacher.

Kavanagh, Patrick. Journalist.

Keats, John. Apothecary.

Kennedy, John Pendleton. Attorney, U.S. congressman from Maryland, secretary of the navy.

Kennedy, William. Journalist, teacher.

Kipling, Rudyard. Journalist.

Lamb, Charles. Clerk for East India Company.

Lanier, Sidney. Flautist, teacher.

Lardner, Ring. Sportswriter.

Larkin, Philip. Librarian.

Lawrence, D. H. Clerk, teacher.

Lewis, C. Day. Teacher.

Lewis, Matthew Gregory. Member of Parliament for Hindon.

Lewis, Sinclair. Journalist.

Liebling, A. J. Journalist.

London, Jack. Longshoreman, sealer, tramp, etc.

Longfellow, Henry Wadsworth. Teacher.

Longstreet, Augustus Baldwin. Newspaper editor, attorney, clergyman, teacher.

Lowell, James Russell. Attorney, editor, teacher, diplomat.

Lytle, Andrew. Farmer, teacher, editor.

McCorkle, Jill. Teacher.

MacDairmid, Hugh. Journalist.

McFee, William. Seaman.

McKay, Claude. Constable, pullman porter.

MacLeish, Archibald. Attorney, teacher, editor, librarian, diplomat.

MacNeice, Louis. Teacher, radio producer.

McPhee, William. Television scriptwriter, journalist.

Malamud, Bernard. Teacher.

Marlowe, Christopher. Spy.

Marquand, J. P. Journalist, advertising writer.

Marvell, Andrew. Member of Parliament for Hull, diplomat.

Masefield, John. Seaman, journalist.

Mason, Bobbie Ann. Teacher.

Masters, Edgar Lee. Attorney.

Maugham, Somerset. Physician.

Melville, Herman. Inspector of customs.

Mencken, H. L. Journalist, magazine editor.

Merwin, W. S. Tutor, translator.

Miller, Arthur. Truck driver, waiter, laborer.

Miller, Henry. Tailor, telegraph company manager, proprietor of speakeasy.

Milton, John. Propagandist and Latin (*i.e.*, Foreign) Secretary.

Moore, Marianne. Teacher, librarian.

More, Sir Thomas. Chancellor of England.

Morris, William. Businessman, designer.

Morris, Wright. Teacher.

Morrison, Toni. Publishing house editor.

Muir, Edwin. Worker in bone factory, journalist, warden of Newbattle Abbey.

Murray, Albert. Air Force officer, teacher.

Nabokov, Vladimir. Teacher.

Nemerov, Howard. Teacher.

Norris, Frank. Journalist.

Oates, Joyce Carol. Teacher.

O'Brien, Flann. Newspaper columnist.

O'Casey, Sean. Railroad laborer.

Odets, Clifford. Actor.

O'Hara, Frank. Museum curator, editor.

O'Hara, John. Journalist.

Olsen, Tillie. Typist.

Olson, Charles. Teacher.

O'Neill, Eugene. Seaman, journalist.

Orwell, George. Member of Indian constabulary, dishwasher, radio broadcaster, factory worker.

Page, Thomas Nelson. Attorney, diplomat.

Parker, Dorothy. Pianist, journalist.

Pater, Walter. Teacher.

Pinter, Harold. Actor.

Poe, Edgar Allan. Magazine editor, soldier.

Porter, Katherine Anne. Actress, journalist.

Price, Reynolds. Teacher.

Prior, Matthew. Government official, diplomat, member of Parliament for East Grinstead.

Pynchon, Thomas. Journalist.

Ransom, John Crowe. Teacher, editor.

Rexroth, Kenneth. Journalist.

Rice, Elmer. Attorney.

Rich, Adrienne. Teacher.

Richardson, Samuel. Printer.

Robinson, Edwin Arlington. Subway worker, customs house employee.

Roethke, Theodore. Teacher.

Rossetti, Dante Gabriel. Painter.

Sandburg, Carl. Journalist.

Sanders, Dori. Farmer, assistant banquet manager of motel.

Schorer, Mark. Teacher.

Schwartz, Delmore. Teacher.

Scott, Sir Walter. Sheriff-deputy, clerk of court, partner in printing company.

Sexton, Anne. Teacher.

Shakespeare, William. Actor, landlord.

Shapiro, Karl. Teacher, editor.

Shaw, George Bernard. Music critic.

Sheridan, Richard Brinsley. Member of Parliament for Stafford, Westminster, Ilchester.

Sherwood, Robert. Journalist.

Simms, William Gilmore. Journalist, editor.

Simpson, Louis. Teacher.

Smith, Dave. Teacher, editor.

Smith, Lee. Teacher.

Smith, Stevie. Radio writer, broadcaster.

Spencer, Elizabeth. Journalist, teacher.

Spender, Stephen. Editor, teacher.

Spenser, Edmund. Government official, sheriff.

Steele, Richard. Justice of the peace, member of Parliament for Boroughbridge, Yorkshire.

Steinbeck, John. Journalist, laborer, surveyor.

Sterne, Laurence. Clergyman.

Stevens, Wallace. Lawyer, vice-president of insurance company.

Stoker, Bram. Actor's manager.

Strand, Mark. Teacher.

Suckling, Sir John. Diplomat.

Swift, Jonathan. Dean of St. Patrick's Cathedral, Dublin.

Tarkington, Booth. State legislator.

Tate, Allen. Editor, teacher.

Taylor, Edward. Clergyman.

Taylor, Peter. Teacher.

Thackeray, William Makepeace. Illustrator.

Thomas, Dylan. Journalist.

Thoreau, Henry David. Pencil maker, surveyor.

Thurber, James. Journalist.

Timrod, Henry. Tutor, journalist.

Tolkien, J. R. R. Teacher.

Trollope, Anthony. Postal clerk.

Twain, Mark (pseud. of Samuel L. Clemens). Printer, steamboat pilot, journalist, publisher.

Vaughan, Henry. Physician.

Walker, Alice. Teacher.

Waller, Edmund. Member of Parliament for Amersham, Ilchester, Chipping Wycombe, St. Ives, Hastings.

Walpole, Horace. Member of Parliament for Callington, Castle Rising, King's Lynn.

Warren, Robert Penn. Teacher.

Wells, H. G. Draper's apprentice, teacher.

Welty, Eudora. Photographer.

West, Nathanael. Hotel clerk, movie scriptwriter.

Wheatley, Phillis. Slave.

White, E. B. Advertising writer, journalist.

Whitman, Walt. Printer, building contractor, newspaper editor, government clerk.

Whittier, John Greenleaf. Journalist.

Wilbur, Richard. Teacher.

Wilder, Thornton. Teacher.

Williams, William Carlos. Pediatrician.

Wilson, Edmund. Magazine editor.

Winters, Yvor. Teacher.

Wolfe, Thomas. Teacher.

Woolf, Virginia. Publisher.

Wordsworth, William. Distributor of stamps.

Wright, Charles. Teacher.

Wright, James. Teacher.
Wright, Richard. Porter, salesman, postal worker, WPA worker, journalist.
Wyatt, Sir Thomas. Diplomat, justice of the peace, sheriff.
Zukofsky, Louis. Teacher.

SOURCES

Barnhart, Clarence L., ed. *The New Century Handbook of English Literature.* New York: Appleton-Century-Crofts, 1956.

Hart, James D., ed. *The Oxford Companion to American Literature.* 4th ed. New York: Oxford University Press, 1965.

New Encyclopaedia Britannica: Micropëdia. 15th ed. Chicago: Encyclopaedia Britannica Co., Inc., 1990.

Vinson, James, ed. *Great Writers of the English Language.* 3 vols. New York: St. Martin's Press, 1979.

Wynne-Davies, Marion, ed. *Prentice-Hall Guide to English Literature.* New York: Prentice-Hall, 1990.

—Ian Crump; LDR

35

EPIC HEROES AND HEROINES

. . . . .

UNTIL ABOUT THREE HUNDRED YEARS OR SO AGO THE EPIC WAS CONSIDERED the ultimate form that literature could assume, to be handled only by the greatest of poets. Today the form is dead; no competent poet in his right mind would think to try writing one. "Epic" now means a Hollywood historical extravaganza.

The formal epic poem as such comes down to us from Homer in the latter years of the eighth century B.C.E., but extended poetic tales chronicling the heroic deeds of warriors, kings, and divinities go far back before that in time. Unlike the *Iliad*, the *Odyssey*, and Virgil's *Aeneid*, such poetry was recited and remembered orally rather than written down.

During the nineteenth century it was thought that there was actually no such person as a single author named Homer, and that both *The Iliad* and *The Odyssey* were transcripts of narrative poems that had been recited by bards for centuries. Nowadays scholars generally agree that there was indeed a poet named Homer, and that he did indeed write the two epics, which are obviously carefully shaped literary narratives and not rote-learned recitations, but that he used traditional oral material and many of the conventions of bardic recitation.

The last major epics of importance were those of John Milton in the seventeenth century. Of *Paradise Lost* Samuel Johnson wrote that "None ever wished it longer than it is." Thereafter the epic form declined, in large part because readers had come to expect more realistic portrayals of characters, and because attitudes toward heroic personages were changing. The epic conventions now seemed too contrived and artificial.

Poets wrote mock epics such as *The Rape of the Lock*, by Alexander Pope. In a sense the development of the historical novel as a literary genre provided a replacement for some of the social functions of the epic, as with *War and Peace, Dr. Zhivago,* and *Gone with the Wind*. James Joyce's *Ulysses* both parodies the Homeric epic poem and uses its theme to show what it means in terms of modern middle-class experience.

The following list of epic heroes and heroines is drawn from twenty-odd works of epic literature spanning 4,000 years of human culture.

Acestes. Trojan chieftain ruling in Sicily before the advent of Aeneas in Virgil's *Aeneid* (19 B.C.E.).

Achilles. Main hero of Homer's *Iliad* (ca. 725 B.C.E.), whose wrath—first toward his leader Agamemnon and later toward his enemy Hector—is the chief motive factor of the poem's plot.

Adam. Principal earthly figure in John Milton's *Paradise Lost* (1667).

Aeneas. Son of the goddess Aphrodite and the human Anchises, leader of the Dardanian troops at the siege of Troy in Homer's *Iliad* and later the main hero of Virgil's *Aeneid* (19 B.C.E.)

Agamemnon. Leader of the Greeks during the ten-year siege of Troy in Homer's *Iliad*. His bullying tactics incur the wrath of Achilles and set the tragic plot in action.

Aias. See **Ajax**.

Aineias. See **Aeneas**.

Ajax. Powerful but slow-witted Greek warrior in Homer's *Iliad*. Ajax is second only to Achilles in strength and martial ability, but he is the only major hero in the poem who receives no help from the gods.

Aladine. Prince of Judea and persecutor of Christians in Torquato Tasso's *Jerusalem Delivered* (1581).

Alexandros. See **Paris**.

Altamore. King of Samarcand, suitor of Armida, and slayer of many in Torquato Tasso's *Jerusalem Delivered*.

Amoret. Sister of Belphoebe captured by the evil Busirane in Edmund Spenser's *The Faerie Queene* (1590–96).

Amphialus. Son of the evil Cecropia and usurper of the throne of his uncle Basilius in Sir Philip Sidney's prose epic, *Arcadia* (1590).

Anchises. Father of Aeneas by the goddess Aphrodite in Virgil's *Aeneid*.

Andromache. Wife of the Trojan hero Hector and mother of Astyanax in Homer's *Iliad*.

Angelica. The great love of Orlando in Matteo Boiardo's *Orlando Innamorato* (1494).

Anzu. Hero of the Mesopotamian *Epic of Anzu* (ca. 800 B.C.E.).

Argantes. Ferocious Circassian opponent of Christians who is finally slain by Tancred in Torquato Tasso's *Jerusalem Delivered*.

Arjuna. Main hero and one of the brothers rival for the throne in the Sanskrit *Mahabharata* (ca. 500 B.C.E.) of ancient India. His discourse with a charioteer makes up a famous subsection known as the *Bhagavat Gita*.

Armida. Circelike seductress of Rinaldo in Torquato Tasso's *Jerusalem Delivered*.

Artegall. Hero of the quest for justice in Edmund Spenser's *The Faerie Queene.*

Arthur, Prince. Chief hero of *The Faerie Queene,* as of other works cited under "Legendary Kings and Knights," elsewhere in this book. Spenser's original plan was to write an epic in twelve books depicting the perfection of Prince Arthur in virtue before he became king; but he lived only to complete six books and fragments of a seventh.

Ascanius. Son of Aeneas and Creusa in Virgil's *Aeneid.*

Basilius. King of Arcadia in Sir Philip Sidney's *Arcadia,* husband of Gynecia, and father of Pamela and Philoclea.

Beatrice. Inspirational lady in much of Dante's poetry, who appears in *The Divine Comedy* (1321) to lead the author into Paradise.

Beelzebub. Satan's chief lieutenant after the fall from heaven in Milton's *Paradise Lost.*

Belphoebe. Beautiful sister of Amoret in Edmund Spenser's *The Faerie Queene.* Sir Walter Raleigh also used the name to designate Queen Elizabeth in several poems he wrote to her in the 1590s.

Beowulf. Hero of the Anglo-Saxon heroic poem *Beowulf* (ca. 725), whose main feats are the slaying of the monster Grendel and of Grendel's mother, a water-hag.

Britomart. Heroine of the quest for chastity in Edmund Spenser's *The Faerie Queene,* Book 3.

Brynhild. Wise and militant valkyrie who loves Sigurd but loses him to Gudrun, after which Brynhild murders him and immolates herself on his funeral pyre in the Icelandic *Volsunga Saga* (ca. 1250).

Caesar. Roman general who triumphs over Pompey at the battle of Pharsalia as represented in Lucan's Latin epic, *Pharsalia* (ca. 63–65).

Calidore. Hero of the quest for courtesy in Edmund Spenser's *The Faerie Queene,* Book 6.

Cambel. Hero, with Telamond, of the quest for friendship in Edmund Spenser's *The Faerie Queene,* Book 4.

Camilla. Warrior-maiden in Virgil's *Aeneid.*

Christ. See **Jesus.**

Clorinda. Warlike and powerful female pagan who, after many battles and much slaughter, accepts baptism on her deathbed in Torquato Tasso's *Jerusalem Delivered.*

Clout, Colin. Poet-hero in several works by Edmund Spenser, especially *The Faerie Queene.*

Cu Chulainn. Semidivine hero of a medieval cycle of Irish myths and legendary tales.

Deiphobus. Son of the Trojan king Priam and one of the more prominent warriors in Homer's *Iliad.*

Deirdre. Heroine in Irish legend whose fate is to bring trouble to all with whom she becomes involved. One version of her story, which dates back to at least the ninth century, is in the twelfth-century *Book of Leinster*.

Dido. Suicidal queen of Carthage, lover of Aeneas in Virgil's *Aeneid*.

Diomedes. Second or third most powerful Greek fighter (after Achilles and possibly Ajax) in Homer's *Iliad*. Diomedes is a young, eager, and flashy warrior, thoroughly and somewhat blindly committed to the heroic code of his culture.

Draupadi. Beautiful wife to all five of a band of brothers in the Sanskrit epic *Mahabharata* of ancient India.

Enkidu. Wild and primitive man created by the goddess Aruru as an opponent of Gilgamesh but later Gilgamesh's ally in the Babylonian *Epic of Gilgamesh* (*ca.* 1800 B.C.E.).

Erra. Hero of the Mesopotamian *Epic of Erra* (*ca.* 800 B.C.E.).

Eve. The first woman, heroine of John Milton's *Paradise Lost*.

Ganelon. Roland's stepfather, undertaker of the dangerous task of envoy to the Saracens, and betrayer of Roland in the French *Song of Roland* (*ca.* 1100).

Gilgamesh. Young ruler of Uruk, semidivine hero of the Babylonian *Epic of Gilgamesh*, bringer of knowledge from before the time of the Great Flood.

Godfrey of Bouillon. Captain and a major hero in Torquato Tasso's *Jerusalem Delivered* who eventually conquers the city of Jerusalem and returns it to Christian rule.

Grendel. See **Beowulf**.

Guyon. Hero of the quest for temperance in Edmund Spenser's *The Faerie Queene*, Book 2.

Hector. Son of Priam, chief Trojan hero of *The Iliad*, whose slaying of Patroclus incurs the wrath and revenge of Achilles.

Hecuba. See **Hekabe**.

Hekabe. Wife of Priam, King of Troy, and mother of Hector, Paris, and numerous other sons in Homer's *Iliad*.

Helen (of Troy). Former wife of the Greek chieftain Menelaus. Her abduction by the Trojan Paris, aided by Aphrodite, occasioned the Trojan War in *The Iliad*.

Helgi. Son of Sigmund and a prominent hero in the Icelandic *Volsunga Saga*.

Herakles. Greek hero (accorded immortality and divine status upon his death in some of the mythological tales) whose twelve heroic labors are recorded in many accounts. They are the strangling of the Nemean lion; the defeat of the many-headed Hydra; the capture of the fleet Cerynithian deer; the netting of the Erymanthian boar; the cleaning out of the filthy Augeian stables; the routing of the Stymphalian birds from their roosting places; the capture of the Cretan bull; the capture of the mares of Diomedes; the capture of the belt of Hippolyta, queen of the Amazons; the herding of Geryon's cattle; the collection of the apples of the Hesperides; and the extraction of the great three-headed hound Cerberus from the underworld.

Hercules. See **Herakles**.

Hiordis. Wife of Sigmund and mother of Sigurd in the Icelandic *Volsunga Saga*.

Hrothgar. Danish king in the Anglo-Saxon heroic poem *Beowulf*.

Humbaba. Forest giant slain by Gilgamesh and Enkidu in the Babylonian *Epic of Gilgamesh*. In some texts the name is Huwawa.

Huwawa. See **Humbaba**.

Idomeneus. Lord of Crete in Homer's *Iliad*, one of the more distinguished of the Greek warriors.

Iulus. See **Ascanius**.

Jason. Captain of the ship *Argo* and leader of the Argonauts in quest of the Golden Fleece, husband of Medea in the *Argonautica* (*ca.* 215 B.C.E.) of Apollonius of Rhodes.

Jesus (Christ). Son of God who takes human form in order to save mankind in Milton's *Paradise Lost* and *Paradise Regained* (1671); also hero of Marco Vida's Latin epic *The Christiad* (1535).

Latinus. King of Latium in Virgil's *Aeneid*.

Mammon. Fallen angel, later to be pagan god of wealth in John Milton's *Paradise Lost*.

Marduk. Hero of the Mesopotamian *Epic of Creation* (*ca.* 1000 B.C.E.), conquerer of the goddess Tiamat; also appears in the Mesopotamian *Epic of Erra* (*ca.* 800 B.C.E.).

Menelaus. Brother of King Agamemnon and first husband of Helen, whose abduction by the Trojan Paris with the aid of Aphrodite occasioned the Trojan War in Homer's *Iliad*.

Moloch. Fallen angel, later to become pagan god of violence and idolatry in John Milton's *Paradise Lost*.

Musidorus. Prince of Thessaly, one of the two main heroes (with Pyrocles) of Sir Philip Sidney's *Arcadia*. Musidorus falls in love with Pamela, daughter of King Basilius.

Nestor. Aged warrior and counselor of the Greeks in Homer's *Iliad*, distinguished both for his wisdom and his garrulousness.

Odysseus. Craftiest and most articulate of the Greeks in Homer's *Iliad*, chief hero of Homer's *Odyssey* (*ca.* 700 B.C.E.), husband of the faithful Penelope, and father of Telemachus. In Roman accounts he is known as Ulysses.

Oliver. Crusader with Roland in the French *Song of Roland*.

Orlando. Italian name for the epic hero Roland, hero of Matteo Boiardo's *Orlando Innamorato* (1494) and Ludovico Ariosto's *Orlando Furioso* (1516).

Palinurus. Aeneas' helmsman in Virgil's *Aeneid*.

Pandarus. Trojan soldier who breaks a truce by shooting Menelaus with an arrow in Homer's *Iliad*.

Paris. Son of Priam and seducer of Helen of Troy, whose abduction is the ultimate cause of the Trojan War in Homer's *Iliad;* also referred to as Alexandros.

Patroclus. Tentmate and close friend of Achilles in Homer's *Iliad.* Patroclus' death at the hands of Hector brings Achilles back into the war to exact revenge.

Penelope. Odysseus' faithful wife in Homer's *Odyssey,* who resists the pressure of numerous suitors during her husband's long absence from their home in Ithaca.

Pompey. Roman general defeated by Caesar at the battle of Pharsalia in Lucan's Latin epic, *Pharsalia.*

Priam. King of Troy in Homer's *Iliad* and Virgil's *Aeneid.* In *The Iliad* his supplication for the body of his slain son Hector brings about his reconciliation with Achilles, the end of Achilles' wrath, and the conclusion of the poem.

Pyrocles. Prince of Macedon, one of the two main heroes (with Musidorus) of Sir Philip Sidney's *Arcadia.* Pyrocles falls in love with Philoclea, daughter of King Basilius.

Quingu. Monster leader of an army, slain by Marduk in the Mesopotamian *Epic of Creation.*

Rama. Prince and hero of the Sanskrit epic *The Ramayana* (ca. 500 b.c.e.) of ancient India.

Raphael. Angel sent to enlighten Adam and explain God's plan before the Fall of Man in John Milton's *Paradise Lost.*

Ravana. Demon-king, abductor of Rama's wife Sita in the Sanskrit epic *The Ramayana;* slain by Rama with the aid of the nation of monkeys.

Raymond. Count of Toulouse, a Christian hero in Torquato Tasso's *Jerusalem Delivered* who eventually places the cross on the tower of David.

Re. Also Ra; Egyptian sun god whose heroic progress through the sky and underworld is charted in the twelve episodes of *The Book of Am-Duat* (ca. 1425 b.c.e.). Shorter versions are *The Book of Gates* (ca. 1300 b.c.e.) and *The Book of Caverns* (ca. 1150 b.c.e.).

Redcrosse Knight, The. Hero of the quest for holiness in Edmund Spenser's *The Faerie Queene,* Book 1.

Rhiannon. Goddess-heroine in the Welsh *Mabinogion* (ca. 1200).

Rinaldo. Warrior and lover of Armida in Torquato Tasso's *Jerusalem Delivered.*

Roland. Hero of the French *Song of Roland,* leader of the crusaders against the Saracens. See **Orlando.**

Satan. Epic fiend, tempter of angels and human beings in John Milton's *Paradise Lost* (1671) and *Paradise Regained* (1697), and instigator of the crucifixion in Marco Vida's *Christiad* (1535).

Satyrane. Satyr-hero in Edmund Spenser's *The Faerie Queene.*

Scipio Africanus. Roman general of the Second Punic War, hero of Francesco Petrarch's neo-Latin epic, *Africa* (1341).

Siegfried. See **Sigurd**.

Sigmund. Major hero in the Icelandic *Volsunga Saga*.

Sigurd. Hero who slays the dragon Fafnir in the *Volsunga Saga*; appears as Siegfried in the operas of Richard Wagner (1813–83).

Sita. Wife of Prince Rama in the Sanskrit epic of ancient India, *The Ramayana*.

Solyman. Turkish hero killed by Rinaldo in Torquato Tasso's *Jerusalem Delivered*.

Talus. Invincible iron man, henchman of Artegall in Edmund Spenser's *The Faerie Queene*.

Tancred. Christian hero and rescuer of Raymond in Torquato Tasso's *Jerusalem Delivered*.

Telamond. See **Cambel**.

Telemachus. Son of Odysseus and Penelope in Homer's *Odyssey*.

Thersites. Ugly and obnoxious member of the Greek camp who speaks ironically and bitterly but with biting accuracy to his comrades in Homer's *Iliad*.

Turnus. Rutulian king slain by Aeneas at the end of Virgil's *Aeneid*.

Ulysses. See **Odysseus**.

Una. Wandering heroine eventually betrothed to the Redcrosse Knight in Edmund Spenser's *The Faerie Queene*, Book 1.

Uriel. Angel appointed as the guardian of the entrance to earth in John Milton's *Paradise Lost*.

Vasco da Gama. Portuguese navigator and voyager to India, epic hero of Luis de Camoens' nationalistic epic *Os Lusiadas* (1572), also called *The Luciad*.

Virgil. Classical poet and author of *The Aeneid* who appears as a character in Dante's *Divine Comedy* (1321) and guides the speaker of the poem (Dante himself) through Purgatory and Hell.

SOURCES

Ariosto, Ludovico. *Orlando Furioso*. Translated by Sir John Harington. Edited by Rudolf Gottfried. Bloomington, Ind.: Indiana University Press, 1963.

Dante Alighieri. *The Divine Comedy*. Transated by H. R. Huse. New York: Rinehart and Co., 1954.

Hart, George. *Egyptian Myths*. Austin: University of Texas Press, 1990.

Homer. *The Iliad*. Translated by Richmond Lattimore. Chicago: University of Chicago Press, 1951.

———. *The Odyssey*. Translated by George Herbert Palmer. Cambridge, Mass.: Harvard University Press, 1912.

Hornstein, Lilian Herlands, and G. D. Percy, eds., *The Reader's Companion to World Literature*. New York: New American Library, 1956.

Lucan. *Pharsalia*. Translated by Robert Graves. Harmondsworth, Eng.: Penguin Books, 1957.

McCall, Henrietta. *Mesopotamian Myths*. Austin: University of Texas Press, 1990.

Spenser, Edmund. *The Faerie Queene.* Edited by Thomas P. Roche, Jr. Harmondsworth, Eng.: Penguin Books, 1978.

Tasso, Torquato. *Jerusalem Delivered.* Translated and edited by Ralph Nash. Detroit, Mich.: Wayne State University Press, 1987.

Tillyard, E. M. W. *The English Epic and Its Background.* London: Chatto and Windus, 1954.

Vida, Marco Girolamo. *The Christiad.* Translated and edited by Gertrude C. Drake. Carbondale, Ill.: Southern Illinois University Press, 1978.

Virgil. *The Aeneid.* Translated by W. F. Jackson Knight. Harmondsworth, Eng.: Penguin Books, 1958.

—J.L.M.

36

KNIGHTS AND KINGS OF CHIVALRIC LEGEND

. . . . .

IT WILL BE RECALLED THAT THE POET EDWIN ARLINGTON ROBINSON'S MINIVER Cheevy "loved the days of old / When swords were bright and steeds were prancing; / The vision of a warrior bold / Would set him dancing," and that he "dreamed of Thebes and Camelot, / And Priam's neighbors." Miniver's trouble was that he was "born too late," and could only scratch his head, cough, and keep on drinking.

The days of medieval knighthood and chivalry have long exercised an imaginative appeal upon writers and readers. By the time of the Renaissance the doings of knights, squires, and ladies in distress had so come to dominate the literary scene that Miguel de Cervantes Saavedra felt impelled to satirize the whole business in *Don Quixote* (1605, 1615). Effective though Cervantes' great work was as literature, it by no means succeeded in eradicating the infamy, however, so that Mark Twain had to try doing it all over again in *A Connecticut Yankee in King Arthur's Court* (1889). (The truth was that neither Cervantes nor Sam Clemens was 100 percent convinced of its foolishness himself, and neither was the creator of Miniver Cheevy, who also wrote several long narrative poems about Arthurian knights.)

Most of our romantic notions about knights and chivalry come not from the actual historical European institution of knighthood itself, but from the chivalric legends of the Middle Ages, almost all of which have something to do with the British king Arthur, the knights associated with him, or his predecessors in the line of legendary rulers of Britain extending back to the supposed first immigrants to the island, Trojan survivors of the Greek siege immortalized by Homer in the *Iliad* (*ca.* 725 B.C.E.).

The Arthurian matter comes down to us in two related but essentially separate traditions. One is the large body of Arthurian stories contained in thirteenth-century French and fourteenth-century English romances, in both prose and verse, culminating in the second half of the fifteenth century in Sir Thomas Malory's huge collection, *Le Morte d'Arthur*.

The other, earlier tradition is the pseudo-historical accounts that attempt to link the early Britons with Troy. These survive from as early as the ninth century but receive their first continuous and coherent treatment in Geoffrey of Monmouth's *History of the Kings of Britain*, written in Latin as *Historia Regum Britanniae* about the year 1137. Geoffrey, a Welsh monk, describes how the nation was founded by one of the nephews of the Trojan king Priam, a warrior named Brute. After the sack of Troy, Brute and his followers voyaged until they reached an unknown island, faced with chalk cliffs and inhabited by a race of giants. After defeating the giants and naming the land after himself ("Brutan" became "Britain"), Brute established a government and a line of kings that reigned, through both peace and turmoil, until the Saxon invasions of the fifth century.

Chief defender of the British against these invaders was King Arthur, who fought valiantly and well until betrayed by the evil Mordred and forced to retreat into obscurity in the mythical fastness of Avalon, which Geoffrey and his countrymen generally understood to be in Wales. It was prophesied (perhaps by Merlin) that Arthur was the "once and future king," destined to return someday to reign again in Britain.

According to Geoffrey's account, the monarchs between Brute and Arthur are as follows, in order of succession:

Locrine. Succeeded his father, Brute, as general monarch while his brothers Albanact and Camber ruled respectively the northern and western divisions of the realm. All three ruled effectively until the land was invaded by Huns. Locrine defeated the invaders and slew Humber, their chieftain. Afterward, however, Locrine fell into a life of sloth and voluptuousness, betraying his wife Gwendolyn for a woman named Elstrid.

Gwendolyn. Dethroned her wayward husband and imprisoned him, slew his mistress Elstrid, and caused Elstrid's innocent daughter, Sabrina, to cast herself into the Severn River.

Madan. Seized the crown from his mother Gwendolyn, ruled shamefully, and proved unworthy of his office.

Memprise. Also unworthy of the throne, he slew his brother Manildus in order to advance his ambitions.

Ebranck. Performed many noble deeds, won military honors against the Germanic tribes, and lived happily with his fifty-two children until his forces were expelled from the Continent and he returned to Britain.

Brute II. Reconquered France for the Britons.

Leill. Sponsored public works such as the building of Carlyle and the repair of Cairleon.

Hudibras. Brought peace by putting an end to the Britons' wars of expansions.

Bladud. Brought arts and sciences from Athens to the British Isles, built the baths at Cairbadon, but was killed, like Icarus, in a presumptuous attempt to fly.

Lear. As in Shakespeare's version of the story, he ruled most of his life in peace but had no male issue, so divided his realm in two parts between his flattering daughters Goneril and Regan, while giving his honest daughter Cordelia in an undowered marriage (in Geoffrey it is to Maglan, king of the Scots, rather than to the king of France). After being abused by Goneril and Regan he went to Cordelia, who restored him to the throne, where (unlike the account in Shakespeare) he eventually died a natural death.

Cordelia. Succeeded her father and ruled well until overthrown by her nephews Cundah and Morgan, and thereafter hanged herself in prison.

Cundah. After usurping the throne he envied his brother Morgan and slew him in order to rule alone.

Rivallus. Ruled badly. During his reign blood rained from heaven.

Gurgustus. Brought peace to the land again.

Caecilius. Continued the peace and ruled justly.

Lago. Mentioned only as having reigned.

Kinmarke. Had an undistinguished rule.

Gorbogud. Ruled until an advanced age but was unseated by his ambitious sons Ferrex and Porrex.

Porrex. Overthrew his father and killed his brother Ferrex out of envy and ambition. He was himself killed by his mother, Wyden, in revenge for Ferrex. Civil chaos followed his death.

Donwallo. Restored law and order and reorganized the realm. He slew the miscreants Ymner, Ruddoc, and Stater and pacified their territories. He gave laws beneficial to all estates and died happy, leaving his two sons Brennius and Belinus.

Brennius and Belinus. Ruled conjointly. They sacked Rome in punishment for a broken treaty and invaded Greece, France, and Germany.

Gurgiunt. Subdued Easterland and Denmark and established a claim to Ireland.

Guitheline. The most just and honorable man of his time, he married the best of wives and lived happily ever after.

Sisillus. Reigned without special distinction.

Kimarus. Reigned without special distinction.

Danius. Reigned without special distinction.

Morindus. A man of great achievements, his virtues were overshadowed by his excessive cruelty. The next five rulers were his sons.

Gorboman. A virtuous ruler.

Archigald. Deposed because of his pride, he was later reinstated, but then deposed again. After the deaths of his brothers he returned to power yet again and this time reigned long and well.

Elidure. A ruler of compassionate nature.

Peridurus. Imprisoned Archigald after deposing him.

Vigent. Reigned with Peridurus after helping him depose Archigald. After this there were thirty-three unnamed descendants of Morindus who reigned in order.

Hely. Came to the throne by natural descent and reigned without special distinction.

Lud. An excellent monarch, he reedified the city of Troynovant (London) and built Ludgate. He died leaving two minor sons, Androgeus and Tenantius, under the regency of his brother Cassibalane.

Cassibalane. Governed well, but was defeated by the Romans under Caesar through the treason of his jealous and impatient nephew Androgeus.

Androgeus. A traitor.

Tenantius. Reigned without special distinction.

Cimbeline. Reigned over the Britons at the time when Christ was born (that "fact" is thematically important in Shakespeare's play *Cymbeline*).

Arviragus. A great military leader who fought the Romans to a standstill and was respected by all. He married the daughter of the Roman emperor Claudius.

Marius. Lived out his reign in tranquility.

Coyll. Ruled without distinction. Either he or the second Coyll (see below) was the "Old King Cole" of the nursery rhyme.

Lucius. First of the British kings to embrace Christianity, he was a good man but died without issue, after which civil strife ensued throughout the land.

Bunduca. A woman of great ability, a warrior-queen who made a heroic attempt during the interregnum to consolidate the country. She made great headway against the Romans, but was betrayed by her own captains and driven to suicide on the field of battle.

Fulgent. Stayed in command long enough to retrieve Bunduca's remains from the field, but was then killed in battle.

Carausius. A tyrant, he held brief sway during the interregnum.

Allectus. Gained power when he overthrew Carausius by treachery.

Asclepiodate. Overthrew Allectus and laid claim to the throne.

Coyll II. First of the true seed of Brute to rule since Lucius, he slew the wicked Asclepiodate and began to renew the realm, building Colchester. He married the great Roman musician Helena and begat a daughter whom he married to Constantius, the Roman ambassador.

Constantine the First. Grandson of Coyll II; a great man, but he lost the realm by dividing his time between Britain and Rome.

Octavius. Usurped the throne and confirmed his possession by defeating the Romans in Britain. Having no male issue, he gave his daughter in marriage to Maximian, but Maximian died before any children could be conceived, and the realm was again torn by war.

Constantine II. Elected by common consent to defend the land. He fortified the north against Scotland and died leaving three underaged sons under the regency of Vortiger, their uncle.

Vortiger. Usurped the rights of his nephews and called in the evil Saxons to help protect his claim.

Hengist (along with Horsa). A Saxon, he wrested the crown from Vortiger.

Vortimer. Son of Vortiger, he restored the kingdom to his father. Hengist repented, and through the wiles of his daughter was received into Vortiger's good graces. Afterward Hengist treacherously slew three hundred British lords, whose tombstones form the place known as Stonehenge.

Ambrose. Son of the second Constantine, he joined with his brother Uther to slay Vortiger and Hengist.

Uther Pendragon. Mainly distinguished for being the father of Arthur.

For the story of Arthur we turn from Geoffrey to Sir Thomas Malory, whose lengthy account of the Round Table, Camelot, and other matters is, as mentioned above, drawn not only from Geoffrey but from a wealth of romance materials in the intervening two centuries between the Welsh monk and the English knight and soldier whose book was first printed in 1485, some dozen years after Malory's death, by William Caxton, the first English printer. (It was after George W. Cable had introduced him to Malory that Mark Twain conceived the idea for his Connecticut Yankee.) Malory treats the story in eight large sections, from the conception of Arthur to the final dissolution of Camelot.

Smitten with desire for Igrayne, the wife of his worst enemy, the Duke of Tintagel, Uther is disguised, through the magic of Merlin his royal magician, as her husband, lying with her in that guise even as her actual husband is slain on the field of combat. After the duke's death is confirmed, Uther marries Igrayne, and Arthur, the product of their union, is born though not conceived in wedlock. He has three half-sisters, Igrayne's daughters by her previous marriage: Morgause, Elayne, and Morgan le Fay, who has learned the arts of sorcery.

While still a child, Arthur proves his prophesied right to rule by being able to extract easily, from the marble stone and anvil in which it is deeply embedded, a great sword that none of the adult claimants to the throne have been able to budge. Thus he succeeds his father in kingship. He eventually takes as his queen Guinevere, daughter of Lodegraunce, and establishes his court at Camelot, where the Knights of the Round Table keep residence and from which they begin a bewildering variety of quests and exploits. Most of the more important of these quests involve a search for the Holy Grail, a chalice used at Christ's Last Supper, said to contain some drops of his blood. Some of the more prominent of Arthur's knights and ladies are these:

Balin. Like Arthur, able to draw out a sword that no one else can move, but is warned that the sword, if he takes it, will kill the person he loves most in the world, and it eventually slays his brother Balan.

Bedivere. One of Arthur's most faithful knights. It is he who, in the end, casts Arthur's sword Excalibur into the lake, where an arm rises to receive it. He then carries the dying Arthur to the shore, where a barge of mystic queens and attendant ladies bears the king off to Avalon and healing.

Bors. One of the three Grail Knights, who eventually achieves the Holy Grail. He is allowed to do so even though he has slipped once from the ideal of chastity that is a usual precondition.

Galahad. Son of Lancelot through a union with Elayne (see **Lancelot**, below), the purest and most morally upright of the knights. He is one of the three who achieve the Grail. He is virtually without flaw and thus lacks the human interest generated by some of the other knights.

Gareth. His story is one of maturation by trial. Serving as a kitchen boy, he earns the right to use his real name and escape the demeaning nickname "fair hands." He fights and defeats a series of differently colored knights, black, blue, red, and green.

Gawain. One of the best and most honorable of the knights. He nonetheless makes mistakes, including the unintended beheading of a lady, whose severed head he is forced to wear about as a penance. He is the hero of a very accomplished fourteenth-century poem of which the author is not known, Sir Gawain and the Green Knight, which also involves an incident of decapitation. In Malory, Gawain is eventually killed by Lancelot.

Isolde (Isoud, Yseut, etc.). Two different ladies, both near to Tristram. Tristram is married to Isolde of the White Hands but has given his heart to Isolde the Fair, wife of King Mark of Cornwall.

Kay. Son of Ector, the man who fostered the young Arthur. Kay has been knighted but is nonetheless a coward.

Lamerok. Winner of the title of third-best knight in the world at a tournament staged by Arthur. In one episode he disguises himself as the cowardly Sir Kay in order to get the only slightly less cowardly King Mark to fight with him. He becomes involved in an adulterous relationship with

Lancelot. Winner, at Arthur's tournament, of the right to call himself the best knight in the world. Many of Lancelot's adventures reveal the problems attendant upon having no room for improvement of his reputation and thus no obtainable goals. Perhaps consequently, he gets into serious troubles, not the least of which are occasioned by his twenty-four-year adulterous relationship with Arthur's queen, Guinevere. (To pursue the Grail, he has to spend twenty-four hours in a steamroom in symbolic cleansing.) Further, he betrays Guinevere with Elayne, with whom he begets Galahad, eventually the best knight of all and one of the three (with Percival and Bors) who will achieve the Grail.

In the final days of Camelot, Arthur finds the adultery between his wife and Lancelot impossible to endure any longer, and he condemns the queen to death. Lancelot has championed and saved her on other occasions, but in attempting to do so again he inadvertently commits the great breach of honor of killing an unarmed knight and has to retreat from the court. This leaves Camelot underdefended as Mordred comes to destroy it, and Lancelot returns too late to save the world of the Round Table.

Mark. King of Cornwall, distinguished for lack of bravery. His wife is Isolde the Fair.

Mordred. Arthur's illegitimate son, born of an incestuous union between the unaware Arthur and his half-sister Morgause. Mordred grows up in hatred of the king and eventually leads the force that destroys Camelot.

Morgan le Fay. Arthur's half-sister. She is a sorceress who uses her powers on several occasions to attempt to embarrass Lancelot and Guinevere by making their adultery public.

Pellinore. Knight who, on a quest to avenge the deaths of Gawain's dogs and Arthur's horse, fails to aid a dying knight whose lady turns out to be Pellinore's own daughter.

Percival. One of the three Grail Knights, he achieves the Grail.

Torre. Son of Sir Pellinore. He beheads Abellus, a herdsman, as a result of making too hastily the knightly pledge to another person that he will accomplish anything that person desires.

Tristram. A Cornish knight, he is winner of the title of second-best knight in the world at Arthur's tournament. He is best known in later versions of his story for his great but adulterous love for Isolde, wife of king Mark (see above).

Neither king nor knight, the magician and seer **Merlin** is a pervasive figure in the legends of Arthur and the Round Table. In Geoffrey of Monmouth's account Merlin enters the story during the time of Vortiger, and Geoffrey interrupts his history to record the "Prophecies of Merlin." In Malory, Merlin assists Uther Pendragon's scheme to seduce Igrayne, then early on prophesies to Arthur the nature of Arthur's death and his own. Merlin himself falls prey to a counterenchantment of Nimue, who shuts him away beneath a rock; in another story, it is Vivien who entangles him in brush. In any case, though removed from the scene, Merlin, like Arthur, may be only sleeping until his time comes again.

SOURCES

Chambers, E. K. *Arthur of Britain.* London: Sidgwick and Jackson, 1923.

Dillon, Bert. *A Malory Handbook.* Boston: G. K. Hall, 1978.]

Geoffrey of Monmouth. *History of the Kings of Britain.* Translated by Sebastian Evans. New York: E. P. Dutton, 1958.

———. *History of the Kings of Britain.* Translated by Lewis Thorpe. Harmondsworth, Eng.: Penguin Books, 1966.

Helterman, Jeffrey. "Sir Thomas Malory." In *Writers of the Middle Ages and Renaissance Before 1660,* by Jeffrey Helterman. Detroit: Gale Research Co., 1992.

Harper, Carrie Anna. *The Sources of the British Chronicle History in Spenser's "Faerie Queene."* Philadelphia: John C. Winston, 1910.

Malory, Sir Thomas. *Le Morte D'Arthur.* Edited by R. M. Lumiansky. New York: Charles Scribner's Sons, 1982.

—J.L.M.

37

LITERARY AND CRITICAL TERMS: A GLOSSARY

· · · · ·

ALL CRITICISM OF LITERATURE IS EITHER PLATONIC OR ARISTOTELIAN—which is to say, it deals with literary works either in terms of their relationship to experience, as Plato did in *The Republic,* or else in terms of how they are constructed and function, as Aristotle did in the *Poetics.* When the Rev. So-and-So urges the school board to ban the reading of J. D. Salinger's *The Catcher in the Rye* because it will corrupt youthful minds, or Professor Such-and-Such advises his political science students to read Robert Penn Warren's *All the King's Men* because it illustrates the nature of political leadership so well, the assumptions of Plato about the uses of imaginative literature are being echoed. When a high school senior, exposed to T. S. Eliot's "The Waste Land" for the first time, objects to the presence of German, French, Greek, Latin, and Sanskrit words in a poem, he is invoking, however innocently, what are essentially Aristotelian criteria.

We study and criticize literary works to try to make sense of an imaginative experience which has been apprehended in language. To do so, we have to develop a vocabulary so that everyone concerned will presumably be talking about the same thing. At various times this vocabulary has become extremely specialized—and as in any other field of specialized knowledge, the demonstrated ability to use it becomes a badge of membership. Thus the successive critical movements, or schools, or whatever have sprouted their own sets of special terms, and the resultant renaming of the phenomena of the world have produced whole new glossaries of words.

The following is a compilation of some of the more commonly used terms in literary history, criticism, and critical theory.

Abstract poetry. Poetry that derives its effect from arrangement of sounds and rhythms rather than from conveying some specific message or meaning.

Absurdist literature. Forms of modern fiction and drama that seek to depict the alienation of human beings from their environments by concentrating on situations lacking logic, consistency, or relation to reasonable causes.

Accent. The emphasis given a syllable in a word, whereby patterns of rhythm are established in poetry.

Accentual-syllabic verse. The standard method of verse in English, which derives its rhythm from patterns involving the number of syllables in a line and the organization, within that line, of accented and unaccented syllables.

Acrostic verse. A poem that contains within itself words or phrases spelled out when certain sequences of letters are noticed; as in the familiar greeting-card poem in which the initial letters of its six lines add up to the word MOTHER.

Act. A main division in a drama, within which there are usually several scenes. Shakespeare and his contemporaries, imitating Roman models, worked with five-act structures. In late nineteenth- and twentieth-century drama a three-act form is more common, with the one-act play occurring frequently as an apprentice form.

Action. The sequence of events that makes up the plot of a work of fiction or drama.

Aesthetic distance. An effect of the author's emotional removal from the events and persons depicted in his work, so that the work does not appear autobiographical or experientially based.

Aestheticism. A movement, usually associated with the late nineteenth century, in which beauty of execution took precedence over moral or philosophical value of content; "art for art's sake."

Aesthetics. The branch of philosophy concerned with the quality of beauty in art and nature.

Affective criticism. An approach to art that is concerned with the effects—especially emotional—that a work may have on a reader or audience; sometimes called "reader-response criticism."

African-American literature. Writings by black American authors of the nineteenth and twentieth centuries; also called *Afro-American literature* or *black literature.*

Age of Reason. See **Neoclassical period.**

Age of sensibility. A term applied to the second half of the eighteenth century and emphasizing the premium on feeling that emerges in some of the literature of that time; also called the *pre-romantic period.*

Agrarian writers. A group of southern writers and critics in the 1920s and 1930s who advocated an agrarian as opposed to an industrial economy and who championed, in literature, values associated with community, regionalism, and a commonality of philosophical assumptions; often termed "Fugitive Agrarians" because of the magazine of poetry and criticism, *The Fugitive*, which some of the group had earlier published. The leading Agrarians were Allen Tate, John Crowe Ransom, Donald Davidson, and Robert Penn Warren.

Alba. Poem of lament by a poet having to part from his lover at dawn.

Alexandrine. In English, a line of iambic hexameter, such as Edmund Spenser's "Fierce wars and faithful loves shall moralize my song"; in France, the alexandrine is a verse of twelve syllables containing three or four accents.

Allegory. A narrative whose characters and events take on meanings that derive from ideas outside the narrative itself, and whose concrete images represent abstract qualities.

Alliteration. Repetition of initial consonant sounds in the stressed syllables of successive words, as in the phrase "rough, raw, ragged rhymes."

Alliterative verse. Poetic forms with rhythms based on alliteration, as with Anglo-Saxon poetry and the various "alliterative romances" of the late Middle Ages, such as *Sir Gawain and the Green Knight* (ca. 1350).

Allusion. A reference within a literary work that brings to mind some other literary work or historical event, usually related in theme to the context in which the allusion occurs. If we call someone a "Napoleonic figure" we define him with a historical allusion; if we call him a "Falstaffian figure" we define him with a literary allusion.

Ambiguity. The use, intentionally or otherwise, of language that leaves room for more than one interpretation of a statement or an image.

Anacreontic verse. Short poems celebrating wine, women, and song in the manner of the Greek poet Anacreon (ca. 575–488 B.C.E.).

Analogue. A version of a story similar enough to imply a literary relationship but incapable of being proved a source or imitation.

Anapest. A three-syllable foot or metrical unit of a poetic line, with the accent on the final syllable: ta-ta-TA.

Anaphora. A rhetorical figure that repeats the same verbal formula at the beginning of successive utterances, as when Shakespeare's Richard II declaims, "How some have been deposed, some slain in war,/Some haunted by the ghosts they have deposed,/Some poisoned by their wives, some sleeping killed."

Anglo-Irish literature. Writings in English by Irish authors, usually dealing with issues of special relevance to Irish culture, as in the works of James Joyce and W. B. Yeats.

Anglo-Norman period. The literary age of strong French influence in England, 1100–1350, a time of chivalric romances (chiefly about King Arthur and his Round Table), ballads, and cycles of religious drama. See **Mystery play**.

Angry Young Men. A group of British antiestablishment writers in the 1950s that included Kingsley Amis, John Osborne, and John Braine.

Annals. Historical chronicles recorded in annual sequence.

Antagonist. Rival or opponent of the principal character (protagonist) in a literary work.

Anterior narration. An episode in poetry or fiction in which events of a time prior to the setting are related as background to the story; a flashback.

Antihero. A protagonist with traits usually regarded as antithetical to the heroic, as when the main character is a criminal, a derelict, a drug addict, or a generally inept person.

Antithesis. A rhetorical figure with strongly contrasting words or ideas, as in the following extended example from John Lyly's *Euphues* (1578): "Alexander valiant in war, yet given to wine. Tully eloquent in his gloses, yet vainglorious. Solomon wise, yet too, too wanton. David holy but yet a homicide."

Aphorism. A concise and memorable formation of an idea, as in Francis Bacon's statement that "he that hath wife and children hath given hostages to fortune."

Apollonian. As used by the German philosopher Friedrich Nietzsche, the artistic or cultural quality of being ordered, reasoned, and formal. *Cf.* Dionysian.

Apostrophe. A rhetorical figure of direct address to a person, object, or abstract quality, as in the hungry fisherman's "Hail to thee, immortal breakfast!"

Apothegm. A very condensed aphorism or pithy comment, such as Francis Bacon's definition of revenge as "a kind of wild justice."

Arcadian. Pastoral, idyllic, Edenic; like the setting of Sir Philip Sidney's *Arcadia* (1590) and other bucolic works.

Archaism. A purposefully old-fashioned word or expression, often used to create a historical atmosphere, as Edmund Spenser uses Chaucerian and other Middle English words in *The Faerie Queene* (1590–96).

Archetype. An image or idea considered to be derived from the collective unconscious or "racial memory" of mankind, as discussed by the Swiss psychologist Carl Jung.

Architectonics. Elements of overall structure in a literary work providing unity, harmony, and proportion.

Arena stage. "Theater in the round," in which the audience surrounds or abuts three sides of a stage where actors perform without benefit of a proscenium arch or curtain. The Globe Theatre of Shakespeare's acting company was such a stage.

Aristotelian criticism. A literary approach deriving from the Greek philosopher Aristotle, emphasizing internal, formal qualities of a work of art as opposed to historical, social, or theoretical contexts.

Assonance. Repetition of similar vowel sounds in the stressed syllables of words: *e.g.,* "goat" and "core," "page" and "labor."

Attic. Literary style characterized by simple but polished and graceful expression, as if modeled on the Athenians.

Aubade. A lyric poem heralding the dawn.

Augustan. In Roman history, the period of the Emperor Augustus (27 B.C.E.–14 C.E.), in which literature was distinguished for polish, grace, and sophistication; in English history, the period of the first half of the eighteenth century, in which the same qualities in literature and society were cultivated.

Autobiography. The narrative of a person's life written by himself or herself.

Baconian theory. The opinion, recurrent in various forms since the mid-nineteenth century, that someone other than Shakespeare actually wrote the plays generally attributed to him. Candidates for their authorship include Francis Bacon, Christopher Marlowe, Queen Elizabeth I, and the seventeenth earl of Oxford.

Ballad. A narrative poem, imitative of song, relating a dramatic event or episode, usually with the use of repetition and refrains. F. J. Child's *The English and Scottish Popular Ballads* (1898) is the standard collection of examples in English.

Ballad stanza. A four-line stanza, common in folk ballads, with the rhyme scheme *abab,* the first and third lines of four stressed syllables and the second and fourth of three. See **Doggerel** (the example quoted there is in ballad form).

Baroque. In literature, a style associated with the period of the late Renaissance (*ca.* 1585–1680), involving strong and often violent contrasts, powerful spatial images, and complex verbal rhythms. The term is sometimes used pejoratively to describe an excess of these qualities. In English literature the chief example is Richard Crashaw (1612–49), who sought to dramatize spiritual concepts through the use of dramatic physical and emotional symbolism and the elaborate adaptation of style to subject matter.

Bathos. A comical effect of anticlimax, usually from failed elevation of style, as in this example cited by Kemp P. Battle, president of the University of North Carolina during the Reconstruction period: "She rushed from her bed like a raging catamount, and in her gigantic tearing strength seized him by the collar and tore his shirt" (*Memories of an Old-Time Tar Heel,* Chapel Hill: University of North Carolina Press, 1945).

Beast fable. A tale, often allegorical or moral in intent, in which animals display human characteristics.

Beat generation. Collective term for a group of American writers of the 1950s who rebelled against social and literary conventions, experimented with drugs and exotic religious practices, and cultivated a variety of literary styles that incorporated spontaneous composition, street slang and argot from the musical subcultures of New York and San Francisco, and rhythms in both poetry and prose based on analogies with jazz. The term *beat* has been variously explained as meaning "down and out," "beatific," and living to the "beat" of cool jazz. Principal figures were the poets Allen Ginsberg, Gregory Corso, and Lawrence Ferlinghetti, and the novelists Jack Kerouac and William S. Burroughs.

Belles-lettres. Imaginative literature of artistic intent as opposed to the exposition of fact and information.

Bestiary tale. See **Beast fable**.

Bildungsroman. German term for the type of novel that charts the development of a young person from adolescence to maturity, or from innocence to experience; also called the "novel of apprenticeship."

Binary signification. The potentiality within a word to imply its opposite, as "blindness" implies the possibility of "sightedness," "oppression" implies the possibility of "freedom," "well done" implies the possibility of "rare," etc.

Biographical criticism. Interpretation of a literary work in light of its author's personal life; called the "biographical fallacy" or "genetic fallacy" by those who oppose it.

Biography. The record of a person's life, written by a second party.

Black humor. A bitter, pessimistic, and often angry humor in the works of such writers as Günter Grass, Thomas Pynchon, Kurt Vonnegut, and Harold Pinter.

Blank verse. Unrhymed iambic pentameter lines organized into verse paragraphs; the basic medium of Shakespeare's plays and Milton's epic poems.

Bloomsbury group. A group of London writers in the 1920s and 1930s, centering around the novelist Virginia Woolf and promoting the values of sophisticated discourse and aesthetic appreciation. E. M. Forster and John Maynard Keynes were among its members.

Bombast. Overblown rhetoric and extravagantly exaggerated language; fustian.

Bowdlerize. To expurgate and remove passages deemed offensive, as the nineteenth-century British editor Thomas Bowdler did in his edition of the works of Shakespeare.

Breton lay. Brief medieval French romance associated with the Celtic culture of Brittany and usually incorporating themes of magic and the supernatural. Chaucer's "Franklin's Tale" imitates the form of the Breton lay.

Bricolage. The assemblage of something out of available materials—*e.g.*, literary works out of familiar forms and conventions—as opposed to truly imaginative conceptualization or creation.

Broadside ballads. Versified accounts of events, meant to be sung to the tunes of old ballads, sold on the streets of sixteenth-century England.

Bucolic. Pastoral writing, usually set in idealized rural settings.

Burlesque. Comedy based on broad exaggeration, often involving travesty of legitimate literary forms.

Caesura. A break or hiatus in the course of a line of poetry, usually in or near the middle.

Canon. A list of literary works (1) constituting the known authoritative writings of a given author or (2) constituting an accepted body representative of a period, type, or quality of literature.

Canto. A subsection or division of a longer poem, such as Ariosto's *Orlando Furioso* (1516) or Spenser's *Faerie Queene* (1590–96).

Canzone. A type of lyrical poem found chiefly in Italy but represented in England by Edmund Spenser's *Epithalamion* (1595) and Milton's *Lycidas* (1637). Its content is usually of an emotional nature (love, grief), and its structure usually consists of lines of varying length and rhyme scheme ending in a coda or *tornada*, in which the poet turns and addresses the reader or someone other than the subject of the main body of the poem.

Caricature. Characterization by exaggeration of salient details of physique or character.

Caroline period. The reign of Charles I in England (1625–49), encompassing both the Cavalier and the Puritan writings of the end of the Renaissance in England.

Carpe diem. Phrase from an ode by Horace, meaning "seize the day," or, in the memorable phrasing of Robert Herrick, "Gather ye rosebuds while ye may"—take advantage of youth and joy while they last.

Catalog. A list of people, places, objects, events, etc., usually associated with epic poetry and abundantly evident in poems such as Homer's *Iliad* (*ca.* 725 B.C.E.) and Milton's *Paradise Lost* (1667).

Catharsis. A purging of the emotions through the witnessing of tragic experiences on the stage or in fiction; Aristotle's *Poetics* (*ca.* 370 B.C.E.) asserts that catharsis by pity and terror is the desired effect of tragic drama.

Cavalier poetry. Light, lyrical poems characteristic of the aristocratic poets (*e.g.*, Richard Lovelace and Sir John Suckling) who supported Charles I during the Puritan revolt in England and wrote of love, humor, war, and the royal cause.

Celtic Renaissance. A movement in Ireland in the late nineteenth and early twentieth centuries emphasizing the preservation of the Gaelic language and the revival of ancient Celtic themes and history in modern works. Writers associated with these impulses included W. B. Yeats, George Moore, John Millington Synge, and Lord Dunsany.

Chanson de geste. The genre of the early French epic, represented by the *Chanson de Roland* (*Song of Roland*) of about the year 1100 and other poems often involving the wars between Christian and Saracen forces.

Character. The aggregate of personality traits an author assigns an individual in his literary representation. A *unique* character is one who stands out from his environment and has an individualized personality. A *representative* character is one whose personality traits are typical of a group or class, or simply illustrate some theory or abstract idea.

Characterization. The creation of character in literature, usually by depiction of episodes involving choice, by anecdotes or illustrative episodes, by comments of the author or character himself, or by symbolic motifs.

Chiasmus. A rhetorical figure whereby the second section reverses the balance of the first, as in the phrase "friendly dogs, and doggedly friendly men."

Chivalric romances. Long poems of the medieval period in Europe and England, treating the deeds, beliefs, and behavior of the knightly class. Many involve King Arthur and the knights of his Round Table.

Choric characters. Persons in drama and other forms of literature who, like the chorus in Greek tragedy, serve to state or exemplify normative, orthodox points of view on the themes and issues of the work.

Chronicle play. Drama created out of the materials of English history, chiefly associated with the Elizabethan and Jacobean periods and with playwrights such as Shakespeare and Christopher Marlowe.

Ciceronian style. A stately prose style, imitative of the oratorical prose of the Roman Cicero, notable for its long periodic sentences and its elaborate employment of balance, parallelism, and antithesis. It was standard in England during the sixteenth and much of the seventeenth centuries.

Classicism. Cultivation of certain values evident in Greek and Roman literature and criticism, including logic, symmetry, balance, restraint, proportion, and unity of parts in a work of art. Classicism as a literary goal surfaces at many points in literary history but is chiefly associated with the eighteenth century or Augustan period in England.

Climax. The turning point in a work of literature, at which the emotion building in the audience reaches its point of greatest intensity and requires the beginning of a resolution.

Closed couplet. A pair of lines with end rhyme containing a complete idea acceptable independently of its context, as in John Dryden's famous couplet from *Absalom and Achitophel* (1681): "Great wits are sure to madness near allied/And thin partitions do their bounds divide."

Closet drama. A play written to be read rather than acted.

Coda. A brief addition at the end of a literary composition, usually reiterating or commenting upon the issues and ideas of the work as a whole.

Colloquialism. An informal expression more common in casual speech than in writing or oratory.

Colloquy. A dialogue or exchange among two or more characters.

Colonial period. The era in American literature *ca.* 1607–1765, when Americans generally thought of themselves as English people in another country. Major themes of this period are religious and philosophical.

Comedy. A literary or dramatic work whose plot reaches a happy or successful conclusion for characters the audience has come to support and wish well.

Comedy of humours. A variety of dramatic comedy associated mainly with Ben Jonson (1572–1637) but employed to some degree by Shakespeare in *2 Henry IV* and *The Merry Wives of Windsor*. Based on the medical theories of the ancient Greek Galen and tending toward the methodology of caricature, the comedy of humours treats interactions among characters whose personalities reflect imbalances of the four humours or bodily fluids— blood, yellow bile (choler), black bile, and phlegm. Too much blood produces the *sanguine* temperament; too much yellow bile, the *choleric* temperament; too much black bile, the *melancholy* temperament; and too much phlegm, the *phlegmatic* temperament. Characterization by these principles is evident also in the General Prologue to Chaucer's *Canterbury Tales* (ca. 1386).

Comedy of manners. A variety of dramatic comedy associated mainly with the Restoration period in English literature (1660–1700) and drawing on social customs and fashions for its situations and conflicts.

Comedy of situation. Comedy depending more on plot and incident than on character or psychology for its humor.

Comic relief. A comical speech or episode injected into a tragic context to provide a temporary lessening of emotional intensity.

Complaint. A poem of lament for some situation of less than mortal significance, such as the indifference of a lady, the stinginess of a patron, or the general corruption of society.

Complication. The "rising action" or developing conflict of a plot, leading eventually to climax and resolution.

Confession. An autobiographical work that reveals some private and, frequently, regretted aspect of the author's life.

Conflict. The struggle of opposing forces that creates interest in a literary plot.

Consonance. A form of partial rhyme in which the final consonants of stressed words are the same but the vowels that precede them are not, as in the relationship of "bail" and "boil," or of "cross" and "grass."

Convention. A theme or literary device so often used that it has become an accepted and even expected element in a certain type of work, such as the runaway stagecoach in a western plot or the attitude of the suffering lover in a love sonnet.

Counterplot. A subplot or subordinate plot which parallels and contrasts with the main action.

Couplet. A two-line stanza of verse, united by end rhyme and usually, though not always, containing a complete thought.

Courtesy book. A manual of education and behavior intended for members of the upper or ruling classes, associated chiefly with the period of the Renaissance in Europe and represented by such works as Baldassare

Castiglione's *The Courtier* (1528) and Sir Thomas Elyot's *Book Named the Governour* (1531).

Courtly love. A stylized code of courtship celebrated frequently (and sometimes satirized) in the Middle Ages and Renaissance, in which the male lover undergoes infinite suffering and frustration from the real or pretended indifference of his lady, which, even while it pains him, inspires him to noble deeds and self-improvement in order to make himself worthy.

Court satire. A type of literature common in monarchical or oligarchical societies, in which the manners of the ruling class are exposed to criticism or ridicule.

Crisis. Often synonymous with climax, the point in a plot at which opposing forces create the necessity for choice and action on the protagonist's part.

Cubist poetry. A movement in poetry parallel to the more familiar one in visual art, in which elements of art are rearranged for novel emphases and relationships. The typographical experiments of e. e. cummings and Kenneth Rexroth fall into this school.

Cultural pluralism. The awareness that modern society consists of numerous ethnic, ideological, cultural, and racial groups whose traditions, social mores and customs, needs, and ideological assumptions are of equal value, and the concomitant educational and critical programs that seek to represent and give voice to this diversity in surveys of literature in colleges and universities, lists of prescribed or suggested readings, media coverage of artistic events, etc.

Dactyl. A three-syllable foot or metrical unit of a poetic line, with the accent on the initial syllable: TA-ta-ta.

Débat. A debate between two spokesmen with the judgment left to a third party or to the reader.

Decadence. Period of decline or overrefinement in a literary tradition after it has reached its apex of development.

Deconstruction. A critical process, postulated upon the instability of language and the cultural basis of what is considered to be truth, that denies the possibility of final or definitive meaning in texts or events and questions traditional valuations such as the distinction between "high" and popular culture, or the concept of a stable canon of "great works" necessary to be studied for the transmission of ideas of permanent value.

Decorum. The concept of the proper relationship of the parts to the whole and of style to content in a literary work; also the behavior and speech appropriate to a given character in order to make that character believable.

Deus ex machina. Literally, the "god from the machine," any artificial device an author might use to solve simply a complicated situation, as when Shakespeare has a traveling evangelist convert an evil brother so that Duke

Senior's dukedom can be restored to him at the end of *As You Like It* (*ca.* 1598).

Diachronic. Relating to development or change as it occurs over a period of time. A diachronic plot in fiction arranges its events as they would occur in history.

Dialogue. Conversation among two or more characters in a literary work; or the particular kind of work, such as the *Dialogues* of Plato or Sir Thomas More, that advances an argument or point of view through such an imagined conversation. See also **Colloquy.**

Didacticism. The intent of moral, ethical, or philosophical instruction in a work of literature.

Différance. French term, from the writings of the critic Jacques Derrida, describing the lack of exact correspondence between words (signifiers) and the ideas they denote (signifieds), and the interrelation and play between the two. The example offered below from Joyce under Plurisignification is dependent upon this *différance.*

Dime novel. A cheap paperback thriller of a type common in nineteenth-century America, such as the western novels of Ned Buntline or Edward Wheeler.

Dionysian. As used by the German philosopher Friedrich Nietzsche, the artistic or cultural quality of being ecstatic, frenzied, imaginative, and creatively suprarational. *Cf.* **Apollonian.**

Distich. A couplet that is especially aphoristic or self-contained, as in Alexander Pope's *Essay on Criticism* (1711): "Whoever thinks a faultless piece to see/Thinks what ne'er was, nor is, nor e'er shall be."

Dithyramb. A form of literary art distinguished by wild, ecstatic language and rhythm.

Doggerel. Crude, choppy verse, overly emphatic in rhyme and cadence, dull and repetitious in diction and sentiment, often descending to bathos: "He loved but her, she loved but him,/With love they both did burn;/She tasted first his hungry lips/And then he tasted hern."

Domestic drama. Comedy or tragedy centered in the daily domestic affairs of ordinary people.

Double entendre. A purposely ambiguous word or statement, usually containing some veiled bawdry.

Dramatic monologue. An extended speech by a character speaking alone but to an assumed listener about some issue of great importance in his life. A distinguished modern example is T. S. Eliot's "The Love Song of J. Alfred Prufrock" (1917).

Dramatis personae. Literally the "people of the play," the cast of characters in any work of literature.

Dream allegory. A medieval poetic form in which the narrator represents himself as falling asleep, having a dream with allegorical implications, then waking up and writing the dream down as a poem. Dante's *Divine Comedy* (1321) and Chaucer's *House of Fame* (*ca.* 1375) are notable examples of this genre.

Dream vision. See **Dream allegory**.

Droll. A brief, usually comic, dramatic skit, often excerpted from a longer play.

Dumbshow. A pantomime incorporated into a play, such as the wordless prologue to the "mousetrap" play in Shakespeare's *Hamlet* (*ca.* 1605).

Early Tudor period. The era from the accession of Henry VII in 1485 to that of Elizabeth I in 1558, including the literary careers of such writers as John Skelton, Sir Thomas Wyatt, Henry Howard, Earl of Surrey, and Sir Thomas More.

Eclogue. A pastoral poem, usually cast as a conversation among shepherds, sometimes arranged in sequences, such as Edmund Spenser's *Shepherd's Calender* (1579) or Michael Drayton's *Shepherd's Garland* (1593).

Écriture. French term denoting, in its most literal sense, the representation of sounds by the letters of the alphabet, and in a more general one representation of abstract ideas or concepts through the use of linguistic signs and literary constructs.

Edwardian period. The era 1901–14, characterized by a certain literary reaction against the strait-laced Victorian period that preceded, encompassing the work of writers such as H. G. Wells, Samuel Butler, and Thomas Hardy.

Effictio. A stylized celebration of a lady's beauty, accomplished by a survey or catalog of her physical charms. Shakespeare's Sonnet CXXX ("My mistress' eyes are nothing like the sun") is a burlesque of the convention. *Cf.* **Notatio.**

Eiron. A comic trickster who appears as a stock character in Greek drama.

Elegiac poetry. Poems of either love or lamentation, so called because the ancient Greek poets treated these themes in elegiac meter, couplets with alternating hexameter and pentameter lines.

Elegy. A poem of meditation on a sober and serious theme, often that of death.

Elizabethan period. The High Renaissance in England during the reign of Elizabeth I (1558–1603), the age of Shakespeare, Marlowe, Spenser, Sidney, and many other great writers.

Emblem. A visual image with direct and specific allegorical associations. The American flag, for example, with its combination of stars and stripes, is an emblem of thirteen original colonies and fifty current states.

Encomium. A poem or oration in praise of a human hero or accomplishment, frequently taking the poetic form of the ode.

End-stopped line. A line of verse containing one complete and independent grammatical structure, as in these lines from Shakespeare's *Venus and Adonis* (1593): "She looks upon his lips, and they are pale;/She takes him by the hand, and it is cold."

Enjambement. "Runover" lines in poetry, in which a sentence is continued over from line to line, the opposite of end-stopped lines. Enjambement is a prominent characteristic of the blank verse of Milton's *Paradise Lost* (1667).

Envoy. A stanza at the end of a poem which closes the subject, usually with an address to a ruler or some prominent personage, or with a summing-up of four lines or so.

Epic. A long narrative in verse of an elevated nature, presenting heroic actions and great events. Twenty-odd examples are cited elsewhere in this book.

Epic simile. An extended comparison, introduced by Homer in the *Iliad* and *Odyssey* (eighth century B.C.E.) and imitated by many subsequent epic poets, in which the second term or vehicle of the comparison is developed at great length.

Epideictic literature. The literature of praise and blame, such as encomium and satire, usually composed for specific occasions.

Epigram. (1) A concise, wittily phrased statement, such as Dorothy Parker's celebrated formulation "Candy is dandy, but liquor is quicker"; (2) a fairly brief poem of condensed wisdom on some moral or philosophical theme, as in the epigrams of the Roman poet Martial and his English imitator, Ben Jonson.

Epigraph. An inscription—usually a quotation—preceding a poem or prose work and intended to suggest something in advance about the theme or subject.

Epilogue. A concluding section or terminal addition to a literary work. In some plays (*e.g.,* Shakespeare's *As You Like It*) it is spoken by an actor to the audience after the conclusion of the play proper.

Epiphany. A sudden revelation or showing forth of truth. James Joyce translated the term from a primarily religious to a literary context, using it as roughly equivalent to the Aristotelian "recognition," a point at which a character (and the reader) suddenly sees reality in a new or more lucid way.

Episode. An incident presented as part of a sequence of events making up a literary plot.

Episodic structure. A loose linear structure consisting simply of a series of episodes strung together in sequence without a rigorous principle of unity to relate them to one another.

Epistle. A poem or other literary composition in the form of a letter on some usually moral or philosophical theme, customarily addressed to a friend or patron of the author.

Epistolary novel. A novel in which narration takes the form of a series of letters written by one or more of the people in the story.

Epitaph. An inscription on a tomb or burial marker, or a poem (usually short) in praise of a deceased person, cast in such a form. The seventeenth-century poets Ben Jonson and Robert Herrick are among the more notable English authors of epitaphs.

Epithalamion. A poem written to celebrate and commemorate a wedding, usu- ally including a highly stylized narrative of the events of the nuptial day. Catullus in ancient Rome and Edmund Spenser in sixteenth-century England occupy high points in the tradition.

Epithet. A descriptive adjectival formula intended to emphasize the main char- acteristic of a person or thing—"Dirty Harry," "babbling brook," "pealing thunder" are examples. In Homer and his followers in the epic mode, the epithet becomes a reiterated rhetorical device: "rosy-fingered dawn," "ox- eyed Athene," "Zeus the cloud-gatherer," etc.

Eponym. The name of a person used to convey a quality with which that person is associated, as when one is said to be a Scrooge (miserly), a Judas (treach- erous), or a Don Juan (adventurously amorous). An "eponymous hero" is a person for whom a place is thought to be named, as the Trojan Brute was once considered eponymous hero of Britain (Brutan) and Sir Walter Raleigh is the eponymous hero of Raleigh, North Carolina.

Epyllion. Literally, "little epic," a term used for a relatively short narrative- heroic poem, such as the individual narratives in Tennyson's *Idylls of the King* (1859–85). In the sixteenth and seventeenth centuries the term was applied to mythological-erotic narratives in the manner of the Roman poet Ovid, such as Shakespeare's *Venus and Adonis* (1593) and Marlowe's *Hero and Leander* (1593).

Ethos. The character of the speaker as it appears via the speech. In Aristotle's rhetorical theory, widely followed in the European Renaissance, orators were advised to appeal through ethos (creating trust in the personality of the orator), pathos (appeal to the audience's emotions), and logos (logical argument.)

Eulogy. A formal tribute to a person, place, or institution.

Euphemism. An indirect, circumlocutory word or phrase substituted for one more direct and painful, as when we work around the mention of death by saying that someone has "passed away," "joined the majority," or "bought the farm." The Anglo-Saxons had many such terms for the Vikings of Scandinavia, whose visits they dreaded in the extreme.

Excursus. A long expository digression within a literary work.

Exegesis. An explication and interpretation of difficult passages or texts.

Exemplum. An "example," a story with a specific moral application.

Existentialism. A broad, variously used term for a complex of philosophical ideas associated with such philosophers as Søren Kierkegaard and Jean-Paul Sartre and such writers as Franz Kafka and Albert Camus. As a literary term it usually denotes the kind of fiction that denies any intrinsic meaning in life but recognizes the free will of human beings to create their meaning through action.

Exordium. The opening section of an oration or other composition, wherein the author addresses his audience and eases gracefully into the body of his work.

Expatriate. An artist who leaves his native country to live and work in another, often for the purpose of gaining proportion and objectivity in his view of home. Prominent expatriate writers include James Joyce, Ezra Pound, Ernest Hemingway, and D. H. Lawrence.

Explication de texte. French term for the process of careful analysis and exegesis of literary passages and texts.

Expressionism. A movement in twentieth-century literature, especially drama, in which the artist abandons usual canons of realism and representational art and distorts his medium to present his own subjective reality with appropriate symbolic emphasis. Tennessee Williams has used the term to describe his method in *The Glass Menagerie* (1945).

Eye-rhyme. Words that look alike but do not sound precisely the same, such as *lover, rover,* and *mover.*

Fable. A fictional story with a moral application.

Fabliau. A humorous, frequently bawdy tale. The genre originated in medieval France and is well represented in Chaucer's *Canterbury Tales* (ca. 1386) by "The Miller's Tale" and several others.

Falling action. The action of a tragic drama after the climax, leading to the catastrophe or final decisive act of the protagonist.

Familiar essay. An essay personal and informal in tone, dealing with ordinary events and issues and usually revealing a good deal about the author's personality.

Farce. A humorous play depending more on situation than on character for its interest and usually dealing with less than weighty issues.

Feminine ending. An unstressed syllable ending a line of poetry.

Feminine rhyme. Rhyme by words each of which has a stressed followed by an unstressed syllable; *e.g., waking* and *forsaking.*

Feminist criticism. Criticism that approaches literature with specific reference to the ways in which it deals with issues of special relevance to women, especially to the roles of women in society.

Fin de siècle. Literally "century's end," a term used to denote the period of restlessness and discomfort with traditional social customs and assumptions often occurring near the turn of a new century. The phrase is often used for the characteristic attitude and ambience of the 1890s in English literature.

Flashback. See **Anterior narration**.

Flyting. A literary exchange of challenges and insults, either in dialogue or in a monologue directed by one speaker against another who is not present.

Foil. A character, especially in drama, whose function is to clarify the personality or situation of another by parallelism or contrast.

Folktale. A story transmitted through oral tradition for an appreciable length of time before being written down.

Foot. The basic metrical unit of a line of poetry. Descriptions of a poem's meter usually consist of one term denoting the form of each foot followed by another specifying the number of feet per line, as in "iambic pentameter," "dactylic hexameter," etc. See **Anapest; Dactyl; Iamb; Spondee; Trochee.**

Foreshadowing. Hints or suggestions in a literary work of events that are to occur later in the narrative or dramatic exposition.

Formal criticism. Criticism that approaches literature in terms of the forms or genres involved.

Fourteener. A line of iambic heptameter verse, such as "Then I went down to London town to seek my fortune there."

Frame story. A tale enclosing another tale or a framework for narrative, such as Chaucer's *Canterbury Tales* (ca. 1386), Boccaccio's *Decameron* (1353), or the Cass Mastern episode in Robert Penn Warren's novel *All the King's Men* (1946).

Free verse. Poetry based on rhythms other than the conventional ones achieved through the use of regular meter.

Fugitives. See **Agrarian writers.**

Fustian. See **Bombast.**

Genre. A conventionally defined type of literary work, such as comedy, epic, etc.; a category.

Georgian age. Period in English literature between the two world wars, 1914–39.

Georgic. A poem about agriculture, rustic in setting but different from the pastoral because of the georgic's emphasis on the practical and realistic duties of country life.

Goliardic verse. The rhyming, robust Latin poetry of the wandering scholars of the Middle Ages, frequently irreverent, celebrating tavern life and conviviality.

Gothic novel. A type of novel, originating in the eighteenth century but still current today, emphasizing terror, suspense, and often romance in morbid or frightening settings.

Grotesque. A technique of literary exposition that makes use of distorted characters or bizarre situations, usually for symbolic or thematically emphatic purposes.

Haiku. A Japanese poetic form consisting of seventeen syllables arranged in three lines and usually concentrating on a specific visual image.

Heptameter. A seven-foot line of verse.

Hermeneutics. Theory of interpretation, including its methods, goals, premises, and limitations.

Heroic couplet. A two-line unit of iambic pentameter lines united by end rhyme and centering a complete, independent thought or idea, as in the following from John Dryden's *MacFlecknoe* (1678): "All arguments, but most his plays, persuade/That for anointed dullness he was made."

Hexameter. A six-foot line of verse.

Historicism. A critical approach that emphasizes the relationship of literary works with their social and historical contexts.

Homeric simile. See **Epic simile**.

Horatian satire. Satire in the vein of the Roman poet Horace, balanced and judicious in tone rather than strongly aggressive.

Iamb. A two-syllable metrical foot with the stress on the second syllable: ta-TA.

Imagery. Use of words or phrases, usually with concrete reference to objects, with emotional connotations to intensify the force of a literary passage or work; thus, "wine-dark sea" or "polar opposites."

Impressionism. A style that presents experience as it appears through the subjective perceptions of a narrator rather than concretely or objectively.

In medias res. Literally "in the middle of things," referring to a structure common to epic poetry in which the narrator begins at some dramatic point well into a story and later fills in the preceding action through anterior narration; thus Homer's *Iliad* (*ca.* 725 B.C.E.) begins with an incident in the tenth year of the Trojan War and restores the background later as occasions present themselves.

Intention. A subject or principal idea of a work of fiction, to the expression of which all elements of the work should, ideally, be directed if the work is to have artistic unity. The term can be used to denote either conscious purpose on the author's part or simply the overall organizing theme.

Interior monologue. A passage representing the direct, unstructured process of thought or inner emotional experience of a character as it passes through his mind; "stream of consciousness."

Internal rhyme. Rhyme that occurs at some point in a line of poetry other than at the end, as in "And the Raven, never flitting, still is sitting, still is sitting."

Irony. An effect produced by a difference and contradiction between appearance and reality, either on a verbal or a situational level.

Italian sonnet. See **Petrarchan sonnet**.

Jacobean period. The reign of King James I (1603–25), which included the literary productions of John Donne, Ben Jonson, and Francis Bacon, as well as the second half of Shakespeare's career as playwright.

Kenning. A formula in Anglo-Saxon poetry used regularly in place of a simple word, such as "whale-road" for "sea."

Künstlerroman. An apprenticeship novel treating the development of a young artist (literary or otherwise), usually in conflict with his family and society, as in James Joyce's *A Portrait of the Artist as a Young Man* (1916).

Lampoon. A work of prose or poetry which attacks, ridicules, or expresses contempt directly toward an individual.

Lay. A short narrative poem, often in the form of a lengthy ballad or narrative song.

Local color. Literature that emphasizes the regional characteristics peculiar to its setting and its inhabitants.

Lyric. A relatively short poem on a predominantly emotional theme.

Machinery. See **Deus ex machina**.

Masculine ending. Rhyme on the stressed syllables of the words involved.

Masque. A short play, usually with an obvious symbolic or allegorical message, often used in the period of the Renaissance as prelude to a dance or fancy-dress ball. Ben Jonson wrote a number of masques for the court of King James I (1603–25).

Melodrama. A play or other literary production aimed at direct stimulation of the audience's emotions, whether of joy, terror, pity, or some combination of strong feelings.

Metafiction. Fiction written about the writing of fiction.

Metaphor. An implied comparison in which the secondary term (the vehicle) is employed to clarify or amplify the primary term (the tenor).

Metonymy. Use of some object often associated with a word to represent the word itself, as when we say "the White House" for the current presidential administration, or print "surf and turf" on a menu to signify a combination of seafood and beef.

Metrics. The science, art, and practice of the creation of poetry through devices of rhythmic organization such as metrical feet, lines, stanzas, etc.

Mimesis. Aristotle's word for "imitation," the process of representing objective reality in fictional forms.

Miracle play. A medieval drama depicting a religious miracle, usually by or on behalf of a saint.

Mock epic. A work that applies the elevated style and conventions of heroic poetry to trivial subjects for comical, satiric, or bathetic effect.

Mock heroic. See **Mock epic**.

Monody. A lament or dirge spoken by a single voice.

Monologue. A soliloquy or extended speech entirely by one person.

Morality play. A medieval play on a moral or homiletic theme, usually presenting its lesson through simple parable or allegory.

Motif. A conventional idea, situation, or combination of events used as a basis for expansion and variation; a quarrel or combat between two great heroes, for example, is a common motif in epic poetry, on which other themes are built.

Mystery play. A medieval play that dramatizes episodes from the Bible, such as the creation of the world or the crucifixion of Christ.

Narrator. The person imagined as relating a poem, novel, or other work of fiction.

Naturalism. A variety of realism in fiction that suggests that human beings are controlled or primarily influenced by their natural or social environments.

Neoclassical. Term applied to work that seeks to imitate or embody the principles of order, balance, and formal grace associated with the art of ancient Greece and Rome.

Neoclassical period. The period 1660–1798, encompassing the Restoration and Augustan periods, in which neoclassical canons of art were in general ascendance.

New Criticism. A critical approach promulgated in the 1930s, 1940s, and 1950s, associated mainly with the opinions of Cleanth Brooks, Robert Penn Warren, and John Crowe Ransom and seeking to analyze literary works as objective, self-contained entities more important for internal than for contextual qualities.

New Historicism. A school of criticism that, like historicism, emphasizes the relationship of literary works with their historical backgrounds, but concentrates on social, economic, and political tensions in that background. It seeks, especially, to discover "embedded texts," or hidden ideological agendas that writers might not have been able to treat openly or candidly in the times in which they wrote.

Notatio. A catalog and celebration of a lady's virtues of spirit, character, and personality, as opposed to the physical attributes celebrated in an efficacio.

Novel. A term defined variously but generally appropriate to any extended fictional narrative in prose.

Novella. A fictional tale in prose, falling in length between a short story and a novel, usually between about ten thousand and twenty thousand words.

Octosyllabic verse. Tetrameter verse, usually in couplets, as in Chaucer's *House of Fame* (*ca.* 1375), but sometimes not, as in W. H. Auden's lyric "Lay your sleeping head, my love" (1940).

Ode. A lyrical poem of praise, celebration, or commemoration, addressed directly to a person, place, institution, or event.

Old English period. The time between *ca.* 450 and 1100, when Anglo-Saxon was the vernacular language of England.

Omniscient viewpoint. The point of view assumed by an author who represents himself as having access to all existing information needed to tell his story, including the private thoughts and past histories, etc., of his characters.

Onomatopoeia. The quality of words whose sounds suggest or define their meaning, such as *gurgle, boom, sneeze.*

Paean. A song of praise or exultation.

Palinode. A retraction or rejection of an opinion formerly held or a work written earlier.

Panegyric. A eulogy or poem of praise for a person or a deed.

Paradox. An apparently self-contradictory statement which may contain more truth than immediately appears.

Parallelism. Alignment of phrases, sentences, characters, or structural units of a literary work for purposes of comparison, contrast, or architectonic rhythm.

Parody. A literary burlesque that satirizes another work by imitating it with exaggerated emphasis.

Paronomasia. A pun.

Pastoral. A literary treatment of rustic life, usually in idealized form.

Pathetic fallacy. The attribution of quasihuman feelings to nonhuman objects, as when a poet says that all nature wept for the sorrowing shepherd, or that the sea wind sang a mournful dirge.

Pentameter. A five-foot line of verse.

Periodic sentence. A sentence whose grammatic order and hence its meaning are not complete until its end, usually employing several clauses dependent on a main verb.

Periphrasis. A circuitous or otherwise indirect locution, such as "indicate the route to my habitual abode" for "show me the way to go home."

Persona. The author's depiction of a version of himself in a literary work when that literary self differs from his actual personality as a participant in real life. In *The Canterbury Tales* (*ca.* 1386), for example, Chaucer depicts himself as a naïve reporter of the pilgrimage through which the tales are framed.

Personification. Representation of animals, inanimate nature, or abstract ideas as having human traits or form, as when a poet personifies the moon as Diana, or as when Uncle Remus attributes human speech and opinions to Br'er Rabbit *et al.* in the story collections of Joel Chandler Harris.

Petrarchan sonnet. Fourteen-line poem divided into an eight-line octave rhymed *abbaabba,* and six-line sestet, usually but not always *cdecde,* developed by the Italian poet Petrarch.

Phenomenological criticism. A critical approach that considers the literary work only as it exists in the consciousness of the perceiver, and so explores the way in which the reader becomes aware of art rather than examining any objective qualities of the work itself. See **Affective criticism**.

Picaresque. A mode of fiction that depicts the wanderings of a central character through a series of settings and experiences which contribute, ultimately, to his education or greater understanding. Henry Fielding's *Tom Jones* (1749) would be an example.

Plot. An ordering of events and episodes into a structure for the literary representation of a story in prose fiction, drama, or narrative verse.

Plurisignification. The capacity of words to suggest several ideas or images at the same time, and the writer's practice of exploiting this ambiguity to enrich the work. James Joyce's title *Finnegans Wake,* for example, by omitting an apostrophe implies several possibilities of interpretation: is it Finnegan's individual wake, as in the song it alludes to; is it the wake of the Finnegans regarded as the Irish nation; does it enjoin the Finnegans to wake up; does it aim that injunction at the Finnish nation, threatened by Soviet Russia in the late 1930s; or does it signify all these meanings at once?

Poetic diction. Word choice based on the supposedly poetic or elevated quality of the words, such as in the choice of *Araby* for *Arabia* or *e'en* for *evening.*

Poetic justice. A quality evident in the outcome of a story in which the good are rewarded and the bad are punished, *i.e.*, a justice that is "poetic" as opposed to realistic.

Poetics. A theory or body of assumptions about the nature and practice of poetry.

Point of view. The position the author assumes relative to the story. He may view the actions and characters as an onlooker (third-person limited); go "inside" them and know all that he can know about them (omniscient); or assume the position of a participatory narrator or character within the story (first-person limited).

Postmodern. A contemporary style of writing that inverts or distorts traditional forms of expression or literature in order to repudiate the sense of order and philosophical coherence most of those forms once implied. Thus antiheroes supplant heroes, modes of representation mix fantasy and realism, and the author's perception usually emerges as enigmatic or even bizarre as it finds itself expressed in the work. The term is usually applied to the period since *ca.* 1965.

Poulter's measure. Couplets of verse each containing a line of iambic hexameter (12 syllables) followed by a line of iambic heptameter (14 syllables), especially popular in the earlier sixteenth century in England. Supposedly so named because poulterers—sellers of chickens and eggs—sometimes gave twelve to the dozen and sometimes fourteen.

Prosopopoeia. See **Personification**.

Protagonist. The main character in a work of fiction, around whose fortunes the principal themes are organized.

Pun. An instance of wordplay involving two words that sound the same but have different meanings—*e.g.*, "when the cattle stampeded the rustlers seemed cowed."

Pyrrhic foot. A metrical foot of verse consisting of two unaccented syllables: ta-ta.

Quantitative verse. Verse, such as that in classical Greek and Latin, whose rhythm derives from duration rather than stress, *i.e.*, from syllables held for short or long times in pronunciation rather than from forceful emphasis. Uncommon in English and the other Germanic languages, it was nonetheless used successfully by Thomas Campion (1567–1620), one of whose verses provides this example of iambic pentameter in quantitative meter: "When thou must home to shades of underground/And there arrived, a new admired guest . . . "

Quatorzain. A fourteen-line stanza or poem, the usual form of the sonnet.

Quatrain. A four-line stanza.

Quibble. A play on words.

Reader-response criticism. See **Affective criticism**.

Realism. A style in fiction that seeks to represent actuality, especially of setting, as it is familiarly experienced.

Recognition scene. The point in a fictional work at which a character comes to the realization of some important truth previously unavailable to or unperceived by him; usually followed by a significant change of direction in the character's behavior and thought. See **Reversal; Epiphany**.

Requiem. A chanted prayer for the dead, or a literary work that resembles such a chant in form and purpose.

Restoration period. The era in English literature and history beginning in 1660 with the restoration of the monarchy and extending to about 1700 and the death of its premier writer, John Dryden; the first half of the neoclassical period in England.

Reversal. The significant change of direction in a character's behavior and thought following the recognition. See **Recognition scene; Epiphany**.

Rhyme. As defined by William Harmon, "the articulatory-acoustic relation between stressed syllables that begin differently and end alike" ("Rhyme in English Verse: History, Structures, Functions," *Studies in Philology*, LXXXIV [1987], 365–93).

Rhyme royale. A stanza form of seven iambic pentameter lines rhyming *ababbcc*; probably invented by Chaucer around 1375 but called "royale" after its later employment by the poetry-writing monarch James I of Scotland in the fifteenth century.

Rococo. Term for a style originating in the late Renaissance period and now used categorically for styles emphasizing a great deal of decorative detail and elaboration; frequently used pejoratively for an overly elaborate or ornate style.

Roman à clef. A novel that presents real persons and happenings under the guise of fiction.

Romantic period. The literary era beginning in England *ca.* 1798 and in America *ca.* 1830 and extending in both countries to *ca.* 1865.

Saga. Term used specifically for the Icelandic heroic tales of the Middle Ages, and more generally to describe a traditional story of adventure and heroic action.

Satire. Literature of any genre whose purpose is to expose vice, folly, or ineptitude by subjecting it to scorn, ridicule, or humorous critical examination.

Scenario. The outline of a plot, intended for later augmentation and elaboration.

Semiotics. The study of ways in which the "signs" of language used in discourse may have meanings determined by the cultures or societies in which such discourse originates.

Sensibility. Term denoting the tendency to trust feelings as opposed to strict rationality as a guide to truth or enlightenment, and denoting literature that maximizes the importance of feeling in human conduct, such as the novel of sensibility of the latter half of the eighteenth century.

Sentimentalism. A quality of promoting emotional over rational criteria in judging people and situations, and a category of literature that does the same; see **Sensibility**.

Setting. The social, historical, or natural background of a story. It may be merely scenic (used as a framework for the action), contributory (adding understanding to the action it frames), or a major factor—for example, the work may be written to explain or examine the setting it uses.

Shakespearean sonnet. The "English" form of the sonnet devised by the Earl of Surrey in the 1540s but gaining its name through use by Shakespeare in the 154 sonnets published in 1609. The Shakespearean form consists of fourteen lines arranged in three quatrains rhyming *ababcdcdefef* and followed by a couplet (*gg*).

Short story. A prose tale of length somewhere between five hundred words (the usual length of the "short short story") and the length of a short novel or novella. There are of course no rigid standards for its size, a matter at least partially governed by the magazines and journals in which it tends to appear.

Signifier. The concrete linguistic sign that evokes a more abstract or general idea. The element signified may be determined by any number of contexts, as the word *course* may signify ideas related to sport, country-club society, college studies, dining, fox hunting, navigation, etc.

Simulacrum. An image, reflection, or representation of something, not necessarily exact.

"Slice of life" fiction. An extreme form of realism that attempts to reproduce setting and behavior in exactly the unselective, unordered, way in which it occurs in daily life.

Soliloquy. Device in which a character speaks alone in a play or other work of fiction, revealing his inner thoughts, conflicts, plans, etc., to the audience.

Sonnet. A form of lyric poem of no rigidly set line length but usually, by tradition, in fourteen lines and appearing in a variety of rhyme schemes and structural patterns. Most sonnets proceed in logical development from the concrete in the first eight lines (the octave) to the more abstract in the last six (the sestet). See also **Petrarchan sonnet**; **Shakespearean sonnet**; **Spenserian sonnet**.

Spenserian sonnet. A sonnet whose rhyme scheme is *ababbcbccdcdee*, developed by Edmund Spenser.

Spondee. A metrical foot of two accented syllables: TA-TA.

Stanza. A group of two or more lines of verse arranged according to a repeated pattern of rhythm and rhyme, usually occurring as one of a number of such units in a larger work, but occasionally standing alone, as in various aphoristic uses of the couplet or in epigrams.

Stream of consciousness. See **Interior monologue**.

Structuralism. An approach to literature that studies ways in which its elements of language, convention, genre, etc., interrelate within a work to give it unity and proportional emphasis.

Structure. The arrangement of parts that constitutes the framework of a literary construct.

Suspension of disbelief. The willingness often required of a reader or audience to grant the author his right to create elements of his art without subjecting them to the canons of ordinary realism—as when we accept a magic carpet or a flying nun in fictional situations. Also, our basic assumption that what we see acted on a stage or written in a story is not "real life" but fiction.

Symbol. An image or object used to represent a complex of ideas and/or emotions.

Synchronic. Happening at the same time. Synchronic arrangement in a literary plot represents events as taking place concurrently, rather than diachronically, as when we follow the progress of Bloom and Dedalus separately through the same hours of the day in James Joyce's *Ulysses* (1922).

Synecdoche. A type of metaphor which uses a part to imply the whole, as when we speak of "head" of cattle or "hands" in a factory.

Tetrameter. A four-foot line of verse.

Text. Anything set apart for special analysis, discussion or elucidation. In current critical usage, "text" is often distinguished from "work of literature" and used to signify the process, instigated by the literary work but not confined to it, in which the reader participates as he reacts and enlarges.

Textuality. The state of constituting a text by possessing a system of signifiers capable of being interpreted; thus we can speak of the "textuality" of religion, or inanimate nature, or marriage, etc.

Theme. The main idea of a literary work, usually established by a series of allusions or illustrative episodes.

Threnody. A death song or dirge.

Topos. A commonplace topic, situation, or convention in a literary work, such as the runaway stagecoach in a western novel or the sexual initiation scene in a *Bildungsroman*.

Tragicomedy. A literary work that combines elements of both tragedy and comedy. Usually it involves a tragic plot with an unexpectedly happy ending, such as Shakespeare's *The Winter's Tale* (ca. 1612); but in Harry Crews's novel *Body* (1990), which its author describes as tragicomic, the process is reversed.

Transcendentalism. A form of idealism that trusts intuition and inner conscience as instruments of knowing moral, ethical, and philosophical truth;

reliance on an inner sense that transcends ordinary logic, and the literature that promotes or embodies this reliance. The American Transcendentalists of the 1830s–50s included Ralph Waldo Emerson, Henry David Thoreau, Bronson Alcott, and Margaret Fuller.

Trimeter. A three-foot line of verse.

Trochee. A metrical foot of two syllables with its accent on the first: TA-ta.

Trope. Term applied to a large variety of figures of speech involving metaphor or comparison.

Unities. Three criteria derived from Aristotle by critics in the European Renaissance for unity and decorum in drama. The unity of *time* requires that the action be confined to a finite period, usually one day; the unity of *place* requires that it all occur in a single locale; and the unity of *action* rules out episodes and incidents not related to the central action.

Unreliable narrator. A narrator in fiction whose character or ability may render him suspect or unreliable as a reporter and judge. When such a narrator is used, his character is usually important to the main subject or theme.

Verisimilitude. The appearance of truth in representation, which allows a reader or audience to accept a literary work without straining credulity.

Victorian. The period in English and American literature extending through the reign of Queen Victoria, 1837–1901.

Well-made plot. A plot in prose fiction or drama that is tightly unified and constructed with concern for logic, causal order, and verisimilitude of incident.

Zeugma. A figure of speech in which two unlike words or concepts are connected through a third term, as in the phrase "the cleanup crew arrived with *sweeping* brooms and generalizations."

SOURCES

Abrams, M. H., *et al. The Norton Anthology of English Literature.* 4th ed. Vol. I. New York: W. W. Norton, 1979.

Beckson, Karl, and Arthur Ganz. *A Reader's Guide to Literary Terms.* New York: Noonday Press, 1960.

Brooks, Cleanth, John Purser, and Robert Penn Warren. *An Approach to Literature.* 3rd ed. New York: Appleton-Century-Crofts, 1952.

Holman, C. Hugh, and William Harmon. *A Handbook to Literature.* 6th ed. New York: Macmillan, 1992.

Hornstein, Lillian H., and G. D. Percy. *The Reader's Companion to World Literature.* New York: New American Library, 1956.

—J.L.M.

38

CURRENT SLANG AND INFORMAL EXPRESSIONS

. . . . .

AT ANY GIVEN TIME THERE IS AN ARRAY OF CURRENT WAYS OF SAYING THINGS that almost everyone in a social community knows quite well, yet would have been next to meaningless even ten years earlier. A decade later and most will have fallen into disuse, while some few will have survived and given promise of becoming reasonably lasting units of discourse.

The process, and the lexicographical problem involved, can be illustrated by this example. What would a young person, reading a newspaper account of a major league baseball game today, make of a sentence of description such as the following? "Big Six applied the Kalsomine brush in the fashion of Togo at Tsushima, permitting the White Elephants but four bingles and nary an Annie Oakley and delighting the Gotham bugs, the meanwhile his fellow Brushmen were denting the dish on three occasions." A baseball fan in 1905 would have recognized at once that New York of the National League had defeated Philadelphia of the American League in the opening game of the World Series by 3–0, with Christy Mathewson pitching, giving up four hits and no bases on balls, and allowing no runs.

Today's fan would be familiar with the term *bingle* for base hit, and he might well recognize that the dish in question was home plate. He might even know that Kalsomine was a form of whitewash. But unless a student of history he would be most unlikely to grasp the reference to the Japanese navy's destruction of the Russian fleet off Korea the previous May; he would not know that *bugs* was the term then commonly used for baseball fans; that an Annie Oakley was a common term for a free pass; that the New York Giants were then owned by John T. Brush; that the star New York pitcher was called Big Six in reference to a famous fire truck; that the Philadelphia team was known as the White Elephants; and so on. (Incidentally, the above is a reasonable facsimile of the way that newspaper sports stories were written at the time.)

No living language can remain immutably fixed. Our language is constantly being enriched by slang and colloquial expressions, and the compilers of new editions of dictionaries are regularly confronted with the need to decide upon which hitherto-unlisted words and expressions should be included, and which are likely to prove ephemeral. In the "Oxen of the Sun" chapter of *Ulysses*, James Joyce parodies the evolution of the English language from its Latin and Germanic origins onward as used by various stylists, ending in a melange of semigibberish. Lexicographers, aware that their decisions about new words and new usages will carry weight among teachers and editors, attempt to negotiate a tricky area between being overly prescriptive—*i.e.*, presuming to decide what *should* be given the respectability of inclusion within a dictionary—and being uncritically descriptive—*i.e.*, declining to make judgments of any kind whatever and thus acquiescing in utter linguistic chaos.

Fortunately, there are dictionaries that are devoted entirely to slang and colloquial speech; their compilers are constantly on the lookout for the advent of new words and expressions, and are greatly interested in watching whether they will survive or drop out of sight. The dictionaries they compile thus constitute a kind of screening process, or perhaps a waiting-out period, for new language, and so help to determine what should be incorporated within the general dictionaries. Such works also perform the valuable historical function of preserving the more ephemeral language of a period that might otherwise be forgotten.

The glossary of some more frequently encountered contemporary slang and informal expressions here presented has been compiled by Connie C. Eble, of the University of North Carolina at Chapel Hill, and is based on four recent lexicographical works, each of which is identified as the authority for the words and expressions included and their earliest-known appearance in print. References to the dictionaries thus consulted are as follows:

Algeo   Algeo, John, ed. *Fifty Years Among the New Words: A Dictionary of Neologisms, 1941–1991*. Cambridge, Eng.: Cambridge University Press, 1991.

Beale   Beale, Paul, ed. *A Dictionary of Slang and Unconventional English*. 8th ed. London: Routledge and Kegan Paul, 1984. (Based on the many editions of Eric Partridge's dictionary of the same title.)

Chapman   Chapman, Robert, ed. *New Dictionary of American Slang*. New York: Harper and Row, 1986. (Based on Harold Wentworth and Stuart Flexner, comps. and eds. *Dictionary of American Slang*. 2nd ed. with supp. New York: T. Y. Crowell, 1975.)

RHD   *The Random House Dictionary of the English Language*. 2nd ed., unabridged. New York: Random House, 1987.

A–1, A Number One. First-rate, the very best, tops. Originally nautical, based on the classification of ships in Lloyd's Register as equipped and maintained to the highest standard. 1830–40. RHD: informal.

Ack-ack. Antiaircraft fire. World War II. RHD: informal.

All get-out. To an extreme degree. Late 1800s. Chapman.

All-nighter. Act of staying up all night, as to study or finish a task. 1890–95. RHD: informal.

All shook up. Excited, shocked, upset. Teenagers, 1950s. Chapman.

All-star. A player selected for a team consisting of athletes chosen as the best at their positions from all teams in a league or region. 1885–90. RHD: sports.

Ambulance chaser. An attorney overly zealous for clients. 1895–1900. RHD: disparaging.

Asphalt jungle. Large city. 1920. Algeo.

Asshole. Stupid, mean, contemptible person. 1350–1400. RHD: slang.

Attaboy! That's the boy! Expression of approval or commendation. 1905–10. RHD: informal.

Baby-sit; baby-sitter. Take care of children while their parents go out; one who does so. 1945–50. RHD.

Back burner. Low priority. 1966. Algeo.

Ball-park, in the. Within a reasonable or acceptable range. 1967. Algeo.

Bananas. Eccentric, excited, crazy, nutty. 1957. Algeo.

Bashing. Malicious, unprovoked attack on. *Ca.* 1955. Beale.

Bat the breeze. Carry on friendly conversation, gossip, etc. Australian army, 1939. Beale.

Bazoo. The mouth, as a device for speaking. Middle 1800s. Chapman.

Bazooka. Over-the-shoulder antitank weapon widely known during World War II. So called because of its resemblance to a musical device used by the radio comedian Bob Burns in the 1930s and 1940s. 1930–35. RHD: military.

Beat (whale) the tar out of. Thrash soundly. *Ca.* 1920. Beale.

Beef up. Strengthen, reinforce. 1860. Algeo.

Belly-ache. Complain. Early 1900s. Chapman.

Bigmouth. Loud, talkative person. 1885–90. RHD.

Big wheel. Person of importance. 1905–10. RHD: informal.

Bird-brain. A person of very little intelligence. 1920–25. RHD: slang.

Bitch. To complain. 1925. Beale.

Bite the dust. Die or be killed; fail or be destroyed. Mid–1800s. Chapman.

Blabbermouth. Person who talks too much, especially indiscreetly. 1935–40. RHD.

Black Hole of Calcutta. Any unusually wretched place of imprisonment or confinement. From a small prison cell in Ft. William, Calcutta, in which, in 1756, Indians are said to have imprisoned 146 Europeans, only 23 of whom were alive the next morning. RHD.

Black market. Place for the sale of contraband or illegal goods. 1930–35. RHD.

Blind date. A social engagement with a member of the opposite sex that one does not already know. 1920–25. RHD.

Blockbuster. Exceptionally large, powerful, or effective person or thing. 1943. Algeo.

Blood brother. Fellow black. *Ca.* 1960. Chapman.

Blowhard. Loud talker, braggard, windbag. 1850–55. RHD: slang.

Blow the whistle on. Provide information, usually to the authorities, about illegal or secret activities. *Ca.* 1960. Beale.

Bomb. Be or make a complete failure. 1960–65. RHD: slang.

Bombed. Drunk. 1935–40. RHD: slang.

Bonkers. Mentally unbalanced, mad, crazy. 1945–50. RHD: slang.

Boob. Stupid person (1905–10); female breast (1945–50). RHD: slang.

Boob-tube. Television. 1965–70. RHD: informal.

Bop on down. Move, go, proceed. 1945–50. RHD: slang.

Bottom line. Definitive argument, statement, answer, summary, etc. 1970. Algeo.

Bozo. Rude, obnoxious, annoying person. 1915–20. RHD: slang.

Bread. Money. 1950–55. RHD: slang.

Broad. Woman. Early 1900s. Chapman.

Brown-nose. Curry favor. 1935–40. RHD: slang.

Brownout. Any curtailment of electric power. 1940–45. RHD: slang.

Buck. A dollar. 1855–60. RHD: slang.

Bull. Exaggeration, lies, nonsense. 1620–30. RHD: slang.

Bull pen. Place where substitute pitchers warm up before entering a baseball game. 1920–25. RHD: baseball.

Bullshit. Exaggeration, lies, nonsense. 1910–15. RHD: slang.

Bump. Displace another with less priority or seniority. 1940s. Algeo.

Bum's rush. Forcible ejection, abrupt dismissal. 1920–25. RHD: slang.

Bum steer. Bad advice, wrong information. Early 1900s. Chapman.

Buns. Buttocks. 1325–75. RHD: slang.

Buzz off. Depart, especially quickly. *Ca.* 1905. Beale.

BYOB, BYO. "Bring your own bottle." An indication on the announcement of a social occasion that guests should provide their own alcoholic beverages. 1970–75. RHD.

By the numbers. In a specified order, by rote. World War I. Chapman.

Call of nature. Need to urinate or defecate. 1850–55. RHD: informal.

Call on the carpet. Reprimand. Early 1800s. Chapman.

Camp it up. Behave effeminately; work in highly stylized, overwrought form. 1930s. Chapman.

Can. Stop, cease, especially some objectionable behavior. Early 1900s. Chapman.

Cancer stick. Cigarette. 1965–70. RHD: slang.

Cheesecake. Magazine photographs of scantily clad women. 1930–35. RHD: informal.

Chew out. Scold, reprimand someone severely. World War II. Chapman.

Chew the fat. Carry on a friendly conversation on far-ranging topics. Late 1800s. Chapman.

Chopper. Helicopter. 1952. Algeo.

Cliff-hanger. Anything exciting and drawn out. *Ca.* 1914. Beale.

Cold shoulder. Deliberate snub. Early 1800s. Chapman.

Cool. Satisfying; sophisticated, unostentatiously fashionable. *Ca.* 1950. Beale.

Copacetic. Quite satisfactory, as it should be. 1920s. Chapman.

Corn pone. Of or characteristic of an unsophisticated, rural person, especially from the South; a hick. 1965–70. RHD: usually disparaging.

Cotton to. Approve of, like, appreciate. Late 1700s. Chapman.

Couch potato. One who spends time lying down watching television. 1982. Algeo.

Countdown. Period immediately preceding a critical decision or turning point. 1959. Algeo.

Country mile. A long distance. 1945–50. RHD: informal.

Crash. Gain admittance though uninvited. 1920–25. RHD: informal.

Cuba Libre. A drink of rum and Coca-Cola. From the toast used in the Cuban uprising against Spain in 1895. RHD.

Deep-six. Throw overboard, get rid of, abandon. 1950–55. RHD: slang.

Dibs. Rights, claims. 1720–30. RHD: informal.

Dicey. Unpredictable, risky, uncertain. 1935–40. RHD: informal.

Dirty old man. Mature or elderly man with lewd or obscene preoccupations. 1930–35. RHD: informal.

Disc jockey. Radio announcer who plays popular music off records, tapes, etc. 1940–45. RHD.

Dive. Vulgar and disreputable haunt, such as a cheap bar or nightclub. Late 1800s. Chapman.

Doozie. Something extraordinary, outstanding. 1925–30. RHD: informal.

Dope. Any narcotic or illicit drug. 1885–90. RHD: slang.

Dork. (1) Stupid person; jerk; nerd; (2) penis (vulgar). 1960–65. RHD.

Drip. A tedious, unimaginative person. Especially students in 1940s. Chapman.

Dry out. Refrain from alcohol. Late 1800s. Chapman.

Egghead. An intellectual. 1915–20. RHD: informal, often disparaging.

Elbow grease. Muscular exertion, physical effort. Late 1700s. Chapman.

Fast lane. The lifestyle of those who desire immediate gratification and lack restraint and commitment. 1978. Algeo.

Fat cat. Wealthy person who makes campaign contributions and gets influence or special privileges in return. 1925–30. RHD: slang.

Fat-head. A stupid person, a fool. 1830–40. RHD: slang.

Filthy lucre. Money. Translation of New Testament Greek in Titus 1:11. 1520–30. RHD.

Flimflam. Trick someone out of money. 1530–40. RHD: informal.

Floozy. A gaudily dressed woman, usually of questionable reputation. 1905–10. RHD: slang.

Flush. Having plenty of money. Late 1600s. Chapman.

Fly off the handle. Lose one's temper. Early 1800s. Chapman.

Four-letter word. An obscene word. 1936. Algeo.

From hunger. Highly undesirable, inferior. 1930s. Chapman.

Fruit salad. Military campaign ribbons worn on chest. World War II. Chapman.

Fuzz. Policeman or detective. 1925–30. RHD: slang.

Get cracking. Begin; work faster. 1920s. Chapman.

Gig. Paid engagement for a musician. 1925–30. RHD: slang.

Girlfriend. Close female friend, with romantic attachment. 1855–60. RHD.

Glitch. An operating defect, a disabling minor problem. 1960s. Chapman.

Go ape. Act in berserk fashion, lose control of one's emotions. Early 1970s. Beale.

Gobbledegook. Pretentious and scarcely intelligible language. 1944. Chapman.

Go Dutch. Pay for one's own meal. Mid-twentieth century. Beale.

Gofer. Employee whose chief duty is running errands. 1965–70. RHD: slang.

Go haywire. Become inoperative, break down unexpectedly. Early 1900s. Chapman.

Go hog wild. Act audaciously and unrestrainedly. Late 1800s. Chapman.

Goldbrick. Shirk responsibility; perform half-heartedly, loaf. 1850–55. RHD: slang.

Goo. Any sticky or viscous substance. Early 1900s. Chapman.

Goof off. Shirk one's responsibilities, be absent from one's post (1915–20); person who habitually makes mistakes, gets in trouble, etc. (1940–45). RHD: slang.

Goose egg. Zero on athletic scoreboard showing no runs, points, etc., scored. 1885–90. RHD: informal.

Got it made. Assured of success. Later twentieth century. Beale.

Gross out. Disgust, offend. 1970s. Chapman.

Hack it. Do what is required. Late 1950s. Beale.

Hair of the dog. Alcoholic drink taken to relieve a hangover. Twentieth century. From hair of the dog that bit, 1546. Beale.

Half-assed. Insufficient, incompetent. 1960–65. RHD: slang (vulgar).

Hassle, hassel. An irritation, problem, struggle. 1946. Algeo.

Have a monkey on one's back. To use drugs habitually. 1945. Beale.

Hell-bent for leather. Rapidly and energetically. Late 1800s. Chapman.

Highfalutin. Overblown and pretentious, bombastic, stilted. Middle 1800s. Chapman.

Hip. Familiar with or informed about the latest ideas, styles, developments. 1900–1905. RHD: slang.

Hit list. List of persons or programs against which some action is to be taken. 1976. Algeo.

Hopped up. Under the influence of drugs. 1920–25. RHD: slang.

Hot stuff. Person of exceptional merit, talents, attractions, etc. Late 1800s. Chapman.

Humdinger. Person or thing that is remarkable, wonderful, superior. Early 1900s. Chapman.

Hung over. In physical distress on morning after drinking liquor. 1945–50. RHD: informal.

Hunky-dory. Satisfactory, fine. Middle 1800s. Chapman.

Hype. Excessive publicity, media attention. 1925–30. RHD: informal.

Hyped up. Intensively or extensively stimulated or exaggerated. 1945–50. RHD: informal.

Iffy. Contingent, doubtful. 1940. Algeo.

In. Accepted by or as a member in a favored or select group. *Ca.* 1920. Beale.

In a swivet. Anxious, concerned. 1890–95. RHD.

Jerk. Contemptibly naïve, fatuous, foolish, or inconsequential person. 1935–40. RHD: slang.

Jerk off. Masturbate. 1540–50. RHD: slang.

Jive. Banter, jest, tease. Early 1900s. Chapman.

Joe Doaks. The average man, any man. 1920s. Chapman.

John. Toilet. 1930s. Chapman.

Jug wine. Any inexpensive wine sold in large bottles. 1970–75. RHD.

Juke box. Coin-operated phonograph. 1915–20. RHD.

Jumping-off place. A point of departure. 1826. Beale.

Kangaroo court. Mock court proceedings within a group; any crudely or irregularly operated court. Mid–1800s. Chapman.

Keep a stiff upper lip. Not show fear or sorrow. *Ca.* 1815. Beale.

Keep tabs on. Keep informed about; keep watch on. Late 1800s. Chapman.

Keep your shirt on. Remain calm, do not lose patience. Mid–1800s. Chapman.

Keister. Human posterior. 1880–85. RHD: slang.

Kick the bucket. To die. Late 1700s. Chapman.

Kick upstairs. Promote to higher position. 1887. Beale.

Kiss of death. An apparently advantageous action which in reality will bring trouble or destruction. *Ca.* 1950. Beale.

Knee-high to a grasshopper. Very small of stature. Early 1800s. Chapman.

Knock it off. Be silent, cease what one is doing. Middle 1800s. Chapman.

Kooky. Crazy, eccentric. 1950s. Chapman.

Lay an egg. Fail. 1940. Algeo.

Lay a trip on. Burden someone with something; accuse. 1960s. Chapman.

Like greased lightning. With high speed. 1833. Beale.

Litterbug. One who strews debris in public places. 1945–50. RHD.

The living end. Perfection, the ultimate, the ideal. *Ca.* 1955. Beale.

Longhair. Devotee of classical music. 1915–20. RHD: informal.

Long in the tooth. Advanced in age. Early 1900s. Chapman.

Looney tunes. Illogical, erratic, absurd, or crazy in behavior. 1985. Algeo.

Loose cannon. Someone or something that has become uncontrollable. 1981. Algeo.

Low-rent. Cheap, crude, tasteless. 1982. Algeo.

Lunatic fringe. An extremist or unbalanced minority of an organization or movement. 1928. Algeo.

Lunkhead. Dull or stupid person. 1850–55. RHD: slang.

Lush. Habitual heavy drinker, an alcoholic. 1780–90. RHD: slang.

Make the grade. Be able to do a thing; meet a standard. Late nineteenth century. Beale.

Make waves. Upset established or accepted routine or procedure. *Ca.* 1972. Beale.

Malarkey. Lies, exaggeration, empty bombastic talk. 1920s. Chapman.

Meal ticket. Someone depended upon to provide a livelihood. 1865–70. RHD: informal.

Mishmash. Many ingredients mixed together, without order or logic. 1425–75. RHD.

Mooch. Beg. 1425–75. RHD: slang.

Moon. Display one's naked posterior. Late 1970s. Beale.

Mug shot. Photograph of a face. 1945–50. RHD: slang.

Musical chairs. Situation or series of events in which jobs, decisions, prospects, etc., are changed with confusing rapidity. 1875–80. RHD: informal.

Nerd. Stupid, irritating, ineffectual, or unattractive person. 1960–65. RHD: slang.

Nerdy. Behaving like a nerd. 1975–80. RHD: slang.

No-show. A person who fails to keep an appointment. 1930s. Chapman.

No spring chicken. Older, more experienced woman. Late 1800s. Chapman.

Oddball. Eccentric, quirky. 1940–45. RHD: informal.

Off the wall. Unusual, not normal. 1960s. Beale.

Old hat. Old-fashioned, trite. 1941. Algeo.

One-horse. Small and unimportant. 1740–50. RHD.

On the fritz. Failing to function properly, broken. 1934. Beale.

On the level. Honest. Early 1900s. Chapman.

On the up-and-up. Strictly legitimate, honest. Mid-1800s. Chapman.

On the (water) wagon. Abstaining from alcohol. Late 1800s. Chapman.

Pain in the neck. Tedious, boring, irritating person. *Ca.* 1910. Beale.

Paint the town red. Go on a spree. Late 1800s. Chapman.

Pan out. Happen as planned. Middle 1800s. Chapman.

Paper trail. Evidence, especially for a decision or of clandestine or improper action. 1987. Algeo.

Park. Place oneself, sit. 1920. Beale.

Party-poop, party pooper. One who leaves a party early in the evening. 1940–45. RHD: slang.

Pass the buck. Escape responsibility by handing on a problem to someone else. 1938. Beale.

Peanuts. Very small salary or fee. 1930. Beale.

Piece of cake. Something that is easy to handle or accomplish. *Ca.* 1938. Beale.

Pill. Unpleasant person. Late 1800s. Chapman.

The pill. Oral contraceptive. *Ca.* 1960. Beale.

Pissed off. Extremely angry. 1935–40. RHD: slang (vulgar).

Play second fiddle to. Be in an inferior position to. Middle 1700s. Chapman.

Podunk. The legendary small town. Early 1900s. Chapman.

Pooped. Exhausted, worn out. 1930–35. RHD: informal.

Prexy. President. 1855–60. RHD: slang.

Pull. Influence. Late 1800s. Chapman.

Put-up job. A prearranged matter. Middle 1800s. Chapman.

Queen. Male homosexual who plays the female role. Late nineteenth century. Chapman.

Railroad. Convict without evidence, push through without discussion or majority vote. Late 1800s. Chapman.

Ralph. Vomit. 1970–75. RHD: slang.

Rap. Discuss, converse. Late 1960s. Beale.

Rhubarb. A loud quarrel or squabble, particularly in baseball. Late 1900s. Chapman.

Rock and roll. Heavily accented popular music usually played on amplified electronic instruments. 1950s. Chapman.

Root-hog or die. Do what is necessary for survival. Early 1800s. Chapman.

Rubberneck. Stare at sights, as a tourist. Late 1800s. Chapman.

Rumble. Fight between rival gangs. *Ca.* 1944. Beale.

The sack. Dismissal from a job. Middle 1800s. Chapman.

Saphead. Fool, stupid person. 1790–1800. RHD: slang.

Scarf. Eat voraciously. 1955–60. RHD: slang.

Schlep. Carry, lug, move slowly. 1920–25. RHD: slang.

Scrambled eggs. Ornamental gold material on the peak of a high-ranking military officer's cap. *Ca.* 1925. Beale.

Screaming meemies. Hysteria; excessive fear, noisily expressed. 1930s. Beale.

Screwball. Eccentric, crazy. 1930s. Chapman.

Scrub. Cancel. 1944. Algeo.

Scuttlebutt. Idle gossip. 1930s. From Navy. Chapman.

Security blanket. Anything affording one a feeling of security, comfort, or safety. 1970. Algeo.

Set-up. Everything needed for a drink of liquor except the liquor itself. 1920s. Chapman.

Shack up. Live together when unmarried; engage in unmarried sexual intercourse. 1920s, but especially World War II, Army. Chapman.

Shindig. Party, event. 1855–60. RHD: informal.

Shit hits the fan. Trouble begins. 1930s. Chapman: slang (vulgar).

Shoo-in. Any winner without serious competition. 1935. Algeo.

Shootout. A hotly fought contest between evenly matched rivals. 1968. Algeo.

Shoot the shit. Engage in idle talk, especially outlandish storytelling or boasting. World War II. Beale.

Show and tell. Any informative presentation or demonstration. 1950–55. RHD: facetious.

Shtick. One's special interest, talent, etc. 1955–60. RHD: slang.

Shuteye. Sleep. 1895–1900. RHD: informal.

Skedaddle. Run away in a panic. 1860–65. RHD: informal.

Skin flick. A motion picture that features nudity and usually scenes of explicit sexual activity. 1965–70. RHD: slang.

Slob. Unattractive, ineffective person. Late 1800s. Chapman.

Slush fund. Illegal or unaccounted-for money used for bribery, influence purchasing, etc. Late 1800s. Chapman.

Smack. Heroin. 1960–65. RHD: slang.

Small potatoes. Meager, minor, unimportant. Middle 1800s. Chapman.

Snap. Something easy to accomplish. Late 1800s. Chapman.

Snatch. Vagina. Late nineteenth century. Beale.

Snooty. Haughty, snobbish. 1930. Beale.

Snow job. Act of convincing by insincere persuasion. 1940–45. RHD: slang.

Soft touch. A person easy to borrow from or sponge off of. *Ca.* 1910. Beale.

Some pumpkins. Highly admirable, impressive. Middle 1800s. Chapman.

Song and dance. Alibi, far-fetched story. 1870–75. RHD.

So's your old man. Contemptuous retort. Early 1900s. Chapman.

Spill the beans. Reveal a secret unintentionally. Early 1900s. Chapman.

Spin doctor. One who interprets political events for public dissemination. 1986. Algeo.

Stacked. (Of a woman) having a voluptuous figure. 1940–45. RHD: slang.

Stir-crazy. Anxious, impatient, as result of close confinement. 1935–40. RHD: informal.

String [someone] along. Extend a relationship through promises. Late 1800s. Chapman.

Stud. A man, especially one who is notably virile and sexually active. 1920–25. RHD: slang.

Suds. Beer. 1900–1905. RHD: slang.

Sugar daddy. A wealthy older man who spends freely on a young woman in return for her companionship or intimacy. 1915–20. RHD.

Sure-fire. Certain, infallible. *Ca.* 1918. Beale.

Take to the cleaners. Swindle thoroughly. *Ca.* 1945. Beale.

Talk turkey. Get to the point, speak directly to the issue (early 1800s, Chapman); talk business or sense (*ca.* 1890, Beale).

Tell it like it is. Be candid. 1960s. Chapman.

Teenager. Adolescent. 1935–40. RHD.

That's the way the cookie crumbles. Philosophical comment on disaster. Early 1950s. Beale.

Tight-assed. Rigidly self-controlled, inhibited, or conservative in attitude. 1965–70. RHD: slang (vulgar).

Turf. Any field, discipline, subject, or area of responsibility that one claims as one's own. 1962. Algeo.

Turn someone on. Arouse strong interest. 1950s. Chapman.

Under one's hat. Secret, not to be mentioned. Early 1900s. Chapman.

Upper crust. The highest social class. 1830–35. RHD: informal.

Veggie. A vegetable; a vegetarian. 1965–70. RHD: informal.

V.I.P. Very important person, of high rank or authority. World War II. Chapman.

Waffle. Remain uncommitted, fail to make unequivocal statements. Late 1800s. Chapman.

Way out. Original and bold; admirable. 1930s. Chapman.

Well-heeled. Rich. Late 1800s. Chapman.

Wheeler-dealer. Person with numerous business or social interests. Later twentieth century. Beale.

Whole shebang. Everything involved in a situation or action. Later twentieth century. Beale.

Wild card. Of, being, or including an unpredictable or unproven participant or team. 1955–60. RHD: sports.

The willies. Nervousness, fright, jitters. 1895–1900. RHD: informal.

Wiped out. Completely exhausted; intoxicated. 1960–65. RHD: slang.

Wire-puller. One who uses private connections to achieve results, especially in politics. Early 1800s. Chapman.

Yak. Talk, gossip. Late 1950s. Beale.

Zap. Kill or shoot. 1940–45. RHD: informal.

Zip. Zero, no runs or points scored. 1895–1900. RHD: slang.

Zonked out. Exhausted; asleep. 1955–60. RHD: slang.

—**Connie Eble**

DRAMA AND THEATER

39

FAMOUS PLAYS OF THE BRITISH, IRISH, AND AMERICAN THEATERS

. . . . .

THE NOVELIST THOMAS WOLFE, HAVING TRIED WITHOUT SUCCESS FOR A half dozen years to write plays before he discovered that prose fiction and not drama was his true account, referred later on to his error in pursuing "the sterile old brothels of the stage, mistaking the glib concoctions of a counterfeit emotion for the very flesh and figure of reality." On the other hand, William Shakespeare, Henrik Ibsen, Eugene O'Neill, and some few other writers have managed in their time to write plays not wholly devoid of reality. So perhaps it depends, to an extent at least, on the particular gifts of the person doing the writing. Besides, theorists from Aristotle through Coleridge and Auerbach (but not contemporary European theorists and their American disciples) have insisted that all art is counterfeit—*i.e.*, imitation, *i.e., mimesis.*

Be all that as it may, drama has been an active art form for 2,500 years or so, albeit with assorted barren periods. Moreover, the legitimate theater—live actors, performing in front of an audience—seems not to have been rendered obsolete by either the movies or television, but instead goes on drawing audiences whenever performed.

What follows is a listing of a number of famous plays of the British, Irish, and American theater. "Famous" as we use it here is a not-quite-neutral term. The great majority of these plays derive their fame from literary and dramatic qualities that have ensured their preservation in the tests of time and fashion, and have accounted for revivals throughout the years. Some, though, exercise claims on our interest apart from their intrinsic quality as drama. Many have titles that have become catch phrases and common terms of reference—*Who's Afraid of Virginia Woolf?, The Iceman Cometh,* and *Tea and Sympathy* are cases in point.

Others are here because of their great popular appeal, despite less than enthusiastic approval by critics in our time—*Abie's Irish Rose, East Lynne, The Drunkard*—and others because they represent "firsts" of one kind or another, such as *The Castle of Perseverance,* the earliest surviving morality play from the Middle Ages, or Royall Tyler's *The Contrast,* the first play staged professionally in America written by a citizen of the then-new (1787) republic. Tom Taylor's *Our American Cousin* has a sadder fame: its Washington, D.C., production was the scene of Lincoln's assassination by John Wilkes Booth.

Information is given below in the following order: Title, author, place and year of first performance, some of the principal actors, when known (for Elizabethan and Jacobean plays, the acting company—*e.g.,* Lord Chamberlain's Men, the Lord Admiral's Men—is usually all that is available). None of Shakespeare's plays is included; they are all treated in a separate section of this book.

Abie's Irish Rose. Anne Nichols. New York, 1922. Robert B. Williams, Marie Carroll, Alfred Wiseman.

Ah, Wilderness! Eugene O'Neill. New York, 1933. George M. Cohan, Marjorie Marquis, Elisha Cook, Jr.

All for Love. John Dryden. London, 1677. Charles Hart, Michael Mohun, Elizabeth Boutell.

All for Money. Thomas Lupton. London, 1577. Actors unknown.

All My Sons. Arthur Miller. New York, 1947. Arthur Kennedy, Karl Malden, Beth Merrill.

American Buffalo. David Mamet. Chicago, 1975. William H. Macy, Bernard Erhard, J. J. Johnson.

Amphitryon. John Dryden. London, 1690. Thomas Betterton, Michael Lee, Elizabeth Barry.

Angel Street. Patrick Hamilton. New York, 1941. Vincent Price, Judith Evelyn, Leo G. Carroll.

Anna Lucasta. Phil Yordan. New York, 1944. Earle Hyman, Hilda Simms, Rosetta LeNoire.

Arms and the Man. George Bernard Shaw. London, 1894. Alma Murray, Florence Farr, Yorke Stephens.

Arsenic and Old Lace. Joseph Kesselring. New York, 1941. Jean Adair, Josephine Hull, Boris Karloff.

Atheist's Tragedy, The. Cyril Tourneur. London, 1609. King's Men.

Barefoot in the Park. Neil Simon. New York, 1963. Elizabeth Ashley, Robert Redford, Kurt Kasznar.

Bartholomew Fair. Ben Jonson. London, 1614. Lady Elizabeth's Men.

Basic Training of Pavlo Hummel, The. David Rabe. New York, 1971. William Atherton, Victoria Racimo, Joe Fields.

Battle of Alcazar, The. George Peele. London, 1589. Lord Admiral's Men.

Beaux' Stratagem, The. George Farquhar. London, 1707. Robert Wilks, Anne Oldfield, John Mills.

Beyond the Horizon. Eugene O'Neill. New York, 1920. Richard Bennet, Edward Arnold, Helen Mae Kellar.

Biography. S. N. Behrman. New York, 1932. Earle Larrimore, Ina Claire, Jay Fassett.

Birthday Party, The. Harold Pinter. Cambridge, Eng., 1958. Willoughby Gray, Beatrix Lehmann, Richard Pearson.

Black-Eyed Susan. Douglas Jerrold. London, 1829. T. P. Cooke, Dibdin Pitt, Mrs. Forrester.

Blind Beggar of Alexandria, The. George Chapman. London, 1596. Lord Admiral's Men.

Blithe Spirit. Noel Coward. New York, 1941. Peggy Wood, Clifton Webb, Leonora Corbett.

Blues for Mister Charlie. James Baldwin. New York, 1964. Al Freeman, Jr., Rip Torn, Diana Sands.

Born Yesterday. Garson Kanin. New York, 1946. Judy Holliday, Paul Douglas, Gary Merrill.

Boy Meets Girl. Bella and Samuel Spewack. New York, 1935. Allyn Joslyn, Jerome Cowan, Joyce Arling, Royal Beal.

Buried Child. Sam Shepard. San Francisco, 1978. Joseph Gistirak, Catherine Willis, Dennis Ludlow, William M. Carr.

Bus Stop. William Inge. New York, 1955. Kim Stanley, Anthony Ross.

Caesar and Cleopatra. George Bernard Shaw. New York, 1906. Jonathan Forbes-Robertson, Adeline Bourne, A. Hylton Allen.

Careless Husband, The. Colley Cibber. London, 1704. Robert Wilks, Anne Oldfield, Colley Cibber.

Caretaker, The. Harold Pinter. London, 1960. Alan Bates, Peter Woodthorpe, Donald Pleasence.

Case Is Altered, The. Ben Jonson. London, 1597. Actors unknown.

Castle of Perseverance, The. Author unknown. England, *ca.* 1425. Actors unknown. [This is the earliest surviving morality play in English.]

Cat on a Hot Tin Roof. Tennessee Williams. New York, 1955. Ben Gazzara, Barbara Bel Geddes, Burl Ives.

Cathleen ni Houlihan. W. B. Yeats. Dublin, 1902. Maude Gonne, Maire ni Bheublagh, W. G. Fay.

Cato. Joseph Addison. London, 1713. Robert Wilks, John Mills, William Mills.

Changeling, The. Thomas Middleton. London, 1622. Lady Elizabeth's Men.

Chaste Maid in Cheapside, A. Thomas Middleton. London, 1611. Lady Elizabeth's Men.

Children's Hour, The. Lillian Hellman. New York, 1934. Katherine Emmet, Eugenia Rawls, Florence McGee, Robert Keith.

Cocktail Party, The. T. S. Eliot. Edinburgh, Scotland, 1949. Alec Guinness, Cathleen Nesbitt, Ursula Jeans.

Come Back, Little Sheba. William Inge. New York, 1950. Sidney Blackmer, Shirley Booth, Joan Loring.

Conquest of Granada, The. John Dryden. London, 1670. Nell Gwynn, Edward Kynaston, Edward Lydall.

Conscious Lovers, The. Sir Richard Steele. London, 1722. John Mills, Robert Wilks, Mrs. Moore.

Constant State of Desire, The. Karen Finley. New York, 1986. Karen Finley. [One-woman performance.]

Contrast, The. Royall Tyler. New York, 1787. Thomas Wignell, John Henry, Lewis Hallam. [This was the first play by a U.S. citizen to be staged professionally in America.]

Country Wife, The. William Wycherly. London, 1675. Charles Hart, Elizabeth Boutell, Michael Mohun.

Crimes of the Heart. Beth Henley. New York, 1981. Lizbeth Mackay, Sharon Ullrick, Raymond Baker.

Crucible, The. Arthur Miller. New York, 1953. Madeleine Sherwood, Don McHenry, Fred Stewart.

Dark at the Top of the Stairs, The. William Inge. New York, 1957. Judith Robinson, Timmy Everett, Pat Hingle.

Dead End. Sidney Kingsley. New York, 1935. Billy Hallop, Bobby Jordon, Theodore Newton, Huntz Hall.

Death of a Salesman. Arthur Miller. New York, 1949. Mildred Dunnock, Lee J. Cobb, Arthur Kennedy.

Deirdre. W. B. Yeats. Dublin, 1906. Arthur Sinclair, F. J. Fay, Miss Darragh.

Deirdre of the Sorrows. John Millington Synge. Dublin, 1910. Sara Allgood, J. A. O'Rourke, Maire O'Neill.

Dial M for Murder. Frederick Knott. New York, 1952. Maurice Evans, Gusti Huber, Anthony Dawson.

Diary of Anne Frank, The. Frances Goodrich and Albert Hackett. New York, 1955. Susan Strasberg, Joseph Schildkraut, Gusti Huber.

Doctor Faustus. Christopher Marlowe. London, 1592. Lord Admiral's Men.

Drunkard, The, or The Fallen Saved. W. H. Smith. Boston, 1844. W. H. Smith and members of The Boston Museum; thereafter, numerous traveling troupes.

Dutchman. Amiri Baraka [LeRoi Jones]. New York, 1964. Robert Hooks, Jennifer West.

East Lynne. John Oxenford. London, 1867. Fred Hastings, John Saunders, Avonia Jones.

Edward II. Christopher Marlowe. London, 1592. Earl of Pembroke's Men.

Elephant Man, The. Bernard Pomerance. New York, 1979. Philip Anglim, I. M. Hobson, Carole Shelley.

Evening's Love, An. John Dryden. London, 1668. Charles Hart, Michael Mohun, Nell Gwynn.

Every Good Boy Deserves Favour. Tom Stoppard. London, 1977. Ian McKellen, John Wood, Barbara Leigh-Hunt.

Everyman. Author unknown. England, *ca.* 1495. Actors unknown.

Every Man in His Humour. Ben Jonson. London, 1598. Lord Chamberlain's Men.

Every Man Out of His Humour. Ben Jonson. London, 1599. Lord Chamberlain's Men. [William Shakespeare is known to have played one of the roles, but the specific character is not recorded.]

Fair Maid of the West, The. Thomas Heywood. London, 1609. Queen Anne's Men.

for colored girls who have considered suicide/when the rainbow is enuf. Ntozake Shange. New York, 1976. Janet League, Aku Kadogo, Trazana Beverley.

Friar Bacon and Friar Bungay. Robert Greene. London, 1589. Lord Strange's Men.

Front Page, The. Ben Hecht and Charles MacArthur. New York, 1929. Lee Tracy, Dorothy Stickney, Osgood Perkins.

Fulgens and Lucrece. Henry Medwell. England, 1497. Actors unknown.

Game at Chess, A. Thomas Middleton. London, 1624. King's Men.

Gay Lord Quex, The. Arthur Wing Pinero. London, 1899. John Hare, Gilbert Hare, Fanny Coleman.

Ghost of Yankee Doodle, The. Sidney Howard. Boston, 1937. Ethel Barrymore, Dudley Digges, Frank Conroy.

Glance at New York, A. Benjamin Baker. New York, 1848. Frank Chanfrau. [This was the first of many plays about New York City folk hero "Mose the Bowery B'hoy," a tradition that continued into the movies a hundred years later with the "Bowery Boys" films of Leo Gorcey and Huntz Hall.]

Glass Menagerie, The. Tennessee Williams. New York, 1945. Laurette Taylor, Julie Haydon, Eddie Dowling.

Gods of the Mountain, The. Lord Dunsany. London, 1911. W. A. Warburton, Claude Rains, H. R. Hignett.

Great Divide, The. William Vaughn Moody. Chicago, 1906. Margaret Anglin, Henry Miller.

Great White Hope, The. Howard Sackler. New York, 1968. James Earl Jones, Jane Alexander, George Mathews.

Green Pastures, The. Mark Connelly. New York, 1930. Richard B. Harrison, Wesley Hill, Tutt Whitney, Alonzo Fenderson.

Hairy Ape, The. Eugene O'Neill. New York, 1922. Louis Wolheim and the Provincetown Players.

Harvey. Mary Chase. New York, 1944. Frank Fay, Janet Tyler, Eloise Sheldon, John Kirk.

"Having Wonderful Time." Arthur Kober. New York, 1937. Katherine Locke, Jules Garfield, Janet Fox.

Homecoming, The. Harold Pinter. London, 1965. Paul Rogers, Ian Holm, Vivien Merchant.

Honest Whore, The. Thomas Dekker. London, 1604. Prince Henry's Men.

Hostage, The. Brendan Behan. New York, 1960. Glynn Edwards, Celia Salkeld, Alfred Lynch.

Iceman Cometh, The. Eugene O'Neill. New York, 1946. Dudley Digges, Morton L. Stevens, E. G. Marshall, Ruth Gilbert.

Idiot's Delight. Robert E. Sherwood. Washington, D.C., 1936. George Meader, Alfred Lunt, Lynn Fontanne.

If It Be Not Good, the Devil Is in It. Thomas Dekker. London, 1611. Queen Anne's Men.

If You Know Not Me You Know Nobody. Thomas Heywood. London, 1604. Queen Anne's Men.

Importance of Being Earnest, The. Oscar Wilde. London, 1895. George Alexander, Allen Aynesworth, Rose Leclercq.

Inherit the Wind. Jerome Lawrence and Robert E. Lee. New York, 1955. Paul Muni, Ed Begly, Tony Randall.

I Remember Mama. John van Druten. New York, 1944. Marlon Brando, Frances Heflin, Mady Christians.

Jew of Malta, The. Christopher Marlowe. London, 1589. Lord Strange's Men.

John Bull's Other Island. George Bernard Shaw. London, 1904. Louis Calvert, F. L. Shine, Harley Granville-Barker.

Johnny Johnson. Paul Green. New York, 1936. Tony Kraber, Phoebe Brand, Lee J. Cobb, Elia Kazan.

King Johan. John Bale. Canterbury, Eng., 1548. Actors unknown.

King's Threshold, The. W. B. Yeats. Dublin, 1903. F. J. Fay, Seamus O'Sullivan, Maire ni Shiubhlaigh.

Kismet. Charles Lederer and Luther Davis. New York, 1953. Joan Diener, Alfred Drake.

Krapp's Last Tape. Samuel Beckett. London, 1958. Patrick Magee. [One-man performance.]

Lady Windermere's Fan. Oscar Wilde. London, 1892. Nutcombe Gould, A. Vane Tempest, Fanny Coleman, Marion Terry, George Alexander.

Life with Father. Howard Lindsay and Russel Crouse. New York, 1939. Dorothy Stickney, John Drew Devereaux, Howard Lindsay.

Little Foxes, The. Lillian Hellman. New York. 1939. Tallulah Bankhead, Carl Benton Reid, Dan Duryea, Patricia Collinge.

London Merchant, The. George Lillo. London, 1731. Colley Cibber, Charlotte Clarke.

Longer Thou Livest the More Fool Thou Art, The. W. Wager. England, 1559. Actors unknown.

Look Back in Anger. John Osborne. London, 1956. Kenneth Haigh, Alan Bates, Mary Ure.

Loot. Joe Orton. London, 1966. Gerry Duggan, Sheila Ballantine, Kenneth Cranham.

Mad World My Masters, A. Thomas Middleton. London, 1606. Paul's Boys.

Malcontent, The. John Marston. London, 1604. The Queen's Revels.

Male Animal, The. James Thurber and Elliott Nugent. New York, 1940. Regina Wallace, Matt Briggs, Ruth Matteson.

Man and Superman. George Bernard Shaw. London, 1902. Harley Granville-Barker, Lillah McCarthy.

Mankind. Author unknown. England, *ca.* 1471. Actors unknown.

Man of Mode, The, or Sir Fopling Flutter. Sir George Etherege. London, 1626. Thomas Betterton, Mary Betterton, William Smith.

Man Who Came to Dinner, The. George S. Kaufman and Moss Hart. New York, 1939. Virginia Hammond, Monty Woolley, Gordon Merrick.

Marriage à la Mode. John Dryden. London, 1672. William Wintershall, Edward Kynaston, Anne Reeve.

Marriage of Wit and Science, The. London, *ca.* 1564. Westminster School Boys.

Massacre at Paris, The. Christopher Marlowe. London, 1592. Lord Admiral's Men.

Member of the Wedding, The. Carson McCullers. New York, 1950. Julie Harris, Ethel Waters, Brandon de Wilde.

Miracle Worker, The. William Gibson. New York, 1959. Anne Bancroft, Patty Duke, Patricia Neal.

Miseries of Enforced Marriage, The. George Wilkins. London, 1606. King's Men.

Mrs. Warren's Profession. George Bernard Shaw. London, 1902. Fanny Brough, Madge McIntosh, Harley Granville-Barker.

Murder in the Cathedral. T. S. Eliot. Canterbury, Eng., 1935. Robert Speaight, E. Martin Browne, Frank Napier.

Native Son. Richard Wright and Paul Green. New York, 1941. Anne Burr, Canada Lee.

New Way to Pay Old Debts, A. Philip Massinger. London, 1621. Lady Elizabeth's Men.

'Night, Mother. Marsha Norman. Cambridge, Mass., 1982. Kathy Bates, Anne Pitoniak.

No Time for Sergeants. Ira Levin. New York, 1955. Andy Griffith, Myron McCormick, Roddy McDowell.

Octoroon, The, or Life in Louisiana. Dion Boucicault. London, 1861. Delman Grace, John Billington, Robert Romer.

Odd Couple, The. Neil Simon. New York, 1965. Walter Matthau, Art Carney, Carole Shelley, Monica Evans.

Old Fortunatus. Thomas Dekker. London, 1599. Lord Admiral's Men.

Old Lady Says "No," The. Denis Johnston. Dublin, 1929. Micheál MacLiammóir, Meriel Moore, Hilton Edwards.

Old Wives' Tale, The. George Peele. London, 1590. Queen's Men.

On Baile's Strand. W. B. Yeats. Dublin, 1904. Frank Fay, George Roberts, G. MacDonald.

Our American Cousin. Tom Taylor. London, 1861. E. A. Sothern, J. B. Buckstone, George Braid. [This was the play at which Abraham Lincoln was assassinated in Washington, D.C., April 14, 1865.]

Our Town. Thornton Wilder. Princeton, N.J., 1938. Frank Craven, Jay Fassett, Evelyn Varden.

Pal Joey. John O'Hara, Richard Rodgers, and Lorenz Hart. New York, 1940. Gene Kelly, Diane Sinclair, Francis Krell.

Passion Play. Peter Nichols. London, 1981. Priscilla Morgan, Billie Whitelaw, Benjamin Whitrow.

Paternoster Play, The. Author unknown. York, Eng., *ca.* 1378. Actors unknown.

Patriot for Me, A. John Osborne. London, 1965. Maximilian Schell, John Castle, Rio Fanning.

Petrified Forest, The. Robert Sherwood. New York, 1935. Humphrey Bogart, Blanche Sweet, Leslie Howard.

Philaster, or Love Lies A-Bleeding. Francis Beaumont and John Fletcher. London, 1609. King's Men.

Playboy of the Western World, The. John Millington Synge. Dublin, 1907. W. G. Fay, Arthur Sinclair, Maire O'Neill.

Plough and the Stars, The. Sean O'Casey. Dublin, 1926. F. J. McCormick, Barry Fitzgerald, Maureen Delaney.

Porgy. Dorothy and Du Bose Heyward. New York, 1927. Percy Verwayne, Frank Wilson, Evelyn Ellis.

Pride of Life, The. Author unknown. England, *ca.* 1450. Actors unknown.

Quare Fellow, The. Brendan Behan. Dublin, 1954. Denis Hickie, Austin Byrne, John McDarby.

Quartermaine's Terms. Simon Gray. London, 1981. Edward Fox, Jenny Quayle, Peter Birch.

Raisin in the Sun, A. Lorraine Hansberry. New York, 1959. Ruby Dee, Glynn Turman, Sidney Poitier.

Rare Triumphs of Love and Fortune, The. Anthony Munday. London, 1582. Lord Derby's Men.

Rehearsal, The. George Villiers *et al.* London, 1671. Anna Reeves, William Wintershall, Joseph Haines.

Revenger's Tragedy, The. Thomas Middleton (?). London, 1606. King's Men.

Richelieu. Edward Bulwer-Lytton. London, 1839. George Bennett, Helen Faucit, William Charles Macready.

Riders to the Sea. John Millington Synge. Dublin, 1904. Honor Lavelle, W. G. Fay, Sarah Allgood.

Rivals, The. Richard Brinsley Sheridan. London, 1775. Edward Shuter, John Quick, Lee Lewes.

Roaring Girl, The, or Moll Cutpurse. Thomas Dekker and Thomas Middleton. London, 1608. Prince Henry's Men.

Roots. Arnold Wesker. London, 1959. Patsy Byrne, Charles Kay, Joan Plowright.

Rose Tattoo, The. Tennessee Williams. New York, 1951. Sal Mineo, Maureen Stapleton, Phyllis Love.

Ruling Class, The. Peter Barnes. London, 1969. Robert Robertson, Dudley Jones, Ann Heffernan.

Saint Joan. George Bernard Shaw. New York, 1923. Winifred Lenihan, Philip Leigh, A. H. Van Buren.

Saved. Edward Bond. London, 1965. John Castle, Tony Selby, Richard Butler.

School for Scandal, The. Richard Brinsley Sheridan. London, 1777. Thomas King, Miss P. Hopkins, Frances Abington.

Second Mrs. Tanqueray, The. Arthur Wing Pinero. London, 1893. George Alexander, Mrs. Patrick Campbell.

Second Shepherd's Play, The. The "Wakefield Master." Wakefield, England, *ca.* 1425. Actors unknown.

Secret Love. John Dryden. London, 1667. Rebecca Marshall, Nell Gwynn, Michael Mohun.

Sejanus His Fall. Ben Jonson. London, 1603. King's Men.

Separate Tables. Terence Rattigan. New York, 1956. Margaret Leighton, Eric Portman.

Sergeant Musgrave's Dance. John Arden. London, 1959. Donal Donnelly, Alan Dobie, Freda Jackson.

Shanwalla. Lady Gregory. Dublin, 1915. H. E. Hutchinson, Sydney J. Morgan, Kathleen Drago.

She Stoops to Conquer. Oliver Goldsmith. London, 1773. Edward Shuter, John Quick, Michael Stoppelaer.

Shoemaker's Holiday, The. Thomas Dekker. London, 1599. Lord Admiral's Men.

Silver Box, The. John Galsworthy. London, 1906. James Hearn, Frances Ivor, A. E. Matthews.

Silver Tassie, The. Sean O'Casey. London, 1929. Charles Laughton, Barry Fitzgerald, Sidney Morgan.

Sir Martin Mar-all, or The Feigned Innocence. John Dryden. London, 1667. James Nokes, Mr. Priest, Madame Davies.

Spanish Fryar, The. John Dryden. London, 1680. Thomas Betterton, Joseph Williams, Elizabeth Barry.

Spanish Tragedy, The. Thomas Kyd. London, 1587. Lord Strange's Men.

Staple of News, The. Ben Jonson. London, 1626. King's Men.

Streetcar Named Desire, A. Tennessee Williams. New York, 1947. Marlon Brando, Kim Hunter, Jessica Tandy.

Street Scene. Elmer Rice. New York, 1929. Leo Bulgakov, Beulah Bondi, Russel Griffin.

Tale of a Tub, A. Ben Jonson. London, 1596. Lord Admiral's Men.

Tamburlaine the Great, Part 1. Christopher Marlowe. London, 1587. Lord Admiral's Men.

Tea and Sympathy. Robert Anderson. New York, 1953. Deborah Kerr, John Kerr, Leif Erickson.

Teahouse of the August Moon, The. John Patrick. New York, 1953. John Forsythe, David Wayne, Paul Ford.

They Knew What They Wanted. Sidney Howard. New York, 1924. Glenn Anders, Richard Bennett, Pauline Lord.

Thomas Muskerry. Padraic Colum. Dublin, 1910. Arthur Sinclair, Sara Allgood, J. M. Kerrigan.

Time of Your Life, The. William Saroyan. New York. 1939. Eddie Dowling, Edward Andrews, Charles de Sheim, Julie Haydon, Curt Conway.

Tiny Alice. Edward Albee. New York, 1964. John Gielgud, William Hutt, Irene Worth.

Tobacco Road. Erskine Caldwell and Jack Kirkland. New York, 1933. Sam Byrd, Margaret Wycherly, Henry Hull.

Tom Thumb. Henry Fielding. London, 1731. William Mullart, Lewis Hallam, Mrs. Jones.

Tooth of Crime, The. Sam Shepard. London, 1972. Malcolm Storey, Petronella Ford, Michael Weller.

Top Girls. Caryl Churchill. London, 1982. Gwen Taylor, Deborah Findlay, Lindsay Duncan.

Trip to Chinatown, A. Charles A. Hoyt. New York, 1891. Henry Conor, George A. Beane, Lillian Barr.

Two Angry Women of Abingdon, The. Henry Porter. London, 1588. Lord Admiral's Men.

Uncle Tom's Cabin. George L. Aiken, adapting Harriet B. Stowe's novel. Troy, N.Y., 1852. Cordelia Howard, Green Germon.

Unicorn from the Stars, The. W. B. Yeats. Dublin, 1907. Arthur Sinclair, J. A. O'Rourke, Maire O'Neill.

Venice Preserved. Thomas Otway. London, 1682. Elizabeth Barry, Thomas Betterton, William Smith.

View from the Bridge, A. Arthur Miller. New York, 1955. Van Heflin, Jack Warden, Gloria Marlowe.

Virginius. James Sheridan Knowles. London, 1820. Mr. Abbott, Mr. Norris, W. C. Macready.

Visit to a Small Planet. Gore Vidal. New York, 1957. Cyril Ritchard, Sibyl Bowan, Eddie Mayehoff.

Volpone, or The Fox. Ben Jonson. London, 1606. King's Men.

Waiting for Godot. Samuel Beckett. Paris, 1953. Roger Blin, Lucien Raimbourg, Pierre Latour.

Waiting for Lefty. Clifford Odets. New York, 1935. Russell Collins, Lewis Leverett, Paula Miller, Herbert Ratner.

Way of the World, The. William Congreve. London, 1700. Jack Verbruggan, Anne Bracegirdle, Thomas Betterton.

Well-Remembered Voice, A. J. M. Barrie. London, 1918. H. V. Esmond, Dawson Milward, Lilian Braithwaite.

West Indian, The. Richard Cumberland. London, 1771. J. Aickin, John Packer, William Parsons.

When You See Me You Know Me. Samuel Rowley. London, 1604. Prince Henry's Men.

White Devil, The. John Webster. London, 1612. Queen Anne's Men.

Whore of Babylon, The. Thomas Dekker. London, 1606. Prince Henry's Men.

Who's Afraid of Virginia Woolf? Edward Albee. New York, 1962. Uta Hagen, Arthur Hill, George Grizzard, Melinda Dillon.

Winged Victory. Moss Hart. New York, 1943. Red Buttons, Henry Slate, Jack Slate.

Woman Hater, The. John Fletcher. London, 1606. Paul's Boys.

Woman Killed With Kindness, A. Thomas Heywood. London, 1603. Worcester's Men.

Women, The. Clare Boothe. New York, 1936. Ilka Chase, Phyllis Povah, Margalo Gillmore.

Women Beware Women. Thomas Middleton. London, 1621. King's Men.

Wounds of Civil War, The. Thomas Lodge. London, 1588. Lord Admiral's Men.

Zoo Story. Edward Albee. New York, 1960. George Maharis, William Daniels.

SOURCES

Barnes, Clive, ed. *Best American Plays.* New York: Crown Publishers, 7th ser., 1975; 8th ser., 1983.

Bradley, David. *From Text to Performance in the Elizabethan Theatre.* Cambridge, Eng.: Cambridge University Press, 1992.

Cerf, Bennett, and Van H. Cartmell, eds. *Sixteen Famous American Plays.* New York: Modern Library, 1941.

Cornish, Roger, and Violet Ketels, eds. *The Plays of the Seventies.* London: Methuen, 1986.

————. *The Plays of the Sixties.* London: Methuen, 1985.

Freedley, George, and John A. Reeves. *A History of the Theatre.* New York: Crown Publishers, 1941.

Gassner, John, ed. *Best Plays of the Modern American Theatre.* 2nd ser. New York: Crown Publishers, 1947.

————. *Twenty Best Plays of the Modern American Theatre.* New York: Crown Publishers, 1939.

Hawkins-Dady, Mark, ed. *International Dictionary of Theatre. Vol. I. Plays.* Chicago: St. James Press, 1992.

Kennelly, Brendan, ed. *Landmarks of Irish Drama.* London: Methuen, 1988.

Moses, Montrose J. *Representative British Dramas, Victorian and Modern.* Boston: Little, Brown and Co., 1920.

Mullin, Donald, comp. *Victorian Plays: A Record of Significant Productions on the London Stage, 1837–1901.* Westport, Conn.: Greenwood Press, 1987.

Richards, Stanley, ed. *The Most Popular Plays of the American Theatre.* New York: Stein and Day, 1979.

Stott, William, and Jane Stott, eds. *On Broadway.* Austin: University of Texas Press, 1978.

Van Lennep, William, and Emmett L. Avery *et al.,* eds. *The London Stage 1660–1800.* 11 vols. Carbondale: University of Southern Illinois Press, 1960–68.

—J.L.M.

40

NOTED ACTORS AND ACTRESSES OF THE AMERICAN AND ENGLISH STAGE

. . . . .

WRITERS HAVE TENDED TO FEEL, AND TO EXPRESS, A CERTAIN AMOUNT OF disdain for actors. Samuel Johnson's retort to James Boswell's insistence that great actors merit respect is famous: "What, Sir, a fellow who claps a hump on his back, and a lump on his leg, and cries 'I am Richard the Third'?" Johnson, however, was always a bit jealous of his friend and former pupil, David Garrick. And of course the greatest of all writers in the English language, William Shakespeare, whose plays Johnson edited, was by trade an actor.

No doubt the reason for the distrust has to do in part with temperament. Writing is a solitary craft; by nature writers tend to be introverted. Acting, by contrast, depends absolutely upon the presence of an audience. An actor's art, and success at it, are founded upon the ability to perform in public, to assume a stage personality, to pretend to *be* someone else. Yet at the same time actors and actresses must keep in mind at all times that they are *not* the characters they are portraying. Even in their most passionate moments they must be fully in control of the impact of their presentation upon the audience.

Still, writers must do that, too. What they write about will be read, and they must carefully calculate the effect of what they are writing upon the reader. There is a very real sense in which authors, too, assume in their writings a personality meant to have an impact upon their audience. So perhaps what it comes down to is that writers and actors are rival operators; and that writers, being the inward-brooding creatures they are, are envious of the outer-directed ways of actors and actresses.

Until the advent of film, there was no way to preserve the performances of great actors and actresses. All that we have to go on are the memories and written descriptions of those who saw them act. The list that follows is of some of the English and American actors and actresses whose names have come down to us as among the luminaries of the stage in their time, along with a few of the most esteemed living players, and a few of the roles that made them famous, when known.

Abington, Frances (1737–1815). Beatrix, Lady Townly, Lady Betty Modish, Millamant (*The Way of the World*), Lady Teazle (*The School for Scandal*).

Alleyn, Edward (1566–1626). Barabas (Marlowe's *Jew of Malta*), Marlowe's Tamburlaine and Faustus, Frederick (*Frederick and Basilea*).

Anderson, Mary (1859–1940). Juliet, Evadne, Bianca (*Fazio*), Julia (*The Hunchback*), Desdemona (*Othello*), Rosalind (*As You Like It*).

Ashcroft, Dame Peggy (1907–91). Beatrice (*Much Ado About Nothing*), Portia (*The Merchant of Venice*), Naomi (*Jew Süss*), Desdemona (*Othello*), Cleopatra (*Antony and Cleopatra*), Imogen (*Cymbeline*), Rosalind (*As You Like It*), Juliet, Nina (*The Seagull*), Miranda (*The Tempest*), Ophelia (*Hamlet*), Cordelia (*Lear*), Hedda Gabler, Agnes (*A Delicate Balance*).

Barrett, Lawrence (1838–91). Clifford (*The Hunchback*), Tressel, Hamlet, Henry Lagardere.

Barry, Spranger (1719–77). Lear, Henry V, Othello, Pierre, Hotspur, Orestes.

Bates, Alan (1934–). Edmund Tyrone (*Long Day's Journey Into Night*), Richard Ford (*Poor Richard*), Cliff (*Look Back in Anger*), Ford (*The Merry Wives of Windsor*), Richard III, Hamlet, Petruchio (*The Taming of the Shrew*), Trigorin (*The Seagull*).

Beerbohm-Tree, Sir Herbert (1853–1917). Grimaldi (*The Life of an Actress*), Marquis de Pontsable (*Madame Favart*), Lambert Streyke (*The Colonel*), Svengali (DuMaurier's *Trilby*).

Bellamy, George Ann (1730–88). Juliet, Cleone.

Bensley, Robert (ca. 1738–1817). Edmund (*Lear*), Buckingham (*Richard III*), Hotspur, Iago (*Othello*), Malvolio (*Twelfth Night*).

Bentley, John (1553?–1585). *Pierce Penilesse, A Knight's Conjuring.*

Betterton, Thomas (1635–1710). *The Loyall Subject, The Mad Lover,* Pericles, Prince Alvaro (*Roscius Anglicanus*).

Betty, William Henry West (1791–1874). Young Norval (*Douglas*), Selim (*Barbarossa*), Hamlet, Romeo, Frederic (*Lover's Vows*), Octavian (*Mountaineers*).

Booth, Edwin (1833–1893). Sir Giles Overreach, Richard III, Shylock (*The Merchant of Venice*), Richelieu, Hamlet, Romeo.

Booth, Junius Brutus (1796–1852). Richard III, Brutus (*Julius Caesar*), Second Actor (*Hamlet*), Sir Giles Overreach, Cassius, Bertram (*All's Well That Ends Well*), Shylock (*The Merchant of Venice*).

Browne, Robert (1583–1620). *Gammer Gurton's Needle.*

Burbage, Richard (ca. 1567–1619). Richard III, Henry V, Brutus (*Julius Caesar*), Lear, Shylock (*The Merchant of Venice*), Romeo, Othello, Hamlet, Ferdinand (*The Duchess of Malfi*), Volpone, *The Alchemist.*

Burton, William E. (1804–60). Doctor Ollapod (*Poor Gentleman*), Doctor Pangloss (*Heir-at-Law*), Launcelot Gobbo (*The Merchant of Venice*).

Clarke, J. S. (1833–99). Doctor Pangloss (*Heir at Law*), Major de Boots (*Everybody's Friend*), Paul Pry, Doctor Ollapod (*Poor Gentleman*), Bob Tyke (*School of Reform*).

Clive, Katherine (1711–85). Chloe, Nell (*Devil to Pay*), Phillidia (*Damon and Phillida*), Mrs. Winifred (*School for Rakes*).

Condell, Henry (?–1627). Sejanus, Volpone, *The Alchemist, The Mad Lover*, the Cardinal (*The Duchess of Malfi*).

Cooke, George Frederick (1756–1812). Othello, Dumont (*Jane Shore*), Octavian (*Mountaineers*), Richard III, Shylock (*The Merchant of Venice*), Sir Archy MacSarcasm, Iago (*Othello*), Macbeth, Kitely.

Cooper, Thomas Abthorpe (1776–1849). Pierre (*Venice Preserved*), Richard III, Shylock (*The Merchant of Venice*), Macbeth.

Cornell, Katharine (1893–1974). Joan of Arc (*Saint Joan*), Elizabeth Barrett (*The Barretts of Wimpole Street*), Juliet (*Romeo and Juliet*), Candida (*Candida*).

Courtenay, Tom (1937–). John Clare (Bond's *The Fool*), Raskolnikov (*Crime and Punishment*), Norman (*The Dresser*), Faulkland (*The Rivals*).

Cummings, Constance (1910–). Alice Overton (*Sour Grapes*), Emma Bovary (*Madame Bovary*), Katherine (*Goodbye, Mr. Chips*), Juliet, Joan (*Saint Joan*), Gabby Maple (*The Petrified Forest*), Lysistrata, Martha (*Who's Afraid of Virginia Woolf?*), Volumnia (*Coriolanus*), Emily Stilson (*Wings*).

Cushman, Charlotte (1816–76). Queen Katherine, Lady Macbeth, Meg Merrilies, Nancy Sikes.

Davenport, Edwin L. (1816–77). Brutus (*Julius Caesar*), Othello, Edgar (*Lear*), Iago (*Othello*), Macduff (*Macbeth*).

Dench, Judi (1934–). Beatrice (*Much Ado About Nothing*), Juliet, Anya (*The Cherry Orchard*), Lady Macbeth, Joan (*Saint Joan*), Viola (*Twelfth Night*), Portia (*The Merchant of Venice*), the Duchess of Malfi, Vilma (*The Wolf*).

Duff, Mary Ann (1795–1857). Juliet, Hermione (*Distrest Mother*), Isabella (*Fatal Marriage*).

Elliston, Robert William (1774–1831). Romeo, Hamlet, Richmond (*Richard III*), Falstaff.

Evans, Dame Edith (1888–1976). Cressida (*Troilus and Cressida*), Serpent and She-Ancient (*Back to Methuselah*), Millamant (*The Way of the World*), Katharina (*The Taming of the Shrew*), Rebecca West (*Rosmersholm*),

Orinthia (*The Apple Cart*), Arkadina (*The Seagull*), Lady Bracknell (*The Importance of Being Earnest*), Mrs. Malaprop (*The Rivals*), Lady Pitts (*Daphne Laureola*), Mrs. St. Maugham (*The Chalk Garden*).

Farren, Elizabeth (1759–1829). Miss Hardcastle (*She Stoops to Conquer*), Belinda (*Old Bachelor*), Millamant (*The Way of the World*), Dorinda, Olivia, Portia (*The Merchant of Venice*).

Faucit, Helen (Lady Martin) (1820–98). Rosalind (*As You Like It*), Juliet, Lady Macbeth, Imogen (*Cymbeline*).

Fechter, Charles (1824–79). Seide (*Mahomet*), Valère (*Tartuffe*), Armand Duval, Ruy Blas.

Field, Nathan (1587–1620). *Cynthia's Revels, The Poetaster,* Humphrey (*The Knight of the Burning Pestle*).

Finney, Albert (1936–   ). Edgar (*Lear*), Billy Liar, Luther, Feste (*Twelfth Night*), Victor Chandebise and Poche (*A Flea in Her Ear*), Macbeth.

Forbes-Robertson, Sir Johnston (1853–1937). Hamlet, Romeo, Mark Embury (M. L. Riley's *Mice and Men*), Caesar (*Caesar and Cleopatra*).

Forrest, Edwin (1806–72). Sir Edward Mortimer, Hamlet, Othello, Richard III, Iago (*Othello*), Cassio, Antony, Macbeth.

Garrick, David (1717–79). Bales (*The Rehearsal*), Othello, Macbeth, Richard III, Lear, Hamlet, Shylock (*The Merchant of Venice*).

Gielgud, John (1904–   ). Raskolnikov (*Crime and Punishment*), Trofimov (*The Cherry Orchard*), *The Vortex,* Hamlet, Richard of Bordeaux, Romeo, Iago (*Othello*), Richard II.

Guinness, Alec (1914–   ). Andrew Aguecheek (*Twelfth Night*), Lorenzo (*The Merchant of Venice*), Hamlet, Bob Acres (*The Rivals*), Ferdinand (*The Tempest*), Abel Drugger (*The Alchemist*), Richard III, Ross, Dylan Thomas (*Dylan*), Macbeth.

Hallam, Lewis, the younger (1740–1808). Mungo (*Padlock*), *Gamester.*

Hayes, Helen (1900–93). Pollyanna Whittier (*Pollyanna*), Elsie Beebe (*To the Ladies*), Constance Neville (*She Stoops to Conquer*), Cleopatra (*Caesar and Cleopatra*), Mary Stuart (*Mary of Scotland*), Queen Victoria (*Victoria Regina*), Portia (*The Merchant of Venice*), Mrs. Antrobus (*The Skin of Our Teeth*), Amanda Wingfield (*The Glass Menagerie*), Mrs. Candour (*The School for Scandal*), Mrs. Grant (*The Front Page*).

Heminges, John (1556–1630). Falstaff (*Henry IV*).

Henderson, John (1747–85). Hamlet, Falstaff.

Heron, Matilda (1830–77). Juliet, Camille.

Holm, Ian (1931–   ). Mutius (*Titus Andronicus*), Fool (*Lear*), Prince Hal (1 *Henry IV*), Henry V, Edward IV, Richard III, Lenny (*The Homecoming*), Voinitsky (*Uncle Vanya*).

Irving, Sir Henry (1838–1905). Joseph Surface, Robert Macaire, Mathias (*Bells*), Dubosc, Richelieu.

Jackson, Glenda (1936–). Alexandra (*The Idiot*), Siddie (*Alfie*), Charlotte Corday (*Marat/Sade*), Hedda Gabler, Stevie, Cleopatra (*Antony and Cleopatra*).

Jacobi, Derek (1938–). Benedick (*Much Ado About Nothing*), Hamlet, Prospero (*The Tempest*), Laertes (*Hamlet*), Angelo (*Measure for Measure*), Orestes (*Electra*), Oedipus Rex, Octavius Caesar (*Antony and Cleopatra*).

Jefferson, Joseph (1829–1905). Doctor Pangloss (*Heir-at-Law*), Asa Trenchard and Lord Dundreary (*Our American Cousin*), Rip Van Winkle, Caleb Plummer.

Jones, James Earl (1931–). Brutus Jones (*The Emperor Jones*), Jack Jefferson (*The Great White Hope*), Claudius (*Hamlet*), Lear, Lennie (*Of Mice and Men*).

Jordan, Dora (1762–1816). Thalia, Juliet, Ophelia (*Hamlet*), Jane Shore.

Kean, Charles (1811–68). Selim (*Barbarossa*), Romeo, Richard III, Titus (*Brutus*), Hamlet, Iago (*Othello*).

Kean, Edmund (1787–1833). Shylock (*The Merchant of Venice*), Richard III, Hamlet, Othello, Iago (*Othello*), Macbeth, Romeo, Sir Giles Overreach.

Kemble, Charles (1775–1854). Laertes (*Hamlet*), Cassio, Falconbridge, Macduff (*Macbeth*), Edgar (*Lear*), Hamlet.

Kemble, Frances Ann (1809–93). Juliet, Bianca (*Fazio*), Julia (*The Hunchback*).

Kemble, John Philip (1757–1823). King John, Lear, Coriolanus.

Kemp, William (?–*ca.* 1603). Dogberry (*Much Ado About Nothing*), Peter (*Romeo and Juliet*), *The Return from Parnassus*.

King, Thomas (1730–1804). Tom (*The Conscious Lover*), Sir Peter Teazle (*The School for Scandal*).

Liston, John (1776–1846). Zekiel Homespun and Sheepface (*Village Lawyer*), Paul Pry, Malvolio.

Lowin, John (1576–1653). Falstaff (*Henry IV*), Volpone, Melantius (*The Maid's Tragedy*).

McCullough, John (1832–85). Laertes (*Hamlet*), Macduff (*Macbeth*), Iago (*Othello*), Edgar (*Lear*), Richmond (*Richard III*), Titus, Virginius.

McKellen, Ian (1939–). Macbeth, Sir Thomas More, Claudio (*Much Ado About Nothing*), Leonidik (*The Promise*), Pentheus (*The Bacchae*), Richard II, Edgar (*Lear*).

Macklin, Charles (1690/9–1797). Macbeth, Richard III, Shylock (*The Merchant of Venice*), Polonius (*Hamlet*), Sir John Daw, Cutbeard.

Macready, William Charles (1793–1873). Rob Roy, Virginius, Othello, Romeo, King John, Shylock (*The Merchant of Venice*).

Matthews, Charles (1776–1835). Risk (*Love Laughs at Locksmiths*), Mr. Pennyman (*At Home*).

Mills, Sir John (1908–). Lord Fancourt Babberley (*Charley's Aunt*), Ross, Otto Moll (*Power of Persuasion*).

Modjeska, Mme. (Helena) (1840–1909). Adrienne Lecouvreur, Camille, Rosalind (*As You Like It*), Viola (*Twelfth Night*), Juliet.

Morris, Clara (1848–1925). Cora (*L'article* 47), Magdalene (*False Shame*), Camille, Miss Multon, Alixe.

Mowatt, Anna Cora (1819–70). Lady Teazle (*The School for Scandal*), Mrs. Haller, Lucy Ashton, Katherine (*The Taming of the Shrew*), Julia (*The Hunchback*), Juliet.

Neilson, Adelaide (1848–80). Lilian (*Life for Life*), Amy Robsart, Juliet, Isabella (*Measure for Measure*), Imogen (*Cymbeline*).

Olivier, Sir Laurence (1907–89). Captain Stanhope (*Journey's End*), Romeo and Mercutio (*Romeo and Juliet*), Iago (*Othello*), Coriolanus, Richard III, Lear, Oedipus the King, Macbeth, Archie Rice (*The Entertainer*), Becket, Solness (*The Master Builder*), Shylock (*The Merchant of Venice*), James Tyrone (*A Long Day's Journey Into Night*), Henry V, Astrov (*Uncle Vanya*).

O'Neill, Eliza (1791–1872). Juliet, Desdemona (*Othello*), Belvidera.

Palmer, John (ca. 1742–98). Captain Absolute, Young Wilding (*Liar*), Joseph Surface (*The School for Scandal*), Dionysius (*Grecian Daughter*).

Payne, John Howard (1791–1852). Young Norval (*Douglas*), Zaphna (Voltaire's *Mahomet*), Octavian (*Mountaineers*), Hamlet, Tancred, Petruchio, Edgar (*Lear*).

Plowright, Joan (1929–   ). Margery Pinchwife (*The Country Wife*), Jean Rice (*The Entertainer*), Major Barbara, Maggie Hobson (*Hobson's Choice*), Katherine (*The Taming of the Shrew*), Josephine (*A Taste of Honey*).

Quin, James (1693–1766). Falstaff, Henry VIII, Jacques, Volpone.

Raymond, John T. (1836–87). Colonel Sellers, Asa Trenchard (*Our American Cousin*).

Redgrave, Sir Michael (1908–85). Macbeth, Hamlet, Antony (*Antony and Cleopatra*), Uncle Vanya, Henry Hobson (*Hobson's Choice*), Samson (*Samson Agonistes*).

Redgrave, Vanessa (1937–   ). Sarah Undershaft (*Major Barbara*), Helena (*A Midsummer Night's Dream*), Katherine (*The Taming of the Shrew*), Nina (*The Seagull*), Jean Brodie (*The Prime of Miss Jean Brodie*), Polly Peachum (*The Threepenny Opera*), Cleopatra (*Antony and Cleopatra*).

Richardson, Ian (1934–   ). Richard II, Berowne (*Love's Labour's Lost*), Richard III, Ford (*The Merry Wives of Windsor*), Prospero (*The Tempest*), Higgins (*My Fair Lady*).

Richardson, Sir Ralph (1902–83). Lorenzo (*The Merchant of Venice*), Caliban (*The Tempest*), Sir Toby Belch (*Twelfth Night*), Petruchio (*The Taming of the Shrew*), Henry V, Othello, Uncle Vanya, Peer Gynt, Falstaff (*Henry IV*), Doctor Sloper (*The Heiress*), Prospero (*The Tempest*), Sir Anthony Absolute (*The Rivals*), Shylock (*The Merchant of Venice*), John Gabriel Borkman, Hirst (*No Man's Land*), Author (*The King Fisher*).

Robeson, Paul (1898–1976). Jim Harris (*All God's Chillun Got Wings*), Brutus Jones (*The Emperor Jones*), Othello, Yank (*The Hairy Ape*).

Scofield, Paul (1922–   ). Konstantin (*The Seagull*), John Tanner (*Man and Superman*), Henry V, Malcolm (*Macbeth*), Lucio (*Measure for Measure*),

Pericles, Hamlet, Sir Thomas More (*A Man for All Seasons*), Lear, Uncle Vanya, Prospero (*The Tempest*).

Sheridan, Thomas (1721–88). Richard III, Othello, Cato, Hamlet, Brutus (*Julius Caesar*).

Siddons, Sarah (1755–1831). Hamlet, Isabella (*Fatal Marriage*), Isabella (*Measure for Measure*), Lady Macbeth, Volumnia (*Coriolanus*).

Smith, Maggie (first appearance, 1952). Daisy (*Rhinoceros*), Lucile (*The Rehearsal*), Doreen (*The Private Ear*), Belinda (*The Public Eye*), Mary (*Mary, Mary*), Desdemona (*Othello*), Beatrice (*Much Ado About Nothing*), Hedda Gabler, Cleopatra (*Antony and Cleopatra*), Lady Macbeth.

Snow, Sophia (1745–86). Cordelia (*Lear*), Fanny (*The Clandestine Marriage*).

Sothern, E. A. (1826–81). Armand Duval, Lord Dundreary (*Our American Cousin*).

Tarlton, Richard (*ca.* 1545–88). Bottom (*A Midsummer Night's Dream*), Dogberry (*Much Ado About Nothing*), First Grave Digger (*Hamlet*), *Pierce Penilesse*.

Terry, Ellen (1847–1928). Gertrude (*Little Treasure*), Clara Douglas (*Money*), Portia (*The Merchant of Venice*), Olivia, Ophelia (*Hamlet*), Beatrice (*Much Ado About Nothing*).

Tooley, Nicholas (?–1623). Nick (*Seven Deadly Sins*), *The Alchemist*, Forobosco (*The Duchess of Malfi*).

Tree, Ellen (Mrs. Kean) (1805–80). Desdemona (*Othello*), Julia (*The Hunchback*), Ion.

Vestris, Eliza Lucy (1797–1856). Mrs. Page, Mrs. Ford, Oberon (*A Midsummer Night's Dream*), Lady Teazle (*The School for Scandal*), Letitia Hardy.

Wallack, James W. (1795–1864). Squire Broadlands (*Country Girl*), James V (*King of the Commoners*), Benedick (*Much Ado About Nothing*).

Wallack, Lester (1820–88). Claude Melnotte, Steerforth, Percy Ardent (*West End*), Young Rapid (*A Cure for the Headache*).

Wilkinson, Tate (1739–1803). Othello, Lear, Hamlet, Richard III, Romeo, Hotspur.

Woffington, Margaret (1719–60). Phillis (*Conscious Lovers*), Lady Macbeth, Cleopatra (*Antony and Cleopatra*).

Woodward, Henry (1714–77). Beggar and Ben Budge (*Beggar's Opera*), Feeble (*2 Henry IV*), Marplot (*Busybody*).

Young, Charles Mayne (1777–1856). Hamlet, Romeo, Othello, Iago (*Othello*), Ford (*The Merry Wives of Windsor*).

SOURCES

Bio-base. Microfiche. Detroit: Gale Research Co., 1984.

Bradbrook, M. C. *The Rise of the Common Player.* London: Chatto and Windus, 1962.

Brook, Donald. *A Pageant of English Actors*. London: Rockliff, 1950.

Gurr, Andrew. *The Shakespearean Stage, 1574–1642*. Cambridge, Eng.: Cambridge University Press, 1970.

Hartnoll, Phyllis, and Peter Found, eds. *The Concise Oxford Companion to the Theatre*: Oxford: Oxford University Press, 1992.

Herbert, Ian, with Christine Baxter and Robert E. Finley. *Who's Who in the Theatre: Biographies*. Detroit: Gale Research Co., 1981.

Matthews, Brander, and Laurence Hutton, eds. *Actors and Actresses of Great Britain and the United States*. 5 vols. New York: Cassell, 1886.

Nunzeger, Edwin. *A Dictionary of Actors*. New Haven: Yale University Press, 1929.

Roberts, Peter, ed. *The Best of "Plays and Players," 1953–1968*. London: Methuen, 1987.

———. *The Best of "Plays and Players," 1969–1983*. London: Methuen, 1989.

—J.L.M.

41

SHAKESPEARE'S PLAYS
AND PRINCIPAL CHARACTERS

· · · · ·

AT LEAST SINCE THE LATER NINETEENTH CENTURY THERE HAS BEEN CONSID-
erable dispute as to who actually wrote the plays of William Shakespeare
(1564–1616), about whom not much more is really known than that he was
an actor who eventually retired to the town he originally came from. The
authorship has variously been credited to Francis Bacon, the Earl of Oxford,
and to somebody else with the same name.

At bottom the reason why people have been so quick to assume that
someone else wrote the plays has less to do with the scantiness of direct evidence linking the living man to the writings than with the fact that, for all
our supposed belief in democracy and equality, we simply can't believe that
an ordinary citizen without aristocratic or otherwise distinguished fore-
bears could possibly have achieved profundity or greatness. It is the same
kind of reasoning that seeks to account for Abraham Lincoln by making
him the illegitimate offspring of Andrew Jackson (but how account for
him?) or John C. Calhoun.

Even if it is conceded that the William Shakespeare of record was the
William Shakespeare who wrote the plays, the sonnets, and assorted other
verse, there is much argumentation among scholars as to the genuineness of
everything published under his name. Here the disputing is based on much
firmer evidence. The central difficulty is that Shakespeare himself never
bothered to publish all his plays in a collected edition during his lifetime.

Of the thirty-seven plays generally accepted nowadays as authentic
Shakespeare, thirty-six were printed (eighteen for the first time ever) in the
collected edition of 1616 now known as the First Folio. Published in London
by the stationers Isaac Jaggard and Edward Blount, its title was *Mr. William
Shakespeare's Comedies, Histories, and Tragedies, Published According to
the True Original Copies*, and it was assembled and edited by two men who
had known the playwright well. These were John Heminge and Henry

Condell, fellow actors and shareholders in the theatrical company to which Shakespeare belonged for almost all of his professional career, a group first known as the Lord Chamberlain's Men and then, after the accession of King James I in 1603, as the King's Men.

Heminge and Condell omitted from their collection only *Pericles, Prince of Tyre,* of those plays considered authentic today, possibly because the first two acts were written by someone else—a common enough occurrence in an age and profession in which collaboration among stage writers was frequent. Shakespeare may have contributed scenes and passages to other plays that are extant—John Fletcher's *Two Noble Kinsmen* and Antony Munday's *Book of Sir Thomas More* are two that are often cited— but there are few reasons to doubt the judgment of Heminge and Condell about what he did and did not write. Their work of selection has withstood several generations of critical examination and revaluation. The First Folio's title and table of contents also established the division of Shakespeare's plays into genres of comedy, history, and tragedy. These divisions, with the probable dates of composition and the settings, are preserved in the listing that follows.

> 1590–91—*The Comedy of Errors*, comedy set at Ephesus in Asia Minor
> 1590–92—*Henry VI* (three parts), history set in England
> 1593—*Richard III*, history set in England
> 1593—*The Taming of the Shrew*, comedy set in England and Italy
> 1594—*Titus Andronicus*, tragedy set in ancient Rome
> 1594—*The Two Gentlemen of Verona*, comedy set in Verona, Milan, and Mantua
> 1594—*King John*, history set in England
> 1595—*A Midsummer Night's Dream*, comedy set in ancient Athens and environs
> 1595—*Richard II*, history set in England
> 1596—*Love's Labour's Lost*, comedy set in Navarre in France
> 1596—*Romeo and Juliet*, tragedy set in Verona and Mantua
> 1597—*The Merchant of Venice*, comedy set in Venice
> 1597–98—*Henry IV* (two parts), history set in England
> 1598—*As You Like It*, comedy set in the Forest of Arden (fictional)
> 1599—*Henry V*, history set in England and France
> 1599—*Julius Caesar*, tragedy set in ancient Rome
> 1599—*Much Ado About Nothing*, comedy set at Messina in Italy
> 1600—*Twelfth Night*, comedy set in Illyria (fictional)
> 1600—*The Merry Wives of Windsor*, comedy set in rural England
> 1601—*Hamlet*, tragedy set in Denmark
> 1602—*Troilus and Cressida*, comedy set in ancient Troy

1603—*All's Well That Ends Well*, comedy set in France and Italy

1604—*Measure for Measure*, comedy set in Vienna

1604—*Othello*, tragedy set in Venice and Cyprus

1605—*King Lear*, tragedy set in ancient Britain

1605—*Macbeth*, tragedy set in ancient Scotland

1606—*Timon of Athens*, tragedy set in ancient Athens

1607—*Pericles, Prince of Tyre*, romance set in ancient Lebanon

1607—*Antony and Cleopatra*, tragedy set in ancient Rome and Alexandria, Egypt

1608—*Coriolanus*, tragedy set in ancient Rome

1609—*Cymbeline*, romance set in ancient Britain and Rome

1610—*The Winter's Tale*, romance set in Sicily and Bohemia

1611—*The Tempest*, romance set on a fictional isle

1613—*Henry VIII*, history set in England

In addition to the plays, Shakespeare wrote several nondramatic works, two of which were dedicated to the young Henry Wriothesley, Earl of Southampton, whose patronage the playwright evidently sought during 1593 and 1594 when a plague epidemic shut down the public theaters along with all other occasions for large and medically inadvisable crowds. These were both long narrative poems: *Venus and Adonis* (1593), a rhetorically lush contribution to the mythological-erotic tradition deriving ultimately from the Roman poet Ovid, and *The Rape of Lucrece* (1594), an equally ornate if more overtly moral tale of crime and retribution. "The Phoenix and the Turtle" (1601) is a complex poem of 67 lines celebrating an ideal relationship between a married couple. The 154 poems of the sequence entitled simply *Sonnets* (1609) constitute indisputably the most brilliant sonnet sequence in English. Also in the 1609 volume was printed a 329-line poem entitled "A Lover's Complaint," whose authenticity is still debated by critics.

Shakespeare was a master of almost all the facets of dramatic art in his time, but what has appealed most widely over the centuries are his characterizations. Altogether the plays contain just over 1,000 characters, not counting unspecified numbers of attendant soldiers, citizens, etc., used to swell a crowd scene or piece out a battle. Some of Shakespeare's characters are so often cited or used in comparisons that they seem to have lives of their own, independently of their original dramatic contexts. Hamlet, Iago, Shylock, and Falstaff, to name a few, are among the Shakespearean names known even to many people who have never read the plays in which they appear. Any good collected edition of Shakespeare's works will contain an index of characters and their appearances. Here are some of the many who appear in Shakespeare's writings.

Aaron. The violent Moor in *Titus Andronicus*, the lover of Tamora.

Abhorson. The executioner in *Measure for Measure*. His name echoes both *abhorrent* and *whoreson* (a common Elizabethan term of insult) and thus shows the disesteem in which his profession was held.

Achilles. Traditionally the bravest and most powerful of the Greeks at Troy. In Shakespeare's *Troilus and Cressida* he kills the unarmed Hector in a cowardly manner.

Adam. The old and faithful servant of Orlando in *As You Like It*. His name reinforces his characterization as one who has the virtues of an earlier and more innocent age. This is one of the roles that Shakespeare is reputed to have played on the stage as actor in his own work.

Agrippa. Proposes the marriage between Antony and Octavia in *Antony and Cleopatra*.

Aguecheek, Sir Andrew. An affected fop in *Twelfth Night*.

Ajax. Among the Greeks at Troy in *Troilus and Cressida*. Shakespeare follows tradition in making him somewhat slow-witted.

Alcibiades. An avenger in *Timon of Athens*.

Alexas. One of Cleopatra's attendants in *Antony and Cleopatra*.

Alice. An attendant on Princess Katherine of France in *Henry V* who gives Katherine a comical lesson in speaking English.

Amiens. One of the banished Duke's followers in *As You Like It*. Because several of the play's songs are assigned to him, we may assume that the role was first acted by one of the better singers of Shakespeare's theatrical company.

Angelo. The man deputized to enforce law and order in *Measure for Measure* who reveals himself as a hypocrite. Another Angelo is a goldsmith in *The Comedy of Errors*.

Antigonus. Servant of Leontes in *The Winter's Tale*. He leaves the stage with a famous stage direction, "Exit pursued by a bear." He is eaten by the bear offstage.

Antonio. A name Shakespeare used for characters in five of his plays. In *The Merchant of Venice* Antonio is the merchant. In *The Two Gentlemen of Verona* Proteus' father bears that name. In *Much Ado About Nothing* Antonio is Leonato's brother. In *Twelfth Night* a sea captain named Antonio lends Sebastian money. Prospero's brother in *The Tempest*, who usurps Prospero's throne, is named Antonio.

Antony, Marc. One of the triumvirs in *Julius Caesar* and the man who makes the famous speech at Caesar's funeral. He is also the hero of *Antony and Cleopatra*. Historically, he lived from about 83 to 30 B.C.E.

Apemantus. An ill-natured misanthrope in *Timon of Athens*.

Armado, Don Adriano de. One of the suitors of Jaquenetta in *Love's Labour's Lost*.

Arragon. One of the suitors of Portia in *The Merchant of Venice*. He chooses the silver casket in the lovers' testing episode, and is rewarded with a picture of a "blinking idiot."

Arthur. King John's nephew in *King John*, over whom John was chosen king.

Arviragus. Cymbeline's son and Imogen's brother in *Cymbeline*.

Aufidius. Military leader of the Volscians in *Coriolanus*. He is first the enemy, then the ally, and finally the slayer of Coriolanus.

Aumerle. A member of the York faction in *Richard II*.

Autolycus. A thief and ballad monger in *The Winter's Tale*. Shakespeare evidently takes the name from Homer's *Iliad*, where an Autolycus is also mentioned as a thief.

Bagot. Along with Bushy and Green, one of the flatterers and bad counselors of Richard in *Richard II*.

Balthasar. A name Shakespeare used for a merchant in *The Comedy of Errors*, for a servant in *The Merchant of Venice*, for a servant in *Much Ado About Nothing*, and for the bearer of the news of Juliet's alleged death in *Romeo and Juliet*.

Banquo. Murdered by order of Macbeth. He appears as a ghost at the banquet in *Macbeth*.

Baptista Minola. The father of Katherina and Bianca in *The Taming of the Shrew*.

Barnardine. A drunken, unrepentant prisoner in *Measure for Measure* who refuses to sober up long enough to be executed.

Bassanio. Angelo's close friend in *The Merchant of Venice*.

Beatrice. The heroine who unsuccessfully tries to conceal her love for Benedick in *Much Ado About Nothing*.

Belarius. A banished lord in *Cymbeline* who rears Cymbeline's sons and restores them to him, even though Cymbeline has wronged him deeply.

Belch, Sir Toby. Olivia's hard-drinking uncle in *Twelfth Night*. His name has become synonymous with revelry, and "toby" mugs bearing his caricature have been used for ale in Britain since Victorian times.

Benedick. A man who relinquishes his resolve to live a bachelor's life to court and bandy wits with the spirited Beatrice in *Much Ado About Nothing*.

Benvolio. Romeo's friend who persuades Romeo to attend the dance where he falls in love with Juliet in *Romeo and Juliet*.

Berowne. One of the King of Navarre's three attending lords in *Love's Labour's Lost*. He is especially distinguished for his fondness for wordplay. In some texts the name is spelled "Biron."

Bertram. Son of the Countess of Rousillon and the chief male character of *All's Well That Ends Well*. He is the reluctant husband of Helena.

Bianca. The nonshrewish daughter of Baptista Minola in *The Taming of the Shrew*, and also the name of Cassio's mistress in *Othello*.

Blanch. King John's niece who marries the French dauphin in *King John*.

Bolingbroke, Henry. Deposer of Richard in *Richard II* and the title king in *Henry IV*, Parts 1 and 2. Historically, his dates are 1367–1413. Another Bolingbroke is the Conjurer in 2 *Henry VI* who is condemned to hanging.

Bottom the Weaver. One of the "rude mechanicals" in *A Midsummer Night's Dream*. Titania, the fairy queen, while under the influence of a mind-altering potion, falls in love with him even though he is wearing an ass's head put on him by Puck.

Brabantio. Desdemona's father in *Othello*. He strongly opposes her marriage to the Moor.

Brutus, Marcus Junius. Despite the play's title, the central character of *Julius Caesar*. He is depicted as an inflexible idealist. Another Brutus in the same play is Decius Brutus. In *Coriolanus* a Junius Brutus helps to stir up the populace against Coriolanus.

Buckingham, Humphrey, Duke of. Nobleman who dupes Cade's rebels into surrendering their cause in 2 *Henry VI*. His grandson, Henry, Duke of Buckingham, appears in *Richard III* and is murdered by Richard. Henry's son, Edward, is an opposer of Cardinal Wolsey in *Henry VIII*.

Bullcalf. A comic character who, despite the hearty appearance his name denotes, bribes his way out of being drafted into the military in 2 *Henry IV*.

Bushy. Along with Green and Bagot, one of the flatterers and bad counselors of Richard in *Richard II*.

Cade, Jack. Leader of a peasant rebellion that figures prominently in 2 *Henry VI*.

Caesar, Julius. Roman dictator slain by conspirators in the play that bears his name. His grandnephew, Octavius Caesar, wins out over Antony and Cleopatra in *Antony and Cleopatra*.

Caius. An irascible French medical doctor who hopes to marry Anne Page in *The Merry Wives of Windsor*. Fenton and the Host trick him into going through a wedding ceremony with a boy in disguise.

Caliban. Monstrous son of the witch Sycorax who embodies the worst possibilities of human character in *The Tempest*.

Calpurnia. Caesar's barren wife in *Julius Caesar*.

Camillo. A Sicilian lord in *The Winter's Tale*. Leontes fails in his attempt to have Camillo poison Polixenes, whom he suspects of adultery with his wife Hermione.

Capulet. Juliet's father and the head of one of the two feuding families in *Romeo and Juliet*.

Cassio. A lieutenant in *Othello* whose promotion by the Moor kindles the murderous jealousy of Iago.

Cassius. Appears with a "lean and hungry look" in *Julius Caesar* as an ally of Brutus.

Catesby, Sir William. A supporter of the king in *Richard III*.

Celia. Rosalind's cousin and close friend in *As You Like It.*

Cesario. The name used by Viola in boy's attire in *Twelfth Night.*

Charmian. Cleopatra's devoted attendant who dies with her in *Antony and Cleopatra.*

Chiron. With his brother rapes and mutilates Lavinia in *Titus Andronicus.* The brothers are ultimately slain and fed to their mother in a pastry dish.

Cinna. A poet first mistaken for Cinna the politician by the mob in *Julius Caesar* and then killed anyway, "for his bad verses."

Cobweb. One of the fairies in *A Midsummer Night's Dream.*

Cominius. A Roman general, counselor, and defender of Coriolanus in the play of that name.

Cordelia. The faithful daughter of King Lear, victimized for her honesty in *King Lear.*

Corin. An old shepherd in *As You Like It.* He represents an unromanticized view of the pastoral life.

Coriolanus. A Roman general much decorated in war but rigid and aloof from the people of the city. In *Coriolanus* he is depicted as uncommonly devoted to and influenced by his fiercely competitive mother, Volumnia.

Cornwall. Husband of Lear's daughter Regan in *King Lear.* He is responsible for the cruel blinding of Gloucester.

Costard. A clown in *Love's Labour's Lost.*

Cressida. The chief female role in *Troilus and Cressida,* a somewhat bitter satire that uses the story of Chaucer's *Troilus* as vehicle for a skeptical examination of human nature, especially on the issue of war. Many scholars believe that the play was written to be performed before an audience of attorneys at one of the Inns of Court (law societies).

Cymbeline. One of the mythical pre-Arthurian kings of Britain. He supposedly reigned at the time of Christ, the historical period of the setting of the play of his name.

Davy. The secretary and steward of Justice Shallow in 2 *Henry IV.*

Demetrius. A name given to three characters in Shakespeare. In *Titus Andronicus* it denotes Chiron's brother; in *A Midsummer Night's Dream* the young man (one of the main characters) in love with Hermia; in *Antony and Cleopatra,* a friend of Antony.

Diomedes. One of the chief Greek soldiers in *Troilus and Cressida.* The name is also used for one of Cleopatra's servants in *Antony and Cleopatra.*

Dogberry. A comic constable in *Much Ado About Nothing.*

Dolabella. A friend of Octavius Caesar in *Antony and Cleopatra.*

Donalbain. The younger of Duncan's sons in *Macbeth.* He flees to Ireland after his father is murdered.

Dorcas. A simple shepherdess in *The Winter's Tale.*

Doricles. Florizel in disguise in *The Winter's Tale.*

Dromio. The name used by the twin slaves in *The Comedy of Errors*.

Duke Senior. Rosalind's father, driven into exile by his brother Frederick in *As You Like It*.

Dumaine. One of the King of Navarre's three attendant lords in *Love's Labour's Lost*. The name is also used for two French brothers in *All's Well That Ends Well*.

Edward IV. Brother and predecessor on the throne of Richard III. He appears in 2 and 3 *Henry VI* and in *Richard III*. Historically he lived 1442–83.

Egeus. Father of Hermia in *A Midsummer Night's Dream*. He creates problems for the four young lovers of the play by insisting on his right to select his daughter's husband.

Elinor. The mother of King John in the play of that name.

Elizabeth. Edward IV's queen in *Richard III*. Shakespeare avoided using the name for fictional characters, perhaps out of deference to Queen Elizabeth I, who reigned during the first half of his career.

Emilia. Iago's wife and Desdemona's attendant/companion in *Othello*. Iago stabs her fatally after she reveals his duplicity.

Enobarbus. Antony's close friend and colleague in arms in *Antony and Cleopatra*. Despairing at Antony's misjudgments, he joins with Caesar against him, but dies of guilt over his disloyalty.

Eros. Antony's servant who kills himself rather than help his master commit suicide as ordered.

Escalus. A name Shakespeare associated with judiciousness, using it both for the Prince in *Romeo and Juliet* and a wise magistrate in *Measure for Measure*.

Evans, Sir Hugh. A Welsh parson in *The Merry Wives of Windsor*.

Falstaff, Sir John. An engaging rogue who appears in both parts of *Henry IV*. His death is reported in *Henry V*, after which, perhaps by popular demand, Shakespeare used him again, as a character in *The Merry Wives of Windsor*. With his combination of wit, agreeability, and pure, exploitive self-interest, he is Shakespeare's most complex comic character and among the greatest comic creations in all of literature.

Faulconbridge, Philip. Illegitimate son of Richard I and known as the Bastard throughout *King John*. He is knighted by John, whom he serves faithfully and well.

Feeble. A commoner whose name denotes his appearance. Feeble also contrasts sharply with some able-bodied cowards in 2 *Henry IV* by his willingness to accept military service when he is recruited by Falstaff.

Fenton. The young man who wins the hand of Anne Page in *The Merry Wives of Windsor*.

Feste. Olivia's professional fool in *Twelfth Night*. Like Touchstone in *As You Like It* and the Fool in *King Lear*, under his disguise he is truly wise.

Flaminius. Timon's loyal servant in *Timon of Athens*.

Fleance. Banquo's son in *Macbeth*. Unlike his father, he escapes Macbeth's murderous intentions, fleeing to Wales.

Florizel. The young Prince of Bohemia, marries Perdita in *The Winter's Tale*.

Fluellen. A Welsh officer in Henry's army in *Henry V*. He is famous for making a far-fetched comparison between Alexander of Macedon and Henry of England on the basis of their both having grown up near rivers, and "there is salmons in both."

Fool. A jester who has no other name in *King Lear*, but as King Lear's faithful adviser, protector, and friend, is among the most important characters in the play and the ultimate development of the character type of the "wise fool," which Shakespeare used earlier in *As You Like It* and *Twelfth Night*.

Fortinbras. A general who typifies the active, unreflective personality (his name in French means "strong-in-arms") in contrast to the hero in *Hamlet*. He is selected to succeed Hamlet on the Danish throne at the end of the play.

France, Kings of. Monarchs appearing in four plays. Philip II is in *King John*, and Charles VI is in *Henry V*. A fictional French king marries Cordelia in *King Lear*, and another presides over part of *All's Well That Ends Well*.

Francis. A boy working in a tavern, the butt of a practical joke by Prince Hal and Poins in 1 *Henry IV*.

Francisco. The name of one of the shipwrecked courtiers in *The Tempest*, and of a watchman at Elsinore in *Hamlet*.

Friar John. A friar who fails to get a crucial message to the hero in *Romeo and Juliet*.

Friar Laurence. The friar who performs the marriage between Romeo and Juliet.

Friar Peter. Assistant of the Duke in *Measure for Measure*. He performs the marriage between Angelo and Mariana.

Friar Thomas. Provider of the disguise (a friar's habit) for the Duke in *Measure for Measure*.

Gadshill. One of the low characters who consort with Falstaff in 1 *Henry IV*. His name is probably a nickname taken from a site near London, where a robbery takes place in the play.

Ganymede. Rosalind's name while she is disguised as a boy in *As You Like It*. It was an Elizabethan slang term for an effeminate man.

Gertrude. Hamlet's mother in *Hamlet*. Her hasty remarriage, after Hamlet's father's death, deeply troubles the prince in the play.

Glendower, Owen. A Welsh lord of a mystic imagination. He is one of the rebels in the Percy rebellion in 1 *Henry IV*.

Gloucester. Father of Edmund and Edgar in *King Lear*. The actions of these three make up the play's subplot, which reflects and comments on several of the themes in the main story.

Gobbo, Launcelot. Shylock's servant who turns against him in *The Merchant of Venice*.

Goneril. Lear's eldest, evil daughter in *King Lear*.

Gower, John (1330–1408). A poet who lived in the time of Chaucer and whom Shakespeare uses as the chorus character in *Pericles*, calling attention to the fact that one of Gower's works is a source for the play. Characters with the name Gower also appear in 2 *Henry IV* and *Henry V*.

Gratiano. Brabantio's brother in *Othello*. Another Gratiano appears in *The Merchant of Venice*.

Green. Along with Bushy and Bagot, one of the flatterers and bad counselors of Richard in *Richard II*.

Gremio. Among the suitors of Bianca in *The Taming of the Shrew*.

Guiderius. The elder son of Cymbeline in the play of that name.

Guildenstern. With Rosencrantz, a college friend of Hamlet who comes to visit him in Denmark and is drawn by King Claudius into a plot to destroy Hamlet.

Hamlet, Prince of Denmark. Quite likely the most written about and critically analyzed character in world literature. He has been viewed variously as a spineless procrastinator, a bloody-minded hothead, and a sufferer from the Oedipus complex. He is, in the play that bears his name, none of these.

Hastings. One of the leaders of the rebellion in 2 *Henry VI*, and one of the partisans of Edward IV in *Richard III*.

Hecate. Patroness of witches and goddess of the underworld who appears briefly in *Macbeth* in a scene that has been attributed to another playwright "doctoring" the text for performance.

Helen. In *Troilus and Cressida* as in the *Iliad* of Homer, the abducted wife of Paris over whom the Trojan War is fought. There is also a Helen in *Cymbeline*, an attendant of Imogen.

Helena. Heroine in *All's Well That Ends Well*. Another Helena features, with Hermia and their respective swains, in the lovers' tangle in *A Midsummer Night's Dream*.

Henry IV (1367–1413). As Henry Bolingbroke, usurps the crown of Richard II in the play of that title. His reign continues in 1 and 2 *Henry IV*, where his chief problems are the Percy rebellion and his own disappointment at the character and what he considers the irresponsibility of his son, Prince Hal. See **Bolingbroke, Henry**.

Henry V (1387–1422). The hero-king, presented as the ideal monarch in *Henry V*. His development as Prince Hal and his exploits with Falstaff in the two parts of *Henry IV* are among the most popular of Shakespeare's stories.

Henry VI (1421–71). Monarch whose reign is the setting of Shakespeare's first tetralogy of history plays and who held on to the throne precariously throughout the Wars of the Roses.

Henry VII (1457–1509). King who, when the Earl of Richmond, defeated Richard III at the battle of Bosworth Field in 1485. Richard's famous words "my kingdom for a horse!" are uttered during the scene of this conflict in *Richard III*.

Henry VIII (1491–1547). King treated in the play of that name, on which Shakespeare seems to have collaborated with another playwright, possibly John Fletcher. Henry is the son of Henry VII and father of Queen Elizabeth I by Anne Boleyn.

Hermia. Daughter of Egeus who loves Lysander in *A Midsummer Night's Dream*. She is frustrated by her father's insistence that she marry Demetrius.

Hermione. Leontes' wife in *The Winter's Tale*. Deeply wronged by her husband, she remains hidden and thought dead for sixteen years, then returns to forgive him.

Holofernes. A pedantic schoolteacher in *Love's Labour's Lost*.

Horatio. Hamlet's close friend, a calming and stabilizing influence in *Hamlet*. Hamlet probably has him in mind when he says that he admires the kind of man who is not subject to the whims of fortune.

Hortensio. Petruchio's friend and Bianca's suitor in *The Taming of the Shrew*.

Hotspur. See **Percy, Henry**.

Iachimo. A Roman met by the exiled Posthumus in *Cymbeline*.

Iago. Antagonist of Othello and among the craftiest and most vicious villains in literature. Motivated initially by jealousy, he seems, as *Othello* progresses, to regard his schemes as works of art to be enjoyed for themselves and for the skill they demonstrate. Like many of the great villains of Renaissance literature (Milton's Satan in *Paradise Lost* is another), Iago is a sophist, an abuser of the great power of rhetoric to sway men to good or evil. The jealousy he stirs in Othello causes Othello to kill his faithful wife; and Iago seems to enjoy the agonies of doubt he creates in the Moor as much as the ultimate outcome of his revenge.

Imogen. Heroine of *Cymbeline*, daughter of the king and wife of Posthumus.

Isabella. Heroine of *Measure for Measure*.

Jaques. Melancholy character of *As You Like It* who exaggerates the pose of world-weary sophisticate (a fashionable attitude in Elizabethan court society) until it becomes an object of satire. Pronounced "jakes" (Elizabethans anglicized most French words in pronunciation), his name puns on the slang word for an outhouse or privy. Another character in the same play, Orlando's brother, is named Jaques de Boys.

Jessica. Daughter of Shylock in *The Merchant of Venice* who takes her usurious father's money and runs away with Lorenzo.

John, Don. Illegitimate brother of the Prince of Arragon, who helps to stir up trouble in *Much Ado About Nothing*.

John, King (1167–1216). Monarch who succeeded Richard I and reigns during the play of his name.

John of Gaunt. Elder statesman, duke of Lancaster, and father of Henry Bolingbroke who represents the old, stable political order that begins to be destroyed in *Richard II.*

Juliet. Daughter of the house of Capulet and heroine of *Romeo and Juliet.* Claudio's pregnant fiancée in *Measure for Measure* is also named Juliet.

Katherina. The Shrew in *The Taming of the Shrew.* Her father decrees that her younger sister, the beautiful and sweet-tempered Bianca, may not be married until someone marries Katherina.

Katherine. The name of the French princess who marries Henry in *Henry V;* of one of the ladies in *Love's Labour's Lost;* and of Katherine of Arragon, the king's first wife, in *Henry VIII.*

Laertes. Brother of Ophelia and son of Polonius who demands the final and fatal duel in *Hamlet.*

Lafew. An old, gracious, and wise lord in *All's Well That Ends Well.*

Launce. A comic servant in *The Two Gentlemen of Verona,* master of a dog named Crab.

Le Beau. A fop in the retinue of Duke Frederick in *As You Like It.*

Leontes, King of Sicily. One of the principal characters in *The Winter's Tale.* His irrational jealousy destroys his family, but his wife and daughter are restored to him after sixteen years of penitential reflection.

Lepidus. A member of the triumvirate in *Julius Caesar.*

Lodovico. Duke who prescribes torture for Iago after his plots are uncovered in *Othello.*

Longaville. One among the lords of the King of Navarre who retreat from women in *Love's Labour's Lost.*

Lord Chief Justice. Judge in 2 *Henry IV* who functions chiefly as a contrast to Falstaff. Both men seek influence over Prince Hal when he becomes king, and Hal chooses the wise Justice as his counselor, rejecting Falstaff.

Lovel. One of Richard's main henchmen in *Richard III.*

Lucentio. Winner of Bianca's hand in *The Taming of the Shrew.*

Lucillius. The name of a friend of Brutus in *Julius Caesar* and of a servant in *Timon of Athens.*

Lucio. A degenerate courtier who provides cynical but accurate commentary on the action in *Measure for Measure.*

Lucius. A name that appears in three plays. It is the name of both Titus' son and his grandson in *Titus Andronicus,* of a sleepy servant boy in *Julius Caesar,* and of a flatterer in *Timon of Athens.*

Lucullus. Another of Timon's flatterers.

Lychorida. Marina's nurse in *Pericles.*

Lysimachus. The governor of Mytilene in *Pericles.*

Macbeth. Eleventh-century king of Scotland, the hero of one of Shakespeare's most famous tragedies. His strong-willed wife, Lady Macbeth, partially motivates him to murder King Duncan (and several others) to obtain the throne in *Macbeth*.

Macmorris. An Irish soldier in *Henry V* who quarrels with the Welsh Fluellen.

Malvolio. The rigid and socially ambitious steward of Olivia in *Twelfth Night*. Shakespeare may be using him to typify the puritans in Elizabethan England, who, in their opposition to the theaters, were natural enemies of playwrights and actors. The name suggests "mal voglio" or "ill will."

Mamillius. Young son of Leontes in *The Winter's Tale* who dies of sorrow at his mother's accusation of adultery.

Marcellus. Watchman who, along with Bernardo, sees the ghost of the slain king at the beginning of *Hamlet*.

Mariana. The betrothed of Angelo in *Measure for Measure*. She substitutes for Isabella in the "bed-trick" that exposes Angelo's hypocrisy. There is also a minor character named Mariana in *All's Well That Ends Well*.

Marina. The heroine, born at sea, of *Pericles*.

Menenius Agrippa. Orator of the famous "fable of the belly" speech in *Coriolanus*, persuading the common citizens to accept the role of the patricians as appropriate managers of the food supply during a period of shortage.

Menteith. Leader of a force of soldiers against Macbeth.

Mercutio. Energetic young friend of Romeo who dies in a quarrel with Tybalt in *Romeo and Juliet*, necessitating the flight of Romeo, who was also involved, from the city.

Messala. Partisan of Brutus in *Julius Caesar*.

Metellus Cimber. A conspirator in *Julius Caesar*.

Miranda. Daughter of Prospero and the heroine of *The Tempest*.

Montano. Governor of Cyprus in *Othello*.

Mopsa. A shepherdess much impressed with the ballads of Autolycus in *The Winter's Tale*.

Morton, John. Bishop in *Richard III* who joins the Earl of Richmond (later Henry VII) in opposing Richard's tyranny.

Moth. Page in *Love's Labour's Lost* and a fairy in *A Midsummer Night's Dream*.

Mouldy. A commoner who, along with Bullcalf, is drafted into the army by Falstaff but buys his way out in *2 Henry IV*.

Mowbray, Duke of Norfolk. Nobleman challenged to a duel by Henry Bolingbroke in the action that begins the conflict in *Richard II*.

Mustard-Seed. One of the fairies in *A Midsummer Night's Dream*.

Mutius. Titus' youngest son in *Titus Andronicus*.

Nestor. Oldest of the Greeks at Troy who appears in *Troilus and Cressida*.

Northumberland. A northern family whose earls figure prominently in the history plays. Henry Percy, first earl and later father of Hotspur, intends to join the rebellion against Henry in 1 *Henry IV* but fails to show up at the crucial battle of Shrewsbury, where Hotspur is defeated and killed by Prince Hal. He reneges on another promise, this time to join the rebellion of Archbishop Scrope, in 2 *Henry IV*. His great-grandson, the third earl of Northumberland, dies in 3 *Henry VI*.

Nym. One of Falstaff's cronies in both *Henry V* and *The Merry Wives of Windsor*.

Oberon. King of the fairies and husband of Titania in *A Midsummer Night's Dream*.

Octavia. Sister of Octavius Caesar who marries Marc Antony in *Antony and Cleopatra*. Antony's abandonment of the marriage, which he had entered only for political purposes, causes war.

Oliver. The churlish elder brother and guardian of Orlando in *As You Like It*.

Olivia. One of the principal characters in *Twelfth Night*. She has vowed to live in seclusion for seven years following the death of her brother, but is drawn back into active life by love.

Orlando. Hero of *As You Like It* who loves Rosalind and marries her in the Forest of Arden.

Page, Anne. Heroine of *The Merry Wives of Windsor*. Despite the efforts of her father and mother to select a husband for her against her will, she marries Fenton, the man of her choice.

Pandarus. Cressida's uncle in *Troilus and Cressida*. In Shakespeare as in Chaucer, he serves as a go-between for the young couple. By Shakespeare's time his name had come into the language as *pander* for procurer or pimp, and Shakespeare so uses it in *Pericles*, where a character named Pandar keeps a brothel.

Parolles. Character whose name means "utterances," a garrulous, cowardly blowhard who follows Bertram and for a while deceives him in *All's Well That Ends Well*.

Patroclus. Closest friend of Achilles in Homer and in *Troilus and Cressida*.

Peaseblossom. One of the fairies in *A Midsummer Night's Dream*.

Percy, Henry. Nicknamed "Hotspur" because of his quick temper, slain by Prince Hal in 1 *Henry IV*.

Perdita. Daughter of Leontes, heroine of *The Winter's Tale*. Her name means "the lost one," and she is lost to her father for sixteen years.

Pericles, Prince of Tyre. Central character of the play of his name.

Peto. One of Falstaff's rowdy companions in the two parts of *Henry IV*. His name suggests French words for both "explosion" and "fart."

Petruchio. Eventual husband (and "tamer") of Katherina in *The Taming of the Shrew*.

Phebe. Shepherdess courted by Silvius in *As You Like It*.

Philario. Host to the banished Posthumus in *Cymbeline*.

Pisanio. Posthumus' servant in *Cymbeline.*

Pistol. Loud, ranting associate of Falstaff, characterized by constant misuse and misquotation of "heroic" language, some of it from the plays of Christopher Marlowe. He appears in 2 *Henry IV, Henry V,* and *The Merry Wives of Windsor.*

Polixenes. King of Bohemia in *The Winter's Tale.*

Polonius. Father of Laertes and Ophelia in *Hamlet.* A self-important and smug old fellow who constantly cites proverbial sayings to make his points, Polonius attempts to spy on Prince Hamlet and is killed by him when mistaken for Claudius, the king, eavesdropping behind a curtain.

Pompey. A pimp or procurer in *Measure for Measure.* Another Pompey, a Roman general, appears in *Antony and Cleopatra.*

Portia. The name of Brutus' wife in *Julius Caesar* and of the heroine of *The Merchant of Venice.*

Priam, King of Troy. Troilus' father in *Troilus and Cressida.*

Proculeius. Partisan of Octavius Caesar in *Antony and Cleopatra.*

Prospero. Banished Duke of Milan and the main character in *The Tempest.*

Proteus. One of the principal male characters in *The Two Gentlemen of Verona.*

Provost. Supervisor of the prison in *Measure for Measure.*

Puck, or Robin Goodfellow. Attendant spirit of *A Midsummer Night's Dream.*

Quickly, Mistress. The hostess of the inn where Falstaff, Prince Hal, and their cronies gather in the two parts of *Henry IV.* She also appears in *The Merry Wives of Windsor* and in *Henry V,* where she reports the death of Falstaff. In 1 *Henry IV* she is called simply Hostess, but in the second part she acquires her punning name ("quick lie," *i.e.,* quick to assume a recumbent position).

Quince, Peter. Organizer and director of the Pyramus and Thisbe play by the "rude mechanicals" in *A Midsummer Night's Dream.*

Regan. Surpassingly evil second daughter in *King Lear,* married to Cornwall.

Richard III (1452–85). Most evil of the kings in Shakespeare's history plays. Shakespeare draws upon and even embellishes the popular image of Richard established by Sir Thomas More's biography two generations earlier.

Romeo. Scion of the house of Montague, the tragic hero of *Romeo and Juliet.*

Rosalind. Beloved of Orlando, heroine of *As You Like It.*

Rousillon, Countess of. Bertram's mother in *All's Well That Ends Well.*

Saturninus. Emperor of Rome in *Titus Andronicus* who slays Titus at the end.

Scarus. A friend of Antony in *Antony and Cleopatra.*

Seleucus. Cleopatra's treasurer in *Antony and Cleopatra.*

Seyton. Announcer of Lady Macbeth's death in *Macbeth.*

Shadow. Citizen conscripted into the army by Falstaff in 2 *Henry IV.*

Shallow. Justice of the peace who imprudently lends Falstaff a large sum of money in 2 *Henry IV.*

Shylock. The moneylender who demands his "pound of flesh" in *The Merchant of Venice*.

Silence. Shallow's cousin, also a justice of the peace in *2 Henry IV*.

Silvius. Shepherd and lover in the Petrarchan mold, fawns on Phebe in *As You Like It*.

Simonides. King of Pentapolis in *Pericles*.

Simple. Servant whose simplicity is evident in *The Merry Wives of Windsor*.

Siward. An English commander in *Macbeth*. His son, also named Siward, is slain in combat by Macbeth.

Slender. A weakling who hopes to marry Anne Page in *The Merry Wives of Windsor*.

Sly, Christopher. Drunken tinker who falls asleep in the first scene of *The Taming of the Shrew*.

Snare. Police officer in *2 Henry IV*.

Snug the joiner (carpenter). One of the "rude mechanicals" in *A Midsummer Night's Dream*.

Solinus. Duke of Ephesus in *The Comedy of Errors*.

Stephano. Drunkard whom Caliban worships as a god in *The Tempest*. There is also a servant named Stephano in *The Merchant of Venice*.

Tearsheet, Doll. One of the low-life women who consort with Falstaff and his friends in *2 Henry IV*.

Thersites. A cynical, bitingly critical member of the Greek force at Troy in Homer's *Iliad* and in *Troilus and Cressida*.

Theseus. Duke of Athens and fiancé of Hippolyta in *A Midsummer Night's Dream*.

Thurio. Cowardly suitor of Silvia in *The Two Gentlemen of Verona*.

Titania. Wife of Oberon and the fairy queen in *A Midsummer Night's Dream*.

Touchstone. Professional fool who accompanies Rosalind and Celia in the Forest of Arden in *As You Like It*. With him, for the first time, Shakespeare develops the figure of the "wise fool" that he uses later in *Twelfth Night* and *King Lear*.

Tubal. Bringer of good and bad news to Shylock in *The Merchant of Venice*.

Tyrrel. Henchman of Richard III in the murder of the little princes in the Tower of London in *Richard III*.

Valeria. Companion of Coriolanus' wife, Virgilia.

Verges. Along with Dogberry, a constable in *Much Ado About Nothing*.

Vincentio. The name of the Duke in *Measure for Measure*, but it occurs only in the list of characters at the beginning and is never used in the text. Another Vincentio is Lucentio's father in *The Taming of the Shrew*.

Virgilia. Coriolanus' wife, in her quiet and retiring nature a marked contrast to her mother-in-law, the martial Volumnia.

Volumnia. Mother of Coriolanus who inculcated in him the values of military conduct and contempt for the plebeians from his earliest years.

Wolsey, Cardinal. In *Henry VIII*, as in history, the opposer of Henry's marriage to Anne Boleyn.

Worcester. One of the rebels against the king in 1 *Henry IV*.

York, Duke of. Uncle of both Richard and Bolingbroke in *Richard II*. Other Dukes of York appear in *Henry V*, the three parts of *Henry VI*, and *Richard III*.

SOURCES

Beckerman, Bernard. *Shakespeare at the Globe, 1599–1609*. New York: Macmillan, 1962.

Bradley, David. *From Text to Performance in the Elizabethan Theatre*. Cambridge, Eng.: Cambridge University Press, 1992.

Halliday, F. E. *A Shakespeare Companion, 1564–1964*. Harmondsworth, Eng.: Penguin Books, 1964.

Harbage, Alfred. *As They Liked It*. New York: Macmillan, 1947.

———, ed. *William Shakespeare: The Complete Works*. New York: Viking, 1969.

Neilson, William Allen, and Charles Jarvis Hill, eds. *The Complete Plays and Poems of William Shakespeare*. Cambridge, Mass.: Houghton Mifflin Co., 1942.

—J.L.M.

VIII

RADIO, TELEVISION, AND FILM

42

THE MOVIES

. . . . .

IN THE HEYDAY OF HOLLYWOOD, BACK IN THE 1930S, 1940S, AND EARLY
1950s before television came along and changed everything, writing
movie scripts for the big studios was a lucrative way for a successful
playwright or novelist to earn money. The movie moguls, not themselves noted for subtlety of artistic discernment, liked the prestige that
came from importing prestigious literary figures to their studios, sometimes without being themselves familiar with what such authors had
actually written. One story is that Samuel Goldwyn fetched Maurice
Maeterlinck to Hollywood in a private railway car, and then, when the
distinguished Belgian author turned in his first film script, was appalled.
"My God, the hero is a bee!" he cried.

Writing for the movies was and still is a subtly different—and all things
considered, cruder—art than writing for the stage, and greatly different from
writing prose fiction. The film script itself is only one of several elements,
and the story is spoken and shown, not told. Suffice it to say that, as more
than one author who sought to make the change in order to earn the
enhanced revenue discovered, writing film scripts required much adaptation of technique, and to do it well wasn't simply a matter of writing in dialogue without description or exposition.

Scott Fitzgerald's frustration with writing film scripts is well known.
He needed the money he earned in Hollywood very badly, but seemingly he
was never able to master the form. One of his problems doubtless was that
he took it too seriously *as writing*—he yearned to be known as a successful
writer of movies. William Faulkner knew better; prose fiction was what
mattered to him, and as far as he was concerned, working on film scripts
was something he did in order to buy time for writing fiction. The result
was apparently that he was considerably better at it than Fitzgerald. But the
best—and most successful—writers of film scripts were for the most part
authors who mainly did that and nothing much else.

The first motion picture to tell a story was Edwin S. Porter's *The Great*

Train Robbery (1903). By the 1910s, directors and producers were developing lengthy feature films, and in the process were learning to exploit the resources of the camera and to emancipate their new medium from the built-in limitations of stage drama. Fade-ins and fade-outs, juxtapositions, close-ups, panoramas, and other devices, and the fact that scenes and segments could be shot separately and spliced together in sequence, offered new dimensions to visual storytelling.

The movie, recorded on film and duplicated in numerous copies, was shipped to theaters throughout the nation and the world, and the cinema quickly began reaching audiences far larger than had ever been possible to stage drama. The big Hollywood studios spent millions of dollars to produce feature films that appealed to the tastes of a mass audience.

In the late 1920s it became possible to use sound, and with the advent of spoken dialogue and the "talkie" the role of the screenwriter became more important. It was then that the Hollywood studios began hiring well-known authors to produce scripts for screen plays.

Paradoxically, it was the advent of television in the 1950s and 1960s, which by bringing film entertainment into the home expanded the demand and broadened the mass audience beyond anything known before, that resulted in the enhancement of film as a serious art form. For by ending the dominance of the Hollywood commercial movie industry in theaters, it made possible greater specialization, and movies that were shaped to the interests of smaller but more sophisticated audiences and shown in small theaters could now be produced.

The following is a sampling of representative movies from across the span of cinema history. It includes classics, modern masterpieces, cult favorites, comedies, musicals, high drama, horror, westerns, sleepers, foreign films: what was popular at the box office, on late-night TV reruns or at college film festivals, and on videocassette—more than three hundred famous films with dates, directors, and principal actors.

Abbott and Costello Meet Frankenstein (1948). Charles Barton, dir.; Bud Abbott, Lou Costello, Lon Chaney, Bela Lugosi.

Ace Hugh (1918). Lynn Reynolds, dir.; Tom Mix, Lloyd Perl, Lewis Sargent, Kathleen Connors.

Adventures of Baron Munchausen, The (1990). Terry Gilliam, dir.; John Neville, Robin Williams.

Adventures of Priscilla, Queen of the Desert (1994). Stephen Elliott, dir.; Terence Stamp, Hugo Weaving, Guy Pearce.

Advise and Consent (1962). Otto Preminger, dir.; Henry Fonda, Walter Pidgeon, Charles Laughton, Don Murray, Franchot Tone.

African Queen, The (1951). John Huston, dir.; Humphrey Bogart, Katharine Hepburn.

Agony and the Ecstasy, The (1965). Carol Reed, dir.; Charlton Heston, Rex Harrison.

Alfie (1966). Lewis Gilbert, dir.; Michael Caine, Shelley Winters, Millicent Martin.

Algiers (1938). John Cromwell, dir.; Charles Boyer, Hedy Lamarr.

Alice Doesn't Live Here Anymore (1974). Martin Scorsese, dir.; Ellen Burstyn, Kris Kristofferson, Diane Ladd, Harvey Keitel.

All About Eve (1950). Joseph L. Mankiewicz, dir.; Bette Davis, Anne Baxter, Marilyn Monroe.

All My Sons (1950). Irving Reis, dir.; Edward G. Robinson, Burt Lancaster.

All Quiet on the Western Front (1930). Lewis Milestone, dir.; Lew Ayres, Louis Wolheim.

All the President's Men (1976). Alan J. Pakula, dir.; Dustin Hoffman, Robert Redford, Jason Robards, Jr.

Amadeus (1984). Milos Forman, dir.; Tom Hulce, F. Murray Abraham, Elizabeth Berridge.

Amarcord (1974). Federico Fellini, dir.; Magali Noel, Bruno Zanin, Pupella Maggio.

American in Paris, An (1951). Vincente Minnelli, dir.; Gene Kelly, Leslie Caron.

Angel at My Table, An (1991). Jane Campion, dir.; Kerry Fox, Alexia Keogh, Karen Fergusson.

Anastasia (1956). Anatole Litvak, dir.; Ingrid Bergman, Yul Brynner, Helen Hayes.

Andrei Rublev (1966). Andrei Tarkovsky, dir.; Andrej Mikhalkov, Andrei Tarkovsky.

And Then There Were None (1945). René Clair, dir.; Barry Fitzgerald, Walter Huston.

Angels with Dirty Faces (1938). Michael Curtiz, dir.; James Cagney, Pat O'Brien, Humphrey Bogart, Ann Sheridan.

Animal Crackers (1930). Victor Heerman, dir.; Groucho, Chico, and Harpo Marx, Margaret Dumont.

Anne of Green Gables (1919). William D. Taylor, dir.; Mary Miles Minter, Paul Kelly, Marcia Harris, Frederick Burton.

Annie Hall (1977). Woody Allen, dir.; Woody Allen, Diane Keaton, Tony Roberts.

Apartment, The (1960). Billy Wilder, dir.; Jack Lemmon, Shirley MacLaine, Fred MacMurray.

Apocalypse Now (1979). Francis Ford Coppola, dir.; Marlon Brando, Robert Duvall, Martin Sheen.

Apollo 13 (1995). Ron Howard. dir.; Tom Hanks, Kevin Bacon, Bill Paxton.

Arsenic and Old Lace (1944). Frank Capra, dir.; Cary Grant, Raymond Massey, Peter Lorre, Josephine Hull.

Asphalt Jungle, The (1950). John Huston, dir.; Sterling Hayden, Louis Calhern, Sam Jaffé.

Auntie Mame (1958). Morton DaCosta, dir.; Rosalind Russell, Peggy Cass, Coral Browne.

Au Revoir, Les Enfants (1987). Louis Malle, dir.; Gaspard Manesse, Raphael Fejto, Francine Racette.

Autumn Sonata (1978). Ingmar Bergman, dir.; Ingrid Bergman, Liv Ullmann, Lena Nyman.

Bad Seed, The (1956). Mervyn Leroy, dir.; Nancy Kelly, Patty MacCormack, Eileen Heckart, Henry Jones.

Bank Dick, The (1940). Eddie Cline, dir.; W. C. Fields, Cora Witherspoon, Una Merkel, Shemp Howard.

Barcelona (1994). Whit Stillman, dir.; Taylor Nichols, Christopher Eigeman, Tushka Bergen.

Barefoot Contessa, The (1954). Joseph Mankiewicz, dir.; Humphrey Bogart, Ava Gardner, Edmond O'Brien.

Barefoot in the Park (1967). Gene Saks, dir.; Robert Redford, Jane Fonda, Charles Boyer, Mildred Natwick.

Basic Instinct (1992). Paul Verhoeven, dir.; Michael Douglas, Sharon Stone, Jeanne Triplehorn.

Batman (1990). Tim Burton, dir.; Michael Keaton, Jack Nicholson.

Battleship Potemkin, The (1925). Sergei Eisenstein, dir.; Alexander Antonov, Vladimir Barsky.

Beat the Devil (1954). John Huston, dir.; Humphrey Bogart, Jennifer Jones, Robert Morley, Peter Lorre.

Beau Geste (1939). William Wellman, dir.; Gary Cooper, Ray Milland, Robert Preston, Brian Donlevy.

Beauty and the Beast (1946). Jean Cocteau, dir.; Josette Day, Jean Marais.

Bella Donna (1923). George Fitzmaurice, dir.; Pola Negri, Conway Tearle, Conrad Nagel, Adolphe Menjou.

Bells of St. Mary's, The (1945). Leo McCarey, dir.; Bing Crosby, Ingrid Bergman.

Beloved Rogue (1927). Alan Crosland, dir.; John Barrymore, Conrad Veldt.

Ben-Hur (1959). William Wyler, dir.; Charlton Heston, Jack Hawkins, Sam Jaffé.

Best Years of Our Lives, The (1946). William Wyler, dir.; Myrna Loy, Fredric March, Dana Andrews, Harold Russell.

Betrayal (1983). David Jones, dir.; Jeremy Irons, Ben Kingsley, Patricia Hodge.

Beverly Hills Cop (1985). Martin Brest, dir.; Eddie Murphy, Judge Reinhold.

Big Parade, The (1925). King Vidor, dir.; John Gilbert, Renée Adorée, Hobart Bosworth.

Big Sleep, The (1946). Howard Hawks, dir.; Humphrey Bogart, Lauren Bacall.

Birgit Haas Must Be Killed (1981). Laurent Heynemann, dir.; Philippe Noiret, Jean Rochefort.

Birth of a Nation (1915). D. W. Griffith, dir.; Henry Walthall, Mae Marsh, Miriam Cooper, Tom Wilson.

Black Stallion, The (1979). Carroll Ballard, dir.; Kelly Reno, Mickey Rooney, Teri Garr.

Black Venus (1983). Claude Mulot, dir.; Josephine Jacquelline Jones, Emiliano Redondo.

Blade Runner (1982). Ridley Scott, dir.; Harrison Ford, Rutger Hauer, Daryl Hannah.

Blazing Saddles (1974). Mel Brooks, dir.; Cleavon Little, Gene Wilder, Mel Brooks, Madeline Kahn, Harvey Korman.

Blow-Up (1966). Michaelangelo Antonioni, dir.; Vanessa Redgrave, David Hemmings, Sarah Miles.

Blue Angel, The (1930). Josef von Sternberg, dir.; Emil Jannings, Marlene Dietrich, Kurt Gerron.

Blue Hawaii (1961). Norman Taurog, dir.; Elvis Presley, Joan Blakman, Nancy Walters, Roland Winter, Angela Lansbury, John Archer, Howard McNeer.

Blue Velvet (1986). David Lynch, dir.; Isabella Rossellini, Dennis Hopper, Laura Dern.

Bob and Carol and Ted and Alice (1969). Paul Mazursky, dir.; Robert Culp, Natalie Wood, Elliott Gould, Dyan Cannon.

Bob le Flambeur (1955). Jean-Pierre Melville, dir.; Roger Duchesne, Isabel Corey, Daniel Cauchy, Howard Vernon.

Body and Soul (1947). Robert Rossen, dir.; John Garfield, Lilli Palmer, Hazel Brooks.

Body Heat (1981). Lawrence Kasdan, dir.; William Hurt, Kathleen Turner.

Bonnie and Clyde (1967). Arthur Penn, dir.; Warren Beatty, Faye Dunaway, Gene Hackman.

Born Yesterday (1950). George Cukor, dir.; Judy Holliday, Broderick Crawford, William Holden.

Boudou Saved from Drowning (1932). Jean Renoir, dir.; Michel Simon, Charles Granval, Max Dalban, Jean Dasté.

Boys Town (1938). Norman Taurog, dir.; Spencer Tracy, Mickey Rooney.

Braveheart (1995), Mel Gibson, dir.; Mel Gibson, Sophie Marceau, Patrick McGoohan, Catherine McCormack.

Breakfast at Tiffany's (1961). Blake Edwards, dir.; Audrey Hepburn, George Peppard, Patricia Neal.

Breaking Away (1979). Peter Yates, dir.; Dennis Christopher, Dennis Quaid, Daniel Stern, Jackie Earle Haley.

Breathless (1959). Jean-Luc Godard, dir.; Jean-Paul Belmondo, Jean Seberg.

Bride of Frankenstein (1935). James Whale, dir.; Boris Karloff, Colin Clive, Elsa Lanchester.

Bridge on the River Kwai, The (1957). David Lean, dir.; William Holden, Alec Guinness, Jack Hawkins, Sessue Hayakawa, James Donald.

Bull Durham (1989). Ron Shelton, dir.; Susan Sarandon, Kevin Costner, Tim Robbins.

Burden of Dreams (1983). Les Blank, dir.; Werner Herzog, Klaus Kinski, Mick Jagger, Jason Robards, Jr., Claudia Cardinale.

Butch Cassidy and the Sundance Kid (1969). George Roy Hill, dir.; Paul Newman, Robert Redford, Katharine Ross.

Cabaret (1972). Bob Fosse, dir.; Liza Minnelli, Michael York, Joel Grey.

Caine Mutiny, The (1954). Edward Dmytryk, dir.; Humphrey Bogart, José Ferrer, Van Johnson, Fred MacMurray.

Call Me Madam (1953). Walter Lang, dir.; Ethel Merman, Donald O'Connor, George Sanders, Vera-Ellen.

Camille (1936). George Cukor, dir.; Greta Garbo, Robert Taylor, Lionel Barrymore.

Captains Courageous (1937). Victor Fleming, dir.; Spencer Tracy, Freddie Bartholomew, Lionel Barrymore, Melvyn Douglas, Mickey Rooney.

Carousel (1956). Henry King, dir.; Gordon MacRae, Shirley Jones, Gene Lockhart, Cameron Mitchell.

Casablanca (1942). Michael Curtiz, dir.; Humphrey Bogart, Ingrid Bergman, Claude Rains.

Catch-22 (1970). Mike Nichols, dir.; Alan Arkin, Martin Balsam, Richard Benjamin, Arthur Garfunkel, Jack Gilford, Orson Welles.

Cat on a Hot Tin Roof (1958). Richard Brooks, dir.; Elizabeth Taylor, Paul Newman, Burl Ives, Jack Carson, Judith Anderson.

Champion (1949). Mark Robson, dir.; Kirk Douglas, Arthur Kennedy, Marilyn Maxwell, Paul Stewart.

Chariots of Fire (1981). Hugh Hudson, dir.; Ben Cross, Ian Charleson, Nigel Havers, Nicholas Farrell, Alice Krigel.

Chikamatsu Monogatari (1954). Kenji Mizoguchi, dir.; Kazuo Hasegawa, Kyoko Kagawa.

Children of a Lesser God (1986). Randa Haines, dir.; William Hurt, Marlee Matlin, Piper Laurie, Philip Bosco.

Children of Paradise, The (1944). Marcel Carne, dir.; Jean-Louis Barrault.

Chinatown (1974). Roman Polanski, dir.; Jack Nicholson, Faye Dunaway, John Huston.

Christmas Carol, A (1951). Brian Desmond Hurst, dir.; Alastair Sim, Kathleen Harrison, Jack Warner, Michael Hoerdern.

Citizen Kane (1941). Orson Welles, dir.; Orson Welles, Joseph Cotten, Everett Sloane, Agnes Moorhead.

City Lights (1931). Charles Chaplin, dir.; Charlie Chaplin, Virginia Cherrill, Harry Myers, Hank Mann.

Claire's Knee (1971). Eric Rohmer, dir.; Jean-Claude Brialy, Aurora Cornu, Beatrice Romand.

Cleopatra (1963). Joseph Mankiewicz, dir.; Elizabeth Taylor, Richard Burton, Rex Harrison.

Cocoanuts, The (1929). Robert Florey and Joseph Santley, dirs.; Groucho, Chico, Harpo, and Zeppo Marx, Margaret Dumont.

Color Purple, The (1985). Steven Spielberg, dir.; Whoopi Goldberg, Danny Glover, Adolph Caesar, Margaret Avery, Oprah Winfrey.

Come Back, Little Sheba (1952). Daniel Mann, dir.; Burt Lancaster, Shirley Booth.

Conversation, The (1974). Francis Ford Coppola, dir.; Gene Hackman, John Cazale, Allen Garfield, Cindy Williams, Harrison Ford.

Cool Hand Luke (1967). Stuart Rosenberg, dir.; Paul Newman, George Kennedy, J. D. Cannon, Lou Antonio.

Cops (1922). Buster Keaton, dir.; Buster Keaton, Virginia Fox, Joe Roberts.

Covered Wagon, The (1923). James Cruze, dir.; Lois Wilson, J. W. Kerrigan, Ethel Wales, Alan Hale.

Cries and Whispers (1972). Ingmar Bergman, dir.; Harriet Andersson, Liv Ullmann, Ingrid Ghulin, Kari Sylwan.

Crimes and Misdemeanors (1989). Woody Allen, dir.; Martin Landau, Woody Allen, Alan Alda, Mia Farrow, Angelica Huston.

Crocodile Dundee (1987). Peter Faiman, dir.; Paul Hogan, Linda Kozlowski.

Cross My Heart (1991). Jacques Fansten, dir.; Sylvain Copans, Nicolas Marodi, Cecilia Rovaud.

Crying Game, The (1992). Neil Jordan, dir.; Forest Whitaker, Miranda Richardson, Stephen Rea.

Cyrano de Bergerac (1991). Jean-Paul Rappeneau, dir.; Gerard Depardieu, Anne Brochet, Vincent Perez, Jacques Weber.

Dances with Wolves (1990). Kevin Costner, dir.; Kevin Costner, Mary McDownnell, Graham Greene, Rodney A. Grant.

Dark Victory (1939). Edmund Goulding, dir.; Bette Davis, George Brent, Humphrey Bogart, Geraldine Fitzgerald, Ronald Reagan.

Das Boot (1982). Wolfgang Petersen, dir.; Jurgen Prochnow, Herbert Gronemeyer.

Day at the Races, A (1937). Sam Wood, dir.; Groucho, Chico, and Harpo Marx, Allan Jones, Maureen O'Sullivan.

Day for Night (1973). François Truffaut, dir.; Jacqueline Bisset, Jean-Pierre Léaud, François Truffaut.

Days of Heaven (1978). Terrence Malick, dir.; Richard Gere, Brooke Adams, Sam Shepard, Linda Mans.

Dead, The (1987). John Huston, dir.; Angelica Huston, Donald McCann, Ingrid Craigie, Dan O'Herlihy.

Dead Man Walking (1995). Tim Robbins, dir.; Susan Sarandon, Sean Penn.

Dead Poets Society, The (1990). Peter Weir, dir.; Robin Williams.

Death of a Salesman (1951). Laslo Benedek, dir.; Fredric March, Mildred Dunnock, Kevin McCarthy, Cameron Mitchell.

Deer Hunter, The (1978). Michael Cimino, dir.; Robert De Niro, John Cazale, John Savage, Meryl Streep, Christopher Walken.

Deliverance (1972). Jon Boorman, dir.; Jon Voight, Burt Reynolds, Ned Beatty, Ronny Cox.

Detective Story (1951). William Wyler, dir.; Kirk Douglas, Eleanor Parker, William Bendix.

Dial M for Murder (1954). Alfred Hitchcock, dir.; Ray Milland, Grace Kelly, Robert Cummings, John Williams.

Dinner at Eight (1933). George Cukor, dir.; John Barrymore, Jean Harlow, Marie Dressler, Billie Burke, Wallace Beery.

Dirty Dancing (1987). Emile Ardolino, dir.; Jennifer Grey, Patrick Swayze, Jerry Orbach, Cynthia Rhodes, Jack Weston.

Dirty Dozen, The (1967). Robert Aldrich, dir.; Lee Marvin, Ernest Borgnine, Charles Bronson, Jim Brown, John Cassavetes, George Kennedy, Donald Sutherland, Robert Ryan.

Dirty Harry (1971). Don Siegel, dir.; Clint Eastwood, Harry Guardino, Reni Santoni.

Distant Voices/Still Lives (1988). Terence Davies, dir.; Freda Dowie, Pete Postlethwaite, Angela Walsh, Dean Williams.

Dr. No (1962). Terence Young, dir.; Sean Connery, Ursula Andress, Jack Lord, Joseph Wiseman.

Dr. Strangelove, or How I Learned to Stop Worrying and Love the Bomb (1964). Stanley Kubrick, dir.; Peter Sellers, Sterling Hayden, George C. Scott, Slim Pickens.

Doctor Zhivago (1965). David Lean, dir.; Omar Sharif, Rod Steiger, Tom Courtenay, Geraldine Chaplin, Julie Christie, Alec Guinness.

Don Quixote (1988). Marius Pettipa, Alexander Gorsky, dirs.; Kirov Ballet.

Double Indemnity (1944). Billy Wilder, dir.; Fred MacMurray, Barbara Stanwyck, Edward G. Robinson, Porter Hall.

Dracula (1931). Tod Browning, dir.; Bela Lugosi.

Dresser, The (1983). Peter Yates, dir.; Albert Finney, Tom Courtenay, Edward Fox, Zena Walker.

Drifting Weeds (1959). Yasujiro Ozu, dir.; Ganjiro Nakamura, Machiko Kyo.

Driving Miss Daisy (1989). Bruce Beresford, dir.; Morgan Freeman, Jessica Tandy.

Duck Soup (1933). Leo McCarey, dir.; Groucho, Chico, Harpo, and Zeppo Marx, Margaret Dumont.

Duel in the Sun (1946). King Vidor, dir.; Jennifer Jones, Joseph Cotten, Gergory Peck, Lionel Barrymore, Walter Huston.

East of Eden (1955). Elia Kazan, dir.; James Dean, Jo Van Fleet, Julie Harris, Raymond Massey, Burl Ives.

Easy Rider (1969). Dennis Hopper, dir.; Peter Fonda, Dennis Hopper, Jack Nicholson.

8 ½ (1963). Federico Fellini, dir.; Marcello Mastroianni, Anouk Aimée, Claudia Cardinale, Barbara Steele, Sandra Milo.

El Norte (1983). Gregory Nava, dir.; Zaide Silvia Gutierrez, David Vilalpando.

Entre Nous (Between Us) (1983). Diane Kurys, dir.; Miou-Miou, Isabelle Huppert, Guy Marchand.

E.T. the Extra-Terrestrial (1983). Steven Spielberg, dir.; Henry Thomas, Drew Barrymore, Peter Coyote.

Exodus (1960). Otto Preminger, dir.; Paul Newman, Eva Marie Saint, Ralph Richardson, Peter Lawford, Lee J. Cobb, Sal Mineo.

Exorcist, The (1973). William Friedkin, dir.; Ellen Burstyn, Linda Blair, Jason Miller, Lee J. Cobb, Max von Sydow.

Experience Preferred . . . But Not Essential (1983). Peter Duffell, dir.; Elizabeth Edmonds, Sue Wallace, Gerraldine Griffith, Karen Meagher.

Exterminating Angel, The (1962). Luis Buñuel, dir.; Silvia Pinal, Enrique Rambal.

Fanny and Alexander (1983). Ingmar Bergman, dir.; Pernilla Allwin, Bertil Guve.

Fantasia (1940). Walt Disney animation.

Farewell to Arms, A (1932). Frank Borzage, dir.; Helen Hayes, Gary Cooper.

Faust (1926). F. W. Murnau, dir.; Emil Jannings, Gosta Ekman, Camilla Horn.

Field of Dreams (1989). Phil Alden Robinson, dir.; Kevin Costner, Amy Madigan, James Earl Jones, Burt Lancaster, Ray Liotta.

Fish Called Wanda, A (1988). Charles Crichton, dir.; Jamie Lee Curtis, Kevin Kline, John Cleese.

Five Heartbeats, The (1991). Robert Townsend, dir.; Robert Townsend, Michael Wright, Leon, Harry J. Lennix, Tico Wells, Diahann Carroll, Harold Nicholas.

Forbidden Games (1951). René Clement, dir.; Brigitte Fossey, Georges Poujouly.

Foreign Correspondent (1940). Alfred Hitchcock, dir.; Joel McCrea, Laraine Day, Herbert Marshall, George Sanders, Edmund Gwenn.

Forrest Gump (1994). Robert Zemeckis, dir.; Tom Hanks, Gary Sinise, Robin Wright, Sally Field.

Four Horsemen of the Apocalypse, The (1921). Rex Ingram, dir.; Rudolph Valentino, Alice Terry, Pomeroy Cannon, Joseph Swickard.

400 Blows (1959). François Truffaut, dir.; Jean-Pierre Léaud, Patrick Auffay, Claire Maurier, Albert Rémy.

Four Weddings and a Funeral (1994). Mike Newell, dir.; Hugh Grant, Andie MacDowell, Simon Callow.

Frankenstein (1931). James Whale, dir.; Colin Clive, Mae Clarke, Boris Karloff.

French Connection, The (1971). William Friedkin, dir.; Gene Hackman, Fernando Rey, Roy Scheider, Edie Egan, Sonny Gross.

French Lieutenant's Woman, The (1981). Karel Reisz, dir.; Meryl Streep, Jeremy Irons, Leo McKern.

Fritz the Cat (1971). Ralph Bakshi, dir. and animation; from the cartoon strip by R. Crumb.

From Here to Eternity (1953). Fred Zinnemann, dir.; Burt Lancaster, Montgomery Clift, Deborah Kerr, Frank Sinatra, Donna Reed, Ernest Borgnine.

Funny Face (1957). Stanley Donen, dir.; Audrey Hepburn, Fred Astaire.

Funny Girl (1968). William Wyler, dir.; Barbra Streisand, Omar Sharif, Walter Pidgeon, Kay Melford.

Funny Thing Happened on the Way to the Forum, A (1966). Richard Lester, dir.; Zero Mostel, Phil Silvers, Jack Gilford.

Gandhi (1982). Richard Attenborough, dir.; Ben Kingsley, Candice Bergen, Edward Fox, John Gielgud, Martin Sheen, John Mills.

General, The (1927). Buster Keaton, dir.; Buster Keaton, Marion Mack, Glen Cavender, Jim Farley, Joseph Keaton.

Gentlemen Prefer Blondes (1953). Howard Hawks, dir.; Jane Russell, Marilyn Monroe, Charles Coburn.

Georgy Girl (1966). Silvio Narizzano, dir.; James Mason, Lynn Redgrave, Charlotte Rampling, Alan Bates.

Get Shorty (1995). Barry Sonnenfeld, dir.; John Travolta, Gene Hackman, René Russo.

Ghostbusters (1985). Ivan Reitman, dir.; Bill Murray, Dan Aykroyd, Sigourney Weaver, Harold Ramis, Rick Moranis.

Gigi (1958). Vincente Minnelli, dir.; Leslie Caron, Maurice Chevalier, Louis Jourdan, Hermione Gingold.

Glass Menagerie, The (1988). Paul Newman, dir.; Joanne Woodward, John Malkovich, Karen Allen.

Glory (1989). Edward Zwick, dir.; Matthew Broderick, Denzel Washington, Cary Elwes, Morgan Freeman.

Godfather, The (1972), *The Godfather, Part II* (1974), *The Godfather, Part III* (1990). Francis Ford Coppola, dir.; Marlon Brando, Al Pacino, Diane Keaton, Robert Duvall.

Gods Must Be Crazy, The (1980). Jamie Uys, dir.; Nixau, Marius Meyers, Sandra Prinsloo.

Godzilla (1955). Inoshiro Honda, dir.; Raymond Burr, Takashi Shimura, Momoko Kochi.

Going My Way (1944). Leo McCarey, dir.; Bing Crosby, Rise Stevens, Barry Fitzgerald.

Golden Boy (1939). Rouben Mamoulian, dir.; William Holden, Barbara Stanwyck.

Goldfinger (1964). Guy Hamilton, dir.; Sean Connery, Gert Frobe, Honor Blackman.

Gold Rush, The (1925). Charles Chaplin, dir.; Charlie Chaplin, Mack Swain, Georgia Hale.

Gone With the Wind (1939). Victor Fleming, dir.; Clark Gable, Vivien Leigh, Leslie Howard, Olivia de Havilland, Thomas Mitchell, Hattie McDaniel.

Goodbye, Mr. Chips (1939). Sam Wood, dir.; Robert Donat, Greer Garson.

Good, the Bad, and the Ugly, The (1966). Sergio Leone, dir.; Clint Eastwood, Eli Wallach, Lee Van Cleef.

Graduate, The (1967). Mike Nichols, dir.; Dustin Hoffman, Anne Bancroft, Katharine Ross, William Daniels, Murray Hamilton.

Grand Illusion (1937). Jean Renoir, dir.; Jean Gabin, Pierre Fesnay, Erich von Stroheim.

Grapes of Wrath, The (1940). John Ford, dir.; Henry Fonda, John Carradine, Jane Darwell, Russell Simpson.

Grease (1978). Randal Kleiser, dir.; John Travolta, Olivia Newton-John, Stockard Channing, Eve Arden, Frankie Avalon, Joan Blondell, Edd Byrnes, Sid Caesar, Alice Ghostley, Sha Na Na.

Great Dictator, The (1940). Charles Chaplin, dir.; Charlie Chaplin, Jack Oakie, Paulette Goddard.

Greed (1924). Erich von Stroheim, dir.; Gibson Gowland, ZaSu Pitts, Jean Hersholt.

Grey Fox, The (1982). Phillip Borsos, dir.; Richard Farnsworth, Jackie Burroughs, Ken Pogue, Timothy Webber.

Guess Who's Coming to Dinner (1967). Stanley Kramer, dir.; Spencer Tracy, Katharine Hepburn, Sidney Poitier.

Gunfight at the O.K. Corral (1957). John Sturges, dir.; Burt Lancaster, Kirk Douglas, Rhonda Fleming.

Gunfighter, The (1950). Henry King, dir.; Gregory Peck, Helen Westcott, Millard Mitchell, Skip Homeier, Jean Parker, Karl Malden.

Gunga Din (1939). George Stevens, dir.; Cary Grant, Victor McLaglen, Douglas Fairbanks, Jr., Sam Jaffé, Joan Fontaine.

Guys and Dolls (1955). Joseph L. Mankiewicz, dir.; Marlon Brando, Jean Simmons, Frank Sinatra, Vivian Blaine.

Hamlet (1948). Laurence Olivier, dir.; Laurence Olivier, Basil Sydney, Eileen Herlie, Jean Simmons.

Hannah and Her Sisters (1986). Woody Allen, dir.; Woody Allen, Michael Caine, Mia Farrow, Carrie Fisher, Barbara Hershey, Maureen O'Sullivan, Dianne Wiest.

Hard Day's Night, A (1964). Richard Lester, dir.; the Beatles, Wilfrid Bramble, Norman Rossington, Victor Spinetti.

Harold and Maude (1971). Hal Ashby, dir.; Bud Cort, Vivian Pickles, Ruth Gordon, Cyril Cusack.

Harry and Tonto (1974). Paul Mazursky, dir.; Art Carney, Ellen Burstyn.

Harvey (1950). Henry Koster, dir.; James Stewart, Josephine Hull.

Hellzapoppin (1942). H. C. Potter, dir.; Ole Olsen, Chic Johnson, Hugh Herbert, Martha Raye.

Help! (1965). Dick Lester, dir.; the Beatles, Leo McKern, Eleanor Bron, Victor Spinetti.

Henry V (1944). Laurence Olivier, dir.; Laurence Olivier, Robert Newton, Leslie Banks, Felix Aylmer.

Henry V (1989). Kenneth Branagh, dir.; Kenneth Branagh, Derek Jacobi, Emma Thompson, Michael Maloney, Paul Schofield, Judi Dench, Ian Holm.

Here Comes Mr. Jordan (1941). Alexander Hall, dir.; Robert Montgomery, Evelyn Keyes, Claude Rains.

High and Low (1963). Akira Kurosawa, dir.; Toshiro Mifune, Tatsuya Nakadai, Tatsuya Mihashi.

Highest Honor, The (1984). Peter Maxwell, dir.; John Howard, Atsuo Nakamura, Stuart Wilson.

High Hopes (1989). Mike Leigh, dir.; Ruth Sheen, Philip Davis.

High Noon (1952). Fred Zinnemann, dir.; Gary Cooper, Grace Kelly, Lloyd Bridges.

His Girl Friday (1940). Howard Hawks, dir.; Cary Grant, Rosalind Russell, Ralph Bellamy, Gene Lockhart.

History of the World—Part I (1981). Mel Brooks, dir.; Mel Brooks, Dom de Luise, Madeline Kahn, Cloris Leachman.

Hobson's Choice (1954). David Lean, dir.; Charles Laughton, John Mills, Brenda de Banzie, Daphne Anderson.

Home and the World (1984). Satyajit Ray, dir.; Soumitra Chatterjee, Victor Banerjee.

Horse Feathers (1932). Norman Z. McLeod, dir.; Groucho, Chico, Harpo, and Zeppo Marx, Thelma Todd, David Landau.

Howards End (1992). James Ivory, dir.; Vanessa Redgrave, Anthony Hopkins, Emma Thompson, Sam Wert, Helena Bonham-Carter, Nicola Duffet.

How Green Was My Valley (1941). John Ford, dir.; Walter Pidgeon, Maureen O'Hara, Roddy McDowall.

How to Succeed in Business Without Really Trying (1967). David Swift, dir.; Robert Morse, Rudy Vallee, Michele Lee, Anthony Teague.

Hud (1963). Martin Ritt, dir.; Paul Newman, Patricia Neal, Melvyn Douglas, Brandon de Wilde.

Hustler, The (1961). Robert Rossen, dir.; Paul Newman, Jackie Gleason, Piper Laurie, George C. Scott.

I Am a Fugitive from a Chain Gang (1932). Mervyn Leroy, dir.; Paul Muni, Glenda Farrell.

In Cold Blood (1967). Richard Brooks, dir.; Robert Blake, Scott Wilson, John Forsythe, Jeff Corey.

Inherit the Wind (1960). Stanley Kramer, dir.; Spencer Tracy, Fredric March, Gene Kelly, Dick York, Claude Akins.

In the Heat of the Night (1967). Norman Jewison, dir.; Sidney Poitier, Rod Steiger, Lee Grant.

Intolerance (1916). D. W. Griffith, dir.; Mae Marsh, Robert Harron, Fred Turner, Lillian Gish.

In Which We Serve (1942). Noel Coward, David Lean, dirs.; Noel Coward, John Mills.

Iphigenia (1978). Michael Cacoyannis, dir.; Irene Pappas.

It Happened One Night (1934). Frank Capra, dir.; Clark Gable, Claudette Colbert, Ward Bond.

It's a Gift (1934). Norman Z. McLeod, dir.; W. C. Fields, Kathleen Howard, Baby LeRoy.

Ivan the Terrible, Part I and Part II (1945). Sergei Eisenstein, dir.; Nikolai Cherkassov, Ludmila Tselikovskaya.

Jailhouse Rock (1957). Richard Thorpe, dir.; Elvis Presley, Judy Tyler, Micky Shaughnessy, Vaughn Taylor, Dean Jones.

Jane Eyre (1944). Robert Stevenson, dir.; Joan Fontaine, Orson Welles.

Jaws (1975). Steven Spielberg, dir.; Roy Scheider, Robert Shaw, Richard Dreyfuss.

Jazz Singer, The (1927). Alan Crosland, dir.; Al Jolson, Warner Oland, Eugene Besserer, William Demarest.

Jean de Florette (1987). Claude Berri, dir.; Yves Montand, Gérard Depardieu, Daniel Auterril.

Jezebel (1938). William Wyler, dir.; Bette Davis, Henry Fonda.

Ju Dou (1990). Zhang Yimou, dir.; Gong Li, Li Baotian.

Jules and Jim (1961). François Truffaut, dir.; Oskar Werner, Jeanne Moreau, Henri Serre.

Julia (1977). Fred Zinnemann, dir.; Jane Fonda, Vanessa Redgrave, Jason Robards, Maximilian Schell.

Juliette of the Spirits (1965). Federico Fellini, dir.; Giulietta Masina, Sandra Milo, Sylvia Koscina.

Jurassic Park (1993). Steven Spielberg, dir.; Sam Neill, Laura Dern, Jeff Goldblum, Richard Attenborough.

Key Largo (1948). John Huston, dir.; Humphrey Bogart, Lauren Bacall, Edward G. Robinson, Lionel Barrymore.

Killing Fields, The (1984). Roland Joffé, dir.; Sam Waterson, Haing S. Ngor, John Malkovich, Julian Sands, Craig T. Nelson.

Kind Hearts and Coronets (1949). Robert Hamer, dir.; Alec Guinness, Dennis Price, Valerie Hobson, Joan Greenwood.

King and I, The (1956). Walter Lang, dir.; Yul Brynner, Deborah Kerr.

King Kong (1933). Merian C. Cooper, Ernest B. Schoedsack, dirs.; Robert Armstrong, Fay Wray, Bruce Cabot, Frank Reicher, Noble Johnson.

King's Row (1941). Sam Wood, dir.; Ann Sheridan, Robert Cummings, Ronald Reagan, Claude Rains.

Kiss of Death (1947). Henry Hathaway, dir.; Victor Mature, Richard Widmark, Brian Donleavy.

Klute (1971). Alan Pakula, dir.; Jane Fonda, Donald Sutherland.

Lady Vanishes, The (1938). Alfred Hitchcock, dir.; Margaret Lockwood, Michael Redgrave, May Whitty.

Last Emperor, The (1987). Bernardo Bertolucci, dir.; John Lone, Peter O'Toole, Joan Chen, Ying Ruocheng, Victor Wong, Dennis Dun.

Last Picture Show, The (1971). Peter Bogdanovich, dir.; Timothy Bottoms, Ben Johnson, Jeff Bridges, Cloris Leachman, Cybill Shepherd, Randy Quaid.

Last Seduction, The (1995). John Dahl, dir.; Linda Fiorentino, Peter Berg, Bill Pullman.

Last Tango in Paris (1972). Bernardo Bertolucci, dir.; Marlon Brando, Maria Schneider, Jean-Pierre Léaud.

La Strada (1954). Federico Fellini, dir.; Giulietta Masina, Anthony Quinn, Richard Basehart.

Late Spring (1949). Yasujiro Ozu, dir.; Setsuo Hara, Chishu Ryu.

Laura (1944). Otto Preminger, dir.; Gene Tierney, Dana Andrews, Vincent Price, Judith Anderson, Clifton Webb.

Lavender Hill Mob, The (1951). Charles Crichton, dir.; Alec Guinness, Stanley Holloway, Sidney James, Alfie Bass.

Lawrence of Arabia (1962). David Lean, dir.; Peter O'Toole, Alec Guinness, Anthony Quinn, Arthur Kennedy, Omar Sharif.

Libeled Lady (1936). Jack Conway, dir.; William Powell, Myrna Loy, Spencer Tracy, Jean Harlow.

Life and Death of Colonel Blimp, The (1943). Michael Powell, Emeric Pressburger, dirs.; Roger Livesey, Deborah Kerr, Anton Walbrook.

Life and Nothing But (1989). Bertrand Tavernier, dir.; Philippe Noiret, Sabine Azema.

Lifeboat (1944). Alfred Hitchcock, dir.; Tallulah Bankhead, William Bendix, Walter Slezak, Hume Cronyn, John Hodiak.

Lion King, The (1994). Roger Allers, dir.; voices of Jonathan Taylor Thomas, Matthew Broderick, James Earl Jones, Moira Kelly (Walt Disney animation).

Little Dorrit (1988). Christine Edzard, dir.; Alec Guinness, Derek Jacobi, Sarah Pickering, Joan Greenwood, Roshan Seth.

Lola Montes (1955). Max Ophuls, dir.; Maxine Carola, Peter Ustinov, Anton Walbrook.

Lolita (1962). Stanley Kubrick, dir.; James Mason, Sue Lyon, Shelley Winters, Peter Sellers.

Long Day's Journey into Night (1962). Sidney Lumet, dir.; Katharine Hepburn, Ralph Richardson, Jason Robards, Jr., Dean Stockwell.

Longest Day, The (1963). Ken Annakin and Andrew Morton, dirs.; John Wayne, Robert Mitchum, Henry Fonda, Richard Burton, Rod Steiger, Sean Connery.

Long Good Friday, The (1980). John Mackenzie, dir.; Bob Hoskins, Helen Mirren, Pierce Brosnan.

Long, Hot Summer, The (1958). Martin Ritt, dir.; Paul Newman, Joanne Woodward, Orson Welles.

Los Olvidados (1950). Luis Buñuel, dir.; Alfonso Meija, Roberto Cobo.

Lost Horizon (1937). Frank Capra, dir.; Ronald Colman, Jane Wyatt, Thomas Mitchell.

Lost Weekend, The (1945). Billy Wilder, dir.; Ray Milland, Jane Wyman, Philip Terry, Howard DaSilva, Frank Faylen.

Love and Anarchy (1973). Lina Wertmuller, dir.; Giancarlo Gianni, Mariangela Melato.

Love Me Tender (1956). Robert D. Webb, dir.; Elvis Presley, Debra Paget.

Love Me Tonight (1932). Rouben Mamoulian, dir.; Jeanette MacDonald, Maurice Chevalier, Myrna Loy, Charles Ruggles.

Love Story (1975). Arthur Hiller, dir.; Ryan O'Neal, Ali McGraw, Ray Milland.

M (1931). Fritz Lang, dir.; Peter Lorre, Gustav Grundgens.

Madame Rosa (1977). Moshe Mizrahi, dir.; Simone Signoret, Sammy Den Youb, Claude Dauphin.

Madness of King George, The (1994). Nicholas Hytner, dir.; Nigel Hawthorne, Helen Mirren, Rupert Everett.

Magnificent Ambersons, The (1942). Orson Welles, dir.; Joseph Cotten, Tim Hold, Agnes Moorhead.

Magnificent Seven, The (1960). John Sturges, dir.; Yul Brynner, Steve McQueen, Eli Wallach.

Malcolm X (1992). Spike Lee, dir.; Denzel Washington, Angela Bassett, Albert Hall, Al Freeman, Jr.

Maltese Falcon, The (1941). John Huston, dir.; Humphrey Bogart, Mary Astor, Sydney Greenstreet, Peter Lorre, Elisha Cook, Jr., Ward Bond.

Man and a Woman, A (1966). Claude Lelouch, dir.; Anouk Aimée, Jean-Louis Trintignant.

Man for All Seasons, A (1966). Fred Zinnemann, dir.; Paul Schofield, Wendy Hiller, Robert Shaw, Orson Welles, Susannah York.

Manhattan (1979). Woody Allen, dir.; Diane Keaton, Woody Allen, Michael Murphy, Mariel Hemingway, Meryl Streep.

Man in the White Suit, The (1952). Alexander Mackendrick, dir.; Alec Guinness, Joan Greenwood, Cecil Parker.

Man of Flowers (1984). Paul Cox, dir.; Norman Kaye, Alyson Best, Chris Haywood, Werner Herzog.

Manon of the Spring (1987). Claude Berri, dir.; Yves Montand, Daniel Auteuil, Emmanuelle Béart, Elisabeth Depardieu.

Man Who Came to Dinner, The (1941). William Keighley, dir.; Monty Woolley, Bette Davis, Ann Sheridan, Jimmy Durante.

Man Who Shot Liberty Valance, The (1962). John Ford, dir.; John Wayne, James Stewart, Vera Miles, Lee Marvin.

Mark of Zorro, The (1920). Fred Niblo, dir.; Douglas Fairbanks, Sr., Noah Beery, Charles Mailes, Claire McDowell.

Marriage Circle, The (1924). Ernst Lubitsch, dir.; Florence Vidor, Monte Blue, Marie Prévost, Adolphe Menjou.

Marty (1955). Delbert Mann, dir.; Ernest Borgnine, Betsy Blair.

M*A*S*H (1970). Robert Altman, dir.; Donald Sutherland, Elliott Gould, Tom Skeritt, Sally Kellerman, Robert Duvall, Jo Ann Pflug, René Auberjonois, Gary Burghof.

Mask (1985). Peter Bogdanovich, dir.; Cher, Sam Elliott, Eric Stotz, Laura Dern.

Mata Hari (1931). George Fitzmaurice, dir.; Greta Garbo, Ramon Novarro, Lionel Barrymore.

Mephisto (1981). Istvan Szabó, dir.; Klaus Marira Brandauer, Krystyna Janda.

Metropolis (1926). Fritz Land, dir.; Brigitte Helm, Alfred Abel.

Midnight Cowboy (1969). John Schlesinger, dir.; Jon Voight, Dustin Hoffman, Sylvia Miles, Bernard Hughes, Brenda Vaccaro.

Miracle on 34th Street (1947). George Seaton, dir.; Natalie Wood, Edmund Gwenn, Maureen O'Hara.

Miracle Worker, The (1962). Arthur Penn, dir.; Anne Bancroft, Patty Duke.

Misfits, The (1961). John Huston, dir.; Clark Gable, Marilyn Monroe, Montgomery Clift.

Missing (1982). Constantin Costa-Gavras, dir.; Jack Lemmon, Sissy Spacek, John Shea, Melanie Mayron.

Mississippi Masala (1992). Mira Nair, dir.; Denzel Washington, Darita Choudbury, Roshan Seth.

Mrs. Doubtfire (1993). Chris Columbus, dir.; Robin Williams, Sally Field, Pierce Brosnan.

Mrs. Miniver (1942). William Wyler, dir.; Greer Garson, Walter Pidgeon, Teresa Wright.

Mr. Deeds Goes to Town (1936). Frank Capra, dir.; Gary Cooper, Jean Arthur.

Mr. Smith Goes to Washington (1939). Frank Capra, dir.; James Stewart, Jean Arthur, Claude Rains.

Modern Times (1935). Charles Chaplin, dir.; Charlie Chaplin, Paulette Goddard, Henry Bergman, Chester Conklin.

Monkey Business (1931). Norman McLeod, dir.; Groucho, Chico, Harpo, and Zeppo Marx, Thelma Todd.

Monty Python and the Holy Grail (1975). Terry Gilliam and Terry Jones, dirs.; Graham Chapman, John Cleese, Terry Gilliam, Eric Idle, Michael Palin.

Moon Is Blue, The (1953). Otto Preminger, dir.; William Holden, David Niven, Maggie McNamara.

Moulin Rouge (1952). John Huston, dir.; José Ferrer, Mel Ferrer, Zsa Zsa Gabor.

Mouse That Roared, The (1959). Jack Arnold, dir.; Peter Sellers, Jean Seberg, David Kosoff, William Hartnett, Leo McKern.

Music Teacher, The (1989). Gérard Corbiau, dir.; José Van Dam, Anne Roussel, Philippe Volter.

Mutiny on the Bounty (1935). Frank Lloyd, dir.; Clark Gable, Charles Laughton, Franchot Tone.

My Bodyguard (1980). Tony Bill, dir.; Chris Makepeace, Matt Dillon, Martin Mull, Ruth Gordon, Adam Baldwin.

My Dinner with André (1981). Louis Malle, dir.; André Gregory, Wallace Shawn.

My Fair Lady (1964). George Cukor, dir.; Rex Harrison, Audrey Hepburn, Stanley Holloway, Wilfred Hyde-White.

My Favorite Wife (1940). Garson Kanin, dir.; Cary Grant, Irene Dunne, Randolph Scott.

My Left Foot (1989). Jim Sheridan, dir.; Daniel Day-Lewis, Ray McAnally, Brenda Fricker, Fiona Shaw.

My Life as a Dog (1987). Lasse Hallstrom, dir.; Anton Glanzelius.

My Little Chickadee (1939). Edward Cline, dir.; Mae West, W. C. Fields.

My Man Godfrey (1936). Gregory LaCava, dir.; Carole Lombard, William Powell, Gail Patrick, Alice Brady, Eugene Pallette.

Napoleon (1927). Abel Gance, dir.; Albert Dieudonné, Antonin Artaud.

Nasty Girl, The (1990). Michael Verhoeven, dir.; Lena Stolze.

Navigator, The (1924). Buster Keaton and Donald Krisp, dirs.; Buster Keaton, Kathryn McGuire, Frederick Vroom, Noble Johnson.

Nazarin (1958). Luis Buñuel, dir.; Francisco Rabal.

Network (1977). Sidney Lumet, dir.; Peter Finch, William Holden, Faye Dunaway, Robert Duvall, Ned Beatty.

Never Give a Sucker an Even Break (1941). Edward Cline, dir.; W. C. Fields, Gloria Jean, Franklin Pangborn, Margaret Dumont.

Never on Sunday (1959). Jules Dassin, dir.; Melina Mercouri, Jules Dassin, Georges Foundas, Titos Vandis, Desapo Diamantidon.

Night at the Opera, A (1935). Sam Wood, dir.; Groucho, Chico, and Harpo Marx, Kitty Carlisle, Allan Jones.

Night of the Iguana (1964). John Huston, dir.; Richard Burton, Ava Gardner, Deborah Kerr, Sue Lyon.

Night of the Living Dead (1968). George A. Romero, dir.; Judith O'Dea, Duane Jones, Karl Hardman, Keith Wayne.

Ninotchka (1939). Ernst Lubitsch, dir.; Greta Garbo, Melvyn Douglas, Bela Lugosi.

Nixon (1995). Oliver Stone, dir.; Anthony Hopkins, Joan Allen, Paul Sorvino.

North by Northwest (1959). Alfred Hitchcock, dir.; Cary Grant, Eva Marie Saint, James Mason, Martin Landau.

Nosferatu (1921). F. W. Murnau, dir.; Max Schrenck, Alexander Granach, Ruth Landshoff.

Notorious (1946). Alfred Hitchcock, dir.; Ingrid Bergman, Cary Grant, Claude Rains, Louis Calhern.

Odd Couple, The (1968). Gene Saks, dir.; Jack Lemmon, Walter Matthau.

Official Story, The (1985). Luis Puenzo, dir.; Norma Aleandro, Hector Alterio, Analia Castro.

Oklahoma! (1955). Fred Zinnemann, dir.; Gordon MacRae, Shirley Jones, Gloria Grahame, Charlotte Greenwood, Rod Steiger.

Once Upon a Time in the West (1969). Sergio Leone, dir.; Claudia Cardinale, Henry Fonda, Charles Bronson, Jason Robards, Jr., Jack Elam.

One-Eyed Jacks (1961). Marlon Brando, dir.; Marlon Brando, Karl Malden, Katy Jurado.

One Flew over the Cuckoo's Nest (1975). Milos Forman, dir.; Jack Nicholson, Louise Fletcher, Will Sampson, Danny DeVito, Christopher Lloyd, Scatman Crothers, Brad Douriff.

On Golden Pond (1981). Mark Rydell, dir.; Henry Fonda, Katharine Hepburn, Jane Fonda, Doug McKeon.

On the Waterfront (1954). Elia Kazan, dir.; Marlon Brando, Eva Marie Saint, Karl Malden, Lee J. Cobb, Rod Steiger.

Ossessione (1942). Luchino Visconti, dir.; Clara Calamai, Massimo Girotti.

Otello (1987). Franco Zeffirelli, dir.; Placido Domingo, Fatia Ricciarelli, Justino Diaz, Urbano Barberini.

Pal Joey (1957). George Sidney, dir.; Rita Hayworth, Frank Sinatra, Kim Novak, Barbara Nichols, Bobby Sherwood.

Paper Moon (1973). Peter Bogdanovich, dir.; Ryan O'Neal, Tatum O'Neal, Madeline Kahn, John Hillerman.

Passage to India, A (1984). David Lean, dir.; Judy Davis, Victor Banerjee, Alec Guinness, Peggy Ashcroft.

Passion of Joan of Arc, The (1928). Carl Dryer, dir.; Maria Falconetti, Eugene Silvain, Antonin Artaud.

Paths of Glory (1957). Stanley Kubrick, dir.; Kirk Douglas, Adolphe Menjou, George Macready.

Patton (1970). Franklin Schaffner, dir.; George C. Scott, Karl Malden.

Pawnbroker, The (1965). Sidney Lumet, dir.; Rod Steiger, Geraldine Fitzgerald, Brock Peters.

Pelle the Conqueror (1988). Bille August, dir.; Max von Sydow, Pelle Hvenegaard.

Perils of Divorce, The (1916). Edwin August, dir.; Edna W. Hopper, Frank Sheridan, Macy Harlan, Ruby Hoffman.

Perils of Pauline, The (1913–14), serial. Louis Gasnier, dir.; Pearl White, Crane Wilbur, Pal Panzer.

Petrified Forest, The (1936). Archie Mayo, dir.; Leslie Howard, Bette Davis, Humphrey Bogart.

Phantom of the Opera (1925). Rupert Julian, dir.; Lon Chaney, Sr., Mary Philbin, Norma Kerry.

Philadelphia Story, The (1940). George Cukor, dir.; Katharine Hepburn, Cary Grant, James Stewart, Ruth Hussey, John Howard.

Piano, The (1993). Jane Campion, dir.; Holly Hunter, Harvey Keitel, Sam Neill.

Pillow Talk (1959). Michael Gordon, dir.; Rock Hudson, Doris Day, Tony Randall.

Pink Panther, The (1964). Blake Edwards, dir.; Peter Sellers, David Niven, Robert Wagner, Capucine.

Pinocchio (1940). Walt Disney animation.

Places in the Heart (1984). Robert Benton, dir.; Sally Field, Ed Harris, Lindsay Crouse, John Malkovich, Danny Glover.

Platoon (1986). Oliver Stone, dir.; Tom Berenger, Willem Dafoe, Charlie Sheen.

Prime of Miss Jean Brodie, The (1969). Ronald Neame, dir.; Maggie Smith, Robert Stephens, Celia Johnson, Pamela Franklin.

Prix de Beauté (Beauty Prize) (1930). Augusto Genina, dir.; Louise Brooks.

Prizzi's Honor (1985). John Huston, dir.; Jack Nicholson, Kathleen Turner, Robert Loggia, John Randolph.

Psycho (1960). Alfred Hitchcock, dir.; Anthony Perkins, Janet Leigh, Vera Miles, John Gavin.

Pulp Fiction (1994). Quentin Tarantino, dir.; John Travolta, Samuel L. Jackson, Uma Thurman, Harvey Keitel, Bruce Willis.

Quiet Man, The (1952). John Ford, dir.; John Wayne, Maureen O'Hara, Victor McLaglen, Barry Fitzgerald.

Raiders of the Lost Ark (1981). Steven Spielberg, dir.; Harrison Ford, Karen Allen, Wolf Kahler, John Rhys-Davies.

Rain Man (1988). Barry Levinson, dir.; Dustin Hoffman, Tom Cruise, Valeria Golino.

Ran (1985). Akira Kurosawa, dir.; Tatsuya Nakadai, Akira Terao.

Rashomon (1951). Akira Kurosawa, dir.; Toshiro Mifune, Machiko Kyo, Masayuke Mori.

Rear Window (1954). Alfred Hitchcock, dir.; James Stewart, Raymond Burr, Grace Kelly.

Rebecca (1940). Alfred Hitchcock, dir.; Laurence Olivier, Joan Fontaine, George Sanders, Nigel Bruce.

Rebel Without a Cause (1955). Nicholas Ray, dir.; James Dean, Natalie Wood, Sal Mineo, Jim Backus, Dennis Hopper.

Red Balloon, The (1956). Albert Lamorisse, dir.; Pascal Lamorisse, Georges Sellier.

Red River (1948). Howard Hawks, dir.; John Wayne, Montgomery Clift, Walter Brennan, Joanne Dru, John Ireland.

Reds (1981). Warren Beatty, dir.; Warren Beatty, Diane Keaton, Jack Nicholson, Gene Hackman, Maureen Stapleton.

Reincarnation of Golden Lotus, The (1989). Clara Law, dir.; Joi Wong.

Reservoir Dogs (1992). Quentin Tarantino, dir.; Harvey Keitel, Tim Roth, Michael Madsen.

Return of the Soldier, The (1983). Alan Bridges, dir.; Glenda Jackson, Julie Christie, Ann-Margaret, Alan Bates, Ian Holm.

Right Stuff, The (1983). Phil Kaufman, dir.; Sam Shepard, Scott Glen, Ed Harris, Dennis Quaid, Barbara Hershey, Fred Ward, Kim Stanley.

Road to Rio, The (1947). Norman Z. McLeod, dir.; Bing Crosby, Bob Hope, Dorothy Lamour.

Rocky (1976). John G. Avildsen, dir.; Sylvester Stallone, Burgess Meredith, Talia Shire, Burt Young, Carl Weathers.

Rocky Horror Picture Show, The (1975). Jim Sharman, dir.; Tim Curry, Susan Sarandon, Barry Bostwick, Meatloaf.

Roman Holiday (1953). William Wyler, dir.; Gregory Peck, Audrey Hepburn, Eddie Albert.

Room at the Top (1959). Jack Clayton, dir.; Laurence Harvey, Simone Signoret, Heather Sears, Hermione Baddeley.

Room with a View, A (1986). James Ivory, dir.; Maggie Smith, Helena Bonham-Carter, Denholm Elliott, Julian Sands, Daniel Day-Lewis.

Rosemary's Baby (1968). Roman Polanski, dir.; Mia Farrow, John Cassavetes, Ruth Gordon, Sidney Blackmer.

Rules of the Game, The (1939). Jean Renoir, dir.; Marcel Dalio, Nora Gregor, Mila Parley.

Samurai Trilogy, The (1954). Hiroshi Inagaki, dir.; Toshiro Mifune, Koji Tsuruta.

Scarface: The Shame of the Nation (1932). Howard Hawks, dir.; Paul Muni, Ann Dvorak, Boris Karloff.

Scenes from a Marriage (1973). Ingmar Bergman, dir.; Liv Ullmann, Erland Josephson, Bibi Andersson.

Schindler's List (1993). Steven Spielberg, dir.; Liam Neeson, Ben Kingsley, Ralph Fiennes, Caroline Goodall.

Searchers, The (1956). John Ford, dir.; John Wayne, Natalie Wood, Jeffrey Hunter, Ward Bond, Vera Miles.

Separate Tables (1983). John Schlesinger, dir.; Julie Christie, Alan Bates, Claire Bloom.

Seven Beauties (1976). Lina Wertmuller, dir.; Giancarlo Giannini, Fernando Rey, Shirley Stoler.

Seven Samurai, The (1954). Akira Kurosawa, dir.; Toshiro Mifune, Takashi Shimura.

Shaft (1971). Gordon Parks, dir.; Richard Roundtree, Moses Gunn, Charles Cioffi, Christopher St John.

Shane (1953). George Stevens, dir.; Alan Ladd, Jean Arthur, Jack Palance, Van Heflin, Ben Johnson.

Ship of Fools (1965). Stanley Kramer, dir.; Vivien Leigh, Oskar Werner, Simone Signoret, José Ferrer, Lee Marvin, George Segal, Michael Dunn.

Showboat (1951). George Sidney, dir.; Kathryn Grayson, Howard Keel, Ava Gardner.

Silence of the Lambs (1991). Jonathan Demme, dir.; Jodie Foster, Anthony Hopkins, Scott Glenn, Ted Levine.

Sin (1915). Robert Brenon, dir.; Theda Bara, Warner Oland, William Shay.

Singin' in the Rain (1952). Gene Kelly, Stanley Donen, dirs.; Gene Kelly, Debbie Reynolds, Donald O'Connor, Jean Hagen, Cyd Charisse, Rita Moreno.

Sleuth (1972). Joseph L. Mankiewicz, dir.; Michael Caine, Laurence Olivier.

Small Change (1976). François Truffaut, dir.; Geary Desmouceaux, Philippe Goldman.

Smiles of a Summer Night (1955). Ingmar Bergman, dir.; Ulla Jacobsson, Gunnar Bjornstrand, Eva Dahlbeck, Harriet Andersson, Jarl Kulle.

Soldier of Orange (1979). Paul Verhoeven, dir.; Rutger Hauer, Peter Faber, Jeroen Krabbe.

Soldier's Story, A (1984). Norman Jewison, dir.; Howard Rollins, Jr., Adolph Caesar.

Some Like It Hot (1959). Billy Wilder, dir.; Marilyn Monroe, Jack Lemmon, Tony Curtis.

Song of Bernadette, The (1942). Henry King, dir.; Jennifer Jones, Charles Bickford, Vincent Price, William Eythe.

Sophie's Choice (1982). Alan J. Pakula, dir.; Meryl Streep, Kevin Kline, Peter MacNicol.

Sound of Music, The (1965). Robert Wise, dir.; Julie Andrews, Christopher Plummer, Eleanor Parker, Richard Haydn.

Spartacus (1960). Stanley Kubrick, dir.; Kirk Douglas, Laurence Olivier, Tony Curtis, Charles Laughton, Peter Ustinov.

Stagecoach (1939). John Ford, dir.; John Wayne, Clair Trevor, Thomas Mitchell, John Carradine, Donald Meek, Andy Devine.

Stalag 17 (1953). Billy Wilder, dir.; William Holden, Robert Strauss, Peter Graves, Otto Preminger.

Stand by Me (1986). Rob Reiner, dir.; River Phoenix.

Star Is Born, A (1954). George Cukor, dir.; Judy Garland, James Mason, Charles Bickford, Jack Carson.

Star Wars (1977). George Lucas, dir.; Alec Guinness, Mark Hamill, Harrison Ford, Carrie Fisher.

Sting, The (1973). George Roy Hill, dir.; Paul Newman, Robert Redford, Robert Shaw, Charles Durning.

The Stone Boy (1984). Christopher Cain, dir.; Robert Duvall, Frederic Forrest, Glenn Close, Wilford Brimley.

Strangers on a Train (1951). Alfred Hitchcock, dir.; Farley Granger, Robert Walker, Ruth Roman, Leo G. Carroll.

Streetcar Named Desire, A (1951). Elia Kazan, dir.; Vivien Leigh, Marlon Brando, Kim Hunter, Karl Malden.

Suddenly Last Summer (1959). Joseph L. Mankiewicz, dir.; Katharine Hepburn, Montgomery Clift.

Sugarcane Alley (1983). Euzhan Paley, dir.; Garry Cadenat, Darling Legitimus.

Sullivan's Travels (1941). Preston Sturges, dir.; Joel McCrae, Veronica Lake, Robert Warwick, William Demarest.

Sunset Boulevard (1950). Billy Wilder, dir.; William Holden, Gloria Swanson, Erich von Stroheim.

Tale of Two Cities, A (1935). Jack Conway, dir.; Ronald Colman, Basil Rathbone, Edna May Oliver, Elizabeth Allen.

Tall T, The (1957). Budd Boetticher, dir.; Randolph Scott, Richard Boone, Maureen O'Sullivan, Henry Silva.

Targets (1968). Peter Bogdanovich, dir.; Tim O'Kelly, Boris Karloff, Nancy Hsueh, Peter Bogdanovich.

Tarzan the Ape Man (1932). W. S. Van Dyke, dir.; Johnny Weissmuller, Maureen O'Sullivan.

Taxi Driver (1976). Martin Scorsese, dir.; Robert De Niro, Harvey Keitel, Cybill Shepherd, Jodie Foster, Peter Boyle.

Tea and Sympathy (1956). Vincente Minnelli, dir.; Deborah Kerr, John Kerr.

Ten Commandments, The (1956). Cecil B. De Mille, dir.; Charlton Heston, Yul Brynner, Anne Baxter, Edward G. Robinson.

Tender Mercies (1982). Bruce Beresford, dir.; Robert Duvall, Tess Harper, Ellen Barkin.

They Shoot Horses, Don't They? (1969). Sidney Pollack, dir.; Jane Fonda, Gig Young, Michael Sarrazin.

Third Man, The (1949). Carol Reed, dir.; Joseph Cotten, Orson Welles, Alida Valli, Trevor Howard.

Thirty-Nine Steps, The (1935). Alfred Hitchcock, dir.; Robert Donat, Madeline Carroll, Lucie Mannheim.

Three Brothers (1980). Francesco Rossi, dir.; Philippe Noiret, Michele Placido, Vittorio Mezzogiorno.

Three Coins in a Fountain (1954). Jean Negulesco, dir.; Clifton Webb, Dorothy McGuire, Jean Peters, Louis Jourdan.

Three Faces of Eve, The (1957). Nunnally Johnson, dir.; Joanne Woodward, Lee J. Cobb, David Wayne, Vince Edwards.

Three Men from Texas (1940). Lesley Selander, dir.; William Boyd, Russell Hayden, Andy Clyde, Morris Ankrum, Dick Curtis.

Three Musketeers, The (1973). Richard Lester, dir.; Michael York, Oliver Reed, Raquel Welch, Richard Chamberlain, Faye Dunaway, Charlton Heston.

Thunder Road (1958). Arthur Ripley, dir.; Robert Mitchum, Gene Barry, Jacques Aubuchon, Keely Smith.

Tightrope (1984). Richard Tuggle, dir.; Clint Eastwood, Geneviève Bujold, Dan Hedaya, Alison Eastwood.

Titanic (1953). Jean Negulesco, dir.; Clifton Webb, Barbara Stanwyck, Robert Wagner.

To Kill a Mockingbird (1962). Robert Mulligan, dir.; Gregory Peck, Mary Badham, Philip Alford, John Megna.

Tom Jones (1963). Tony Richardson, dir.; Albert Finney, Susannah York, Hugh Griffith, Edith Evans.

Tomorrow (1972). Joseph Anthony, dir.; Robert Duvall, Olga Berlin, Sudie Bond.

Tootsie (1982). Sidney Pollack, dir.; Dustin Hoffman, Bill Murray, Jessica Lange, Dabney Coleman.

Top Hat (1935). Mark Sandrich, dir.; Fred Astaire, Ginger Rogers.

Topper (1937). Norman Z. McLeod, dir.; Cary Grant, Roland Young, Constance Bennett.

Touch of Class, A (1972). Melvin Frank, dir.; George Segal, Glenda Jackson, Paul Sorvino, Hildegard Neil.

Touch of Evil (1958). Orson Welles, dir.; Charlton Heston, Janet Leigh, Orson Welles, Akim Tamitoff.

Treasure of the Sierra Madre, The (1948). John Huston, dir.; Humphrey Bogart, Tim Holt, Walter Huston, Bruce Bennett.

Tree of the Wooden Cross, The (1978). Ermanno Olmi, dir.; Luigi Ornaghi, Francesco Moriggi, Omar Brigroli.

Trouble in Paradise (1932). Ernst Lubitsch, dir.; Miriam Hopkins, Herbert Marshall, Kay Francis, Edward Everett Horton, Charles Ruggles.

True Grit (1969). Henry Hathaway, dir.; John Wayne, Glen Campbell, Kim Darby.

True Lies (1994). James Cameron, dir.; Arnold Schwarzenegger, Jamie Lee Curtis, Tom Arnold, Charlton Heston.

Tunes of Glory (1960). Ronald Neame, dir.; Alec Guinness, John Mills, Susannah York, Dennis Price, Duncan Macrae.

Twelve Angry Men (1957). Sidney Lumet, dir.; Henry Fonda, Lee J. Cobb, Ed Begley, Sr., E. G. Marshall, Jack Klugman, Jack Warden, Martin Balsam.

Twentieth Century (1934). Howard Hawks, dir.; John Barrymore, Carole Lombard, Roscoe Karns, Walter Connolly, Etienne Giradot, Ralph Forbes.

Twice in a Lifetime (1985). Bud Yorkin, dir.; Gene Hackman, Ann-Margaret, Ellen Burstyn, Amy Madigan, Ally Sheedy, Brian Dennehy.

2001: A Space Odyssey (1968). Stanley Kubrick, dir.; Keir Dullea, William Sylvester, Gary Lockwood.

UTU (1985). Geoff Murphy, dir.; Anzac Wallace, Bruno Lawrence, Kelly Johnson, Tim Elliot.

Umberto D (1955). Vittorio De Sica, dir.; Carlo Battisti, Maria Pia Casilio.

Unbearable Lightness of Being, The (1987). Phil Kaufman, dir.; Daniel Day-Lewis, Juliette Binoche, Lena Olin, Derek de Lint, Erland Josephson.

Un Chien Andalou (1928). Luis Buñuel, dir.; Salvador Dali, Luis Buñuel.

Unmarried Woman, An (1978). Paul Mazursky, dir.; Jill Clayburgh, Michael Murphy, Alan Bates, Pat Quinn.

Vampyr (1931). Carl Dryer, dir.; Julian West, Sybille Schmitz.

Vanishing, The (1988). George Sluizer, dir.; Bernard Pierre Donnadieu, Gene Bervoets, Johanna ter Steege.

Variety (1926). E. A. Dupont, dir.; Emil Jannings, Lya de Putti.

Virginian, The (1946). Stuart Gilmore, dir.; Joel McCrea, Brian Donleavy.

Virgin Spring, The (1960). Ingmar Bergman, dir.; Max von Sydow, Birgitta Pettersson, Gunnel Lindblom.

Viridiana (1961). Luis Buñuel, dir.; Silvia Pinal, Fernando Rey, Francisco Rabal, Margarita Lozano.

Wages of Fear, The (1953). Henri-Georges Clouzot, dir.; Yves Montand, Charles Vanel, Peter Van Eyck, Vera Clouzot.

War and Peace (1956). King Vidor, dir.; Audrey Hepburn, Henry Fonda, Mel Ferrer, Herbert Lom, John Mills, Oscar Homulka.

Way Down East (1920). D. W. Griffith, dir.; Lillian Gish, Joseph Bernard, Patricia Fruen.

Way Out West (1937). James W. Horne, dir.; Stan Laurel, Oliver Hardy, Sharon Lynn.

Wedding in Galilee, A (1987). Michel Kheiti, dir.; Ali Mohammed, El Akili.

West Side Story (1961). Robert Wise, Jerome Robbins, dirs.; Natalie Wood, Richard Beymer, Rita Moreno, George Chakiris, Russ Tamblyn.

White Christmas (1954). Michael Curtiz, dir.; Bing Crosby, Danny Kaye, Rosemary Clooney, Vera-Ellen, Dean Jagger, Mary Wickes, Sig Rumann, Grady Sutton.

White Heat (1949). Raoul Walsh, dir.; James Cagney, Virginia Mayo.

White Men Can't Jump (1992). Ron Shelton, dir.; Wesley Snipes, Woody Harrelson, Rosie Perez.

Who Framed Roger Rabbit? (1988). Robert Zemeckis, dir.; Bob Hoskins, Christopher Lloyd.

Who's Afraid of Virginia Woolf? (1966). Mike Nichols, dir.; Elizabeth Taylor, Richard Burton, Sandy Dennis, George Segal.

Wild Bunch, The (1969). Sam Peckinpah, dir.; William Holden, Ernest Borgnine, Robert Ryan.

Wild One, The (1954). Laslo Benedek, dir.; Marlon Brando, Lee Marvin, Mary Murphy.

Wild Strawberries (1957). Ingmar Bergman, dir.; Victor Sjostrom, Ingrid Thulin, Gunnar Bjornstrand, Bibi Andersson, Naima Wifstrand, Jullan Kindahl.

Witness for the Prosecution (1957). Billy Wilder, dir.; Tyrone Power, Charles Laughton, Marlene Dietrich, Elsa Lanchester.

Wizard of Oz, The (1939). Victor Fleming, dir.; Judy Garland, Ray Bolger, Bert Lahr, Jack Haley.

Woman in the Dunes (1964). Hiroshi Teshigahara, dir.; Eiji Okada.

Woman of the Year (1942). George Stevens, dir.; Spencer Tracy, Katharine Hepburn, Fay Bainter, Reginald Owen, William Bendix.

Wuthering Heights (1939). William Wyler, dir.; Merle Oberon, Laurence Olivier, David Niven.

Yellow Submarine (1968). George Dunning, dir.; animated film with music by the Beatles.

Yojimbo (1961). Akira Kurosawa, dir.; Toshiro Mifune, Ejiro Tono.

You Can't Cheat an Honest Man (1939). George Marshall, Edward Clive, dirs.; W. C. Fields.

You Can't Take It with You (1938). Frank Capra, dir.; James Stewart, Lionel Barrymore, Jean Arthur, Edward Arnold, Spring Byington, Mischa Auer, Ann Miller.

Young Frankenstein (1974). Mel Brooks, dir.; Gene Wilder, Marty Feldman, Peter Boyle, Madeline Kahn.

Ziegfeld Follies (1946). Vincente Minelli, dir.; Fred Astaire, Lucille Ball, Fanny Brice, Esther Williams, Judy Garland, Jimmy Durante.

Zorba the Greek (1964). Michael Cacoyannis, dir.; Anthony Quinn, Alan Bates.

SOURCES

Annual Index to Motion Picture Credits. Beverly Hills, Calif.: Academy of Motion Picture Arts and Sciences, 1988–95.

Boussinot, Roger, ed. *L'Encyclopédie du Cinema.* Paris: Bordas, 1967.

Gardner, Gerald, ed. *I Coulda Been a Contender: A Collection of Hollywood's All-Time Classic Lines and Outstanding Witticisms.* New York: Warner Books, 1992.

Halliwell, Leslie, *Halliwell's Film Guide.* 8th ed. New York: Harper and Row, 1990.

Martin, Mick, and Marsha Porter. *Video Movie Guide, 1992.* New York: Ballantine, 1991.

Monush, Barry, William Pay, and Patricia Thompson, eds. 1991 *International Motion Picture Almanac.* New York: Quigley, 1991.

The Motion Picture Guide Annual(s). New York: Cine Books, 1986–1995.

Munden, Kenneth W., ed. *The American Film Institute Catalog. Vols. F1, F2.* New York: R. R. Bowker, 1971.

Pallot, James, ed. *The Motion Picture Guide, 1992 Annual.* New York: Baseline, 1992.

———. *The Motion Picture Guide, 1993 Annual.* New York: Baseline, 1993.

Scheuer, Steven H., ed. *Movies on TV and Videocassette, 1990.* New York: Bantam, 1989.

Variety International Film Guide, 1995. London: Hamlyn; Boston: Focal Press, 1996.

—**John Sepich; J.L.M.**

43

FAMOUS FILM STARS

The witch that came (the withered hag)
To wash the steps with pail and rag
Was once the beauty Abishag

The picture pride of Hollywood.

. . . . .

THUS THE POET ROBERT FROST ON THE EVANESCENCE OF FAME. ON THE
other hand, another ex-Hollywood luminary was elected to two terms as
president of the United States. So it all depends.

The great divide in movie acting, of course, came in the late 1920s, with
the advent of talkies. Before words could actually be spoken, the technique
of the performer was perhaps closer to that of the mime than of the stage
actor. The enhanced gesture had always been a part of acting, as for example the celebrated "start" of David Garrick upon espying Banquo's ghost in
Macbeth. But for black-and-white cinema without dialogue, produced for a
mass audience and with only occasional titles to communicate what was
being said, extravagant exaggeration of expression and action became a
necessity—which may be why most of the silent movies that have become
classics are comedies, not tragedy or even melodrama.

Some actors and actresses made the transition without undue difficulty.
Others couldn't master the demands for greater subtlety of technique, or
their voices simply didn't fit their visual personalities. W. C. Fields was
undoubtedly funnier once he was able to use his voice, while Laurel and
Hardy thrived for many years under the new dispensation, even though several of their earlier two-reeler silents were among their most hilarious performances. But for all the fanfare that accompanied Charlie Chaplin's several
talkies, it was on the silent screen that he did his best work, while Buster
Keaton's art was decisively for the silents. For various reasons matinee idols

such as John Gilbert, Mae Murray, Pola Negri, Clara Bow, and Mary Pickford did not become stars of the talkies, while others such as Greta Garbo, Wallace Beery, Janet Gaynor, Gloria Swanson, Jean Hersholt, and Adolphe Menjou, to name only a few, did very nicely when using their voices.

Hollywood itself is not quite what it was in the years before television, when the major studios—Paramount, Metro-Goldwyn-Mayer, RKO, Twentieth-Century Fox, United Artists, Columbia, Warner Brothers, Universal, a few others—completely dominated the film business. Independent producers and small companies are now of considerably greater importance in the scheme of things, and many are based, and their movies are made, in locales throughout the nation and even the world. To be a film star, however, is still to be known to millions of viewers.

The list which follows is of some of the more prominent film actors and actresses and several of the films for which they are noted. Dates are occasionally supplied with titles to indicate which of two or more versions (*e.g.,* of *Mutiny on the Bounty,* or *Hamlet*) of a movie is intended. Actors whose work was primarily or exclusively in westerns are not included; they are listed in a separate section.

Abbott, Bud (1895–1974) and **Lou Costello** (1906–59). *Abbott and Costello in the Foreign Legion, Abbott and Costello Meet Frankenstein, Buck Privates.*

Alda, Alan (1936–). *Crimes and Misdemeanors, The Four Seasons, Kill Me If You Can, Same Time Next Year, Sweet Liberty.*

Allen, Woody (1935–). *Annie Hall, Hannah and Her Sisters, Manhattan, Sleeper, Zelig.*

Ameche, Don (1908–93). *Alexander's Ragtime Band, Heaven Can Wait, Midnight, Wing and a Prayer.*

Andrews, Julie (1935–). *The Americanization of Emily, Mary Poppins, The Sound of Music, Victor/Victoria.*

Arbuckle, "Fatty" (Roscoe) (1887–1933). *The Cook, The Life of the Party, Out West.*

Arkin, Alan (1934–). *Catch-22, The In-Laws, Wait Until Dark, Woman Times Seven.*

Arlen, Richard (1898–1976). *Call of the Yukon, Hurricane Smith, Santa Fe Trail.*

Arliss, George (1868–1946). *Disraeli, The House of Rothschild, The Iron Duke.*

Arthur, Jean (1905–91). *Mr. Deeds Goes to Town, Only Angels Have Wings, Shane, You Can't Take It with You.*

Ashcroft, Dame Peggy (1907–). *Madame Sousatzka; The Nun's Story; Passage to India; Sunday, Bloody Sunday.*

Astaire, Fred (1899–1987). *Easter Parade, Funny Face, The Gay Divorcee, Holiday Inn, Roberta, Shall We Dance?, Top Hat.*

Ayres, Lew (1908–). *All Quiet on the Western Front, Advise and Consent, State Fair.*

Bacall, Lauren (1924–). *The Big Sleep, How to Marry a Millionaire, Key Largo, The Shootist, To Have and Have Not.*

Bancroft, Anne (1931–). *Agnes of God, Demetrius and the Gladiators, The Graduate, The Miracle Worker.*

Bankhead, Tallulah (1903–68). *The Devil and the Deep, Lifeboat, Stage Door Canteen.*

Bara, Theda (1890–1955). *A Fool There Was, The Darling of Paris, The Hunchback of Notre Dame, Camille, Sin.*

Bardot, Brigitte (1934–). *And . . . God Created Woman, Contempt, Viva Maria.*

Barrymore, Ethel (1879–1959). *The Farmer's Daughter, Rasputin and the Empress, The Spiral Staircase.*

Barrymore, John (1882–1942). *A Bill of Divorcement, Dinner at Eight, Grand Hotel, Rasputin and the Empress, The Tempest, Twentieth Century.*

Barrymore, Lionel (1878–1954). *Camille, A Free Soul, Grand Hotel, Key Largo, Rasputin and the Empress, You Can't Take It with You.*

Barthelmess, Richard (1897–1963). *The Bright Shawl, The Cabin in the Cotton, The Dawn Patrol.*

Bates, Alan (1934–). *Far from the Madding Crowd, Georgy Girl, An Unmarried Woman, Zorba the Greek.*

Beatty, Warren (1938–). *Bonnie and Clyde, Heaven Can Wait, McCabe and Mrs. Miller, Reds, Shampoo, Splendor in the Grass, Dick Tracy.*

Beery, Noah (1884–1945). *The Girl of the Golden West, The Mark of Zorro, The Sea Wolf.*

Beery, Wallace (1885–1949). *The Champ, Dynamite Smith, Grand Hotel, A Message to Garcia, Robin Hood (1922), Tugboat Annie.*

Belmondo, Jean-Paul (1933–). *Breathless (1959), Le Doulos, Two Women, A Woman Is a Woman.*

Bennett, Constance (1905–65). *Code of the West, Moulin Rouge, Topper.*

Bennett, Joan (1910–90). *Bulldog Drummond, Confirm or Deny, Little Women, The Man I Married.*

Bergman, Ingrid (1915–82). *Anastasia, Casablanca, For Whom the Bell Tolls, Gaslight, Joan of Arc, Murder on the Orient Express.*

Blondell, Joan (1909–79). *Blond Crazy, Gold Diggers of 1933, Will Success Spoil Rock Hunter?*

Bloom, Claire (1931–). *The Brothers Karamazov, Look Back in Anger, Richard III, The Spy Who Came in from the Cold.*

Bogart, Humphrey (1899–1957). *The African Queen, The Big Sleep, Casablanca, Key Largo, The Maltese Falcon, The Treasure of the Sierra Madre.*

Boone, Richard (1917–81). *Dragnet, The Garment Jungle, The Shootist.*

Borgnine, Ernest (1917–　). *Bad Day at Black Rock, The Dirty Dozen, From Here to Eternity, Marty.*

Bow, Clara (1905–65). *The Ancient Mariner, Dangerous Curves, Whispering Smith* (1926).

Boyer, Charles (1899–1978). *Algiers, Around the World in Eighty Days, The Constant Nymph, Gaslight, Love Affair, Mayerling.*

Brando, Marlon (1924–　). *Apocalypse Now, The Godfather, Julius Caesar (1953), Last Tango in Paris, On the Waterfront, A Streetcar Named Desire, The Ugly American.*

Brennan, Walter (1894–1974). *Banjo on My Knee, Red River, Tammy and the Bachelor.*

Bronson, Charles (1920–　). *The Dirty Dozen, The Great Escape, Hard Times, Jubal, The Magnificent Seven, The Mechanic.*

Brynner, Yul (1915–85). *Anastasia, The Brothers Karamazov, The King and I, The Magnificent Seven, The Ten Commandments.*

Bujold, Geneviève (1942–　). *Anne of the Thousand Days, Coma, Obsession, King of Hearts.*

Burke, Billie (1885–1970). *A Bill of Divorcement, The Man Who Came to Dinner, The Young Philadelphians.*

Burton, Richard (1925–84). *Becket, Dr. Faustus, The Sandpiper, The Spy Who Came In from the Cold, The Taming of the Shrew, Who's Afraid of Virginia Woolf?*

Bushman, Francis X. (1883–1966). *Dawn and Twilight, Hollywood Boulevard, Modern Marriage.*

Caan, James (1939–　). *Brian's Song, Cinderella Liberty, Comes a Horseman, The Godfather, The Godfather Part II, The Rain People.*

Cagney, James (1899–1986). *Mr. Roberts, Public Enemy, The Seven Little Foys, Yankee Doodle Dandy.*

Caine, Michael (1933–　). *Alfie, Dirty Rotten Scoundrels, Educating Rita, Hannah and Her Sisters, The Man Who Would Be King.*

Carrillo, Leo (1881–1961). *The Gay Amigo, Phantom of the Opera (1943), The Valiant Hombre.*

Carroll, Nancy (1906–65). *Chicken à la King, The Man I Killed, Wayward.*

Chaney, Lon (1883–1930). *The Hunchback of Notre Dame, The Phantom of the Opera (1925), West of Zanzibar.*

Chaplin, Charlie (1889–1977). *City Lights, The Gold Rush, The Great Dictator, Modern Times, Monsieur Verdoux, Tillie's Punctured Romance, The Tramp.*

Christie, Julie (1941–　). *Darling, Dr. Zhivago, Far from the Madding Crowd, McCabe and Mrs. Miller, Petulia, Separate Tables.*

Clift, Montgomery (1920–66). *From Here to Eternity, The Heiress, Judgment at Nuremberg, The Young Lions.*

Colbert, Claudette (1905–). Cleopatra, Drums Along the Mohawk, The Egg and I, It Happened One Night, Since You Went Away.

Colman, Ronald (1891–1958). Beau Geste, A Double Life, Kismet, Lost Horizon, Stella Dallas, A Tale of Two Cities.

Connery, Sean (1930–). Goldfinger, The Hill, The Hunt for Red October, The Name of the Rose, The Russia House, The Untouchables.

Coogan, Jackie (1914–84). Skinner's Baby, Peck's Bad Boy, The Kid, The Rag Man.

Cooper, Gary (1901–61). Beau Geste, A Farewell to Arms, High Noon, Sergeant York, The Virginian, Wings.

Cooper, Jackie (1921–). The Champ, Skippy, Treasure Island.

Costello, Lou. See **Abbott, Bud.**

Cotten, Joseph (1905–1994). Citizen Kane, The Magnificent Ambersons, Petulia, The Third Man.

Crawford, Broderick (1910–86). All the King's Men, Born Yesterday, Not as a Stranger.

Crawford, Joan (1908–77). Grand Hotel, Mildred Pierce, Possessed (1931), The Women.

Crosby, Bing (1903–77). The Bells of Saint Mary's, Going My Way, The Greatest Show on Earth, The Road to Rio, White Christmas.

Cruise, Tom (1962–). Born on the Fourth of July, The Color of Money, Rain Man, Top Gun.

Curtis, Tony (1925–). The Boston Strangler, Some Like It Hot, Spartacus.

Daniels, Bebe (1901–71). Dangerous Money, Feel My Pulse, Take Me Home.

Davies, Marion (1897–1961). Blondie of the Follies, Ever Since Eve, Peg o' My Heart.

Davis, Bette (1908–89). All About Eve, The Corn Is Green, Dangerous, Jezebel, The Little Foxes, Now Voyager, Of Human Bondage.

Dean, James (1931–55). East of Eden, Rebel Without a Cause.

De Camp, Rosemary (1914–). Bowery to Broadway, On Moonlight Bay, Scandal Sheet.

Dee, Ruby (1924–). The Balcony, The Jackie Robinson Story, A Raisin in the Sun.

De Havilland, Olivia (1916–). The Charge of the Light Brigade, Gone With the Wind, The Heiress, Hush . . . Hush, Sweet Charlotte, To Each His Own.

De Niro, Robert (1943–). Bang the Drum Slowly, The Deer Hunter, Raging Bull, The Godfather Part II, Taxi Driver.

Dietrich, Marlene (1901–92). Around the World in Eighty Days, The Blue Angel, Destry Rides Again, Touch of Evil, Witness for the Prosecution (1957).

Dix, Richard (1894–1949). The Arizonian, The Kansan, The Whistler.

Donat, Robert (1905–58). Goodbye, Mr. Chips, The Private Life of Henry VIII, The 39 Steps, The Young Mr. Pitt.

Donlevy, Brian (1899–1972). *Beau Geste, Kiss of Death, Song of Sheherazade.*

Douglas, Kirk (1916–   ). *Detective Story, Lust for Life, Spartacus.*

Douglas, Melvyn (1901–81). *The Americanization of Emily, Being There, Hud, Mr. Blandings Builds His Dream House, Hotel.*

Douglas, Paul (1907–59). *It Happens Every Spring, A Letter to Three Wives, Solid Gold Cadillac.*

Dressler, Marie (1869–1934). *Bringing Up Father, Min and Bill, Tugboat Annie.*

Dreyfuss, Richard (1947–   ). *American Graffiti, The Goodbye Girl, Jaws, Postcards from the Edge, What About Bob?*

Dru, Joanne (1923–   ). *Dark Avenger, Mr. Belvedere Rings the Bell, Thunder Bay.*

Dunaway, Faye (1941–   ). *Bonnie and Clyde, Chinatown, The Eyes of Laura Mars, Mommie Dearest, Network.*

Dunn, James (1905–67). *Bad Boy, Pride of the Navy, A Tree Grows in Brooklyn.*

Dunne, Irene (1904–90). *Back Street, Cimarron, Life with Father, My Favorite Wife, Showboat* (1936).

Durante, Jimmy (1893–1980). *Melody Ranch, One in a Million, What! No Beer!*

Duvall, Robert (1931–   ). *Apocalypse Now, The Godfather, The Great Santini, Tender Mercies, True Confessions.*

Duval, Shelley (1950–   ). *Annie Hall, The Godfather, McCabe and Mrs. Miller, Popeye, The Shining, Tender Mercies, Three Women.*

Eastwood, Clint (1930–   ). *Dirty Harry; The Good, the Bad, and the Ugly; Outlaw Josey Wales; Play Misty for Me.*

Eddy, Nelson (1901–67). *Maytime, Naughty Marietta, Rose Marie.*

Fairbanks, Douglas (1883–1939). *The Mark of Zorro* (1920), *The Private Life of Don Juan, Robin Hood* (1922), *The Thief of Baghdad.*

Fairbanks, Douglas, Jr. (1909–   ). *Green Hell, Gunga Din, The Prisoner of Zenda.*

Farrow, Mia (1946–   ). *Alice, Crimes and Misdemeanors, Hannah and Her Sisters, Radio Days, Rosemary's Baby, Zelig.*

Ferrer, José (1912–92). *Cyrano de Bergerac, Lawrence of Arabia, Moulin Rouge, Ship of Fools.*

Field, Sally (1946–   ). *Norma Rae, Places in the Heart, Steel Magnolias, Sybil.*

Fields, W. C. (1879–1946). *The Bank Dick, The Fatal Glass of Beer, David Copperfield, My Little Chickadee.*

Flynn, Errol (1909–59). *Adventures of Robin Hood* (1938), *Captain Blood, The Charge of the Light Brigade, The Dawn Patrol, The Sea Hawk, The Sun Also Rises.*

Fonda, Henry (1905–82). *The Grapes of Wrath, Jesse James, The Lady Eve, Mister Roberts, On Golden Pond, The Ox-Bow Incident.*

Fonda, Jane (1937–   ). *Barbarella, Barefoot in the Park, Cat Ballou, Coming Home, Hurry Sundown, Julia, Klute.*

Fontaine, Joan (1917–   ). *The Constant Nymph, Gunga Din, Rebecca, Suspicion.*

Fontaine, Lynn (1892–1983). *The Man Who Found Himself, Second Youth.*

Ford, Glenn (1916–   ). *The Blackboard Jungle, Gilda, Jubal, The Man from Colorado, 3:10 to Yuma.*

Ford, Harrison (1942–   ). *Blade Runner, The Conversation, Raiders of the Lost Ark, Star Wars, Witness.*

Forsythe, John (1918–   ). *Destination Tokyo, In Cold Blood, The Trouble with Harry.*

Foster, Jodie (1962–   ). *Alice Doesn't Live Here Anymore, Five Corners, Silence of the Lambs, Taxi Driver.*

Francis, Kay (1903–68). *British Agent, Divorce, Play Girl.*

Gable, Clark (1901–60). *Gone With the Wind, Idiot's Delight, Mutiny on the Bounty* (1935), *It Happened One Night.*

Gabor, Eva (1924–1995). *Don't Go Near the Water, It Started with a Kiss, Youngblood Hawke.*

Gabor, Zsa Zsa (1920–   ). *Jack of Diamonds, Moulin Rouge, Touch of Evil.*

Garbo, Greta (1905–90). *Anna Christie* (1930), *Anna Karenina* (1935), *Camille, Grand Hotel, The Kiss, Ninotchka, Queen Christina, A Woman of Affairs.*

Gardner, Ava (1922–90). *The Barefoot Contessa, The Killers, The Long Hot Summer, On the Beach, The Snows of Kilimanjaro.*

Garfield, John (1913–52). *Body and Soul, Gentleman's Agreement, The Postman Always Rings Twice.*

Garland, Judy (1922–69). *Easter Parade, Judgment at Nuremberg, Meet Me in St. Louis, A Star Is Born* (1954), *The Wizard of Oz.*

Garson, Greer (1914–1996). *Mrs. Miniver, Pride and Prejudice, The Valley of Decision.*

Gaynor, Janet (1906–84). *Seventh Heaven, A Star Is Born, State Fair, Sunrise, The Young in Heart.*

Gere, Richard (1949–   ). *Days of Heaven, An Officer and a Gentleman, Power, Pretty Woman.*

Gibson, Mel (1956–   ). *Gallipoli, Hamlet* (1990), *Lethal Weapon, The River, The Year of Living Dangerously.*

Gielgud, John (1904–   ). *Around the World in Eighty Days, Becket, Brideshead Revisited, Chariots of Fire, Gandhi, The Loved One, Plenty, Richard III, The Shooting Party.*

Gilbert, John (1897–1936). *The Big Parade, Queen Christina, A Woman of Affairs.*

Gish, Dorothy (1898–1968). *Home Sweet Home, Nell Gwynn, Romola.*

Gish, Lillian (1896–1993). *The Birth of a Nation, The Night of the Hunter, Orphans of the Storm, Romola, The Scarlet Letter* (1926).

Glenn, Scott (1942–   ). *The Right Stuff, The River, Silence of the Lambs, Urban Cowboy.*

Goddard, Paulette (1911–90). *Hold Back the Dawn, The Great Dictator, The Women.*

Gould, Elliott (1938–   ). *Bob and Carol and Ted and Alice, The Long Goodbye, Little Murders, M*A*S*H.*

Grable, Betty (1916–73). *The Farmer Takes a Wife, The Gay Divorcee, Follow the Fleet, Million-Dollar Legs, Pin-Up Girl, A Yank in the RAF.*

Grant, Cary (1904–86). *Arsenic and Old Lace, His Girl Friday, My Favorite Wife, Holiday, Notorious, She Done Him Wrong, Topper.*

Guinness, Sir Alec (1914–   ). *The Bridge on the River Kwai, The Horse's Mouth, Kind Hearts and Coronets, The Ladykillers, The Lavender Hill Mob, Lawrence of Arabia, Dr. Zhivago.*

Hackman, Gene (1931–   ). *Bonnie and Clyde, The Conversation, The French Connection, Hoosiers, Postcards from the Edge.*

Hanks, Tom (1956–   ). *Big, Forrest Gump, The Man with One Red Shoe, The Money Pit, Philadelphia, Splash.*

Hardy, Oliver. *See* **Laurel, Stan.**

Harlow, Jean (1911–37). *Bombshell, City Lights, Dinner at Eight, Hell's Angels, Riffraff.*

Harrison, Rex (1908–90). *Anna and the King of Siam, Blithe Spirit, Major Barbara, My Fair Lady, Night Train to Munich.*

Harvey, Laurence (1928–73). *Of Human Bondage, I Am a Camera, The Manchurian Candidate, The Wonderful World of the Brothers Grimm.*

Hayes, Helen (1900–93). *Airport, Anastasia, Sin of Madelon Claudet, What Every Woman Knows.*

Hayward, Susan (1919–75). *Beau Geste, I Want to Live, The Lost Moment, The Snows of Kilimanjaro.*

Hayworth, Rita (1918–87). *Gilda, Only Angels Have Wings, Pal Joey, You Were Never Lovelier, Separate Tables.*

Heflin, Van (1910–71). *Battle Cry, Shane, They Came to Cordura.*

Hepburn, Audrey (1929–93). *Breakfast at Tiffany's, Charade, My Fair Lady, Roman Holiday, Sabrina Fair, War and Peace.*

Hepburn, Katharine (1907–   ). *The African Queen, Guess Who's Coming to Dinner?, The Lion in Winter, Long Day's Journey into Night* (1962), *Morning Glory, On Golden Pond, The Philadelphia Story.*

Heston, Charlton (1924–   ). *Ben-Hur, El Cid, The Ten Commandments, Touch of Evil.*

Hoffman, Dustin (1937–   ). *All the President's Men, The Graduate, Hook, Kramer vs. Kramer, Lenny, Little Big Man, Midnight Cowboy, Rain Man, Tootsie.*

Holden, William (1918–82). *The Bridge on the River Kwai, Network, Picnic, Stalag 17, Sunset Boulevard.*

Hope, Bob (1904–   ). *The Greatest Show on Earth, The Paleface, Road to Morocco, Road to Rio, Monsieur Beaucaire.*

Hopkins, Anthony (1937–   ). *A Chorus of Disapproval, The Lion in Winter, Silence of the Lambs.*

Hopkins, Miriam (1902–72). *All of Me, Barbary Coast, Fanny Hill.*

Horton, Edward Everett (1886–1970). *Bluebeard's Eighth Wife, I Married an Angel, Sex and the Single Girl.*

Howard, Leslie (1893–1943). *Gone With the Wind, Intermezzo, Of Human Bondage, Pygmalion, The Scarlet Pimpernel* (1934).

Howard, Trevor (1916–88). *Around the World in Eighty Days, Gandhi, Outcast of the Islands, Sons and Lovers.*

Hudson, Rock (1925–85). *All That Heaven Allows, Giant, Pillow Talk.*

Hurt, William (1950–). *The Accidental Tourist, Body Heat, Children of a Lesser God, The Elephant Man, Kiss of the Spider Woman.*

Huston, Walter (1884–1950). *Dodsworth, The Maltese Falcon, The Treasure of the Sierra Madre.*

Jackson, Glenda (1936–). *Marat/Sade; The Rainbow; Sunday, Bloody Sunday; A Touch of Class; Turtle Diary.*

Jannings, Emil (1886–1950). *The Blue Angel, The Last Command, The Way of All Flesh.*

Jones, Allan (1907–92). *A Night at the Opera, Showboat* (1936), *The Firefly.*

Jones, James Earl (1931–). *Field of Dreams; Gardens of Stone; The Great White Hope; Dr. Strangelove, or How I Learned to Stop Worrying and Love the Bomb; Star Wars.*

Jourdan, Louis (1921–). *Bird of Paradise, Made in Paris, Three Coins in the Fountain.*

Karloff, Boris (1887–1969). *The Body Snatcher, Frankenstein, Mr. Wong, Detective, Scarface: The Shame of a Nation.*

Karns, Roscoe (1893–1970). *Alibi Ike, They Drive by Night, 20,000 Years in Sing Sing.*

Kaye, Danny (1913–87). *Hans Christian Andersen, The Court Jester, The Inspector General, The Secret Life of Water Mitty.*

Keaton, Buster (1895–1966). *Blue Blazes, The Frozen North, The Navigator, Sidewalks of New York.*

Keaton, Diane (1946–). *Annie Hall, Crimes of the Heart, The Godfather, The Godfather Part II, Interiors, Reds.*

Keaton, Michael (1951–). *Batman, Clean and Sober, Mr. Mom, Pacific Heights.*

Kelly, Gene (1912–1996). *An American in Paris, Brigadoon, For Me and My Gal, On the Town, Singin' in the Rain.*

Kelly, Grace (1929–82). *The Country Girl, Dial M for Murder, High Noon, Rear Window.*

Kerr, Deborah (1921–). *The Adventuress, Bonjour Tristesse, From Here to Eternity, Night of the Iguana, The Sundowners.*

Kinski, Klaus (1926–). *Aguirre: Wrath of God, Fitzcarraldo, Nosferatu* (1979), *The Secret Diary of Sigmund Freud.*

Kitt, Eartha (1928–). *Anna Lucasta, Friday Foster, The Saint of Devil's Island.*

Ladd, Alan (1913–64). *Branded, Shane.*

Lahr, Bert (1895–1967). *DuBarry Was a Lady, The Wizard of Oz, Zaza.*

Lake, Veronica (1921–73). *So Proudly We Hail, This Gun for Hire, Variety Girl.*

Lamarr, Hedy (1914–). *Algiers; Ecstasy; The Female Animal; H. M. Pulham, Esq.; Samson and Delilah.*

Lancaster, Burt (1913–94). *Atlantic City, Elmer Gantry, From Here to Eternity, Judgment at Nuremberg, The Professionals, Separate Tables.*

Langdon, Harry (1884–1944). *A Chump at Oxford, Double Trouble, The Shrimp.*

Laughton, Charles (1899–1962). *Captain Kidd, The Hunchback of Notre Dame (1939), Mutiny on the Bounty (1935), Private Life of Henry VIII.*

Laurel, Stan (1890–1965) and **Oliver Hardy** (1892–1957). *Charlie's Aunt, An Elephant Never Forgets, Hello Trouble, Way Out West.*

Lawford, Peter (1923–84). *Exodus, Julia Misbehaves, Ocean's 11.*

Leigh, Vivien (1913–67). *Caesar and Cleopatra, Gone With the Wind, A Streetcar Named Desire, Waterloo Bridge.*

Lemmon, Jack (1925–). *The Apartment, The China Syndrome, Days of Wine and Roses, JFK, Mister Roberts, The Odd Couple, Save the Tiger, Some Like It Hot, A Touch of Class.*

Lewis, Jerry (1926–). *My Friend Irma, The Nutty Professor, Sailor Beware.*

Lockhart, June (1925–). *Adam Had Four Sons, Meet Me in St. Louis, The Yearling.*

Lollobrigida, Gina (1927–). *Beat the Devil, Solomon and Sheba, Woman of Rome.*

Lombard, Carole (1909–42). *My Man Godfrey, To Be or Not to Be, We're Not Dressing.*

Loren, Sophia (1934–). *The Condemned of Altona, Desire Under the Elms, Two Women.*

Lorre, Peter (1904–64). *Beat the Devil; Casablanca; The Maltese Falcon; The Mysterious Mr. Moto; Think Fast, Mr. Moto.*

Loy, Myrna (1905–93). *Arrowsmith, The Best Years of Our Lives, The Great Ziegfeld, Love Me Tonight, The Thin Man.*

Lugosi, Bela (1882–1956). *The Corpse Vanishes, Dracula, Frankenstein Meets the Wolf Man, The Wolf Man.*

McCrea, Joel (1905–40). *Buffalo Bill, Foreign Correspondent, Ride the High Country, Stars in My Crown, Union Pacific, Wichita.*

MacDonald, Jeanette (1903–65). *Love Me Tonight, Maytime, The Merry Widow, Naughty Marietta.*

McLaglen, Victor (1886–1959). *Gunga Din, The Informer, The Quiet Man.*

MacLaine, Shirley (1934–). *The Apartment, Irma la Douce, Some Came Running, Terms of Endearment.*

MacMurray, Fred (1908–91). *The Apartment, The Caine Mutiny, Double Indemnity, The Trail of the Lonesome Pine.*

Mansfield, Jayne (1932–67). *The Girl Can't Help It, The Wayward Bus, Will Success Spoil Rock Hunter?*

March, Fredric (1897–1975). *Anna Karenina* (1935), *The Best Years of Our Lives, Death of a Salesman* (1951), *Dr. Jekyll and Mr. Hyde, Les Miserables* (1935).

Marshall, Herbert (1890–1966). *A Bill of Divorcement, Crack-Up, Zaza.*

Martin, Dean (1917–1995). *Ocean's 11, Some Came Running, That's My Boy.*

Martin, Steve (1945–   ). *All of Me, Dead Men Don't Wear Plaid, Dirty Rotten Scoundrels, The Jerk, Parenthood, Roxanne.*

Marvin, Lee (1924–87). *Bad Day at Black Rock, Cat Ballou, The Iceman Cometh, Raintree County.*

Marx, Groucho (Julius) (1890–1977), **Harpo (Arthur) Marx** (1888–1964), and **Chico (Leonard) Marx** (1891–1961). *A Night at the Opera, Animal Crackers, Duck Soup, Monkey Business* (1931).

Mason, James (1909–1984). *Face to Face, Five Fingers, Georgy Girl, Lolita, North by Northwest, The Shooting Party, A Star Is Born* (1954), *Voyage of the Damned.*

Mastroianni, Marcello (1924–   ). *La Dolce Vita, 8 ½, Everybody's Fine, Ginger and Fred, Macaroni, The Organizer.*

Mature, Victor (1916–   ). *Kiss of Death, The Robe, Samson and Delilah.*

Menjou, Adolphe (1890–1963). *The Front Page, The Hucksters, State of the Union.*

Merrill, Dina (1928–   ). *Butterfield 8, Don't Give Up the Ship, Operation Petticoat.*

Mifune, Toshiro (1920–   ). *High and Low, The Samurai Trilogy, The Seven Samurai, Yojimbo.*

Milland, Ray (1905–86). *Forever and a Day, The Lost Weekend, Dial M for Murder, The Thief.*

Minnelli, Liza (1946–   ). *Cabaret; New York, New York; Tell Me That You Love Me, Junie Moon.*

Mitchum, Robert (1917–   ). *Blood on the Moon, Cape Fear* (1962), *Farewell My Lovely, Home from the Hill, The Night of the Hunter, Out of the Past.*

Monroe, Marilyn (1926–62). *All About Eve, The Asphalt Jungle, Bus Stop, Gentlemen Prefer Blondes, How to Marry a Millionaire, The Misfits, The Seven-Year Itch, Some Like It Hot.*

Montgomery, Robert (1904–81). *Hide-out, Night Must Fall, Riptide.*

Muni, Paul (1895–1967). *I Am a Fugitive from a Chain Gang, The Life of Emile Zola, Scarface: The Shame of a Nation, The Story of Louis Pasteur, The Valiant.*

Murray, Mae (1885–1965). *The Bride's Awakening, The Gilded Lily, Peacock Alley* (1930).

Neal, Patricia (1926–   ). *Breakfast at Tiffany's, A Face in the Crowd, Hud.*

Negri, Pola (1894–1987). *Bella Donna, East of Suez, Forbidden Paradise.*

Newman, Paul (1925–). *Butch Cassidy and the Sundance Kid, Cat on a Hot Tin Roof, The Color of Money, Hud, The Hustler, The Sting.*

Nicholson, Jack (1937–). *Batman* (1989), *Chinatown, One Flew over the Cuckoo's Nest, Ironweed, Prizzi's Honor, Terms of Endearment.*

Niven, David (1910–83). *The Dawn Patrol, The Guns of Navarone, Wuthering Heights.*

Novak, Kim (1933–). *Bell, Book, and Candle; The Man with the Golden Arm; Picnic; Vertigo.*

Oberon, Merle (1907–79). *The Dark Angel, A Song to Remember, Wuthering Heights.*

O'Brien, Pat (1899–1983). *Ceiling Zero, The Front Page, Knute Rockne: All-American, The Last Hurrah, Some Like It Hot.*

O'Hara, Maureen (1920–). *How Green Was My Valley, The Quiet Man, Sentimental Journey.*

Oland, Warner (1880–1938). *Charlie Chan Carries On, Daughter of the Dragon, The Mysterious Dr. Fu Manchu.*

Oliver, Edna May (1883–1942). *David Copperfield, Drums Along the Mohawk, Lydia.*

Olivier, Sir Laurence (1907–89). *The Divorce of Lady X, The 49th Parallel, Hamlet* (1948), *Henry V* (1945), *Rebecca, Wuthering Heights* (1939).

O'Sullivan, Maureen (1911–). *The Barretts of Wimpole Street, Pride and Prejudice, Tarzan the Ape Man, A Yank at Oxford.*

Pacino, Al (1940–). *Dog Day Afternoon, Frankie and Johnny, The Godfather, Scent of a Woman, Serpico.*

Parker, Fess (1926–). *Davy Crockett, The Jayhawkers, Old Yeller.*

Peck, Gregory (1916–). *Cape Fear* (1962), *Gentleman's Agreement, The Gunfighter, The Guns of Navarone, Roman Holiday, The Snows of Kilimanjaro, To Kill a Mockingbird, Twelve O'Clock High.*

Pfeiffer, Michelle (1957–). *Dangerous Liaisons, The Fabulous Baker Boys, Married to the Mob, Sweet Liberty.*

Pickford, Mary (1893–1979). *Coquette, Esmeralda, Kiki, Little Annie Rooney, The Little Princess, The Poor Little Rich Girl* (1917), *Stella Maris.*

Pidgeon, Walter (1887–1984). *Advise and Consent, How Green Was My Valley, Madame Curie, Mrs. Miniver.*

Poitier, Sidney (1927–). *The Blackboard Jungle, The Defiant Ones, In the Heat of the Night, Lilies of the Field.*

Powell, Dick (1904–63). *Christmas in July, Colleen, 42nd Street, I Want a Divorce, Mrs. Mike, You Never Can Tell.*

Powell, William (1892–1984). *The Great Ziegfeld, Mister Roberts, My Man Godfrey, Street of Chance, The Thin Man.*

Power, Tyrone (1913–58). *In Old Chicago, Jesse James, Nightmare Alley, This Above All, Witness for the Prosecution.*

Price, Vincent (1911–93). *Laura, The Three Musketeers, The Ten Commandments.*

Raft, George (1895–1980). *The Bowery, Each Dawn I Die, Johnny Angel, Scarface: The Shame of a Nation.*

Rains, Claude (1889–1967). *Angel on My Shoulder* (1946), *Casablanca, Here Comes Mr. Jordan, The Invisible Man, King's Row, Notorious.*

Randall, Tony (1920–   ). *The Mating Game, Pillow Talk, Will Success Spoil Rock Hunter?*

Rathbone, Basil (1892–1967). *The Adventures of Robin Hood* (1938), *The Adventures of Sherlock Holmes, Anna Karenina* (1935), *The Hound of the Baskervilles* (1939), *A Tale of Two Cities* (1935).

Reagan, Ronald (1911–   ). *Brother Rat, Dark Victory, King's Row, Knute Rockne: All-American, Santa Fe Trail.*

Redford, Robert (1937–   ). *All the President's Men, Barefoot in the Park, Butch Cassidy and the Sundance Kid, Electric Horseman, Jeremiah Johnson, The Sting, Three Days of the Condor.*

Redgrave, Sir Michael (1908–85). *David Copperfield, The Lady Vanishes, The Loneliness of the Long Distance Runner, Oh! What a Lovely War.*

Redgrave, Vanessa (1937–   ). *Blow-Up, The Devils, Howards End, Julia, A Man for All Seasons, Murder on the Orient Express.*

Reynolds, Burt (1936–   ). *At Long Last Love, Deliverance, The Longest Yard, Smokey and the Bandit.*

Reynolds, Debbie (1932–   ). *The Affairs of Dobie Gillis, The Mating Game, Singin' in the Rain, Tammy and the Bachelor.*

Richardson, Sir Ralph (1902–83). *The Divorce of Lady X, A Doll's House* (1973), *The Fallen Idol, The Four Feathers* (1939), *Richard III, Things to Come.*

Robards, Jason, Jr. (1922–   ). *All the President's Men, The Ballad of Cable Hogue, Julia, Long Day's Journey into Night, Melvin and Howard, A Thousand Clowns.*

Robinson, Bill (Bojangles) (1878–1949). *Dimples, Harlem Is Heaven, The Littlest Rebel.*

Robinson, Edward G. (1893–1973). *Brother Orchid, The Hatchet Man, Kid Galahad, Key Largo, The Red House, A Slight Case of Murder.*

Rogers, Ginger (1911–95). *Carefree, The Gay Divorcee, Kitty Foyle, Shall We Dance?, Stage Door, Top Hat.*

Romero, Cesar (1907–94). *Captain from Castile, Coney Island, Donovan's Reef.*

Rooney, Mickey (1922–   ). *Baby Face Nelson, Boys Town, Love Finds Andy Hardy, A Midsummer Night's Dream.*

Ruggles, Charles (1890–1970). *Bringing Up Baby, The Farmer's Daughter, Ruggles of Red Gap.*

Russell, Jane (1921–   ). *Gentlemen Prefer Blondes, His Kind of Woman, The Outlaw, The Paleface, The Revolt of Mamie Stover.*

Russell, Rosalind (1907–76). *Auntie Mame, China Seas, The Citadel, His Girl Friday, Mourning Becomes Electra, My Sister Eileen.*

Sanders, George (1906–72). *All About Eve, Foreign Correspondent, Rebecca.*

Schwarzenegger, Arnold (1947–). *Commando, Predator, The Terminator, Total Recall, Twins.*

Scott, George C. (1927–). *The Changeling; Dr. Strangelove, or How I Learned to Stop Worrying and Love the Bomb; The Hospital; The Hustler; The New Centurions; Patton; Petulia; They Might Be Giants.*

Scott, Randolph (1903–87). *Belle of the Yukon, Colt 45, Follow the Fleet, Jesse James, Ride the High Country, The Texans, Wagon Wheels.*

Sellers, Peter (1925–80). *Being There; Dr. Strangelove, or How I Learned to Stop Worrying and Love the Bomb; Lolita; The Party; The Return of the Pink Panther; The World of Henry Orient.*

Shearer, Norma (1902–83). *The Barretts of Wimpole Street, The Divorcee, Romeo and Juliet, The Women.*

Sheen, Martin (1940–). *Apocalypse Now, Badlands, Catholics, Gandhi.*

Sheridan, Ann (1915–67). *King's Row, The Man Who Came to Dinner, The Unfaithful.*

Simmons, Jean (1929–). *Great Expectations, Hamlet* (1948), *Spartacus.*

Smith, Maggie (1934–). *California Suite, Lily in Love, The Lonely Passion of Judith Hearne, The Prime of Miss Jean Brodie, A Room with a View.*

Stack, Robert (1919–). *Good Morning, Miss Dove; The High and the Mighty; To Be or Not to Be; Written on the Wind.*

Stallone, Sylvester (1946–). *F.I.S.T., Paradise Alley, Rambo, Rocky.*

Stanwyck, Barbara (1907–90). *Annie Oakley, Banjo on My Knee, Double Indemnity, The Lady Eve, Stella Dallas.*

Steiger, Rod (1925–). *The Chosen, The Harder They Fall, In the Heat of the Night, The Loved One, On the Waterfront.*

Stewart, James (1908–). *Destry Rides Again, The Greatest Show on Earth, Harvey, How the West Was Won, It's a Wonderful Life, Mr. Smith Goes to Washington, The Philadelphia Story, Rear Window, You Can't Take It with You.*

Stone, Fred (1873–1959). *The Goat, Johnny Get Your Gun, The Trail of the Lonesome Pine.*

Stone, Lewis (1878–1953). *Grand Hotel, Mata Hari, State of the Union.*

Streep, Meryl (1949–). *The Deer Hunter, The French Lieutenant's Woman, Ironweed, Julia, Out of Africa, Postcards from the Edge, Silkwood, Sophie's Choice.*

Streisand, Barbra (1942–). *Funny Girl, Hello Dolly, The Way We Were.*

Sullavan, Margaret (1911–60). *Back Street, Cry Havoc, Three Comrades.*

Sutherland, Donald (1934–). *The Day of the Locust, JFK, Klute, M*A*S*H, Ordinary People.*

Swanson, Gloria (1889–1983). *Bluebeard's Eighth Wife, Her Gilded Cage, Queen Kelly, Sadie Thompson, Sunset Boulevard.*

Talmadge, Norma (1893–1957). *Camille, The Dove, Fogg's Millions.*

Taylor, Elizabeth (1932–). *Butterfield 8, Cat on a Hot Tin Roof, Cleopatra, Suddenly Last Summer, The Taming of the Shrew, Who's Afraid of Virginia Woolf?*

Taylor, Robert (1911–69). *Billy the Kid, Escape, Camille, Flight Command, Quo Vadis, Stand Up and Fight, Waterloo Bridge.*

Temple, Shirley (1928–). *Captain January, Little Miss Marker, The Little Princess, The Littlest Rebel, Poor Little Rich Girl (1936).*

Tierney, Gene (1920–91). *Belle Starr, Heaven Can Wait, Laura, Whirlpool.*

Tone, Franchot (1905–68). *Dangerous, Lives of a Bengal Lancer, Mutiny on the Bounty.*

Tracy, Lee (1898–1968). *The Best Man, The Lemon Drop Kid, Private Jones.*

Tracy, Spencer (1900–67). *Bad Day at Black Rock, Boys Town, Captains Courageous, Guess Who's Coming to Dinner?, Inherit the Wind, The Last Hurrah, The Power and the Glory.*

Turner, Lana (1920–1995). *The Bad and the Beautiful, DuBarry Was a Lady, Imitation of Life, The Postman Always Rings Twice.*

Ullmann, Liv (1939–). *Cries and Whispers, The Emigrants, Face to Face, The New Land.*

Valentino, Rudolph (1895–1926). *Alimony, Blood and Sand (1922), The Four Horsemen of the Apocalypse, The Sheik.*

Von Sydow, Max (1929–). *The Exorcist, Hannah and Her Sisters, The Seventh Seal, Virgin Spring, Voyage of the Damned.*

Wayne, John (1907–79). *Hondo, The Quiet Man, Red River, Rio Bravo, She Wore a Yellow Ribbon, The Shootist, Stagecoach (1939).*

Welch, Raquel (1940–). *Fantastic Voyage, Myra Breckinridge, One Million Years B.C.*

Welles, Orson (1916–85). *Citizen Kane, The Long, Hot Summer, Macbeth (1948), A Man for All Seasons, Othello, The Stranger (1946), The Third Man, Touch of Evil.*

West, Mae (1892–1980). *Diamond Lil, I'm No Angel, My Little Chickadee, She Done Him Wrong.*

White, Pearl (1889–1938). *Perils of Paris, The Perils of Pauline, A Woman's Revenge.*

Widmark, Richard (1915–). *The Alamo, Judgment at Nuremberg, Kiss of Death.*

Wilding, Michael (1912–79). *The Egyptian, Torch Song, Trent's Last Case.*

Williams, Robin (1952–). *The Dead Poets Society, Hook, Moscow on the Hudson, Popeye, The World According to Garp.*

Winters, Jonathan (1925–). *The Fish That Saved Pittsburgh, The Loved One, The Russians Are Coming! The Russians Are Coming!*

Winters, Shelley (1922–   ). *The Big Knife, The Chapman Report, The Diary of Anne Frank, The Night of the Hunter, A Patch of Blue.*

Woodward, Joanne (1930–   ). *The Long Hot Summer; Rachel, Rachel; The Three Faces of Eve.*

Wyman, Jane (1914–   ). *Johnny Belinda, The Lost Weekend, My Man Godfrey, The Yearling.*

Young, Loretta (1912–   ). *Born to Be Bad, Bulldog Drummond Strikes Back, The Farmer's Daughter, The Hatchet Man, Platinum Blonde.*

Young, Robert (1907–   ). *Northwest Passage, Remember Last Night?, Sweet Rosie O'Grady.*

Young, Roland (1887–1953). *Sherlock Holmes, Tales of Manhattan, Topper.*

SOURCES

Martin, Mick, and Marsha Porter. *Video Movie Guide, 1992.* New York: Ballantine, 1991.

Scheuer, Steven H., ed. *Movies on TV and Videocassette, 1990.* New York: Bantam, 1989.

Thomson, David. *A Biographical Dictionary of Film.* 2nd ed., rev. New York: William Morrow, 1981.

Truitt, Evelyn Mack. *Who Was Who on Screen.* 3rd ed. New York: R. R. Bowker, 1983.

Vinson, James, Christopher Lyon, and Greg S. Faller, eds. *The International Dictionary of Films and Filmmakers, Vol. III: Actors and Actresses.* Chicago: St. James, 1986.

—J.L.M.

44

STARS OF THE
CELLULOID WEST

. . . . .

IN THE HEYDAY OF HOLLYWOOD, THERE WERE BASICALLY TWO KINDS OF western movies. By far the more common was the low-budget "hoss opera" or "oater," ground out in relentless numbers by studios such as Universal and Republic, and designed basically for edification of the young, who took them in on Fridays and Saturdays along with the episode of a serial, a cartoon, a newsreel, and perhaps a bouncing-ball sing-along. There were, to be sure, degrees of the oater; a somewhat more subtle version, designed for adult as well as child viewing, was also made.

The other kind of western was the adult variety, with a more complex plot, somewhat more intricacy of characterization, and usually featuring a more torrid romance than was considered appropriate for the very young. This wasn't budgeted so tightly, and it starred such consummate masters of facial expression and intonation as John Wayne (who began his film career in oaters), Randolph Scott, Gary Cooper, and so on.

Once movies began to be produced for commercial viewing, the western movie was inevitable. Ever since James Fenimore Cooper invented Leatherstocking (alias Natty Bumppo, Hawkeye, Le Longue Carabine, Deerslayer, etc.) and his Indian sidekick Chingachgook (pronounced Chicago, Mark Twain suggested) in the 1820s, the American imagination, and indeed that of western Europe as well, has been captivated with the story of the alert, high-minded, hard-riding hero on the frontier, skilled at outdoor pursuits.

William S. Hart was the first western movie star to enjoy widespread renown. Then Tom Mix came along with his great horse Tony, and his fame eclipsed Hart's. Mix, who had actually been a working cowboy at one time, even made his way into children's folklore, as in:

Shave and a haircut: two bits
Who's going to pay for it? Tom Mix.
Who did he marry? Marie.
Why did he marry? For money.

A galaxy of other Hollywood knights of the western range followed. In the mid–1930s the singing cowboy appeared, to the disgust of no small number of red-blooded American youths, and at about the same time the double feature: two full-fledged oaters for the price of one.

The names of many of the western actors and actresses fell from view after the great era of Saturday-morning double and triple features of black-and-white western movies came to its end sometime in the mid–1950s. Others went on to play in later films, western and otherwise.

The arrival of television in the 1950s, with the resultant demand for old movies to fill out the program schedule, gave them renewed life. Once again the air rang with the pounding hooves, the blazing away of six-guns equipped with seemingly inexhaustible magazines, shouts of "reach!" and "head 'em off at the pass!" and hearts and flowers at the end, though this time in the living room rather than the Bijou, the Majestic, the Rex, the Odeon, the Palace, or whatever the now-defunct hoss opera emporium was entitled. The supply of such movies was abundant, for in their heyday stars such as Bob Steele, Tom Tyler, Johnny Mack Brown, Hoot Gibson, Buck Jones, Ken Maynard, Roy Rogers, and Charles Starrett could turn out up to a half dozen oaters per annum for decades apiece.

Here now are some of the toughest hombres who ever rode the celluloid range, with several representative films in which each starred. If what they did wasn't really how the West was won, it was undeniably how a great deal of southern California was paid for. (When you say that, smile.) Dates are occasionally supplied to indicate which of two or more versions of the same movie is intended.

Allen, Rex (1923–). *The Arizona Cowboy, Old Oklahoma Plains, Shadows of Tombstone.*

Autry, Gene (1907–). *Back in the Saddle, Bells of Capistrano, Call of the Canyon, Mexicali Rose, Red River Valley, Riders in the Sky, Stardust on the Sage, Winning of the West.*

Barry, Donald ("Red") (1912–80). *The Adventures of Red Ryder* (serial); *The Dalton Gang, Phantom Cowboy, The Shakiest Gun in the West.*

Beery, Noah, Jr. (1913–). *The Carson City Kid, The Daltons Ride Again, Stormy, The Story of Will Rogers, Under Western Skies, White Feather.*

Boone, Richard (1917–81). *Against a Crooked Sky, Big Jake, Hombre,* "Have Gun Will Travel" (television).

Boyd, William (1895–1972). *Border Patrol, The Frontiersman, Hopalong Cassidy, Hoppy Serves a Writ, In Old Mexico, Law of the Pampas.*

Brennan, Walter (1894–1974). *Brimstone; Long, Long Trail; My Darling Clementine, The Westerner* (1940).

Brown, Johnny Mack (1904–74). *Billy the Kid, Bury Me Not on the Lone Prairie, Ghost Guns, Law of the Range, Sheriff of Medicine Bow, Valley of the Lawless, Wild West Days* (serial).

Carey, Harry (1878–1947). *The Ace of the Saddle, The Devil Horse* (serial), *Knight of the Range, Powdersmoke Range, Roped, Wagon Train.*

Carson, Sunset ("Kit") (1927–). *Alias Billy the Kid, Call of the Rockies, Rough Riders of Cheyenne, Sunset Carson Rides Again.*

Cooper, Gary (1901–61). *Alias Jesse James* (1939), *Arizona Bound, The Cowboy and the Lady, High Noon, The Texan, The Virginian* (1929), *Wild Horse Mesa.*

Crabbe, Larry ("Buster") (1908–83). *The Arizona Raiders, Billy the Kid Wanted, Devil Riders, Gunfighters of Abilene, The Thundering Herd.*

Devine, Andy (1905–77). *Law and Order, The Man Who Shot Liberty Valance, Springtime in the Sierras, Stagecoach.*

Dix, Richard (1894–1949). *The Arizonian, The Kansan, The Vanishing American, West of the Pecos.*

Eastwood, Clint (1930–). *Ambush at Cimarron, High Plains Drifter, Paint Your Wagon.*

Elliott, William ("Wild Bill") (1903–65). *Boots and Saddles, Fargo, The Great Adventures of Wild Bill Hickok* (serial), *The Great Stagecoach Robbery, Wyoming.*

Farnum, Dustin (1874–1929). *Call of the North, Davy Crockett, The Virginian* (1914, 1923).

Farnum, William (1876–1953). *The Spoilers, Last of the Duanes, Brass Commandments.*

Ford, Glen (1916–). *Advance to the Rear, The Americano,* "Cade's County" (television), *Cimarron, The Fastest Gun Alive, Texas.*

Garner, James (1928–). *Duel at Diablo,* "Maverick" (television), *Support Your Local Sheriff.*

Gibson, Hoot (1892–1962). *Ace High, Frontier Justice, The Hurricane Kid, Powdersmoke Range, Spirit of the West, Wild Horse.*

Hale, Monte (1921–). *Home on the Range, California Firebrand, San Antone Ambush, The Missourians.*

Hart, William S. (1870–1946). *The Bargain, The Darkening Trail, The Gunfighter, The Silent Man, Wild Bill Hickok, Wolves of the Trail.*

Hayes, George ("Gabby") (1885–1969). *Heart of the Golden West, Helldorado, Riders of Destiny, West of the Divide.*

Holt, Tim (1918–73). *Fighting Frontier, Gold Is Where You Find It, The Law West of Tombstone, Masked Raiders, My Darling Clementine, Stagecoach, The Treasure of the Sierra Madre, Under the Tonto Rim.*

Johnson, Ben (1922–). *Chisum, Hondo, The Rare Breed, Shane, She Wore a Yellow Ribbon, Will Penny.*

Jones, Buck (1889–1942). *The Arizona Express, California Trail, Chain Lightning, Empty Saddles, Gordon of Ghost City* (serial), *Not a Drum Was Heard, The Overland Express, Sundown Rider, White Eagle.*

Lancaster, Burt (1913–). *Gunfight at the O.K. Corral, The Kentuckian, The Scalphunters, The Unforgiven.*

Lane, Allan ("Rocky") (1904–73). *Bells of Rosarita, Daredevils of the West* (serial), *Desperadoes of Dodge City, King of the Royal Mounted* (serial), *Silver City Kid, Stagecoach to Monterey, Thundering Caravans.*

LaRue, Alfred ("Lash") (1921–). *Law of the Lash, Song of Old Wyoming, The Thundering Trail.*

McCoy, Colonel Tim (1891–1978). *Beyond the Law, The Fighting Marshal, The Frontiersman, The Overland Telegraph, The Prescott Kid, Requiem for a Gunfighter, Square Shooter, The Westerner* (1934).

McCrea, Joel (1905–90). *Colorado Territory, Stranger on Horseback, Union Pacific, The Virginian* (1946), *Wells Fargo, Wichita.*

Maynard, Ken (1895–1973). *California Mail, Cheyenne, Gun Gospel, In Old Santa Fe, The Lone Avenger, Somewhere in Sonora, The Strawberry Roan, Unknown Cavalier, Wild Horse Stampede.*

Maynard, Kermit (1898–1971). *The Fighting Trooper, Timber War, Wildcat Trooper, The Fighting Texans.*

Mix, Tom (1880–1940). *The Arizona Wildcat, The Coming of the Law, Destry Rides Again* (1932), *The Heart of Texas Ryan, The Miracle Rider* (serial), *Tony Runs Wild, The Wilderness Trail.*

Murphy, Audie (1924–71). *The Cimarron Kid, The Duel at Silver Creek, Posse from Hell, Walk the Proud Land.*

O'Brien, George (1900–85). *Cheyenne Autumn, Hard Rock Harrigan, The Iron Horse, O'Malley of the Mounted, Riders of the Purple Sage, Whispering Smith Speaks.*

Ritter, Tex (1905–74). *Deep in the Heart of Texas, King of Dodge City, Rollin' Plains, Song of the Gringo, The Utah Trail.*

Robertson, Dale (1923–). "Death Valley Days" (television), *Golden Girl,* "Tales of Wells Fargo" (television), *Two Flags West.*

Rogers, Roy (1912–). *In Old Caliente, King of the Cowboys, My Pal Trigger, The Mysterious Avenger, The Ranger and the Lady, Roll On, Texas Moon, The Yellow Rose of Texas.*

Scott, Randolph (1903–87). *Belle Starr, Canadian Pacific, Colt .45, Heritage of* the Desert, Jesse James (1939), *The Last of the Mohicans* (1936), Santa Fe, The Virginian (1929).

Starrett, Charles (1904–86). *Bandits of El Dorado, Blazing across the Pecos, The Blazing Trail, Colorado Trail, Dodge City Trail, The Durango Kid, Return of the Durango Kid, Snake River Desperadoes.*

Steele, Bob (1907–88). *The Amazing Vagabond, Billy the Kid Outlawed, Doomed at Sundown, Hidden Valley, Powdersmoke Range, Requiem for a Gunfighter, Westward Ho!, The Wild Westerners.*

Stewart, James (1908–). *Destry Rides Again, The Far Country, How the West Was Won, The Shootist.*

Thomson, Fred (1890–1928).*Thundering Hoofs, Ridin' the Wind, Jesse James* (1927), *Pioneer Scout.*

Tyler, Tom (1903–54). *The Arizona Streak, Born to Battle, Drums Along the Mohawk, The Flying U Ranch, Laramie Kid, Mystery Ranch, The Phantom of the West* (serial), *Return of the Badmen, She Wore a Yellow Ribbon, Silver Bullet, The Westerner* (1940.)

Wayne, John (1907–79). *Big Jake, The Big Stampede, The Big Trail, Hondo, How the West Was Won, Randy Rides Alone, She Wore a Yellow Ribbon, Stagecoach, True Grit.*

SOURCES

Fenin, George N., and William K. Everson. *The Western: From Silents to the Seventies.* Rev. ed. New York: Grossman, 1973.

Holland, Ted. *B Western Actors Encyclopedia: Facts, Photos and Filmographies for More than 250 Familiar Faces.* Jefferson, N.C.: McFarland & Co., 1989.

Lenihan, John H. *Showdown: Confronting Modern America in the Western Film.* Urbana: University of Illinois Press, 1987.

McDonald, Archie P., ed. *Shooting Stars: Heroes and Heroines of Western Film.* Bloomington: Indiana University Press, 1987.

Martin, Mick, amd Marsha Porter. *Video Movie Guide, 1992.* New York: Ballantine, 1991.

Miller, Lee O. *The Great Cowboy Stars of Movies and Television.* New Rochelle, N.Y.: Arlington House, 1979.

Nye, Douglas E. *Those Six-Gun Heroes: 25 Great Movie Cowboys.* Spartanburg, S.C.: ETV Endowment of South Carolina, 1982.

—John Sepich; J.L.M.

45

POPULAR RADIO SHOWS

. . . . .

Next to popular music of the big band era, radio programming of the pretelevision era probably constitutes the most immediately available source of nostalgia today. Few American citizens indeed who are in late middle age or older are unable to recite the lineup of network radio shows on Sunday evenings, or that of children's serials of late weekday afternoons, during the 1930s, 1940s, and into the 1950s. Give such a person a couple of drinks and he or she will willingly sing all the words to the theme song of Ovaltine's Little Orphan Annie: "Who's that little chatterbox / The one with pretty auburn locks/etc. etc."

The first commercial radio stations to begin regular programming did so in the early 1920s, when radio was still a luxury to be enjoyed by the few and radio receiving sets were costly, complex affairs occupying entire cabinets. Within a few years, however, radio sets became considerably less expensive and less complicated, radio stations were established in most cities and towns, and the average middle-class American family was tuning in regularly to hear its favorite programs.

The first American radio network was the National Broadcasting Company, beginning in 1926. There were two NBC networks, the Red and the Blue. In 1927 the Columbia Broadcasting System—CBS—was formed, and in 1934 the Mutual Broadcasting System. NBC's massive linkage of chain broadcasting came under federal scrutiny in the early 1940s, and the Blue network was sold, becoming the American Broadcasting Company—ABC—in 1943.

The decades of the 1930s and 1940s were network radio's "golden years." Certain radio shows achieved enormous popularity. Housewives listened to soap operas (so called because their sponsors tended to be the major manufacturers of soap flakes) as they performed their household duties. In the late afternoon, the children came in from play to hear their favorite 15-minute serials. Following the network news, there were comedy, drama, and musical programs for the family. On Saturday afternoons the networks vied for attention with college football, and after World War II the NBC and CBS major league baseball games of the week. Sunday evening was the time for the comedians—Joe Penner, Jack Benny, Fred Allen, Edgar Bergen and Charlie McCarthy, others—and for musical and variety programs.

It was the coming of television in the 1950s that ended the hegemony of network radio programming. Televison now took over the function of providing family entertainment, and radio became what it is today—primarily recorded music, broadcast on a local basis. The networks' role became principally that of providing news broadcasts. The development of Frequency Modulation—FM—broadcasting in the 1950s and 1960s virtually eliminated static interference, and the relative inexpensiveness of broadcasting on a local scale made it possible for classical music and programming of greater depth and sophistication to be aired throughout the nation.

The listing of network radio programs that follows is for the years before TV took over, when radio was the supreme form of family entertainment in the home. The names of some of the more popular shows are given, together with the years during which they flourished, the networks broadcasting them, their commercial sponsors (when available), and some of the principal personalities they featured. When a particular role on a show was played by more than one person in different periods, the names of the performers are separated by slashes.

Abbott and Costello Show. 1942–46 (NBC); 1947–48 (ABC). Sponsor: Camel Cigarettes. Starring Bud Abbott and Lou Costello.

Aldrich Family (Henry Aldrich). 1939 (NBC Blue). Sponsor: Jell-O. Featuring Ezra Stone/Norman Tokar/Raymond Ives/Dickie Jones/Bobby Ellis, Clyde Fillmore/House Jameson/Tom Shirley, and Lea Penman/Katharine Raht/Regina Wallace.

Allen's Alley. See **Fred Allen Show**.

Al Pearce and His Gang. 1935–36 (NBC); 1937–38 (CBS); 1938–39 (NBC); 1939–42 (CBS); 1943 (NBC Blue); 1945–46 (ABC). Sponsors: Pepsodent, Ford Motor Company, Grape Nuts, Dole Pineapple, Camel Cigarettes. Comedy starring Al Pearce and cast including Arlene Harris, Kitty O'Neil, Bill Comstock, Jennison Parker, Monroe Upton, and Harry Stewart.

American Album of Familiar Music. 1931–51 (NBC Red). Songs and music presented by cast of regulars as well as guest stars, headed by Frank Munn.

American Forum of the Air. 1937–43 (Mutual); 1949–50s (NBC). Discussion with guests moderated by Theodore Granik.

Amos 'n Andy. 1929–48 (NBC Red); 1948–54 (CBS). Sponsors: Pepsodent, Campbell Soups, Rinso, Rexall. Comedy starring Charles J. Correll and Freeman F. Gosden.

Arthur Godfrey's Talent Scouts. 1946–53 (CBS). Sponsor: Lipton Tea. Variety show hosted by Arthur Godfrey with performances by undiscovered talent.

Arthur Godfrey Time. 1945–72 (CBS). Sponsors: Chesterfield Cigarettes and approximately 60 other sponsors. Variety show with host Arthur Godfrey and regulars including Patti Clayton, Julius LaRosa, Tony Marvin, Marshall Young, Frank Parker, LuAnn Simms, the Symphonettes, the Polka Dots.

Atwater Kent Hour. 1926–31 (NBC). Sponsor: Atwater Kent. Classical music, with numerous Metropolitan Opera stars. Frances Alda frequently performed; Josef Pasternak and Donald Voorhees conducted orchestra.

Aunt Jenny's True-Life Stories. 1937–56 (CBS). Sponsor: Spry. Serial with Edith Spencer/Agnes Young and Dan Seymour.

Baby Snooks Show. 1939–48 (CBS); 1949–51 (NBC). Sponsors: Post Cereals, Sanka Coffee. Comedy with Fanny Brice, Hanley Stafford, Lalive Brownell/Lois Corbett/Arlene Harris.

Bachelor's Children. 1936–46 (CBS). Sponsor: Old Dutch Wonder Bread. Serial drama with Hugh Studebaker, Marjorie Hannan, Patricia Dunlap, and Olan Soule.

Believe It or Not. 1930 (NBC); 1932, 1935 (Blue); 1939 (CBS); 1942 (Blue); 1943 (Mutual); 1947 (NBC). Variety drama with host Robert L. Ripley.

Bell Telephone Hour. 1940–58 (NBC). Sponsor: Bell Telephone. Musical show with Donald Voorhees and the Bell Telephone Orchestra.

Ben Bernie, the Old Maestro. 1930 (WJZ New York); 1931 (CBS); 1932–35 (NBC); 1935 (Blue); 1937–39 (CBS); 1940 (Blue); 1941 (CBS). Sponsors: Mennen, Pabst Blue Ribbon, American Can, U.S. Rubber, Half & Half Tobacco, Bromo Seltzer, Wrigley's Gum. Variety show starring Ben Bernie with regulars Lew Lehr, Mary Small, Manny Prager, Buddy Clark, Jackie Heller, Jane Pickens, Pat Kennedy, Dick Stabile, Frank Prince.

The Big Story. 1947–55 (NBC). Sponsor: Pall Mall Cigarettes. Drama with narrator Bob Sloane.

Big Town. 1937–48 (CBS); 1948–52 (NBC). Sponsors: Rinso, Ironized Yeast, Bayer Aspirin, Lifebuoy Soap. Drama series with Edward G. Robinson and Claire Trevor.

Bing Crosby Show. 1931–34 (CBS); 1935–46 (NBC); 1947–54 (ABC). Sponsors: General Electric, Philco, Chesterfield Cigarettes. Variety show starring Bing Crosby. See also **Kraft Music Hall**.

Blondie. 1939–50 (CBS). Sponsors: Camel Cigarettes, Ford Motor Company, Super Suds. Situation comedy based on Chic Young's comic strip with Arthur Lake, Penny Singleton, and Hanley Stafford.

Bob and Ray Show. 1946–89 (NBC). Various sponsors. Comedy with Bob Elliott and Ray Goulding.

Bob Burns Show. 1941 (CBS); 1942–47 (NBC). Sponsors: Campbell Soups, Lever Brothers, American Foods. Comedy starring Bob Burns.

Bob Hope Show. 1934–55 (NBC). Sponsor: Pepsodent. Variety show starring host Bob Hope, with Jerry Colonna and others.

Box 13. 1948 (syndicated). Adventure action series with Alan Ladd.

Breakfast at Sardi's (later known as **Tom Breneman's Hollywood** and **Breakfast in Hollywood**). 1941–49 (NBC Blue/ABC). Early-morning interview show at Sardi's restaurant with Tom Breneman/Garry Moore (1949).

Breakfast Club. 1933–68 (NBC/ABC). Variety show with host Don McNeill.

Buck Rogers in the 25th Century. 1931–45 (CBS); 1946–47 (Mutual). Sponsors: Kellogg's, Cocomalt, Cream of Wheat, Popsicle. Science-fiction adventure show with Matt Crowley/Curtis Arnall/Carl Frank/John Larkin, Adele Ronson, Elaine Melchoir, and Edgar Stehli.

Captain Midnight. 1940–49 (Mutual/NBC Blue). Sponsor: Ovaltine. Children's adventure series with Ed Prentiss.

Carnation Contented Hour. 1932 (NBC Blue); 1933–49 (NBC Red); 1949–51 (CBS). Sponsor: Carnation. Musical variety show with host Tony Marvin and regulars Jo Stafford, Buddy Clark, and the Ken Lane Singers.

Cavalcade of America. 1935–39 (CBS); 1939–53 (NBC). Sponsor: DuPont Corporation. Drama anthology of famous Americans in history with narrator Gabriel Heatter.

Chandu the Magician. 1932–36, 1948–49 (Mutual); 1949–50 (ABC). Sponsor: White King Soap. Juvenile adventure show with Gayne Whitman/Tom Collins.

Charlie Chan. 1932–33 (NBC Blue); 1937–39, 1944–46 (Mutual); 1945–47 (ABC); 1947–48 (Mutual); 1950 (syndicated). Sponsors: Lever Brothers, Pharmaco, Inc. Mystery with Walter Connolly/Ed Begley/Santos Ortega/William Rees, and Leon Janney/Rodney Jacobs.

Cheerio. 1927–late 1930s (NBC). Talk show with "Cheerio"—Charles K. Field.

Cities Service Concerts. 1927–56 (NBC). Sponsor: Pillsbury Flour. Concert music/discussion with Graham McNamee, Jessica Dragonette/Lucille Manners, and band of Edwin Franko Goldman/Rosario Bourdon/Frank Parker and the Cavalier Quartet/Paul LaValle.

Clara, Lu, and Em. 1931–36 (Blue); 1942 (CBS). Sponsor: Pillsbury Flour. Serial drama with Louise Starkey/Fran Allison, Isabel Carothers/Dorothy Day, and Helen King/Harriet Allyn.

Counterspy. 1942–50 (NBC Blue); 1950–53 (NBC); 1954–57 (Mutual). Sponsors: Pepsi-Cola, Gulf/Gulf Oil, and others. Adventure show with House Jameson, Don MacLaughlin, and Mandel Kramer.

Crime Doctor. 1940–47 (CBS). Sponsor: Philip Morris. Crime drama with Roy Collins/House Jameson/Everett Sloane/John McIntire, Edgar Stehli, and Walter Greaza.

Death Valley Days. 1930–41 (NBC Blue); 1941–45 (CBS). Sponsor: Pacific Borax Company. Western adventure show with Tim Daniel Frawley/George

Rand/Harry Humphrey/John MacBryde, Harvey Hays, John White, Edwin Bruce, Robert Haag, and Olyn Landick.

Dick Tracy. 1935 (Mutual); 1937–39 (NBC). Adventure serial based on comic strip by Chester Gould with Ned Wever/Matt Crowley, Barry Thompson, and Andy Donnelly/Jackie Kelk.

Dr. Christian. 1937–53 (CBS). Sponsor: Vaseline. Medical drama with Jean Hersholt, Lurene Tuttle/Helen Claire/Rosemary DeCamp.

Double or Nothing. 1940–46 (Mutual); 1947 (CBS); 1947–52 (NBC). Sponsor: Feenamint, Campbell Soups. Quiz show with host Walter Compton/John Reed King/Todd Russell.

Dragnet. 1949–56 (NBC). Sponsors: Fatima Cigarettes, Chesterfield Cigarettes. Police drama with Jack Webb, Barton Yarborough, Richard Boone, and Ben Alexander.

Duffy's Tavern. 1941 (CBS); 1942–51 (NBC). Sponsors: Schick, Ipana, Blatz Beer. Comedy with Ed Gardner and Shirley Booth/Florence Halop/Gloria Erlanger/Florence Robinson/Sandra Gould/Hazel Shermet.

Easy Aces. 1930 (KMBC, Kansas City, Mo.); 1931–43 (NBC); 1943–45 (CBS); 1948 (CBS—under name **Mr. Ace & Jane**). Sponsor: Anacin. Comedy serial with Goodman Ace and Jane Ace.

Eddie Cantor Show. 1931–34 (NBC); 1935–40 (CBS); 1940–49 (NBC). Sponsors: Chase and Sanborn, Pebeco Toothpaste, Texaco Oil, Camel Cigarettes, Sal Hepatica. Comedy/variety show starring Eddie Cantor.

Edgar Bergen and Charlie McCarthy Show (Chase and Sanborn Hour). 1937–48 (NBC); 1949–56 (CBS). Sponsors: Chase and Sanborn, Coca-Cola, Hudnut, Kraft Cheese. Comedy/variety show with ventriloquist Edgar Bergen, dummies Charlie McCarthy, Mortimer Snerd, and Effie Klinker; W. C. Fields; and emcee Don Ameche.

Ellery Queen (Adventures of Ellery Queen). 1939–40 (CBS); 1941–44 (NBC); 1945–47 (CBS); 1947–48 (ABC). Sponsors: Bromo Seltzer, Anacin. Mystery with Hugh Marlowe/Carleton Young/Sidney Smith/Larry Dobkin.

Escape. 1947–54 (CBS). Sponsor: Richfield Oil Company (briefly). High-adventure anthology with narrator William Conrad/Paul Frees.

Ethel and Albert. 1944–50 (ABC). Comedy with Peg Lynch, Richard Widmark/Alan Bunce, and Madeleine Pierce.

Eveready Hour. 1923 (local New York); 1926–29 (NBC). Sponsor: National Carbon Company. Variety show featuring George Gershwin, the Flonzaley String Quartet, Eddie Cantor, Julia Marlowe, Will Rogers, Pablo Casals, and others.

Family Theater. 1947–57 (Mutual). Drama anthology with guest hosts and performers including Walter Brennan, Ethel Barrymore, Bing Crosby, Irene Dunne, J. Carrol Naish.

Famous Jury Trials. 1936–37 (Mutual); 1940–49 (NBC Blue/ABC). Sponsors:

Mennen Aftershave, O. Henry, General Mills. Drama with Maurice Franklin and Roger DeKoven/DeWitt McBride.

Father Knows Best. 1949–54 (NBC). Sponsor: General Foods, including Maxwell House and Post Toasties. Situation comedy starring Robert Young, June Whitley, Rhoda Williams, Ted Donaldson, and Norma Jean Nilson.

The Fat Man. 1946–51 (ABC). Sponsor: Pepto-Bismol. Crime drama with J. Scott Smart, Ed Begley, and Mary Patton.

FBI in Peace and War. 1944–58 (CBS). Sponsors: Lava Soap, Wildroot Cream Oil, Lucky Strike, Nescafe, Wrigley's Gum. Crime adventure starring Martin Blaine.

Fibber McGee and Molly. 1935–52 (NBC). Sponsors: Johnson Wax, Pet Milk, Reynolds Aluminum, Alka-Seltzer. Comedy starring Jim Jordan and Marian Jordan.

First Nighter. 1929–38 (NBC Blue); 1938–41 (CBS); 1942–44 (Mutual); 1945–49 (CBS); 1952–53 (NBC). Sponsors: Campana Balm, Miller High Life. Drama and comedy anthology with Charles P. Hughes/Bret Morrison/Marvin Miller/Don Briggs/Rye Billsbury.

Fitch Bandwagon. 1937–48 (NBC). Sponsor: Fitch Shampoo. Variety show with Phil Harris and Alice Faye Harris.

Ford Sunday Evening Hour. 1934–42 (CBS); 1945–46 (ABC). Sponsor: Ford Motor Company. Classical music with host John Charles Thomas/Lawrence Tibbett and the Eugene Ormandy Orchestra/Detroit Symphony Orchestra.

Fred Allen Show. 1932–37 (CBS); 1938–39 (NBC); 1940–49 (CBS). Sponsors: Hellmann's Mayonnaise, Ipana and Sal Hepatica, Blue Bonnet Margarine, Tenderleaf Tea, Shefford's Cheese, Ford Motor Company, V–8 Vegetable Juice, Texaco Gasoline. Comedy/variety show with host Fred Allen and cast of Allen's Alley—Charles Cantor, Alan Reed, Kenny Delmar, Minerva Pious, Parker Fennelly, and Peter Donald.

Fred Waring Show. 1938–50 (NBC). Sponsors: Bromo Quinine, Chesterfield Cigarettes, American Meat Company, General Electric. Musical variety show with host Fred Waring and his band.

Gangbusters. 1936–39 (CBS); 1940–44 (NBC Blue); 1945–48 (ABC); 1948–55 (CBS); 1955–57 (Mutual). Sponsors: Palmolive Brushless Shaving Cream, Cue Magazine, Sloan's Liniment, Waterman Pens, General Foods, and others. Drama with Phillips H. Lord/Colonel H. Norman Schwarzkopf/John C. Hilley/Dean Carlton, and Lewis J. Valentine.

Gene Autry's Melody Ranch. 1940–56 (CBS). Sponsor: Wrigley's Gum. Western variety show with Gene Autry and featuring Pat Buttram, Jim Boles, and Tyler McVey.

George Burns and Gracie Allen Show. 1932–36 (CBS); 1937 (NBC); 1938–39 (CBS); 1940 (NBC); 1941–45 (CBS); 1945–49 (NBC); 1949–50 (CBS). Sponsors:

Robert Burns Cigars, White Owl Cigars, Campbell's Soups, Grape Nuts, Chesterfield Cigarettes, Hinds Cream, Hormel Packing, Lever Brothers, Swan Soap, Maxwell House Coffee. Variety show starring George Burns and Gracie Allen with regulars including Mel Blanc, Elvia Allman, Sara Berner, and Dick Crenna.

The Goldbergs. 1929–34 (NBC); 1937–45 (CBS/Mutual); 1949 (CBS). Sponsors: Pepsodent, Oxydol, General Foods. Comedy/drama series with Gertrude Berg, James R. Waters, Roslyn Siber, Alfred Ryder/Everett Sloane.

Grand Ole Opry. 1925–present (WSM Nashville); 1939–57 (NBC). Sponsors: Prince Albert Tobacco, Schick, Coca-Cola, Kellogg's, Lava, Pet Milk. Country-western music/variety show with host George D. Hay, Whitey Ford, Minnie Pearl, Ernest Tubb, Gene Autry *et al.*

Grand Slam. 1943–53 (CBS). Sponsors: Wesson Oil, Continental Baking. Daytime quiz show with host Irene Beasley.

Great Gildersleeve. 1941–54 (NBC). Sponsor: Kraft Foods. Situation comedy with Hal Perry/Willard Waterman, Walter Tetley, Lurene Tuttle/Marylee Robb.

Green Hornet. 1936 (WXYZ Detroit); 1938 (Mutual); 1939–50 (NBC Blue/ABC); 1952 (Mutual). Sponsors: General Mills, Orange Crush. Mystery adventure with Al Hodge/Donovan Faust/Bob Hall/Jack McCarthy, Raymond Hayashi/Rollon Parker/Mickey Tolan.

Guiding Light. 1938–47 (NBC Red); 1947–56 (CBS). Serial drama with original cast of Ed Prentiss, Sarajane Wells, Ruth Bailey, Reese Taylor, Eloise Kummer, Norma Jean Ross, Laurette Fillbrandt, and Gladys Heen.

Gunsmoke. 1952–61 (CBS). Sponsors: Chesterfield and L&M Cigarettes, Kellogg's. Western with William Conrad, Parley Baer, Georgia Ellis, and Howard McNear.

Hallmark Playhouse. 1948–55 (CBS). Drama anthology with host James Hilton.

Hardy Family. 1950 (syndicated). Comedy/drama with Mickey Rooney, Lewis Stone, Jean Parker, Dick Crenna.

Hop Harrigan. 1942–45 (NBC Blue); 1946–48 (Mutual). Sponsor: General Foods. Adventure serial with Chester Stratton/Albert Aley, Mitzi Gould, Kenny Lynch/Jackson Beck.

Hour of Charm. 1935–38, 1940–46 (NBC); 1946–48 (CBS). Sponsor: General Electric. Performances by all-girl orchestra headed by Phil Spitalny.

House Party. 1945–67 (CBS). Sponsors: General Electric, Pillsbury, Lever Brothers. Audience participation with host Art Linkletter.

I Love a Mystery. 1939–44 (NBC); 1949–52 (Mutual). Sponsors: Fleischmann's Yeast, Procter & Gamble. Adventure show with Barton Yarborough/Jim Boles, Michael Raffetto/Russell Thorson/Jay Novello/John McIntire, Walter Paterson/Tony Randall, and Gloria Blondell.

Information, Please. 1938–48 (NBC Blue/ABC). Sponsors: Canada Dry, Mobil Oil. Panel quiz with moderator Clifton Fadiman and panel members Oscar Levant, John Kieran, Franklin P. Adams, and guests.

Inner Sanctum Mysteries (The Squeaking Door). 1941–42 (NBC Blue); 1943–50 (CBS); 1950–52 (ABC). Sponsors: Carter's Pills, Colgate, Lipton Tea and Soup, Bromo Seltzer, Mars Candy. Mystery with host Raymond Edward Johnson/Paul McGrath/House Jameson and guest stars.

It Pays to Be Ignorant. 1942–44 (WOR New York); 1944–49 (CBS). Sponsors: Philip Morris, others. Comedy panel quiz with quizmaster Tom Howards and panelists George Shelton, Lulu McConnell, Harry McNaughton.

Jack Armstrong, the All-American Boy. 1933–36 (CBS); 1937–41 (NBC); 1941–42 (Mutual), 1942–50 (ABC). Sponsor: Wheaties. Adventure serial with St. John Terrell/Jim Ameche/Stanley Harris/Charles Flynn/Michael Rye.

Jack Benny Program. 1932 (NBC Blue); 1932 (CBS); 1933–49 (NBC); 1949–55 (CBS). Sponsors: Chevrolet, Canada Dry, Jell-O, Grape Nuts Flakes, Lucky Strike. Comedy/variety show starring Jack Benny with Mary Livingstone, Dennis Day, Eddie Anderson, Don Wilson, and others.

Jack Pearl Show. 1932–36 (NBC); 1936 (NBC Blue); 1942 (Mutual); 1948 (NBC). Sponsors: Lucky Strike, Royal Gelatin, U.S. Treasury Department. Comedy starring Jack Pearl.

Jimmy Durante–Garry Moore Show. 1943 (NBC); 1943–47 (CBS); 1947–50 (NBC as the *Jimmy Durante Show*). Sponsors: Camel Cigarettes, Rexall. Comedy/variety show starring Jimmy Durante and Garry Moore (until 1947).

Joe Penner Show (also known as the *Baker's Broadcast*). 1933–34, 1936–40 (CBS). Sponsor: Fleischmann's Yeast. Situation comedy with Joe Penner.

Jungle Jim. Early 1940s, exact date unknown (syndicated). Sponsor: Comic Weekly-Hearst Newspapers. Adventure with Matt Crowley, Juano Hernandez, Franc Hale, Irene Winston.

Kraft Music Hall. 1933–49 (NBC). Sponsor: Kraft Foods. Variety show with host Deems Taylor/Al Jolson/Bing Crosby/Eddie Foy/John Scott Trotter/Bob Burns, etc. See also *Bing Crosby Show*.

Ladies Be Seated. 1944–50 (ABC). Sponsor: Quaker Oats. Half-hour variety show with music, games, interviews hosted by Ed East/Johnny Olson/Tom Moore.

Land of the Lost. 1943–45 (ABC); 1945–47 (Mutual); 1947–48 (ABC). Sponsor: Bosco chocolate-flavored syrup. Children's fantasy with Betty Jane Tyler, Ray Ives, Junius Matthews/William Keene.

Let's Pretend. 1930–34 (as *Adventures of Helen & Mary*); 1939–54 (CBS). Sponsor: Cream of Wheat. Children's drama with Bill Adams, Harry Swan/Brad Baker, Marilyn Erskine, Miriam Wolfe.

Life Can Be Beautiful. 1938–54 (CBS). Sponsor: Spic and Span. Serial drama with Alice Reinheart/Teri Keane, Ralph Locke, Earl Larrimore/John Holbrook, Carl Eastman, Richard Kollmar/Dick Nelson.

Life of Riley. 1943–51 (NBC). Sponsors: American Meat Institute, Prell Shampoo, Pabst Blue Ribbon. Situation comedy with Lionel Stander/William Bendix, Grace Coppin/Paula Winslow/Georgia Backus.

Life with Luigi. 1948–53 (CBS). Sponsor: Wrigley's Gum. Ethnic situation comedy with J. Carrol Naish, Jody Gilbert, Alan Reed, Mary Shipp, Joe Forte, Hans Conried, Ken Peters.

Lights Out. 1934 (WENR Chicago); 1935–39 (NBC Red); 1942–43 (CBS); 1945, 1946 (NBC); 1947 (Mutual). Sponsor: Ironized Yeast (CBS years only). Horror anthology with announcer George Stone/Bob Lemond and guest stars.

Little Orphan Annie. 1931–43 (NBC Blue). Sponsor: Ovaltine. Adventure serial adapted from Harold Gray's comic strip with Shirley Bell/Janice Gilbert, Allan Barruck/Mel Torme, Jerry O'Mera.

Lone Ranger. 1933 (WXYZ Detroit); 1934–42 (Mutual); 1942–55 (NBC Blue/ABC). Sponsors: Silvercup Bread, Bond Bread, General Foods. Western adventure show starring George Seaton/Jack Deeds/Earle Graser/Brace Breemer/John Todd/Jim Jewell and John Todd.

Lorenzo Jones. 1937–55 (NBC). Sponsors: Sterling Drugs for Philips' Milk of Magnesia and Bayer Aspirin, Procter & Gamble. Comedy serial with Karl Swenson, Betty Garde/Lucille Wall, Jean McCoy, Joseph Julian, John Brown, Nancy Sheridan/Mary Wickes/Grace Keddy, Elliott Reid, Colleen Ward, Ann Shepherd, and Art Carney.

Lum and Abner. 1931–38 (NBC); 1938–40 (CBS); 1941–47 (ABC); 1948–49 (CBS); 1950–53 (ABC). Sponsors: Quaker Oats, Horlick's Malted Milk, Postum, Alka Seltzer, Frigidaire, Ford Motor Company. Comedy with Chester Lauck, Norris Goff, and Andy Devine.

Lux Radio Theater. 1934–48 (NBC); 1935–55 (CBS); appeared on two networks for a period at same time. Sponsor: Lux. Adaptations of films with host Cecil B. DeMille/William Keighley and guest actors.

Major Bowes' Original Amateur Hour. 1934 (WHN New York); 1935 (NBC); 1936–45 (CBS); 1948–52 (ABC). Sponsors: Chase and Sanborn, Chrysler Corporation, Old Gold Cigarettes. Talent contest and variety show hosted by Major Edward Bowes/Jay C. Flippen/Ted Mack.

Ma Perkins. 1933–60 (CBS). Sponsor: Oxydol. Serial drama with Virginia Payne, Rita Ascot/Marjorie Hannan/Cheer Brentson/Laurette Fillbrandt/Margaret Draper, Gilbert Faust, Charles Egleston/Edwin Wolfe.

March of Time. 1931–37 (CBS); 1937–44 (NBC); 1945 (ABC). Sponsors: Time Magazine; Rennington-Rand and Wrigley's Gum (between 1933 and 1936). News documentary with actors including Dwight Weist, Orson Welles, Agnes Moorhead, Martin Gabel, and Kenny Delmar.

Meet Corliss Archer. 1943–52 (CBS); 1952–53 (ABC); 1954–55 (CBS). Sponsors: Anchor Hocking Glass, Campbell Soups, Electricity Co-Ops. Situation comedy with Janet Waldo/Priscilla Lyon/Lugene Sanders, Fred Shields/Bob Bailey, Irene Tedrow/Helen Mack, and Sam Edwards/David Hughes/Irwin Lee.

Mercury Theater on the Air (also known as the **Campbell Playhouse, Orson Welles Theater, Mercury Wonder Show**). 1938–43 (CBS). Sponsor: Campbell Soups. Drama anthology with host Orson Welles.

Metropolitan Opera Broadcasts. 1931–present (NBC). Sponsor: Texaco. Opera, long hosted by Milton Cross.

Mr. and Mrs. North. 1942–47 (NBC); 1947–54 (CBS). Sponsors: Woodbury Soap, Jergens Lotion, Colgate-Palmolive. Crime drama starring Joseph Curtin/Richard Denning and Alice Frost/Barbara Britton.

Mr. District Attorney. 1939–51 (NBC); 1951–52 (ABC). Sponsors: Vitalis and Sal Hepatica, Bristol-Myers. Crime drama with Dwight Weist/Raymond Edward Johnson/Jay Jostyn/David Brian, Vicki Vola, Jay Jostyn/Walter Kinsella, and Eleanor Silver/Arlene Francis.

Mr. Keen, Tracer of Lost Persons. 1937–42 (NBC Blue); 1942–51 (CBS); 1951–52 (NBC); 1952–54 (CBS). Sponsors: California Syrup of Figs, Bisodol, Kolynos, Whitehall Drug Company, Chesterfield Cigarettes, others. Mystery adventure starring Bennett Kilpack/Philip Clarke/Arthur Hughes, Florence Malone, Jim Kelly.

My Friend Irma. 1947–54 (CBS). Sponsors: Lever Brothers, Camel Cigarettes, others. Situation comedy starring Marie Wilson.

Myrt and Marge. 1931–45 (CBS); 1946 (syndicated). Serial drama starring Myrtle Vail and Donna Damerel Flick/Helen Mack.

National Barn Dance. 1924–33 (WLS Chicago); 1933–46 (NBC); 1948–50 (ABC). Sponsors: Alka Seltzer, Philips' Milk of Magnesia. Country-western music and variety show starring Joe Kelly.

National Farm and Home Hour. 1928–1950s (NBC). Sponsors: Montgomery Ward, U.S. Department of Agriculture. Variety show with crop and agricultural information, with Everett Mitchell, Don Ameche/Raymond Edward Johnson, and orchestra of Harry Kogen and the Homesteaders.

Nick Carter, Master Detective. 1943–55 (Mutual). Sponsors: Lin-X Home Brighteners, Cudahy Meats. Crime drama with Lon Clark, Helen Choate/Charlotte Manson, Ed Latimer, and John Kane.

One Man's Family. 1932–59 (NBC). Sponsors: Wesson Oil-Snowdrift, Kentucky Winner Tobacco, Royal Gelatin, Tenderleaf Tea, Miles Laboratories. Serial drama featuring J. Anthony Smythe and Minetta Ellen/Mary Adams.

Our Miss Brooks. 1948–57 (CBS). Sponsors: Colgate, Toni Home Permanent. Situation comedy with Eve Arden, Jeff Chandler, Gale Gordon, and Dick Crenna.

Ozzie and Harriet (Adventures of Ozzie and Harriet). 1944–47 (CBS); 1948–49 (NBC); 1949–54 (ABC). Sponsors: International Silver, Heinz Foods. Situation comedy starring Ozzie Nelson and Harriet Hilliard Nelson.

People Are Funny. 1942–51 (NBC); 1951–54 (CBS); 1954–59 (NBC). Sponsors: Wings Cigarettes, Raleigh Cigarettes, Mars Candy. Audience participation/comedy with host Art Baker/Art Linkletter.

Perry Mason. 1943–55 (CBS). Sponsor: Procter & Gamble. Crime drama starring Bartlett Robinson/Santos Ortega/Donald Briggs/John Larkin.

Phil Baker Show. 1933–40 (CBS). Sponsors: Gulf Oil, Dole Pineapple. Comedy/variety show with Phil Baker and regulars Harry McNaughton, Ward Wilson, the Andrews Sisters, and the Seven G's.

Philip Morris Playhouse. 1939–43, 1948 (CBS); 1951 (NBC); 1952–53 (CBS). Sponsor: Philip Morris. Drama anthology hosted by Charles Martin.

Queen for a Day. 1945–57 (Mutual). Audience participation/interview show hosted by Dud Williamson/Jack Bailey.

Quiz Kids. 1940–42 (NBC); 1942–46 (NBC Blue/ABC); 1946–51 (NBC); 1952–53 (CBS). Sponsor: Alka Seltzer. Juvenile quiz show with host Joe Kelly.

Radio Hall of Fame. 1943–46 (NBC Blue). Sponsor: Philco. Variety performances of guest stars with Paul Whiteman, Deems Taylor, and Martha Tilton.

Railroad Hour. 1948 (ABC); 1949–54 (NBC). Sponsor: Association of American Railroads. Music and drama with Gordon MacRae and guest stars.

Red Ryder. 1942–50s (Mutual). Sponsor: Langendorf Bread. Western adventure show based on Fred Harmon's comic strip with Reed Hadley/Carlton KaDell/Brooke Temple and Tommy Cook/Henry Blair.

Red Skelton Show. 1941–44, 1945–49 (NBC); 1949–51 (CBS); 1952–53 (NBC). Sponsors: Raleigh Cigarettes, Tide, Norge, others. Comedy with Red Skelton, Harriet Hilliard, Lurene Tuttle, and GeGe Pearson.

Road of Life. 1937–54 (NBC); 1952–59 (CBS); ran on two networks at same time for a period. Sponsor: Proctor & Gamble. Serial drama with Ken Griffin/Matt Crowley/Don MacLaughlin/David Ellis, Lesley Woods/Louise Fitch/Marion Shockley, Muriel Bremner, Reese Taylor, Donald Kraatz/Lawson Zerbe/David Ellis, Elizabeth Lawrence, Barbara Becker, and Julie Stevens/Helen Lewis.

Romance of Helen Trent. 1933–60 (CBS). Sponsors: American Home Products, Whitehall Drug Company, others. Serial drama with Virginia Clark/Betty Ruth Smith/Julie Stevens, Audrey McGrath, David Gothard, Marilyn Erskine *et al.*

Roy Rogers Show. 1944–46 (Mutual); 1946–48 (NBC); 1948–51 (Mutual); 1951–55 (NBC). Sponsors: Goodyear Tires, Miles Laboratories, Quaker Oats, General Foods, Dodge. Western variety show starring Roy Rogers, Sons of the Pioneers/Foy Willing and the Riders of the Purple Sage, Dale Evans, and Pat Brady.

Rudy Vallee Show. 1929–47 (NBC). Sponsors: Standard Brands for Fleischmann's Yeast and Royal Gelatin, Sealtest. Variety hour with Rudy Vallee and regulars including Virginia Gregg, Andy Devine, Mary Boland, Abe Reynolds, Billie Burke, Sara Berner, John Barrymore.

Sam Spade. 1945–49 (CBS); 1949 (NBC). Sponsor: Wildroot Cream-Oil. Detective show starring Howard Duff/Steve Dunne and Lurene Tuttle.

Saturday Night Serenade/Pet Milk Show. 1936–48 (CBS); 1948–50 (NBC). Sponsor: Pet Milk. Music with maestro Howard Barlow/Sammy Kaye/Gustave Haenschen, Jessica Dragonette, and Vic Damone.

Screen Guild Theater. 1939–48 (CBS); 1948–50 (NBC); 1950–51 (ABC). Sponsors: Gulf Oil, Camel Cigarettes. Anthology with host Roger Pryor, and guest stars including Bing Crosby, Ronald Colman, Ingrid Bergman, Vincent Price.

Sergeant Preston of the Yukon. 1947–50 (CBS); 1950–55 (Mutual). Sponsor: Quaker Oats. Juvenile adventure show with Jay Michael, Paul Sutton, and John Todd.

The Shadow. 1930–32 (CBS); 1932–34 (NBC); 1934–36 (CBS); 1937–54 (Mutual). Sponsors: Blue Coal, Goodrich Tires, Grove Laboratories, Wildroot Cream-Oil. Mystery drama starring Frank Readick/George Earle/Robert Hardy Andrews/Orson Welles/Bill Johnstone/Bret Morrison.

Show Boat. 1932–37 (NBC). Sponsor: Maxwell House. Variety hour with Lanny Ross and guest stars.

Smilin' Ed McConnell Show (Buster Brown Gang). 1944–52 (NBC). Sponsor: Buster Brown Shoes. Children's program with Ed McConnell, Jerry Marin, Bud Tollefson.

Stella Dallas. 1937–56 (CBS). Serial drama based on Olive Higgins Prouty's novel with Anne Elstner, Frederick Tozere, Vivian Smolen, Joy Hathaway, Jane Houston *et al.*

Stop the Music. 1948–52 (ABC); 1954 (CBS). Musical quiz with Bert Parks/Bill Cullen.

Superman (Adventures of Superman). 1940–49 (Mutual); 1949–51 (ABC). Sponsor: Kellogg's Pep. Adventure serial with Clayton "Bud" Collyer/Michael Fitzmaurice and Joan Alexander.

Suspense. 1942–62 (CBS). Sponsors: Roma Wines, Autolite. Drama anthology of mystery and suspense stories with Joe Kearns, Paul Frees, and guest stars.

Tarzan. 1932–35 (syndicated); 1951–52 (ABC). Sponsor: General Foods. Adventure show starring James Pierce/Calton KaDell/Lamont Johnson and Joan Burroughs.

Terry and the Pirates. 1937–39 (NBC); 1943–48 (NBC Blue). Sponsors: Dari-Rich, Quaker Oats. Adventure show with Jackie Kelk/Cliff Carpenter/Owen Jordan, Clayton "Bud" Collyer/Larry Alexander/Warner Anderson/Bob Griffin, Agnes Moorhead/Adelaide Klein/Marion Sweet, and Frances Chaney.

Texaco Star Theater. 1938–40, 1944–46, 1947 (CBS); 1948 (ABC). Sponsor: Texaco. Variety show hosted by Ken Murray with James Melton, Annamary Dickey, Ed Wynn, Gordon MacRae, Evelyn Knight, Alan Young, and guest stars.

Theater Guild of the Air. 1945–49 (ABC); 1949–53 (NBC). Sponsor: U.S. Steel. Drama anthology with host Lawrence Langner/Roger Pryor/Elliott Reid.

The Thin Man (Adventures of the Thin Man). 1941–42 (NBC); 1942–47 (CBS); 1948 (NBC); 1948–50 (ABC). Sponsors: Post Toasties, Pabst Blue Ribbon. Crime drama starring Lester Damon/Les Tremayne/Joseph Curtin/David Gothard/Bill Smith and Claudia Morgan.

This Is Your FBI. 1945–53 (NBC Blue/ABC). Sponsor: Equitable. Drama starring Stacy Harris and Frank Lovejoy/Dean Carlton.

Tom Mix Ralston Straightshooters. 1933–37 (NBC); 1937–42 (NBC Blue); 1944–50 (Mutual). Sponsors: Ralston, Kellogg's. Western juvenile adventure show with Artells Dickson/Russell Thorson/Jack Holden/Curley Bradley and Percy Hemus.

Truth or Consequences. 1940–50 (NBC); 1950–52 (CBS); 1952–57 (NBC). Sponsors: Ivory Soap, Proctor & Gamble, Philip Morris, Pet Milk, others. Quiz show with host Ralph Edwards.

Twenty Questions. 1946–54 (Mutual). Sponsor: Ronson Lighters. Quiz show with panel members Fred Van Deventer, Florence Rinard, Bobby McGuire, Herb Polesie, and one rotating guest.

University of Chicago Round Table. 1933–55 (NBC). Round-table discussion among three college professors and guests.

Vic and Sade. 1932–44 (NBC); 1946 (Mutual). Sponsor: Procter & Gamble's Crisco. Comedy serial with Art Van Harvey, Bernadine Flynn, Billy Idelson/Johnny Coons/Sid Kross, Clarence Hartzell, Ruth Perrott, and Carl Kroenke.

Voice of Firestone. 1928–54 (NBC); 1954–55 (ABC). Sponsor: Firestone Tire and Rubber Company. Music with Hugh James, Firestone Symphony Orchestra, and guest artists.

Vox Pop (debuted as **Sidewalk Interviews**). 1935–38 (NBC); 1939–46 (CBS); 1947 (ABC). Sponsors: Mollé, Kentucky Club Tobacco, Bromo Seltzer, Lipton Tea, American Express. Quiz/interview show hosted by Parks Johnson and Jerry Belcher/Wally Butterworth/Warren Hull.

Walter Winchell's Journal. 1932–55 (NBC Blue/ABC). Sponsors: Jergens Lotion, Lucky Strike, Richard Hudnut. News and commentary with Walter Winchell.

Waltz Time. 1933–48 (NBC Red). Music from Abe Lyman's Orchestra.

We, the People. 1936–37 (NBC); 1937–49 (CBS); 1949–51 (NBC). Sponsors: Calumet Baking Soda, Sanka Coffee, Gulf Oil. Human interest show with host Gabriel Heatter/Eddie Dowling/Milo Boulton/Dwight Weist/Burgess Meredith/Danny Seymour.

The Whistler. 1942–55 (CBS). Sponsor: Signal Oil. Mystery drama with Bill Forman/Marvin Miller/Everett Clarke.

The Witch's Tale. 1931 (WOR); 1935–38 (Mutual). Horror starring Adelaide Fitzallen.

You Bet Your Life. 1947–49 (ABC); 1949–51 (CBS); 1951–59 (NBC). Sponsors: Elgin-American, DeSoto, and Plymouth. Game/quiz show hosted by Groucho Marx.

Your Hit Parade. 1935–59 (NBC). Sponsor: Lucky Strike. Pop music featuring guest vocalists and orchestras, including Kay Kyser and Frank Sinatra.

Yours Truly, Johnny Dollar. 1949–62 (CBS). Sponsors: Pepsi-Cola, Ex-Lax, Kent Cigarettes. Adventure show starring Charles Russell/Edmond O'Brien/John Lund/Bob Bailey/Bob Readick/Mandel Kramer.

Ziegfeld Follies of the Air. 1932, 1936–1940s (CBS). Sponsor: Palmolive. Variety show featuring guest stars and Al Goodman orchestra and hosted by James Melton.

SOURCES

Buxton, Frank, and Bill Owen. *The Big Broadcast, 1920–50.* New York: Viking, 1972.

Dunning, John. *Tune in Yesterday.* Englewood Cliffs, N.J.: Prentice-Hall, 1976.

Pitts, Michael R. *Radio Soundtracks: A Reference Guide.* 2nd ed. Metuchen, N.J.: Scarecrow Press, 1986.

Swartz, Jon D., and Robert C. Reinehr. *Handbook of Old-Time Radio.* Metuchen, N.J.: Scarecrow Press, 1993.

Terrace, Vincent. *Radio's Golden Years: The Encyclopedia of Radio Programs, 1930–60.* New York: A. S. Barnes and Co., 1981.

—**Jesma Reynolds; L.D.R.**

46

POPULAR TELEVISION SHOWS

. . . . .

SEVERAL DECADES AGO H. M. McLUHAN CAUSED CONSIDERABLE EYEBROW raising in intellectual circles when he proclaimed that the age of Gutenberg—the printed word—was swiftly drawing to an end, and the age of television was currently taking over. Most people laughed at the prophecy. Today, from a literary standpoint at least, it doesn't seem so funny.

The impact of TV has been immense. Few areas of American life have not been touched by it. As a medium of family entertainment it has replaced radio, closed out the general circulation magazine, demolished the afternoon newspaper in all but the largest of cities, and relegated the movie theater to a subordinate status within the community. At the same time, it has made the production of movies for television into a major industry. Television has replaced newspapers as the principal source of spot and breaking news. It has changed political strategies and reshaped allegiances. Anybody in the book publishing industry knows that almost the only way to get a book launched into best-sellerdom is to get an endorsement by a TV personality.

Whether the role of TV in American life has been for the better or worse, or some of both, is a matter of opinion. What H. L. Mencken once contended, however—that nobody had ever gone broke from underestimating the intelligence of the American people—has at this juncture in our history yet to be disproved.

The history of commercial television in the United States properly begins in the late 1940s, although some telecasting was done in the metropolitan New York area in the years before World War II. The development of TV as home entertainment can be divided into three stages: the early black-and-white days, lasting through the 1950s and into the 1960s; the development of color television in the late 1950s and early 1960s; and, in the 1980s, the coming of CATF—cable television.

The first two stages were dominated by the three major networks, NBC, CBS, and ABC. Cable TV not only introduced a number of additional networks but made possible more specialized programming. With the advent of CNN—Cable News Network—news was aired twenty-four hours a day. Networks concentrating entirely on sports, country and western music, weather reports and forecasts, movies, business news and financial reports, government, education, and other specialized fields were developed. The *World Almanac* for 1994 estimates that 98 percent of all U.S. households own at least one television set.

The compilation below is concerned with television as a home entertainment medium. The listing is of some of the more popular and longer-lived television shows, with dates, network affiliation, brief description, and some principal performers. Reruns are not included. When a particular role on a show was played by more than one person in different periods, the names of the performers are separated by slashes.

Adam-12. 1968–75 (NBC). Crime drama starring Martin Milner and Kent McCord.

Addams Family. 1964–66 (ABC). Situation comedy starring Carolyn Jones, John Astin, Lisa Loring, Ken Weatherwax, Jackie Coogan, Blossom Rock, Ted Cassidy, and Felix Silla.

Alfred Hitchcock Presents (Alfred Hitchcock Hour). 1955–60 (CBS); 1960–62 (NBC); 1962–64 (CBS); 1964–65, 1985–86 (NBC); 1987–92 (USA). Anthology of mystery and suspense stories; hosted by Alfred Hitchcock.

Alice. 1976–85 (CBS). Situation comedy starring Linda Lavin, Vic Tayback, Polly Holliday, and Beth Howland.

All in the Family. 1971–83 (CBS). Situation comedy starring Carroll O'Connor, Jean Stapleton, Sally Struthers, and Rob Reiner.

American Bandstand. 1957–87 (ABC); 1987–89 (syndicated); 1989 (USA). Rock and roll music variety hosted by Dick Clark.

Andy Griffith Show. 1960–68 (CBS). Rural situation comedy starring Andy Griffith, Don Knotts, Ron Howard, Frances Bavier, and Elinor Donahue.

Andy Williams Show. 1957 (NBC); 1958 (ABC); 1959 (CBS); 1962–63, 1967, 1969–71 (NBC); 1976 (syndicated). Variety show with music and comedy starring Andy Williams.

Armstrong Circle Theater. 1950–57 (NBC); 1957–63 (CBS). Dramatic anthology hosted by Nelson Case/Douglas Edwards/Ron Cochran/Henry Hamilton and featuring performances by actors including Cara Williams, Cloris Leachman, Patty Duke, Leslie Nielsen, Grace Kelly, and Darren McGavin.

Arthur Godfrey and Friends. 1949–57 (CBS). Hour variety show with host Arthur Godfrey and regulars including Pat Boone, Janette Davis, Marion Marlows, Julius LaRosa, Allen Dase, Carmel Quinn, and Lu Ann Simms.

Arthur Godfrey's Talent Scouts. 1948–58 (CBS). Variety show of amateur performers hosted by Arthur Godfrey.

Arthur Murray Party (Arthur Murray Show). 1950 (ABC); 1950–51 (Dumont); 1951, 1951–52 (ABC); 1952 (CBS); 1952–53 (Dumont); 1953 (CBS); 1953–54, 1954, 1955 (NBC); 1956 (CBS); 1957, 1958–60 (NBC). Variety show featuring ballroom dance hosted by Arthur Murray and Kathryn Murray.

Barnaby Jones. 1973–80 (CBS). Crime drama starring Buddy Ebsen and Lee Merriwether.

Barney Miller. 1975–82 (ABC). Situation comedy with Hal Linden, Abby Dalton/Barbara Barrie, Abe Vigoda, Max Gail, Gregory Sierra, Jack Soo.

Beat the Clock. 1950–58 (CBS); 1958–62 (ABC); 1969–74 (syndicated); 1979–80 (CBS). Game show hosted by Bud Collyer/Monty Hall during network years and Jack Narz/Gene Wood during syndication.

Bell Telephone Hour. 1959–68 (NBC). Music featuring the Bell Telephone Orchestra conducted by Donald Voorhees.

Beverly Hillbillies. 1962–71 (CBS). Rural situation comedy with Buddy Ebsen, Irene Ryan, Donna Douglas, Max Baer, Raymond Bailey, and Harriet MacGibbon.

Bewitched. 1964–72 (ABC). Situation comedy with Elizabeth Montgomery, Dick York/Dick Sargent, Agnes Moorhead, and David White.

The Big Story. 1949–57 (NBC). Dramatic anthology based on actual news stories with host William Sloane/Ben Grauer/Norman Rose/Burgess Meredith.

Big Town. 1950–54 (CBS); 1954–56 (NBC). Crime drama starring Patrick McVey/Mark Stevens, Margaret Hayes/Mary K. Wells/Jane Nigh/Beverly Tyler/Trudy Wroe/Julie Stevens.

Bob Newhart Show. 1972–78 (CBS). Situation comedy with Bob Newhart, Suzanne Pleshette, and Bill Daily.

Bonanza. 1959–73 (NBC). Western starring Lorne Greene, Pernell Roberts, Dan Blocker, and Michael Landon.

Brady Bunch. 1969–74 (ABC). Situation comedy starring Robert Reed, Florence Henderson, Ann B. Davis, Maureen McCormick, Eve Plumb, Susan Olsen, Barry Williams, Christopher Knight, and Michael Lookinland.

Break the Bank. 1948–49 (ABC); 1949–52 (NBC); 1952 (CBS); 1953 (NBC); 1954–56, 1976 (ABC); 1985 (syndicated). Game show with host Bert Parks/Tom Kennedy/Jack Barry/Gene Rayburn/Joe Farago.

Bugs Bunny Show/Bugs Bunny, Road Runner Hour (Bugs Bunny and Tweety Show). 1960–67 (ABC); 1968–73 (CBS); 1973–75 (ABC); 1975–present (CBS). Cartoon, voice by Mel Blanc until 1989.

Bullwinkle Show. 1961–64 (NBC); 1964–73 (ABC). Cartoon with voices by June Foray and Bill Scott.

Candid Camera. 1948 (ABC); 1949 (NBC); 1949–51 (CBS); 1951–56 (ABC); 1960–67, 1990 (CBS); 1974–80 (sydicated). Comedy/human interest with host Allen Funt.

Captain Kangaroo. 1955–84 (CBS). Children's hour starring Bob Keeshan and Lumpy Brannum.

Captain Video. 1949–55 (Dumont); 1953–56 (syndicated). Space adventure show starring Richard Coogan/Al Hodge, Don Hastings, and Hal Conklin.

Car 54, Where Are You? 1961–63 (NBC). Police comedy starring Joe E. Ross, Fred Gwynne, Paul Reed, and Beatrice Pons.

Carol Burnett Show. 1967–78 (CBS). Variety hour starring Carol Burnett with regulars Lyle Waggoner, Vicki Lawrence, Tim Conway, and Harvey Korman.

Charlie's Angels. 1976–81 (ABC). Crime drama starring Kate Jackson (1976–79), Farrah Fawcett (1976–77), Jaclyn Smith (1976–81), Cheryl Ladd (1977–81), and Shelley Hack (1979–80).

Cheers. 1982–94 (NBC). Situation comedy starring Ted Danson, Shelley Long (1982–87), Rhea Perlman, George Wendt, John Ratzenberger, and Kirstie Alley (1987–94).

Cheyenne. 1955–63 (ABC). Western starring Clint Walker and Jack Elam.

Chico and the Man. 1974–78 (NBC). Situation comedy starring Jack Albertson and Freddie Prinze.

Coke Time with Eddie Fisher (Eddie Fisher Show). 1953–57, 1957–59 (NBC). Variety show hosted by Eddie Fisher with regulars including Don Ameche, Jaye P. Morgan, George Gobel, and Debbie Reynolds.

The Colgate Comedy Hour. 1950–55 (NBC). Comedy/variety hour with guest hosts including Abbott and Costello, Dean Martin and Jerry Lewis, Donald O'Connor, Bob Hope, Eddie Cantor, Jimmy Durante, and Fred Allen.

Columbo. 1971–78 (NBC); 1989–90 (ABC). Crime drama starring Peter Falk and Bill Zuckert.

Concentration. 1958–73 (NBC); 1973–79 (syndicated). Daytime game show with host Hugh Downs (1958–65)/Jack Berry/Art James/Bill Mazer/Ed McMahon/Bob Clayton (1969–73).

Cosby Show/Bill Cosby Show/Cos. 1969–71 (NBC); 1972–73 (CBS); 1976 (ABC); 1984–92 (NBC). Comedy starring Bill Cosby.

Dallas. 1978–91 (CBS). Serial drama with Jim Davis, Barbara Bel Geddes/Donna Reed, Larry Hagman, Patrick Duffy, Linda Gray, and Victoria Principal.

Daniel Boone. 1964–70 (NBC). Adventure starring Fess Parker, Ed Ames, Patricia Blair, and Albert Salmi.

Dark Shadows. 1966–71 (ABC). Gothic serial with Jonathon Frid and Alexandre Moltke/Betsy Durkin/Carolyn Groves.

Dean Martin Show. 1965–74 (NBC). Comedy/variety hour with host Dean Martin and regulars Dom deLuise, Tom Bosley, Nipsey Russell, Kay Medford, Marian Mercer, and Lou Jacobi.

December Bride. 1954–59 (CBS). Domestic comedy starring Spring Byington, Frances Rafferty, and Dean Miller.

Designing Women. 1986–94 (CBS). Situation comedy with Dixie Carter, Delta Burke, Annie Potts, and Jean Smart.

Dick Van Dyke Show. 1961–66 (CBS). Situation comedy starring Dick Van Dyke, Mary Tyler Moore, and Larry Matthews.

Dinah Shore Show. 1951–62 (NBC). Musical variety show with host Dinah Shore.

Dr. Kildare. 1961–66 (NBC). Medical drama starring Richard Chamberlain, Raymond Massey, Lee Kurty, and Jud Taylor.

Donna Reed Show. 1958–66 (ABC). Situation comedy starring Donna Reed, Carl Betz, Shelley Fabares, and Paul Petersen.

Doris Day Show. 1968–73 (CBS). Situation comedy starring Doris Day, Denver Pyle, Philipo Brown, and Todd Starke.

Dragnet. 1951–59, 1967–70 (NBC). Crime drama starring Jack Webb, Barton Yarborough, and Ben Alexander/Harry Morgan.

Dynasty. 1981–89 (ABC). Prime-time serial drama starring John Forsythe, Linda Evans, and Joan Collins.

Eddie Fisher Show. See *Coke Time with Eddie Fisher*.

Ed Sullivan Show (Toast of the Town). 1948–71 (CBS). Variety show with host Ed Sullivan.

Ernie Kovacs Show/New Ernie Kovacs Show. 1952–53 (CBS); 1955–56 (NBC); 1961–62 (ABC). Comedy show featuring Ernie Kovacs with various others; in 1955–56 his wife Edie Adams took part.

Face the Nation. 1954–61; 1963–present (CBS). Weekly news series with panel of interviewers moderated by George Herman (1969–83)/Lesley Stahl (1983–present).

Family Affair. 1966–71 (CBS). Situation comedy with Brian Keith, Sebastian Cabot, Kathy Garver, Johnny Whitaker, and Anissa Jones.

Family Ties. 1982–89 (NBC). Family situation comedy with Meredith Baxter Birney, Michael Gross, Michael J. Fox, and Justine Bateman.

Fantasy Island. 1978–84 (ABC). Adventure anthology starring Ricardo Montalban and Herve Villechaize (1978–83).

Fat Albert and the Cosby Kids. 1972–84 (CBS); 1989 (NBC). Cartoon with host Bill Cosby and voices of characters by Bill Cosby and Jan Crawford.

Father Knows Best. 1954–55 (CBS); 1955–58 (NBC); 1958–62 (CBS). Situation comedy starring Robert Young, Jane Wyatt, Elinor Donahue, Billy Gray, and Lauren Chapin.

The FBI. 1965–74 (ABC). Crime drama starring Efrem Zimbalist, Jr., and Philip Abbott.

Fireside Theater. 1949–55 (NBC). Anthology of drama hosted by Gene Raymond/Jane Wyman.

Flintstones. 1960–66 (ABC); 1967–70 (NBC); 1972–74 (CBS); 1979–84 (NBC);

1986–89 (ABC). Prime-time cartoon series with voices by Alan Reed, Jean vander Pyl, Mel Blanc, and Bea Benaderet/Gerry Johnson.

Flipper. 1964–68 (NBC). Adventure series starring Brian Kelly, Luke Halpin, Tommy Norden, and dolphins.

Ford Theater. 1948–51 (CBS); 1952–56 (NBC); 1956–57 (ABC). Dramatic anthology series with stars including Ernest Borgnine, Shelley Winters, Donna Reed, Tab Hunter, Vince Edwards, and Michael Connors.

Frontline. 1983–present (PBS). Independently produced documentaries series hosted by Jessica Savitch/Judy Woodruff.

Garry Moore Show. 1950–58, 1958–64, 1966–67 (CBS). Music and comedy variety with host Garry Moore.

General Electric Theater. 1953–62 (CBS). Dramatic anthology series with host Ronald Reagan (1954–62) and featuring performers including Myrna Loy, Groucho Marx, Bette Davis, James Stewart, Anne Baxter, Alan Ladd, Rosalind Russell, and Joan Crawford.

George Burns and Gracie Allen Show. 1950–58 (CBS). Comedy series with George Burns, Gracie Allen, Ronnie Burns, Harry Von Zell, and others.

The George Gobel Show. 1954–59 (NBC); 1959–60 (CBS). Comic variety series with host George Gobel and regulars Peggy King, Eddie Fisher, and Jeff Donnell.

Get Smart. 1965–69 (NBC); 1969–70 (CBS). Spy comedy starring Don Adams, Barbara Feldon, and Edward Platt.

Gillette Cavalcade of Sports. 1948–60 (NBC). Friday night boxing with commentary by Jimmy Powers.

Gilligan's Island. 1964–67 (CBS). Situation comedy starring Bob Denver, Alan Hale, Jr., Jim Backus, Tina Louise, Natalie Schafer, Dawn Wells, and Russell Johnson.

Golden Girls. 1985–93 (NBC). Situation comedy starring Bea Arthur, Rue McClanahan, Betty White, and Estelle Getty.

Gomer Pyle, USMC. 1964–69 (CBS). Situation comedy starring Jim Nabors and Frank Sutton.

Goodyear Playhouse. 1951–57 (NBC). Hour-long dramatic anthology with actors including Julie Harris, Leslie Nielsen, Paul Newman, Steve McQueen, and Raymond Massey.

Great Performances. 1974–present (PBS). Classical music, dance, drama. Jac Venza, executive producer.

Green Acres. 1965–71 (CBS). Situation comedy starring Eddie Albert and Eva Gabor.

Guiding Light. 1952–present (CBS). Daytime drama series.

Gunsmoke. 1955–75. Western series starring James Arness, Amanda Blake, Milburn Stone, and Dennis Weaver.

Happy Days. 1974–84 (ABC). Situation comedy starring Tom Bosley, Marian Ross, Ron Howard, Erin Moran, and Henry Winkler.

Have Gun, Will Travel. 1957–63 (CBS). Western starring Richard Boone, Kam Fong, and Lisa Lu.

Hawaii Five-O. 1968–80 (CBS). Crime drama starring Jack Lord, James MacArthur, Kam Fong, and Zulu.

Hee Haw. 1969–71 (CBS); 1971–present (syndicated). Country-western variety hour with cohosts Buck Owens and Roy Clark.

Here's Lucy. 1968–74 (CBS). Situation comedy starring Lucille Ball, Gale Gordon, Lucie Arnaz, and Desi Arnaz, Jr.

Hogan's Heroes. 1965–71 (CBS). World War II situation comedy starring Bob Crane, Werner Klemperer, John Banner, Robert Clary, and Richard Dawson.

Hollywood Palace. 1964–70 (ABC). Hour variety series with guest host and guest performers including Bing Crosby, Mickey Rooney, Dean Martin, and Fred Astaire.

Hollywood Squares. 1966–80 (NBC); 1972–80, 1986–89 (syndicated). Celebrity game show with host Peter Marshall and regulars including Wally Cox, Paul Lynde, Rose Marie, Karen Valentine, and George Gobel.

Honeymooners (Jackie Gleason Show). 1952–59, 1961, 1962–70 (CBS); 1977 (syndicated). Situation comedy starring Jackie Gleason, Audrey Meadows/Sheila MacRae, Art Carney, Joyce Randolph/Jane Kearr.

Howdy Doody. 1947–60 (NBC); 1976 (syndicated). Children's show with Bob Smith and Bob Keeshan/Henry McLaughlin/Bob Nicholson/Lew Anderson.

I Dream of Jeannie. 1965–70 (NBC). Situation comedy starring Barbara Eden, Larry Hagman, Bill Daily, and Hayden Rorke.

I Love Lucy. 1951–57 (CBS). Situation comedy starring Lucille Ball, Desi Arnaz, William Frawley, and Vivian Vance.

In Living Color. 1990-present (FOX). Comedy series with host Keenen Ivory Wayans and regulars including Damon Wayans, Kim Wayans, Jim Carrey, and Tommy Davidson.

Inside Washington. 1988–present (syndicated). Weekly news analysis hosted by Gordon Peterson.

Ironside. 1967–75 (NBC). Crime drama starring Raymond Burr, Barbara Anderson, Don Galloway, and Don Mitchell.

I've Got a Secret. 1952–67 (CBS); 1972 (syndicated); 1976–78 (CBS). Prime-time game show with host Garry Moore/Steve Allen/Bill Cullen.

Jack Benny Program. 1950–64 (CBS); 1964–65 (NBC). Variety show/situation comedy starring Jack Benny, Mary Livingston, Eddie Anderson, Don Wilson, Dennis Day, and Mel Blanc.

Jackie Gleason Show. See ***Honeymooners***.

The Jeffersons. 1975–85 (CBS). Situation comedy starring Sherman Hemsley, Isabel Sanford, Franklin Cover, and Roxie Roker.

Jeopardy. 1964–75 (NBC); 1974 (syndicated); 1978–79 (NBC); 1984–present (syndicated). Game show hosted by Art Fleming/Alex Trebek.

The Jetsons. 1962–63, 1963–64 (ABC); 1964–65 (CBS); 1965–67 (NBC); 1969–71 (CBS); 1971–76, 1979–81, 1982–83 (NBC); 1985 (syndicated). Space-age cartoon with voices by George O'Hanlon, Penny Singleton, Janet Waldo, and Daws Butler.

Jonny Quest (Adventures of Jonny Quest). 1964–65, 1967–70 (CBS); 1970–72 (ABC); 1979, 1980–81 (NBC). Cartoon with voices by Tim Mattheson and John Stephenson.

Kojak. 1973–78 (CBS); 1989–90 (ABC). Crime drama starring Telly Savalas, Dan Frazer, and Kevin Dobson.

Kraft Television Theater. 1947–58 (NBC); 1953–55 (ABC). Dramatic anthology series with performers including Jack Lemmon, Lee Remick, Elizabeth Montgomery, Sal Mineo, Patty Duke, Anne Bancroft, Edgar Bergen, Tony Perkins, and George Peppard.

Kukla, Fran, and Ollie. 1948–54 (NBC); 1954–57 (ABC); 1961–62 (NBC); 1969–71 (PBS). Children's series featuring puppets of Burr Tillstrom and human friend Fran Allison.

L.A. Law. 1986–93 (NBC). Legal/crime drama starring Harry Hamlin, Susan Dey, Corbin Bernsen, Jill Eikenberry, Richard Dysart, Alan Rachins, and Jimmy Smits.

Lassie. 1954–71 (CBS); 1971–74 (syndicated). Adventures starring collie dogs.

Late Night with David Letterman. 1982–93 (NBC); 1993–present (CBS). Late-night talk and variety show with host David Letterman.

Laugh-In (Rowan and Martin's Laugh-In). 1968–73 (NBC). Comedy/variety show with hosts Dan Rowan and Dick Martin.

Laverne and Shirley. 1976–83 (ABC). Situation comedy starring Penny Marshall and Cindy Williams.

Lawrence Welk Show. 1955–71 (ABC); 1971–82 (syndicated). Variety of music, songs, and dances with host Lawrence Welk.

Leave It to Beaver. 1957–58 (CBS); 1958–63 (ABC). Family situation comedy starring Hugh Beaumont, Barbara Billingsley, Tony Dow, and Jerry Mathers.

Let's Make a Deal. 1963–68 (NBC); 1968–76 (ABC); 1971–76, 1980, 1984–85 (syndicated); 1990–91 (NBC). Game show hosted by Monty Hall.

Life Begins at 80. 1950 (NBC); 1950–52 (ABC); 1952–55 (Dumont); 1955–56 (ABC). Panel discussion by octogenarians with host Jack Barry.

Life of Riley. 1949–50 (Dumont); 1953–58 (NBC). Situation comedy with Jackie Gleason/William Bendix, Rosemary DeCamp/Marjorie Reynolds, Gloria Winters/Lugene Sanders, Lanny Rees/Wesley Morgan.

Little House on the Prairie. 1974–82 (NBC). Drama series starring Michael Landon, Karen Grassle, Melissa Gilbert, and Melissa Sue Anderson.

Live from Lincoln Center. 1976–present (PBS). Concerts, operas, ballets, chamber music. John Goberman, executive producer; Kirk Browning, director.

Lone Ranger. 1949–65 (ABC). Western starring Clayton Moore/John Hart, Jay Silverheels.

Loretta Young Show (A Letter to Loretta). 1953–61 (NBC). Half-hour dramatic anthology hosted by Loretta Young.

Love Boat. 1977–86 (ABC). Comedy-drama starring Gavin MacLeod, Bernie Kopell, Fred Grandy, Ted Lange, Lauren Tewes, and Pat Klous.

Love of Life. 1951–80 (CBS). Daytime drama series.

Lucy Show. 1962–68 (CBS). Situation comedy starring Lucille Ball, Vivian Vance, Gale Gordon, and Charles Lane.

Lux Video Theater. 1950–54 (CBS); 1954–57 (NBC). Half-hour dramatic anthology series hosted by James Mason/Otto Kruger/Gordon MacRae and appearances by actors including Grace Kelly, Peter Lorre, Edward G. Robinson, and Esther Williams.

McCloud. 1970–77 (NBC). Crime drama starring Dennis Weaver and featuring J. D. Cannon, Terry Carter, Diana Muldaur, Sharon Gless/Nancy Fox, and Ken Lynch.

MacNeil-Lehrer Report (MacNeil-Lehrer News Hour). 1976–present (PBS). In-depth newscast hosted by Robert MacNeil and Jim Lehrer.

Make Room for Daddy (Danny Thomas Show). 1953–57 (ABC); 1957–64 (CBS); 1970–71 (ABC). Situation comedy starring Danny Thomas, Jean Hagan, Sherry Jackson/Penny Parker, Rusty Hamer.

Mama (I Remember Mama). 1949–56, 1956–57 (CBS). Situation comedy starring Peggy Wood, Judson Laire, Rosemary Rice, and Dick Van Patten.

Man Against Crime. 1949–53 (CBS); 1953–54 (Dumont); 1953–54, 1956 (NBC). Crime drama starring Ralph Bellamy/Robert Preston/Frank Lovejoy.

The Man from U.N.C.L.E. 1964–68 (NBC). Spy adventure starring Robert Vaughn and David McCallum.

Mannix. 1967–75 (CBS). Crime drama starring Mike Connors, Joseph Campanella, and Gail Fisher.

Marcus Welby, M.D. 1969–76 (ABC). Medical drama starring Robert Young, James Brolin, Elena Verdugo, and Sharon Gless.

Mary Tyler Moore Show. 1970–77 (CBS). Situation comedy starring Mary Tyler Moore, Edward Asner, Gavin MacLeod, Ted Knight, Valerie Harper, and Cloris Leachman.

M*A*S*H. 1972–83 (NBC). Comedy/drama starring Alan Alda, Wayne Rogers, McLean Stevenson, Loretta Swit, Larry Linville, Gary Burghoff, and Jamie Farr.

Masquerade Party. 1952 (NBC); 1953, 1954 (CBS); 1954–56 (ABC); 1957 (NBC); 1958 (CBS); 1958–59 (NBC); 1959–60 (CBS); 1960 (NBC); 1974 (syndicated). Game show hosted by Bud Collyer/Douglas Edwards/Peter Donald/Eddie

Bracken/Robert Q. Lewis/Bert Parks/Richard Dawson and starring a panel of celebrities.

Masterpiece Theatre. 1971–present (PBS). Dramatic anthology with host Alistair Cooke/Russell Baker (since 1993).

Medical Center. 1969–76 (CBS). Medical drama starring James Daly and Chad Everett.

Meet the Press. 1947–present (NBC) News/interview show with moderator Martha Rountree/Ned Brooks/Bill Monroe/Marvin Kalb/Garrick Utley/Tim Russert.

Merv Griffin Show. 1962–63 (NBC); 1965–69 (syndicated); 1969–72 (CBS); 1972–86 (syndicated). Variety/talk show hosted by Merv Griffin.

Miami Vice. 1984–89 (NBC). Crime drama starring Don Johnson and Philip Michael Thomas.

Mickey Mouse Club. 1955–59 (ABC). Children's series with music, songs, cartoons, and adventure hosted by Jimmie Dodd and featuring the Mouseketeers.

Mike Douglas Show. 1963–82 (syndicated). Talk show hosted by Mike Douglas.

Milton Berle Show. 1953–55, 1955–56 (NBC); 1966–67 (ABC). Variety show with music and slapstick comedy hosted by Milton Berle.

Mission: Impossible. 1966–73 (CBS). Adventure series starring Steven Hill, Peter Graves, Barbara Bain, Martin Landau, Greg Morris, and Peter Lupus.

Mister Ed. 1961 (syndicated); 1961–65 (CBS). Sitcom featuring talking horse with voice by Allan "Rocky" Lane and regulars Alan Young and Connie Hines.

Mister Rogers' Neighborhood. 1967–present (PBS). Children's program hosted by Fred Rogers.

Mod Squad. 1968–73 (ABC). Crime drama starring Michael Cole, Peggy Lipton, Clarence Williams III, and Tige Andrews.

Mork & Mindy. 1978–82 (ABC). Comedy starring Robin Williams, Pam Dawber, and Conrad Janis.

Muppet Show. 1976–81 (syndicated). Comic variety hour featuring the puppets of Jim Henson, including Kermit the Frog, Miss Piggy, Rowlf, and Fozzie.

Murder, She Wrote. 1984–present (CBS). Whodunit drama starring Angela Lansbury.

Murphy Brown. 1988–present (CBS). Situation comedy starring Candice Bergen, Grant Shaud, Faith Ford, Joe Regalbuto, and Charles Kimbrough.

My Favorite Martian. 1963–66 (CBS). Situation comedy starring Bill Bixby, Ray Walton, and Pamela Britton.

My Three Sons. 1960–65 (ABC); 1965–72 (CBS). Situation comedy starring Fred MacMurray, Tim Considine, Don Grady, and Stanley Livingston.

Name That Tune. 1953–54 (NBC); 1954–59 (CBS); 1974–75, 1977 (NBC); 1974–80 (syndicated). Music-identification game show hosted by Red Benson/Bill Cullen/George DeWitt/Dennis James/Tom Kennedy.

Nature. 1982–present (PBS). Documentaries on biological subjects.

Night Court. 1984–92 (NBC). Situation comedy with Harry Anderson, John Larroquette, Richard Moll, Paula Kelly/Elen Foley/Markie Post.

Nova. 1974–present (PBS). Science show produced by WGBH, Boston; Paula S. Apsell, executive producer; Bill Grant, executive editor.

The Odd Couple. 1970–75 (ABC). Situation comedy with Tony Randall and Jack Klugman.

One Day at a Time. 1975–84 (CBS). Situation comedy with Bonnie Franklin, Mackenzie Phillips, Valerie Bertinelli, and Pat Harrington, Jr.

Oprah Winfrey Show. 1986–present (syndicated). Daytime talk show with host Oprah Winfrey.

Our Miss Brooks. 1952–56 (CBS). Situation comedy with Eve Arden, Gale Gordon, Richard Crenna, Gloria McMillan, and Jane Morgan.

Ozzie and Harriet (Adventures of Ozzie and Harriet). 1952–66 (ABC). Situation comedy with Ozzie Nelson, Harriet Nelson, Ricky Nelson, and Dave Nelson.

Password. 1961–67 (CBS); 1967–69 (syndicated); 1971–75 (ABC); 1979–82 (NBC); 1984–89 (NBC). Game show hosted by Allen Ludden/Tom Kennedy/Bert Convy.

Patty Duke Show. 1963–66 (ABC). Situation comedy starring Patty Duke, William Schallert, Jean Byron, Paul O'Keefe, Eddie Applegate.

Perry Como Show (Chesterfield Supper Club). 1948–50 (NBC); 1950–55 (CBS); 1955–63 (NBC). Variety show hosted by Perry Como.

Perry Mason. 1957–66 (CBS). Crime drama with Raymond Burr, Barbara Hale, and William Hopper.

Petticoat Junction. 1963–70 (CBS). Rural situation comedy with Bea Benaderet, Edgar Buchanan, Linda Kay Henning, Jeanine Riley/Gunilla Hutton/Meredith MacRae, and Pat Woodell/Lori Saunders.

Peyton Place. 1964–69 (ABC). Prime-time serial with cast including Mia Farrow, Ryan O'Neal, Dorothy Malone, Ed Nelson, Frank Ferguson, Christopher Connelly, Barbara Parkins, Patricia Morrow, and Paul Langston.

Philco Television Playhouse. 1948–55 (NBC). Dramatic anthology series with appearances by actors including Lillian Gish, Grace Kelly, Eli Wallach, Jack Grant, James Dean, and Walter Matthau.

Phil Donahue Show. 1970–present (syndicated). Daytime talk show with host Phil Donahue.

Pink Panther Show. 1969–78 (NBC); 1978–79 (ABC). Cartoon with voices by John Byner, Paul Frees, Dave Barry, Rich Little, Marvin Miller, Athena Ford, June Foray, and Mel Blanc.

Price Is Right. 1956–63 (NBC); 1963–65 (ABC); 1972–74, 1985–present (syndicated). Game show hosted by Bob Barker.

Queen for a Day. 1956–60 (NBC); 1960–64 (ABC); 1970 (syndicated). Game show hosted by Jack Bailey/Dick Curtis and cohost Jeanne Cagney.

Rawhide. 1959–66 (CBS). Western with Eric Fleming, Clint Eastwood, Sheb Wooley, Paul Brinegar, Steve Raines, Raymond St. Jacques.

The Real McCoys. 1957–62 (ABC); 1962–63 (CBS). Rural situation comedy with Walter Brennan, Richard Crenna, Kathleen Nolan, Lydia Reed, and Michael Winkleman.

Red Skelton Show. 1951–53 (NBC); 1953–70 (CBS); 1970–71 (NBC). Variety half-hour and hour hosted by Red Skelton and regulars including Chanin Hale, Stanley Adams, Dorothy Lowe, Mike Wagner, Peggy Rea, Ida Moe McKenzie, Lloyd Kino, and Jan Davis.

Rin Tin Tin (Adventures of Rin Tin Tin). 1954–61 (ABC). Adventure starring Lee Aaker, James L. Brown, and dogs.

Robert Montgomery Presents. 1950–57 (NBC). Dramatic anthology series hosted by Robert Montgomery with appearances by actors including Helen Hayes, Joanne Woodward, Peter Falk, James Cagney, and Jack Lemmon.

Rockford Files. 1974–80 (NBC). Crime drama with James Garner, Noah Berry, and Joe Santos.

Roseanne. 1988–present (ABC). Situation comedy with Roseanne Barr and John Goodman.

Sanford and Son. 1972–77 (NBC). Situation comedy with Redd Foxx and Demond Wilson.

Saturday Night Live. 1975–present (NBC). Comedy and music with weekly guest host and regulars through the years including Chevy Chase, Dan Aykroyd, John Belushi, Jane Curtin, Garret Morris, Laraine Newman, Gilda Radner, Joe Piscopo, Eddie Murphy, Joan Cusack, Robert Downey, Jr., Nora Dunn, Jon Lovitz, Dana Carvey, Victoria Jackson, Chris Rock, Chris Farley, and Dennis Miller.

Schlitz Playhouse of the Stars. 1951–59 (CBS). Half-hour dramatic anthology series hosted by Irene Dunne/Robert Paige and performances by actors including Helen Hayes, James Dean, Janet Leigh, John Payne, and Anthony Quinn.

Scooby-Doo. 1969–76 (CBS); 1976–86 (ABC). Cartoon with voices of Don Messick, Casey Kasem, Frank Welker, Heather North, and Nicole Jaffe.

Search for Tomorrow. 1951–82 (CBS); 1982–86 (NBC). Daytime serial with Mary Stuart, Larry Haines *et al.*

Sesame Street. 1969–present (PBS). Children's educational show with performers including Loretta Young, Matt Robinson/Roscoe Orman, Bob McGrath, Will Lee, Northen J. Calloway, Emilio Delgado, and Sonai Manzano and also featuring the muppets of Jim Henson.

Sid Caesar Show. See **Your Show of Shows**.

The Simpsons. 1990–present (Fox). Prime-time cartoon with voices by Nancy Cartwright, Dan Castellaneta, Julie Kavner, and Yeardley Smith.

Sing Along with Mitch. 1961–64 (NBC). Musical series with host Mitch Miller.

Siskel & Ebert (Siskel and Ebert at the Movies). 1978–present (syndicated). Movie criticism with Gene Siskel and Roger Ebert.

Six Million Dollar Man. 1973–78 (ABC). Action adventure show with Lee Majors, Richard Anderson, Alan Oppenheimer/Martin E. Brooks.

60 Minutes. 1968–present (CBS). Hour news magazine with hosts including Mike Wallace (1968–present), Harry Reasoner (1968–70)/Morley Safer (1970–present), Dan Rather (1975–81)/Ed Bradley (1981–present), Diane Sawyer (1981–89) and commentary by Andy Rooney (1978–present).

Sonny and Cher Comedy Hour (Sonny and Cher Show). 1971–74, 1976–77 (CBS). Variety show with Sonny Bono and Cher.

Soul Train. 1971–present (syndicated). Dance/music hour hosted by Don Cornelius.

Star Trek. 1966–69 (NBC). Science fiction with William Shatner, Leonard Nimoy, DeForest Kelley, Nichelle Nichols, and James Doohan.

Star Trek: The Next Generation. 1987–present (syndicated). Science fiction with Patrick Stewart, Denise Crosby, Jonathan Frakes, and LeVar Burton.

Steve Allen Show. 1950–52 (CBS); 1956–60 (NBC); 1961 (ABC); 1962–64 (syndicated); 1967 (CBS); 1967–69 (syndicated). Variety show hosted by Steve Allen.

Strike It Rich. 1951–58 (CBS). Game show with host Warren Hull.

Studio One. 1948–58 (CBS). Dramatic anthology series with featured presentations including performances by Lorne Greene, Charlton Heston, Mike Wallace, Inger Stevens, Mary Wickes, E. G. Marshall, and Valerie Cossart.

Superman. 1951–57 (syndicated). Adventure serial with George Reeves, Phyllis Coates, and Jack Larson.

Suspense. 1949–54, 1964 (CBS). Half-hour anthology of thrillers with Paul Frees as narrator (1949–54) and Sebastian Cabot as host (1964).

Taxi. 1978–82 (ABC); 1982–83 (NBC). Situation comedy with Judd Hirsch, Jeff Conaway (1978–81), Tony Danza, Marilu Henner, Danny DeVito, and Andy Kaufman.

Ted Mack's Original Amateur Hour. 1948–49 (Dumont); 1949–54 (NBC); 1955–57 (ABC); 1957–58 (NBC); 1959 (CBS); 1960 (ABC); 1960–70 (CBS). Talent show hosted by Ted Mack.

Tennessee Ernie Ford Show. 1956–61 (NBC); 1962–65 (ABC). Variety show hosted by Tennessee Ernie Ford and with regulars Anita Gordon, Dick Noel, and Billy Strange.

$10,000 Pyramid ($20,000 Pyramid/$25,000 Pyramid/$50,000 Pyramid/$100,000 Pyramid). 1973–74 (CBS); 1974–80 (ABC); 1974–79, 1981 (syndicated); 1982–88 (CBS); 1985–89, 1991 (syndicated). Game show with host Bill Cullen/Dick Clark/John Davidson.

Texaco Star Theater. See ***Milton Berle Show***.

That Girl. 1966–71 (ABC). Situation comedy with Marlo Thomas and Ted Bessell.

This Is Your Life. 1952–61 (NBC); 1970, 1983 (syndicated). Tribute/human interest show hosted by Ralph Edwards.

Three's Company. 1977–84 (ABC). Situation comedy with John Ritter, Joyce DeWitt, Suzanne Somers, Norman Fell, and Audra Lindley.

Today. 1952–present (NBC). Morning news and features show with hosts including Dave Garroway/Frank Blair, Barbara Walters, Hugh Downs, Jane Pauley, Tom Brokaw, Bryant Gumbel, Deborah Norville, Katie Couric.

Tom and Jerry. 1965–72 (CBS); 1975–77 (ABC); 1980–82 (CBS). Cartoon with vocal effects by Paul Frees, Mel Blanc, June Foray, and Allen Swift.

Tonight Show. 1954–present (NBC). Late-night variety show hosted by Steve Allen/Ernie Kovacs/Jack Paar/Johnny Carson/Jay Leno.

To Tell the Truth. 1956–68, (CBS); 1969–77, 1980 (syndicated); 1990 (NBC). Game show hosted by Bud Collyer/Garry Moore/Joe Garagiola/Alex Trebek.

Truth or Consequences. 1950–51 (CBS); 1952–56, 1956–65 (NBC); 1966–74 (syndicated). Game show hosted by Ralph Edwards/Jack Bailey/Bob Barker.

Twentieth Century (Twenty-First Century). 1957–69 (CBS). Documentary series hosted by Walter Cronkite.

Twilight Zone. 1959–62, 1963–64, 1985–86, 1987 (CBS); 1988 (syndicated). Science-fiction anthology series hosted by Rod Serling/Charles Aidman.

Unsolved Mysteries. 1988–present (NBC). Unsolved real-life cases hosted by Robert Stack.

Untouchables. 1959–63 (ABC). Crime drama with Robert Stack, Jerry Paris, Nicholas Georgiade, and Abel Fernandez.

U.S. Steel Hour. 1953–55 (ABC); 1955–1963 (CBS). Dramatic anthology series with appearing actors including Johnny Carson, Anne Francis, Walter Sleazak, Andy Griffith, and Keenan Wynn.

The Virginian (Men from Shiloh). 1962–70 (NBC). Western with James Drury and Doug McClure.

Wagon Train. 1957–62 (NBC); 1962–65 (ABC). Western with Ward Bond, John McIntire, and Robert Horton.

Wall Street Week. 1972–present (PBS). Stock market news and views; moderated by Louis Rukeyser; John David, executive producer.

Walt Disney (Disney's Wonderful World/Disneyland/Walt Disney Presents/Walt Disney's Wonderful World of Color/Wonderful World of Disney). 1954–61 (ABC); 1961–81 (NBC); 1981–83 (CBS); 1984–86, 1986–88 (ABC); 1988–90 (NBC). Family series.

Waltons. 1972–81 (CBS). Drama with Richard Thomas, Jon Walmsley, Judy Norton, Eric Scott, Michael Learned, Mary Elizabeth McDonough, David W. Harper, Kami Cotler, Ralph Waite.

Washington Week in Review. 1967–present (PBS). Half-hour news review produced by WETA, Washington; moderated by Paul Duke (after March 1994, Ken Bode); among regular participants have been Peter Lisagor, Charles McDowell, Charles Corddry, Jack Nelson, Hedrick Smith, Haynes Johnson, Neil McNeil, Georgie Anne Geyer.

What's My Line? 1950–67 (CBS); 1968–75 (syndicated). Prime-time game show hosted by John Daly.

Wheel of Fortune. 1975–89 (NBC); 1989–91 (CBS); 1991–present (NBC); 1993–present (syndicated). Game show with host Chuck Woolery/Pat Sajak and cohost Susan Stafford/Vanna White.

Who Said That? 1948–51, 1952, 1953–54 (NBC); 1955 (ABC). Game show with celebrity panel and host Robert Trout/Walter Kiernan.

Wild Kingdom. 1963–71 (NBC); 1971–88 (syndicated). Animal documentary series hosted by Marlin Perkins.

Wyatt Earp (Life and Legend of Wyatt Earp). 1955–61 (ABC). Adult western with Hugh O'Brian, Douglas Fowley/Myron Healy, and Morgan Woodward.

Yogi Bear (Yogi's Gang/Yogi's Space Race). 1961–63, 1973–75; 1978–79 (syndicated). Cartoon with voices by Daws Butler and Don Messick.

You Asked for It. 1950–51 (Dumont); 1951–59 (ABC); 1972 (syndicated). Human interest show with host Art Baker/Jack Smith.

You Bet Your Life. 1950–61 (NBC); 1980 (syndicated). Game show hosted by Groucho Marx/Buddy Hackett (1980s version).

Young and the Restless. 1973–present (CBS). Daytime serial drama.

Your Hit Parade. 1950–58 (NBC); 1959, 1974 (CBS). Variety show with regulars Dorothy Collins, Giselle Mackenzie, Jill Corey, Virginia Gibson, Johnny Desmond, Chuck Cassey, Ray Cooke, and Bob Sands.

Your Show of Shows (Caesar's Hour/Sid Caesar Show). 1950–54, 1954–57, 1958 (NBC). Variety hosted by Sid Caesar and with regulars Imogene Coca/Nanette Fabray, Carl Reiner, and Howard Morris.

Zane Grey Theater (Dick Powell's Zane Grey Theater). 1956–62 (CBS). Western dramatic anthology hosted by Dick Powell.

SOURCES

Brooks, Tim, and Earl Marsh. *The Complete Directory of Prime Time TV Shows, 1946-Present.* 5th ed. New York: Ballantine Books, 1992.

Halliwell, Leslie. *Halliwell's Television Companion.* 3rd ed. London: Grafton Books, 1986.

Les Brown's Encyclopedia of Television. 3rd ed. Detroit: Gale Research, Co., 1992.

McNeil, Alex. *Total Television—A Comprehensive Guide to Programming from 1948 to the Present.* New York: Penguin Books, 1991.

Steinberg, Cobbett. *TV Facts.* New York: Facts on File, 1985.

Terrace, Vincent. *The Complete Encyclopedia of Television Programs.* Vols. I and II. New York: A. S. Barnes and Co., 1979.

———. *Fifty Years of Television.* New York: Cornwall Books, 1991.

—Jesma Reynolds; L.D.R.

IX

RELIGION, FOLKLORE, AND LEGEND

47

MAJOR RELIGIONS OF THE WORLD: CALENDARS AND FESTIVALS

The World is trying the experiment of attempting to form a civilized but non-Christian mentality. The experiment will fail; but we must be very patient in awaiting its collapse; meanwhile redeeming the time; so that the Faith may be preserved alive through the dark ages before us; to renew and rebuild civilization, and save the World from suicide.
—T. S. ELIOT, "THOUGHTS AFTER LAMBETH"

I say, we good Presbyterian Christians should be charitable in these things, and not fancy ourselves so vastly superior to other mortals, pagans and what-not, because of their half-crazy conceits on these subjects. There was Queequeg, now, certainly entertaining the most absurd questions about Yojo and his Ramadan;— but what of that? Queequeg thought he knew what he was about, I suppose; he seemed to be content, and there let him rest. All our arguing with him would not avail; let him be, I say: and heaven have mercy on us all— Presbyterians and Pagans alike—for we are all somehow dreadfully cracked about the head, and sadly need mending.
—HERMAN MELVILLE, *Moby-Dick*

· · · · ·

THOSE TWO OBSERVATIONS BY AMERICAN WRITERS, ALTHOUGH NOT THEO-
logically contradictory, may be said to exemplify two contrasting attitudes
toward the nature of religious belief. Eliot's comment, made in 1931,
assumes a certainty about the unique authority of Christian truth that
Melville, writing in 1855, obviously does not share. Yet the two approaches
are equally "religious"—which is to say, both exhibit a belief in the existence of a Supreme Being. Both concede that Christianity is not universally
accepted by the world.

The difference lies in what the two see as the appropriate human
response to that belief and that fact. Eliot's response leaves no room for
questioning the human interpretation of the divine will. Melville's
assumes a considerable gulf between divine truth and what humans may
make of it. The difference in approach is essentially psychological. All
writing about religion can be thought of as embodying one or the other
response.

Matthew Arnold, in the 1850s, regretted the "melancholy, long, withdrawing roar" of the Sea of Faith, which had once been at full tide. Yet
undoubtedly there are more Christians, and they make up a larger percentage of the world's population, than ever before. Christianity as a
whole is the most numerous religion in the world, with roughly 33 percent of the global population. (From Arnold's standpoint, of course, genuine religious faith and religious affiliation are by no means the same
thing.)

There are thousands of different religions in the world. In the United
States, Roman Catholicism is the largest single denomination—the 1993
World Almanac and Book of Facts cites a membership of 58,568,015; the
total for all Protestant sects is 86,684,476, which for some churches does
not include unbaptized children.

The following is a listing of the calendars of festivals and holy days of
major world religions. (See also the section on gods and goddesses, elsewhere in this book.)

PROTESTANT (EPISCOPAL CHURCH, U.S.A.)

The Episcopal church recognizes two cycles of feast days and holy days. Fixed
feasts are calculated in relation to Christmas Day (properly, the Feast of the
Nativity of Our Lord), commemorating the birth of Christ, which is fixed on
December 25. Movable feasts are holy days calculated from the date of Easter,
the Feast of the Resurrection. Easter is always the first Sunday after the first full
moon on or after March 21. Easter cannot fall earlier than March 22 or after
April 25.

Fixed Feasts and Their Dates

All Saints' Day. November 1.
Christmas Day. December 25.
Epiphany. January 6.

Movable Feasts and Their Anchors

Easter Day. As above.
Ascension Day. The Thursday that falls forty days after Easter, commemorating the ascension of Christ to heaven.
Day of Pentecost. The seventh Sunday after Easter, commemorating the descent of the Holy Spirit on the Apostles.
Trinity Sunday. The first Sunday after Pentecost.

Seasons of the Church Year and Their Principal Holy Days

Advent. The four Sundays before Christmas, a season of prayer and fasting that runs through Christmas Eve and ends on Christmas Day.
Christmas. The major fixed feast of the Episcopal church, running from Christmas Day to Epiphany. Holy days: Feast of the Nativity of Our Lord, Christmas Day, December 25; Holy Name of Our Lord Jesus Christ, January 1.
Epiphany. The Manifestation of Christ to the Gentiles, running from Epiphany through the last (ninth) Sunday of Epiphany. Holy days: Epiphany, January 6; first Sunday after Epiphany, the Baptism of Christ.
Lent. A season of fasting commemorating Christ's forty days of temptation in the wilderness; runs from the last (ninth) Sunday after Epiphany through the fifth Sunday of Lent, preceding Palm Sunday. Holy day: Ash Wednesday, the first day of Lent.
Holy Week. A week commemorating Christ's Passion, running from Palm Sunday through Easter Eve. Holy days: Palm Sunday, the Sunday of the Passion (one week before Easter); Maundy Thursday, the commemoration of Christ's washing the feet of the disciples and the Last Supper (Eucharist); Good Friday, the commemoration of Christ's death; Holy Saturday (Easter Eve), commemorating Christ's body lying in the tomb.
Easter. The major movable feast of the church year, commemorating Christ's Resurrection, running from Easter Day through Whitsunday. Holy days: Easter Day, the Sunday of the Resurrection (calculated as above); Ascension Day (calculated as above); the Day of Pentecost, Whitsunday (calculated as above).
Season after Pentecost. Runs from Trinity Sunday through the last (twenty-eighth) Sunday after Pentecost. Holy day: Trinity Sunday, the first Sunday after Pentecost.

Major Holy Days and Saints' Days and Their Dates

St. Andrew the Apostle, November 30
St. Thomas the Apostle, December 21
St. Stephen, Deacon and Martyr, December 26
St. John, Apostle and Evangelist, December 27
Holy Innocents, December 28
Confession of St. Peter the Apostle, January 18
Conversion of St. Paul the Apostle, January 25
Presentation of Our Lord Jesus Christ in the Temple (also called
     the Purification of St. Mary the Virgin), February 2
St. Matthias the Apostle, February 24
St. Joseph, March 19
Annunciation of Our Lord Jesus Christ to the Blessed Virgin Mary,
     March 25
St. Mark the Evangelist, April 25
St. Philip and St. James, Apostles, May 1
Visitation of the Blessed Virgin Mary, May 31
St. Barnabas the Apostle, June 11
Nativity of St. John the Baptist, June 24
St. Peter and St. Paul, Apostles, June 29
St. Mary Magdalene, July 22
St. James the Apostle, July 25
Transfiguration of Our Lord Jesus Christ, August 6
St. Mary the Virgin, Mother of Our Lord Jesus Christ, August 15
St. Bartholomew the Apostle, August 24
Holy Cross Day, September 14
St. Matthew, Apostle and Evangelist, September 21
St. Michael and All Angels, September 29
St. Luke the Evangelist, October 18
St. James of Jerusalem, Brother of Our Lord Jesus Christ,
     and Martyr, October 23
St. Simon and St. Jude, Apostles, October 28
All Saints' Day, November 1.

National Days

Independence Day, July 4
Thanksgiving Day, the fourth Thursday in November (U.S.)

ROMAN CATHOLIC

The Roman Catholic calendar consists of a series of liturgical seasons and com-
memorations with special honors to the Blessed Mary, Mother of God. Sunday
is the holy day of obligation and original Christian feast day. The commemoration of a saint is observed on the day of death with the following exceptions. St.
John the Baptist is commemorated on the day of his birth. Sts. Basil the Great
and Gregory Nazianzen, and the brother saints Cyril and Methodius, are commemorated in joint feasts.

Observances of feasts and holy days are ranked according to dignity:
"solemnity" is the highest rank and corresponds to former first-class feasts,
"feast" corresponds to second-class feasts, "memorial" corresponds to former
third-class feasts, and "optional memorial" refers to those days celebrated by
choice but not universally under the Roman rite.

Seasons

Advent. A period of four weeks associated with the coming of Christ.

Christmas Season. Season that begins with the observance of Christmas and
continues until the Sunday following January 6.

Lent. A season of penitence that begins Ash Wednesday and lasts until the Mass
of the Lord's Supper (Holy Thursday) with six Sundays.

Easter Triduum. Period that begins with the evening Mass of the Lord's Supper
and ends with the Evening Prayer of Easter Sunday.

Easter Season. A period of fifty days from Easter to Pentecost.

Ten Holy Days of Obligation

There are ten holy days of obligation as prescribed under church law. Six of these
days are observed in the United States: Christmas, the Nativity of Jesus,
December 25; Solemnity of Mary the Mother of God, January 1; Ascension of
the Lord; Assumption of Blessed Mary the Virgin, August 15; All Saints' Day,
November 1; Immaculate Conception of Blessed Mary the Virgin, December 8.
The other four holy days of obligation are: Epiphany, January 6; St. Joseph,
March 19; Corpus Christi; Sts. Peter and Paul, June 29.

All Saints' Day. November 1, solemnity. Commemoration of all the blessed in
heaven, particularly honoring those martyrs and saints with no special
feasts set for them.

Ascension of the Lord. Movable observance occurring forty days after Easter,
solemnity. Marks the ascension of Christ into heaven forty days after his
resurrection from the dead.

Assumption of Blessed Mary the Virgin. August 15, solemnity. Celebration of the ascent of Mary's body and soul into heaven at the time of her death on the earth. One of the oldest and most solemn of feasts of Mary.

Christmas, Nativity of Jesus. December 25, solemnity. Commemorates the birth of Jesus Christ.

Corpus Christi. Movable, celebrated on Thursday, or in the United States on Sunday, following Trinity Sunday, solemnity. Commemoration of the Holy Eucharist.

Epiphany of the Lord. January 6, or in the United States on a Sunday between January 2 and 8, solemnity. One of the oldest Christian feasts, it originally recognized the manifestations of the divinity of Christ—his birth, the visits by the wise men, and his baptism by John the Baptist. The central focus is now on Christ's baptism.

Immaculate Conception of Blessed Mary the Virgin. December 8, solemnity. Honors Mary, who was preserved from original sin at the time of her conception and filled with grace from the beginning of her life.

St. Joseph. March 19, solemnity. Honors the husband of Blessed Mary the Virgin. Recognizes Joseph as the protector and patron of the universal church as proclaimed by Pius IX.

Sts. Peter and Paul. June 29, solemnity. Honors the chief apostles Peter, who was crucified, and Paul, who was beheaded during the Neronian persecution.

Solemnity of Mary the Mother of God. January 1, solemnity. Formerly the Feast of Circumcision that marked the initiation of Jesus Christ, it now focuses on the initiation of persons into Christianity through baptism and honors Mary.

Other Holy Days and Feasts

All Souls. November 2. Recognizes and honors the dead, the faithful departed. Three Masses are celebrated for this commemoration.

Annunciation of the Lord. March 25, solemnity. Formerly the Annunciation of the Blessed Virgin Mary, it celebrates the delivery of the message by Gabriel the Archangel to the Virgin Mary that she was to be the Mother of Christ.

Ash Wednesday. Movable, occuring six and a half weeks before Easter. Marks the beginning of Lent and is a day of fasting and penitence, symbolized by marking foreheads of worshipers with ashes in the Sign of the Cross.

Baptism of the Lord. Movable, usually occurring on the Sunday after January 6 (Epiphany), feast. Associated with the liturgy of Epiphany, it celebrates the baptism of Christ by John the Baptist.

Birth of Mary. September 8, feast. Commemorates the birth of the Blessed Virgin Mary.

Candlemas Day. February 2. See **Presentation of the Lord**.

Chair of Peter. February 22, feast. Expression of belief in the hierarchy and order of the church.

Christ the King. Movable, occuring on the last Sunday of the liturgical year, solemnity. Recognizes Christ as one deserving homage, service, and fidelity from all men in all phases of life.

Conversion of St. Paul. January 25, feast.

Dedication of St. John Lateran. November 9, feast. Commemorates the first public consecration of a church. The church was the Basilica of the Most Holy Savior, consecrated by Pope St. Sylvester on November 9, 324, and was a gift of the Emperor Constantine along with the Lateran Palace. It has been known as St. John Lateran since the twelfth century, honoring St. John the Baptist.

Dedication of St. Mary Major. August 5, optional memorial. Commemorates the rebuilding and consecration of the Basilica of St. Mary Major in Rome by Pope Sixtus III.

Easter. Movable, occurring on the first Sunday after the full moon following the vernal equinox (between March 22 and April 25), solemnity. Marks the resurrection of Christ from the dead. The observance extends through the Easter Season of fifty days.

Easter Vigil. The night before Easter. Ceremonies held after sunset and relate to Christ's resurrection and the renewal theme of Easter.

Good Friday. The Friday before Easter, the second day of Easter Triduum. Celebration takes place in the afternoon, preferably at 3:00 P.M., and commemorates the Passion and Death of Christ in the reading of the Passion, offers special prayers for the church and people, venerates the Cross, and offers a service of Communion.

Guardian Angels. October 2, memorial. Honors the angels who protect people from spiritual and physical dangers.

Holy Family. Movable, occurring on the Sunday after Christmas, feast. Commemorates the Holy Family of Jesus, Mary, and Joseph, recognizing them as the model of society in their holiness and virtue.

Holy Innocents. December 28, feast. Honors the infants killed by Herod's soldiers who sought to kill the child Jesus.

Holy Saturday. The day before Easter. Neither Mass nor Communion is celebrated, and the Easter fast is observed until the Easter Vigil.

Holy Thursday. The Thursday before Easter. The Mass of the Lord's Supper in the evening marks the beginning of the Easter Triduum, and the day commemorates the institution of the sacraments of Eucharist and Holy Orders as well as Jesus' washing the Apostles' feet at the Last Supper.

Immaculate Heart of Mary. The Saturday following the second Sunday after Pentecost, optional memorial. Celebrates Mary's title as her Most Pure Heart and what Pius XII ordered in 1944 as "peace among nations, freedom for the Church, the conversion of sinners, the love of purity and the practice of virtue."

Joachim and Ann. July 26, memorial. Commemorates the parents of Mary.

John the Baptist, Birth of. June 24, solemnity. Only saint besides Blessed Virgin Mary whose birthday is celebrated.

Michael, Gabriel, and Raphael, Archangels. September 29, feast.

Octave of Christmas. January 1. See **Solemnity of Mary the Mother of God**.

Our Lady of Guadalupe. December 12, feast in the United States. Commemorates the appearances of the Blessed Virgin to Juan Diego, an Indian, on Tepayac Hill outside Mexico City in 1531.

Our Lady of Sorrows. September 15, memorial. Recognizes the sorrowful experiences associated with Mary in her relation to Christ.

Our Lady of the Rosary. October 7, memorial. This feast commemorates the Virgin Mary through the Rosary, which recounts the events of her and Jesus' lives.

Passion Sunday. Formerly called Palm Sunday, the Sunday before Easter. Marks the beginning of Holy Week by recounting Christ's entry into Jerusalem the last week of his life. Includes full liturgical observance with blessing of palms and reading of the Passion, by Matthew, Mark, or Luke.

Pentecost. Also known as Whitsunday, movable, occuring fifty days after Easter, solemnity. Regarded as the birthday of the Catholic church, it commemorates the Holy Spirit's descent upon the Apostles, the Apostles' preachings in Jerusalem to Jews, and the baptism of several thousand people as noted in Acts.

Presentation of the Lord. Formerly called Purification of the Blessed Virgin Mary, also Candlemas Day, February 2, feast. Based on the prescriptions of Mosaic Law, it commemorates the presentation of Jesus in the Temple and the purification of Mary forty days following his birth.

Queenship of Mary. August 22, memorial. Honors Mary as queen of heaven, angels, and all people. Originally, the date was May 31.

Sacred Heart of Jesus. Movable, occurring on the Friday after the second Sunday after Pentecost, solemnity. Commemorates the divine Person of Christ, whose heart symbolizes love for all people, for whom he sought redemption.

Transfiguration of the Lord. August 6, feast. Commemorates Christ's revelation of his divinity to Peter, James, and John on Mount Tabor.

Trinity, Most Holy. Movable, occurring on the Sunday after Pentecost, solemnity. Commemorates the Trinity of Christian faith—Father, Son, and Holy Spirit—in one God.

Triumph of the Cross. September 14, feast. Marks the recovery of the cross on which Christ was crucified in 326 as well as the consecration of the Basilica of the Holy Sepulchre and the recovery of a major part of the cross in either 628 or 629 after Persians removed it from Jerusalem.

Visitation. May 31, feast. Recalls Mary's visit to her cousin Elizabeth following the Annunciation and prior to the birth of John the Baptist.

EASTERN ORTHODOX CHURCH

The Orthodox church uses both the Gregorian and the Julian calendars. The Gregorian Calendar has been thirteen days ahead of the Julian since the beginning of this century. In 1923, all of the Greek Orthodox churches (withstanding a small minority in Greece) chose to adopt the Gregorian Calendar, following centuries of refusal. However, the Russian, Serbian, Georgian, Bulgarian, and Jerusalem churches retained the old calendar. Since then, the Church of Bulgaria has changed to the new calendar. However, all Orthodox churches observe Easter on the same day as they do the dates, which vary relative to the calendar in use.

The liturgical calendar begins on September 1, the feast of St. Simon Stylites, which recognizes Christ's entry into public life by preaching in the synagogue at Nazareth. The "feast of feasts" in the Orthodox Christian year is Easter Day, standing above all the rest. Next in importance are the Twelve Great Feasts, divided into two groups: Feasts of the Mother of God and Feasts of the Lord.

Feasts of the Mother of God

Birth of the Theotokos. September 8. Celebrates the birth of the Blessed Virgin Mary unto her parents, Joachim and Ann. From her birth, she was specially designated by God to be the Mother of God and is thus recognized on this day for this title.

Entry of the Theotokos into the Temple. November 21. Celebrates Mary's entry into the temple to dedicate her life to God, in preparation for her future role as Mother of the Incarnate Lord.

Meeting of Our Lord. February 2. Festival commemorating Christ's meeting of the people in the form of Simeon the Elder and Ann the Prophetess. Serves as the conclusion of the Nativity sequence, which began approximately eighty days earlier with the start of the Christmas fast.

Annunciation. March 25. Recognizes both the active participation of the Virgin Mary in accepting Gabriel's announcement to her to be the Mother of the Lord and the divine work of the Lord in the Incarnation.

Dormition of the Theotokos. August 15. Honors the death of the Virgin Mary on earth and her assumption into heaven, remaining forever linked to all men on earth.

Feasts of the Lord

Exaltation of the Cross. September 14.

Christmas. Also known as the Nativity of Christ, December 25. Commemorates the birth of Christ, the adoration of the shepherds, and the arrival of the Magi with their gifts of gold, frankincense, and myrrh. The story of the Three Wise Men is read at this time.

Theophany. January 6, also known as the Feast of Lights. Celebration of Christ's baptism in Jordan and literally of the manifestation of God through Christ. The day is marked by the Great Blessing of the Waters, performed both on January 5 and 6, culminating in the priest immersing the Cross into the body of water three times, recalling Christ's triple immersion in the Jordan as well as the baptism of every Orthodox Christian.

Palm Sunday. Occurring one week before Easter. Marks the beginning of Holy Week.

Ascension of Our Lord. Occurring forty days after Easter. Commemorates the Lord's resurrection and ascension into heaven.

Pentecost. Also known as Trinity Sunday. Occurring fifty days after Easter.

Transfiguration of Our Lord. August 6.

Other Feasts and Fasts

A period of preparation precedes the Great Feast, known as the Forefeast, and varies in the amount of time. Two of the Great Feasts are preceded by a special fast in the Greek Orthodox church, while the Russian Orthodox observes four special fasts. Three of the Great Feasts are followed on the next day by what is known as a Synaxis, generally meaning "assembly for worship" and more specifically a special commemoration of a saint connected with the feast.

Awakening of Lazarus. Occurring the Saturday before Palm Sunday.

The Conception. December 9. Ann's bearing of her child, the future Mother of the Lord, the Theotokos.

All Saints' Day. Occurring on the Monday eight days after Pentecost.

Feast of Sts. Peter and Paul. June 29.

Memorial of Sts. Joachim and Ann. September 9. Commemorates the parents of the Theotokos.

Synaxis of Theotokos. December 26. Commemorates the Mother of the Lord.

Synaxis of St. John the Baptist. January 7.

Memorial of Sts. Simeon and Ann. February 3.

Synaxis of Archangel Gabriel. March 26.

Four Special Fasts Observed

Christmas Fast. Beginning November 15.

Great Fast (Lent). Beginning seven weeks before Easter and ending on the Saturday of Lazarus, the day before Palm Sunday.

Fast of the Apostles. Beginning on Monday after All Saints' Day, and varying in time from one to six weeks, ending on the eve of the feast of Sts. Peter and Paul, June 28.

Dormition Fast. Beginning August 1 and ending on the eve of the Feast of the Dormition, August 14.

JUDAISM

There are twelve months commencing at the new moon in the Jewish lunar calendar. The months comprise 29 or 30 days and are:

Nisan: March/April
Iyar
Sivan
Tamuz
Av
Ellul
Tishri
Cheshvan
Kislev
Teveth
Shevat
Adar

Festivals and Days of Fasting

Rosh Hashanah/New Year. Literally meaning "head of the year," Rosh Hashanah occurs in Tishri (September/October) and recognizes God's creation of the world and his reign over the earth. Ten days of penitence and self-examination begin during this observance. These days are known as the Ten Days of Penitence.

Atonement/Yom Kippur. Considered the most holy day in the Jewish religious year, Yom Kippur comes at the end of penitence that began at Rosh Hashanah. The day is characterized by fasting and contrition, and by a continuing service the entire day in the synagogue.

Sukkoth/Tabernacles. Beginning on the 15th of Tishri and lasting nine days, it is one of three harvest festivals (Passover and Pentecost being the other two). It celebrates the autumn harvest and is a remembrance of God's grace and his protection of the Jewish people during their forty-year journey from Egypt to Israel. Each family constructs a sukkah, temporary structure, to recreate the conditions experienced during the Hebrews' wanderings.

Simchat Torah/Rejoicing of the Torah. The cycle of reading the Torah begins with the first five books of the Hebrew Bible being read in the synagogue. There is singing, dancing, and exuberant joy.

Hanukkah/Festival of Lights. Beginning on the 25th of Kislev, this observance lasts eight days and commemorates the victory of Judas Maccabeus over the Syrians, who wanted to destroy the Jewish faith; however, rather than celebrating the military victory, it pays tribute to the rebuilding of the

Temple in Jerusalem in 164 B.C.E. A candelabrum of eight candles (menorah) is lit each of the eight days.

Purim. This festival occurs on the 14th of Adar and recalls the story in the *Book of Esther* when Jews were saved from persecution and massacre from Haman (seen as the persecutor of Jews). Gifts are given to the impoverished at this time.

Passover/Pesach. This spring festival begins on the 15th of Nisan and lasts eight days. Once marking the barley harvest, it now chiefly celebrates the deliverance of the Israelites from slavery in Egypt. It is also known as the Feast of the Unleavened Bread, and matzah (unleavened bread) is eaten as a reminder of the bread of affliction eaten by the Jewish slaves. The seder, a festive meal that features the retelling of the Exodus by the head of each family, is also celebrated.

Shavuot/Pentecost. Beginning on the 6th of Sivan, this observance lasts seven weeks and is celebrated fifty days after the second day of Passover. It commemorates the giving of the Torah, or the Law, to Moses; it is also associated with the failed Jewish revolt against Rome in the second century C.E.

Ninth Day of Av. This day of fasting and mourning, held in commemoration of the destruction of the Jewish Temple in both 586 B.C.E. and C.E. 70, is also used to commemorate the death of six million Jews during World War II.

In addition to these festivals, the **Sabbath** or day of rest is the most important day in the Jewish calendar. It begins on Friday evening, the evening of the seventh day. In the home, sabbath candles are lit and kiddush (sanctification) is recited. The day is characterized by abstention from work and the study of the Torah.

ISLAM

The Islamic calendar is dated from the New Year, the Day of Hijra. All dates are noted as occurring on a certain day of a certain month AH ("After Hijra"). Each festival falls eleven or twelve days earlier during the solar year, since the Islamic calendar follows the lunar cycle: each month begins with the sighting of the new moon. These are the months of the Islamic year:

Muharram: 30 days
Safar: 29 days
Rabi I (Rabi ul-Awwal): 30 days
Rabi II: 29 days
Jumad I: 30 days
Jumad II: 29 days
Rajab: 30 days
Shaban: 29 days

Ramadan: 30 days
Shawwal: 29 days
Dhu al-Aa'dah: 30 days
Dhu al-Hijja: 29 or 30 days

Principal Islamic Religious Festivals and Holy Days

Day of Hijra. Fixed in the calendar by caliph 'Umar, this festival commemorates the journey of Muhammad and his followers from Mecca to Medina in C.E. 622. It falls on the first day of Muharram, and begins the new year. All other dates in the Islamic calendar are based on this holy day.

10th Muharram. Muhammad observed this day of fasting to mark Moses' leading the Israelites out of bondage in Egypt, but it has become a symbol of the division between the majority Sunni Muslims and the minority Shi'ite Muslims. On this day Shi'ites observe the death in battle of Muhammad's grandson Husain, who perished while fighting the Sunnis under his brother Ali. This date marks the beginning of the schism between the two main branches of Muslims. This period of mourning continues for forty days. On the tenth day of Muharram, a mourning procession is held in Husain's memory, and on this day no public entertainments or television broadcasts are permitted.

Mawlid ul-Nabi. The 12th of Rabi ul-Awwal (Rabi I), this day is also known as the Birth of the Prophet. It commemorates Muhammad's birth in C.E. 570 and celebrates his life and work. The festivities include readings from the Qur'an and prayers. The whole month of Rabi ul-Awwal is traditionally known as "birth month."

Lailat ul-Isra. Celebrated on the 27th of Rajab, this feast is also called the Night Journey. It commemorates Muhammad's journey to Jerusalem, from where he was taken to heaven and then returned to earth.

Lailat ul-Bara'h. This festival, also called the Night of Forgiveness, celebrates the preparations for Ramadan. It is observed on the night of the full moon two weeks before the beginning of Ramadan, during the month of Shaban. Quarrels and disagreements are settled and special prayers are offered so that the coming year will be a holy one.

Ramadan. A month of fasting from sunup to sundown, in which neither food nor drink may be taken during daylight hours. Ramadan's fasts begin on the new moon at the beginning of the month and end with the sighting of the new moon that begins Shawwal.

Lailat ul-Qadr. Also called the Night of Power, this festival commemorates the revelation of the Qur'an to Muhammad. It takes place during the month of Ramadan.

'Id ul-Fitr. This feast marks the end of Ramadan and occurs on the first day of
Shawwal with the sighting of the new moon. During this period of happiness
and rejoicing, people greet each other with the traditional greeting " 'Id
Mubaraq" ("Happy 'Id"). The festivities include ritual bathing, new clothes,
prayers, visits to the mosque, and the eating of samosas (meat and potato
dumplings).

Hajj. The Pilgrimage, traditionally undertaken during the month of Dhu al-Hijja.
Every Muslim aspires to travel to Mecca, the most sacred site in the Islamic
faith, for visits to many holy places, especially Bayt ul-haram, the mosque in
which the Black Stone of the Ka'ba is kept. There are a number of ceremonies associated with the pilgrimage, including prayers on Mount Arafat
and Jamrat, the ceremony of stoning the Devil. Pilgrims who return from the
Hajj may take the name "al-hajji" ("One who has made the Pilgrimage").

'Id ul-Adha. Also called the Feast of the Slaughter or Festival of Sacrifice, this four-
day celebration traditionally comes at the end of the Hajj, once the pilgrims
have begun to return home and visit their local mosques. Each Muslim tries
personally to sacrifice a cow, sheep, goat, or camel; those who cannot do so send
money to relatives who will do it on their behalf. Gifts of all kinds, including
meat sacrificed but not eaten during the festival, are given to the poor.

HINDUISM

The Hindu sacred year consists of twelve lunar months with a leap year calculated every two and a half years. There is no universal festival calendar.
Furthermore, the new year begins in either spring or late autumn, depending on
the location. Months begin at full moon in northern India and at new moon in
southern India.

There are many divisions and sects of Hinduism, each devoted to worshiping one of several gods. The three main gods of Hinduism are Brahma, Vishnu,
and Shiva, who carry out the activities of the supreme, single being (Ishvara) or
reality (Brahman). Brahma has the power to create, Vishnu maintains and preserves life, and Shiva is the great destroyer. Along with these three, there are
many other manifestations whose importance varies regionally and within certain sects. Thus there are many local festivals held in celebration of specific
deities. There are several festivals that are widely recognized by all Hindus,
though the significance of these festivals may depend on the region, caste, and
religious affinities of the people. The major festivals are as follows:

Holi. Spring festival (February) that occurs during the last month of the Indian
traditional calendar. *Holi* literally means "it is all over, it is all past."
Dedicated to Krishna, Holi was once strictly a fertility ceremony but has
now also come to signify the dissolution of social barriers, as caste and

taboo are ignored at this time. It is celebrated in a carnival atmosphere, with street dancing and dousing of colored water or powder on everyone.

Divali. Also known as the festival of lights, occurring at the onset of winter (November) and associated with Kali, Shiva's female counterpart, and Lakshmi, Vishnu's female counterpart, who is the goddess of wealth and beauty. Lakshmi is believed to bestow good fortune on every house that is lit by a lamp or light.

Dasara. Ten-day celebration held in late autumn (October) commemorating the triumph of Rama, the hero of the *Ramayana,* over the demon army and honoring Kali the Destroyer, a manifestation of the god Shiva. Presents are exchanged, and there are dances and processions.

Shivaratri. Celebration held in late February that is devoted to Shiva, who along with Vishnu and Brahma constitutes the Hindu Trinity. Known as the great destroyer, Shiva is also associated with fertility and energy.

Janamashtami. Krishna's birthday, celebrated at the end of the summer. The god Krishna, a manifestation of Vishnu, is an important figure in the *Bhagavad Gita.*

BUDDHISM

The Buddhist religious year celebrates important events in the life of its founder as well as of the early religious communities. The year varies within particular cultures; many are closely tied with the cycle of rice cultivation and other economic activities. There are several types of Buddhism: Chinese, Tibetan, Japanese, Thai, Sri Lankan, and Burmese.

Important Events Throughout the Year and Approximate Time of Occurrence

Wesak/Vesak. April/May, commemorates the birth, death, and enlightenment of Buddha.

Dhammacakka. July/August, commemorates preaching of Buddha's first sermon.

Vassa. July, celebrates onset of monsoon season (in areas where applicable).

Vassa. October, celebrates end of monsoon season.

Bodhi Day. November/December, celebrates Buddha's enlightenment.

Other religious days include observances of saints' anniversaries and the monastic order as well as seasonal changes and the cycle of life and death.

In Japan, the following seasonal dates are observed:

Joya-e. New Year's Eve, December 31.

Oshogatsu. New Year's Day, January 1.

Setsubun-e. Heralding of Spring, February 3.

Higan-e. Spring Equinox, March 21.
Obon. Festival of the Dead, July 13–15.
Higan-e. Fall Equinox, September 21.
Buddhist Thanksgiving. Sometime in summer.
   In Thailand:
Songkran. New Year celebration, mid-April, end of dry season.
   In Sri Lanka:
Festival of the arrival of the eyetooth relic. July/August, lasts twelve days and
   honors the particular relic of Buddha that was given to the Sri Lankan ruler
   following Buddha's death.

SHINTO

Shinto, the independent religion of Japan, stresses unity with nature.
Traditionally it has emphasized obedience and loyalty to the emperor. Since
there are no weekly religious services, festivals are popular. Many relate to rites
of passage and daily life.

Major Rites of Passage Commemorations

First Shrine Visit of Newborn Children. Occurs on the 30th or 100th day following birth.
Schichigosan Rite. November 15; children ages three, five, and seven are taken
   to shrine to give thanks for healthy, expedient growth.
Seijin no Hi. January 15; originally considered the day of attaining adulthood;
   today commemorates Japanese young people who are twenty and have the
   right to vote.

Rites relating to professional and daily life are highly individualistic. For example, there will be a ceremony for the completion of a construction site or to
purify a building site.

   There are also shrine festivals. Annual ones are called "grand" and were
originally tied to the harvest. These occur in the spring and fall. The spring festivals are dedicated to reaping a good harvest and achieving success in various
businesses. The fall festivals are a time for thanksgiving. Occasional shrine festivals occur to dedicate or remove a shrine.

CHINESE FOLK RELIGION

The followers of traditional Chinese folk religion, comprising over 236 million
people, combine elements of Confucian ethics, Taoism, veneration of ancestors,
worship of local deities, universism, and some Buddhist elements.
Traditionally, religious dates were issued by the Bureau of Astronomy in the

Ministry of Rites to demonstrate the divine mandate of the ruling dynasty. Calculations were based on both lunar and solar calendars.

Some of the more well-known (and widespread) religious festivals are:

Chinese New Year. January/February, commemorates return of Kitchen god to heaven.
Dragon Boat Festival. June, commemorates Chinese martyr.
Moon Festival. September, recognizes Chinese hero.
Winter Festival. December, time of feasting.

SOURCES

The Book of Common Prayer and Administration of the Sacraments and Other Rites and Ceremonies of the Church, According to the Use of the Episcopal Church. New York: Oxford University Press, 1979.

Eerdman's Handbook to the World's Religions. Grand Rapids, Wis.: W. B. Eerdman's Co., 1982.

Eliade, Mircea, ed. *The Encyclopedia of Religion.* 16 vols. New York: Macmillan, 1987.

Fortescue, Adrian. *The Orthodox Eastern Church.* New York: Burt Franklin, 1969.

Foy, Felician A. 1991 *Catholic Almanac.* Huntington, Ind.: Our Sunday Visitor, Inc., 1991.

Hinnells, John R. *The Facts on File Dictionary of Religions.* New York: Facts on File, 1984.

Kennedy, Richard. *The International Dictionary of Religion.* New York: Crossroads Publ. Co., 1984.

Mother Mary and Archimandrite Kallistos Ware. *The Festal Menaion* (service book of the Orthodox church). London: Faber and Faber, 1969.

Paden, William E. *Religious Worlds.* Boston: Beacon Press, 1988.

Parrinder, Edward Geoffrey. *World Religions: From Ancient History to the Present.* New York: Facts on File, 1971.

Sutherland, Stewart, *et al.*, eds. *The World's Religions.* London: Routledge and Kegan Paul, 1988.

Webster's New World Encyclopedia. 9th ed. New York: Prentice-Hall, 1990.

The World Almanac and Book of Facts, 1993. New York: Pharos Books, 1994.

—David Sisk; Jesma Reynolds; L.D.R.

48

BIBLICAL CHARACTERS

· · · · ·

In Mark Twain's Adventures of Tom Sawyer, it will be recalled that Tom succeeds in cornering the local market on Bible tickets, supposedly awarded for diligence in memorizing Scriptural passages, and proudly goes forward at Sunday School to cash them in. Quizzed upon his apparent knowledge of the Good Book, he is asked to name the first two disciples. "David and Goliath," he replies.

Writers even so could once assume a reasonable acquaintance with the characters and events of the Bible on the part of their readers—writers, that is, within the Western cultural tradition. That this is no longer a safe assumption is undeniable. How many readers, for example, of Walker Percy's novel *The Last Gentleman* will automatically recognize the allusion when Sutter Vaught, encountering Will Barrett out in the desert Southwest, asks him, "Are you Philip?"

Whether this is a good thing or a bad thing, or merely a cultural fact, we leave to the individual judgment. But since one can't assume that readers will know who even the major characters in the Bible are, we thought it would be useful to provide a roster of some of the best-known figures. Chapter references are to the Revised Standard Version.

OLD TESTAMENT

Aaron. Moses' brother, a priestly figure during the Exodus (Exod. 4 ff.).

Abel. Adam's second son, killed by his brother Cain (Gen. 4).

Abraham. A patriarchal figure whose faith saves his son Isaac from sacrificial death (Gen. 12–13, 16, 21).

Absalom. Son of David, kills his half-brother for raping his sister (2 Sam. 13–18).

Adam. The first human figure (Gen. 1–5).

Ahab. Regarded as a type of the wicked king (1 Kings 17–21; 2 Kings 21).

Ahasuerus. King of Persia, husband of Esther (Esther).

Balaam. Seer, diviner, accused of excessive greed (Num. 22–24).

Bathsheba. Solomon's mother, so desired by David that he arranges her husband's death (2 Sam. 11–12; 1 Kings 1–2).

Belshazzar. A king of Babylon; at a feast God's words written in flame appear on his wall (Dan. 5).

Benjamin. Jacob's youngest son, Joseph's full brother (Gen. 42–45).

Bildad. One of Job's three comforters (Job 2).

Cain. His brother Abel's killer, given divine protection (Gen. 4).

Daniel. Interpreter of dreams, divinely protected in a den of lions (Dan.).

David. Heroic king, psalmist, passionate man; slays the Philistine giant Goliath, unites Israel and Judah (1 Sam. 16–31; 2 Sam. 1–5, 6–20).

Deborah. Female prophet and judge of Israel who incites Barak against Sisera (Judg. 4–5).

Delilah. Samson's betrayer (Judg. 16).

Elijah. A prophet (1 Kings 17 through 2 Kings 2).

Elisha. Successor to Elijah; after his death his bones continue to work miracles (1 Kings 19; 2 Kings 2–9, 13).

Esau. Son of Isaac, outwitted of his inheritance by his younger brother Jacob (Joseph's father) (Gen. 25).

Esther. A heroine; by her courage she saves the Jews from massacre: the Jewish feast of Purim is related to this success (Esther).

Eve. The first mother (Gen. 2–3).

Ezekiel. Priest and prophet, mysterious; his is the vision of fiery wheels in the sky (Ezek.).

Gabriel. An archangel, he explains mysteries to Daniel (Dan. 8–9); in the New Testament he greets both Elizabeth and Mary the mother of Jesus (Luke 1).

Gideon. Judge who delivers Israel from Midianites (Judg. 6–8; Isa. 9–10); in the New Testament, Paul cites his example (see Heb. 10).

Goliath. The Philistine giant killed by David early in his rise to prominence (1 Sam. 17; 2 Sam. 21).

Hagar. The maid of Abraham's wife Sarah, mother of Abraham's firstborn, the nomadic Ishmael (Gen. 16, 21).

Ham. Noah's son who "saw the nakedness of his father" (Gen. 5, 9).

Haman. Chief minister of King Ahasuerus, who conspires against the Jews and is hanged (Esther 3–7).

Immanuel. Isaiah's name for the child who would save Israel, an Old Testament prophecy taken to prefigure Jesus' birth (Isa. 7).

Isaac. Abraham's son nearly sacrificed by his father, an obedient son (Gen. 22).

Isaiah. The prophet with the greatest influence on later Christian thought; taken to have prophesied Jesus' birth (Isa.).

Ishmael. Hagar's son, driven away after the birth of Isaac to Sarah and Abraham (Gen. 16).

Israel. The name given to Jacob after his wrestling with an angel (Gen. 32).

Jacob. As Israel, is held to be the founder of the people; a subtle man who often advances through deceptions (Gen. 25, 27–28, 31).

Jehoiakim. Wicked king of Judah who rebels against Nebuchadnezzar (2 Kings 23–25; Jer. 1, 22, 35–36; Dan. 1).

Jeremiah. A grim prophet whose words and life filter into the New Testament. (Jer.; Heb. 8; Matt. 16).

Jesse. Father of David (1 Sam. 16–20; Ruth 4).

Jezebel. Wife of Ahab who introduces worship of Baal into kingdom of Israel (1 Kings 16, 18–19, 21; 2 Kings 9).

Job. A righteous man afflicted with sorrow, a universal figure (Job).

Jonah. God's greatness, in the story of this prophet, is found in all the world, even in the enemies of his people (Jon. 1).

Jonathan. A son of Saul and great friend of David (1 Sam. 13–14, 19–20).

Joseph. A son of Jacob, his brothers sell him into slavery; yet in Egypt he rises after adversity to Pharaoh's favor and saves his family from starvation (Gen. 37–50).

Joshua. Leads the invasion of Palestine, which sees the fall of Jericho (Josh.).

Judith. The heroine who cuts off the head of Nebuchadnezzar's general Holofernes when he is drunk, demoralizing his army (Jth. 8–16).

Leah. Daughter of Laban and sister of Rachel, who marries Jacob and bears children to him (Gen. 29–35).

Lot. Spared as Sodom is destroyed; his wife, looking back, is transformed into a pillar of salt (Gen. 11–19).

Melchizedek. A mysterious priest figure taken, later, to prefigure Christ's priesthood (Gen. 14).

Methuselah. His 969-year life span is the greatest of any of those living in the preflood, golden-age time (Gen. 5).

Mordecai. Queen Esther's cousin, whose advice on how to handle Haman saves the Jewish people (Esther).

Moses. Taken as the author of the first five books of the Bible; born an Israelite in Egyptian slavery, he is raised in Pharaoh's house; leading the Israelites from Egypt, he receives the Ten Commandments directly from God; during forty years of desert wanderings, he brings his people to God's promised land of Canaan (Exod. 2–18; Deut. 34).

Nebuchadnezzar. Ruler of the Babylonian Empire, in 587 B.C.E. he takes Jerusalem and razes it, the beginning of the Babylonian captivity (2 Kings 24; Jer. 27; Ezek. 26, 29; Dan. 4).

Noah. The hero of the Bible's flood story, a righteous man at a time of great wickedness (Gen. 6–9).

Potiphar. Steward to Pharaoh and Joseph's master; the story of Potiphar's wife's unsuccessful temptation of Joseph ends with Joseph in prison (Gen. 37, 39).

Rachel. Jacob's favorite wife, Joseph and Benjamin's mother; her father tricks Jacob into marrying Rachel's sister Leah first (Gen. 29, 35).

Reuben. Oldest son of Jacob, who helps save Joseph's life (Gen. 29, 35, 37–50).

Ruth. Moabite woman devoted to her mother-in-law, Naomi; widowed, she marries Boaz (Ruth).

Samson. A man of legendary strength, the last of the great judges (Judg. 13–16).

Samuel. The prophet who anoints David to succeed to Saul's throne (1 Sam. 1–16, 25:1, 28).

Sarah. Abraham's wife; aged and previously barren, she miraculously bears Isaac (Gen. 11–23).

Satan. That Biblical figure that opposes God's will (Zech. 3; Job 1; 1 Chron. 21).

Saul. First king of Israel (1 Sam. 9–31).

Solomon. David's wise son; as king he builds the great temple in Jerusalem (1 Kings 3–11).

Tobias. Son of the pious Jew Tobit who is afflicted by troubles, Tobias both eventually cures Tobit and frees the character Sarah from an evil spell (Tob.).

Uriah. Bathsheba's husband; his death is set in motion at David's command (2 Sam. 11).

Uriel. An archangel, with Gabriel, Michael, and Raphael (2 Esd. 4 ff.).

Zadok. High priest who is loyal to King David (2 Sam. 15, 17–19; 1 Kings 1).

NEW TESTAMENT

Ananias. Liar who with his wife Sapphira dies when confronted by Peter (Acts 5); another Ananias is high priest at Paul's trial (Acts 23–24).

Barnabas. Companion of Paul on his missionary voyage (Acts 4, 9, 11–15; Gal. 2).

Caiaphas. High priest at Jesus' trial (John 18).

Elizabeth. A relative of Mary the mother of Jesus, John the Baptist's mother (Luke 1).

Herod Antipas. Tetrarch of Judea, who causes the death of John the Baptist (Mark 6, 8; Luke 3, 9, 23; Acts 4).

Herod the Great. King of Judea at the time of Jesus' birth, he orders the slaughter of the innocents (Matt. 2).

James the Greater. One of the apostles, brother of John the Evangelist (Mark 1, 3, 6, 9–10, 14; Acts 1, 12).

Jesus. The redeemer, the Christ; firsthand accounts of his life are collected in the four gospels (Matt., Mark, Luke, John).

John. Beloved disciple of Jesus, author of the Gospel of John.

John the Baptist. Ascetic figure of the wilderness who baptizes Jesus (Mark 1; Luke 1, 3; Acts 1).

Joseph. The carpenter of Nazareth, husband of Mary the mother of Jesus (Matt. 1–2; Luke 1–3).

Judas (Iscariot). Disciple and betrayer of Jesus (Matt. 26–27).

Lazarus. A man four days dead, raised to life by Jesus (John 11).

Luke. Author of one of the gospels; possibly the unnamed man to whom Christ appears on the road to Emmaus (Luke 24; Mark 16).

Mark. Evangelist, author of one of the gospels (Mark).

Martha. One of two sisters at whose house Jesus stays; mildly reprimanded by Jesus (Luke 10; John 11–12).

Mary. Jesus' virgin mother (Matt. 1–2; Luke 1–2, 8; John 2, 19).

Mary Magdalene. Possibly a prostitute, she is at the cross as Jesus dies and is the first to see him resurrected (Matt. 28; Mark 16; Luke 8, 24; John 20).

Matthew. Disciple of Jesus, author of one of the gospels (Matt.).

Paul. Turns miraculously from his persecution of the early Christians; the second most powerful presence in the New Testament and writer of at least thirteen of the epistles (1 Cor. 15).

Pontius Pilate. Roman governor of Judea C.E. 26–36; delivers Jesus over for execution (Matt. 27; Mark 15; Luke 23; John 18–19; Acts 3–4; 1 Tim. 6).

Salome. Daughter of Herodias; she demands and receives the head of John the Baptist on a platter (Mark 6).

Silas. Paul's companion on his second missionary journey (Acts 15–18).

Simon Magus. Regarded as a magician, converts to Christianity; he is reprimanded by Peter for trying to buy the power to work miracles (Acts 8).

Thomas. One of the twelve apostles; he doubts the Resurrection until he sees and feels Jesus' wounds (Mark 3; John 11, 14, 20; Acts 1).

Timothy. Timotheus, disciple of apostle Paul (Acts 16, 18–20; Rom. 16; 1 Cor. 4, 16; 2 Cor. 1; Phil. 2; Col. 1; 1 Thess. 1; 2 Thess. 1; 1 Tim.; 2 Tim.; Philem.).

Zacharias. Father of John the Baptist (Luke 1).

SOURCES

Coggins, Richard. *Who's Who in the Bible.* Totowa, N.J.: Barnes and Noble, 1981.

Deen, Edith. *All of the Women of the Bible.* New York: Harper and Row, 1955.

"Glossary of Biblical Terms." In *The Bible Designed to Be Read as Living Literature,* edited by Ernest Sutherland Bates. New York: Simon and Schuster, 1943.

Jeffrey, David Lyle, ed. *A Dictionary of Biblical Tradition in English Literature.* Grand Rapids, Mich.: W. B. Eerdman's Co., 1992.

Sims, Albert, and George Dent. *Who's Who in the Bible.* New York: Philosophical Library, 1960.

—John Sepich; J.L.M.

49

ANCIENT GODS, GODDESSES, DEMIGODS, AND OTHER MYTHICAL HEROES AND HEROINES

. . . . .

"WHERE IS THE GRAVEYARD OF DEAD GODS?" H. L. MENCKEN ASKED. "WHAT lingering mourner waters their mounds?" Not himself a believer in a revealed Supreme Being, the Sage of Baltimore worked up a lengthy list of now-forgotten divinities, "gods of the highest dignity—gods of civilized people—worshipped and believed in by millions. All were omnipotent, omniscient and immortal. And all are dead."

Elsewhere in this volume is a section devoted to the calendars and activities of the world's major religions. The present section has to do with those divinities whose constituencies have since deserted them. Foremost in our pantheon come the gods and goddesses of the classical Greeks and Romans. So important were these to writers that it was customary to begin epic poems by asking their intervention: "Sing, goddess, of the wrath of Achilles," etc., etc. This was done even as late as the nineteenth century; Herman Melville worked an invocation to what he referred to as "thou great democratic god" (he spelled it with a small *d*) into the text of *Moby-Dick*. The extent to which Greeks actually believed in the specific doings of Zeus & Co. by the time that they got into the writing business is debatable; it depends upon what is meant by "believed in," and also on which Greeks. But beyond doubt the Greco-Roman pantheon, with attendant mythology, has exercised an impact upon our literature second only to that of the Judeo-Christian dispensation.

The Norse gods have been considerably less influential. Once the various Teutonic, Gallic, Scandinavian, and other northern European migrations settled down and were converted to Christianity, their older divinities were dropped from public view for purposes other than of designating the

745

days of the week. A thirteenth-century Icelandic poet tried to stem the tide, for literary purposes at least, by compiling a handbook of the vanishing Nordic pantheon (see below), but was unable to halt the process. Except for a brief vogue for Nordic mythology during the latter nineteenth century, which inspired the likes of Richard Wagner, William Morris, and Henrik Ibsen (briefly), not much has been done literarily and artistically with Fafnir, Freyr, Thor, Odin, Loki, and co. for some time now.

As for the other traditions, their memory has long since departed except among scholars. The only Egyptian divinities that most people have heard of, for example, are Isis and Osiris, because Mozart put them into an aria.

We take no editorial position in all this, you understand. Far be it from us to offend Balder, Horus, Quetzalcoatl, Pan, Amun-re, Acanum, Dana, or any of the others. Mencken said they're dead; we didn't. We say only that nobody much worships them any more, and not that they are not—or are—certified divine entities fully worthy of respect. (Knock on wood.)

The compilation that follows is divided into three parts, each with its list of reference sources.

GREEK AND ROMAN GODS

The deities of the ancient Greeks and Romans fell into two broad groups or generations: the Titans, offspring of Gaia and Uranus not long after the beginning of the world, and the more numerous Olympians, their descendants who eventually defeated them in battle and took over their domain, banishing the Titans into Tartarus, a region far beneath the earth. In the list that follows the spelling follows common English practice, Latin rather than Greek in form—*e.g., Hades* rather than *Haides, Apollo* rather than *Apollon.* When the Roman name differs greatly from the Greek—*e.g.,* Mars for Ares, Neptune for Poseidon—it is given in parentheses after the Greek form and cross-referenced. Titans are specified as such when cited; others may be assumed to be of the Olympian generation.

Amor. See **Eros**.

Amphitrite. A sea goddess who rejected Poseidon's advances for a time and then gave in to produce Triton, who dwelled with his parents in their palace beneath the sea.

Aphrodite (Venus). Goddess of sexual love. Her parentage differs in various accounts, but the most memorable story is that she rose from the genitals of Uranus after his son, the Titan Cronus, severed and cast them into the sea. In the myths she usually appears in the company of Eros.

Apollo. Son of Zeus and the Titaness Leto, brother of Artemis. Apollo was god of music, poetry, rationality, and intellectual endeavors in general.

Ares (Mars). God of war, son of Zeus and Hera and sometime lover of Aphrodite. Because of his love of carnage and destruction most of the other gods disliked him.

Artemis (Diana). Virgin daughter of Zeus and the Titaness Leto, huntress and goddess of wild beasts and human childbirth. She disdained males for the most part and punished many of them for making advances.

Athene (Minerva). Virgin goddess of wisdom, war, and the arts, patroness of the city of Athens. Athene "sprang full-panoplied" from Zeus's brow (Hesiod) after he swallowed his first wife, Metis, to keep her from bearing a male child. Athene became her father's favorite of all his offspring.

Aurora. See **Eos**.

Bacchus. See **Dionysos**.

Ceres. See **Demeter**.

Cronus (Saturn). Titan, son of Uranus and Gaia. Cronus castrated his father and threw his genitals into the sea. From the resulting foam sprang Aphrodite, in some versions of her genesis. Afterward, fearing deposition by one of his own children, Cronus began swallowing his children by his wife Rhea.

Cupid. See **Eros**.

Demeter (Ceres). Goddess of grain and agricultural abundance, daughter of Cronus and Rhea and mother of Persephone through a union with Zeus.

Diana. See **Artemis**.

Dionysos (Bacchus). God of wine, son of Zeus and a mortal lover, Semele. His followers included the Maenads (female) and Satyrs (male); both groups were given to wild celebration and emotional excess.

Dis. See **Hades**.

Eos (Aurora). Goddess of the dawn.

Eros (Cupid, Amor). God who personified the creative power of sexual love. He was present at the creation of the world and helped to bring it about, and he persisted into the age after the Titans to inspire desire in both gods and human beings.

Gaia. Original Mother Earth who emerged out of chaos when the world came into being. She was Uranus' mother and also his lover, and with him she produced Oceanus, first of the Titans. Among her other children was Cronus, who would eventually destroy his father Uranus.

Hades (Pluto, Dis). God of the underworld, keeper of dead souls, and the most relentless of the gods—the only one who would never give back what he had claimed for his own.

Hebe. Daughter of Zeus and Hera, goddess of youth and beauty and cupbearer to the gods on Mt. Olympus.

Hephaestus (Vulcan). Lame god of fire and the metal-working crafts, son of Hera, but fatherless (see **Hera**). Though physically unattractive, he had Aphrodite for a wife.

Hera (Juno). Sister and wife of Zeus. As a child she was swallowed by her father, the Titan Cronus, but was later regurgitated and raised to adulthood by the Titans Oceanus and Tethys. With Zeus she became mother of Hebe and Ares. She produced Hephaestus without a male partner in retaliation for Zeus's giving birth to Athene from his own brow. She and Zeus lived a stormy domestic life: their quarrels figure prominently in Greek myth and in Homer's *Iliad.*

Heracles (Hercules). Originally a mortal but admitted, upon his earthly death, to immortality and the pantheon on Mt. Olympus.

Hercules. See **Heracles**.

Hermes (Mercury). God of thieves and herdsmen and messenger of the Olympians. He alone among them was allowed to pass at will among the realms of Olympus, earth, and the underworld, to which it was his job to escort the souls of the dead. Hermes was the father of Pan, god of shepherds.

Hestia (Vesta). Virgin goddess, daughter of the Titans Cronus and Rhea. Hestia was a guardian deity of hearth, home, and family.

Juno. See **Hera**.

Jupiter. See **Zeus**.

Leto. A Titaness, mother of Artemis and Apollo by Zeus.

Maenads. See **Dionysos**.

Mars. See **Ares**.

Mercury. See **Hermes**.

Metis. A sea-nymph, first wife of Zeus, who tricked her into assuming miniature size so that he could swallow her to prevent her from having male children to threaten him in later life.

Minerva. See **Athene**.

Neptune. See **Poseidon**.

Oceanus. First of the Titans, son of Gaia and her own son Uranus.

Ops. See **Rhea**.

Pan. God of shepherds, usually depicted in satyr form, human from the waist up but with legs and feet of a goat.

Persephone. Daughter of Zeus and Demeter, doomed by Hades' abduction of her to spend a third part of each year in his abode in the underworld.

Pluto. See **Hades**.

Plutus. God of wealth.

Poseidon (Neptune). God of the sea, over which he gained control when he and his brothers Zeus and Hades drew lots for the three divisions of the universe. Poseidon was partial to horses and also to bulls, whose bellowing duplicated the sound of the raging sea.

Prometheus. Titan who fashioned humankind out of clay and later gave them the gift of fire against Zeus's proscription. As punishment, Zeus caused him to be chained to a rock and have his liver gnawed daily by an eagle. The first man he created was Phaemon, the first woman Pandora, who brought with her all the troubles of the world.

Rhea (Ops). A Titaness, wife of Cronus and mother of Hestia, Demeter, Hera, Hades, Poseidon, and Zeus—all Olympians.

Saturn. See **Cronus.**

Satyrs. See **Dionysos; Pan.**

Tethys. A Titaness, foster mother of Hera.

Thetis. A sea goddess who married a mortal, Peleus, and bore him Achilles, greatest of the heroes at Troy.

Triton. A sea god, son of Poseidon and Amphitrite.

Venus. See **Aphrodite.**

Vesta. See **Hestia.**

Vulcan. See **Hephaestus.**

Zeus (Jupiter). God of the sky, most powerful of the Olympians and ruler over the other gods, a position he won by distinguishing himself in the battle against the Titans. Zeus married Metis, a sea nymph, but swallowed her (see **Metis**). Later he married Hera, his sister; but the myths are filled with accounts of his seductions of both goddesses and mortal women and of the many offspring these unions produced.

NORSE GODS AND HEROES

The Norse myths come down to us through three sources, the most comprehensive of which is, interestingly enough, a writer's handbook from about the year 1220. This is the *Prose Edda* of Snorri Sturleson, an Icelandic farmer and poet who compiled his book as an aid to Christian poets seeking to flesh out their works with allusions and figures of speech out of their country's pagan past and its heroic traditions. Snorri's sources were chiefly poems, many now lost but some preserved in one form or another in the second major repository, the *Poetic Edda* from the second half of the thirteenth century in Iceland. A third source is a body of poetic texts known as skaldic verse (a skald was a bard or composer of heroic poems), by various poets both named and anonymous, written down in the early years of Christianization but extending back in oral tradition to a considerably earlier age. From this combined body of material come the following names, places, and events.

Gods

Aesir. Most populous of the two families or races of gods (the other is the Vanir), including the most powerful members of the pantheon, Odin and Thor. Some details in the various sources imply that the Aesir and Vanir were once hostile to each other; but on the whole they live together with no more difficulty than the Aesir among themselves.

All-father. Predecessor of Odin as chief deity in the age in which the world was created. References to the All-father in the sources are sparse and vague.

Asgard. Home of the gods and goddesses, located at the center of the created world hard by the giant ash tree Yggdrasil.

Balder. Son of Odin and Frigg and husband of Nanna. Through arrangements made by his mother, Balder was rendered immune in his youth to wounds by plants, metals, and woods that grow on the earth—*i.e.,* from poisons and weapons of violence. Because of this invulnerability he played games with the younger children of the gods in which he served as a willing target for their spears and arrows. But the evil Loki had an arrow crafted from the wood of mistletoe, which grows not on earth but in the tops of trees. He then persuaded Balder's blind brother Hoder to shoot the arrow and unintentionally slay his sibling.

Berserks. Warriors in Valhalla who fight in a wild, frenzied trance, wearing animal skins and howling in the fray like wolves, or, since *serkr* means "bear hide," like bears.

Bragi. Husband of Idun and a patron of poets and eloquent people.

Fenrir. A huge wolf, offspring of one of Loki's unnatural unions, brought to Asgard as a cub and fated to participate in the final destruction of the world by attacking the gods and by joining with other wolves to eat up the moon. During his stay in Asgard Fenrir bit off the hand of Tyr, who attempted to tether him with a leash.

Freyja. A Vanir, daughter of Niord and sister of Freyr, associated, like the Greek Aphrodite, with beauty and sexuality.

Freyr. Member of the Vanir, second family of the gods, son of Niord and brother of Freyja. Freyr once experienced a great passion for Gerd, a daughter of the odious race of Frost Giants.

Frigg. Wife of Odin and mother of Balder and Hoder.

Frost Giants. A race of creatures, bitter enemies of both gods and human beings, who live near the ocean at the edge of the world.

Garm. A great hound prophesied to slay the god Tyr at Ragnarok, the cataclysmic end of the world.

Gerd. A daughter of the Frost Giants, sometimes involved sexually with Freyr. She seems to have been associated with the principle of fertility, since the root word of her name is the same as "garden."

Gungnir. Odin's great spear, which he uses to influence the outcome of battles by casting it in the direction of the side he decrees will lose.

Heimdall. Watchman or sentry for Asgard. His trumpet, like Gabriel's horn in the Christian Last Judgment, will signal the beginning of the end at the time of Ragnarok. Heimdall will be killed even as he slays his mortal enemy, Loki, on that day.

Hel. Goddess and keeper of the bleak underworld (also called Hel), which lies to the north of Midgard.

Hoder. Blind son of Odin and Frigg who was tricked into slaying his brother Balder.

Hymir. A sea giant with whom Thor was fishing when he narrowly missed catching and destroying the World Serpent, thus losing an opportunity to avert the fated downfall of Asgard while at the same time establishing a precedent for the One That Got Away, which fishermen have followed religiously ever since.

Idun. Wife of Bragi and keeper of the all-important apples of youthfulness, which the gods eat to remain impervious to the ravages of time.

Loki. Strangest of the gods to the modern mind, more demonic than divine. He is the master trickster, endlessly resourceful and without principles. At times he allies himself—usually through necessity—with the other gods, but more often he opposes them vindictively. With a giantess as his mistress he fathered the wolf Fenrir, the World Serpent, and the goddess of Hel—abundant proof of his ability to visit trouble upon the world. Norse mythology is filled with tales of his malice and coersion. Wagner makes him the God of Fire in the Ring operas.

Midgard. An enclosed terrain that constitutes the created world, inhabited by gods and human beings alike. At its center is Asgard, home of the gods; to its north lies Hel; and its outer boundary is an encircling ocean stream.

Mjollnir. Thor's mighty hammer, a short-handled throwing weapon rather than a work tool such as a modern hammer.

Nanna. Wife of Balder.

Niord. Patriarch of the Vanir, father of Freyr and Freyja, and god of fisheries.

Norns. The three goddesses who live by the Well of Fate and determine the destinies of gods and human beings.

Odin. Chief deity of the Norse pantheon, one-eyed god of warriors who keeps a hall within Asgard called Valhalla, to which the bravest of the men who die in battle are transported by fierce demigoddesses known as valkyries. Odin is not to be trusted, for he allows his favorites as well as others to go down in defeat when he desires their company in Valhalla, where he knows he will need them for impending wars with giants and monsters. His most devoted followers are the Berserks. Odin rides an eight-legged flying horse named Sleipnir, carries a huge spear named Gungnir, and keeps about him wolves, eagles, and ravens—creatures that feed on battlefield corpses. Despite his fondness for war and carnage, he also patronizes poets and musicians. With his wife Frigg he begat Balder, Hoder, Vidar, and other gods.

Ragnarok. The period of destruction at the end of the world when, after three years of uninterrupted winter and social turmoil, wolves will eat the sun and moon and the order of the stars and planets will fall apart. A ship of giants commanded by Loki will invade Asgard as the World Serpent emerges from the sea and the great wolf Fenrir begins to attack and mangle Odin. The world will go up in flames, leaving only two human beings to survive in Midgard—possibly to begin a new cycle when Balder returns from the dead to set it in motion.

Sif. Yellow-haired wife of Thor.

Sleipner. Odin's airborne, eight-legged horse, descended from the cart-horse of the giants who built Asgard's wall, through a union with Loki in the shape of a mare.

Thor. God of the sky, red-haired and physically the strongest of the gods though second to Odin in authority and overall power. Thor is responsible for thunder, lightning, and storm. With his great hammer Mjollnir he defends the gods against their principal enemies, the Frost Giants, and against the World Serpent, one of the destined agents of the end of the world. Thor drives a chariot drawn by goats which he can slaughter, eat, and then resurrect from their bones and hides. He is married to Sif of the yellow hair. His name is preserved in *Thur*sday, fifth day of the week.

Tyr. A war god nonetheless known as a giver of civil order and the rule of law. He does not appear extensively in the Norse myths except in the story of how the wolf Fenrir once bit off his hand. The weekday *Tues*day reflects his name.

Valhalla. Odin's hall, located within Asgard, where fallen warriors of exceptional courage go in the afterlife. At Valhalla they spend each day in combat and each evening in revelry with flagons of ale and platters of pork.

Valkyries. Demigoddesses who retrieve the fallen heroes chosen by Odin from the battlefield and carry them to Valhalla.

Vanir. The second and by far the least numerous family or race of gods (the other is the Aesir), consisting only of Niord, his son Freyr, and his daughter Freyja. The son and daughter enjoy an incestuous relationship that is accepted, though not practiced, by the other gods.

Vidar. Odin's son who is to kill the wolf Fenrir after Fenrir slays Odin at the time of Ragnarok.

Well of Fate. A spring in Asgard where the Norns, or fates, dwell.

World Serpent. An immense reptile who threatens Asgard and is destined to be one of the destroyers of the world at Ragnarok.

Yggdrasil. A great ash tree at the center of Asgard, whose limbs, trunk, and roots connect earth and sky and hold the cosmos together. A well or spring between its roots contains an elixir of wisdom and insight, for a single drink of which Odin once traded one of his eyes.

Heroes

In the thirteenth century Norse myth combined with central European tales of kings and heroes in the long prose Volsunga saga, which charts the dynastic line of King Volsung of Hunland, his son Sigmund, and his daughter Signy, a story adapted in part in the operas of Richard Wagner (1813–83). The Volsung family history links back to an episode in Snorri and other eddic sources, the story of the otter's blood ransom. According to this tale, Loki, traveling one day with Odin and another god, killed an otter who turned out to be Otr, the shape-shifting son of a human farmer, Hreidmar. Hreidmar and his surviving sons Fafnir and Regin held the three gods captive, demanding a huge ransom in gold. Loki, released to raise the funds, tricked a dwarf, Andvari, out of his hoard of gold, including a gold ring with magical properties; but not before the dwarf placed a curse on the treasure. This curse operates throughout the span of time covered by the cycle of events.

Andvari. The dwarf who, being cheated out of a hoard of gold by the god Loki, laid a curse upon the treasure affecting anyone who possessed it.

Atli. Brother of Brynhild who gains the widowed Gudrun against her will in the story that ends the cycle.

Borghild. Wife of Sigmund after Sigmund's return to Hunland.

Brynhild. Wise valkyrie who loves Sigurd but loses him to Gudrun, after which she concocts a complex and successful plot to murder Sigurd and immolate herself on his funeral pyre.

Fafnir. Son of the farmer Hreidmar and brother of the slain Otr. Fafnir kills his father in order to obtain the dwarf's hoard of gold and changes himself into a dragon in order to guard it. He is eventually slain by Sigurd.

Grani. Sigurd's horse, sired by Odin's great steed Sleipnir.

Gudrun. Wife of Sigurd whose marriage to him triggers the fatal machinations of Brynhild.

Helgi. Son of Sigmund and Borghild, husband of the valkyrie Sigrun. Helgi is eventually killed by partisans of King Hoddbrodd, Sigrun's first husband, whom he had slain.

Hiordis. Wife of Sigmund after the death in exile of Borghild, mother of Sigurd, who dominates the last long section of the Volsunga saga.

Hoddbrodd. An ineffectual king, first husband of Sigrun.

Hreidmar. Farmer, father of Otr, whose fate begins the cycle of stories in the Volsunga saga.

Hunding, King. Monarch slain by Sigmund and his father Helgi.

Otr. Son of Hreidmar, brother of Fafnir and Regin.

Regin. Fafnir's brother. Regin becomes the tutor of Sigurd and contrives to use Sigurd as an instrument of his revenge against Fafnir. Regin is killed by Sigurd after his intentions become evident but not before his scheme has met with success.

Siggeir. Swedish warrior who becomes engaged to Volsung's daughter Signy. At the wedding, the god Odin, in disguise, thrusts his sword deep into a great tree's trunk and invites any guest who wishes to try to extract the blade and keep it as a prize. In this parallel to the sword-in-the-stone motif of the Arthurian stories, many try but only Sigmund proves strong enough to succeed. His refusal to sell the sword to Siggeir begins a period of enmity and finally a war between the two families after Siggeir carries Signy away, against her wishes, to Sweden.

Sigmund. Brother of Signy and enemy of Siggeir after the episode described above (see **Siggeir**). With his sister, who has decided that only he is capable of begetting a son strong enough to accomplish her revenge on Siggeir, he fathers a child named Sinfiotli, with whom he eventually destroys Siggeir in a fire.

Signy. Daughter of King Volsung, sister of Sigmund, wife of Siggeir, and mother (through incest with Sigmund) of Sinfiotli.

Sigrun. A valkyrie, wife first of Hoddbrodd and then of Helgi.

Sigurd. Posthumous son of Sigmund by his second wife Hiordis. Sigurd (this is the hero who appears as Siegfried in Wagner's operas) slays the dragon Fafnir, falls in love with the valkyrie Brynhild, marries Gudrun, and dies through the jilted valkyrie's machinations.

Sinfiotli. Son of an incestuous union between Sigmund and Signy.

Volsung, King. Father of Sigmund and Signy, whose family history provides the essential matter of the Norse heroic cycles.

OTHER TRADITIONS

It would be impossible to track down all the gods, demigods, spirits, sprites, demons, specters, and supernatural beings of primitive peoples. The following is a compilation of six of the major pantheons.

Aztec (Nahuatlan)

The religion of the Aztec, Mexica, or Nahuatlan people of pre-Spanish Mexico incorporated various gods of their predecessors, including the Maya, adding an especially bloodthirsty god of war named Huitzilopochtli. Almost all their deities were believed to delight in human sacrifice, a practice which had grown in magnitude to the mass spectacles witnessed by the troops of Cortes when they invaded the region in 1519. These were the principal members of the Aztec pantheon:

Chalchihuitlicue. Goddess of water whose jeweled robe bespoke her importance in Aztec life.

Chantico. Goddess of the hearth.

Chicomecoatl. Goddess of maize and grain.

Cihuacoatl. Serpentine goddess of childbirth and of women who died in labor.

Cinteotl. Maize god, husband of Xochiquetzal.

Huehuecoyotl. The old coyote god, patron of mischief and discord.

Huitzilopochtli. Chief deity of the capital city, Tenochtitlan. He was god of the sun and of war, envisioned as a young warrior whose death at the end of each day was balanced by his morning rebirth after fighting all night with his siblings, the moon and stars. His rise to the high point of noon each day had to be fueled by the blood of sacrificial victims or of warriors who died in battle.

Itzli. God of the obsidian-bladed sacrificial knife.

Ixcuina. See **Tlazolteotl**.

Mayauel. Goddess of the maguey plant and of fertility.

Mictlantecuhtli. A god of death, overseer of the region of the dead.

Mixcoatl. The "cloud serpent," god of stars and numerology, sometimes of war.

Patecatl. God of medicine.

Paynal. Huitzilopochtli's messenger.

Quetzalcoatl. The feathered serpent, the fair god, main god of learning, life, the priesthood, morning, and wind. Unfortunately the Aztecs briefly but fatally mistook Hernando Cortes' advent for the fair god's return.

Teteoinnan. See **Tlazolteotl**.

Tezcatlipoca. The "smoking mirror," god of death and evil, the moon and the nighttime sky. He was Quetzalcoatl's main enemy and the patron of nocturnal criminals.

Tlaloc. God of rains and storms, a variation of the Mayan Chac. His children made up a group known as the Tlaloques, embodying various aspects of himself.

Tlazolteotl. Fertility goddess and Earth Mother, patroness of the soil known also as Teteoinnan and Ixcuina.

Tloque Nahuaque. God of creativity and abstract thinking.

Tonacatecuhtli. Chief of the gods, the creator.

Xipe Totec. God of spring, of planting, and of jewelry making, envisioned as having been flayed or skinned, as were the victims sacrificed to him.

Xiuhtecuhtli. God of fire and of the progression of the year.

Xochipilli. God of pleasure, feasting, and merriment.

Xochiquetzal. Goddess of flowers and patroness of craftsmen, wife of Cinteotl.

Celtic

The religion of the ancient Celts of western Europe and the British Isles had distinctly local orientations; objects of veneration were more often than not regional and tribal gods thought to inhabit certain physical features of the landscape, especially springs and wells. Others were ancestral kings of godlike status. The names of nearly four hundred such deities survive, but only about a fourth of them are mentioned more than once in surviving materials. Therefore there is no "standard" pantheon. The following are some of the gods who enjoyed wider recognition than the great majority.

Annis. See **Dana**.

Boann. A river goddess associated with fertility.

Cailleach. See **Dana**.

Cu Chulainn. A prominent figure of Irish myth, which is generally ambiguous as to whether he was human or divine. There are numerous tales of his exploits.

Dagda. Father-protector of the Irish Celts, god of abundance and fertility and husband of Dana.

Dana (Danu). Earth Mother, embodiment of the female principles of fruitfulness and abundance but also goddess of death and slaughter in battle. She is the wife of Dagda and also known, in various regions, as Annis, Cailleach, and Magog.

Epona. The horse goddess, object of a European cult, especially in Gaul. She was one of several goddesses—Medb and Rhiannon are others—who were envisioned as divine consorts of human kings.

Fintan. Patron deity of tale telling and narrative poetry.

Lug(h). Irish correspondent to the Greek Hermes, associated with poetry and medicine.

Mabon. Main godly figure in the Welsh collection of myth and legend known as the *Mabinogion*.

Magog. See **Dana**.

Medb. Goddess of sovereignty and ruling lineages.

Morrigan. Irish demigoddess, a slayer of men.

Rhiannon. Welsh goddess prominent in the *Mabinogion*.

Sequanna. A river goddess.

Tuatha. A group of demigods, patrons of music and fine arts, analogous to the Greek muses.

Egyptian

The pantheon of ancient Egyptian deities is complicated by variations that occurred in names and other details from region to region, especially the three areas surrounding the great cities of Heliopolis, Hermopolis, and Memphis, each of which developed versions specific to its culture. The following list of the principal gods and goddesses reflects the most common accounts.

Amaunet. See **Amun**.

Amun. God who, paired with Amaunet, personified the latent power in the world.

Anat. Daughter of Re and sister of Astarte, given with Astarte as brides to Seth as consolation when he lost sovereignty over Egypt.

Anhur. A god of warriors in the region of Abydos.

Anubis. Jackal god, guardian of Isis after Osiris' death, son of Osiris and his sister Nephthys.

Apophis. Serpent god, representative of the potential return of chaos, chief enemy of the sun god Re, whom he recurrently tried to swallow.

Astarte. See **Anat**.

Atum. Creator of the universe who rose up out of nonbeing and generated the world. From the beginning he contained within himself the potentials of all the subsequent gods and goddesses, who began to appear when he produced, through solitary ejaculation, the twin deities Shu (male) and Tefnut (female). From a union between these two came Geb and Nut, who begat Osiris, Isis, Seth, and Nephthys. Atum was the original sun god, the monad or single element from which all elements derive.

Djeheuty. See **Thoth**.

Geb. The earth god, personification of the land of Egypt, brother and husband of Nut.

Hapy. God of caverns and floods in the region of Thebes.

Hathor. Goddess of love and pleasure, guardian of royal persons.

Hauhet. See **Heh**.

Heh. God who, paired with Hauhet, personified the power of floods.

Horus. The hawk god, son of Isis and Osiris and unseater of his uncle Seth as god of the land of Egypt. In one account he beheaded his mother for sparing Seth's life, was blinded by Re in retaliation but had his sight restored by Hathor, who administered gazelle milk to his eyes.

Isis. Daughter of Geb and Nut, sister and wife of Osiris, attributed with great cleverness and manipulative ability and with skill in medicine, especially the treatment of worms and gastrointestinal ailments. See **Osiris**; **Horus**.

Kauket. See **Kek**.

Kek. God who, paired with Kauket, personified darkness.

Khepri. A form of the son god Re, envisaged as a scarab beetle as he emerged from the underworld each morning.

Khnum. Ram-headed god attributed, in the Theban region, with creating mankind by making the human form out of clay on a potter's wheel.

Meretseger. Serpent goddess who protected and tended the tombs in the Valley of the Kings on the west bank of Thebes.

Meskhenet. Goddess of childbirth.

Min. One of the fertility gods in the Theban area.

Naunet. Goddess who, paired with Nu, personified the original waters of nonbeing.

Neith. Goddess associated in some areas with the power of creation of the world.

Nephthys. Sister of Osiris and the mother of his son, the jackal god Anubis.

Nu (Nun). The original being or substance before the creation of the world, personifying nonbeing as an ocean of dark, lifeless water. Nu's consort was Naunet.

Nut. Sky goddess, keeper of the barrier between the world and Nu, or nonbeing, sister and wife of Geb.

Osiris. Firstborn son of Geb and Nut, brother and husband of Isis. Osiris was originally god of the land of Egypt but became god of Duat, the underworld, after he was slain by his brother Seth, who wanted his realm. After his death Isis brought him back to life long enough to have him beget Horus, the son whose mission was eventually to gain revenge on Seth by dispossessing him.

Ptah. Principal god of the region of Memphis, where attributes elsewhere ascribed to Atum are given to him. In Memphis it was Ptah who rose from Nu and created the other gods, in his case by simply ordering them into existence. See **Ta-tenen**.

Re. Also Ra; the sun god who moved by boat on an elaborate journey, through the sky by day and the underworld by night. During his passage he took many forms, and his name sometimes appears as a prefix (*Re-*) with other words that denote his various powers and manifestations.

Sakhmet. Ferocious lion goddess employed by the sun god Re as an agent of punishment for humankind.

Serket. Scorpion goddess who helped control Apophis, or the threat of chaos.

Seth. Second son of Geb and Nut, brother and husband of Nephthys, ruler of Egypt after he murdered his brother Osiris. When Osiris' posthumous son Horus grew up to challenge his claim to Egypt, a lengthy trial or judgment occurred in which several deities offered opinions (most of them in favor of Horus), generating a large number of stories in Egyptian mythology about events that occurred during or as a result of the trial. After being unseated as god of the land, Seth was permitted to accompany the sun god Re in the sky. His voice caused the sound of thunder.

Shu. Lion-headed son of Atum, brother and husband of Tefnut, associated with the region and element of air.

Sokar. A manifestation of the sun god Re in the underworld.

Ta-tenen. Another name for Ptah.

Tefnut. Lioness-headed goddess, daughter of Atum, sister and wife of Shu, associated with the element and realm of moisture.

Thoth. God of wisdom, a name derived from Greek for the god known more commonly in Egypt as Djeheuty. It was he who gave to human beings the method of writing in hieroglyphs.

Inca

Ancient Peruvian religion was originally a combination of totemism and animism, wherein the spirits (called "mamas") of nature were worshiped through the places, plants, and animals they were thought to inhabit. With the political development of the Inca empire there grew up a more codified, state-directed religion in which the origins of the people were celebrated through veneration of ancestors and a handful of "official" gods considered instrumental in the founding of the race. The moon and planets were deified, and the ruling Inca or governor of the people was venerated as a representative of the sun on earth.

Acsumama. The "potato mother," spirit that made the potato grow.

Cocamama. Spirit of the coca shrub.

Coniraya Viracocha. A nature spirit, a trickster who claimed to have created the world and went about disguised in it as a ragged indigent deceiving human beings.

Copacahuana. Fish-shaped, human-headed goddess of the sacred lake now known as Titicaca (previously Mamacota), the spirit of the water in its function of providing fish. See **Copacati**.

Copacati. Serpent goddess of Lake Titicaca, representative of water as an element. See **Copacahuana**.

Cuycha. Spirit of the rainbow.

Huamantantac. An agricultural spirit who caused the cormorants and other sea birds to flock together each year and deposit the fertilizing guano.

Mamapacha. Spirit of the world of visible objects and of the soil itself.

Pachacamac. Supreme divinity of the Incas, great spirit of the earth that animates all things, flora and fauna, that emerge and occur there.

Pachamama. Spirit of mountains, plains, and geological phenomena.

Pachayachachic. Creator and ruler of the earth, a later god who emerged in the religion near the end of the Inca empire.

Quinuamama. Spirit of the quinua plant.

Saramama. Spirit of the corn or maize, most important of the "mamas" or animating powers of individual plants, worshiped as a doll made of corn husks.

Thonapa. A hero-god, civilizer of the people, with characteristics similar to those of Viracocha.

Viracocha. God who arose from Lake Titicaca to people the earth and give it the arts of civilization.

Mayan

The religion of the Central American Mayans was ultimately monotheistic, but the various powers and aspects of the Deity were represented and personified as individual god-figures. These are many and often confusing, since each god embodied qualities of its opposite and could be, for example, simultaneously good and evil, male and female, etc. Many of their names are now unknown because our information in many cases is limited to what can be interpreted from carvings and other visual representations. Here are the principal figures:

Acanum. God of hunters and the chase.

Ahau gods. Patrons of the final day (Ahau) in each twenty-day period.

Ah Chicum Ek. God of the North Star, guide to merchants and travelers.

Ah Kak Nexoy. God of fishing and fishermen.

Ah Kin. Apparently an aspect of Itzamna, he is a sun god associated with the jaguar.

Bolontiku. Collective term for nine gods (names unknown) of the lower world, actually nine aspects of a single force. See **Oxlahuntiku**.

Bolon Tzacab. A reptilian deity, patron and protector of ruling families.

Buluc Chabtan. God of war, violence, and human sacrifice.

Chac. The rain god, reptilian in appearance with long fangs, honored as a bringer of life and especially venerated by farmers. He was usually represented as a four-fold in nature, corresponding to the compass directions; those who held the victims during human sacrifices dressed as four Chacs.

Cit Chac Coh. A god of war.

Ek Chuah. Scorpion god, patron of merchants, especially dealers in cacao.

Hobnil. God of honey and beekeeping.

Hunab Ku. See **Itzamna**.

Itzamna. The chief deity of the Mayas, inhabiter of earth and sky, creator of the universe, source and patron of knowledge and medicine. He invented and gave to human kind the arts of writing and record keeping, and he laid out the boundaries of the various districts of Yucatan. Often represented as a double-headed snake, he may be the same god as Kukulcan, the plumed serpent known in Mexico as Quetzalcoatl. In his role as earth-creator he was known also by the name of Hunab Ku.

Ix Chebel Yax. A patron goddess of weaving.

Ix Chel. Moon goddess associated with cloth making, childbirth, prophecy, and the healing arts. She is the spouse or consort of Itzamna.

Ixtab. Goddess of suicide, represented as hanging from the sky in a decomposing state.

Katun gods. Thirteen gods (names unknown), each associated with one of the Katuns or twenty-year periods in the Mayan cycle.

Kinich Ahau. A sun god, probably the aspect of Itzamna that governed the passage of the sun through the heavens by day. He was patron of the number 4.

Kukulcan. See **Itzamna**.

Mam. A god of the underworld, also known as Pauahtun, whose functions cannot now be determined.

Month gods. Nineteen gods, names unknown, each associated with one of the nineteen months of the annual calendar.

Numeral gods. Patrons, names mostly unknown, of the fourteen main numerals.

Oxlahuntiku. Collective term for thirteen gods, names unknown, of the upper world, actually thirteen aspects of a single force. See **Bolontiku**.

Pauahtun. See **Mam**.

Yum Cimil. A death god represented as a skeletal person with shreds of rotten flesh. He may have been involved at ceremonies of human sacrifice.

Yum Kaax. God of agriculture, especially corn, represented with a head that resembles an ear of corn. He represents life and abundance but needs the protection and support of the rain god.

Mesopotamian

The Mesopotamian deities derive from the land between the Tigris and Euphrates rivers, extending from the mountains of eastern Asia Minor to the Persian Gulf, comprising the ancient lands of Assyria, Babylonia and Sumer and containing such fabled cities as Ashur, Babylon, Baghdad, Nineveh, and Ur.

Adad. God of precipitation, both benevolent (crop-stimulating rain) and destructive (violent storms).

Annukki. Sumerian gods of fertility, dwellers in the underworld.

Antum. Wife of Anu.

Anu. God of the sky, husband of Antum and father of Ishtar, chief god in the Sumerian pantheon until replaced by his son Ellil.

Aruru. Another name for Mammi.

Damkina. Wife of Ea.

Dumuzi. An earlier name for Tammuz.

Ea. Lord over the subterranean reservoirs of water, instructor of human beings in arts, sciences, and magical lore.

Ellil. Anu's son who succeeded him as chief deity, keeper of the tablets that record the destinies of gods and mortals alike, head of the Igigi, or sky gods.

Enki. Sumerian name for Ea.

Ereshkigal. Goddess of the underworld.

Erra. Another name for Nergal.

Igigi. See **Ellil**.

Inanna. Sumerian name for Ishtar.

Ishtar. Goddess of love and sex and sometimes war, attributed in the myths with prodigious sexual feats such as exhausting over one hundred consecutive lovers.

Mammi. Nurturing mother goddess, wife of Nergal.

Marduk. Son of Ea, chief god in the Babylonian regions.

Mulliltu. Wife of Ellil.

Mylitta. Another name for Mulliltu.

Nabu. Son of Marduk and god of scribes and wise men.

Namtar. Like Nergal, a god of plagues. Namtar served as administrative officer for Ereshkigal and controlled a large number of pandemic diseases, which he used as instruments of threat and discipline.

Nergal. A god of war and plagues.

Nin-hursag. Another name for Mammi.

Ninurta. A goddess of hunting and war.

Shamash. God of the sun, judge of gods and human beings.

Sin. God of the moon and the calendar of months.

Tammuz. God of fertility and lover of Ishtar.

Utu. Sumerian name for Shamash.

SOURCES

Greek and Roman Gods

Bellingham, David. *An Introduction to Greek Mythology.* Secaucus, N.J.: Chartwell Books, 1989.

Graves, Robert. *The Greek Myths.* 2 vols. Baltimore: Penguin Books, 1959.

Smith, Sir William. *Smaller Classical Dictionary.* New York: E. P. Dutton, 1958.

Norse Gods and Heroes

Branston, Brian. *Gods of the North.* London: Thames and Hudson, 1980.

Davidson, H. R. Ellis. *Scandinavian Mythology.* London: Paul Hamlyn, 1969.

Grimm, Jacob. *Teutonic Mythology.* 4th ed. Translated by James Steven Stallybrass. New York: Dover Publications, 1966.

Page, R. I. *Norse Myths.* Austin, Tex.: British Museum Publications, 1990.

Other Traditions

Duran, Fray Diego. *Book of the Gods and Rites and the Ancient Calendar.* Translated and edited by Fernando Horcasitas and Doris Heyden. Norman, Okla.: University of Oklahoma Press, 1971.

Hart, George. *Egyptian Myths.* Austin, Tex.: University of Texas Press, 1990.

Henderson, John S. *The World of the Ancient Maya.* Ithaca, N.Y.: Cornell University Press, 1981.

McCall, Henrietta. *Mesopotamian Myths.* Austin, Tex.: University of Texas Press, 1990.

MacCana, Proinsias. *Celtic Mythology.* Rev. ed. New York: P. Bedrick Books, 1985.

Morley, Sylvanus G., and George W. Brainerd. *The Ancient Maya.* 4th ed. Stanford, Calif.: Stanford University Press, 1983.

Oaks, Laura S. "The Goddess Epona: Concepts of Sovereignty in a Changing Landscape." In *Pagan Gods and Shrines of the Roman Empire,* edited by Martin Henig and Anthony King. Oxford: Oxford University Committee for Archaeology, 1986.

Shorter, Alan W. *The Egyptian Gods: A Handbook.* London: Kegan Paul, Trench, Turner and Co., 1937.

Spence, Lewis. *Myths and Legends: Mexico and Peru.* Boston: Nickerson and Co., 1909.

Squire, Charles. *Celtic Myth and Legend, Poetry and Romance.* New York: Bell Publ. Co., 1979.

Vaillant, George C. *Aztecs of Mexico: Origin, Rise and Fall of the Aztec Nation.* New York: Doubleday and Co., 1941.

Weaver, Muriel Porter. *The Aztecs, Maya, and Their Predecessors.* New York: Seminar Press, 1972.

—J.L.M.

50

FAMOUS FIGURES OF
LEGEND AND FOLKLORE

. . . . .

WAS KING ARTHUR A FIGURE OF HISTORY OR OF FOLKLORE AND LEGEND? Robin Hood? Blackbeard? Davy Crockett? Casey Jones?

Distinctions among historical, literary, and legendary figures are not always easy to make. Much of folklore is based ultimately on historical persons and events, and many of these, in turn, have found their ways into our written culture and literary heritage. The heroes of Homer's *Iliad* (*ca.* 725 B.C.E.) provide an excellent illustration. The soldiers at the siege of Troy, a historical event several hundred years before Homer's time, had long since become part of the traditional, communal lore of the ancient Greeks; but we know about them today because of the literary status conferred by Homer's great epic poem.

Is Achilles a historical, legendary, or literary character? The answer is, most likely, all three, yet the force and permanence of Homer's treatment has fixed his image indelibly, removing a great deal of that fluidity and capacity for variation we associate with folk tradition.

What follows is a listing of heroes and heroines that we know about primarily in terms of folklore and legend, not through literature or history. Those heroes we know primarily through the "high" literary accounts of Homer, the medieval Arthurian romances, the Norse Volsunga Saga, and other epics, appear elsewhere in this book. Even in the list below there is some overlapping; cross-references occur where appropriate.

Abominable Snowman, the (Tibetan). A large, apelike creature said by inhabitants of the high Himalayas to inhabit the hidden recesses of that area. Sightings are reported from time to time, but no authentication exists based on examination of a specimen dead or alive. Called *yeti* ("rock dweller") by the natives, the Abominable Snowman is alleged to be omnivorous, filthy, and shy of human contact. See also **Bigfoot.**

Aino. (Finnish). Beautiful Laplander who refused to marry Wainamoinen, the great bard, causing him to go to the northern region of Pohjola, where he met the Maid of the North and her mother, Louhi.

Appleseed, Johnny (American). Character based on John Chapman of Massachusetts (1774–1847), eccentric promoter of orchard culture who distributed seeds and scions to families migrating to Ohio Valley homesteads and whose extensive travels on foot, combined with his disheveled appearance and visionary religious propensities, earned him legendary status and the central role in a variety of tall tales.

Beaver, Tony (American). Lumberjack of West Virginia, like Paul Bunyan a giant of a man capable of fantastic feats of strength, skill, and ingenuity, such as inventing peanut brittle by stopping an icy flood with peanuts and molasses.

ben Dosa, Hanina (Hebrew). Rabbi celebrated for various miracles and supernatural cures, so potent in magical power that a scorpion that bit him fell dead.

Bigfoot (North American). Legendary creature very similar to the Himalayan Abominable Snowman, said to inhabit forested regions of the extreme northwestern United States and western Canada. Called Sasquatch by the Native Americans of those regions, it supposedly walks erect, stands over six feet tall, and emits a repulsive odor.

Blackbeard (American). Character developed from the historical Edward Teach, pirate of the southeastern coast, especially the North Carolina Outer Banks, who was beheaded in 1718, after which his headless body is said to have swum three laps around his executioner's ship. Various legends surround Blackbeard's swashbuckling and amatory adventures, his thirteen wives, and his hoards of buried treasure.

Bludso, Jim (American). Engineer of the steamboat *Prairie Belle* on the Mississippi River, who saved many lives at the expense of his own when his boat caught fire.

Boru, Brian (Irish). King of a region along the River Shannon, driver of the Norsemen out of his territories and thereafter ruler of all Ireland; killed after successfully opposing later Norse invaders under Sigurd.

Bran (Welsh and Irish). A great monarch at Harlech, brother of the beautiful Branwen and possessor of a magical life-restoring cauldron. After Bran was decapitated his head continued to talk for eighty-seven years.

Branwen (Welsh and Irish). Beautiful sister of Bran. Her marriage to King Mathol of Ireland made her queen of that country and united the two regions for a time but incurred the bitter enmity of her half-brother Evnissyen.

Brieriu (Irish). Boastful chieftain in Ulster, famed for building a fabulous guest house to promote his reputation, but infamous as an instigator of quarrels and contentions among his guests.

Bunyan, Paul (American). Hero of the logging industry from the upper Midwest to Washington and Oregon, celebrated for immense size, endurance, and logging ability. Accompanied by his blue ox, Babe, he performed many outlandish exploits, such as inventing a pancake griddle of such size that it had to be greased by men skating over it with bacon attached to their feet.

Christmas, Annie (American). Seven-foot, mustachioed lady of New Orleans in the early 1800s, mother of twelve, a woman of prodigious strength and defeater of all comers, including Mike Fink, in weight-lifting contests and brawls; said to have committed suicide after her lover's death at a roulette wheel.

Cid Campeador, or El Cid (Spanish). National hero of Spain, spectacular fighter in the Christian-Moorish wars and defeater of five Moorish kings to end the Arab domination of Spain. The real-life model was Rodrigo Diaz de Bivar (1040–99), a knight and soldier of fortune.

Conan Baldhead (Irish). Ugly, uncouth, and sharp-tongued member of the followers of Finn MacCoul; an Irish counterpart of Homer's character Thersites in the *Iliad.*

Concobar, King (Irish). Monarch of Ulster, sometime consort of Maeve, and major figure in numerous Irish comic and heroic tales; name sometimes given as "Conor."

Conor. See **Concobar, King**.

Cormac, King (Irish). Grandson of Conn of the Hundred Battles, raised by wolves and later elevated to king of Ireland, celebrated for strength and wisdom and for building the most magnificent structure at Tara, the legendary royal seat at Meath.

Crockett, Davy (American). Born in Tennessee in 1786, real-life hero elevated to legendary status as frontiersman, Indian fighter, U.S. congressman, and soldier through many tall tales, a panegyrical biography published in 1833, and his heroic death as a defender at the Alamo in 1837. Among his many fabled attributes was the ability to drive raccoons out of trees by grinning at them and to keep whole communities stocked with bear grease through his hunting prowess.

Cu Chulainn (Irish and Welsh). Major hero of Celtic legend both written and oral, sometimes accorded divine or semidivine status. See earlier essays in this book on epic heroes and heroines; ancient gods and goddesses.

Daddy Mention (American). Fabled African-American inmate of various Florida prisons, famous for escapes and triumphs of wit over guards and law officers.

David of Sassoun (Armenian). Benevolent and amatory hero of adventures during the Saracen occupation of Armenia in the Middle Ages, frequently at odds with his half-brother Misra Melik, whom he eventually slew.

Deirdre (Irish and Welsh). See earlier essay "Epic Heroes and Heroines." In Irish versions she was fostered up by King Concobar and raised to become his bride; often cited as Deirdre of the Sorrows.

Diarmaid. See **Grania**.

Don Juan (Spanish). Legendary lover, seducer of the daughter of the Commander of Seville. Don Juan slew the commander, but his memorial statue came to life and dragged Don Juan down to hell.

Duttabaung, King (Burmese). Legendary Buddhist hero and ruler, owner of over 30 million elephants and a huge bell and drum, at whose sounds lesser potentates would send tribute. The king was carried away by spirits at the age of 105.

El Cid. See **Cid Campeador**.

Evnissyen. See **Branwen**.

Faust (German). Magician and astrologer, whose legend is perhaps based on a historical person who died around 1540. Faust purportedly sold his soul to the devil in exchange for knowledge and power. His story has been the subject of many literary treatments, such as the plays of the English Marlowe (1564–93) and the German Goethe (1749–1832).

Fergus (Irish and Scots). Bard and ambassador to foreign powers, a son of Finn MacCoul distinguished for his chivalrous behavior.

Feridun (Persian). Slayer of the evil Zohak to avenge his father's death in a cycle of stories involving the royal Iranian family line in the Middle Ages.

Fink, Mike (American). Indian scout and riverboatman on the Mississippi and Ohio rivers in the early 1800s, famous for marksmanship, riotous behavior, and brawling; victim of a revenge murder in 1833 after he killed a friend while trying to shoot a cup of whiskey off his head. Many of the tales surrounding Fink are wildly humorous, while others suggest a dark, even sadistic side to his personality.

Gallans (French). Gallic name for the Anglo-Saxon Wayland.

Ganelon (French and Spanish). See earlier essay "Epic Heroes and Heroines."

Gilgamesh (Mesopotamian). See earlier essay "Epic Heroes and Heroines."

Girty, Jim (American). Flatboatman on the Tennessee River in the early 1800s, famous knife fighter whose ribs were said to have grown together into shields of bone that protected him from blade and bullet wounds.

Golem, the (Hebrew). Monster of medieval Jewish tradition, a mute and shapeless creature.

Gonzales, Speedy (Mexican). Elusive trickster in Mexican and Mexican-American tall tales, expert at outwitting the authorities for his own not-always-upright purposes.

Grainne. See **Grania**.

Grateful Dead, the (European). Term used by scholars for a motif, widespread in medieval folklore, in which a character makes some gesture of respect for a dead person and is later assisted in time of need by the grateful soul or spirit.

Grania (Irish). Daughter of King Cormac, sought for marriage by Finn MacCoul but won by Dermott (Diarmaid) O'Duivna instead, beginning a long feud. Dermott was eventually mangled by a wild boar and died after Finn refused to save him. Grania then became Finn's consort. "Grainne" is another spelling of her name.

Grettir the Strong (Icelandic). Powerful hero of both folk and literary tradition in Scandinavia. So strong was he that in one tale he defeated Odin's own special forces, the Berserks.

Hanina. See **ben Dosa, Hanina**.

Harun al-Rashid (Persian). Historical Caliph of Baghdad about whom legends developed in the Middle Ages. He was said to patrol his city in disguise to protect the citizens at night.

Hatim the Generous (Arabian). Hero of a series of legends that illustrate his generosity in the course of several quests and adventures.

Henry, John (American). African-American hero of numerous tales and ballads, a steel-driver for the railroad who, with his forty-pound hammer (nine pounds in some versions) bested a steam drill in a steel-driving contest in West Virginia around 1870 but lost his life through the effort.

Honi (Hebrew). Rabbi whose prayers could not only bring rain but also adjust the rate and volume of it.

Hot Biscuit Slim (American). Paul Bunyan's cook, renowned for the fabulous amounts of food he prepared for the giant logger.

Hushing (Persian). Leader of both men and animals into battle, the first human being to generate fire from flint.

Igor (Russian). Grandson of Oleg, hero in wars against pagans.

Ilmarin (Finnish). Fabulous smith and metalworker, brother of Wainamoinen and creator of Sampo, a magic mill that ground out endless resources of food and other goods. Like his brother, he was refused by the Maid of the North, but, unlike him, he eventually won her hand.

Jemshid (Persian). Civilizing monarch of Iranian legend, a great builder and inventor who ruled for seven hundred years but became guilty of pride and was killed by his enemy, Zohak.

John the Bear (European). Human son of a bear who figures in a widely dispersed cycle of legends.

Jones, Casey (American). Historically, John Luther Jones, engineer on the Illinois Central Line who died with his hand on the brake lever in a train wreck in 1900; famed for his size, strength, affability, and concern for others.

Kresnik (Eastern Europe). Slovenian national hero, slayer of monsters and practitioner of magic who eventually met his death at the hands of a jealous woman.

Krishna (Hindu). Chief hero of Hindu mythology, performer of numerous exploits displaying his ingenuity and propensity for tricks, deceits, and subterfuges.

Krpàn, Martin (Eastern European). Peasant, salt smuggler, and hero of Slovene folklore.

Laveau, Marie (American). Voodoo queen of old New Orleans, famed for powers of conjuration, prophecy, and supernatural cure.

Lemminkainen (Finnish). Like Wainamoinen and Ilmarin, a seeker of the hand of the Maid of the North. He was dismembered and thrown into a river, but restored to life by his mother's magic songs.

Lilith (Hebrew). Adam's first wife, who rejected submission to her husband and left him to roam through history as a seductress and misleader of men.

Lohengrin (German). Son of Parsifal, champion of Elsa, Duchess of Brabant, whom he married but abandoned when she asked his name after being told never to do so.

Louhi (Finnish). Hag of the North, mother of a beautiful maid sought by the brothers Wainamoinen and Ilmarin and by another hero, Lemminkainen.

MacCoul, Finn (Irish and Scots). Also known as Fingal, leader of the Fenians, a warrior band dedicated to the defense of Ireland; father of Fergus and Oisin and possessor of prophetic insight from having eaten a magical salmon. There are many stories of his exploits. Finn was eventually killed by his own rebellious followers. "McCohal" and "McCool" are common variants of the name.

Maeve (Irish and Welsh). Queen of the west, wife of Ailill and sometime consort of King Concobar or Conor; major figure in the long and complicated Cattle Raid of Cooley story; sometimes regarded as divine or semidivine. Her name occurs also as "Medb" and is so cited in the earlier essay "Ancient Gods, Goddesses, Demigods. . . ."

Magarac, Joe (American). Giant steelworker from Pittsburgh famous for shaping ingots of molten steel with his bare hands.

Maid of the North, the. See **Wainamoinen**.

Mathol, King. See **Branwen**.

Maui (Polynesian). Trickster figure and culture-giver whose feats included raising the South Pacific Islands from the sea and forcing the sun to move at a slower pace through the sky.

Mose the Bowery B'hoy (American). East Side fireman and gutter tough of mid-nineteenth-century New York City, one of the first urban folk heroes of America, celebrated in a series of stage plays featuring the colorful slang and cocky manner that concealed a heart of gold and a willingness to champion the oppressed. Mose's real-life counterpart was probably Moses Humphreys, a famous brawler, like most of the New York volunteer firemen of that era (*b'hoy* was a slang term for such a character).

Mpu Barada (Malaysian). A magician capable of raising the dead.

Murometz, Ilya (Russian). Defender of the Christian faith after Jesus restored his paralyzed limbs; with his horse Cloudfall, a figure in numerous heroic tales.

O'Duivna, Dermott. See **Grania**.

Oisin (Irish). One of the sons of Finn MacCoul. In one of the many tales about him, Oisin met Saint Patrick.

Oleg (Russian). A prince of Kiev granted immunity to most wounds by a sorcerer, but killed by a snake after conquering Constantinople.

Oliver (French and Spanish). See earlier essay "Epic Heroes and Heroines."

Ossian. Scots variant of "Oisin."

Patch, Sam (American). Cotton-mill worker from Rhode Island who performed a number of spectacular jumps from rooftops, cliffs, and, in 1829, from Niagara Falls. In his attempt to duplicate his feat at Genessee Falls he was killed, but stories consistently reported sightings and more exploits around the country as his name became associated with both fearlessness and foolish presumption.

Pecos Bill (American). Fabled teacher of cowboy skills and culture to the wranglers of the Old West. Among his feats were the digging of the Rio Grande, the invention of the revolver, the taming of a mountain lion to saddle and bridle, and the use of rattlesnakes for lariats.

Prester John (British and Western European). Supposed descendant of one of the Three Magi, a medieval Christian ruler somewhere in the Far East, owner of a magical mirror and other wonders in his realm of Edenic peace and splendor.

Qat (Melanesian). Main hero in a cycle of legends of New Guinea and neighboring islands, a magician and trickster like the Polynesian Maui.

Railroad Bill (American). African-American Robin Hood figure of Alabama legend, whose ghost, it is said, continues to steal goods from freight cars and leave them on the doorsteps of poor people's shacks. A number of legends concern Bill's ability to outwit the sheriff, in one instance by turning himself into a black bloodhound and trailing himself to his girlfriend's cabin.

Rama (Hindu). See earlier essay "Epic Heroes and Heroines."

Robin Hood (English). Leader of the medieval band of Merry Men in Sherwood Forest who lived outside the law, constantly opposed the oppressive Sheriff of Nottingham, stole from the rich, and gave generously to the poor.

Roland (French and Spanish). See earlier essay "Epic Heroes and Heroines."

Rustum or Rustam (Persian). Main legendary hero of ancient Iran, warrior and performer of heroic labors on the order of those of the Greek Herakles; husband of the beautiful Tahmineh and father of Sohrab, whom he tragically slew in heroic combat, unaware of his identity.

Sadko (Russian). Great harpist whose music the Lake King rewarded with great riches and whom the Ocean King allowed to return to earth after drowning.

Sasquatch. See **Bigfoot**.

Sohrab (Persian). Son of Rustum and Tahmineh, a mighty warrior slain tragically by his father, not knowing his identity, in heroic combat.

Stackolee (American). Also known as Stagger Lee, a notoriously belligerent African American of twentieth-century urban legend, who, in several versions of a song or oral poem, heartlessly shot a character named Billy Long or Lyons or Billy the Lion.

Stagger Lee. See **Stackolee.**

Stig, Marsk (Danish). Champion of the common people against an oppressive monarchy, hero of several ballads.

Tannhäuser (German). Knight and bard granted the privilege of having sex with the goddess Venus. He returned to find that his human love, Lisaura, had committed suicide after he left her.

Teach, Edward. See **Blackbeard.**

Wainamoinen (Finnish). National folk hero of Finland, a great bard or singer of tales who won the beautiful Aino in a poetry contest with her brother. Aino, however, refused to marry him, causing him to retreat to the northern regions, where he was also rejected by the Maid of the North. See also **Ilmarin; Lemminkainen.**

Waldemar (Danish). Hero-king of a group of medieval ballads involving him, his wife Sophie, and his mistress Tove.

Wayland (Anglo-Saxon). An accomplished smith who created such fabulous artifacts as a magical boat and a winged garment. He was crippled and imprisoned by a wicked king but avenged his wrongs by killing the king's sons, raping his daughter, and sending objects beautifully wrought from the sons' skulls, teeth, and eyes to members of the royal family.

Wieland (German). Teutonic version of the Anglo-Saxon Wayland.

Yamato Date (Japanese). Wandering hero-prince of early medieval Japan and model for the later Samurai ethic; a slayer of monsters and men, a relentless and disciplined warrior who was turned into a white bird after his death.

Yankee Jonathan (American). Unlettered but crafty New Englander whose fame arose in the 1830s and 1840s as a naïve and rustic but proud and patriotic supporter of the new republic.

Yeti. See **Abominable Snowman.**

Zal (Persian). Hero whose hair was white even in youth. Abandoned on a rocky mountain as a child, he managed to return to court and eventually became a wise and effective ruler.

SOURCES

Abrahams, Roger D. *Deep Down in the Jungle.* New York: Aldine, 1970.

Botkin, B. A. *A Treasury of Southern Folklore.* New York: Crown Publishers, 1949.

Cavendish, Richard, ed. *Legends of the World.* New York: Schocken Books, 1982.

Colum, Padraic. *A Treasury of Irish Folklore.* New York: Crown Publishers, 1954.

Delany, Frank. *Legends of the Celts.* London: Hodder and Stoughton, 1989.

Dorson, Richard M. *America in Legend.* New York: Pantheon Books, 1973.

Leach, Maria, and Jerome Fried, eds. *Funk and Wagnalls' Standard Dictionary of Folklore, Mythology, and Legend.* 2 vols. New York: Funk and Wagnalls, 1950.

Robinson, Herbert Spencer, and Knox Wilson. *Myths and Legends of All Nations.* New York: Garden City Publ. Co., 1950.

—J.L.M.

X

NATIVE AMERICANS

51

NATIVE AMERICAN TRIBES

. . . . .

THE FIRST ENGLISH-LANGUAGE WRITER TO HOLD FORTH AT LENGTH ON THE ways of Native Americans was Captain John Smith (1608). The story of how Pocahontas saved his life by interceding just as Powhatan's executioners were about to dispatch him became part of our national mythology. Whether it ever actually happened has been questioned; scholars now think that it probably did, but that the incident may have been part of an initiation ritual that the doughty captain mistook for the real thing.

If so, the precedent was significant, because in the years since then, Native Americans—mistakenly dubbed Indians by Columbus, who thought he had reached India, and thereafter called that for 450 years or so—have been the subject of a vast body of writing, a great deal of which has involved misinterpretation and misunderstanding.

In popular culture, as developed in James Fenimore Cooper's enormously popular Leatherstocking Tales, there were two kinds of Native Americans: Good Indians, who helped the white man take over the North American continent, and Bad Indians, who resisted the takeover. Cooper's Good Indian (named Chingachgook, which Mark Twain suggested should be pronounced "Chicago") still flourishes in the person of the Lone Ranger's sidekick, Tonto.

This is not the place to recite the long history of the Native Americans in North America, and the largely shameful way in which they were victimized by whites. In recent years Native American authors such as Scott Momaday and William Least-Heat Moon have arisen to tell the story of what happened from the viewpoint of the encroached upon rather than the encroachers.

Anthropologists and paleontologists still dispute the question of how long ago Native Americans first arrived on the American continent from Asia. It was long believed to have happened fairly recently, within 9,000 years or so, but the possible date has now been pushed back to as many as 25,000 years ago. Indeed, one school of thought has it that they have been here for as long as 100,000 years. By the time of Columbus' arrival they were in place from the Arctic region of North America to Tierra del Fuego at the southern tip of South America.

Nobody knows, of course, just how many Native Americans were living in North America when the Europeans arrived; there were no written records by the Native Americans themselves, and they were encountered in stages, over the course of several hundred years, as the westward movement of European civilization progressed. They spoke numerous languages; in 1891 the ethnologist John Wesley Powell estimated that there were 58 language families spoken in the United States and Canada, of which five were by then extinct. In 1929 Edward Sapir suggested a regrouping into six major linguistic divisions.

The compilation below lists the Indian tribes for the United States and Canada, their locations, the linguistic phylum for each, and the particular language family if known. In addition, individual tribes spoke their own dialects, with the same names as the tribes themselves. What are thought to be among the more important tribes and confederations within their geographical areas at the time of Columbus' arrival are given in capital letters: *i.e.*, ALEUT, ASSINIBOIN, etc. Needless to say, by no means are all anthropologists or linguistic scholars in agreement over such matters; there is room for a great deal of dispute on all counts.

ABNAKI (also called *Abenaki* or *Wabanaki*). The Eastern tribes, including the Abenaki proper, the Kennebec, and the Penobscot, were located along the major rivers of central Maine; the Western tribes, including the Winnipesaukee and Pennacook, along the major rivers of New Hampshire and Vermont as well as on the borders of Massachusetts and Quebec. (Macro-Algonquian phylum—Algonquian family)

Achomawi. Northeastern California. (Hokan phylum—Palaihnihan family)

Acoma. A pueblo and branch of the Keres, located in west-central New Mexico. (Undetermined phylum—Keres Language Isolate)

Adai. See Caddo.

Ahtena (also known as the *Copper River Indians*). South-central Alaska, concentrated in the Copper River area, and along Yukon Territory border. (Na-Dene phylum—Athapascan family)

Akwa'ala. Northern Baja peninsula, a branch of the Tipai-Ipai. (Hokan phylum—Yuman family—Southern and Baja California Yuman group)

Alabama (also called *Alibamu*). Southern Alabama. (Macro-Algonquian phylum—Muskogean family)

ALEUT. Southwestern mainland Alaska and Aleutian Islands. (American Arctic-Paleo-Siberian phylum—Eskimo-Aleut family)

ALGONQUIN (also *Algonkin, Algonquian*). Ontario and Quebec, concentrated in the Ottawa Valley. Other Algonquin tribes were located as far south as coastal North and South Carolina and as far west as Colorado. "Algonquian" is more properly the name of a language phylum and one of its families: any of the numerous tribes speaking such a language can be called "Algonquin," which can be extremely confusing. "Algonquin" as a tribal name most frequently refers to the Canadian Algonquins and to the Algonquin tribes of coastal North Carolina, the Pamlico and the Secotan (both of which are also called the *Carolina Algonquin*). (Macro-Algonquian phylum—Algonquian family)

Alsea (also *Alsi*). Central coastal Oregon, concentrated around Alsea Bay and the Yaquina River. Includes Yaquina. (Penutian phylum—Yakonan family)

Angmagssalik Inuit. See **East Greenland Inuit**.

APACHE, EASTERN. See **Chiricahua**; **Jicarilla**; **Kiowa Apache**; **Lipan**; **Mescalero**.

APACHE, WESTERN. See **Coyotero**; **Northern Tonto**; **San Carlos**; **Southern Tonto**.

Apalachee. Northwestern Florida panhandle. (Macro-Algonquian phylum—Muskogean family)

ARAPAHO. Between the Platte and Arkansas rivers in eastern Colorado and southeastern Wyoming. (Macro-Algonquian phylum—Algonquian family)

Arikara. Northern South Dakota. (Macro-Siouan phylum—Caddoan family)

ASSINIBOIN (*Yanktonai Nakota*). Northern Montana, Alberta, and Saskatchewan, concentrated between Lake of the Woods and Lake Winnipeg. (Macro-Siouan phylum—Siouan family—Nakota dialect group)

Atakapa. Southwestern Louisiana and southeastern Texas coastal region. (Macro-Algonquian phylum—Atakapa Language Isolate)

Atsina. Colorado–Nebraska–Kansas border region. Related to Gros Ventre. (Macro-Algonquian phylum—Algonquian family)

Atsugewai. Northeastern California. (Hokan phylum—Palaihnihan family)

Avoyel. See **NATCHEZ**.

Baffinland Inuit. Baffin Island, in Canada's Northwest Territories. (American Arctic-Paleo-Siberian phylum—Trans-Arctic Inuit family)

Bannock. Southern Idaho. Related to the Northern Paiute and Shoshoni. (Aztec-Tanoan phylum—Uto-Aztecan family)

Beaver. North-central Alberta and British Columbia to southern Alberta. (Na-Dene phylum—Athapascan family)

Bellabella. Central-western coastal British Columbia around Milbank Sound. A branch of the Kwakiutl. (Mosan phylum—Wakashan family)

Bella Coola. Central and northwestern coastal British Columbia, around the shores of the Bella Coola River and its tributaries. (Mosan phylum—Salishan family)

BEOTHUK. Newfoundland. (Undetermined phylum—Beothuk Language Isolate)

Biloxi. Southern coastal Mississippi around Biloxi Bay. (Macro-Siouan phylum—Siouan family)

BLACKFOOT. A confederacy of tribes (more properly called the *Siksika*) composed of the Blackfoot proper, the Blood, the Kainah, and the Piegan. Located on the Montana–Alberta border region. (Macro-Algonquian phylum—Algonquian family)

Blood. Montana-Alberta border region. See **BLACKFOOT**. (Macro-Algonquian phylum—Algonquian family)

Brulé (*Dakota Sioux*). Located near the White and Niobrara rivers in South Dakota and Nebraska. (Macro-Siouan phylum—Siouan family—Dakota dialect group)

Bungi. See **OJIBWA**.

Caddo. A loose confederacy of tribes that includes the Adai, the Eyish, the Haisinai (located in eastern Texas), the Kadohadacho, or Caddo proper (found in Louisiana and Arkansas), and the Natchitoches (located around Louisiana's Red River). (Macro-Siouan phylum—Caddoan family)

Cahuilla. Southeastern California, near the San Bernardino Mountains. (Aztec-Tanoan phylum—Uto-Aztecan family)

Calusa. An extinct tribe of southern Florida's Everglades area. (Macro-Algonquian phylum—Muskogean family)

Caribou Inuit. A group of tribes located in the southern part of Canada's Barren Grounds, west of Hudson Bay. (American Arctic-Paleo-Siberian phylum—Trans-Arctic Inuit family)

Carolina Algonquin (or *Algonquin*). Northern coastal North Carolina. See **ALGONQUIN; Pamlico; Secotan**.

Carrier. South-central British Columbia. Includes Takuilli. (Na-Dene phylum—Athapascan family)

Catawba. Central North Carolina–South Carolina border region along the Catawba River. (Macro-Siouan phylum—Catawba Language Isolate)

Cayuga (Iroquois). Western New York (Lake Ontario coast). (Macro-Siouan phylum—Iroquoian family)

Cayuse. Northeastern Oregon and southeastern Washington, around the headwaters of the Walla Walla, Umatilla, and Grand Ronde rivers. The Cayuse called themselves Waiilatpus. (Penutian phylum—Cayuse Language Isolate)

Chastacosta. Southwestern coastal Oregon. (Na-Dene phylum—Athapascan family)

Chehalis. Coastal Washington, around the Chehalis River. (Mosan phylum—Salishan family)

Chemehuevi. A nomadic tribe that wandered throughout southeastern California, southwestern Nevada, and northwestern Arizona. They called themselves Nuwu. (Aztec-Tanoan phylum—Uto-Aztecan family)

CHEROKEE. Northern Georgia–western North Carolina–eastern Tennessee border region, with a few tribes in southwest Virginia and northeastern Alabama (later forcibly moved to Oklahoma). The Cherokee called themselves the Ani-Yunwiya and were one of the Five Civilized Tribes. (Macro-Siouan phylum—Iroquoian family)

CHEYENNE, NORTHERN. Northeastern Wyoming–southwestern South Dakota border region, especially along the Yellowstone and Platte rivers. Both branches of the Cheyenne called themselves Tsitsista. (Macro-Algonquian phylum—Algonquian family)

CHEYENNE, SOUTHERN. Eastern Colorado–western Kansas border region, especially along the Arkansas River. (Macro-Algonquian phylum—Algonquian family)

Chickahominy. A tribe belonging to the Powhatan confederacy located along Virginia's Chickahominy River. (Macro-Algonquian phylum—Algonquian family)

CHICKASAW. Northeastern Mississippi and western Alabama border region. One of the Five Civilized Tribes. (Macro-Algonquian phylum—Muskogean family)

Chilcotin (also *Tsilkotin*). South-central British Columbia near the Chilcotin River/Anahim Lake area. (Na-Dene phylum—Athapascan family)

Chimakum. Northeastern coastal Washington, on the Juan de Fuca Strait. (Undetermined phylum—Chimakum family)

Chimariko. Northwestern coastal California. (Hokan phylum—Chimariko Language Isolate)

Chinook. Two distinct groups, the Upper and Lower Chinook, both located in southwestern coastal Washington along the Columbia River. (Penutian phylum—Chinookan family)

CHIPEWYAN. Northern Saskatchewan, Alberta, Manitoba, and the Northwest Territories. (Na-Dene phylum—Athapascan family)

Chippewa. See **OJIBWA**.

Chiricahua (*Eastern Apache*). Southwestern New Mexico, southeastern Arizona, northern Chihuahua Mexico. (Na-Dene phylum—Athapascan family)

Chitimacha. Southern Louisiana on the Gulf Coast, centered around Grand Lake. (Macro-Algonquian phylum—Chitimacha Language Isolate)

CHOCTAW. Central and southern Mississippi and southwestern Alabama border region. One of the Five Civilized Tribes. (Macro-Algonquian phylum—Muskogean family)

CHUMASH. South-central coastal California from Estero Bay to Malibu Canyon, concentrated in the Santa Barbara region (including the islands of San Miguel, Santa Rosa, Santa Cruz, and Ancapa). The Chumash included the Barbareño, the Obispeño, the Purisimeño, the Ventureño, and the Ynezeño. (Hokan phylum—Chumashan family)

Coahuiltec. Southern Texas–Mexico border region. (Hokan phylum— Coahuiltecan Language Isolate)

Cochiti. A pueblo and branch of the Keres, located south of Santa Fe, New Mexico. (Undetermined phylum—Keres Language Isolate)

Cocopa. Southwestern Arizona–northwestern Baja Mexico border region. The Cocopa called themselves the Xawil Kunyavaei. (Hokan phylum—Yuman family—Delta River Yuman group)

Cœur d'Alene. North-central Idaho, along the headwaters of the Spokane River and Cœur d'Alene Lake. (Mosan phylum—Salishan family)

Columbia. North-central Washington, along the eastern bank of the Columbia River. Includes the Sinkiuse. (Mosan phylum—Salishan family)

Colville. Northeastern Washington–northwestern Idaho–southern British Columbia border region. See **Okanagan**. (Mosan phylum—Salishan family)

COMANCHE. Northern Texas and Oklahoma border region, especially in the panhandles of both states. The Comanche called themselves Numinu and were related to the Shoshoni. (Aztec-Tanoan phylum—Uto-Aztecan family)

Comox. Western coastal British Columbia, along the eastern coast of Vancouver Island. (Mosan phylum—Salishan family)

Conestoga. See **Susquehanna**.

Coos. Southwestern coastal Oregon along the Coos River and Coos Bay. (Penutian phylum—Coos family)

Copper Inuit. Victoria Island and Coronation Gulf in Canada's Northwest Territories. (American Arctic-Paleo-Siberian phylum—Trans-Arctic Inuit family)

Costano. Central coastal California around San Francisco Bay. (Penutian phylum—Miwok-Costanoan family)

Cowichan. Western coastal British Columbia along the southeastern coast of Vancouver Island and the lower Fraser River. Includes the Stalo (also called *Fraser River Cowichan*). (Mosan phylum—Salishan family)

Cowlitz. Southwestern Washington. (Mosan phylum—Salishan family)

Coyotero (*Western Apache*). Southern Kansas, eastern Arizona, New Mexico, and western Texas. (Na-Dene phylum—Athapascan family)

CREE. South-central Saskatchewan and Manitoba south of Hudson Bay, later expanding from Labrador in the east to the Great Slave Lake in the west and south into northern Montana and North Dakota. (Macro-Algonquian phylum—Algonquian family)

CREEK (also called *Muscogee* or *Muskogee*). Central Alabama–Georgia border region. One of the Five Civilized Tribes. The Creek confederacy included the Alabama, the Apalachicola, the Hitchiti, the Koasati, the Ocmulgee, the Tuskegee, and the Yuchi. (Macro-Algonquian phylum—Muskogean family)

CROW. Southwestern Montana and northern Wyoming. The Crow called themselves the Absaroke. (Macro-Siouan phylum—Siouan family)

Cupeno. Extreme southeastern California. (Aztec-Tanoan phylum—Uto-Aztecan family)

Cusabo. A loose group of tribes located from northeastern Georgia (the Savannah River and its tributaries) to central South Carolina (Charleston Harbor). The Cusabo included the Ashepoo, Combahee, Coosa, Edisto, Escamacu, Etiwa, Kiawa, Stono, Wando, and Wimbee subtribes. (Macro-Algonquian phylum—Muskogean family)

DAKOTA (*Sioux*). One of the three great divisions of the Sioux people, based on differences in their languages. The Santee, or Eastern Dakota Sioux, included the Mdewakanton, Sisseton, Wahpekute, and Wahpeton tribes, all speaking the Dakota dialect of the Siouan family language. They called themselves the Oceti Sakowin. See **SIOUX** and capitalized tribe names for location. (Macro-Siouan phylum—Siouan family—Dakota dialect group)

DELAWARE. An Algonquian confederacy located along the Delaware River basin, including New Jersey, Delaware, eastern Pennsylvania, and southeastern New York. This confederation had three divisions: the Munsee (in the highlands), the Unami (downstream), and the Unalachtigo (on the coast). All members of this group called themselves Lenni Lenape. (Macro-Algonquian phylum—Algonquian family)

Diegueño. Southern California–Baja border region, a branch of the Tipai-Ipai. (Hokan phylum—Yuman family—Southern and Baja California Yuman group)

DOGRIB. A nomadic group that wandered between the Great Slave and Great Bear lakes in Canada's Yukon and Northwest Territories. They called themselves Thlingchadinne. (Na-Dene phylum—Athapascan family)

Duwamish. Northwestern coastal Washington, on Juan de Fuca Strait near present-day Seattle. (Mosan phylum—Salishan family)

East Greenland Inuit (*Angmagssalik*). Southeastern coastal Greenland. (American Arctic-Paleo-Siberian phylum—Eskimo-Aleut family)

Edisto. Southern South Carolina coast along the Edisto River. See **Cusabo**. (Macro-Algonquian phylum—Muskogean family)

Erie. Along the southern shores of Lake Erie. (The Erie spoke an Iroquoian language similar to Huron.)

Eskimo. See **INUIT**.

Esselen. Central California. (Hokan phylum—Esselen Language Isolate)

Eyak. Southern Alaskan peninsula. (Na-Dene phylum—Athapascan family)

Eyish. See **Caddo**.

Five Civilized Tribes. See **CHEROKEE; CHICKASAW; CHOCTAW; CREEK; Seminole**.

Flathead. Northeastern Idaho-west-central Montana border region. This grouping includes the Salish proper (Flatheads), the Spokan, and the Kalispel (or Pend d'Oreilles). They called themselves Se'lic. (Mosan phylum—Salishan family)

Fox. North-central Wisconsin, near Lake Winnebago. They called themselves Meskwakihug or Meskakwi. (Macro-Algonquian phylum—Algonquian family)

Gabrielino. Located in west-central California near present-day Los Angeles, and also on the coastal islands of Santa Catalina, San Nicholas, and San Clemente. (Aztec-Tanoan phylum—Uto-Aztecan family—Takic division)

Gosiute. West-central Utah, southwest of the Great Salt Lake. See **SHOSHONI, WESTERN**. (Aztec-Tanoan phylum—Uto-Aztecan family)

Gros Ventre. Northern Montana. Often called the *Gros Ventre of the Prairie*, to distinguish themselves from the Hidatsa (who are sometimes called the *Gros Ventre of the Missouri*). (Macro-Siouan phylum—Siouan family)

HAIDA. Queen Charlotte Islands, British Columbia, and Prince of Wales Island, Alaska. They called themselves Xa'ida. (Na-Dene phylum—Haida Language Isolate)

Haisimai. See **Caddo**.

Haisla. Central coastal British Columbia. (Mosan phylum—Wakashan family)

Halchidhoma. West-central Arizona. (Hokan phylum—Yuman family—Upriver Yuman group)

Han. Border of Alaska and Yukon Territory along the Yukon River. (Na-Dene phylum—Athapascan family)

Hano (also *Tano*). A branch of the Tewa located in central New Mexico, south of present-day Santa Fe in the Gallisteo Basin. (Aztec-Tanoan phylum—Kiowa-Tanoan family)

HARE (also called *Kawchodinne*). Yukon and Northwest Territories, western Alberta. (Na-Dene phylum—Athapascan family)

Havasupai. Northwest Arizona, in Cataract Canyon (a branch of the Grand Canyon). (Hokan phylum—Yuman family—Upland Yuman group)

Hidatsa. Western North Dakota near the confluence of the Missouri and Knife rivers, including the Hidatsa proper, the Awatixa, and the Awaxawi. See *Gros Ventre*. (Macro-Siouan phylum—Siouan family)

Hitchiti. Western Georgia–eastern Alabama border region, on the eastern bank of the Chattahoochee River. This group originally belonged to the Creek confederacy and later fled to Florida, becoming both a language group and a tribe of the Seminole. (Macro-Algonquian phylum—Muskogean family)

Hoh. See **Quileute**.

HOPI. Northeastern Arizona. They were also called the Moqui, but referred to themselves as the Hopitu. (Aztec-Tanoan phylum—Uto-Aztecan family)

Hualapai (also called *Walapai*). Northwestern Arizona. (Hokan phylum—Yuman family—Upland Yuman group)

Hunkpapa (*Lakota Sioux*). Located from the Big Cheyenne River to the Yellowstone River and west to South Dakota's Black Hills. (Macro-Siouan phylum—Siouan family—Lakota dialect group)

HUPA. Southwestern coastal Oregon to northwestern coastal California along the Trinity River. (Na-Dene phylum—Athapascan family)

HURON (also *Wyandot*). South-central Ontario. This confederation of four tribes called themselves the Wendat, which became corrupted to Wyandot. (Macro-Siouan phylum—Iroquoian family)

Iglulik Inuit. North of Hudson Bay, in Canada's Northwest Territories. (American Arctic-Paleo-Siberian phylum—Eskimo-Aleut family)

ILLINOIS. A confederacy of tribes that stretched across southern Wisconsin and northern Illinois, from the west bank of the Missouri River as far south as the Des Moines River. The confederation included the Cahokia, Kaskaskia, Michigamea, Moingwena, Peoria, and Tamora. (Macro-Algonquian phylum—Algonquian family)

INGALIK. South-central Alaska and along Yukon Territory border. (Na-Dene phylum—Athapascan family)

INUIT (also called *Eskimo*). A large group of linguistically and culturally related peoples that ranged along the Arctic coasts of North America from Greenland to the Bering Strait. All spoke languages of the American Arctic-Paleo-Siberian phylum, specifically the Eskimo-Aleut family.

IOWA. Eastern Iowa and southwestern Minnesota. The Iowa called themselves Pahoja. (Macro-Siouan phylum—Siouan family)

IROQUOIS. A confederation of tribes centered around the southern shores of Lake Ontario in New York. See **Cayuga; Mohawk; Oneida; Onondaga; Seneca; Tuscarora**.

Isleta. A pueblo and branch of the Tiwa located in central New Mexico on the banks of the Rio Grande River. (Aztec-Tanoan phylum—Kiowa-Tanoan family)

Jemez (also *Towa*). Central New Mexico. (Aztec-Tanoan phylum—Kiowa-Tanoan family)

Jicarilla (*Eastern Apache*). Southeastern Colorado and northeastern New Mexico. (Na-Dene phylum—Athapascan family)

Juaneño. See **Luiseño**.

Kadohadacho. See **Caddo**.

Kainah. See **BLACKFOOT**.

KALAPUYA. A group of tribes in western Oregon's Willamette River valley. (Penutian phylum—Kalapuyan family)

Kalispel (also called *Pend d'Oreilles*). Northern Idaho. See **Flathead**. (Mosan phylum—Salishan family)

Kamia. Southern California-Baja border region, a branch of the Tipai-Ipai. (Hokan phylum—Yuman family—Southern and Baja California Yuman group)

KANSA. Central and northeastern Kansas, near the Kansas and Missouri rivers. Later split into five separate tribes, four of which moved to different areas:

the Kansa proper, the Omaha, the Osage, the Ponca, and the Quapaw. (Macro-Siouan phylum—Siouan family)

Karankawa. Southeastern Texas Gulf Coast. (Undetermined phylum—Karankawa Language Isolate)

Karok. Northwestern California near the Klamath River. (Hokan phylum—Karok Language Isolate)

Kaska. Northern British Columbia. See NAHANE.

Kaskaskia. Southern Wisconsin, northern Illinois, eastern Iowa. See ILLINOIS. (Macro-Algonquian phylum—Algonquian family)

Kato. Northwestern California. (Na-Dene phylum—Athapascan family)

Kawaiisu. A branch of the Chemehuevi, located farther to the west in southeastern California. (Aztec-Tanoan phylum—Uto-Aztecan family)

Kennebec. See ABNAKI; **Norridgewock.**

Keres. A group of closely related pueblo tribes of central New Mexico. See **Acoma; Cochiti; Laguna; San Felipe; Santa Ana; Santo Domingo; Zia.**

Kichai. See **Wichita.**

Kickapoo. Located around the Fox and Wisconsin rivers in Wisconsin, calling themselves Kiwegapaw. (The Kickapoo spoke an Algonquian language similar to Sauk and Shawnee.)

Kiliwa. Northern Baja peninsula, a branch of the Tipai-Ipai. (Hokan phylum—Yuman family—Southern and Baja California Yuman group)

KIOWA. From western Montana to central and western Oklahoma, especially the panhandle. They called themselves the Gaigwu, or Kaigwu, corrupted into Kiowa. (Aztec-Tanoan phylum—Kiowa-Tanoan family)

Kiowa Apache (*Eastern Apache*). Southwestern Oklahoma. Closely related to the Kiowa except linguistically. (Na-Dene phylum—Athapascan family)

Klallam. Northwest coastal Washington, on the southern bank of Juan de Fuca Strait. (Mosan phylum—Salishan family)

Klamath. South-central Oregon–northern California border region, along Upper Klamath Lake, Klamath Marsh, Williamson and Sprague rivers. (Penutian phylum—Klamath-Modoc Language Isolate)

Klikitat. Occupied the headwaters of the Cowlitz, Lewis, White Salmon, and Klikitat rivers in central Washington. They called themselves Qwulh-hwai-pum. (Penutian phylum—Sahaptin-Nez-Perce family)

Koasati. Northern and central Alabama. See CREEK. (Macro-Algonquian phylum—Muskogean family)

Koroa. See **Tunica.**

KOYUKON (also called *Koyukhotana*). Border of Alaska and Yukon Territory. (Na-Dene phylum—Athapascan family)

KUTCHIN. Border of Alaska and Yukon Territory, along the Yukon, Mackenzie, and Peel rivers. (Na-Dene phylum—Athapascan family)

KUTENAI. Southern British Columbia to Washington and Idaho. (Undetermined phylum—Kutenai Language Isolate)

KWAKIUTL. South-central coastal British Columbia, including northern Vancouver Island and the mainland coast from Douglas Channel to Bute Inlet. (Mosan phylum—Wakashan family)

Labrador Inuit. Along the Labrador-Ungava coast. (American Arctic-Paleo-Siberian phylum—Trans-Arctic Inuit family)

Laguna. A branch of the Keres, located on the south bank of the San Jose River, west of present-day Albuquerque, New Mexico. (Undetermined phylum—Keres Language Isolate)

Lake (also *Senijextee*). Southeastern British Columbia in the valley of the Kettle and Kutenai rivers to Washington and the Columbia River. See **Okanagan**. (Mosan phylum—Salishan family)

LAKOTA (*Sioux*). One of the three great divisions of the Sioux people, based on differences in their languages. The Lakota dialect of the Siouan language family was spoken by the Teton, or Western, group: Brulé, Hunkpapa, Miniconjou, Oglala, Sans Arcs, Sihasapa (or Blackfoot), and Two Kettle (or Oohenonpa). See **SIOUX** and capitalized tribe names for location. (Macro-Siouan phylum—Siouan family—Lakota dialect group)

Lillooet. Southwestern British Columbia. (Mosan phylum—Salishan family)

Lipan (*Eastern Apache*). South-central Texas. (Na-Dene phylum—Athapascan family)

Luiseño. Southwestern coastal California. Includes the Juaneño. (Aztec-Tanoan phylum—Uto-Aztecan family)

Lummi. Southwestern coastal British Columbia–northwestern coastal Washington border region, especially on San Juan and the other islands of Puget Sound. (Mosan phylum—Salishan family)

Mackenzie Inuit. Located in the delta of the Mackenzie River in the northwestern part of Canada's Northwest Territories. (American Arctic-Paleo-Siberian phylum—Trans-Arctic Inuit family)

Mahican. A confederacy of subtribes located on the Hudson River in upstate New York. One branch, the Westenhuck, survived as the Stockbridge. (Macro-Algonquian phylum—Algonquian family)

Maidu. Composed of four distinct bands, all located in northeastern California: the Southern Maidu, the Northwest Maidu, the Mountain Maidu, and the Valley Maidu. (Penutian phylum—Maidu family)

Makah. Washington, on Cape Flattery and along the shores of Juan de Fuca Strait. The Makah called themselves the Kwe-net-che-chat. (Mosan phylum—Wakashan family)

Malecite. The St. John River valley in New Brunswick, Canada. (Macro-Algonquian phylum—Algonquian family)

MANDAN. South-central South Dakota, concentrated along the Missouri River. (Macro-Siouan phylum—Siouan family)

Maricopa. Central southwestern Arizona, along the Gila River. (Hokan phylum—Yuman family—Upriver Yuman group)

Massachuset. Located along Massachusetts Bay from Plymouth to Salem and along the Neponset and Charles rivers to present-day Boston. (The Massachuset spoke an Algonquian language similar to Narraganset.)

Mdewakanton (*Dakota Sioux*). Nebraska's plains. (Macro-Siouan phylum—Siouan family—Dakota dialect group)

Menominee. Wisconsin and Michigan along the Menominee River. (Macro-Algonquian phylum—Algonquian family)

Mescalero (*Eastern Apache*). Southern New Mexico, western Texas, northern Chihuahua Mexico. (Na-Dene phylum—Athapascan family)

MIAMI (also *Twightwee*). Originated around Green Bay, Wisconsin; migrated to northern and central Indiana around the southern end of Lake Michigan in the seventeenth century. Includes the Atchatchakangouen, Kilkatika, Mengakonkia, Pepicokia, Piankashaw, Wea. (Macro-Algonquian phylum—Algonquian family)

Miccosukee. South-central Georgia–Alabama border region. (Macro-Algonquian phylum—Muskogean family)

MICMAC. Northern Maine to northern New Brunswick, including Nova Scotia, Cape Breton, Prince Edward Island, and Quebec's Gaspé peninsula. (Macro-Algonquian phylum—Algonquian family)

Mikasuki. See **Seminole**.

Miniconjou (*Lakota Sioux*). South Dakota, from the Black Hills south to the Platte River. (Macro-Siouan phylum—Siouan family—Lakota dialect group)

Missisauga. See **OJIBWA**.

Missouri. Located near the junction of the Missouri and Grand rivers. They called themselves Niutachi. (Macro-Siouan phylum—Siouan family)

MIWOK. Three distinct bands located in central coastal California, between present-day San Francisco and Monterey: the Sierra Miwok, the Coast Miwok, and the Lake Miwok. (Penutian phylum—Miwok-Costanoan family)

Mobile. Southern Alabama–western Florida border region. (Macro-Algonquian phylum—Muskogean family)

Modoc. Northern California–southern Oregon border region. (Penutian phylum—Klamath-Modoc Language Isolate)

Mohave (also *Mojave*). Southeastern California–west-central Arizona border region around the lower Colorado River. (Hokan phylum—Yuman family—Upriver Yuman group)

Mohawk (*Iroquois*). Central New York, along the Hudson and Mohawk river valleys in the south to the St. Lawrence River in the north. They called themselves Kaniengehaga. (Macro-Siouan phylum—Iroquoian family)

Mohegan (also *Mohican*). See **Pequot**.

Molale (also *Molala*). North-central Oregon. (Penutian phylum—Molale Language Isolate)

Mono (also *Monache*). Central California–western Nevada border region, concentrated in the Sierra Nevada. (Aztec-Tanoan phylum—Uto-Aztecan family)

Montagnais. North-central Quebec and western Labrador. (Macro-Algonquian phylum—Algonquian family)

Montauk. A loose confederacy located at the eastern end of New York's Long Island. (The Montauk spoke an Algonquian language similar to Niantic.)

Munsee. See **Delaware**.

Nabesna. See **Tanana**.

Nahane. Northern British Columbia and southern Yukon Territory. Includes Kaska, Tahltan. (Na-Dene phylum—Athapascan family)

Nakota (*Sioux*). One of the three great divisions of the Sioux people, based on differences in their languages. The Nakota dialect of the Siouan language family was spoken by the Wiciyela, or Middle group of the Sioux, the Yankton, and the Yanktonai. See **Sioux** and capitalized tribe names for location. (Macro-Siouan phylum—Siouan family—Nakota dialect group)

Nambe. A pueblo and branch of the Tewa located in central New Mexico. (Aztec-Tanoan phylum—Kiowa-Tanoan family)

Nanticoke. Located on the peninsula between the Chesapeake and Delaware bays. Related to the Delaware. (Macro-Algonquian phylum—Algonquian family)

Narraganset. Most of Rhode Island and southern Massachusetts. Includes Niantic. (Macro-Algonquian phylum—Algonquian family)

Naskapi. South-central Saskatchewan and Manitoba, closely tied to the Montagnais. (Macro-Algonquian phylum—Algonquian family)

Natchez. Southwestern Mississippi. Includes Avoyel, Taensa. (Macro-Algonquian phylum—Muskogean family—Natchez Language Isolate)

Natchitoches. See **Caddo**.

Navajo. North-central Arizona, New Mexico, and Utah. (Na-Dene phylum—Athapascan family)

Nawunena. Colorado–Nebraska–Kansas border region. (Macro-Algonquian phylum—Algonquian family)

Nespelem. See **Sanpoil**.

Netsilik Inuit. North of Hudson Bay. (American Arctic-Paleo-Siberian phylum—Trans-Arctic Inuit family)

Neutral. Ranging from the northern shore of Lake Erie to the Niagara River in the east to the Grand River in the west. (The Neutral spoke an Iroquoian language similar to Huron.)

Nez Perce. Northeastern Oregon–north-central Idaho region and southwestern Washington, especially along the lower Snake River and its tributaries. (Penutian phylum—Sahaptin-Nez Perce family)

Niantic. See **Narraganset**.

Nipmuc. Between the Merrimack and Connecticut rivers in central Massachusetts. (Macro-Algonquian phylum—Algonquian family)

Nisqualli. West-central Washington along the Nisqualli River. (Mosan phylum—Salishan family)

Nitinant. Northwest coastal Washington. (Mosan phylum—Wakashan family)

Nootka. The western coast of Vancouver Island. (Mosan phylum—Wakashan family)

Norridgewock. An eastern group of the Abnaki in the Kennebec Valley of southern Maine, later dispersed into Canada. See **Abnaki**. (Macro-Algonquian phylum—Algonquian family)

North Alaska Inuit. Located along the northern Alaskan coast between Point Hope and Point Barrow. (American Arctic-Paleo-Siberian phylum—Kuskokwim family)

Northern Tonto (*Western Apache*). Northeastern Arizona. (Na-Dene phylum—Athapascan family)

Ntlakyapamuk (also called *Thompson*). Southwestern British Columbia, in the valleys of the Fraser, Thompson, and Nicola rivers. (Mosan phylum—Salishan family)

Nyakipa (also *Nakipa*). Northern Baja peninsula, a branch of the Tipai-Ipai. (Hokan phylum—Yuman family—Southern and Baja California Yuman group)

Oglala (*Lakota Sioux*). South Dakota, north of the North Platte River (including the Black Hills). (Macro-Siouan phylum—Siouan family—Lakota dialect group)

Ojibwa (or *Ojibway*). Ontario north of Lake Huron and northeast of Lake Superior. Includes the Bungi, Chippewa, Missisauga. (Macro-Algonquian phylum—Algonquian family)

Okanagan. Northern Washington–southern British Columbia border region. This loose group of tribes included the Colville, Lake, Okanagan proper, and Sanpoil. (Mosan phylum—Salishan family)

Omaha. Northeastern Nebraska. See **Kansa**. (Macro-Siouan phylum—Siouan family)

Oneida (*Iroquois*). Central New York (Lake Ontario coast). (Macro-Siouan phylum—Iroquoian family)

Onondaga (*Iroquois*). West-central New York (Lake Ontario coast), also south to the upper Susquehanna River. (Macro-Siouan phylum—Iroquoian family)

Osage. Southern Kansas–western Missouri border region. See **Kansa**. (Macro-Siouan phylum—Siouan family)

Oto. Southeastern Nebraska along the Platte River. (Macro-Siouan phylum—Siouan family)

Ottawa. Ontario; Manitoulin Island and Bruce Peninsula on northern Lake Huron. (Macro-Algonquian phylum—Algonquian family)

PAIUTE, NORTHERN. Northern Nevada–southeastern Oregon–southwestern Idaho border region. (Aztec-Tanoan phylum—Uto-Aztecan family)

PAIUTE, SOUTHERN. Southwestern Utah, northern Arizona, southern Nevada, and southeastern California. This loose group called itself the Nuwu and included the Kaibab, Kaiparowits, Las Vegas, Moapa, Panaca, Panguitch, Paranigets, Saint George, San Juan, and Shivwits subtribes. (Aztec-Tanoan phylum—Uto-Aztecan family)

Palouse. Located along the Palouse River in Washington and Idaho. (Penutian phylum—Sahaptin-Nez Perce family)

Pamlico (also called *Carolina Algonquin*). Coastal North Carolina, concentrated along the Pamlico River and the Pamlico Sound. (Macro-Algonquian phylum—Algonquian family)

Pamunkey. A member tribe of the Powhatan confederation, located in eastern tidewater Virginia. (Macro-Algonquian phylum—Algonquian family)

Panamint. A branch of the Western Shoshoni located in the southwestern Nevada–southeastern California border region. (Aztec-Tanoan phylum—Uto-Aztecan family)

PAPAGO. Northern Sonora Mexico–southern Arizona border region. (Aztec-Tanoan phylum—Uto-Aztecan family)

Passamaquoddy. Maine and New Brunswick coasts. (Macro-Algonquian phylum—Algonquian family)

Patwin. Northwest California. (Penutian phylum—Wintun family)

PAWNEE. Central and southern Nebraska, concentrated in the Platte River valley. (Macro-Siouan phylum—Caddoan family)

Pend d'Oreilles. See **Kalispel; Flathead**.

Pennacook. A small Algonquian confederacy in the Merrimack River valley of central New Hampshire, northeastern Massachusetts, and southern Maine. This confederation included the Agawam, Amoskeag, Nashua, Wamesit, and Winnipesaukee. See **ABNAKI**. (Macro-Algonquian phylum—Algonquian family)

Penobscot. Central Maine, along the Penobscot River. See **ABNAKI**. (Macro-Algonquian phylum—Algonquian family)

Peoria. See **ILLINOIS**.

PEQUOT (later called *Mohegan*). Central and southeastern Connecticut. (Macro-Algonquian phylum—Algonquian family)

Piankashaw. See **MIAMI**.

Picuris. A pueblo and branch of the Tiwa located in central New Mexico, north of present-day Santa Fe. (Aztec-Tanoan phylum—Kiowa-Tanoan family)

Piegan. Montana–Alberta border region. See **BLACKFOOT**. (Macro-Algonquian phylum—Algonquian family)

PIMA. South-central Arizona in the Gila and Salt River valleys. They called themselves Aatam. (Aztec-Tanoan phylum—Uto-Aztecan family)

Pima Bajo. Northwestern Mexico, on the Gulf of California. (Aztec-Tanoan phylum—Uto-Aztecan family)

Piro. A pueblo tribe of northern New Mexico. (Aztec-Tanoan phylum—Kiowa-Tanoan family)

Pojoaque. A pueblo and branch of the Tewa located on the Rio Grande just north of present-day Santa Fe. (Aztec-Tanoan phylum—Kiowa-Tanoan family)

Polar Inuit. Northwestern coastal Greenland. (American Arctic-Paleo-Siberian phylum—Trans-Arctic Inuit family)

POMO. Comprised of four distinct groups, all of which occupied the northern and coastal California area: the Coast Pomo, the Northeast Pomo, the Western Clear Lake Pomo, and the Southeast Clear Lake Pomo. (Hokan phylum—Pomo family—each spoke a mutually unintelligible dialect)

Ponca. Northeastern Nebraska. See **KANSA**. (Macro-Siouan phylum—Siouan family)

Potawatomi. Central Michigan, along the eastern shore of Lake Michigan. (Macro-Algonquian phylum—Algonquian family)

POWHATAN. An Algonquian confederacy along the eastern shore of Chesapeake Bay in Virginia. Included the Powhatan proper, Pamunkey, and Chickahominy. (Macro-Algonquian phylum—Algonquian family)

PUEBLO. Not a distinct tribe, but a term referring to all tribes who lived in permanent stone or adobe villages (pueblos). Pueblo groups of the American southwest include the Hopi, Jemez, Keres, Piro, Tewa, Tiwa, and Zuñi.

Puyallup. Lived along the Puyallup River and Commencement Bay in northwestern Washington. (Mosan phylum—Salishan family)

Quapaw (also called *Arkansea*). Northern Arkansas. See **KANSA**. (Macro-Siouan phylum—Siouan family)

Quileute. Northwest coastal Washington. Includes Hoh. (Undetermined phylum—Chimakuan family)

QUINAULT. Northwestern coastal Washington along the Quinault River. (Mosan phylum—Salishan family)

Salina. Central coastal California. (Hokan phylum—Salinan family)

Salish. See **Flathead**.

San Carlos (*Western Apache*). South-central Arizona. (Na-Dene phylum—Athapascan family)

Sandia. A pueblo and branch of the Tiwa located in central New Mexico, north of present-day Albuquerque on the eastern bank of the Rio Grande. (Aztec-Tanoan phylum—Kiowa-Tanoan family)

Sanetch. See **Songish**.

San Felipe. A pueblo and branch of the Keres, located southwest of present-day Santa Fe, New Mexico. (Undetermined phylum—Keres Language Isolate)

San Ildefonso. A pueblo and branch of the Tewa located in central New Mexico. (Aztec-Tanoan phylum—Kiowa-Tanoan family)

San Juan. A pueblo and branch of the Southern Paiute located in central New Mexico. (Aztec-Tanoan phylum—Kiowa-Tanoan family)

Sanpoil. Northeastern Washington near the confluence of the Columbia and Sanpoil rivers. Includes Nespelem. See **Okanagan**. (Mosan phylum—Salishan family)

Sans Arcs (*Lakota Sioux*). Located west of the Missouri River between the Grand and Heart rivers. They called themselves Itazipcho—the French corrupted this to "Sans Arcs," "without bows." (Macro-Siouan phylum—Siouan family—Lakota dialect group)

Santa Ana. A pueblo and branch of the Keres, located in central New Mexico. (Undetermined phylum—Keres Language Isolate)

Santa Clara. A pueblo and branch of the Tewa located in central New Mexico. (Aztec-Tanoan phylum—Kiowa-Tanoan family)

Santee. Another name for the Eastern Dakota Sioux, who remained for the most part in Minnesota, Wisconsin, and the eastern Dakotas.

Santo Domingo. A pueblo and branch of the Keres, located in south-central New Mexico. (Undetermined phylum—Keres Language Isolate)

SARSI. North-central Alberta and British Columbia to southern Alberta. (Na-Dene phylum—Athapascan family)

SAUK (also *Sac*). Eastern Michigan to north-central Wisconsin. They called themselves Osakiwug, corrupted to Sauk. (Macro-Algonquian phylum—Algonquian family)

Saulteaux. Ontario. Possibly related to the Ojibwa. (Macro-Algonquian phylum—Algonquian family)

Secotan (also called *Carolina Algonquin*). An extinct tribe located between the Pamlico River and the Albemarle Sound in eastern coastal North Carolina. (Macro-Algonquian phylum—Algonquian family)

Seechelt. British Columbia, on Jervis and Seechelt inlets as well as Nelson Island and southern Texada Island in the Strait of Georgia. (Mosan phylum—Salishan family)

Sekani. North-central Alberta and British Columbia to southern Alberta. (Na-Dene phylum—Athapascan family)

Seminole. Southeastern Florida. Originally formed from refugee Oconee, Yamasee, Creek, and others fleeing Georgia and South Carolina. One of the Five Civilized Tribes. Includes Hitchiti, Mikasuki, Muskogee. (Macro-Algonquian phylum—Muskogean family)

Seneca (*Iroquois*). Southwestern New York (Lake Ontario coast). (Macro-Siouan phylum—Iroquoian family)

Serrano. South-central California along the San Bernardino Mountains and into the Mojave Desert. (Aztec-Tanoan phylum—Uto-Aztecan family)

Shasta. Northern California–southern Oregon border region. (Hokan phylum—Shastan family)

SHAWNEE. The Ohio Valley, ranging from northern Kentucky to the Cumberland River in Tennessee. (Macro-Algonquian phylum—Algonquian family)

Shinnecock. New York's Long Island between Shinnecock Bay and Montauk Point. Part of the Montauk confederacy. (The Shinnecock spoke an Algonquian language similar to Niantic.)

SHOSHONI, NORTHERN. Eastern Idaho, northern Utah, and western Montana. Includes the Snake. (Aztec-Tanoan phylum—Uto-Aztecan family)

SHOSHONI, WESTERN. Central Nevada, Idaho, Utah, California. Includes the Gosiute. (Aztec-Tanoan phylum—Uto-Aztecan family)

Shoshoni, Wind River. Western Wyoming. (Aztec-Tanoan phylum—Uto-Aztecan family)

SHUSWAP. Southeastern British Columbia. (Mosan phylum—Salishan family)

Sihasapa (*Dakota Sioux*). A branch of the Teton Dakota, located west of the Missouri River between the Heart and Grand rivers, South Dakota. (Macro-Siouan phylum—Siouan family—Dakota dialect group)

Siksika. The proper name for the Blackfoot confederacy. See **BLACKFOOT**.

Sinkiuse. See **Columbia**.

SIOUX. A large group of tribes speaking three different dialects of the same language. All originated in northern Minnesota and Wisconsin, but migrated to the Great Plains—as far west as eastern Wyoming and Montana, including the Dakotas, Nebraska, and parts of Idaho. See **DAKOTA** (Sioux); **LAKOTA** (Sioux); **NAKOTA** (Sioux). (Macro-Siouan phylum—Siouan family)

Sisseton (*Dakota Sioux*). The western plains of the Dakotas, northwestern Nebraska, northeastern Wyoming, southeastern Montana. (Macro-Siouan phylum—Siouan family—Dakota dialect group)

Siuslaw. Southern coastal Oregon. (Penutian phylum—Yakonan family)

Skagit. Located along the Skagit River and Whidbey Island in northwest Washington. They called themselves Hum-a-luh. (Includes Swinomish.) (Mosan phylum—Salishan family)

Skokomish. See **Twana**.

SLAVE. Northwestern Alberta to the Northwestern Territories. (Na-Dene phylum—Athapascan family)

Snake. See **SHOSHONI, NORTHERN**.

Snohomish. Located at the southern end of Whidbey Island and at the mouth of the Skagit River in Washington. (Mosan phylum—Salishan family)

Snuqualmi. Northwestern coastal Washington (Juan de Fuca Strait). (Mosan phylum—Salishan family)

Songish. Vancouver Island, British Columbia, and San Juan Islands, Washington. Includes Sanetch. (Mosan phylum—Salishan family)

South Alaskan Inuit. Kodiak Island to Controller Bay. (American Arctic-Paleo-Siberian phylum—Unalaska family)

Southampton Inuit. Southampton Island, Hudson Bay, Canada's Northwest Territories. (American Arctic-Paleo-Siberian phylum—Trans-Arctic Inuit family)

Southern Tonto (*Western Apache*). Southeastern Arizona. (Na-Dene phylum—Athapascan family)

Spokan (also *Spokane*). Southeastern Washington, in the Spokane River valley. See **Flathead**. (Mosan phylum—Salishan family)

Squamish. Southwestern coastal British Columbia. (Mosan phylum—Salishan family)

Stalo (also called *Fraser River Cowichan*). See **Cowichan**.

Stockbridge. See **Mahican**.

Susquehanna. Located along the Susquehanna River in New York, Pennsylvania, and Maryland. Variously known as the Andaste, Minquas, and Sasquehannock. Includes Conestoga. (Macro-Siouan phylum—Iroquoian family)

Swinomish. See **Skagit**.

Taensa. See **NATCHEZ**.

Tahltan. See **NAHANE**.

Takelma. Southwestern Oregon along the middle Rogue River. (Penutian phylum—Takelma Language Isolate)

Takuilli. See **CARRIER**.

Taltushtuntude. South-western coastal Oregon. (Na-Dene phylum—Athapascan family)

Tanaina. South-central Alaska and along Yukon Territory border. (Na-Dene phylum—Athapascan family)

TANANA. Border of Alaska and Yukon Territory. Includes Nabesna. (Na-Dene phylum—Athapascan family)

Tano. See **Hano**.

Taos. A pueblo and branch of the Tiwa located in central New Mexico, on both sides of Taos Creek. (Aztec-Tanoan phylum—Kiowa-Tanoan family)

Tawakoni. See **Wichita**.

Tesuque. A pueblo and branch of the Tewa located in central New Mexico. (Aztec-Tanoan phylum—Kiowa-Tanoan family)

Teton (*Sioux*). A division of the Dakota originating in northern Minnesota that later migrated to western North and South Dakota, northwest Nebraska, northeast Wyoming, and southeastern Montana. (Macro-Siouan phylum—Siouan family)

Tewa. See **Hano; Nambe; Pojoaque; San Ildefonso; Santa Clara; Tesuque**.

Thompson. See **Ntlakyapamuk**.

Tigua. See **Tiwa**.

Tillamook. Northwestern coastal Oregon. (Mosan phylum—Salishan family)

Timucua. North-central Florida. (Undetermined phylum—Timucua Language Isolate)

Tionontati. A branch of the Huron confederacy, located just east of Lake Huron in Ontario. (Macro-Siouan phylum—Iroquoian family)

Tipai-Ipai. A group of related tribes in southern and Baja California. See **Akwa'ala; Diegueño; Kamia; Kiliwa; Nyakipa**.

Tiwa (also *Tigua*). See **Isleta; Picuris; Sandia; Taos**.

Tlingit. Southeastern coastal Alaska to northwestern coastal British Columbia. (Na-Dene phylum—Tlingit Language Isolate)

Tolowa. Northwestern coastal California from the Oregon border to Wilson Creek. (Na-Dene phylum—Athapascan family)

Tonkawa. A nomadic tribe that ranged through central and eastern Texas. (Macro-Algonquian phylum—Tonkawa Language Isolate)

Towa. See **Jemez**.

Tsimshian. Coastal west-central British Columbia, along the Nass and Skeena rivers. (Penutian phylum—Tsimshian Language Isolate)

Tubatulabal. South-central California, in the Sierra Nevada foothills. (Aztec-Tanoan phylum—Uto-Aztecan family)

Tunica. A loose confederation in the northeastern Louisiana–Mississippi border region; includes Koroa, Yazoo. (Macro-Algonquian phylum—Tunica Language Isolate)

Tuscarora (*Iroquois*). Originally central North Carolina along the Tar, Pamlico, Roanoke, and Neuse rivers; later moved to join the Huron confederacy in central New York. Called themselves Skaroo'ren, which was corrupted to Tuscarora. (Macro-Siouan phylum—Iroquoian family)

Tutchone. Border of Alaska and Yukon Territory, along the course of the Yukon River. (Na-Dene phylum—Athapascan family)

Tutelo. West-central Virginia along the upper James and Rappahannock rivers. They were related to a number of other tribes, including the Keyauwee, Occaneechi, and Saponi. (Macro-Siouan phylum—Siouan family)

Tututni. South-western coastal Oregon. (Na-Dene phylum—Athapascan family)

Twana. South-central coastal Washington. Includes Skokomish. (Mosan phylum—Salishan family)

Two Kettle (*Lakota Sioux*). A branch of the Lakota Sioux that lived along South Dakota's Cheyenne, Moreau, and Grand rivers. They called themselves Oohenonpa. See **Lakota** (Sioux). (Macro-Siouan phylum—Siouan family—Lakota dialect group)

Umatilla. Lived along the Umatilla and Columbia rivers in Oregon. (Penutian phylum—Sahaptin-Nez Perce family)

Umpqua. Lived along the course of the North Umpqua River in Oregon. (Na-Dene phylum—Athapascan family)

Unalachtigo. See **Delaware**.

Unami. See **Delaware**.

Ute. Western Colorado–eastern Utah border region. (Aztec-Tanoan phylum—Uto-Aztecan family)

Waco. See **Wichita**.

Wahpekute (*Dakota Sioux*). Northern Nebraska. (Macro-Siouan phylum—Siouan family—Dakota dialect group)

Wahpeton (*Dakota Sioux*). Around the mouth of the Minnesota River. (Macro-Siouan phylum—Siouan family—Dakota dialect group)

Wailaki. Northwestern California along the Eel River. (Na-Dene phylum—Athapascan family)

Walapai. See **Hualapai**.

Wallawalla. Oregon and Washington along the Walla Walla and Columbia rivers. (Penutian phylum—Sahaptin-Nez Perce family)

Wampanoag (also *Pokanokets*). Southeastern Massachusetts from Cape Cod to Narraganset Bay, including Nantucket and Martha's Vineyard. (Macro-Algonquian phylum—Algonquian family)

Wappinger. A loose confederacy of Algonquian tribes along the eastern bank of the Hudson River from Manhattan to Poughkeepsie and east into the lower Connecticut River valley. Included the Kitchawank, Manhattan, Mattabesec, Nochpeem, Sitsink, Siwanoy, Tankiteke, Wappinger proper, and Wecquaesgeek. (Macro-Algonquian phylum—Algonquian family)

Wappo. North-central California and the Napa Valley. (Undetermined phylum—Yuki family)

Wasco. See **Wishram**.

Washo. Western Nevada–southeastern California border region around Lake Tahoe. (Hokan phylum—Washo Language Isolate)

Wea. See **Miami**.

Wenatchee. North-central Washington. (Mosan phylum—Salishan family)

Wenrohronon. New York, south of Lake Ontario. (Macro-Siouan phylum—Iroquoian family)

West Alaska Inuit. Along the Alaskan coast from Point Hope south to Kodiak Island. (American Arctic-Paleo-Siberian phylum—Kuskokwim family)

West Greenland Inuit. Along the western coast of Greenland. (American Arctic-Paleo-Siberian phylum—Trans-Arctic Inuit family)

Wichita. A loose grouping of related tribes, all of them offshoots of the Caddo confederacy, in the northeastern Texas–south-central Oklahoma border region. They called themselves Kitikiti'sh. Includes the Kichai, Tawakoni, and Waco. (Macro-Siouan phylum—Caddoan family)

Winnebago. Eastern Wisconsin, around Green Bay. They called themselves Hotcangara. (Macro-Siouan phylum—Siouan family)

Winnipesaukee. See **Abnaki**.

Wintun (also *Wintu*). Northwestern coastal California. (Penutian phylum—Wintun family)

Wishram. The north bank of the Columbia River in Washington. They called themselves Tlakluit. Includes Wasco. (Penutian phylum—Chinookan family)

Wyandot. See Huron.

Yakima. Located along the Columbia, Yakima, and Wenatchee rivers in Washington. They called themselves Waptailmim. (Penutian phylum—Sahaptin-Nez Perce family)

Yamasee (also *Yemasee*). Southeastern coastal Georgia and South Carolina to northeastern coastal Florida. Some Yamasee later fled to join the Seminoles. (Macro-Algonquian phylum—Muskogean family)

Yana. Northeastern California in the upper Sacramento Valley. (Hokan phylum—Yanan family)

Yankton (*Nakota Sioux*). Southeast South Dakota–northwestern Iowa border region. (Macro-Siouan phylum—Siouan family—Nakota dialect group)

Yanktonai (*Nakota Sioux*). Southeastern North Dakota. (Macro-Siouan phylum—Siouan family—Nakota dialect group)

Yaquina. See **Alsea**.

Yavapai. Western and central Arizona. (Hokan phylum—Yuman family—Upland Yuman group)

Yazoo. See **Tunica**.

Yellowknife. Northwest Territories/Great Slave Lake area. See Chipewyan. (Na-Dene phylum—Athapascan family)

Yokuts. Three distinct bands located in central California, especially the San Joaquin Valley and the western foothills of the Sierra Nevada, between the Fresno and Kern rivers. Included the North Foothill group, the South Foothill group, and the Valley group. (Penutian phylum—Yokuts family)

Yuchi. Eastern Tennessee, with some bands in northeastern Georgia. (Macro-Siouan phylum—Yuchi Language Isolate)

Yuki. North-central coastal California along the upper Eel River. (Undetermined phylum—Yuki family)

Yuma. South-central Arizona, along both banks of the Colorado River to the Gila River. (Hokan phylum—Yuman family—Upriver Yuman group)

Yurok. Northwest California coast to the Klamath River. They called themselves Olekwo'l. (Macro-Algonquian phylum—Yurok Language Isolate)

Zia. A pueblo and branch of the Keres, located on the north bank of the Jemez River in central New Mexico. (Undetermined phylum—Keres Language Isolate)

Zuñi. Western New Mexico–eastern Arizona border region. They called themselves Ashiwi. (Penutian phylum—Zuñi Language Isolate)

SOURCES

Dictionary of Indian Tribes of the Americas: I. Newport Banks, Calif.: American Indian
    Publications, Inc., 1980.
Irvine, Keith, ed. *Encyclopedia of Indians of the Americas.* St. Clair Shores, Mich.:
    Scholarly Press, Inc., 1974.
Kehoe, Alice Beck. *North American Indians: A Comprehensive Account.* Englewood
    Cliffs, N.J.: Prentice-Hall, 1992.
Leitch, Barbara A. *A Concise Dictionary of Indian Tribes of North America.* Algonac,
    Mich.: Reference Publications, Inc., 1979.
Nichols, Roger L., ed. *The American Indian, Past and Present.* 3rd ed. New York: Alfred
    A. Knopf, 1986.
Waldman, Carl, and Molly Brown (cartographer). *Atlas of the North American Indian.*
    New York: Facts on File, 1985.

—**David Sisk; L.D.R.**

XI

BUSINESS AND FINANCE

52

WHEN CONSUMER PRODUCTS CAME INTO GENERAL USE

. . . . .

SEVERAL OF THE NOVELISTS WHO WERE QUERIED ABOUT COMPILATIONS THAT they might find especially useful in a writer's companion cited a need to be able to find out when consumer products came into general use in the United States. They could usually discover without undue trouble when something was invented or first patented, but not when the average middle-class consumer might have been able to purchase it at an affordable price. Often a considerable interval elapsed before certain commonly used items reached the general retail market. Safety pins, for example, were being made centuries before they became available commercially at low prices in the 1850s. Cameras were being used in the 1830s, and by the 1870s commercial photographers were active everywhere, but not until the early 1900s did inexpensive snapshot cameras become widely used consumer items.

The impact of technology upon our daily lives has been as pervasive as it has been subtle. We have become so accustomed to the advent of new products that we often fail to take note of their arrival, or to notice the disappearance of other products from store shelves. When, for example, was the last time that most people purchased a bottle of writing ink? How often do most writers use carbon and onionskin paper to make copies any more?

A young person growing up in the mid–1990s would find it difficult to understand that refrigerated soft drinks in aluminum cans became widely available only in the 1960s, or that a business shirt or a pair of trousers that could be left overnight to dry in the bathtub and be ready for use, wrinkle-free, the next day was unknown before World War II.

How many persons remember that in the 1950s anyone purchasing color film to use in a camera did not take the exposed roll to a store for developing and printing? Instead, the buyer of such film received a cloth bag with label attached in the box along with the film, and after taking photographs mailed it off to the manufacturer for processing.

When might someone who wasn't well-fixed financially expect to be able to go into a shop and find an item at an affordable price, or to order it by mail? In many instances the best way to find out was to check through the catalogs of mail-order firms such as Sears, Roebuck and Co. and Montgomery Ward. We also passed out questionnaires to various friends and acquaintances of our own vintage or older (there were not many of the latter available). And there were fascinating books, in particular those by Charles Panati, which, though not concerned primarily with when it was that various things became available in stores, nonetheless frequently offered valuable clues. And of course James Trager's ever-useful *People's Chronology*.

The compilation that follows is an attempt to indicate the specific decade in which the items listed in it can be said to have become *generally accessible* to consumers, at a price that middle-class citizens could afford to pay.

Acetate. Late 1920s.

Adding machines. 1900s.

Aerosol spray cans. 1950s.

Air conditioners, home. 1950s.

Alarm clocks. Wind-up, 1910s; electric, 1920s.

Alka-Seltzer tablets. 1930s.

Aluminum foil. 1950s.

Animal crackers. Mid–1900s.

Antiperspirants. 1970s.

Aspirin tablets. 1920s.

Automobiles. 1900s; enclosed cars, 1920s; station wagons, 1930s; minivans, 1960s; utility vehicles, 1970s; self-starters, mid–1910s; storage batteries, 1910s; generators, 1920s; electric windshield wipers, 1920s; safety glass windshields, 1930s; radiator antifreeze, 1930s; radios, early 1930s; automatic shift transmissions, 1940s; air conditioning, 1960s; alternators, 1960s; cruise control, 1980s.

Baby carriages. 1860s.

Baby foods, in jars. 1930s.

Baby powder. 1890s.

Bakelite products. 1910s.

Bandaids. 1920s.

Barbed wire. 1870s.

Barbie dolls. 1960s.

Baseball cards. Cigarettes, 1900s; chewing gum, 1930s.

Bathtubs, with hot running water. Gas-heated, 1890s; heated by electricity, 1920s.

BB guns. 1900s.

Beer. Bottled, 1900s; canned, 1940s; aluminum cans, 1960s; lite, 1970s.

Bicycles. 1890s; lightweights with caliper brakes and adjustable gears, 1950s; trail bikes, 1980s.

Bifocal eyeglasses. 1820s.

Bikinis. Mid–1940s.

Binoculars. 1900s.

Birth control pills. 1960s.

Blankets, electric. Late 1940s.

Blenders, kitchen. Late 1940s.

Blue jeans. 1870s.

Bobby pins. 1820s.

Bowties, clip-on. 1920s.

Brassieres, elastic. 1920s.

Bread. Sliced, 1920s; packaged, 1930s.

Breakfast food. Packaged, 1890s; pre-cooked, 1900s.

Bridge tables, folding. 1920s.

Brillo pads. Mid–1910s.

Bubble gum. 1920s.

Bumper stickers. Early 1960s.

Button-down collars. 1910s.

BVD's underwear. 1880s.

Cake flour, packaged. 1900s.

Calculators, pocket. Early 1970s.

Cameras. Snapshot, 1900s; 35 mm, 1930s; home movie, 1930s.

Candy confections, packaged. 1920s.

Canned goods. 1860s.

Can openers, wall. 1870s.

Cardboard cartons. 1880s.

Carpet sweepers. 1880s.

Cellophane-wrapped packages. 1920s.

Celluloid products. 1880s.

Cheese, packaged processed. Mid–1910s.

Chewing gum. 1890s.

Chlorine bleach. 1830s.

Cigarette lighters. 1920s.

Cigarettes, factory-made. 1890s.

Citizens Band radios. Mid–1970s.

Cleansers, home, packaged. 1890s.

Clothes, ready-made. 1860s; "wash-and-wear" with synthetic fabrics, 1950s.

Coffee. 1700s; packaged ground, 1930s; instant, 1940s; decaffeinated, 1960s; Sanka, 1930s.

Comic books. Mid–1930s.

Comic strips, newspaper. 1900s.

Computers and word-processors, home. 1970s.

Condensed milk, canned. 1870s.

Condoms, latex. 1930s.

Contact lenses. 1960s.

Corn flakes, packaged. 1910s.

Crackerjack. 1900s.

Credit cards. Gasoline, 1940s; general sales, mid–1950s.

Crossword puzzles. Mid–1910s.

Cough drops, packaged. 1870s.

Detergents, packaged. 1920s; for clothes washing, late 1940s.

Diapers, disposable. 1960s.

Dishwashers, electric. Late 1940s.

Disposals. 1950s.

Dixiecups. 1920s.

Dry cell batteries. 1890s.

Dry cleaning. 1860s.

Dryers, electric clothes. 1950s.

Electric trains, Lionel and American Flyer. Mid–1910s.

Epoxy glues. 1950s.

Erector sets. Mid–1910s.

Ex-Lax. 1910s.

False teeth, porcelain. 1860s.

Fans, electric. 1910s.

Film, color. 1930s; developed and printed locally, 1960s.

Firecrackers. 1860s.

Fishing reels, geared. 1890s.

Flashguns. 1930s.

Flashlights, electric. 1900s.

Flower seeds, packaged. 1880s.

Fluorescent light fixtures. 1940s.

Formica products. Late 1930s.

Frisbees. Late 1950s.

Frozen food. 1940s.

Garden hoses, rubber. 1880s.

Gas lighting fixtures, domestic. 1860s.

Graham crackers. 1810s.

Hair dryers, electric. 1920s.

Harmonicas. 1880s.

Hearing aids, electric. 1930s; ear-sized, 1950s.

Ice cream, ready-made. 1850s; packaged in bulk, 1920s.

Ice cream cones. Late 1910s.

Innerspring mattresses. Early 1900s.

Insect sprays. 1930s; in aerosol cans, 1950s.

Intercoms. 1930s.

Irons, electric. 1910s.

Irons, electric steam. 1940s.

Jell-O. 1910s.

Jigsaw puzzles, interlocking. 1900s.

Jockey shorts. 1930s.

Jogging togs. 1970s.

Kewpie dolls. 1910s.

Kitchen ranges. Wood, 1800s; gas, late 1910s; electric, 1930s.

Kitchen utensils. Iron, eighteenth century; porcelain, 1790s; aluminum, 1890s; teflon, 1960s.

Kleenex. 1920s.

Kotex. 1920s.

Lawnmowers. Hand, 1890s; power, 1940s.

Lego blocks. 1960s.

LifeSaver mints. Mid–1920s.

Light bulbs, electric. 1900s.

Lincoln logs. 1920s.

Linoleum. 1900s.

Listerine mouthwash. 1890s.

Locks, cylinder. 1860s.

Mah-Jongg sets. 1920s.

Margarine. 1910s.

Mason jars. 1870s.

Matches. Kitchen, 1840s; safety, 1860s; paper book, late 1890s.

Mayonnaise, packaged in jars. Mid–1910s.

Milk bottles. Glass, 1910s; in paper cartons, 1950s.

Milk chocolate. 1880s; packaged bars, 1900s.

Milk of magnesia. 1880s; tablets, 1930s.

Mimeograph machines. 1890s.

Monopoly sets. Late 1930s.

Motorcycles. 1910s.

Nylon hose. Late 1940s.

Orange juice, frozen. 1940s.

Organs, electric. 1950s.

Ouija boards. 1910s.

Outboard motors. 1910s.

Ovens. Electric, 1920s; microwave, 1960s.

Paints, ready-mixed. 1880s.

Panama hats. Mid–1910s.

Pancake mixes. Mid–1890s.

Pantyhose. 1950s.

Paperback books. Late 1930s.

Paper bags. 1890s.

Paper drinking cups. 1910s.

Paper towels. 1910s.

Pencils. 1820s; with erasers, 1860s.

Pens. Steel-pointed, 1830s; fountain, late 1880s; cartridge, 1950s; ballpoint, 1950s; felt-tip, 1960s.

Percolators, coffee. 1900s.

Phonograph records. Cylinder, 1890s; wax disk, 1900s; long-playing, late 1940s; compact discs, 1980s.

Phonographs. 1890s; electric, 1920s; stereo, 1950s.

Photocopiers. 1960s; dry paper, 1970s.

Pianos, upright. 1880s.

Picture windows. 1940s.

Pistols, multishot. Revolvers, 1840s; automatics, 1900s.

Pizza. Mixes, 1950s; delivered to homes, 1970s.

Plexiglas. 1930s.

Polyester products. 1940s.

Popcorn, packaged. 1920s.

Popsicles. 1930s.

Postage stamps. 1850s.

Postcards. 1870s; picture, 1890s.

Potato chips, packaged. 1920s.

Power tools. 1930s.

Radiators, steam. 1900s.

Radios. Crystal, 1910s; electric, early 1920s; portables, 1930s; fm, 1950s; transistor, 1960s.

Raincoats, rubberized (macintoshes). 1850s.

Razors. Safety, 1900s; electric, 1930s.

Refrigerators, electric home. 1930s.

Ritz crackers. 1930s.

Road maps. 1910s.

Roller skates, ball-bearing. 1890s.

Safety pins. 1850s.

Saws, electric, portable. 1950s.

Scotch tape. 1930s.

Scrabble sets. 1950s.

Screens, window. Wire, 1900s; plastic, 1970s.

Scuba-diving equipment. 1960s.

Sewing machines. 1840s; electric, 1910s.

Shampoos, liquid. 1920s.

Shaving cream, in aerosol cans. 1950s.

Shirley Temple dolls. Mid–1930s.

Shortening, vegetable, solid. 1910s.

Shotguns, breech-loading. 1840s.

Showers, stall, in homes. 1920s.

Skateboards. Mid–1970s.

Sneakers. Late 1910s.

Soap, floating, packaged. 1870s.

Soft drinks, bottled. 1880s; Hires Root Beer, mid–1880s; Coca-Cola, 1890s; Dr. Pepper, 1890s; Pepsi-Cola, 1900s; Cliquot Club ginger ale, 1920s; Orange Crush, 1920s; Nehi, 1920s; Canada Dry ginger ale, 7-Up, mid–1930s; Royal Crown Cola, 1930s; Tab, mid–1960s.

Spam. Canned, 1940s.

Sports shirts. 1930s.

Stereopticons. 1880s.

Storm windows, aluminum. 1940s.

Stoves and furnaces, heating, residential. Wood, 1820s; coal, 1850s; gas, 1860s; kerosene, 1870s; oil, 1920s; electric, 1910s.

Sunglasses. 1930s; wraparounds, 1960s.

Suntan lotion. 1940s.

Tabasco sauce, bottled. 1870s.

Tampax. 1930s.

Tape recorders. 1950s; cassette, 1960s.

Tea. Early eighteenth century; Pekoe, 1840s; teabags, 1920s.

Teddy bears. 1900s.

Telephones. Late 1870s; one-piece, 1920s; dial, 1930s; punch, 1970s; cordless, 1970s; answering machines, 1970s; cellular, late 1980s; toll-free calls, 1970s.

Television sets. Late 1940s; color, 1960s.

Thermos bottles. Mid–1900s.

Tinkertoys. Mid–1910s.

Toasters, electric. 1910s; pop-up, late 1920s.

Toilet paper, rolls. 1880s.

Toilets, flush. 1890s.

Tomato juice, canned. Mid–1920s.

Toothbrushes. Eighteenth century; nylon, 1940s; electric, 1960s.

Toothpaste tubes. 1900s.

Top hats. 1800s.

TV dinners. 1960s.

Typewriters. 1880s; portable, 1900s; electric, 1950s; electronic, 1970s.

Vacuum cleaners. 1910s.

Valium. 1960s.

Vaseline. 1890s.

VCRs. 1980s.

Vegetable oil, packaged. 1900s.

Velcro. 1970s.

Vinyl products. 1930s.

Waffle iron, electric. 1920s.

Walkie-talkies. 1940s.

Wallpaper. Eighteenth century.

Washing machines, electric. 1930s.

Watches. Inexpensive pocket, 1850s; wrist, 1910s; battery-powered, 1960s; digital display, 1980s.

Waterbeds. 1970s.

Yo-yos. 1920s.

Zippers. 1930s.

SOURCES

Hawke, David Freeman. *Nuts and Bolts of the Past: A History of American Technology, 1776–1860.* New York: Harper and Row, 1989.

Montgomery Ward catalog for 1923.

Panati, Charles. *Extraordinary Origins of Everyday Things.* New York: Harper and Row, 1987.

———. *Panati's Browser's Book of Beginnings.* Boston: Houghton Mifflin Co., 1984.

———. *Panati's Parade of Fads, Follies and Manias.* New York: Harper-Perennial, 1991.

Robinson, Patrick. *The Book of Firsts.* New York: Clarkson N. Potter, 1974.

Sears, Roebuck and Co. catalogs for 1897, 1898, 1900, 1909, 1928–29, 1936–37, 1947–48, 1951–52, 1957–58, 1961, 1967, 1972, 1975–76.

Trager, James, ed. *The People's Chronology: A Year-by-Year Record of Human Events From Prehistory to the Present.* New York: Holt, Rinehart and Winston, 1979.

—**L.D.R.**

53

ECONOMIC AND FINANCIAL TERMS: A GLOSSARY

. . . . .

MOST WRITERS ARE NOT VERY GOOD BUSINESSMEN OR BUSINESSWOMEN. (There are exceptions.) Elsewhere in this compendium is a listing of the occupations of a number of American, British, and Irish authors. Since very few good writers can earn a livelihood from their writings alone, they have had to do various kinds of work. What is surprising is how very few authors have engaged in business. Indeed, they would seem to have tried almost everything else *except* business. President Calvin Coolidge declared that "the business of America is business," and Napoleon Bonaparte once described the English as a "nation of shopkeepers." If Coolidge and Napoleon were right, then most English-language writers would appear to be averse to dealing with the principal kind of activity going on around them, for their writings tend to mirror Napoleon's attitude toward business. How many good novels are there about businessmen? *Buddenbrooks, The Rise of Silas Lapham*—the trouble is that in fiction the measure of a businessman's sensibility appears to be his liability for failure, which doesn't seem fair.

Life magazine, back before it fell victim to its advertisers' preference for television, once lamented the fact that American authors failed to write about the positive side of the national experience, including business. *Life* complained that our nation was "producing a literature which sounds sometimes as if it were written by an unemployed homosexual living in a packing-box shanty on the city dump while awaiting admission to the county poorhouse." Tsch tsch.

However reluctantly, writers do have to deal with business and business people in their daily lives, if not in their writings. After all, *publishers* are business people; and a good thing that they are, too, for if not they soon cease to be publishers. (What our literature badly needs are publishers who are not *just* businessmen; there are all too few such.)

To aid writers in their dealings with the business-minded world around them, we have compiled a glossary of some of the more commonly used economic and financial terms.

Acceleration principle. Theory that there is a direct relationship between the level of investment and the rate of change of output, because investment must increase to meet increased demands for goods or services and must decrease if there is a decline in demand.

Acquisition. Purchase of one company by another.

Ad valorem. Latin for "according to value"; calculated as a percentage of the total value of goods rather than the goods' quantity when determining tax, duty, charge, commission, etc., due.

American Stock Exchange. Second largest organization that provides a marketplace for buying and selling stocks, bonds, and other securities; located in New York City.

Amortization. Payment of debt in installments, usually in the means of a sinking fund, reducing the principal of the debt.

Antidumping duty. Import tariff intended to raise the domestic price of a product that has been exported by another country at an "unjustifiably low" price.

Applied economics. Branch of economics that deals with translating theories and principles into action.

Appreciation. The increase in the value of an item.

Asset. Anything owned by an individual or company and that has a monetary value.

Balanced budget. Budget for which receipts equal current expenditures.

Balance of payments. Difference between all payments to and from foreign countries over a period of time; payments include visible trade (trade in tangible goods and merchandise) and invisible trade (tourist expenditures, transportation, insurance, and other services), repayment of principal on loans, and interest and dividend payments; a favorable balance exists when more payments are received than are going out, and an unfavorable balance is the reverse situation.

Balance of trade. Difference between exports and imports in both actual funds and credits; a trade surplus, or a favorable balance, exists when exports are greater than imports, and a trade deficit denotes an unfavorable balance, *i.e.*, when imports exceed exports.

Bankruptcy. Formal declaration by a court that an individual is unable to pay his debts and is thus insolvent.

Bearer bonds. Bonds in which ownership is determined by possession and are thus transferred in ownership without change of registration.

Bear market. A stock market in which prices are falling.

Bilateral trade agreements. Trade agreements between two countries, regarded as being disruptive to world trade as a whole; multilateral agreements have been promoted to replace bilateral trade agreements.

Black economy. Economic activity that is unrecorded in national statistics of income because payment is made in cash and is not declared for income tax; believed to constitute a large portion of the gross national product in economies of high unemployment and economic hardship.

Bond. Security issued by a government, government agency, or private corporation as a means of raising money; most usually have a fixed interest rate payable at semiannual or some other intervals.

Bretton Woods. Conference in June 1944, attended by forty-four nations in Bretton Woods, New Hampshire, to plan reconstruction after the end of World War II; out of this conference came the International Monetary Fund and the International Bank for Reconstruction and Development.

Broker. Agent employed by a client (principal) to buy and/or sell goods or services in securities, commodities, etc., for the principal's account; this person usually possesses specialized knowledge of his market and receives a commission for his services.

Brokerage fee. Fee charged to the client by a broker for buying or selling goods or services under the client's orders in securities, commodities, insurance, etc.

Bullion. Gold and silver in the form of bars; also, large quantities of coins by weight.

Bull market. Stock market in which prices are rising.

Buyer's market. Market economy in which supply is greater than demand, so buyers can dictate prices to a certain extent.

Capital. One of the basic components of an economy and includes everything that is manufactured for the purpose of helping man to increase and become more efficient in production; includes machinery, roads, buildings, etc.; also known as *capital goods.*

Capital gains. Income resulting from sale of a capital asset for a price higher than that originally paid.

Capitalism. Economic system characterized by private ownership of property and the means of production, minimum government involvement, and the freedom of choice of consumers who, in essence, determine production.

Centrally planned or command economy. Economy in which central authorities make basic economic decisions such as what and how many items should be produced, prices of goods and services, etc., in the interest of overall economic growth as opposed to allowing the market to decide; opposite of capitalism.

Certificate of deposit (CD). A deposit that cannot be withdrawn before a certain date, usually available for purchase from savings and commercial banks.

Chronic deficit. Reoccurrence of a negative balance of payments several consecutive years with no improvement in the foreseeable future.

Circular flow of money. Flow of income from households to businesses through spending on goods and services and from businesses into factors of production to continue to produce the resources.

Collateral. Property or item of value used to obtain a loan; can be sold by the lender in the event of default on the loan by the borrower.

Commodity. A tangible good that can be transported; in commerce, a commodity is more specifically a raw material (sugar, coffee, grain, rubber, tea, metals, jute, sisal, etc.).

Commodity exchange. Market dealing with transactions of commodities, usually with both a spot market for actual physical exchange and a futures market; the futures market is an attempt to achieve some form of price stabilization over the fluctuations of supply and demand (see **Futures markets**).

Commodity Exchange Authority. U.S. organization responsible for controlling the transactions of commodities, licensing brokers, and regulating special trades.

Common stock. Stock, ownership shares of a corporation, that carries voting privileges but does not include any promise regarding payment of dividends; compare with Preferred stock.

Conglomerate. Business enterprise that exists in several unrelated markets.

Consolidation. Joining of two or more corporations, resulting in a new organization.

Constant dollars. Statistical measure determined by dividing current dollars by an appropriate price index to demonstrate how the dollar would have been valued with a constant purchasing power.

Consumer price index (CPI). Statistical measure of the change in prices of goods and services bought by consumers, or wage earners; covers the change in price of everything except income and personal property taxes and is used in labor management to adjust wages.

Consumption. Using up of goods and services by the consumer.

Convertible bond. Corporate bond that may be converted into a stated number of shares of common stock.

Corporation. Group or body of persons recognized as an individual entity with its own rights, privileges, and liabilities that are separate from those of its members.

Cost of living. Cost of maintaining a standard of living measured in terms of purchased goods and services; also a good indicator of the rate of inflation.

Credit crunch. Situation whereby cash for lending to businesses and individuals is in short supply.

Debenture. Long-term debt obligation that is secured only by the credit of the issuing corporation.

Debt. Obligation, usually money, owed by debtor to a creditor.

Deficit spending. Practice whereby a government goes into debt in order to finance some of its expenditures; also known as *deficit financing.*

Deflation. Decline in prices in both the product and resource markets owing to the decrease in economic activity of a nation.

Demand curve. Curve relating the amount of the good a consumer will buy along with the maximum price he is willing to pay.

Depression. Long period of economic decline characterized by low prices, high unemployment, lack of confidence, and numerous business failures.

Devaluation. Official lowering of a nation's currency that reduces the value of the currency in relation to other nations' currencies.

Discount rate. Rate of interest charged to member banks by the Federal Reserve when they borrow money through the federal reserve system.

Disposable income. After-tax income available to individuals for spending and savings.

Dividend. Payment to shareholders by a corporation, usually in the form of stock shares, cash, or other property.

Dow-Jones Industrial Average. Measure of stock market prices, based on thirty leading companies on the New York Stock Exchange.

Dumping. Flooding of a market (usually the international market) with a large amount of a certain product at an unjustifiably low price.

Durable goods. Goods intended for use over a relatively long period of time.

Economic growth. Expansion of a nation's economic output, hence increasing its national income.

Economic sanctions. Embargoes on the export of goods, services, and capital to a particular nation.

Economy of scale. The decline in the average cost of production as output increases.

Elastic demand. Demand schedule that illustrates the inverse relationship of price to demand; a relatively small increase (decrease) in price will cause a large decrease (increase) in demand.

Eurodollar. Name for international currency; a deposit made in dollars that is placed in a bank outside of the United States and is effectively beyond the control of any public monetary authority.

European Economic Community (EEC). Largest regional trade bloc in the world, founded in 1957 to promote free economic activity and remove restrictions on trade, labor, and capital among its members.

Exchange rate. Price of a currency in the foreign exchange market, *i.e.*, the rate at which one currency can be exchanged for another.

Excise tax. Tax on the sale or manufacture of a specified product, usually reflected in higher prices for the product and thus passed along to the ultimate buyer.

Federal Deposit Insurance Corporation (FDIC). Government-sponsored organization that insures accounts of depositors in national banks and other qualifying institutions.

Federal Reserve Board. Officially known as Board of Governors of the Federal Reserve System; a U.S. agency that formulates national monetary policy and regulates banking operations.

Federal reserve notes. Form in which all paper currency is issued by the United States.

Federal reserve system. The entire banking system of the United States that regulates the flow of money and credit and sets monetary policy with four specific objectives: to achieve a high level of employment; to provide stability in overall price levels; to promote economic growth; to maintain a sound balance of payments in the international arena.

Federal Trade Commission. U.S. government agency that enforces laws related to competition in business activities.

Franchise. Arrangement, usually in retail trade, whereby a license is issued allowing a product with an established trade name or service to be marketed and manufactured by another person.

Free trade. International trade free of tariffs or quotas on imports by individual countries.

Full employment. Condition in an economy whereby everyone who wishes to work at the going wage rate is employed, with only fractional unemployment existing.

Fungible. Exchangeable; product for which one quantity may be exchanged for another, as with money, wheat, salt, etc.; an oil painting or a particular musical composition, by contrast, would not be fungible.

Futures markets. Markets in which consumers and dealers of commodities can buy and sell for future delivery; the futures markets allow for hedging, or protecting from price variations in which individuals have no control, as well as allow for speculation, therefore helping to reduce the effects of fluctuations that result from gluts and shortages of raw materials.

General Agreement on Tariffs and Trade (GATT). International organization of over eighty nations that serves as a center for multilateral negotiation on tariffs and trade among member states; accounts for over 80 percent of world trade.

Government bonds. Bonds issued by the U.S. Treasury as a form of I.O.U. and consisting of the following types: savings bonds, treasury bills, treasury notes, and treasury bonds; all have different conditions surrounding the purchase and selling of the bonds.

Gross domestic product (GDP). Market value of all goods and services produced in the economy during a year within the nation's borders; the official measure of the U.S. economy.

Gross national product (GNP). Total sales value of all goods (consumer and investment) and services produced in a year, as determined from national income and product accounts, covering all American residents regardless of location.

Hidden tax. Tax included in the price of a product.

Holding company. Company that exerts management control over another company or companies.

Horizontal integration. Situation whereby a company has control of an industry or a good in a particular stage of production.

Hostile takeover. Acquisition of the control of a corporation achieved despite the opposition of the former management.

Hyperinflation. Extremely high rate of inflation, lasting usually only several months but bringing with it economic collapse and social disorder.

Income tax. A tax whose amount is a function of the taxpayer's income.

Individual retirement account (IRA). Self-funded retirement plan that allows employees to put a portion of annual income into a special fund; the interest earned on the money set aside is tax deferred.

Industrial sector. Portion of the economy consisting of privately owned enterprises.

Inflation. Decrease in purchasing power of a nation's money, and within the nation, an increase in the average level of prices over a period of time.

Insider information. Important facts about a company that have not been released to the general public.

Insolvency. Inability of an individual or a company to pay debts as they become due; not the same thing as bankruptcy but can lead to it.

Intangible assets. Things that are valuable to a company but cannot be measured in physical terms, *e.g.*, goodwill or intellectual property, such as a patent or trademark.

Interest. Money paid by a borrower for use of the lender's money, of two types: simple interest is interest calculated upon the principal sum, while compound interest includes interest calculated on the principal along with any interest due at the due date of the outstanding loan.

International Monetary Fund (IMF). Fund established by the United Nations in 1947 as a result of the Bretton Woods conference to help stabilize exchange rates, expand world trade by breaking down trade barriers, and make funds available to lesser-developed countries.

Investment. Spending or purchasing of capital goods.

Investment Tax Credit. Provision of income tax that allows companies to receive a tax credit for a percentage of total expenditures for capital goods.

Junk bonds. High-yield, high-risk securities that sell at relatively low prices.

Key leading indicators (leading economic indicators). Eleven indicators from different areas of the U.S. economy used by the Commerce Department to predict the future of the economy.

Lesser developed country (LDC). Country unable to generate savings and investment in further industrialization; usually characterized by an economy based on goods produced by a large supply of low-wage labor, or dependent on a single product.

Leveraged buy-out. Acquisition of a company characterized by a high degree of debt financing in the purchase.

Limited partnership. Type of partnership wherein each partner's maximum risk is equal to his total investment in the venture (see **Partnership**).

Liquid assets. Items that can be converted to money quickly with very little or no loss in value.

Merger. Fusion of two or more corporations whereby operations of individual companies no longer exist and a new corporation is created.

Monopoly. Market situation in which there is only one producer for many consumers.

Monopsony. Market situation in which there is only one buyer but many producers.

Multinational. Firm or company with operations in several countries.

New York Stock Exchange (NYSE). Largest organization in the United States providing a marketplace for buying and selling of securities; located in New York City.

North American Free Trade Agreement (NAFTA). Agreement that forms the largest regional common market in the world, linking North, Central, and South America in trade.

Oligopoly. Industry consisting of a small number of large-scale suppliers, thus decreasing competition.

Partnership. Business association that is bound together by an agreement of two or more individuals, each of whom assumes full liability for all debts.

Per capita income. Nation's total income divided by the number of people in the nation.

Preferred stock. Stock that does not have voting privileges but guarantees payments of regular dividends by the corporation.

Prime interest rate. Rate charged by banks on loans to customers with highest credit ratings.

Producer price index. Statistic that measures the change in the price of wholesale goods; reported for three stages of production: crude, intermediate, and finished goods.

Progressive tax. A form of taxation whose rate increases with increased income (see **Regressive tax**).

Public debt. Total of the nation's debts owed by all levels of government combined.

Rate of return. Earnings as a percentage of investment from an enterprise.

Recession. Mild decrease in economic activity characterized by a decline in real gross national product (*i.e.*, measured in constant dollars rather than current dollars), employment, and trade.

Reciprocity. Agreement between nations to reduce import tariffs.

Regressive tax. A form of taxation whose average rate declines as income increases (see **Progressive tax**).

Seasonal adjustments. Changes made in data to allow comparison between identical periods in a cycle in order to present a more accurate projection of long-term economic trends, *e.g.*, taking into account the increase in farm income following summer harvest or the increase in consumer spending during the holiday season.

Securities and Exchange Commission (SEC). Organization that regulates security transactions within the various exchange systems in the United States.

Security. (1) Generic term for stocks, bonds, or other documents used as collateral for a loan by a borrower; (2) income-yielding instrument that may be traded on a recognized exchange system.

Seller's market. Market situation whereby demand is greater than supply; thus sellers can, in essence, dictate prices.

Shareholder. An owner of a corporation, control of which is based on the percentage of shares or stocks owned.

Sole proprietorship. Business owned by one person.

Stagflation. Combination of stagnation with rising unemployment and inflation.

Stagnation. Period of economic slowdown in which there is little growth in gross domestic product, capital investment, and real income.

Stock option. A plan whereby an individual is given the right to purchase a given number of shares of a corporation at a fixed price per share.

Subsidy. Economic assistance by the federal government given to a particular firm or industry in the private sector to ensure its international economic competitiveness.

Supply and demand, laws of. Laws stating that if demand for a product increases, the price will rise, and if the demand decreases, the price will fall; accordingly, if the supply of a product exceeds its demand, the price will fall, and vice versa.

Takeover. The acquisition of the control of one company by another company or group by sale or merger.

Tariff. Tax applied by the federal government to imports based upon their value or upon some other rate.

Tender offer. Public offer to purchase a company's stock at a price above the current market value.

Trade barrier. Any government measure that hinders free trade.

Underemployment. Employment situation in which workers' skills are not fully utilized or the number of hours are not sufficient to satisfy them.

Underwriter. Middleman who issues securities of a company to the public in return for a commission.

Unearned income. Income earned from capital investment, such as dividend from stocks or increase in property value of land.

Venture capital. Capital invested in an asset or a venture possessing a certain degree of risk.

Vertical integration. Situation whereby one company controls the manufacture of a good in successive stages of production from start to finish.

Wasting asset. Something that decreases in value over a period of time; more specifically, often used in reference to natural resources that have been removed from nature, reducing the original land value where they were taken.

Welfare state. A nation that provides goods and services to its residents at public expense.

Windfall profit. Profit that comes from an unforeseen event.

SOURCES

"Economic and Financial Glossary." *World Almanac and Book of Facts, 1994.* New York: Pharos Books, 1994.

Heilbroner, Robert L., and Lester C. Thurow. *Economics Explained.* New York: Simon and Schuster, 1987.

Moffat, Donald W. *Economics Dictionary.* New York: Elsevier, 1976.

Stiegler, S. E. *Dictionary of Economics and Business.* 2nd ed. Hants, Eng.: Market House Books, Ltd., 1976.

—**Jesma Reynolds; L.D.R.**

XII

THE ANIMAL
KINGDOM

54

DISTINGUISHED DOGS,
EMINENT CATS,
AND NOTABLE HORSES

. _ . . . .

IN MY QUARTER-CENTURY-OLD EDITION OF *BARTLETT'S FAMILIAR QUOTATIONS* there are 102 references to dogs, as compared with 99 to horses and only 52 for cats. Since until quite recently the horse has been far more important to civilization than the dog, this important statistical fact can only be said to show that people are less interested in what is important than in what is companionable and affectionate. However, the comparison may merely indicate that many more writers have been personally acquainted with dogs than with horses. As for cats, well—no statistic or theory can properly account for cats.

The aptitude of dogs for getting along with people has been ascribed to the fact that in the wild state they traveled in packs. The notion of hierarchy was clearly established, and it was comparatively easy for a dog to transfer its allegiance and affection from the *alpha* pack dog to a human master. Whatever the explanation, canine ties with humans go far back into prehistory; dogs were undoubtedly the first animal to have been domesticated. A rough drawing of a dog appears in a cave painting believed to be at least 50,000 years old, although there is some question as to whether it was a dog or a wolf, from which dogs are thought to have descended.

Dogs were originally domesticated because of the assistance they could render in hunting, and they have also been put to other uses, but their principal virtue is that they are good company. This of course varies from individual dog to individual dog, but on balance they have done quite well. Given the interrelationship of dogs and people, it is not surprising that dogs have figured in myth and legend from early times onward, and that they have been written about often and at considerable length.

As contrasted with dogs (which they often are), cats have established relationships with humans fairly recently. The first cats to take up with people did so about 3000 B.C.E., when the Egyptians tamed a variety of the African wild cat in order to police the mice in their granaries. This the cats were quite willing to do, since they would have done it anyway. In the 5,000 years or so since that time, no cat has shown the slightest willingness to help out in any other way, except perhaps to guard temples in Siam.

Persons who prefer cats to dogs say that dogs are fawning; those who prefer dogs say that cats are stupid. It is undeniable that, not having a pack heritage, cats are by nature independent-minded (if the word *mind* may be applied to a cat). Their ways of doing things have earned the affection of cat lovers, including writers, for several millennia. Whether it is possible to generalize about the personalities of writers in terms of their preference for cats or dogs is dubious; Edgar Allan Poe, Mark Twain, Samuel Johnson, and T. S. Eliot, for example, were cat owners, while William Faulkner, William Wordsworth, Lord Byron, and Sir Walter Scott were dog owners—as also was Henry Adams, when surely one would have expected a cat.

There seem to have been *fewer* cats than dogs written about by name. On the other hand, the Egyptians considered the cat to be a god, while dogs have never been accorded divine rank on their own, though at the Festival of Diana they were crowned, and several were named for gods.

Be that as it may, there can be no question that the most important animal in history has been the horse; after all, nobody is ever known to have cried, "My kingdom for a dog!" In the words of the *Encyclopedia Britannica,* "all the great early civilizations were the products of horse-owning, horse-breeding and horse-using nations . . . and those in which the horse was either unknown or in the feral state remained longest sunk in savagery." When we consider that from the dawn of history until almost within the time of people still alive, other than shank's mare the horse was the principal means of travel on land, the chief element of mobility in warfare, and the most important beast of burden in agriculture, some idea of the magnitude of the changes that our own century has undergone can be comprehended. Today the horse is principally to be seen at race tracks, on riding paths, and hauling tourists around colonial districts; barely a century ago existence in human society was next to inconceivable without its presence.

It has been omnipresent in literature. The oldest passage in the Bible, the "Song of Moses" in the Book of Exodus, which goes back to the twelfth century B.C.E., contains the lines "I will sing unto the Lord, for he has triumphed gloriously: The Horse and his rider hath he thrown into the sea." An interesting search would be to find a novel written before, say, 1900, in which there was no trace of horses of any kind whatever. (Even in the tiny Boston settlement in Hawthorne's *Scarlet Letter,* where everybody walks, there is a blacksmith present.)

What, however, will be the horse's future place, whether in literature or life? William Faulkner, facing the economic extinction of the horse, was sure that it would survive, because "what the horse supplies to man is something deep and profound in his emotional nature and need." He wrote that encomium in a magazine article on the Kentucky Derby, and it may well be that the horse's best hopes for continued notice rest with the $2 window.

Herewith are the names of some better-known dogs, cats, and horses.

Dogs

Aibe. Famous Irish hunting wolfhound for which King Connaught offered 6,000 cows.

Alce, Aello, Agre, Agrodius, Asbolus, Canace, Cyprias, Dorcas, Harpalus, Harpyia, Hylactor, Hylæus, Ichnobates, Lachne, Lacon, Lælap, Leocon, Lodon, Lysisce, Melampus, Nape, Nebrophonous, Oribasus, Pamphagus, Pœmenis, Pterelas, Sticte, Theron, Tigrus, Thous. The hounds of Actæon, as listed by Ovid.

Andrew Jackson. Dog in Mark Twain's "The Celebrated Jumping Frog of Calaveras County."

Anubis. Companion of the god Thoth in Egyptian myth.

Arctophonos and Ptoophagos. Orion's dogs.

Argus. Ulysses' dog in *The Odyssey.*

Asta. Mr. and Mrs. Charles' dog in the Thin Man detective series.

Athos. Leopold Bloom's father's dog in James Joyce's *Ulysses.*

Ball. Henry VIII's dog.

Bally Shannon. Irish wolfhound that won fame as the Red Cross dog in World War I.

Balthasar. Young Jolyon's dog in John Galsworthy's *A Forsyte Saga.*

Balto. Eskimo dog that led a dog team with diphtheria serum 600 miles through a blizzard from Nemani to Nome, Alaska, in 1925.

Barry. St. Bernard dog that rescued 40 persons lost in snow, *ca.* 1800.

Baskervilles, Hound of the. Dread mastiff in Arthur Conan Doyle's novel of that name.

Baudelaire. Christian Gauss' mongrel dog.

Bauschen. Short-haired "deutscher hühnerhund" in Thomas Mann's *Herr und Hund.*

Beau. William Cowper's dog.

Beaumont. Greyhound of Charles IX of France.

Beauregard Bugleboy. Noble hound of Walt Kelly's "Pogo" comic strip.

Beautiful Joe. Dog in Marshall Saunders' novel of that name.

Becerillo. "Friendly dog" given to Charlemagne by Haroun al-Raschid.

Bevis. Sir Henry Lee's greyhound in Walter Scott's *Woodstock.*

Big Red. Dog in Kim Kjelgaard's novel of that name.

Bijou. Mary Stuart's dog.

Bingo. Dog in American and English folk song.

Black Dog. Ernest Hemingway's dog.

Blondi. Adolf Hitler's dog.

Blue, or Old Blue. Dog in American folk song.

Blue Bell. Dog in English nursery rhyme.

Boatswain. Lord Byron's dog.

Bob. Dog in Lee Smith's story "Bob: A Dog."

Bob, Son of Battle. Dog in Alfred Ollivant's novel by that name.

Boojum and Polliwog. Henry and Clover Adams' Skye terriers.

Boru. Irish wolfhound in the novel by J. Allan Dunn.

Bounce. Alexander Pope's Danish dog.

Boy. Prince Rupert of Hentzau's white dog that died at Marston Moor.

Bran. Fingal's dog in Gaelic mythology.

Brumus. Robert Kennedy's dog.

Bruno. Dog in the Disney movie *Cinderella*.

Brutus. Sir Edwin Landseer's greyhound.

Buck. Dog that leads wolves in Jack London's *The Call of the Wild*.

Buddy. German shepherd, first seeing eye dog, 1928.

Bugle Ann. Hound dog in Mackinlay Kantor's novel *The Voice of Bugle Ann*.

Bullseye. Bill Sykes' dog in Dickens' *Oliver Twist*.

Caesar. King Edward VII's terrier; bulldog that was set upon Jack in Marryat's *Midshipman Easy*.

Camp. Walter Scott's favorite terrier.

Carlo and Pilot. Dogs in Charlotte Bronte's *Jane Eyre*.

Cavall. King Arthur's favorite hound.

Cerberus. Three-headed dog guarding the gates of the underworld in Greek myth.

Charlie. Poodle companion of John Steinbeck in *Travels with Charlie*.

Checkers. Cocker spaniel that Republican vice-presidential candidate Richard Nixon declined to return to its donor during Eisenhower's 1952 presidential campaign.

Chips. Collie-shepherd wardog with U.S. Seventh Army in Europe in World War II.

Chopper. Pluck the Butcher's dog in George Farquhar's *The Recruiting Officer*.

Chowder. Tabitha Bramble's cur in Smollett's *Humphry Clinker*.

Chriss. John Galsworthy's black cocker spaniel.

Countess, Jupiter, Juno, Mopsey, Music, Rover, Singer, Sweetlips, Lady, and Truelove. George Washington's hounds.

Crab. Launce's dog in Shakespeare's *Two Gentlemen of Verona*.

Cromwell. Ford Madox Ford's dog.

Daisy. Dagwood and Blondie Bumstead's dog in the comic strip.

Dash. First Thomas Hood's, then Charles Lamb's dog.

Diamond. Sir Isaac Newton's dog.

Dido. Edith Sitwell's dog.

Diogenes. Very nice dog in Charles Dickens' *Dombey and Son.*

Dragon. Dog belonging to Aubry of Montdidier whose hostility to his master's murderer, Richard of Macaire, caused Richard to undergo trial by combat with the dog in 1371; Dragon won, and Richard confessed all.

Dugdale. Anti-Indian dog in William Gilmore Simms's *The Yemassee.*

Escamillo. Joseph Conrad's dog.

Fag and Monk. Dogs in George Eliot's *Middlemarch.*

Fala. President Franklin Delano Roosevelt's Scottie.

Falcon. Dog of sixteenth-century Italian scholar Agostino Nifo.

Fido. Maggie's dog in George McManus' comic strip, "Bringing Up Father."

Fleet. General George C. Marshall's dog.

Flush. Elizabeth Barrett Browning's dog.

Fossil. Gattling-Fenn's dog in Stephen Potter's *Oneupmanship.*

Gargittios and Two-Headed Orthos. Dogs slain by Hercules.

Garm. Bull terrier in Rudyard Kipling's story "Garm—A Hostage."

Garryowen. Dog accompanying the Citizen in James Joyce's *Ulysses.*

Geist and Kaiser. Matthew Arnold's dachshunds.

Gelert. Llewellyn's great hound in Welsh folklore.

Ginger Pye. Dog in Eleanor Estes' Pye family series.

Grayfriars Bobby. Terrier that watched over its master's grave in Grayfriar's kirkyard, Edinburgh, from 1851 to 1872.

Grzmilas. Dog named for the Polish thunder god, as reported by Jacob Grimm.

Gyges. Alec Maury's dog in Caroline Gordon's *Alex Maury, Sportsman.*

Hamlet. Sir Walter Scott's black greyhound.

Hector. Natty Bumppo's dog in James Fenimore Cooper's *The Pioneers* and *The Prairie.*

Hiidi. Dog belonging to the legendary Finnish giant Kiidin Kissar.

Him and Her. Lyndon Johnson's beagles.

Hodain (or Leon). Tristram's dog.

Hrmiles. Dog named for the Bohemian thunder god, as reported by Jacob Grimm.

Iasa. Maltese dog of the first century, celebrated by the poet Martial.

Igloo. Rear Adm. Richard Evelyn Byrd's fox terrier, which accompanied him on polar flights.

Jack. Dog in Virginia folk song.

Jane. Lord Birkinhead's cairn terrier.

Jed. P. G. Wodehouse's dachshund.

Jip. Doctor Doolittle's dog friend in the stories by Hugh Lofting; Dora's dog in Dickens' *David Copperfield.*

Juneau. Sleigh dog in the novel by West Lathrop.

Juno, Skulker, and Throttler. Dogs in Emily Bronte's *Wuthering Heights.*

Katmir. Dog of the *Seven Sleepers of Ephesus.*

Kazan. Dog in James Oliver Curwood's *Kazan, the Wolf Dog.*

Lady and Tramp. Dogs in the Walt Disney movie *Lady and the Tramp.*

Laelaps. Hound that Zeus turned into stone, along with a fox, because one was fated to catch whatever it pursued, the other to elude its pursuer.

Laska. First dog sent into space, aboard a Russian rocket in 1957; likewise the first canine space fatality.

Lassie. Collie in Eric Knight's story; also the star of the television series.

Linda, Turk, and Sultan. Charles Dickens' dogs.

Lion. Dog in William Faulkner's "The Bear."

Luath. Cuchulain's hound in Irish mythology; Robert Burns's dog; Sheila Burnford's dog in *The Incredible Journey.*

Lufra. Douglas' hound in Walter Scott's *The Lady of the Lake.*

Lupetto. Stendhal's café au lait–colored dog.

Lycas. Female hunting dog, subject of an epitaph attributed to Simonides.

Maida. Sir Walter Scott's favorite deerhound.

Malapaca. Adm. Chester Nimitz' schnauzer.

Marco. Queen Victoria's Pomeranian.

Margarita. Hunting dog to which its Roman owners erected a tombstone (now in the British Museum).

Marquis. Henry Adams' dog.

Mathe. Richard II's greyhound, which abandoned him for Henry of Lancaster.

Mauthe dog. Ghostly spaniel that haunted Peel Castle on the Isle of Man.

Millie. Barbara Bush's White House dog.

Mr. Gooser. John Dos Passos' poodle.

Mœra. Icarius' dog in Greek myth; became the star Procyon.

Monsieur. Dog of Agrippa von Nettesheim.

Montmorency. Jerome K. Jerome's dog.

Muggs. James Thurber's dog that bit people.

Music. William Wordsworth's dog.

Mustard and Pepper. Terriers of Dandy Dinmont in Walter Scott's *Guy Mannering.*

Nana. Dog in James M. Barrie's *Peter Pan.*

Nipper. Anthony Eden's dog.

Old Bob. Ty Cobb's dog.

Old Drum. Foxhound eulogized in Senator George Vest's famous tribute to "man's best friend" during a Missouri trial in 1870.

Old Napper and Old Trailer. Dogs in Mississippi folk songs, as collected by Arthur Palmer Hudson.

Paddy. Harold Wilson's dog.

Peritas. Dog owned by Alexander the Great, who supposedly named a city after it.

Perun. Dog named for the Slavic thunder god, as reported by Jacob Grimm.

Pete. William Faulkner's pointer.

Phil. David Garrick's spaniel.

Phoebe. Lapdog of Catherine de Medici.

Pinkerton. Great Dane of Stephen Kellogg's series of Pinkerton stories.

Pluto. Mickey Mouse's dog (also known as Dippy and Goofy).

Pomero and Giallo. Dogs owned by Walter Savage Landor.

Ponto. Jerry Melford's drowned Oxford dog in Smollett's *Humphry Clinker*.

Presto. Hester Thrale's dog.

Punch. Dante Gabriel Rossetti's Pomeranian.

Quoodle. G. K. Chesterton's dog.

Rab. Mastiff in John Brown's *Rab and His Friends*.

Rin-Tin-Tin. German police dog star of 1920s movies.

Robber. Richard Wagner's Newfoundland.

Rockwood, Jowler, Ringwood, Thunder, Plunder, Wonder, Blunder, and Fairmaid. Pack of dogs attacking Parson Adams in Henry Fielding's *Joseph Andrews*.

Roswal. Sir Kenneth's hound in Walter Scott's *The Talisman*.

Rover. Dog owned by Sir Walter Scott.

Rufus. Winston Churchill's poodle.

Sandy. Little Orphan Annie's dog in the comic strip.

Scamp. U.S. Army World War II shepherd wardog.

Semiramis. Osbert Sitwell's mastiff.

Shock. Belinda's lapdog in Alexander Pope's *The Rape of the Lock*.

Silver Chief. Hero of Jack O'Brien's *Silver Chief, Dog of the North*.

Sirius. Dog-star in Greek myth.

Skean. Charles A. Lindbergh's dog.

Snoopy. Charlie Brown's beagle in Charles Schulz's comic strip.

Sponge and Flannel. Stephen Crane's dogs.

Stickeen. Little black dog accompanying John Muir on his wilderness trips.

Stubby. Heroic half-terrier, half-boxer wardog of World War II.

Tang. Francis Starwick's dog in Thomas Wolfe's *Of Time and the River*.

Tartar. Part-mastiff, part-bulldog in Charlotte Bronte's *Shirley*.

Telek. Gen. Dwight D. Eisenhower's Scottie.

Theron. Roderick the Goth's dog.

Thuner. Dog named for the thunder god, as reported by Jacob Grimm.

Tige. Buster Brown's dog in the early comic strip.

Tiger. Arthur Gordon Pym's dog in Poe's *Arthur Gordon Pym*.

Toby. Dog of Punch in traditional Punch and Judy shows.

Tonton. Spaniel given to Horace Walpole by Mme. du Deffand.

Toto. Dorothy's dog in Frank Baum's *Wizard of Oz*.

Tracy. Dog in Robert Herrick's poem "Upon His Spaniel Tracy."

Tray. Ever-faithful dog of Stephen Foster's song.

Tray, Blanche, and Sweetheart. Dogs in Shakespeare's *King Lear*.

Troy. Leslie Stephen's dog.

Trump. Painter William Hogarth's dog, depicted in his paintings.

White Fang. Half-dog, half-wolf of Jack London's story.

Willie. Gen. George Patton's bull terrier.

Wolf. Rip Van Winkle's dog in Washington Irving's story.

Zemire. Catherine the Great's greyhound.

Cats

Agrippina. Agnes Repplier's cat.

Atossa and Buchanan. Edmund Gosse's cats.

Bast. Cat-headed goddess of Egyptian mythology.

Bates, Blindy, Boissy d'Anglais (Boise), Dillinger, Friendless, Friendless's Brother, Good Will, Dillinger, Pony, and Tester. Ernest Hemingway's cats at the Finca Vigia.

Bill the Cat. Deranged cat in "Bloom County" comic strip.

Black Annie. Cat demon of the Dane Hills, Lincolnshire.

Blackmalken, Greymalkin, and Nibbins. Cats (and witch's familiars) in John Masefield's *Midnight Folk*.

Brer Puss. Cat of Caribbean folklore.

Calvin. Charles Dudley Warner's cat.

Caterina. Edgar Allan Poe's cat.

Cat in the Hat. Dr. Seuss's cartoon cat.

Cecus Becus Berneusz. Cat of Hungarian folklore.

Chapalu. Monster cat of French Arthurian legend.

Cheshire Cat. Disappearing cat in Alice in Wonderland.

Chessie. Cat featured in Chesapeake and Ohio Railway advertisements.

Dinah. Alice's cat in Alice in Wonderland.

Father Gatto. Cat of Sicilian folklore.

Felix the Cat. Pat Sullivan's cartoon cat.

Figaro. Cat in Walt Disney film Pinocchio.

Foss. Edward Lear's cat and model for the cat in *The Comic Alphabet*.

Fritz the Cat. Cat in Ralph Bakshi's cartoon movie.

Garfield. Cat in the cartoon strip of that name.

Geoffrey. Christopher Smart's cat.

Gib Hunter. Cat in the fifteenth-century fable by Robert Henryson.

Glass Cat. Cat in Frank Baum's *Wizard of Oz*.

Heathcliff. Cat in the cartoon strip of that name.

Hodge. Samuel Johnson's cat.

Irusan. King-cat of Irish myth.

Kisa. Cat of Scandinavian folklore.

Krazy Kat. Brickbat-tossing cat of the 1920s comic strip.

Lucifer. Cat in the Walt Disney movie *Cinderella.*

Lulu. Edmund Wilson's cat.

Macavity. Master criminal cat in Eliot's *Old Possum's Book of Practical Cats.* Other Eliotian cats include **Jennyanydots, Growltiger, Rum Tum Tugger, Mungojerrie, Rumpleteazer, Old Deuteronomy, Mr. Mistoffelees, Gus (Asparagus), Bustopher Jones,** and **Skimbleshanks**.

Mehitabel. Concupiscent cat in Don Marquis' *archy and mehitabel.*

Minneloushe. W. B. Yeats's dancing cat.

Morris. Finicky cat of television advertisements.

Muezza. Cat of prophet Mohamet.

Nelson. Winston Churchill's cat.

Old Frank. Cat in Andrew Lang's *My Own Fairy Book.*

Palug Cat. Spotted-headed cat goddess, one of the Three Plagues of Anglesey, in Welsh myth.

Pansie. Walter Pater's cat.

Peter. Cat to which Tom Sawyer feeds painkiller in *Adventures of Tom Sawyer.*

Polar Bear. Cleveland Amory's Siamese cat.

Puss in Boots. Cat in the fairy tale by Charles Perrault.

Pussy-cat. Cat in Edward Lear's "The Owl and the Pussy-cat."

Pyewacket. Cat in John Van Druten's play *Bell, Book and Candle.*

Saha. Cat in Colette's *The Cat.*

Samson. Cat in Graham Oakley's churchmice books for children.

Sathan. Devil-cat of the convicted witch Elizabeth Francis.

Selima. Cat drowned in a tub of goldfish in Thomas Gray's poem "Ode on the Death of a Favorite Cat."

Simpkin. Cat hero of Beatrix Potter's *Tailor of Gloucester.*

Sir Pertinax. Edward and Constance Garnett's cat.

Socks. President and Mrs. Bill Clinton's cat.

Sylvester. "Looney Tunes" cartoon cat.

Tiddles. Cat with Horatio Nelson at Trafalgar.

Tobermory. Saki (H. H. Munro)'s storied cat.

Tom. Cartoon cat paired with mouse Jerry.

Tom Kitten. Hero of Beatrix Potter tale.

Tomlyn. Cat in C. S. Lewis' *The Last Battle.*

Webster. Ecclesiastical cat in P. G. Wodehouse's fiction.

Horses

Aarvak. Horse drawing the sun's chariot in Norse mythology.

Abaster, Abatos, Æton, and Nomos. Horses of Pluto.

Abraxa, Eèos, and Phæthon. Horses of Aurora.

Actæon, Æthon, Amathea, Bronte, Erythreos, Lampos, Phlegos, and Purosis. Horses of Helios, the Sun.

Aganippe. See **Pegasus**.

Alfana. Gradasso's horse in Ariosto's *Orlando Furioso.*

Allycrocker and Caractacus. Horses of Thomas Jefferson.

Alsvid or Alwider. Horse drawing the chariot of the moon in Norse mythology.

Anzac. Horse of George V.

Aquiline. Raymond's horse in Tasso's *Jerusalem Delivered.*

Arion. Hercules' horse, formerly owned by Neptune.

Arundel. Horse of Bevis of Hampton.

Baldy. Horse of Gen. George Gordon Meade.

Balios. Horse given to Peleus by Neptune.

Barbary Roan. Horse of Richard II.

Bavieca. Horse of El Cid.

Beauty. Horse of George III.

Billy. Horse of Gen. George H. Thomas.

Black Agnes and Rosabelle. Horse of Mary, Queen of Scots.

Black Beauty. Horse in Anna Sewell's story of that name.

Black Bess. Dick Turpin's horse, in Harrison Ainsworth's *Rookwood.*

Black Saladin. Horse of the Earl of Warwick.

Brigadore. Horse of Govon, in Spenser's *Faerie Queene.*

Brigliadoro and Vegliantino. Orlando's horse in Ariosto's *Orlando Furioso.*

Broiefori. Horse of Ogier the Dane.

Brown Adam. Horse of Sir Walter Scott.

Bucephalus. Horse of Alexander the Great.

Carman. Horse of the Chevalier Bayard.

Celer. Horse of Emperor Lucius Verus.

Cerus. Horse of Adrastus.

Champion. Gene Autry's horse.

Chancellor, Highfly, Lady Margrave, Skylark, and Virginia. Gen. J. E. B. Stuart's horses.

Cincinnati, Egypt, Jeff Davis, and Jack. Gen. Ulysses S. Grant's horses.

Clavileño. Wooden horse on which Sancho Panza took his magical ride in *Don Quixote.*

Copenhagen and Diomed. Duke of Wellington's horses.

Cylarus and Harpagus. Horses of Castor and Pollux.

Daisy and Prince. Henry and Clover Adams' horses.

Dan Webster and Black Burns. Gen. George Brinton McClellan's horses.

Dapple. Sancho Panza's donkey in *Don Quixote.*

Désiré, Embelli, Ingénu, Marengo, and Roitelet. Napoleon's horses.

Dinos and Lampon. Horses of Diomedes.

Duke. John Wayne's horse.

El Morzillo. Hernando Cortes' horse.

Ethon, Galathe, and Podarge. Hector's horses.

Fadda. White mule of Mohamet.

Ferrant d'Espagne. Oliver's horse.

Fire-Eater. Gen. Albert Sidney Johnston's horse.

Glencoe. Gen. John Hunt Morgan's horse.

Grani. Siegfried's horse.

Gringolet. Gawain's horse, in *Gawain and the Green Knight*.

Grizzle. Dr. Syntax's horse, in William Combe's *Three Tours of Dr. Syntax*.

Haizum. Archangel Gabriel's horse.

Hippocambus. Neptune's horse.

Hrimfaxi. Horse of Night in Scandinavian mythology.

Incitatus. Caligula's horse.

Kantaka. Horse of Gautama, the Buddha.

King Philip. Gen. Nathan Bedford Forrest's horse.

Lamri. King Arthur's horse.

Little Sorrel. Gen. Thomas J. "Stonewall" Jackson's horse.

Lookout. Gen. Joseph Hooker's horse.

Marocco. Trick horse of Elizabethan England, belonging to Banks.

Moscow, Bayard, Monmouth, and Decatur. Gen. Philip Kearny's horses.

Nelson and Magnolia (Magnolio). George Washington's horses.

Old Charlie. Horse of William F. Cody, "Buffalo Bill."

Old Whitey. Gen. Zachary Taylor's horse.

Peanuts. Stephen Crane's horse.

Pegasus. Winged horse of Bellerophon; also known as *Aganippe*.

Phallus. Heraclius' horse.

Phrenicos. Horse of Hiero of Syracuse.

Rain-in-the-Face and Texas. Theodore Roosevelt's horses.

Raksh. Horse of Rustum (Rustam).

Rienzi. Gen. Philip Sheridan's horse.

Rosinante. Don Quixote's horse.

Sam and Lexington. Gen. William Tecumseh Sherman's horses.

Savoy. Horse of Charles VIII of France.

Scout. Tonto's horse.

Set. Red-headed ass of the Egyptian Saturnalia.

Shibdiz. Horse of Chosroes II.

Silver. Buck Jones's horse; Lone Ranger's horse.

Sleipnir. Odin's horse.

Sorrel. William III's horse.

Strymon. Horse burned by Xerxes before the Persian invasion of Greece.

Swallow. Horse of Hereward the Wake.

Tarzan. Ken Maynard's horse.

Tendencur. Charlemagne's horse.

Tony. Tom Mix's horse.

Traveller and Lucy Long. General Robert E. Lee's horses.

Trebizond. Horse of Guarinos.

Veillantif. Roland's horse.

Vic. Gen. George A. Custer's horse.

White Surrey. Richard III's horse.

Xanthus and Balios. Achilles' horses.

SOURCES

Dogs

Brewer, Ebenezer Cobham. *Brewer's Dictionary of Phrase and Fable: Centenary Edition, Revised.* Edited by Ivor H. Evans. New York: Harper and Row, 1981.

Fiske, John. *Old Virginia and Her Neighbours.* 2 vols. Boston: Houghton Mifflin Co., 1901. (For George Washington's hounds, courtesy Mr. Julian Scheer, Catlett, Va.)

Graves, Robert. *The White Goddess.* New York: Farrar, Straus and Giroux, 1978.

Harvey, Sir Paul, comp. and ed. *The Oxford Companion to English Literature.* 3rd ed. Oxford: Clarendon Press, 1946.

Leach, Maria. *God Had a Dog: Folklore of the Dog.* New Brunswick, N.J.: Rutgers University Press, 1961.

Cats

Brewer, Ebenezer Cobham. *Brewer's Dictionary of Phrase and Fable: Centenary Edition, Revised.* Edited by Ivor H. Evans. New York: Harper and Row, 1981.

Briggs, Katherine M. *Nine Lives: Cats in Folklore.* London: Routledge and Kegan Paul, 1980.

Graves, Robert. *The White Goddess.* New York: Farrar, Straus and Giroux, 1978.

Mery, Fernand. *The Life, History and Magic of the Cat.* Translated by Emma Street. New York: Grosset and Dunlap, 1968.

Saunders, Nicholas J. *The Cult of the Cat.* London: Thames and Hudson, 1991.

Zistel, Era. *The Golden Book of Cat Stories.* Chicago: Ziff-Davis, 1946.

Horses

Boatner, Mark Mayo, II. *The Civil War Dictionary.* New York: David McKay Co., 1959.

Brewer, Ebenezer Cobham. *Brewer's Dictionary of Phrase and Fable: Centenary Edition, Revised.* Edited by Ivor H. Evans. New York: Harper and Row, 1981.

Graves, Robert. *The White Goddess.* New York: Farrar, Straus and Giroux, 1978.

Harvey, Sir Paul, comp. and ed. *The Oxford Companion to English Literature.* 3rd ed. Oxford: Clarendon Press, 1946.

—L.D.R.

55

WHERE ARE THE BIRDS?

· · · · ·

The nineteenth-century American poet William Cullen Bryant wrote a much-anthologized poem, "To a Waterfowl," describing its northward migration in eight stanzas of four lines each, and closing with an inspirational moral—

> He who, from zone to zone,
> Guides through the boundless sky thy certain flight,
> In the long way that I must tread alone,
> Will guide my steps aright—

without ever identifying what particular kind of waterfowl he had in mind. Was it a duck? A goose? A swan? A loon? A grebe? If so, which variety? From the details of the poem, somebody like Roger Tory Petersen, Chandler Robbins, Richard Pough, Ann Whitman, or John K. Terres might be able to narrow down the possibilities, but only to an extent.

It is possible that the particular kind of waterfowl that Bryant had in mind went unspecified because to give the actual name would have seemed insufficiently poetic for the inspirational moral to be derived from it: "To a Loon," say, or "To a Goose." A good deal of American poetry in the nineteenth century tended toward the evocation of the poetic ideal, with the idea being to ennoble vernacular American middle-class experience through elevation. The poet's job was to cleanse everyday life of its mundane particulars and put it into properly abstract language. How inspirational and noble can a mallard duck be made to seem? Or perhaps the waterfowl was too far off for Bryant to tell for sure.

In any event, not only poets but novelists and other writers of prose frequently concern themselves with birds, and it is important to make certain that the particular bird chosen for description is in the right place at the right time. A novelist who purported to have one of his characters observe an indigo bunting, say, in western Pennsylvania during the winter would lose all credibility with readers who happened to be birdwatchers.

With this in mind, we have attempted to provide a guide to the general areas in which some of the more common species of birds might be found within the United States and Canada. The kind of environment typically frequented by the bird is given first, followed by the regions in which the bird customarily ranges. *Summer* is used to designate the range during warm weather, including breeding and nesting periods. *Intermediate* denotes the area normally traversed during fall and spring migrations. When no *winter* range is given, it is outside the United States and Canada. If no season is designated, the bird is a permanent resident. To quote Peterson's *Field Guide,* "Within these broad outlines may be many gaps—areas that are ecologically unsuited for the species. A marsh wren must have a marsh, a meadowlark a meadow, a ruffed grouse a woodland or a forest."

For geographical purposes "U.S." does not include Alaska or Hawaii. We regret this inconvenience, but very few migrating birds are willing to adhere to political divisions.

Anhinga (also known as *snake-bird, water-turkey*). Quiescent freshwater swamps, marshes. Southeast and Gulf coasts year-around; lower Southwest, Gulf states, Southeast, and Florida year-around.

Avocet, American. Shallow western lakes, marshes of plains. Western U.S. into Canada in summer.

Bittern, American. Freshwater marshland. Throughout upper U.S. and most of Canada to sub-Arctic in summer; Pacific Coast, Great Basin, lower eastern Southwest, lower Louisiana, west Tennessee and Kentucky, Chesapeake Bay, and northern Florida year-around; western Southwest, Deep South, east Tennessee, and Carolinas in winter.

Bittern, least. Freshwater marsh with dense cattails and reed grass, also salt marsh in South. Pacific Coast, Mississippi Valley, East Coast to Canada in summer; Florida and southwest Texas in winter.

Blackbird, Brewer's. Meadows and prairies. Lower western Canada and upper U.S. Midwest to Great Lakes in summer; California and central Far West and Rockies year-around; Southwest, lower Great Plains, and Deep South in winter.

Blackbird, red-winged. Marshes, fields, lake shores. Throughout Canada to sub-Arctic from upper Northwest to Atlantic Coast, U.S. Great Lakes and Northeast in summer; British Columbia and throughout rest of U.S. year-around.

Bluebird, eastern. Open woodlands, farms, orchards, fields. East of Great Plains throughout lower Canada and upper U.S. Midwest and Northeast in summer; lower Midwest, Texas, and South year-around.

Bobolink (also known as *rice-bird*). Meadows, fields, marshes. Throughout lower Canada and northern U.S. east of Pacific Coast in summer; upper Great Plains and throughout lower Midwest, Middle Atlantic and South intermediate.

Bobwhite, northern (also known as *quail, partridge*). Farmlands, fields, edges of woods. Southwest, Mississippi Valley, lower Midwest, Middle Atlantic, and South year-around.

Bunting, indigo. Fields, woodland edges, clearings. Lower Canada and eastern half of U.S., except lower Southeast coast, in summer; southernmost Florida in winter.

Bunting, lazuli. Woodland edges, streams. Lower western Canada and U.S. Pacific Northwest in summer; far Southwest in winter; Southwest intermediate.

Cardinal. Woods and fields, especially woodland margins, residential districts. U.S. South, Southwest, Midwest, Northeast year-around.

Catbird, gray. Dense shrubbery and moist thickets. Lower Canada and most of U.S. except Pacific Coast and far Southwest in summer; U.S. East and inland Gulf states year-around; Gulf Coast, Florida, lower Southeast coast in winter.

Chickadee, black-capped. Fields, mixed and deciduous forests, open woodlands. Alaska, Canadian Great Plains to sub-Arctic eastward to maritime provinces, upper U.S. from Washington to Maine throughout year.

Chickadee, Carolina. Fields and wooded areas. Eastward from Texas through lower Midwest, Middle Atlantic, South, except Florida, year-around.

Coot, American. Ponds, marshes, bay shores. Canadian Great Plains to St. Lawrence River, most U.S., except lower Midwest, inland Middle Atlantic, New England, in summer; Pacific Coast, Southwest, western Gulf states year-around; Southeast to New England coast in winter.

Cormorant, Brandt's. Coastal. Pacific Coast in winter.

Cormorant, double-crested. Coasts, inland lakes, and rivers. Pacific, Atlantic, eastern Gulf coasts year-around; areas of St. Lawrence River, Great Lakes, center of continent west of Great Lakes in summer.

Cowbird, brown-headed. Woodlands, pastures, farmland, suburbs. Western Canada except Pacific Coast eastward to Great Lakes, Ontario, Quebec, and maritime provinces, U.S. Pacific Northwest eastward through Great Plains, Midwest to Middle Atlantic and New England in summer; southern California, lower Southwest, and South year-around; Florida in winter.

Crane, sandhill. Prairies, open land. Throughout North America to Arctic eastward to Great Lakes in summer; Florida, coast of southern California in winter.

Creeper, brown. Forests. Across lower Canada in summer; U.S. Pacific Coast, Rockies, upper Midwest, Northeast, and Appalachians year-around; Great Plains, Midwest, and South except Florida in winter.

Crow, American. Woods, orchards, fields, suburbs, parks. Canadian Great Plains eastward to sub-Arctic, upper U.S. Great Plains in summer; throughout U.S. except lower Southwest year-around.

Crow, fish. Tidal rivers and bays. Lower Gulf coast, Florida, East Coast tidewater to New England.

Cuckoo, black-billed. Woodlands. East of Rockies, across Canada, U.S. Midwest and Northeast in summer; southern states intermediate.

Cuckoo, yellow-billed. Woodlands. Pacific Coast, Southwest, Great Plains, Gulf Coast, entire eastern half of U.S. to Connecticut in summer.

Curlew, long-billed. Moist meadows, river valleys, sea coast. Great Plains in summer; southern California, western Gulf coast in winter.

Dickcissel. Fields, open habitats. Mississippi Valley, Southwest, and Appalachians in summer; East and Gulf coasts in winter; lower Mississippi river year-around.

Dipper, American. Mountain streams. Western mountains, Alaska to Southwest year-around.

Dove, ground. Coastal plain and tidewater. Lower South, Texas to South Carolina, southern California, and Arizona.

Dove, mourning. Farmlands and suburbs. Throughout U.S. except upper Great Plains, Great Lakes, and northern New England year-around; Canadian Pacific Coast and Great Plains, lower eastern Canada in summer.

Dove, rock (also known as *domestic pigeon*). Everywhere in U.S. and lower Canada.

Dowitcher. Mudflats and edges of sea. Florida, Louisiana, lower California in winter; along ocean coasts and sometimes inland intermediate.

Duck, American wigeon. Shallow bodies of water and shorelines. Alaska, western Canada to Arctic, northwest U.S. in summer; Pacific Coast, lower Texas, Gulf and Southeast coasts in winter; U.S. lower Midwest, inland Middle Atlantic, and Northeast, eastern Canada intermediate.

Duck, black. Coastal marshes, estuaries, shallows, and ponds. U.S. lower Great Lakes to Atlantic Coast and south to Chesapeake year-around; Canada to Arctic from east of Hudson's Bay to northern Atlantic coast in summer; lower Midwest and South in winter.

Duck, blue-winged teal. Ponds, marshes, bays. Throughout Canada to sub-Arctic, U.S. upper Northwest and north-central states in summer; Gulf and Florida coasts in winter; throughout U.S. and maritime Canadian provinces intermediate.

Duck, bufflehead (also known as *butterball*). Large lake and rivers, coastal waters. Throughout western U.S. and Pacific Coast to Alaska, Southwest, lower deep South, upper Southwest of mountains, East Coast in winter; central Alaska, much of northwestern Canada in summer; eastern Canada, Appalachians, upper Mississippi valley intermediate.

Duck, canvasback. Coastal bays and river mouths. U.S. Pacific, Gulf, and Atlantic coasts in winter; Pacific Northwest and western Canada inland from coast in summer; intermediate throughout U.S. and lower eastern Canada.

Duck, cinnamon teal. Ponds, marshes, bays. U.S. Pacific Coast and mountain states in summer; along Mexican border in winter; U.S. Southwest intermediate.

Duck, goldeneye (also known as *whistler*). Forest lakes and rivers, coastal bays. Throughout most of U.S. and Pacific Coast of Canada in winter; Alaska, central and upper northwestern Canada to Arctic east to maritime provinces in summer.

Duck, green-winged teal. Ponds, lakes, mudflats, wet fields. Pacific Northwest and northwest-central U.S. throughout year; Alaska, western Canada to Arctic east to maritime provinces, U.S. upper Great Plains in summer; inland California, central and southern Rockies, Gulf and Atlantic coasts in winter; U.S. Midwest and Northeast intermediate.

Duck, lesser scaup. Lakes, ponds, bays, and rivers, especially inland. Along Mid-Atlantic, Southeast, Gulf, and Pacific coasts and inland, Mexican border, lower Mississippi river and Great Lakes in winter; Pacific Northwest and upper Rockies northward to Alaska and northwest Canada to Arctic in summer; eastern and central Canada, rest of U.S. intermediate.

Duck, mallard. Ponds, marshes, bays, beaches. Alaska, Canada to Arctic eastward to southern Quebec in summer; much of northern half of U.S. year-around; U.S. Southwest, South, lower Midwest in winter.

Duck, common merganser (also known as *goosander*). Freshwater lakes and ponds. Northwest U.S. and Canada to sub-Arctic in summer; U.S. except South and Southwest in winter; west-central Canada intermediate.

Duck, pintail. Shallow bays, lakes, ponds. Everywhere in North America, but especially central and southern U.S. in winter; northwest U.S., Alaska, and Canada to Arctic in summer; eastern Canada, upper northeast U.S. intermediate.

Duck, red-breasted merganser. Lakes, ponds, rivers, sea coast. Sub-Arctic to Arctic Canada north from Great Lakes in summer; U.S. Gulf and Atlantic coasts, Canadian East Coast in winter; intermediate throughout U.S. and Canada except Rockies.

Duck, redhead (also known as *American pochard*). Coastal bays, lakes. Lower California, Atlantic and Gulf coasts in winter; west-central Canada and north-central U.S. in summer; intermediate through U.S.

Duck, ring-necked. Swamps, ponds, coastal bays. U.S. Southeast seaboard, Middle Atlantic Coast, lower South, Southwest, lower Pacific coast in winter; lower Canada in summer; intermediate throughout U.S.

Duck, shoveler. Ponds, marshes, mudflats. Pacific Coast year-around; U.S. Gulf Coast and lower Southwest in winter; inland Alaska and western Canada to sub-Arctic, U.S. upper Northwest in summer; intermediate throughout U.S.

Duck, surf scoter. Ocean shores, interior lakes. Range similar to white-winged scoter (see below) but does not include Great Lakes or southwestern Canada.

Duck, white-winged scoter (also known as *American velvet scoter*). Ocean shores and woodland lakes. Along Pacific and northern Atlantic coasts and Great Lakes in winter; Alaska and western Canada to Arctic in summer; intermediate throughout Canada.

Duck, wood. Woodland near freshwater lakes and streams. Northwest Pacific coast, South throughout year; eastern U.S. in summer.

Dunlin (also known as *red-backed sandpiper*). Ocean beaches and inlets. All U.S. coastlines in winter; Alaskan and Canadian Arctic coast in summer; sometimes intermediate inland east of Mississippi.

Eagle, bald. Shores of sea coasts, lakes, rivers, marshes. California and Atlantic coasts, most of U.S. except Southwest, upper-central Midwest, and Appalachians in winter; Florida and northern Pacific coast year-around; Alaska, northern Canada to Arctic and eastward to maritime provinces, upper U.S. eastward to Great Lakes and New England in summer.

Eagle, golden. Mountains and remote areas. Alaska, Canada to Arctic in summer; eastern U.S. along Appalachians in winter; western U.S. and British Columbia year-around.

Egret, cattle. Originally European; pastures near coast and thence inland. Lower seaboard and Gulf South and along U.S. Northeast coast in summer; western Gulf coast and Florida in winter.

Egret, common (also known as *American egret, great egret*). Shallow waters, tidal flats, lagoons, and marshes along coasts and inland. Mississippi Valley, Deep South, Middle Atlantic, and northern California coast in summer; southern California, lower east Texas, Florida, Gulf and Southeast coasts year-around; lower Southwest in winter.

Egret, snowy. Marshes, ponds, swamps. East and Gulf coasts in winter; areas of southern Texas and Arkansas, lower Mississippi river in summer; southwestern U.S. intermediate.

Falcon, prairie. Plains, wooded areas. Pacific Coast and lower Southwest in winter; Northwest to Canada in summer; intermediate area year-around.

Finch, house. Towns and city suburbs in East, desert scrub and chapparal in West. Western U.S. and into Canada, Great Plains, and Texas, upper Southeast, below eastern Great Lakes, and Middle Atlantic year-around.

Finch, purple. Pine woods, open canyons, suburbs. Northwest Canada and across lower Canada to Atlantic Coast in summer; Pacific Coast, Great

Lakes, and New England year-around; western mountains, Midwest, and South except Florida in winter.

Flicker, common. Open country near trees. Three varieties. *Yellow-shafted:* Central Alaska, throughout Canada east of Rockies to sub-Arctic in summer; Great Plains to East Coast year-around; western Gulf northward along west of range in winter. *Red-shafted:* Far West and Rockies year-around; Pacific Coast to Alaska summer; west Texas along east of range in winter. *Gilded:* lower Southwest year-around.

Flycatcher, Acadian. Swampy woodlands, forests. Throughout U.S. eastward from Great Plains in summer except for western Gulf coast and Florida.

Flycatcher, great crested. Orchards and forests. Eastern half of U.S. and Canada in summer.

Flycatcher, least. Groves, orchards, woodlands. Northern U.S. and Canada east of Rockies to sub-Arctic in summer; South and Southwest intermediate.

Gallinule. See **Moorhen, common**.

Gannet, northern. Ocean, offshore islands. Gulf and South Atlantic coasts in winter; North Atlantic Coast intermediate.

Gnatcatcher, blue-gray. Bottomlands and moist forests. Northern California east to South, Midwest, and Middle Atlantic in summer; southern California, lower Southwest, Gulf Coast, Florida, and south Atlantic coast year-around.

Goldfinch, American. Weedy grasslands, thickets, deciduous woodlands, residential areas. Lower British Columbia, Pacific Northwest, California, Nebraska, Oklahoma eastward through lower Midwest and upper South to New England and Atlantic Coast year-around; Canadian Great Plains and lower Canada to maritime provinces in summer; rest of U.S. in winter.

Goldfinch, lesser. Fields, thickets, woodlands, residential areas. Pacific Coast, California, and Great Basin, lower Southwest year-around; southern Rockies in summer; central-southwest Texas in winter.

Goose, Canada. Marshes, harvested fields, bays, rivers, ponds. Alaska, Arctic, and throughout northern Canada to Atlantic Coast in summer; northern Pacific coast, middle of U.S. west of Pacific slope year-around; Southwest, lower Mississippi valley, Atlantic Coast from Nova Scotia to Georgia in winter.

Goose, snow. Fresh and salt water. Pacific, western Gulf and mid-Atlantic coasts in winter; Arctic Alaska and Canada in summer; Alaska and throughout Canada to maritime provinces, U.S. Mississippi Valley intermediate.

Goose, white-fronted. Lakes, coastal areas, marshes. Arctic Alaska and Canada in summer; U.S. north Pacific coast and western Gulf coast in winter; Great Plains and northwest Canada intermediate.

Grackle, boat-tailed. Near salt and brackish water. Atlantic and Gulf coasts, Florida year-around.

Grackle, common (also known as *purple grackle*). Open fields, pines, parks, and gardens. Canadian and U.S. upper Great Plains to Nova Scotia, Appalachians in summer; U.S. lower Great Plains, lower Midwest, Middle Atlantic, and South year-around.

Grebe, horned. Lakes, bays, ponds, sloughs. Alaska, northwest and central Canada to Arctic in summer; Atlantic, Pacific, and Gulf coasts in winter; U.S. Northeast and Mississippi Valley intermediate.

Grebe, western. Borders of large lakes, shallow sloughs. Pacific Coast in winter; southern California, much of U.S. Northwest and west-central Canada in summer.

Grosbeak, black-headed. Woodlands and orchards. U.S. western Great Plains to Pacific Coast, British Columbia, California, southwestern Rockies in summer.

Grosbeak, evening. Spruce and pine woods. Across lower Canada, New England, Pacific Coast, and much of Far West year-around; northeast Canada to sub-Arctic, Canadian and U.S. Great Plains, Southwest, lower Midwest, Middle Atlantic, and upper South in winter.

Grosbeak, pine. Coniferous forests. Alaska, western Canada and maritime provinces, U.S. Pacific Northwest and Rockies year-around; west-central, central, and eastern Canada to sub-Arctic in summer; Great Plains, upper Midwest, and northeast U.S. in winter.

Grosbeak, rose-breasted. Mature deciduous forests, orchards. West-central Canada, Manitoba to Great Lakes and Atlantic Coast, U.S. upper Midwest, Northeast, Appalachians in summer.

Grouse, blue. Woodlands. Rockies and westward to Pacific Coast of U.S. and Canada.

Grouse, ruffed. Woods and forests. Alaska and Canada to sub-Arctic, southward to Mid-Atlantic states, Appalachians to Georgia, Alabama, upper Mississippi valley, Pacific Northwest.

Gull, Bonaparte's. Lakes, river valleys, tidal flats. Alaska and northwest Canada to Arctic in summer; U.S. Atlantic, Pacific, and Gulf coasts in winter; intermediate through center and eastern half of continent and Canadian Pacific coast.

Gull, California. Along coast and well inland. Pacific Coast and inland to northwest Canada and U.S. Great Plains in summer; U.S. Pacific Coast in winter; Northwest intermediate.

Gull, Franklin's (also known as *prairie-dove*). Western prairies. Alaska and west-central Canada to Arctic in summer; western Gulf coast in winter; western and Great Plains areas intermediate.

Gull, great black-backed. Coastal regions. Canadian maritime provinces, St. Lawrence seaway to Great Lakes, northeast coast of U.S. year-around; eastern Arctic Canada in summer.

Gull, herring. Sea coasts, lakes, rivers. Along all U.S. and Canadian coastlines and waterways in winter; U.S. Great Lakes, U.S. and Canada to Arctic except Canadian Great Plains in summer.

Gull, laughing. Sea coast. Gulf and South Atlantic coasts year-around; Middle Atlantic Coast in summer.

Gull, ring-billed. Shorelines and ploughed fields. Canadian Great Plains and inland Pacific Northwest, lower eastern Canada and eastern Arctic coast in summer; Atlantic, Pacific, Gulf coasts, Mississippi River to Great Lakes in winter; intermediate throughout U.S. and much of Canada.

Gull, western. Beaches and islands. U.S. Pacific Coast throughout year.

Harrier, northern. See **Hawk, marsh**.

Hawk, broad-winged. Dry forests and groves. Eastern U.S. and Canada to sub-Arctic in summer; south Florida in winter.

Hawk, marsh (also known as *northern harrier*). Meadows, open fields, and marshes. Alaska, most of Canada to sub-Arctic, upper U.S. Great Plains in summer; U.S. West Coast to Rockies, lower Great Plains, Midwest to Middle Atlantic and New England year-around; Texas, Deep South, and Southeast in winter.

Hawk, red-shouldered. Moist woodlands, river timber. Southeast, Mid-Atlantic, Midwest to Great Lakes, California coast year-around; New England and upper Midwest summer.

Hawk, red-tailed. Forests, open country, tundra, deserts with trees. Throughout most of U.S., British Columbia year-around; Alaska and Canada to Arctic in summer.

Hawk, sharp-shinned. Open woods, especially conifer forests, and adjacent fields. Throughout northern U.S. and Canada to sub-Arctic in summer; seaboard South and California in winter; balance of U.S. year-around.

Hawk, sparrow (also known as *American kestrel*). Open and broken areas, farmlands, city parks. U.S. Pacific Coast and Far West, upper Southwest, lower Great Plains, Midwest below Great Lakes, Middle Atlantic, South year-around; Alaska, Canada to sub-Arctic eastward to Atlantic Coast, U.S. upper Great Plains to Great Lakes, New England in summer; lower southwest Texas in winter.

Hawk, Swainson's. Woods, but especially prairie. Alaska, western Canada to Arctic, western U.S. east to Mississippi Valley in summer; lower Southwest intermediate.

Heron, black-crowned night. Marshes, freshwater swamps. Atlantic, Gulf, Pacific coasts, lower Mississippi river, southern California throughout year; Great Plains and midcontinent, Pacific Northwest, lower South, inland east of Appalachians to New England in summer.

Heron, great blue. Streams, meadows, lake shorelines. Pacific Coast, Great Basin, lower Southwest, Texas, and lower Mississippi Valley, lower Deep South, and Atlantic Coast year-around; Pacific Northwest interior, U.S. and

Canadian Great Plains eastward to Maritime Provinces, New England, and Appalachians in summer.

Heron, great white. Marshes and swamps. Southern Florida and Keys.

Heron, green. Ponds and streams. Florida and lower California in winter; Pacific Coast and throughout eastern U.S. in summer.

Heron, little blue. Marshes, rivers, ponds. Carolina, Florida, Gulf coasts year-around; Middle Atlantic and New England coasts in summer.

Heron, Louisiana. Seashores and bays. Coasts of Florida and Gulf year-around; Atlantic Coast and lower California in summer.

Hummingbird, black-chinned. Meadows and woods. Pacific Coast, western mountains, Southwest in summer.

Hummingbird, broad-tailed. Gardens and woods. Rocky Mountains to upper Northwest in summer.

Hummingbird, ruby-throated. Gardens and woods. Throughout Canada east of Rockies to sub-Arctic eastward to Atlantic Coast, eastern half of U.S. in summer; southern Florida in winter.

Hummingbird, rufous. Pacific Northwest to Alaska summer; intermediate California, southern Rockies, and Southwest.

Ibis, white. Coastal marshes, swamps. Tidewater areas from South Carolina to Texas.

Jay, blue. Woodlands. Throughout eastern two-thirds of U.S. and Canada to sub-Arctic year-around.

Jay, Canada (also known as *gray jay*). Spruce forests. Throughout Alaska and Canada to Arctic, U.S. Pacific Northwest, and central Rockies throughout year.

Jay, Steller's. Conifer forests. Rocky Mountains and Pacific Coast to Alaska year-around.

Junco, slate-colored (also known as *dark-eyed junco*). Clearings, fields, edges of woods. Through Alaska and Canada to Arctic in summer; Pacific Coast, Great Lakes, Appalachians, and New England year-around; most of U.S. except south Florida in winter.

Kestrel, American. See **Hawk, sparrow**.

Killdeer. Meadows, ponds, croplands, beaches. Pacific Coast, Southwest, below Great Lakes, South and Atlantic coasts to New England throughout year; Canada to sub-Arctic, U.S. upper Midwest, northern Rockies, and Appalachians in summer.

Kingbird, eastern. Rural country. U.S. and Canada to sub-Arctic from Great Plains east to Atlantic Coast in summer.

Kingbird, western (also known as *Arkansas kingbird*). Farms, stream valleys. Throughout U.S. west of Mississippi.

Kingfisher, belted. Sandbanks, river bluffs, streams, ponds. Most of Canada and Alaska to sub-Arctic in summer; Pacific Northwest, Great Plains eastward throughout U.S. except Florida year-around; Southwest, Rockies, Florida in winter.

Kinglet, golden-crowned. Conifer forests. Southern Alaska coast across Canada to sub-Arctic and Maritime Provinces in summer; Pacific Northwest, Sierras and Rockies, northern Appalachians, and coastal New England year-around; rest of U.S. except Florida in winter; west-central Canada intermediate.

Kinglet, ruby-crowned. Conifers. Throughout Alaska and Canada to Arctic, U.S. Pacific Northwest and northern Rockies in summer; Sierras and southern Rockies year-around; Southwest and lower South in winter; Great Plains, central Midwest, and Middle Atlantic intermediate.

Kite, swallow-tailed. Coastal forests, swamps, cypress lagoons. Florida, Gulf and Atlantic coasts to South Carolina.

Lark, horned. Prairies, plains, open spaces, shore. Alaska, Arctic Canada, and lower Canada in summer; New England, Midwest, western U.S. year-around; Northwest Pacific coast and South except coasts and Florida in winter.

Limpkin. Wooded swampland. Florida.

Loon, common. Northern freshwater lakes; winters on salt water. Alaska and Canada north of Great Plains and British Columbia to Arctic, Great Lakes in summer; along oceans and Gulf Coast in winter; interior of U.S. intermediate.

Loon, red-throated. Lakes and salt water. Alaska, Arctic Canada in summer; Pacific Coast, Atlantic Coast north of Florida in winter; central Canada to Virginia intermediate.

Magpie, American (also known as *black-billed magpie*). Open country near brush. Northwest U.S. and lower northwest Canada except coastline year-around.

Martin, purple. Residential areas, open woodland, farms. Lower Canadian Great Plains, Great Lakes to Maritime Provinces, U.S. Pacific Coast, Rocky Mountains eastward in summer.

Meadowlark, eastern. Fields, grasslands, and meadows. Great Lakes, lower eastern Canada, and northern New England in summer; lower Southwest, eastern half of U.S. year-around.

Meadowlark, western. Meadows and fields. U.S. upper Midwest, Canadian and upper U.S. Great Plains, Great Lakes, British Columbia in summer; U.S. Pacific Coast, central and southern Rockies, lower Great Plains year-around; southwest Texas and lower Mississippi valley in winter.

Mockingbird (also known as *northern mockingbird, eastern mockingbird*). Woodland edges, deserts, towns, and farmland. California, Texas, South, lower Midwest, and Middle Atlantic year-around; northern California eastward across Rockies and Great Plains to Great Lakes to New England in summer.

Moorhen, common (also known as *gallinule*). Freshwater marshes. Southeast, Gulf, California coasts year-around; eastern half of U.S. in summer.

Nighthawk, common. Cities and suburbs, towns, sagebrush plains, and orchards. Throughout U.S. and most of Canada to sub-Arctic in summer.

Nuthatch, red-breasted. Evergreen forests. Across lower Canada in summer; U.S. Pacific Coast, Rockies, upper Midwest, Northeast, and Appalachians year-around; lower Great Plains, lower Midwest, and South, except Florida, in winter.

Nuthatch, white-breasted. Woodlands, orchards, swamps. Everywhere in U.S. except prairies, arid Southwest areas, Gulf Coast, and Florida, throughout year.

Oriole, northern (also known as *Baltimore oriole, Bullock's oriole*). Shade trees, especially near rivers. (1) Eastern (Baltimore) from west-central Canada, U.S. northern plains, Mississippi Valley, Midwest, and Northeast in summer; Gulf and Southeast coasts and Florida in winter; southwest Texas and lower Deep South intermediate. (2) Western (Bullock's) throughout West and Southwest in summer; Gulf Coast and southernmost Florida in winter.

Osprey. Coastal marshes, rivers, bays, lakes. Along Atlantic, Pacific, and Gulf coasts, across upper center of continent to sub-Arctic in summer; southern Florida, lower California in winter; rest of U.S. intermediate.

Ovenbird. Dry hilly forests. Across Canada east of Rockies to sub-Arctic, throughout upper U.S. Great Plains, Midwest, Northeast, and upper South in summer; Gulf and Southeast coasts in winter; lower Plains, Texas, and lower South intermediate.

Owl, barn. Old buildings, farm areas, marsh, prairies, woodlands, suburbs. Throughout U.S. except upper Great Plains, Great Lakes, and New England, year-around.

Owl, barred. Swamps, rivers, deciduous woodlands. Eastern half of continent to sub-Arctic and westward across lower Canada, except British Columbia, year-around.

Owl, eastern screech. Towns, farms, groves, and woods. Throughout eastern two-thirds of U.S. to New England year-around.

Owl, great horned. Woodlands, swamps, deserts. Throughout North America to Arctic year-around.

Owl, long-eared. Woods, especially evergreens, near open country. Canadian Great Plains and central Canada to sub-Arctic and northern New England in summer; U.S. Pacific Coast, Northwest, upper Midwest, and upper Middle Atlantic states throughout year; Southwest, upper South into Virginia in winter.

Owl, northern pygmy. Woodlands. Western U.S. and Canadian Pacific Coast to Rockies year-around.

Partridge. See **Bobwhite, northern**.

Pelican, brown. Coastal. Pacific, Gulf, and Southeast coasts throughout year.

Pelican, white. Coasts and lakes. California, Gulf, and eastern Florida coasts in winter; Canadian Great Plains in summer; west of Mississippi, except Pacific Coast, intermediate.

Petrel, fork-tailed storm (also known as *Leach's petrel*). Offshore, coastal islands. Pacific Coast summers.

Petrel, Wilson's storm. Offshore. Pacific Coast, Atlantic Coast north of Cape Hatteras in summer; Pacific Coast off lower California in winter.

Pewee, eastern wood. Forests, orchards, groves. Canadian Great Plains to maritime provinces, U.S. Mississippi Valley eastward to Atlantic Coast, except Florida, in summer.

Pewee, western wood. Forests and woods along streams. Western U.S., Alaska, and Canada to sub-Arctic in summer.

Pheasant, ring-necked. Asiatic bird; grassy areas, farmlands. Agricultural areas of U.S. Pacific Northwest, upper Midwest to southern New England, lower Great Plains, Canadian Great Plains year-around.

Phoebe, black. Farms and streams. Southern California and lower western and central Southwest year-around.

Phoebe, eastern. Farms, open woodlands, under small bridges, usually near water. Canadian Great Plains, Great Lakes, eastern Canada to maritime provinces, northeastern U.S. Mississippi Valley, Midwest, and Northeast in summer; upper Deep South, Tennessee to Chesapeake Bay year-around; lower South in winter.

Phoebe, Say's. Plains, bluffs, cliffs. U.S. Southwest, Rockies, and Great Plains, Canadian Great Plains to Arctic in summer; Mexican border year-around.

Pigeon, domestic. See **Dove, rock**.

Pipit, water. Ploughed open fields, damp soil. Western mountains north to Arctic Alaska and Canada in summer; lower California and lower Southwest and South in winter; most of Canada and across U.S. intermediate.

Plover, mountain. Prairie, open ground. Western plains in summer; Southwest in winter.

Plover, ringed (also known as *semipalmated plover*). Tidal flats and salt marshes; inland shorelines during migration. Alaskan and Canadian Arctic regions in summer; Southeast and Gulf coasts in winter; intermediate everywhere except Rockies.

Poorwill, common. Arid country. U.S. Southwest and West to Canada in summer; lower California and along Mexican border throughout year.

Ptarmigan, willow. Thickets and tundra. Northmost Arctic Alaska and Canada in summer; lower Alaska and sub-Arctic Canada in winter; Alaska and Arctic Canada year-around.

Quail. See **Bobwhite, northern**.

Quail, scaled. Arid, semidesert areas. Southwest.

Rail, king. Freshwater marshes. Eastern half of U.S. in summer; coastal South in winter.

Rail, Virginia. Fresh and brackish water marshland. Southeast, Gulf, and Pacific coasts in winter; throughout U.S. and lower Canada in summer.

Raven. Forests. Throughout Alaska and Canada to Arctic, Great Lakes region, U.S. Pacific Coast and Rockies, southern Appalachians year-around.

Redstart, American. Second-growth woodlands and deciduous forests. Lower and Great Plains Canada to sub-Arctic, U.S. northern Rockies, Midwest, and upper South to Middle Atlantic and New England in summer; southernmost Florida in winter.

Roadrunner, greater. Arid country. California, Southwest.

Robin, American. Residential areas, swamps, woodland. Alaska and Canada to Arctic in summer; most of U.S. year-around; Florida, Gulf Coast, and semidesert areas of Southwest in winter.

Sanderling. Water's edge along beaches. Arctic Canada in summer; Southeast Atlantic, Gulf, and Pacific coasts in winter; intermediate throughout much of U.S.

Sandpiper, purple. Rocky shores and jetties. Atlantic Coast north of Florida in winter.

Sandpiper, solitary. Freshwater shorelines. Alaska, northwest and north-central Canada to Arctic in late spring and early summer; Gulf and Southeast coasts and Florida in winter; intermediate throughout lower Canada and U.S.

Sandpiper, spotted. Shorelines. Throughout Alaska and Canada to Arctic, U.S. except lower South in summer; Pacific, Gulf, and Southeast coasts in winter; lower South and Southwest intermediate.

Sapsucker, yellow-bellied. Woods and orchards. Throughout Canada to sub-Arctic, Pacific Northwest, interior of Far West in summer; most of California, southern Rocky Mountains, southern Appalachians year-around; valley of southern California and lower Southwest, central Texas eastward across South and lower Midwest to Atlantic Coast in winter; western Great Plains intermediate.

Shearwater, sooty. Offshore. Both oceans intermediate in summer.

Shrike, loggerhead. Open country, scattered trees, telephone wires, fences. Pacific Northwest, Canadian plains to sub-Arctic, across Canada and northern U.S. to eastern mountains in summer; Canadian and northern U.S. Pacific coast and eastward across continent year-around; Middle Atlantic and southern New England coasts, lower southwest Texas in summer.

Siskin, pine. Evergreen forests. Canada from far northwest eastward across lower Canada to maritime provinces, northern U.S. Rockies in summer; Pacific Coast, central Rockies, and upper Northeast year-around; rest of U.S. except northern Great Plains and south Florida in winter.

Skimmer, black. Seacoast. New England, Middle Atlantic coast in summer; Southeast and Gulf coasts year-around.

Snipe, common (also known as *Wilson's snipe*). Meadows, ponds, marshes, bogs. Alaska and most of Canada to Arctic in summer; British Columbia and upper U.S. Northwest year-around; most of U.S. except Appalachians in winter; lower Canada and inland Middle Atlantic states intermediate.

Sora. Marshes and rice fields. Northern U.S. and Canada into sub-Arctic in summer; Northwest Pacific Coast year-around; California, Gulf and Southeast coasts in winter; lower half of U.S. intermediate.

Sparrow, field. Roadsides, pastures, fields with trees. Upper Midwest and Northeast in summer; lower Midwest and Northeast, most of South year-around; Florida, Gulf Coast, portions of Southwest in winter.

Sparrow, grasshopper. Fields, pastures, meadows. West-central and lower Canada, California and inland Pacific Northwest, Midwest, and Middle Atlantic in summer; lower Mississippi Valley and mid-central South year-around; lower Southwest, South, and Southeast in winter.

Sparrow, house. European bird; farmland, towns, and cities. Throughout U.S. and Canada to Arctic year-around.

Sparrow, savannah. Fields and short grass. Northern U.S., including northern Rockies, Alaska, and Canada to Arctic in summer; Pacific and Atlantic coasts, lower Southwest and South in winter; upper South and central U.S. intermediate.

Sparrow, song. Hedgerows, edges of fields, ponds and streams. Across Canada to sub-Arctic, U.S. upper Great Plains and Midwest in summer; Pacific Coast, Pacific Northwest, far Southwest, central Great Plains, lower Midwest, Northeast, and Appalachians year-around; South and Southwest in winter.

Sparrow, tree. Fields, clearings, thickets. Arctic Alaska and Canada in summer; upper U.S. except Pacific Coast in winter; throughout sub-Arctic and lower Canada intermediate.

Sparrow, white-crowned. Brushy areas near fields, hedgerows. Across Canada to Arctic from Great Plains to Atlantic Coast in summer; Southwest, South, lower Midwest, and Middle Atlantic in winter; Great Plains and upper Midwest intermediate.

Starling, European. Everywhere except dense woods and mountains. Throughout U.S. and lower Canada year-around.

Stilt, black-necked. Fresh and brackish lakes, ponds, flooded fields. California and U.S. Southwest, western Gulf Coast, coastal South Carolina, and Florida in summer.

Surfbird. Along rocky shorelines, mountains above timberline. Pacific Coast in winter.

Swallow, barn. Farmlands. Throughout Canada to sub-Arctic, throughout U.S. except Florida in summer.

Swallow, cliff. Cliffs, bridges, outside of barns. Alaska, Canada to Arctic, all of U.S. except lower South and Southeast coast in summer; South and along Southern coast intermediate.

Swallow, tree. Near water. Canada to Arctic, upper Midwest and New England, Pacific Coast, and western U.S. in summer; Gulf, Southeast, and California coasts in winter; mid-U.S. from Pacific Coast to Eastern Seaboard intermediate.

Swan, whistling (also called *tundra swan*). Fresh and brackish water. Arctic Alaska and Canada in summer; northern California, western Gulf coast, Chesapeake Bay, and North Carolina coast in winter; Alaska, west Canada, Pacific Northwest, Great Lakes southward intermediate.

Swift, chimney. Cities, towns, farms. Throughout eastern U.S. and lower Canada eastward from Great Plains in summer.

Swift, white-throated. Cliffs and canyons. Southwest, Rockies to eastern Washington.

Tanager, scarlet. Groves and forests. Eastern half of lower Canada, eastern U.S., except lower South, in summer; lower South intermediate.

Tanager, summer. Open and broken woods; along streams. Lower Midwest, Middle Atlantic, South, and Texas in summer.

Tanager, western. Forests. Canadian and U.S. Far West including Rockies in summer; lower Southwest and western Great Plains intermediate.

Tern, black. Inland marshes, shallow lakes, ploughed fields. Western and central Canada to sub-Arctic, U.S. Pacific Northwest, and upper Midwest in summer; intermediate throughout U.S.

Tern, common. Seashore and inland lakes. Canadian Great Plains to sub-Arctic, eastward across Canada and New England in summer; Florida, lower Southwest, and eastern Gulf coast in winter; rest of eastern half of continent intermediate.

Thrasher, brown. Fields, woodland borders, residential areas. Midwest and eastern U.S., lower Canada from Great Plains to Atlantic Coast in summer; west Texas in winter; southern states year-around.

Thrush, hermit. Forests. Across Canada to sub-Arctic, western U.S., and New England in summer; southern and southwest U.S. in winter; Pacific Coast year-around; lower Midwest and upper Mississippi Valley intermediate.

Thrush, Swainson's. Evergreen forests. Summer range almost same as that of hermit thrush; most of U.S., except Northwest, intermediate.

Thrush, wood. Woodlands. Throughout U.S. east of Mississippi to lower eastern Canada in summer; Florida and Southwest intermediate.

Titmouse, tufted. Woodlands, thickets, gardens, and parks with dense cover. U.S. east of Great Plains to Atlantic Coast, except northern New England and Florida, year-around.

Towhee, rufous-sided (also known as *chewink*). Thickets, edges of woods, residential shrubbery. Across lower Canada and upper U.S. in summer; Pacific Northwest, Rockies, lower Midwest, Northeast, and South year-around; far Southwest, Texas, and lower Great Plains in winter.

Turkey, wild. Swamps, marshes, forest clearings. Throughout southern half of U.S., Mid-Atlantic states year-around.

Turnstone, black. Rocky shorelines. Alaskan coast in summer, Pacific Coast in winter.

Turnstone, ruddy. Rocky tidal shorelines. Arctic shores in summer; California, Gulf, and Southeast coasts in winter; Pacific Coast, central and eastern Canada, U.S. east of Mississippi intermediate.

Veery. Moist woods, bottomlands, mountains, forests. U.S. Northwest, upper Midwest and Northeast, Appalachians, across lower Canada to maritime provinces in summer; rest of U.S. intermediate.

Vireo, red-eyed. Deciduous forests, suburbs with shade trees. Canadian Great Plains to sub-Arctic across lower Canada, U.S. upper Northwest inland from coast eastward to Mississippi Valley and throughout eastern half of U.S. in summer.

Vireo, solitary (also known as *blue-headed vireo*). Mixed evergreen-hardwood forests. Across Canada to sub-Arctic, western U.S., upper Northeast and New England and Appalachians in summer; lower Southwest, Gulf, and Southeast coasts and inland in winter; lower central Canada, Midwest, Middle Atlantic, and South intermediate.

Vireo, white-eyed. Moist thickets and swamps. Eastern half of U.S., Atlantic Coast to Nova Scotia in summer; Gulf and lower Southeast coasts and Florida year-around.

Vulture, black (also known as *turkey buzzard*). Farmland, open country, woods. Lower Southwest, South and Eastern seaboards, California coast year-around; throughout U.S. and lower western Canada, except New England, in summer.

Warbler, American redstart. See **Redstart, American**.

Warbler, Audubon's. See **Warbler, yellow-rumped**.

Warbler, black-and-white. Forests and damp woodlands. From upper Canadian Great Plains across Canada to Atlantic Coast, U.S. upper Midwest, Middle Atlantic, and upper South in summer; Gulf Coast and southern Florida in winter; U.S. Great Plains and lower Southwest and South intermediate.

Warbler, blackpoll. Stunted spruce, northern pine forests. Alaska and upper Canada to Arctic in summer; lower Canada east of Rockies, upper Great Plains, and eastern half of U.S. intermediate.

Warbler, black-throated blue. Streams, springs in evergreen forests. Upper Midwest and lower Canada from Great Lakes through New England, Appalachians in summer; lower eastern Midwest and South intermediate.

Warbler, common yellow-throat. See **Yellowthroat, common**.

Warbler, myrtle. See **Warbler, yellow-rumped**.

Warbler, northern waterthrush. See **Waterthrush, northern**.

Warbler, ovenbird. See **Ovenbird**.

Warbler, pine. Pines and orchards. Great Lakes east to lower New England, Middle Atlantic, and upper-central South in summer; Southeast and Deep South year-around; western Gulf coast in winter.

Warbler, prothonotary. Swamps, lake and stream borders. Midwest, South, and Middle Atlantic except southern Florida in summer; southern Florida and western Gulf coast intermediate.

Warbler, yellow. Shrubs and low trees, thickets, and woodlands. Throughout Alaska and Canada to Arctic, across U.S., except central and north Texas and lower South, in summer; latter are intermediate.

Warbler, yellow-rumped (also known as *Audubon's warbler, myrtle warbler*). Mixed and coniferous forests. Alaska and throughout Canada to Arctic east to Atlantic Coast, U.S. Great Basin and Rockies, Great Lakes, and Northeast in summer; Pacific Coast except southern California and parts of lower Southwest year-around; Texas, lower Mississippi Valley, lower Midwest, Middle Atlantic, and South in winter.

Warbler, yellow-throated. Swamps, bottomlands, pine and sycamore forests. Midwest below Great Lakes, Middle Atlantic to Connecticut in summer; Gulf and Southeast coasts and northern Florida year-around; southern Florida in winter; western Gulf coast intermediate.

Waterthrush, northern. Swamps and brooks. Alaska and Canada to Arctic, Canadian Rockies, and Great Plains eastward, Great Lakes, New York State, northern Appalachians, and New England in summer; southern Florida in winter; U.S. Great Plains and east of Mississippi River to Atlantic Coast intermediate.

Waxwing, cedar. Orchards, residential areas, woods where berries are abundant. Throughout Canada to sub-Arctic, New England in summer; across northern U.S. to Appalachians, Middle Atlantic coast year-around; rest of U.S. in winter.

Whimbrel (also known as *Hudsonian curlew*). Coastal areas near freshwater. Alaska and Canadian Arctic shores in summer; California and Florida coasts in winter; intermediate along both ocean coasts and eastern Canada.

Whippoorwill. Woodlands, especially near fields. U.S. Northeast, Midwest, western Southwest, lower central and eastern Canada in summer; lower Southeast and Gulf coasts in winter.

Willet. Coastal marshes east, lakes west of Mississippi. Canadian and upper U.S. Great Plains, Nova Scotia, northeast Atlantic coast, areas in Oregon and Colorado in summer; Southeast and Gulf year-around; lower California coast in winter; intermediate throughout western U.S. and along East Coast.

Woodcock, American. Moist bottomlands. Central and eastern states, Canadian maritime provinces in summer; southeast U.S. to Middle Atlantic coast year-around; Florida, Gulf Coast, southeast Texas winter.

Woodpecker, downy. Forests, woods, orchards, residential areas and parks. Lower Alaska, most of lower half of Canada, throughout U.S., except lower Southwest, year-around.

Woodpecker, hairy. Forests. Throughout all of U.S., Canada, and Alaska to sub-Arctic year-around.

Woodpecker, pileated. Woodlands. Central Texas throughout South to Atlantic Coast, interior of Middle Atlantic states to Canadian Maritime Provinces, westward across Canada to British Columbia, ranging extensively to north-western Canada (but excluding Rocky Mountains, western plains, southern California, and Southwest) throughout year.

Woodpecker, red-bellied. Woodlands. Throughout east half of U.S. except upper Appalachians, New York, New England year-around.

Woodpecker, red-headed. Open woodland. Throughout South and lower Midwest year-around; Great Plains and upper Midwest in summer.

Wren, Carolina. Thickets and undergrowth. Mississippi Valley eastward to Atlantic Coast, except upper Midwest and New England, throughout year.

Wren, house. Woodland edges, orchards, farms, and residential areas. British Columbia, Canadian Great Plains and lower Canada, across U.S., except upper South, in summer; California year-around; lower South in winter.

Wren, marsh. Marshes. Canadian Northwest except Pacific Coast eastward through lower Canada to maritime provinces, U.S. Pacific Northwest and central West to Mexican border, California coast, upper Mississippi Valley and New England in summer; northern Pacific Coast and Great Basin year-around; lower Southwest, Gulf, and Atlantic Coasts in winter; areas of lower western Canada and rest of U.S. intermediate.

Yellowthroat, common. Marshes, swamps, moist thickets, forest edges near water. North Pacific Coast, California, lower Southwest, Gulf and Southeast coasts year-around; throughout Canada to sub-Arctic, rest of U.S. in summer.

SOURCES

Peterson, Roger Tory. *A Field Guide to the Birds: A Completely New Guide to All the Birds of Eastern and Central North America.* 4th ed. Boston: Houghton Mifflin Co., 1980.

Potter, Eloise F., James F. Parnell, and Robert P. Teulings. *Birds of the Carolinas.* Chapel Hill: University of North Carolina Press, 1980.

Pough, Richard W. *Audubon Water Bird Guide: Eastern and Central North America.* Garden City, N.J.: Doubleday and Co., 1951.

Robbins, Chandler S., Bertel Bruun, and Herbert S. Zim. *Birds of North America.* Rev. ed. New York: Golden Press, 1983. (Ranges have been drawn primarily from this work, *Familiar Birds of North America,* cited below, and Peterson's *Field Guide to the Birds.*)

Sprunt, Alexander, Jr., and E. Burnham Chamberlain. *South Carolina Bird Life.* Rev. ed. Columbia, S.C.: University of South Carolina Press, 1970.

Whitman, Ann H., ed. *Familiar Birds of North America: Eastern Region.* Audubon Society Pocket Guide. New York: Alfred A. Knopf, 1986.

—**L.D.R.**

XIII

SCIENCE AND THE
NATURAL WORLD

56

HOW THE EARTH DEVELOPED

. . . . .

THE NOTION THAT OUR PLANET IS SOMEWHAT OLDER THAN WAS THOUGHT by those who fixed its date of creation at 4004 B.C.E. is now generally accepted. Without getting involved in the scientific nonsense called "creationism," it is safe to say that at a minimum the earth is more like four and a half billion years old, and very possibly even older.

Although the Greeks had deduced something of what was involved in the formation of the earth's structures, it was not really until the seventeenth century that the geological evidence of the earth's formation began to be thought about scientifically. That the earth had evolved, rather than simply come into full existence, was until then not assumed; thus the phenomenological evidence was read only biblically—for example, persons who observed belts of sea shells high up in the mountains assumed that they had been deposited there during the biblical flood described in Genesis and folklore.

Even after it began to be understood that the formation of the earth and the development of life could not possibly have occurred within the traditional framework, but was necessarily a process taking place over a far greater expanse of time, the assumption was that there had been a period during which geological change occurred with relative swiftness and violence, as a result of catastrophic processes no longer operative. It was the eighteenth-century English scientist James Hutton who formulated the so-called Law of Uniformity, which eventually won general credence: that the processes which have been at work on the earth in the past are the same as those now in operation, so that the formation of topographical features—mountains, valleys, plains, coastal areas, bodies of water, and the like—could have come about only over a period of time that involved millions and even billions of years.

As the theory of biological evolution took hold, paleontologists were able to trace, through fossil evidence, the development of life forms from primitive bacterialike organisms toward the complexity of plant and animal forms of the present day. It was not until the twentieth century, however, that certain observations that had long been made—that the shape of the continents, in particular of Africa and South America, suggested that they had broken off from each other—were formulated, by Alfred Lothar Wegener, into a long-controversial theory of continental drift, which held that there had once been a single solid land mass which subsequently divided as the crust of the earth split apart. This was followed closely by the theory, now generally accepted, that the earth's crust is in the form of plates, and that these have been engaged in shifting.

Working with the evidence of sedimentary rock strata, and on the theory that when similar fossils appear in different rock layers they were all deposited during a given period, geologists have been able to develop a chronology of the planet's development. Beginning with the Precambrian era, when the earth's crust was formed and its atmosphere first grew able to sustain life, so that organisms developed, it advances thereafter through vast but roughly identifiable periods, each more specifically detailed than its predecessor, culminating with the emergence, in what geologically is only a brief sector in the earth's timeline, of humanlike creatures.

Within that general framework of agreement, however, there are questions that produce broad and sometimes heated disagreement among scientists. Compared to other sciences such as physics, astronomy, biology, and chemistry, geology is still a "young" science, and many of its assumptions are under constant examination.

The table that follows is a chronology of the earth's past as generally schematized nowadays.

Precambrian era. 4,600,000,000–570,000,000 years ago.

Seas form, mountains grow, oxygen builds up in atmosphere; immense volcanic activity, lava flows form metamorphic rocks; bacterialike life forms at sea; first jellyfish, algae appear; microfossils are deposited.

. . . .

Paleozoic era. 570,000,000–225,000,000.

Cambrian period. 570,000,000–500,000,000.
Shallow seas cover areas of continental mass; extensive deposits are made on inland seas; thin rocks are deposited on continental margins; trilobites, brachiopods, snails, sponges, seaweed, other marine invertebrates appear.

. . . .

Ordovician period. 500,000,000–430,000,000.
Much of present-day North America is flooded; Appalachian Mountains are formed; volcanic activity occurs; jawless fish appear; invertebrates dominate in seas.

. . . .

Silurian period. 430,000,000–395,000,000.
Warm, shallow seas cover much of North America; eastern U.S. is desert; Caledonian Mountains of Scandinavia are formed; there are extensive coral reefs; land plants and animals—spiders, scorpions—appear; jawed fish and air-breathing animals develop in seas.

. . . .

Devonian period. 395,000,000–345,000,000.
Continents now exist as two land masses; erosion of mountains deposits thick sediment in seas; New England mountains are formed; forests grow in swampy areas; fish are dominant form; sharks, amphibians, insects develop.

. . . .

Carboniferous period. 345,000,000–280,000,000 (divided for North America into Mississippian, 345,000,000–325,000,000, and Pennsylvanian, 325,000,000–280,000,000).
Large areas of globe are covered by ice; coal-forming forests and swamps exist through much of Europe and North America; reptiles and giant insects appear; seed-bearing ferns develop.

. . . .

Permian period. 280,000,000–225,000,000.
Extensive glaciation; ice age in South America; deserts in western U.S.; Ural Mountains of Russia rise; many marine invertebrates, including trilobites, become extinct; ferns, fish, amphibians, reptiles flourish.

. . . .

Mesozoic era. 225,000,000–65,000,000.

Triassic period. 225,000,000–190,000,000.
Atlantic Ocean, continents of Africa and South America are formed; Caucasus Mountains of Russia and Palisades of Hudson River rise; dinosaurs and mammals appear; modern fish, corals, insect types evolve; tropical evergreens develop.

. . . .

Jurassic period (also known as Spielburg period).
190,000,000–136,000,000.
Sierra Nevada and Pacific Coast ranges are formed; volcanoes appear in western North America; palms, cone-bearing trees spread; large dinosaurs are dominant; birds appear; primitive mammals develop.

. . . .

Cretaceous period. 136,000,000–65,000,000.
Rocky Mountains and Colorado Plateau uplift begins; dinosaurs and numerous sea reptiles disappear; flowering plants develop.

. . . .

Cenozoic era. 65,000,000 to present.

Tertiary period. 65,000,000–2,500,000 (Paleocene epoch, 65,000,000–55,000,000; Eocene epoch, 55,000,000–38,000,000; Oligocene epoch, 38,000,000–25,000,000; Miocene epoch, 25,000,000–6,000,000; Pliocene epoch, 6,000,000–2,500,000).
Western U.S. uplift continues, coal forming in West; Alps, Himalayas, Andes Mountains rise; many new mammals appear; angiosperm plants now dominant; ancestors of modern horse appear; elephants appear in Africa; grasses and grazing animals flourish; primates, humanlike creatures appear; modern horse and camel develop.

. . . .

Quaternary period. 2,500,000 to present (Pleistocene epoch, 2,500,000–less than 5,000; Holocene epoch, 5,000 to present).
Ice ages; ice covers large areas of U.S. and Europe; Grand Canyon is formed; Great Lakes are formed as ice melts; western U.S. uplift continues; woolly mammoths become extinct; primitive human beings appear; humans become dominant; civilization begins.

Sources

Coble, Charles R., et al., eds. *Prentice Hall Earth Science.* Englewood Cliffs, N.J.: Prentice-Hall, 1988.

Cooney, Timothy N., Jay M. Paschoff, and Naomi Paschoff. *Earth Science.* Glenview, Ill.: Scott, Foresman and Co., 1990.

Hester, Dale N., and Susan S. Leach. *Focus on Life Science.* Columbia, Ohio: Merrill Publ. Co., 1989.

—L.D.R.

57

THE PRINCIPAL COLORS

. . . . .

WRITERS OF ADVERTISING COPY HAVE A WAY OF GOING ALL OUT WHEN IT comes to describing the colors of clothes. Here are a few colors as taken from the Christmas edition of one well-known catalog: teal, teal blue, slate blue, French blue, mallard blue, ink blue, powder blue, blueberry, burgundy, "old tan," chestnut, sage, salmon, periwinkle, raspberry, light coral, bright mulberry, charcoal heather, rust heather, blue heather, heather gray, oatmeal heather, light gray heather, purple heather, light plum heather, cobalt, eggplant, oatmeal, seabreeze, birch, rose mauve, forest, steel green, hunter green, icy green, street green, spruce green, soft mallard, jade, icy pink, stone, camel, sapphire, oyster, taupe emerald, raisin.

This, needless to say, is an improvement upon the way that Henry Ford used to sell automobiles—"they can have any color they want, so long as it's black"—though one does wonder sometimes whether the garments advertised are meant to be worn or eaten. The names are chosen, of course, in terms of their connotations for potential purchasers; one finds no fabrics advertised as being turnip green or fishbelly white. The same phenomenon arises when one goes into a store to purchase house paint and finds oneself having to decide whether goldenrod yellow or tropical banana will better match what is now on the bathroom wall.

To get down to fundamentals, there are seven basic colors of visible light; all the variations come from these. (We take our text from *A Dictionary of Color,* by A. Mertz and M. Rea Paul.) Beginning with the shortest wavelengths of light, there are the "warm" colors—red, orange, and yellow. Next is green, a transitional hue formed by equal parts of yellow and blue. Then come the "cool" colors—blue, indigo ("You ain't been blue 'til your mood's indigo"), and violet. There are also the neutral colors—white, which actually is not a single color, but is composed equally of all colors in the lightest color visible to the human eye; black, which technically is the absence of all color and light, and is the darkest color visible to the human eye; and gray, which is any hue composed by mixing only black and white.

(In actuality, the color of something is that of the light rays it reflects rather than absorbs, so that when we say that a firetruck, for example, is red, technically speaking the object itself contains any color *except* red.)

To list all the varieties of color possible from combining the above colors would take many pages. Below are a few of the more commonly encountered varieties. The rest we leave to the clothing and paint industries.

Amber. Bright golden yellow; natural amber ranges from nearly white to yellow to red to quasibrown.

Amethyst. Clear purple or bluish violet.

Apple green. Soft green with yellowish tints.

Apricot. Soft-tone brown and orange with yellow tones.

Azure. Deep blue.

Beige (also *écru*). Natural color of unbleached woolen or cotton cloth.

Blood red. Deep red.

Brick red. Darker red with violet and brown tones.

Bronze. Deep metallic red-yellow.

Bronze green. Metallic brownish green; the color of bronze patina.

Brown. From the Anglo-Saxon "bryn," "to burn"; reddish red-yellow to yellowish red-yellow, of low saturation and brilliance.

Canary yellow. Deep yellow, as the bird.

Carmine (also *carmine lake*). Rich crimson or scarlet, somewhat softened with small amounts of white and yellow.

Cherry. Bright red with slight purplish tone.

Chestnut. Brown, red-yellowish in hue, the color of chestnut hulls.

Chocolate. Dark brown, of low saturation and brilliance, often mixed with red and black.

Cinnamon. Deep yellow-reddish-brown with orange tones.

Clay. Lighter yellowish-red brown like that of clay soil.

Copper red (also *Indian red*). Deep metallic reddish orange.

Coral. Very light red, shading toward pink.

Cornflower blue. Reddish blue with a delicate greenish tone.

Cream. White with light undertones of brown and yellow, of very high brilliance.

Crimson. Deep bluish red, of low brilliance.

Dun. Dingy grayish brown.

Emerald green. Deep yellow-green.

Fawn. Very light brown, almost tan.

Flesh. Mixture of pink, white, and very light brown; the flesh in question is presumably Caucasian.

Gold. Metallic, highly polished yellowish red-yellow.

Golden. Same as gold, but without the polished metallic overtones.

Grass green. Dark green with yellow undertones.

Havana brown. Darker yellow-brown with green undertones, like a maduro-wrapped cigar.

Hazel. Light, clear brown, the color of ripe hazelnuts.

Honey. Deep yellow with brown and golden undertones.

Ivory. Whitish yellow.

Lead. Dull, bluish metallic gray.

Lemon yellow. Bright yellow, slightly greenish.

Lilac. Lavender; a very light, pale purple.

Magenta. Reddish-blue red.

Moss green. Deep green with brown and yellow overtones.

Mouse gray. Light gray with whitish tinge.

Myrtle green. Light yellow-green.

Navy blue. Dark glossy blue.

Nut brown. Light brown, reputedly the color of an ale consumed exclusively by English Renaissance poets.

Ochre. Yellowish brown with green undertones.

Olive green. Darker, brownish-yellow green.

Peach. Light reddish-yellow pink.

Peacock blue. Bright, deep blue with a faint greenish metallike sheen.

Pea green. Light yellowish green.

Pearl gray. Almost purely neutral gray.

Pink. Pale red tone made by mixing red and white.

Plum. Dark bluish purple, semiviolet.

Red lead. Somewhat grayish red.

Rose. Pure light red.

Russet. Generally a light reddish brown.

Rust red. Orange-red, somewhat burnt.

Saffron yellow. Delicate orange-yellow, like the flower.

Salmon. Reddish pink.

Sandstone. Dark whitish yellow.

Scarlet. Brilliant deep red with an orange undertone.

Sea green. Deep bluish green with yellow overtones.

Sepia. Color of cuttlefish ink; dark brown with yellowish undertones.

Silver. Metallic light gray.

Silver gray. Similar to silver, but duller and lighter.

Sky blue. Deep blue lightened with white; "Carolina blue."

Slate. Dark gray with violet overtones.

Smoke gray. Vague term covering most medium grays.

Steel gray. Light, highly polished gray with silver overtones.

Stone. Any dull light gray.

Straw. Brownish yellow with green tints.

Sulphur yellow. Deep yellow tinged with orange.

Tan. Very light brown, often with yellow highlights.

Terra cotta. Brownish red, with purplish tint, as of fired clay.

Turquoise blue. Lighter blue with greenish undertones.

Umber. Dark burnt brown softened with white.

Verdigris. Light whitish green; color of copper patina.

Vermilion. Dark red with purple or indigo overtones.

Wine red. Dark purplish red.

SOURCE

Maerz, A., and M. Rea Paul. *A Dictionary of Color.* New York: McGraw-Hill, 1930.

—**David Sisk; L.D.R.**

58

SCIENTIFIC TERMS:
A GLOSSARY

· · · · ·

THE LATE EDGAR ALLAN POE, POET, STORYTELLER, CRITIC, AND JOURNALIST, was not very flattering to science. Addressing it in a sonnet, he described it as a vulture with peering eyes, with wings that were "dull realities," and claimed that it specialized in preying upon the hearts of poets. At the same time, Poe tried his hand at what is now called SciFi—science fiction—and might even be thought of as one of its inventors. Meanwhile science has gone right along on its business and has managed to change our daily lives in near-incalculable ways.

Almost until Poe's time—the first half of the nineteenth century—it was possible for gifted individuals to be more or less fully conversant with the sciences while also being professional literary persons. Such things as the "scientific temperament" and the "artistic temperament" were not seen as being mutually exclusive. Nowadays the enormous amount of specialized knowledge and training required to attain professional competence in a science has made doing that and anything else on other than a casual basis extremely difficult, if not impossible. Seemingly the most that a writer can hope to have—unless he is a scientific writer, which is a specialized talent, and an extremely valuable one—is a very general idea of what science is all about.

What follows is a listing of a few of the more elementary scientific concepts and terms that are likely to turn up in everyday discourse. They are meant for scientific illiterates like the editor of this book. See also the section entitled "Certain Immutable Laws" in this book.

Aberration of light. Alteration in the position of a heavenly body as seen from earth because of the motion of the earth during the time that light takes to reach the viewer; see also **Lens aberration**.

Absolute zero. Lowest temperature theoretically attainable, where molecules of a substance cease all motion and thus possess no heat energy. See **Thermodynamics; Entropy**.

Archimedes' principle. Principle stating that the buoyant force acting on a submerged object is equal to the weight of the displaced fluid.

Atavism. Inherited characteristic not evident in a plant's or animal's immediate ancestors, derived from earlier ancestors or caused by reappearance of a recessive trait or a recombination of genes.

Atom. Particle consisting of two basic structures, the nucleus and a set of electrons that orbit it; within the nucleus are electrically charged protons and neutral particles or neutrons, made up of quarks. See **Quarks; Elementary particles; Nuclear energy; Nuclear force**.

Big bang theory. Cosmological theory that all matter and energy in the universe originated from an explosion of a highly dense cosmic egg at a finite moment in the past, from which the universe has been expanding ever since.

Biogenesis. Opposite of spontaneous generation; belief that all living things come from other living things.

Biological clock. Mechanism that controls the cycles and rhythms of animal and plant activities such as reproduction and migration in animals and photosynthesis and leaf movement in plants; most activities follow the rhythm of a 24-hour period, called the "circadian rhythm."

Biosphere. The part of the earth, oceans, and atmosphere which consists of living organisms; see **Ecosystem**.

Black hole. Term coined by John A. Wheeler in 1967 for a region of space formed by the gravitational collapse of a massive star or galaxy where matter and energy cannot escape owing to the tremendous mass and density of the object.

Boyle's law. Law stating that the volume of a gas is related inversely to the pressure exerted upon it.

Catalyst. A substance which speeds up a chemical reaction but is itself unchanged at the end of the reaction.

Cell theory. Theory stating that all living tissue is composed of cells, the smallest independently functioning units in an organism, and that all cells come from other cells.

Chromosomes. Threadlike structures of genetic materials within the nuclei of all living cells, which transmit all inherited characteristics. Chromosomes are long molecules consisting of proteins and the nucleic acid DNA (and sometimes RNA), constant within each species of plant or animal; there are 46 chromosomes in human beings.

Clone. The duplicate aggregate of an organism produced by asexual reproduction such as parthogenesis, as in unfertilized eggs, through splitting, budding, etc.

Comet. Celestial body moving about the solar system in elongated, near-round or near-parabolic orbit, often developing a long gaseous or dusty tail, which points away from the sun.

Continental drift. Hypothesis proposed in 1912 by Alfred Lothar Wegener that the earth's continents at one time formed a single mass called Pangaea (Greek for "all earth"), which slowly broke and drifted apart; see **Plate tectonics**.

Corpuscular theory of light. Isaac Newton's (1642–1727) theory that light is composed of a stream of particles.

Deoxyribonucleic acid (DNA). Nucleic acid whose molecules are responsible for storing the genetic code and whose structure consists of a double helix located in the nucleus of a cell.

Doppler effect. The change observed in the frequency of sound, light, and other waves due to the relative motion of the source and the observer; thus the whistle of an approaching train appears to have a higher pitch, and a receding train a lower pitch, because of the speed of the train toward, then away from, the observer. In the case of light, the Doppler effect explains the red shift (see **Red shift**) of distant galaxies and stars that are receding from the Milky Way. Doppler radar is used to distinguish moving from stationary targets and to determine their speed.

Ecosystem. Community of living organisms balanced within a physical environment, joined in feeding relationships that continuously recycle raw materials such as nitrogen, carbon, oxygen, and hydrogen.

Einstein's theory of general relativity (1916). Theory that analyzes gravity by working with accelerated systems; explains that gravitational force is caused by the presence of matter in space (*e.g.*, planets), which makes space curve in a way that produces gravitational attraction; to quote John Wheeler, "matter tells space how to curve; space tells matter how to move."

Einstein's theory of special relativity (1905). Theory that explains the dynamics of matter and energy in nonaccelerating systems. A few simple precepts and conclusions concerning the four dimensions of motion, space, time, and mass: (1) There is no absolute rest or absolute motion; (2) the measurement of space is relative; (3) relative motion and relative time are intimately related, *i.e.*, the hands of a clock moving relative to you appear to run slow when compared to the hands of a clock at rest relative to you; (4) mass and energy are equivalent and may be turned from one form to the other, with the transformation obeying $e = mc^2$.

Electromagnetism. Study of the relationship between magnetism and electricity; the basis for everything from the light bulb to television and the computer. See **Grand Unified Theory (GUT)**.

Elementary particles. Fundamental units of which all matter in the universe is composed. In current theories, there are two classes of particles: leptons—

those with no internal structure and which interact by electromagnetic or weak interactions; and hadrons—those with complex internal structure and which interact by strong interaction. The latter are thought to be composed of quarks; see **Quarks**.

Entropy. Measurement of the unavailable energy within a system, often seen as the function of the "disorder" within the system. All systems have a finite and positive entropy, but as a system approaches absolute zero the system's entropy approaches zero; see **Absolute zero; Thermodynamics (third law)**.

Enzyme. Biochemical catalyst that accelerates chemical change produced in living cells.

Equinox. Occurs twice a year, in spring and in autumn, when the sun rises and sets above the equator and day and night are equal in length; the differences in other days are due to the tilt of the earth's axis.

Escape velocity. The speed necessary for an object to escape a gravitational field. Escape velocity for a given object increases with the mass and density of its attracting object, and inversely with its proximity to the object.

Galaxy. A self-gravitating group of stars, gas, and interstellar dust. There are spiral galaxies such as our own disc-shaped Milky Way, where the center or nucleus bulges with stars and is surrounded by spiral arms or streams; and elliptical galaxies, which lack spiral arms and rotate more slowly.

Gas laws. Three laws explaining the relationship between volume, pressure, and temperature of gases, which are substances possessing low density and viscosity compared to solids and liquids: (1) Boyle's law—as pressure on gas increases, the volume of the gas decreases if kept at a constant temperature; (2) Charles' law—as temperature rises, the volume of a gas increases if kept at a constant pressure; and (3) Avogadro's law—different gases of equal volumes at equal temperatures and pressures contain the same number of molecules.

Gene. A small segment of a chromosome that determines an inherited characteristic.

Genetic engineering. Biochemical alteration of the DNA in cells by conscious human design, to produce new organisms.

Geocentrism. Ptolemy's view that the earth is the center of the universe, with all planets revolving around it in circular motions.

Grand Unified Theory (GUT). An attempt to describe the four fundamental forces of the universe with several sets of mathematical equations: The four forces are: (1) gravitation—graviton particles (see **Graviton**) transmit the force of gravity; (2) electromagnetism—photons (see **Photon**) transmit this force, which holds together every atom and molecule by both attraction and repulsion; (3) weak nuclear force—W and Z particles transmit this force, usually in the atomic nucleus; and (4) strong nuclear force—particles called gluons hold together parts of the nucleus of an atom (see **Nuclear force; Elementary particles**).

Gravitation (gravity). Mutual attracting force between all particles of matter in the universe; it keeps the planets and moons in their orbits in relation to one another and to the sun. See **Einstein's theories; Newton's laws**.

Graviton. Hypothetical massless particle that transmits the force of gravity, traveling at the speed of light.

Greenhouse effect. Accumulation of carbon dioxide and other gases in the atmosphere, which traps heat from solar radiation and results in an increase in the temperature of the earth's surface.

Greenwich Mean Time (GMT). Time standard used throughout the world based on the local mean time along the Greenwich or zero meridian of longitude; it was based on the observatory in Greenwich, England.

Heisenberg's uncertainty principle. See **Uncertainty principle**.

Heliocentrism. Copernicus' revolutionary theory that the sun is the center of the solar system and the planets revolve around it; first advanced by the third century B.C.E. Greek astronomer Aristarchus of Samos.

Hubble's constant. Named after American astronomer Edward P. Hubble (1889–1953); a quantity representing the rate at which the velocity of a receding galaxy increases with its distance from the observer, determined by the red shift of the distant galaxy; in other words, it is the ratio of the rate of speed at which a typical galaxy recedes divided by the distance to that galaxy, and is used to determine the rate of the expansion of the universe. The Hubble Space Telescope is named after E. P. Hubble.

Hubble's law. Law stating that a distant galaxy recedes at a velocity proportional to its distance from the observer (on earth) as shown by its red shift (see **Red shift**).

Hydrologic cycle. Water cycle; circulation of water from the clouds to the land and oceans of earth in the form of precipitation, and back to the atmosphere again via evaporation.

Inverse square law. Law stating that unhindered energy from a source spreads out evenly and equally in all directions with its intensity diminishing as the inverse square of its distance from the source; gravity, sound, and electromagnetic radiation all behave in this manner.

Ion. Electrically charged atom or group of atoms.

Isotope. One of several or more species of a chemical element, containing an identical number of electrons arranged identically about a nucleus, but with different mass or mass number and different physical properties.

Kepler's laws of planetary motion. Laws concerning the ways in which planets in a solar system behave: (1) planets orbit the sun in an elliptical manner; (2) planetary speed depends on the distance from the sun, with those closest to the sun moving fastest; (3) the square of the time it takes for a planet to orbit the sun is proportional to the cube of its mean distance from the sun.

Laser. Light amplification by simulated emission of radiation; a means of controlling light, discovered in 1960, so that the beam of light consists of an orderly progression of in-phase, monochromatic energy waves.

Latent heat. The amount of heat needed to change matter into another physical form without a change in temperature; the energy is either absorbed in the form of latent heat, or released as a material changes from, for instance, a solid to a liquid or a liquid to a gas; there is no temperature increase during the process. For example, boiling water is at 212° Fahrenheit throughout the boiling transition; the energy the water absorbs goes into turning the liquid into steam.

Law of conservation of mass. Law stating that the total mass within a closed system remains the same no matter what physical or chemical changes occur; matter can be neither created nor destroyed in any system. This principle is strictly accurate only when the energy of the process is much less than mc^2.

Law of conservation of momentum. Law stating that the momentum within a closed system will remain constant so long as no external forces are acting upon that system. For example, the momentum of two colliding bodies before impact equals the momentum after impact.

Law of constant (definite) proportions (also called *Proust's law*). Law stating that the proportions of elements in a chemical compound are always the same no matter how they are combined.

Lens aberration. Failure of a lens to focus light properly.

Light year. Amount of distance that light travels in one year.

Liquid. Intermediate state between a solid and a gas. A liquid resembles a gas in that molecules are relatively free to move about, but its volume remains nearly constant when faced with changes in pressure; liquids take the shape of their containers.

Local group. Astronomical term denoting the galaxies closest to our own Milky Way; the Magellanic Clouds and Andromeda are part of the local group.

Lunar eclipse. Occurrence at the time of the full moon only, when the moon passes into the umbra, or completely dark section, of the shadow of the earth; compare with Solar eclipse.

Matter. Substance that has extension in space and time, or anything that has mass and is made up of atoms; exists in four physical states: solid, liquid, gas, plasma.

Meiosis. A two-step process of reproductive cell division resulting in production of half the number of chromosomes by splitting the double helix into two single helices, so that during fertilization the combined chromosomes will reach the complete number within a cell, thus making possible genetic variation and change.

Mendelian laws of inheritance. These constitute the foundation of genetics as developed by Gregor Johann Mendel regarding the inheritance of certain characteristics in plants and animals: (1) law of segregation—each characteristic is inherited independently and with equal probability; later determined to be controlled by alleles, which are paired contrasting factors of a gene that determine particular characteristics of an organism and which can be dominant or recessive; if both a dominant and a recessive characteristic appear in an individual, the dominant form will be expressed, *e.g.*, brown eyes over blue eyes, but either can be passed on with equal likelihood; (2) law of recombination or independent assortment—successive generations of crossbred offspring will exhibit all possible combinations of inherited characteristics; later found to mean that alleles segregate independently of each other when forming germ cells.

Mercator projection. A cylindrical projection of a portion or all of the earth, which is spherical in shape, onto the flat surface of a map; meridian lines stay parallel, as do latitude lines, and the two still meet at right angles; however, distances become increasingly distorted as one moves toward the poles. Mercator maps marked the beginning of modern geography; the first Mercator books displayed Atlas on the cover, thus providing a name for map books.

Meteorite. Small body of matter within the solar system, which on intersecting the earth survives passage through the atmosphere and reaches the surface of the earth.

Mitosis. Process of normal cell division where a nucleus divides to form two new nuclei, each containing the same number of chromosomes as the original.

Mutation. Sudden variation in genetic material of a cell causing appearance or behavior that is different from the normal type, thus providing a mechanism for evolutionary change; the antithesis of heredity.

Mutualism. Interaction between two species that benefits both; *symbiosis* is often used as a synonym.

Natural selection (also know as *Darwinism*). First suggested by Charles Darwin to explain biological evolution. Darwin proposed that those life forms will survive that are best adapted to their environment—the "survival of the fittest"—and therefore will reproduce in the greatest numbers; we now think of them as transmitting genetic information within their species.

Neutron. Neutral particle within the atom; see **Atom**.

Neutron star (also known as *pulsar*). Collapsed star consisting of tightly packed neutrons; they are millions of times denser than white dwarf stars.

Newton's law of universal gravitation. Mathematical expression developed to show the relationship between the mass and distance of two objects and their gravitational attraction; reliant on two factors: (1) the attraction between two objects is directly proportional to the product of their masses;

the more matter contained in an object, the greater the gravitational force it feels and the greater the force it exerts; (2) gravitational attraction is inversely proportional to the square of the distance between two bodies; as two bodies move farther apart, attraction diminishes.

Newton's laws of motion. Three laws that provide the basis of classical mechanics: (1) the principle of inertia—a material particle or body, if left to itself, will maintain its condition, either of rest or of motion, unchanged; (2) an acceleration is the result of a force acting on a body, with the magnitude of that force equal to *ma*, the body's mass times the acceleration; accelerations from multiple forces are additive; (3) to every force there is an equal and opposite reaction, so that an object will exert a force equal in magnitude and opposite in direction to any force applied to it.

Nova. Star that shows a sudden increase in brightness, followed by a decrease.

Nuclear energy. Formerly called atomic energy; has to do with the conversion of matter into energy by the release of the energy in the nucleus of the atom, through releasing some of the binding energy that holds the nucleus together. There are two nuclear energy-releasing processes: (1) fission—the splitting or breaking apart of very heavy atoms into approximately equal parts, resulting in the release of radiation; used in the atomic bomb and nuclear reactors; and (2) fusion—the assemblage or forcing together of very light atoms (usually hydrogen) to form heavier atoms (usually helium) with an enormous release of radiation in the form of heat and radiant energy; this is the source of energy in the sun and hydrogen bombs. See **Nuclear Force**.

Nuclear force. The strong nuclear force is within the atom and holds it together; when released by fission or fusion, it produces the heat and light of the sun and other stars. It makes possible atom and hydrogen bombs and nuclear reactors. The weak nuclear force, also within the atom, is produced by the slow process of the natural decay of nuclear particles. Its radiation is the source of the heat of the earth's core and the glow of a radium watch dial. It is the source of danger in radioactivity and nuclear wastes.

Parallax. The apparent change in observed direction and distance between two objects caused by the difference in position of the observer; as objects become more distant, the parallax decreases.

Pascal's law of fluid pressure. Law stating that when pressure is exerted on a fluid in an enclosed body, it is transmitted equally in all directions and acts at a right angle to all surfaces of the container; this law is the basis for the hydraulic press. See also **Archimedes' principle**.

Photon. A massless particle which travels at the speed of light that is the quantum of electromagnetic radiation such as light, radio waves, and X-rays.

Photosynthesis. Process by which plant cells convert carbon dioxide and water in the presence of chlorophyll and light into carbohydrates, releasing oxygen as the by-product.

Plate tectonics. Science dealing with forces that shape the major land masses and oceans of the earth in terms of the movement of large plates of the upper part of the earth's crust and mantle (lithosphere) that are carried along by the slow movement of plastic rock (asthenosphere) underneath. The theory of plate tectonics is fundamental to modern geology and has explained continental drift, earthquake zones, volcanic belts, mountain building, and sea-floor spreading.

Polymer. Chemical compound or mixture of compounds formed by linking small molecules together to form a large, reduplicating long-chain molecule.

Precession of the equinoxes. The uniform shift of stars over the centuries from west to east, due to the fact that the earth's axis is precessing like a spinning top. It will take 26,000 years to complete one cycle.

Principle of buoyancy. Principle that an object immersed in a fluid displaces the volume of the fluid equal to its own weight; see **Archimedes' principle**.

Pulsar. See **Neutron star**.

Punctuated evolution. Theory put forth in 1972 by Stephen Jay Gould and Niles Eldridge proposing that evolution is a matter of stability interrupted or punctuated by occasional periods of rapid change that result in the development of new species. This view presents a challenge to James Hutton's Law of Uniformity upon which the Darwinian view of slow, steady change is based; not a widely accepted view.

Quantum mechanics. Method for interpreting small-scale physical phenomena such as properties of atoms and molecules; explains how atoms release and absorb photons, which contain both particle and wave characteristics, incorporating the uncertainty principle (see **Uncertainty principle**); explains how all particles have wavelike properties. It incorporates the Pauli exclusion principle (important for developing the periodic table) based on the idea of characterizing each electron in an atom as possessing one of four quantum numbers and states that no two electrons within an atom can have the same set of four quantum numbers. In the large size limit, its predictions agree with those of Newtonian physics.

Quantum theory (1895–1930). Max Planck explained the relationship between energy and wavelengths by showing that energy is not infinitely divisible but exists in pieces (quanta). Albert Einstein used this theory to explain the dual nature of light—sometimes behaving as waves and other times as particles (see **Quantum theory of light**). The size of the quanta is inversely proportional to the wavelength of energy, or the larger the quanta, the shorter the wavelength.

Quantum theory of light (also called *quantum electrodynamics*). This theory explains how atoms and electrons interact with radiation, demonstrating the dual nature of light.

Quarks. Elementary particles that occur in six "flavors" (not implying taste) and are thought to possess "color change," and a fraction of the charge of an electron ⅓ or ⅔). Along with leptons, quarks are considered to be the only truly elementary particles (see **Elementary particles**). The name comes from a phrase in James Joyce's *Finnegans Wake,* "Three quarks for Muster Mark," and was introduced by Murray Gell-Mann in the 1960s. Recently (1994) the sixth, top quark, hitherto unobserved, is believed to have been found.

Radar (radio detection and ranging). System for determining the positions of long-range objects by transmitting radio waves and measuring the time it takes for them to travel to the object and be reflected back to the source; developed just before and during World War II.

Red shift. The observed shift to the red, or the long-wave, end of the light spectrum as a galaxy or star moves away from our galaxy; this is the principal evidence for the big-bang theory of an expanding universe. See **Doppler effect**.

Relativity, theories of. See **Einstein's theories**.

Respiration. Process by which living organisms take oxygen from water or the air, metabolize it (or use it to burn carbon), and release carbon dioxide.

Retrograde motion. Observed motion of a planet in a sense opposite to that of the other planets; Venus' rotation is said to be retrograde because it spins the opposite way from the other eight planets.

Ribonucleic acid (RNA). A single-strand molecule of nucleic acid similar to DNA (see **Deoxyribonucleic acid [DNA]**) that carries instruction for protein synthesis in the body.

Royal Society. First formal group of scientists that met to share information; it published a journal, *Philosophical Transactions;* chartered by Charles II of England in 1662.

Solar eclipse. Occurrence when the moon comes between the sun and the earth to block the passing of light from the sun either partially or completely.

Solid. Substance of densely packed atoms that is resistant to force and has a definite shape.

Speed of light. Velocity of electromagnetic waves in a vacuum (see **Vacuum**); defined to be exactly 186,282.5 miles or 299,792.8 kilometers per second.

Spontaneous generation. Belief that new forms of life can arise from nonlife, particularly the popular belief about microorganisms prior to Pasteur.

Standard Model. Current accepted working hypothesis about the nature of force; see **Electromagnetism; Gravitation; Nuclear force; Grand Unified Theory (GUT)**.

String theory. Controversial hypothesis, held as yet only by a minority of scientists, which posits all phenomena and matter in the universe as caused by the vibrations of minute, unobservable "strings."

Supernova. Exploding star that has used up all of its nuclear fuel and whose core collapses violently, then explodes; its brightness is far greater than that of an ordinary nova and lasts several years at such an intensity. It is believed that a supernova may eventually form a black hole or a neutron star.

Thermodynamics. Branch of physics dealing with heat and its relation to mechanical, chemical, and other forms of energy based on the following laws concerning systems (any defined collection of matter), the three famous laws of thermodynamics: (1) Quantities of heat may be converted into energy, and vice versa, with the total amount of energy being always conserved; (2) when heat or energy is exchanged between two bodies at different temperatures, the hotter body loses heat and the colder body gains heat; and (3) every substance has an available entropy that approaches zero as its temperature approaches absolute zero. The laws of thermodynamics specify that if two systems are in thermal equilibrium with a third body, then all three bodies will be in thermal equilibrium with each other, the underlying concept for temperature.

Uncertainty principle. Principle in quantum mechanics that it is impossible to determine both the position and the velocity (speed) of a particle simultaneously; also known as Heisenberg's uncertainty principle (1927).

Vacuum. Any region of space lacking atoms and molecules, where sound waves cannot be transmitted.

Wave theory of light. Theory that light is composed of waves that move in and out perpendicularly to the same direction in which they travel, like waves in a shaken rope or plucked rubber band; used to explain reflection and refraction of light.

SOURCES

Asimov, Isaac. *Asimov's Chronology of Science and Discovery*. New York: Harper and Row, 1989.

Barnhardt, Robert K., ed. *The American Heritage Dictionary of Science*. Boston: Houghton Mifflin Co., 1986.

Isaacs, Allen, John Daintith, and Elizabeth Martin, eds., *Concise Science Dictionary*. 2nd ed. New York: Oxford University Press, 1991.

Pears Cyclopedia. 101st ed. London: Pelham Books Ltd., 1992.

Schneider, Herman, and Leo Schneider. *The Harper Dictionary of Science in Everyday Language*. New York: Harper and Row, 1988.

Uvarov, E. B. *The Penguin Dictionary of Science*. 6th ed. New York: Viking, 1986.

Walker, Peter M. B., ed. *Chambers's Science and Technology Dictionary*. Cambridge, Eng.: W & R Chambers Ltd. and Cambridge University Press, 1988.

Yule, John-David, ed. *Concise Encyclopedia of the Sciences*. New York: Facts on File, 1976.

—Jesma Reynolds; L.D.R

XIV

PSYCHOANALYSIS

59

PSYCHOANALYTIC TERMS:
A GLOSSARY

. . . . .

SIGMUND FREUD, WHO INVENTED PSYCHOANALYSIS, WAS QUICK TO SAY THAT it was not he who was the discoverer of the workings of the unconscious mind. "The poets and philosophers before me discovered the unconscious," he declared. "What I discovered was the scientific method by which the unconscious can be studied."

What Freud made of the workings of the unconscious has been much argued about and considerably revised by others over the course of what is now almost a century since publication of *The Interpretation of Dreams* in 1900. It has even been questioned whether psychoanalysis is actually a science, rather than an art; there are good arguments for the latter view. But whether science or art, its basic assumptions about the workings of the mind, and the language used to describe them, have proved extraordinarily useful in telling us about the way we think and write.

Freud's own writings about works of literature are not notably insightful. Assuming that all writers tended to be neurotic, which was and is by no means an untenable hypothesis, he failed to take in the corollary, which was that all neurotics are not writers. So he viewed literature as a form of daydream, or wish fulfillment. As the late Lionel Trilling pointed out, however, Freudian theory itself is by no means incompatible with the literary imagination; on the contrary, Freud's assumptions about the nature of thought are essentially those that underlie artistic creativity. Whatever the limitations of psychoanalytical literary criticism, as practiced by Freud himself and others, the mind as Freud sees it functions as literature does: metaphorically. Psychoanalytical criticism of literature became useful once its practitioners ceased using it to psychoanalyze the author and began using it to explore the dynamics of the literary work.

The terminology used in psychoanalysis has become part of our vocabulary. Regrettably, although Freud himself was a masterly writer, those who first translated his work from German into English were by no means as skilled with language, and much of the burdensome terminology they employed remains with us.

The following is a glossary of some of the more common psychoanalytical and related terms.

Abreaction. Process of remembering a repressed experience and experiencing the strong feelings associated with it. This concept was developed early in the history of psychoanalysis as part of a theory of cure.

Acting out. The enacting of prior experiences without awareness of their memorial nature. This term is usually limited to behaviors associated with great conflict occurring during psychotherapy. It is often misused as a synonym for "misbehavior."

Adaptation. The process of meeting one's needs within the demands, limitations, and opportunities of the environment.

Adultomorphic error. The erroneous attribution of adult forms of mental activity to infants or children.

Aetiology (also *etiology*). The causes of a patient's illness or difficulties.

Affective disorder. Mental illness characterized by abnormally intense or persistent alterations of moods of depression and/or mania.

Affects. States of feeling or experienced emotion.

Aggressive instinct (also *aggressive drive*). In psychoanalytic theory, the innate urge to act in ways that appear destructive in intent. This and the sexual instinct are the instinctual bases of behavior in early psychoanalytic theory. Transformations of the aggressive drive are seen to be bases for healthy self-assertion and competitiveness.

Alexithymia. A condition characterized by difficulty in discerning and describing feelings.

Alloeroticism. Sexual pleasure involving others; its opposite is autoeroticism.

Ambivalence. Condition of having conflicting or contradictory feelings for an object.

Amnesia. Inability to bring memories of experiences or events to consciousness.

Anaclitic depression. A syndrome in infants characterized by a profound loss of vitality that can imperil survival. It appears during deprivation of needed human contact.

Anal-sadistic phase. A hypothesized stage of psychosexual development occurring when children are about two years old, during which time they take pleasure in the sensations of anal functioning such as withholding and expelling. This stage is hypothesized to be associated with characteristic ways of relating to others, including gift giving and obstructionism.

Analysand. Person undergoing psychoanalysis.

Analysis (also *psychoanalysis*). Process directed toward a deepening and transforming self-awareness which uses free association and requires a relationship between doctor and patient that has great emotional force.

Analyst. Person who conducts a psychoanalytic treatment.

Analytic psychology. Study of human psychology developed by Carl Jung.

Anhedonia. Inability to enjoy that which once brought pleasure.

Anima. Term from analytic psychology referring to hypothesized inborn predispositions to behave and give meanings to experience in ways associated with the feminine.

Animus. Term from analytic psychology referring to hypothesized inborn predispositions to behave and give meanings to experience in ways associated with the masculine.

Anorexia nervosa. An eating disorder with self-starvation characterized by an inability to see the deforming effects of low weight and by fear of gaining weight. It is often associated with excessive exercise and, in women, amenorrhea.

Anxiety. A frightened feeling accompanying a perception of danger. Commonly distinguished from fear, with fear referring to realistic dangers and anxiety to fear without an apparent realistic basis.

Apathy. State of indifference.

Archetype. Term from analytic psychology signifying a theorized prototypical idea or concept that shapes behaviors and holds great emotional and spiritual meaning and is an innate aspect of being human.

Association. A thought prompted by an antecedent thought.

Autoeroticism. Sexual pleasures obtained by the use of one's own body and without interaction with other people.

Bisexuality. Erotic interest in both sexes.

Borderline personality disorder. Disorder characterized by a persistent instability of affects, volatile and intense relationships with others, and a dread of abandonment and being alone, which may lead to self-destructive behavior such as cutting on one's body.

Boredom. Unpleasant emotional state marked by dissatisfaction and absence of specific ideas about what to do.

Bulimia nervosa. An eating disorder in which the individual rapidly consumes a large amount of food in a short period of time, feels a loss of control during the binges, and then engages in attempts to minimize the caloric intake through purging (*i.e.*, self-induced vomiting or abuse of laxatives or diuretics) or fasting and exercise.

Castration anxiety. A male's fear that his genitals will be cut off or injured in retaliation for his sexual wishes. Freud theorized that females when confronted with the anatomical differences between the sexes react with humiliation and have the fantasy that they once possessed a penis but were castrated. It is now recognized that in healthy female development, females react with pride and pleasure in the discovery of their genitals. Their reactions to sexual differences is varied, but if the mother-daughter relationship is strong and the father is emotionally available, intense penis envy and fantasies of their genitals as mutilated or damaged will not typically develop.

Cathexis. An emotional investment in or attention to an object. Term is associated with the theory of instinctual drives.

Cloacal theory. Childhood fantasy that a woman's digestive, genital, and urinary tracts are convergent. It arises from ignorance of the existence of the vagina and may lead to theories that children are born in the same manner that feces are excreted.

Collective unconscious. In the analytic psychology of Jung, inborn templates for the shaping or focus of perceptions and motivations.

Complex. A stable mental interrelating of certain memories, ideas, and images manifested in one idea or experience regularly evoking implications of certain other ideas.

Compromise formation. A term denoting the finding in psychoanalysis that thoughts and behaviors are generated as compromises among urges of need, moral standards, and reality.

Condensation. A mental activity whereby an entity can embody multiple significances simultaneously.

Consciousness. Reflective self-awareness manifested in experiencing of sensations.

Conversion disorder. Illness characterized by a disturbance of body functioning, which results from psychological conflict. The symptom is symbolic, embodying in this way the patient's ideas. The individual is generally not anxious or disturbed by the symptom, a state known as *la belle indifférence*.

Counter-transference. Feelings and thoughts a therapist has about a patient. The therapist may or may not be aware of these responses. More narrowly, the term refers to the therapist's responses to the patient's transferences or, alternatively, the therapist's transference reactions to the patient. Because of varying denotations, the term has been associated with forms of the therapist's understanding and also with the therapist's responses to the treatment.

Daydream. A story created in imagination during a reverielike state. Like dreams at night, daydreams are seen to fulfill wishes.

Day-residue. Recent thoughts or experiences that appear as dream elements within a few days of their occurrence.

Death instinct. Also known as thanatos in early psychoanalytic theory; a life tendency seeking stillness and death. It was thought to be in constant opposition with the life instinct, Eros.

Defense mechanism. An unconscious mental act protecting the self from the awareness of a thought or event that is anticipated or experienced as being unwelcome.

Déjà vu. The sense that a current experience has previously occurred in precisely the same way.

Denial. The unconscious avoidance of awareness of some painful aspect of reality.

Depersonalization. A feeling of estrangement or disturbance in one's sense of self.

Depression. May refer either to a feeling state or to a diagnosis of a disorder. Associated with a sense of lowered self-worth, guilt, hopelessness, low energy, and a diminished interest in activities that once brought pleasure. If diagnosed as a mood disorder, there will be associated physical symptoms. Depression occurs in association with an imagined or actual loss.

Depth psychology. Psychology concerned with the nature of unconscious mental life.

Displacement. Defense mechanism wherein meanings associated with one object are attributed instead to a substitute object.

Distortion. A product of the dream work whereby the wish within the dream is disguised.

Dream. An experience during sleep characterized by reflective self-awareness and sensory perceptions.

Dream work. Described by Freud as the royal road to the unconscious, dreams are a figuration of the wishes and desires that have been active during waking life. The thinking active in this figuration is primary process thinking, and it is seen in condensation and displacement. The dream is accorded a narrative quality by a process termed secondary revision. Dream work is the sum of this process.

Dysfunctional. Not serving adaptation constructively.

Ego. A subdivision of the mind defined by its functions, including sensory perception, language, muscular control, and defense. In the structural model, the other divisions are the *id*, and the *superego* (q.v.).

Ego ideal. An aspect of the superego, both conscious and unconscious, with images of the self that one aspires to realize. It is created by identification (a change in one's self through taking on of qualities of others) with loved and idealized parents.

Ego instincts. In an early psychoanalytic model, a portion of the self-preservative instincts that inhibit some sexual urges as well as impel actions assuring the survival of the individual.

Ego psychology. Study of the properties, strengths, and deficits of the ego.

Eros. The instinctual basis of urges toward life and love.

Erotogenic zone (also *erogenous zone*). Area of the body whose stimulation is associated with a high degree of sexual pleasure.

Exhibitionism. Pleasurable display of oneself to others. May also refer to a sexual perversion in which individuals, usually males, are sexually gratified by display of their genitals to unsuspecting strangers.

Externalization. The attribution of origins of one's behavior to agents other than oneself.

Family romance. A fantasy that one's real parents are not the parents one is reared by, usually associated with ideas that the real parents are ideal persons. The fantasy is seen to arise out of the child's disillusionment with his parents.

Fetish. An inanimate object or body part that is the focus of great erotic interest and needed for sexual gratification. These objects may take a variety of forms such as hair, a foot, or shoes, and are highly specific for each individual.

Fixation. A point of arrest in development characterized by persisting immature sexual wishes or immature attachment to others from childhood.

Free association. Process in psychoanalysis in which the patient lets his mind wander and does not interfere, meanwhile reporting his thoughts to the analyst.

Frigidity. Lack in a woman of expectable sexual responsiveness or pleasure. It may be the result of mental conflicts, mood disorder, anatomical abnormality, hormonal disorder, other medical illness, or a conflictual relationship.

Genital phase. The final stage of psychosexual development characterized by mature sexuality with high concern for the welfare of the partner.

Group psychology. The study of the actions and dynamics of groups and the individual's experiences within them.

Guilt. An unpleasant feeling that accompanies the sense that one has done something that is morally wrong or destructive to others.

Hallucination. A sensory perception in the absence of an external stimulus. This may involve any of the senses and may be due to a mental illness or to an interference with brain functioning.

Heterosexuality. Sexual desire directed to those of the opposite sex

Homosexuality. Sexual desire directed to those of the same sex. Psychoanalytic understanding of homosexuality has changed, often amidst controversy. It is viewed as part of the spectrum of human sexuality in which biological, developmental, and environmental factors play pivotal roles.

Hysteria. An early psychoanalytic diagnostic entity, specifically a neurosis characterized by alteration of certain bodily functions, including disturbances of movement and sensation, and arising from mental conflicts.

Id. In the structural theory, the division of mind that is the domain of the mental representations of instinctual drives and thus of impulsion toward activity and gratification.

Idealization. Attribution of qualities of perfection to another.

Identification. A process whereby an individual takes on attributes of another person. This can occur in areas of ideals and in ways of behaving.

Identification is an important element in psychological development as well as a mechanism by which symptoms are developed.

Identification with the aggressor. Defense mechanism described by Anna Freud wherein an individual who has felt menaced by another behaves like that other in dealings with people.

Imago. Term coined by Carl Jung to refer to a child's unconscious concepts of parents, as well as other family members, as perceived by the child and subject to distortions by the child's own conflicts and urges.

Imitation. The consciously intentional act of copying qualities of another. This differs from identification, which is a more enduring and less conscious process.

Incorporation. The fantasy of taking another into one's body by eating or insertion. It may serve to acquire abilities or wishes to other powers of an admired or feared person and to destroy the other.

Individuation. Process described by Margaret Mahler whereby a child in the first three years of life grows to capacities of independence and a basic sense of safety.

Inferiority complex. A nontechnical term referring to a person's belief in his inadequacy, insignificance, or unworthiness.

Inhibition. Restraining of urges in order to protect against feared consequences of their indulgence.

Intellectualization. Defense mechanism whereby one considers or speaks about areas of one's life in a manner that stresses explanations and ignores evidence from feeling states or needs.

Internalization. General term that includes introjection, identification, and incorporation and denotes changes in the self wherein qualities of interactions with others persist as experiences of one's self.

Isolation of affect. The unconscious restriction of the development of feelings that people would ordinarily expect a person to have in a given situation.

Latency period. Stage of development beginning approximately at age six and lasting until puberty, during which there is a putative diminution of sexual concerns.

Latent content. The dream as interpreted through the use of free associations and understood as an expression of desires.

Libido. The mental representative of the motivational force of the sexual instinct.

Mania. Aberrant mental state characterized by a great overestimation of one's achievements or capabilities, excessive physical activity, rapid thoughts, pressured speech, instability of mood ranging from euphoria to violent outbursts, heightened sexual interest, and poor impulse control and judgment as demonstrated by excessive spending or risk-taking behavior.

Manic depressive disorder (also *bipolar disorder*). A mental illness characterized by periods of mania and, in some cases, periods of depression as well.

Manifest content. The dream as remembered. Distinguished from latent content, which is the dream as interpreted.

Masochism. Pleasure in experiencing pain or punishment. Also, a sexual perversion in which pain is required for erotic pleasure.

Narcissism. Self-love; also used to designate mental processes involved in experiences of self-esteem, self-consciousness, and shame. Also, a quality of exploitativeness in dealings with others.

Neurosis (also *psychoneurosis*). A mental disorder characterized by symptoms but not by misperceptions of reality and which is seen to arise from mental conflicts.

Object. In psychoanalytical understanding of relationships, an "object" is anything that is accorded interest or concern, usually denoting an entity in the environment.

Object constancy. The sense that a needed person remains a source of love and safety even when not present.

Object permanence. The ability to know that entities in the environment survive when they are not perceived.

Object relations theory. A body of psychoanalytic observations and theories involved with the psychology of relations of an individual with others and with their transforming and enduring influences in the mental life of that individual. Also, the school of psychoanalysis begun by the discoveries made by Melanie Klein.

Object representation. A persisting mental image of an object, drawn from attributes of that object, as well as one's experiences of that object.

Obsession. Recurrent, intrusive, and persistent thoughts that are unwelcome and difficult to stop and that may be associated with recurrent, intrusive, and persistent urges to behave in a rigid and stereotyped manner of which the significance is unknown to the person, as in a compulsion.

Oedipus complex. Hypothesized universal conflictual experience occurring generally by the time the child reaches three to six years of age in which love for one parent ignites rivalry and hostility toward the other.

Oral stage. Hypothesized early stage of psychosexual development occurring in the first year of life in which the child's needs, pleasures, and developing capacity for love involve the mouth and ideas about the mouth.

Paranoia. Term used in the past to designate a mental illness characterized by enduring grandiose or persecutory delusions.

Parapraxis. A mistake in speech or deed that is motivated by thoughts and feelings outside the individual's awareness, *e.g.*, slips of the tongue and lapses in memory.

Persona. Term from analytic psychology signifying a way in which one presents oneself in order to engender a particular impression on others or to conceal one's true self.

Perversion. Term used in the past to denote aberrant sexual behavior.

Phallic mother. Fantasy that the mother or other woman has a penis.

Phallic stage. Hypothesized developmental period occurring between the ages of three and six in which children have a growing awareness of and interest in their genitals and physical prowess as well as the beginning of romantic thoughts about the opposite sex.

Phobia. Persistent and apparently irrational dread of certain objects or situations.

Pleasure principle. The overarching mental tendency to press toward the meeting of instinctual needs.

Preconscious. Thoughts or memories one is at the moment not aware of but which can easily be brought into awareness.

Primal fantasies. Common myths and fantasies of childhood regarding sexuality and one's origin that may persist into adulthood.

Primal scene. Sexual intercourse, witnessed or imagined, usually referring to a child's observations or ideas about the sexual life of the parents.

Primary process. Thinking that is defined in contrast to secondary process and denoting imaginative and spontaneous thinking and poetical capacities.

Projection. Defense mechanism in which one attributes to another person one's own wishes and qualities and thereby does not experience them as one's own.

Psychic apparatus. A figuration given the mind in which thoughts, emotions, and motivations are considered to be properties and products of fixed psychic agencies, *i.e.*, the id, ego, and superego.

Psychic determinism. The point of view that all mental events are products of mental forces that operate in scientifically lawful ways.

Psychoanalysis. See **Analysis**.

Psychodynamic. Of or relating to the interplay of psychic forces.

Psychosis. A severe mental affliction disturbing in great degree one's experience of the external world or oneself and characterized variously by hallucinations, bizarre behaviors, delusions, and disruption of the capacity for rational or orderly thinking and the capacity for grasping reality.

Rationalization. Defense mechanism wherein a person offers a reasonable justification for a particular experience or behavior and does not seek to discern more fundamental origins.

Reality principle. The overarching tendency to realize one's needs in a manner that takes into account the opportunities and limitations of the environment and the consequences of one's actions.

Regression. The return while under stress to chronologically earlier ways of thinking or earlier patterns of need.

Repetition compulsion. The overarching tendency to recreate traumas independent of pleasure needs, seen in intrusive thoughts, repetitive dreams, and behavioral reenactments. This tendency was seen by Freud as more fundamental than the pleasure principle.

Repression. The unconscious banishing from awareness of a thought or experience.

Resistance. Actions by a patient in psychotherapy that serve to impede deepening self-awareness.

Sadism. Sexual gratification accompanying the inflicting of physical or emotional pain on others.

Schizoid personality. An enduring set of personal attributes of persistent detachment from others and restricted emotional expression in relationships with others.

Schizophrenia. Severe mental illness characterized by one or more psychotic symptoms and a deterioration in the person's relationships and capacities for work and self-care. The onset generally occurs in a person's late teenage years or early twenties.

Scopophilia (also voyeurism). Sexual gratification attained through secretly viewing a person in a state of undress or in sexual activity.

Screen memory. A childhood memory that embodies representations of various additional important memories and fantasies. Its form is believed by some to be a defensive disguise of important mental constructs.

Secondary process. Primarily conscious thought that is governed by logic and rules of language.

Sexual instinct. Basic urge to satisfy oneself sexually and to procreate.

Shadow. Term from analytic psychology for attributes of the self that may be unrecognized or suppressed and therefore exist outside of the person's awareness, but may be revealed to the person through dreams; to be distinguished from the collective unconscious.

Somatization. The generation by emotional distress or conflict of certain bodily sensations and discomfort.

Sublimation. The transformation of sexual or aggressive impulses into productive and creative behaviors and interests.

Superego. One's moral standards, goals, and ideals for oneself. A party to conflicts that can be experienced in fluctuations in self-esteem and feelings of guilt.

Suppression. The conscious attempt to drive certain thoughts from awareness.

Thanatos. See **Death instinct**.

Transference. The experiencing of another person in ways that embody antecedent experiences with important people.

Transitional object. An inanimate object that a child imbues with powerful emotional significance and with which it forms an emotional bond. An example is the special blanket the child regularly turns to for a sense of comfort and safety.

Trauma. A dreadful experience that overwhelms a person's ability to cope.

Unconscious. Adjective referring to the state of mental events outside awareness; noun referring to a division of mind in early psychoanalytic theory, characterized by activity of the instincts and primary process thinking.

Vagina dentata fantasy. Fantasy that the vagina has teeth.

Voyeurism. See **Scopophilia**.

Working through. Thoughts, feelings, and behaviors that constitute the accommodation to some new self-understanding.

SOURCES

First, Michael B., ed. *Diagnostic and Statistical Manual of Mental Disorders.* 4th ed. Washington, D.C.: American Psychiatric Association, 1994.

Freud, Sigmund. *The Standard Edition of the Complete Psychological Writings.* Translated and edited by James Strachey. 24 vols. London: Hogarth Press, 1953–74.

Hendricks, Ives. *Facts and Theories of Psychoanalysis.* New York: Alfred A. Knopf, 1958.

Jung, Carl Gustav. *Collected Works.* 20 vols. to date. New York: Pantheon Books, 1953– .

———. *Man and His Symbols.* Garden City, N.Y.: Doubleday and Co., 1964.

Laplanche, J., and J. B. Pontalis. *The Language of Psycho-analysis.* New York: W. W. Norton, 1973.

Moore, Burness E., and Bernard D. Fine, eds. *Psychoanalytic Terms and Concepts.* New Haven, Conn.: American Psychiatric Association and Yale University Press, 1990.

Nagera, Humberto, ed. *Basic Psychoanalytic Concepts on Metapsychology, Conflicts, Anxiety, and Other Subjects.* London: George Allen and Unwin, 1970.

———. *Basic Psychoanalytic Concepts on the Libido Theory.* London: George Allen and Unwin, 1969.

———. *Basic Psychoanalytic Concepts on the Theory of Dreams.* London: George Allen and Unwin, 1969.

———. *Basic Psychoanalytic Concepts on the Theory of Instincts.* London: George Allen and Unwin, 1970.

A Psychiatric Glossary. Washington, D.C.: American Psychiatric Association, 1975.

Schafer, Roy. *Aspects of Internalization.* New York: International Universities Press, 1968.

Tyson, Phyllis, and Robert L. Tyson. *Psychoanalytic Theories of Development: An Integration.* New York: Yale University Press, 1990.

—Marc S. Litle, M.D.

XV

LAW AND LAWS

60

LEGAL TERMS:
A GLOSSARY

. . . . .

"IF THE LAW SUPPOSES THAT," SAID DICKENS' MR. BUMBLE, "THEN THE LAW
is a ass, a idiot." The law, as is well known, supposes a great many things,
and its language, in an effort to be as specific as possible, tends to be somewhat on the conservative side so far as changing its terminology goes. Much
of it dates back to the Middle Ages, and there is also no small amount of
Latinate diction, as well as some outright Latin itself, involved.

Judges also used to be fond of quoting Latin proverbs and sayings in
their opinions, such as *A piratis et latronibus capto dominium non
mutant*—"The ownership of things taken by pirates and thieves does not
change" (Chancellor Kent's *Commentaries*). Or *Ne lites sint immortales
dum litantes sunt mortales*—"Let not lawsuits last forever, seeing that the
litigants are but mortal." Somehow, saying it in Latin supposedly made it
more authoritative.

I haven't the statistics to prove it, but it's my impression that relatively
few imaginative writers—*i.e.*, novelists, poets, or dramatists—earned their
livings as practitioners of law. Not a few studied law, then gave it up. But
the Edgar Lee Masters, Henry Fieldings, Wallace Stevenses, and Louis
Auchinclosses seem few and far between. Why this is so may be explained
in part by the joke that the antebellum Charlestonians used to tell about
John C. Calhoun: he was, they said, the only man ever to write a love poem
beginning with the word *Whereas*.

But writers, and editors, and even readers find themselves having to
deal with lawyers and the law from time to time. To help with such transactions, the compilation that follows attempts to define for nonlawyers
what some commonly encountered legal terms mean. However, *ignorantis
juris no excusat* ("Ignorance of the law is no excuse"). Therefore *caveat
emptor* ("Let the buyer of this book beware").

Alienate. (1) To transfer property to someone else; (2) to cause estrangement, as in "alienation of affections."

Allegation. The statement of facts in a pleading that a plaintiff intends to prove in the trial. See **Pleading**.

Allege. To assert or state.

Appeals court (also *appellate court*). Federal or state court that rehears or reviews the outcome or actions of a lower, district or superior court, to correct mistakes or injustices. State and United States supreme courts are types of appeals courts. See **Court; District court; Superior court; Supreme court**.

Assault. An intentional show of force, a threat, or an action meant to cause another person to fear actual physical harm. Assault can be a crime defined by statutory law or a tort. See **Statutory law; Tort**.

Assign. To transfer or formally give ownership or ownership rights to another person. One can have ownership rights in property yet not own the property. See **Estate; Life Estate**.

Assignee. One to whom ownership or rights are formally transferred. See **Assign**.

Assignment. Formal transfer of ownership rights, property, or money to another person or legal entity, *e.g.*, a corporation.

Assignment of risk (also *assigned risk*). A type of insurance, especially automobile insurance, which an insurance company handles only because the government requires it to do so.

Assumption of risk. A legal rule of defense. Those who knowingly expose themselves or their property to a known or appreciated danger cannot then recover damages if harmed. See **Damages**.

Bankruptcy. (1) A state of being unable to pay debt obligations as they come due; (2) proceedings in federal court under the Federal Bankruptcy Act in which the debtor may be relieved of personal responsibility for debt obligations by allowing the court to supervise all of his property and money to pay off the debts. This process can be initiated by the debtor or the creditor. See **Chapter Seven; Chapter Eleven; Chapter Thirteen**.

Bar. (1) Those licensed to practice law, all members of the legal profession, lawyers. In Great Britain only barristers, those licensed to argue before a court, are members of the bar; (2) a prohibition, to be prohibited from doing something.

Battery. An intentional act or action that results in harmful or unwelcome physical contact with another person, or that causes an object to come into harmful or unwelcome physical contact with another person. Battery can be a crime defined by statutory law or a tort. See **Statutory law; Tort**.

Beneficiary. The person who stands to gain from the act or actions of another. See also **Third-party beneficiary**.

Beyond a reasonable doubt. The degree of proof required to convict someone of a crime. While it is not a standard of complete certainty, it comes close. It is the highest standard of proof required in any trial. See also **Standard of proof; Clear and convincing evidence; Preponderance of the evidence**.

Black letter law. (1) The basic principles of law that most judges in most states accept; (2) the fundamentals in any specific area of law.

Breach. (1) The breaking of a law or failure to perform a duty; (2) the violation of an obligation like a contract, or of a law.

Burden of proof. The responsibility of showing that the evidence supporting the facts or fact contested in a dispute favors one's case. See **Evidence; Standard of proof**.

Burglary. Generally unlawful entry into someone's house in order to commit a felony, usually theft. See **Felony; Intent**.

Carrier. A person or business that transports people, goods, or information for hire. A common carrier performs this function for the general public.

Case law. (1) All recorded judicial decisions, outcomes of trials; (2) any new law established in judicial opinions.

Causation. The origination of something, or the act that produces the result.

Cause of action. (1) Sufficient facts to warrant or support a lawsuit; (2) the basis in legal theory for a lawsuit.

Caveat emptor. "Let the buyer beware"; the buyer's duty to inspect property before purchasing it.

Certiorari. "To be informed of"; (1) the request for certiorari (often referred to as *cert.*) is like an appeal, but the higher court chooses whether to hear the case. Only supreme courts are petitioned by certiorari, (2) literally, a writ asking a lower court for a certified copy of the court record. See **Appeals court; Court; Court record; Supreme court; Writ**.

Chapter Eleven. The reorganization of a corporation that is insolvent, or unable to pay its debts, which is supervised by the federal bankruptcy court. A new corporation is created in which the owners are both the creditors and the owners of the old corporation. The new corporation agrees to pay the debts of the old corporation.

Chapter Seven. Bankruptcy proceedings for an individual, corporation, or business in which the federal bankruptcy court supervises the sale of that person's or business' assets and property, and the disbursement of the proceeds from the sale to the person's or business' creditors. When the creditors receive the proceeds from a bankruptcy sale, the debtor's obligation is discharged.

Chapter Thirteen. Federal bankruptcy court's supervision of a person or a small business that agrees to repay a portion of its debt, or is granted extra time to repay debts, or both. The process is called rehabilitation.

Civil suit (also *civil action*). The opposite of a criminal suit or criminal action. A lawsuit in which someone sues another person to enforce a right or redress a wrong. See **Redress**.

Clear and convincing evidence. A degree of proof stronger than the preponderance of the evidence, but less than beyond a reasonable doubt. The jury must firmly believe the truth of the allegation based on the facts presented at the trial. See **Beyond a reasonable doubt; Preponderance of the evidence; Standard of proof**.

Collective bargaining. Negotiations between an employer and the union to which the employees belong. A collective bargaining agreement is the contract that results from the negotiations. Wages, hours of work, and work conditions are usually the subject of collective bargaining.

Common law. (1) Judge-made law, often based on custom, as opposed to statutory, legislative-made law; (2) the body of unwritten law based on custom, tradition, case law, and statutory law going back to the earliest years of English history, and which was transferred to most of the present-day United States through English settlement before 1776.

Comparative negligence. A rule of law that allows for an assessment of the degree of fault or carelessness on both sides in a dispute over the cause of injury. If the plaintiff is less at fault than the defendant, then the plaintiff may still recover damages from the defendant. The defendant is then responsible only for the percentage of the plaintiff's injury caused by the defendant's fault or carelessness. See **Damages; Defendant; Plaintiff; Contributory negligence; Rule of law**.

Complaint. The first necessary document filed by a plaintiff with the court in a civil suit. The document sets out the alleged wrong, harm, or injury to the plaintiff caused by the defendant, and asks the court to help the plaintiff to recover damages. See **Civil suit; Damages; Defendant; Plaintiff**.

Compliance. The act of adhering to or obeying the law or the terms of an agreement. See **Substantial compliance**.

Conclusion of law. A statement by the court of the law that applies to the facts in the case. The truth of the facts is determined by the jury or by the trial judge in a nonjury trial.

Consideration. Something of value given, exchanged, promised, or bargained for when making a contract. To be valid all contracts must have consideration.

Contract. A legally binding agreement negotiated and agreed to by two parties in which one or both parties consent to do or not to do a specific act. To be valid a contract must have at least one promise, consideration, legally competent parties, and reasonably certain terms. See **Consideration**.

Contributory negligence. A rule of law. A plaintiff's own carelessness or fault that is a part of the cause of the injury caused by another person's, the defendant's, carelessness. A plaintiff who is found to be contributorily negligent cannot recover damages from the defendant. See **Defendant; Plaintiff; Rule of law**.

Corporation. An artificial person or legal entity created under state or federal law, which exists separately from its owners, the shareholders or stockholders. A corporation may be a business or may perform almost any legal activity.

Court. A tribunal supervised by one or more judges in which disputes of law and fact are decided according to state or federal law. Courts decide civil and criminal lawsuits. Cases may be decided by a jury or by a judge without a jury. Courts from which a plaintiff or a defendant can appeal a decision are referred to as lower courts. The court that hears the appeal is called a higher court. See **Appeals court; District court; Superior court; Supreme court**.

Court record. The formal written account of a trial including all actions, papers filed, written opinions, etc.

Damages. (1) Monetary compensation for loss due to injury to a person or property when the injury is caused by another person. The person who caused the injury makes the restitution; (2) actual and compensatory damages are equal to the amount of the loss, or the dollar value assigned to the loss. This is often referred to as making the plaintiff, the injured party, whole; (3) punitive damages are above and beyond actual damages and are assessed to punish the wrongdoer.

Deed. The document used to transfer property or ownership rights, usually in land, to another person. To be valid a deed must be properly signed by the person transferring the property and witnessed by at least two people who are not named in the deed.

De facto. "That which is in fact"; actual, real, as opposed to an assumption or an opinion.

Default. Failure to act or carry out a duty or responsibility.

Default judgment. A judgment against a defendant because he failed to respond to the complaint properly, or appear before the court to make a defense. See **Complaint; Defendant**.

Defendant. A person against whom charges of wrongdoing are brought in a lawsuit, and against whom recovery is sought. The one who denies or pleads guilty to the charges.

De jure. "As a matter of law"; in accordance with the law.

District court. United States district courts are federal trial courts where initial lawsuits under federal laws are brought, often referred to as the court of first instance. State district courts may be trial courts or appeals courts. See **Appeals court; Court**.

Due care. Proper, just, reasonable degree of care in a particular situation. See also **Standard of care**.

Due process. Fundamental fairness in the administration of law. Every person against whom legal proceedings are initiated is entitled to notice of the legal proceedings, a real opportunity to defend against the charges, and assurance that no law and no government procedure is unfair or arbitrary.

Easement. A right granted by the owner of property to a particular person who is not the owner that allows the person to use a part of the land in a specific and limited way. Easements usually stay with the land when it is sold. See also **Right of way**.

Equity. What is fair and right; the court's ability in a particular situation to "do justice" when specific laws do not apply to the situation at hand.

Escheat. The passing of property to the state because no owner can be found to claim it. This happens especially in cases of inheritance when no living heir can be found. See **Heir**.

Estate. (1) The property a person owns. Land is real estate, and personal effects are personal property or a personal estate; (2) ownership rights; the right to possess and use property as an owner would, but not actual legal ownership. See **Life estate**.

Estoppel. A legal defense which can prohibit a plaintiff from claiming rights against a defendant because the defendant relied on the plaintiff's prior actions or words.

Evidence. All types of proof or information presented at a trial or hearing to substantiate the truth or falsity of disputed facts.

Ex post facto. "After the fact"; ex post facto laws are passed in an effort to make an action a crime, though it was not a crime when it was done. Ex post facto laws are prohibited by the U.S. Constitution.

Extradition. The surrender of someone in state (or country) A to state (or country) B because the person who is in A is wanted in B to defend criminal charges or to serve a sentence for a criminal conviction.

Fannie Mae. F.N.M.A.: Federal National Mortgage Association.

Federalism. The governmental structure in the United States in which city, state, and national governments coexist, with the state and city governments having some independence from the national—federal—government.

Fee simple absolute, or fee simple. An estate in land with no restrictions or conditions on ownership. See **Estate**.

Felony. Any serious crime, usually statutory, that carries the punishment of a prison term of more than a year or the death penalty. See **Statutory law**; see also **Misdemeanor**.

Fiduciary. (1) Any person in whom someone can place great trust and from whom one should expect great loyalty; (2) any relationship of trust in which someone acts on behalf of another.

First Amendment. The freedom of speech, religion, press, assembly, and petition of the government, contained in the Bill of Rights, which is a part of the U.S. Constitution.

Fixture. Anything attached to land or a building which is considered a permanent part of the property, *e.g.*, timber or a heat pump.

F.O.B. Free on Board; (1) in the Uniform Commercial Code, F.O.B. means that the price of the goods being shipped includes transportation costs to the named place of delivery; (2) generally, the seller of goods has fulfilled his contractual responsibilities when the goods are placed aboard the carrier. See **Carrier; Uniform commercial code**.

Forbearance. Refraining from taking action, especially collecting debt that is due or overdue.

Foreclosure. A process through which mortgaged property is repossessed or sold by the person holding the mortgage to pay the mortgage debt. The person holding the mortgage can foreclose only if the person possessing the property defaulted on the loan. See **Mortgage**.

Forfeit. To lose the right to something or to a privilege because of an offense, *e.g.*, breach of contract, default, or error. See **Breach; Default**.

Go up on appeal. Refers to the process of requesting that a higher court review the actions of a lower court. See **Appeals court; Court**.

Grand Jury. A group of people selected by law to hear criminal complaints and preliminary evidence of the prosecutor. The grand jury is responsible for deciding whether there is enough evidence to file a formal indictment so that a trial can be held. See **Complaint; Indictment; Prosecutor**.

Guarantor. Someone who agrees, usually in writing, to pay the debt of another should the original debtor default. See **Default**.

Habeas corpus. "You have the body"; a judicial order which requires an official, like a sheriff, who is holding a person in custody to bring that person to court so that the legality of the person's detention or imprisonment can be decided.

Habendum clause. The part of a deed that describes the property or ownership rights being transferred. The clause often begins with the words "to have and to hold." See **Deed**.

Hatch Act. The federal law which makes political activity such as holding an elected office illegal for federal and some state employees.

Hearsay. (1) A statement made, usually in court, about what someone else, who is not in court, said, wrote, or communicated; (2) secondhand information.

Heir. (1) Someone who inherits property; (2) the person(s) legally entitled to receive a dead person's property, if the latter dies with a valid will. Heirs cannot be determined until someone dies.

Holder. (1) Someone who possesses something; (2) someone who has legally acquired possession of a negotiable instrument, *e.g.*, a check or promissory note. See **Negotiable instrument**.

Holder in due course. According to the Uniform Commercial Code, someone who buys a negotiable instrument in good faith, thinking it is valid, without notice that it is overdue or has been dishonored. See **Holder; Negotiable instrument; Uniform commercial code; Valid**.

Homicide. The killing of another person. It is a crime if done intentionally or through carelessness, negligence, or without justification.

Indictment. A sworn accusation of a crime made against a person or several people by a grand jury upon the request of the prosecutor. See **Grand jury; Prosecutor**.

Injunction. A prohibition ordered by the court to prevent someone from doing something or from continuing to do something. Temporary injunctions are granted until the issue can be settled in court. Or an injunction may be final and permanent.

Intent. The resolve, purpose, aim, or goal of a person to cause the consequences of an action, or the knowledge that the consequences will result. Intent explains the means by which someone wants to do something and what he wants done.

Intestate. (1) Without a will; (2) someone who dies without a will.

Issues of fact (also called *questions of fact*). The questions that come up in a trial concerning the truth of the facts or events in dispute. The law is not disputed. Juries decide issues of fact.

Issues of law (also called *questions of law*). The questions that come up in a trial concerning how the law should be applied or interpreted when the facts are not disputed. The judge decides issues of law.

J.N.O.V. Judgment Notwithstanding the Verdict; a judgment rendered by the judge that is the opposite of the jury's verdict. When the judge decides to issue a J.N.O.V., he must decide that the jury acted unreasonably given the evidence in the case.

Joint tenants. Two or more people who have equal ownership rights in the same property. If one tenant dies, his ownership rights automatically pass to the other tenant(s). See **Estate**.

Judgment. The final and official decision of the court about the rights and duties of all parties in the trial.

Jurisdiction. (1) The power of the court to decide cases brought before it; (2) the geographic region within which the court may hear cases.

Jury. A group of people, often twelve, sometimes six, who are selected legally and sworn to hear testimony about contested facts in a trial. They must decide, based on the facts presented in court, what is the truth.

Laches. A legal defense when the plaintiff has delayed in pursuing or enforcing a claim or right so long that he may be harmed by the delay itself. The plaintiff may lose the lawsuit.

Leveraged buy-out. A leveraged buy-out occurs when a purchaser borrows money to buy out the stock of a company and thus gains control of the corporation, and then uses the liquid assets and/or liquidates other assets of the corporation to pay off the loan. The result is a reduction in the value of the bought-out corporation, because the value of the assets sold is not replaced.

Liability. (1) Responsibility; (2) debt.

Lien. A claim, charge, or security on specific property for payment of a judgment or debt. See **Judgment**.

Life estate. An estate that lasts only as long as the person to whom it is granted lives. A life estate in property allows the person holding the estate the right to possess and/or use the property, but he does not own the property. Life estates can be transferred. If a life estate is transferred, it lasts only as long as the life of the original holder of the life estate. See **Estate**. See also **Quitclaim deed**.

Malfeasance. (1) Wrongdoing; (2) committing an act one should not. Used especially in reference to public officials.

Malice. (1) Ill will; (2) intentionally harming someone without an excuse.

Malice aforethought. The deliberate intention to harm someone or to commit a serious crime. See **Intent**.

Merger. The fusion of one thing with another. Often the smaller or less important thing ceases to exist when it becomes a part of the other. Used most often in reference to one corporation buying out another.

Miranda Warning or Miranda Rights. Rights accorded a person who is arrested: He must be advised of the right to remain silent, and that if he speaks, what is said may be used as evidence; of the right to have an attorney present during questioning; and of the right to an attorney provided by the government if he wants an attorney but cannot afford one. Based on the decision by the U.S. Supreme Court in *Miranda v. Arizona* (1966).

Misdemeanor. A crime less serious than a felony, which carries a punishment of less than a year in prison and a fine. See **Felony**.

Monopoly. (1) Virtually complete control by a few companies of the manufacture, sale, distribution, or price of a good or commodity; (2) the exclusion of all competition.

Mortgage. The pledging of property, usually land or buildings, as security or collateral for a loan. The person who lends the money is the mortgagee; the person who borrows the money is the mortgagor.

Motion. A request asking the judge in a case to make a decision or take some other action.

Negotiable instrument. A signed document containing an unconditional promise to pay a specified amount of money on demand or at a specific date in the future. A check is a negotiable instrument payable on demand. A bank note is a negotiable instrument due at a specific date in the future.

Nolo contendere. "I will not contest it"; a plea by a defendant in a criminal case that neither admits guilt nor denies the charges, but submits to sentencing or punishment. The judge must agree to a defendant's use of the plea. See **Pleading**.

Nonfeasance. (1) Neglect of a required duty, especially in reference to public officials; (2) nonperformance of a required act or duty.

Notice. Knowledge of certain facts or formal receipt of certain facts, *e.g.*, to give notice of a lawsuit. See **Service of process**.

Order. A written decree or command given by a judge.

Par. The face value or stated value of stocks or bonds.

Parties. The participants in any trial or proceeding.

Plaintiff. (1) The person who initiates or starts the lawsuit against another person; (2) the one who brings legal action.

Pleading. (1) The formal written statement in which claims and defenses are made in a civil case; (2) the process of making and filing with the court formal written statements on each side of a lawsuit. See also **Complaint**.

Power of appointment. A part of a will, deed, or other document that authorizes someone to distribute the property or money, or to decide how it will be used.

Power of attorney. A document that authorizes someone to act as the agent or the attorney for the person signing the document.

Precedent. A court opinion in which the judge uses an older, analogous case, decided by another court, to help decide the case presently being heard. The judge relies on the first court's analysis and interpretation of the law to decide the case presently being tried. Court decisions on issues of law are binding authority on lower courts. See **Court; Issues of law**.

Preponderance of the evidence. The degree of proof required in civil cases; the greater weight of the evidence in terms of its quality. Evidence that is more convincing than that presented in opposition to it; more probable than not.

Probable cause. Circumstances that would lead one to believe that a crime has been committed by the person the police wish to arrest. The police must have probable cause before a judge will issue an arrest warrant.

Probate. (1) The process by which the validity of a will is proved and the property in the will distributed according to the terms of the will; (2) the name given to the court in which this process takes place.

Proceeding. The process of trying a case before a court or an administrative board.

Prosecutor. The attorney who indicts and brings a defendant to trial on criminal charges on behalf of the county, state, or federal government. See **Indictment**.

Proxy. (1) A representative, one who acts for another; (2) the document authorizing such action. See also **Fiduciary**.

Quash. To vacate, overthrow, or annul.

Quitclaim deed. A deed that transfers to the buyer whatever ownership rights the seller has in the property. The seller may have less than full ownership rights. See **Fee simple absolute; Estate; Life estate**.

Recovery. The satisfaction or award given by a judgment at the termination of a lawsuit. See **Judgment**.

Redress. (1) Satisfaction for harm done; (2) damages.

Release. (1) To relinquish rights or claims that could have been enforced against another person; (2) the written document by which claims or rights are given up.

Reliance. The belief in something and dependence upon that belief when acting.

Remedy. (1) The means used to enforce a right or to prevent the violation of a right; (2) the means used to gain satisfaction.

Res judicata. "A thing decided"; the final judgment rendered on the merits of the case which prohibits the parties from retrying the same issue(s).

Revocation. The act of making something void, *e.g.*, a will, or the termination of some power or authority.

Right of way. The right to cross over another person's land. See also **Easement**.

Rule of law. A well-established legal principle, standard, or guide.

Security. Something of monetary value pledged to the lender by the borrower to assure that a loan will be repaid. If the borrower defaults, the lender has the right to take possession and sell the security. See also **Default; Mortgage**.

Service of process. The delivery of a legal document by an authorized person according to prescribed requirements so that the person who receives the document knows to appear in court and for what reasons. See **Notice**.

Standard of care. In a negligence case, the degree of care a reasonable person would have used in similar circumstances. The standard of care is used by the jury to determine whether the plaintiff and/or the defendant was negligent.

Standard of proof. The degree of certainty to which something must be proved in order for a plaintiff to win the lawsuit. See **Beyond a reasonable doubt; Clear and convincing evidence; Preponderance of the evidence**.

Stare decisis. "Let the decision stand"; the doctrine that cases with similar fact situations should be decided by applying the same rule of law unless the court has good reason not to do so. Lower courts must apply principles of law established by higher courts. See **Court; Precedent; Rule of law**.

Statute of limitation. The statutorily specified period of time, usually a number of years, in which lawsuits must be initiated. The complaint that commences the lawsuit must be filed within the statute of limitation. If the statute of limitation runs (expires) before the complaint is filed, a plaintiff cannot sue the defendant. See **Complaint**.

Statutory law. Law created by state or federal legislatures. See also **Common law**.

Subpoena. A court order requiring a person to appear in court to give testimony in a trial. The court can also subpoena documents. See also **Summons**.

Substantial Compliance. (1) Satisfactory adherence to or obeyance of an agreement, adherence that is complete enough; (2) adherence to the essential requirements. See **Compliance**.

Summary judgment. A final judgment rendered in a lawsuit without completing the trial, or in a lawsuit without a trial at all. The judge must decide that there are no issues of genuine fact to be decided. Either the plaintiff or the defendant may file a motion for summary judgment. See **Issues of fact; Judgment; Motion**.

Summons. A written notice informing someone that a lawsuit has been filed, that he has been named a party to it, and when to appear in court. A person can be summoned as a defendant or as a witness. If the person has been named as the defendant in the lawsuit, failure to appear at the specified time can result in a default judgment. See **Default Judgment; Notice; Parties; Writ**.

Superior court. State trial court where initial lawsuits under state law are brought, often referred to as the court of first instance. See **Court; Appeals court; District court**.

Supreme court. The highest court in a state or federal court system. The United States Supreme Court is the highest court in all of the United States. The United States and state supreme courts are sometimes referred to as courts of final resort. See **Court; Appeals court; District court; Superior court**.

Temporary restraining order (T.R.O.). A command of the court issued in an emergency, prohibiting someone from doing something that is dangerous or causes harm or damage. The T.R.O. remains in effect only until the conclusion of a hearing requesting an injunction. See **Injunction**.

Tenants by the entirety. Husband and wife who hold ownership rights jointly. The law treats the couple as a single legal entity. When one spouse dies, the other inherits full ownership rights in the property to the exclusion of other heirs. See **Heirs**.

Tenants in common. Two or more people who possess undivided, but not necessarily equal, ownership rights in the same single piece of property. Each tenant's portion can be passed through a will. There is no right of survivorship as with joint tenants. See **Estate; Joint tenants**.

Third-party beneficiary. The person for whose benefit a contract is created, but who is not one of the people who signs the contract. See also **Beneficiary**.

Title. (1) Formal ownership property, or the document proving ownership; (2) the name for a part of a statute, *e.g.*, Title VII of the 1964 Civil Rights Act.

Tort. A civil wrong (other than breach of contract) that causes harm, injury, or damage to another person or property. See **Breach**.

Tortfeasor. The person who commits the civil wrong that causes harm, injury, or damage to another person or property.

Trespass. Unauthorized or unlawful interference with a person's property or rights.

Trust. (1) Property or property rights held by one person, the trustee, for the benefit of another person, the beneficiary. The person who creates the trust is the settlor; (2) a group of people or companies with the intention of creating a monopoly or with the intention of interfering with the free flow of trade. See **Beneficiary; Monopoly**.

Uniform Commercial Code (UCC). A comprehensive law governing business transactions. The UCC has been adopted virtually without change in whole or in part in most states.

Valid. (1) Legally sufficient; (2) binding.

Venue. The local area or specific place within a larger geographic region where a case may be tried. The court system may have jurisdiction over the larger geographic area, but proper venue would be the place most convenient to the parties of the lawsuit. See **Jurisdiction**.

Vest. (1) To give an immediate, fixed right; (2) to take effect.

Warrant. A precept or writ issued by a magistrate authorizing an officer to make an arrest, seizure, or search.

Watered stock. Shares of stock that were sold at less than par value; drawn from the practice of letting cattle drink before being weighed for sale. See **Par**.

Writ. A judge's order requiring that something be done outside the courtroom, or granting the authority for it to be done. See **Order; Summons**.

SOURCES

Black, Henry Campbell. *Black's Law Dictionary*. 6th ed. St. Paul, Minn.: West Publishing Co., 1990.

Grilliot, Harold J. *Introduction to Law and the Legal System*. 4th ed. Boston: Houghton Mifflin Co., 1988.

Rush, George E. *The Dictionary of Criminal Justice*. 3rd ed. Guilford, Conn.: Dushkin Publishing Group, 1991.

— **Clair Sanders; L.D.R.**

61

CERTAIN IMMUTABLE LAWS, BOTH SERIOUS AND NOT SO

· · · · ·

MY DESK DICTIONARY, AN OLD WEBSTER'S COLLEGIATE, DISTINGUISHES between various kinds of laws, including enforced rules of conduct and "a statement of an order or relationship of phenomena which, so far as known, is invariable under the given conditions." It is the latter kind of laws that will concern us here.

Over the course of time, humankind has evolved, discovered, or identified certain laws that serve to express an immutable order or relationship of phenomena. Given identical circumstances or conditions, such laws, insofar as is known, are invariable. Nobody, for example, can permanently repeal the law of gravitation. Typically such laws are scientific, but they can be philosophical, artistic, economic, philological, or whatever.

Some widely accepted immutable laws are believed to be not wholly serious in intent: *e.g.,* Murphy's law. (See, for example, Arthur Bloch's two compendia, *Murphy's Law and Other Reasons Why Things Go Wrong* and *Murphy's Law, Book Two,* cited in the Sources.) It should be pointed out, however, that some authorities question the validity of the distinction. Whether this is so is not for us to say. However, for purposes of convenience and to avoid misleading the young or the pure in heart, the laws below have been grouped into the classifications of "Serious" and "Not So Serious."

What follows is a compilation of some of the better-known laws of various kinds. When ascertainable the author of the law is given.

Serious

Absorption, law of (logic). If of two aggregants one contains the other as a component, the aggregate is identical with the former ($a + ab = a$).

Acceleration, law of (embryology). The development of an organ is accelerated in proportion to its importance. (sociology) Cultural evolution, especially in its material effects, becomes more and more rapid.

Amontons' law (chemistry). The pressure of a given amount of gas at a fixed volume is proportional to the absolute temperature. (Guillaume Amontons)

Averages, law of (also known as *Bernoulli's theorem*)(statistics). When the number of trials (n) of an event or probability (p) is increased indefinitely, the probability of any assigned deviation from the value np approaches zero. (Jacob Bernoulli)

Avogadro's law (physics). Equal volumes of different gases, under like conditions of pressure and temperature, contain the same number of molecules. (Amadeo Avogadro)

Beer's law (also known as *Lambert-Bouguer-Beer law*) (physical chemistry). The absorption of light by different concentrations of the same solute dissolved in the same solvent is an exponential function of the concentration, provided that the thickness of the absorbing medium remains constant. (A. Beer)

Bernoulli's theorem. See **Averages, law of**.

Blass's law (classical languages). Demosthenes avoids a succession of more than four short syllables. (Friedrich Blass)

Boyle's law (also known as *law of Boyle and Marriotte*) (physics). When a gas is subjected to compression and kept at a constant temperature, the product of the pressure and volume is a constant quantity; *i.e.*, the volume is in inverse proportion to the pressure. (Robert Boyle, Jr.)

Buys Ballot's law (meteorology). Wind will blow along the lines of constant pressure (isobars) with a speed that is proportional to the horizontal pressure gradient (the slope of a constant pressure surface) and that depends on the latitude. (C. D. H. Buys Ballot)

Causality, law of (*law of causation*) (philosophical). Every change in nature is produced by some cause.

Charles' law (physics). The volume of a given mass of gas increases for a given rise of temperature, or decreases for a given fall, (provided that the pressure is unchanged) by a definite fraction of its volume. (J. A. C. Charles)

Comte's law of the three stages (sociology). Each of our leading conceptions, each branch of human knowledge, passes successively through three different phases: theological, metaphysical, and positive. (Auguste Comte)

Conservation of angular motion, law of (physics). The angular momentum of an object is unchanged unless a net external torque acts on it.

Conservation of baryons, law of (physics). When a baryon (a subatomic particle with a large rest mass) decays or reacts with another particle, the number of baryons is the same on both sides of the equation.

Conservation of energy, law of (chemistry). Energy may be converted from one form to another, but the total quantity of energy remains constant.

Conservation of hypercharge, law of (physics). Hypercharge is conserved in strong and electromagnetic interactions, but not in weak interactions.

Conservation of leptons, law of (physics). In a reaction involving leptons (sub-atomic particles with a small rest mass), the arithmetic sum of the lepton numbers is the same on each side of the equation.

Conservation of mass, law of (chemistry and physics). The total mass within a closed system remains the same no matter what physical or chemical changes occur; matter can be neither created nor destroyed in any system. This law is strictly accurate only when the energy of the process is much less than mc^2.

Conservation of mass-energy, law of (physics). Energy increases with the increased mass of a body; mass is thus a measure of energy content; *i.e.,* $e = mc^2$.

Conservation of mechanical energy, law of (physics). The sum of the potential and kinetic energies of an ideal energy system is constant.

Conservation of momentum, law of (physics). The momentum within a closed system will remain constant so long as no external forces are acting upon that system. For example, the momentum of two colliding bodies before impact equals the momentum after impact.

Constant angles, law of (chemistry and physics). The angles between the various faces of a crystal remain unchanged throughout its growth. (Romé d'Isle)

Constant (definite) proportions, law of (also known as *Proust's Law*) (chemistry). The proportions of elements in a compound are always the same no matter how they are combined. (Joseph-Louis Proust)

Continuity, law of (biology). There is no break in nature; nothing passes from one state to another without passing through all the intermediate states. (Gottfried Wilhelm von Liebniz) See also **Haeckel's law**.

Coulomb's law of electrostatics (physics). The force between two point charges is directly proportional to the product of their magnitudes and inversely proportional to the square of the distance between them. (Charles Augustin de Coulomb)

Coulomb's law of magnetism (physics). The force between two magnetic poles is directly proportional to the strengths of the poles and inversely proportional to the square of their distance apart. (Charles Augustin de Coulomb)

Cross-cutting relations, law of (geology). If one rock type or rock structure cuts across or in some way truncates another, then the cross-cutting rock must be the younger.

Dalton's law. See **Partial pressures, law of**.

Darcy's law. See **Permeability, law of**.

Demand, law of (economics). The demand for an economic product varies inversely with its price; see also **Supply, law of**.

Diminishing return, law of (economics). An increase in expenditure of capital and labor will eventually cause an increase in product proportionally smaller than the increase in expenditure.

Dulong and Petit, law of (chemistry). Elements in the solid state have nearly the same atomic heat—about 6.4. (P. L. Dulong and A. P. Petit)

Effect, law of (also known as *Thorndike's law*) (psychology). Of several responses made to the same situation, those accompanied or clearly followed by satisfaction to the animal will, other things being equal, be more firmly connected with the situation . . . the greater the satisfaction or discomfort, the greater the strengthening or weakening of the bond. (Edward L. Thorndike)

Electrostatics, basic law of (physics). Similarly charged objects repel each other; oppositely charged objects attract each other.

Engels' law (sociology). The lower the total consumption, the greater the percentage of food consumption. (F. Engels)

Entropy, law of (physics). A natural process always takes place in such a direction as to increase the entropy—the measure of available energy—of the universe.

Error, law of (mathematics). The square of any accidental error varies as to the logarithm of its frequency.

Faegri's laws (meteorology). (1) The shorter the duration of a climatic function, the smaller the area similarly affected; the longer the cycle, the greater the area in which it is felt in the same way; (2) the longer the period of climatic change, the more complete is the reaction of all indicators. (Knut Faegri)

Falling bodies, law of (physics). All freely falling bodies accelerate at an identical rate of 32 feet per second during each second of the fall.

Faraday's laws (electrolysis). (1) The quantity of substance liberated at the anode or the cathode is proportional to the quantity of the current passed; (2) the quantities of different substances liberated by the same quantity of current are proportional to their chemical equivalents. (Michael Faraday)

Faunal succession, law of (geology). Fossils will always succeed one another in the same sequence; thus the rocks in which these fossils may be contained can be sequenced in time relative to one another by the fossils contained therein.

Fechner's law (psychophysics). The intensity of stimulation in the middle ranges increases as the logarithm of the stimulus. (G. T. Fechner)

Ferrel's law (meteorology). Winds in the northern hemisphere are deflected to the right, and winds in the southern hemisphere are deflected to the left. (William Ferrel)

Frontality, law of (artistic). In two-dimensional early Egyptian art, the body stands rigidly so that an axial plane cutting the figure vertically would pass through the mouth, nose, chin, torso, and juncture of legs, dividing it into two symmetrical portions.

Gay-Lussac's law (chemistry and physics). When two or more gaseous substances combine to form a gaseous compound, the volume of the product is either equal to the sum of the factors or is less than, and bears a simple ratio to, this sum. (Joseph L. Gay-Lussac)

Graham's law of effusion (chemistry). The rate of effusion of gas molecules from a given hole, at constant temperature and pressure, is inversely proportional to the square root of the molecular weight of the gas. (Thomas Graham)

Gravitation, law of (physics). Any two material bodies, if free to move, will be accelerated toward each other; the force of attraction is proportional to the masses of the two bodies, and inversely proportional to the square of the distance between them. (Isaac Newton)

Gresham's law (economics). When two coins are equal in debt-paying value but unequal in intrinsic value, the one with the greater intrinsic value will be hoarded; *i.e.*, bad money drives out good. (Thomas Gresham)

Grimm's law (philology). A regular shift of groups of consonants takes place between the early classical Indo-European languages—Sanskrit, Greek, Latin—and German and English, as follows: (1) Classical voiceless stops (*k, t, p*) become voiceless aspirates (*h, th, f*) in English and mediae (*h, d, f*) in German, as in Latin *pater*, English *father*, German *Vater*; (2) classical unaspirated voice stops (*g, d, b*) become voiceless stops (*k, t, p*) in English and voiceless aspirates (*kh, th, f*) in German, as in Latin *decem*, English *ten*, German *zehn*; (3) classical aspirated voice stops (*gh, dh, bh*) become unaspirated voice stops (*g, d, b*) in English and voiceless stops (*k, t, p*) in German, as in Sanskrit *dhar*, English *draw*, German *tragen*. (Jacob Grimm)

Grotthuss' law (physical chemistry). Only those rays of light that are absorbed can produce chemical change. (Theodor Grotthuss)

Group conflict, law of (sociology). The greater the rate of conflict between groups, the greater the rate of in-group cohesion, all else being equal.

Gyration, law of (meteorological). The wind generally shifts in its direction with the sun. (Heinrich Dove)

Haeckel's law (biology). Every individual organism, in its development from the ovum, goes through a series of evolutionary changes in each of which it represents a stage of the class to which it belongs—*i.e.*, ontogeny recapitulates phylogeny. Also, every such organism breeds true insofar as it is influenced by heredity, and becomes modified insofar as it is influenced by conditions of environment. (Ernst Heinrich Haeckel)

Hardy-Weinberg law (biology). The frequency of dominant and recessive genes in a population remains the same from generation to generation, provided that no new genes enter the gene pool and mating is random. (Godfrey Hardy and Wilhelm Weinberg)

Heat exchange, law of (physics). In any heat transfer system, the heat lost by hot materials equals the heat gained by cold materials. See also **Thermodynamics, laws of**.

Henry's law (chemistry). The solubility of a gas is directly proportional to the partial pressure of the gas above the solution. (Joseph Henry)

Hess's law (physical chemistry). The heat sum—the algebraic totals of the amounts of heat evolved or absorbed in a given chemical process—is constant regardless of the number of stages in which the process is effected. (V. F. Hess)

Holmes's law (criminology). When all other possible explanations have been ruled out, the one that remains, however seemingly improbable, must be true. (attributed to Sherlock Holmes by Sir Arthur Conan Doyle)

Homogeneity, law of (mathematics). In every arithmetical calculation, the logical nature of the things numbered must remain unaltered.

Hooke's law (physics). Below the elastic limit, strain is directly proportional to stress. (Robert Hooke)

Hubble's law (astronomy). The galaxies in the universe are receding from earth and from each other at a velocity proportional to their distance from one another. (E. P. Hubble)

Hutton's law. See **Uniformity, law of**.

Ideal gas law (chemistry). For an ideal gas, the product of pressure and volume is proportional to the product of the number of molecules and temperature.

Independent assortment, law of (also known as *Mendel's law*) (genetics). Different gene pairs separate independently from one another in all possible combinations in second and later generations during formation of sex cells.

Inverse square law (physics). Unhindered energy from a source spreads out evenly and equally in all directions with its intensity diminishing expressed as the inverse square of its distance from the source; electromagnetism, gravity, sound, radiation, and magnetism all operate under this law.

Joule's law (physics). The heat produced in a conductor is directly proportional to the resistance of the conductor, the square of the current, and the time the current is maintained. (James Prescott Joule)

Jurin's law (physics). The ascent of a given liquid in a capillary tube is inversely proportional to its diameter. (James Jurin)

Kepler's laws of planetary motion (astronomy). (1) Planets orbit the sun in an elliptical manner; (2) planetary speed depends on the distance from the sun, with those closest to the sun moving fastest; (3) the square of the time it takes for a planet to orbit the sun is proportional to the cube of its mean distance from the sun.

Kirchhoff's laws (physics). (1) The algebraic sum of the currents at any circuit junction is equal to zero; (2) the algebraic sum of all charges in a potential occurring around any loop in a circuit equals zero. (Gustav Robert Kirchhoff)

Koch's postulates. See **Specificity of bacteria, laws of**.

La Fontaine's law. See **Strongest, law of the**.

Lambert-Bouguer-Beer law. See **Beer's law**.

Le Chatelier's law (physical chemistry). The equilibrium of a system, when displaced by a stress, is displaced in such a way as to tend to relieve that stress. (Henri-Louis Le Chatelier)

Leibig's law. See **Minimum, law of.**

Lenz's law (physics). An induced current is in such a direction that its magnetic property opposes the charge by which the current is induced. (Heinrich Lenz)

Marx's law of capitalist accumulation (economics). The value of the commodities purchasable by a worker's wages is less than the value of the commodities produced by the worker; the surplus value represents the profit of the capitalist. (Karl Marx)

Mass action, law of (chemistry). The chemical action of a reacting substance is proportional at any moment to its active mass. (Guldberg and Waage)

Mendelian laws of inheritance (biology). (1) Law of segregation—each characteristic is inherited independently and with equal probability; later determined to be controlled by alleles, which are paired contrasting factors of a gene that determine particular characteristics of an organism and which can be dominant or recessive; if both a dominant and a recessive characteristic appear in an individual, the dominant form will be expressed, *e.g.*, brown eyes over blue eyes, but either can be passed on with equal likelihood; (2) law of recombination or independent assortment—successive generations of crossbred offspring will exhibit all possible combinations of inherited characteristics; later found to mean that alleles segregate independently of each other when forming germ cells. (Gregor Johann Mendel)

Mersenne's law (physics). The time of vibration of a string varies directly in accordance with the length and the square root of its density, and inversely as the square root of the tension. (Marin Mersenne)

Minimum, law of (also known as *Leibig's law*) (biology). Those essential elements for which the ratio of supply to demand reaches a minimum will be the first to be removed from the environment by life processes. (J. von Leibig)

Monodromy, law of (mathematics). A function of a complex variable whose only singularities in a simply connected region of the complex plane are poles is one-valued in that region.

Multiple proportions, law of (chemistry). When the same elements form more than one proportion, the masses of one element in those compounds for a fixed mass of the other element are in ratios of small whole numbers.

Newton's laws of motion (physics). (1) A material particle or body, if left to itself, will maintain its condition, either of rest or of motion, unchanged; (2) a change in motion indicates a force due to the presence and effect of another body, and the change due to one force is the same even if there are other forces acting; (3) to every force there is an equal and opposite reaction. (Isaac Newton)

Octaves, law of (chemistry). When a number of elements are arranged in the order of their atomic weight, each one resembles the eighth one below or after it.

Ohm's law (electricity). The strength of an electric current, or the quantity of electricity passing through a section of the conductor in a unit of time, is directly proportional to the whole electromotive force in operation, and inversely proportional to the sum of all the resistances in the circuit. (Georg Simon Ohm)

Okun's law (economics). A reduction of one percentage point in unemployment is associated with a 3 percent increase in gross national product. (Arthur Okun)

One price, law of (economics). In a given market at a given moment, with knowledgeable buyers and sellers, a homogenous goodwill sell for one price only.

Organic evolution, law of (geology). Organisms have developed in a certain definite order of progression, from less organized to more organized types and from lower to higher forms of life.

Original horizontality, law of (geology). Sedimentary rocks are originally deposited horizontally.

Partial pressures, law of (also known as *Dalton's law*) (chemistry). In a mixture of gases, the sum of the partial pressures of all the different gases is equal to the total pressure of the mixture. (John Dalton)

Pascal's law of fluid pressure (chemistry and physics). When pressure is exerted on a fluid in an enclosed body, it is transmitted equally in all directions and acts at a right angle to all surfaces of the container; this law is the basis for the hydraulic press. (Blaise Pascal)

Periodic law (chemistry). When the chemical elements are arranged by atomic number, their physical and chemical properties vary periodically.

Permeability, law of (also known as *Darcy's law*) (physics). The velocity of flow of water through a rock is a function of permeability, hydraulic head, and the distance between the two points of interest.

Photoelectric emission, laws of (physics). (1) The rate of emissions of photoelectrons is directly proportional to the intensity of the incident light; (2) the kinetic energy of photoelectrons is independent of the intensity of the incident light; (3) within the region of effective frequencies, the maximum kinetic energy of photoelectrons varies directly with the difference between the frequency of the incident light and the cutoff frequency.

Planck's law (quantitative mechanics). Energy associated with electromagnetic radiation is emitted or absorbed in discrete amounts that are proportional to the frequency of radiation. (Max Planck)

Porson's law (classical languages). When a Greek tragic trimeter ends in a word forming a cretic (long/short/long), this is regularly preceded by a short trisyllable or by a monosyllable. (Richard Porson)

Priority, law of (biology). In taxonomy, the first published name of a species of genus takes precedence over any subsequently published.

Proust's law. See **Constant (definite) proportions, law of**.

Raoult's law (chemistry). The partial pressure of solvent over a solution equals the vapor pressure of pure solvent times the mole fraction of solvent in the solution. (François-Marie Raoult)

Reflection, law of (optics). When light falls on a plane surface, it is so reflected that the angle of reflection is equal to the angle of incidence, and the incident ray, reflected ray, and normal all lie in the plane of incidence.

Say's law (economics). Supply creates its own demand. (Jean-Baptiste Say)

Segregation, law of (genetics). The pair of factors for each trait of an organism separate as sex cells are formed.

Signs, law of (mathematics). The product or quotient of two numbers is positive if the numbers have the same sign, negative if they have opposite signs.

Snell's law (optics). The ratio of the sines of the angles of incidence and refraction is constant for all incidences in any given pair of media for waves of a definite frequency. (Willebrord Snell)

Specificity of bacteria, laws of (also known as *Koch's postulates*) (biology). (1) A microorganism identified as the etiologic agent (the cause of a disease) must be present in every case of the disease; (2) the etiologic agent must be isolated and cultivated in pure culture; (3) the etiologic agent must produce the disease when inoculated in pure culture into susceptible animals; (4) the organism must be present in the animal after recovery from the disease. (Robert Koch)

Stefan-Boltzmann's law (astronomy). The energy emitted per unit time by each unit area of the surface of a blackbody is proportional to the fourth power of the absolute temperature of the blackbody. (Josef Stefan and Ludwig Boltzmann)

Strings, laws of vibrating (physics). (1) *Lengths:* the frequency of a vibrating string is inversely proportional to its length if all other factors are constant; (2) *diameters:* the frequency of a string is inversely proportional to its diameter if all other factors are constant; (3) *tensions:* the frequency of a string is directly proportional to the square root of the tension on the string if all other factors are constant; (4) *densities:* the frequency of a string is inversely proportional to the square root of its density if all other factors are constant.

Strongest, law of the (Loi du plus fort) (also known as *La Fontaine's law*) (general). Might makes right.

Sufficient reason, law of (logic). For every given fact or event, there is a reason why it is as it is rather than otherwise.

Superposition, law of (geology). Where there has been no subsequent disturbance, sedimentary strata were deposited in ascending order, younger beds successively overlying older beds.

Supply, law of (economics). The quantity of an economic product offered for sale varies directly with its price; see also **Demand, law of**.

Thermodynamics, laws of (chemistry and physics). (1) Quantities of heat may be converted into energy, and vice versa, with the amount of energy being always equal to the amount of heat; (2) when heat or energy is exchanged between two bodies at different temperatures, the hotter body loses heat and the colder body gains heat; (3) every substance has an available entropy that approaches zero as its temperature approaches absolute zero.

Thermoneutrality, law of (chemistry). When dilute solutions of neutral salts are mixed, and no precipitate is formed, no thermal effect is produced.

Thorndike's law. See **Effect, law of**.

Thought, laws of (logic). (1) *Identity*—entity *A* is always the same as *A*; (2) *contradiction*—entity *A* cannot be both *B* and not-*B*; (3) *excluded middle*—entity *A* must be either *B* or not-*B*. (Aristotle)

Uniformity, law of (also known as *Hutton's law*) (geology). The processes that have been at work on the earth in the past are the same as those now in operation; no agent of change can be evoked that cannot now be seen and proved to be effective. (James Hutton)

Variable proportions, law of (economics). In the short run, output will change as one input is varied while the others remain constant.

von Baer's law (biology). The development of an organism is a product from the general to the special; the embryos belonging to various classes closely resemble one another in their earlier stages, but diverge more or less as their development proceeds. (K. E. von Baer)

Weber's law (psychology). The least noticeable change in a stimulus is a constant proportional of the original stimulus. (Ernst Heinrich Weber)

Not So Serious

Acheson's rule of the bureaucracy (administrative). A memorandum is written not to inform the reader but to protect the writer.

Algren's laws for the conduct of human life on earth (general). (1) Never eat at a place called "Mom's"; (2) never play poker with a man called "Doc"; (3) never, never get into bed with someone who has worse problems than you do. (Nelson Algren)

Augustine's law number one (administrative). The best way to make a silk purse from a sow's ear is to begin with a silk sow. The same is true of money. (Norman R. Augustine)

Avery's rule of three (general). Trouble strikes in series of threes, but when working around the house the next job after a series of three is not a fourth job, but the start of a new series of three.

Bagdikian's observation (journalism). Trying to be a first-rate reporter on the average American newspaper is in a direct ratio to trying to play Bach's *St. Matthew Passion* on a ukelele.

Bernstein's laws of acquisition (library science). (1) If you buy a hardcover edition of a book, the paperback edition will appear next week, at a much lower price; (2) if you buy a paperback edition of a book, the hardcover will be remaindered next week, at a much lower price; (3) if you buy a paperback edition, or a hardcover edition, or a remaindered copy of a book, the next week you will find the book in excellent condition in a used-book shop—at a much lower price.

Bloch's corollary (authorship). The first page an author turns to upon receiving an advance copy will be the one containing the worst error. (Arthur Bloch)

Bombeck's rule (medicine). Never go to a doctor whose house plants have died. (Irma Bombeck)

Brockington's law of presidential politics (politics). No matter how incompetent the candidates, there must be a new president. (D. L. Brockington)

Bursey's law (general). The time required to complete a task exceeds the time carefully alloted to it by a factor equal to the square root of seven. (Maurice M. Bursey)

Calkin's law of menu language (gourmetship). The number of adjectives and verbs that are added to the description of a menu item is in inverse proportion to the quality of the dish.

Canada Bill Jones's law (gambling). A Smith and Wesson beats four aces.

Combat, laws of armed (war). (1) If the enemy is in range, so are you; (2) incoming fire has the right of way; (3) try to look unimportant; they may be low on ammo; (4) the enemy diversion you have been ignoring will be the main attack; (5) make it tough enough for the enemy to get in and you won't be able to get out; (6) never share a foxhole with anyone braver than yourself; (7) if the sergeant can see you, so can the enemy; (8) whenever you have plenty of ammo, you can't miss; whenever you are low on ammo, you can't hit the broad side of a barn; (9) for every action, there is always an equal and opposite criticism; (10) the complexity of a weapon is inversely proportional to the IQ of the weapon's operator; (11) if it's stupid but it works, it isn't stupid; (12) the only thing more accurate than incoming enemy fire is incoming friendly fire; (13) when both sides are convinced they are about to lose, they are both right; (14) the most dangerous thing in the world is a second lieutenant with a map and a compass.

Completion time, law of (general). The first 90 percent of a project takes 10 percent of the time needed to complete it; the last 10 percent takes the other 90 percent of the time needed to complete it.

Computer memory, law of (computers). Any given program will expand to more than fill the available memory.

Computer programming, law of (computers). Inside every large program there is a small program struggling to get out.

Cooke's law (administrative). In any decision situation, the amount of relevant information is inversely proportional to the importance of the decision.

Disk error, law of (computers). A bad sector disk error occurs only after several hours' work without a backup.

Drazen's law of restitution (general). The time it takes to rectify a situation is inversely proportional to the time it took to do the damage.

Drew's law of highway biology (transportation). The first bug to hit a clean windshield lands directly in front of your eyes.

Drury's laws (zoology). (1) An animal is presumed to be smart until proved stupid; (2) people who study animals are presumed to be stupid until proved smart. (William Drury)

Ettore's observation (shopping). The other line moves faster.

Finagle's creed (science). Science is true. Don't be misled by the facts.

Frisbee, laws of the (athletics). (1) The most powerful force in the world is that of a disc straining to get under a car; (2) the higher the quality of the catch, the greater the possibility of a crummy rethrow; (3) the greatest single aid to distance is for the disk to be traveling in the wrong direction; (4) the most difficult move with a disc is to put it down (also known as the *law of just one more throw*).

Hanlon's razor (interpersonal relations). Never attribute to malice that which is adequately explained by stupidity.

Historical research, first law of (also known as *Faber's second law*) (scholarship). The number of errors in any piece of writing rises in proportion to the writer's reliance on secondary sources.

Judgment and experience, law of (general). Judgment comes from experience; experience comes from bad judgment.

Kramer's law (transportation). You can never tell which way the train went from looking at the track.

Liebling's law (journalism). If you are smart enough you can kick yourself in the pants, grab yourself by the back of the collar, and throw yourself out on the sidewalk. (A. J. Liebling)

Long's law (political economy and general). Worry is a constant. The things you worry about change, but not the amount of worrying done about them. *Alternate version:* The volume of worry (w) within a given individual remains constant, whatever the rate of and occasion for variation (v) in its daily causes (c); thus, $w = vc$. (Clarence D. Long)

Lynch's law (general). When the going gets tough, everyone leaves.

Mencken's law (social reform). Whenever A annoys or injures B on the pretense of saving or improving X, A is a scoundrel. (H. L. Mencken)

Murphy's laws (general). (1) If anything can go wrong it will; (2) nothing is ever as simple as it seems; (3) if there is a possibility of several things going wrong, the one that will do the most damage will go wrong first; (4) left to themselves, all things go from bad to worse; (5) if you play with something long enough, you will surely break it; (6) if everything seems to be going well, you have obviously overlooked something; (7) nature always sides with the hidden flaw; (8) Mother Nature is a bitch; (9) everything east of the San Andreas fault will eventually fall into the Atlantic Ocean; (10) Murphy was an optimist. (Arthur Bloch)

Oliver's law of location (transportation). No matter where you go, there you are.

Parkinson's law (administrative). The work load of an organization expands to accommodate the personnel available. (C. Northcote Parkinson)

Perkins' postulate (general). The bigger they come, the harder they hit.

Probable dispersal, law of (general). Whatever hits the fan will not be evenly dispersed. (Arthur Bloch)

Product assembly, law of (general). When all else fails, read the instructions.

Ralph's observation (technology). It is a mistake to let any mechanical object realize that you are in a hurry.

Reece's second law (highwaymanship). The speed of an oncoming vehicle is directly proportional to the length of the parking zone.

Ross's law (general). Bare feet magnetize sharp metal objects so that they always point upward from the floor, especially in the dark.

Rubin's laws. (1) (literature) All writers are neurotics, but not all neurotics are writers; (2) (fishing) whenever two fishing lines are contiguous, they will become continuous. (L.D.R.)

Seits's law (higher education). The one course you must take to graduate will not be offered during your last semester.

Sex, Ten laws of (biology). (1) Sex has no calories; (2) virginity can be cured; (3) sex is hereditary; if your parents never had it the chances are you won't, either; (4) the game of love is never called off on account of darkness; (5) it was not the apple on the tree but the pair on the ground that caused the trouble in the garden; (6) before you find your handsome prince you've got to kiss a lot of frogs; (7) love is a matter of chemistry; sex is a matter of physics; (8) never stand between a fire hydrant and a dog; (9) never go to bed mad; stay up and fight; (10) it is better to be looked over than overlooked.

Simmons' law (sociology). The desire for racial integration increases with the square of the distance from the actual event.

Success, laws of (general). Never tell everything you know.

von Braun's law (science). Research is what I'm doing when I don't know what I am doing. (Wernher von Braun)

Yardley's law (dining). No matter how many good tables are free, you will always be given the worst available. (Jonathan Yardley)

SOURCES

For assistance in compiling various of the immutable laws cited above, the editor is grateful to Maurice M. Bursey, P. Geoffrey Feiss, M. David Galinsky, Robert E. Gallman, Stirling Haig, William Harmon, George Kennedy, Barbara B. Moran, John Sheldon Reed, Jack M. Sasson, Lee T. Shapiro, George B. Tindall, and Bruce Winterhalder.

Bloch, Arthur. *Murphy's Law and Other Reasons Why Things Go Wrong*. Los Angeles: Price Stern Sloan, 1977.

———. *Murphy's Law, Book Two*. Los Angeles: Price Stern Sloan, 1980.

Bridgwater, William, and Seymour Kurtz, eds. *Columbia Encyclopedia*. 3rd ed. New York: Columbia University Press, 1963.

Century Dictionary of the English Language. Rev. ed. New York: Century Co., 1914.

Clayton, Gary E., and James E. Brown. *Economics: Principles and Practices*. Columbus, Ohio: Merrill Publ. Co., 1988.

Crampton, Jean E. "Murphy, Parkinson, and Peter: Laws for Libraries." *Library Journal*, October 15, 1988.

Ebbing, Darrell D. *General Chemistry*. 3rd ed. Boston: Houghton Mifflin Co., 1990.

Fairbanks, Rhodes W., ed. *The Encyclopedia of Atmospheric Sciences and Astrogeology*. New York: Reinhold Publishing Corp., 1967.

Gottfried, Sandra, *et al.*, eds. *Prentice Hall Biology*. 5th ed. Englewood Cliffs, N.J.: Prentice-Hall, 1983.

Jevons, W. Stanley. *The Principles of Science: A Treatise on Logic and Scientific Method*. New York: Dover Publications, 1958.

McGraw-Hill Dictionary of Scientific and Technical Terms. New York: McGraw Hill, 1974.

Trinklein, Frederick E. *Modern Physics*. Austin, Tex.: Holt, Rinehart and Winston, 1990.

Webster's New International Dictionary of the English Language. 2nd ed., unabridged. Vols. I–III. Springfield, Mass.: G. and C. Merriam Co., 1959.

—L.D.R.

PHILOSOPHY

PHILOSOPHICAL TERMS:
A GLOSSARY

· · · · ·

SOMEONE ONCE LIKENED THE PHILOSOPHER'S QUEST FOR KNOWLEDGE TO that of a blindfolded person in a dark room looking for a black cat that is not there. An extreme view, perhaps; but one to which extensive exposure to philosophical discourse might reasonably lead.

To aid in such quests, we offer the following dictionary, with the warning that individual philosophers, like any other specialists, often adapt and give special meanings to words within the contexts of their own agendas. Our definitions are gauged, on the whole, to provide a sense of the most general acceptation of the terms in question, with specialized uses noted where appropriate.

Absolute. The quality of being free from contingency, dependence, limitations, or reservations; existing in pure and unconditional form. In philosophical usage, *absolute* is the opposite of *relative*.

Abstract. The form in which a concept (*e.g.*, beauty) exists apart from its embodiment in concrete examples (*e.g.*, beautiful objects).

Abstraction. The process by which we derive concepts from experience or from other information, as when we form an abstract concept of ugliness from experience of many ugly things.

Accident. A nonessential or temporary quality of something, as opposed to that which is essential or part of its substantial being; see **Substance**.

Acosmism. The theory that an objective physical world does not exist.

Actualization. The concept of a transition in existence from potential to real.

Aesthetics. A branch of philosophy dealing with the values of art and beauty.

Affectivity. The property of being able to affect the organs of sense.

Agnosticism. The doctrine or belief that the universe is not knowable; in common usage, the idea that it is not possible to know or refute the idea of the existence of God.

Alogism. An attitude that rejects logic as a way of arriving at truth and promotes instead the process of intuition and belief in revelation.

Amoralism. Rejection of laws of morality as having no philosophical ground.

Amphibology. A fallacy that results from grammatical ambiguity or vagueness of phrasing rather than from the ambiguity of individual words.

Analysis. The breaking down of a thing or idea into its component parts for the purpose of examination and understanding.

Anarchism. A philosophical and political attitude that rejects all civil authority and the political state.

Animism. A belief, often found in primitive societies, that spirits affect the lives of people and animals, and objects in the external world. Most religions contain animistic elements.

Anthropomorphism. The attribution of human form and qualities to forces or phenomena in nature, which in many religions are personified as gods.

Antinomy. The coexistence of two apparently contradictory but equally valid inferences; for example, the assertion that the universe is both finite and infinite.

Antithesis. An apparent opposition to an idea or assertion.

Apathia. Freedom from emotion that results, in the Stoic and Epicurean philosophies, in inner peace and philosophical calm.

Apollonian. In the philosophy of Friedrich Nietzsche (1844–1900), the variety of artistic or philosophical experience that strives for balance, harmony, order, and a classical sense of proportion, as opposed to the *Dionysian* experience (see below).

Apologetics. A set of arguments intended to defend a doctrine or system of philosophical positions.

A posteriori. A term for mental data that owes its existence to observed fact in the outside world rather than to logic or insight; a form of reasoning that is inductive (see **Inductive logic**). See also **A priori**.

A priori. A term for concepts acquired without any necessary experience of fact or observation; concepts prior to experience and affecting our evaluation of experience. *Deductive logic* (see below) is based on arguing from *a priori* concepts whose validity is accepted as a given.

Arche. The first item in a series, the origin of what comes after; an *archetype*.

Argumentum ad hominem. An argument that attacks the character or personality of the opposing party rather than that party's facts and logic.

Aristotelianism. The philosophy of the ancient Greek thinker Aristotle (384–322 B.C.E.) and of various groups influenced by his work, such as the scholastic philosophers of the Middle Ages in Europe (see **Scholasticism**). Much of Aristotle's complex thinking is concerned with ways in which form or idea combines with matter to produce being in the observable world. See **Form; Being**.

Associationism. A psychological theory evident in the thought of, among others, David Hume (1711–76), David Hartley (1705–57), and John Stuart Mill (1806–73), which holds the mind's association of ideas and images to be the fundamental principle of intellectual process.

Ataraxia. Tranquility of mind, the goal of Greek skeptical thought.

Atomism. The theory that all matter is made up of atoms. The Greek philosopher Democritus (*ca.* 460–360 B.C.E.) is among the earliest proponents of atomism.

Axiom. A statement for which no proof is necessary, usually the basis for a succession of arguments or proofs.

Begging the question. Taking for granted the very idea or issue that is under dispute.

Being. Existence; the most broadly based property of reality.

Bivalence, principle of. The principle that any given statement must be true or false.

Buddhism. An Indian religion originating in the thought of Siddhartha Gautama (*ca.* 563–483 B.C.E.), the "Buddha" or "enlightened one." Buddhism emphasizes the seeking of the state of *nirvana* (the achievement of complete wisdom and compassion) through meditation and the inducing of contemplative trances.

Cambridge Platonists. A group of thinkers around Cambridge, England, in the second half of the seventeenth century, including Ralph Cudworth (1617–88), Joseph Glanville (1636–80), and Benjamin Whichcote (1609–83), who looked to Plato in order to formulate a rational basis for Christian religious faith.

Cartesian. Pertaining to the philosophy of the French philosopher René Descartes (1596–1650), who sought to establish the existence of the thinking self with the famous assertion *cogito, ergo sum:* "I think, therefore I am."

Casuistry. Application of broad and general principles or laws to specific cases in morals or politics; now usually employed pejoratively to denote the evasion of specific questions or issues.

Categorical imperative. A term coined by the German philosopher Immanuel Kant (1724–1804) to denote a moral injunction, such as one or another of the Ten Commandments, that could be regarded as an absolute requirement independent of individual feelings or opinions.

Categories. The widest, most universal concepts of which the mind is capable; for Kant, the *a priori* forms under which the human imagination must function.

Causation. The relationship between two or more events wherein the first brings about those subsequent to it.

Chain of Being, the Great. A metaphor for the harmony and completeness of creation, extending from the Creator hierarchically to the smallest grain of matter. The metaphor was especially popular during the Middle Ages and Renaissance in Europe.

Cognitive process. Mental activity associated with understanding, acquiring knowledge, and formulating concepts.

Common sense. Traditional formulations of truth and opinions about life in general, taken for granted by ordinary people and philosophers alike.

Concept. A principle of discrimination or classification, *e.g.*, tallness, redness, freedom, etc.; a generic term for a class; a general, abstract representation.

Confucianism. A philosophy inaugurated by the Chinese sage Confucius (551–479 B.C.E.), in which moral values are cultivated as bases for social and political behavior and regarded as part of the natural order of the universe.

Contextualism. A theory in aesthetics wherein works of art must be interpreted in their historical and cultural contexts.

Cosmogony. An account, scientific or fanciful, of the origin of the universe.

Cosmology. A branch of philosophy that attempts to discern order and relation among the totality of phenomena making up the universe.

Cosmos. The ancient Greek idea of the universe as a rational and orderly entity.

Cybernetics. The study of self-regulatory systems, either mechanical or organic, which perform purposeful activity, such as communication or calculation.

Cynics. The philosophical sect centered around the teachings of the ancient Greek Diogenes (ca. 412–323 B.C.E.), who advocated living in the simplest and most basic manner and rejected notions that anything beyond physical gratification was of value. The goal of cynicism was freedom and independence from encumbering philosophical systems and imagined obligations.

Darwinism. Theories that emphasize evolution through natural selection, formulated in biology by the English scientist Charles Darwin (1809–82) but expanded variously by critics in other fields to describe developments in culture, literature, music, etc.

Deductive logic. Argumentative logic in which conclusions are derived from premises accepted or agreed upon though not necessarily proven at the beginning of the argument. *Cf.* **Inductive logic.**

Deism. The doctrine, usually regarded as originating in eighteenth-century Europe, that religious belief can be held reasonably without support from supernatural assumptions or revelations.

Demiurge. The creator of the physical world in various cosmogonies, especially the account in Plato's *Timaeus*.

Deontology. A theory in ethics in which duty is seen as the basis of moral behavior.

Determinism. A form of thought that holds that the progress of events is determined in advance by divine or natural laws.

Dialectic. A process of reasoning, usually through verbal discourse and/or logical steps; often used to denote a particular plan of reasoning, such as "Hegelian dialectic" or "Marxist dialectic."

Dialectical materialism. A doctrine associated with the thinking of Karl Marx (1818–83) and opposed to various forms of idealism. Dialectical materialism posits that matter and its physical motion are fundamental to any understanding of reality.

Dionysian. The variety of artistic or philosophical experience that emphasizes frenzy, passion, release, and intense reexperience of the pains and joy of life; opposed to *Apollonian* (see above).

Double truth. The idea that something false in philosophy or science may be nonetheless true in religion.

Dualism. A philosophical position in which all substances are divided into either mental or material categories, *i.e.*, into categories of ideas or objects.

Eidos. Greek term used by Plato (427–347 B.C.E.) to denote an idea or abstract form as opposed to its concrete manifestation in objects.

Empiricism. The idea that knowledge must be based on experience of concrete objects and observable events. Empiricism is at the basis of experimental science.

Entelechy. Actuality, or that which is realized, as opposed to something that exists only in potentiality.

Epistemology. The area of philosophy that is concerned with knowledge and the question of how we know what we believe we know.

Eschatology. The branch of philosophy concerned with the ends of things, such as the Last Judgment and the idea of an afterlife.

Essence. The internal principle or inner nature of a thing that determines what it is and will become.

Eternity. That which exists outside of duration and is timeless.

Ethics. A branch of philosophy dealing with theories of behavior based on obedience to principles or moral obligations.

Etiology. Study or inquiry into the causes of things.

Existentialism. A philosophical view usually associated, in its modern forms, with such thinkers as Søren Kierkegaard (1813–55), Jean-Paul Sartre (1905–80), and Albert Camus (1913–60) and in which the individual is regarded as having no essence or intrinsic identity apart from that established by the act of choosing. For existentialists the universe has no rational plan or moral framework; but an individual can, through the exercise of his free will and his acceptance of responsibility for his choices, create his own moral truth.

Faculty. A power or ability of the mind or soul.

Fatalism. The idea that the form and end taken by all events is necessitated by forces beyond human control.

Fideism. The doctrine that religious truth rests in faith rather than in logic or individual knowledge; and, usually, that faith is superior to other means of attempting to gain knowledge of reality.

First cause. The uncaused causer (usually the Deity) of a chain of events bringing about the existence and operation of the universe.

First principles. Self-evident laws or statements in a system of knowledge or belief.

Form. Word usually employed in the same sense as *essence* (see above), especially in discourse deriving from Platonic or Aristotelian traditions.

Formalism. Any philosophical system based upon the existence of rules or laws or *first principles* (see above).

Free will. Belief that the will can function independently of all determination; opposite of *determinism*.

Gestalt. A school of thought that regards most external reality as consisting of organized wholes capable of being broken down and analyzed, as opposed to existing in complete and non-reducible form.

Hedonism. A philosophy, usually associated with Epicurus (341–270 B.C.E.) in the ancient Greek world and with Walter Pater (1839–94) in Victorian England, in which life's highest goals are the pursuit of rational pleasure and freedom from pain and vexation.

Heuristic. Helping to solve a problem or elucidate truth.

Historicism. A mode of thought that seeks to explain things in terms of their historical development or background.

Humanism. Any of various modes of thought in which the individual human being, his welfare and creative development, are regarded as of paramount value apart from religious or supernatural contexts.

Idea. A mental image or concept resulting from an act of awareness, usually existing prior to its concrete manifestation in the observable world.

Idealism (also *immaterialism*). A term for various doctrines in which all reality is regarded as mental and the external world is not thought to exist apart from the mind's ability to conceptualize.

Inductive logic. Form of logic in which general conclusions are derived from observed, objective phenomena; the "scientific method" opposed to *deductive logic* (see above).

Inference. The process of reaching a conclusion through observation or logic.

Isomorphism. Similarity of form or structure establishing the relationship and, therefore, the classes of things that are similar.

Law, natural. See **Natural law**.

Logic. The process of attempting to make valid inferences from reality or its representation in discourse. See **Inductive logic** and **Deductive logic** as different forms of procedure.

Logical positivism. A belief in logic, reason, and scientific method as the sources of true knowledge of reality, involving the rejection of all hypothetical construction of entities apart from the sensible universe; associated with Auguste Comte (1797–1857).

Logicism. The position that mathematics is a form of logic.

Logos. A Greek word with multiple meanings, usually understood in philosophy to denote the rationale or underlying set of principles for a thing or a process.

Materialism. A term applied to various forms of thought that endorse the concept that nothing really exists except matter in motion; materialism denies supernatural or spiritual agency in the world.

Matter. The physical makeup of something; that which occupies space and can be experienced by the human organs of sense perception.

Meliorism. The belief that the world and humanity are gradually becoming better over time.

Metaphysics. Most generally, the study of spiritual, intellectual, and abstract matters not capable of being understood by means peculiar to the physical sciences.

Mind. The capacity to think, reason, experience awareness, conceive ideas, etc.

Monad. A single indestructible and indivisible entity.

Monism. The theory that everything in the universe relates to the activity of a single entity, principle, or cause, such as God, energy, the movement of atoms, etc.; the opposite of *dualism* (see above) and *multiplicity* (see **Multiplicity, doctrine of**).

Multiplicity, doctrine of. The belief that reality is comprised of a variety of components that cannot be reduced to a single principle; the opposite of *monism* (see above).

Mysticism. Belief that truth can be gained by suprarational or intuitive means, which transcend logic and science. John Cardinal Newman observed that religious mysticism "begins in mist and ends in schism."

Naturalism. A term applied to a variety of philosophical perspectives that have in common the ideas that natural phenomena constitute the only reality and that there is no supernatural realm.

Natural law. The rules, principles, laws, etc., considered to exist as part of the structure of the universe and to which physical properties and human conduct are obliged to conform; see **Materialism**.

Natura naturans. Nature regarded as an ongoing process.

Natura naturata. Nature regarded as an aggregate of existing, created things.

Necessitarianism. Determinism; the concept that all events are predetermined by immutable causes.

Nescience. A state of ignorance or not-knowing.

Nihilism. The denial of objective truth, usually with the accompanying belief that all knowledge is ultimately false.

Noetic. Concerning the reason and the powers of the intellect.

Nominalism. The theory that only particular things, and not universal or general essences, exist; the opposite of *realism* (see below).

Object. Something capable of being singled out and referred to in thought or discussion.

Occam's razor. A principle derived from the writings of the medieval scholastic William of Occam (1280–1348), which insists that the simplest explanation for a natural phenomenon is the one most likely to be accurate.

Ontology. The branch of philosophy that studies the idea of essential being or existence, as distinguished from individual things that exist; see **Metaphysics**.

Organicism. A theory that attempts to explain the universe as a functioning whole with contributing and coordinated parts, as is the case with a biological organism.

Organon. The collective term for the various works of logic by Aristotle (384–322 B.C.E.).

Pantheism. The belief that God and the universe are identical.

Paradox. A statement that is apparently absurd or self-contradictory but nonetheless possibly true.

Percepts. Data supplied by acts of perception.

Phenomenology. The study of relationships between concrete objects of sense and human awareness of those objects; or of self-awareness as a function of human consciousness.

Phenomenon. An object of perception; a fact or event that can be observed or experienced.

Platonism. The philosophy of the ancient Greek Plato (427–347 B.C.E) or one of the philosophical systems built upon it, such as the various forms of neo-Platonism. Basically, Platonism deals with the concept that the real world is the unseen realm of ideas and perfect forms capable of being known only by the mind, as distinguished from the actual and imperfect world available to the perceptions of sense.

Pluralism. The doctrine that more than one kind of reality exists.

Postulate. A statement accepted as true without proof.

Pragmatism. The belief that knowledge is best derived from experience and experimental procedure, and that it is most properly applied to the solution of practical problems in life.

Prima facie. "On first view," as something appears on the surface.

Prime mover. The original cause (usually regarded as God) of all activity in the universe; see also **First cause**.

Pyrrhonism. An extreme form of skepticism that denies the possibility of obtaining true knowledge of reality and seeks a state of intellectual indifference as the source of calmness in life.

Pythagoreanism. The philosophy constructed from reports of the doctrines of

Pythagoras (*ca.* 572–10 B.C.E), who did not write down his thoughts, emphasizing the rational and mathematical organization of the universe, the possession of souls by all things, and the transmigration after death of souls
from one body to another.

Quality. Something that two or more individuals may hold in common or by
which they may be differentiated, as the quality of strength relates and dif-
ferentiates individual athletes.

Quiddity. The *essence* (see above) of a thing.

Quintessence. Generally used to denote the highest or most nearly pure version
of a thing.

Rationalism. The philosophical approach that emphasizes reason, as opposed to
sensory impressions, as the best means of discovering truth.

Realism. The position that abstractions or universal essences exist independently
of objects that we can perceive with our senses and that these abstractions
constitute the true reality; the opposing view to *nominalism* (see above).

Reincarnation. The investment of the soul in another body after death, as in
Pythagorean philosophy (see **Pythagoreanism**).

Relativism. The doctrine that truth does not exist apart from individual per-
ceivers, and that perceptions are so colored by our personalities that no
absolute truth can be said to exist.

Scholasticism. The Christian philosophy of the European Middle Ages, derived
chiefly from Aristotle. The most notable of the scholastics, in output and
influence, was St. Thomas Aquinas (1225–74). Chief among the goals of
scholasticism was the reconciliation of faith and reason.

Semantics. The study of relationships between linguistic symbols (*i.e.*, words)
and the things they signify.

Semiotics. The study of the nature and kinds of linguistic signifiers.

Sensationalism. The doctrine that all knowledge has its basis in sense perception.

Sign. In semiotics, anything that stands for or denotes anything other than itself.

Skepticism. A term for a range of philosophical positions having in common an
endorsement of doubt or suspension of judgment.

Sophistry. Manipulative rhetoric and intentionally misleading logic, used to
advance a cause or win an argument regardless of its lack of worth.

Stoicism. A school of ancient Greek philosophy, founded by Zeno (*ca.* 340–270
B.C.E.) of Cyprus, that posited a rational order in the universe and advocated
acceptance of one's fate within that order with calmness and philosophical
resignation.

Subjectivism. The theory that all knowledge originates in the knowing party's
inner mental states, and that these states condition perception so thoroughly that an external reality cannot be said to exist; subjectivism is a
form of *relativism* (see above).

Substance. Something that exists in itself, and not as part of or related to anything else.

Summum bonum. The highest or ultimate good, toward which human life should be directed; one of the uses of philosophy is to determine what it is.

Synthesis. The reconstitution of a whole from the parts revealed during the process of *analysis* (see above).

Tabula rasa. As used by the English philosopher John Locke (1632–1704), a characterization of the human mind as a "blank tablet" before being altered and impressed by experience from the external world. The purpose of the term is to suggest that knowledge is acquired rather than innate, and that it is initially gained from sense experience, which is then reflected upon and refined by the mind (see **Associationalism**).

Teleology. The study of purposes and desired ends.

Theodicy. The attempt, through philosophy, to justify the ways of God to humankind.

Timology. The study of worth or value.

Transcendentalism. A type of philosophy that values spirituality and intuition over experiential or empirical means of seeking truth.

Utilitarianism. The theory that life should be organized and led so as to promote the greatest amount of good to the greatest number of people, and that the value of actions is determined by their practical consequences.

Vitalism. Belief in autonomous forces that inform nature and humankind and determine the growth and behavior of animate beings. Like souls, these forces survive the deaths of the organisms they inhabit and exist as principles in nature.

World soul. A spirit believed, especially in philosophies based on Platonic thought (see **Platonism**), to inhabit nature in the same way that the human soul inhabits the individual being, governing animate activity in the cosmos.

SOURCES

Angeles, Peter A. *Dictionary of Philosophy*. New York: Barnes and Noble, 1981.

Barwick, Daniel. *Intentional Implications: The Impact of a Reduction of Mind on Philosophy*. New York: University Press of America, 1994.

Flew, Antony, ed. *A Dictionary of Philosophy*. New York: St. Martin's Press, 1979.

Kiernan, Thomas. *Who's Who in the History of Philosophy*. New York: Philosophical Library, 1965.

Lacey, A. R. *A Dictionary of Philosophy*. 2nd ed. London: Routledge and Kegan Paul, 1986.

Runes, Dagobert D., ed. *Dictionary of Philosophy*. New York: Philosophical Library, 1983.

Saifalin, Murad, and Richard R. Dixon, eds. *Dictionary of Philosophy*. New York: International Publishers, 1989.

—**J.L.M.**

XVII

GASTRONOMY

63

GASTRONOMY:
AN INTERNATIONAL GLOSSARY

> We may live without poetry, music and art;
> We may live without conscience, and live without heart;
> We may live without friends; we may live without books;
> But civilized man cannot live without cooks.
>
> —Owen Meredith (E. R. Bulwer-Lytton), Lucile

. . . . .

Nor civilized woman. Nor would either want to. Or without cook-books. Food and drink, decently prepared, have been the subject of many an author's fondest meditations. Consider the delight that Samuel Johnson took in wolfing down food, the prize turkey that a reformed Scrooge buys for the Crachit family, the turkey that the Dedalus family consumes in *A Portrait of the Artist as a Young Man*, the groaning table of edibles at the family dinner in Wolfe's *Look Homeward, Angel*, the cold jellied beef spiced with carrots that François prepares for M. de Norpois in Proust's *Remembrance of Things Past*, numerous bottles of wine and restaurant meals in the fiction of Ernest Hemingway, the family reunion spread in Eudora Welty's *Losing Battles*, the shore dinner that Mrs. Hosea Hussey serves up in Melville's *Moby-Dick*, and many another literary repast old and new.

Decades ago I read a popular novel entitled *The World, the Flesh and Father Smith*. I can remember nothing about it except that at one point Father Smith goes into a butcher shop and purchases a large steak. Cook it with plenty of butter, the butcher counsels him. And that vivid piece of advice has remained with me ever since, long after everything else about the book has been forgotten. Such is the imaginative power of food in fiction.

Some authors seem to be more interested in food and eating than others. Can anyone recall a really vivid description of an appetizing meal in William Faulkner, for example? I can recall Lena Grove eating sardines, V. K. Ratliff ordering a slice of pie at a restaurant, the Texas cowboy eating ginger snaps, Chick Mallison being fed underdone biscuits by Lucas Beauchamp, and so on. But a genuinely scrumptious imaginative repast, such as Hemingway repeatedly serves up to his readers? There are doubtless some, but they don't leap readily into mind. By contrast, the lunch that Jake Barnes and Bill Gorton consume when fishing at Burguete, with the hard-boiled eggs and chicken and the wine that was "icy cold and tasted faintly rusty," is, as Wright Morris said of the trout placed between layers of ferns in the creel upon the same occasion, immortal, as sensuously vivid as a painting by Braque. (Maybe Maud Butler Faulkner wasn't much of a cook.)

It goes almost without saying that most writers will at one time or the other need to know something about food and cookery. For the benefit of those who haven't a copy of *Larousse gastronomique* or any of the compendia listed under Sources below handy, we offer this abbreviated glossary of some terms employed in the art of gastronomy in various countries.

Achar. East Indian term for any pickled and salted relish.

Acidulated water. Mixture of water and vinegar or citric juice applied to cut fruit to keep it from discoloring.

Aïoli. Provençal mayonnaise made with olive oil and garlic.

À la. Abbreviation of the French phrase "à la mode de," meaning "in the manner of."

À la bourguignonne. Dish that is cooked in wine and served with mushrooms and onions.

À la carte. French phrase meaning that each item on the menu ("carte") is priced separately.

À la florentine. Dish served upon spinach and covered with mornay sauce.

À la king. Dish of diced food covered with a creamy mushroom sauce.

À l'alsacienne. Dish prepared with sauerkraut, sausage, and potatoes.

À la lyonnaise. Dish served with sautéed onions.

À l'américaine. Dish prepared with a spicy tomato and brandy sauce.

À la mode. American phrase for "topped with ice cream."

À l'andalouse. Dish prepared with tomatoes, pimentos, and often rice or sausage.

À l'anglais. Dish in which the food has been boiled or poached.

À la niçoise. Dish served with tomatoes, black olives, garlic, and anchovies.

À la périgourdine. Dish prepared with truffles.

À la Provençal. Dish prepared with tomatoes, garlic, olives, and olive oil.

Al dente. Italian term referring to the degree of doneness of a food, usually pasta or vegetables; meaning "to the tooth," it indicates that the food is barely tender.

Alla. Italian phrase meaning "in the manner of" or "as done by."

Alla carbonara. Pasta sauce made with cream, eggs, Parmesan cheese, and bacon.

Allemande sauce. A velouté sauce thickened with egg yolks; also known as *Parisienne sauce.*

Amandine. Dish garnished with almonds.

Antipasto. Italian appetizer course, served "before the pasta."

À point. French phrase for meat cooked "to the point (of doneness)," *i.e.,* medium rare.

Appetizer. Food or foods served before the main meal; also called *hors d'oeuvres.*

Arborio rice. High-starch Italian rice used for making risotto.

Argenteuil. French term for dish prepared with asparagus (named for the main French asparagus-growing center).

Aspic. Usually a molded salad made from vegetable or meat stock and a natural gelatin; also a flavored glaze for meat, fish, or poultry.

Au bleu. French method of cooking freshly killed fish.

Au gratin. Food combined and/or covered with grated cheese or bread crumbs and then baked.

Au jus. French term for serving a dish of cooked meat along with its natural, unthickened juices.

Au naturel. French term for any food served in its "natural" state.

Avgolemono. Greek soup made from chicken broth, egg yolks, and lemon juice.

Baba. French yeast cake generally flavored with fruit juice or rum.

Baba ghanoush. Middle Eastern spread made from puréed eggplant, tahini, olive oil, garlic, and lemon juice.

Bagel. Jewish yeast roll that is boiled and then baked.

Baguette. Long, narrow loaf of crusty bread; a French staple.

Bain marie. Saucepan or baking pan half-filled with water in which a smaller pan or pot rests; an in-oven double boiler, designed to give more even heat over a large surface.

Baking powder. Leavening agent made from baking soda and an acid such as cream of tartar; when mixed with water it produces carbon dioxide, which causes dough to rise.

Baking soda. Sodium bicarbonate, used as a leavening agent.

Baklava. Middle Eastern filo dessert soaked in honey and lemon juice.

Barbeque (or *barbecue*). The technique of roasting meat over an open wood or charcoal fire; also, the meat so cooked; in the South barbeque signifies pork barbeque; in the Southwest it can be beef or pork.

Bard. Practice of wrapping meat in thin strips of fat, both to baste the meat while it cooks and to keep its delicate parts, such as drumsticks, from drying out and burning.

Basmati rice. Fragrant Himalayan rice used in Indian cooking.

Baste. Technique of brushing roasting or baking meats with a mixture of liquids, including the meat's own juices.

Béarnaise sauce. Sauce made by reducing wine, vinegar, tarragon, pepper, and shallots.

Béchamel. Basic white sauce made from butter, flour, and cream or milk.

Beurre blanc. Sauce made by adding butter to a reduced liquid of white wine, vinegar, and shallots.

Bind. To thicken a hot liquid by stirring in such ingredients as eggs, cheese, flour, butter, or cream.

Bisque. Thick cream soup made from puréed fish or vegetables.

Blacken. Cajun practice of coating meat with spices and then quickly broiling it over high flames to seal in the juices; the spices blacken as they char and form a protective outer layer that keeps the meat from burning while also flavoring it.

Blanch (or *blanche*). To plunge a food (usually vegetables) briefly into boiling water in order to preserve its hard or crunchy texture and also retain its juices.

Blanquette. Creamy, light-colored stew made from veal, chicken, or lamb.

Bombe. Frozen confection or dessert made by lining a mold with one kind of ice cream or sherbet and then filling the mold with a second flavor.

Borscht. Russian beet soup.

Bouillabaisse. Provençal fish soup.

Bouillon. Clear broth made from boiled beef or chicken.

Bouquet garni. Small bundle of herbs, including bay leaves, thyme, and parsley, tied in cheesecloth and added to simmering soups or stews for flavoring.

Braise. To brown a meat and then simmer it in a small amount of liquid in a covered pot.

Broil. To cook food over open flames or close to intense heat.

Brown. To cook meat briefly over an intense heat so that its exterior turns brown, but it retains most of its juices.

Bulgur. Starch made from cracked whole wheat; it is used extensively in Balkan and Middle Eastern cooking.

Burrito. Flour tortilla folded to enclose a combination of refried beans, meat, and cheese.

Butterfly. Technique of cutting a food into connected halves for cooking.

Cacciatore. Italian dish prepared in the hunter ("cacciatore") style with tomatoes, mushrooms, onions, herbs, and wine.

Calzone. Folded-over pizza, originating in Naples.

Can. Technique of preserving food by sealing it hermetically in glass jars.

Canapé. French term for any small, open-faced sandwich, usually served as an appetizer.

Cannellini. White kidney beans used in Italian cooking.

Cannelloni. Italian dish of tubes of pasta stuffed with a meat and béchamel filling and baked.

Cannolli. Italian dessert of pastry tubes filled with whipped cream.

Capelli d'angelo. Very thin pasta that resembles "angel hair."

Capers. Pickled flower buds of a Mediterranean shrub; used as a condiment or flavoring agent.

Casing. Translucent intestinal membrane stuffed with meat to form sausage.

Casserole. Dish baked in an earthenware pot inside an oven.

Cassoulet. Southwestern French casserole of goose or pork and beans.

Caviar. Sturgeon or salmon roe.

Cellophane noodles. Thin mung bean noodles, used in several Southeast Asian recipes; also known as *bean threads.*

Cèpes. Wild mushrooms of the Boletus edulis species; Italians call them porcini.

Chafing dish. Pot that includes its own source of heat; used to prepare fondues.

Challah. Braided Jewish holiday bread.

Chalupa. Fried corn tortilla shaped into a boat ("chalupa") and filled with meat, cheese, or vegetables.

Champignon. French term for mushroom.

Chanterelle. Funnel-shaped wild mushroom of the *Cantharellus cibarius* species.

Chapati. Flat bread; a staple of Indian cuisine.

Charlotte. French dessert made from ladyfingers, cream, and fruit.

Chasseur sauce. Brown sauce made with mushrooms, shallots, and white wine; it is served with game (*chasseur* is the French word for *hunter*).

Chitterlings (also *chitlins*). Small intestines of pigs, which have been simmered until tender.

Chowder. Thick soup usually made with seafood or vegetables.

Chutney. Spicy, slightly sweet East Indian relish made from fruits, nuts, and vegetables, and served with curried dishes.

Clarify. To skim cloudy fat particles from a soup, stew, gravy, or butter.

Coddle. To cook a food in liquid just below the boiling point.

Colander. Perforated bowl used to drain off liquids.

Compote. Dish of cooked fruit served in a sugar syrup.

Condiment. Sauce or relish used as an accompaniment to food.

Confit. French term referring to any preserved food.

Consommé. Clear meat broth similar to bouillon.

Convection oven. Oven that cooks faster than a regular oven because it uses a fan to circulate the heat.

Cooling rack. Slightly raised grill on which freshly baked items are placed so that they will not become soggy as they cool.

Coquilles. Shells, or dishes in the shape of shells, used for baking and serving sauced meat and seafood dishes.

Corning. Method of preserving fresh meat by drawing its juices out with a mixture of salt and spices.

Cornstarch. Powdered corn derivative used as a thickening agent.

Court bouillon. Concentrated stock made from fish and herbs.

Couscous. North African dish consisting of semolina covered with a lamb or chicken stew.

Crème-fraîche. Thick, rich cream that has been aged.

Crêpe. Very thin light pancake in which meats, cheeses, fruits, or jams are rolled.

Croquettes. Cakes, patties, or balls of seasoned cooked meat and vegetables.

Croutons. Small wedges or cubes of toasted bread added to soups and salads.

Crumb. Term referring to the texture, consistency, and degree of moisture within a loaf of bread.

Curing. Process of preserving a meat by smoking, pickling, corning, or salting it.

Curry. Any dish cooked with a blend of Indian spices. Curry powder—a misnomer—is not a single spice, but an idiosyncratic mixture of turmeric, fenugreek, chili peppers, ginger, cumin, cardamom, nutmeg, cinnamon, cloves, lemon grass, and curry leaves.

Custard. Dessert made by boiling or baking a mixture of eggs, milk, sugar, and flavoring.

Dal. Spicy Indian dish made with lentils, tomatoes, and onions.

Decant. To pour a wine, liquor, or liqueur from its original bottle into another vessel to separate out sediment; older beverages are also decanted so that they can "breathe" and release the complexity of their flavors and aromas.

Deep-fry. To cook a food by immersing it completely in very hot fat or oil.

Deglaze. To remove meat drippings from a roasting pan by adding wine or some other liquid and scraping; this mixture forms the base for a gravy or sauce.

Degrease. Process of skimming fat from a liquid.

Dehydrate. Practice of preserving food by slowly drying it to remove all water.

Demitasse. The term for both a serving of very strong black coffee given after dinner and the small cup in which the coffee is served.

Dolma. Balkan and Middle Eastern appetizer consisting of grape leaves stuffed with a combination of lamb, rice, and vegetables.

Dredging. Technique of rolling pieces of dampened or moist food in flour, spices, meal, or another dry, finely ground agent before cooking them; if ground crackers or bread crumbs are used, the process is called *breading*.

Dress. Term for the preparation of game or fowl for cooking.

Dressing. Sauce used to coat and flavor foods, especially salads.

Drippings. Melted fat, bits of meat, and juices found at the bottom of a pan that has been used for roasting; deglazed, they become the base for a gravy.

Emulsion. Mixture of two liquids that do not combine on their own.

En brochette. French phrase for food cooked on skewers.

Enchilada. Meat-, bean-, or cheese-filled tortilla covered with a salsa, sour cream, and/or grated cheese.

Enology (or *œnology*). Science of wines and wine making.

Entrée. In the United States, the main dish of a meal.

Espanole sauce. Brown sauce made from meat stock, diced vegetables, and a brown roux.

Fajitas. A Tex-Mex dish consisting of grilled steak or chicken placed in a soft tortilla with guacamole and grilled onions and peppers.

Falafel. Middle Eastern dish consisting of balls of mashed chickpeas and spices that are deep-fried and served in pita bread with dipping sauces.

Farci. French term for *stuffed.*

Farfalle. Bowtie- or butterfly-shaped noodle.

Feijoada. Brazilian dish of assorted sliced meats, black beans, rice, orange slices, peppers, and shredded greens.

Fettuccine. Flat egg noodle.

Fideo. Vermicellilike noodle used in Spanish and Mexican cooking.

Figaro sauce. Hollandaise sauce into which puréed tomatoes and parsley have been mixed.

Filé. Powdered thickening agent used in gumbo and jambalaya.

Fillet (or *filet*). Cut of meat or fish from which the bones have been removed.

Filo (also *phyllo*). Paper-thin pastry sheets used in many Greek and Middle Eastern recipes.

Finnan haddie. Scottish smoked haddock dish.

Fish and chips. English dish consisting of pieces of deep-fried white fish and French fries.

Flambé. Food served with a flaming sauce; the food is drenched with an alcoholic liquid that is then ignited.

Flan. Spanish caramel egg custard.

Flauta. Corn tortilla filled and rolled into the shape of a flute ("flauta") and then fried.

Foie gras. French delicacy of goose liver.

Fold. Method of gently blending an ingredient into a mixture.

Fondue. Swiss dish consisting of a heated mixture of Gruyere or Emmenthaler cheese and white wine into which bread cubes on skewers are dipped.

Fool. English dessert of puréed fruit and whipped cream.

Forcemeat (also *farce*). Mixture of meats, herbs, and bread crumbs that can be served alone or as part of the stuffing for meats, fish, and poultry.

Frappé. Diluted, sweetened fruit juice that is frozen until slushy.

Fricassée. The French term for any dish in which the meats are first sautéed and then simmered in a liquid (compare with **Stew**).

Frittata. Italian open-faced omelet.

Fromage. French word for *cheese.*

Fusille. Corkscrew-shaped noodle.

Gado gado. Indonesian dish consisting of raw or cooked vegetables served with a spicy peanut sauce.

Galette. Round, short French cake.

Garam masala. Mixture of "warm" spices that can include black pepper, cardamom, cinnamon, coriander, cumin, cloves, dried chilies, fennel, or nutmeg; it is a staple of Indian cooking.

Gâteau. French word for cake.

Gazpacho. Cold Spanish soup made from a purée of tomatoes, cucumbers, onions, vinegar, and green peppers.

Gelato. Italian ice cream.

Ghee. Indian clarified butter.

Giblets. Liver, heart, gizzard, and sometimes the lungs of poultry; these are often used in making gravy for the cooked fowl.

Glace. French ice cream.

Glacé. French term for a food that is frozen or glazed.

Glaze. Thick coating brushed on both hot and cold foods.

Gnocchi. Italian dumplings.

Gorp. Mixture of nuts, dried fruits, and seeds consumed for quick energy.

Goulash. Hungarian beef or veal stew flavored with paprika and often served with sour cream.

Grand cru. French phrase, meaning "great growth," for a wine from an officially classified vineyard.

Granola. Breakfast cereal consisting of a toasted mixture of oats, nuts, and dried fruit.

Guacamole. Mexican dip made from mashed avocado and salt and often cilantro, chilies, and lemon juice.

Gumbo. Thick Creole soup or stew containing various game meats, shellfish, okra, tomatoes, and onions.

Gyro. Greek pita bread sandwich of roasted lamb, onions, and peppers.

Haggis. Scottish dish consisting of a mixture of sheep or calf organs, suet, and oatmeal, boiled in the animal's stomach.

Halva (or *halvah*). Middle Eastern dessert made from ground sesame-seed paste and honey.

Hard sauce. Whipped mixture of butter, sugar, and alcohol served as an accompaniment to plum pudding; the British call it brandy butter. "Caught between a rock and a hard sauce"—Edmund Fuller.

Harissa sauce. Hot Tunisian sauce made from hot peppers, garlic, coriander, cumin, and caraway.

Hash. Dish of chopped meat and potatoes fried together.

Hasty pudding. Dish made from cornmeal mush, milk or water, and honey, maple syrup, or molasses; it was popular in colonial America.

Hero sandwich. Long sandwich that can include several kinds of meat and cheese, peppers, pickles, lettuce, onions, and tomatoes.

Hoisin sauce. Reddish-brown sauce made from sweetened bean paste, garlic, peppers, and hot spices; used in many Asian recipes.

Hollandaise sauce. Creamy yellow sauce made from butter, egg yolks, and lemon juice.

Hominy. Dried corn with the hull and germ removed; when ground, it constitutes hominy grits.

Hors d'oeuvre. French phrase for any appetizer.

Horseradish. Bitter white root from which horseradish sauce is made.

Hummus *(or houmos).* Middle Eastern appetizer made from mashed chickpeas, garlic, and spices.

Hushpuppy. Small fried cornmeal dumpling.

Irish stew. Stew made from lamb or mutton chops, potatoes, and onions.

Jambalaya. Creole dish made with rice, poultry and/or sausage, and vegetables.

Julienne. Technique of cutting food into thin strips.

Kasha. Russian porridge made from buckwheat kernels or hulled oats.

Kebab (or *kabob*)**.** Arabic term for food cooked on a skewer.

Kefir. Sour, yogurtlike drink brewed from cow's milk.

Kimchee (also *kim chee or kimchi*)**.** Hot Korean pickle made from salted cabbage, turnips, and spices.

Kippering. To preserve fish (usually herring) by splitting it, salting it dry, then smoking it.

Kosher. Term for foods prepared in accordance with Jewish dietary laws.

Ladyfinger. Small spongecake shaped like a fat woman's finger.

Lard. Originally, to insert slivers of solid fat or lard into meats to keep them from drying out during cooking. Now slivers of garlic, onion, or spices are used to flavor the cooking meats.

Lasagna. Wide, long, flat egg noodle.

Latke. Potato and matzo meal pancake traditionally served during Hanukkah.

Leaven. Agent that makes dough rise, usually through carbon dioxide production caused by the chemical interaction of yeast, baking soda, and baking powder.

Lefse. Norwegian griddle-fried potato bread.

Legumes. Term for vegetables that bear their fruits or seeds in pods, including beans, peas, and lentils.

Lemongrass. Long, scallionlike herb used extensively in Thai cooking.

Linguine. Long, flat, narrow noodle shaped like a little tongue ("linguine").

Litchi (or *leechee*). Fruit of a tree native to Southeast Asia and used extensively in Chinese cooking.

Macaroni. Small, curved tube of pasta; among the different types are elbow macaroni, penne (quill shaped), rigatoni (ridged), and ziti (unridged).

Macaroon. Small cookie made from almond paste.

Maceration. Process of immersing food, especially fruit, in a liquor for flavoring.

Madeleine. Small, spongy cake often dipped in tea or coffee before being eaten.

Manicotti. Long, broad tubes of pasta filled with cheese and a béchamel sauce.

Marinara sauce. Italian pasta sauce made from tomatoes, onions, garlic, and oregano.

Marinate. Process of soaking uncooked meats for a time in spicy liquids or marinade, thereby tenderizing and adding flavor.

Marzipan. European confection made from shaped sweetened almond paste.

Matzo (or *matzoh*). Loaves of unleavened bread traditionally eaten during Passover.

Mayonnaise. Emulsion of vegetable oil, egg yolks, and lemon juice or vinegar.

Menudo. Spicy Mexican soup made from tripe, calf's feet, green chilies, and hominy.

Meringue. Mixture of egg whites and sugar beaten until stiff.

Milanese. Dish in which the meat is dipped in beaten eggs, bread crumbs, and Parmesan cheese, then fried in butter.

Mille-feuille. French dessert made with puff pastry, cream, custard, and jam.

Minestrone. Italian vegetable soup, sometimes served cold.

Mirepoix (or *mirepois*). Small cubes of carrots, onions, celery, and ham sautéed and then served as a garnish.

Miso. Fermented soybean paste used extensively in Japanese cooking.

Mocha. Generally, a beverage made from mixing coffee and chocolate; also refers to any coffee-flavored substance.

Mock turtle soup. Soup made by boiling a calf's head in water.

Mole sauce. Spicy, rust-colored Mexican sauce most frequently used as an accompaniment to poultry.

Mornay sauce. Béchamel sauce made with Parmesan or Swiss cheese.

Mousse. Most commonly, a light, airy chocolate dessert served chilled; mousses may also be made with meat, fish, or cheese and served hot.

Muddle. Process of simultaneously stirring and crushing, especially fresh fruits or herbs, to release juices, flavors, and aromas.

Muesli. Swiss breakfast cereal, developed by Dr. Bircher-Benner; a mixture of toasted cereals, dried fruits, nuts, and wheat germ.

Mull. Practice of heating a beverage, such as cider or wine, with spices.

Mulligan stew. Stew made from any ingredients which happen to be available.

Mulligatawny soup. Curried soup that originated in southern India and Sri Lanka.

Naan. Flat bread; a staple in India, Pakistan, and Afghanistan.

Nachos. Mexican appetizer consisting of crisp tortilla chips covered with a spicy melted cheese.

Neat. Term for a liquor beverage served without ice, water, or a mixer.

Nockerl. Austrian dumpling.

Olive oil. Monounsaturated oil obtained from pressed olives; extra-virgin olive oil is obtained from the first pressing of the olives.

Omelet (or *omelette*). Baked or fried egg dish usually containing several fillings.

On the rocks. Term for a liquor beverage served with ice cubes.

Orzo. Type of pasta consisting of small round or oval tablets.

Oyster sauce. Thick, salty brown sauce made from pulverized oysters and soy sauce; it is often used in Southeast Asian recipes.

Paella. Spanish dish generally consisting of seafood, baked rice, tomatoes, olive oil, and saffron.

Pancetta. Italian bacon that has been salted rather than smoked.

Parboil. To boil a food briefly before cooking in some other manner.

Pare. Process of removing the outer skin of a vegetable or fruit.

Pasta. Italian word for any type of paste made from water and ground grain (generally wheat) that is formed into one of a variety of shapes and then dried for storage before being cooked.

Pâté. Preparation of ground meat, usually liver.

Pesto. Italian sauce made by grinding together fresh basil leaves, garlic, pine nuts, Parmesan cheese, and olive oil.

Petit four. Small French cake or cookie, decoratively iced.

Pilaf. Middle Eastern dish in which a mixture of rice and other grains is briefly sautéed, then cooked in a stock.

Piroshki (or *pirozhki*). Russian pastries stuffed with a variety of fillings, including meat or cabbage.

Pita. Middle Eastern flat bread cut open to form pockets.

Pizza. Neopolitan baked dish consisting of a round flat crust covered with tomato sauce and a combination of meats, peppers, cheeses, onions, and anchovies.

Poach. Process of cooking foods in liquid.

Poi. Hawaiian dish of mashed taro root and water.

Polenta. Italian cornmeal and cheese dish often served beside cooked meats.

Pot-au-feu. Clear meat broth usually served in the earthenware pot in which it was cooked (and from which it takes its name); it is the national dish of France.

Pot stickers. Chinese appetizers made by frying stuffed wonton skins.

Praline. Confection made from a mixture of caramelized sugar and ground almonds or pecans; it is popular in the South.

Prix fixe. French phrase for a complete meal served at a "fixed price."

Proof. Term for the amount of alcohol in a liquor; in the United States, proof is twice the percentage of alcohol.

Pulse. Dried, edible seeds of any legume.

Purée. Method of reducing a food to a mushy, pastelike consistency.

Quatre épices. The French term for the "four spices"—pepper, ground cloves, ginger, and nutmeg—that are considered essential.

Quenelle. Poached dumpling made from ground meat or fish.

Quesadilla. Tortilla folded around cheese or beans and fried.

Quiche. French pie made from eggs, cheese, and other ingredients.

Ragout. French, thick meat or vegetable stew, highly seasoned.

Ramekin. Small, individual baking dish.

Ramen. Japanese dish of rice or wheat noodles, usually served with meat or vegetables and a broth.

Ratatouille. Provençal dish made from eggplant, zucchini, onions, garlic, and tomatoes.

Ravioli. Small squares of pasta stuffed with meat or cheese.

Reconstitute. To add water to a dehydrated food.

Reduce. To cook a liquid in an uncovered pan so that evaporation carries away moisture and thickens the liquid.

Refried beans. Mexican dish of red or pinto beans that have been simmered, mashed, and then fried.

Render. To separate fat from meat while over heat.

Rijsttafel. Dutch-Indonesian meal of hot rice served with several side dishes and condiments.

Risotto. Italian dish of rice that is sautéed and then has stock added.

Rotelle. Wheel-shaped pasta.

Rotini. Small, corkscrew spaghetti.

Rotisserie. Spit which rotates so that meats are evenly cooked.

Roulade. Thin strip of meat wrapped about a filling, browned, and then baked or braised.

Roux. Heated mixture of flour and butter used as a thickener for sauces and gravies.

Rumaki. Japanese appetizer consisting of chestnuts wrapped in chicken livers and bacon, skewered, and broiled with teriyaki sauce.

Sake. Japanese rice wine, usually drunk warm.

Salsa. In the United States, typically an appetizer or condiment made with tomatoes, onions, cilantro, and peppers; but in Mexico it refers to any fresh or cooked sauce.

Samosa. Stuffed triangular pastry popular in India.

Sashimi. Japanese dish of sliced raw fish and condiments.

Satay (or *saté*). Indonesian dish of skewered meats grilled and served in a peanut sauce.

Sauté. Method of quickly frying meats or vegetables in oil.

Scalding. Process identical to blanching; it is often used for milk.

Shiitake. Dark-brown flavorful mushroom.

Simmer. Method of cooking food slowly in liquid or in its own juices.

Sopaipilla. Deep-fried puff-pastry dessert popular in the Southwest.

Soufflé. Dish based on egg whites beaten until fluffy and then baked until the mixture rises into a delicate airy puff.

Souvlaki. Greek dish of grilled lamb served with a yogurt sauce in pita bread.

Soy sauce. Condiment made from fermented soybeans; used extensively in Asian cooking.

Spaetzle. German dish of tiny dumplings.

Spaghetti. Long, thin strands or strings ("spaghetti") of pasta.

Spanakopita. Greek dish made with filo crust, spinach, feta cheese, and eggs.

Steaming. Practice of cooking foods with steam, which seals in juices without burning the outer layers of the food.

Stew. Dish in which meats are cooked in a liquid for a long time.

Stir-fry. Asian technique designed to fry foods quickly over high heat in a minimum of oil or other liquid.

Stock. Highly flavored liquid resulting from slowly cooking meats, bones, or vegetables in water.

Sukiyaki. Japanese dish of meats, tofu, and vegetables stir-fried in the same pan.

Sushi. Japanese dish of boiled rice, often flavored with vinegar or seaweed, served with raw fish.

Sweetbreads. The thymus glands and the pancreas of lambs or calves.

Tabasco sauce. Spicy red condiment made from tabasco peppers, vinegar, and salt.

Tabouleh (also *tabouli*). Middle Eastern dish made from bulgur, tomatoes, onions, olive oil, mint, and lemon juice.

Tahini. Thick sesame-seed paste used in many Middle Eastern recipes.

Tamale. Highly seasoned Mexican dish of ground meat and beans rolled in oiled cornhusks and steamed or boiled.

Tandoori. Properly speaking, any food cooked in a tandoor, an Indian clay oven with a live coal or wood fire.

Tapas. Spanish appetizers traditionally served with sherry.

Tapenade. Provençal condiment; a paste of capers, anchovies, olives, lemon juice, and tuna.

Tempura. Japanese dish of finger foods dipped in a special egg, flour, and cornstarch batter, then deep-fried.

Teriyaki. Term for the Japanese technique of marinating foods in a spiced mixture of wine and soy sauce.

Terrine. Term that refers both to the dish in which fish, meat, or poultry pâtés are cooked, and to those pâtés.

Tex-Mex. Style of cooking from Texas that combines Texan and Mexican elements.

Timbale. Custard dish of chicken, lobster, or fish baked in a mold.

Tisane. Herbal tea, especially when taken as a tonic or a medicine.

Tofu. Solidified soybean curd, often used in Asian cooking.

Torte. Any of a number of rich European cakes made from nuts, eggs, crumbs, or meringue.

Tortellini. Small ring- or triangle-shaped dumplings.

Tortilla. Thin round cake of bread made from cornmeal or wheat flour.

Tostada. Crispy tortilla "bowl" filled with a combination of beans, meat, lettuce, tomato, cheese, sour cream, and guacamole.

Trifle. English dessert of sponge cake soaked with liquor, then covered with jam and custard.

Truffle. Fragrant fungus that grows underground; trained pigs or dogs are used to sniff out truffles.

Velouté sauce. White sauce made with stock.

Vichysoisse. Cold French soup of creamed potatoes and leeks.

Vinaigrette. Sauce or dressing based on vinegar and spices.

Wasabi. Japanese horseradish used as a condiment for sushi and sashimi.

Wok. Curved cooking dish used for stir-frying.

Wonton. Asian dumpling filled with vegetables and/or meats, then deep-fried.

Worcestershire sauce. Popular English bottled sauce based on garlic, anchovies, soy sauce, tamarinds, molasses, and lime.

Yogurt. Fermented and coagulated milk product.

Zabaglione. Italian dessert custard made with Marsala, a sweet dessert wine.

Zest. Colorful and pungent outer layer of citrus peel.

SOURCES

Betty Crocker's International Cookbook. New York: Random House, 1980.

Child, Julia, Louisette Bertholle, and Simone Beck. *Mastering the Art of French Cooking.* New York: Alfred A. Knopf, 1967.

Coyle, L. Patrick. *The World Encyclopedia of Food.* New York: Facts on File, 1982.

Hazan, Marcella. *More Classic Italian Cooking.* New York: Ballantine Books, 1984.

Herbst, Sharon Tyler. *The Food Lover's Companion: Comprehensive Definitions of over 3000 Food, Wine, and Culinary Terms.* New York: Barron's, 1990.

Johnson, Frank E. *The Professional Wine Reference.* Rev. ed. New York: Harper and Row, 1983.

Rombauer, Irma S., and Marion Rombauer Becker. *The Joy of Cooking.* Rev. ed. New York: New American Library, 1973.

Simon, Andre L. *A Concise Encyclopedia of Gastronomy.* Woodstock, N.J.: Overlook Press, 1981.

—Ian Crump; David Sisk; L.D.R.

XVIII

SPORTS

64

PENNANT CONTENDERS

*Which Major League Baseball Teams Have Been Most, and
Also Least, Competitive over the Years?*

. . . . .

MORE BOOKS HAVE PROBABLY BEEN WRITTEN AND PUBLISHED ABOUT BASE-
ball than about all other professional sports in America combined. The
game seems to lend itself to the literary mind, much as cricket does in
England. It may be because of the way in which the individual players are
made to stand out, with their personality traits in clear view, over the
course of a season that extends across more than half a year. The availabil-
ity of statistics and records probably has something to do with it, too; they
can measure individual performance, and with certain adjustments are
comparable through the decades. A player's batting and pitching performance at the turn of the 20th Century can thus be compared, however
roughly, with another player's in the 1990s. So there is continuity, and individual and team records can be contemplated the year around.

Whatever the reason or reasons, there can be no gainsaying that the
game has intrigued writers of various temperaments, ranging from newspaper reporters to novelists and poets. In recent years it has spawned a host of
SABRmetricians, who belong to a Society for American Baseball Research
and, aided by computer technology, work out complicated mathematical
formulas and graphs to compare and contrast the relative abilities of a century and more of major league players. The measurable nature of individual
statistics has even facilitated the development of elaborate tabletop games,
whose devotees divide up the player talent past and present, form teams and
leagues, and play out entire seasons—on which statistics are equally kept.
They take these things seriously, and write newsletters and even books
about their doings.

The loyalties to various teams that fans acquire, usually at a tender age,
often endure for the course of a lifetime, and cause them to become partisans of their favorite franchises over the years. Depending upon the teams

involved, this can become a matter of sustaining joy or abiding frustration. There are major league franchises that seem to be able to field pennant contenders with heartening regularity, and others that offer mediocrity year after year.

All major league baseball teams have as their goal the winning of league championships and the World Series. But what is of greater significance, from the standpoint of baseball fans purchasing tickets and therefore of the owners of franchises, is that a team be in pennant contention. The knowledge that the team has a chance to win the pennant sustains spectator interest and keeps the turnstiles active. What makes a baseball organization successful and memorable, and therefore profitable, is the extent to which it is able, season after season, to keep its club in contention. It is for precisely that reason that for playoff purposes, beginning with the 1994 season the two major leagues, taking their cue from the National Football League, divided themselves into three divisions apiece and added a wild card team to the total playoff lineup—thus including eight instead of four teams in post-season play. Needless to say, this expanded the number of teams in contention for the league championship, and produced more sellout crowds—until the well-paid players and well-heeled owners of major league baseball together produced a strike and lock-out that blew the 1994 season skyhigh.

In the the tabulation which follows, when no team finished within ten games of the league or division champion, the second place team is given in parentheses. For 1969 and thereafter, teams winning divisional playoffs are in bold type. For the 1995 season, when the leagues were grouped into three divisions each and a wild card team added to the playoffs, the wild card team is indicated by the symbol #, and the team winning in the first round of the playoffs but losing the championship series between the divisional playoff winners is in *italics*. World Series winners are asterisked: *.

NATIONAL LEAGUE, 1901 TO PRESENT

1901—Pittsburgh, Philadelphia 7½, Brooklyn 9½
1902—Pittsburgh, (Brooklyn 27½)
1903—Pittsburgh, New York 6½, Chicago 8
1904—New York, (Chicago 13)
1905—New York*, Pittsburgh 9
1906—Chicago, (New York 20)
1907—Chicago*, (Pittsburgh 17)
1908—Chicago*, New York and Pittsburgh 1
1909—Pittsburgh*, Chicago 6½

1910—Chicago, (New York 13)

1911—New York, Chicago 7½

1912—New York, Pittsburgh 10

1913—New York, (Philadelphia 12½)

1914—Boston*, (New York 10½)

1915—Philadelphia, Boston 7, Brooklyn 10

1916—Brooklyn, Philadelphia 2½, Boston 4, New York 7

1917—New York, Philadelphia 10

1918—Chicago, (New York 10½)

1919—Cincinnati*, New York 9

1920—Brooklyn, New York 7

1921—New York*, Pittsburgh 4, St. Louis 7

1922—New York*, Cincinnati 7, St. Louis and Pittsburgh 8

1923—New York, Cincinnati 4½, Pittsburgh 8 ½

1924—New York, Brooklyn 1½, Pittsburgh 3, Cincinnati 10

1925—Pittsburgh*, New York 8½

1926—St. Louis*, Cincinnati 2, Pittsburgh 4½, Chicago 7

1927—Pittsburgh, St. Louis 1½, New York 2, Chicago 8½

1928—St. Louis, New York 2, Chicago 4, Pittsburgh 9

1929—Chicago, (Pittsburgh 10½)

1930—St. Louis, Chicago 2, New York 5, Brooklyn 6

1931—St. Louis*, (New York 13)

1932—Chicago, Pittsburgh 4, Brooklyn 9

1933—New York*, Pittsburgh 5, Chicago 6, Boston 9, St. Louis 9½

1934—St. Louis*, New York 2, Chicago 8

1935—Chicago, St. Louis 4, New York 8½

1936—New York, Chicago and St. Louis 5, Pittsburgh 8

1937—New York, Chicago 3, Pittsburgh 10

1938—Chicago, Pittsburgh 2, New York 5, Cincinnati 6

1939—Cincinnati, St. Louis 4½

1940—Cincinnati*, (Brooklyn 12)

1941—Brooklyn, St. Louis 2½

1942—St. Louis*, Brooklyn 2

1943—St. Louis, (Cincinnati 18)

1944—St. Louis*, (Pittsburgh 14½)

1945—Chicago, St. Louis 3

1946—St. Louis*, Brooklyn 2 (St. Louis won championship playoff with
          Brooklyn, 2 games to 0)

1947—Brooklyn, St. Louis 5, Boston 8

1948—Boston, St. Louis 6½, Brooklyn 7½, Pittsburgh 8½

1949—Brooklyn, St. Louis 1

1950—Philadelphia, Brooklyn 2, New York 5, Boston 8

1951—New York, Brooklyn 1 (New York won championship playoff with Brooklyn, 2 games to 1)

1952—Brooklyn, New York 4½, St. Louis 8½, Philadelphia 9½

1953—Brooklyn, (Milwaukee 13)

1954—New York*, Brooklyn 5, Milwaukee 8

1955—Brooklyn*, (Milwaukee 13½)

1956—Brooklyn, Milwaukee 1, Cincinnati 2

1957—Milwaukee*, St. Louis 8

1958—Milwaukee, Pittsburgh 8

1959—Los Angeles*, Milwaukee 2 (Los Angeles won championship playoff with Milwaukee, 2 games to 0), San Francisco 4, Pittsburgh 9

1960—Pittsburgh*, Milwaukee 7, St. Louis 9

1961—Cincinnati, Los Angeles 4, San Francisco 8, Milwaukee 10

1962—San Francisco, Los Angeles 1 (San Francisco won championship playoff with Los Angeles, 2 games to 1), Cincinnati 3½, Pittsburgh 8

1963—Los Angeles*, St. Louis 6

1964—St. Louis*, Cincinnati and Philadelphia 1, San Francisco 3, Milwaukee 5

1965—Los Angeles*, San Francisco 2, Pittsburgh 7, Cincinnati 8

1966—Los Angeles, San Francisco 1½, Pittsburgh 3, Philadelphia 8, Atlanta 10

1967—St. Louis*, (San Francisco 10½)

1968—St. Louis, San Francisco 9

1969—East—**New York***, Chicago 8
West—Atlanta, San Francisco 3, Cincinnati 4, Los Angeles 8

1970—East—Pittsburgh, Chicago 5, New York 6
West—**Cincinnati**, (Los Angeles 14½)

1971—East—**Pittsburgh***, St. Louis 7
West—San Francisco, Los Angeles 1, Atlanta 8

1972—East—Pittsburgh, (Chicago 11)
West—**Cincinnati**, (Houston 10½)

1973—East—**New York**, St. Louis 1½, Pittsburgh 2½, Montreal 3½, Chicago 5
West—Cincinnati, **Los Angeles** 3½

1974—East—Pittsburgh, St. Louis 1½, Philadelphia 8, Montreal 8½
West—Los Angeles, Cincinnati 4

1975—East—Pittsburgh, Philadelphia 6½
West—**Cincinnati***, (Los Angeles 20)

1976—East—Philadelphia, Pittsburgh 9
West—**Cincinnati***, Los Angeles 10

1977—East—Philadelphia, Pittsburgh 5
West—**Los Angeles**, Cincinnati 10

1978—East—Philadelphia, Pittsburgh 1½
West—**Los Angeles**, Cincinnati 2½, San Francisco 6

1979—East—**Pittsburgh***, Montreal 2

West—Cincinnati, Houston 1½

1980—East—**Philadelphia***, Montreal 1, Pittsburgh 8

West—Houston, Los Angeles 1 (Houston won divisional championship playoff with Los Angeles, 1 game to 0), Cincinnati 3½

1981—Because of players' strike, pennant races were divided into two half seasons, with winners in playoffs to determine divisional championships. Teams finishing within five games of first place in either half season are rated as pennant contenders.

East—(1) Philadelphia, St. Louis 1½, Montreal 4; (2) Montreal, St. Louis and Philadelphia 4½ (Montreal won playoff with Philadelphia to determine divisional championship, 3 games to 2)

West—(1) Los Angeles, Cincinnati ½; (2) Houston, Cincinnati 1½, San Francisco 3½ (**Los Angeles*** won playoff with Houston to determine divisional championship, 3 games to 2)

1982—East—**St. Louis***, Philadelphia 3, Montreal 6, Pittsburgh 8

West—Atlanta, Los Angeles 1, San Francisco 2, San Diego 8

1983—East—**Philadelphia**, Pittsburgh 6, Montreal 8

West—Los Angeles, Atlanta 3, Houston 6, San Diego 10

1984—East—Chicago, New York 6½

West—**San Diego**, (Atlanta and Houston 12)

1985—East—**St. Louis**, New York 3

West—Los Angeles, Cincinnati 5½

1986—East—**New York***, (Philadelphia 21½)

West—Houston, Cincinnati 10

1987—East—**St. Louis**, New York 3, Montreal 4

West—San Francisco, Cincinnati 6

1988—East—New York, (Pittsburgh 15)

West—**Los Angeles***, Cincinnati 7

1989—East—Chicago, New York 6, St. Louis 7

West—**San Francisco**, San Diego 3, Houston 6

1990—East—Pittsburgh, New York 4, Montreal 10

West—**Cincinnati***, Los Angeles 5, San Francisco 6

1991—East—Pittsburgh (St. Louis 14)

West—**Atlanta**, Los Angeles 1, San Diego 10

1992—East—Pittsburgh, Montreal 9

West—**Atlanta**, Cincinnati 8

1993—East—**Philadelphia**, Montreal 3, St. Louis 10

West—Atlanta, San Francisco 1

1994—season cancelled because of strike

1995—East—**Atlanta***, (New York 21)

Central—*Cincinnati*, Houston 9

West—Los Angeles, Colorado 1# (lost to Atlanta in playoffs), San Diego 8

AMERICAN LEAGUE, 1901 TO PRESENT

1901—Chicago, Boston 4, Detroit 8½, Philadelphia 9

1902—Philadelphia, St. Louis 5, Boston 6½, Chicago 8

1903—Boston*, (Philadelphia 14½)

1904—Boston, New York 1½, Chicago 6, Cleveland 7½

1905—Philadelphia, Chicago 2

1906—Chicago*, New York 3, Cleveland 5

1907—Detroit, Philadelphia 1½, Chicago 5½, Cleveland 8

1908—Detroit, Cleveland ½, Chicago 1½, St. Louis 6½

1909—Detroit, Philadelphia 3½, Boston 9½

1910—Philadelphia*, (New York 14½)

1911—Philadelphia*, (Detroit 13½)

1912—Boston*, (Washington 14)

1913—Philadelphia*, Washington 6½, Cleveland 9 ½

1914—Philadelphia, Boston 8½

1915—Boston*, Detroit 2½, Chicago 9 ½

1916—Boston*, Chicago 2, Detroit 4

1917—Chicago*, Boston 9

1918—Boston*, Cleveland 2½, Washington 4

1919—Chicago, Cleveland 3½, New York 7½, Detroit 8

1920—Cleveland*, Chicago 2, New York 3

1921—New York, Cleveland 4½

1922—New York, St. Louis 1

1923—New York*, (Detroit 16)

1924—Washington*, New York 2, Detroit 6

1925—Washington, Philadelphia 8½

1926—New York, Cleveland 3, Philadelphia 6, Washington 8, Chicago 9 ½

1927—New York*, (Philadelphia 19)

1928—New York*, Philadelphia 2½

1929—Philadelphia*, (New York 18)

1930—Philadelphia*, Washington 8

1931—Philadelphia, (New York 13½)

1932—New York*, (Philadelphia 13)

1933—Washington, New York 7

1934—Detroit, New York 7

1935—Detroit*, New York 3

1936—New York*, (Detroit 19½)

1937—New York*, (Detroit 13)

1938—New York*, Boston 9½

1939—New York*, (Boston 17)

1940—Detroit, Cleveland 1, New York 2, Boston and Chicago 8

1941—New York*, (Boston 17)

1942—New York, Boston 9

1943—New York*, (Washington 13½)

1944—St. Louis, Detroit 1, New York 6

1945—Detroit*, Washington 1½, St. Louis 6, New York 6½

1946—Boston, (Detroit 12)

1947—New York*, (Detroit 12)

1948—Cleveland*, Boston 1 (Cleveland won championship playoff with Boston,
     1 game to 0), New York 2½

1949—New York*, Boston 1, Cleveland 8, Detroit 10

1950—New York*, Detroit 3, Boston 4, Cleveland 6

1951—New York*, Cleveland 5

1952—New York*, Cleveland 2

1953—New York*, Cleveland 8½

1954—Cleveland, New York 8

1955—New York, Cleveland 3, Chicago 5

1956—New York*, Cleveland 9

1957—New York, Chicago 8

1958—New York*, Chicago 10

1959—Chicago, Cleveland 5

1960—New York, Baltimore 8

1961—New York*, Detroit 8

1962—New York*, Minnesota 5, Los Angeles 10

1963—New York, (Chicago 10½)

1964—New York, Chicago 1, Baltimore 2

1965—Minnesota, Chicago 7, Baltimore 8

1966—Baltimore*, Minnesota 9, Detroit 10

1967—Boston, Detroit and Minnesota 1, Chicago 3, California 7 ½

1968—Detroit*, (Baltimore 12)

1969—East—**Baltimore**, (Detroit 19)
     West—Minnesota, Oakland 9

1970—East—**Baltimore***, (New York 15)
     West—Minnesota, Oakland 9

1971—East—**Baltimore**, (Detroit 12)
     West—Oakland, (Kansas City 16)

1972—East—Detroit, Boston ½, Baltimore 5, New York 6½
     West—**Oakland***, Chicago 5½

1973—East—Baltimore, Boston 8
     West—**Oakland***, Kansas City 6

1974—East—Baltimore, New York 2, Boston 7
     West—**Oakland***, Texas 5, Minnesota 8, Chicago 9

1975—East—**Boston**, Baltimore 4½

West—Oakland, Kansas City 7

1976—East—**New York**, (Baltimore 10 ½)

    West—Kansas City, Oakland 2 ½, Minnesota 5

1977—East—**New York***, Baltimore and Boston 2 ½

    West—Kansas City, Texas 8

1978—East—**New York***, Boston 1 (New York won championship playoff with
        Boston, 1 game to 0), Milwaukee 6 ½, Baltimore 9

    West—Kansas City, California and Texas 5

1979—East—**Baltimore**, Milwaukee 8

    West—California, Kansas City 3, Texas 5, Minnesota 6

1980—East—New York, Baltimore 3

    West—**Kansas City**, (Oakland 14)

1981—Because of players' strike, pennant races were divided into two half sea-
        sons, with winners in playoffs to determine divisional champi-
        onships. Teams finishing within five games of first place in either half
        season are rated as pennant contenders.

    East—(1) **New York**, Baltimore 2, Milwaukee 3, Detroit 3 ½, Boston 4,
        Cleveland 5; (2) Milwaukee, Boston and Detroit 1 ½, Baltimore 2,
        Cleveland and New York 5 (New York won playoff with Milwaukee
        to determine divisional championship, 3 games to 2)

    West—(1) Oakland, Texas 1 ½, Chicago 2 ½; (2) Kansas City, Oakland 1,
        Texas 4 ½ (Oakland won playoff with Kansas City to determine divi-
        sional championship, 3 games to 0)

1982—East—**Milwaukee**, Baltimore 1, Boston 6

    West—California, Kansas City 3, Chicago 6

1983—East—**Baltimore***, Detroit 6, New York 7, Toronto 9

    West—Chicago, (Kansas City 20)

1984—East—**Detroit***, (Toronto 15)

    West—Kansas City, California and Minnesota 3, Oakland 7, Chicago and
        Seattle 10

1985—East—Toronto, New York 2

    West—**Kansas City***, California 1, Chicago 6

1986—East—**Boston**, New York 5 ½, Detroit 8 ½, Toronto 9 ½

    West—California, Texas 5

1987—East—Detroit, Toronto 2, Milwaukee 7, New York 9

    West—**Minnesota***, Kansas City 2, Oakland 4, Seattle 7, Chicago 8,
        California and Texas 10

1988—East—Boston, Detroit 1, Toronto and Milwaukee 2, New York 3 ½

    West—**Oakland**, (Minnesota 13)

1989—East—Toronto, Baltimore 2, Boston 6, Milwaukee 8

    West—**Oakland***, Kansas City 7, California 8

1990—East—Boston, Toronto 2, Detroit 9

West—**Oakland**, Chicago 9

1991—East—Toronto, Boston and Detroit 7, Milwaukee 8

West—**Minnesota***, Chicago 8, Texas 10

1992—East—**Toronto***, Milwaukee 4, Baltimore 7

West—Oakland, Minnesota 6, Chicago 10

1993—East—**Toronto***, New York 7, Baltimore and Detroit 10

West—Chicago, Texas 8, Kansas City 10

1994—season cancelled because of strike

1995—East—Boston, New York 7#(lost to Cleveland in playoffs)

Central—**Cleveland**, (Kansas City 30)

West—*Seattle*, California 1, Texas 4½

NUMBER OF SEASONS IN PENNANT CONTENTION

The figures below show the number of times, the years, and the percentage of seasons in which a team has been in pennant contention. Years in bold face indicate league championships. Teams are listed in order of highest percentage of successful contention. Unless otherwise indicated, teams were members of the league from the 1901 season onward.

National League

Colorado Rockies *(joined league in 1993)*. 1 (1994)—100%

San Francisco (New York, 1901–57) Giants. 45 (1903–**04–05**; 1908; **1911–12–13**; 1916–**17**; 1919–20–**21–22–23–24**–25; 1927–28; 1930; **1933**–34–35–**36–37**–38; 1950–**51–52**; **1954**; 1959; 1961–**62**; 1964–65–66; 1968–69; 1971; 1978; 1981–82; 1987; 1989–90; 93)—48%.

Pittsburgh Pirates. 43 (**1901–02–03**; 1905; 1908–**09**; 1912; 1921––22–23–24–**25**–26–**27**–28; 1932–33; 1936–37–38; 1948; 1958–59–**60**; 1962; 1965–66; 1970–**71**–72–73–74–75–76–77–78–**79**–80; 1982–83; 1990–91–92)—46%.

Los Angeles (Brooklyn, 1901–57) Dodgers. 41 (1901; 1915–16; 1920; 1924; 1930; 1932; **1941**–42; 1946–**47**–48–**49**–50–51–**52–53**–54–**55**–56; **1959**; 1961–62–**63**; **1965–66**; 1969; 1971; 1973–**74**; 1976–**77–78**; 1980–**81**–82–83; 1985; **1988**; 1990–91)—44%.

St. Louis Cardinals. 37 (1921–22; **1926**–27–**28**; **1930–31**; 1933–**34**–35–36; 1939; 1941–**42–43–44**–45–**46**–47–48–49; 1952; 1957; 1960; 1963–**64**; **1967–68**; 1971; 1973–74; 1981–**82**; 1985; **1987**; 1989; 1993)—40%.

Cincinnati Reds. 31 (**1919**; 1922–23–24; 1926; 1938–**39–40**; 1956; **1961**–62; 1964–65; 1969–**70**; **1972**–73–74–**75–76**–77–78–79–80–81; 1985–86–87–88; **1990**, 1992)—33%.

Chicago Cubs. 26 (1903; **1906–07–08**–09–10–11; **1918**; 1926–27–28–**29**–30; 1932–33–34–**35**–36–37–**38**; **1945**; 1969–70; 1973; 1984; 1989)—28%.

Atlanta (Boston, 1901–52; Milwaukee, 1953–65) Braves. 23 (**1914**–15–16; 1933; 1947–**48**; 1950; 1954; 1956–**57–58**–59–60–61; 1964; 1966; 1969; 1971; 1982–83; **1991–92**–93)—25%.

Philadelphia Phillies. 18 (1901; **1915**–16–17; **1950**; 1952; 1964; 1966; 1974–75–76–77–78; **1980**–81–82–**83**, **1993**)—19%.

New York Mets (*joined league in 1962*). 10 (**1969**–70; **1973**; 1984–85–**86**–87–88–89–90)—31%.

Montreal Expos (*joined league in 1969*). 11 (1973–74; 1979–80–81–82–83; 1987; 1990, 1992–93)—44%

Houston Astros (*joined league in 1962*). 6 (1979–80–81; 1983; 1986; 1989)—19%.

San Diego Padres (*joined league in 1969*). 5 (1982–83–**84**; 1989; 1991)—20%.

Florida Marlins (*joined league in 1993*). 0.

American League

New York Yankees (*joined league in 1903*). 55 (1904; 1906; 1919–20–**21–22–23**–24; **1926–27–28**; **1932**–33–34–35–**36–37–38–39**–40–**41–42–43**–44–45; **1947**–48–**49–50–51–52–53**–54–**55–56–57–58**; **1960–61–62–63–64**; 1972; 1974; **1976–77–78**; 1980–**81**; 1983; 1985–86–87–88, 1993)—60%.

Chicago White Sox. 33 (**1901**–02; 1904–05–**06**–07–08; 1915–16–**17**; **1919**–20; 1926; 1940; 1955; 1957–58–**59**; 1964–65; 1967; 1972; 1974; 1981–82–83–84–85; 1987; 1990–91–92–93)—35%.

Boston Red Sox. 32 (1901–02–**03–04**; 1909; **1912**; 1914–**15–16**–17–**18**; 1938; 1940; 1942; **1946**; 1948–49–50; **1967**; 1972–73–74–**75**; 1977–78; 1981–82; **1986**; 1988–89–90–91)—34%.

Oakland (Philadelphia, 1901–54; Kansas City, 1955–70) Athletics. 30 (1901–**02**; **1905**; 1907; 1909–**10–11**; **1913–14**; 1925–26; 1928–**29–30–31**; 1969–70–71–**72–73–74**–75–76; 1981; 1984; 1987–**88–89–90**; 1992)—32%.

Detroit Tigers—29 (1901; **1907–08–09**; 1915–16; 1919; 1924; **1934–35**; **1940**; 1944–**45**; 1949–50; 1961; 1966–67–**68**; 1972; 1981; 1983–**84**; 1986–87–88; 1990–91, 1993)—31%.

Baltimore Orioles (St. Louis Browns, 1902–53; *joined league in 1902*). 25 (1902; 1922; **1944**–45; 1960; 1964–65–**66**; **1969–70–71**–72–73–74–75; 1977–78–**79**–80–81–82–**83**; 1989, 1992–93)—27%.

Cleveland Indians. 22 (1904; 1906–07–08; 1913; 1918–19–20–21; 1926; 1940; **1948**–49–50–51–52–53–**54**–55–56; 1959; 1981)—24%.

Minnesota Twins (Washington Senators, 1901–59). 21 (1913; 1918; **1924–25**–26; 1930; **1933**; 1945; 1962; **1965**–66–67; 1969–70; 1974; 1976; 1979; 1984; **1987**; **1991**–92)—23%.

Kansas City Royals (*joined league in 1969*). 14 (1973; 1975–76–77–78–79–80–81–82; 1984–**85**; 1987; 1989; 1993)—56%.

Toronto Blue Jays (*joined league in 1977*). 10 (1983; 1985–86–87–88–89–90–91–**92–93**)—59%.

California Angels (Los Angeles Angels, 1961–66; *joined league in 1961*). 10 (1962; 1967; 1978–79; 1982; 1984–85–86–87; 1989)—30%.

Milwaukee Brewers (Seattle Pilots, 1969; *joined league in 1969*). 9 (1978–79; 1981–**82**; 1987–88–89; 1991–92)—36%.

Texas Rangers (Washington Senators, 1961–71; *joined league in 1961*). 9 (1974; 1977–78–79; 1981; 1986–87; 1991; 1993)—27%.

Seattle Mariners (*joined league in 1977*). 2 (1984; 1987)—18%.

CONSECUTIVE SEASONS IN WHICH TEAM WAS IN PENNANT CONTENTION

14 seasons
New York Yankees (1932–45)

12 seasons
New York Yankees (1947–58)

11 seasons
Los Angeles (Brooklyn) Dodgers (1946–56)
Pittsburgh Pirates (1970–80)

10 seasons
Cincinnati Reds (1972–81)

9 seasons
St. Louis Cardinals (1941–49)
Cleveland Indians (1948–56)
Toronto Blue Jays (1985–93)

8 seasons
Pittsburgh Pirates (1921–28)
Oakland (Philadelphia, Kansas City) Athletics (1969–76)
Kansas City Royals (1975–82)

7 seasons
San Francisco (New York) Giants (1919–25)
Chicago Cubs (1932–38)
Baltimore Orioles (St. Louis Browns) (1969–75; 1977–83)
New York Mets (1984–90)

6 seasons
Chicago Cubs (1906–11)
New York Yankees (1919–24)
San Francisco (New York) Giants (1933–38)
Atlanta (Boston, Milwaukee) Braves (1956–61)

5 seasons
Chicago White Sox (1904–1908)
Boston Red Sox (1914–18)
Chicago Cubs (1926–30)
New York Yankees (1960–64)
Baltimore Orioles (St. Louis Browns) (1979–83)
Montreal Expos (1979–83)
Philadelphia Phillies (1974–78)
Chicago White Sox (1981–85)

CONSECUTIVE SEASONS IN WHICH TEAM FAILED TO BE IN PENNANT CONTENTION

37 seasons
Oakland (Philadelphia, Kansas City) Athletics (1932–68)

32 seasons
Philadelphia Phillies (1918–49)

23 seasons
Chicago Cubs (1946–68)

21 seasons
Baltimore Orioles (St. Louis Browns) (1923–43)
Cleveland Indians (1960–80)

20 seasons
St. Louis Cardinals (1901–20)

19 seasons
Baltimore Orioles (St. Louis Browns) (1903–21)
Boston Red Sox (1919–37)

18 seasons
Cincinnati Reds (1901–18)

17 seasons
Houston Astros (1962–78)

16 seasons
Atlanta (Boston, Milwaukee) Braves (1917–32)
Boston Red Sox (1951–66)
Minnesota Twins (Washington Senators) (1946–61)

15 seasons
Cincinnati Reds (1941–55)

14 seasons
Baltimore Orioles (St. Louis Browns) (1946–59)
Chicago White Sox (1941–54)

13 seasons
Atlanta (Boston, Milwaukee) Braves (1901–13; 1934–46)
Los Angeles (Brooklyn) Dodgers (1902–14)
Philadelphia Phillies (1902–14)
Chicago White Sox (1927–39)
Cleveland Indians (1927–39)
Texas Rangers (Washington Senators) (1961–73)
San Diego Padres (1969–81)

12 seasons
Minnesota Twins (Washington Senators) (1901–12)
New York Yankees (1907–18)
Cleveland Indians (1982–93)

11 seasons
Cincinnati Reds (1927–37)
Minnesota Twins (Washington Senators) (1934–44)
San Francisco (New York) Giants (1939–49)
Philadelphia Phillies (1953–63)

10 seasons
Oakland (Philadelphia, Kansas City) Athletics (1915–24)
Detroit Tigers (1951–60)
California Angels (1968–77)
Atlanta (Boston, Milwaukee) Braves (1972–81)
Chicago Cubs (1974–83)
New York Mets (1974–83)

9 seasons
Detroit Tigers (1925–33)
Pittsburgh Pirates (1939–47; 1949–57)
Milwaukee Brewers (Seattle Pilots) (1969–77)
Philadelphia Phillies (1984–92)

8 seasons

Pittsburgh Pirates (1913–20)
Los Angeles (Brooklyn) Dodgers (1933–40)
Detroit Tigers (1973–80)

7 seasons

Chicago Cubs (1919–25)
Cleveland Indians (1941–47)
New York Mets (1962–68)
New York Yankees (1965–71)
Philadelphia Phillies (1967–73)
Seattle Mariners (1977–83)
Atlanta (Boston, Milwaukee) Braves (1984–90)

6 seasons

Chicago Cubs (1912–17; 1939–44)
Chicago White Sox (1909–14)
San Francisco (New York) Giants (1972–77)
Chicago White Sox (1975–80)
St. Louis Cardinals (1975–80)
Toronto Blue Jays (1977–82)
Pittsburgh Pirates (1984–89)
Seattle Mariners (1988–93)

5 seasons

Detroit Tigers (1902–1906; 1910–14)
Minnesota Twins (Washington Senators) (1919–23)
Chicago White Sox (1921–25)
Los Angeles (Brooklyn) Dodgers (1925–29)
Baltimore Orioles (St. Louis Browns) (1984–88)
Chicago Cubs (1900–95)
Houston Astros (1990-95)

SOURCES

Neff, David S., and Richard M. Cohen. *The Sports Encyclopedia: Baseball: 1992 Edition.*
    New York: St. Martin's Press, 1992.
Reichler, Joseph L., ed. *The Baseball Encyclopedia.* 7th ed. New York: Macmillan, 1988.
Thorn, John, and Pete Palmer, with Joseph Reuther. *Total Baseball.* 2nd ed. New York:
    Times Warner, 1991.
The World Almanac and Book of Facts, 1993. New York: Pharos Books, 1992.
The World Almanac and Book of Facts, 1994. New York: Pharos Books, 1993.

—**L.D.R.**

65

THE PRO QUARTERBACKS

. . . . .

IT WAS IN THE YEARS AFTER THE CLOSE OF WORLD WAR II THAT PROFES-
sional football began its ascent to a popularity comparable only to that of
major league baseball. The simultaneous emergence of the pro quarterback
as the leading focus of interest is not a coincidence. Three factors contributed to the pro quarterback's elevation: the rediscovery of the T-formation in 1940 by the Chicago Bears; an end that same year to the rule requiring that forward passes be thrown from at least five yards behind the line of
scrimmage; and the introduction, in 1949, of the platoon system, so that
players were no longer forced to perform both on offense and defense.

The professional game increasingly offered considerably more skilled
specialization, finesse, and razzle-dazzle offense, with quarterbacks concentrating on passing and hand-offs, and running with the ball only very occasionally. The almost simultaneous development of network television
helped to convert pro football into a sport of nationwide interest. The leading quarterbacks of the National Football League became celebrities. Fans
throughout the country now debated the merits of Johnny Unitas, Y. A.
Tittle, Otto Graham, Bobby Layne, Bart Starr, Don Meredith, Sonny
Jurgensen, Fran Tarkenton, John Brodie, Len Dawson, and others.

As the pro game's popularity spread throughout the land, so did the
expansion of franchises into new cities. Immediately after the war the NFL
faced competition from the All-America Conference, formed in 1946. When
the latter folded after the 1949 season, three of its teams joined the NFL.
The advent of the American Football League in 1960 proved considerably
more enduring; competition for fan support, and the higher salaries that
came when the NFL and AFL made rival offers to graduating collegiate
stars, brought about an agreement in 1966 to join forces, with the league
champions meeting in the Super Bowl for the national championship. In
1970 the leagues became conferences of the NFL, with several NFL teams
moving over into the American Conference and regular season interconference play introduced.

The compilation below is designed to show the continuity of the pro quarterbacks, beginning with the 1946 season, by which time most NFL teams had moved from single-wing to T-formation offense. Of the three All-America Conference franchises—the Cleveland Browns, San Francisco Forty-Niners, and Baltimore Colts—that continued in existence after the AAC folded, Cleveland and San Francisco survived to become permanent NFL teams; the Colts dropped out after a year, and the franchise bearing that name began in 1952 as the Dallas Texans, moving to Baltimore the year following. The quarterback continuity of the Cleveland and San Francisco organizations during their AAC years is shown, along with that of all NFL teams surviving into the modern era. AFL teams are identified as such prior to the full merger of the NFL into conferences with interconference play in 1970.

The pro quarterbacks—usually only one—who lead each team's offense during a season are listed. When, whether because of injuries or changes of personnel, the season's quarterbacking was divided between two or more players, these are listed in order of number of passes thrown. For the years 1946 through 1969, the years in which teams won NFL, AAC, or AFL league championships are given in bold type; thereafter the years when teams won NFL conference championships are in bold. When teams from 1946 through 1969 won conference championships but lost league playoff games, the years are listed in italic type; thereafter teams which lost playoff games for NFC or AFC conference championships are listed by year in italic type. The winners of Super Bowl games, which are played in January of the year following the championship season, are noted by an asterisk.

Arizona Cardinals (Chicago Cardinals, 1946–59; St. Louis Cardinals, 1960–87; Phoenix Cardinals, 1988–93)

1946—Paul Christman	1958—Lamar McHan,
1947—Paul Christman	M. C. Reynolds
1948—Ray Mallouf, Paul Christman	1959—King Hill
1949—Paul Christman, Jim Hardy	1960—John Roach
1950—Jim Hardy	1961—Sam Etcheverry
1951—Frank Tripucka	1962—Charley Johnson
1952—Charlie Trippi	1963—Charley Johnson
1953—Jim Root	1964—Charley Johnson
1954—Lamar McHan	1965—Charley Johnson
1955—Lamar McHan	1966—Charley Johnson,
1956—Lamar McHan	Terry Nofsinger
1957—Lamar McHan	1967—Jim Hart

1968—Jim Hart
1969—Charley Johnson
1970—Jim Hart
1971—Jim Hart
1972—Gary Cuozzo,
    Jim Hart
1973—Jim Hart
1974—Jim Hart
1975—Jim Hart
1976—Jim Hart
1977—Jim Hart
1978—Jim Hart
1979—Jim Hart
1980—Jim Hart
1981—Jim Hart,
    Neil Lomax

1982—Neil Lomax
1983—Neil Lomax
1984—Neil Lomax
1985—Neil Lomax
1986—Neil Lomax
1987—Neil Lomax
1988—Neil Lomax
1989—Gary Hogeboom
1990—Timm Rosenbach
1991—Tom Tupa
1992—Chris Chandler
1993—Steve Beuerlein
1994—Steve Beuerlein,
    Jay Schroeder
1995—Dave Krieg

Atlanta Falcons

1966—Randy Johnson
1967—Randy Johnson
1968—Randy Johnson, Bob Berry
1969—Bob Berry
1970—Bob Berry
1971—Bob Berry
1972—Bob Berry
1973—Bob Lee
1974—Bob Lee
1975—Steve Bartkowski
1976—Kim McQuilken,
    Steve Bartkowski,
    Scott Hunter
1977—Scott Hunter,
    Steve Bartkowski
1978—Steve Bartkowski
1979—Steve Bartkowski

1980—Steve Bartkowski
1981—Steve Bartkowski
1982—Steve Bartkowski
1983—Steve Bartkowski
1984—Steve Bartkowski
1985—David Archer
1986—David Archer
1987—Scott Campbell
1988—Chris Miller
1989—Chris Miller
1990—Chris Miller
1991—Chris Miller
1992—Chris Miller
1993—Bobby Hebert
1994—Jeff George
1995—Jeff George

Baltimore Ravens (Cleveland Browns 1946-1995)

1994—Vinny Testaverde
1995—Vinny Testaverde

Buffalo Bills

1960 (AFL)—Johnny Green
1961 (AFL)—M. C. Reynolds
1962 (AFL)—Warren Rabb,
　　　　　Jack Kemp
1963 (AFL)—Jack Kemp
1964 (AFL)—Jack Kemp
1965 (AFL)—Jack Kemp
1966 (AFL)—Jack Kemp
1967 (AFL)—Jack Kemp
1968 (AFL)—Dan Darragh
1969 (AFL)—Jack Kemp
1970—Dennis Shaw
1971—Dennis Shaw
1972—Dennis Shaw
1973—Joe Ferguson
1974—Joe Ferguson
1975—Joe Ferguson
1976—Gary Marangi
1977—Joe Ferguson

1978—Joe Ferguson
1979—Joe Ferguson
1980—Joe Ferguson
1981—Joe Ferguson
1982—Joe Ferguson
1983—Joe Ferguson
1984—Joe Ferguson
1985—Vince Ferragamo,
　　　　Bruce Mathison
1986—Jim Kelly
1987—Jim Kelly
1988—Jim Kelly
1989—Jim Kelly
1990—Jim Kelly
1991—Jim Kelly
1992—Jim Kelly
1993—Jim Kelly
1994—Jim Kelly
1995—Jim Jelly

Carolina Panthers

1995—Kerry Collins,
　　　Frank Reich

Chicago Bears

1946—Sid Luckman
1947—Sid Luckman
1948—Sid Luckman
1949—Johnny Lujack
1950—Johnny Lujack
1951—Johnny Lujack
1952—George Blanda,
　　　Steve Romanik
1953—George Blanda
1954—George Blanda
1955—Ed Brown
1956—Ed Brown

1957—Ed Brown
1958—Ed Brown
1959—Ed Brown
1960—Zeke Bratkowski,
　　　Ed Brown
1961—Billy Wade
1962—Billy Wade
1963—Billy Wade
1964—Billy Wade
1965—Rudy Bukich
1966—Rudy Bukich
1967—Jack Concannon

1968—Jack Concannon,
   Virgil Carter
1969—Jack Concannon,
   Bobby Douglass
1970—Jack Concannon
1971—Bobby Douglass
1972—Bobby Douglass
1973—Bobby Douglass
1974—Gary Huff
1975—Gary Huff
1976—Bob Avellini
1977—Bob Avellini
1978—Bob Avellini
1979—Mike Phipps
1980—Vince Evans
1981—Vince Evans
1982—Jim McMahon

1983—Jim McMahon
1984—Jim McMahon
*1985—Jim McMahon
1986—Mike Tomczak,
   Jim McMahon
1987—Jim McMahon,
   Mike Tomczak
1988—Jim McMahon,
   Mike Tomczak
1989—Mike Tomczak
1990—Jim Harbaugh
1991—Jim Harbaugh
1992—Jim Harbaugh
1993—Jim Harbaugh
1994—Steve Walsh
1995—Erik Kramer

Cincinnati Bengals

1968 (AFL)—John Stofa
1969 (AFL)—Greg Cook
1970—Virgil Carter
1971—Virgil Carter
1972—Ken Anderson
1973—Ken Anderson
1974—Ken Anderson
1975—Ken Anderson
1976—Ken Anderson
1977—Ken Anderson
1978—Ken Anderson
1979—Ken Anderson
1980—Ken Anderson,
   Jack Thompson
1981—Ken Anderson

1982—Ken Anderson
1983—Ken Anderson
1984—Ken Anderson
1985—Boomer Esiason
1986—Boomer Esiason
1987—Boomer Esiason
1988—Boomer Esiason
1989—Boomer Esiason
1990—Boomer Esiason
1991—Boomer Esiason
1992—Boomer Esiason
1993—David Klingler
1994—Jeff Blake,
   David Klingler
1995—Jeff Blake

Cleveland Browns

1946 (AAC)—Otto Graham
1947 (AAC)—Otto Graham

1948 (AAC)—Otto Graham
1949 (AAC)—Otto Graham

1950—Otto Graham
1951—Otto Graham
1952—Otto Graham
1953—Otto Graham
1954—Otto Graham
1955—Otto Graham
1956—Tom O'Connell
1957—Tom O'Connell
1958—Milt Plum
1959—Milt Plum
1960—Milt Plum
1961—Milt Plum
1962—Frank Ryan,
      Jim Ninowski
1963—Frank Ryan
1964—Frank Ryan
1965—Frank Ryan
1966—Frank Ryan
1967—Frank Ryan
1968—Bill Nelsen
1969—Bill Nelsen
1970—Bill Nelsen
1971—Bill Nelsen
1972—Mike Phipps

1973—Mike Phipps
1974—Mike Phipps
1975—Mike Phipps
1976—Brian Sipe
1977—Brian Sipe
1978—Brian Sipe
1979—Brian Sipe
1980—Brian Sipe
1981—Brian Sipe
1982—Brian Sipe,
      Paul McDonald
1983—Brian Sipe
1984—Paul McDonald
1985—Bernie Kosar
1986—Bernie Kosar
1987—Bernie Kosar
1988—Bernie Kosar
1989—Bernie Kosar
1990—Bernie Kosar
1991—Bernie Kosar
1992—Bernie Kosar
1993—Vinny Testaverde,
      Bernie Kosar,
      Todd Philcox

Dallas Cowboys

1960—Eddie LeBaron
1961—Eddie LeBaron
1962—Don Meredith
1963—Don Meredith
1964—Don Meredith
1965—Don Meredith
1966—Don Meredith
1967—Don Meredith
1968—Don Meredith
1969—Craig Morton
1970—Craig Morton
*1971—Roger Staubach
1972—Craig Morton
1973—Roger Staubach

1974—Roger Staubach
1975—Roger Staubach
1976—Roger Staubach
*1977—Roger Staubach
1978—Roger Staubach
1979—Roger Staubach
1980—Danny White
1981—Danny White
1982—Danny White
1983—Danny White
1984—Gary Hogeboom
1985—Danny White
1986—Steve Pelleur
1987—Danny White

1988—Steve Pelleur
1989—Troy Aikman
1990—Troy Aikman
1991—Troy Aikman

*1992—Troy Aikman
*1993—Troy Aikman
1994—Troy Aikman
*1995—Troy Aikman

Denver Broncos

1960 (AFL)—Frank Tripucka
1961 (AFL)—Frank Tripucka
1962 (AFL)—Frank Tripucka
1963 (AFL)—Mickey Slaughter
1964 (AFL)—Jacky Lee
1965 (AFL)—John McCormick
1966 (AFL)—John McCormick,
    Mick Choboian
1967 (AFL)—Steve Tensi
1968 (AFL)—Marlin Briscoe
1969 (AFL)—Steve Tensi
1970—Pete Liske
1971—Steve Ramsey,
    Don Horn
1972—Charley Johnson
1973—Charley Johnson
1974—Charley Johnson
1975—Steve Ramsey
1976—Steve Ramsey
1977—Craig Morton

1978—Craig Morton
1979—Craig Morton
1980—Craig Morton
1981—Craig Morton
1982—Steve DeBerg
1983—John Elway,
    Steve DeBerg
1984—John Elway
1985—John Elway
1986—John Elway
1987—John Elway
1988—John Elway
1989—John Elway
1990—John Elway
1991—John Elway
1992—John Elway
1993—John Elway
1994—John Elway
1995—John Elway

Detroit Lions

1946—(tailback in single wing)
    Dave Ryan
1947—Clyde LaForce
1948—Fred Enke
1949—Frank Tripucka,
    Fred Enke
1950—Bobby Layne
1951—Bobby Layne
1952—Bobby Layne
1953—Bobby Layne
1954—Bobby Layne

1955—Bobby Layne
1956—Bobby Layne
1957—Tobin Rote
1958—Tobin Rote
1959—Tobin Rote,
    Earl Morrall
1960—Jim Ninowski
1961—Jim Ninowski
1962—Milt Plum
1963—Earl Morrall
1964—Milt Plum

1965—Milt Plum
1966—Karl Sweetan
1967—Karl Sweetan,
    Milt Plum
1968—Bill Munson
1969—Bill Munson,
    Greg Landry
*1970—Bill Munson,
    Greg Landry
1971—Greg Landry
1972—Greg Landry
1973—Bill Munson,
    Greg Landry
1974—Bill Munson
1975—Joe Reed
1976—Greg Landry
1977—Greg Landry
1978—Gary Danielson
1979—Jeff Komio
1980—Gary Danielson

1981—Eric Hipple
1982—Gary Danielson
1983—Eric Hipple
1984—Gary Danielson
1985—Eric Hipple
1986—Eric Hipple
1987—Chuck Long
1988—Rusty Hilger
1989—Bob Gagliano,
    Rodney Peete
1990—Rodney Peete
1991—Erik Kramer,
    Rodney Peete
1992—Erik Kramer,
    Rodney Peete
1993—Rodney Peete,
    Eric Kramer
1994—Scott Mitchell,
    Dave Krieg
1995—Scott Mitchell

Green Bay Packers

1946—(tailback in single wing)
    Irv Comp, Cliff Aberson
1947—Jack Jacobs
1948—Jack Jacobs
1949—Jug Girard
1950—Tobin Rote
1951—Tobin Rote,
    Bobby Thomason
1952—Babe Parilli,
    Tobin Rote
1953—Tobin Rote,
    Babe Parilli
1954—Tobin Rote
1955—Tobin Rote
1956—Tobin Rote
1957—Bart Starr
1958—Babe Parilli,
    Bart Starr

1959—Bart Starr,
    Lamar McHan
1960—Bart Starr
1961—Bart Starr
1962—Bart Starr
1963—Bart Starr
1964—Bart Starr
1965—Bart Starr
***1966**—Bart Starr
***1967**—Bart Starr
1968—Bart Starr,
    Zeke Bratkowski
1969—Don Horn,
    Bart Starr
1970—Bart Starr
1971—Scott Hunter
1972—Scott Hunter
1973—Jerry Tagge

1974—John Hadl
1975—John Hadl
1976—Lynn Dickey
1977—Lynn Dickey
1978—Dave Whitehurst
1979—Dave Whitehurst
1980—Lynn Dickey
1981—Lynn Dickey
1982—Lynn Dickey
1983—Lynn Dickey
1984—Lynn Dickey
1985—Lynn Dickey

1986—Randy Wright
1987—Randy Wright
1988—Don Majkowski
1989—Don Majkowski
1990—Don Majkowski
1991—Mike Tomczak,
    Don Majkowski
1992—Brett Favre
1993—Brett Favre
1994—Brett Favre
1995—Brett Favre

Houston Oilers

1960 (AFL)—George Blanda
1961 (AFL)—George Blanda
1962 (AFL)—George Blanda
1963 (AFL)—George Blanda
1964 (AFL)—George Blanda
1965 (AFL)—George Blanda
1966 (AFL)—George Blanda
1967 (AFL)—Pete Beathard
1968 (AFL)—Pete Beathard
1969 (AFL)—Pete Beathard
1970—Charley Johnson
1971—Dan Pastorini
1972—Dan Pastorini
1973—Dan Pastorini
1974—Dan Pastorini
1975—Dan Pastorini
1976—Dan Pastorini
1977—Dan Pastorini
1978—Dan Pastorini
1979—Dan Pastorini

1980—Ken Stabler
1981—Ken Stabler
1982—Gifford Nielsen,
    Archie Manning
1983—Oliver Luck,
    Gifford Nielsen
1984—Warren Moon
1985—Warren Moon
1986—Warren Moon
1987—Warren Moon
1988—Warren Moon
1989—Warren Moon
1990—Warren Moon
1991—Warren Moon
1992—Warren Moon,
    Cody Carlson
1993—Warren Moon
1994—Billy Joe Tolliver,
    Bucky Richardson
1995—Chris Chandler

Indianapolis Colts (Dallas Texans, 1952; Baltimore Colts, 1952–83)

1952—Frank Tripucka
1953—Fred Enke
1954—Gary Kekorian

1955—George Shaw
1956—Johnny Unitas
1957—Johnny Unitas

1958—Johnny Unitas
1959—Johnny Unitas
1960—Johnny Unitas
1961—Johnny Unitas
1962—Johnny Unitas
1963—Johnny Unitas
1964—Johnny Unitas
1965—Johnny Unitas
1966—Johnny Unitas
1967—Johnny Unitas
1968—Earl Morrall
1969—Johnny Unitas
*__**1970**—Johnny Unitas
1971—Johnny Unitas,
    Earl Morrall
1972—Marty Domres
1973—Marty Domres
1974—Bert Jones
1975—Bert Jones
1976—Bert Jones

1977—Bert Jones
1978—Bill Troup
1979—Greg Landry
1980—Bert Jones
1981—Bert Jones
1982—Mike Pagel
1983—Mike Pagel
1984—Mike Pagel
1985—Mike Pagel
1986—Jack Trudeau
1987—Jack Trudeau
1988—Chris Chandler
1989—Jack Trudeau
1990—Jeff George
1991—Jeff George
1992—Jeff George
1993—Jeff George,
    Jack Trudeau
1994—Jim Harbaugh
1995—Jim Harbaugh

Jacksonville Jaguars

1995—Mark Brunell

Kansas City Chiefs (Dallas Texans, 1960–62)

1960 (AFL)—Cotton Davidson
1961 (AFL)—Cotton Davidson
1962 (AFL)—Len Dawson
1963 (AFL)—Len Dawson
1964 (AFL)—Len Dawson
1965 (AFL)—Len Dawson
1966 (AFL)—Len Dawson
1967 (AFL)—Len Dawson
1968 (AFL)—Len Dawson
*__**1969** (AFL)—Len Dawson,
    Mike Livingston
1970—Len Dawson
1971—Len Dawson

1972—Len Dawson
1973—Mike Livingston,
    Len Dawson
1974—Len Dawson
1975—Mike Livingston,
    Len Dawson
1976—Mike Livingston
1977—Mike Livingston
1978—Mike Livingston
1979—Steve Fuller
1980—Steve Fuller
1981—Bill Kenney
1982—Bill Kenney

1983—Bill Kenney
1984—Bill Kenney,
    Todd Blackledge
1985—Bill Kenney
1986—Bill Kenney
1987—Bill Kenney
1988—Steve DeBerg
1989—Steve DeBerg

1990—Steve DeBerg
1991—Steve DeBerg
1992—Dave Krieg
1993—Joe Montana,
    Dave Krieg
1994—Joe Montana
1995—Steve Bono

Los Angeles Raiders (Oakland Raiders, 1960–81)

1960 (AFL)—Tom Flores
1961 (AFL)—Tom Flores
1962 (AFL)—Cotton Davidson
1963 (AFL)—Tom Flores,
    Cotton Davidson
1964 (AFL)—Cotton Davidson
1965 (AFL)—Tom Flores
1966 (AFL)—Tom Flores
1967 (AFL)—Daryle Lamonica
1968 (AFL)—Daryle Lamonica
1969 (AFL)—Daryle Lamonica
1970—Daryle Lamonica
1971—Daryle Lamonica
1972—Daryle Lamonica
1973—Daryle Lamonica
1974—Ken Stabler
1975—Ken Stabler
***1976**—Ken Stabler
1977—Ken Stabler
1978—Ken Stabler
1979—Ken Stabler

***1980**—Jim Plunkett
1981—Marc Wilson
1982—Jim Plunkett
***1983**—Jim Plunkett
1984—Marc Wilson,
    Jim Plunkett
1985—Marc Wilson
1986—Jim Plunkett,
    Marc Wilson
1987—Marc Wilson
1988—Jay Schroeder,
    Steve Beuerlein
1989—Steve Beuerlein,
    Jay Schroeder
1990—Jay Schroeder
1991—Jay Schroeder
1992—Jay Schroeder
1993—Jeff Hostetler
1994—Jeff Hostetler
1995—Jeff Hostetler

Los Angeles Rams

1946—Bob Waterfield
1947—Bob Waterfield
1948—Jim Hardy,
    Bob Waterfield
1949—Bob Waterfield

1950—Norm Van Brocklin,
    Bob Waterfield
1951—Norm Van Brocklin,
    Bob Waterfield
1952—Norm Van Brocklin

1953—Norm Van Brocklin
1954—Norm Van Brocklin
1955—Norm Van Brocklin
1956—Billy Wade,
        Norm Van Brocklin
1957—Norm Van Brocklin
1958—Billy Wade
1959—Billy Wade
1960—Billy Wade
1961—Zeke Bratkowski
1962—Zeke Bratkowski
1963—Roman Gabriel
1964—Bill Munson
1965—Bill Munson
1966—Roman Gabriel
1967—Roman Gabriel
1968—Roman Gabriel
1969—Roman Gabriel
1970—Roman Gabriel
1971—Roman Gabriel
1972—Roman Gabriel
1973—John Hadl
1974—James Harris

1975—James Harris
1976—James Harris
1977—Pat Haden
1978—Pat Haden
1979—Pat Haden
1980—Vince Ferragamo
1981—Pat Haden
1982—Vince Ferragamo
1983—Vince Ferragamo
1984—Jeff Kemp
1985—Dieter Brock
1986—Jim Everett,
        Steve Dils,
        Steve Bartkowski
1987—Jim Everett
1988—Jim Everett
1989—Jim Everett
1990—Jim Everett
1991—Jim Everett
1992—Jim Everett
1993—Jim Everett,
        T. J. Rubley

Miami Dolphins

1966 (AFL)—Dick Wood
1967 (AFL)—Bob Griese
1968 (AFL)—Bob Griese
1969 (AFL)—Bob Griese
1970—Bob Griese
1971—Bob Griese
* **1972**—Earl Morrall
* **1973**—Bob Griese
1974—Bob Griese
1975—Bob Griese
1976—Bob Griese
1977—Bob Griese
1978—Bob Griese
1979—Bob Griese
1980—David Woodley
1981—David Woodley

1982—David Woodley
1983—Dan Marino
1984—Dan Marino
1985—Dan Marino
1986—Dan Marino
1987—Dan Marino
1988—Dan Marino
1989—Dan Marino
1990—Dan Marino
1991—Dan Marino
1992—Dan Marino
1993—Scott Mitchell,
        Steve DeBerg
1994—Dan Marino
1995—Dan Marino

Minnesota Vikings

1961—Fran Tarkenton
1962—Fran Tarkenton
1963—Fran Tarkenton
1964—Fran Tarkenton
1965—Fran Tarkenton
1966—Fran Tarkenton
1967—Joe Kapp
1968—Joe Kapp
1969—Joe Kapp
1970—Gary Cuozzo
1971—Gary Cuozzo
1972—Fran Tarkenton
1973—Fran Tarkenton
1974—Fran Tarkenton
1975—Fran Tarkenton
1976—Fran Tarkenton
1977—Fran Tarkenton
1978—Fran Tarkenton
1979—Tommy Kramer

1980—Tommy Kramer
1981—Tommy Kramer
1982—Tommy Kramer
1983—Steve Dils
1984—Tommy Kramer,
    Wade Wilson
1985—Tommy Kramer
1986—Tommy Kramer
1987—Wade Wilson
1988—Wade Wilson
1989—Wade Wilson
1990—Rich Gannon
1991—Rich Gannon
1992—Rich Gannon
1993—Jim McMahon,
    Sean Salisbury
1994—Warren Moon
1995—Warren Moon

New England Patriots (Boston Patriots, 1960–70)

1960 (AFL)—Butch Songin
1961 (AFL)—Babe Parilli,
    Butch Songin
1962 (AFL)—Babe Parilli
1963 (AFL)—Babe Parilli
1964 (AFL)—Babe Parilli
1965 (AFL)—Babe Parilli
1966 (AFL)—Babe Parilli
1967 (AFL)—Babe Parilli
1968 (AFL)—Tom Sherman,
    Mike Taliaferro
1969 (AFL)—Mike Taliaferro
1970—Joe Kapp,
    Mike Taliaferro
1971—Jim Plunkett
1972—Jim Plunkett
1973—Jim Plunkett
1974—Jim Plunkett

1975—Steve Grogan
1976—Steve Grogan
1977—Steve Grogan
1978—Steve Grogan
1979—Steve Grogan
1980—Steve Grogan
1981—Matt Cavanaugh,
    Steve Grogan
1982—Steve Grogan
1983—Steve Grogan
1984—Tony Eason
1985—Tony Eason
1986—Tony Eason
1987—Steve Grogan,
    Tom Ramsey
1988—Doug Flutie,
    Steve Grogan
1989—Steve Grogan

1990—Marc Wilson   1993—Drew Bledsoe
1991—Hugh Millen   1994—Drew Bledsoe
1992—Hugh Millen,   1995—Drew Bledsoe
       Tommy Hodson

New Orleans Saints

1967—Gary Cuozzo,   1981—Archie Manning,
       Billy Kilmer   Dave Wilson
1968—Billy Kilmer   1982—Ken Stabler
1969—Billy Kilmer   1983—Ken Stabler
1970—Billy Kilmer   1984—Richard Todd
1971—Edd Hargett,   1985—Dave Wilson
       Archie Manning   1986—Dave Wilson
1972—Archie Manning   1987—Bobby Hebert
1973—Archie Manning   1988—Bobby Hebert
1974—Archie Manning   1989—Bobby Hebert
1975—Archie Manning   1990—Steve Walsh
1976—Bobby Douglass,   1991—Bobby Hebert
       Bobby Scott   1992—Bobby Hebert
1977—Archie Manning   1993—Wade Wilson
1978—Archie Manning   1994—Jim Everett
1979—Archie Manning   1995—Jim Everett
1980—Archie Manning

New York Giants

1946—Frankie Filchock   1960—George Shaw,
1947—Paul Governali   Chuck Conerly
1948—Chuck Conerly   1961—Y. A. Tittle
1949—Chuck Conerly   1962—Y. A. Tittle
1950—Chuck Conerly   1963—Y. A. Tittle
1951—Chuck Conerly   1964—Y. A. Tittle
1952—Chuck Conerly   1965—Earl Morrall
1953—Chuck Conerly   1966—Gary Wood,
1954—Chuck Conerly   Earl Morrall
1955—Chuck Conerly   1967—Fran Tarkenton
1956—Chuck Conerly   1968—Fran Tarkenton
1957—Chuck Conerly   1969—Fran Tarkenton
1958—Chuck Conerly   1970—Fran Tarkenton
1959—Chuck Conerly   1971—Fran Tarkenton

1972—Norm Snead
1973—Randy Johnson,
     Norm Snead
1974—Craig Morton
1975—Craig Morton
1976—Craig Morton
1977—Joe Pisarcik
1978—Joe Pisarcik
1979—Phil Simms
1980—Phil Simms
1981—Phil Simms
1982—Scott Brunner
1983—Scott Brunner

1984—Phil Simms
1985—Phil Simms
*1986—Phil Simms
1987—Phil Simms
1988—Phil Simms
1989—Phil Simms
*1990—Phil Simms
1991—Jeff Hofstetler
1992—Jeff Hofstetler,
     Phil Simms
1993—Phil Simms
1994—Dave Brown
1995—Dave Brown

New York Jets (New York Titans, 1960–62)

1960 (AFL)—Al Dorow
1961 (AFL)—Al Dorow
1962 (AFL)—Johnny Green
1963 (AFL)—Dick Wood
1964 (AFL)—Dick Wood
1965 (AFL)—Joe Namath
1966 (AFL)—Joe Namath
1967 (AFL)—Joe Namath
*1968 (AFL)—Joe Namath
1969 (AFL)—Joe Namath
1970—Al Woodall,
     Joe Namath
1971—Bob Davis,
     Al Woodall
1972—Joe Namath
1973—Al Woodall
1974—Joe Namath
1975—Joe Namath
1976—Joe Namath
1977—Richard Todd

1978—Matt Robinson
1979—Richard Todd
1980—Richard Todd
1981—Richard Todd
1982—Richard Todd
1983—Richard Todd
1984—Pat Ryan,
     Ken O'Brien
1985—Ken O'Brien
1986—Ken O'Brien
1987—Ken O'Brien
1988—Ken O'Brien
1989—Ken O'Brien
1990—Ken O'Brien
1991—Ken O'Brien
1992—Browning Nagle
1993—Boomer Esiason
1994—Boomer Esiason
1995—Boomer Esiason

Philadelphia Eagles

1946—Tommy Thompson,
     Roy Zimmerman
1947—Tommy Thompson

1948—Tommy Thompson
1949—Tommy Thompson
1950—Tommy Thompson

1951—Adrian Burk
1952—Bobby Thomason
1953—Bobby Thomason
1954—Adrian Burk,
    Bobby Thomason
1955—Adrian Burk,
    Bobby Thomason
1956—Bobby Thomason
1957—Bobby Thomason,
    Sonny Jurgensen
1958—Norm Van Brocklin
1959—Norm Van Brocklin
1960—Norm Van Brocklin
1961—Sonny Jurgensen
1962—Sonny Jurgensen
1963—King Hill,
    Sonny Jurgensen
1964—Norm Snead
1965—Norm Snead
1966—Norm Snead
1967—Norm Snead
1968—Norm Snead
1969—Norm Snead
1970—Norm Snead
1971—Pete Liske

1972—John Reaves
1973—Roman Gabriel
1974—Roman Gabriel
1975—Roman Gabriel
1976—Mike Boryla
1977—Ron Jaworski
1978—Ron Jaworski
1979—Ron Jaworski
1980—Ron Jaworski
1981—Ron Jaworski
1982—Ron Jaworski
1983—Ron Jaworski
1984—Ron Jaworski
1985—Ron Jaworski
1986—Ron Jaworski,
    Randall Cunningham
1987—Randall Cunningham
1988—Randall Cunningham
1989—Randall Cunningham
1990—Randall Cunningham
1991—Jim McMahon
1992—Randall Cunningham
1993—Bubby Brister
1994—Randall Cunningham
1995—Rodney Peete

Pittsburgh Steelers

1946—(tailback in single wing)
    Bill Dudley
1947—(tailback in single wing)
    Johnny Clement
1948—(tailback in single wing)
    Ray Evans
1949—(tailback in single wing)
    Joe Geri,
    Jim Finks
1950—(tailback in single wing)
    Joe Geri
1951—(tailback in single wing)
    Chuck Ortmann
1952—Jim Finks

1953—Jim Finks
1954—Jim Finks
1955—Jim Finks
1956—Ted Marchibroda
1957—Earl Morrall
1958—Bobby Layne
1959—Bobby Layne
1960—Bobby Layne
1961—Rudy Bukich,
    Bobby Layne
1962—Bobby Layne
1963—Ed Brown
1964—Ed Brown
1965—Bill Nelsen

1966—Ron Smith
1967—Kent Nix
1968—Dick Shiner
1969—Dick Shiner
1970—Terry Bradshaw,
    Terry Hanratty
1971—Terry Bradshaw
1972—Terry Bradshaw
1973—Terry Bradshaw
*1974—Joe Gilliam
*1975—Terry Bradshaw
1976—Terry Bradshaw
1977—Terry Bradshaw
*1978—Terry Bradshaw
*1979—Terry Bradshaw
1980—Terry Bradshaw

1981—Terry Bradshaw
1982—Terry Bradshaw
1983—Cliff Stoudt
1984—Mark Malone
1985—Mark Malone,
    David Woodley
1986—Mark Malone
1987—Mark Malone
1988—Bubby Brister
1989—Bubby Brister
1990—Bubby Brister
1991—Neil O'Donnell
1992—Neil O'Donnell
1993—Neil O'Donnell
1994—Neil O'Donnell
1995—Neil O'Donnell

St. Louis Rams (Los Angeles Rams, 1946–1994)

1994—Chris Miller
1995—Chris Miller

San Diego Chargers (Los Angeles Chargers, 1960)

1960 (AFL)—Jack Kemp
1961 (AFL)—Jack Kemp
1962 (AFL)—John Hadl
1963 (AFL)—John Hadl
1964 (AFL)—John Hadl
1965 (AFL)—John Hadl
1966 (AFL)—John Hadl
1967 (AFL)—John Hadl
1968 (AFL)—John Hadl
1969 (AFL)—John Hadl
1970—John Hadl
1971—John Hadl
1972—John Hadl
1973—Dan Fouts
1974—Dan Fouts
1975—Dan Fouts
1976—Dan Fouts

1977—James Harris
1978—Dan Fouts
1979—Dan Fouts
1980—Dan Fouts
1981—Dan Fouts
1982—Dan Fouts
1983—Dan Fouts,
    Ed Luther
1984—Dan Fouts
1985—Dan Fouts
1986—Dan Fouts
1987—Dan Fouts
1988—Mark Malone
1989—Jim McMahon
1990—Billy Joe Tolliver
1991—John Friesz
1992—Stan Humphries

1993—Stan Humphries,   1994—Stan Humphries
      John Friesz   1995—Stan Humphries

San Francisco Forty-Niners

1946 (AAC)—Frankie Albert   1973—John Brodie,
1947 (AAC)—Frankie Albert   Steve Spurrier
1948 (AAC)—Frankie Albert   1974—Tom Owen
1949 (AAC)—Frankie Albert   1975—Steve Spurrier,
1950—Frankie Albert   Norm Snead
1951—Frankie Albert   1976—Jim Plunkett
1952—Y. A. Tittle   1977—Jim Plunkett
1953—Y. A. Tittle   1978—Steve DeBerg
1954—Y. A. Tittle   1979—Steve DeBerg
1955—Y. A. Tittle   1980—Steve DeBerg,
1956—Y. A. Tittle   Joe Montana
1957—Y. A. Tittle   *1981—Joe Montana
1958—John Brodie,   1982—Joe Montana
      Y. A. Tittle   1983—Joe Montana
1959—Y. A. Tittle   *1984—Joe Montana
1960—John Brodie   1985—Joe Montana
1961—John Brodie   1986—Joe Montana
1962—John Brodie   1987—Joe Montana
1963—Lamar McHan   *1988—Joe Montana
1964—John Brodie   *1989—Joe Montana
1965—John Brodie   1990—Joe Montana
1966—John Brodie   1991—Steve Young,
1967—John Brodie   Steve Bono
1968—John Brodie   1992—Steve Young
1969—John Brodie   1993—Steve Young
1970—John Brodie   *1994—Steve Young
1971—John Brodie   1995—Steve Young
1972—Steve Spurrier

Seattle Seahawks

1976—Jim Zorn   1981—Jim Zorn
1977—Jim Zorn   1982—Jim Zorn
1978—Jim Zorn   1983—Dave Krieg,
1979—Jim Zorn   Jim Zorn
1980—Jim Zorn   1984—Dave Krieg

1985—Dave Krieg
1986—Dave Krieg
1987—Dave Krieg
1988—Dave Krieg,
    Kelly Stouffer
1989—Dave Krieg

1990—Dave Krieg
1991—Dave Krief
1992—Stan Gelbaugh
1993—Rick Mirer
1994—Rick Mirer
1995—Rick Myrer

Tampa Bay Buccaneers

1976—Steve Spurrier
1977—Gary Huff
1978—Doug Williams
1979—Doug Williams
1980—Doug Williams
1981—Doug Williams
1982—Doug Williams
1983—Jack Thompson
1984—Steve DeBerg
1985—Steve DeBerg

1986—Steve Young
1987—Steve DeBerg
1988—Vinnie Testaverde
1989—Vinnie Testaverde
1990—Vinnie Testaverde
1991—Vinnie Testaverde
1992—Vinnie Testaverde
1993—Craig Erickson
1994—Craig Erickson
1995—Trent Dilfer

Washington Redskins

1946—Sammy Baugh
1947—Sammy Baugh
1948—Sammy Baugh
1949—Sammy Baugh
1950—Sammy Baugh,
    Harry Gilmer
1951—Sammy Baugh
1952—Eddie LeBaron
1953—Eddie LeBaron
1954—Al Dorow,
    Jack Scarbath
1955—Eddie LeBaron
1956—Eddie LeBaron,
    Al Dorow
1957—Eddie LeBaron
1958—Eddie LeBaron
1959—Eddie LeBaron

1960—Ralph Guglielmi
1961—Norm Snead
1962—Norm Snead
1963—Norm Snead
1964—Sonny Jurgensen
1965—Sonny Jurgensen
1966—Sonny Jurgensen
1967—Sonny Jurgensen
1968—Sonny Jurgensen
1969—Sonny Jurgensen
1970—Sonny Jurgensen
1971—Billy Kilmer
1972—Billy Kilmer
1973—Billy Kilmer
1974—Billy Kilmer
1975—Billy Kilmer
1976—Billy Kilmer
1977—Billy Kilmer,
    Joe Theismann

1978—Joe Theismann

1979—Joe Theismann

1980—Joe Theismann

1981—Joe Theismann

*1982—Joe Theismann

1983—Joe Theismann

1984—Joe Theismann

1985—Joe Theismann

1986—Jay Schroeder

*1987—Jay Schroeder

1988—Doug Williams

1989—Mark Rypien

1990—Mark Rypien

*1991—Mark Rypien

1992—Mark Rypien

1993—Mark Rypien

1994—Heath Shuler,
        John Friesz

1995—Gus Frerotte

SOURCES

Jim Feist's Pro Football 1994 Annual. Las Vegas, Nev.: National Sports Services, Inc., 1994.

Neff, David S., and Richard M. Cohen. *The Football Encyclopedia: The Complete History of Professional NFL Football From 1892 to the Present.* New York: St. Martin's Press, 1991.

———. *The Sports Encyclopedia: Football: 6th Edition: The Modern Era, 1960 Through 1987.* New York: St. Martin's Press, 1988.

Preview Sports Pro Football Preview '96.

Roberts, Reggie, and Chuck Garrity, Jr., eds. *The Official National Football League 1993 Record and Fact Book,* New York: Workman Publishing Co., 1993.

Sports Illustrated 1996 Sports Almanac. Boston and New York: Little Brown & Co., 1996.

—L.D.R.

XIX

REFERENCE

66

SOME REFERENCE BOOKS
THAT WRITERS USE

· · · · ·

Everyone who writes or edits has certain favorite reference works. When the idea for this book was first conceived, I wrote to a number of authors in the United States and Great Britain and asked them to list reference books they found particularly useful in their writing. The result, from some fifty respondents, was a plenitude of useful volumes that could fill several floor-to-ceiling bookcases. (The names of the writers making suggestions are listed in the introduction to this book.)

What follows is neither a bibliography nor a checklist with pretensions to thoroughness, but a presentation of some of the favorite reference sources drawn upon by a number of professional authors of various kinds, including novelists, poets, journalists, and scholars in a number of fields. For more specialized works—and almost everybody queried cited works of particular appropriateness to their own interests and predilections—the ready is referred to the titles listed under "Sources" for the various compilations in this volume.

In noting the books cited below, the reader should keep in mind that except perhaps in the physical sciences, most references books do not necessarily become outdated with age. Several writers queried expressed a fondness for the eleventh edition of the *Encyclopaedia Britannica*, because of the quality and length of its literary and philosophical essays. An encyclopedia of United States history published in, say, 1953 would omit certain important information about World War II that became known only later, such as the fact that the Ultra wireless interceptions permitted the English and Americans to know about every German troop and naval movement in advance. But the account of New Deal legislation in the 1930s, and the events of World War I, would continue to offer accurate information decades after publication.

I mention this because the responses to the questionnaire indicate that authors tend to hold on to their earlier reference works and continue to use them, without usually bothering to replace them with more up-to-date editions. Indeed, not a few writers reported that they were continuing to make considerable use of the textbooks they studied back in college. Unless a book has been thoroughly revised and rewritten, however, the reader would in most instances do much better to seek the latest version of that book rather than the one mentioned.

Indeed, this goes for the writers who mention them as well, as I know from experience. I wonder how many of them had examined more recent editions of favorite reference works? Example: When I was twelve or thirteen I was given a copy of *Roget's Thesaurus*, which I used for the next half century. Then a few years ago I happened to look at the most recent Roget; it was so much more inclusive and informative that I bought one at once, and have used it almost daily ever since. This might seem only common sense, but we do tend to keep on using our older, familiar reference books without realizing their limitations.

As noted in the introduction, almost all the American authors said they relied upon an almanac—usually *The World Almanac and Book of Facts*, sometimes the *Information Please Almanac*. An almanac, a dictionary, and a thesaurus—these were almost everyone's standbys. Among dictionaries there was no universal favorite, but as might be expected, at least a dozen writers cited the *OED*—the multivolumed *Oxford English Dictionary*, particularly for its etymologies and citations of earliest recorded usage. It should be noted, however, that several writers made a point of saying that they preferred the 1933 12-volume *OED*, rather than the 20-volume edition of 1989. The same is even more true for the unabridged Merriam-Webster, also widely named—several respondents cited *Webster's Third New International Dictionary of the English Language* (1961), but several others expressed a strong preference for the second edition, which is markedly more prescriptive and less descriptive in its approach to contemporary language. *The Random House Dictionary of the English Language*, second edition unabridged (1987), also has its strong proponents. The French *Larousse* was frequently cited, as were dictionaries for other languages. One respondent listed Mathews' *Chinese-English Dictionary*.

It should not be assumed, however, that every time the possessor of a set of the *OED* or another multivolumed unabridged dictionary wishes to check the definition of a word, he gets up from the typewriter or word-processor, goes over to a bookcase, and hauls down the volume containing that word. Most of the writers queried also listed desktop dictionaries. Among those cited were the *American Heritage Dictionary of the English Language*,

Merriam-Webster's *New Collegiate, Webster's New World Dictionary of American English*, and the *Shorter Oxford English Dictionary.* (Several respondents even listed Samuel Johnson's *Dictionary.*)

The late Howard Nemerov, however, wrote that when he was at work on a poem he *never* looked anything up, because doing so "is a sure way, sometimes a handy way, to stop work that morning." His Merriam-Webster, second edition, "lies open on the radiator cover, drying out its glue and being slowly digested by learned cats," he reported, adding that "I'd be proud to say that my copy of the *OED* was tattered as Auden's is said to have been; but I don't have a copy of the *OED.*"

Eric Partridge's *Dictionary of Slang and Unconventional English* (the 1984 edition is edited by Paul Beale) was variously cited as a source for off-beat terms. Partridge's *Origins* and Morris' *Dictionary of Word and Phrase Origins* were praised by several writers, as was C. T. Onions' *Oxford Dictionary of English Etymology.* Another Eric Partridge compilation, *A Dictionary of Clichés,* was noted. At least a dozen persons regularly consult Fowler's *Dictionary of Modern English Usage.* For synonyms and antonyms, *Roget's International Thesaurus* was most often cited, but *Sisson's Synonyms,* Soule's *Dictionary of English Synonyms,* and J. I. Rodale, *The Synonym Finder,* have their admirers.

A reference work, unique of its kind, that was named by numerous writers is *Brewer's Dictionary of Phrase and Fable,* edited in its most recent edition by Ivor H. Evans. This unusual volume, first published in 1870 by Dr. Ebenezer Cobham Brewer, is a gold mine of facts about words, literary characters, myth, colloquial expressions, figures of speech, and whatever; Brewer himself called it a "Treasury of Literary Bric-a-brac"; where else could one find lists of the names of historical, mythological, and literary horses and dogs (present volume excepted, of course), or the last words of famous people, or a list of public-house signs with their explanations?

Another useful work, which few American writers seem to know about, is *Pears Cyclopedia,* a British publication which has been distributed in the United States by Viking-Penguin. Its random contents range from Greek myths and thumbnail biographies of important people to cooking, gardening, medical information, the care and feeding of domestic pets, a lengthy listing of general information, and an atlas and gazetteer. Although much of its contents is of use mainly for Great Britain, there is a great deal that any writer anywhere will find extremely handy for reference.

Encyclopedias, of course, are much used, among them the *Americana, Chambers's,* and the *Britannica,* the last not only for its latest, fifteenth, edition, which has a new format, but for the fourteenth edition and the great eleventh edition of 1903. One respondent even expressed a fondness for the 1771 edition. The one-volume *Columbia Encyclopedia,* which though scarcely pocket-sized (9" x 12", 3,000+ pages) can be kept nearby on the desk, also had numerous devotees.

Other general works esteemed by the writers who responded included the *Guinness Book of World Records,* the *New York Public Library Desk Reference,* and Jacques Barzun's and Henry F. Graff's *The Modern Researcher.*

William L. Langer's *Encyclopedia of World History* is a much-used guide to when things happened; it includes an extraordinary amount of easily consulted historical information. Bernard Grun's *The Timetables of History,* cited by several authors, is arranged year by year in parallel columns, so that one can see various kinds of events, discoveries, inventions, etc., in various civilizations in chronological juxtaposition. James Trager's *The People's Chronology* offers quite lengthy year-by-year developments, including many areas such as business and popular history that other compilations omit. Although the *New York Public Library Book of Chronologies* appeared too late to be cited by the respondents, undoubtedly it would have been, for it contains vast amounts of information broken down handily into categories. Several persons stressed their dependence upon Lois and Alan Gordon's *American Chronicle,* and several others named Paul Prucha's *Handbook for Research in American History* and the *Harvard Guide to American History.*

Various writers indicated a strong reliance on atlases. There was little unanimity or near-unanimity here; among those cited were the *Times Atlas,* the *National Geographic Atlas,* the *Rand-McNally Atlas,* and the *Reader's Digest Atlas of the World.* Among historical atlases were *Shepherd's Historical Atlas,* Hermann Kinder and Werner Hilgemann's *Anchor Atlas of World History,* Rand-McNally's *Historical Atlas of the World,* and *The West Point Atlas of American Wars.* Webster's *Geographical Dictionary* was listed by several writers. (A compendium which no respondent thought to cite, but which the editor of this book is willing to bet that many of them frequently use, is the *Road Atlas* of the American Automobile Association.)

For biographical information, several of the American scholarly writers responding use the *Dictionary of American Biography,* with its several supplements, and the British scholars the *Dictionary of National Biography* and supplements. In addition to those multivolumed works, *Chambers's Biographical Dictionary, Webster's Biographical Dictionary,* Justin Wintle's *Makers of Modern Culture,* the British *Who's Who, Who's Who in America,* the *Dictionary of American Negro Biography* and *Encyclopedia of Black America,* Jennifer S. Uglow's *Continuum Dictionary of Women's Biography,* and biographical dictionaries within various fields were used.

In important respects, reference works, as already noted, do not necessarily become obsolete. One respondent reported that she kept three different editions of *Bartlett's Familiar Quotations*—1915, 1955, 1976. H. L. Mencken's *The American Language*, with its several supplements, does certain things in ways that more recently compiled works do not. I have a dilapidated six volume set of *Appleton's Cyclopedia of American Biography* (1888) which contains sketches of people then considered of much importance, but long since eliminated from newer compilations, and a 118-year-old *Centennial Gazetteer of the United States*, by A. von Steinwehr, "A. M. (Author of Eclectic Series of School Geographies, and Topographical Map of the United States)," which can be used to locate places as they once were, including some which no longer exist.

Collections of familiar—and not-so-familiar—quotations obviously receive much use. *Bartlett's* remains the favorite, but the *Oxford Dictionary of Quotations* and Edward F. Murphy's *Crown Treasury of Relevant Quotations* are also popular. Two respondents prefer H. L. Mencken's *Dictionary of Quotations* (1942). There is also the *Viking Book of Aphorisms.*

Among reference books having to do with literature and publishing, *Benét's Reader's Encyclopedia*, C. Hugh Holman and William Harmon's *A Handbook to Literature*, Alex Preminger's *Princeton Encyclopedia of Poetry and Poetics*, Karl Shapiro and Robert Beum's *Prosody Handbook*, the *Literary Market Place*, J. A. Cuddon's *A Dictionary of Literary Terms*, the *Chicago Manual of Style*, Karl Beckson's *Literary Terms: A Dictionary*, Hiram Haydn and Edmund Fuller's *Thesaurus of Book Digests*, and the Magill *Masterplots* volumes were given. A book I find myself frequently consulting is Frank Luther Mott's *Golden Multitudes: A History of Best-Sellers in the United States* (1947). Books chronicling and describing literature in other languages, such as Wallace Fowlie's excellent *French Literature: Its History and Meaning*, were cited by various respondents.

Almost every writer queried keeps a Bible close by, usually the King James but sometimes the Revised Standard Version. Other works having to do with religion that were cited included *The Book of Common Prayer*, *The Jerome Biblical Commentary*, *Harper's Bible Dictionary*, the *Bible Almanac*, Strong's *Exhaustive Concordance of the Bible*, Burton Stevenson's *The Home Book of Bible Quotations*, the *Oxford Dictionary of the Christian Church*, the *Penguin Dictionary of Saints*, K. S. Latourette's *History of Christianity*, and the *New Catholic Encyclopedia.*

Books on mythology get frequent use. Among those cited were Robert Graves's *Greek Myths*, Sir James G. Frazer's *The Golden Bough*, Gayley's *Classic Myths*, Daniel S. Norton and Peters Rushton's *Classical Myths in*

English Literature, the *Oxford Classical Dictionary,* G. M. Kirkwood's *Short Guide to Classical Mythology,* Edith Hamilton's *Mythology,* and, most often of all, *Brewer's Dictionary of Phrase and Fable,* noted above.

For philosophy and philosophers, books cited included the *Fontana Dictionary of Modern Thought* and the Fontana/Collins *Biographical Companion to Modern Thought.* I find myself frequently consulting my college textbook, B. A. G. Fuller's *History of Philosophy,* not least for its succinct little "Glossary of Common Terms."

Certain books seem essential for various writers concerned with politics and government. These include the *Congressional Directory,* Spaeth and Smith's *Constitution of the United States,* with case summaries, the *Public Papers of the Presidents,* Michael Barone and Grant Ujifusa's *Almanac of American Politics,* the *Statesman's Year-Book,* and *Historical Statistics of the United States.*

The mysteries of technology, machinery, and the things of the everyday world find explanation for the writers queried in such books as Macauley's *The Way Things Work* and Bragonier and Fisher's *What's What,* Patrick Robinson's *The Book of Firsts,* and the several volumes by Charles Panati, including *Panati's Browser's Book of Beginnings* and *Extraordinary Origins of Everyday Things.*

The Sources listed throughout this book after each section can be consulted for useful books about the various topics described; many were cited by the writers queried. There were also, however, some off-the-beaten-path works (within the context) that those responding reported finding useful that merit mention.

One novelist finds the name-books on sale at newsstands, designed to afford parents assistance in naming babies, useful for choosing names for her characters, and *Dr. Spock's Baby and Child Care* for describing what fictional children do when they come down with assorted ailments.

A historian of British culture lists the *Oxford Dictionary of Nursery Rhymes.* A journalist says he makes frequent recourse to Ambrose Bierce's *The Devil's Dictionary.* An author of books on baseball cites Hugh Rawson's *Wicked Words* and Shari and Bernard Benstock's *Who's He When He's at Home: A James Joyce Directory.* A military historian cites David Chandler's *Military Maxims of Napoleon.*

A scholar in French literature cites Mary McCarthy's *Stones of Florence.* A journalist and a literary scholar both cite Leo Rosten's *The Joys of Yiddish.* A novelist suggests *Psychiatry for Medical Students;* another lists *The Merck Manual of Diagnosis and Therapy* and Gray's *Anatomy.* A journalist cites *Black's Medical Dictionary.* A writer on fishing recommends *McClane's New Standard Fishing Encyclopedia* and the Audubon Society Field Guides. And I recommend the *New Glénans Sailing Manual,*

Anthony Storr's *Music and the Mind,* and Katie Letcher Lyle's *Scalded to Death by the Steam: The True Stories of Railroad Disasters and the Songs That Were Written About Them.*

Following are citations to the works given above and others.

American Heritage Dictionary of the English Language. 3rd ed. Boston: Houghton Mifflin Co., 1992.

Attwater, Donald. *Penguin Dictionary of Saints.* 2nd ed. New York: Penguin, 1984.

Auden, W. H., ed. *Viking Book of Aphorisms.* New York: Viking, 1966.

Audubon Society Field Guides. A series of guidebooks to the North American outdoors, published by Alfred A. Knopf, New York. A 16-volume set was published by Chanticleer Press in New York, 1988.

Barone, Michael, and Grant Ujifusa, eds. *Almanac of American Politics,* 1992. Washington, D.C.: National Journal, 1991.

Bartlett, John. *Familiar Quotations.* 15th ed. Boston: Little, Brown and Co., 1980.

Barzun, Jacques, and Henry F. Graff. *The Modern Researcher.* 5th ed. New York: Harcourt, Brace and Co., 1992.

Beckson, Karl E. *Literary Terms: A Dictionary.* 3rd ed. New York: Noonday Press, 1989.

Benét, William Rose. *The Reader's Encyclopedia.* 2nd ed. New York: T. Y. Crowell, 1955.

Benstock, Shari, and Bernard Benstock. *Who's He When He's at Home: A James Joyce Directory.* Urbana: University of Illinois Press, 1980.

Bierce, Ambrose. *The Devil's Dictionary.* New York: Dell Publishing Co., 1991.

The Book of Common Prayer and Administration of the Sacraments and Other Rites and Ceremonies of the Church, According to the Use of the Episcopal Church. New York: Oxford University Press, 1979.

Bragonier, Reginald, and David Fisher. *What's What: A Visual Glossary of the Physical World.* Rev. ed. Maplewood, N.J.: Hammond, 1990.

Brewer, Ebenezer Cobham. *Brewer's Dictionary of Phrase and Fable.* Edited by Ivor H. Evans. 14th ed. New York: Harper and Row, 1989.

Bridgwater, William, and Seymour Kurtz, eds. *Columbia Encyclopedia.* 3rd ed. New York: Columbia University Press, 1963.

Brown, Raymond Edward, Joseph A. Fritzmyer, and Rowland Edmund Murphy, eds. *The Jerome Biblical Commentary.* Englewood Cliffs, N.J.: Prentice-Hall, 1968.

Bullock, Alan, and Stephen Trombley, eds. *The Fontana Dictionary of Modern Thought.* Rev. ed. London: Fontana, 1988. (American edition is titled *Harper Dictionary of Modern Thought.*) Copublished with this work is *The Fontana Biographical Companion to Modern Thought*. London: Collins, 1983.

Chambers's Encyclopaedia. New rev. ed. 15 vols. Oxford: Pergamon Press, 1987.

Chandler, David G., ed. *The Military Maxims of Napoleon*. Translated by Lt.-Gen. Sir George C. D'Aguilar. London: Greenhill Books, 1987.

Chapman, Robert L., ed. *Roget's International Thesaurus*. 5th ed. New York: HarperCollins, 1992.

The Chicago Manual of Style. 13th ed. Chicago: University of Chicago Press, 1982.

Congressional Directory. Biennial volumes. Washington, D.C.: U.S. Government Printing Office.

Cross, F. L., and E. A. Livingstone, eds. *Oxford Dictionary of the Christian Church*. 2nd ed. New York: Oxford University Press, 1974.

Cuddon, John A. *A Dictionary of Literary Terms*. New York: Viking-Penguin, 1982.

Dictionary of American Biography. 20 vols. with 10 Supplements. New York: Charles Scribner's Sons.

The Dictionary of National Biography. 22 vols. London: Smith, Elder, 1908–1909. Supplements 2–8. Oxford University Press, 1912–81. *DNB for 1981–1985*. Oxford: Oxford University Press, 1990.

Encyclopaedia Britannica. 14th ed. Chicago: Encyclopaedia Britannica Co., Inc., 1957. (See also **New Encyclopaedia Brittannica**.)

Encyclopedia Americana. 30 vols. Chicago: Encyclopedia Americana, 1982.

Esposito, Col. Vincent J., ed. *The West Point Atlas of American Wars*. New York: Frederick A. Praeger, 1959.

Fowler, Henry Watson. *Dictionary of Modern English Usage*. 2nd ed. Revised by Sir Ernest Gowers. New York: Oxford University Press, 1991.

Fowlie, Wallace. *French Literature: Its History and Meaning*. Englewood Cliffs, N.J.: Prentice-Hall, 1973.

Frazer, James G. *The Golden Bough*. Avenal, N.J.: Outlet Book Co., 1987. (The 13-volume set [1890] was reprinted by St. Martin's Press, New York.)

Freidel, Frank, and Richard K. Showman, eds. *Harvard Guide to American History*. 2 vols. Cambridge, Mass.: Belknap Press, 1974.

Fuller, B. A. G. *A History of Philosophy*. Rev. ed. New York: Henry Holt and Co., 1945.

Gayley, Charles Mills. *Classic Myths in English Literature and Art, Based Originally on Bulfinch's "Age of Fable."* Boston: Ginn and Co., 1939.

Gordon, Lois, and Alan Gordon. *American Chronicle: Seven Decades in American Life, 1920–1989*. New York: Crown Publishers, 1990.

Graves, Robert. *Greek Myths*. 2 vols. New York: Viking-Penguin, 1990.

Gray, Henry. *Anatomy of the Human Body.* 30th ed. Philadelphia, Pa.: Lee and Febiger, 1985.

Grun, Bernard. *The Timetables of History: A Horizontal Linkage of People and Events.* 3rd ed. New York: Simon and Schuster, 1991.

Guinness Book of World Records, 1990–1991. New York: Bantam Books, 1991.

Hamilton, Edith. *Mythology: Timeless Tales of Gods and Heroes.* New York: NAL-Dutton, 1989.

Hammond, N. G. L., and H. H. Scullard, eds. *Oxford Classical Dictionary.* 2nd ed. New York: Oxford University Press, 1970.

Harris, William H., and Judith S. Levey, eds. *The New Columbia Encyclopedia.* 4th ed. New York: Columbia University Press, 1975.

Havard, C. W. H., ed. *Black's Medical Dictionary.* 35th ed. Totowa, N.J.: Barnes and Noble, 1987.

Haydn, Hiram, and Edmund Fuller, eds. *Thesaurus of Book Digests.* New York: Crown Publishers, 1949. Continued in Irving Weiss and Anne de la Vergne Weiss's *Thesaurus of Book Digests, 1950–1980.* New York: Crown Publishers, 1981.

Holman, C. Hugh, and William Harmon. *A Handbook to Literature.* 6th ed. New York: Macmillan, 1992.

Information Please Almanac. Annual editions.

Johnson, Samuel. *A Dictionary of the English Language.* 2 vols. London, 1755. Various reprints and abridgements of this classic exist, among them McAdam, E. L., Jr., and George Milne, *Samuel Johnson's Dictionary: A Modern Selection.* New York: Pantheon Books, 1981.

Kinder, Hermann, and Werner Hilgemann. *Anchor Atlas of World History.* Translated by Ernest A. Menze. 2 vols. New York: Anchor Books, 1978.

Kirkwood, G. M. *A Short Guide to Classical Mythology.* New York: Holt, Rinehart and Winston, 1959.

Langer, William L., comp. and ed. *An Encyclopedia of World History.* 5th ed. Boston: Houghton Mifflin Co., 1972.

Larousse Dictionnaire de Français. Paris: Larousse, 1986.

Latourette, Kenneth Scott. *History of Christianity.* 2 vols. Rev. ed. New York: Harper and Row, 1975.

Literary Market Place. 1993 ed. New York: R. R. Bowker, 1992.

Logan, Rayford W., and Michael R. Winston, eds. *Dictionary of American Negro Biography.* New York: W. W. Norton, 1982.

Low, W. Augustus, and Virgil A. Clift, eds. *Encyclopedia of Black America.* New York: McGraw-Hill, 1981.

Lyle, Katie Letcher. *Scalded to Death by the Steam: The True Stories of Railroad Disasters and the Songs That Were Written About Them.* Chapel Hill, N.C.: Algonquin Books, 1983.

Macaulay, David. *The Way Things Work.* Boston: Houghton Mifflin Co., 1988.

McCarthy, Mary. *Stones of Florence.* New York: Harcourt, Brace and Co., 1987.

McClane, A. J. *McClane's New Standard Fishing Encyclopedia and International Angling Guide.* Rev. ed. New York: Holt, Rinehart and Winston, 1974.

Magill, Frank, ed. *Masterpieces of World Literature in Digest Form.* Ser. 1–4. New York: Harper and Bros., 1952–69. Also *Masterplots Annuals,* 22 vols., 1954–76; and *Masterplots II,* published by Salem Press, Englewood Cliffs, N.J.

Mathews, Robert Henry. *Mathews' Chinese-English Dictionary.* Cambridge, Mass.: Harvard University Press, 1943.

Mencken, H. L., *The American Language, Abridged.* Edited by Raven McDavid, Jr. New York: Alfred A. Knopf, 1963.

———. *A New Dictionary of Quotations on Historical Principles from Ancient and Modern Sources.* New York: Alfred A. Knopf, 1942.

The Merck Manual of Diagnosis and Therapy. 14th ed. Rahway, N.J.: Merck Sharp and Dohme, 1982.

Miller, Madeleine Sweeney, and J. Lane Miller. *Harper's Bible Dictionary.* 8th ed. New York: Harper and Row, 1973. 1985 edition, San Francisco: Harper and Row, 1985.

Morris, William, and Mary Morris. *Morris' Dictionary of Word and Phrase Origins.* 2nd ed. New York: Harper and Row, 1988.

Mott, Frank Luther. *Golden Multitudes: A History of Best-Sellers in the United States.* New York: Macmillan, 1947.

Murphy, Edward F., ed. *Crown Treasury of Relevant Quotations.* New York: Crown Publishers, 1978.

National Geographic Atlas of the World. 6th ed. Washington, D.C.: National Geographic Society, 1990.

New Catholic Encyclopedia. 17 vols. New York: McGraw-Hill, 1967–79. Reissued by Publishers Guild, Palatine, Ill., 1981.

New Century Dictionary of the English Language. Rev. ed. 2 vols. New York: Appleton-Century-Crofts, 1953.

New Encyclopaedia Britannica: Micropëdia. 15th ed. Chicago: Encyclopaedia Britannica Co., Inc., 1990. (See also **Encyclopaedia Britannica**.)

New English Dictionary on Historical Principles. 10 vols. and Supplement. Oxford: Clarendon Press, 1888–1933. (See also **Oxford English Dictionary**.)

New Glénans Sailing Manual. Translated by James MacGibbon and Stanley Caldwell. Boston, Mass.: Sail, 1978.

New York Public Library Desk Reference. Englewood Cliffs, N.J.: Prentice-Hall, 1989.

Norton, Daniel S., and Peters Rushton. *Classical Myths in English Literature.* Westport, Conn.: Greenwood, 1969.

Office of the Federal Register, National Archives and Record Service. *Public Papers of the Presidents of the United States.* Vols. published for U.S. presidents from Washington to Reagan. Washington, D.C.: U.S. Government Printing Office.

Onions, C. T., ed. *Oxford Dictionary of English Etymology.* Oxford: Clarendon Press, 1966.

Opie, Iona. *Oxford Dictionary of Nursery Rhymes.* Edited by Iona and Peter Opie. New York: Oxford University Press, 1951.

Oxford English Dictionary. 20 vols. Oxford: Clarendon Press, 1989.

Packer, James I., Merrill C. Tenney, and William White, Jr., eds. *The Bible Almanac.* Nashville, Tenn.: Thomas Nelson, 1980.

Palmer, Robert R., ed. *Historical Atlas of the World.* Chicago: Rand-McNally, 1991.

Panati, Charles. *Extraordinary Origins of Everyday Things.* New York: Harper and Row, 1987.

———. *Panati's Browser's Book of Beginnings.* Boston: Houghton Mifflin Co., 1984.

Partington, Angela, ed. *Oxford Dictionary of Quotations.* New York: Oxford University Press, 1992.

Partridge, Eric. *A Dictionary of Clichés.* 5th ed. London: Routledge and Kegan Paul, 1978.

———. *A Dictionary of Slang and Unconventional English.* Edited by Paul Beale. London: Routledge and Kegan Paul, 1984.

———. *Origins.* 4th ed. London: Routledge and Kegan Paul, 1966.

Pears Cyclopedia. 101st ed. London: Pelham Books Ltd., 1992.

Preminger, Alex, *et al.*, eds. *Princeton Encyclopedia of Poetry and Poetics.* Rev. ed. Princeton: Princeton University Press, 1974.

Prucha, Francis Paul. *Handbook for Research in American History.* Lincoln, Nebr.: University of Nebraska Press, 1987.

Rand-McNally New International Atlas. Chicago: Rand-McNally, 1991.

The Random House Dictionary of the English Language. 2nd ed., unabridged. New York: Random House, 1987.

Rawson, Hugh. *Wicked Words: A Treasury of Curses, Insults, Put-downs, and Other Formerly Imprintable Terms from Anglo-Saxon Times to the Present.* New York: Crown Publishers, 1989.

Reader's Digest Atlas of the World. Chicago: Rand-McNally, 1990.

Robinson, Patrick. *The Book of Firsts.* New York: Clarkson N. Potter, 1974.

Rodale, Jerome Irving. *The Synonym Finder*. Revised by Laurence Urdang and Nancy La Roche. Emmaus, Pa.: Rodale Press, 1978.

Rosten, Leo. *The Joys of Yiddish*. New York: Simon and Schuster, 1991.

Shapiro, Karl, and Robert Beum. *A Prosody Handbook*. New York: Harper and Row, 1965.

Shepherd, William Robert. *Shepherd's Historical Atlas*. 9th ed. New York: Barnes and Noble, 1964.

The Shorter Oxford English Dictionary on Historical Principles. 2 vols. Oxford: Clarendon Press, 1973.

Sisson, A. F. *Sisson's Synonyms: An Unabridged Synonym and Related-Terms Locator*. Englewood Cliffs, N.J.: Prentice-Hall, 1969.

Soule, Richard, and G. Howson, eds. *Dictionary of English Synonyms and Synonymous Parallel Expressions*. Rev. ed. of a nineteenth-century work by Soule. Smith's Grove, Ky.: Shalom Publishing Co., 1993.

Spaeth, Harold J., and Edward C. Smith. *Constitution of the United States*. 13th ed. New York: Harper-Perennial, 1991.

Spock, Benjamin M., and Michael Rothenberg. *Dr. Spock's Baby and Child Care: Fortieth Anniversary Edition*. New York: NAL-Dutton, 1985.

Statesman's Year-Book. 129th ed. New York: St. Martin's Press, 1992.

Stevenson, Burton E. *The Home Book of Bible Quotations*. New York: Harper and Bros., 1949.

Storr, Anthony. *Music and the Mind*. New York: Free Press, 1992.

Strong, James. *Exhaustive Concordance of the Bible*. London: Hodder and Stoughton; New York: Hunt, 1894. Various reprints.

Thorne, J. O., ed. *Chambers's Biographical Dictionary*. Rev. ed. New York: St. Martin's Press, 1969.

The Times Atlas of the World. 8th ed. New York: New York Times Books, 1990.

Trager, James, ed. *The People's Chronology: A Year-by-Year Record of Human Events from Prehistory to the Present*. New York: Holt, Rinehart and Winston, 1979.

Uglow, Jennifer S. *The Continuum Dictionary of Women's Biography*. New York: Continuum Publishing Co., 1989.

United States, Bureau of the Census. *Historical Statistics of the United States: Colonial Times to 1970*. Washington, D.C.: U.S. Department of Commerce, Bureau of the Census, 1975.

von Steinwehr, A. *The Centennial Gazetteer of the United States*. Philadelphia: J. C. McCurdy and Co., 1876.

Waldinger, Robert J., ed. *Psychiatry for Medical Students*. 2nd ed. Washington, D.C.: American Psychiatric Press, 1991.

Webster's New Biographical Dictionary. Springfield, Mass.: Merriam-Webster, 1988.

Webster's New Geographical Dictionary. Rev. ed. Springfield, Mass.: G. and C. Merriam Co., 1984.

Webster's New International Dictionary of the English Language. 2nd ed., unabridged. Vols. I-III. Springfield, Mass.: G. and C. Merriam Co., 1959. See also **Webster's Third New International Dictionary**.

Webster's New World Dictionary of American English. 3rd. college ed. New York: Webster's New World, 1988.

Webster's Ninth New Collegiate Dictionary. Springfield, Mass.: G. and C. Merriam Co., 1990.

Webster's Third New International Dictionary of the English Language. Unabridged. Springfield Mass.: G. and C. Merriam Co., 1976. See also **Webster's New International Dictionary**.

Wetteran, Bruce, ed. *New York Public Library Book of Chronologies.* New York: Prentice-Hall, 1990.

Who's Who. Annual volumes published in U.S. by St. Martin's Press, New York.

Who's Who in America. Biennial editions published by Marquis Who's Who, New Providence, N.J.

Wilson, James Grant, and John Fisher, eds. *Appleton's Cyclopedia of American Biography.* 6 vols. New York: D. Appleton and Co., 1888.

Wintle, Justin, ed. *Makers of Modern Culture.* New York: Facts on File, 1981.

The World Almanac and Book of Facts. New York: Pharos Books, annual editions.

—**L.D.R.**